LOUIS L. SNYDER'S
HISTORICAL GUIDE TO
WORLD WAR II

LOUIS L. SNYDER'S HISTORICAL GUIDE TO WORLD WAR II

LOUIS L. SNYDER

 GREENWOOD PRESS
WESTPORT, CONNECTICUT • LONDON, ENGLAND

Copyright Acknowledgments

Grateful acknowledgment is given for permission to use the following:

William L. Shirer broadcast over CBS on June 22, 1940 about the surrender of France to the Germans at Compiègne. Courtesy of William L. Shirer.

Copyright MCMXXXIX by The Peter Maurice Music Co. Ltd. London, England/RENEWED Sole Selling Agents-Skidmore Music Co. Inc. 10 East 53 Street, N.Y., N.Y. 10022. Used by Permission of Shapiro, Bernstein & Co. Inc. on behalf of Skidmore Music Co. Inc.

Library of Congress Cataloging in Publication Data

Snyder, Louis Leo, 1907–
   Louis L. Snyder's Historical guide to World War II.

   Bibliography: p.
   Includes index.
   1. World War, 1939–1945—Dictionaries.   I. Title.
II. Title: Historical guide to World War II.   III. Title:
Historical guide to World War Two.
D740.S65   940.53'03'21   81-13433
ISBN 0-313-23216-4 (lib. bdg.)   AACR2

Copyright © 1982 by Louis L. Snyder

Library of Congress Catalog Card Number: 81-13433
ISBN: 0-313-23216-4

First published in 1982

Greenwood Press
A division of Congressional Information Service, Inc.
88 Post Road West
Westport, Connecticut 06881

Printed in the United States of America

10 9 8 7 6 5 4 3 2 1

pd
7-27-83

CONTENTS

PREFACE

World War II was the greatest prolonged mass tragedy in the history of civilization. This historical guide presents a compendium of facts about that war but avoids the narrow presentation of campaigns and battle entries preferred by the military historian. Details of battles, weapons, and weapon systems, which may be desirable for the classrooms of West Point, Annapolis, and Sandhurst, are too specialized for a complete history of the war arranged in reference form. The emphasis here is on non-military aspects of the war, including economic, political, social, cultural, and psychological phases.

There are literally millions of facts related to the events of 1939–1945. The compiler is faced with constant decisions of what is important and what can be eliminated. In this sense a work of this kind mirrors the experiences of its editor, who must make every effort to avoid personal likes and dislikes in favor of presenting plain facts.

Another typical problem is the wide divergence among authorities on casualties and battle losses. Even "official" sources often present varying statistics. Military and naval historians such as B. H. Liddell Hart and Samuel E. Morison give altogether different estimates of such losses.

For reader convenience the entries are arranged alphabetically to enable quick reference to any subject. The style is consistent for each category.

Causes, Development, Results. An effort has been made to break essentials down to component parts. For example, the reader interested in economic motivations will find entries on economic clashes leading to war, resources, supplies, Lend-Lease, and material losses due to the war.

Individuals. These entries are selective and condensed, with space allocated on the basis of importance to the war effort.

Weapons of War. Descriptions are given of all the major tools of war from small guns to big artillery to massive tanks. Because of the vital role of air power, special attention is devoted to aircraft, with specifications from wing span to recognition nicknames.

Code Names. Every code or cover name of consequence is included with identification of secret names designed to hide major strategies and minor tactics.

Allied War Conferences. The meetings of top war leaders from Argentia Bay to Potsdam are treated in detail, with attention to participants, background, decisions, and significance.

Catastrophes. War on a large scale brings with it many catastrophes for one side or the other. There are entries on the sinking of the *Athenia, Royal Oak, Graf Spee,* and *Bismarck,* the bombings of Rotterdam, Coventry, Hamburg, Cologne, and Dresden; the massacres at the Ardentine Cave and at Malmédy; and the tragic events of the Final Solution. In each case attention is directed to background and consequences.

Social Aspects. Added to the facts of combat are parallel developments on the home front of each belligerent. These include such diverse subjects as population movements, forced labor, propaganda, and entertainment.

Cultural. Attention is given to such subjects as wartime art, the confiscation of art treasures, wartime literature, songs of war, and war reporting.

Spies, Counterspies, and Hoaxes. The war years saw a plethora of strange, bizarre, and mysterious happenings. Many of these are described, including the Gleiwitz Raid, Black Tuesday and Black Thursday, the Oslo Letter, Kilroy Was Here, and the "phony" corpse of *Mincemeat.*

Cross References. Because of the interrelationships of many topics, liberal use has been made of cross references for the reader who wants more details.

Bibliographies. Recommendations for further reading are chosen from the voluminous literature of the war.

I should like to express my warm thanks to the staffs of the Wiener Library in London, the British Museum, the *Bibliothèque Nationale* in Paris, the University of Cologne Library, the New York Public Library, the Princeton Public Library, especially Eric Greenfeldt, and the Firestone Library of Princeton University. The assistance of these librarians has been invaluable.

Once again, as in all my previous work, this volume would have been impossible without the collaboration of my wife, Ida Mae Brown Snyder. It is an understatement to pay tribute to her talent for insisting on clarity, for finding the exact word, and for eliminating the runaway clichés.

For the professional historian, the armchair scholar, the World War II buff, and especially for the student essayist—good hunting!

ABBREVIATIONS

WORLD WAR II ACRONYMS

ABDA	Australian-British-Dutch-American Command
AEAF	Allied Expeditionary Air Force
AIF	Australian Imperial Force
ANZAC	Australian-New Zealand-Fijis-New Hebrides-New Caledonia Command
ARP	Air Raid Precautions
ATC	Air Transport Command
AVG	American Volunteer Group (*see* FLYING TIGERS)
BBC	British Broadcasting Corporation
BCRA	*Bureau Central de Reseignement et d'Action* (Central Bureau of Intelligence and Action)
BEF	British Expeditionary Force
BEW	Board of Economic Warfare
BSC	British Security Coordination
CBI	China-Burma-India Theater
CCS	Combined Chiefs of Staff
CGS	Chief of General Staff
CIC	Combined Intelligence Committee
CIGS	Chief of Imperial General Staff
CINCAF	Commander-in-Chief, Allied Forces
CINCMED	Commander-in-Chief, Mediterranean
CINCPAC	Commander-in-Chief, Pacific Area
CNAC	China National Aviation Corporation
CSF	Combined Striking Force
DP	Displaced Persons
DUKW	Amphibious truck (duck)
E-BOAT	Enemy boat, German or Italian motor torpedo boat
EAM	Greek National Liberation Movement
EDES	Greek Liberation Army

ETO	European Theater of Operations
ETOUSA	European Theater of Operations, U.S. Army
FBI	Federal Bureau of Investigation
FCNL	French Committee of National Liberation
FF	Free French
FFI	French Forces of the Interior
FTP	*Francs-Tireurs et Partisans Français* (French Sharpshooters and Partisans)
GCCS	Government Code and Cipher School
GESTAPO	*Geheime Staats Polizei* (Secret State Police)
GHQ	General Headquarters
GOC	General Officer Commanding
GRU	*Glavnoe Razvedivatelnoe Upravlenie* (Chief Administration for Intelligence), Division of the General Staff of the Soviet Army, USSR
IMF	International Monetary Fund
INA	Indian National Army
IRRA	Imperial Rule Assistance Association (Japan)
JCS	Joint Chiefs of Staff
JIC	Joint Intelligence Committee
JPS	Joint Planning Staff
JSC	Joint Security Council
KGB	*Komitet Gossudarstvennoi Bezopastnosti* (Committee of State Security). Russian secret police
LCA	Landing Craft Assault
LCS	London Controlling Section
LRDG	Long-Range Desert Group
LRPG	Long-Range Penetration Group (*see* CHINDITS)
LSD	Landing Ship Dock
LSI	Landing Ship Infantry
MAAF	Mediterranean Allied Air Force
MAC	Mediterranean Air Command
MED	Mediterranean Engineers District
MTO	Mediterranean Theater of Operations
NATO	North Africa Theater of Operations
NEI	Netherlands East Indies
NKVD	*Narodnyi Kommissariat Vnutrennykh Del* (Soviet People's Commissariat of Internal Affairs
OCD	Office of Civilian Defense
OCTA	Office of the Coordinator of Inter-American Affairs
ODT	Office of Defense Transportation
OEM	Office of Emergency Management
OES	Office of Economic Stabilization
OKH	*Oberkommando des Heeres* (High Command of the Army)

OKW	*Oberkommando der Wehrmacht* (High Command of the Armed Forces)
OPA	Office of Price Administration
OPM	Office of Production Management
OSRD	Office of Scientific Research and Development
OSS	Office of Strategic Services
OWI	Office of War Information
OWM	Office of War Mobilization
PCNL	Polish Committee of National Liberation
PT	U.S. motor torpedo boat
PWE	Political Warfare Executive
RAAF	Royal Australian Air Force
RAF	Royal Air Force
RCAF	Royal Canadian Air Force
RFSS	*Reichsführer SS* (Reich Leader *SS*—Heinrich Himmler)
RN	Royal Navy
RSHA	*Reichssicherheitshauptamt* (Reich Security Office)
SA	*Sturmabteilungen* (Storm Troopers)
SACEUR	Supreme Allied Commander in Europe
SACMED	Supreme Allied Commander, Mediterranean Theater
SAS	Special Air Service
S-BOOT	German motor torpedo boat
SCAEF	Supreme Commander of Allied Expeditionary Force
SCAP	Supreme Commander of Allied Powers
SD	*Sicherheitsdienst* (Security Service)
SEAC	Southeast Asia Command
SHSAC	Supreme Headquarters of Supreme Allied Commander
SIS	*Servizio Informazione Segneto* (Secret Information Service), Italy
SOE	Special Operations Executive
SOS	Service of Supply
SS	*Schutzstaffel* (Elite Guard)
TAF	Tactical Air Force
UP	United Press
USAAF	U.S. Army Air Forces
USMC	U.S. Marine Corps
USN	U.S. Navy
USO	United Service Organizations
USS	U.S. Ship
USSTAF	U.S. Strategic Air Force
WAAC	Women's Auxiliary Army Corps
WAAF	Women's Auxiliary Air Force
WAC	Women's Army Corps
WAFFEN-SS	Armed *SS*

WAFS	Women's Auxiliary Ferrying Squadron
WASP	Women's Air Force Service Pilot
WAVE	Women Accepted for Voluntary Emergency Service (Navy)
WMC	War Manpower Commission
WPB	War Production Board
WPD	War Plans Division
WRNS	Women's Royal Naval Service
WSA	War Shipping Administration

LOUIS L. SNYDER'S HISTORICAL GUIDE TO WORLD WAR II

THE HISTORICAL GUIDE

A

A-4 ROCKET. German long-range rocket, commonly known as the *V-2*, used late in the war. (*See V-2.*)

AARHUS RAID. An attack by the Royal Air Force (*q.v.*) on *Gestapo* (*q.v.*) headquarters in Copenhagen on October 31, 1944. (*See* SHELL HOUSE RAID.)

ABC PLANS. Plans drafted for cooperation between the United Kingdom and the United States in the event that the U.S. joined the war.

In January–March 1941, at a time when the United States was supposed to be neutral, a staff mission from London visited Washington, D.C., to draw up plans for mutual action in the event that both countries found themselves at war with Germany and with Japan. It was agreed that Germany would be dealt with first, while Japan would be given second priority.

ABWEHR. Secret intelligence and counterespionage agency of the German General Staff.

The term was a popular designation for (*Amt Auslandsnachrichten und Abwehr*), the foreign and counterintelligence department of the High Command. At the head of the *Abwehr* was Adm. Wilhelm Canaris (*q.v.*), who was a leader in the conspiracy against Hitler. He was arrested after the July Plot (*q.v.*) of 1944 against Hitler and was hanged on April 9, 1945. After the arrest of Canaris, Hitler had little faith in the *Abwehr*.

ADMIRAL GRAF SPEE. German pocket battleship (*Panzerschiff*) scuttled in Montevideo harbor in late 1939.

DESIGN. Symbol of Hitler's rising naval power, the *Graf Spee* was named for Graf Maximilian von Spee (1861–1914), German naval hero of World War I who went down with his flagship in the Battle of the Falkland Islands on December 8, 1914. With her sister ships the *Lützow* (originally named

5

Deutschland) and the *Admiral Scheer*, the *Graf Spee* was the third and last of the German pocket battleships designed to circumvent the Treaty of Versailles.

Speedy, heavily armored, the *Graf Spee* had the weight of a cruiser but the firing power of a battleship. As long as three New York City blocks and as wide as a four-lane superhighway, she could outrun any warship she could not outshoot. German technicians made her a miracle of naval construction. When she was launched at Wilhelmshaven in 1934, a correspondent of *The New York Times* reported: "She was a sight to stir a seaman's heart—the lean strength of her fine flowing lines and her unbroken main deck sweeping abaft the after turret."

SPECIFICATIONS.
   Measurements. Length 609.3 ft.
   Standard Displacement. Over 12,000 tons.
   Maximum Speed. 28 knots.
   Armor. 4-in. side with 1.5-in. internally.
   Armament. Six 11-in. Krupp guns, firing a 670-lb. projectile at a range of 30,000 yds. at
      full 60° elevation. Guns mounted in two triple turrets, one fore, one aft. Eight 5.9-in.
      50 cal. in single mounts behind armored shields.
   Complement. 1,107 on final voyage.
   Special Features. Carried fuel of 3,500 tons of diesel oil; two seaplanes and one catapult;
      external bulges; horsepower 54,000; complete underwater protection.

RAIDER. Between August 21 and 24, just a few days before the outbreak of World War II, the *Graf Spee* moved into the Atlantic before the British blockade and northern patrols were organized. She crossed the North Atlantic trade routes undetected and accompanied by an auxiliary vessel to replenish fuel and stores. Soon she was far south of the Azores. On September 30, 1939, she sank the British liner *Clement* off the coast of Brazil. Hurried into action by the unwelcome news, the British Admiralty immediately ordered hunting groups, comprising 23 powerful ships, to search for the *Graf Spee* and the *Lützow*.

The *Graf Spee* became the terror of the South Atlantic. Between September 30 and early December 1939 she sank nine British ships. Under Capt. Hans Langsdorff, described by Churchill as "a high-class person," she would make a brief appearance at one point, claim a victim, and then vanish. The South American countries had drawn a safety belt of 300 miles off their shores, an area into which no belligerent ship was supposed to enter, but Adm. Erich Raeder (*q.v.*), Commander-in-Chief of the German Navy, undoubtedly under Hitler's orders, paid no attention to the safety belt.

BRITISH REACTION. For the British Admiralty the *Graf Spee* in South American waters posed a serious problem. The Admiralty assigned Commodore Henry Harwood to special duty to cover British shipping off the River Plate and Rio de Janeiro. It also gave permission to authorities in Brazilian ports to sell British fuel to German merchant ships in the hope that these fuel-laden freighters would lead British shadowing warships to German raiders being refueled at sea.

When Harwood received word that the British ship *Doric Star* had been sunk by the *Graf Spee* on the Cape-Freetown route on December 2, 1939, he was convinced that sooner or later the German raider would come toward the Plate to sink the rich prizes waiting for her there. It was an accurate guess, even though at the time the *Graf Spee* was more than 3,000 miles away.

TRAP. To await the *Graf Spee,* Harwood, on orders of the Admiralty, deployed a force of three cruisers, the *Exeter* (8,390 tons), the *Achilles* (7,030 tons), and the *Ajax* (6,985 tons), plus several smaller ships. The task force moved to the center of the shipping routes off the mouth of the river. Harwood guessed that the *Graf Spee* might arrive by December 13.

ACTION. At 6:14 A.M. on December 13, 1939, British lookouts sighted smoke to the east. The moment for collision had come. Harwood ordered his cruisers to attack the German ship from divergent quarters and thereby confuse her fire. Langsdorff, mistakenly believing he was facing a light cruiser and two accompanying destroyers, ordered full speed ahead. When he recognized the strength of his opponents, it was too late.

From the beginning of the fight salvoes from the *Exeter* struck the *Graf Spee*. Meanwhile other cruisers also hit hard and effectively. Below deck on the German pocket battleship some 60 British seamen, who had been captured by the German raider, cheered lustily as shells rained on the decks above them. Soon the *Exeter* received a direct hit that temporarily put her out of action. At the critical moment Langsdorff turned away to strike at the other ships, a move that gave respite to the hard-pressed *Exeter*.

The *Graf Spee* was doing well in the confrontation, but Langsdorff feared that heavier British battlewagons were in the vicinity. He turned away with the apparent intention of seeking a haven. Aboard, 30 of his crew had been killed and 60 wounded. The *Ajax* and *Achilles* continued the attack despite considerable damage inflicted by the big guns of the *Graf Spee*. To this point the action had lasted one hour and 20 minutes.

MONTEVIDEO. Shortly after midnight, the *Graf Spee* entered Montevideo harbor. Damage crews were set to work; the wounded were landed; stores were taken aboard; reports were sent to Hitler. Langsdorff asked Uruguayan authorities for 15 days to complete needed repairs, but he was informed that he had to leave within two days or be interned with his crew. He protested the decision and ordered that supplies be taken to his ship from the German merchant ship *Tacoma*.

Meanwhile, both the British Admiralty and the German Naval Command were busily at work. London ordered the *Ajax* and *Achilles* to lay outside the harbor and wait for the German ship. At the same time it dispatched the cruiser *Cumberland* from the Falklands to replace the battered *Exeter*. British radio staff filled the air with crackling messages to and from non-existent cruisers "converging on the spot." Langsdorff was convinced that he would soon be the victim of an overwhelming British naval force.

Langsdorff cabled to his base that escape was impossible. At a conference presided over by Hitler, it was decided to advise Langsdorff to extend the time in neutral waters, fight through to Buenos Aires if possible, not to accept internment in Uruguay, and attempt effective destruction if the ship was scuttled.

SCUTTLING. Langsdorff decided with bitterness that the Uruguayan refusal "makes it necessary for me to sink my ship near the coast and save my crew." On the afternoon of December 17, he transferred 700 men to the *Tacoma*. At 6:15 P.M., watched by enormous crowds ashore, the *Graf Spee* weighed anchor, left harbor, and steamed slowly seaward. Before she reached the three-mile limit, she suddenly stopped and the tugboats accompanying her moved away. There were bursts of flames as explosions shattered the hull of the ship. Within three minutes she sank to the bottom of the harbor.

SIGNIFICANCE. The scuttling of the *Graf Spee* was one of the first great sensations of the war. Langsdorff and his crew were immediately interned. Deeply distressed by the loss of his ship, Langdorff wrapped himself in the flag of the Imperial Navy and shot a bullet into his head.

Thus ended Germany's first surface challenge to the British Navy. It also effectively demolished the "pocket battleship myth," for the *Graf Spee* was not fast enough to evade British cruisers. For the British public it was a comforting victory at a time when news from the battlefronts was discouraging.

Bibliography. E. P. Von den Porten, *The German Navy in World War II* (1969); and P. Kemp, *Victory at Sea* (1976).

ADMIRAL HIPPER. German heavy cruiser, named after Adm. Franz von Hipper, of World War I Battle of Jutland fame.

DESIGN. Construction on the *Hipper* began on January 18, 1935, and she was launched in 1937. Together with her sister ships, the *Prinz Eugen* and the *Blücher*, she was designed to add strength to the new German Navy. Throughout her career she was burdened by faulty engines.

WORLD WAR II. In December 1940 the *Hipper* slipped unnoticed through the Denmark Strait to prey on merchant ships in the North Atlantic. Thereafter, she became a constant threat to Channel shipping and Mediterranean-bound convoys. From February 1 to 15, 1941, she sank 7 out of 9 ships in an unescorted North Atlantic convoy. In February 1942 she was chased away by a Royal Navy escort of an Arctic convoy, a defeat that led to the retirement of Adm. Erich Raeder (*q.v.*). In July 1942 she operated with the *Tirpitz* (*q.v.*) against Convoy *PQ-17* (*q.v.*). In December 1942 she was badly damaged by a British task force. On May 3, 1945, after suffering heavy bombing damage, she was scuttled in Kiel.

SPECIFICATIONS.
  Measurements. Length 655 ft.; beam 69 ft. 11 in.
  Displacement. Standard 10,000 tons; actual 14,000 tons.
  Maximum Speed. 32 knots.
  Armor. Belt: 4 in.
  Armament. Eight 8-in. guns in twin turrets; twelve 4-in. guns; twelve antiaircraft guns.
  Special Features. One catapult; three seaplane scouts.

ADMIRAL SCHEER. German pocket battleship (*Panzerschiff*), sister to the *Lützow* (ex-*Deutschland*) and the *Admiral Graf Spee* (*q.v.*).

DESIGN. Construction of the *Scheer* began on September 6, 1931, and was completed on November 12, 1934. Because Article 181 of the Treaty of Versailles limited the German Navy to six battleships, the *Scheer* was designed as a battleship with the 10,000-ton weight of a cruiser.

WORLD WAR II. On November 5, 1940, the *Admiral Scheer,* on patrol in the North Atlantic, attacked an Allied convoy homeward bound from Halifax, Nova Scotia, sinking five merchant ships and her sole escort. The Royal Navy auxiliary cruiser *Jervis* sacrificed herself by holding the *Scheer* while the convoy scattered. (*See* JERVIS BAY.) In mid-January 1941 the *Scheer* captured three British freighters. Later she was sent to Norway where she was assigned to training duty. She was sunk by RAF (*q.v.*) bombers in Kiel, her home port, on April 8, 1945.

SPECIFICATIONS.
  Measurements. Length 617 ft. 8 in.; beam 71 ft. 1 in.
  Displacement. Standard 10,000 tons; actual 13,483.
  Maximum Speed. 28 knots.
  Armor. Belt: 4 in. tapering to 2 in. foreward and aft.
  Armament. Six 11-in. guns in triple turrets; eight 5 ft. 9 in.; fourteen antiaircraft guns.
  Special Features. One catapult; two float planes.

AFRICA, NORTH, CAMPAIGNS IN. *See* NORTH AFRICA, CAMPAIGNS IN and *TORCH.*

AFRIKA KORPS (DEUTSCHES AFRIKA KORPS-DAK). German elite motorized force that took part in the North African campaign from 1941 to 1943. It was the nucleus of and component of Gen. Erwin Rommel's (*q.v.*) later Italo-German *Panzer* Army.

Under Rommel's command the *Afrika Korps* arrived in Tripoli in February

1941 and speedily changed Axis fortunes there. At the time Rommel had only two units, which he hurried to the front. In mid-March the first *Panzer* (tank) regiment arrived on the scene. Within a fortnight it altered the balance in favor of the Axis, driving the British to their Egyptian bases and besieging the garrison left at Tobruk.

Then began a seesaw struggle between the *Afrika Korps* and the British 8th Army. (*See* EIGHTH ARMY.) In December 1941 the British struck and forced the Germans back to El Agheila, liberating Tobruk in the process. In early 1942 the *Afrika Korps* moved again. In a slashing counterattack, it took Tobruk and went on toward Egypt. On October 23, 1942, the British under Gen. Bernard Law Montgomery (*q.v.*) struck at El Alamein (*q.v.*) and finally inflicted a disastrous defeat on the *Afrika Korps*.

Bibliography. K. J. Macksey, *Afrika Korps* (1972).

AIRCRAFT. (See Aircraft Data Charts, pp. 9–19.)

ALAMEIN, BATTLE OF. *See* EL ALAMEIN, BATTLE OF.

ALEUTIAN ISLANDS CAMPAIGNS. Struggle in 1942–1943 between the Japanese and Americans for control of the northern flank in the Pacific.

BACKGROUND. The Aleutian Islands, a chain extending about 1,100 miles southwest from the peninsula of Alaska toward Kamchatka, did not seem to have any strategic importance because the bitterly cold climate and the barren, rocky land made air bases of dubious value. Both sides, however, were aware that occupation of the islands would put Japan within 1,000 miles of the Alaskan Peninsula. Americans wanted the psychological assurance that California would be safe from enemy attack.

JAPANESE OCCUPATION. In early June 1942, as a cover for the Midway (*q.v.*) operation, the Japanese sent out a task force whose planes made a diversionary raid on Dutch Harbor at the eastern end of the archipelago. At the same time they sent two landing forces to take Attu and Kiska, westernmost of the fogbound Aleutians, American territory nearest to Japan (1,200 miles). Because of the humiliating defeat at Midway, Tokyo's propaganda machine proclaimed the Aleutian operation highly successful.

COUNTERATTACK. The Americans countered by the rapid construction of an air station on one of the Andreanof group at Adak, 200 miles east of Kiska. American bombers frequently bombed Kiska, but for the moment little more could be done because American naval, land, and air strength was concentrated in the Southwest Pacific. In January 1943 the Americans set up another air base at Amchitka, 90 miles east of Kiska. The goal was to recapture the only U.S.-owned territories in North America that had fallen to the Japanese.

AMERICAN AIRCRAFT DATA CHART

Name	Nickname	Category	Manufacturer	Wing Span	Length	Height	Engine	Top Speed	Ceiling	Range	Armament	Bomb Load
P-38 Lightning	"Three Bullets on a Knife"	Fighter	Lockheed	52'	37' 10"	9' 10"	2 Allison	415	39,000	1200	1 20mm. cannon; 4 fixed .50	1000
P-39 Airacobra	"Flying Bullet"	Pursuit	Bell	34'	29' 9"	9' 3"	1 Allison	394	35,000	675	1 37mm. cannon; 6 fixed .50	500
P-40 Warhawk	"Sharkmouth"	Fighter	Curtiss	37'4"	31' 9"	10' 7"	1 Allison	360	34,400	910	4 fixed .50	720
P-47 Thunderbolt	"Supercharged Milk Bottle"	Fighter	Republic	40' 10"	35' 4"	12' 5"	1 Pratt & Whitney	430	45,000	750	6 fixed .50	
P-51 Mustang	"Rodeo Special"	Fighter	North American	37'	32' 3"	8'	1 Rolls-Royce Merlin	400	30,000	500	6 fixed .50	1,000
A-20 Havoc or Boston	"Junior B-17"	Light Bomber-Fighter	Douglas	61' 4"	48'	17' 11"	2 Wright Cyclone	337	24,000	1010	6 fixed .50; 3 flex. .50	1000-2000
A-29 Hudson	"Old Boomerang"	Light Bomber	Lockheed	65' 6"	44' 4"	11' 10"	2 Pratt & Whitney	275	24,500	2090	2 fixed .50; 2 flex. .50	1200
A-30 Baltimore	"Maryland Mosquito"	Light Bomber	Martin	61' 4"	48' 6"	17' 8"	2 Wright Cyclone	315	22,000		4 fixed .30; 8 flex. .30	1500
A-35 Vengeance	"Bat Wing"	Dive Bomber	Vultee	48'	40'	12' 10"	1 Wright Cyclone	280	20,000	1200	4 fixed .50; 1 flex. .50	1000-2000
B-25 Mitchell	"Twin-Breasted Gull"	Medium Bomber	North American	67' 6"	54' 1"	15' 9"	2 Wright-Cyclone	300	25,000	2050	1 fixed .50; 5 flex. .50	2000-5900

AMERICAN AIRCRAFT DATA CHART *Continued*

Name	Nickname	Category	Manufacturer	Wing Span	Length	Height	Engine	Top Speed	Ceiling	Range	Armament	Bomb Load
B-26 Marauder	"White Owl Cigar"	Medium Bomber	Martin	71'	58' 3"	21' 6"	2 Pratt & Whitney	300	23,000	1840	4 fixed .50; 7 flex. .50	2000-5800
B-34 Ventura	"Bite in the Belly"	Medium Bomber	Vega	65' 6"	51' 5"	11' 10"	2 Pratt & Whitney	300	32,000	2000	2 fixed .50; 2 flex. .50; 2 fixed .30; 2 flex. .30	1750-2500
B-17 Flying Fortress	"The Big Tale"	Heavy Bomber	Boeing	103' 10"	74' 9"	19' 1"	4 Wright-Cyclone	310	35,000	2000	10 flex. .50	5000-15200
B-24 Liberator	"Flying Prostitute" (no visible means of support)	Heavy Bomber-Transport	Consolidated	110'	66'	18'	4 Pratt & Whitney	310	30,000	3100	9 flex. .50	4000-15200
B-29 Superfortress		Heavy Bomber	Boeing	141.2'	76' 4"	19' 1"	4 Wright radial	358	30,000	5333	12 .50; 20mm. cannon	20000
C-46 Commando	"Moby Dick"; "Flying Whale"	Transport; glider tug	Curtiss	108'	64' 5"	16' 11"	2 Pratt & Whitney	310	25,000	2500		
C-47 Skytrain	"Stream-liner"	Transport; glider tug	Douglas	95'	93' 10"	27' 9"	2 Pratt & Whitney	230	23,700	2125		
C-54 Skymaster	"Flying Pullman"	Transport	Douglas	117' 6"	49' 9"	11' 10"	4 Pratt & Whitney	282	22,200	2080		
C-60 Lode-star		Transport	Lockheed	65' 6"			2 Wright-Cyclone	265	30,000	2000		

S03C Seagull	"Eyes of the Fleet"	Reconnaissance	Curtiss	28'	35' 8"	16' 7"	1 Ranger	190	23,000	1200	1 fixed .30; 1 flex. .30	200–650
OS2U Kingfisher	"Three-braced Floater"	Reconnaissance	Vought Sikorsky	35' 11"	33' 10"	15'	1 Pratt & Whitney	170	13,900	1200	1 fixed .30; 1 flex. .30	200–650
F4F Wildcat	"Shorty Stubb"	Fighter	Grumman	38'	28' 11"	9' 2"	1 Wright-Cyclone	310	27,000	925	4 fixed .50	
F6F Hellcat		Fighter	Grumman	42' 10"	33' 6¼"		1 Pratt & Whitney	400				
F4U Corsair	"Upside Down Bird"; "Leon Errol"	Fighter	Vought Sikorsky	41'	33' 4"	16' 1"	1 Pratt & Whitney	400	34,200	970	6 fixed .50	
SBD Dauntless	"Coco Cola Bottle"	Dive Bomber	Douglas	41' 6"	32' 1"	12' 11"	1 Wright-Cyclone	252	25,200	975	2 fixed .50	700–1600
SB2A Buccaneer	"Long Greenhouse"	Scout and Dive Bomber	Brewster	47'	39' 1"	10' 10"	1 Wright-Cyclone	314	25,600	950	4 fixed .50; 1 flex. .50	500–1000
SB2C Helldiver	"Pepsi Cola Bottle"	Dive Bomber	Curtiss	49' 9"	36' 8"		1 Wright-Cyclone	304	23,000	1200	2 20mm. cannon; 1 flex..50	300–1000
TBF Avenger	"Tin Bellied Fish"	Torpedo Bomber	Grumman	54' 2"	40'	16' 5"	1 Wright-Cyclone	253	21,700	1000	1 flex. .50; 1 fixed .30; 1 flex. .30	2000–3000
PBY Catalina	"The Cat"; "Skinny Legs"	Patrol Bomber	Consolidated	104'	63' 10"	19' 8"	2 Pratt & Whitney	184	19,000	1000	2 flex. .50; 2 flex. .30	2000–4000
PB2Y Coronado	"Seagoing B-24"	Patrol Bomber	Consolidated	115'	79' 3"	27' 6"	4 Pratt & Whitney	225	19,700	4000	6 fixed .50	8000–10000
PBM Mariner	"Cross-eyed Tail"	Patrol Bomber-Transport	Martin	118'	80'	27' 6"	2 Wright-Cyclone	210	19,000	1825	8 fixed .50	4000

BRITISH AIRCRAFT DATA CHART

Name	Nickname	Category	Manufacturer	Wing Span	Length	Height	Engine	Top Speed	Ceiling	Range	Armament	Bomb Load
Spitfire	"Straight Nose"; "Guardian Angel"	Fighter	Supermarine	36' 10"	29' 11"	11' 5"	1 Rolls Royce	406	40,700	472	2 20mm. cannon; 4 fixed .303	500–1000
Hurricane	"Flying Humpback"	Fighter	Hawker	40'	31' 5"	13' 2"	1 Rolls Royce	335	36,600	540	4 20mm. cannon; 12 fixed .303	
Typhoon	"Cleaned Up Hurricane"	Fighter	Hawker	41'	32'		1 Napier Sab.	414	34,600	610	2 20mm. cannon	
Wellington	"Flying Basket"	Medium Bomber	Vickers-Armstrong	86'	61' 3"	17' 5"	2 Bristol	265	24,000	1490	7 fixed .303	4500
Halifax	"Halibag"	Heavy Bomber	Handley-Page	99'	70' 1"	21' 7"	4 Rolls Royce	270	23,000	1810	6 flex. .303	4950–13000
Stirling	"Flying Florist Box"; "Dachshund"	Heavy Bomber	Short	99'	87' 3"		4 Bristol	285	22,000	2000	10 flex. .303	5000–14000
Lancaster	"Lank"	Heavy Bomber	Avro	102'	69' 4"	20'	4 Rolls Royce	291	25,000	1075	10 flex. .303	3900–12750
Beaufighter	"Tank Buster"; "Barney Ross"	Night Fighter	Bristol	57' 10"	41' 6"		2 Bristol	333	28,000	880	4 fixed .50; 6 fixed .303	

Beaufort	"Rhineland Castle"	Torpedo Bomber	Bristol	58'	44' 2"		2 Bristol	275	17,000	1510	6 fixed .303 2 flex. .303	1000–2000
Blenheim	"Tank-Buster"; "Streamlined Bristol"	Medium Bomber	Bristol	56' 4"	42' 9"	9' 10"	2 Bristol	244	19,500	1230	3 fixed .50; 2 fixed .303	1000–1600
Mosquito	"Wooden Wonder"; Flying Champagne Glass"	Night Fighter	DeHavilland	54' 2"	40' 9"	15' 3"	2 Rolls Royce	379	29,500	1700	4 fixed .50; 4 fixed .303	2000–2500
Sunderland	"Pregnant Motorboat"	Patrol Bomber	Short	112' 9"	85' 4"	32' 11"	4 Bristol	264	18,500	2850	7 flex. .303	1900–4000

GERMAN AIRCRAFT DATA CHART

Name	Category	Manufacturer	Wing Span	Length	Engine	Top Speed	Ceiling	Range	Armament	Bomb Load
Me-109	Fighter	Messerschmitt	32' 9"	29' 10"	1 Daimler-Benz	370	38,000	360–1030	2 7.9; 1 2mm. cannon	1100
Ju-87 Stuka	Attack and Dive Bomber	Junkers	45' 4"	35' 6"	1 Junkers Juno	242	27,000	500	3 7.9 guns	1320
FW-190	Fighter	Focke-Wulf	34' 6"	29' 1"	1 BMW	392	36,000	380–820	2 7.9 guns; 1 20mm. cannon	
Me-110	Fighter-Bomber	Messerschmitt	53' 5"	40'	2 Daimler-Benz	365	34,000	740	5 7.9 guns; 2 20mm. cannon	
He-111	Dive Bomber	Heinkel	73' 11"	53' 8"	2 Daimler-Benz	255	26,000	2140	2 7.7 guns	5500
Ju-88	Medium Bomber-Fighter	Junkers	65' 6"	47' 2"	2 Daimler-Benz	321	32,200	1620	3 7.9 guns; 3 20mm. cannon	2200
He-177	Heavy Bomber	Heinkel	103' 4"	67' 3"	2 Daimler-Benz	295	23,500	3400	15mm. or 20mm. cannon	2200–16000
Do-217	Heavy Bomber	Dornier	62' 5"	56' 6"	2 BMWs	309	29,000	2150	1 20mm. Oerlikon; 5 varied machine guns	4400–5500
He-115	Torpedo Bomber-Reconnaissance	Heinkel	72' 10"	56' 8"	Twin radial	206	27,000			
D-26	Patrol Bomber	Dornier	98' 6"	80' 6"	4 Diesel in tandem	200	16,000			
Ju-52	Transport-Glider Tug	Junkers	95' 11"	62'	3 BMWs	207	21,000	250–780	2 7.9mm. guns	
FW-200	Heavy Bomber-Transport	Focke-Wulf	108'	78' 3"	4 BMWs	279	30,000	4000	4 7.9 guns; 1 20mm. cannon	3300–11000

Arado-196	Reconnaissance	Arado	41'	36'1"	1	195	21,500			
HA-138	Patrol Bomber	Blohm & Voss	88' 7"	65' 5"	2	170	18,000			7700
Ju-90	Transport-Heavy Bomber	Junkers	115' 6"	85'	4 radial or in-line	260	15,000	1960		22000 cargo
Ju-290	Transport-Heavy Bomber	Junkers	137' 6"	90'	4 radial	270	22,000	1700		5300 freight
Gotha-242	Glider	Gotha	79'	52' 6"		149 (towing speed)				
Me-210	Fighter-Light Bomber	Messerschmitt	53' 6"	40' 3"	2	368	28,500			3300
FW-189	Reconnaissance	Focke-Wulf	60' 4"	39' 4"	2	210	27,550	620	5 7.9	440

ITALIAN AIRCRAFT DATA CHART

Name	Category	Manufacturer	Wing Span	Length	Engine	Top Speed	Ceiling
Fiat G-50	Fighter	Fiat	35' 9"	25' 6"	1 radial	300	32,500
Mc-202	Fighter	Macchi	34' 8"	29' 1"	1 in-line	360	36,000
Re-2001	Fighter	Reggiane	36'	27' 4"	1 in-line	350	34,000
SM-79	Medium Bomber-Transport	Savoia-Marchetti	69' 6"	54' 6"	3 radial	255	23,000
Z-1007	Medium Bomber	Cantiere	81' 10"	61' 3"	3 radial	280	26,500
Br-20	Medium Bomber	Fiat	70' 6"	52' 10"	2 radial	255	25,000

JAPANESE AIRCRAFT DATA CHART

Name	Category	Manufacturer	Wing Span	Length	Engine	Top Speed	Ceiling	Range	Armament	Bomb Load
NATE Type 97-F	Fighter	Nakajima	35' 10"	24' 4"	1 radial	280	33,000		4 7.7	
ZEKE (ZERO) Type 0 MK-1F	Fighter	Mitsubishi	39' 5"	30' 3"	1 Mitsubishi Sakae 12	345	38,500	750	2 fixed 7.7; 1 20mm. cannon	Normally none
RUFE Type 0 MK-1F	Fighter-Reconnaissance	Mitsubishi	39' 5"	30' 3"	1 radial	326	38,500			
HAP Type 0 MK-2F	Fighter	Mitsubishi	36'	28"	1 Nakajima	338	38,800		2 7.7; 2 20mm. cannon	
TONY	Fighter		38' 5"	30'	1 in-line	363	37,500		2 12.7	
OSCAR	Fighter	Nakajima	37' 7"	28' 7"	1 radial	342	17,000		2 7.7	
KATE Type 97 MK-3TB	Torpedo Bomber	Nakajima	52'	34'	1 radial	225	27,000	495	2 fixed 7.7; 1 flex. 7.7	
VAL Type 99 DB	Dive Bomber	Aichi	47' 7"	32' 10"	1 Mitsubishi radial Golden Star	240	26,000	875	2 fixed 7.7; 1 flex. 7.7	814
NELL Type 96 MK-4MB	Medium Bomber	Mitsubishi	82'	54'	2 underslung	225	28,000		5 7.7; 1 20mm. cannon	
SALLY Type 97 MB	Medium Bomber	Mitsubishi	72'	52'	2 Mitsubishi radial Golden Star	230	22,000	1850	4 flex. 7.7	2000–4400
BETTY Type 1 MB	Medium Bomber	Mitsubishi	79' 8"	66' 5"	2 radial Mitsubishi Mars	273	30,000	1450	3 flex. 7.7; 1 20mm. cannon	1700–2000
LILY	Medium Bomber		56' 11"	47' 3"	2 underslung	278	28,000			800
DAVE Type 95 O-F/P	Reconnaissance	Nakajima	36'	28' 4"	1 radial	225	23,000		1 fixed 7.7; 1 flex. 7.7	500

JAPANESE AIRCRAFT DATA CHART *Continued*

Name	Category	Manufacturer	Wing Span	Length	Engine	Top Speed	Ceiling	Range	Armament	Bomb Load
MAVIS Type 97 F/B	Patrol Bomber	Kawanishi	131'	82'	4	205	25,000		4 7.7	3300
TOPSY	Transport	Mitsubishi	74'	25' 8"	2	266	23,000	1020		
PETE Type 0 O-F/P	Reconnaissance	Sasebo	37'	34' 6"	1 radial	198	29,000		1 fixed 7.7; 1 flex. 7.7	500
DINAH	Reconnaissance		50' (est.)	68' (est.)	2 radial	343	34,700			
JAKE	Reconnaissance- Bomber	Aichi and Watanabe	47' 6"	35' 4"	1 radial	216	24,400		1 7.7	520
EMILY	Patrol Bomber		118'	90'	4 radial					

RUSSIAN AIRCRAFT DATA CHART

Name	Category	Manufacturer	Wing Span	Length	Engine	Top Speed	Ceiling
YAK-1 (I-26)	Fighter	State-Russia	32' 10"	27' 11"	1 in-line; probably Hispano-Suiza type	435	30,000
MIG-3 (I-18)	Fighter	State-Russia	34' 6"	26' 8"	1 in-line	375	34,000
I-16	Fighter	State-Russia	29' 2"	20' 4"	1 radial	300	32,000
Il-2 STORMOVIK	Fighter-Bomber	State-Russia	47' 11"	38'	1 in-line	275	28,000
PE-2	Attack Bomber	State-Russia	56' 1"	41' 5"	2 in-line	300	32,000
DB-3F	Medium Bomber	State-Russia	70' 2"	47' 7"	2 radial	295	29,000
SB-3	Medium Bomber	State-Russia	66' 11"	21'	2 liquid-cooled	360	28,000
YAK-4	Light Bomber	State-Russia	45' 11"	32' 10"	2 in-line	320	27,500
SU-2	Attack Bomber	State-Russia	47' 2"	31' 10"	1 radial	320	27,500
TB-7	Heavy Bomber	State-Russia	131' 2"	73' 10"	4 in-line	275	36,000

American strategy called for bypassing Kiska and an assault on Attu. On May 11, 1943, two U.S. forces landed on Attu, where the defending Japanese were entrenched on mountainsides covered by tundra and snow and protected by land mines and booby traps. The Americans suffered heavy casualties, but by June 3 they had wiped out most of the Japanese garrison.

The capture of Attu resulted in the biggest *banzai* charge (*q.v.*) of the war. In a grotesquely carnal scene, frustrated Japanese made a last suicide attack on the American lines. Hundreds of Japanese pressed hand grenades against their bodies. Only a few snipers managed to escape to the hills. About 2,350 Japanese were killed and only 28 captured alive. The Americans lost 550 killed and more than 1,000 wounded, in addition to many casualties due to cold conditions.

EVACUATION. The capture of Attu meant the isolation of Kiska, the main Japanese base in the islands 170 miles to the east. After preliminary bombardment, a strong Allied force (29,000 Americans, 5,300 Canadians) invaded Kiska on August 15, 1943. In what seemed to be a magic trick but what was actually a combination of daring, American bungling, and the Aleutian fog, the Japanese evacuated 5,183 officers, men, and civilians. Within a few hours the garrison successfully avoided American scouting planes and a destroyer blockade and vanished under cover of the mid-summer fog.

SIGNIFICANCE. The Aleutians were finally cleared, but it had taken a large ground force, supported by strong naval and air forces, to accomplish the task. Some military experts criticized the operations in the Aleutians as trivial and useless. Others judged that this diversionary attack forced the enemy to abandon an early conquest and that the threat to Alaska and the West Coast was now removed.

Bibliography. B. Garfield, *The Thousand-Mile War: World War II in Alaska and the Aleutians* (1969).

ALEXANDER, FIELD MARSHAL, SIR HAROLD (1891-1969). One of the war's outstanding commanders, who played an important role in virtually every Allied operation involving British troops.

Maj. Gen. Alexander commanded the 1st Division of the British Expeditionary Force (BEF) in France in 1939. With great skill and gallantry he covered the final stages of the Dunkirk evacuation (*q.v.*) in 1940. After holding the Southern Command for a time, he was appointed to head the army in Burma. In August 1942 he was named to succeed Gen. Claude Auchinleck (*q.v.*) as Commander-in-Chief Middle East.

Alexander's planning contributed much to the great victory of the British 8th Army under Gen. Bernard Law Montgomery at the Battle of El Alamein (*qq.v.*), which led to a reversal of the situation in Libya and Egypt. Alexander commanded the 18th Army Group in Tunisia when the entire Axis army was destroyed or taken prisoner. As deputy to Gen. Dwight D. Eisenhower (*q.v.*), he helped complete the successful operations in North Africa.

Alexander commanded the Allied armies that defeated the Germans and Italians in Sicily and Italy. After the capture of Rome on June 4, 1944, he was promoted to Field Marshal. In December 1944 he was appointed Supreme Allied Commander of the Mediterranean. In 1945 he launched the final Allied offensive in the Po Valley. On April 29, 1945, he accepted the first unconditional surrender signed by the Germans.

Bibliography. J. North (ed.), *The Alexander Memoirs, 1940–1945* (1962); and W.G.F. Jackson, *Alexander of Tunis as Military Commander* (1971).

ALSOS MISSION. American project for nuclear intelligence.

The Alsos Mission was a cooperative project of the Office for Scientific Research and Development (*q.v.*) and the U.S. Army and Navy. Because of the fear that Germany might succeed in developing an atomic bomb, the Alsos Mission collected information about the development of German nuclear research. It also sent teams to the Continent to take over enemy research installations and capture scientists. (*See also MANHATTAN PROJECT.*)

ALTENFJORD RAID. Attack by British midget submarines on the giant German battleship *Tirpitz* (*q.v.*) in Altenfjord, Norway, in 1943.

BACKGROUND. In January 1942 the *Tirpitz,* one of the heaviest warships ever built, slipped into Norwegian waters and anchored near Trondheim within reach of British land-based bombers. During the next several months, the Royal Air Force (*q.v.*) made five separate attacks on the battleship, only to lose 14 planes on the missions. The Germans then moved the *Tirpitz* to Altenfjord, some 1,000 miles from the nearest British bomber base. British dive-bomber pilots were faced with formidable natural barriers, including snow-streaked cliffs around Altenfjord.

The Germans further fortified the area with an ingenious system of obstacles: an extensive mine field, antisubmarine booms, metal nets hanging from buoys, floodlights, patrol boats with sonar devices, radar warning stations (*see* RADAR, WARTIME), and coastal guns. Two sentry islands and a smoke-screen system protected Altenfjord from air assault.

PREPARATION. For the Allies it became a matter of highest priority that the *Tirpitz* be neutralized. At Altenfjord she was only 50 miles from Allied convoy routes to Murmansk in the Soviet Union, and she posed an immediate threat to that crucial life line. "The whole strategy of the war," said Churchill, "turns at this time on this ship."

In late 1942 the Royal Navy began a project to which the code or cover name *Operation Source* was given. Because a successful air attack was unlikely, it was decided to send a group of midget submarines, called X-craft, through the

German defenses to reach the *Tirpitz*. The crew would place explosive charges under the ship and escape before they exploded. The project would be helped by decoded *Ultra* (*q.v.*) signals.

The Admiralty commissioned Vickers Armstrong to build six midget submarines, which were constructed quickly and delivered in January 1943. These were small, primitive undersea craft, just 51 feet in length, resembling large boilers more than submarines. The aft compartment of each submarine contained the main fan motor run by batteries for underwater propulsion. For surface operation they utilized a 40-horsepower diesel engine taken from a London bus. The small control room housed a mass of equipment including motor controls, hydroplane, periscope, air purifier, pump, and other machinery. From the Wet-and-Dry chamber well forward, a diver could leave or reenter a craft while she was submerged. The forward compartment held the main batteries covered with sleeping pallets. Outside the hull the craft carried two 2-ton detachable bombs to be fired by clockwork fuses, especially designed by British engineer Wallis Barnes. Because their range was only 1,200 miles, X-crafts had to be towed to their target for the 2,000-mile round trip.

CREW. For the crews the Admiralty sent out a call for young officers "who are able to swim" to volunteer for a secret mission. After tests the selected crews were put through a severe training process in six midget subs numbered *X-5* to *X-10*. Donald Cameron (*q.v.*), a 24-year-old Scotsman who had been in the merchant navy since his teens, was given command of *X-6*, and Godfrey Place, a 22-year-old officer, was assigned to *X-7*. Each captain acted as navigator, strategist, and tactician of his craft, and each worked with three crewmen. The men trained diligently from January to late Summer 1943.

RAID. On September 11, 1943, just two days after the *Tirpitz* had returned from the Spitzbergen raid (*q.v.*), the six X-craft, towed by 300-foot nylon towlines, left home port for Norway. For six days the crews endured appalling bouts of seasickness in the rolling craft. The *X-8* had to be scuttled because of mechanical difficulties, and the *X-9* broke loose and sank with its crew. The *X-10*, which was assigned to attack the *Scharnhorst* (*q.v.*) had to abandon the mission. The remaining three continued on.

The three midget craft reached the mine fields on September 17, 1943. They then left their parent submarines and proceeded on their own through the mine fields. Slowly they made their way through a narrow 15-mile funnel of water. Diving to avoid gun batteries and torpedo tubes, they passed the entrance undetected by patrol boats and harbor guns. Heading straight for the *Tirpitz*, the *X-6* and the *X-7* were able to set their charges. Their crews were quickly captured. The *X-5* surfaced to be blown to bits by guns from the *Tirpitz*.

RESULTS. Four explosive charges did tremendous damage to the *Tirpitz*. The warship trembled as oil flowed from her hull and the lower decks were flooded. The damage was so great that repair crews had to be rushed from Germany. Not until April 1944 could the *Tirpitz* be moved south to Tromsö. The Royal Air Force (*q.v.*) completed her destruction on November 12, 1944.

Cameron and Place completed one of the most daring missions of the war. Both were awarded the Victoria Cross, Britain's highest military decoration. Their feat can be compared with the sinking of the *Royal Ark* at Scapa Flow by U-Boat commander Günther Prien (*q.v.*) on October 14, 1939, and the rescue of Mussolini on the Grand Sasso d'Italia in the Abruzzi Apennines on September 13, 1943. (*See* SKORZENY, OTTO.)

Bibliography. T. J. Waldron and J. Gleason, *The Frogmen* (1950); T. N. Gallagher, *X-Craft Raid* .(1963); E. P. Von der Porten, *The German Navy in World War II* (1969); and L. Kennedy, *The Death of the Tirpitz* (1979).

ALTMARK RAID. German supply ship and fleet oiler boarded by the British in 1940 to rescue their comrades.

BACKGROUND. In the early days of the war the German battleship *Admiral Graf Spee* (*q.v.*) roamed the South Atlantic and sank one merchant ship after another. She transferred many of the captured enemy crewmen to her supply ship, the *Altmark,* which was to bring them as prisoners of war to Germany.

ENCOUNTER. In February 1940 the *Altmark* arrived in what was supposed to be neutral Norwegian waters after slipping through the Iceland-Faeroes patrol line. Just south of Bergen she was sighted by British warships. Two destroyers moved in to board the *Altmark,* but her captain refused to stop and instead headed for sanctuary in Jössingfjord. The British destroyer *Cossack,* under command of Capt. Philip Vian (*q.v.*), followed her in, only to be told by the Norwegian authorities that the *Altmark* was unarmed and entitled to use neutral waters. Vian withdrew to ask for instructions from London.

Winston Churchill (*q.v.*), then First Lord of the Admiralty, sent a direct order to Vian to board the *Altmark.* On February 16th the *Cossack* moved into the fjord again. Vian requested the Norwegians to join him in escorting the *Altmark* back to Bergen for inspection. When the Norwegians refused, Vian turned his ship toward the *Altmark.* The *Altmark* attempted to push the destroyer into the shore with her stern, but Vian turned and moved into a position alongside the German ship.

BOARDING. Suddenly a British boarding party leaped to the deck of the *Altmark.* In the encounter six German sailors were killed and six wounded. The British then released 299 men with the cry, "The navy's here!" The prisoners were transferred quickly to the *Cossack* and brought to England.

AFTERMATH. The Norwegian Government protested the British action. It allowed the *Altmark* to return to Germany. An angry Hitler denounced the raid and the British lack of respect for Norwegian neutrality. He overlooked the fact that the *Altmark* with her human cargo was also violating Norwegian waters. Norway, he charged, had revealed herself as Britain's accomplice. He decided to occupy the country as punishment.

The successful venture was greeted by the British public with jubilation. It added immensely to Churchill's popularity and helped pave the way to his post as Prime Minister. Vian's report that the *Altmark* was armed with machine guns contradicted German propaganda that the ship was unarmed.

Bibliography. J.M.K. Srabolgi, *The Battle of the River Plate* (1940); and H. Dau, *Unentdeckt über die Meere: die Fahrt der "Altmark"* (1941).

AMERICA FIRST COMMITTEE. Group organized in the United States to keep the country out of World War II.

BACKGROUND. After September 1939 a bitter debate took place between those who favored and those who opposed American entry into the war. Interventionists believed that it was a struggle between the authoritarian and the democratic ways of life. At first they called for aid to Britain "short of war" and then for outright intervention. Isolationists demanded that the United States avoid taking part in "cynical European quarrels." Among such isolationists were Senator Gerald P. Nye of North Dakota, Senator Burton K. Wheeler of Montana, the La Follette brothers of Wisconsin, Congressman Hamilton Fish of New York, William Randolph Hearst and his newspaper chain, and Col. Robert R. McCormick of the Chicago *Tribune.* They were joined by Norman Thomas, Socialist leader and pacifist, as well as by pro-Germans, Irish, and others who bore grudges against the British.

THE COMMITTEE. The isolationist movement was bolstered by the formation in September 1940 of a well-financed organization that called itself the America First Committee. The committee was headed by Gen. Robert E. Wood, Chairman of Sears, Roebuck Co. Its most important convert was Charles A. Lindbergh, Jr. (*q.v.*). American Public Hero No. 1. Lindbergh spoke for the Committee: "War is not inevitable for this country. Such is defeatism in the true sense. No one can make us fight abroad unless we ourselves are willing to do so. No one will attempt to fight us here if we ourselves as a great nation should be armed. Over a hundred million people in this nation are opposed to entering the war."

AFTERMATH. The America First Committee was disbanded immediately on news of the Japanese attack on Pearl Harbor on December 7, 1941.

Bibliography. W. S. Cole, *America First: The Battle Against Intervention, 1940–41* (1953); and M. F. Stenehjem, *An American First: John T. Flynn and the America First Committee* (c. 1976).

"AMERICAN SHOOTING SEASON." Name given by German submariners to the period beginning in January 1942 when they successfully attacked American shipping. Adm. Karl Doenitz (*q.v.*) sent a half-dozen U-Boats to operate between the St. Lawrence River and Cape Hatteras. Waiting outside American harbors, the U-Boats picked targets, preferably tankers silhouetted by city lights, and sent their deadly torpedoes against them. Other smaller ships were dispatched by gunfire. Shore dwellers heard the explosions and the next day saw bodies and wreckage drift into the shores.

For German submariners it was their second "happy time," almost as successful as the attacks on British shipping off England in 1940. One U-Boat captain sent home an enthusiastic jingle:

> *The new-moon night is black as ink,*
> *Off Hatteras the tankers sink,*
> *While sadly Roosevelt counts the score—*
> *Some fifty thousand tons—by Mohr.*

Much of the German success was due to American negligence in the opening months of war. Continued coastal lighting and radio chatter proved valuable to U-Boat commanders. The Americans soon adopted British tactics—a convoy system, air cover, destroyer escorts—and the submarine menace was eventually overcome.

AMERY, LEOPOLD (1873–1955). British politician noted for his role in the fall of the Chamberlain Government in 1940.

Amery was a strong critic of the Munich Agreement (*q.v.*), which sacrificed Czechoslovakia to Nazi Germany. A supporter of Winston Churchill (*q.v.*), he spoke often in the House of Commons for the rearmament of Britain in the face of Hitler's intransigence. In 1940 he made a devastating attack on Prime Minister Neville Chamberlain (*q.v.*), applying to him Cromwell's bitter injunction to the Long Parliament: "In the name of God, go!" As Secretary of State for India in Churchill's War Cabinet, Amery formulated a plan for India's self-government. In 1945 he was made a Companion of Honour. He died in London on September 16, 1955.

Bibliography. Amery was noted as a writer as well as a politician. Among his many works were *The Times History of the South African War* (1900–1909); *The Empire versus the New Era* (1928); *India and Freedom* (1942); *Thoughts on the Constitution* (1947); *The Elizabethan Spirit* (1948); and *My Political Life* (3 vols., 1953–1955), an account of his professional career.

ANDERS, WLADYSLAW (1892–1970). Polish war leader.

After the invasion of Poland by Germany and the Soviet Union in 1939, Anders was captured by the Russians. Released in 1941, he led Polish prisoners-of-war in Persia, where the British armed them to fight the Germans in the Western Desert. The 2nd Polish Corps, led by Anders, captured Monte Cassino on May 18, 1944, after attempts by other troops had failed. In 1945 the Polish government-in-exile (*see* GOVERNMENTS-IN-EXILE) appointed Anders commander in chief of the Polish Army.

ANDERSON, JOHN (1882–1958). British civil servant and member of the War Cabinet.

As Home Secretary and Minister of Home Security, Anderson gave his name to the inexpensive Anderson shelters (*q.v.*) which were used extensively in the summer of 1940 for protection against air raids. (*See* ANDERSON SHELTER.) He entered the War Cabinet of Prime Minister Winston Churchill (*q.v.*) as Lord President of the Council. From 1940 to 1943 he chaired the committee coordinating economic policy. In 1943 he became the Cabinet representative on the British project for developing the atomic bomb. From 1943 to 1945 he was Chancellor of the Exchequer and in this post inaugurated a pay-as-you-go withholding policy.

Bibliography. See J. Gunther, *Inside Europe* (1940), p. 345, for a sketch of Anderson.

ANDERSON SHELTER. British air-raid refuge.

BACKGROUND. In 1938 the possibility of war brought attention of British officialdom to the fact that tens of thousands of homes had no cellars and those that did were apt to prove death traps. In November 1938 Home Secretary John Anderson (*q.v.*) launched a household word in wartime Britain with his special type of air-raid shelters.

PROTECTION. The Anderson shelter was a simple shell of corrugated steel, 6 feet high, 4½ feet wide, and 6½ feet long. It was designed to support the earth above it and was buried to a depth of 4 feet; at least 15 inches of soil were heaped over its curved roof. In effect the celebrated contraption consisted merely of a few sheets of corrugated iron sunk a few feet into the earth, forming a kind of cubbyhole. People who had their shelters built on sloping ground could gain access quite easily, but others had to slide down a kind of trench to reach the low entry. Inside there was nothing other than the cold steel shell and the feeling of being in a tomb.

Altogether more than 2 million Anderson shelters were built. They were issued free to all those with an income of less than 250 pounds a year and at a charge of 7 pounds for those with larger incomes. During the last months before the outbreak of war, they were universally disliked by Britons who regarded them as "proper death traps."

USE. In the first autumn of the war, however, Anderson shelters, although unpopular, were put to use. Many people went to considerable pains to make their shelters as comfortable and safe as possible, with gay flowers on the outside and ingenious decorations in the interior. Critics still ridiculed them as suited only for growing mushrooms and insisted that they could not possibly take the place of reinforced concrete structures. Defenders claimed that Anderson shelters saved many lives especially in the Battle of Britain (*q.v.*).

ANDRUS, BURTON C. (1893–1977). U.S. Army officer and jailer at Nuremberg and Spandau.

As an army colonel, Andrus was charged with security during the Nuremberg Trials (*q.v.*). He also served as commanding officer at Spandau, the fortress prison in West Berlin at the mouth of the Spree River, where convicted Nazi leaders served their sentences. In the mid-1970s he led an unsuccessful campaign for the release of Rudolf Hess (*q.v.*), the last remaining inmate of Spandau. Later Andrus was a military attaché in Israel and Brazil. He died in Tacoma, Washington, on February 2, 1977.

Bibliography. B. C. Andrus, *The Infamous of Nuremberg* (1969).

ANKARA COMMITTEE. Allied organization responsible for intelligence in the Balkans, the Middle East, and the Eastern Mediterranean. Formed under the authorization of MI-5, the British counterintelligence and security service, the Ankara Committee supervised political warfare, sabotage, and deception in the areas assigned to it. It had a coordinating organization in Turkey. (*See* ESPIONAGE.)

ANZIO ANNIE. Name given by American troops to the German *K5(E)*, 28-cm. railway gun (also called Anzio Express). It was brought into action after the Anglo-American amphibious assault at Anzio. (*See* ANZIO BEACHHEAD.) Several of the huge guns, 28 of which were built, rained heavy shells accurately. The Allied Bomber Command sent aircraft to destroy them, but the missions were unsuccessful. The massive weapons were silenced only when they were surrounded and captured by ground troops.

> *SPECIFICATIONS.*
> *Measurements.* Length 135 ft.; weight 215 tons.
> *Range.* 39 mi.; rocket shells 54 mi.
> *Special Features.* Shell had curved ribs to produce spin.

ANZIO BEACHHEAD. An important subsidiary front in the Allied campaign against the Germans in the Italian Peninsula in early 1944. (*See also* ITALIAN FRONT, CAMPAIGNS ON THE.)

BACKGROUND. In late December 1943 the Allied advance in Italy was practically halted. The Germans held the Gustav Line (*see* DEFENSIVE LINES, GERMAN, CASSINO LINE), a defensive position with Cassino at its center, to hold off an assault on Rome from the south. "The Gustav Line," said Hitler, "must be held at all costs for the sake of the political consequences which would follow a completely successful defense. The *Fuehrer* expects the most bitter struggle for every yard."

The Allied Supreme Command was also interested in the Gustav Line. It devised *Operation Shingle* (*see* CODE NAMES, ALLIED, SHINGLE) as a means of breaking the winter deadlock. Allied forces would make an end run around the Gustav Line followed by a speedy breakthrough to the Alban Hills and the road to Rome. The target was Anzio, ancient Antinum, a popular coastal resort on the Tyrrhenian Sea, 33 miles south of Rome.

ASSAULT. On January 22, 1944, under an umbrella of bombers, 50,000 U.S. and British troops landed on the beaches of Anzio. The 1st British Division went ashore just north of Anzio, while the U.S. 3rd Division landed south of Nettuno. Within a few days 70,000 men and 18,000 vehicles were on the beaches. But instead of proceeding inland, the Allied forces paused to consolidate their beachheads. That was a nearly fatal mistake.

REACTION. The Germans were caught by surprise but recovered quickly. Opposed to a general withdrawal, Field Marshal Albert Kesselring (*q.v.*) reacted with a display of unexpected strength. Within days he had three Axis divisions across bridges that the Allies believed they had destroyed. The Germans commanded the heights around the beachheads and gradually increased their forces to eight divisions. They trapped the Allied troops on the open, rocky beaches with no place to hide. It was almost impossible to build foxholes, and those that were finished were soon filled with water. Allied troops were protected only by a few buildings that had escaped destruction. Meanwhile, the *Luftwaffe* (*q.v.*) rained death from the skies and German *88s* (*see* ARTILLERY WEAPONS, GERMANY EIGHTY-EIGHT GUN) hurled a mass of steel down on the immobilized men.

LOSSES. For almost four months the Allied troops remained stranded on the beaches, every foot of which was vulnerable to German attack. Thousands of men were lost at Anzio, of whom many succumbed to disease, starvation, and exhaustion.

BREAKTHROUGH. The men at Anzio were not able to break out of their trap until May 11, 1944, when a massive offensive was mounted by the 5th and 8th Armies along the Gustav Line. On May 18 other Allied troops stormed Cassino and broke through the Gustav Line to effect a junction with them.

AFTERMATH. "I had hoped," said Winston Churchill (*q.v.*), "that we were hurling a wildcat onto the shore, but all we got was a stranded whale." Early in the campaign when the landings bogged down, Maj. Gen. John P. Lucas, commander of the U.S. 6th Corps, was criticized for not moving rapidly from the beach after the invasion. He was replaced on February 23, 1944, by Lt. Gen. Lucian Truscott (*q.v.*), who was known for his aggressiveness. Lucas was defended by colleagues who insisted that he did not have enough men to effect the breakthrough.

Foreign correspondent Eric Sevareid (*q.v.*) reported the landing "a stupid mistake." Churchill had more to say: "The story of Anzio was a story of high opportunity and shattered hopes, of skillful inception on our part and swift recovery by the enemy, of valor shared by both.'' Gen. Dwight D. Eisenhower (*q.v.*) was optimistic: ''In the final outcome the Anzio operation paid off handsomely. . . . The move undoubtedly convinced Hitler that we intended to push the Italian campaign as a major operation.''

For the miserable troops caught at Anzio it was concentrated hell. It took much blood and sweat to break the trap at Anzio.

Bibliography. C. Buckley, *Road to Rome* (1945); Albert Kesselring, *Memoirs of Field Marshal Kesselring* (1953); M. Blumenson, *Anzio: The Gamble That Failed* (1963); and C. Hibbert, *The Battle of Anzio* (1970).

ARDEATINE CAVES MASSACRE. Reprisal execution of 335 Italian civilians by the Germans in the spring of 1944.

BACKGROUND. On March 23, 1944, a small band of Communist-dominated Italian Partisans, after learning that a detachment of German police troops marched each day at the same time down the same street in the heart of Rome, planted a bomb that killed 33 Germans in a *Waffen-SS* (*q.v.*) unit. Gen. Kurt Maelzer, the German commandant immediately ordered the execution of every Italian living on the Via Rasella, the street on which the explosion had taken place. Dissuaded by the German Embassy, Maelzer referred the matter to Berlin. Hitler, through Heinrich Himmler (*q.v.*), directed that every able-bodied male in Rome be deported to forced labor (*q.v.*) camps in Germany.

Gen. Albert Kesselring (*q.v.*), the ranking officer in Italy, regarded the new order as placing an intolerable burden on his rail and supply system. Instead, he ordered that 10 Romans be executed for every German who had died. Not enough prisoners were on the scene to meet the quota, so German officers charged with the execution made up the difference with Jews, criminals, and suspected Italians. Exactly 330 were called for by Kesselring's order: The jailers rounded up 335 males, five more than the number in the order.

EXECUTION. On March 24, 1944, a detachment of German soldiers herded the prisoners into one of the Fosse Ardeatine caves and shot them to death in a systematic plan worked out the night before. The bodies were covered with lime and the entrance to the tunnel sealed with a blast of dynamite.

WARNING. After the slaughter the German High Command published a notice in Rome's newspapers denouncing ''this brutally violent act committed by the Communists of Badoglio's party.'' (*See* BADOGLIO, PIETRO.) It hinted at the possibility of Anglo-American influence. It gave notice that for every German who was murdered, ''ten of Badoglio's Communists will be shot.'' (*See* HOSTAGE SYSTEM.)

AFTERMATH. Italians, shocked and angered by the slaughter of innocents in the reprisal action, later set up a memorial for the victims as a national shrine. Kesselring, who was tried after the war for his part in the massacre, insisted that he had acted humanely by scaling down Hitler's demand that all Italian males thenceforth be sent to forced labor camps. He was sentenced to death, but the verdict was commuted and he was freed in 1952.

Herbert Kappler, the German SS (*q.v.*) colonel in charge of the massacre, was arrested by the Italians and sentenced to life imprisonment. In mid-August 1977, at the age of 70 and suffering from terminal cancer, he was spirited away from a military hospital near Rome by his wife and returned to Germany. The Italian Government requested Kappler's extradition, but the West German constitution prohibited turning a German citizen over to foreign prosecution. Kappler, who became known as ''the Hangman of the Ardeatine Caves,'' died in Soltau, West Germany, on February 9, 1978.

Bibliography. R. H. Adleman and G. Walton, *Rome Fell Today* (1968).

ARDENNES CAMPAIGN. *See* BULGE, BATTLE OF THE.

ARGENTIA.
Scene of the conference held in August 1941 by President Franklin D. Roosevelt and Prime Minister Winston Churchill (*qq.v.*) to discuss war aims. (*See* ATLANTIC CHARTER.) Argentia is on the east shore of Placentia Bay, Newfoundland. In World War II it was an American military and naval base.

ARK ROYAL. British aircraft carrier crippled by a German U-Boat in 1941.

DESIGN. HMS *Ark Royal* was completed in 1938 and commissioned in 1939. Named after the British flagship in the Spanish Armada (1588), she was the third of her name in the annals of the British Navy. Designed for speed and a superb fighting ship in every way, she was destined for an active role in the war.

> *SPECIFICATIONS.*
> *Standard Displacement.* 22,000 tons.
> *Maximum Speed.* 30.75 knots.
> *Horsepower.* 102,000.
> *Main Armament.* Sixteen 4.5-in. guns.

DUTY. In early December 1939 the *Ark Royal* disconcerted the German Navy by appearing at Cape Town in search of the *Admiral Graf Spee* (*q.v.*). In the spring of 1940 her bombers pressed home an attack on German ships berthed at Trondheim, Norway, against stiff fighter opposition. She played an important role in the destruction of the *Bismarck* (*see* BISMARCK, SINKING OF THE) in May 1941. Planes from the carrier *Ark Royal* heavily damaged ships of the Italian Navy and accounted for the loss or damage to 67 Italian aircraft.

Again and again German propaganda claimed the destruction of the *Ark Royal*, and she was frequently "sunk" by the propaganda machine of Paul Joseph Goebbels (*q.v.*).

SINKING. On November 13, 1941, German U-Boat *U-81*, commanded by Friedrich Guggenberger, slipped past Gibraltar on the surface and spent the day dodging aircraft and destroyers. Ordered to search for a British force heading from the east, Guggenberger found it and loosed a four-torpedo salvo. One torpedo hit the *Ark Royal*, which listed heavily. She headed back toward Gibraltar. Hours later a fire broke out. After ineffective damage control, she sank early the next morning, just 25 miles from safety. Only one man of the crew was lost.

Bibliography. Great Britain: Admiralty, His Majesty's Stationery Office, *Ark Royal* (1943); and E. P. von der Porten, *The German Navy in World War II* (1969).

ARMED FORCES NETWORK. Radio broadcasting stations used to boost morale of American troops during the early months of the occupation of Germany in 1945.

Bored with the news, GIs (*q.v.*) much preferred to listen to hours of jazz music. Their wishes were met by disc jockeys who played records by Benny Goodman, Glenn Miller, Duke Ellington, Tommy Dorsey, and Jimmy Dorsey. Two of the most popular programs were "Bouncing in Bavaria" and "Bedlam in Bremen." (*See also* UNITED SERVICES ORGANIZATIONS-USO.)

ARMY OF THE NILE. Original British armed force stationed in Egypt and called Army of the Delta at the start of the war. At that time it numbered only 36,000 men under command of Gen. Archibald Wavell (*q.v.*), but it was considerably enlarged for the Western Desert campaign. Churchill often used the term Army of the Nile to describe the Western Desert Force. (*See* NORTH AFRICA, CAMPAIGNS IN.)

ARMY OF THE WESTERN DESERT. Alternate name for the British 8th Army formed in September 1941. Under command of Gen. Alan Cunningham (*q.v.*), it was later turned over to Gen. Bernard Law Montgomery (*q.v.*). The 8th Army played a central role in the seesaw battle in North Africa between Montgomery and Gen. Erwin Rommel (*q.v.*). (*See* NORTH AFRICA, CAMPAIGNS IN; and EIGHTH ARMY.)

ARNHEM, BATTLE OF. Code or cover name *Market-Garden*. A combined Allied parachute and glider landing (*Operation Market*) and a British ground advance (*Operation Garden*), launched September 17, 1944. The plan was to secure crossings over the great Dutch rivers, Maas, Waal, and Lower Rhine, and thereby open the way for an advance into the north German plain before the onset of winter. As the largest airborne operation in the European theater, the plan failed.

BACKGROUND: TACTICAL DISPUTE. The Normandy invasion (*q.v.*) was a turning point of the war. After the breakout from Normandy came what was, perhaps, the most serious tactical dispute of the war. Gen. Dwight D. Eisenhower (*q.v.*), Supreme Allied Commander, leaned toward a so-called broad front advance to the Rhine, which was advocated by Gen. Omar Bradley (*q.v.*), commander of the 12th Army Group. But Gen. Bernard Law Montgomery (*q.v.*), hero of El Alamein (*q.v.*) and commander of the British 21st Army Group, insisted that after crossing the Seine, the two groups should keep together as a mass of 40 divisions and advance northward to Antwerp and Aachen with their right flank on the Ardennes. Wishing to please the experienced Montgomery, Eisenhower agreed to a compromise, giving Montgomery priority for the moment for his "concentrated thrust" northward. Once Antwerp was won, the Allied armies would revert to the pre-invasion plan of advancing to the Rhine on a broad front north and south of the Ardennes.

PREPARATIONS. Senior Allied officers were carefully briefed for the great combined airborne and ground operation in the north. The American 101st and 82nd Airborne Divisions were assigned to capture the bridges at Eindhoven and Nijmegen respectively. The British 1st Airborne Division was to take those at Arnhem. Meanwhile, as parachute and glider landings were taking place, the British 30th Corps would advance some 60 miles from the Meuse-Escaut Canal to combine *Market* and *Garden*.

In August 1944 Gen. Lewis Brereton was appointed first commander of the 1st Allied Airborne Army, with his deputy Lt. Gen. Frederick ("Boy") Browning (*qq.v.*). Brig. Gen. James M. Gavin (*q.v.*) and his 82nd Airborne Division were assigned the area between Grave and Nijmegen. Maj. Gen. Robert E. Urquhart and his Red Devils (*q.v.*), assisted by Maj. Gen. Stanislaw Sosnbowski and his Polish Parachute Brigade, were to capture the bridge over the Lower Rhine at Arnhem.

OPERATION MARKET. The imaginative plan went sour in the very beginning. U.S. airborne landings on September 17, 1944, were a success, but British paratroopers ran into difficulties from the start. They could not be dropped close to the Arnhem bridges because of the polderlands bordering the river, an area of woods, heathland, villages, and country estates. Urquhart had no alternative but to drop his men in open country flanked by woods about six miles from Arnhem. "We can hold the Arnhem bridge for four days," Browning reported, "but I think we might be a bridge too far." His men ran into fierce counterattacks on the first day and succeeded only in capturing the north end of one of the bridges at Arnhem. The Red Devils were thrust up against two seasoned SS *Panzer* divisions.

OPERATION GARDEN. The airborne drop was in trouble, but so was the armored drive on the ground. The weather turned bad and air support for the British 30th Corps was steadily reduced. On September 19 about 30 Polish gliders were sent in with reinforcements only to be decimated by antiaircraft fire. Allied aircraft swarmed in to drop tons of supplies, but the food and ammunition missed the targets and much of it ended in German hands.

Desperate fighting continued for more than a week. Finally, on the night of September 25–26, 1944, about 2,000 of the trapped troops managed to break out.

LOSSES. Approximately 16,500 paratroops and 3,500 glidermen had been landed on September 17. The total number of Allied casualties, including ground troops, was 11,850. More than 5,000 men, including 3,000 wounded, were taken prisoners. The Poles alone suffered 3,000 casualties.

SIGNIFICANCE. Operation Market-Garden was a failure, one of the worst examples of faulty Allied strategy in the European theater. The culmination of the advance from Normandy, Operation Market-Garden was undertaken at precisely the wrong time. Lack of transportation had created a supply shortage. Allied troops were worn out after their dash across France and Belgium. Moreover, German reaction was a classic of "flexible response."

Montgomery's argument for a single and concentrated thrust was excellent in principle, but he had to face a number of difficulties: the delay in opening the port of Antwerp; the six-day stoppage of air supply; lack of gasoline; and defective British trucks. Despite its failure, Montgomery called the operation a success.

Bibliography. R. E. Urquhart, *Arnhem* (1958); S. Sosabowski, *Freely I Served* (1960); C. Hibbert, *The Battle of Arnhem* (1962); C. Bauer, *The Battle of Arnhem* (1966); B. Gregory, *British Airborne Troops* (1974); and C. Ryan, *A Bridge Too Far* (1974).

ARNOLD, HENRY HARLEY ("Hap") (1886–1950). Commanding General of the U.S. Army Air Forces.

At the outbreak of World War II in 1939, Arnold held the record for the longest continuous flying time in the army. In 1941 he was made Deputy Chief of Staff for Air. After the entry of the United States into the war, he arrived in Britain to set up the U.S. 8th Air Force, which was to play an important role in future air operations. In March 1942, as a lieutenant-general, he was made commander of all Army Air Forces throughout the world. Arnold was responsible for the organization and training of what eventually became the largest and most powerful air force among the belligerent powers. Under his command were 2.5 million men and 95,000 aircraft. During the war he also served on the U.S. Joint Chiefs of Staff and on the Allied Combined Chiefs of Staff. In March 1943 he was made the first full aviation General in American military history.

In September 1942 Arnold was awarded the Distinguished Service Medal for leading a 77-hour flight from Brisbane, Australia, to San Francisco. He was also presented with the Distinguished Flying Cross. In 1944 he established the 20th Air Force composed of *B-29*'s (*see* SUPERFORTRESS) which wreaked havoc on most German cities. In December 1944 he was raised to five-star rank as General of the Army, along with Gens. Marshall, Eisenhower, and MacArthur.

Bibliography. Together with Gen. Ira Eaker (*q.v.*), Arnold wrote several books on his flying career, including *Winged Warfare* (1941); *Army Flyer* (1942); and *Global Mission* (1949). *See also* F. O. Dupre, *Hap Arnold: Architect of American Air Power* (1972).

ARSENAL OF DEMOCRACY. Term used to describe American productive capacity from September 1, 1939, to December 7, 1941. It was first used by President Franklin D. Roosevelt in a fireside chat on December 29, 1940. The United States, with its enormous industrial potential, provided aid that for the British was a powerful and decisive barrier against defeat. (*See also* LEND-LEASE.)

ART, WARTIME. Art forms during the war were produced at two levels. On the one hand there was a considerable body of serious and even great civilian and combat art adding to the contributions of prewar years; and on the other hand, wartime art in all belligerent countries was utilized to serve the propaganda machine.

BACKGROUND. New art forms, including expressionism, surrealism, cubism, and futurism, were developed throughout the early 20th century. In one form or another each of these approaches was continued during the war. The war also stimulated the production of great works, thereby following the tradition of creativity during times of stress, like Goya's early 19th century *Disasters in War,* inspired by the horrors of the French occupation of Spain. Picasso's *Guernica* was a powerful protest against German bombing from the air during the Spanish civil war.

The occupation of Paris by Germany in 1940 cut the city off as the main magnet for artists from all over the world. Paris had continued to draw students from Europe and the Americas during the time between the impressionist movement of 1867–1886 and the opening of World War II. The French capital had been the center of art experiments in the Western world primarily because of the pioneering work of Cézanne, Seurat, van Gogh, Gauguin, and the *fauves*. Munich, the other main point of study and new departure, was also isolated from artists of the world. Such creative artists as the Spaniard Picasso, the Italian Modigliani, and the Rumanian sculptor Brancusi stayed on in Paris, but other great artists destined to make history had to remain in their native lands. Some artists, however, came to the United States as refugees.

COMBAT ART. To boost both military and civilian morale each belligerent government sent artists to combat zones to use paint, watercolor, pen, or pencil to record great events of the war. Activity on the American side is attested by the *Time-Life* collection of serious war art. Added to professional production was a vast array of amateur art sponsored by each army. Such art resulted from the need to embellish bare walls of recreation buildings, the interiors of which were nothing more than shelters from the weather. Those with artistic experience were enlisted to make the buildings more attractive. Local commanding officers established studio workshops in numerous camps. Here soldier artists would gather together in their off-duty time to discuss interiors for service clubs, recreation rooms, day rooms, and other places of general assembly. Classes in painting were held in many camps, the artists planning and producing murals and easel pictures. Instructors were usually the most advanced artists.

In combat areas soldier-artists and conscripted professional artists transferred to canvas the speed of planes, the roar of tanks, the boom of guns, and all the modern aspects of war. Much of this work has been retained in private and public collections.

BRITISH. As in other countries, British artists conscripted for war service enjoyed a military status much like that of war correspondents. Government control of art was greater than in World War I. There were exceptional organizations, such as the War Artists and Illustrators, Limited, which included W. Krogman and Frank Wootton, and the Royal Society for the Prevention of Accidents, which worked for the Ministry of Labour. A War Artists' Advisory Committee, under the chairmanship of Kenneth Clark, was established in the early months of the war. Some artists were employed full time by governmental agencies, others were given assignments, and still others were posted to the services.

Exhibitions of war art held in London and the provinces were popular. The style often drifted to neo-romanticism, induced by the tradition of Blake and Palmer and continental surrealism. John Piper and Graham Sutherland specialized in blitzed ruins and ghostly wrecks. Henry Moore found ideal subjects for his drawings in the London tubes. Francis Bacon reveled in the violence of war. Amateurs, like Winston Churchill, turned to painting as a relief from the strains of war. "Painting," said Noël Coward, "was the best means of escape from the trials of life and work."

British poster art was of unusual excellence. The humorous tradition of World War I was continued by survivors such as Bert Thomas and Bruce Bairnsfather, the creator of "Old Bill," a middle-aged cartoon character with a walrus mustache. Humor was more generally used in World War II, as shown in the cartoons of Cyril Kenneth Bird, who went by the name of Fougasse, Carl Giles, and David Low, who deflated the images of Hitler and Nazism. Posters urged secrecy, *Even the Walls . . .* ; health, *Keep the Nation Fighting Fit*; and loyalty, *All Behind You, Winston!* The malicious "Squander Bug" by Phillip Boydel helped the German war effort by encouraging the British housewife to spend her money on luxuries.

RUSSIAN. Just as German war art was animated by Hitler's taste, so did Russian art reflect the wishes of dictator Stalin. Once in power Stalin decreed realistic postcard art as the Russian ideal, and that remained the model throughout World War II. Paintings, posters, and cartoons leaned heavily on one theme—hatred of Germans. (*See* RUSSIA AT WAR.) Russian art emphasized the barbarity of German armies, looting, devastation, mass burial, and executions. The typical Russian war painting was like that of D. Shmaridov depicting the suffering of a mother holding her child killed by the Germans. There were many historical allusions: V. Ivanov and O. Burova showed the defeat of Napoleon in 1812 with the warning: "This, Hitler will learn in our days."

In the Bolshevik Revolution of 1917 the Russians produced an original method of poster production by stencil, which lent itself to a style close to that of Daumier in 19th century France. In World War II a trio of popular illustrators, using the collective name of Kukryniksi, poured out 200 posters designed "to arouse wrath and contempt for the enemy." These fierce cartoons were much admired in Britain and the United States, where they were reproduced with English captions.

AMERICAN. Refugee artists, such as the German Max Beckmann and the Austrian Oskar Kokoschka, came to the United States and devoted their talents to the Allied cause. Unlike the British, however, the American public preferred illustration in the mode of Norman Rockwell, its most successful exponent. During the war era little support was given to the social realism of such artists as Ben Shahn, although he was officially employed for war work.

American war posters reached the high level won by British artists. Typical slogans were *Time is Short* and *A Slip of the Lip Can Sink a Ship*, and American imagery prevailed in *We Won't Let Them Catch Us With Our Plants Down* and *My Girl's a Wow!* The Graphic Division of the Office of War Information (*q.v.*) produced a series promoting the purchase of war bonds using the slogan *Let 'Em Have It, Buy Extra Bonds*. The War Department encouraged painters in war zones. Such cartoonists as Bill Mauldin (*q.v.*) and Sgt. George Baker won enormous popularity among GIs (*q.v.*). (*See* SAD SACK.)

GERMAN. Under the Nazi dictatorship German art took the realistic form decreed by Hitler, himself a frustrated artist. The *Fuehrer* denounced all modern art as *entartete kunst* ("degenerate art") and forbade it on German soil. Instead he fixed the intellectual level of German art at a common denominator "confined to a few essentials." All art in the Third Reich was placed under the jurisdiction of the Reich Chamber of Creative Artists supervised by Paul Joseph Goebbels (*q.v.*), Reich Minister for Public Enlightenment and Propaganda. Goebbels, at Hitler's bidding, discouraged or banned all experimental art.

Instead, Nazi art during World War II depicted exactly what Hitler wanted.

It showed "mothers of the nation" surrounded by domestic happiness, so-called Aryan women working at the lathes in munitions factories, and war as a great adventure in which men could prove their value. As Henri Nannen said in 1937, "Art is ideology in concrete form, it is contagious, draws people along in its spell, and fires them with enthusiasm. . . . Art is one of the most effective elements of order and leadership in a nation's existence."

In conformity with this point of view Nazi wartime art stressed virtues of patriotism, the rhythm of nature, heroic deeds, and concepts of nation and race. War artists in the pay of state and party were expected to paint what the population "needed"—security, order, and a harmonious existence.

Typical of Nazi-approved war art was Siebert's *Meine Kameraden in Polen* (*My Comrades in Poland*) and Bergen's *Im Atlantik* (*On the Atlantic*). Even in wartime, along with grandiloquent combat scenes, a favorite motif was farm life—idylls of sunburned laborers working freshly turned earth. By painting agricultural workers, snorting cart horses, and freshly turned earth, Hitler's artists believed that they were producing what he called "the new and true German art."

The triptych by Hans Schmitz-Wiedenbrück, titled *Arbeiter, Bauern und Soldaten* (*Workers, Peasants and Soldiers*), typified Nazi war art. With extraordinary clarity it proclaimed the hierarchy of a society at war. The centerpiece, painted from a worm's eye view, revealed the trinity of the armed forces with the air force as the most aggressive combatant. To the left and right miners and peasants bow to fate and accept their captive existence. The idea was to emphasize the camaraderie of those who engaged in war and those who worked in industry. In reality, the painting revealed the way the Nazi economy revolved around arms production and the exploited workers.

Although most German war art was propagandistic in nature, side by side with it was the production of paintings of high quality. In its drive through Germany the U.S. Army gathered a voluminous collection of serious German war art. German posters, superb in idealization, symbols, and strong colors, were of a consistently high order. During his campaign to power Hitler had used the extraordinary talent of Leni Riefenstahl to produce a series of superior films. Although much of it was propaganda during the war years, German film retained a high level of craftsmanship. In order to convince the German people as he moved against Poland that Germany was secure in the west, the *Fuehrer* had films of the West Wall (*q.v.*) shown in all cinemas. (*See* FILMS IN THE WAR.)

HITLER'S MASSIVE PLUNDER. The most noteworthy development in art during the war years was Hitler's large-scale plunder of Europe's art treasures and his plan to make Linz, the provincial Austrian city of his childhood, the cultural art center of the world. Nazi looting of art from museums and private collections all over the continent reached enormous proportions during the war. It is popularly believed that Hermann Goering (*q.v.*), second-ranking Nazi, was the greatest Nazi plunderer of art treasures, but actually it was Hitler who ordered the looting. Quietly and without seeking the limelight, as had Goering, Hitler amassed an extraordinarily valuable collection of art, which, he claimed, was a national possession.

Unlike Goering, who wanted works of art because they were beautiful and because they satisfied his aesthetic taste, Hitler showed little interest in them once they passed into his possession. He preferred to store them in air-raid shelters, dark rooms, and deep inside salt mines. He designated Alfred Rosenberg (*q.v.*), with his Rosenberg Task Force (*Einsatz Rosenberg*), to confiscate great art treasures of Poland and France, as well as other occupied countries. The conquest of France offered unparalleled opportunities for further plundering. Because he wanted the French people to accept the occupation, Hitler at first had seized primarily art treasures from Jewish collections. Rosenberg's official report later stated that between 1940 and 1944 he had appropriated 21,903 art objects of all kinds, which were brought to Germany in 29 shipments requiring 137 freight cars.

Nazi plundering of art was throughout Europe. In the art market of The Hague, prices rapidly rose as triumphant Nazis bid furiously against one another for works of art. Hitler's agents, paying in German money, made large-scale purchases even though a large part of Dutch art had been removed to America. In Italy there was no organized looting until after September 1943, when Italian resistance collapsed. Hitler's purchases of Italian art were on such a scale that on May 9, 1942, Mussolini's Government was forced to publish a new law restricting exportation of works of art.

In addition to collecting paintings, sculpture, armor, and coins, Hitler intended to build a great library and a huge theater in Linz, the city of his childhood, which he hoped to transform from an uninteresting industrial community to the cultural capital of the Nazi New Order and the world. His special agents gathered works by da Vinci, Goya, Rembrandt, Tintoretto, and Vermeer as well as such priceless masterpieces as Michelangelo's *Madonna and Child,* Brueghel's *The Hay Harvest,* and the Ghent altarpiece by the van Eycks.

Within seven years, either by forced sale or by direct confiscation, the Nazis appropriated more than 100,000 works of art, much of it of priceless value. The hoard included paintings, sculptures, rare books, coins, and other *objets d'art* with a value greater than the combined collections of the British Museum in London, the Louvre in Paris, the Metropolitan Museum of Art in New York City, and Moscow's Tretyskov Gallery.

During the later years of the war, when Allied bombing of Germany increased, Hitler issued orders to have his works of art moved to places of safety. The overflow was stored in Schloss Thuerntal near Kremamünster, the Hohenfurth monastery inside the Czech border, the Schloss Neuschwanstein near Fuessen, and a huge salt mine at Alt Aussee. The largest part, earmarked for Linz, was stored at Alt Aussee, which was transformed into a series of chambers. Of the 10,000 paintings finally stored, 6,755 belonged to Hitler. Of these, 5,350 were old masters, of priceless value.

RETURN OF ART WORKS. After the war Allied officials were faced with the stupendous task of returning the treasures that had been confiscated by Hitler and his agents. At Nuremberg Alfred Rosenberg explained that what he had done was only historical justice, because after World War I billions of marks in German property had been expropriated by the Allies. His actions, he insisted, were designed to protect great art from the vicissitudes of war, to make an inventory of it, and see that the treasures were not destroyed. The art was not intended, he said, for Goering's private collection. The Dutch paintings found in his home, he explained, were antique gifts to his wife. Unimpressed, Allied authorities traced all the looted art and returned it to the original owners.

Trained investigators rooted out Nazi storehouses in castles, farms, and salt mines. In the Munich area alone more than 175 caches of Nazi art loot were discovered. Experts from all over Europe helped identify both the works of art and their rightful owners. Restitution was swift and efficient in the case of great masterpieces. There were many frustrations and delays in identifying and returning lesser-known works. The situation was complicated in the case of Jewish collections whose owners had been exterminated.

The Rosenberg confiscations, housed at Neuschwanstein, were returned to their owners. Of the 200 collections represented, the Rothschilds headed the list with 3,978 of their looted art treasures. In addition to oil paintings there were engravings, watercolors, miniatures, valuable antique furniture, Gobelin tapestries, jewelry, rare coins, rare gems, porcelains, and ivories. The total value was phenomenal.

Bibliography. A. Crane (ed.), *Art in the Armed Forces* (1944); C.G.E. Bunt, *Russian Art* (1947); D. Roxan and K. Wanstall, *The Rape of Art* (1964); A.A. Hoehling, *Home Front. U.S.A.* (1966); A. Calder, *The People's War, Britain, 1939-1945* (1969); D. Judd, *Second World War Posters* (1971); M. Simon, *The Battle of the Louvre* (1971).

ARTIFICIAL PORTS. *See* MULBERRIES.

ARTILLERY WEAPONS. Land service weapons of various calibers, small and large, used in most of the major theaters of war.

MEANING. In the general sense, artillery refers to offensive weapons of war, whether small or large. It also means the use and management of large guns.

Field artillery: artillery designed to be taken with an army to the field of battle.

Flying artillery: artillery, the gunners of which are trained to rapid revolutions, in order to change positions speedily.

Park artillery: a body or force of artillery with all carriages and stores necessary for its use.

Siege artillery: heavy guns used to destroy fortifications.

Train of artillery: cannon pieces mounted on carriages with equipment.

Artillery was at the heart of all major war efforts from the era of Napoleon through World War I. From 1914 to 1918 it took a place second only to infantry.

WORLD WAR II. The opening German *Blitzkrieg* (*q.v.*) abandoned static warfare. Technically, the new artillery weapons were merely an extension of preceding forms, but new demands of mobility brought an important change. To ensure better accuracy, longer range, and more powerful velocity, artillery combined the mobility of the tank with the power of the old artillery. It could now follow the course of mobile battle.

This basic change amounted to a veritable revolution in weaponry. Hitherto untried scientific principles were being applied to the technology of land warfare. Novel forms of self-propelled guns were used for assault or close support of infantry. Special attention was given to the development of the antitank gun, with a fire power varying from 2- to 170- pound shells, the latter of which could stop an enemy heavy tank at a range of 3,000 yards.

FIELD ARTILLERY. A new tactical development in World War II was the use of field artillery in close cooperation and coordination with infantry, tanks, and other units of aggression. There was a rapid massing of field artillery fire through the help of fire-direction finders and improved communications. There were new developments in design: improved sights, carriages, and operating equipment. Basic range was improved to more than 13,000 yards as compared with the 7,500-yard range of World War I. A new recoil-control feature was the muzzle brake, which used some of the discharged gas to reduce the coil of the gun.

MORTARS. Short-range, high-angled weapons were popular in the trench warfare of World War I and were also used in World War II. The guns were set up for high-angle fire: Shells were dropped down the muzzle, the primer of the propellant charge struck the fixed firing pin, and exploded. The rate of fire was as fast as the shells could be dropped down the muzzle. The extreme range was 3,000 yards with shells weighing from 3 to 14 pounds.

ROCKET WEAPONS. The unguided artillery rocket was a new feature of World War II. The types varied from the American bazooka (*q.v.*) to the long-range German *V-2* (*q.v.*). In the early stage of the war the British introduced small rockets fired from coastal vessels against enemy dive bombers.

ANTIAIRCRAFT ARTILLERY (AA). Large antiaircraft guns, with bores ranging from 3 to 5 inches, were introduced. Batteries of four guns had electrical controls and radar aiming devices. Among the best of the ground-mount antiaircraft automatic guns was the 40-mm. Swedish-produced *Bofors*.

AMMUNITION. Ammunition was improved by the use of smokeless powder, high explosives including TNT, fragmentation shells, and delayed-action percussion fuses. The proximity fuze, (*q.v.*), introduced by the Americans, used a miniature radio set that sent out a continuous radio impulse as the shell moved to its target. The impulse echo returned to the fuze as it arrived in bursting range, operated the firing mechanism, and exploded the shell.

BRITISH ARTILLERY. The first British attempts to produce self-propelled guns were not encouraging. The *Bishop,* which mounted a 25-pounder on a moving hull, with a crew of four, was weak in design and construction. The *Sexton,* with more reliable components, was somewhat better. During the war a succession of British antitank guns appeared, firing shells varying from 2 to 17 pounds. An effective *Panzer*-killer was the 17-pounder, which could knock out a German *Tiger* at 1,000 yards.

For antiaircraft purposes the British preferred the Swedish originated *Bofors* and *Oerlikon* antiaircraft guns. Many versions of these pieces were manufactured during the war.

BRITISH 25-POUND GUN HOWITZER

The most dependable British piece of artillery was the 25-pound gun howitzer, which came under the category of light and medium field artillery. Weighing 4,048 pounds in firing position, it could be depressed 5 degrees, elevated 40 degrees, and could traverse 360 degrees on a platform. It fired four rounds per minute with a maximum horizontal range of 12,500 yards, using high explosive, armor-piercing shells.

One of the great artillery pieces of the war, the British 25-pounder was used in concentration on every Allied front in Europe and Asia. It played an important role in October 1942 in the thunderous artillery barrage during the Battle of El Alamein (*q.v.*), when 400 stationary 25-pounders were among the thousand artillery pieces set 30 yards apart on a 10,000-yard stretch. The continuous hail of metal made the Axis lines a boiling strip of explosions and flying sand.

GERMAN ARTILLERY. The Germans developed artillery to a fine art. Virtually all German weapons, from field artillery pieces to self-propelled guns to large mortars and long-range field guns were products of first-rate design and craftsmanship.

GERMAN EIGHTY-EIGHT GUN

The German 88-mm. artillery piece was considered by both sides to be the most effective single weapon of its kind used during the war. Weighing 5.5 tons, it fired a projectile of 22 pounds at a rate of 15 to 20 per minute and a range of 11,500 to 16,000 yards.

The *88* was originally designed as an antiaircraft gun, but later it won fame as an antitank gun. It made its first appearance in the late days of World War I and was continually improved in succeeding versions until the final year of World War II.

The *88* was introduced in World War II in June 1940 by Gen. Erwin Rommel's *Afrika Korps* (*qq.v.*) in the headlong German drive toward Egypt. Firing a 22-pound shell from camouflaged emplacements, the *88*s took a quick toll of British lives.

Until the Americans introduced the *Sherman* tank, the British 8th Army (*q.v.*) in North Africa was at the mercy of the *88*. The Germans used it to deadly effect both on the ground and mounted on Tiger tanks. In February 1944, German *88*s placed on hillsides around the monastery at Monte Cassino picked off Allied armor with deadly efficiency and provided one of the main reasons for the Allied decision to destroy the monastery from the air. (*See* MONTE CASSINO, BOMBING OF.)

GERMAN SELF-PROPELLED 75-MM. GUN

The Germans were the first to build and use self-propelled guns on a large scale. The self-propelled 75-mm. gun mounted on a *PzKwIV* medium tank weighed 25.6 tons and moved at a top speed of 25 miles per hour with a 300-horsepower Maybach V-12 cylinder engine. There were varied designs of this powerful mobile weapon. Low in silhouette, it presented a difficult target to the enemy.

The 75-mm. gun, with its stubby nose giving the appearance of a half-extended pocket telescope, was used in all the major German campaigns, first in the invasion of Poland, then the Low Countries and France. Later it served with the *Afrika Korps* (*q.v.*) in North Africa as well as on the eastern front against the Soviet Union.

GERMAN *NEBELWERFER*

The German rocket launcher, the *Nebelwerfer,* was one of the most effective pieces of artillery used in the war. Weighing 1,195 pounds, it fired six rounds every 90 seconds, with a range varying from 2,700 to 7,723 yards.

The original version of the *Nebelwerfer* was a five-barreled, 150-mm. rocket launcher firing chemical or smoke shells. Later designs, using six 51-inch-long barrels and wheel mounts, were fired electrically by remote control.

The *Nebelwerfer* was first used in large numbers in the North African desert campaign and later at the battle for Monte Cassino (*q.v.*). Here they were set in emplacements on the hillsides surrounding the monastery, from which they rained death on the Allied troops below. They were used in many other campaigns, especially in the attempt to halt the Allied offensive after the Normandy landings. (*See* NORMANDY INVASION.) Allied troops learned to have great respect for German rocket launchers, which they called "Screaming Meemies" because the cluster of rockets made a shrieking sound when in flight.

GERMAN *GUSTAV*

In the closing stage of the war the Germans developed many new pieces of artillery, including large mortars and long-range field guns, some of the latter with rocket-assisted shells. The *Hunting Tiger* was a 120-mm. gun mounted on a *Tiger* chassis.

In both world wars German ordnance designers produced a variety of railway guns. In World War I their *Big Bertha* hurled shells at Paris from 75 miles. In 1937 Krupp conceived the idea of a railway gun of monster proportions. The orthodox mounting comprised a box-girder lower carriage set on four twin trucks each of five axles, with a total of 80 wheels running on two parallel tracks. When traveling, the upper parts were removed by cranes and loaded on transport cars.

Gustav was test fired on the Rugenwalde Range in 1942. A delighted Hitler inspected it there in March 1943. Weighing 1,328 tons, it could fire a five-ton high explosive up to 23 miles. Its shell could pierce heavy concrete fortifications. The huge gun required more than 1,000 men for maintenance and firing. Construction or dismantling required four to six weeks of work. After trials it was used at Sevastopol in 1942, where it fired between 30 and 40 shots, one of which penetrated into 100 feet of earth to destroy a Russian ammunition dump. (*See* SEVASTOPOL, SIEGE OF.). It was also used at Pruskov, 18 miles from Warsaw, in September 1944, firing 30 rounds during the Warsaw confrontation. (*See* WARSAW UPRISING.). *Gustav* was not heard of again after this appearance. It is believed to have fallen into Russian hands after a counterattack.

RUSSIAN. "Artillery," said Stalin, "is the God of war." The Russians were its undisputed masters during the war. Because of the enormous loss of men and equipment after the German invasion, Russian ordnance experts concentrated on simple designs that could be mass produced. They were the first to use the "artillery division," a large independent unit equipped with guns of all calibers that could be used *en masse* to bring pressure in strength at any given part of the front.

Late in the war the Russians introduced several monster guns, including 240-mm. and 305-mm. howitzers and 12- to 15-inch guns, but not on the same scale as the Germans. These giant guns joined a concentration of 22,000 pieces of artillery in the final assault on Berlin. (*See* BERLIN, BATTLE OF.).

RUSSIAN *KATYUSHA* ROCKET LAUNCHER

The general term *Katyusha* was used to describe one of the most devastating weapons of the war. Weighing 7.3 tons, it fired 16 94-pound rockets by electrical impulse with a range of 8,435 yards. The "Stalin Organ" was feared and respected by the Germans.

The early *Katyusha*, produced by Russian ordnance technicians, was crude and simple but effective. It was really only a metal rack on which as many as 26 rockets ranging up to 16 inches were placed. Later there were more sophisticated models. American ordnance experts, building on Russian experience, invented even more refined versions, which could be mounted on *Sherman* tanks, fired in 30 seconds, and then jettisoned.

The *Katyushas* of the early days in the war were not altogether accurate, but they wrought havoc when fired in unison. They were especially effective against tanks and artillery. German troops who experienced the first *Katyusha* attacks after the invasion of the Soviet Union on June 22, 1941, turned and fled from the whining rockets.

AMERICAN. The Americans also specialized in the mass production of artillery. U.S. ordnance designers produced a wide variety of self-propelled artillery. The most used howitzer was the 105-mm. and the accurate 155-mm., which had a range of 16,000 yards at a rate of two rounds per minute. The 37-mm. antitank gun fired an antipersonnel canister and had a range of 12,800 yards. The 155-mm. mortar, used as a substitute for a field gun, could throw a 60-pound bomb accurately at various ranges from 200 to 2,205 yards.

At the 1944 Normandy invasion (*q.v.*) the Americans used large batteries of *M-12* Gun Motor Carriages, which carried a 155-mm. gun to soften enemy fortifications. Full-tracked, half-tracked, and self-propelled guns were used in the dash across France into Germany. (*See* GERMANY, BATTLE OF.)

AMERICAN *M-18* HELLCAT

The tank destroyer (TD) was essentially a powerful high velocity gun mounted on a standard tank chassis. The *M-18 Hellcat* had a weight of 19.5 tons with its 76-mm. gun mounted in an open turret. It was lightly armored, but it had the advantage of speed. It could be used both as a moving tank and as a stationary artillery piece.

The *M-18* inflicted severe damage on German *Panzer* units all the way from Normandy to eastern Germany. It was a standard weapon used by Gen. George S. Patton, Jr., (*q.v.*) in the sensational dash of his 3rd Army across Europe. American statisticians claimed that in eight months of fighting the 3rd Army's *M-18*s knocked out 648 German tanks as well as thousands of other vehicles and hundreds of artillery pieces, bunkers, and pillboxes.

By 1945 American ordnance designers were working on recoilless guns, rocket launchers, and ballistic missiles.

AMERICAN *M-40 LONG TOM*

Late in the war the Americans introduced the *M-40 Long Tom,* a 150-mm. gun placed on a *Sherman* tank. The tank itself weighed 40.5 tons and had a top speed of 24 miles per hour. The gun could hurl a 95-pound projectile up to 14 miles.

BOFORS ANTIAIRCRAFT GUN

This Swedish-designed 40-mm. antiaircraft gun was adopted by most European countries before the war, but for some reason American ordnance experts rejected it. The scintillating success of the *Bofors* in the Battle of Britain (*q.v.*) led to its adoption as the standard Anglo-American light AA weapon. Weighing 2.4 tons in wheel-mount with outriggers, it could fire 2-pound shells at the rate of 120 per minute at a maximum range of 5,100 yards. It used four-round clips.

The *Bofors* was designed to be used not only against aircraft but also against fortifications and other ground targets. Mounted on a wheeled carriage with attached folding outriggers, it could be depressed to six degrees and elevated to 90 degrees, with a full 360-degree traverse.

The *Bofors,* one of the most widely used weapons of the war, provided saturating fire against aircraft. Most of the 2,000 AA guns defending England in the summer of 1940 were *Bofors* guns. In the fall of 1942 they were used in the Battle of El Alamein (*q.v.*) during night attacks to fire tracers as a guideline for advancing infantry. They were employed during the late days of the war to fire on German *V-1*s (*q.v.*) sent over London.

OERLIKON ANTIAIRCRAFT GUN

Swiss-originated, the fine 20-mm. *Oerlikon* AA gun was adopted by the Allies in the early years of the war. With 60-round drums, it could fire at the rate of 600 to 650 rounds per minute.

The *Oerlikon* could be used in single and multiple mounts. It served in various ways—to give teeth to amphibious landing craft, for antiaircraft purposes, and for mounting on tanks. It was light, easy to operate, and fired an explosive shell. The mounting was well adapted for shipboard use. The British equivalent was the *Pom-Pom,* a rapid-fire gun used in multiple mounts.

At the start of the war, the British desperately needed light automatic guns to defend ships against low-flying aircraft. They acquired a license so that the *Oerlikon* could be made in England. Both the U.S. Army and Navy adopted the gun for their own use. In the later stages of the war, the *Oerlikon* became less effective because of new heavily armored aircraft then in service.

JAPANESE. Among the variety of artillery weapons supplied by the Japanese to their troops was the 50-mm. mortar. Light and portable, it could fire smoke grenades or demolition bombs weighing approximately two pounds about 700 yards. This weapon was used in great quantities against American troops in the island jungle fighting of the Pacific war. American troops nicknamed it the "knee mortar" in the mistaken belief that it was fired while braced just above the knee. American GIs (*q.v.*) who tried to use the weapon in this fashion had their legs broken by the powerful recoil.

Bibliography. G. M. Barnes, *Weapons of World War II* (1947); J. Kirk and R. Young, *Great Weapons of World War II* (1961); I. V. Hogg, *The Guns, 1939-1945* (1961); K. Mackey, *Panzer Division: The Mailed Fist* (1968); and A. Kershaw (ed.), *Weapons of War* (1973).

ASDIC (SONAR). British antisubmarine detector. The name is an acronym for the 1917 *A*llied *S*ubmarine *D*etection *I*nvestigation *C*ommittee. Later its American name was Sonar.

DESIGN. The device operated similar to the method used by a bat to navigate. If a U-Boat was suspected to be in the vicinity, then a surface ship would transmit a signal of an electric alternating current through a quartz crystal. The vibration sent sound pulses through the water. When the signal struck an object, it bounced back to the receiver. The range of the object could then be calculated from the time the signal took to return to the ship. The longer the interval, the longer the range. At his instrument the operator swept signals 360 degrees around his ship while watching the dotted cones of his search area.

WORLD WAR II. British destroyers were fitted with Asdic early in the war. The Germans learned of the secret device when they captured units of the French Navy in 1940. Meanwhile, Asdic played a major role in sea warfare. (*See* ATLANTIC, BATTLE OF THE.) A powerful weapon in the war against U-Boats, Asdic accounted for 246 German submarines. (*See also* RADAR, WARTIME.)

ASQ. French village in the Département du Nord.
    On April 2, 1944, 86 residents of Asq were killed by German troops in revenge for a guerrilla attack on railroads.

ATHENIA. Passenger liner sunk by a German U-Boat within hours after the British and French declared war.

BACKGROUND. In the critical days before the Germans invaded Poland on September 1, 1939, thousands of tourists in Europe frantically sought early return to the United States and Canada. One of the passenger ships brought into service to accommodate the rush was the 13,500-ton *Athenia* of the Donaldson Line, Captain James Cook in command. The ship hurriedly took on passengers at Glasgow, Belfast, and finally Liverpool and sailed on September 2, 1939, for Quebec and Montreal. The unarmed ship had on board 1,102 passengers, a majority of whom were British, and a crew of 315.

CONFRONTATION. On September 3, 1939, the *U-30*, a 350-ton German U-Boat, was poised at a point 200 miles west of the Hebrides. Its commander, Senior Lt. Fritz-Ludwig Lemp, was anxious to strike a quick blow for his country. Through his periscope he sighted a ship in an ideal position for attack. Within seconds he sent four torpedoes hurtling toward the oncoming vessel. One torpedo struck home, and the *Athenia* began to go down. Fortunately for passengers and crew, the ship was properly fitted with lifeboats and rafts. Immediate calls went out for help, whereupon other vessels quickly reached the scene and took survivors to Glasgow, Belfast, and Halifax. Of the 1,417 on board, 112 were lost. Of these, 68 were women and 16 children. Twenty-eight American lives were lost.

AFTERMATH. Public opinion in Britain, Canada, and the United States was outraged by the sinking without warning of an unarmed passenger ship. The British and American press denounced the attack as a renewal of German tactics inaugurated in World War I. The incident was the first of several that helped drive the United States into the war.

In Berlin Paul Joseph Goebbels (*q.v.*), Reich Minister for Public Enlightenment and Propaganda, denied that a German U-Boat was involved. What had happened, he charged, was that a time bomb had been placed in the vessel on orders of Prime Minister Winston Churchill (*q.v.*) in a typically perfidious British scheme to create a new *Lusitania* incident and bring the United States into the war. On word from Berlin, Adm. Karl Doenitz (*q.v.*), head of the German submarine fleet, ordered the commander of *U-30* to remove from his war diary the page describing the sinking and to substitute another page omitting any mention of the attack. This was to avoid a possible leak when the usual eight pages of U-Boat war diaries were prepared for future training of submarine crews.

U-Boat commander Lemp later claimed that he had mistaken the *Athenia* for an armed merchantman because it was off the normal shipping lanes and was zigzagging suspiciously. But he maintained radio silence and did not ask his home base for a directive. Not until September 30, 1939, when he returned to port, did he inform Adm. Doenitz verbally that he had sunk the *Athenia.* Lemp later lost his life in an attack by a convoy escort on his submarine.

Bibliography. D. Mason, *U-Boat: The Secret Menace* (1968); and E. P. Von den Porten, *The German Navy in World War II* (1969).

ATLANTIC, BATTLE OF THE. Contest between the Allies and Germany for control of the sea routes important for success on land. By its U-Boat campaign, Germany sought to deny the Allies the use of the Atlantic Ocean and other seas.

BACKGROUND. The shadow of World War I hung heavily over World War II. More than 12.75 million tons of merchant shipping had been sunk during the earlier conflict, most of it by German U-Boats. Only when a system of escorted convoys was devised was the sinking of precious cargo ships overcome. In 1939, as well as in 1914, the British were dependent for their very existence upon safe sea routes. To protect their lines of communication they maintained a powerful naval force and a large merchant marine.

Fortunately for the British, Hitler, like Napoleon, paid more attention to ground than to sea warfare. The war broke out before the new German Navy was ready. Adm. Karl Doenitz (*q.v.*), the World War I U-Boat commander now heading Hitler's submarine force, had only 56 U-Boats at his disposal in 1939 and was not ready for action on the scale necessary for a successful campaign.

On October 18, 1939, Hitler delivered a directive including these provisions:

The Navy may attack passenger ships in convoy or proceeding with lights.

The *Fuehrer* will decide on all further measures to intensify the trade war against England. . . .

The attacks on English naval units at sea and in naval bases are to be kept up whenever a suitable opportunity offers and in close liaison between Navy and Air Force.

BEGINNING. The Battle of the Atlantic began in earnest as soon as the war started. Only hours after its outbreak a German U-Boat sank the passenger liner *Athenia* (*q.v.*). Both sides instituted a blockade, laying magnetic mines at strategic areas. During the winter of the so-called Phony War (*see SITZKRIEG*), both the Royal Navy and German U-Boats halted and inspected hundreds of merchant ships in the Atlantic.

Of his available U-Boats, Doenitz could count on only 22 as fully equipped for Atlantic action. These were mostly Type VII of 600 to 1,000 tons displacement, surface speed of 16 to 17 knots, and submerged speed of 8 knots. Of the original 56, at least 30 were "North Sea Ducks," unsuitable for service in the Atlantic. It was a modest fleet but it could cause serious damage. Hitler ordered the construction of more U-Boats.

On September 15, 1939, the first Allied transatlantic convoy was attacked and the *Aviemore* was sunk the next day. By the end of the first week almost 40 merchant ships had been sunk by U-Boats and mines. On September 17 the British aircraft carrier *Courageous* was torpedoed with the loss of 514 men and 48 aircraft. On October 14, 1939, in an extraordinarily skillful action, Capt. Günther Prien (*q.v.*) guided his *U-47* into the defenses of Scapa Flow in the Orkney Islands and sank the British battleship *Royal Oak* (*q.v.*). The English Channel was closed to U-Boats after the sinking of three submarines in the Straits of Dover.

On December 17, 1939, the German pocket battleship *Admiral Graf Spee* (*q.v.*), which had caused much destruction in the South Atlantic, was trapped and scuttled in Montevideo harbor. Elsewhere Allied losses at sea continued.

FIRST PHASE, 1940–1941. Using Doenitz's wolf-pack tactics (*q.v.*), U-Boats took a heavy toll. By April 1940 the total losses to Allied and neutral shipping amounted to 688,000 gross tons, and the rate of loss continued to mount after the fall of France enabled Doenitz to use bases on the Bay of Biscay. In November 1940 the German pocket battleship *Scheer* attacked a convoy and sank the *Jervis Bay* (*q.v.*).

By now the Battle of the Atlantic had assumed grim proportions. Between April 10, 1940, and March 7, 1941, Allied losses amounted to 2,314,000 tons.

In February–March 1941 the German battleships *Scharnhorst* and *Gneisenau* sank or captured 22 Allied ships totaling 115,000 tons. (*See SCHARNHORST.*)

On April 11, 1941, Roosevelt announced that the United States was extending its security zone and patrol areas to a line covering all North Atlantic waters west of West Longitude 26°. This was to be the new "sea frontier" of the United States. On May 21, 1941, a German U-Boat sank the American merchant ship *Robin Moor* in the South Atlantic off the coast of Brazil. On May 24, 1941, the German battleship *Bismarck,* on patrol in the North Atlantic, sank the British warship *Hood.* The *Bismarck* herself was sunk on May 27, 1941, while attempting to return to port. (*See* BISMARCK, SINKING OF THE.)

On September 4, 1941, a German U-Boat attacked the USS *Greer,* a destroyer on duty off Iceland. A week later Roosevelt announced a "shoot-on-sight" order to U.S. forces in defensive waters. On October 17, 1941, the U.S. destroyer *Kearney* was torpedoed and damaged by a German U-Boat off Iceland, with the loss of 11 American lives. On October 30, 1941, the U.S. destroyer *Reuben James* (*q.v.*), on convoy duty off Iceland, was sunk with the loss of 115 lives. The U.S. Congress then authorized the arming of American merchant vessels and allowed them to carry cargoes to belligerent ports.

SECOND PHASE: 1942. The entry of the United States into the war changed the course of sea warfare. Immediately, the entire Atlantic, including American coastal waters, became a hunting area for German U-Boat wolf packs. Sinkings increased. In January 1942 about 31 merchant ships were sunk off the coasts of the United States and Canada. By the summer of 1942 an additional 3,000,000 tons of shipping were lost. By now Doenitz had more U-Boats at his disposal: During the last six months of 1942 the Germans produced 101 submarines. In this period the U-Boats sank 585 ships with a tonnage of more than 5 million. Using refined wolf-pack tactics, the Germans made many heavy attacks on convoys, including Convoy *PQ-17* (June 27); *SC-94* (August 5); *ON-127* (September 10); and *PQ-18* (September 12) (*qq.v.*).

WANING SUPREMACY: 1943. The year 1943 marked the beginning of the end of German U-Boat power. It started off with the sinking of 86 ships in 20 days. But Allied antisubmarine measures were beginning to get results. Air protection, provided by the U.S. Army Air Forces and the Royal Air Force (*qq.v.*), was intensified. New corvettes and frigates provided stronger escorts. Techniques were developed to identify and track down U-Boats on the prowl. (*See* ASDIC; and RADAR, WARTIME.) Allied countermeasures forced U-Boats to remain below the surface, as a result of which they often missed the convoys. Meanwhile, American shipyards produced Liberty Ships (*q.v.*) and Victory Ships at an extraordinary rate. (*See also* KAISER, HENRY J.)

In March 1943 German U-Boats sank more than 100 ships, but the sinkings began to decline dramatically thereafter. In May Doenitz called all U-Boats back to port. Although he was sending out bigger and better submarines, the rate of loss was high. In December 14, 1943, Doenitz admitted, "The enemy has rendered the U-Boat ineffective. He has torn our sole defensive weapon in the war against the Anglo-Saxons from our side." For every 10,000 tons of shipping sunk the Germans were losing one U-Boat. It was an unbearable rate of loss.

At this time Germany navy yards were working on advanced types of U-Boats equipped with *Schnörkels* (*q.v.*) and hydrogen peroxide engines. But it was too late. The Battle of the Atlantic continued spasmodically until the German surrender in May 1945.

SIGNIFICANCE. Despite the tremendous damage inflicted on the Allies, the Germans clearly lost the sea battle. By their own figures they counted 2,232 Allied and neutral ships destroyed in the Atlantic, Mediterranean, and Indian Oceans, a total of nearly 12 million tons. For this they paid with the loss of 785 U-Boats and 32,000 seamen. The British lost about the same number of seamen. But in overcoming the German U-Boat menace, they assured final victory. "The only thing that ever frightened me during the war," Churchill admitted, "was the U-Boat peril. It was our worst evil." It was a long, grueling, cold, and dirty fight, but its outcome helped turn the scales of war.

Bibliography. C. D. Bekker, *Swastika at Sea* (1953); H. Busch, *U-Boats at War* (1955); J. Brennecke, *The Hunters and the Hunted* (1958); K. Doenitz, *Memoirs* (1959); D. Mason, *U-Boat: The Secret Menace* (1968); T. Hughes and J. Costello, *The Battle of the Atlantic* (1977); J. Wade, *The Battle of the Atlantic* (1977); and L.-G. Buchheim, *U-Boat War* (1978).

ATLANTIC CHARTER. Joint Anglo-American statement of war aims and basic principles for the postwar years.

BACKGROUND. In August 1941 the war was almost two years old in Western Europe and just a few weeks in progress in the Soviet Union. There was much gloom in Allied countries: The Russians seemed to be on the verge of defeat; the *Luftwaffe* (*q.v.*) was smashing London; and convoys in the North Atlantic were reeling under heavy U-Boat assault. In the United States isolationists called for "hands off." Though still nonbelligerent, the country was far from neutral. From March 1941 on, it had been helping Britain under Lend-Lease (*q.v.*) and was planning to do the same thing for the Soviet Union.

MEETING. In this grim situation, President Franklin D. Roosevelt and Prime Minister Winston Churchill (*qq.v.*) met "at sea" off Placentia Bay, Newfoundland, for three days, August 9–12, 1941. The purpose was to consider their cooperation in the problems of war and peace. They discussed especially the Battle of the Atlantic (*see* ATLANTIC, BATTLE OF THE); aid to the Soviet Union (*see* LEND-LEASE); and the problem of Japan. The two leaders formulated plans for a new era based on an end to "Nazi tyranny," the disarming of aggressors, and the "fullest cooperation between all nations" for social and economic gain.

DECLARATION. On August 12, 1941, the Atlantic Charter was issued, as a "Joint Declaration by the President and the Prime Minister . . . to make known certain common principles in the national policies of their respective countries on which they base their hopes for a better future for the world."

There were eight provisions:

FIRST, Their countries seek no aggrandizement, territorial or other;

SECOND, They desire to see no territorial changes that do not accord with the freely expressed wishes of the people concerned;

THIRD, They respect the right of all peoples to choose the form of government under which they will live; and they wish to see sovereign rights and self-government restored to those who have been forcibly deprived of them;

FOURTH, They will endeavor with due respect for their existing obligations, to further the enjoyment by all states, great or small, victor or vanquished, of access, on equal terms, to the trade and to the raw materials of the world which are needed for their economic prosperity;

FIFTH, They desire to bring about the fullest collaboration between all nations in the economic field with the object of securing, for all, improved labor standards, economic adjustment and social security;

SIXTH, After the final destruction of the Nazi tyranny, they hope to see established a peace which will afford to all nations the means of dwelling in safety within their own boundaries, and which will afford assurance that all the men in all the lands may live out their lives in freedom from fear and want;

SEVENTH, Such a peace should enable all men to traverse the high seas and oceans without hindrance;

EIGHTH, They believe that all of the nations of the world, for realistic as well as spiritual reasons, must come to the abandonment of the use of force. Since no future peace can be maintained if land, sea, or air armaments continue to be employed by nations which threaten, or may threaten, aggression outside of their frontiers, they believe, pending the establishment of a wider and permanent system of general security, that the disarmament of such nations is essential. They will likewise aid and encourage all other practicable measures which will lighten for peace-loving peoples the crushing burden of armaments.

SIGNIFICANCE. Although it was not an official document, the announcement of the Atlantic Charter had an electric effect upon the peoples of the Allied countries. At a time of pessimism and discouragement, it expressed the war aims by two powers, one belligerent and one technically neutral. (*See* WAR AIMS.) The phraseology of the document was cautious, but it held out hope for a world in which political and economic equality would prevail among nations.

The meeting in the Atlantic actually meant the birth of the United Nations. The Soviet Union and nine governments in exile soon endorsed the Atlantic Charter. Sometimes compared to the Wilsonian Fourteen Points agenda of World War I, the Charter differed from the previous statement on two points:

First, nothing was said about specific territorial changes, and second, this was a joint statement by Britain and the United States, assented to by ten other Allied nations.

Bibliography. J. F. Dulles, *Long-Range Peace Objectives* (1941); H. Morton, *Atlantic Meeting* (1943); and T. A. Wilson, *The First Summit* (1969).

ATLANTIC WALL. Highly publicized German system of fixed and field fortifications along the North Sea, the English Channel, and the Atlantic coastline to act as a defensive wall against Allied attack. It was planned and built after the German capture of France in June 1940.

BACKGROUND. Fearing an Allied assault in the West, Hitler in 1942 decreed the construction of a fortified coastline running in a great arc from Norway to Holland to the Channel and Biscay coasts. The plan was to concentrate heavy forces in each major port and between them set up a system of strong points, many of them miles apart. At each of the outmost ramparts hedgehog obstacles would be set in the turf to sink or disable landing craft. Ashore there would be concrete bunkers, barbed wire, and pillboxes, from which machine gunners could stop invaders who managed to get ashore.

CONSTRUCTION. Hitler assigned construction of the Atlantic Wall to the Todt Organization, a semi-military governmental unit set up in 1938 to build military installations and special highways for armored vehicles. (*See* TODT, FRITZ.) After November 1943 Gen. Erwin Rommel (*q.v.*) supervised work on the wall. Tens of thousands of laborers were assigned to the task. German planners were handicapped by the fact that they had no idea where the Allies planned to strike and not enough manpower to complete a continuous line of fortifications. Nevertheless, Goebbels' Propaganda Ministry attempted to create the illusion of an impregnable Atlantic Wall. There were strong as well as weak sections, as indicated by success of the Allied invasion on June 6, 1944. (*See* NORMANDY INVASION.)

ATLANTIS. Germany's deadliest sea raider during the first two years of the war until she was trapped by a British cruiser and sunk in late 1941.

DESIGN. Built by the Bremen Hansa Line as the freighter *Goldenfels,* the *Atlantis* was converted in 14 weeks into an armed merchant carrier known to the Germans as *Hilfskreuzer No. 2* and later to the British Admiralty as Raider ''C.'' Her designers completely altered her appearance for use as a carrier. A dummy funnel could be erected or stowed away on command. Her real funnel could be lengthened or shortened. Her masts were telescopic like the legs of a camera tripod. She was outfitted with false platforms, huge crates that could be mistaken for deck cargo, and contraptions to hold torpedo-tubes on either side of the waterline amidships. She was the last word in a camouflaged warship.

SPECIFICATIONS.

Measurements. Length 500 ft.; width 65 ft.

Standard Displacement. 6,860 tons.

Maximum Speed. 17½ knots.

Armament. Six 6-in. guns; a 3-in. warning gun; two twin 3.7-cm. AA guns; four 2-cm. automatics.

Complement. 104 elite seamen.

Special Features. Mine compartment with storage space for 92 magnetic mines; one *Heinkel-111* (*see* AIRCRAFT: GERMAN AIRCRAFT DATA CHART) fully assembled and a reserve plane in crates.

RAIDS. On December 19, 1939, under the command of Capt. Bernhard Rogge, the *Atlantis* set out disguised as a Norwegian freighter. At night she dropped her disguise and became "the Soviet auxiliary warship *Kim.*" Negotiating the narrows between western Norway and the Shetlands, which were closely guarded by the Royal Navy, she moved into the Atlantic. On orders from the German Naval Staff she proceeded to the South Atlantic to operate on the Capetown-Freetown route.

Thus began an extraordinary cruise. One day the *Atlantis* was Japanese, another day she might be Dutch, Norwegian, or even British. She roamed the Atlantic until May 1940, the Indian Ocean from May to December 1940, and cruised around the world from January to November 1941. Her mission was to find unsuspecting Allied merchant ships and send them to the bottom. Altogether she sank 22 ships of 145,067 tons of Allied shipping while logging 622 days at sea and 102,000 miles.

ENTRAPMENT. The British Admiralty believed it essential that the *Atlantis* be removed as a hazard to Allied shipping. It ordered a close search for the shadowy German raider. On November 22, 1941, the British cruiser *Devonshire* finally caught up with her. One of the cruiser's reconnaissance aircraft sighted the *Atlantis* in the South Atlantic. Then began a tug-of-war as the raider tried to maneuver the cruiser into the path of an accompanying U-Boat. The *Devonshire* moved in from 18,000 yards to 12,000 and then at 10,000 opened fire. The *Atlantis* sustained eight direct hits, listed to port, and began to sink stern first. Many of her crew were rescued and brought 5,000 miles through Allied controlled waters to home port.

Bibliography. W. Frank and B. Rogge, *The German Raider Atlantis,* trans. by R.O.B. Long (1956).

ATLAS. A special German train that housed Hitler's field headquarters (*Fuehrerhauptquartier*) during the early campaign in Poland in September 1939. (*See also Fuehrer's* Headquarters.)

The *Fuehrer* continued to use this convenient mobile command post during the attacks on the Low Countries and France in 1940. He ordered the locomotive engineers of *Atlas* not to exceed a speed of 35 miles per hour. He never forgot an accident in 1936 when his then special train, traveling at a speed of 80 miles per hour, collided at a crossing with a coach carrying a theatrical touring company and killed all its occupants.

ATOMIC BOMB. *See* MANHATTAN PROJECT.

ATTLEE, CLEMENT RICHARD (1883–1967). British statesman and leader of the Labour Party during the war.

In 1939 Attlee gave his support to the war but refused to serve in the Cabinet of Prime Minister Neville Chamberlain (*q.v.*). After May 10, 1940, when Winston Churchill (*q.v.*) took office as Prime Minister, Attlee was given a post in the Coalition Government and served throughout the war. He was able to minimize many problems facing Churchill during the conflict. He took over Churchill's duties whenever the Prime Minister was out of the country on official business. In 1943 Attlee was named Lord President of the Council. In 1945 he went to San Francisco as a member of the British delegation to the Conference on World Security.

Bibliography. Among Attlee's own works were: *Social Worker* (1924); *The Will and Way to Socialism* (1935); *The Labour Party in Perspective* (1937); *Purpose and Policy: Selected Speeches by C. R. Attlee* (1946); *The Labour Party in Perspective and Twelve Years Later* (1954); *As It Happened* (1954); *Purpose and Policy* (1954); and *A Prime Minister Remembers* (1962). *See also* the biography by R. Jenkins, *Mr. Attlee: An Interim Biography* (1948).

AUCHINLECK, CLAUDE JOHN EYRE (1884–   ). British commander during the early days of the war.

In May–June 1940 Auchinleck commanded British forces in the unsuccessful campaign in Norway. He was then made chief of the Southern Command in England with responsibility for supervising defense against a threatened German invasion. In December 1940 he was posted again to India as Commander-in-Chief.

In May 1941 Auchinleck led an Indian division to the Near East to support Gen. Archibald P. Wavell's (*q.v.*) campaign against the Axis. The next month he was ordered to replace Wavell as Commander-in-Chief Middle East. On November 18, 1941, he launched an offensive, which was successful at Sidi Rezegh, relieved Tobruk, and captured Benghazi. However, Auchinleck's drive broke down at El Agheila, as a German counteroffensive drove the British back to Gazala in the middle of Cyrenaica. After several months of inactivity, the Germans under Gen. Erwin Rommel (*q.v.*) smashed through to Tobruk. The British retreated to El Alamein, where Auchinleck began to fortify a strong defensive line. (*See* NORTH AFRICA, CAMPAIGNS IN.)

At this time Churchill replaced Auchinleck with Gen. Bernard Law Montgomery (*q.v.*). Auchinleck's Middle East command was given to Gen. Harold Alexander (*q.v.*). In 1943 Auchinleck was transferred to his old post in India, where he was given responsibility for the British campaign in Burma. In this post he performed his greatest service in the course of the war.

AUSCHWITZ. *See* EXTERMINATION CAMPS.

AXIS. Term originated by Mussolini to describe the common ideology and goals of Fascist Italy and National Socialist Germany.

Believing that Britain and France were hostile regarding his claim to the Mediterranean as *mare nostrum* ("our sea"), the *Duce* turned to Hitler for support. After withdrawing from the League of Nations, Italy formed the Rome-Berlin Axis on October 25, 1936, made formal on May 22, 1939 (Pact of Steel). On September 27, 1940, it was extended into the Berlin-Rome-Tokyo Axis (*q.v.*), also called the Tripartite Pact, when the Japanese joined. The Russians refused to enter the Axis. The pact described the circumstances under which the members would cooperate in event of war.

Bibliography. R. Wiskemann, *The Rome-Berlin Axis* (1940).

AXIS SALLY (1900–   ). American-born radio propagandist for the Germans in World War II.

American-born Mildred Gillars, called Axis Sally by her listeners, studied at Ohio Wesleyan University and then went to Germany in the 1920s as a music student. During World War II she was hired by the Germans to broadcast propaganda talks along with music from a Berlin studio. She urged American troops to go home and forget the war. American GIs (*q.v.*) enjoyed the jazz records she played as a disc jockey, but they paid little attention to her accompanying propaganda line.

After the war Gillars was arrested by American authorities, tried, and sentenced to 12 years in prison. She taught for a while in a Roman Catholic convent in Columbus, Ohio, and then returned to her old college, Ohio Wesleyan, and received a bachelor's degree in speech in 1973 at the age of 73.

Paul Joseph Goebbels (*q.v.*), Reich Minister for Public Enlightenment and Propaganda, regarded radio as a major war weapon, and engaged a number of other Britons and Americans to present the Nazi cause on the air. He supplemented broadcasts with leaflets fired by artillery or dropped from bombers. In addition to Gillars, for the Nazi cause he recruited Lord Haw Haw (*q.v.*), Jane Anderson, Fred Kaltenbach, and several other foreigners.

AYRES, LEW (1908–   ). American film star and conscientious objector.

Lew Ayres first gained acclaim as the young hero of *All Quiet on the Western Front* (1930), an eloquent antiwar film. If the First World War helped launch Ayres in his work, World War II virtually destroyed it. The career of the young star was fading when he was rescued by the role of Dr. James Kildare, assistant to Dr. Gillespie, a crusty old physician played by Lionel Barrymore. When called up for military service, Ayres pronounced himself a conscientious objector, reminding the nation that he had made his name in an antiwar picture and still believed in that picture's viewpoint.

Ayres's decision brought down upon him the wrath of public, press, and of

Louis B. Mayer, the Hollywood tycoon. Mayer replaced Ayres with Van Johnson in the Kildare series. Ayres performed noncombatant work during the war, but his career was shattered. A small minority respected him for his conscientious objection to the war.

B

BABI YAR. Scene of the execution of Ukrainian Jews and Soviet prisoners of war.

On September 19, 1941, a German Army group, after hammering at the Soviet defenses at Kiev for forty-five days, finally managed to enter the city. Several days later a tremendous explosion rocked the German command post in the Continental Hotel. In the ensuing fire many German soldiers lost their lives.

The German military command held local Jews responsible for the loss of German lives. In reprisal Jews were marched in groups to the outer limits of the city to the Babi Yar ravine. Here thousands of Jews, as well as Soviet prisoners of war, were slaughtered in two days of summary executions.

At the Nuremberg Trials (*q.v.*) Gen. Alfred Jodl claimed that land mines had been planted in Kiev by Russian troops before their retreat. Investigators later claimed that evidence had been discovered implicating Russians in the Babi Yar massacre, but the facts have never been ascertained.

The Babi Yar massacre was the subject of an emotional poem by Yevgeny Yevtushenko, who expressed his distress not only because of German behavior but also because of Russian Anti-Semitism. "Today I am a Jew," he wrote, though no drop of Jewish blood flowed in his veins. Anti-Semites, he charged, detested him as if he were a Jew.

BADER, DOUGLAS ROBERT (1910–   ). Legendary British war hero who had lost both legs in a flying accident in 1931.

On the outbreak of war Bader joined the RAF (*q.v.*) as a flying officer. He fought his first action during the evacuation of the British Expeditionary Force (*q.v.*) from Dunkirk (*q.v.*) in May–June 1940. In the Battle of Britain (*q.v.*) he commanded the first Canadian Fighter Squadron (242) of the RAF and was credited with 20 "kills." Promoted to Wing Commander in March 1941, he was captured on August 9, 1941, following a collision with an enemy aircraft over occupied France. After one escape he spent the rest of the war in prison and was released from Colditz (*q.v.*) on April 15, 1945, by the U.S. 1st Army. After the war he worked for the Shell Petroleum Company as managing director of its aircraft division.

Bibliography. Bader told the story of the *Spitfire* and the *Hurricane* in *Fight for the Sky* (1973).

BADOGLIO, PIETRO (1871–1956). Italian Chief of the General Staff and Mussolini's successor.

At the beginning of the war Badoglio was convinced that Italy was not ready for war on a major scale and needed time to digest its conquest of Ethiopia. He was unsuccessful, however, in preventing Italy's entrance into the war on June 10, 1940, as Hitler's partner. He sought to persuade Mussolini not to attack Greece, but he was overruled and ordered to lead the invasion of Greece. Blamed for the defeat, he was dismissed in December 1940. (*See* GREECE, BATTLE FOR.)

On July 25, 1943, after the fall of Mussolini, Badoglio was appointed Premier. On September 3, 1943, he negotiated an armistice with the Allies. He fled behind the Allied lines to Brindisi in the south, to join the king and government there. Badoglio managed to get the Allies to declare Italy's "cobelligerency" against the Germans. He resigned on June 10, 1944.

Bibliography. P. Badoglio. *The War in Abyssinia* (1937); and S. Bertholdi, *Badoglio* (1967).

BAEDEKER RAIDS. Hitler's reprisal air strikes at British cities following Royal Air Force (*q.v.*) attacks on Lübeck on March 28–29, 1942, and subsequently on the Rhineland. The name *Baedeker* was taken from the famous series of German guide books, often carried by tourists visiting cathedral towns.

On May 30–31, 1942, the British made their first 1,000-bomber air assault on Cologne. (*See* COLOGNE, BOMBING OF.) Shortly afterward came another devastating raid on Mainz. Angered, Hitler ordered his reprisal campaign by the weakened *Luftwaffe* (*q.v.*) stepped up to appease the German public. On May 31, 1942, came an attack on Canterbury, and on October 31 a raid on York in reprisal "for Cologne and Mainz respectively."

BALBO, ITALO (1896–1940). Father of the Italian air force.

Balbo returned home from posts abroad after Italy declared war on June 10, 1940. Eighteen days later, together with nine other airmen, he was killed in a plane crash during a British bombardment of Tobruk, the Italian naval and air base in North Africa. The British Foreign Office denied the Italian announcement that Balbo had died in action against the Royal Air Force (*q.v.*) and claimed that he had been killed accidentally by his own antiaircraft fire.

Bibliography. R. Cupini, *Balbo* (1973).

BALKANS, CAMPAIGNS IN THE. Axis mastery of the Balkans in the early stage of the war.

BACKGROUND. After the fall of France in June 1940, Hitler turned his attention to the Balkans, where important developments were soon to take place.

The area was critical for him because it was necessary to guard his flank before an all-out assault on the Soviet Union. At the same time control of the Balkan peninsula would give him another bridge to North Africa and his goal—the Suez Canal. He was also angered by Greek support of the British and by Yugoslav defiance.

The Russians were considerably disturbed by the rapid collapse of France. Despite their partnership with the Third Reich, they had little trust in it and were not comfortable with a powerful Hitler in control of the Continent.

RUMANIA. There was a growing rift between Moscow and Berlin on Rumania. On June 26, 1940, without consulting the Germans, the Kremlin compelled Rumania to cede Bessarabia and northern Bukovina to the Soviet Union. Disturbed by the possible loss of Rumanian oil, Hitler decided to forestall any further moves in the area. He forced the Rumanians to cede half of Transylvania to Hungary and a portion of Dobrudja to Bulgaria, evidently regarding both these satellites as more trustworthy. Rumanian King Carol, who was held responsible for these disasters, had to abdicate and flee abroad. Control of Rumania was vested in a frankly Fascist and pro-German regime under Gen. Ion Antonescu, with Carol's son, Michael, as puppet ruler.

By October 1940, German troops were moving into Rumania to protect the Ploesti oil fields. The Kremlin was effectively blocked from the Balkans.

GREECE. At this time a gross blunder by Mussolini opened the Balkans to the British. On October 28, 1940, without consulting Hitler and without provocation, the Italian dictator went off on an adventure of his own. His invasion of Greece collapsed ingloriously in the face of energetic Greek resistance and his troops were forced back into Albania. Encouraged by the Italian disaster, London sent troops from the British Middle Eastern Command in Egypt to Crete and landed several squadrons of the Royal Air Force (*q.v.*) on Greek soil. The Greeks needed little help at the time and were able to take care of themselves. (*See* GREECE, BATTLE FOR.)

DIPLOMATIC INTERLUDE. Infuriated by the ineptitude of his Italian partner, Hitler ordered preparations for *Marita* (*see* CODE NAMES, GERMAN, MARITA), an operation for the invasion of the Balkans in the spring of 1941. Before proceeding, he attempted to ascertain the intentions of Moscow. He offered the Russians membership in the Axis (*q.v.*), to which there was no reply. The Russians countered by asking that the Balkans be divided into two spheres of influence, the western Balkans (Yugoslavia) for Germany and the eastern Balkans (Bulgaria and the Straits) for Russia. Now it was Hitler's turn to maintain a contemptuous silence. Instead, he resolved on *Barbarossa* (*q.v.*), his plan to attack the Soviet Union.

YUGOSLAVIA. Hitler moved simultaneously on Greece and Yugoslavia. First he demanded free passage through Yugoslavia. Belgrade quickly accepted. But two days later, on March 27, 1941, Yugoslav military chiefs repudiated the bargain, deposed Prince Paul, and proclaimed young Peter II as king. Angered, Hitler ordered a *Panzer* (*q.v.*) attack (April 6, 1941) on the countryside and a *Luftwaffe* (*q.v.*) strike at the capital. (*See* BELGRADE, BOMBING OF.) The Yugoslavs capitulated after the savage attack and formally surrendered on April 17, 1941. The country was carved into different states and partitioned among the Germans, Italians, Hungarians, and Bulgarians. Only an independent Croatia ruled by pro-Axis politicians survived.

YUGOSLAV RESISTANCE. The Yugoslavs, one of the most fiercely independent people of Europe, refused to take their defeat as final. In villages, forests, and mountains throughout the country, guerrilla bands rallied to harry the invaders. One group, the Chetniks (*q.v.*), Serbians led by Gen. Draja Mikhailovich (*q.v.*), worked zealously to break Axis rule and restore the monarchy. Another, the Partisans (*q.v.*), headed by Josip Broz, known as Tito (*q.v.*), favored a Yugoslav republic and a Communist-oriented society. A bitter struggle broke out between these two factions. In time Allied backing went to Tito. (*See* GOVERNMENTS-IN-EXILE.)

CRETE. Meanwhile, in the middle of May 1940, the Germans launched an offensive on the strategic island of Crete. It was the first major airborne invasion in history and a clear-cut victory of air power over sea power. (*See* CRETE, BATTLE OF.) Hitler was now in a favorable position to seize the Near and Middle East by a leap from Crete or a drive from Libya. With his Balkan flank cleared, he could now turn on the Soviet Union. But in 1942 the tide of war began to change against the Axis. Eventually, the entire Balkans were cleared of Axis control. (*See* EASTERN FRONT, CAMPAIGNS ON THE.)

LIBERATION OF THE BALKANS, 1944-1945. The Russian offensive into Rumania began in August 1944. On August 23 Rumanian dictator Antonescu was arrested and his government dissolved. King Michael announced the end of hostilities and agreed to an armistice. Meanwhile, the Russians moved on to the Ploesti oil fields. At the end of the month they took Bucharest. They disregarded a Bulgarian proclamation of neutrality, marched into the country in early September, and took Sofia.

Triumphant Russians moved on to Belgrade and Budapest as Germans retreated from the Balkans. The entire Danubian valley was now in Russian hands. Tito's Yugoslav Partisans, helped by Allied arms, moved into Belgrade on October 20, 1944.

Bibliography. L. White, *The Long Balkan Night* (1944); D. Martin, *Ally Betrayed: The Uncensored Story of Tito and Mihailovich* (1946); L. S. Stavrianos, *Greece: The War and Aftermath* (1947); C. Buckley, *Greece and Crete, 1941* (1952); T. Higgins, *The Soft Underbelly* (1968); D. Orlow, *The Nazis in the Balkans* (1968); and Bantes, E., *et al., Romania in the War against Hitler's Germany, August 1944-May 1945* (1970).

BANZAI CHARGES. Attacks by Japanese troops in combat. The interjection *banzai* means literally "Ten Thousand Years, Forever!" It was a shout of honor or a hurrah often dedicated to the life of the Emperor. The word was shouted by trapped troops in a final desperate assault on a superior enemy force.

BACKGROUND. The philosophy behind *banzai* reflected the traditional *samurai* code. Despite the rapid modernization of Japan after the mid-19th century, vestiges of the feudal system were retained by the *samurai* class of retainers under feudal lords. These warriors were trained to refuse defeat in combat under any circumstances and to accept death rather than capture—the ultimate dishonor. The custom persisted among the 20th-century militarists (*gumbatsu*) and was encouraged by elder statesmen (*genro*) and business interests (*zaibatsu*).

WORLD WAR II. The *banzai* charge was used after 1931 on the Chinese mainland and throughout World War II. Both officers and enlisted men were trained to accept death rather than inadmissible surrender. Officers who held themselves responsible for defeat often chose death in battle or ceremonial suicide. (*See HĀRĀ-KĪRI.*) A few enlisted men abandoned the practice, but officers were virtually unanimous in accepting death. A typical case of the officers' syndrome occurred on August 9, 1942, at the Battle of Savo Island, when American crewmen on destroyers attempted to rescue floating Japanese seamen. When Japanese enlisted men tried to grasp the outstretched arms of the Americans, their officers slashed with knives at the arms of their men breaking the code.

So powerful was the fear of disgrace that there have been many cases of Japanese troops retreating into the jungles and living there for years because they had not been given an order to surrender. Isolated instances occurred in the postward period of such Japanese troops returning to civilization.

ATTU. On June 2, 1943, American troops, after a fierce struggle, occupied Attu in the Aleutian Islands. In the closing stage of the battle, 1,000 Japanese men, trapped on a ridge between Chichagov Harbor and Saranh Bay, made a wild charge on the American lines with shouts of *"Banzai!"* and "Japanese drink blood like wine!"

The Americans took only 28 prisoners at Attu. From the corpses of dead men they took letters, which included such comments as "Voices of *banzai* would make a wild god weep," and "I will become a deity with a smile in this heavy fog. I am only waiting for the day of death." In Tokyo the incident was compared in headlines to the British Charge of the Light Brigade, when 500 cavalrymen rode to their death before Sevastopol on October 25, 1854 (*See* ALEUTIAN ISLANDS CAMPAIGNS.)

TARAWA. On November 21, 1943, U.S. Marines stormed ashore on Tarawa in the Gilbert Islands and overwhelmed the Japanese garrison in a few days. The defenders, dug in under pillboxes covered with five feet of concrete, were flushed out with grenades and flame throwers. Many, stupefied with *sake,* a rice wine, sought death in a *banzai* charge.

KWAJALEIN. At Kwajalein in the Marshall Islands Americans were astonished by the unpredictable actions of the enemy. Japanese officers, brandishing swords in a *banzai* charge, frantically beat their weapons against the armor plate of tanks, with no effect other than to make themselves perfect targets. Others would approach a tank, hold a grenade against it, and keep it there until it exploded, taking an arm but causing no damage to the armored vehicle.

ENIWETOK. Similar suicidal charges took place at Eniwetok Atoll in the Marshalls. A detachment of Japanese troops was trapped on the air base there. "We cornered fifty or so at the end of the island," wrote Lt. Cord Meyer, "where they attempted a *banzai* charge. But we cut them down like overripe wheat, and they lay like tired children with their faces in the sand."

SAIPAN. The biggest *banzai* land attack of the war took place in Saipan in the Marianas on July 6–7, 1944. The two Japanese commanders ordered the remaining troops on the island to kill at least 10 Americans each before taking their own lives. The commanders then committed *härä-kïri* in ceremonial fashion.

Meanwhile, more than 3,000 Japanese swarmed into a 200-yard gap between two battalions of the 27th Division. Some were armed with guns, others carried only bayonets, still others had no weapons at all. They overran command posts and inflicted heavy casualties in their wild charge, but eventually all were killed in the desperate attack.

Another grisly episode occurred after the capture of Saipan. Japanese civilians on the island had been showered with surrender leaflets guaranteeing them honorable treatment. Refusing to accept the word of the enemy, hundreds took their own lives in a macabre display of hysteria. Like lemmings, they gathered on the northern cliffs. Parents dashed their babies to death on the rocks below and then, one after another, screaming and shouting, jumped off the cliffs. Some cut the throats of others. Others took their lives with hand grenades. Still others piled in the caves and ravines from which they were blasted by flame throwers.

OKINAWA. In Spring 1945 the suicide mania reached incredible heights in the *kamikaze* attacks around Okinawa. *Kamikaze* tactics were, in effect, a streamlined, air-minded version of the *banzai* charge. The grisly practice suggested ritual obedience, veneration of the Emperor, loyalty to country and family, and belief in the life of the spirit after death. The attacks caused large casualties, but had no effect on the outcome of the war. (*See KAMIKAZE.*)

BARBAROSSA. Early name *Fritz*. German code or cover name for the attack on the Soviet Union on June 22, 1941. The operation was named after Frederick I (c. 1122–1190), Holy Roman Emperor who was called Barbarossa, or Redbeard, and popularly remembered by the German people as a just and beneficent ruler.

The massive German invasion crossed the Russian borders and headed in three great waves toward Leningrad in the north, Moscow in the center, and Kiev in the south. At first the invasion seemed to be crowned with success, but it soon slowed to a crawl and was eventually smashed by the Russians. (*See* EASTERN FRONT, CAMPAIGNS ON THE.)

Bibliography. A. Clark, *Barbarossa: The Russo-German Conflict, 1941–1945* (1965); A. M. Nekrich, *"June 22, 1941"* (1968); and J. Keegan, *Barbarossa; Invasion of Russia, 1941* (1971).

BARUCH, BERNARD (1870–1965). American financier, philanthropist, and presidential adviser.

After the United States entered the war against Germany in 1941, Baruch was offered the post of war mobilization director but declined it. He, nevertheless, took part in the construction of a massive war industry. From 1943 to 1945 he had an unpaid post as personal adviser to James Byrnes (*q.v.*), Director of Economic Stabilization and later Director of War Mobilization. Although he held no administrative post, Baruch performed important services during the war emergency. He also headed a special fact-finding commission for President Franklin D. Roosevelt.

Bibliography. See biographies by C. Field (1944); W. L. White (1950); M. V. Rosenbloom (1953); and M. L. Coit (1957).

BASTOGNE. Small but important road center in the Ardennes region of Belgium and scene of a major German counteroffensive in December 1944. The key to the southern Ardennes, Bastogne commanded a network of roads spread out like the spokes of a wheel.

BACKGROUND. On December 16, 1944, Field Marshal Gerd von Rundstedt (*q.v.*) launched a well-planned and executed offensive in the Ardennes along a 70-mile front. Taking advantage of the foggy, snowy weather, the move quickly gained momentum as the Germans pushed ahead for a dozen miles the first day. British and American troops attempted to stem the attack, but they soon saw a huge gash cut into their lines. The German *Blitzkrieg* (*q.v.*) of the 5th Panzer Army seemed to be on the verge of a giant breakthrough.

The Allies held the shoulders of the wedge at Mondschau and Bastogne. At Bastogne the Germans collided head-on with big *Sherman* tanks (*q.v.*) of the American 10th Armored Division. The armored vehicles crashed through the cobblestone streets of Bastogne, paused, and then turned east to meet three enemy spearheads. Both sides traded lives for time. Perceiving the danger created by the salient, Gen. Dwight D. Eisenhower (*q.v.*) ordered relief from the south. Gen. George S. Patton (*q.v.*) and his tanks of the 4th Armored Division broke through to end the encirclement and rescued the trapped Americans at Bastogne.

THE "NUTS!" INCIDENT. On December 21, 1944, in the midst of furious fighting, two German officers, a major and captain, were sent into Bastogne under a flag of truce to demand surrender. They described the hopeless position of the Americans. "Capitulate immediately—or be destroyed."

The message was handed to Brig. Gen. Anthony C. McAuliffe (*q.v.*), temporarily in command of the 101st Airborne Division. Through an aide, McAuliffe gave a one-word reply: "Nuts!" The puzzled Germans asked for an explanation. The aide snapped: "If you do not understand what 'Nuts!' means, in plain English it is the same as 'Go to Hell!' And I tell you something else—if you continue to attack, we will kill every goddam German who tries to break into this city." The Germans clicked their heels, saluted, while one said, "We will kill many Americans. This is war." "On your way, bud!" growled the American.

AFTERMATH. Instead of strangling Bastogne, von Rundstedt found his forces trapped by powerful American divisions on both sides. By the middle of January 1945 the Ardennes salient was reduced. The last German offensive only delayed the end of the war.

The "Nuts!" story, like that of the Patton slapping incident (*see* PATTON, GEORGE SMITH, JR.), was only a minor event in the war, but it became a *cause célèbre* both in military and civilian circles throughout the world. German historians recorded the Bastogne story in serious terms: "Our demand for surrender was refused." American GIs (*q.v.*) were delighted by the response given by their scrappy general and deemed it a perfect reflection of the American way of life. Combat correspondents reported that American troops fought with renewed vigor when they learned about the incident. From then on McAuliffe was known as the "Hero of Bastogne," and his name was inseparably linked with the one-word reply. He was promoted to Major General.

SIGNIFICANCE. The Allies were near to disaster at the beginning of the Ardennes battle, primarily because they had neglected to protect their defensive flank. In the end, however, Hitler made the more serious mistake. He believed that "attack is the best defense," but it turned out to be the worst defense. Rundstedt wanted to withdraw his forces from the nose of the German salient, but Hitler forbade any retreat. "Hitler," said Rundstedt, "insisted that it must go on. It was Stalingrad No. 2." (*See also* BULGE, BATTLE OF THE.)

Bibliography. F. Mackenzie, *The Men of Bastogne* (1968); and P. Elstob, *Bastogne: The Roadblock* (1970).

BATAAN, BATTLE OF.

U.S. stand on Bataan Peninsula, west of Manila Bay, which extended the defense of the Philippines for four months in early 1942.

BACKGROUND. The Japanese attack on Pearl Harbor (*q.v.*) on December 7, 1941, immediately placed the Philippines in jeopardy. The U.S. Command there had a total of 111,000 troops, including 31,000 regulars (Americans and Filipino Scouts) and the rest undertrained Filipinos used to guard the coastlines. On December 22, 1941, Lt. Gen. Masaharu Homma (*q.v.*), commander of the Japanese 14th Army, led 85 transports carrying 57,000 seasoned veterans of the Chinese fighting, on main landings in the Lingayen Gulf, 120 miles north of Manila. Two days later another force of 7,000 troops landed near Lamon Bay on the east coast opposite Manila.

The U.S. commander in the Philippines, Gen. Douglas MacArthur (*q.v.*), was informed through faulty intelligence that the Japanese had double their real strength. He decided to withdraw his men into the Bataan Peninsula. By January 6, 1942, about 43,000 Americans and Filipino Scouts finished the step-by-step withdrawal without any attempt by Homma to stop them.

BATAAN. Bataan Peninsula, 25 miles long and 20 miles wide across its base, juts out from Luzon like a great finger pointed at the Cavite naval base a dozen miles away. Protected from sea attack by the heavy guns on the nearby island of Corregidor, crossed by ravines and mountain streams, Bataan seemed to be an ideal spot for defense. Its two roads adequate for a mobile force were covered with tank traps and barbed-wire entanglements.

SIEGE. During the first week of January 1942, American and Filipino troops retreated from both ends of Luzon while fighting delaying actions. The two files joined at San Fernando and began the last stage of the journey into Bataan. Here the Japanese invaders subjected them to every kind of attack—frontal onslaught, flank actions, concentrated artillery bombardment, and seaborne infiltration. MacArthur had counted on feeding only his own troops, but was soon faced with the problem of taking care of tens of thousands of civilians.

Conditions rapidly worsened on Bataan. Japanese warships sank all the supply ships sent to Luzon. By the end of January rations were cut in half and the food supply dwindled further. Hungry men ate the meat of dogs, iguanas, monkeys, mules, carabaros, and snakes, and whatever berries and roots they could find in the jungle. The besieged troops and civilians were stricken with malaria, dengue fever, scurvy, beriberi, and amoebic dysentery, while the supply of drugs ran out. Thousands were placed in makeshift hospitals. Gaunt, undernourished, disease-ridden, the garrison fought on.

In early February 1942 the Japanese, too, had to suspend operations because their own men were struck down by malaria. In addition, the crack Japanese 48th Division was withdrawn to be sent to the Dutch East Indies. By early March the Japanese had only 3,000 troops in the Bataan campaign, but the besieged Americans, unaware of the lightened enemy forces, and suffering badly from disease, were in no shape to take the offensive. Morale fell when MacArthur was ordered to Australia. The commander left on March 11 for Mindanao and thence by plane to Australia, leaving Lt. Gen. Jonathan M. Wainwright (*q.v.*) in command.

CAPITULATION. At the end of March 1942 the Japanese on Bataan were reinforced by 22,000 fresh troops, more guns, and additional aircraft. They moved again on April 3, this time pushing the Americans back down the peninsula. On April 8 Wainwright withdrew with a small force to Corregidor. (*See* CORREGIDOR, FALL OF.) The next day the 35,000 men left on Bataan were surrendered unconditionally "to avoid mass slaughter." (*See also* BATAAN DEATH MARCH.)

Bibliography. W. L. White, *They Were Expendable* (1942); J. Redmond, *I Served on Bataan* (1943); J. Hersey, *Men on Bataan* (1943); J. M. Wainwright, *General Wainwright's Story* (1946); R. Conroy, *The Battle of Bataan* (1970); and R. C. Mallonée, *The Naked Flagpole: Battle for Bataan* (1980).

BATAAN DEATH MARCH. Trek of American and Filipino troops to prison camps at Cabanatuan in April 1942.

The Bataan Death March began six days after the surrender at Bataan on April 9, 1942. (*See* BATAAN, BATTLE OF.) The captured troops, who had surrendered to avoid certain annihilation, were required by their captors to march for 60 miles in the excruciatingly hot tropical sun from Mariveles in the south of Bataan to railroad sidings at San Fernando.

Under brutal conditions, with little food or water, the prisoners were forced to move in columns of four under the blinding sun, over the hot earth, and through the grayish-white dust. Filthy, dazed, nearly mad with thirst and hunger, the men staggered forward. Sadistic Japanese guards beat to death any prisoner caught with Japanese currency or articles presumed to have been stolen from Japanese dead. Marchers were robbed of their own money, watches, and fountain pens, or taunted as they watched helplessly while Japanese guards threw food away. Behind the main lines mop-up squads killed those who dropped out because of illness, exhaustion, or abuse. Filipino natives who tried to help the prisoners were driven off. A few prisoners managed to escape.

On the sixth day the remaining captives reached barbed-wire compounds in the railroad sidings at San Fernando. Here they were packed into antique boxcars with only tiny slits in the walls for ventilation. Many were overcome by the foul air and stench of vomit. After a three-hour ride and another seven-mile hike, the survivors reached Camp O'Donnell in the jungles of Arlac Province, where they were interned.

CASUALTIES. Estimates vary, but it is believed that at least 10,000 lives were lost, of whom 2,300 were Americans, through summary execution, sickness, and starvation.

AFTERMATH. Lt. Gen. Masaharu Homma (*q.v.*), who commanded the Japanese troops at Bataan, was held responsible for the brutal behavior of the guards on that Death March. Arrested in September 1945, he was tried in Manila and executed by firing squad in April 1946.

Bibliography. See bibliography on BATAAN, BATTLE OF.

BATTALION OF HEAVEN. A force of French guerrillas dropped behind German lines by parachute before and after D-Day. (*See* NORMANDY INVASION.)

Trained by the British, the Battalion of Heaven was composed of agents who served behind enemy lines. It was trained to set up armed redoubts in France, and to arm, train, and lead local guerrillas of the *Maquis* (*q.v.*)

BAZOOKA. American 2.36-inch recoilless antitank rocket launcher. The bazooka got its name from a gas pipe horn made famous by entertainer Bob Burns.

DESIGN. The bazooka was produced to give the American foot soldier a powerful defense weapon against the German *Panzer* (*q.v.*) (tank). It was a simple device made of a section of metal tubing open at both ends, fitted with hand grips, a wooden shoulder stock, a breech guard, and a dry-cell battery to ignite the rockets electrically. The sight was set atop the tube near the muzzle. The hollow-charged weapon was operated by two men, one loading and the other aiming and firing. It fired a 3-½ pound projectile up to about 400 yards.

WORLD WAR II. The bazooka made its first combat appearance in Tunisia after Allied landings in North Africa in 1942. The effect was devastating. German tankmen were astonished to find their heavy armor penetrated by the outlandish weapon. German designers attempted to defend their tanks from bazooka fire by using heavy wire mesh for side screens. Eventually, they put into production their own version, the 88-mm. *Raketenwerfer.*

SPECIFICATIONS.
Measurements. Length 54 in.; weight 12 lbs.
Range. Sight aimed for fire from 100 to 400 yds.
Special Features. Breech loaded; fired by electrical impulse; no recoil; could use high explosives.

BCRA. (*Bureau Central de Renseignement et d'Action.*) Secret intelligence service suggested originally by Gen. Charles de Gaulle (*q.v.*) to direct the Free French (*See* FREE FRANCE) in its underground work in occupied France. Led by André de Wavrin ("Colonel Passy"), it worked with British and American intelligence units in organizing the French Resistance to Nazi occupation.

BEAVERBROOK, WILLIAM MAXWELL AITKEN, 1st BARON
(1879–1964). British financier, newspaper proprietor, and Cabinet Minister
in World War II.

As World War II approached, Beaverbrook continued to assert that there
would be no war. He supported the Munich Agreement (*q.v.*), which led to the
destruction of Czechoslovakia's independence. But when war came, he turned
all his energy to promotion of Britain's war effort. In May 1940 Churchill appointed Beaverbrook Minister for Aircraft Production. With characteristic drive
and efficiency, Beaverbrook promoted the production of the *Spitfires* and *Hurricanes* (*qq.v.*), which played so important a role in the Battle of Britain (*q.v.*).
In 1941 he became Minister of Supply and served until 1942. He visited
Washington as British Lend-Lease (*q.v.*) co-ordinator, and also led an Anglo-
American mission to Moscow to arrange for the supply of war materials to the
Soviet Union.

Beaverbrook did not survive the Cabinet crisis of February 1942 and resigned. In 1943 he came back into office as Lord Privy Seal and for the rest of
the war served as Churchill's personal trouble-shooter.

Bibliography. Among Beaverbrook's books were: *Success* (1921); *Politicians and Press* (1926);
Friends (1960); and *The Decline and Fall of Lloyd George (1963)*. Biographies of Beaverbrook were written by F. A. Mackenzie (1931); E. Middleton (1941), and T. Driberg (1956).

BECK, LUDWIG (1880–1944). German General who led the resistance
against Hitler.

Beck was one of the original members of the anti-Nazi Wednesday Club.
Convinced that Hitler was ruining the name of the old Germany, Beck became
leader of the Resistance movement. Together with Carl Friedrich Goerdeler,
the civilian leader of the Resistance movement, Beck worked assiduously for the
overthrow of Hitler. Toward the end of the war, Beck decided that resistance
was not enough. He turned to conspiracy to get rid of the *Fuehrer*. He was
groomed as a possible new head of state following the removal of Hitler.

On July 20, 1944, a bomb exploded in Hitler's eastern headquarters at
Rastenburg, but the *Fuehrer* escaped with his life. (*See* JULY PLOT.) Beck was
in the War Office at the time. Knowing that he faced certain execution after
failure of the plot, Beck made two unsuccessful attempts to commit suicide. At
his request a Sergeant gave him the *coup de grâce*.

Bibliography. On Beck's role in the Resistance, *see* A. W. Dulles, *Germany's Underground*
(1945) and H. Rothfels, *The German Opposition to Hitler* (1961). On Beck's part in the
July Plot, *see* R. Manvell and H. Fraenkel, *The July Plot* (1944); and C. Fitzgibbon, *Officers' Plot to Kill Hitler* (1956). *See also* W. Foerster, *Generaloberst Ludwig Beck* (1953).

BEF. British troops sent to Norway and France. (*See* BRITISH EXPEDI-
TIONARY FORCE.)

BELGIUM, INVASION OF. The German conquest of Belgium in May
1940. (*See* LOW COUNTRIES, CAMPAIGNS IN THE.)

BELGRADE, BOMBING OF. German air assault on the capital of Yugoslavia in 1941.

TARGET. Belgrade, ancient Singedunum and Serbo-Croatian Beograd, was built on seven hills on the right bank of the Danube and the Sava at the junction of the two rivers. In 1940 it was a commercial center. Its manufactures included textiles, machinery, leather goods, and foodstuffs. The city was undefended by antiaircraft guns.

BACKGROUND. In the spring of 1941 Hitler concluded an ''alliance'' with Yugoslavia to help secure his Balkan flank in preparation for his coming attack on Soviet Russia. (*See* BALKANS, CAMPAIGNS IN THE.) Angered at the prospect of becoming a German satellite, the Yugoslavs, who never took lightly to outside pressure, overthrew their government and repudiated the treaty. The *Fuehrer* flew into a violent rage. He ordered *Operation Punishment* to teach the Yugoslavs a lesson for upsetting his timetable for the Russian campaign.

The *Luftwaffe* (*q.v.*) had been badly battered in the Battle of Britain (*q.v.*) the previous summer, but it was still a formidable air arm superior to any other in Europe. From the western front, a thousand miles from the Balkans, Hitler ordered 600 additional aircraft for *Operation Punishment*.

ATTACK. On April 6, 1941, Hitler hurled 33 divisions against the Yugoslavs. At the same time a force of 150 low-level and dive bombers knocked out the weak fighter and ground defenses, after which the *Luftwaffe* worked unmolested. For three days and three nights German bombers attacked the undefended city at low level.

LOSSES. The result was catastrophic for the Yugoslav capital. More than 17,000 people lay dead and thousands more were injured. The center of the city—public buildings, apartment houses, churches, stores—was reduced to rubble.

AFTERMATH. After delivering the knockout blow on Belgrade, the *Luftwaffe* shifted its attention to targets in support of ground troops, namely, lines of communications and battle areas. Twelve days after the assault began, Yugoslavia surrendered. The simultaneous German attack on Greece was equally successful. Yugoslavia was dismembered among the Axis, portions going to Germany, Italy, Hungary, and Bulgaria. Hitler created a new puppet state in Yugoslavia, which lasted from 1941 to 1944 under constant assault from Yugoslav guerrillas.

Hitler's bombardment of Belgrade and his assault on Yugoslavia forced him to postpone his invasion of the Soviet Union for four weeks. That was sufficient to bring him into a winter campaign against the Russians—and eventual defeat. (*See also* BALKANS, CAMPAIGNS IN THE.)

BENEŠ, EDUARD (1884–1948). Head of the Czechoslovak Government-in-exile. At the start of the war Beneš set up a Czechoslovak National Council and military unit in France. After the collapse of France he began again in London. In 1941 the British recognized the Czechsoslovak Government-in-exile, with Beneš as its President. Beneš organized the Czech Army and Air Force from refugees and placed them at the service of the Allies. He persuaded Britain and France to renounce the Munich Agreement (*q.v.*). On December 11, 1943, he arrived in Moscow to sign a treaty of alliance with the Russians. On April 3, 1945, he reentered Prague and reestablished his government.

Bibliography. Beneš wrote *My Fears and My Hopes* (1940). His unfinished memoirs appeared in 1954 under the title *Memoirs from Munich to New War and New Victory. See also* the biographies: P. Grabites, *Beneš: Statesman of Central Europe* (1936); E. B. Hitchcock, *I Built a Temple for Peace: The Life of Eduard Beneš* (1940); and C. Mackenzie, *Dr. Beneš* (1946).

BERGEN-BELSEN. German concentration camp.

Bergen-Belsen was opened in 1941 specifically for Allied prisoners-of-war. Many thousands of Russian prisoners died there during the next year. In 1943 the camp was placed under control of Heinrich Himmler (*q.v.*), who transformed it into a concentration camp for Jews. The Jewish girl Anne Frank (*q.v.*) was one of the victims who died in Bergen-Belsen.

On April 24, 1945, Patrick Gordon-Walker, British Broadcasting Corporation commentator, went into liberated Bergen-Belsen. He reported that hundreds of bodies had been shoveled into mass graves by bulldozers. ''People died before my eyes, scarcely human, moaning skeletons, many of them gone mad. Bodies were just piled up.'' (*See* CONCENTRATION CAMPS.)

BERIA, LAVRENTI PAVLOVICH (1899–1953). Head of the Soviet secret police.

In late June 1941, after the Nazi attack on the USSR, Beria was designated a member of the State Committee on Defense of the Soviet Union. The following week Stalin combined all internal affairs and state security in the NKVD (*Narodnyi Kommissariat Vnutrennykh Del*—Soviet People's Commissariat of Internal Affairs), and assigned the directing post to Beria. Beria's main task was to enforce Stalin's scorched-earth policy of destroying everything in the Germans' path before surrendering any territory. He was highly decorated for his ''military and revolutionary merits'' in this assignment.

Bibliography. See W. Duranty, *The Kremlin and the People* (1941).

BERLIN, BATTLE FOR. Final assault by the Russian armies on the German capital in April 1945.

BACKGROUND. For several years, Berlin had been the target of sustained bombing from the air by the combined Allied Air Commands. By day U.S. bombers plastered the city and at night British planes maintained the pace of destruction. (*See* BERLIN, BOMBING OF.) By the spring of 1945 the great metropolitan center was three-quarters destroyed and the remaining inhabitants lived in ruin and rubble. The city was ready for capture.

Already, in February 1945, the Russians had arrived within 35 miles of Berlin. Three Russian armies, totaling 2.5 million men, supported by more than 6,000 tanks, moved on the German capital. The 1st Ukrainian, led by Gen. Ivan S. Konev (*q.v.*) was on the southeast; the 1st Belorussian, commanded by Gen. Georgi K. Zhukov (*q.v.*) was at Kustrin on the Oder; and the 2nd Belorussian, led by Gen. Konstantin K. Rokossovsky, headed for the northern part of the Oder.

At this point came one of the major operational decisions of the war. The U.S. 9th Army reached the Elbe, just 70 miles from Berlin, on April 11, 1945. Gen. Dwight D. Eisenhower (*q.v.*) ordered his troops to halt and allow the Russians first chance at Berlin.

FINAL ASSAULT. Zhukov moved first, ordering his men to attack bridgeheads over the Oder and the Neisse. Konev sent his army surging forward from the southeast. Two days later the Russians held a rough circle around the city at a radius of 25 miles. Both armies moved to close the trap.

What remained of German artillery attempted to halt the Russians, but with little success. The Russians themselves used one of the greatest concentrations of artillery in the battle for any city in history—41,600 artillery pieces. Red infantrymen moved like quicksilver through the suburbs. Overhead Russian *Stormoviks* plastered the Germans in low-level attacks. Terrorized civilians tried to flee to the west away from the gun and firepower and from the vengeful Russians. On April 25 the armies of Zhukov and Konev joined northeast of Potsdam, cutting off all roads leading to the west.

The Russians then moved to the center of Berlin. Scattered bands of fanatical youngsters and rounded-up old men fought from the ruins in a suicide stand. Huge columns of smoke rose from the center of the city as Russians scurried through the ruins in search of defenders. German soldiers threw their weapons away and some officers stripped insignia from their uniforms.

On April 27 the Russians took Spandau, Potsdam, and Rathenau in Berlin proper, and at the same time captured the industrial district of Neukölln and the airport at Tempelhof. The next day Russian troops hoisted a victory banner inside the shattered city. The garrison in Berlin surrendered on May 2, 1945.

Bibliography. H. R. Trevor-Roper, *The Last Days of Hitler* (1947); G. Blond, *The Death of Hitler's Germany* (1945); V. I. Chuikov, *The Fall of Berlin* (1968); V. Sevruk (ed.), *How Wars End: Eye Witness Accounts of the Fall of Berlin* (1969); and E. Ziemke, *Battle for Berlin* (1969).

BERLIN, BOMBING OF. Allied air attacks on the capital of Germany from 1940 to early 1945. The result was one of the most devastating assaults by air on any metropolitan center in the history of warfare.

TARGET. Berlin, the largest German city and center of the government, lay in the northeast of the country on the river Spree, which flowed through it from southeast to northwest. Greater Berlin included an area of 340 square miles, embracing populated areas, lakes, and cornfields. Hitler intended to make the city the focus of German life and culture and had grandiose plans for its rebuilding. For the Allies, angered by the bombing of London, Berlin became a target of prime importance.

BACKGROUND. Because of its geographic position, remote from the battlefields of World War I, Berlin was untouched during that conflict. In the postwar era inhabitants of the German capital were warned that they could not expect to be favored in the event of another European war. After Hitler came to power in 1933, the people of Berlin, nevertheless, came to believe that their city was invulnerable. Gen. Hermann Goering (*q.v.*), head of the *Luftwaffe* (*q.v.*) assured them with the comforting words: "If a single bomb falls on Berlin, you can call me Meyer!" The people of Berlin later recalled with much bitterness that boastful remark.

FIRST PHASE. When the Battle of Britain (*q.v.*) was in full force in the summer of 1940, the British Bomber Command, under pressure of public opinion, decided to use its remaining 200 long-range bombers to strike back at Berlin. British reserve was abandoned after the German air assaults on Warsaw (*See* WARSAW, BOMBING OF), Rotterdam (*See* ROTTERDAM, BOMBING OF), and London (*See* BRITAIN, BATTLE OF). The first Royal Air Force (*q.v.*) raid on Berlin took place on the night of August 25–26, 1940, when 22 tons of bombs were dropped on the German capital. There were seven more attacks by the end of the summer of 1940. Paul Joseph Goebbels (*q.v.*), German propaganda chief, denounced the raids as "killing and wounding civilians and causing fire and other damage." By the end of the year there were 27 additional night raids. The most effective attack was in September when 656 British bombers flew in to bomb the capital, but not all reached the target.

PAUSE. Throughout 1941 and 1942 the British Bomber Command paid little attention to Berlin. Its main concern at this time was to build a strong strategic bomber force for later use. In the fall of 1941 there were several token attacks mainly to appease the Russians. A raid on September 7–8, 1941, damaged the Potsdam Railway station and the Potsdamer Platz, both in the center of Berlin. Another raid on November 7–8, 1941, resulted in hits on the residential districts of Spandau and Moabit, but it was costly to the British. Air Marshal Arthur "Bomber" Harris (*q.v.*) was dissatisfied with the results. Raids in early 1942 cost so many planes that Harris decided to discontinue attacks for the time being, concentrating instead on Lübeck, Cologne, and Essen in the west.

RESUMPTION. Raids were resumed in early 1943, including heavy assaults on January 18–19, March 1–2, and March 29. Additional attacks came in June and July. The great mass attacks on Hamburg from July 23 to August 4, 1943, with accompanying terrible firestorms, marked a turning point in the air war as well as a grim warning to the people of Berlin.

Concerned by increasing casualties, Hitler began to transfer governmental agencies to other cities. He moved the central office of the *Gestapo* (*q.v.*) to Prague and the Foreign Ministry to Vienna. Meanwhile, in London news of the Hamburg bombing brought public clamor for similar raids on Berlin. On the night of August 23, 1943, a British force of 700 bombers manned by 5,000 airmen broke through the *Luftwaffe* defense and dropped 1,700 tons of bombs within one hour. The British lost 58 bombers and 1 fighter, but the damage to Berlin was tremendous. The center was hit hard as well as the outlying factory districts.

By this time the people of Berlin were angered and alarmed. Goebbels's propaganda could do little to comfort them. It was now decided to clear the city of as many unnecessary people as possible. By the fall of 1943 at least 1 million people had left. Schools were closed and young people were moved to other cities and to the countryside.

CLIMAX. British raids on November 22–23, 1943, turned most of the city from Potsdamer Platz through the Wilhelmstrasse to the Tiergarten into a mass of flame and smoke. In January 1944 there were six more heavy attacks, two of them with more than 400 bombers each. On the night of February 15–16, 1944, came the heaviest air assault of the war. From British airfields 891 bombers, chiefly *Halifaxes* and *Lancasters* (*See* AIRCRAFT; BRITISH AIRCRAFT DATA CHART), took off for Berlin. The 806 planes that reached the target dropped 2,642 tons of bombs in 30 minutes. *Mosquitos* (*q.v.*) followed to hamper the work of Berlin's fire brigades.

On March 4, 1944, came the first experimental daylight attack by the U.S. Air Force (*See* U.S. ARMY AIR FORCES), with 30 *Flying Fortresses* escorted by strong fighter protection. Two days later 672 *Flying Fortresses* and *Liberators,* supported by *Lightnings, Thunderbolts,* and *Mustangs,* dropped 1,600 tons of bombs, mostly on industrial targets. Only 200 *Luftwaffe* fighters were available to strike back. The Americans lost 43 aircraft. From then on the Americans hammered the city by day, the British by night.

LOSSES. It is impossible to give the exact number of casualties during the years of the bombing of Berlin. The incomplete figure of the Reich Statistical Office recorded a total of 14,186 formally registered as dead. Others put the total at 50,000.

The material losses were tremendous. Berlin's City Council reported the destruction of 612,000 houses. The center of the city was a wasteland. About 75 percent of Berlin was literally destroyed. Most of the rest of the city was dilapidated or partly damaged. The main arteries were burnt out and in the Tiergarten only a few trees survived the bombs. Planes flying over the city took photographs that showed mile after mile of utter desolation. Berlin had become a modern Carthage, a city of cave and cellar dwellers.

AFTERMATH. In early April 1945 the bombing of Berlin merged into the Battle for Berlin. Three huge Russian armies, poised outside the city, finally smashed their way into the stricken city and forced its surrender on May 2, 1945. (*See* BERLIN, BATTLE FOR.)

Bibliography. A. T. Harris, *Bomber Offensive* (1947); and H. Rumpf, *The Bombing of Germany* (1963).

BERLIN-ROME-TOKYO AXIS. Ten-year military-economic treaty among Germany, Italy, and Japan, signed on September 27, 1940, also called Tripartite Pact.

BACKGROUND. Concerned with the possibility of the United States entering the war, Hitler was determined to add the power of the Japanese Empire to that of Germany and Italy. He proposed to extend the 1936 Rome-Berlin Axis and thereby discourage the United States from entering the war.

AGREEMENT. Representatives of the three nations met in Berlin on September 27, 1940, and signed an agreement by which they pooled their armaments and promised to assist each other if any one of them became involved in a war with the United States.

TEXT. The official text:*

The governments of Germany, Italy, and Japan, considering it as a condition precedent of any lasting peace that all nations of the world be given each its proper place, have decided to stand by and cooperate with one another in regard to their efforts in Greater East Asia and regions of Europe respectively wherein it is their prime purpose to establish and maintain a new order of things calculated to promote the mutual prosperity and welfare of the peoples concerned.

Furthermore, it is the desire of the three governments to extend cooperation to such nations in other spheres of the world as may be included to put forth endeavors along lines similar to their own, in order that their ultimate aspirations for world peace may thus be realized.

Accordingly, the governments of Germany, Italy and Japan have agreed as follows:

ARTICLE 1. Japan recognizes and respects the leadership of Germany and Italy in establishment of a new order in Europe.

---

*The official English translation of the treaty, quoted in *World Almanac* (New York, 1942), p. 273.

ARTICLE 2. Germany and Italy recognize and respect the leadership of Japan in the establishment of a new order in Greater East Asia.

ARTICLE 3. Germany, Italy and Japan agree to cooperate in their efforts on aforesaid lines. They further undertake to assist one another with all political, economic and military means when one of the three contracting powers is attacked by a power at present not involved in the European war or in the Chinese-Japanese conflict.

ARTICLE 4. With the view of implementing the present pact, joint technical commissions, members of which are to be appointed by the respective governments of Germany, Italy and Japan, will meet without delay.

ARTICLE 5. Germany, Italy and Japan affirm that the aforesaid terms do not in any way affect the political status which exists at present as between each of the three contracting parties and Soviet Russia.

ARTICLE 6. The present pact shall come into effect immediately upon signature and shall remain in force ten years from the date of its coming into force. At the proper time before expiration of said term the high contracting parties shall at the request of any of them enter into negotiations for its renewal.

In faith whereof, the undersigned, duly authorized by their respective governments, have signed this pact and have affixed hereto their signatures.

Done in triplicate at Berlin, the 27th day of September, 1940, in the eighteenth year of the Fascist era, corresponding to the 27th day of the ninth month of the fifteenth year of Showa [the reign of Emperor Hirohito].

AFTERMATH. Hungary joined the Axis on November 20, 1940; Rumania on November 23, 1940; Slovakia on November 24, 1940; and Bulgaria on March 1, 1941. Yugoslavia signed on March 25, 1941, but stipulated that Axis troops should not march through the country and that its territorial integrity be respected. Two days later, the Yugoslav regime that signed the agreement was overthrown, and the new Cabinet refused to ratify the pact. The Axis powers then marched into Yugoslavia. Croatia, a part of conquered Yugoslavia, joined the Axis on June 15, 1941.

Bibliography. V. Israelian and L. Kutsov, *Diplomacy of Aggression: Berlin, Rome, Tokyo Axis— Its Use and Fall* (1970).

BERMUDA STATION. A satellite security base in Bermuda, the British crown colony 650 miles southeast of Cape Hatteras.

The New York City headquarters of British Security Coordination (BSC) (*q.v.*), run by master spy William Stephenson (*q.v.*), grew so large that bases were needed elsewhere. Bermuda Station was selected along with Camp X (*q.v.*) in Canada as extension bases for undercover operations. More than 1,200 British experts worked in dungeon-like cellars of the Princess Hotel. They were assigned to read postal, telegraph, and radio traffic between German embassies in the Western Hemisphere and German-occupied European countries.

Bibliography. W. Stevenson, *A Man Called Intrepid* (1976).

BERN INCIDENT. Circumstances surrounding the first peace feeler in the Italian theater.

In November 1944 a high-ranking German Catholic dignitary came to Bern, Switzerland, to see Allen W. Dulles (*q.v.*), who since 1942 represented the American Office of Strategic Services (*q.v.*) there as head of an intelligence center inside German-occupied Europe. Several Swiss and Italian citizens approached a friend of Dulles's about acting as an intermediary with the Allies in arranging a German surrender in Italy.

After these initial talks, intermediaries met in Lugano with German SS (*q.v.*) officers. Dulles informed Allied headquarters of the negotiations. When Nazi officials in Berlin became suspicious, Allied headquarters ordered Dulles in April 1945 to break off the negotiations. In the meantime Roosevelt and Churchill informed Stalin of the "Bern incident," but Stalin reacted by claiming that they were seeking to negotiate a separate peace with the Germans. The Italian unconditional surrender took place on May 2, 1945.

BERNHARD, OPERATION. Code or cover name for the counterfeiting of more than £100 million in English bank notes from 1941 to 1945. *Operation Bernhard* (*Unternehmen Bernhard*) was given its name after Bernhard Krüger, head of the workshop in which the Nazi Secret Service produced forged passports, bogus motor licenses, university degrees, and other documents used by espionage agents. (*See* ESPIONAGE.)

PLOT. The scheme was proposed by Alfred Naujocks (*q.v.*), a charter member of the main Reich Security Office (*Reichssicherheitshauptamt*) in Berlin. Naujocks suggested to his superior officers that forged British pounds be dropped by plane over England and also used in neutral countries to undermine the British economy. The word was given to go ahead.

German experts had three problems: (1) to produce paper identical with that of the British bank notes; (2) to forge plates that could print notes identical in color and design; and (3) to work out a proper numbering system. Workers cut genuine 5-pound notes into slivers and used the clean batches for paper analysis. After months of painstaking labor, they were able to match the paper by employing Turkish rags that had been made thoroughly dirty before use. They finally produced a paper, which, both to the naked eye and under the microscope, was identical with the original British bank notes.

Other workers enlarged the British notes 20 times and after seven months made a plate that matched the originals almost perfectly. Still others worked out a suitable numbering system. The forged notes were produced in quantity in a concentration camp near Berlin.

USAGE. The first 5-pound counterfeit notes were so well done that they were passed without question by banks in Switzerland and even reached the Bank of England without detection. The forged notes were distributed in limited quantities throughout Europe. The Reich Security Office even paid salaries in this spurious money to its agents in enemy countries. The adventurer

Otto Skorzeny (*q.v.*) used these counterfeit bills in his rescue of Benito Mussolini (*q.v.*) from the Gran Sasso d'Italia, high in the Abruzzi Appenines, on September 13, 1943.

AFTERMATH. As Allied victory approached in the spring of 1945, officers in the Reich Security Office deemed it imperative to destroy every evidence of the forged bank notes. Boxes of packed notes were dropped in Austrian lakes for safekeeping, but they were eventually recovered. Fifteen years later, on July 27, 1959, Austrian peasants watched in amazement as waterlogged British notes in large quantities were brought to the surface.

In due course most of the forged notes were returned to England. Infrequently, some of the "Bernhard" forgeries appeared in many countries around the world. In 1955 the Bank of England replaced the large black and white 5-pound note with a colored smaller one. By 1961 the old notes ceased to be legal tender. The market persisted. People behind the Iron Curtain, convinced that their Communist regime would not last, transferred their fortunes into what they mistakenly believed to be sound, hard currency, but were actually forged Bernhard notes.

Bibliography. W. Hagen, *Unternehmen Bernhard* (1955); W. Schellenberg, *The Schellenberg Memoirs* (1956); and A. Pirie, *Operation Bernhard* (1961).

BERNHARD, PRINCE OF THE NETHERLANDS (1911–   ).

German-born prince consort of Queen Juliana.

When the Germans invaded Holland in 1940, Bernhard fled with the royal family to England. Trained as a pilot, he engaged actively in the Allied war effort. He helped gather information of refugees escaping from Holland to England. He also reorganized Dutch Intelligence into an efficient operations unit. In 1944 he was made Commander-in-Chief of the Dutch armed forces and returned secretly to Holland to work with the Dutch Resistance for the liberation of the Netherlands.

BEVAN, ANEURIN (1897–1960). British statesman, one of the leaders of the British Socialist movement.

Throughout the conflict Bevan remained a strong critic of the Churchill Government, which, he said, was fighting the war for the benefit of capitalism. He also denounced what he called Britain's subservience to U.S. policy. He opposed the Allied invasion of North Africa, but called loudly for the establishment of a second front in Europe. (*See* SECOND FRONT).

Bibliography. See biographies by M. M. Krug, *Aneurin Bevan: Cautious Rebel* (1961); M. Foot, *Aneurin Bevan: A Biography* (1962); and V. Brome, *Aneurin Bevan: A Biography* (1963).

BEVERIDGE, WILLIAM HENRY (1879–1963). Author of the Beveridge Report, a landmark in British social history.

In 1942, in the midst of the war, Beveridge served on a national committee of experts who undertook a survey of the existing schemes of social insurance. The outcome of these labors was the celebrated Beveridge Report, which provided for a Social Security system for all British citizens from cradle to grave. The plan provided for a Ministry of Social Security to unify the administrative work of combining provisions for unemployment, disability, retirement, training benefits, maternity grants, childrens' and widows' allowances, and a national health service. In addition to its merits, the plan symbolized the stability and confidence of Britain while engaged in total war. Engaged in a conflict in which its very existence was at stake, the country nevertheless could concern itself with bettering social conditions.

Bibliography. Among Beveridge's many works is *Full Employment in a Free Society* (1944), written in the midst of the war and advocating planned public spending, control of private investment, and full employment measures. *See also* his *Voluntary Action* (1948) and his autobiography *Power and Influence* (1953).

BEVIN, ERNEST (1881–1951). Trade-union leader in the British war effort.
Unlike Aneurin Bevan (*q.v.*), Bevin played a critical role in administration during the war. In May 1940 Churchill called Bevin to his Coalition Government as Minister of Labour and National Service. In this key position Bevin became virtual dictator of Britain's domestic war effort. The Emergency Powers (Defense) Act gave him complete control over industry, while the Restriction on Engagement Order permitted him to organize the country's entire labor force in the way he thought best. Bevin persuaded the unions to accept voluntary suspension of their safeguards during the war emergency, while at the same time working to gain benefits for labor. He was responsible for introducing a number of measures protecting the status of workers. He supported the Female Conscription Act of 1941, which released thousands of men for the fighting fronts. In 1945 he helped draft plans well in advance which led to the smooth demobilization of British fighting forces.

Bibliography. Bevin's early war speeches and broadcasts were published in *The Job to Be Done* (1942). *See also* the biographies by A. Bullock, *The Life and Times of Ernest Bevin*, vol. 1 (1960), vol. 2 (1967); and F. Williams, *Ernest Bevin: Portrait of a Great Englishman* (1952).

BIAK ISLAND. *See* NEW GUINEA, CAMPAIGNS IN.

BIG FOUR. Extension of the term *Big Three* (*q.v.*) to include Generalissimo Chiang Kai-shek (*q.v.*) of China. The term was also used to denote the four Allied countries—the United States, Great Britain, Soviet Russia, and China. The Big Four nations played a major role in the establishment of the United Nations.

BIG SIX. Popular term for the top governing committee of the Japanese cabinet during the war years. On June 22, 1945, the Emperor summoned the Big Six to an Imperial Presence Conference and asked that they consider a way to end the war as quickly as possible.

BIG THREE. The three top Allied war leaders after the summer of 1941: U.S. President Franklin D. Roosevelt, British Prime Minister Winston Churchill, and Soviet Premier Joseph Stalin (*qq.v.*). Roosevelt and Churchill worked in close harmony. Their relations with Stalin were formal and correct but were tinged with suspicion on both sides. Roosevelt believed incorrectly that he could use his personal charm to goad Stalin into cooperation.

The term *Big Three* was also used to describe the three major powers—the United States, Great Britain, and the Soviet Union.

BIG WEEK. Name given by American pilots to a series of air raids on German targets, especially air-frame manufacturing and assembly plants, beginning the third week in February 1944.

From air bases in England, bombers of the U.S. 8th Air Force made several thousand sorties over Germany. During the same week bombers from the U.S. 15th Air Force made more than 500. Losses were approximately 5 percent. Also during that same week aircraft sent out by the RAF Bomber Command made night attacks against major cities.

BISMARCK SEA, BATTLE OF THE. Devastating Allied attack on a large Japanese convoy headed for New Guinea on March 3–4, 1943.

BACKGROUND. In early 1943 Allied operations in the Pacific were hampered by the strategic decision to concentrate first on Germany. But slowly the Allies began to work their way from points on the Solomon Islands in a northwesterly direction toward Japan. Avoiding a direct attack on Rabaul (*q.v.*), the key Japanese base in New Britain, they would outflank it by a two-pronged offensive up the Solomons and New Guinea ladder.

The Japanese, too, considered New Guinea to be of vital importance. On March 1, 1943, a strong Japanese convoy with 7,000 troops in 8 transports and an equal number of destroyers, left Rabaul for Lae, New Guinea. Allied aircraft based on Papua kept the convoy under observation. On March 3 U.S. and Australian planes moved in to attack the convoy.

AIR ATTACK. The Battle of the Bismarck Sea was a stunning victory for the Allies. As the Japanese transports and warships scattered in all directions, Allied aircraft dropped great clusters of bombs on them. Of the first 37 bombs dropped at least 28 scored. The attack continued all afternoon. The next day the aircraft were joined by American PT-Boats.

LOSSES. The Japanese lost all their transports and 4 of their 8 destroyers, as well as 102 of 150 aircraft. About 3,000 troops (half the total) were killed or drowned. Their last transport still afloat the second day was sunk by U.S. motor torpedo boats, and a Japanese submarine taking on survivors was also sunk. The Allies lost only 2 bombers and 3 fighters out of 300 attacking aircraft and fewer than 20 dead.

SIGNIFICANCE. Gen. Douglas MacArthur (*q.v.*) said the Battle of the Bismarck Sea was one of the decisive battles of the war. Following this grave defeat the Japanese dared to send reinforcements to New Guinea only in submarines or barges. They found it highly unprofitable to risk loaded transports in waters shadowed by Allied aircraft.

Bibliography. S. E. Morison, *The Two-Ocean War* (1963); R. J. Francillon, *U.S. Army Air Forces in the Pacific* (1969); and B. Adams, *Battleground: South Pacific* (1970).

BISMARCK, SINKING OF THE. German battleship destroyed by the British in 1941. Believed to be unsinkable, she was sent to the bottom of the Atlantic by units of the Royal Navy and the Royal Air Force (*q.v.*) after a pursuit of five days covering 1,750 miles.

DESIGN. The *Bismarck* was commissioned in August 1940 and built by Blohm and Voss in Hamburg. Together with her sister ship, the *Tirpitz* (*q.v.*), she was to be the basis for the new German fleet-in-being, which was supposed to reach top strength in 1944 or 1945 (*See* Z-Plan.) Her designers intended her not as a part of the German battle fleet, but as a lone raider on British commerce, as a surface ship to break up the convoy system. They gave her a high speed plus a powerful secondary armament and a superb optical control system. Ingeniously compartmentalized, she could resist tremendous battering. In the beginning of 1941 she was tested with a complement of more than 2,000 men. Churchill pronounced her "a masterpiece of naval construction."

SPECIFICATIONS.
  Measurement. Length 791 ft.
  Displacement. 42,000 tons.
  Maximum Speed. 30½ knots.
  Armor. 7.9-in. sides with 2-in. main deck.
  Armament. Eight 15-in. guns firing at a range of 43,000 yds. at a maximum of 45° elevation; twelve 5-in. guns in twin turrets; sixteen 4.1-in. guns in twin AA shield.
  Complement. 2,200 on final voyage.
  Special Features. Four seaplane scouts; two catapults (athwartships); six 21-in. torpedo tubes; 150,000 h.p.

DUTY. The *Bismarck* was berthed in heavily defended Norwegian waters, where she was 1,000 miles away from the nearest British air base but only 50 miles from the convoy lanes to the Soviet Union. Her mere presence was a threat to British shipping. At any moment she might make her appearance off Iceland or Greenland and could have profoundly altered British naval dispositions in all oceans. The British Admiralty was forced to withdraw strong naval forces from the Mediterranean to keep close watch on the giant German battleship.

After the beginning of the Battle of the Atlantic (*q.v.*) in 1939–1940, there was a lull in naval action. By January 1941 Adm. Erich Raeder (*q.v.*), Commander-in-Chief of the German Navy, decided that it was time to begin the raids again. He planned *Operation Rheinübung* (*See* CODE NAMES, GER-MAN, RHEINÜBUNG) for the following May. The *Bismarck* and the *Prinz Eugen*, protected by a screen of smaller vessels, would move into the Atlantic and attack convoys bound for the Soviet Union. Fleet Commandant Günther Lütjens was ordered to repeat his earlier successes in the Atlantic. Adm. Lütjens would have preferred to wait until the *Tirpitz* was ready within a few months, but he had to follow orders.

COLLISION. On May 18, 1941, the *Bismarck* and the *Prinz Eugen*, accompanied by 6 U-Boats, sailed from Gdynia in occupied Poland through the British blockade. British secret agents reported the move to London. Three days later a British reconnaissance aircraft took photographs of German ships lying in Korsfjord near Bergen taking on fuel oil. The next day the fleet was on its way through fog and clouds.

Alerted, the British Admiralty ordered all naval forces to the vicinity to prevent a breakthrough into the Atlantic. Deployed to the area from Scapa Flow was a battle squadron comprising the new battleship *Prince of Wales,* the battle cruiser *Hood,* and escorts. The following day, the Home Fleet, with the battleship *King George V,* the carrier *Victorious,* and numerous cruisers and destroyers under Admiral John Tovey, Commander-in-Chief of the Home Fleet at Scapa Flow, also put to sea.

On the evening of May 23, 1941, British cruisers *Norfolk* and *Suffolk* sighted the German fleet passing through the Denmark Strait. Lütjens, realizing that any attempt at concealment was now impossible, attacked the *Norfolk,* which disappeared into the mist. The British warships, fortified with their new radar (*See* RADAR, WARTIME), were able to maintain contact.

The next day, the fleets clashed. The *Bismarck* rained heavy shells on the *Hood,* one of which penetrated her aft-magazine, and exploded. The *Hood* sank in three minutes, leaving only three survivors. All that was left was a patch of smoke on the water and some small bits of wreckage. The *Prince of Wales,* badly damaged, limped away. The *Bismarck,* also seriously wounded, slowed down and began to lose oil. She turned back at reduced speed to seek a haven at Saint-Nazaire in occupied France. Taking advantage of the snow, mist, and squalls, Lütjens headed for France.

CHASE. From London the British Admiralty ordered every big naval unit from the Mediterranean to Newfoundland to the vicinity. The fast German battleship, its radio silent, knifed through the water on its dash south. On the morning of May 26, a Royal Air Force plane, an American-built *Catalina* flying boat, spotted the *Bismarck* 700 miles off the French coast and apparently in trouble. British torpedo planes, sent to delay the escape, struck the *Bismarck* twice, once in the rudder. Soon the giant battle wagon began to turn in uncontrollable circles. Other British naval units caught up with the floundering monster and closed in for the kill. The big ship could do nothing more than wait to fight and die.

FINISH. The next morning the battleships *King George V* (flagship of the Home Fleet) and *Rodney* appeared on the scene. Training their guns on the helpless target, they sent salvoes of shells that bored their way through Krupp armor as if it were cheese. The *Bismarck* was now a battered wreck, her superstructure mangled, her giant guns pointed crazily in all directions. Sheets of flame poured from jagged holes in her sides. Hundreds of crewmen, faced with death in the blazing inferno, leaped into the sea. The *Dorsetshire* closed in and fired her last three torpedoes into the mortally wounded ship. At 10:40 P.M. on May 27, 1941, the *Bismarck* heeled over to port, turned upside down, and sank.

TOLL. The sea was rough, but the *Dorsetshire* and the *Maori* moved in to rescue the survivors floating in life boats or holding on to wreckage. Because the water was too rough to lower boats, British crews dropped ladders and threw out life lines. They rescued 100 men, but broke off when word came that a German U-Boat was rushing to the spot. Some 2,100 men perished with the *Bismarck.* Total British casualties, apart from the loss of the *Hood,* were 27 killed and 13 wounded.

SIGNIFICANCE. Hitler had lost the *Admiral Graf Spee* (*q.v.*) in the first dramatic confrontation of the war on December 17, 1939. Now in the second great sea encounter he had lost his most powerful and irreplaceable battleship. The British achieved a great victory and took a giant step in driving the German surface fleet from the seas. But they paid heavily for the triumph, losing their most powerful vessel, the *Hood,* and suffering damage to other battleships, a destroyer, and many planes. To catch the *Bismarck,* the Admiralty had diverted much of its Mediterranean Fleet, thus weakening the defense of Crete. Disappointed Germans claimed that the *Bismarck* sank only because her crew had detonated scuttling charges.

Bibliography. For an ingenious reenactment, *see* C. S. Forester, *Sink the Bismarck* (1959), and *Hunting the Bismarck* (1980); B. B. Schofield, *The Loss of the Bismarck* (1972); and B. von Mühlenheim-Rechberg, *Battleship Bismarck* (1980).

BLACK DAY. Name given by the Japanese to August 17, 1943, when U.S. aircraft, based on Port Moresby, destroyed virtually all the Japanese planes on airfields near Wewak, New Guinea.

BLACK MARKET. Term for illegal trade in goods without regard to rationing.

Black markets quickly appeared in countries occupied by Germans after the outbreak of war. Because of the scarcity of goods, prices were pushed up to extraordinarily high levels. German troops stationed in occupied countries bought strictly rationed goods for themselves and to send them back to their families in Germany.

BLACK MAY. Name given by German submariners to May 1943. During that month 41 U-Boats, fully one-third of all those at sea, failed to return to home base and were presumed lost through combat or accident. Adm. Karl Doenitz (*q.v.*) ordered all remaining U-Boats to withdraw from the North Atlantic and take stations southwest of the Azores, where they were less vulnerable.

Black May marked the turning point in the Battle of the Atlantic (*q.v.*) and, indeed, in the war itself. The U-Boat campaign had come close to victory. "It was our worst evil," said Churchill. "It would have been wise for the Germans to stake all on it."

BLACK ORDER. Heinrich Himmler's (*q.v.*) elite guard. (*See SS* [*SCHUTZ-STAFFEL*].)

BLACK PIT. Allied name for the Mid-Atlantic Gap beyond air-patrol range. Convoys moving to and from Britain were protected on either side of the Atlantic by air patrols, which took a deadly toll of German U-Boats. But in the center of the Atlantic the slow-moving convoys did not have the advantage of air protection.

The Black Pit gradually closed as the range of protective aircraft increased and as small aircraft carriers were put into use. With stronger escorts, U-Boats could be chased for a longer period of time in the Mid-Atlantic Gap. (*See* ATLANTIC, BATTLE OF THE.)

BLACK SATURDAY. Name given by British survivors to Saturday, October 14, 1939, a few weeks after the outbreak of World War II, when the battleship *Royal Oak* was sunk at Scapa Flow by a German U-Boat. (*See ROYAL OAK.*)

BLACK SHIRTS. Armed uniformed Fascist followers of Italian *Duce* Benito Mussolini (*q.v.*).

Mussolini used his Black Shirts in the battle of the streets against Communists in his drive to political power. Later they were granted status as the Militia of Volunteers.

BLACK THURSDAY. Name given by American airmen to Thursday, October 14, 1943, the day of the second major bombing raid on the ball-bearing works at Schweinfurt in southern Germany. Out of the 260 American aircraft (excluding abortives) that pressed the attack, only 195 landed safely. Only 62 were relatively unscathed. (*See* SCHWEINFURT RAIDS.)

BLACK TUESDAY. Name given by Allied troops to Tuesday, September 19, 1944, when 35 Polish gliders sent to Arnhem were destroyed by German antiaircraft fire. In addition, food and ammunition dropped from the air missed the target and fell into German hands. (*See* ARNHEM, BATTLE OF.)

BLACKOUT. Complete darkening of cities by extinguishing all lights and using curtains on windows and other openings. Blackouts were used in both Allied and Axis cities as a precaution against night air raids.

BLACKOUT ROUTE. Sea route used by Britain and the United States in bringing supplies to the Soviet Union. Allied convoys were heavily hit and many lives were lost in the process. (*See* LEND-LEASE; and CONVOY *PQ-17.*)

BLAMEY, THOMAS ALBERT (1884–1951). Australian General who served in both world wars.

At the outbreak of war in 1939 Blamey was Chairman of the Australian Man-power Commission. After serving in several army posts, he was named to command the Anzac Corps in Greece in 1941. Following the British evacuation of Greece, he became next in command to Field Marshal Archibald Wavell (*q.v.*), who led the British forces in the Middle East. In this capacity Blamey attempted unsuccessfully to hold Crete. (*See* CRETE, BATTLE OF.) Shortly after Pearl Harbor, Blamey returned to Australia as commander of the military forces there. He served under Gen. Douglas MacArthur (*q.v.*) in the Southwest Pacific after 1942. He led the first attacks on the Japanese in New Guinea in September 1942 and assisted in the recapture of Papua.

BLETCHLEY PARK. Site of the British Government Code and Cipher School (GCCS).

The school was set up in 1939 to house a small army of experts too valuable to be kept in London where they would be exposed to German bombs and British curiosity. Bletchley was in a shallow basin in Buckinghamshire, 60 miles from the nearest invasion beach. To the villagers of the tiny, quiet town, the GCCS mathematicians, linguists, chemists, physicists, and crossword-puzzle experts were known as the "Golf, Cheese, and Chess Society," whose members strode through the village in gray flannels and tweed shirts.

Bletchley was the home of *Ultra* (*q.v.*), the cryptanalysis section that broke the German intelligence code and learned German operational plans throughout the war. (*See also* ESPIONAGE.)

BLITZKRIEG **(LIGHTNING WAR).** German term used to describe a new form of rapid warfare distinguished by mobility and fluidity. It was defined by Gen. Erwin Rommel (*q.v.*), one of its most able practitioners: "The act of concentrating strength at one point, forcing a breakthrough, rolling up and securing the flanks on either side, and then penetrating like lightning, before the enemy has time to react, deep into his rear." Another observer described its overall effect: "The whole battlefield becomes an amorphous permeation like a plague of vermin in a garden."

ORIGINS. The concept of the *Blitzkrieg* technique was originated by German Gen. Hans von Seeckt as commander of the German *Reichswehr* in the

1920s. Later, a young French officer, Charles de Gaulle (*q.v.*), while teaching military history at St. Cyr, expressed similar views, which brought him into conflict with orthodox military opinion. In World War I, Gens. Ferdinand Foch and Joseph Joffre favored traditional tactics of parceling out armored units as tank brigades in a supporting role. This view persisted after the war along with trust in the immobility of fortifications expressed in the Maginot Line (*q.v.*) and the defensive military mentality. De Gaulle suggested mechanization of the infantry with emphasis on wholesale use of tanks. Armored mobility and air power, he argued, manned by a corps of professional specialists, would provide more effective defenses than fixed fortifications. De Gaulle projected these views in a book titled *Vers l'armée de métier* (1934) (*The Army of the Future,* 1941). The suggestions were rejected by the French military. Ironically, German *Panzer* ("tank") units utilized de Gaulle's theories when they attacked France in the *Blitzkrieg* of 1940. (*See* PANZER.)

Other military experts presented similar views. British theorists B. H. Liddell Hart and J.F.C. Fuller (*qq.v.*) predicted mobility and fluidity in future warfare. De Gaulle was unable to obtain support from his fellow French officers, but in Germany his book was read in military circles with admiration and rapt attention. Gen. Heinz Guderian (*q.v.*) also advocated *Blitzkrieg* tactics in his book *Achtung Panzer* (1938).

CHARACTERISTICS. Blitzkrieg tactics underwent several modifications during the course of World War II, but they involved a number of basic characteristics:

1. *Preparation.* The new type of warfare was to be prepared carefully by agents behind enemy lines.

2. *Surprise.* The main element was psychological—an overwhelming mobile attack that would startle the enemy and create such chaos that there would be little or no effective retaliation.

3. *Teamwork.* Tactical co-ordination between air assault and mobile armored units was essential.

4. *Air Strikes.* Concentrated bombing from the air would cripple enemy air strength, render communications and transportation ineffective, and throw ground troops into disarray.

5. *Speed.* Tank units and self-propelled artillery would thrust forward with overwhelming speed without stopping for regrouping.

6. *Firepower.* These units would concentrate on a narrow front to achieve superiority in firepower and then move forward.

7. *Backup.* Then there would follow infantry in trucks, armored carriers, mechanized engineers, and motorized supply trains.

8. *Sweep.* Finally, the armored units would turn in wide sweeps to trap and immobilize isolated enemy units.

USE. The Germans used *Blitzkrieg* tactics with complete success at the outbreak of war on September 1, 1939, in the invasion of Poland. Following the pattern precisely, they were able to subjugate Poland within a month. Hitler immediately integrated his share of Poland into the Third Reich. *(See* POLAND, CAMPAIGN IN.) He used similar tactics when the *Sitzkrieg (q.v.)*, the Sitdown War, ended in 1940, in invading the Netherlands, Belgium, and Luxembourg. *(See* LOW COUNTRIES, CAMPAIGNS IN THE.) The same type of *Blitzkrieg* was used in the defeat of France. *(See* FRANCE, FIRST BATTLE OF.)

AMERICAN ADAPTATION. American military experts adopted and refined *Blitzkrieg* tactics and put them to effective use during the later stages of the war. The Normandy invasion *(q.v.)* on D-Day, June 6, 1944, was a gigantic *Blitzkrieg*. German targets were softened by air assault and then armored units under Gen. George Patton *(q.v.)* broke through at St. Lô *(q.v.)*. One spearhead spread into Brittany while the other moved toward Paris and the Seine. *(See* FRANCE, SECOND BATTLE OF.) Patton's armored units smashed forward into Germany until they outdistanced their supply lines. It was a classic textbook version of the German-initiated *Blitzkrieg*. *(See* GERMANY, BATTLE OF.)

Bibliography. J.F.C. Fuller, *Memoirs of an Unconventional Soldier* (1936); H. Guderian, *Actung Panzer* (1938); C. de Gaulle, *The Army of the Future* (1941); F. O. Miksche, *Attack: A Study of Blitzkrieg Tactics* (1942); B. H. Liddell Hart, *The German Generals Talk* (1956); Maj. Gen. F. W. Mellenthin, *Panzer Battles: A Study of the Employment of Armor in the Second World War*, trans. by H. Betzler (1956); and *Second World War*, trans. by H. Betzler (1956); H. Addington, *The Blitzkrieg Era and the German General Staff* (1971); and L. Deighton, *Blitzkrieg* (1980).

BLOCKBUSTERS. Popular nickname for large demolition bombs. Both the Americans and British produced several kinds of blockbusters.

The RAF *(q.v.)* used blockbusters of as much as 11 tons. The huge bombs caused the destruction of whole blocks of buildings. Heavy explosives were contained in thin casings on the assumption that a blast would be more effective than fragmentation. British heavy bombers dropped blockbusters on Berlin with devastating effect. A variation called the "Tall Boy" was used on November 12, 1944, to sink the German super battleship *Tirpitz (q.v.)*.

"BLOOD, TOIL, TEARS, AND SWEAT." Highly publicized phrase from a Winston Churchill war speech on May 13, 1940. *(See* CHURCHILL'S WAR SPEECHES.)

BLUM, LÉON (1872–1950). French Socialist leader and Premier.

In 1936 Blum became Premier of France, the first Socialist and the first Jewish premier in the nation's history. His government, which lasted 13 months, was beset by a wave of sitdown strikes. In 1940 he adamantly refused to share in any compromise with the Germans after the defeat of France. He would not leave France, was arrested, and tried in 1942 by the Vichy Government. He utilized his trial for a brilliant attack on the Vichy French. The charges were withdrawn. In 1943 he was sent to Buchenwald concentration camp, from which he was rescued by British troops in 1945.

Lean, bent, with a long face and walrus mustache, Blum was seldom seen without his spectacles. He had a high-pitched voice and was stubborn in the face of disaster. "For 30 years," he said, "I have done the things for which I was least fitted. What I really love is solitude and books."

Bibliography. Blum's wartime essay, *For All Mankind* (1946) revealed his faith in democracy, democratic socialism, and internationalism. *See also* biographies by R. L. Stokes (1937) and J. Colton (1966).

BLÜCHER. German heavy cruiser, named after Gebhard Leberecht von Blücher, Prussian Field Marshal of the Napoleonic era. She was a sister ship of the *Admiral Hipper* (*q.v.*).

WORLD WAR II. On April 8, 1940, the *Blücher* was part of a task force, which, on the German invasion of Norway, attempted to take Oslo. The defenders at the coastal fortress of Oskarsborg spotted the German cruiser and fired shells that demolished her control tower and bridge. Afire, the *Blücher* attempted to move out of range, only to be hit by two torpedoes fired from ashore. The cruiser rolled over and sank with the loss of more than 1,000 men. The event was one of the few in naval warfare by which coastal fortifications successfully countered an offshore attack.

SPECIFICATIONS. See ADMIRAL HIPPER.

BOCK, FEODOR VON (1880–1945). German General of the old school who despised National Socialism.

On the outbreak of war in 1939, von Bock, at the age of 59, was third in seniority among the officer corps. He commanded Army Group North in the invasion of Poland. He later served in the Netherlands, Belgium, and France. On July 19, 1940, after the defeat of France, he and 11 other high officers were promoted by Hitler to General Field Marshal. He commanded Army Group Center in the Russian campaign. When his offensive broke down, he was dismissed by an angered *Fuehrer,* only to be recalled in early 1942 to lead Army Group South and then again be removed. He was killed in an air raid on May 4, 1945.

Bibliography. A. W. Turney, *Disaster at Moscow: Field Marshal von Bock's Campaigns in Russia, 1941–1942* (1970).

BOHR, NIELS HENRIK DAVID (1885–1962). Danish physicist and key figure in the production of the atomic bomb.

During the winter of 1938–1939, Bohr worked with Albert Einstein at the

Institute for Advanced Study in Princeton, New Jersey. He returned to Denmark in April 1940 but halted his work in protest against the Nazi invasion. In September 1943 he was forced to flee, taking with him his invaluable atomic data. He landed on the Swedish coast from a fishing boat and was taken into custody by the Swedish police. Nineteen days later he was flown to Scotland in a *Mosquito* bomber. (*See* BOHR MISSION.) Later he was called to the United States, where he worked with J. Robert Oppenheimer (*q.v.*) and other scientists at the atomic bomb laboratory at Los Alamos, New Mexico. He played a major role in the final development of the atomic bomb. (*See* MANHATTAN PROJECT.)

Bibliography. W. Pauli (ed.), *Niels Bohr and the Development of Physics* (1955); and R.E. Moore, *Niels Bohr: The Man, His Science, and the World They Changed* (1966).

BOHR MISSION. Clandestine transfer of an important Danish scientist from Stockholm to Edinburgh in 1943 to assist in Allied bomb research.

BACKGROUND. In 1943 research on the atomic bomb in the United States was in a critical stage. The assistance of Professor Niels Bohr, Danish physicist, was considered to be vital, and it was decided at the highest Allied level to bring him to the United States. Bohr agreed. He managed to escape from German-occupied Denmark to Stockholm. A special plane was dispatched to bring him to Scotland. (*See* MOON PLANES.)

MOON FLIGHT. On October 7, 1943, the 58-year-old scientist was brought to an abandoned airstrip near Stockholm. He was fitted into a kind of snow suit and, accompanied by a black-suited pilot, entered the bomb bay of a *Mosquito*. (*See* AIRCRAFT: BRITISH AIRCRAFT DATA CHART). The powerful Rolls Royce engines roared, and with a great blue sheet of flame the black-painted plywood plane pulled into the night sky.

The pilot climbed to a height where enemy interception was difficult and where oxygen was needed. Two hours of flight lay ahead. There was an accident as the plane took off: An intercom plug linking pilot and passenger pulled out of its jack and the oxygen flow to Bohr was cut off. The scientist lapsed into unconsciousness. Immediately the pilot pushed the nose of his plane down to a risky low altitude. At maximum speed he headed for the sea, turning northward to approach Scotland beyond the range of German fighters. Northeast of the Orkney Islands he switched on his Iffy, Identification/Friend or Foe, (*q.v.*) which told British radar that he was harmless.

The *Mosquito* landed at a squadron base near Edinburgh. An ambulance sped across the field to meet the plane. The limp form of Dr. Bohr was lowered to the waiting stretcher. Fortunate to be alive, the scientist quickly recovered and was brought to the United States to assist in work on the atomic bomb.

Bibliography. R. E. Moore, *Niels Bohr: The Man, His Science, and the World They Changed* (1966); and S. Rozental, *Niels Bohr* (1967).

"BOMBS ON ENGLAND." Popular song in Germany in the early days of the war when it was believed that the *Luftwaffe* (*q.v.*), the German Air Force, would bring quick victory.

"Bombs on England" was a streamlined version of the old *"Hasslied"* ("Song of Hate") of World War I. The new song lost its popularity in Germany after the Battle of Britain (*q.v.*) and the subsequent mass raids by Allied bombers on German cities.

The text:

> We challenge the lion of Britian,
> For the last and decisive cup.
> We judge and we say
> An Empire breaks up.
>
> This sure is our proudest day,
> Comrade, Comrade,
> The orders are here,
> We start right away.
>
> Go, get on, get on,
> The motto is known;
> Get on to the foe,
> Get on to the foe!
> BOMBS ON ENGLAND!
>
> Listen to the engine singing,
> Get on to the foe!
> Listen, in your ears it's ringing.
> Get on to the foe.
> BOMBS, OH BOMBS, OH BOMBS ON ENGLAND!

BONHOEFFER, DIETRICH (1906–1945). German theologian executed by the Nazis.

From the beginning of the war Bonhoeffer worked zealously to bring peace. He opposed the Hitler regime with stubborn courage even during wartime. In 1942 he carried proposals to Sweden for peace terms with the Allies. He was arrested on April 5, 1943 and charged with "subversion of the Armed Forces." The full range of his activities was exposed by the failure of the 1944 July Plot (*q.v.*) on Hitler's life. He was sent to Buchenwald concentration camp and eventually to Flossenbürg Prison, where he was hanged on April 9, 1945. Those who came into contact with him, prisoners and guards alike, spoke admiringly of his noble bearing and cheerfulness under most painful conditions. He is to-day regarded both inside and outside Germany as a great 20th century German martyr.

Bibliography. E. Bethge, *Dietrich Bonhoeffer* (1970).

BORIS III (1894-1943). King of Bulgaria.

Aware of what had happened to the Czechs and Poles, Boris did his best to keep his country out of the war. Unable to resist German pressure, he signed the Tripartite Pact (*see* BERLIN-ROME-TOKYO AXIS) in March 1941 and allowed Hitler to use his country as a base to attack Greece and Yugoslavia. On Hitler's insistence, he declared war on Britain and the United States in December 1941.

Hitler made ever-increasing demands on Bulgaria for more manpower. On August 28, 1943, the *Fuehrer* and Boris had a meeting in which Hitler presented his demands in stormy fashion. Boris returned to Sofia, where he died under mysterious circumstances, either from a heart attack or by murder.

Bibliography. J. S. Roucek, *The Politics of the Balkans* (1939); and F.W.L. Kovacs, *The Untamed Balkans* (1941).

BORMANN, MARTIN (1900-?1945). Hitler's private secretary and closest adviser during the declining years of the Third Reich.

The son of a sergeant in a cavalry regiment, Bormann served in World War I and after the war joined the rightist *Freikorps* ''to help liberate Germany from the traitors who had stabbed her in the back.'' He became attached to Hitler after the flight of Rudolf Hess (*q.v.*) to Britain in May 1941. (*See* HESS FLIGHT.) Next to Heinrich Himmler (*q.v.*), Bormann was one of the most powerful men in Nazi Germany. His Party comrades dubbed him the ''Brown Eminence,'' and his enemies called him ''the Machiavelli behind the office desk.''

During the final days Bormann exerted almost total power in the Third Reich. At a time when others deserted, Bormann remained faithful to Hitler, who called him ''my most loyal Party comrade.'' Bormann was in the *Fuehrerbunker* (*See* FUEHRER'S BUNKER) when Hitler committed suicide. He disappeared after Hitler's death. He may have been killed during the breakout from the Chancellery, but his body was never found.

Bibliography. W. Stevenson, *The Bormann Brotherhood* (1973).

BOSE, SUBHAS CHANDRA (1897-1945). Indian nationalist leader who turned his support to the Axis during the war.

In September 1939 the British Viceroy declared India a co-belligerent in the war against Nazi Germany—without the approval of the Indian people. In July 1940 Bose was jailed on the charge of plotting to raze the famed Black Hole monument at Calcutta but in reality for his propaganda attempts to use Britain's preoccupation with the war as an opportunity to win independence for India. Transferred to his home after a hunger strike, he disappeared in January 1941 and later that year showed up in Germany.

In Berlin Bose organized the nucleus of an Indian National Army (INA) and at the same time headed the so-called Provisional Government of India. The Japanese-controlled radio at Bangkok beamed phonograph records of his voice to India. By June 1943 he was in Tokyo to organize troops among prisoners of war. He claimed Japanese support for Burmese and Philippine independence. He took part in actions of the INA on the Japanese side on the India-Burma frontier. He died in a plane crash in Formosa on August 18, 1945.

Bibliography. S. C. Bose, *The Indian Struggle, 1920–1934* (1935).

BOUGAINVILLE. Location of battle between the Japanese and the Allies for a key island in the northern Solomon Islands in late 1943.

BACKGROUND. The struggle for the control of the northern Solomons centered around Bougainville, the last Japanese stronghold in the archipelago. For both sides it was a desirable base. After capturing New Georgia, the Allies decided to bypass Kolombangara and head for Bougainville. In late September the Japanese Imperial General Headquarters (GHQ) gave orders to abandon the Central Solomons and fall back on Bougainville.

CONFRONTATION. On October 27, 1942, the New Zealand 3rd Division landed on Treasury Island and took it after more than a week of heavy fighting. Meanwhile, at dawn on November 1, Lt. Gen. Alexander A. Vandegrift (*q.v.*) led his U.S. Marines ashore at Empress Augusta Bay. The 60,000-man garrison, including the Japanese 17th Army, did not react immediately in the belief that this was a diversionary move before the main attack. Most of the defenders moved into the jungle. While the landings went on, Allied planes operating from carriers and from New Guinea struck at Rabaul to discourage possible enemy reinforcements for Bougainville.

As soon as several miles of Bougainville were secured, U.S. engineers built an airstrip. The very next day Allied planes began bombing Rabaul (*q.v.*) from the new base. The Japanese removed their carriers from the vicinity.

The Allied buildup continued until by November 14 there were 34,000 troops ashore, by mid-December 44,000. By this time there were 4 new airfields on the island.

NEUTRALIZATION. The struggle for Bougainville was now in a stalemate. In March 1944 the Japanese made two major attempts to dislodge the Americans in bitter fighting but without success. About 5,000 Japanese moved out of the jungle to attack the Americans. Allied dead numbered 263. The remainder of the Japanese withdrew to several southern bases, where they were left without supplies, ammunition, or equipment.

SIGNIFICANCE. Once again the Americans, Australians, and New Zealanders demonstrated that they could meet and defeat the Japanese in jungle warfare. The Allies now had a new forward base in their island-hopping campaign to Tokyo.

Bibliography. S. E. Morison, *The Two-Ocean War* (1963); and S. Denliger and C. Carey, *War in the Pacific* (1970).

BRACKEN, BRENDAN RANDALL (1901–1958). British newspaperman and Minister of Information in World War II.

When Winston Churchill (*q.v.*) became Prime Minister in May 1940, he made Bracken his private secretary. In July he appointed his secretary to the post of British Minister of Information. In this capacity Bracken remained one of Churchill's closest advisers and associates. In 1944 he was named to the Emergency Housing Commission. In 1945 he briefly held the post of First Lord of the Admiralty.

Bespectacled, carrot-haired, jerky in manner, Bracken was one of the most outspoken of "Winston's Glamour Boys." He shared Churchill's taste for voluminous reading, energetic talk, and big black cigars. As British Minister of Information he added a dash of showmanship to his routine work.

BRADLEY, OMAR NELSON (1893–1981). Senior American field commander in the war in Europe.

When the United States entered the war in 1941, Bradley, then a Brigadier General, commanded the Infantry School at Fort Benning, Georgia. In February 1943 he was assigned to head the U.S. Second Corps in the North African campaign. After his troops captured Bizerta in May 1943, he was promoted to Lieutenant General. He added further to his growing reputation by leading his men in the invasion of Sicily.

Taken by Gen. Dwight D. Eisenhower (*q.v.*) to England to prepare for the Normandy landing, Bradley commanded the U.S. First Army, all the American forces, in the D-Day landings. This army was later joined by Gen. George Patton's (*q.v.*) Third Army to form the 12th Army Group under Bradley's command. Bradley directed the operations of this group, the largest army ever commanded by an American General, until the end of the war.

Bradley's 12th Group invaded Normandy, solidified its position, broke through at St. Lô (*q.v.*), and liberated Paris. It contained the German counterattack at the Battle of the Bulge (*q.v.*) in late 1944. Bradley's men were the first across the Rhine at Remagen bridge (*q.v.*). They went on to central Germany to make the first Allied contact with Russian troops on April 25, 1945.

General Bradley died on April 8, 1981, at the age of 88.

Bibliography. O. N. Bradley, *A Soldier's Story* (1951); and C. Whiting, *Bradley* (1971).

BRAUCHITSCH, WALTHER VON (1881–1948). Commander-in-Chief of the German Army from 1938–1941.

Von Brauchitsch won temporary prestige by the victories in Poland, Western Europe, and in the first stages of the Russian invasion. These almost uncanny triumphs removed all hope that he would support any plot against Hitler. He attempted to persuade Hitler to strike directly at Moscow instead of supporting the diversionary thrust toward Kiev. Hitler realized too late that von

Brauchitsch had judged the situation correctly. The German armies were soon caught in the Russian winter.

Von Brauchitsch suffered a series of heart attacks at the time of the setbacks in Russia. Hitler on December 19, 1941 finally accepted von Brauchitsch's request for resignation and himself took over command of the armed forces. From then on von Brauchitsch lived with a cloud over his name. When he learned of the 1944 July Plot (*q.v.*), he publicly condemned the conspirators.

BRAUN, WERNHER VON (1912–1977). German-born engineer and rocket expert who played an important role in the development of the *V-1s* and *V-2s* (*qq.v.*).

With the outbreak of the war in 1939, Hitler ordered all advanced rocketry research stopped. But on October 3, 1942, a launching at Peenemünde was so successful that the *Fuehrer* assigned a higher priority to rocket research. He promoted von Braun to full professor and ordered the mass production of *V-2s*. In February 1944 Heinrich Himmler (*q.v.*) tried to take over the Peenemünde project. When von Braun refused to join in the plan, he was arrested on charges that he had planned to fly to England with secret documents. He was freed on Hitler's direct order. In the final nine months of the war more than 3,000 *V-2s* were released on Allied targets.

In March 1945, as the Russian Armies advanced to within 100 miles of Peenemünde, von Braun and several hundred of his colleagues surrendered to the American forces.

Bibliography. See D. K. Huzel, *Peenemünde to Canaveral* (1962).

BRERETON, LEWIS HYDE (1890–1967). Commander of the 1st Allied Airborne Army in the bitter Battle of Arnhem (*q.v.*) in September 1944.

Although a graduate of the U.S. Naval Academy at Annapolis, Brereton chose an army career. When the United States entered World War II, he was in command of the U.S. Far East Air Force. His units suffered great damage during the Japanese attack on the Philippines in 1941. He was sent to India in 1942, and then to the Middle East in 1941–1943, where U.S. units operated with RAF (*q.v.*) squadrons. He was transferred to England in 1943 as commander of the U.S. 9th Air Force. There he built the American air arm into one of the war's most powerful tactical units. He planned and organized many of the raids that devastated German cities and industrial targets. In August 1944 he was placed in command of the 1st Allied Airborne Army, which played an important role in the battle of Arnhem.

Bibliography. L. H. Brereton, *The Brereton Diaries* (1946).

BRETAGNE. French battleship completed in 1915 and partially modernized in the late 1920s and early 1930s. On July 3, 1940, a British task force off Alexandria turned on the French fleet there after its ultimatum was rejected. (*See*

ORAN NAVAL ENCOUNTER.) The old *Bretagne* was set afire before she could get under way. Eleven minutes after the first shot she capsized and sank, taking with her 977 lives.

BRETTON WOODS CONFERENCE. Also termed the United Nations Monetary and Financial Conference. A meeting of representatives of the United Nations in the summer of 1944 to work out provisional understandings to restore financial health to its members and to facilitate postwar reconstruction.

BACKGROUND. Even before the war began, international competition in trade and banking had been rife. The Depression years after 1929 and economic policies of the totalitarian states disrupted the financial balance in international currencies. World War II brought even greater economic and financial problems. Toward the end of the war the United States and Britain took the initiative in an effort to remedy war dislocations and provide for a more balanced economic relationship between nations.

PARTICIPANTS. Economic and financial experts of 44 members of the United Nations met at a rambling summer hotel in the middle of exquisite mountain scenery in Bretton Woods, New Hampshire, during the first 21 days of July 1944. The outstanding delegates were Henry Morgenthau, who led the American delegation, and Lord John Maynard Keynes, the famed British economist. After long and detailed discussions, two major provisional understandings were reached.

INTERNATIONAL MONETARY FUND. This fund, soon to be known as IMF, consisted of U.S. $8.8 billion, a kind of international "kitty," into which the member nations would put their contributions. The contributions were to be worked out on a complicated formula that weighed several elements in a nation's strength. According to the adjustable quotas, the United States would put up U.S. $2.75 billion, about a quarter of the burden, because it was at the time the world's richest nation. The United Kingdom, although grievously bombed during the war, came next, the Soviet Union, also severely damaged, next, and so on.

The fund was to be manipulated by the United Nations to maintain exchange stability, avoid competitive exchange depreciations, ease sudden fluctuations, and encourage a multilateral system of payments. The conferees agreed that each national currency would be assigned a value in terms of either the American dollar or gold.

In fact, the IMF was designed as a kind of teeter-totter, to keep currencies balanced against each other. The idea was to strike a blow at the prevalent financial anarchy by which one nation would take advantage of another. It was a decided advantage when various national governments, or their central banks, could buy another nation's currencies needed to clear trade balances.

International Monetary Fund—Quotas for Each Nation (in Millions of U.S. Dollars)

Australia	200.0	India	400.00
Belgium	225.0	Iran	25.0
Bolivia	10.0	Iraq	8.0
Brazil	150.0	Liberia	0.5
Canada	300.0	Luxembourg	10.0
Chile	50.0	Mexico	90.0
China	550.0	Netherlands	275.0
Colombia	50.0	New Zealand	50.0
Costa Rica	5.0	Nicaragua	2.0
Cuba	50.0	Norway	50.0
Czechosolvakia	125.0	Panama	0.5
Denmark*		Paraguay	2.0
Dominican Republic	5.0	Peru	25.0
Ecuador	5.0	Philippine Commonwealth	15.0
Egypt	45.0	Poland	125.0
El Salvador	2.5	Union of South Africa	100.0
Ethiopia	6.0	USSR	1,200.0
France	450.0	UK	1,300.0
Greece	40.0	US	2,750.0
Guatemala	5.0	Uruguay	15.0
Haiti	5.0	Venezuela	15.0
Honduras	2.5	Yugoslavia	60.0
Iceland	1.0		
		TOTAL	8,000.0

*Denmark, which had no government-in-exile at the time, would wait for a reconstituted government, after which its quota would be set for the Fund.

INTERNATIONAL BANK FOR RECONSTRUCTION AND DEVELOP-MENT. A second agreement set up a World Bank with a capitalization of U.S. $9 billion. Its purpose was to extend loans to nations that required economic rehabilitation. Those billions were also to be contributed on a complicated formula that weighed the economic strength of the member nations. About 35 percent was to be supplied by the United States.

When a country needed a loan to reenter world trade, it could apply to the World Bank. Such a loan had four characteristics: (1) It was to be a loan for a constructive purpose which had a chance of earning an income and repaying itself; (2) It would allow a long time to repay; (3) It would pay a low rate of interest; and (4) It was a loan that no private banking interests would want to assume because of the slow and low rate of repayment.

AFTERMATH. Thirty-five nations ratified the agreement by the Spring of 1946. At that time the Soviet Union had not signed, explaining that more time was needed. The Soviets were reluctant to disclose their gold holdings, as required by the agreement. Eventually, membership was extended to 77 countries.

International Bank for Reconstruction and Development—Subscriptions
(in Millions of U.S. Dollars)

Australia	200.0	India	400.0
Belgium	225.0	Iran	24.0
Bolivia	7.0	Iraq	6.0
Brazil	105.0	Liberia	0.5
Canada	325.0	Luxembourg	10.0
Chile	35.0	Mexico	65.0
China	600.0	Netherlands	275.0
Colombia	35.0	New Zealand	50.0
Costa Rica	2.0	Nicaragua	0.8
Cuba	35.0	Norway	50.0
Czechosolvakia	125.0	Panama	0.2
Denmark*		Paraguay	0.8
Dominican Republic	2.0	Peru	17.5
Ecuador	2.0	Philippine Commonwealth	15.0
Egypt	3.2	Poland	125.0
El Salvador	1.0	Union of South Africa	100.0
Ethiopia	3.0	USSR	1,200.0
France	450.0	UK	1,300.0
Greece	25.0	US	3,175.0
Guatemala	2.0	Uruguay	10.5
Haiti	2.0	Venezuela	10.5
Honduras	1.0	Yugoslavia	40.0
Iceland	1.0		
		TOTAL	9,100.0

*Denmark was permitted to wait for reconstituted government.

SIGNIFICANCE. Together, the IMF and the World Bank represented the financial side of the emerging United Nations structure. Both were designed primarily to forestall future economic warfare between nations by discouraging competitive currency manipulations and financial penetration of other countries.

Bibliography. V. P. Young, Conference at Bretton Woods (1944); C. Morgan, Bretton Woods (1945); and C. O. Watts, The Bretton Woods Agreements (1945).

BRITAIN AT WAR.
Nearly twenty-one years after World War I the British were again at war with the Germans. It was an unwanted war, but, as in the first, the British home front went to work zealously to cope with the emergency.

FIRST REACTIONS. The British public witnessed the early events of the war with stunning disbelief. There was much pessimism during the first few weeks. In his diary Harold Nicolson noted on September 24, 1939:

September 24, 1939:

The effect of the blackout, the evacuation and general dislocation has been bad for morale. . . . The Government has not foreseen a situation in which boredom and bewilderment could be the main elements. . . . We have all the apparatus of war conditions without war conditions. The result is general disillusion and grumbling, from which soil defeatism may grow.

There was dismay as the Nazis overwhelmed five nations and drove British forces from Dunkirk (*see* DUNKIRK EVACUATION) and Norwegian ports. It seemed that nothing could prevent Nazi domination of Europe.

These were, however, initial reactions and they were to be followed by a dramatic about-face. Britons had no intention of following the lead of the French and bowing to Nazi occupation. They would fight to the end. They applauded when their government contemptuously dismissed Hitler's proposed "favorable terms." A British wit put it bluntly, "We have reached the final round and we now play for the championship on the home grounds."

POLITICAL GEAR CHANGE. The public soon lost its confidence in the Chamberlain Government that had tried to appease Hitler in the immediate pre-war days. Winston Churchill (*q.v.*) was accepted by the House of Commons because there was no alternative. He was much distrusted because he had changed sides in Parliament twice. He formed a national government and brought Labour into it. He was also eloquent: "The whole of the warring nations are engaged, not only soldiers but the entire population, men, women, and children. The fronts are everywhere. The trenches are dug in the towns and in the streets. Every village is fortified. Every road is barred. The front lines run through the factories. The workmen are soldiers with different weapons but with the same courage." For the British this was "a people's war," and they were determined to fight it to the end.

The British public, much as the ancient Athenians in time of war, temporarily abandoned its rights and privileges in favor of demands of the hour. The traditional system of local government was replaced by centralized administration from London. The sweeping Emergency Powers (Defense) Act of May 22, 1940, enacted in a single day, indicated that Britain was girding for survival. Those civil rights that had been won at bitter cost over the centuries were suspended for the duration. Within a year after passage of the Act, some 2,000 orders and regulations were issued as necessary for prosecution of the war. A citizen could be ordered to leave his home or stay in it. If he owned a farm he could be told which crops to cultivate and when to plant them. Everything in his daily life—food, clothing, shelter, journeys, and entertainment—was now subject to wartime controls.

The order that created greatest confusion for citizens, and with little or no inconvenience to the Germans, was that which decreed the obliteration of all signs that could identify a locality. Designed to confuse enemy parachutists, the order remained in effect until six months before the end of the war. It created more havoc for bewildered Britons than for imaginary parachutists.

WAR ECONOMY. Early in the conflict the entire British economy was geared to the sole purpose of winning the war. Everything in the economic life of the nation—administrative structure, control techniques, war production, and economic stabilization—was subjected to strict centralized control. Churchill and his colleagues could count on cooperation from every level of the economy—the new capitalism of paternalist corporations, the managerial class, workers, and state bureaucracy. The Prime Minister set up a body called the Production Executive to bring about better co-ordination in war industries and war supplies. The office also had the power to allocate raw materials, fix priorities, and see to the proper distribution of productive capacity and labor. It supervised all ministries concerned with war production, worked closely with military strategists, and integrated British with U.S. production. British production in industrial plants had an output during the war of 100,000 cannon, 26,000 tanks, 900,000 naval mines, and 3,000 miles of pipeline.

Labor was fully employed in the war effort. The Ministry of Labour used its wide powers to shift workers to places where they were most needed. Strikes and lockouts were outlawed for the duration. Workers were frozen in their jobs. By 1943 the work week rose to 54 hours for men and 46 for women. Elderly men, women, and even children flocked to the new factories to give a hand to war production. Skilled trades were heavily diluted by use of semi-skilled workers.

During the opening months of the Churchill administration precious steel was reserved mostly for heavy factory machines and for structural beams; tanks and guns would come later. The corner was turned in the spring of 1940, when the main weight of the British effort went into weapons instead of weapons plants. By the summer of 1940 the stream of guns, tanks, and planes was swelling into a torrent of production.

The crucial problem of meeting the need for fighting planes in 1940 was solved by the efforts of British workers. Lord Beaverbrook (q.v.), appointed head of the new Ministry of Aircraft Production, assumed general responsibility for co-ordination of production hitherto exercised by the Air Ministry. In this capacity he delivered the fighters that won the critical Battle of Britain (q.v.).

FOOD PROBLEM. The British public realized that the very life of the nation depended on handling the food problem. The population of the United Kingdom had risen to 47,750,000 in 1939, but the extent of arable land under crops had fallen by 4,500,000 acres.

The government inaugurated a campaign for enlarged farm production. To ease the strain on shipping and importation of foodstuffs, greatly increased crops of wheat, potatoes, legumes, and other foods were encouraged. More than 1,000 clubs to raise pigs were organized, one by the royal household at Windsor.

The problem of food on the home front was divided into three parts: those foods almost totally absent; those available in reasonable quantities; and those placed on ration. Foods almost wholly unavailable included bananas, oranges, and other tropical fruits; tomatoes, onions, and other vegetables imported by sea; and deep-sea fish, nuts, fruit juices, chocolate, and many canned goods that had been imported before the war. In gardens all over the island, onions and tomatoes were raised.

Food available in reasonable quantities included bread, oatmeal, whole-wheat flour, dried beans, rice, carrots, potatoes, cocoa, and packaged cereals. Supplies of most of these foods dwindled as the war continued. There was sufficient milk at first, but later only one pint a day was allotted to each child.

RATIONING. The war was nearly 5 months old before food rationing was introduced tentatively. The government's desire for rationing arose less from any fear of shortages than from a belief that all should be treated equally. The public willingly accepted the system of "bread crumbs in battle dress." Into the category of rationed goods fell meat (but not poultry or fish), butter, oleo-margarine, cooking fats, sugar, jam, tea, and cheese. Eggs, too, were placed under a control scheme. To stop profiteering, the price of eggs was rigidly fixed, and sales allowed only under license.

Eventually, rationing became a part of everyday life. Most people had to do with one shilling and tuppence worth of meat per week, supplemented by American Spam (*q.v.*), a canned meat. Weekly rations for each individual included: four ounces of bacon or ham; one-half pound of sugar; one-half pound of fats; and one-half pound of cheese.

Britons were also eating foods they had never accepted before, such as whale meat, shark meat, seabirds, and seabirds' eggs. Those who worked in heavy industries or farming, as well as British merchant seamen, were given an extra food allowance. There were strains, but in general the public bore up well. Most people considered it a patriotic duty to pay attention to rationing orders. Some minor black-market operations and under-the-counter deals occurred, but on the whole the distribution of food was managed in a fair and equitable manner.

MORALE. After the first few weeks of pessimism and self-doubt, British morale soared to a high level. Inspired by Churchill's war speeches (*q.v.*), the public plainly and simply refused to accept defeat. Even when standing virtually alone, with Hitler in control of the Continent, British morale never wavered. Day after day, men and women working in factories, offices, and in their own homes, fought human fears with a brave show of indifference. Children sang in the shelters. The entire nation displayed an unquenchable vigor of spirit, enduring emotional sacrifices in parting from their loved ones, abandoning homes, closing down businesses, and terminating professions. The average Briton paid one-third of his income in taxes, and his unearned income of 1,000 pounds was taxed at 94 percent. Despite such tax rates, the British bought more than 8 billion pounds worth of national bonds. Britons accepted the dictum that there was no alternative to victory.

The calm behavior of the British public during the Battle of Britain (*q.v.*)

impressed foreign observers. Londoners under aerial bombardment revealed extraordinary qualities of courage, humor, and kindliness. To those who expressed admiration there came a low-keyed reply: "It isn't heroism at all. It's just that we British lack imagination!" Complaints were also in the tradition of British understatement. An elderly retired officer living in Great Snoring wrote a letter to the editor suggesting that the war bulletins were bad for the nerves. "Let us instead have lecturers on our historical and gallant fights for freedom and also a few calming nature talks."

The survival of Britain in the struggle against Hitler's war machine was due in large part to the Royal Navy, which protected the home islands and which convoyed vital cargoes through submarine-infested seas. Equally as important was the Royal Air Force (q.v.), which against great odds blunted Hitler's pre-invasion air assault. These factors were added to the extraordinary morale on the home front.

CIVILIAN DEFENSE. The object of the Air Raid Precautions (ARP) system was not only to protect the public but also to make possible an effective resistance to the Germans. All over the country, householders prepared to descend reluctantly into musty cellars, judging the risk of pneumonia as preferable to high explosives. In November 1938 John Anderson (q.v.), Home Secretary, had introduced his Anderson shelters (q.v.), which were used after the outbreak of war.

In the large cities, especially London, fear of attack by poison gas was strong, dominating all other concerns. Gas masks were distributed to the public. Ordinary men and women in steel hats patrolled the streets during raids, helped fight fires, rescued victims from the debris of buildings, and worked at first-aid posts. During the worst raids, civilian defense forces in London directed men, women, and children with their bedding through the dusk to the Tubes (subways) to join huddled thousands on the platforms below. There was nowhere else to go. Londoners underground were noted for their resolute comradeship, community spirit, and adjustability to discomfort.

EVACUATION OF CHILDREN. In early September 1939 the mainline railway stations of the great cities were swamped with thousands of young children and mothers. About 1.5 million women and children were evacuated to safe areas. There were many conflicts between hosts and guests, especially in the attempt of slum children to adapt themselves to free life in the open country.

SOCIAL CURRENTS. Traditional British democracy in the past had united different social groups, each of which was aware of its position in the social order. Aerial bombardment and the threat of invasion meant that both privileged and unprivileged classes had to work together to face the common danger. The establishment, whether it liked it or not, was dependent on the cooperation of workers, farmers, and women. All worked together in their common contempt for Hitler and Nazism.

Never before in British history had there been such an intermixture of population and such a confrontation of social mores. The average Briton, after a lifetime of social isolation, found himself part of a community-with-a-purpose. Strangers began to work together in close cooperation. London typists found themselves at benches in northern factories; villagers in the countryside attempted to evaluate the customs of Cockney lads from the East End of London; Welshmen tried to understand the accents of Poles and Danes; citizens from the coastal cities in the south who were moved to Scotland to help manufacture tanks found it most difficult to communicate with unfamiliar natives. Some 60 million changes of address were recorded for the civil population alone, 12 million more than the population of the country.

In return for their cooperation the unprivileged classes were rewarded during the war years by concessions for a higher standard of living, greater social recognition, and better welfare services. The Beveridge Report, issued in 1942 in the midst of the war, provided for a minimum level of security. (*See* BEVERIDGE, WILLIAM HENRY.) This report led eventually to creation of the postwar welfare state.

ENTERTAINMENT. During the war years, ordinary Britons managed to cope with the banalities of daily life. At the start of the war all places of mass entertainment were closed to lessen casualties during bombing raids, but it was not long before they were reopened. Entertainers serving both armed forces and home front included such noted actors and actresses as Laurence Olivier, Noël Coward, and Sybil Thorndike, songstress Vera Lynn, comedian Arthur Ashley, comedienne and singer Gracie Fields, and the Americans Ben Lyon and Bebe Daniels. The public relied heavily on the British Broadcasting Corporation (BBC) for accurate war news. Films, especially the American *Gone With the Wind*, were popular with the public throughout the war years.

Despite air raids, Britishers enjoyed their public houses (pubs). Those who before the war would never have dreamed of setting foot into such an establishment now found themselves part of a group with no such inhibitions. The British pub in wartime presented an oasis of warmth and hospitality in a blacked-out world.

Official entertainment was organized on a gigantic scale. J. B. Priestley described one incident; "The other day I saw two thousand people put aside what remained of the meat pies and fried plaice and chips they'd had for lunch, lift their eyes toward an orchestra consisting of four young women in green silk and then, all two thousand of them, roar out '*Oh Johnny, Oh Johnny, how you can love.*' And having paid tribute to Johnny and applauding the four young women in green silk these two thousand people returned, much heartened, to another five or six hours at their machines.''

British song writers greeted the war with a flood of patriotic numbers. The German *Fuehrer* was the target of derision:

> *Heil Hitler, yah, yah, yah,*
> *O what a horrid little man you are!*

The song titled *We're Gonna Hang Out the Washing on the Siegfried Line* (*q.v.*) caused great offense to Germans, who responded in kind: "*We're Gonna Cry Out Stinking Fish Until the End of Time.*"

BRITAIN AT END OF THE WAR. Britain was weakened considerably during the closing months of the war. The Battle of the Atlantic (*q.v.*) had been won, and although it ended in victory, the time was past when the Royal Navy ruled the waves. The financial situation was precarious: By this time the national debt was three times the national income. In 1945 the national debt stood at £22 billion, a burden weighing heavily on the average citizen. Foreign assets were reduced by half. A quarter of the population needed housing because of devastation by German bombing. Food was in such short supply that the government offered free cartridges to anyone wanting to shoot grey squirrels.

British morale remained high in the days when it became increasingly obvious that victory was near. The country was shaken, but the stubborn courage of its people, embodied in the words and actions of Winston Churchill, persisted. Their old standard of living had been lowered, but their wealth lay in tenacity, skill, and optimism. They had already won global admiration by saving democratic institutions from totalitarian aggression. Now they were determined to see the war through to its end.

HUMAN LOSSES. British losses in human lives were fewer than in other countries. In the four years of World War I the British Empire lost nearly a million dead. In the 6 years of World War II its losses on battle fronts and home front were under 400,000. Strangely, the British had a lighter loss of life in the longer and more desperate of the two wars.

MATERIAL LOSSES. Property damage strained Britain's resources to the limit. More than half her 21 million tons of merchant marine was destroyed. Wide areas in many cities were devastated by German bombs. Railways, factories, and docks were smashed wholly or in part. More than 4 million houses, 1 out of every 3 in the United Kingdom, were demolished or damaged. The national economy was almost throttled. Cut off from the outside world, Britain had lost its best customers. Balance of payments was weakened because invisible exports no longer could make up the usual trade deficit. As in previous wars, Britain had poured out subsidies to numerous allies, few of which were collectible. The country was on the verge of a crippling inflation.

AFTERMATH. At the general election of July 5, 1945, the Labour Party won 393 seats against the Conservatives' 198, thus achieving a clear-cut majority in the 640-member House of Commons. Churchill was defeated after waging a weak campaign. The Labour Government nationalized Britain's major industries, extended social services, and instead of removing wartime controls, maintained them in a policy of austerity. The pound was devalued, thereby forcing the British consumer to pay more for his essential needs, but stimulating foreign trade by reducing export prices. Loans from the United States helped in this program of reconstruction.

For the first time in modern history Britain became a debtor country. The British had played a critical role in smashing the Hitler menace, but the cost of World War II was enormous. The liquidation of foreign investments, decline of the carrying trade, and loss of invisible income eventually cost the leadership of the world economy. With its dollar shortage, Britain could no longer earn enough to keep its people on high Western living standards. Defeated Germany went on eventually to become the Continent's most prosperous nation, while victorious Britain faced one economic crisis after another. This unexpected result illustrates the strange odds and vicissitudes in the results of modern war.

Bibliography. H. Nicolson, *Diaries and Letters, 1939-1945* (1947); A. Calder, *The People's War* (1969); M. G. Henrey, *London Under Fire* (1969); N. Longmate, *How We Lived Then* (1971); M. Panter-Downes, *London War Notes* (1971); H. M. Pelling, *Britain and the Second World War* (1971); and M. Yass, *The Home Front: Britain 1939-45* (1971).

BRITAIN, BATTLE OF. Air battle over Britain between the German *Luftwaffe* and the British Royal Air Force (*qq.v.*) in the summer of 1940. British victory in this confrontation in the skies was the first great turning point of the war.

BACKGROUND. Following the defeat of France (*See* FRANCE, FIRST BATTLE OF), and the armistice at Compiègne (*q.v.*) on June 22, 1940, Britian stood alone against German power. On July 19 Hitler made a speech before the *Reichstag* in which he said that he could see no reason why the war should go on: "I am not the vanquished seeking favors, but the victor speaking in the name of reason." He offered the British a last chance for "a common-sense peace through negotiations." London maintained silence. Hitler then decided to go ahead with the invasion plan he had ordered in a war directive three days earlier (*See* SEA LION). His first goal was to eliminate the RAF as a fighting force and to strangle Britain's overseas trade by attacks on ports and shipping.

GERMAN PREPARATIONS. Hitler gave specific orders to Hermann Goering (*q.v.*), head of the *Luftwaffe:* "The task will be to prevent interference by the enemy Air Force, to destroy coastal fortresses that might operate against our disembarkation points, to break the first resistance of enemy land forces, and to disperse the reserves on the way to the front." Goering had two air fleets (*Luft-flotten II* and *III*) with 2,800 aircraft ready, including 200 low-level bombers, 380 dive bombers, 700 single-engined fighters, 22 twin-engined fighters, and 140 reconnaissance planes plus 190 aircraft of Air Fleet V stationed in Norway. He was ordered to win command of the air within two weeks.

BRITISH PREPARATIONS. In the brief interval of six weeks after the fall of France, the British worked to transform their island into a powerful fortress. Every individual, every shilling was placed at the disposal of the government. Civil defense, including fire fighters, repair units, and demolition squads, was speedily organized, with special efforts made to protect water, sewer, electricity, gas, and telephone services in London and other cities. Labor in the factories went to work on a round-the-clock basis. From concerned Americans came Springfield rifles, Browning machine guns, and artillery pieces.

The key to defense was the Royal Air Force. The British had only about 700 fighter planes available, but they also had several advantages. Their pilots had gained invaluable experience at Dunkirk (*See* DUNKIRK EVACUATION). Their planes, *Spitfires* and *Hurricanes* (*qq.v.*), were well-armed and maneuverable, and their pilots were distinguished by great spirit and resolve. British engineers and physicists had already perfected radar as a defense tool. (*See* RADAR, WARTIME). The defenders also had the advantage of a code-breaking machine. (*See* ULTRA.)

FIRST PHASE. In mid-July 1940 the Germans opened their attack with light probing and mine-laying sorties. On August 13, *Adlertag* (Eagle Day), the *Luftwaffe* made 485 bomber and 1,000 fighter sorties, concentrating on Southampton and other Channel ports and airfields in Hampshire and Kent. In a great display of air power, wave after wave of shrieking *Stuka* dive bombers, fast *Me-109s* and *Fw-190s*, and heavy *Dorniers* appeared over British targets. RAF pilots, including Poles, Czechs, French, and Belgians, rose to meet the invaders. There were incredibly fierce dogfights, a jamboree of twisting, tangling, flame-spitting craft in the din of splattering machine-gun fire. The opening air fights cost the Germans 45 planes and 53 men, the British 13.

Two days later came another mass attack. This time the Germans concentrated on fighter bases. Reacting vigorously, the RAF shot down 75 enemy aircraft while losing 34 planes. On August 18 the *Luftwaffe* lost 71 planes. In two weeks the Germans lost 602 aircraft to an RAF loss of 260.

LONDON. When the RAF retaliated by a raid on Berlin, Hitler ordered London as a primary target to break British morale. On September 7 a German force of 372 bombers attacked the British capital, smashing the dock areas and destroying oil storage tanks. That evening Goering reported, "London is in flames!" Two days later a follow-up attack cost the Germans 28 aircraft.

The assault on London continued for 23 consecutive days as German planes roared in from Calais and up the Thames Valley in large and small formations to drop both high explosives and incendiary bombs. The Germans unveiled a new weapon, the UXB (*q.v.*), a delayed action bomb that buried itself into the ground and exploded later.

By this time it became obvious that this was one battle the *Luftwaffe* was not going to win. Hitler had expected a quick and complete collapse, only to find a spirited and successful resistance. Britain remained alive under the terrific bombing.

SECOND PHASE. Hitler now shifted his tactics to night bombing, from London to the rest of England. On the night of November 14–15, 1940, German bombers smashed the center of Coventry. (*See* COVENTRY, BOMBING OF.) In December the *Luftwaffe* returned to a savage pounding of London, starting 1,500 fires in the center of the city. In the spring of 1941 the attacks concentrated on the seaports in the south and on such cities as Liverpool, Manchester, and Birmingham. The assault persisted until late June 1941, when Hitler turned on the Soviet Union and transferred most of the *Luftwaffe* to the eastern front. He had lost the Battle of Britain.

LOSSES. In the mass bombing of London 29,890 people were killed and more than 120,000 injured. British sources claimed the destruction of 1,733 German aircraft and admitted the loss of 915 planes, although the Germans claimed many more. Estimates vary, but it is believed the Germans lost 1,389 aircraft and the RAF 790 fighters. Damage to London and other British cities was extensive.

SIGNIFICANCE. Failure to subdue the RAF cost Hitler the war. He lost the Battle of Britain first because of British resistance and second because he made a basic military mistake: By shifting his air attack indiscriminately from target to target, instead of concentrating on one target at a time, he scattered his strength. He discovered to his dismay that the *Luftwaffe* could not cope with both the RAF and the unbreakable British spirit, which hardened under massive blows. Churchill paid tribute to the RAF with a famous line: "Never in the field of human conflict was so much owed by so many to so few." (*See* CHURCHILL'S WAR SPEECHES.)

Bibliography. S. St.G. Saunders, *The Battle of Britain* (1941); N. Macmillan. *The Royal Air Force in World War II* (1956); P. Collier, *The Battle of Britain* (1962); A. Price, *Luftwaffe* (1969); E. Bishop, *Their Finest Hour, The Story of the Battle of Britain* (1969); D. H. Wood and D. D. Dempster, *The Narrow Margin: The Battle of Britain and the Rise of Air Power, 1930–1940* (1969); A. Calder, *The People's War: Britain, 1939–1945* (1969); C. FitzGibbon, *The Blitz on London* (1970); and P. Townsend, *Duel of Eagles* (1970).

BRITISH EXPEDITIONARY FORCE (BEF). British Territorials and other troops ordered outside the country for temporary service.

A British military force of 10 divisions was dispatched to France at the start of the war. Commanded by Gen. John Standish Gort (*q.v.*), this BEF was hit by the Germans in May 1940 and driven back into a trap at Dunkirk. (*See* DUNKIRK EVACUATION.)

BRITISH SECURITY COORDINATION (BSC). An organization, with headquarters in New York, that was the hub for all branches of British intelligence.

BSC was headed by William Stephenson (*q.v.*), the master agent code-named *Intrepid*, who was Churchill's secret envoy to the United States. The innocuous-sounding organization was set up on June 16, 1940. After American entry into the war, the BSC worked in close coordination with the American Office of Strategic Services (OSS), headed by William Donovan (*qq.v.*). By its nature the work was obscure and secret. A vast hidden army of agents played an important role in the final overthrow of the Axis. When the Germans surrendered in May 1945, the BSC dismantled its labyrinthine apparatus and silently passed out of existence. (*See also* ESPIONAGE.)

BROOKE, FIELD MARSHAL SIR ALAN, 1ST VISCOUNT ALAN-BROOKE (1883–1963). Distinguished British gunnery officer.

When the war broke out in 1939, Brooke went to France as commander of an army corps. In this post he covered the withdrawal from Dunkirk. (*See* DUNKIRK EVACUATION.) From 1940–1941 he commanded the Home Forces, with the responsibility of organizing the British Army to resist a possible Nazi invasion.

In late 1941 Brooke succeeded Sir John Dill (*q.v.*) as Commander-in-Chief of the Imperial General Staff (CIGS), and served in that capacity for the remainder of the war. He became Churchill's principal strategic adviser, and was said to have retained the Prime Minister's respect and confidence throughout the war. He regarded his own role as one of transforming Churchill's many inspirations into realistic military sense. In 1943 it was believed that he would command the European invasion, but this plan was later changed because of major American participation. Gen. Brooke took part in all the important war meetings. (*See* CONFERENCES, ALLIED WAR.)

Bibliography. A. Bryant, *Turn of the Tide* (1957).

BROOKE-POPHAM, ROBERT MOORE (1878–1953). Commander-in-Chief of British forces in the Far East.

Soon after the start of the war, Brooke-Popham was sent to Canada to establish the Empire Air training scheme. He served on a similar mission to South Africa in 1940. In mid-November 1940 he was made the first British Commander-in-Chief of the Far Eastern Station. His duties were to consult and cooperate with the navy in Far Eastern waters, keep in touch with the command in India, and communicate with the governments of Australia and New Zealand.

Brooke-Popham was told that the defense of British possessions in the Far East would be strengthened by air power, but in fact his requirements ran a hopeless second to those of the hard-pressed British forces in Egypt. He was unable to meet the Japanese anywhere in the Far East on equal terms. Although he was not held responsible for losses to the Japanese, on December 27, 1941, he was replaced by Lt. Gen. Henry Pownall.

BROWN, CECIL (1907–   ). American radio news correspondent.

In January 1940 Brown joined the staff of the Columbia Broadcasting System. During the first Mediterranean fighting, he spoke to the American public. But in March 1941 he came into international prominence when he was expelled from Italy because of "his continued hostile attitude to Fascism." From Italy he made his way to Belgrade to report the war in the Balkans. After narrowly missing being shot by advance Nazi motorcycle squads, he reported from Belgrade the harrowing tale of the German assault on the city. After reporting from Ankara, Syria, and Cairo, he proceeded to Singapore by way of Rangoon and the Malayan jungle.

HMS REPULSE. On December 8, 1941, a day after Pearl Harbor (*q.v.*), Brown sailed from Singapore on the British battle cruiser *Repulse.* He sent a cable to his home office: OUTTOWNING FOUR DAYS SWELL STORY.

A British task force, without air cover, had set out to sea in an effort to smash Japanese transports and landing craft which were disembarking troops to reinforce Japanese bridgeheads on the north coast of Malaya. The plan was to strike the Japanese before they could attack Singapore by land. When only 50 miles off the coast of Malaya, and 150 miles from Singapore, the 35,000-ton battleship *Prince of Wales* and the *Repulse* were sunk in a major victory at sea. (*See PRINCE OF WALES.*)

In one of the great journalistic scoops of the war, Brown broadcasted dramatic report of the fierce air attack by the Japanese on the British task force. He was aboard the *Repulse* and escaped with hundreds of others. Swimming in thick oil, he saw the *Prince of Wales* turn over on her side "like a tired war horse and slide beneath the waters." Captain Tennant of the *Repulse* shouted through the ship's communication system: "All hands on deck, prepare to abandon ship. May God be with you!"

Jumping twenty feet to the water, Brown smashed his stop watch. The first torpedo had just struck. "It felt like the ship had crashed into a well-rooted dock." All around Brown men were stripping off their shoes and tossing aside their clothes. Some were running alongside the exposed hull of the ship to reach a spot where they could slide down without injuring themselves on the jagged side of the ship.

Brown felt a strong tide and a very powerful suction. "It was extremely difficult to make any progress away from the ship in the thick oil. The gentle quiet manner in which these shell-belching dreadnoughts went to their last resting place without explosion was a tribute of gratitude from two fine ships for their fine sailors.''

Brown was picked up by a destroyer and brought back to Singapore. He later criticized the British leaders in Malaya for their complacency and defensive psychology.

Tall, thin, with a beak-like nose, Brown was known as a persistent news reporter who managed to get into and out of one catastrophe after another and lived to tell the tale. A dogged pursuer of facts, he fought unending battles with British censors and colonial officials.

Bibliography. C. Brown, *Suez to Singapore* (1942).

BROWNING, FREDERICK ARTHUR MONTAGU (1896–1965).
Organizer of the British Red Devils (*q.v.*).

At the outbreak of war Browning commanded the Small Arms School. In October 1941 he was named Chief of the Airborne Command, handling problems of supply, organization, and training of the famous outfit later called the Red Devils. Starting with several parachute and glider-borne brigades, Browning built the Red Devils into an imposing combat force of 17 brigades. He led the 1st Airborne Corps at Arnhem in September 1944. (*See* ARNHEM, BATTLE OF.) In the final months of the war he served as Chief of Staff to Lord Louis Mountbatten (*q.v.*) in the Far East.

BROZ, JOSIP. *See* TITO.

BRUNEVAL RAID. Code or cover name *Biting.* A commando-style assault on the northern coast of France in late February 1942 to obtain secrets of German expertise in radar.

BACKGROUND. The giant German Würzburg radar sent out medium-length waves accurate enough to enable flak gunners to engage unseen British aircraft on the English Channel. British scientists were anxious to study sample components of this superior radio-location equipment. Aerial photographs pinpointed one such station on a cliff edge 12 miles north of Le Havre near the village of Bruneval. British Combined Operations designed *Biting,* involving a company of parachute troops, a naval evacuation force, an infantry unit landed from the sea to cover the beach evacuation, and members of the French underground.

ASSAULT. The drop was made on February 27, 1942, when 200 men touched down from 12 planes near Bruneval. The commandos moved silently to the Würzburg radar device, which looked like an enormous saucer, killed or captured its crew, and removed all the necessary component parts. Two raiders were killed and six were lost, but the remaining men, plus six wounded and the radar booty, were transferred on the open sea to naval gunboats. At dawn a squadron of *Spitfires* (*q.v.*) escorted Maj. John Frost and his commandos to Portsmouth harbor.

SIGNIFICANCE. Operation Biting was declared a tremendous success. The captured radar equipment was studied meticulously and disclosed technological aspects that the Germans wanted to be kept secret. (*See* RADAR, WARTIME.)

Bibliography. G. Millar, *The Bruneval Raid* (1974).

BUDËNNY, SEMYON MIKHAILOVICH (1883–1973). Marshal of the Soviet Union.

In 1939 Budënny held the post of Deputy Commissar for Defense. Two weeks after Hitler's invasion on June 22, 1941, Budënny was appointed Commander-in-Chief of Soviet Armies on the southwestern front, in the Ukraine and Bessarabia. In one month the invading Germans cut his forces at Kiev and Uman in two. Most of his troops at Uman were surrounded and captured.

Budënny withdrew across the Dnieper River while carrying out Stalin's scorched-earth policy, destroying everything in his path. In August 1941 he gave orders for the destruction of the Dnieper River dam. In the campaign he lost over 1.5 million men. He was relieved of his command on October 23, 1941. Shifted to the rear to recruit and train new armies, he was not given another command during the war.

BULGE, BATTLE OF THE. Final German counteroffensive in mid-December 1944 in a wooded hills area in south Belgium. It is also known as the Ardennes offensive.

BACKGROUND. In late 1944 Hitler's Third Reich was bleeding from every vein. On each front—west, south, and east—Allied power was headed toward Germany. In the west Anglo-American forces were poised on the Siegfried Line (*q.v.*); in the south they were surging northward up the Italian Peninsula; and in the east the Russians were hammering the Germans in East Prussia and headed toward Berlin via Warsaw and Budapest.

It was a disastrous situation for Nazi Germany, but Hitler, against the advice of his generals, called for a massive counterattack in an operation code-named *Herbstnebel* (*Autumn Fog*). He would send all available forces to his West Wall (*q.v.*) and strike at Belgium's Ardennes Forest, the favorite hunting ground of German strategists. His intelligence experts informed him that in this area Allied forces, mostly inexperienced young troops and veterans in rest areas, were thinly spread. He would hit them a surprise blow in bad weather when their planes were grounded, smash through in open country, seize the bridgeheads over the Meuse, bypass Brussels, and drive on to Antwerp, main port of the Allies. That this would mark a turn to victory, Hitler said, was a "guaranteed certainty."

PREPARATIONS. The *Fuehrer* began his preparations as early as September 1944. On December 11–12 he summoned his top officers to the Eagle's Nest at Berchtesgaden and outlined his plan. Now stooped, with pale, puffy face and trembling hands, the result of the attempt on his life (*See* JULY PLOT), he spoke for an hour and a half. He named Field Marshal Gerd von Rundstedt (*q.v.*) to lead the counterattack. He ordered 20,000 troops, "fresh, completely battleworthy," many of them transferred from the eastern front, to be ready for the assault. He would hit the Allies with 20 (later 25) divisions, including the 7th Army and the 5th and 6th *Panzer* units. Von Rundstedt was hestitant and openly advised against the operation. Hitler replied adamantly: "Nevertheless, I am determined to go ahead with this attack."

ASSAULT. At 5 A.M. on December 16, 1944, three German Armies (5th, 6th, and 7th) with 25 divisions struck at 6 American divisions. Von Rundstedt unleashed his forces with an emotional Order of the Day: "Soldiers of the Western front! Your great hour has struck! Everything is at stake!" The weather was bad, which was just as Hitler had wanted it. After a massive artillery barrage, German troops pushed forward on a 70-mile front to meet the Americans commanded by Gen. Omar Bradley (*q.v.*). Germans in American uniforms had already penetrated the Allied lines. (*See* GREIF.)

Von Rundstedt's offensive utilized all the experiences of the first German *Blitzkrieg* (*q.v.*) in the Ardennes. It took the Americans by surprise. Within 48 hours the Germans pushed 15 miles into the enemy lines. American infantrymen desperately tried to stem the advance, but they were engulfed by the German avalanche. Fog, snow, and freezing temperatures added to the chaos. The whole front disintegrated. Some days neither side knew which one held a given town or village. The Germans claimed that Bradley's 12th Army Group was cut into two parts.

At the center of the German advance was Bastogne, key to the southern Ardennes. Here the Germans collided with contingents of the 10th Armored Division and their big *Sherman* (*q.v.*) tanks. Von Rundstedt's troops bypassed Bastogne, leaving it deep in German-controlled territory as the Germans swung northwest to Liège and the Meuse. (*See* BASTOGNE, and McAULIFFE, ANTHONY CLEMENT for a description of the "Nuts!" incident.)

By December 24 the Germans had cut into Allied-held land to a depth of 65 miles on a fluid front ranging from 10 to 25 miles. The prognosis was good for a major German victory.

ALLIED REACTION. The breakthrough was due more to German efficiency than to Allied negligence. Allied air power was grounded by the weather. Angered by news of the capture of 8,000 American ground troops, the Allied Supreme Command acted with dispatch. Gen. Dwight D. Eisenhower (*q.v.*) named British Gen. Bernard Law Montgomery (*q.v.*) to command all the Allied forces north of the Ardennes salient and appointed Bradley to command those in the south. He then dispatched Lt. Gen. George S. Patton (*q.v.*) and his battering ram of U.S. 3rd Army tanks to the bulge. Von Rundstedt soon found both sides of his salient squeezed by powerful American forces.

When the weather cleared, more than 5,000 Allied aircraft took to the air to smash at the Germans and cripple their supply system. On the ground the Germans were pounded by artillery shells equipped with proximity fuses (*q.v.*). Hitler desperately threw more troops, mostly old men and ill-trained youngsters, into the gap. It was too late.

By January 1945 the Ardennes front was reestablished to the point at which it had been in early December. On the news that the Russians had started a gigantic offensive in the east, Hitler ordered a massive withdrawal from the Ardennes and transferred the bulk of his troops to the eastern front. He had lost the Battle of the Bulge.

LOSSES. A million men were involved in the chaotic battle. The Germans lost 120,000 men, whether killed, wounded, prisoners, or missing; more than 500 tanks; and 1,600 planes. The American casualties were approximately 76,800 killed, wounded or missing.

SIGNIFICANCE. Little was changed. The massive German counteroffensive only delayed the end of the war. Military strategists were puzzled by Hitler's thinking. He had withdrawn valuable veteran units from the Eastern Front, where they were desperately needed, and sent them on a questionable mission to the west. It was not clear what he intended to do with Antwerp once he had taken it or how he proposed to hold a long corridor to the North Sea between increasingly powerful enemy forces. He was confident of his military genius, even if his generals were not.

The Battle of the Bulge cost many American lives, but it demonstrated that American troops could hold their own with picked *Panzer* (*q.v.*) units. Churchill called it "the greatest American battle of the war."

Bibliography. R. E. Merriam, *Dark December* (1949); H. M. Cole, *The Ardennes: Battle of the Bulge* (1965); J. Nobécourt, *Hitler's Last Gamble: The Battle of the Bulge* (1967); and J. Strawson, *The Battle for the Ardennes* (1972).

BUNA. *See* NEW GUINEA, CAMPAIGNS IN.

BURKE, ARLEIGH (1901–   ). Outstanding U.S. naval officer in the Pacific campaigns.

Burke was promoted to Captain on May 1, 1943. In September of that year he was named commander of Destroyer Squadron 23, which won quick attention for its exploits. On November 2, 1943, he applied new tactics at the Battle of Augusta Bay, sweeping around the Solomon bastion of Bougainville (*q.v.*) and attacking Japanese airfields while marines stormed ashore at Augusta Bay. At the same time his ships sank a cruiser and four destroyers of a Japanese task force. After this clash, Burke, who had been ordered to prevent the Japanese from evacuating Buka Island, headed his destroyers up "The Slot" and reached Buka in time to sink three enemy transports.

From March 1944 to July 1945 Burke served as Chief of Staff to Adm. Marc A. Mitscher (*q.v.*), commander of Task Force 58. In May 1945 Burke was aboard the flagship *Bunker Hill* when she was severely damaged by two *kamikaze* (*q.v.*) dive bombers off Okinawa. He succeeded in evacuating the entire crew. He was also aboard a second flagship a few days later when she was hit by a suicide plane, and once again he arranged for transfer of the crew to another vessel.

BURMA ROAD. Supply route to China.

BACKGROUND. In its invasion of China before World War II, Japan severed rail lines from French Indo-China, Hong Kong, and the Soviet Union. The main supply route to China then became the British-built Burma Road that ran from Lashio in Burma to Kunming in Yunnan Province behind the nationalist lines.

In July 1940 the British, who were momentarily expecting a German invasion, consented under pressure from Tokyo to close the Burma Road for three months. This was one of Generalissimo Chiang Kai-shek's (*q.v.*) few remaining connections with the outside world. After closing it for the monsoon period, the British opened it three months later.

When the Japanese 15th Army invaded Burma from Thailand in January 1942, Chiang Kai-shek sent the Chinese 5th and 6th Armies into Burma under command of his Chief of Staff, U.S. Maj. Gen. Joseph W. Stilwell (*q.v.*) to defend the Burma Road. The Allies were unable to withstand the Japanese assault and by mid-May 1942 Burma was lost. (*See* BURMA, CAMPAIGNS IN.)

One of the main objectives of the Allied campaigns in Burma was to reopen the treacherous Burma Road. Sealed off by the Japanese, it was not opened to Allied convoys until early 1945, when it was linked up with the newly constructed Ledo Road (*q.v.*). By June 1945, with Japan on the verge of defeat, the entire route from China to Burma was cleared.

Bibliography. N. Smith, *Burma Road* (c. 1940); and P. Tan, *The Building of the Burma Road* (1945).

BURMA, CAMPAIGNS IN. Clashes in Burma told a story of Allied defeat transformed into victory.

BACKGROUND. For the Japanese, control of Burma was a critical necessity. At the start of the war they intended to cut off the Burma Road (*q.v.*) that supplied Chiang Kai-shek's (*q.v.*) China. They assigned the conquest of Burma to their 15th Army.

For the Allied Chiefs of Staff the China-Burma-India (CBI) theater was for the time being of lesser importance in the Pacific area. It was nearly two years after the fall of Burma before the Allies could undertake a major offensive there. The main problem was the difficulty of sending reinforcements and supplies to a country where ground operations were limited from May to October by the monsoon season. The Allies had to be content with halfway improvised measures to contain the Japanese until a full-scale assault could be launched.

First, the doorway to India had to be closed. Disturbed by evidence of rebellion, Field Marshal Archibald Wavell (*q.v.*), Viceroy of India, imprisoned as a safety measure Mahatma Gandhi and Jawaharlal Nehru as well as other members of the Indian National Congress. He then reorganized the Anglo-Indian forces.

FALL OF BURMA. The surrender of Thailand gave the Japanese an overwhelming advantage over the British in Burma. The Japanese 15th Army moved into Burma from Thailand in January 1942. Under the command of Lt. Gen. Shojiro Iida, the troops took advantage of captured airfields on Rangoon. At this time the Burma theater came under the ABDA (American, British, Dutch, Australian Command), with Wavell as Supreme Commander operating from Java. The British had only the 1st Burma Division and the newly arrived 17th Indian Brigade. Wavell ordered his troops to make a stand as far east as possible as a means of allowing reinforcements to be brought in. The British had only 30 planes, most of which were from the American Volunteer Group sent by Chiang Kai-shek. The Japanese, on the other hand, had 200 aircraft, to be doubled after the fall of Manila.

On January 15, 1942, the Japanese seized the airfield at Tennaserim. British and Indian troops, unable to cope with Japanese efficiency in jungle warfare, were forced back. Meanwhile, Inda's planes bombed Rangoon, forcing the population to flee into the jungle and creating problems for the defenders.

To defend his overland supply route, the Burma Road, Chiang Kai-shek sent his 5th and 6th Armies into Burma under command of U.S. Maj. Gen. Joseph W. Stilwell (*q.v.*) while holding his 6th Army in reserve on the border. Despite these reinforcements, the Allies found it impossible to contain the Japanese assault. When additional Japanese troops arrived, the position of the Allies became hopeless.

The long retreat began on April 25, 1942. It was important for the Allies to reach the border of India before the mid-May monsoon. Mandalay was evacuated on April 30. With the Japanese in pursuit, the British forces under Gen. Harold Alexander (*q.v.*) just managed to reach across the Indian border to Imphal before the monsoon. Stilwell led his men out to Imphal while the Chinese 6th Army retreated into China. The operation had cost the British-Indians-Chinese 13,500 men.

The loss of Burma was a grave misfortune for the Allies. Not only did it put India in danger, but it might also have a deleterious effect on Chinese morale. Burma was rich in raw materials; it had excellent communications and fine airfields. Most important of all, it was a strategic reentry point in Southeast Asia for a possible later counteroffensive. The Allies would have to wait for an opportune moment to strike back.

RENEWAL OF FIGHTING, 1942-1943. Operations in Burma almost ceased until the winter of 1942–1943, when British and Indian troops fought along the length of the Arakan Peninsula. At the same time the Chindits (*q.v.*), under command of Brig. Gen. Orde C. Wingate (*q.v.*), began guerrilla operations in Burma. The Arakan campaign failed. Wingate's raiders, a long-range jungle force supplied entirely by air, did considerable damage in Japanese-controlled areas, penetrating as far as the Shan States. The Chindits caused some destruction but incurred heavy casualties. Their main importance was an effect on Allied morale. (*See* CHINDITS.)

The British offensive in the dry season of 1942–1943 failed because of superior Japanese tactics in jungle warfare, lack of resources, and administrative difficulties. In January 1943 it was decided at the Casablanca Conference (*q.v.*) to mount a seaborne assault on Rangoon (*Operation Anakim*). The British and Chinese would strike in north Burma and capture key points on the coast. Another move was contemplated against Sumatra (*Operation Culverin*). Both projected operations were abandoned.

JAPANESE OFFENSIVE, 1943. Although the Allies were advancing rapidly in the Central Pacific, the situation in Burma caused them much worry. The British still hoped to drive the Japanese out of northern Burma. Instead, the Japanese mounted another offensive, the only one of the war that saw them crossing the Indian frontier into southern Assam. The purpose of the Japanese attack was to forestall and discourage a possible British offensive. It did achieve the strategic success of causing postponement of a major British advance in Burma until 1945.

BRITISH COUNTEROFFENSIVE, 1943. The Allied objective was still northern Burma as the shortest way to renew direct contact with China and resume supplies over the Burma Road. A renewed attack was planned in the Arakan plus a diversionary move by the Chindits in the north. For this campaign a new and unified Southeast Asia Command was set up under Adm. Louis Mountbatten (*q.v.*) in August 1943. A newly formed 14th Army was placed under command of Gen. William Joseph Slim (*q.v.*). Slim's air strength was increased to 67 squadrons, of which 19 were American.

The Japanese, too, reorganized their command system under Lt. Gen. Masakazu Kawabe, their top commander in the Burma theater. Each side planned a limited offensive in the Arakan before a major thrust on the central front. By this time the British had adopted new jungle tactics: They created strongholds into which their troops would withdraw and be maintained by air supply while reserves were brought up to crush the enemy between them and the stronghold. The new tactics worked. Running short of ammunition and supplies the Japanese now found themselves at a disadvantage.

RAIDERS. Meanwhile, the Chindits continued to hit at the Japanese. Since their withdrawal Wingate's raiders remained relatively quiescent. But Churchill, who was intrigued by the activities of the Chindits, saw to it that they were reinforced. Wingate was promoted and the Chindits given their own special air force of 11 squadrons, under the American commander Philip Cochran, called Cochran's Circus. The raiders were now trained to fight it out with the Japanese instead of merely harassing their lines.

The Chindits were joined by Merrill's Marauders (*q.v.*), tough American jungle fighters. While Stilwell's Chinese troops held the Japanese in position in the hill country to the north and west of Myitkyina, the Marauders struck at the enemy's flanks and set up roadblocks in his rear. Throughout 1943 the Chindits and Maurauders ranged far and wide behind enemy lines. This small-scale fighting kept the Japanese off balance and prevented them from moving their forces in strength into India.

Wingate did not see the results of his work. On March 24, 1944, at the age of 41 he was killed in a plane crash. Churchill hailed him as "a man of genius who might well have become also a man of destiny." His work, which had proven successful, was carried on.

TURNING POINT. In mid-January 1944 Mountbatten ordered a new offensive against the Japanese. The new 14th Army under Gen. Slim advanced into the Arakan. At first the British campaign was stopped by a Japanese counterattack aimed at taking Chittagong, but by the middle of February the Japanese were disorganized and defeated. The Japanese lost 50,000 of their 84,000 men, the Allies, with total air control, some 17,000. The Japanese march on Delhi via the Arakan was abandoned.

The Arakan battle, while not of great magnitude, was a historic success for British arms and the turning point of the Burma campaign. For the first time the British had met, held, and decisively defeated a major Japanese attack, and followed this up by driving the enemy out of a strong natural position they had prepared for months and were determined to hold at all costs. The effect on Allied morale was highly favorable.

JULY–DECEMBER 1944. While the repulse of the Japanese was a severe setback it did not break Nipponese control of Burma. The Allies now set up two operations: *Capital,* an overland thrust at north-central Burma, and *Dracula,* an amphibious assault to take southern Burma. The emphasis was placed on *Capital.*

The Allies devoted the second half of 1944 to improvement of land communications and inland water transport, supplying Slim's 14th Army, and reorganizing the commands. In mid-October, after the end of the monsoon season, Slim's forces began to advance on the central front, where the Allies with eight divisions faced four understrength Japanese divisions. Meanwhile, there were additional Allied advances in Arakan and northern Burma.

LEDO ROAD. In January 1945 the Ledo Road (*q.v.*), running 300 miles through some of the most difficult country in the world, was opened. Cut through jungle and over mountains, the new road now linked up with the Burma Road (*q.v.*), the main supply route into China.

BATTLE OF BURMA ENDED. In February 1943 the 14th Army crossed the Irrawady and seized the ancient city of Pagan, giving the Allies a new bridge into the Burma oil fields. Now some 40,000 Japanese defending the Mandalay area were cut off. On April 22, 1945, after an advance of 50 miles in one week, the 14th Army trapped the Japanese in the Rangoon area between two Allied forces in a pincers movement. Rangoon was entered on May 2nd. The Japanese, with no guns, no air support, and little equipment, were driven into pockets and were unable to penetrate the Allied lines.

The work of the liberation of Burma now took on the appearance of a mopping-up process, which was finished in the early summer. The war with Japan ended abruptly in mid-August following the dropping of atomic bombs on Hiroshima and Nagasaki (*qq.v.*). The final instrument of surrender was signed in Rangoon by Japanese envoys on September 13, 1945.

Bibliography. HMSO, *The Campaign in Burma* (1946); M. Collis, *Last and First in Burma* (1946); W. Slim, *Defeat into Victory* (1956); F. Dorn, *Walkout with Stilwell in Burma* (1971); F. N. Trager (ed.), *Burma: Japanese Military Administration* (1971); I. Fellows-Gordon, *The Burma War* (1972); D. Moser, *China, Burma, India* (1978).

BUSH, VANNEVAR (1890–1974). Main American coordinator of scientific research in World War II.

Born in Massachusetts, Bush was the dean of the School of Engineering at the Massachusetts Institute of Technology from 1932–1938. In 1940 President Franklin D. Roosevelt appointed him chairman of the National Defense Research Committee whose purpose it was to supplement the work of the Army and Navy in developing war materials. The next year he was made director of the Office of Scientific Research and Development (*q.v.*), charged with mobilization of the scientific resources of the nation. This included coordinating all aspects of atomic research. (*See* MANHATTAN PROJECT.)

BUTT REPORT. A study made in 1941 on the effectiveness of British strategic bombing.

The report presented the opinion that such bombing was highly inaccurate because bombing planes were not coming close enough to their targets. It recommended instead a technique of area bombing which was then adopted.

BYRNES, JAMES FRANCIS (1879-1972). U.S. public official and war leader.

In 1940 Byrnes supported Roosevelt for a third term. In 1941 he was appointed to the U.S. Supreme Court. He resigned after Pearl Harbor to become Director of the Office of Economic Stabilization. In May 1943 he was named Director of War Mobilization. He accompanied Roosevelt to the Yalta Conference (*q.v.*) on February 4-12, 1945, and acted as the President's adviser there. He resigned shortly before Roosevelt died on April 12, 1945.

In July 1945 the new President, Harry S Truman (*q.v.*) named Byrnes, an old friend, Secretary of State. Byrnes accompanied Truman to the Potsdam Conference (*q.v.*) from July 17 to August 2, 1945, where he played a major role in decision making. He called for the unconditional surrender of Japan and advocated use of the atomic bomb.

Bibliography. Byrnes described his career in *Speaking Frankly* (1947) and *All in One Lifetime* (1957).

C

CABINET INFORMATION BOARD. Japanese agency responsible for coordinating propaganda and censorship inside Japan and psychological warfare abroad.

Created in December 1940, the Cabinet Information Board worked on publicity, supervised all films and radio, operated Radio Tokyo, and censored all publications. One of its main goals was to prevent the organization of resistance movements in Japan. The board was disbanded shortly after the end of the war.

CABINET PLANNING BOARD. Japanese agency responsible for coordination of national economic policies during the war.

An object of much criticism from financial leaders because of its rigid controls and regulations, the Cabinet Planning Board was disbanded in 1943. Direct control of all economic planning was then taken over by the army.

CAIRO CONFERENCE. Allied conference, code-named *Sextant,* meeting from November 22 to 26, 1943, to formulate policy on China. The main participants were President Roosevelt, Prime Minister Churchill, and Generalissimo Chiang Kai-shek.

For the first time Generalissimo Chiang Kai-shek was brought into planning of the war. The meeting was probably the worst-kept secret of the war, with rumors of its imminence spread all over the world. The agenda was confined to the war against Japan. A carefully worded communiqué for the press left out mention of Soviet Russia, which was not yet at war with Japan.

DECISIONS. The communiqué from Cairo announced: The three great Allies "are fighting this war to restrain and punish the aggression of Japan." It reaffirmed that Britain would continue its struggle against Japan after the defeat of Germany, a matter of concern to the Americans. Furthermore, China, although hard pressed, would maintain its guerrilla activity until it could be granted full assistance.

The communiqué further stated that the three Allies "in harmony with those of the United Nations at war with Japan will continue to persevere in the serious and prolonged operations necessary to procure the unconditional surrender of Japan." There would be no negotiated peace in the Far East.

In addition, it was agreed at Cairo that Japan would be stripped of all the conquests it had made since 1894. China would be given Manchuria and Formosa and "in due course" Korea would regain its independence. It was intimated that the Soviet Union would obtain the Kurile Island chain and the southern half of Sakhalin, while the United States would acquire the Japanese-mandated islands in the Central Pacific.

SIGNIFICANCE. In effect the Cairo Conference assured Chiang Kai-shek of full support and additional operations in the Far East. The Western powers were careful to renounce their special rights and interests in China after its reconquest.

CALEDONIA. German clandestine broadcasting station used in early 1940 in conjunction with *Operation Sea Lion* (*q.v.*), the projected invasion of England. (*See also* NEW BRITISH BROADCASTING STATION.)

CALLAGHAN, DANIEL J. (1890-1942). U.S. Admiral killed in action.

Callaghan was Commander of the cruiser *San Francisco* in Pearl Harbor on the day the Japanese struck at the U.S. naval base. Later he took the warship to the South Pacific, but left her to become Chief of Staff to the commander of the U.S. naval forces there. In early November 1942 he commanded a task force that attacked a concentration of Japanese battleships, cruisers, and destroyers screening a large group of transports attempting to land troops on Guadacanal. An enemy cruiser was the first victim of Callaghan's flagship, which opened fire with her big guns and caused the Japanese ship to explode. Callaghan's ship then sank a destroyer with her secondary batteries.

Callaghan then closed in on a Japanese battleship coming up to 2,000 yards range. In the fight that followed, Callaghan's cruiser scored 18 hits on the battleship with her main batteries, but she herself was hit by several 14-inch shells that struck the bridge. In this part of the action Callaghan was killed. His cruiser had so damaged the Japanese battleship that it was later easily sunk by torpedoes.

Tall, beetle-browed, and handsome, Callaghan was a familiar figure at the side of President Roosevelt on numerous military and social functions. One of the best liked men in the service, he was known as "Uncle Dan" to hundreds of navy men.

CAMERON, DONALD (1919–   ). Young British naval officer who completed his midget-submarine mission in attacking the German battleship *Tirpitz* (*q.v.*) at Altenfjord in September 1943. (*See* ALTENFJORD RAID.)

In January 1943 Cameron was one of the volunteers for "a special and hazardous service,'' the only requirement for which was the ability to swim. With other crews of six X-craft (*q.v.*) he entered a period of concentrated training for six months. A lean Scotsman, Cameron had served in the merchant navy since he was 16 years old, and in his training revealed extraordinary qualities of cool courage. He was given command of the *X-6*, a tiny, misshapen lump of metal, which was to serve as his ship for the raid. As Captain, he was navigator and tactician, while his three crewmen were assigned other critical tasks.

Cameron and Lt. Godfrey Place (1914–   ), who commanded *X-7*, were the only ones to penetrate into the formidable natural and constructed defenses around the giant German battleship. They were successful on September 23, 1943, after wild mishaps, in placing explosive charges under the *Tirpitz*. Cameron and his three crewmen and Place plus one crewman survived surrender to the Germans. The explosives put the *Tirpitz* out of action for months and eventually led to her destruction. Both Cameron and Place received the Victoria Cross, Britain's highest combat decoration, for their extraordinary feat.
Bibliography. L. Kennedy, *The Death of the Tirpitz* (1979).

CAMP X. Special camp in Canada for training agents of the British Security Coordination (BSC) and the U.S. Office of Strategic Services (OSS) (*qq.v.*).

Located in closely guarded acres near the Toronto-Kingston highway on the shores of Lake Ontario 300 miles northwest of New York City, Camp X was an ideal secret spot for training purposes. Here trainees were taught the art of killing opponents silently, how to use guerrilla devices, and how to transmit information to home base. They were provided with forged papers for operations in Nazi-occupied countries. All were given L-pills; if swallowed by accident the pills passed through the body without causing harm, but if crushed between the teeth their contents of potassium cyanide caused instant death. Hundreds of agents trained at Camp X were sent on espionage missions. (*See also* BERMUDA STATION; and ESPIONAGE.)

CAMUS, ALBERT (1913–1960). French novelist, playwright, and Resistance leader.

Camus joined the French Resistance movement in 1942. At this time he produced his first major novel, *The Outsider,* which stressed the irrationalities and absurdities of his time—a favorite theme. World War II reminded him of the image of Sisyphus, rolling a rock forever up a hill in hell, always seeing it fall down again. His articles for the underground newspaper *Combat* bridged the gap between journalism and literature. (*See* RESISTANCE MOVEMENTS.)
Bibliography. Camus's works have been translated into more than 30 languages. A collection in English is titled *Resistance, Rebellion, and Death* (1961). Among biographies are those by R. de Lippé (1959); J. C. Brisville (1959); J. Cruickshank (1959); N. A. Scott (1962); and G. Brée (1964).

CANARIS, WILHELM (1887–1945.) Head of the *Abwehr* (*q.v.*), the counterintelligence unit of the armed forces in the Third Reich.

It is believed, although there is no evidence to prove it, that from the beginning of the war Canaris provided the Allies with information about Hitler's invasion plans. Although sympathetic with the aims of the Resistance, he discouraged any attempts to assassinate Hitler. He remained in close contact with Gen. Ludwig Beck (*q.v.*), military head of the conspiracy. He was an arch enemy of Heinrich Himmler (*q.v.*), who believed that all intelligence services should be handled by his own SS (*q.v.*). Himmler won the ensuing struggle and managed to obtain Canaris's dismissal in February 1944.

Canaris was among those arrested after the failure of the 1944 July Plot (*q.v.*) on Hitler's life. He was brought before the People's Court, found guilty of treason, and hanged at Flossenbürg on April 9, 1945.

Bibliography. H. B. Gisevius, *To the Bitter End* (1947); C. Amort and M. Jedlicka, *The Canaris File* (1970); and A. Brissand, *Canaris* (1970).

CAPE ESPERANCE, BATTLE OF. *See* GUADALCANAL CAMPAIGNS.

CAPE MATAPAN, BATTLE OF. *See* MATAPAN, BATTLE OF CAPE.

CASABLANCA CONFERENCE. Under the code or cover name *Symbol* a conference of Allied leaders was held in Morocco, North Africa, in January 1943, at which it was resolved to carry on the war until the complete defeat of the Axis.

PARTICIPANTS. Present at the conference, held from January 14 to 24, 1943, were President Franklin D. Roosevelt and Prime Minister Winston Churchill (*qq.v.*) and their Chiefs of Staff. Marshal Joseph Stalin (*q.v.*) was invited but declined to attend because of the forthcoming Russian offensive. Among the Americans were Gen. George C. Marshall, Gen. Dwight D. Eisenhower, Adm. William D. Leahy, Adm. Ernest J. King, Lt. Gen. Brehon B. Somervell, presidential advisers—Harry Hopkins and W. Averell Harriman (*qq.v.*) and Lt. Gen. Henry H. Arnold (*q.v.*). The British contingent included Admiral of the Fleet Alfred Dudley Pound, Field Marshal John Dill, Gen. Alan Brooke, Air Chief Marshal Charles Portal, Vice Adm. Louis Mountbatten, and Maj. Gen. Hastings Ismay (*qq.v.*). The meetings were held at a hotel about five miles from Casablanca, at a knoll overlooking the sea.

ANGLO-AMERICAN DIFFERENCES. The British arrived at the conference on a 6,000-ton liner with an elaborate staff, cipher experts, and planning organizers who had already worked out statistics and plans to the last detail. Churchill soon made it clear that he preferred a peripheral operation, as in World War I, a stab at the "soft underbelly" (*q.v.*) of Europe from the south. This attack, he said, would shatter an already crumbling Italian morale, throw the Balkans into ferment, and encourage Turkey's entrance into the war. Assistance would be given to the Soviet Union while Germany would be bombed incessantly from the air. Then in 1944 would come a gigantic invasion across the English Channel.

General Marshall dissented on the ground that Churchill's plan would weaken the Allied buildup in Britain and also delay attending to Allied needs in the Pacific. While the British wanted priority for the European theater, the Americans were concerned about Japan. The British called for first things first—Mussolini, then Hitler, then Tojo.

OPERATION HUSKY. In the end a compromise was reached—to invade Sicily. It was agreed that the time had not yet come for the main drive across the Channel, and that a thrust through Sicily would secure the Mediterranean supply route, lift German pressure from the Russians, and knock Italy out of the war.

DE GAULLE AND GIRAUD. On the political side much time was taken to compose differences between Gen. Charles de Gaulle (*q.v.*), supported reluctantly by the British, and Gen. Henri Giraud (*q.v.*), favored by the Americans. "My job," said Roosevelt, "was to produce the bride in the presence of General Giraud, while Churchill was to bring in General de Gaulle to play the role of bridegroom in a shotgun wedding."

Both Churchill and Roosevelt found it difficult to work with the temperamental de Gaulle. Churchill was angered: "Here he was—a refugee, an exile from his own country under sentence of death, in a position entirely dependent upon the good will of the British Government, and also now of the United States. The Germans had conquered his country. He had no real foothold anywhere. Never mind; he defied all." To Roosevelt, de Gaulle was an egoist who regarded himself as the living embodiment of Joan of Arc, "with whom it is said one of his ancestors served as a faithful adherent." "Yes," Churchill was said to have rejoined, "but my bishops won't let me burn him!"

Churchill and Roosevelt settled the issue by making de Gaulle and Giraud sit in a row of chairs alternating with the two top war leaders. It was a light note in the heavily charged atmosphere of Casablanca. But the two generals were induced to agree to a declaration of common purpose.

"UNCONDITIONAL SURRENDER." There was a surprising development at the final press conference held on January 24, 1943. President Roosevelt spoke frankly to the reporters present, stating that peace could come to the world only by total elimination of German and Japanese war power. He then told a story familiar in American history:

Some of you Britishers know the old story—we had a general named U.S. Grant. . . . In my, and the Prime Minister's early days, he was called 'Unconditional Surrender' Grant. The elimination of German, Japanese, and Italian war power means the unconditional surrender by Germany, Italy, and Japan. That means a reasonable assurance of future world peace. It does not mean the destruction of Germany, Italy, and Japan, but it does mean the destruction of the philosophies in those countries which are based on conquest and the subjugation of other peoples.

This was the first public reference to "unconditional surrender," although the term was used at the conference itself. Churchill agreed to its use publicly, as he later said, because any public divergence would be damaging to the war effort. Critics denounced the phrase as dangerous for Allied war policy because it would induce the Germans to fight to the end. German propagandists immediately seized the term to convince the German public that it was necessary to continue their war effort. Roosevelt apparently emphasized the term because he wanted no recapitulation of the situation after World War I, when the Germans claimed that they had surrendered on the basis of the Wilsonian Fourteen Points and had been cheated in the deal.

Bibliography. A. Armstrong, *Unconditional Surrender: The Impact of the Casablanca Policy Upon World War II* (1961); Foreign Relations of the United States, *The Conferences at Washington and Casablanca* (1968); and R. G. O'Connor, *Diplomacy for Victory: FDR and Unconditional Surrender* (1971).

CASSINO. See MONTE CASSINO, BOMBING OF.

CASUALTIES, WAR. No satisfactory statistics are available on casualties of World War II. Any claim of accuracy should be viewed with suspicion.

The figures given here are only approximate. The best estimate is that from 35 million to 55 million lost their lives in the global conflict. Added to this inexact but appalling figure were the wounded, permanently disabled, prisoners of war, and missing. Many civilian deaths resulted from bombing from the air. There was a heavy toll by starvation and disease. Wherever the tide of war shifted, millions of combatants and civilians disappeared. No one knows the exact figures.

The following list, compiled from the U.S. Department of Defense and a dozen other sources, gives approximate figures in round numbers. Varied reputable sources give different figures because several methods of classifying and computing casualties are used. Available estimates of Soviet and German casualties vary widely. It must be emphasized again that, due to fragmentary and sometimes unreliable data, these figures are only approximate. (*See* p. 124.)

CAUSES OF WORLD WAR II. Most historians attribute the fundamental causes of World War II to the general milieu and to Hitler the greater share of responsibility for the spark that ignited the explosion.

1. FUNDAMENTAL CAUSES

UNDERLYING ISSUES

Bidding farewell to the Allied Armistice Commission in 1919, a German representative remarked: "See you again in 20 years!" The accuracy of his

Allied Casualties in World War II (in approximate round figures)

NATION	PEAK STRENGTH*	BATTLE DEATHS	WOUNDED	CIVILIAN DEATHS	PRISONERS OR MISSING
Australia	680,000	23,000–26,000	39,000–180,000	—	32,000
Belgium	650,000	7,760–9,500	55,500	60,000–76,000	—
Canada	780,000	32,400–37,000	53,000	—	11,000
China	3,800,000–5,000,000	1,324,000–2,200,000	1,753,000	—	—
Denmark	25,000	3,000–4,300	—	2,000–3,000	—
France	5,000,000	200,000–400,000	400,000	200,000–350,000	—
Greece	414,000	17,000–73,700	47,000	325,000–391,000	—
India	2,150,000	24,000–32,000	64,000	—	—
Netherlands	300,000–440,000	6,500	2,800	200,000	—
New Zealand	157,000	10,900	17,000	—	10,550
Norway	45,000	1,000–2,000	—	7,000–8,200	—
Poland	1,000,000	123,000–600,000	530,000	5,000,000–plus	420,000
USSR	12,500,000–plus	6,000,000–7,500,000	Unknown	2,000,000–plus	5,000,000–plus
Union of South Africa	140,000	2,400–11,000	—	—	16,000
United Kingdom	5,100,000	244,000–264,000	370,000	60,000–93,000	214,000
United States	12,300,000	292,000	670,000	6,000	139,000
Yugoslavia	500,000	305,000–410,000	425,000	1,200,000	—

Axis Casualties in World War II (in approximate round figures)

NATION	PEAK STRENGTH*	BATTLE DEATHS	CIVILIAN DEATHS
Bulgaria	450,000	6,600–10,000	10,000
Finland	250,000	79,000–82,000	2,000–11,000
Germany (including Austria)	10,200,000	3,275,000–4,400,000	780,000–plus
Hungary	350,000	140,000–180,000	280,000–290,000
Italy	4,000,000	77,500–162,000	146,000
Japan	6,095,000	1,219,000–2,000,000	280,000–plus
Rumania	600,000	300,000–350,000	200,000

*Peak strength means the greatest strength reached at any one time during the war and is to be distinguished from total strength, which refers to total personnel in armed forces. Thus, the United States had a peak strength of 12,300,000 but a total strength of 16,353,000.

prophecy was not so striking as the fact that it reflected a widespread belief in the inevitability of another war. The era from 1919 to 1939, which in reality was a long armistice, witnessed an extension of most of the motivating factors that had led to the Great War of 1914. It became increasingly clear that the blood bath of World War I had brought neither peace nor security, and was not a war "to make the world safe for democracy." If anything it revealed that the European system was undergoing additional social and moral disintegration.

ECONOMIC TIME FUSES

The failure of the triumphant democracies to achieve economic stability, together with the deleterious effects of the world Depression, led to a sense of panic among the major and minor nations of the world. Three dissident powers—Germany, Italy, and Japan—designated themselves as have-not nations, as peoples cut off from a position of affluence. They complained that they had not been allowed a fair share of the world's raw materials, markets, and capital-investment areas. They accused Britain, France, and the United States—democratic Allies of World War I—of having appropriated more global wealth than they deserved.

The democracies, disunited and unprepared for war, remained indifferent to criticism. All they wanted was to maintain their economic status and be left in peace. For a time they were willing to make concessions to clamoring have-not nations in the hope that an awkward appeasement would prevent war. But their efforts to maintain the peace were fruitless when it became apparent that the Axis would not be satisfied with anything less than greater access to raw materials, markets, and investment areas.

In a world in which all nations wanted a favorable balance of trade, some were to be left behind. To assure economic self-sufficiency, most nations resorted to economic warfare, including protective tariffs, managed currencies, subsidized trade, and ruthless competition. The economic milieu was not conducive to peace. The next steps after economic warfare were to be taken on battlefields.

INTERNATIONAL ANARCHY

Added to economic strains were political differences. The failure of the League of Nations to establish a system of collective security led individual members to revert to the traditional system of diplomatic alignments and alliances. Nationalism became stronger than ever. Unfulfilled national ambitions again were to bring death to many millions of people in World War II, with millions more injured, scarred, or crippled for life. (*See* CASUALTIES, WAR.)

Even the friends of the League of Nations admitted that it was unable to assure security in a chaotic world. Its troubles were to be found in the Covenant that rendered it impotent. The public had exaggerated hopes that the League would function as a police unit and enforce the laws. It was not equipped for this task. The Nazis ridiculed the League as "a joint-stock company for the preservation of the booty won in the war." No world opinion was strong enough to protect the League against such criticism.

MILITARISM: RACE TO ARMS

Once the peace machinery broke down, there was a renewed armament race. Each country suspiciously eyed the armed strength of its neighbors and began to strengthen its own military machine. Where the dictators saw rearmament as the means to alter the global map to their advantage, the democracies, over-burdened with economic troubles, tried with little success to stave off the expense of new armaments. In 1933, the last effective year of the League of Nations system, the armies of the world numbered 7 million men, its navies totaled 3 million tons, its air forces 14,000 planes, and $4 billion went into armaments. By 1938, the year of Munich (*See* MUNICH AGREEMENT), the figures had skyrocketed to 10 million men, 8 million naval tons, 50,000 military planes, and $17 billion for armaments. The French Army alone had 800,000 men with a trained reserve of 5.5 million, in a total population of just over 40 million. Everywhere men feared the consequences of war, yet they felt it was necessary to be prepared for it.

CLASH OF IDEOLOGIES

In the 1930s a new challenge to the West emerged in the strategic goals and tactical flexibility of Nazi Germany, Fascist Italy, and militarist Japan. Hitler expressed the philosophy in six words: "War is eternal. War is life." The dictators poured vituperation upon the democracies and chided them for failure to solve the economic dilemma. They pointed to their own totalitarianism as the only logical order in a technological world approaching mid-century. "We are riding the wave of the future." To the democracies this claim was nothing but a renascence of ancient tyranny.

It was becoming clear that something more than the "sweetness and light" of Locarno was necessary to solve critical issues. (In 1925 an international conference held at Locarno produced a number of treaties, the most important of which guaranteed the inviolability of the Franco-German frontier.) Neither side—not the dictatorships or the democracies—was willing to accept the view of the other. The choice lay between appeasement or armed force. The Soviet Union, pursuing its own ideology, did what it considered to be in its own interest: It had a nonaggression pact with Hitler but turned to the Allied side after the German invasion of 1941. The global conflict was to make strange bedfellows.

PSYCHOLOGICAL CLIMATE

Added to powerful economic, political, and ideological factors making for war was a psychological sentiment of vital importance. Those of good will hoped that the periodic descents into barbarism would be ended for all time in

1918, but theirs was a vain wish. The peace settlements of 1919 remade the map of the world along national lines and gave little heed to supporting a psychology directed toward the common interests of mankind.

Many who lived through the horrors of World War I said that never again would they support a war under any circumstances. But they soon forgot, just as human beings tend to forget the pains of illness and push annoying thoughts deep into the subconscious. Impressionable youngsters were still nourished on tales of comradeship, heroism under fire, the glory of victory, the inadmissibility of defeat. Veterans forgot the horrors and filth and boasted to their sons about their feats on the battlefield.

In this milieu of illusion, irrationality, and aggression, the civilized world had to face a burning question: "What to do about Hitler?" Words were admittedly ineffective. The response was, reluctantly but firmly, "Regrettably, we shall have to use force."

2. IMMEDIATE CAUSES

GERMANY'S BID FOR POWER

The problem of war guilt for World War I was never satisfactorily solved. Most of the blame for starting World War II, however, is generally attributed to Hitler and Nazi Germany. Admittedly, the politico-economic and psychological climate was such that war could be expected, but the immediate sparks for the conflagration came from inside the Third Reich. No amount of strained revisionist theory can counteract the fact of Nazi aggression. It is clear from his writings, speeches, and actions that Hitler intended to change by military means what he regarded as the wrongs of Versailles. Obsessed with the idea that the German-Aryan-Nordic-Teutonic "race" was destined for a top role in world society, he was ready to smash his way to domination or ruin. "For the good of the German people," Hitler wrote, "we must wish for a war every 15 or 20 years. An army whose sole purpose is to preserve peace leads only to playing at soldiers—compare Sweden and Switzerland." At the time Hitler insisted (for political reasons), "I am not crazy enough to want a war." Despite his claim of innocence, his documented actions made war certain.

STAGES OF AGGRESSION

A series of aggressive actions by Japan, Italy, and Germany led to the explosion of 1939. The initial stage came in 1931 when Japan seized Manchuria and established the puppet state of Manchukuo. The failure of the League of Nations to solve the subsequent dispute was followed by the withdrawal of Japan from the League in 1933.

The next stage in aggression was Italy's invasion of Ethiopia in 1935 and its annexation in 1936. The League reacted by imposing economic sanctions on Italy, but Mussolini paid no attention. After the annexation of his country by Italy, Haile Selassie I, Emperor of Ethiopia, made a prophetic speech before the

Assembly of the League of Nations on June 30, 1936. "It is my duty," he said while pro-Mussolini newsmen tried to drown him out with catcalls, "to inform the governments of the deadly peril which threatens them." The League found itself unable to deal with a premeditated attack.

The League lost additional prestige in 1937 when Italy resigned. Italo-German cooperation with the insurgent Gen. Francisco Franco (*q.v.*) in the Spanish Civil War of 1936–1939 was another stride toward major conflict. When the Japanese in 1937 opened hostilities in China with the goal of establishing a New Order in Asia, no attempt was made to halt the aggressor. Meanwhile, the French extended their system of security by signing a Franco-Russian Mutual Assistance Pact on May 2, 1935.

At the Seventh World Congress of the Communist International, meeting in Moscow in July 1935, the Russians passed resolutions condemning Japanese imperialism in the Far East and Hitler's actions in the West. On November 25, 1936, Germany and Japan replied by concluding an Anti-Comintern Pact. Germany and Italy then laid the foundation for the Rome-Berlin Axis, an agreement transformed into a formal tripartite political and military treaty among Germany, Italy, and Japan on September 27, 1940. (*See* AXIS and BERLIN-ROME-TOKYO AXIS.)

HITLER'S FOREIGN POLICY

Although the statesmen of the Weimar Republic bitterly resented the Treaty of Versailles, they, nevertheless, adopted a policy of conciliation. They cooperated in the system of collective security, managed to obtain drastic reductions in reparations, accepted membership in the League of Nations, and effected the evacuation of the Rhineland in 1930. Hitler, on assuming power in 1933, abruptly reversed this policy. He insisted that Germany had never been defeated on the battlefields in World War I, but that it had been stabbed in the back (*Dolchstoss*) by traitors at home, notably Jews and Social Democrats.

The Nazi *Fuehrer* struck one crippling blow after another at the system of Versailles. On October 13, 1934, he withdrew Germany from the League of Nations. His aggressive actions in Austria led on July 25, 1934, to the assassination of Chancellor Engelbert Dollfus by Austrian Nazis. He repudiated the military and naval clauses of the Treaty of Versailles in 1935. The next year he demilitarized the Rhineland and denounced international control of the Rhine, Elbe, Oder, and Danube rivers. On March 12–15, 1938, he occupied and then annexed Austria.

With these moves Hitler revealed his contempt for international agreements of any kind. He moved independently, without discussion, without notice. It became increasingly clear that he intended eventually to change the territorial provisions of the Treaty of Versailles by military action if necessary.

APPEASEMENT

Defenders of the system of Versailles, paralyzed into inaction by Hitler's bold moves, did not attempt to thwart the German dictator. There was even some sympathy for his use of the liberal slogan of national self-determination. But gradually, Hitler's tactics, added to the Italian conquest of Ethiopia and Japan's war against China, made it clear that a general war was imminent, despite the *Fuehrer's* claim of peaceful intentions. On September 26, 1938, Hitler delivered a speech in Berlin assuring British Prime Minister Neville Chamberlain (*q.v.*) that if the Sudeten problem—the German minority in Czechoslovakia—were solved, he would have no more territorial claims in Europe. "The Czech state originated in a huge lie and the name of that liar is Beneš." (*See* BENEŠ, EDUARD.)

Unprepared for a major war, England and France hurriedly signed the Munich Agreement with Germany and Italy on September 29, 1938. The new democratic republic of Czechoslovakia, dating from 1919, was dismembered partially—betrayed by its sponsors. The Sudentenland was annexed to Germany. Chamberlain returned to London from Munich waving a piece of paper and assuring his people that it had brought "peace in our time." (*See* MUNICH AGREEMENT.)

After announcing in March 1939 that his territorial demands in Europe had been achieved, Hitler invaded and annexed the whole of Czechoslovakia, with the exception of the Carpatho-Ukraine (given to Hungary), and also seized Memel. It was becoming more and more obvious that the policy of appeasement was bankrupt.

PRELUDE TO WAR

The next month, April 1939, Italy occupied and annexed Albania. At last awakened to the danger, Britain hastened preparations for war, while France gave Premier Édouard Daladier (*q.v.*) dictatorial powers to prepare for the expected conflict. The British, in a reciprocal treaty of mutual assistance, gave a guarantee against aggression to Poland, Greece, and Rumania. Its terms were explicit:

Should one of the Contracting Parties become engaged in hostilities with a European Power in consequence of aggression by the latter against that Contracting Party, the other Contracting Party will at once give the Contracting Party engaged in hostilities all the support and assistance in its power.

The warning to Hitler was clear: Any further territorial change would mean war. Both Britain and France now began negotiations with the Soviet Union. In this confused situation, both the Western democracies and the Russians accused each other of wanting to turn the weight of Axis aggression to the other side. In the midst of negotiations, despite the mutually hostile ideologies of the two dictators, the Russo-German Nonaggression Pact (*q.v.*) was signed on August 23, 1939. Hitler believed that the agreement would remove the danger of having to fight a war on two fronts, while Stalin suspected that Britain and France were concerned primarily with getting Soviet Russia and Nazi Germany involved in a war in which both would bleed to death.

Although the democracies had warned Hitler that there was a point beyond which they could no longer tolerate German aggression, the *Fuehrer*, nevertheless, sent his armies crashing into Poland on September 1, 1939. Two days later, Britain and France declared war on Germany. The second world war of the 20th century was on.

Bibliography. D. E. Lee, *Ten Years: The World on the Way to War* (1942); J. W. Gantenbein, *Documentary Background of World War II, 1931–1941* (1948); L. B. Namier, *Europe in Decay, 1936–1940* (1953); G. A. Craig and F. Gilbert (eds.) *The Diplomats, 1919–1939* (1953); A.J.P. Taylor, *The Origins of the Second World War* (1961); J. W. Wheeler-Bennett, *Munich: Prologue to Tragedy* (1966); J. E. McSherry, *Stalin, Hitler and Europe: The Origins of World War II, 1933–1939* (1968); H. H. Adams, *Years of Deadly Peril: The Coming of the War, 1939–1941* (1969); K. Eubank, *The Origins of World War II* (1969); E. M. Robertsom (ed.), *The Origins of the Second World War* (1970); R. Parkinson, *The Origins of World War II* (1969); M. Beaumont, *The Origins of the Second World War* (1978); J. C. Stoessinger, *Why Nations Go to War* (1978); and G. C. Weinberg, *The Foreign Policy of Hitler's Germany: Starting World War II* (1981).

CAVALERRO, UGO (1880–1943). Italian Army officer ousted from his posts by Mussolini.

In the winter of 1941, following Italian defeats in Greece and Libya, Cavallero was called on by Mussolini to defend Albania and coordinate German intervention in North Africa. As Marshal of Italy and Chief of the Italian General Staff, he attempted a new iron rule to bolster Italian fighting strength. He was always subordinate to the Germans who had little faith in him or his predecessors, Marshals Pietro Badoglio and Rodolpho Graziani (*qq.v.*). Cavallero's reputation declined along with that of the Italian Army. He was ousted on January 31, 1943, as Chief of the High Command following the loss of Tripoli and was replaced by Gen. Vittorio Ambrosio.

Mussolini imprisoned Cavallero in early 1943. On September 10, 1943, *The New York Times* reported that Cavallero had been executed for treason. Five days later the German press announced that he had died by suicide at Frascati (Rome) "because of Italy's treachery." Italian papers also reported the suicide but attributed it to Cavellero's depression caused by his country's ill fortune and fear that his anti-Fascist motives might be discovered.

CHAMBERLAIN, ARTHUR NEVILLE (1869–1940). British statesman who saw appeasement as the only alternative to a second war with Germany.

Chamberlain's policy of appeasement touched off a lively debate that has continued to the present day. His supporters felt that he had no other choice in a critical situation. Britain, they said, was unprepared for war, and Chamberlain performed a priceless service by buying desperately needed time. Chamberlain's part in the Munich Agreement (*q.v.*), they said, gave Britain a year in which to prepare its defense. They believed that Hitler would not have been influenced by a tougher line.

Critics, on the other hand, denounced appeasement as ineffective. Instead of discouraging the Axis leaders, Chamberlain in fact unconsciously gave them the signal to go ahead with their aggressive plans. Furthermore, charged the critics, far from giving Britain time to prepare its defenses, he gave the Germans more time to complete their infinitely greater rearmament program.

On September 3, 1939, after Germany invaded Poland, Chamberlain announced Britain's declaration of war in a moving broadcast. His government did not last much longer. Britons were depressed by the failure of the Allied campaign in Norway. There were heated attacks on Chamberlain in the House of Commons. He tried to meet the storm by reshuffling his Cabinet, but it was too late. The Labour Party refused to serve in any government under him. On May 10, 1940, the day when the Germans invaded the Low Countries, Chamberlain resigned.

Chamberlain served in the Churchill Government as President of the Council and supported Churchill in his war efforts. After serious illness, he died at his estate in Hampshire on November 9, 1940, and was buried in Westminster Abbey.

Bibliography. Keith Feiling, *Life of Neville Chamberlain* (1946); I. MacLeod, *Neville Chamberlain* (1961). *See also* J. W. Wheeler-Bennett, *Munich* (1948); and C. L. Mowat, *Britain Between the Wars, 1918–1940* (1955).

CHANNEL DASH. Escape of three German warships, the *Gneisenau, Prinz Eugen,* and *Scharnhorst* from Brest to Norway on February 12, 1942. (*See SCHARNHORST.*)

CHANSON D'AUTOMNE **(SONG OF AUTUMN).** Poem by Paul Verlaine, two lines of which were to be used to alert the French underground about imminent Allied assault on Fortress Europe in June 1944. (*See* NORMANDY INVASION.) German intelligence had advance knowledge of *Chanson d'Automne,* but it was not enough to outwit Allied deception measures.

CHAPLAINS, FOUR. *See* FOUR CHAPLAINS.

CHENNAULT, CLAIRE LEE (1890–1958). U.S. Air Force General and leader of the Flying Tigers (*q.v.*) in China.

Throughout the fall and winter of 1941, Chennault's Flying Tigers continued to strike at the Japanese. After Pearl Harbor Chennault's airmen sparked Allied resistance throughout the Chinese mainland. By July 1942 they had destroyed 284 Japanese planes in seven months with as many more probable losses, while losing ten pilots in combat and nine in accidents.

Recalled to active duty on July 4, 1942, Chennault served the U.S. Army and headed the U.S. war in China until July 25, 1945, when the Flying Tigers were replaced by the regular Army Air Forces. In May 1943 Chennault was called to Washington to attend a conference on Far Eastern strategy. In the next several months his forces won uncontested supremacy in China. He resigned in late July 1945 rather than agree to disband the Chinese-American wing of the Chinese air force.

Bibliography. C. E. Chennault, *Way of a Fighter* (1949). *See also* R. L. Scott, *Flying Tiger: Chennault of China* (1959).

CHERNYAKHOVSKY, IVAN DANILOVICH (1906–1945). Russian Army commander noted for defeats he inflicted on the Germans.

Following the German invasion of the Soviet Union, Chernyakhovsky helped defend Voronezh in 1942. He led a crossing of the Dnieper in October 1943 and was named a Hero of the Soviet Union. He was promoted to major general and to colonel general in March 1944. He was given command of his own army in June 1944.

In the final campaign against the Germans, Chernyakhovsky led the 3rd White Russian Army across the Beresina River and in nine days covered more than a third of the 360 miles from northwest of Orsha to East Prussia. By July 10, 1944, he had surrounded Vilna and cut off the German escape route through Poland to the Balkans. When he took Vilna after five days of house-to-house fighting, Moscow celebrated with a salute of 24 salvoes from 324 guns. His troops weathered one German counterattack after another. In October 1944, when the weather turned cold, his men smashed into East Prussia. By this time he was leading an army of 500,000 men on an 87-mile front and captured 400 towns and villages. He headed toward Königsberg, the capital of East Prussia.

On February 19, 1945, *The New York Times* reported that Chernyakhovsky had died of wounds received on the battlefield in East Prussia.

CHESHIRE, LEONARD (1917–   ). One of the aces of the Royal Air Force (*q.v.*).

Cheshire qualified for his wings in December 1939 and thereafter was assigned to several squadrons, including the 102nd, 35th, and 67th. In 1944 he was appointed to command the famed 617th Squadron, the "Dambusters," to succeed Wing Commander Guy Gibson (*q.v.*), who was killed while returning from a mission. Cheshire made many dangerous low-level attacks with his *Mosquito* (*q.v.*). His pinpoint method of bombing helped to cripple German flying bombs and rockets at their source. He was awarded the Victoria Cross for gallantry.

Cheshire completed his 100th mission in 1944, after which he was assigned posts in the South East Asia Command and with the British Joint Staff Mission in Washington. He was the official British observer at the dropping of the atomic bomb on Nagasaki on August 9, 1945.

Bibliography. Cheshire wrote *Bomber Pilot* (1942); *Pilgrimage to the Shroud* (1955); and *The Face of Victory* (1961). See also C. Hughes, *Leonard Cheshire, V.C.* (1961).

CHETNIKS. Serbian guerrilla force.

The Chetniks (Serbian, *četnići*) served in the Balkan Wars and in World War I. After the conquest of Yugoslavia by the Germans in 1941, the Chetniks were revived to fight against the Germans. Led by Draja Mikhailovich, they also clashed with the Partisans of Marshal Tito. In 1941 they received considerable acclaim and support from the Allies, but later they were displaced by Tito's

Partisans (*q.v.*). (*See* MIKHAILOVICH, DRAJA; TITO, JOSIP BROZ; and UNDERGROUND.)

CHIANG KAI-SHEK (1887–1975). Chinese military leader and statesman and one of the top war leaders.

Generalissimo Chiang Kai-shek emerged as China's most powerful political leader in the mid-1920s. His Nanjing (Nanking) Government was recognized by the United States and Great Britain in 1928. When his country was invaded by Japanese forces in 1937, he moved his capital to Chungking in the belief that if he held on powerful allies would come to his aid.

The Chinese-Japanese war continued from 1937 to 1945. After the Japanese attack on Pearl Harbor (*q.v.*), President Roosevelt sent Maj. Gen. Joseph W. ("Vinegar Joe") Stilwell (*q.v.*) to China in January 1942, as chief of staff to the Generalissimo. Stilwell commanded a large body of Chinese as well as American troops, but Chiang was the supreme commander of the Allied air and land forces in China. Although he had American backing, Chiang proved difficult to work with. The Americans, fearing growing Communist strength in China, attempted to extend their strength on the mainland. Chiang refused to allow Chinese forces to be unified under American command. Growing differences led to the recall of Stilwell in November 1944.

Bibliography. *The Collected Wartime Messages of Chiang Kai-shek 1937–1945* (2 vols., 1946). For biographies, *see* B. W. Miller, *Generalissimo and Madame Chiang Kai-shek* (1943); H. H. Chang, *Chiang Kai-shek, Asia's Man of Destiny* (1944); T. H. White and A. Jacoby, *Thunder Out of China* (1946); H. Hsiung, *Life of Chiang Kai-shek* (1948); and J. B. Michener, *Voice of Asia* (1951).

CHINDITS. Special Long-Range Penetration Group operating in Burma against the Japanese.

BACKGROUND. The name Chindit was given by its initiator Maj. Gen. Orde C. Wingate (*q.v.*), after a mystical beast, half lion and half eagle, called Chinthe, of which numerous statues were in Burmese pagodas. The griffin-like beast symbolized close ground-and-air cooperation of the Chindits.

Impressed by Wingate's novel ideas of conducting guerrilla fighting, Allied strategists gave him the signal to go ahead with his plans. He trained British and Indian troops into tough, resilient units the size of a brigade to operate behind Japanese lines in Burma. His men became experts in ground-to-air cooperation, demolition, and radio communication. He divided Chindits into two sections—a Northern Group of five columns, with 2,200 men and 850 mules, and a Southern Group of two columns, with 1,000 men and 250 mules.

ACTION IN BURMA. In early 1943 Wingate sent his Chindits to strike at Japanese communications on the upper Irrawaddy River, destroy bridges, demolish supply dumps, and smash railway lines. They ranged far and wide behind enemy lines, crossed mountain ranges, and pushed through deep valleys.

By mid-March 1943 Chindits crossed the Irrawaddy, but they encountered tough Japanese resistance and most of the unit withdrew to India. The operation had little effect, and it was deplored by professional soldiers. It was, however, praised by the British public and it was important for Allied morale. Later, Chindits were joined by Merrill's Marauders (*q.v.*), a similar American unit. (*See* BURMA, CAMPAIGN IN.)

Although Winston Churchill pronounced Orde Wingate "a man of genius who might have become a man of destiny," a recent book by Richard Rhodes James, a veteran of Wingate's second expedition against the Japanese, charged that Wingate's Chindits were a failure. While they won some local successes, they took hideous casualties (of one brigade only 120 of 2,500 men managed to return to India, most rotting away in the jungle from malnutrition, disease, and sheer exhaustion). According to James, almost every aspect of Wingate's Chindits went wrong and the whole enterprise was a waste of human effort and sacrifice.

Bibliography. C.J. Rollo, *Wingate's Raiders* (1944); M. Calvert, *Chindits: Long-Range Penetration* (1973); and R. R. James, *Chindits* (1980).

CHRISTIAN PEACE MOVEMENT. A German clandestine broadcasting station used in early 1940 in conjunction with Operation Sea Lion (*q.v.*), the projected invasion of England. (*See* NEW BRITISH BROADCASTING STATION.)

CHRISTIAN X (1870–1947). King of Denmark.

During the German occupation of Denmark from 1940 to 1945, Christian continued on the throne on sufferance. On occasion he defied German authority and in 1943 was placed on house arrest by the German authorities. He did what he could to maintain a show of independence in his relations with the Germans. Also King of Iceland since 1912, Christian sent the Icelandic Government a message of good will when it declared its independence in 1944.

CHUIKOV, VASILI IVANOVITCH (1900–   ). Russian Army officer and hero of Stalingrad.

Chuikov fought in the Russo-Finnish War (*q.v.*) from 1939 to 1940. Relieved of his duties, he acted as military aide to Generalissimo Chiang/Kai-shek in China. On the invasion of the USSR by Germany in June 1941 he was recalled to assume charge of a division on the central front. In September 1942 he was named to command the 6th Army in the defense of Stalingrad and in this post won national attention. In November he launched a successful counterattack and struck hard at the core of Nazi power. By the time the siege of Stalingrad was lifted, the Germans had lost 300,000 men. Outnumbered and outgunned, Chuikov stood fast and eventually broke the German attack. (*See* STALINGRAD, BATTLE OF.)

CHURCHILL, WINSTON LEONARD SPENCER (1874-1965).

British Prime Minister during World War II. He was born at Blenheim Palace on November 30, 1874, the eldest son of Lord Randolph Churchill. He was educated at Harrow and Sandhurst, and entered the army in 1895.

EARLY CAREER. Churchill reported the war of independence from Spain in Cuba in 1895. After serving in India, he fought at Omdurman in Egypt under Lord Kitchener in 1898. He was a war correspondent for the *Morning Post* in the South African War. His escape after being captured by the Boers thrust him into the forefront of British journalists. Turning to politics, he was elected to Parliament as a Conservative in 1900.

Churchill advanced rapidly in his political career, serving in a succession of important posts including President of the Board of Trade (1908-1910), Home Secretary (1910-1911), and First Lord of the Admiralty (1911-1915). He lost the latter position in 1915 when he was discredited by failure of the Dardanelles campaign. In July 1917 he became Minister of Munitions and was instrumental in supplying the shells that helped the Allies to victory.

Among his postwar posts were Secretary of State for War and Air (1918-1921), Colonial Secretary (1921), and Chancellor of the Exchequer (1924-1929). For the next 10 years he remained out of ministerial office, lecturing and writing.

WORLD WAR II. From the floor of the House of Commons Churchill issued strong warnings about the Hitler threat to peace, but his words went unheeded. On September 3, 1939, Prime Minister Neville Chamberlain (*q.v.*) appointed him First Lord of the Admiralty. On May 10, 1940, after having held nearly every great office of state, Churchill finally achieved that of Prime Minister on the resignation of Chamberlain following the collapse of the Norwegian campaign.

Churchill stubbornly refused to make peace during the grim years of 1940-1942. His stirring oratory was a prime factor in maintaining British morale in the face of imminent defeat. (*See* CHURCHILL'S WAR SPEECHES.) The British had to fight on alone "as the sole champions now in arms to defend the world cause. . . . We shall do our best to be worthy of that honor."

Churchill's most valuable contribution to Allied victory was his Mediterranean strategy. His defense of that vital artery and his brilliant direction of the campaign against Gen. Erwin Rommel (*See* NORTH AFRICA, CAMPAIGNS IN) were vital in the outcome of the war. He directed the strategy of night bombing by the Royal Air Force (*q.v.*) on German cities.

Churchill's relations with President Franklin D. Roosevelt (*q.v.*) were on the basis of perfect mutual understanding and confidence. "Give us the tools, and we will do the job." The two met before the U.S. entry into the war (*see*

ATLANTIC CHARTER) and attended a long series of international conferences (*see* CONFERENCES, ALLIED WAR).

Churchill's conduct of the war never went unchallenged, but he managed to overcome any opposition to his "dictatorial rule." He supported the USSR strongly after it was attacked by Hitler in June 1941, but he never lost his mistrust of communism and warned against future danger.

POSTWAR. Only two months after the end of the war Churchill lost an election to the Labour Party. It was a bitter and humiliating personal blow. In 1946, in a controversial speech at Fulton, Missouri, he originated the expression "the Iron Curtain" and warned of Russian expansionism. He became Prime Minister again in 1951. He died in London on January 24, 1965, at the age of 90. Acclaimed as a citizen of the world, he was given the funeral of a hero.

PERSONALITY AND CHARACTER. Of medium height, with pugnacious nose and strong chin, Churchill was noted for his phenomenal energy. Fearless, unconquerable, gifted with driving zeal, he was one of the great war leaders of history. Extraordinary boldness characterized both his political and military careers. With his bulldog manner, grotesque array of hats, and knack for looking crumpled, he was a prime favorite with the British public. His strength and weaknesses reflected the same source—an indomitable will to maintain Britain as a great power and the beacon for democracy.

Bibliography. Among Churchill's many works were such collections of speeches as *Blood, Sweat, and Tears* (1941); *The Unrelenting Struggle* (1942); *The End of the Beginning* (1943); *Onwards to Victory* (1944); and *Victory* (1946). His *The Second World War* (6 vols., 1948–1954) is considered to be an important source book. *See also* biographies by G. Arthur (1940); R. Sencourt (1940); R. L. Taylor (1952); E. Hughes (1955); C. L. Broad (1956); and R. Churchill (2 vols., 1966).

CHURCHILL TANK. *See* TANKS.

"CHURCHILL'S BUNKER." *See* WAR ROOMS, BRITISH.

CHURCHILL'S WAR SPEECHES. British morale in 1940, at a critical moment in British history, was stimulated by a series of eloquent speeches made by Prime Minister Winston Churchill (*q.v.*). Following are passages from three of these famous war speeches.

"BLOOD, TOIL, TEARS AND SWEAT," May 13, 1940. In his first speech as Prime Minister, Churchill addressed the House of Commons in words that drew global attention.

In this crisis I hope I may be pardoned if I do not address the House at any length today. I hope that any of my friends and colleagues, or former colleagues, who are affected by the political reconstruction, will make allowance, all allowance, for any lack of ceremony with which it has been necessary to act. I would say to the House, as I said to those who have joined this Government; "I have nothing to offer but blood, toil, tears and sweat."

We have before us an ordeal of the most grievous kind. We have before us many, many long months of struggle and of suffering. You ask, what is our policy? I will say: It is to wage war, by sea, land, and air, with all our might and with all the strength that God can give us: to wage war against a monstrous tyranny, never surpassed in the dark, lamentable catalogue of human crime. That is our policy. You ask, what is our aim? I can answer in one word: It is victory, victory at all costs, victory in spite of all terror, victory, however long and hard the road may be; for without victory there is no survival. Let that be realized; no survival for the British Empire; no survival for all that the British Empire has stood for, no survival for the urge and impulse of the ages, that mankind will move forward towards its goal. But I take up my task with buoyancy and hope. I feel sure that our cause will not be suffered to fail among men. At this time I feel entitled to claim the aid of all, and I say, "Come, then, let us go forward together with our united strength."

"THEIR FINEST HOUR," June 18, 1940. The collapse of France moved Churchill to another great speech, delivered before the House of Commons. In ringing terms he linked the coming struggle with the survival of Christian civilization. (See BRITAIN, BATTLE OF.)

What General Weygand called the "Battle of France" is over. I expect that the battle of Britain is about to begin. Upon this battle depends the survival of Christian civilization. Upon it depends our own British life and the long continuity of our institutions and our Empire. The whole fury and might of the enemy must very soon be turned on us. Hitler knows that he will have to break us in this island or lose the war. If we can stand up to him all Europe may be free and the life of the world may move forward into broad, sunlit uplands; but if we fail then the whole world, including the United States, and all that we have known and cared for, will sink into the abyss of a new dark age made more sinister, and perhaps more prolonged, by the lights of a perverted science. Let us, therefore, brace ourselves to our duty and so bear ourselves that if the British Commonwealth and Empire lasts for a thousand years men will still say, "This was their finest hour."

"SO MUCH OWED BY SO MANY TO SO FEW," August 10, 1940. Churchill's tribute to the Royal Air Force (q.v.) was made in a speech to the House of Commons.

The gratitude of every home in our Island, in our Empire, and indeed throughout the world, except in the abodes of the guilty, goes out to the British airmen, who undaunted by odds, unwearied in their constant challenge and mortal danger, are turning the tide of world war by their prowess and by their devotion. Never in the field of human conflict was so much owed by so many to so few. All hearts go out to the fighter pilots, whose brilliant actions we see with our own eyes day after day, but we must never forget that all the time, night after night, month after month, our bomber squadrons travel far into Germany, find their targets in the darkness by the highest navigational skill, aim their attacks, often under the heaviest fire, often with serious loss, with deliberate, careful discrimination, and inflict shattering blows upon the whole of the technical and war-making structure of the Nazi power.

CIANO, GALEAZZO (1903–1944). Italian politician and Fascist diplomat.

When Germany went to war in 1939, Ciano helped convince Mussolini to stay out of the conflict. By June 1940 the Italian dictator could not be restrained and Italy declared war on the Allies. Ciano took command of a bomber squadron for a time and flew on several missions. In early February 1943, after heated arguments with his son-in-law, Mussolini dismissed him from his post as Minister of Foreign Affairs. Ciano became Ambassador to the Holy See.

Ciano took part in the coup of July 25, 1943, as a result of which Mussolini was overthrown and Italian fascism collapsed. He voted against the *Duce* in the dramatic session of the Fascist Grand Council, which was thoroughly disgusted with the war. Mussolini was arrested and Ciano narrowly escaped by seeking refuge in Germany. When the *Duce* was rescued by the Germans, Ciano on the order of Hitler was sent back to Verona to serve in the new Fascist puppet state. After a mock trial he was found guilty of treason. On January 11, 1944, he was given a traitor's death, shot in the back while tied to a chair by a German firing squad. The fact that he was Mussolini's son-in-law did not save him from execution.

Bibliography. Ciano's *Diaries* (1946), published from notes kept by his wife, provide a valuable record of Fascist meetings from 1939 to 1945. *See also* M. Muggeridge (ed.), *Ciano's Diplomatic Papers* (1948).

"CICERO." Alias used by Elyea Bazna (also spelled Elias Basna), an Albanian espionage agent for the Germans in Ankara, Turkey.

Little is known about Bazna's life. In October 1943 he called at the German Embassy in Ankara and offered photographs of secret British documents for £10,000. He was then hired as a valet by the British Ambassador to Turkey, Sir Hughe Knatchbull-Hugessen. In this capacity Bazna managed to obtain a key to his employer's safe and apparently was able to provide Berlin with valuable information, including several hundred photographs of secret British documents. Over a period of six months Bazna was paid a total of £300,000 by his employers. German intelligence agents in Berlin apparently did not realize the value of the documents sent to them by their Albanian spy.

Bazna gave the Germans the exact date of the Teheran Conference (*q.v.*), which was to start on November 28, 1943. He also forwarded information on planned Allied raids on German cities. (*See* ESPIONAGE.)

POSTWAR. After the war Bazna started to build a hotel with his espionage earnings, only to learn that the Germans had paid him in counterfeit money. He disappeared when his name was reported by a woman to the British authorities. He was not seen again in Ankara.

CIGS. Chief of the Imperial General Staff, the highest military post in Great Britain.

CLARK, MARK WAYNE (1896–   ). Allied commander in Italy in 1944.

On the night of October 21–22, 1942, Clark led a small commando group to contact anti-Nazi officers in enemy-held North Africa. After leaving a British submarine and being met ashore by friends, the expedition nearly ended in disaster when the local police learned about it. From 1943 to 1944 he commanded the U.S. 5th Army in North Africa. He led the same army in the invasions of Sicily and Italy. His troops, aided by naval bombardment and an air umbrella, stormed ashore near Salerno (*see* SALERNO BEACHHEAD). Here they met stubborn resistance and were nearly thrown back into the sea.

Clark commanded the unsuccessful Anzio operation and later made the reluctant decision to bomb the monastery at Monte Cassino (*see* MONTE CASSINO, BOMBING OF). On June 5, 1944, his men captured Rome and then continued their drive north. Promoted to full General in 1945, he served (1945–1947) as head of the U.S. occupation forces in Austria.

Bibliography. M. W. Clark, *Calculated Risk* (1950); and *From the Danube to the Yalu* (1954).

CLAY, LUCIUS DU BIGNON (1897–1978). American engineering officer active in procurement.

In 1940 Clay organized the enlargement of 277 older airports and the construction of 197 new ones in the United States, Alaska, and the Philippines. Shortly after American entry into the war, he was sent to Brazil on a mission to establish airports there. In 1942, promoted to Brigadier General, he was made Chairman of the Army Procurement Program. In 1944 he closed the logistics bottleneck after the Normandy invasion (*q.v.*). In the spring of 1945 he was named Director of the Office of War Mobilization to expedite delivery of supplies to all theaters of war.

In the postwar era Clay was Military Governor of the U.S. Zone in Germany. In 1947 he was promoted to four-star rank. When Soviet Russia in June 1948 began its blockade of West Berlin, Clay supervised the American airlift, which brought food and fuel to the city. He retired from the army in May 1949 to enter private business. He died April 17, 1978 at the age of 81.

Bibliography. Clay's *Decision in Germany* (1950) is the definitive account of the U.S. zone in Germany.

"CLIMB MOUNT NIKATA." Japanese code or cover phrase that meant "Proceed with attack."

This radio signal was given by Adm. Isoruku Yamamoto (*q.v.*) on December 2, 1941, for the task force assembled for the raid on Pearl Harbor. (*See* PEARL HARBOR.)

COASTWATCHERS. An organization composed mostly of Royal Australian Navy Intelligence officers and local citizens to watch for the approach of Japanese task forces in 1942.

CODE NAMES, ALLIED

ACCOLADE	Proposed British assault on the Dodecanese Islands, 1941
ACROBAT	Planned British strike on Tripolitania, 1941–1942.
ANAKIM	Seaborne assault on Rangoon, Spring 1943
ANVIL	Early name for DRAGOON, the Allied invasion of southern France, August 1944
ARCHERY	British commando raid on Vaagsø, Norway, December 27, 1941
ARGUMENT	Air raids on German aircraft industry, February 20–25, 1944
AVALANCHE	Amphibious Allied assault on Salerno, in Campania, southern Italy, September 9, 1943
BATTLEAXE	British attempt to relieve Tobruk in North Africa, June–September 1941
BAYTOWN	British crossing of the Strait of Messina into Calabria, September 3, 1943
BIGOT	Security classification for planning papers dealing with cross-Channel attack
BITING	Proposed raid on German radar device near Le Havre, February 1942
BODYGUARD	Deception operations to conceal plans for the invasion of Normandy, June 1944
BOLERO	Movement of combat forces from the United States to England in preparation for invasion of northern France, 1942–1944
BREVITY	British attack in Western Desert, mid-May 1941
BRIMSTONE	Projected Allied invasion of Sardinia, 1944
BRISSEX	British intelligence agents to be dropped by parachute just before Normandy invasion, June 1944
BULLFROG	Proposed attack in Burma, January 1945
BUTTRESS	British operation around Calabria on the toe of Italy, September 3, 1943
CAPITAL	British operation in North Burma, 1944
CATAPULT	British attack on the French Fleet in North African ports, July 1940
CATCHPOLE	U.S. operations in Marshall Islands, 1944
CHAMPION	Offensive in Burma, 1944
CHARIOT	British commando raid on port of St. Nazaire, March 28, 1942

CHASTISE	British raids on Möhne, Eder, and Sorpe dams, May 16–17, 1943
CIRCUS	British air operations against Continental coastal areas, 1941–1942
CLARION	All-out Allied air assault on German communications, late February 1945
COBRA	American breakout at St. Lô in Summer 1944
COCKADE	Plan to convince the Germans that an Allied invasion was imminent, 1943
COLOSSUS	British raid on the Italian coast south of Salerno in Winter 1941
COMET	Original plan to capture all three of the Maas, Waal, and Rhine crossings. Scrapped September 10, 1944, in favor of MARKET-GARDEN
COMPASS	British thrust at the Italians in Egypt, December 1940
CORKSCREW	Occupation of Pantelleria by British, June 1943
CORONET	Invasion of Japan, 1945
CROMWELL	Invasion alert to be sounded on attempt by Germans to invade England, 1940
CROSSBOW	Measures to be taken against German V-weapons, 1944. *See also* DIVER
CULVERIN DEMON	Move against Sumatra, 1944. Abandoned British evacuation of Greece, April 1941
DIADEM	Allied full-scale offensive to take Rome, May 12, 1944
DIVER	Measures to be taken against German V-weapons, 1944
DRACULA	Amphibious attack on Rangoon, May 1945
DRAGOON	Allied invasion of southern France, Summer 1944
DYNAMO	British evacuation of Dunkirk, May 26–June 4, 1940
ENIGMA	Cover name for reproduction of a German coding machine
EPSOM	Allied attack west of Caen, July 18, 1944
EXPORTER	Occupation of Syria, June 1941
FANFARE	Generic name to cover all Allied operations in the Mediterranean
FIREBRAND	Proposed Allied invasion of Corsica, 1944
FLINTLOCK	Operations in Marshall Islands, 1944
FORAGER	Operation in Mariana Islands, 1944
FORTITUDE	Deception tactics for invasion of northern France, 1944
FORTITUDE NORTH	In Scandinavian countries
FORTITUDE SOUTH	Channel coast of France and Belgium
FORTITUDE SOUTH II	Operations after D-Day. Also termed ROSEBUD
FRANTIC	Allied shuttle bombing of Germany from England, Italy, and the Soviet Union, 1944–1945

FRESHMAN	Glider-borne attempt to destroy Vermork heavy water plant in eastern Norway, November 2, 1942
GAFF	Operation of Allied agents to kill Field Marshal Erwin Rommel, 1944
GALVANIC	U.S. attack on Gilbert Islands, 1943
GARDEN	Allied armored drive to capture bridges to take place simultaneously with MARKET, the airborne drop, September 1944
GLIMMER	Deception operation on D-Day by large "invasion" fleet off Boulogne
GOMORRAH	Allied bombing assault on Hamburg, July 24–August 3, 1943
GOODWOOD	British armored breakout from Caen, July 18, 1944
GRAPEFRUIT	Planned offensive in north Italy in closing months of war, 1945
GRENADE	American offensive toward the Rhine, early 1945
GYMNAST	Allied attack on Casablanca in North Africa in late 1942. Renamed SUPERGYMNAST and later TORCH
HABBABUK	Projected airfields of ice in the Atlantic, abandoned as impractical
HANDS UP	Projected assault on Germans at Vannes after D-Day. Cancelled
HARPOON	British convoy to Malta, 1942
HERCULES	Allied plan to capture Rhodes, 1943
HUSKY	Invasion of Sicily, Summer 1943
ICEBERG	Amphibious attack on Okinawa, April 1945
IMPERATOR	Heavy air raids on northern France, 1942
INDIGO	Plan to move U.S. troops to Iceland, 1942
JAEL	Operation to conceal intentions for invasion of France from north, 1943. Replaced by BODYGUARD, 1944
JUBILEE	Raid on Dieppe, August 1942
JUGGLER	Allied air raids on Schweinfurt and Regensburg
JUPITER	Planned invasion of northern Norway
LIGHTFOOT	British offensive in North Africa, October 1942
LUMBERJACK	Allied attack north of the Moselle between Koblenz, Bonn, and Cologne, February 1945
LUSTRE	Allied aid to Greece
MADELEINE	Noor Inayat Khan, British agent in France
MAGNET	Movement of U.S. troops in northern Ireland, 1942
MANHATTAN	Allied atomic energy project
MANNA	British plan to help Greece after German withdrawal on October 4, 1944

MARKET	Airborne drop on Arnhem, September 1944 to take place simultaneously with GARDEN, the armored drive
MARKET-GARDEN	Combined armored drive and air drop to outflank Germans on West Wall, September 1944
MATADOR	Proposed British move into Kra Isthmus, 1941–1942
MATTERHORN	American air assaults on Japan from China, 1944
MENACE	Unsuccessful Anglo-French operation to take Dakar in North Africa, September 1940
MINCEMEAT	Deception operation by British in 1943 to mislead Germans on invasion area
MULBERRIES	Artificial harbors constructed outside French coast in conjunction with OVERLORD
MUSKET	Projected landing by British on heel of Italy near Taranto, November 11, 1943
NEPTUNE	Internal code word for OVERLORD to signal Normandy invasion, June 6, 1944
NOAH'S ARK	Plan for the proposed occupation of Greece, 1944
OLYMPIC	U.S. plan for a landing in Japan, 1945
ORANGE	U.S pre-war plans for possible war with Japan
OVERLORD	All-out invasion of Normandy, June 6, 1944
PAPER CLIP	American search for enemy technical experts in closing days of the war, 1945
PILGRIM	Proposed attack on the Canary Islands, 1942
PLUNDER	Allied plan to cross the Rhine north of the Ruhr, early 1945
PLUTO	Under-Channel oil supply for invasion of Normany, June 1944
POINTBLANK	Combined air bomber offensive against Germany, 1943
PRICELESS	Allied invasion of Italy, 1943
PRINCES	Underground secret intelligence network in Denmark
PUGILIST GALLOP	British attack on the Mareth Line, North Africa, March 1943
PUMA	Projected invasion of the Canary Islands, 1942
RAINBOW	American code word for operations against the Axis, 1939–1941
RANKIN	Overall plan to occupy Continent in event of a German collapse
RATWEEK	Allied project to strike at the German withdrawal from Yugoslavia, 1944
RAVENOUS	Advance into upper Burma, 1944
ROSEBUD	Deception tactics for June 1944 invasion of France. Also code named FORTITUDE SOUTH II

ROUNDHAMMER	Early (1943) code name for invasion of France
ROUND-UP	American buildup in the United Kingdom as preliminary to Normandy invasion, 1944
RUPERT	British Narvik expedition, 1940
RUTTER	Proposed Allied raid on Dieppe in July 1942. Later changed to JUBILEE
SATIN	Proposed U.S. operation in North Africa, December 1942. Cancelled
SATURN	Allied proposal to send troops into Turkey, 1944
SHINGLE	Allied operation to outflank Gustav Line in Italy, late January 1944
SICKLE	Movement of U.S. Air Forces to England, 1942
SKYE	Non-existent U.S. force supposed to train in Scotland for invasion of Norway. Part of FORTITUDE NORTH
SLAPSTICK	British parachute landings in lower Italy, early September 1943
SLEDGEHAMMER	Alternate limited operation to invade European continent, 1942
SOAPSUDS	Contemplated air strikes on Rumanian oil fields, May 24, 1943. Final code name TIDAL WAVE
SOURCE	British cover name for attack by six midget submarines on German battleship *Tirpitz,* September 22, 1941
SPRINGBOARD	Proposed invasion of Madeira, 1942
STARKET	Deception operation to mystify Germans on Allied invasion of Europe, September 1943
STATESMAN	Original code name for projected air attack on Rumanian oil fields. Superseded by SOAPSUDS and TIDAL WAVE
STRANGLE	Allied air attack to seal off Germans in Italy, early 1944
SUNRISE	Operation by U.S. Office of Strategic Services (OSS) leading to surrender of Italian forces in northern Italy, 1945
SUPERCHARGE	British plan to strike at Germans at El Alamein, October 1942. Successor to LIGHTFOOT
SUPERGYMNAST	*See* GYMNAST
TARZAN	Advance in Burma, 1944
TAXABLE	Deception operation for supposed British-American fleet near Le Havre, June 1944
THRUSTER	Planned attack on the Azores, 1942
THUNDERCLAP	Combined bomber offensive on German cities, 1944
THURSDAY	Chindit operation, Burma, 1944
TIDAL WAVE	Contemplated air strike on Rumanian oil fields, August 1, 1943. Succeeded STATESMAN and SOAPSUDS
TINDALL	Deception operation for invasion of Norway, 1943, part of COCKADE

TORCH	Invasion of northwest Africa, November 8, 1942
TOTALIZE	Canadian assault on Falaise, August 1944
TRANSFIGURE	Proposed Anglo-American airborne bid for Paris 1944. Cancelled.
TRINITY	Atomic bomb project
TROJAN HORSE	British deception operation, 1943. *See* MINCEMEAT
TROOPERS	Allied military communications center in London
TUBE ALLOYS	British project to develop an atomic bomb. Counterpart of American Manhattan Project
ULTRA	Intelligence produced by deciphering messages sent by Enigma machine
VANGUARD	Proposal to take Rangoon from the sea
VARSITY	Allied airborne operation at the Rhine, March 1945
VENETTA	Deception operation in southern France, 1944
VERITABLE	Canadian airborne operation on the Rhine, early 1945
VIGOROUS	British Malta convoy, June 1942
WATCHTOWER	Allied plan to take the Solomons and New Guinea, July 1942. Later nicknamed *Operation Shoestring* because of hastiness of preparation
WILD OATS	Cover plan after D-Day for attack on St. Malmo. Cancelled
WINDOW	RAF drop of tinfoil to confuse German radar
ZEPPELIN	General deception operations in countries of southern and southwestern Europe, 1943 and 1944
ZIPPER	Invasion of Malaya, 1945

CODE NAMES, ALLIED WAR CONFERENCES

ARCADIA	First Anglo-American conference, Washington, December 24, 1941 to January 14, 1942.
ARGONAUT	Yalta, February 4–12, 1945
EUREKA	Teheran, November 28–December 1, 1943
OCTAGON	Quebec, September 12–16, 1944
QUADRANT	Quebec, August 17–24, 1943
SEXTANT	Cairo, November 22–26, 1943
SYMBOL	Casablanca, January 14–23, 1943
TERMINAL	Potsdam, July 17–August 2, 1945
TRIDENT	Washington, May 11–27, 1943

CODE NAMES, ALLIED WAR LEADERS

BRAID	Gen. George C. Marshall
CARGO	President Franklin D. Roosevelt

EAGLE	Gen. Mark W. Clark
FORMER NAVAL PERSON	Prime Minster Winston Churchill
KINGPIN	Gen. Henri Giraud
LOOK	Gen. Dwight D. Eisenhower
TELEGRAPH	Gen. Walter Bedell Smith

CODE NAMES, GERMAN

A-DAY (ANGRIFFSTAG— ATTACK DAY)	Offensive in the West, 1940
ACHSE (AXIS)	Plan for disarming of Italians on Allied invasion of Italy, September 1943. Also known as ALARICH
ADLERHORST (EAGLE'S NEST)	Hitler's headquarters in the winter of 1944
ADLERTAG (EAGLE DAY)	Goering's code or cover name for air action, which became Battle of Britain, Summer 1940
AIDA	Advance into Egypt in late January 1942
ALARICH (ALARIC)	Another version of ACHSE
ALPENVEILCHEN (ALPINE VIOLET)	Planned intervention in Albania, 1941
ANTON	Plan for the occupation of the unoccupied zone of France, November 11, 1942. Known earlier as ATTILA
ATTILA	Original plan for occupation of unoccupied zone of France
AUGSBURG	Delay in western offensive in late 1939
BARBAROSSA	Invasion of Soviet Union, June 22, 1941
BIRKE (BIRCH TREE)	Evacuation of Finland, Summer 1944
BIRKHAHN (BLACK COCK)	Evacuation of Norway, 1945
BLAU (BLUE)	Offensive at Voronezh, June 1942. Also code name for air operations against Britain, 1939, code named FALL BLAU (CASE BLUE)
BLÜCHER	Attack on the Caucasus to begin in April 1942
BLUME (FLOWER)	Alert for an Allied invasion of the Continent from either the English Channel or the Mediterranean coast
BODENPLATTE (BASE PLATE)	Air assault on Allied airfields in Holland and Belgium, January 1945
BRAUNSCHWEIG (BRUNSWICK)	Attack on the Caucasus, July 1942
BÜFFELBEWEGUNG (BUFFALO STAMPEDE)	Plans for operations on the central front in the Soviet Union, 1943
CERBERUS	Breakthrough of German capital ships from Brest, February 12, 1942

DANZIG	Order to proceed with offensive in late 1939. *See* AUGSBURG
DONNERSCHLAG (THUNDERBOLT)	Proposed breakout of the 6th Army from Stalingrad, December 1942
EDELWEISS	Proposed attack on the oil fields of Baku in the Caucasus, July 1942
ELBE	Earlier version of AUGSBURG, delay offensive in west, late 1939
ENDLÖSUNG (FINAL SOLUTION)	Plan to exterminate the Jews of Europe
FELIX	Plan for an attack on Gibraltar, 1940
FELSENNEST (EYRIE)	Hitler's field headquarters (*Fuehrerhauptquartier*) on the western front from May 10 to June 6, 1940
FEUERZAUBER (FIRE MAGIC)	Earlier verson of NORDLICHT, plan for the capture of Leningrad, 1942
FISCHREIHER (HERON)	Plan for attack on Stalingrad, 1942
FRITZ	Early code name for the proposed invasion of the Soviet Union, 1941
GELB (YELLOW)	Projected attack on the West in 1939
GERTRUD (GERTRUDE)	Plan to invade Turkey if it joined the Allies
GISELA	Plan for the occupation of Spain and Portugal, 1942
GREIF (GRIFFIN)	Plan to employ troops dressed in American uniforms to capture bridges at the Meuse River during the Ardennes campaign, Winter 1944
GRÜN (GREEN)	Plan to conquer Czechoslovakia, 1938
HAIFISCH (SHARK)	Deception tactics to hide the invasion of the Soviet Union, June 1941
HERBSTNEBEL (AUTUMN FOG)	Early code name for massive counteroffensive in the Ardennes, December 1944. Also used to describe evacuation of the Po plain in Italy, 1944
HERBSTREISE (AUTUMN JOURNEY)	Projected dummy fleet for diversion off Scottish coast in connection with SEELÖWE, the invasion of England, Summer 1940
HERKULES (HERCULES)	Plan for operations against Malta, 1940–1942
HEU AKTION (HAY ACTION)	Order issued by Alfred Rosenberg for quota of foreign workers to be sent from the East to Germany, June 12, 1944
ICARUS	Proposed invasion of Iceland in conjunction with SEELÖWE. Plan was scrapped.
ILONA	Projected attack on Spain, 1942
ISABELLA	Earlier version of ILONA
KAMELIE	Projected invasion of Corsica, 1942

KATHLEEN	Projected invasion of Ireland, 1940
LACHSFANG (SALMON TRAP)	Proposed seizure of the Murmansk Railway, 1943
LÜTTICH	Plan for counteroffensive in August 1944 to throw back Allied invaders of the Continent
MARGARETHE I (MARGARET I)	Projected occupation of Hungary, March 1944
MARGARETHE II (MARGARET II)	Projected invasion of Rumania, March 1944
MARITA	Plan for the occupation of Greece, Spring 1941
MAUS (MOUSE)	Offensive in the Caucasus, Summer 1942
MERKUR (MERCURY)	Invasion of Crete, May 1941
MITTELMEER (MEDITERRANEAN)	*Luftwaffe* operations in the Mediterranean, 1940–1941
MORGENRÖTE (DAWN)	Counteroffensive against Anzio beachhead, January 1944
NORD (NORTH)	Original plan for the invasion of Norway, April 9, 1940
NORDLICHT (NORTHERN LIGHTS)	Intended capture of Leningrad, July 1942
OLDENBOURG	Plan for economic exploitation of conquered Soviet territory after invasion of June 1941
PASTORIUS	Plan for espionage operations in the United States, 1942
REGENBOGEN (RAINBOW)	Attack by battleships on northern Allied convoy, December 31, 1942
RHEIN (RHINE)	Earlier version of DANZIG, to proceed with offensive in west, 1940
RHEINÜBUNG (RHINE EXERCISE)	Plan for prosecution of antimerchant ship campaign, May 1941
RÖSSELSPRUNG (KNIGHT'S MOVE)	Plan for attack on Allied convoy on northern route, July 1942
ROT (RED)	Plan for the latter part of the Battle of France, June 1940
SCHAMIL	Projected parachute drop on Maikop oil field in the Caucasus, 1942
SCHWARZ (BLACK)	Plan for military takeover of Italy, 1943
SEELÖWE (SEA LION)	Hitler's proposed invasion of England and the British Isles, 1940
SIEGFRIED	Offensive on the central front from Kharkov to Stalingrad, July 1942
SILBERFUCHS (SILVER FOX)	Invasion of Soviet Russia from Finland, June 1941
SONNENBLUME (SUNFLOWER)	Plan for rescue operation in North Africa, early 1941
STRAFE (PUNISHMENT)	Hitler's plan to "punish" Bulgaria, 1941
TAIFUN (TYPHOON)	Projected attack on Moscow, October 1941

TANNENBERG	Hitler's field headquarters in the Black Forest, 1940
TROJANISCHES PFERD (TROJAN HORSE)	Plan for the occupation of Budapest, March 1944
VALKYRIE	Plan for use of Home Army in event of rebellion by foreign workers. Also used to describe conspirators' plan to kill Hitler, July 20, 1944
WACHT AM RHEIN (GUARD ON THE RHINE)	Operation designed to pierce Allied lines in Ardennes Forest, December 1944
WEISS (WHITE)	Plan for attack on Poland, September 1939
WERWOLF	Hitler's headquarters at Vinnitsa, Ukraine, Winter 1942–1943
WESERÜBUNG (WESER EXERCISE)	Plan for invasion of Denmark and Norway, April 1940
WIESENGRUND (MEADOW LAND)	Plan for the seizure of Fisherman's Peninsula in Arctic Ocean, 1941
WINTERGEWITTER (WINTER STORM)	Projected relief of the 6th Army at Stalingrad. *See also* DONNERSCHLAG
WOLFSSCHLUCHT (WOLVES' GLEN)	Hitler's headquarters at Givet, Belgium, during invasion of France, June 1940
WOLFSSCHANZE (WOLF'S LAIR)	Hitler's field headquarters (*Fuehrerhauptquartier*) in Rastenburg, East Prussia, Summer 1944
Z-PLAN	Plan to match Britain's naval power, 1939
ZITADELLE (CITADEL)	Plan for attack on the Russian bulge at Kursk, July 4, 1943

CODE NAMES, JAPANESE

A-GO	Projected plan for battle at the Philippines, June 1944
HA-GO	Diversionary move to hide Imphal offensive
I	Air assault from Rabaul against American ships in the Solomons, April 1943
KETSU-GO	Overall plan for home islands defense
DETSU-GO	Overall plan for home islands defense, 1945
KON	Reinforcement of New Guinea, Spring 1944
MO	Plan for offensive, Coral Sea, May 1942
RO	Plan for the defense of Rabaul, Winter 1943
SHO-GO	Plan for battle against Americans at Leyte Gulf, October 1944
TA	Attack at Bougainville, November 1943
TEN-GO	Offensive at Iwo Jima and Okinawa, Spring and Summer 1945
U-GO	Imphal offensive, Spring and Summer 1944

CODES AND CODE BREAKING. Science of secret communications during the war.

MEANING. Cryptology, from the Greek *kryptos* ("hidden") and *logos* ("word"), deals with the clandestine methods and devices used to camouflage messages and to penetrate enemy interchanges.

Cryptography, from the Greek *kryptos* ("hidden") and *graphein* ("to write"), is the art of writing messages in such a way that they can be read only by those possessing the key to understanding the communications.

Ciphers and codes are two systems of cryptography, both of which transform messages from the text status into secret form. Ciphers use many techniques to convert plain texts into cryptograms by memory, print, or cipher machine. Codes are lists of words, numbers, syllables, or letters, which are matched with their secret equivalents, usually groups of three, four, or five letters or numbers.

Cryptanalysis, or code breaking, is the science of solving cryptograms by the use of computers, tabulators, or statistical tests of letter frequency.

BACKGROUND. Cryptography has a long historical background going back to Plutarch, who told of a system used by Spartan generals in 450 B.C. to write and decipher messages. Poor cryptography, or correspondingly good cryptanalysis, has often affected the course of wars. The failure of cryptographical communication cost the Russians the Battle of Tannenberg in August 1914.

The most important solution of a cryptogram in World War I was the decoding of the Zimmermann note. On January 17, 1917, German Foreign Minister Alfred Zimmermann, sent a coded telegram offering Mexico its "lost territory" of Texas, New Mexico, and Arizona if it would join the war on the German side. British intelligence intercepted the message, solved it, and passed it along to President Woodrow Wilson, who presented it to an outraged public. Six weeks later the United States was at war.

WORLD WAR II. Throughout World War II all the belligerents used cipher systems for tactical messages and code systems for high command and diplomatic communications. Cryptanalysis was further mathematicized and mechanized. There were considerable advances in the making of cipher machines.

In the early days of the war the Germans solved the British merchant shipping code, as a result of which their U-Boats took a tremendous toll of enemy shipping. Not until the Allies solved the cipher used by the German U-Boat fleet did they begin to thwart the undersea menace by attacking German submarines at their rendezvous points. (*See* ATLANTIC, BATTLE OF THE.) Meanwhile, the British scored a major cryptanalysis coup by reproducing the German-built Enigma machine, which enabled them to intercept and decode most secret radio messages between Hitler and his generals. (*See* ULTRA.)

Shortly before Pearl Harbor, American cryptanalysts reconstructed the

Japanese cipher machine used for high-level diplomatic and operational communications. Breaking the Japanese code was a major factor in winning the Battle of Midway, June 4–5, 1942. With full information on the size and location of Japanese forces, the numerically inferior Americans were able to set up a successful ambush. It was a turning point in the war.

SIGNIFICANCE. Allied successes in codes and code breaking proved to be a significant factor in eventual victory. According to Gen. George C. Marshall (*q.v.*), U.S. Chief of Staff, operations in Normandy (*See* NORMANDY INVASION) and in the Pacific were "closely related in conception and timing to the information we secretly obtained from secret codes. They contributed greatly to victory."

Bibliography. H. F. Gaines, *Cryptanalysis* (1956); B. Tuchman, *The Zimmermann Telegram* (1958); and D. Kahn, *The Codebreakers* (1967).

COLDITZ. German prisoner-of-war camp.

BACKGROUND. Colditz Castle was in a cluster of buildings overlooking the town of the same name astride the Mulde River in Saxony. Built originally as a hunting lodge for the kings of Saxony, it was converted in 1800 into a prison and in 1838 into a lunatic asylum. Before World War II it was used as a camp for the Hitler Youth.

WORLD WAR II. During the early days of the war German administrators decided to use Colditz to confine important prisoners and habitual escapers. It was redesigned for this purpose and made "escape-proof." Polish prisoners of war were followed by Dutch, Belgian, French, British, and others. The maximum figure was set at 200, but many more were held in the cells. The prisoners were graded according to their rank. About 20 were designated *Prominente,* or more important prisoners, including Capt. Earl Haig, Lt. Viscount Lascelles, and Lt. Romilly, who was related to Churchill.

ESCAPES. On the afternoon of April 12, 1941, a French officer was missing—the first escape from Colditz. Most persistent of the escapers was Lt. Michael Sinclair (*q.v.*), known as the Red Fox, who was eventually killed by his guards. In all 130 prisoners escaped, of which only 32 (14 French, 8 British, 9 Dutch, and 1 Pole) managed to cross the frontiers.

LIBERATION. As the German war machine ground to a halt, conditions at Colditz worsened. By this time only elderly guards could be found to work at the prison. Food and fuel were in short supply. In mid-April 1945, American troops pushed their way to Colditz and freed the remaining prisoners. They found evidence of a bizarre attempt at escape: In the upper attic over the chapel the prisoners had built a glider in sections for launching.

Bibliography. P. R. Reid, *The Colditz Story* (1952); R. Eggers, *Colditz* (1961); and J. M. Green, *From Colditz in Code* (1971).

COLLINGWOOD, CHARLES CUMMINGS (1917–   ). U.S. radio commentator and newspaper correspondent.

A Rhodes scholar at Oxford, Collingwood left in June 1940 to work full time for the United Press (UP) in London. In March 1941 he was hired by Edward R. Murrow (*q.v.*), head of Columbia Broadcasting System (CBS) correspondents in Europe. At first he broadcast from London to the United States and then was sent to North Africa. Here he managed to penetrate the screen of censorship and provide his audience at home with a realistic and straightforward account of battle actions. He was one of the most successful and highly regarded American journalists of the war.

Tall, blond, curly-haired, Collingwood was known for his vigor, skepticism, and sense of humor. A scrupulous dresser, he was said to be "the only man in Africa who knows where to get a suit pressed."

COLLINS, JOSEPH LAWTON (1896–1963). U.S. Army officer known as "Lightning Joe" because he commanded in the Pacific the 25th "Lightning" Division (his men wore a shoulder patch depicting a bolt of lightning).

Collins's first assignment in the war was to Hawaii, where he reorganized and revised the defense of the islands. He took part in the assault on Guadalcanal in September 1942. In December 1943 he was transferred to England and the following February assumed command of the 7th Corps during its training for the coming amphibious assault on the European mainland. He landed with his men on Utah Beach (*q.v.*), captured Cherbourg, and led the breakout from Normandy and the drive into Germany.

Attaining a reputation in Europe for aggressiveness, he was picked by Gen. Bernard Law Montgomery (*q.v.*) to lead the counterattack into the north shoulder of the "bulge."

COLOGNE, BOMBING OF. Devastating assault on the Rhineland city by Allied aircraft in 1942 in the first 1,000-bomber attack of the war (*Operation Millenium*).

TARGET. Cologne (German Köln, Roman Colonia Agrippina) was then the third largest city in Germany. The chief town of the Rhineland, it was in North Rhine-Westphalia. Its commercial importance was due largely to its situation in a lignite-mining area and to its chief industries, including the manufacture of metals, machinery, textiles, chemicals, and foodstuffs. For the British Bomber Command it was strategically important as the center of river, road, and rail communications in the Rhineland. The problem was to bomb the city without destroying the world-famous archiepiscopal Gothic catherdral, one of the most splendid buildings in Europe, and thereby risk global condemnation.

BACKGROUND. Like many other West German cities, Cologne until the end of May 1942 had been raided frequently by British planes. It experienced

268 alerts and 107 actual raids. Gen. Arthur T. (''Bomber'') Harris, (*q.v.*), chief of the British Bomber Command, in early 1942 broached the plan for a demonstrative giant attack on one German city—either Hamburg, Essen, or Cologne. Opponents believed that an increase from 228 planes, the biggest concentration until that time, to a 1,000-bomber raid, was far too risky for the Allies. Harris had his way because he won the consent of Churchill.

ATTACK. At the last moment, on the basis of weather reports, Cologne was chosen as the target. On the night of May 30, 1942, pathfinder planes released floating flares over the city. Then came squadron after squadron to unload their bombs. In all, 1,047 aircraft took off from 52 British airfields. Within the space of 90 minutes, 900 attacking planes dropped 1,455 tons of bombs on the city, two-thirds of them incendiaries. Other planes hit at antiaircraft positions and night-fighter airfields.

LOSSES. In this one raid 460 Germans lost their lives. The total would have been much higher but for the fact that the people of Cologne had had much experience with Allied raids and had developed a strong civil-defense discipline. More than 45,000 people lost their homes, and thousands of fugitives began to surge out of the city.

The material damage was great. More than 12,000 fires were started, and 1,700 of them became local conflagrations. Nearly one-tenth of the entire metropolitan area was devastated and practically the entire Old Town was destroyed. Whole industrial areas were wrecked, including cable works, shell-fuse factories, chemical plants, and an aluminum foundry. Factories turning out internal combustion engines, trucks, submarine batteries, and wire hawsers were badly damaged.

The cost to the Royal Air Force (*q.v.*) was 39 planes, considerably less than the 100 predicted by Churchill.

CATHEDRAL. Bomber Harris had briefed his men well. He gave firm instructions to avoid damaging the great Cologne cathedral and his orders were followed to the letter in an amazing display of precision bombing. The cathedral suffered some damage to its walls, but the main structure survived. Important contents, such as the 15th-century painting *Adoration of the Magi,* by Stefan Lochner, and the 14th-century stained glass of the choir windows, were taken to places of safety, along with the archives and the library. Also saved were such treasures as the medieval gold reliquary of the Three Magi, whose bones were supposed to have been brought to Cologne by Emperor Frederick I in 1162.

AFTERMATH. The giant raid on Cologne was a severe blow to German morale. It indicated the rapidly increasing strength of Allied air power, now dedicated to strategic bombing with navigation aids. It was first assumed that

American bombers had taken part in the raid, and when that was not confirmed there was shock at the extraordinary strength of the Royal Air Force. An astonished Hermann Goering (*q.v.*) refused to believe it. "Impossible," he said, "that many bombs cannot be dropped in a single night."

To appease public opinion Hitler ordered a reprisal campaign, which ended with two small "Baedeker" raids, one of which was on Canterbury on May 31, 1942, and the other on October 31, 1942, on York as a reprisal for a British raid on Mainz. (*See* BAEDEKER RAIDS.)

The 1,000-plane raid on Cologne on May 30–31, 1942, was not the last on that Rhineland city. In all Cologne had 2,300 alerts and 252 raids. In succeeding raids the RAF (*q.v.*) destroyed over 80 percent of the central city and 75 percent of the districts on the west bank of the Rhine. Nearly 100 factories were hit, railway communications smashed, and U-Boat equipment plants destroyed. In 1943 Cologne suffered more than any other city in the Rhine district. Further attacks in 1944 and 1945 leveled more of the city and 2,000 acres lay in ruins. (*See also* AIR RAIDS.)

Bibliography. N. MacMillan, *The Royal Air Force in the World War,* 4 vols. (1949–1950); A. T. Harris, *Bomber Offensive* (1947); G. Bowman, *Strategic Bombing* (1956); and Hans Rumpf, *The Bombing of Germany,* trans. by Edward Fitzgerald (1963).

COMBINED INTELLIGENCE COMMITTEE (CIC). U.S. intelligence evaluation committee established in Washington by the Combined Chiefs of Staff. (*See* ESPIONAGE.)

COMET LINE. An underground escape route in Belgium through which hundreds of downed British airmen and escaped Allied prisoners were able to reach freedom. (*See* JONGH, ANDRÉE.)

COMINCH. Commander-in-Chief U.S. Navy.

The old abbreviation, CINCUS, pronounced Sink Us, was dropped for obvious reaons after Pearl Harbor (*q.v.*). Twelve days after the disaster, Adm. Ernest J. King (*q.v.*), then 63 years old and on the verge of retirement, was summoned to Washington and named COMINCH.

COMMISSAR ORDER. Instructions issued by Hitler shortly before the opening of his Russian campaign in 1941, according to which captured Russian commissars were to be shot.

Early in March 1941 Hitler convoked chiefs of staff of the three armed services and the top Army field commanders and informed them how he intended to fight the campaign against the Russians. His hatred of Bolshevism was so great that on June 6, 1941, he ordered his field commanders to liquidate all captured commissars. Gen. Franz Halder (*q.v.*) recorded the words and repeated them in his testimony at Nuremberg:[*]

---

[*]Halder affidavit, November 22, 1945, at Nuremberg. *See Nazi Conspiracy and Aggression,* (10 vols., 1940), vol. 8, pp. 645–646.

The war against Russia will be such that it cannot be conducted in a knightly fashion. This struggle is one of ideologies and racial differences and will have to be conducted with unprecedented, unmerciful, and unrelenting harshness. All officers will have to rid themselves of obsolete ideologies. I know that the necessity for such means of waging war is beyond the comprehension of you generals. . . .

I insist absolutely that my orders be executed without contradiction. The commissars are the bearers of ideologies directly opposed to National Socialism. Therefore the commissars will be liquidated.

COMPIÈGNE. Scene of the surrender of France to the Germans on June 22, 1940.

BACKGROUND. On November 11, 1918, the armistice that brought an end to World War I was signed in a railway coach in the forest near Compiègne, a French town on the left bank of the Oise. The forest, covering 30,000 acres, had once been the favorite hunting ground of French royalty. Here Marshal Ferdinand Foch, on behalf of the Allies, handed the stiff terms of the armistice to German plenipotentiaries.

Elated by his victory of the French in June 1940, Hitler ordered that the surrender be taken at the precise spot in the forest of Compiègne and in the same railway car that had been used in 1918. Hitler regarded a gesture of this kind as historical justice: In 1919 the Allies had chosen the Hall of Mirrors at Versailles to dictate peace terms to Germany—the same hall in which the Second German Empire had been proclaimed by Bismarck on January 18, 1871. Later the *Fuehrer* would be just as historical minded.

The ceremony at Compiègne was described in a dramatic broadcast by William L. Shirer over the Columbia Broadcasting System. Phrasing his reactions speedily, with no opportunity to polish his delivery, Shirer improvised from notes in what turned out to be one of the most memorable reporting events of World War II:*

ANNOUNCER: At this time, as the French government considers Germany's terms for an armistice, Columbia takes you to Berlin for a special broadcast by William Shirer in Germany. We take you now to Berlin. Go ahead, Berlin.

SHIRER: Hello, America! CBS! William L. Shirer calling CBS in New York.

William L. Shirer calling CBS in New York, calling CBS from Compiègne, France. This is William L. Shirer of CBS. We've got a microphone at the edge of a little clearing in the forest of Compiègne, four miles to the north of the town of Compiègne and about forty-five miles north of Paris. Here, a few feet from where we're standing, in the very same old railroad coach where the Armistice was signed on that chilly morning of November 11, 1918, negotiations for another armistice—the one to end the present war between France and Germany—began at 3:30 P.M., German summer time, this afternoon. What a turning back of the clock, what a reversing of history we've been watching here in this beautiful Compiègne Forest this afternoon! What a contrast to that day

*Courtesy of William L. Shirer.

twenty-two years ago! Yes, even the weather, for we have one of those lovely warm June days which you get in this part of France close to Paris about this time of year.

As we stood here, watching Adolf Hitler and Field Marshal Göring and the other German leaders laying down the terms of the armistice to the French plenipotentiaries here this afternoon, it was difficult to comprehend that in this rustic litle clearing in the midst of the Forest of Compiègne, from where we're talking to you now, that an armistice was signed here on the cold, cold morning at five A.M. on November 11, 1918. The railroad coach—it was Marshal Foch's private car—stands a few feet away from us here, in exactly the same spot where it stood on that gray morning twenty-two years ago, only—and what an "only" it is, too—Adolf Hitler sat in the seat occupied that day by Marshal Foch. Hitler at that time was only an unknown corporal in the German army, and in that quaint old wartime car another armistice is being drawn up as I speak to you now, an armistice designed like the other that was signed on this spot to bring armed hostilities to halt between those ancient enemies—Germany and France. Only everything that we've been seeing here this afternoon in Compiègne Forest has been so reversed. The last time the representatives of France sat in that car dictating the terms of the armistice. This afternoon we peered through the windows of the car and saw Adolf Hitler laying down the terms. That's how history reversed itself, but seldom has it done so as today on the very same spot. The German leader in the preamble of the conditions which were read to the French delegates by Colonel General von Keitel, Chief of the German Supreme Command, told the French that he had not chosen this spot at Compiègne out of revenge but merely to right a wrong.

The armistice negotiations here on the same spot where the last armistice was signed in 1918, here in Compiègne Forest, began at 3:15 P.M., our time; a warm June sun beat down on the great elm and pine trees and cast purple shadows on the hooded avenues as Herr Hitler with the German plenipotentiaries at his side appeared. He alighted from his car in front of the French monument to Alsace-Lorraine which stands at the end of an avenue about two hundred yards from the clearing here in front of us where the armistice car stands. That famous Alsace-Lorraine statue was covered with German war flags, so that you cannot see its sculptured works or read its inscriptions. I had seen it many times in the postwar years, and doubtless many of you have seen it—the large sword representing the sword of the Allies, with its point sticking into a large, limp eagle, representing the old empire of the Kaiser, and the inscription underneath in front saying, "To the heroic soldiers of France, defenders of the country and of right, glorious liberators of Alsace-Lorraine."

Through our glasses, we saw the Führer stop, glance at the statue, observe the Reich war flags with their big swastikas in the center. Then he strolled slowly toward us, toward the little clearing where the famous armistice car stood. I thought he looked very solemn: his face was grave. But there was a certain spring in his step, as he walked for the first time toward the spot where Germany's fate was sealed on that November day of 1918, a fate which, by reason of his own being, is now being radically changed here on this spot.

And now, if I may sort of go over my notes—I made from moment to moment this afternoon—now Hitler reaches a little opening in the Compiègne woods where the Armistice was signed and where another is about to be drawn up. He pauses and slowly looks around. The opening here is in the form of a circle about two hundred yards in diameter and laid out like a park. Cypress trees line it all around, and behind them the great elms and oaks of the forest. This had been one of France's national shrines for twenty-two years. Hitler pauses and gazes slowly around. In the group just behind him are the other Germans plenipotentiaries—Field Marshal Göring, grasping his Field Marshal baton in one hand. He wears the blue uniform of the air force. All the Germans are in uniform, Hitler in a double-breasted gray uniform with the Iron Cross hanging from his left breast pocket. Next to Göring are the two German army chiefs, Colonel General von Keitel, Chief of the Supreme Command, and Colonal General von Brauchitsch, Commander-in-Chief of the German Army. Both are just approaching sixty, but look younger, especially General von Keitel, who has a dapper appearance, with his cap slightly cocked on one side. Then we see there Dr. Raeder, Grand Admiral of the German Fleet. He has on a blue naval uniform and the invariable upturned still collar which German naval officers usually wear. We see two nonmilitary men in Hitler's suite—his Foreign Minister, Joachim von Ribbentrop, in the field-gray uniform of the Foreign Office, and Rudolf Hess, Hitler's deputy, in a gray party uniform.

The time's now, I see by my notes, 3:18 P.M., in the Forest of Compiègne. Hitler's personal standard is run up on a small post in the center of the circular opening in the woods. Also, in the center, is a great granite block which stands some three feet above the ground. Hitler, followed by the others, walks slowly over to it, steps up, and reads the inscription engraved in great high letters on that block. Many of you will remember the words of that inscription. The Führer slowly reads them, and the inscription says, "Here on the eleventh of November, 1918, succumbed the criminal pride of the German Empire, vanquished by the free peoples which it tried to enslave." Hitler reads it, and Göring reads it. They all read it, standing there in the June sun and the silence. We look for the expression on Hitler's face, but it does not change. Finally he leads his party over to another granite stone, a small one some fifty yards to one side. Here it was that the railroad car in which the German plenipotentiary stayed during the 1918 armistice negotiations stood from November 8 to 11. Hitler looks down and reads the inscription, which merely says: "The German plenipotentiary." The stone itself, I notice, is set between a pair of rusty old railroad tracks, the very ones that were there twenty-two years ago.

It is now 3:23 P.M., and the German leaders stride over to the armistice car. This car, of course, was not standing on this spot yesterday. It was standing seventy-five yards down the rusty track in the shelter of a tiny museum built to house it by an American citizen, Mr. Arthur Henry Fleming of Pasadena, California. Yesterday the car was removed from the museum by the German army engineers and rolled back those seventy-five yards to the spot where it stood on the morning of November 11, 1918. The Germans stand outside the car, chatting in the sunlight. This goes on for two minutes. Then Hitler steps up into the car, followed by Göring and the others. We watch them entering the drawing room of Marshal Foch's car. We can see nicely now through the car window.

Hitler enters first and takes the place occupied by Marshal Foch the morning the first armistice was signed. At his sides are Göring and General Keitel. To his right and left at the ends of the table we see General von Brauchitsch and Herr Hess at the one end, at the other end Grand Admiral Raeder and Herr von Ribbentrop. The opposite side of the table is still empty, and we see there four vacant chairs. The French have not yet appeared, but we do not wait long. Exactly at 3:30 P.M. the French alight from a car. They have flown up from Bordeaux to a near-by landing field and then have driven here in an auto.

They glance at the Alsace-Lorraine memorial, now draped with swastikas, but it's a swift glance. Then they walk down the avenue flanked by three German army officers. We see them now as they come into the sunlight of the clearing—General Huntziger, wearing a brief khaki uniform; General Bergeret and Vice-Admiral Le Luc, both in their respective dark-blue uniforms; and then, almost buried in the uniforms, the one single civilian of the day, Mr. Noël, French Ambassador to Poland when the present war broke out there. The French plenipotentiaries passed the guard of honor drawn up at the entrance of the clearing. The guard snapped to attention for the French but did not present arms. The Frenchmen keep their eyes straight ahead. It's a grave hour in the life of France, and their faces today show what a burden they feel on their shoulders. Their faces are solemn, drawn, but bear the expression of tragic dignity. They walked quickly to the car and were met by two German officers, Lieutenant Colonel Tippelskirch, Quartermaster General, and Colonel Thomas, Chief of the Paris Headquarters. The Germans salute; the French salute; the atmosphere is what Europeans call "correct"; but you'll get the picture when I say that we see no handshakes—not on occasions like this. The historic moment is now approaching. It is 3:32 by my watch. The Frenchmen enter Marshal Foch's Pullman car, standing there a few feet from us in Compiègne Forest. Now we get our picture through the dusty windows of the historic old *wagon-lit* car. Hitler and the other German leaders rise from their seats as the French enter the drawing room. Hitler, we see, gives the Nazi salute, the arm raised. The German officers give a military salute; the French do the same. I cannot see Mr. Noël to see whether he salutes or how. Hitler, so far as we can see through the windows just in front of here, does not say anything. He nods to General Keitel at his side. We can see General Keitel adjusting his papers, and then he starts to read. He is reading the preamble of the German armistice terms. The French sit there with marblelike faces and listen intently. Hitler and Göring glance at the green table top. This part of the historic act lasts but a few moments. I note in my notebook here this—3:42 P.M.—that is, twelve minutes after the French arrived—3:42—we see Hitler stand up, salute the three with hand upraised. Then he strides out of the room, followed by Göring, General von Brauchitsch; Grand Admiral Raeder is there, Herr Hess, and, at the end, von Ribbentrop. The French remain at the green-topped table in the old Pullman car, and we see General Keitel remains with them. He is going to read them the detailed conditions of the armistice. Hitler goes, and the others do not wait for this. They walk down the avenue back towards the Alsace-Lorraine monument. As they pass the guard of honor, a German band strikes up the two national anthems *Deutschland über Alles* and the *Horst Wessel Song*.

The whole thing has taken but a quarter of an hour—this great reversal of a historical armistice of only a few years ago.

CBS ANNOUNCER: You have just heard a special broadcast from the Compiègne Forest in France, where on the historic morning of November 11, 1918, representatives of the German army received from the Allies the terms of the armistice which ended the First World War, and where today, June 22, 1940, representatives of the French government received from Führer Adolf Hitler the terms under which a cessation of hostilities between Germany and France may be reached. As you know, the actual terms presented to the French plenipotentiaries have not yet been made public.

MUSIC: *Organ.*

ANNOUNCER: This is the Columbia Broadcasting System.

CONCENTRATION CAMPS. Nazi system of permanent detention camps in which millions of opponents and so-called undesirables were held without trial or sentence.

DISCOVERY. Rumors of horrors about concentration camps leaked out from Germany before the end of the war. Few people believed the stories at the time. Most remembered the exaggerated Allied propaganda of World War I with its tales of dismembered victims and infants boiled in oil to make grease for the Kaiser's war machine. But then came the ghastly facts of Nazi brutality revealed by Allied liberating forces. Battle-hardened veterans, inured to the sight and smell of death, were sickened by what they saw. Staggering out to meet them were walking skeletons, their bodies stripped of flesh and their minds crippled by disease and starvation. Gen. Dwight D. Eisenhower (*q.v.*) recorded that he had "never at any other time experienced an equal sense of shock." He urged Washington and London to send observers to see the indisputable evidence.

BACKGROUND. The term *concentration camp* was first used in the 20th century to describe centers in South Africa where Boer civilians were interned from 1900 to 1902 to prevent them from helping guerrillas. The camps had a notorious reputation because of inefficient administration and bad hygienic conditions.

Hitler regarded concentration camps as a prime necessity for the survival of Nazism. The Germans, he said before assuming political power, must be purged of "softness and sentimental philistinism. . . . We have no time for fine sentiments. I don't want the concentration camps transferred into penitentiary institutions. Terror is the most effective instrument."

CONSTRUCTION. Shortly after he became Chancellor in early 1933, Hitler began building a system of concentration camps. The public was informed that the purpose was to "reform" and "educate" political opponents and to turn "anti-social members of society into useful members." A law promulgated on February 28, 1933, suspended those clauses of the constitution which guaranteed personal liberties, and provided for *Schutzhaft* ("protective custody") for dissenters.

LOCATION. The first three extermination camps (*q.v.*) were Dachau in the south, Buchenwald near Weimar in central Germany, and Sachsenhausen near Berlin in the north. Scores of others followed, including Netzweiler in the south; Flossenbürg, Theresienstadt, and Gross-Rosen in central Germany; and Neuengamme, Belsen, and Ravensbruck in the north. Mauthausen was set up in Austria, Vught in the Netherlands.

INMATES. The first inmates were Communists and Jews, who were followed by democrats, Catholics, Protestants, and dissident Nazis. Others sent to the camps included trade union leaders, clergymen, monks, priests, nuns, pacifists, Gypsies, and Jehovah's Witnesses. Prisoners were divided into four categories: political opponents; "inferior races"; criminals; and "asocial shiftless elements." Political opponents included anti-Nazis, foreign exchange violators, illegal radio listeners, grumblers, and Jehovah's Witnesses. The latter refused to take an oath to Hitler. "Inferior races," embracing Jews and Gypsies, were marked for "special attention." Segregated in separate barracks, they were either worked to death or allowed to starve. Ordinary criminals were mixed with other political prisoners. The "shiftless elements" included homosexuals.

IDENTIFICATION. Inmates were identified by elaborate and prescribed markings. Political prisoners wore a red triangle; criminals, green; shiftless elements, black; homosexuals, pink; Gypsies, brown; and Jews, yellow (the yellow triangle pointed up and an additional triangle below formed the Star of David). Foreigners were identified by letters: *P* for Poland and *F* for France. The letter *K* indicated a war criminal; the letter *A* (from *Arbeit,* "work") identified those selected for labor. The term *Blöd* ("stupid") was worn by the feeble-minded. Anyone trying to escape was required to wear a red-and-white target sewn on both front and back of his jacket. Under this thorough identification system, some inmates were decked out in a variety of colors.

CONDITIONS. The situation in the camps varied widely throughout Germany. Conditions became progressively worse during the war. Allied blockade and the resultant lack of food affected all concentration camps. New camp leaders, including Josef Kramer, who worked at Belsen, and Rudolf Hoess (*q.v.*), who was attached originally to Dachau, introduced severe measures in dealing with inmates. Prisoners were beaten and kicked as a routine part of their daily life. Many lost their lives in cesspools, on electric barbed wires, or by medical experimentation.

In the midst of the war, several camps inside Germany, notably Dachau and Buchenwald, were converted into extermination centers with gas chambers and crematoria. Several of these death camps were constructed in Poland. (*See* EXTERMINATION CAMPS; and FINAL SOLUTION.)

SIGNIFICANCE. Cruelties in Nazi concentration camps were such as to be incomprehensible to the normal human mind. Knowledge of concentration camp horrors was responsible in large part for creation of the Allied Military Tribunal to try Nazi leaders. (*See* NUREMBERG TRIALS.)

Bibliography. N. Levin, *The Holocaust* (1968); P. Julitte, *Block 26: Sabotage at Buchenwald* (1971); and G. Reitlinger, *The Final Solution* (1971).

CONFERENCES, ALLIED WAR. A series of conferences held by Allied war leaders for the purpose of agreement on the next steps to be taken in the war effort. (*See individual entries for details*). The table is limited to conferences that concerned the European theater of operations. (*See* pp. 162–163.)

CONINGHAM, ARTHUR (1895–1948). British Air Marshal.

In 1941 Coningham was made Air Vice-Marshal and given command of the No. 4 Group of the RAF Bomber Command in support of the 8th Army in North Africa. He served in this post during the Libya campaign from 1940 to 1942. He took part in the Allied drive in Tunisia in 1943 and in the Mediterranean from 1943 to 1944 as commander of the 1st Tactical Air Force of the RAF. In early 1944 he was selected as commander of the 2nd Tactical Air Force of British and American units which took part in the invasion of Fortress Europe. (*See* NORMANDY INVASION.) A month after the landings he moved to Normandy to command 100,000 airmen of seven nations. Directly after the war Coningham was made Commander-in-Chief of the Flying Command of the RAF. He was named Air Marshal in 1946 and was created a Knight Commander of the Order of the British Empire that same year. He died in an air crash on a flight from the Azores to Bermuda on January 30, 1948.

CONVOY SYSTEM. Groups of merchant ships sailing together under protection of warships.

The convoy system was adopted in World War I as a desperate measure to combat the success of the German U-Boat campaign. Although strategy, tactics, and weapons changed, the convoy system was preserved in its essentials. Organization of convoys called for careful planning on both sides of the Atlantic and elsewhere. Gun crews were provided and regular schedules of sailings organized. Convoys were protected near shore by patrolling planes overhead and in the mid-Atlantic by escorts of destroyers and other warships.

The convoys suffered heavy losses in the spring of 1943, but the balance tilted in dramatic fashion against U-Boats and their wolf-pack tactics (*q.v.*). Without the convoy system the Allies might well have lost the war.

Bibliography. G. Bennett, *Naval Battles of World War II* (1975).

CONVOY *ON-127*. A westbound convoy attacked by German U-Boats in 1942.

Convoy *ON-127* set out from ports in southern England with 32 merchant ships. Beginning on September 10, 1942, a wolf pack of 13 U-Boats moved on the convoy and pressed the attack for four days. (*See* WOLF-PACK TACTICS.) German submarines sank 12 freighters and an accompanying destroyer. The wolf pack retreated with only one of its U-Boats damaged. The remainder of the convoy reached the vicinity of Newfoundland, where it came under a protective air umbrella.

Allied War Conferences (European Theater of Operations)

PLACE	DATE	CODE NAME	MAIN PARTICIPANTS	MAJOR DECISIONS
ARGENTIA BAY	Aug. 14, 1941	—	Roosevelt, Churchill	Agreement on war aims. Atlantic Charter.
WASHINGTON (First)	Dec. 24, 1941–Jan. 14, 1942	ARCADIA	Roosevelt, Churchill	Combined Chiefs of Staff agree on priority for Atlantic theater of war. Twenty-five nations sign United Nations Declaration.
WASHINGTON (Second)	June 25–27, 1942	—	Roosevelt, Churchill	Subjects discussed: war production; shipping; aid for China; diversion of German strength from eastern front; North African invasion.
CASABLANCA	Jan. 14–23, 1943	SYMBOL	Roosevelt, Churchill	Plans for invasion of Sicily. Decision for cross-Channel invasion in 1944. Stepped-up Battle of the Atlantic. "Unconditional surrender" declaration by Roosevelt.
WASHINGTON (Third)	May 11–27, 1943	TRIDENT	Roosevelt, Churchill	Plans for further pressure in Italy. Increased air attack on Germany. Stepped-up war in the Pacific. Invasion of France.
QUEBEC (First)	Aug. 17–24, 1943	QUADRANT	Roosevelt, Churchill	"Final" decision to invade France. Reorganization of Southeast Asia command.
MOSCOW	Oct. 18–Nov. 1, 1943	—	Foreign ministers Hull, Eden, Molotov	Declaration with China on post-war security and cooperation. Establishment of European Advisory Council. Advisory Council for Italy. Democratic regime for Austria. Punishment of war criminals.
CAIRO	Nov. 22–26, 1943	SEXTANT	Roosevelt, Churchill. Chiang Kai-shek	Agreement on military operations against the Japanese in China. Manchuria promised to China. Free Korea.

PLACE	DATE	CODE NAME	MAIN PARTICIPANTS	MAJOR DECISIONS
TEHERAN	Nov. 28–Dec. 1, 1943	EUREKA	Roosevelt, Churchill, Stalin	Agreement on date of invasion of Western Europe. Declaration on Iran. Aid for Tito and Yugoslav Partisans.
BRETTON WOODS	July 1–22, 1944	—	Representatives of 44 nations	Agreement on International Monetary Fund. Establishment of International Bank for Reconstruction and Development.
DUMBARTON OAKS	Aug. 21–Sept. 28, 1944	—	Representatives of U.S., U.K., and USSR	Agreement on an international organization.
QUEBEC (Second)	Sept. 12–16, 1944	OCTAGON	Roosevelt, Churchill	Plans for completion of European war. Plans for Pacific war.
YALTA	Feb. 4–12, 1945	ARGONAUT	Roosevelt, Churchill, Stalin	Plans dealing with defeat of Germany. Declaration of policy for liberated Europe. Recommendations on establishment of new Polish Provisional Government. Formation of new Yugoslav Government. Permanent machinery for consultation of foreign ministers. Decision to call Conference of United Nations at San Francisco on April 25 to prepare United Nations Charter. Kurile Islands and South Sakhalin to be handed over to the Soviet Union for aid in war against Japan (secret agreement).
POTSDAM	July 17–Aug. 2, 1945	TERMINAL	Truman, Churchill, Attlee, Stalin	Potsdam Declaration. Agreement on Council of Ministers. Agreement on political and economic principles to govern treatment of Germany during control period. Agreement on reparations. Statement on Poland. Statement on peace with the satellites.

CONVOY *PQ-17*. Allied merchant ship convoy that was heavily hit by the Germans when it was proceeding to the Soviet Union.

BACKGROUND. In the summer of 1942 Stalin, concerned about the German assault on Russia, was not only demanding a Second Front (*q.v.*) to relieve pressure on the Red Army, but also huge amounts of supplies and war materials from the West. To meet requests of their new ally, the Western Allies organized great convoys of merchant ships to deliver supplies and war matériel to the Soviet Union. The convoys sailed into dangerous waters patrolled by German sea and air units. Starting in September 1941 the first of the so-called *PQ* convoys sailed for the Soviet Union.

PQ-17. On June 27, 1942, the 17th *PQ* convoy, consisting of 35 merchant ships, left Hvalfjord, Iceland, for Archangel. The convoy was to cross 1,000 miles of the Arctic Ocean, head due east, pass between Spitzbergen and Bear Island in the direction of the Barents Sea, and then turn south in a wide sweep into the ports of Archangel and Murmansk (*q.v.*). With the convoy went an escort of 6 destroyers, and 11 smaller craft. On July 1, 1942, a U-Boat commander flashed word to German Naval Headquarters, which ordered more submarines to the scene to intercept the rich prize.

BATTLE FLEETS. The British Admiralty countered by deploying northward from Scapa Flow a large naval force, including the aircraft carrier *Victorious*, the battleships *Duke of York* and USS *Washington*, and a dozen destroyers. The Germans sent out a strong naval force of their own, including the battleship *Tirpitz* (*q.v.*), the pocket battleships *Lützow* and *Admiral Scheer* (*q.v.*) and 10 destroyers. It seemed for a time that a major naval engagement was about to take place, when the German High Command, on Hitler's orders, signalled the surface fleet to return to home port. Even though the Allied covering force might not have been able to reach the convoy in time, the *Fuehrer* decided not to risk his battle fleet.

The merchant ships, now scattered over a wide area, were defenseless against German attack. A hide-and-seek battle continued for several days.

LOSSES. When it was over, convoy *PQ-17* had lost 24 of its 35 ships, 140,000 tons of shipping, and many lives. Cargo losses were estimated at more than 200 aircraft, 400 tanks, 3,300 vehicles, and large supplies of war equipment. The remaining ships reached Archangel with 70,000 of the original 200,000 tons of supplies.

Bibliography. H. Busch, *U-Boats at War* (1955); P. Lund and H. Ludlum, *PQ-17: Convoy to Hell* (1968); and D. Irving, *The Destruction of Convoy PQ-17* (1969); and L. Kennedy, *The Death of the Tirpitz* (1979).

CONVOY *PQ-18*. Allied convoy of merchant ships headed for the Soviet Union and damaged by German attack in 1942.

BACKGROUND. The disastrous fate of convoy *PQ-17* (*q.v.*) in early July 1942 convinced the British Admiralty that it had to give more protection to its merchant ships. The 43 ships of convoy *PQ-18,* which sailed 10 weeks later, were given an escort of 20 destroyers, a cruiser, 2 antiaircraft ships, 2 submarines, and such smaller craft as 4 corvettes, 3 minesweepers, and 4 trawlers. Behind this escort was a covering force of 3 heavy cruisers, 2 battleships, a light cruiser, and 5 additional destroyers. The Admiralty believed this covering power to be more than enough to ward off any attack on convoy *PQ-18.*

ATTACK. On September 12, 1942, German reconnaissance planes found the convoy and reported back to base. The next day a coordinated plane and U-Boat attack on the ships began. The assault continued sporadically for the better part of a week. From bases in Britain pilots of the Royal Air Force (*q.v.*) set out to engage attacking *Luftwaffe* planes.

LOSSES. Both sides suffered losses. Thirteen out of the 43 merchant ships were sunk. The Germans lost 27 planes and 3 U-Boats.

CONVOY *SC-94.* An eastbound convoy of merchant ships attacked by German U-Boats in 1942.

Convoy *SC-94* set out from Canadian ports with 36 ships protected by a strong escort. U-Boat attacks lasted from August 5 to 10, 1942. The convoy lost 13 of its 36 ships. The Germans lost two U-Boats sunk and two damaged.

CONVOY *SG-19.* Convoy attacked by German U-Boats on February 3, 1943. (*See* FOUR CHAPLAINS.)

COONEYS. Special teams trained by the Allies to disrupt German communication in Brittany in northern France during the invasion of June 6, 1944. The Cooneys served along with the Jedburghs (*q.v.*) for these special missions. (*See* NORMANDY INVASION.)

COOPER, ALFRED DUFF (1890–1954). British statesman and Minister of Information in World War II.

From 1940 to 1941 Cooper was Minister of Information in the Churchill Government. After the Allied disaster in France in May 1940, he broadcast a hopeful message to the British people, quoting Shakespeare's lines about St. Crispin's day from *Henry V* counseling against not only panic itself but the very idea of panic as well. An ardent Francophile, he worked unceasingly for Anglo-French cooperation and gave his support to Gen. Charles de Gaulle (*q.v.*). He was appointed Ambassador to France in 1944.

Bibliography. A. D. Cooper, *Second World War* (1939) and *Selected Papers* (1957). *See also* Watchman, pseud., *Right Honorable Gentleman* (1939).

CORAL SEA, BATTLE OF THE. Major naval battle between the Japanese and Allied navies in May 1942. It was the first of a series of sea-air confrontations that were to become common in the Pacific theater of war between 1942 and 1945.

BACKGROUND. For six months after Pearl Harbor (*q.v.*) the triumphant Japanese pushed their way through the Pacific and set up strong perimeters of defense. Australia was an attractive target. Possession of this huge continent, almost helpless at the time, would round out Japan's Greater East Asia Co-Prosperity Sphere (*q.v.*). As early as February 1942, Japanese planes bombed Port Darwin, Australia's only major naval base in the north. For the next two months the Japanese methodically attempted to isolate Australia from the north, occupying New Britain, New Ireland, the Admiralty Islands, the Gilbert Islands, and parts of New Guinea.

In the spring of 1942 the Japanese Imperial GHQ decided on a major two-pronged thrust. A great task force would be sent to capture Midway Island as a threat to Hawaii. (*See* MIDWAY, BATTLE OF.) At the same time another task force would extend the Japanese hold on the Solomon Islands in the south by taking Port Moresby on New Guinea and isolating Australia from the United States. Japanese forces had been trying to take Port Moresby by land, but they had bogged down in New Zealand's virtually impassable mountain ranges.

DEFENSE. Gen. Douglas MacArthur (*q.v.*), who had been ordered to leave the Philippines, arrived in Australia on March 17, 1942, with explicit instructions to set up a defense system in the Pacific. He decided for strategic reasons to base his operations north of the great continent and set up his headquarters at Port Moresby. By this time military and naval reinforcements and supplies began to flow from the United States. Washington had broken the Japanese code and was aware that the decision had been made to send a huge invasion fleet down past the Solomon Islands and into the Coral Sea.

PREPARATIONS. For the southern thrust a large naval force with carriers was gathered at Rabaul (*q.v.*), the Japanese stronghold in the south, and made ready for action. It was commanded by Vice-Adm. Shigeyoshi Inouye, who was to be assisted by the carriers *Shokaku* and *Zuikaku* with 125 naval aircraft. To meet the Japanese a task force of American and Australian ships, under command of Rear Adm. Frank Jack Fletcher (*q.v.*), headed for the Coral Sea. Fletcher had at his disposal two huge flattops, the *Lexington* and *Yorktown*, with 141 aircraft (99 bombers, 42 fighters).

CONFRONTATION. On May 3, 1942, the Japanese captured the Australian island of Tulagi in the Solomons. The next day the *Yorktown*, then 100 miles from Tulagi, launched several strikes but succeeded only in sinking a Japanese destroyer. Vice-Adm. Takeo Takagi's carrier group, then came south, passing to the east of the Solomon Islands and into the Coral Sea. Meanwhile,

the *Lexington* and the *Yorktown* moved north to intercept the Japanese invasion force on the way to Port Moresby. The opposing admirals, almost as if
blindfolded, groped toward each other, at one time only 70 miles apart.

Early on May 7, 1942, Japanese planes sank an American destroyer and an oil
supply ship. The pilots mistakenly reported to Tokyo that they had accounted
for an American carrier and a cruiser. That same day planes from the *Yorktown*
sank the Japanese light carrier *Shoho* in 10 minutes—one of the quickest sinkings in the entire war, while losing 3 planes. On that day the Japanese lost 26
planes in aerial combat and accidents, 6 of which tried to land on the *Yorktown*
in the gathering darkness.

The two evenly matched carrier forces finally came to grips the next day, May
8. Each side had approximately 120 planes available, while their escorts were
almost equal in strength—4 heavy cruisers and 6 destroyers on the Japanese
side, 5 heavy cruisers and 7 destroyers on the American. The Japanese flattop,
Shokaku, was hit by 3 bombs and, unable to launch its aircraft, had to retire
from the action. The *Lexington* suffered 2 torpedo and 2 bomb hits, and after
internal explosions, had to be abandoned. The Americans came off better in
aircraft losses—74 against more than 80 Japanese. The Japanese lost more than
1,000 men in the action, the Americans 343.

SIGNIFICANCE. The Battle of the Coral Sea was the first in history between
fleets that never came within sight of one another. It was also the first battle in
which the rival senior commanders transferred tactical command to their
aircraft-carrier commanders. There was no conventional naval artillery because
the ships never came close enough to exchange fire. As a result of the battle the
aircraft carrier became the great innovation of naval warfare after its first major
test in the Pacific.

The Japanese retired from the scene in the belief that both American carriers
had been sunk. They had been thwarted in the strategic object of capturing
Port Moresby in New Guinea. They now had cause to regret that U.S. carriers
had not been present at Pearl Harbor on December 7, 1941. For the first time
since Pearl Harbor (*q.v.*), the Japanese advance to the south was checked.

The Americans, too, retired from the Coral Sea, but they had achieved their
objective of corking up the Japanese fleet. They had lost a full fleet carrier, but
they had the satisfaction of knowing that the *Shokaku* and *Zuikaku* could not
be used at Midway. Moreover, the *Yorktown* was put into operation shortly
afterward and was able to take part in the action at Midway.

Bibliography. S. Johnston, *Queen of the Flattops: The U.S.S. Lexington and the Coral Sea Battle*
(1942); and S. E. Morison, *The Two-Ocean War* (1963).

CORREGIDOR, FALL OF. Capture of the American fortress in the Philippines by the Japanese in May 1942.

TARGET. Originally a lighthouse station, the island of Corregidor, just 26
miles from Manila, controlled Manila Bay. Among its advantages over the

Philippine capital was its salubrious climate, with offshore breezes bringing welcome relief from the heat.

The Americans regarded Corregidor as their Gibraltar in the Far East. By 1941 they had constructed formidable defenses on the island, including an elaborate tunnel system protected from both air and artillery attack. U.S. engineers drove a shaft from a rock quarry at Bottomside directly through a hill, thereby creating the famous Malinta Tunnel. In this underground stronghold were housed the U.S. and Filipino command headquarters, a 1,000-bed hospital, and a vast quantity of supplies. American and Filipino officials, officers, enlisted men, workers, nurses, and convalescents, all rubbed elbows in a mole-like existence.

For the Japanese, Corregidor was a target of high priority. They regarded control of the island as absolutely necessary for the building of their Greater East Asia Co-Prosperity Sphere (*q.v.*).

BACKGROUND. In the gloom of the early months of the Pacific war between December 7, 1941, and April 1942, the one satisfaction for the Allies had been the spirited defense of American and Filipino forces in the Philippines under Gen. Douglas MacArthur (*q.v.*). The fall of Bataan (*See* BATAAN, BATTLE OF), however, in April 1942 ended formal American resistance on Luzon. But as long as Corregidor and its sister forts remained in U.S. hands, the Japanese were denied the use of Manila Bay in their goal of conquering the southwest Pacific.

On Corregidor Gen. Jonathan M. Wainwright (*q.v.*) had a garrison of 15,000 Americans and Filipino scouts, plus many civilians. Japanese Imperial Headquarters assigned 200,000 of its best troops to take the island.

SIEGE. In April 1942 Japanese heavy artillery hidden on the peninsula began a massive bombardment of the island fortress. Attacks from the air increased in intensity. Inside Corregidor the defenders endured the pounding week after week. As the battle raged, the work of running the garrison went on underground amid heat, dust, flies, and dwindling hope. The defenders braced themselves for the inevitable amphibious assault.

During the night of May 3, 1942, Japanese troops stormed from the beaches toward the Malinta Tunnel. For 12 hours the besieged garrison fought the Japanese to a standstill in hand-to-hand fighting. The next day the Japanese rained 15,000 shells on the island. Two thousand picked Japanese troops crossed the straits and landed at Cavalry Point on the night of May 5, but were unable to reach the tunnel because of strong currents.

The Japanese continued to cover Corregidor with tons of shells and bombs. Neither concrete and steel nor flesh and blood, could withstand this continuous pounding. One by one the last emplacements and pillboxes were knocked out. The garrison now began to destroy everything that might be of use to the enemy. At Mariveles Bay the Dewey floating dry dock, which had served the

U.S. South Asiatic fleet for many years, was blown up. Nearby ships were scuttled, all arms were smashed, code books were burned.

CAPITULATION. On May 6, 1942, Gen. Wainwright surrendered his entire garrison to Japanese Lt. Gen. Masaharu Homma (*q.v.*). The gaunt and weary troops now filed out of the Malinta Tunnel.

SIGNIFICANCE. For the Japanese it was a stunning victory. Homma had put a powerful enemy army out of action and had driven U.S. sea and air power back to the Malaya barrier. Now the Japanese had one of the best harbors in the Orient, from which they could supply their bases to the south and southeast and drive on to the wealth of the Dutch East Indies. Equally important, they now presented a formidable obstacle to any Allied thrust to cut the line between Tokyo and the critical oil and tin supplies of the East Indies.

The loss of Corregidor plunged the Allied world into gloom. True, the Americans had upset the Japanese timetable by denying them the use of Manila Bay for six months. In addition, the U.S. defenders on the Rock had succeeded in holding a large force of Japanese troops who could well have been used elsewhere and had immobilized a strong proportion of the Nipponese fleet and transports for several months. The stand at Corregidor also slowed the pace of Japanese operations in New Guinea and the Solomons, and helped the Americans take Guadalcanal. Tokyo had designated its crack 4th Division for the Solomons campaign, but it was held up at Corregidor. Racked with malaria, it had to be returned to Japan for demobilization.

For these reasons the stand of the American-Filipino garrison at Corregidor was regarded as vital for the future course of the war. Corregidor became a hallowed name in U.S. military history.

AFTERMATH. Corregidor was recaptured in 1945 in an equally hard-fought campaign. Despite dangerous high winds, U.S. paratroopers surprised the Japanese garrison with a daring drop at the island's highest point. After two weeks, the Americans blasted the Japanese out of the caves and tunnels, and smashed the by now common *banzai* (*q.v.*) attacks. Only 29 of 5,000 Japanese defenders were taken prisoner. The first battle for Corregidor had been fought by U.S. Army and Navy regulars, U.S. Marines, and Filipino scouts. The second was won by a citizen army of GIs.

Bibliography. J. H. and W. M. Belote, *Corregidor: The Saga of a Fortress* (1967); and R. L. Underbrick, *Destination Corregidor* (1971).

COSTS, WAR. *See* CASUALTIES, WAR; and ECONOMIC CONSEQUENCES OF THE WAR.

COVENTRY, BOMBING OF. Air assault by the German *Luftwaffe* (*q.v.*) in late 1940. Along with the attacks on Warsaw and Rotterdam (*qq.v.*), this was one of the first examples of unrestricted bombing in World War II.

TARGET. Coventry, ancient Coventre, in Domesday Coventreu, is located in Warwickshire, England, 18 miles southeast of Birmingham and 18 miles northeast of Stratford-on-Avon. The historic city, made famous by Lady Godiva, was a tourist attraction because of the magnificent church of St. Michael, the spire of which rested on an octagonal tower rising to 300 feet. For the Germans it was a prime target because of its factories producing aircraft engines, motor cars, motorcycles, tractors, machine tools, gauges, and instruments.

BACKGROUND. Hitler's goal of preparing for invasion of England was frustrated in 1940. (*See* BRITAIN, BATTLE OF.) His angry reaction was to order the bombing of key British cities in an effort to cow the people into submission. In his estimation London covered too much ground. He ordered Hermann Goering (*q.v.*), chief of the *Luftwaffe,* to turn his attention to small, more vulnerable towns. Coventry was the first victim of the new tactics.

DILEMMA. Although the point is disputed, it was asserted after the war that Hitler's decision to attack Coventry presented Churchill with a deadly dilemma. On November 14, 1940, it was said, British Intelligence learned through *Ultra* (*q.v.*), its secret code-breaking machine, that Coventry would be bombed four hours later. If the Prime Minister ordered the evacuation of Coventry, he would arouse German suspicions that he had broken the German code. Instead, it was claimed that he made the difficult decision to alert only the Royal Air Force (*q.v.*) and the Coventry city services. That decision cost lives but preserved the secret of *Ultra.* *

ATTACK. German pathfinder planes started marker fires around the aiming points. Then came 449 bombers in a ten-hour attack moving in on the city from all directions. One "crocodile" (group) of planes flew in over the Wash, another over the Isle of Wight, and a third over Brighton. Each had its special target—the Standard Motor Company, the Coventry Radiator and Press Company, the Daimler works. In all the Germans dropped 56 tons of incendiaries, 394 tons of high explosives, and 127 parachute mines.

LOSSES. About 559 people were killed in the bombing and 865 wounded. The city of 200,000 was left a smoking waste with a large part of the center in ruins. Some 70,000 homes were destroyed. Among the buildings shattered were the quadrangle of quaint half-timbered houses of the Palace Yard, the Great Hall of St. Mary's Hall built at the end of the 14th century, and Ford's hospital, one of England's finest Tudor buildings. The cathedral of St. Michael, one of England's proudest possessions, was almost completely destroyed.

---

*See F. W. Winterbotham, *The Ultra Secret* (1940), pp. 60–61.

AFTERMATH. The bombing of Coventry meant the beginning of a new German strategy. The *Luftwaffe* now turned from London to such smaller towns as Birmingham and Southampton. The bombing was regarded in Britain as an inexcusable and unnecessary act. It convinced Air Marshall Charles Portal (*q.v.*), then Chief of Air Staff, that the British, too, would drop their bomb loads on the center of German cities.

Bibliography. F. W. Winterbotham, *The Ultra Secret* (1940); and Alfred Price, *Luftwaffe* (1969).

CRERAR, HENRY DUNCAN GRAHAM (1888–1965). Canadian Army officer.

In 1939 Crerar was Commandant at the Royal Military College. He was ordered to take charge of the training of 100,000 Canadian troops for service in Britain. In 1941 he was made General Officer Commander-in-Chief of the Canadian General Staff. He resigned the next year, accepting a demotion so that he could serve overseas. He led the 1st Canadian Corps in the invasions of Sicily and Italy. In 1944 he was made Commander-in-Chief of the Canadian Army, and under him for the first time Canadian troops marched into battle as a unit commanded by a Canadian General. He led his troops in a dash across northern Europe and eventually freed Antwerp. In early 1945 his men isolated the Germans in the Netherlands.

Crerar had a close-cropped mustache and gray-blue eyes and was known as a loner, so reticent that he had few close friends. A born strategist and an efficient military administrator, he was described as having ''a department store mind on a Napoleonic scale.''

CRETE, BATTLE OF. Capture of the strategic islands in the Mediterranean by the Germans in 1941 in the first large-scale airborne invasion in history.

LOCATION. Crete, called Khandah by the Arabs, Kirid by the Turks, and Candia by the Italians, was the main island of the chain that divided the Greek archipelago from the eastern basin of the Mediterranean. Some 160 miles long, its width varying from 7½ to 35 miles, it was the largest of the Greek islands. Its northern coastline was a long stretch of beach, while the rugged south was difficult of access.

At the outbreak of World War II, Crete lay in a strategic position for both the Allies and Axis. For the British, who controlled the island, Crete was a strong point on the life line to India, protecting both Palestine and Egypt. They assigned elements of the Royal Navy to be sheltered in the great natural harbor of Suda Bay. But despite its importance, the British maintained only a small garrison there, consisting of three infantry battalions, armed with several heavy and light antiaircraft guns, coast-defense artillery, and searchlights. Sensing a coming Axis attack, they began to reinforce Crete with men and supplies. But it was too late. Because of persistent attacks by the *Luftwaffe* (*q.v.*), they could send only a few thousand tons of supplies to the island.

For the Axis, too, Crete was of vital importance. It stood as a barrier in the way of Hitler's grand design for a sweep across North Africa to take Egypt. For Mussolini Crete was a menace for his communications to the Eastern Mediterranean. Hitler decided that he must take the island.

BACKGROUND. On October 28, 1940, the Italians invaded Greece from Albania. Britain promised immediate support for Greece and three days later landed army and Royal Air Force (*q.v.*) units on Crete. When Italian troops bogged down in Greece, Hitler sent in strong reinforcements after smashing Yugoslavia (April 1941). The British, who traditionally fought to save their expeditionary troops anywhere in the world, went ahead to rescue their trapped men in Greece. The evacuation began on April 24, 1941. The next day Hitler issued a directive calling for the capture of Crete. On April 27 the Greek Government surrendered and the King of Greece fled to Crete.

In Greece the British left 11,000 men and tons of equipment, but managed to rescue about 43,000 of their troops. On May 4, 1941, Gen. Bernard Freyberg (*q.v.*) was put in command of Britons, New Zealanders, and Greeks who manned the meager defenses of Crete. On May 19 the last RAF fighters left the island.

AIR ASSAULT. At 8 A.M. on May 20, 1941, the Germans made the first massive airborne invasion of the war with 500 transport aircraft, 72 gliders, supported by 500 bombers and fighters. Some 3,500 elite paratroopers were dropped in waves over Crete. Most of the initial force who jumped in the Suda Bay region and the Candia area were killed in what was a kind of duck shoot for the defenders. Germans dangled in their parachutes, some fell into the sea and were drowned, others were slaughtered in the fields and beaches by Cretans armed with knives.

The next day swarms of German parachutists came, some 3,000 more shock troops jumping from heights varying from 300 to 600 feet. They came in gliders carrying 12 to 30 men each, towed by lumbering old transports with as many as 10 gliders strung out behind each plane. In an incredibly short time the Germans landed more than 20,000 men on the island, together with light and heavy guns, medical supplies, and radio equipment. Included among the troops was Max Schmeling, the former heavyweight boxing champion of the world.

British and New Zealand (that is, Anzac) troops under Freyberg, aided by Greek soldiers and Cretan hillsmen, held the airfields in a desperate display of courage. After another day's furious fighting, the Germans gained a foothold on the one airfield at Máleme, 10 miles southwest of Canea. Almost immediately German reinforcements and supplies began to come in at the rate of 20 planes per hour. With control of the air, the Germans pushed across Crete from the west while the Italians moved in from the east in a classic pincers movement.

SEABORNE INVASION. While the air battle raged, convoys bearing German and Italian troops—small boats, torpedo boats, and kayaks—set out from Greek ports for Crete. The British Admiralty ordered a task force under Adm. Andrew Browne Cunningham (*q.v.*), head of the British Mediterranean Fleet, to intercept the convoys. British warships, including three battle cruisers and four destroyers knifed through the overloaded tramp fleet, and within minutes some 4,000 invasion troops were drowned. Another 5,000 men in the second convoy escaped and landed on Crete.

The Germans, this time with heavy air cover, made another surface invasion attempt. British ships took a heavy pounding from German aircraft. The Germans continued their pressure and by the end of May established superiority on both land and sea. The RAF, in African bases 350 miles to the south, was too far away to help.

EVACUATION. Orders came from London for complete evacuation of Crete. By June 3, 1941, 18,000 men of the British, Anzac, and Greek garrison were taken from the island, leaving behind 10,000 men of the British force, consisting of 3,102 Australians, 1,692 New Zealanders, and 5,000 Greek troops.

LOSSES. Casualties were heavy on both sides. The Royal Navy suffered 1,828 men killed and 183 wounded, as well as the loss of 1 aircraft carrier sunk, as well as 3 cruisers, 6 destroyers, and 29 smaller craft. The commander of the British destroyer *Kelly*, Lord Louis Mountbatten (*q.v.*), was rescued from the sea after his ship was sunk. In addition, one British battleship, four cruisers, and seven destroyers were damaged.

The Germans, too, incurred heavy casualties—some 2,000 men killed, 2,000 wounded, and 2,000 missing, as well as 220 aircraft, including 170 troop-carrying aircraft. Gen. Hermann Goering's crack 7th Air Division was so badly mauled that it was of no further use in the Middle East campaign.

AFTERMATH. The brief campaign was a tremendous victory won by German thoroughness in organization and ingenuity. It was a sensational display of teamwork, with clock-like precision and strategic planning. For the first time in warfare a country had been captured by airborne troops dropped by parachute and opposed by a navy in full control of the seas. But the price was heavy in men and planes. This was the last such large-scale operation ever attempted by the German High Command. Although victorious, Hitler was so appalled by his losses in Crete that he forbade any large-scale parachute operations in the future.

For the British it was a severe defeat and a blow to their prestige. The strategic situation in the eastern Mediterranean was now changed to their disadvantage. Holding Crete, the Germans could easily develop coastal traffic through the Dardanelles and Greek territorial waters up to Trieste. The question now arose: If the British could not hold off an assault from Greece, some

100 miles away, what would happen if Hitler mounted an attack on England from Calais, only 20 miles away? There was cause for consternation in the Allied camp.

Bibliography. A. Moorehead, *Mediterranean Front* (1942); C. Buckley, *Greece and Crete, 1941* (1952).

CRIMEAN CONFERENCE. Allied war conference held at Yalta from February 4 to 12, 1945. (*See* YALTA CONFERENCE.)

CRIPPS, RICHARD STAFFORD (1889–1952). British statesman who served in several important posts during the war.

In May 1940 Churchill sent Cripps to Moscow as British Ambassador. Cripps remained in that post until January 1942. The next month he joined Churchill's Cabinet as Lord Privy Seal and was made Leader of the House of Commons. Later he was transferred from the Cabinet to the Ministry of Aircraft Production. He held this position until the end of the war. (*See also* Cripps Mission.)

Bibliography. E. Estorick, *Stafford Cripps* (1940); and C. Cooke, *The Life of Richard Stafford Cripps* (1957).

CRIPPS MISSION. British delegation to India in 1942, which marked an important step on the Indian road to independence.

BACKGROUND. At the outbreak of World War II, the Indian National Congress, the largest political party in India, declined to join the British in the war. It claimed that only an independent India could give proper and effective support for the Allied side. Following Japanese entry into the war, it was decided in London to send a mission to rally Indian support for the defense of India against Japanese invasion.

NEGOTIATIONS. The British sent Sir Stafford Cripps, a left-wing member of the British War Cabinet, to Delhi from March 22 to April 12, 1942, in an effort to win cooperation of India for the war effort. Cripps proposed the election after the war of a constituent assembly that would draw up a new constitution. A treaty would arrange for a British withdrawal from India in the postwar era.

Many in India, however, had little faith in a promise of independence after the war. Indian leaders countered by asking why the British, if they were sincere in their intentions, did not grant immediate independence. A statement by the Indian National Congress said: "British policy toward India seems to be based on delaying every advance and attempting to create new problems and fresh complications." The Congress called for immediate independence, while the Muslim League insisted on a separate Muslim state. Mahatma Gandhi was opposed to the offer, while Jawaharlal Nehru, second in Congress leadership, supported it.

FAILURE. The failure of the Cripps proposal led to intensified distrust on both sides. During the crisis, which came in August 1942, Gandhi was arrested.

POSTWAR. After the war the situation in India deteriorated rapidly. After intensified antagonism between Hindus and Muslims, the British, unsuccessful in settling the differences, decided that whatever happened they would transfer power to Indian hands. On August 15, 1947, the British flag was hauled down all over India after 200 years of British rule. Two new nations, the Republic of India and the Dominion of Pakistan, emerged.

Bibliography. H. G. Alexander, *India Since Cripps* (1944).

CRYPTANALYSIS. *See* CODES AND CODE BREAKING.

CRYPTOGRAPHY. *See* CODES AND CODE BREAKING.

CRYPTOLOGY. *See* CODES AND CODE BREAKING.

CUNNINGHAM, ALAN GORDON (1887-   ). British Army officer who defeated the Italians in Ethiopia.

At the start of the war Cunningham served successively as commander of the 66th, 9th, and 51st divisions. In November 1940 he was given command of the British forces in Kenya. Marching north in February 1941, he led his troops through severe geographical obstacles and occupied the Red Sea ports of Chisimaio (Kismayu) and Mogadiscio (Mogadishu). Pursuing the Italians into the mountainous interior, he entered Addis Ababa, the capital of Ethiopia, on April 6, 1941. On May 20, 1941, he received the surrender of the main Italian armies.

In August 1941 Cunningham left for Egypt to command the 8th Army in the offensive in Libya. Early British failures were attributed to his preference for defensive tactics, and he was recalled to England. From 1944 to 1945 he headed the Eastern Command.

CUNNINGHAM, ANDREW BROWNE, (1883-1963). British naval commander, older brother of Alan Gordon Cunningham (*q.v.*).

During World War II Cunningham won recognition for his aggressive tactics. At the beginning of hostilities he commanded a cruiser squadron in the Mediterranean and was responsible for protecting the life line from Gibraltar to Malta to the Suez. He was transferred in October 1939 to the North Sea, where his warships took part in the blockade of Germany. On November 11, 1940, ships under his command crippled Italy's fleet at Taranto (*q.v.*) and in March 1941 inflicted further severe damage on the Italian Fleet at the Battle of Cape Matapan (*q.v.*).

In 1942 Cunningham went to Washington as head of the British Admiralty delegation to the Combined Chief of Staffs Committee; he stayed there for six months. He returned to action on November 8, 1942, when he commanded a convoy of some 800 vessels for the combined British and American expeditionary forces in the landings on the Algerian and Moroccan coasts. In January 1943 he was promoted to Admiral of the Fleet.

As Commander-in-Chief, Mediterranean, Cunningham directed a great part of the assault forces for the attack on Sicily on July 9, 1943. He also commanded the naval forces in the dangerous Anzio (*q.v.*) landings as well as the assault on southern France in August 1944. From 1943 to 1946 he served as First Sea Lord and Chief of the Naval Staff at the Admiralty.

Bibliography. A. B. Cunningham, *A Sailor's Odyssey* (1951); and O. Warner, *Admiral of the Fleet: Cunningham of Hyndhope* (1967).

CUNNINGHAM, JOHN (1915–   ). British fighter-pilot hero of the Battle of Britain. (*See* BRITAIN, BATTLE OF.)

Cunningham flew with the 604th Squadron in the summer of 1940 and became its commander from 1941 to 1942. In 1943–1944 he commanded the 85th Squadron and became a group captain in 1944. He was credited with 20 victories, 19 of which were at night. For this feat he became known as "Cat's Eyes" Cunningham.

After the war Cunningham set an international record with a direct flight from London to Khartoum, a distance of 3,064 statute miles in 5 hours and 51 minutes.

CURZON LINE. Boundary laid down by the Allied Supreme Council in 1919 as the tentative eastern frontier of Poland.

Corresponding roughly to national claims, the boundary came to be known as the "Curzon Line" after George Nathaniel Curzon, then British Foreign Secretary. After the Russo-German Nonaggression Pact (*q.v.*), signed on August 23, 1939, and the subsequent invasion of Poland, the Curzon Line, with minor variations, became the boundary between the German and Russian spheres of occupation. Throughout World War II it was a subject of dispute between the Polish Government-in-exile (*see* GOVERNMENTS-IN-EXILE) and the Russians. In 1945 it was accepted by the Polish Government as its frontier line with the Soviet Union.

D

D-DAY. June 6, 1944, the day of the Allied invasion of northern France. (*See* NORMANDY INVASION.)

DAKAR EXPEDITION. Unsuccessful Allied attempt to place a liberating French force ashore in West Africa in late 1940.

BACKGROUND. The capital of French West Africa and the best port on the West African coast, Dakar had great strategic importance. It was the nearest point in Africa to South America and midway between South Africa and South America. President Roosevelt referred to this vital military, naval, and air base as "the Atlantic fortress of Dakar." In World War II it became of critical importance because it commanded the large federation that France had created in West Africa. After the collapse of France in 1940, the question became paramount as to whether Dakar would stay with Vichy France or turn to the Free French (*see* FREE FRANCE).

PREPARATION. Gen. Charles de Gaulle (*q.v.*), head of the Free French forces operating from London, was anxious to establish an operations base in North Africa. He erroneously believed that most of the French in Senegal would support him as they had done in French Equatorial Africa. He decided to take Dakar. When the Vichy Government heard about the project, it dispatched from Toulon three cruisers, which managed to pass through the Straits of Gibraltar and reach Dakar (*See* CODE NAMES, ALLIED *OPERATION MENACE*.)

CLASH. On the morning of September 23, 1940, representatives of de Gaulle attempted to land at Dakar, but they were fired upon by French guards. Shore batteries also opened fire on both French and British warships in the harbor. The French battleship *Richlieu* joined the fracas. The Vichy forces lost two of the three submarines they sent out to attack the British ships.

WITHDRAWAL. The small Free French and British units were unable to make a landing. By now it had become evident that only a major operation could result in the fall of Dakar. Churchill decided on political grounds to abandon the attempt to establish an Allied base on the African mainland at that time. *See* NORTH AFRICA, CAMPAIGNS IN.)

Bibliography. D. Whittlesey, "Dakar and Other Cape Verde Settlements," *Geographical Review* (1941).

DALADIER, ÉDOUARD (1884–1970). French statesman during the critical days before the war.

Daladier's name is associated with that of Prime Minister Neville Chamberlain (*q.v.*) in the policy of appeasement preceding World War II. He was one of the signatories of the Munich Agreement (*q.v.*) in September 1938. At this time he was regarded as France's "strong man," ruling by decree and supporting a two-year postponement of French general elections in July 1939.

In early September 1939 Daladier waited until the British declared war and on September 3 joined the British. He dissolved the French Communist Party when the Soviet Union invaded Poland. In March 1940 he became Minister of War in Paul Reynaud's Government, and in June, Minister of Foreign Affairs. In September 1940 he was arrested by the Vichy Government and in February 1942 was brought to trial accused of "leading France into war unprepared." He denounced Vichy at his public trial at Riom, as a result of which he was interned in Germany as a political prisoner. He remained a prisoner until the end of the war.

Bibliography. Daladier wrote *In Defense of France* (1939). *See also* S. B. Leeds, *These Rule France* (1940); O. Ray, *Life of Édouard Daladier* (1940); J. Romains, *Seven Mysteries of Europe.* (1940); and A. Simone, *J'Accuse* (1940).

DAM BUSTERS SQUADRON. Famed squadron of the Royal Air Force (*q.v.*) organized especially for low-level attacks on the Ruhr Dams on May 16–17, 1943. The Dam Busters were led originally by Wing Commander Guy Gibson and later by Group Captain Leonard Cheshire (*qq.v.*). (*See also* RUHR DAMS.)

DANISH RESISTANCE. *See* SHELL HOUSE RAID.

DARLAN, JEAN LOUIS XAVIER FRANÇOIS (1881–1942). French naval officer and political leader prominent during the early years of World War II.

On the outbreak of World War II in 1939, Darlan was designated Commander-in-Chief of all naval and military forces in France. When Hitler attacked France in 1940, Darlan assured Churchill that under no circumstances would he allow the French Navy to fall into German hands. On the capitulation of France, he declined the appeal to sail the French Navy to British ports, a move which led to a tragic clash between British and French warships. (*See* ORAN NAVAL ENCOUNTER.)

After the fall of France, Darlan held a series of important posts in the Vichy Government of Marshal Henri Pétain (*q.v.*)—Minister of Marine, Vice-Premier, Foreign Minister, Minister of the Interior—and was also designated Pétain's heir as Chief of State. Now the real power in France, he kept in close touch with German leaders. In May 1940 he met Hitler and agreed to the German request to use French ports.

In November 1942, when the Allies invaded North Africa, Darlan was by chance in Algiers, where he had been posted as French High Commissioner. For the Allies he was just the man to win over the dissident pro-Vichy elements. "If I could meet Darlan," Churchill remarked, "much as I hate him, I would cheerfully crawl on my hands and knees for a mile if by so doing I could get him to bring that fleet of his into the circle of Allied forces." Darlan allowed himself to be convinced. When he was told that the Germans had occupied all of France, he announced that Hitler had violated the armistice of 1940, and that he, Darlan, was now ready to work with the Americans. He ordered a cease fire and assumed the role of chief representative of French North Africa in the name of Pétain.

Gen. Dwight D. Eisenhower (*q.v.*), the American Commander-in-Chief, gave Darlan temporary political status. There was a stormy reaction from Gen. Charles de Gaulle (*q.v.*) and his followers, who denounced the "Darlan deal with this notorious Vichy character." Roosevelt defended the appointment as "a temporary expedient."

On December 24, 1942, Darlan was assassinated by a young French anti-Fascist in Algiers.

Bibliography. A. D. Montmorency, *The Enigma of Admiral Darlan* (1943); and P. Tompkins, *The Murder of Admiral Darlan* (1965).

DAVIS, ELMER HOLMES (1871–1958). Well-known American newscaster during the war.

On August 23, 1939, just as the big war news was breaking, Davis was engaged by the Columbia Broadcasting System when its ace commentator, H. V. Kaltenborn (*q.v.*) was in Europe. Within a short time he won nationwide repute as a news analyst. The American public was attracted by his clear, well-reasoned talks. Even in times of war crises, Davis maintained a calm, unhurried manner, checking all information and sorting conflicting reports. He remained with CBS until 1942, when he was made Director for the Office of War Information (*q.v.*) (1942–1945).

Tall, well-proportioned, and energetic, Davis had strong features, gray hair, and thick black brows. Blunt and witty, he was known for his scholarly approach to the news.

Bibliography. Among Davis's books are *History of The New York Times* (1921); *Morals for Moderns* (1930); *But We Were Born Free* (1945); and *Two Minutes Till Midnight* (1955).

DECLARATION OF UNION. Proposal for a permanent union of the British and French governments and empires in June 1940, just before the fall of France.

The proposal was originated by Jean Monnet and Charles Corbin as a means of keeping France in the war. On June 12, 1940, Winston Churchill flew to Tours in a last-minute attempt to persuade the French Cabinet to honor its promise not to sue for a separate peace. Paul Reynaud (*q.v.*) agreed but by this time his colleagues were certain that the situation was hopeless. Gen. Maxime Weygand (*q.v.*), defeatist, predicted that "England's neck would be wrung like a chicken's."

On June 14 the triumphant Germans entered Paris. On June 16, with the French front cracking and the Maginot Line (*q.v.*) pierced, Churchill proposed that France and Britain combine, an astonishing proposal in view of Britain's traditional policy of splendid isolation from the Continent. The suggested Declaration of Union called for joint organs of defense and joint foreign, financial, and economic policies. Every citizen of France would have immediate British citizenship, and every British citizen would become a citizen of France. Both countries would share responsibility for repairing the devastation of war.

The British proposal suggested a single war cabinet, with all the armed forces of Britain and France under its direction. The two parliaments would be formally associated. "The Union appeals to the United States to fortify the economic resources of the Allies, and to bring her powerful material aid to the common cause. . . . The Union will concentrate its whole energy against the powers of the enemy, no matter where the battle may be. And thus we shall conquer."

Churchill's purpose was political. Behind the gesture was the hope that Premier Reynaud's position would be strengthened in an important meeting of the French Cabinet held at 5 P.M. on June 16. Although their situation was desperate, members of the Cabinet began to search for hidden motives in the French offer. "*A quoi sert de la faire!*" ("What good would it do?") From all sides came calls for surrender, from Marshal Pétain, from Laval, even from Reynaud's circle of friends.

The British offer was rejected. Nothing came of the proposed Declaration of Union.

DECLARATIONS OF WAR. Formal announcements by belligerent countries of the existence of a state of war.

Following are the dates on which the major belligerents declared war:

GERMANY. Germany invaded Poland (1939), the Scandinavian countries (1940), the Low Countries (1940), France (1940), and the Soviet Union (1941) without declarations of war. Germany declared war on the United States on December 11, 1941.

GREAT BRITAIN

On Germany, September 3, 1939

On Italy, June 11, 1940.

On Finland, Rumania, and Hungary, December 7, 1941.

On Japan, December 8, 1941.

On Bulgaria, December 13, 1941.

On Thailand, January 25, 1942.

FRANCE

On Germany, September 3, 1939.

On Italy, June 11, 1940.

On Japan, December 8, 1941. (Declared by Free French [*q.v.*].)

ITALY

On Great Britain and France, June 10, 1940.

On the United States, December 11, 1941.

On Germany, October 13, 1943.

On Japan, July 14, 1945.

JAPAN

On the United States, Great Britain, Australia, Canada, New Zealand, and the Union of South Africa, December 7, 1941.

On the Netherlands, January 11, 1942.

SOVIET RUSSIA

Invaded Poland (1939) and Finland (1939) without a declaration of war. Finland declared war on Soviet Russia on June 25, 1941.

On Japan, August 8, 1945.

UNITED STATES

On Japan, December 8, 1941.

On Germany and Italy, December 11, 1941.

On Bulgaria, Hungary, and Rumania, June 5, 1942.

LATIN AMERICA

From January 15–28, 1942, delegates of all 21 American republics met at Rio de Janeiro and voted to recommend to their respective governments a break in diplomatic relations with the Axis nations. All the governments, excepting Chile and Argentina, severed relations. Chile broke off relations (January 20, 1943, Argentina on January 26, 1944).

DEFENSIVE LINES, GERMAN. Series of five defensive lines set up in the Italian peninsula to halt Allied advances.

GUSTAV LINE. Also called Cassino Line. A line set up by the Germans in early 1944 to defend Rome against Allied attack from the south. At its center was the monastery of Monte Cassino (*q.v.*).

ADOLF HITLER LINE. Organized by Field Marshal Albert Kesselring (*q.v.*), this line stretched across the Liri Valley.

CAESAR LINE. Defensive line 20 miles south of Rome.

ALBERT LINE. Temporary position halfway from Rome to the final Gothic Line, July 1944.

GOTHIC LINE. Natural defensive barrier running from Pisa across Italy to Rimini on the heights above the Arno River, about 150 miles north of Rome. This was the penultimate line of defense before the Po Valley. (*See* ITALIAN FRONT, CAMPAIGNS ON THE.)

DE GAULLE, CHARLES ANDRÉ JOSEPH MARIE (1890–1970). French soldier and statesman and leader of the French Resistance.

When the war broke out in 1939, de Gaulle was an obscure general commanding a brigade in Alsace. During the 1940 campaign against Germany, he was given command of the 4th Armored Division, but by this time it was far too late to test the effectiveness of his theories on a new type of armored warfare. (*See* BLITZKRIEG.) On June 6, 1940, he was named Under Secretary of State for War. On June 18, when Marshal Pétain was negotiating the surrender of France, de Gaulle flew to London. Immediately on his arrival he broadcast his famous appeal to the French people to continue the battle. A few days later a French court-martial at Toulouse sentenced him to death.

FREE FRENCH LEADER. In October 1940 de Gaulle formed the Council of Defense for the French Empire, which in 1941 became the Free French National Committee. Soon 45,000 troops rallied to his cause, and he had at his disposal 20 French warships and supplies from several French colonies. Churchill recognized de Gaulle as the source of future assistance, but in the meantime was forced to accept him as a difficult and tiresome ally. Roosevelt regarded de Gaulle as an annoying prima donna.

De Gaulle presided over the Free French (or Fighting French) Council in London with total disregard for all opposition. (*See* RESISTANCE MOVEMENTS.) From 1942 on he gained immeasurably in power and influence. He maintained close ties with the underground in occupied France. Despite his known conservative-clerical views, he was able to win the support of many French liberal leaders. Although he did not actually represent France in Allied affairs, he acted as if he were the unchallenged leader of the nation.

In November 1942, after the American landings in North Africa, the Allied High Command persuaded Adm. Jean François Darlan (*q.v.*), head of the Vichy armed forces and Marshal Pétain's representative in North Africa, to order a cease fire. In return Darlan was named High Commissioner for French North Africa. De Gaulle objected violently to this procedure. When Darlan was assassinated a month later, the Allies named Gen. Henri Giraud (*q.v.*) as High Commissioner. De Gaulle and Giraud became co-presidents of the newly formed French Committee of National Liberation. After bitter disagreement, de Gaulle forced Giraud out of the committee.

VICTORY. De Gaulle was now recognized as the political leader of the French Resistance. All former French colonies, except for Japanese-occupied French Indo-China, were under his control. In June 1944 he transformed the Committee of National Liberation into the Provisional Government of France. He insisted upon leading the Allied forces into France during the invasion starting on June 6, 1944, but was turned down brusquely by Churchill and Roosevelt. Together with Gen. Jacques Philippe Leclerc (*q.v.*), de Gaulle entered Paris in August 1944. His rule was formally recognized by the principal Allies by October. Because Stalin was opposed to French claims, de Gaulle was not invited to the critical conferences at Yalta (February 4–12, 1945) or later at Potsdam (July 17–August 2, 1946) (*qq.v.*).

Bibliography. De Gaulle's two most important military works: *Au fil de l'épée* (1932) (trans. as *The Philosophy of Command*); and *Vers l'armée de métier* (1934) (trans. as *The Army of the Future*, 1940). His memoirs were translated as *The Call to Honor, 1940-1942* (1955). See also P. Barrès, *Charles de Gaulle* (1942); J. Lacouture, *De Gaulle*, trans. by F. K. Price (1966); D. Schoenbrunn, *The Three Lives of Charles de Gaulle*; and A. Werth, *De Gaulle: A Political Biography* (1966).

DEGAUSSING. Use of an electric current to neutralize a ship's magnetism.

At the start of the war British, American, and German scientists were experimenting with devices to protect ships against enemy weapons. The early apparatus, named after a German mathematician and the unit of magnetism, the gauss, used an electric current to neutralize a ship's magnetism. This was done by running a cable around the outside of the hull and sending a low voltage current through it. Sophisticated refinements were later added to warships. (*See also* SCIENCE AND THE WAR.)

DEGRELLE, LÉON (1906–   ). Belgian Fascist politician.

A convinced monarchist, nationalist, and anti-Semite, Degrelle in 1930 founded the Rex movement in imitation of Mussolini's fascism. Violently anti-Communist, he utilized the approved trappings of German and Italian fascism. Belgians in general were unimpressed. When the Germans occupied Belgium in 1940, they allowed Degrelle to revive his Rexist movement. In 1941 he joined a legion of Walloon volunteers to fight for the Germans on the Russian front. Only three of the 850 Belgians in this unit survived. In 1945 Degrelle fled to Spain. After the war a Belgian court sentenced him to death *in absentia* for treason. He declined to return to his homeland and lived in Madrid.

Degrelle's personality appealed to Hitler, who said: "If I had a son I would want him to be like Degrelle." In exile Degrelle praised the German dictator: "He was the greatest statesman of his time."

Bibliography. C. d'Ydewalle, *Degrelle* (1968).

DE HAVILLAND, GEOFFREY (1882–1965). British aircraft designer and manufacturer.

De Havilland's work for the Royal Air Force (*q.v.*) was critically important throughout the war. His most successful product was the speedy, plywood *Mosquito* (*q.v.*), a twin-engined, high mid-wing monoplane that became operational during the latter part of 1942. The *Mosquito* attracted attention when it was used on the first daylight bombing raid on Berlin and later night attacks on the German capital. De Havilland was knighted in 1944.

DE JONGH, A. (1916–   ). Belgian girl who fashioned an underground escape route for downed British airmen and escaped Allied prisoners of war.

For more than two years she supervised her so-called Comet Line, by which some 115 Allied pilots and troops managed to reach England. She was arrested and interrogated again and again by the *Gestapo* (*q.v.*), but at first escaped punishment. Her father, not as fortunate, was arrested, tortured, and executed. She was arrested in France in 1943 and imprisoned for the remainder of the war. Her captors never learned about her activities for the Comet Line.

DEMPSEY, MILES CHRISTOPHER (1896–1969). Army officer who led the British 2nd Army on D-Day (*q.v.*).

In the early part of the war Dempsey was one of the most rapidly promoted officers of the British Army. He distinguished himself in rear-guard actions, which gained valuable time in a critical three-day battle for the evacuation from Dunkirk (*q.v.*). Back in England he helped train the hastily organized armies that were to meet the threatened German invasion. When that danger passed, he was sent to North Africa. In December 1942 he commanded the 13th Army Corp that pursued Gen. Erwin Rommel (*q.v.*) and his *Afrika Korps* (*q.v.*) through Libya after the battle of El Alamein. He also led his corps in the Sicilian and Italian campaigns (*qq.v.*).

Gen. Bernard Law Montgomery (*q.v.*) selected Dempsey to command the 2nd Army for the invasion of Europe. For six months Dempsey was engaged in training his troops. After the landings at Normandy, he successfully delayed powerful German tank forces at Caen, while the Allied west flank moved around to push into France. Subsequently he led his victorious troops across the Rhine and the Elbe.

Dempsey was tall and slim, always neatly dressed, with boots polished to mirror brightness. Modest and shy, he spoke vigorously when addressing his troops. Known to his men as "Lucky," he was a brilliant tactician who in September 1944 sliced through the heart of Belgium and into Holland in 48 hours.

DENMARK, INVASION OF. German conquest of Denmark in April 1940. (*See* SCANDINAVIA, CAMPAIGNS IN.)

DESERT FOX. Name given to Gen Erwin Rommel, commander of the German *Afrika Korps* (*q.v.*) in North Africa. Rommel was highly respected by Allied strategists. (*See* ROMMEL, ERWIN.)

DESERT RATS. The British 7th Armored Division that won attention with its combat record in North Africa. Led by Gen Allan Francis (John) Harding (*q.v.*), the Desert Rats in 1943 pushed the Germans back in a spectacular campaign lasting three months. (*See* NORTH AFRICA, CAMPAIGNS IN.)

DEVERS, JACOB LOUCKS (1887–1979). Commanding officer of the U.S. 6th Army Group in the European theater of war.

An expert in mechanized and armored warfare, Devers early in World War II was assigned to supervise the rapid expansion of the U.S. armored forces. He commanded American forces assembling in England for the invasion of France. (*See* NORMANDY INVASION.) He next served as Deputy Supreme Allied Commander in the Mediterranean theater of operations. He was given command of the 6th Army Group, composed of U.S. and French forces, which invaded southern France in August 1944, and in this post advanced rapidly northward to link up with the forces that had driven into Normandy. Devers commanded the right wing of the Allied forces that moved through Germany into Austria. He was five-feet-ten-inches tall and had hazel eyes and unruly mouse-colored hair. He was noted for his extraordinary energy and broad grin, as well as for what was called "one of the most virile vocabularies in the whole Army." He died in Washington on October 15, 1979.

DIEPPE RAID. Allied combined operations assault in a key point in the West Wall (*q.v.*) in the summer of 1942. The original code or cover name was *Rutter,* but this action was postponed and later named *Jubilee.*

BACKGROUND. In early 1942 Stalin, who was concerned with the power of the German assault on his country, became more and more demanding in his call for an Allied Second Front (*q.v.*). He suspected that the West was deliberately delaying a cross-Channel invasion in the hope that Germany and Russia would destroy each other. It was grievous military judgment, he said, to attack German targets from the air. Wars had to be fought and won on the ground and Russia was doing more than its share there. He deplored British "reluctance" to fight the Germans.

In fact, both Churchill and Roosevelt were very much in favor of a Second Front and for some time had been discussing plans for it. But it was obvious that the Western Allies at that time had neither the troops nor the equipment necessary for a massive assault on Fortress Europe. The British were not yet strong enough militarily and the Americans were heavily engaged in the Pacific.

PLAN. Nevertheless, in April 1942 the Target Committee of Combined Operations, with headquarters in London, set up a limited operation pending a later full-scale invasion of the Continent. They agreed on a strong commando sortie on the port of Dieppe on the English Channel. The intent was to strike a blow at Hitler, test the strength and weaknesses of the defenses, shake the complacency of the German High Command, and convince Stalin of the seriousness of the West's war effort. At the same time much could be learned about conditions to be expected in a future attack on a strongly held Channel port.

The plan envisioned five major steps:

1. German defenses would be weakened by a heavy naval bombardment, especially on the well-defended *Goebbels* battery at Berneval east of Dieppe and the *Hess* battery at Varengeville-Quiberville west of Dieppe.

2. Dive bombers and fighters of the Royal Air Force (*q.v.*) would continue the softening-up process and destroy the airfield at St. Aubryn.

3. Commandos would be landed at a dozen points to the east and west of Dieppe.

4. Tanks would be sent ashore to support the infantry.

5. The commandos would then destroy enemy defenses, radar installations, power stations, dock and railway facilities, and oil dumps. They would remove 40 invasion barges held at Dieppe since the summer of 1940 for *Sea Lion* (*q.v.*), the projected German invasion of England. They would also take documents from German Division headquarters. They would capture prisoners and then return home on the waiting fleet.

PREPARATIONS. To carry out this plan, what was thought to be a strong combined operations force was assigned for the mission. The navy contributed

13 groups, escorted by 8 destroyers and supported in turn by smaller ships, including 9 Infantry Landing Ships (LSIs), a total of 252 vessels of all shapes, sizes, and varying speeds, but none larger than a destroyer. The Royal Air Force (*q.v.*) assigned 69 squadrons of aircraft, including four squadrons of American-built *Mustangs* and other British bombers and fighters. The total assault force consisted of 6, 086 officers and men in ranks, of whom 298 officers and 4,663 men in ranks were from the 4th and 6th Canadian Infantry. There was also a force of British commandos and a detachment of 50 American Rangers.

RAID. On the night of August 18, 1942, the invading flotilla moved out of four British ports—Southampton, Portsmouth, Shoreham, and New Haven. After clearance of their path by mine sweepers, signaled by the raising of green flags, the ships arrived off Dieppe as planned. At 3 A.M. the destroyers fanned out in wide arcs and the LSIs were ready. No aircraft were heard overhead, the radar screens were clean, visibility was 2,000 yards, and everything seemed to be working according to plan. Forty-five minutes after emerging from the mine field, most of the attacking force was safely in the landing craft and awaiting the order to storm ashore.

Then suddenly at 3:47 A.M. flashes of gunfire came from the east. Four German trawlers had discovered the raid and opened fire. The commandos stormed the beaches under heavy fire but with an umbrella of Allied air power. The first men on the beaches cut away barbed wire, cleaned out snipers' nests, and pushed forward to their objectives. The attack on the *Goebbels* battery at Berneval was thrown back almost immediately. The raiders were more successful at Varengeville, where they blew up all six guns of the *Hess* Battery but at high cost in lives. The commandos destroyed one other battery as well as a radio-location station.

Meanwhile, the Germans replied with the heavy thunder of artillery shells and the clatter of machine guns, mortars, and snipers' rifles. As assault boats scraped the beaches and commandos headed for the concrete pillboxes, the defenders raked them with deadly crossfire. The Allies managed to land 28 tanks, which were not enough to overcome the antitank defenses. Several tanks managed to reach the promenade and some troops filtered into town.

AIR BATTLE. At 4:45 P.M. the British *Spitfires* (*q.v.*) dived in to fire their first shots at Dieppe. For a quarter of an hour the planes strafed the coast in coordination with the landings. *Hurricanes* (*q.v.*) and *Bostons* joined the air attack on the *Rommel, Goering,* and *Hitler* batteries. The *Luftwaffe* (*q.v.*), with many of its pilots out on late passes, got its first alert at 6:00 A.M. By 7 A.M. 30 German planes, mostly *FW-190s,* were in the air. Not until 10 A.M. did the German airmen begin to challenge in strength.

By this time the two air forces were locked in a major air battle. Many British pilots had already flown two or more sorties and although exhausted found themselves engaged in deadly dogfights. Both German and Allied planes were shot down into the Channel and on land. At 10:30 A.M. the Allied side was helped immeasurably when 24 American *Flying Fortresses* (*q.v.*) flew in to assist the British. Four squadrons of *Spitfires* attacked the German airfield at Abbeville, choking off German attack at a critical moment.

By noon losses were extremely heavy on both sides. The British lost 112 pilots killed and missing, 40 wounded, and 70 planes. The Germans lost between 40 and 80 bombers and had 150 of their aircraft damaged.

RESULTS. As a military operation, the raid was a disappointing failure. At Dieppe the Allies lost one-half of their attacking force, 3,379 men killed, wounded, or captured. Of the invading 252 ships, about 34 were lost. Despite great gallantry, the assaulting troops who intended to deliver a swift, smashing blow at Dieppe had instead faced a pitiless blizzard of steel from an enemy safely entrenched above and around them. The invaders were caught in a trap. They had attacked an enemy strong point without a heavy advance bombardment and without complete superiority in the air.

The British regretted the heavy loss of life but also felt that much had been accomplished. The raid gave Allied leaders an accurate idea of the kind of tactics needed to break through German defenses. On an invasion of the Continent they could not hope to capture port facilities and would have to develop other means of supply over open beaches. The lesson learned at Dieppe was of great importance in the eventual assault on Hitler's Fortress Europe. (*See* NORMANDY INVASION.)

The raid on Dieppe, although driven back, threw a scare into the German High Command. On Hitler's orders, Field Marshal Erwin Rommel (*q.v.*) was assigned to inspect Atlantic defenses. Rommel found them inadequate and, convinced that the war would be won or lost on the beaches, did everything he could to make the fortifications impregnable. The Pas de Calais area, which Hitler though the likeliest spot for an Allied invasion, was strengthened for mile after mile with underwater obstacles and mines.

Bibliography. For a dramatic account, *see* R. W. Thompson, *Dieppe at Dawn* (1955). *See also* T. Robertson, *Dieppe: The Shame and the Glory* (1962); and C. P. Couture, *Operation "Jubilee": Dieppe* (1969).

DIETRICH, MARLENE (1904–   ). Film actress and singer.

Born in Berlin, Dietrich trained for the stage at Max Reinhardt's School of Drama. Distressed by what was happening in her homeland when the United States entered the war in 1941, she abandoned her motion picture career to concentrate on entertaining American troops overseas. For three years she performed near the front lines and became a favorite of GIs (*q.v.*). In some 500 appearances she rendered songs from her films, performed feats of mind reading, and took a turn on the musical saw (an ordinary large carpenter's saw with the handle held under right knee and played with a violin bow over the left knee with the blade bent to make different notes.) Her audiences were even more appreciative of the famed "Dietrich legs." They knew her sultry voice, instantly recognizable in such songs as *Lili Marlene* (*q.v.*).

Bibliography. L. Frewin, *Dietrich: The Story of a Star* (1967); and C. Higham, *Marlene: The Life of Marlene Dietrich* (1977).

DILL, JOHN GREER (1881–1944). British Field Marshal recognized as Britain's foremost strategist.

In 1939 Dill was appointed commander of the 1st Expeditionary Corps in France. Returning home in April 1940, he was made Chief of the Imperial General Staff (CIGS). He remained the top governmental military adviser until late 1941. Promoted to Field Marshal, he was sent to Washington, where he gained the confidence of President Roosevelt and Gen. George C. Marshall (*qq.v.*). He died in Washington on November 4, 1944.

Dill's integrity and breadth of view made him a vital link between the Allies. He won popularity in high military circles as head of the British Joint Staff Mission. A monument to his memory stands in the national cemetery in Arlington, Virginia.

DISPLACED PERSONS. Enforced movement of peoples, usually called DPs, during and after the war.

BACKGROUND. As armies moved into combat, local populations were forced to gather whatever belongings they could and take to the roads in search of sanctuary. Millions of refugees moved endlessly and at times hopelessly in this vast process of displacement. The problem was a major one in both world wars.

POPULATION MOVEMENTS. From 1939 to 1945 wholesale migrations were on an almost unprecedent scale. In mid-1940 millions of Frenchmen moved to escape from German invaders and in 1944–1945 millions of Germans in east Germany tried to flee from the Soviet armies. In the opening phase and during the first two years of Axis domination, millions of prisoners of war from conquered countries were hauled into Germany to work for the Nazi war machine. (*See* FORCED LABOR.) At the same time tens of thousands of refugees fled before the invading Germans. Poles, Yugoslavs, Greeks, and others were forced to leave their homes because of Nazi occupation.

GERMAN MIGRATIONS. During the war the main migrations concerned the *Volksdeutsche,* who were repatriated by Hitler to Germany through a series of enforced bilateral agreements. German-speaking minorities were brought back from South Tyrol, the Baltic states, Bukovina, North Dobrudja, Croatia, and Bulgaria. Some 600,000 Germans in all were transferred in this way. German communities in Hungary and Transylvania largely stayed where they were.

In the reverse direction, Hitler attempted to colonize Alsace-Lorraine by ex-pelling Lorrainers into France and sending Alsatians to Germany. In the east the Germans sent in settlers to displace 3 million Poles, 70,000 Czechs from the Sudetenland, and 80,000 Slovenes from Carinthia.

RUSSIAN IMPETUS. The Russians also instigated mass population movements. Stalin allowed the Germans to move out of territories annexed by the Soviet Union in 1939–1940. Later he deported to Siberia the Germans on the Volga, Tartars from the Crimea, and Kalmuks from the Caucasus. He transferred Poles, Estonians, and Lithuanians to areas all over the Soviet Union.

POSTWAR ERA. The problem was aggravated after the collapse of Nazi Germany in 1945. Millions of Germans had become displaced. Those who had fled eastward to escape Allied bombing of their cities now began to return home. They were joined by Germans expelled from their ancestral homes in eastern Germany and the Czech Sudetenland. Millions of DPs clogged the roads, crowded the cities, or lived in the countryside. Displaced Germans posed an enormous problem for Allied authorities, whose supply lines were already overtaxed.

At the same time, men, women,and children who had been brought to Germany to work in war factories began to move homeward. Many laborers and prisoners, Ukrainians, Estonians, Latvians, and Lithuanians, preferred to stay in war-torn Germany than to return to Soviet rule. Thousands of East Europeans, who had fled their native countries before or after the arrival of the Russians, also moved to Germany because they feared punishment for collaboration with the Germans or because of hatred of communism.

Russian policy helped to intensify the displaced persons problem. Now the Russians set into motion a vast transfer of peoples. They expelled Finns and Germans from annexed territories. They exchanged Poles left in land annexed from Poland for Russians still remaining in Poland. At the Potsdam Conference (*q.v.*), held in mid-summer 1945, Soviet Russia, with the reluctant approval of the Western Allies, authorized Poland, Hungary, and Czechoslovakia to expel millions of Germans from these countries.

SIGNIFICANCE. It has been estimated that the number of displaced persons was at least 30 million. No European country was unaffected by the migrations. Even Swedes and Norwegians moved out of Lapland when fighting began there. More than 1.5 million Germans were evacuated from Poland where they had settled. Some 200,000 Rumanians moved out of Bessarabia, and 140,000 Magyars out of Transylvania. At times the same populations ebbed and flowed over the same territory. The story was one of cruelty, barbaric behavior, and disregard of human rights. One of the most intensive mass movements of history, it reflected the misery of modern warfare. (*See also* SOCIAL IMPACT OF THE WAR.)

Bibliography. E. M. Kulischer, *The Displacement of Population in Europe* (1943); S. Duggan, *The Rescue of Science and Learning* (1948); U.S. Congress, Senate. *Displaced Persons*

(1950); H. Carter, *The Refugee Problem in Europe and the Middle East* (1950); H.B.M. Murphy, *Flight and Resettlement* (1955); K. Fry, *Rescue* (1968); N. Tolstoy, *The Secret Betrayal* (1978); and D. Zayas, *Nemesis at Potsdam* (1979).

DOENITZ, KARL (1891–1980). Director of Germany's U-Boat strategy during the war and short-time successor to Hitler as head of the Third Reich.

Early in the war Doenitz developed the wolf-pack tactics (*q.v.*) that initially took a heavy toll of Allied shipping. Although he caused tremendous damage, he was unable to drive the Allies from the sea. Promoted to Admiral in 1942, he was named Commander-in-Chief of the German Navy on January 30, 1943.

By May 1943 the tables were turned and the Allies got the upper hand in the Battle of the Atlantic (*q.v.*). Doenitz was forced to withdraw most of his U-Boats from the seas. Hitler said: "There must be no letup in such warfare. The Atlantic is my first line of defense in the West." But the toll of U-Boats continued to be heavy. By Fall 1943 Doenitz was losing a U-Boat for every freighter sunk. At this time he complained that the Allies held "every trump card," especially the new microwave radar (*see* RADAR, WARTIME), which was deadly to German submarines. "The enemy," Doenitz complained, "knows all our secrets and we know none of his."

NEW FUEHRER. On April 30, 1945, the last day of his life, Hitler made Doenitz his successor as *Fuehrer* of the Third Reich. Doenitz retained this post for 23 days. He organized a new government in the Baltic enclave of Flensburg in Schleswig-Holstein. He offered surrender to the British and Americans provided that Germany was allowed to continue its struggle against the Soviet Union. His proposal was rejected. He urged an end to Hitler's policy of demolition and called for immediate German reconstruction.

NUREMBERG TRIAL. Doenitz was arrested by the British on May 23, 1945, and held for trial as a war criminal before the International Military Tribunal at Nuremberg. (*See* NUREMBERG TRIALS.) His judges found that, although he had built and trained the German U-Boat arm, the evidence did not show that he was privy to the conspiracy to wage aggressive wars or that he prepared and initiated such wars. The Tribunal found him guilty on count 2, crimes against peace, and count 3, war crimes. He was sentenced to 10 years' imprisonment and was released in 1956. Doenitz died on December 24, 1980.

Bibliography. See H. Busch, *U-Boats at War*, trans. by L.P.R. Wilson (1955); and D. Mason, *U-Boat: The Secret Menace* (1968).

DOIHARA, KENJI (1883–   ). Commmander-in-Chief of the Japanese Air Force.

Doihara served for many years as an adviser of the Chinese Ministry of War, but was finally dismissed under suspicion. He became closely associated with the Kwantung Army clique, which dominated the Japanese Government through Premier Hideki Tojo (*q.v.*). He was credited with creating the plan that resulted in the "Mukden incident" and the subsequent occupation of Manchuria. He played a leading role in the war against China, leading Japanese armies and making North China a direct sphere of Japanese influence.

In April 1941 Doihara was appointed to leadership of the Japanese Air Force. In this post he was largely responsible for training the airmen who scored repeated gains at Pearl Harbor, Malaya, and Hong Kong in the early days of the Pacific war. He also served as Supreme War Councilor and head of the Military Academy.

DONOVAN, WILLIAM JOSEPH (1883-1959). U.S. organizer and director of the Office of Strategic Services (*q.v.*). He was known as "Wild Bill."

In 1940 Donovan was sent to England as an unofficial observer to study British strength and intelligence methods. From December 1940 to March 1941 he was on a secret government mission to Yugoslavia, Greece, and the Middle East. His observation of Resistance movements (*q.v.*) was to prove valuable for his later career. On June 13, 1942, the Office of Strategic Services was created by executive order and Donovan was appointed its director. From its beginning the OSS was a military agency responsible only to the Joint Chiefs of Staff. Under Donovan's leadership it played a major role in the organization and supply of Resistance groups throughout Occupied Europe. He sent his agents into Germany, Occupied France, and northern Italy equipped with radios to send back information on troop movements, bomb damage, and morale. The OSS was responsible for propaganda, sabotage, and underground activities. (*See* ESPIONAGE.) Donovan received many decorations for his work.

Bibliography. C. Ford, *Donovan of OSS* (1970).

DOOLITTLE, JAMES HAROLD (1896–   ). U.S. Army officer who led the first aerial attack on Tokyo in World War II.

Doolittle reported for active duty in 1940 and was assigned the task of helping automobile manufacturers convert their plants for production of airplane parts. In January 1942 he was posted to Air Force headquarters in Washington, D.C. He volunteered to lead a top-secret mission, for which he prepared for three months.

On April 18, 1942, Doolittle led 16 *B-25 Mitchell* bombers from the deck of the USS *Hornet* on the first aerial raid on the Japanese mainland. (*See* DOOLITTLE RAID.) This extraordinary feat slowed the Japanese offensive in the Pacific, bolstered American morale, and won Doolittle the Congressional Medal of Honor.

In February 1943 Doolittle headed the Northwest Africa Strategic Air Force, made up of both British and American heavy bombers. The next November he was named Commanding General of the U.S. 15th Air Force operating in North Africa and Sicily. From January 1944 to the end of the fighting in Europe, he was in England directing attacks on German cities. He then moved with the 8th Air Force to Okinawa.

Bibliography. Q. Reynolds, *The Amazing Mr. Doolittle* (1953).

DOOLITTLE RAID. First American aerial attack on the Japanese mainland in the spring of 1942.

BACKGROUND. The Japanese surprise air raid on December 7, 1941 (*see* PEARL HARBOR) as well as a series of additional targets from Korea down to Burma, effectively neutralized American naval power temporarily in the Pacific. Recovery was rapid. What Washington needed was a bold move to bolster morale at a time of Japanese military success.

Only a few weeks after Pearl Harbor, a 45-year-old peacetime flyer, Lt. Col. James H. Doolittle (*q.v.*) suggested to his superior officers that he be allowed to lead a bombing raid on Tokyo. At first his idea was dismissed as preposterous, but the aviator was deadly serious. In January 1942 he was assigned to Air Force headquarters in Washington.

PREPARATIONS. Doolittle's call for volunteers to work on an unnamed secret mission was answered by many times the men he could take with him. He chose the North American *B-25 Mitchell,* a medium bomber of excellent speed, gas consumption, and ability to take rough handling. He trained his men with hundreds of take-offs on a short, white-lined landing field. Crewmen studied maps, pictures, and silhouettes for instant recognition of course and objectives. To foil enemy capture, Doolittle provided his planes with a simple 20-cent sight to replace the top-secret Norden bomb sights. The aircraft were fitted with extra fuel tanks.

Flyers and men were loaded aboard the aircraft carrier *Hornet,* commanded by Adm. William F. ("Bull") Halsey (*q.v.*). Training continued on the flat-top, including lectures on navigation, meteorology, and the topography of Japan. Gunners practiced shooting at kites flying above the carrier. The men were carefully briefed: They would move to a point about 550 miles off Tokyo to avoid enemy picket boat patrol; the planes would be launched just before dark, the strike would be made at night; landings would be made on the Chinese mainland in the early morning.

MISSION. The *Hornet* was more than 650 miles from Tokyo when a small Japanese ship was sighted. Fear of a radio warning to Tokyo (later proved to be groundless), led Halsey to sink the vessel. Take-off time was moved up ten hours, a decision that added considerably to the danger of the mission.

At 8:20 A.M. on April 18, 1942, with Doolittle in the lead plane, the crewmen of 16 *B-25*s took off on the mission. One by one the planes rose from a bobbing and slanting deck and began to hedge-hop over the waves to avoid enemy radar. The planes were not spotted until they had almost reached their objective within four hours. Roaring in at tree-top level, the planes rose to 1,500 feet and then dropped their bombs on selected targets in Tokyo, Osaka, Kobe, and Nagoya. Japanese planes that took off from a nearby training field could not stop the attack. The antiaircraft fire, furious but ineffective, brought down only a barrage balloon. The raiders hit a large naval vessel under construction, a flying school, armaments plants, dockyards, an aircraft factory, and the Yokosuka naval base. An American pilot observed a baseball game in progress with players and spectators running for cover. The bombardiers carefully avoided hitting the Emperor's palace.

Japanese radio reported the astounding news that planes had appeared over Tokyo for the first time, inflicting damage on schools and hospitals. "Invading planes failed to cause any damage on military establishments, although casualties in the schools and hospitals are as yet unknown. The inhuman attack is causing widespread indignation among the people."

ESCAPE. After releasing their bombs, the raiders dived again to tree-top level and headed for the coast. This was the most hazardous part of the mission. All planes got away safely, but as they scattered they ran into a storm. Bucking head winds in darkness above strange territory, their gasoline lines drained, most of the men bailed out. Eight who landed in Japanese-occupied areas of China were taken prisoner. The rest, helped by Chinese civilians, were able to make their way to Chungking (Chong-qing). Of the 82 airmen on the mission, 70 eventually reached home. Three were executed by the Japanese for bombing civilians targets. The *Hornet* escaped and returned to Pearl Harbor on April 25, 1942.

AFTERMATH. The Japanese public was stunned and shaken by this thrust into their supposedly impregnable defenses. Without air-raid shelters, mobs panicked, running in all directions, pushing, shouting, screaming. High Japanese officials apologized to the Emperor for their "negligence." The officer in charge of Tokyo's antiaircraft defense committed suicide. Military authorities were mystified by the raid.

No clues came from Washington about the raid. Two days later the U.S. War Department issued a communiqué describing the raid but not disclosing its base. President Roosevelt remarked that the airmen had taken off from Shangri-La, the fictional Tibetan retreat of James Hilton's novel, *Lost Horizon* (1933). The Berlin radio reported: "Doolittle carried out his attack from the air base Shangri-La, which was otherwise not described by Roosevelt."

The Tokyo radio announced that some of the airmen had been executed but gave no names. "The same policy," it added with a dash of American slang, "will be continued in the future. And by the way, don't forget, America, make sure that who comes here has a special pass to hell, and rest assured that it will be a one-way ticket." Roosevelt told the Americans about the executions "with a feeling of deepest horror."

SIGNIFICANCE. It was a spectacular, if near suicidal, feat. An American reporter started his story: "The Doolittle raid, though hardly decisive. . . ." It was, indeed, a raid of small military impact, but its strategic results were important. There was comparatively little damage, but the effect on American and

Japanese morale was great. For Americans it was a tremendous boost, the opening reply to Pearl Harbor, and a portent of things to come. Significantly, the Japanese naval command, ashamed of having allowed an attack on the imperial homeland, was prompted to seek a confrontation with the U.S. Navy as early as May 1942. That led to the defeats at the Battles of Coral Sea and Midway (*qq.v.*), as a result of which the Japanese were never able to meet the Americans again on equal terms.

Bibliography. Q. Reynolds, *The Amazing Mr. Doolittle* (1953); and R. Jackson, *Famous Bomber Raids of World War II* (1980).

DORCHESTER. U.S. Army transport sunk in February 1943.

Formerly a passenger ship, the *Dorchester* was detailed in 1942 for carrying troops and supplies to Newfoundland and Greenland. On February 2, 1943, she was sunk by a German U-Boat with heavy loss of life. (*See* FOUR CHAPLAINS.)

DOUBLE CROSS SYSTEM. British counterintelligence service that caught German spies in England and converted them into double agents. These spies succeeded in misleading the Germans without arousing their suspicions. *See* ESPIONAGE; MASTERMAN, JOHN C.; *MINCEMEAT*; and XX-COMMITTEE.)

Bibliography. J. Masterman, *The Double Cross System of the War of 1939–1945* (1972).

DOUGLAS, WILLIAM SHOLTO (1893–1969). British Air Marshal.

On May 1940 Douglas was named Deputy Chief of Staff. The next November he succeeded Gen. Hugh Dowding (*q.v.*) as Commander of the RAF (*q.v.*) fighter Command. He was made Air Marshal in December. Under his command the RAF turned to the offensive and began attacking German targets in France. His strategy was to force the Germans to keep as many planes as possible on the western front, thereby relieving pressure on the Russians. He initiated two methods of attack: the low-level strike relying mainly on surprise, and the high-level attack with top squadrons operating above 20,000 feet. In 1943 Douglas commanded the RAF in the Middle East. In 1944 he was assigned to lead the Coastal Command for the assault on Fortress Europe. (*See* NORMANDY INVASION.)

Short, powerfully built, athletically inclined, Douglas was known throughout his career as a dynamic leader. He was one of the most popular officers in the Fighter Command.

Bibliography. See his autobiography, *Years of Combat* (1963).

DOWDING, HUGH CASWALL TREMENHEERE (1882–1970). Chief Marshal of the British Royal Air Force (*q.v.*) and architect of victory in the Battle of Britain (*q.v.*).

Although he was trained as an artillery officer, Dowding in the 1930s was a research and development member of the governing body of the Royal Air Force. He vigorously promoted the development of radar (*q.v.*) as well as *Spitfire* and *Hurricane* fighters (*q.v.*). He was appointed head of the Fighter Command in 1936 and was made Air Chief Marshal in 1937.

When the Germans struck at the Low Countries and France in May 1940, Dowding withdrew his fighters and brought them home to defend Britain. Directing his squadrons in the Batttle of Britain from July to October 1940, he is regarded as the victor of the air battle. Although his pilots were outnumbered, his brilliant skill enabled him to win air superiority and thwart Hitler's invasion plans.

Noted for his unsmiling wit and stubborn temper, Dowding was a somewhat inscrutable figure. His junior officers nicknamed him "Stuffy" because of his reserved manner and university don appearance. He was not promoted after 1940. In November 1942 he retired and was succeeded by William Sholto Douglas (*q.v.*) as commander of the RAF Fighter Command. He became Lord Dowding in 1943.

Bibliography. R. Wright, *The Man Who Won the Battle of Britain* (1970).

DRESDEN, BOMBING OF. Air-fire attack on the German city in early 1945.

TARGET. Former capital of Saxony, Dresden was on the Elbe 98 miles southeast of Berlin. The city was called "the German Florence" because of its magnificent rococo art collections and splendid baroque buildings. The British Bomber Command was more interested in Dresden as a major communications and industrial center.

BACKGROUND. In the early stages of the war there was a controversy in England on the relative effectiveness of high explosives and incendiaries in the bombing of German cities. Eventually, Gen. Arthur T. Harris (*q.v.*), Commander-in-Chief of the British Bomber Command, accepted the idea of knockout attacks by incendiaries. The decision was to be fateful for Dresden.

Until the last months of the war Dresden escaped the Allied air assault that was smashing one German city after another. The Russians called for more bombing. The Allied Supreme Command agreed that Dresden was now the main communications and transportation center serving the Russian front and hence was open to attack. The city was filled with some 200,000 refugees who had fled from the advancing Russians to join the 630,000 inhabitants.

FIRESTORM. By far the worst raid came on the night of February 13–14, 1945, Dresden was caught in a firestorm that engulfed people and buildings. Similar in effect to the Hamburg firestorm (*see* HAMBURG, BOMBING OF), it was one of the most terrible events of the war.

LOSSES. Little is known with certainty about the number of victims. Estimates vary from 30,000 to 300,000. For a long time the figure of 225,000 was quoted internationally. Objective accounts based on expert evidence give a figure of 60,000 dead and at least 30,000 more injured. The property damage was enormous, with more than 7,000 public buildings and 30,000 houses destroyed, including many churches and schools. The center of the city was gone; over 1,600 acres of the inner town wrecked. Russian troops who entered Dresden on May 8, 1945, found the Prager, Moritz, Augustus, and Ring Strassen to be the only paved roads between ruins.

AFTERMATH. Germans bitterly denounced the bombing of Dresden as an inexcusable act of barbarism. The Allies replied that the city was a legitimate target and pointed to *Luftwaffe* raids on Warsaw, Rotterdam, and Coventry. (*See* ROTTERDAM, BOMBING OF; and COVENTRY, BOMBING OF.)

Bibliography. H. Rumpf, *The Bombing of Germany*, trans. by E. Fitzgerald (1963); and D. Irving, *The Destruction of Dresden* (1964). Irving's book is highly controversial.

DROP-TANK. An auxiliary fuel container tank used under the wing of combat aircraft and jettisoned when empty.

This simple American invention was introduced several months after raids by the 8th Air Force on ball-bearing plants in Regensburg and Schweinfurt. (*See* REGENSBURG RAID; and SCHWEINFURT RAIDS.) The drop-tank greatly extended fighter-escort range and enabled American and British heavy bombers to fly into the heart of Germany while protected by accompanying fighters using the device. With it American *Thunderbolts* and *Mustangs* could fly half again as far as the lumbering *Flying Fortresses* (*q.v.*) and *Liberators*. (*See* BERLIN, BOMBING OF.)

DULLES, ALLEN WELSH (1893–1966). U.S. Government official and leading American espionage agent during the war.

From October 1942 until the end of the war Dulles served as Chief of the Office of Strategic Services (*q.v.*) in Switzerland. His office on the Herrengasse in Bern became a center of European resistance to Hitler and was used by many agents from the occupied countries. Through Adm. Wilhelm Canaris (*q.v.*), Dulles managed to penetrate the *Abwehr*, the German Intelligence Bureau. He was also assisted by Gerd von Gavernitz, a German-American living in Switzerland who had many connections inside Germany. In his discussions with German emissaries, Dulles stressed the unacceptability of any postwar German Government that included Nazi leaders. Members of the German underground who visited him urged him to convince his superiors that the policy of unconditional surrender would drive the Germans into the Russian camp.

Among Dulles's exploits was the engineering of a revolt in the Italian village of Campione, which caused a change from a Fascist to a pro-Allied regime and enabled OSS agents to use this border town as a point of entry into Italy. His activities helped lead to the capitulation of Italy effective September 8, 1943. He played a leading role in *Operation Sunrise,* which led to the surrender of German troops in northern Italy in 1945. Until late 1945 he headed the OSS mission to Germany.

Bibliography. Dulles was the author of *Can America Stay Neutral?* (1938) (with H. F. Armstrong); *Germany's Underground* (1947); and *The Craft of Intelligence* (1963). For his biography, see R. Edwards, *A Study of a Master Spy, Allen Dulles* (1961).

DUMBARTON OAKS CONFERENCE. Allied war conference held in the summer of 1944 to lay the groundwork for a postwar international organization.

BACKGROUND. On January 1, 1942, the Declaration of the United Nations was signed at the First Washington Conference, reaffirming the principles of the Atlantic Charter (*qq.v.*). From time to time statesmen pointed to the necessity for the formation of a world organization. But it was not until the Moscow Conference (*q.v.*) of October 18–November 1, 1943, that an official communiqué dealt with the subject and proposed "the necessity of establishing at the earliest practicable date a general international organization." A month later the proposal was reaffirmed at the Teheran Conference (*q.v.*).

PARTICIPANTS. To implement the Moscow Declaration, U.S. Secretary of State Cordell Hull (*q.v.*) invited representatives of the United Kingdom, the Soviet Union, and China to join in exploratory conversations. The conference was held at an estate called Dumbarton Oaks near Washington, D.C. The delegates met in two shifts. From August 21 to September 28, 1944, they discussed a draft plan. Then the Chinese replaced the Russians and the discussions continued until October 7, 1944. The Russians did not want to jeopardize their neutrality policy toward Japan and hence declined to particpate at the same conference table with the Chinese.

DECISIONS. General agreement was reached on the so-called Dumbarton Oaks Proposals or the Dumbarton Oaks Plan, but not on the matter of voting procedure.

DUMBARTON OAKS PLAN

By formation of a postwar international organization, the plan projected for prevention of future wars and promotion of world economic and social stability and progress.

VETO

At Dumbarton Oaks the first sharp differences arose over voting procedures in the world organization. Russia demanded separate representation for each of the 16 Soviet Republics, and also the right of veto for Great Powers, even in disputes to which they were a party. Working formulas for voting were agreed upon later at the Yalta Conference (*q.v.*).

Despite differences in the matter of the veto, the Allies issued a declaration that this would not affect their solidarity in the war against Germany.

SIGNIFICANCE. The Dumbarton Oaks Conference was an important step in the formation of the United Nations. The proposals were submitted at the general meeting held in San Francisco in the spring of 1945. (*See* SAN FRANCISCO CONFERENCE.) A working formula on the veto problem was reached at the Yalta Conference (*q.v.*), but the veto remained a stumbling block for the new world organization.

Bibliography. V. N. Dean, *The Four Cornerstones of Peace* (1946).

DUNKIRK EVACUATION. Code or cover name *Dynamo*. Rescue of a large British Expeditionary Force (*q.v.*) from the port of Dunkirk in 1940.

BACKGROUND. Toward the end of May 1940 there was confusion in the French and British ranks as German mechanized forces pushed ahead in an overwhelming *Blitzkrieg* (*q.v.*). On May 27 Leopold III, King of the Belgians, sent word to the British that he would be forced to capitulate to avoid a ruinous collapse. Leopold's decision placed the BEF in acute danger with its left flank almost completely open. The Germans surged in for the kill.

For the British the only hope for escape was through the port of Dunkirk, the most northerly seaport of France at the entrance to the Strait of Dover. To delay the enemy they opened the sluice gates around Dunkirk. The French fought rear-guard delaying actions at Lille and Cassel. Meanwhile, *Luftwaffe* (*q.v.*) bombers and German artillery hammered at the almost trapped enemy.

PREPARATION. Over the radio the British Admiralty requested all owners of self-propelled pleasure craft between 30 and 100 feet in length to prepare their boats for immediate service. The idea was to use civilian assistance in one of the strangest rescue operations in history. The response was immediate and effective.

RESCUE. Starting on May 26, 1940, Britain's armada set sail for Dunkirk. In all there were 848 vessels, naval and civilian craft—British, French, Dutch, and Belgian—carrying 338,226 men. Included were destroyers, mine sweepers, Channel ferries, passenger steamers, pleasure boats, drifters, merchantmen, and yachts. There were tugs with strings of barges, speedboats, coasters, colliers, even car ferries. Never in history had there been such a unique conglomeration of boats and ships. They were manned by every kind of Englishman from the fictional Mrs. Miniver's husband (in *Mrs. Miniver* [1940] by Jan Struthers [Joyce Maxtone Graham]) to Sea Scouts and cockney taxicab drivers, clerks with bowler hats, and bankers with umbrellas. All were wet, chilled, and hungry; they sailed on toward the pillars of smoke and fire rising from Dunkirk.

Traffic in the Channel was a nightmare as sleek destroyers dashed in and out, their wash nearly capsizing the smaller vessels. There was one collision after another. But this amazing flotilla pushed on toward the target. The beaches at Dunkirk were black with lines of weary troops, who staggered into the shallows and boarded the small boats.

For nine days the impromptu fleet moved back and forth rescuing the 338,226 men, of whom 139,911 were French and Belgian and the rest British. Out of the rescue boats to the soil of England staggered an army of fatigued, famished troops. Many were blood-covered or oil-spattered. One reporter noted that they brought with them "half the canine population of France."

SIGNIFICANCE. The retreat at Dunkirk would have been impossible without Hitler's action in halting his *Panzer* (*q.v.*) forces outside the port before the evacuation. In this sense the achievement was due to Hitler's error. German propaganda pronounced Dunkirk a major Allied defeat, but were shocked and perplexed by what was actually a miracle of deliverance. The desperate adventure had been forced upon the British by potential disaster. It was carried out under the eyes of an enemy flushed with victory and certain of conquest. It revealed once again the British genius for improvisation in critical moments of their history. A great army was saved to fight again. It was, said John Masefield, a "Nine Days' Wonder."

Bibliography. E. K. Chatterton, *The Epic of Dunkirk* (1940); J. Masefield, *The Nine Days' Wonder* (1941); and R. Carse, *Dunkirk, 1940* (1970).

E

E-BOAT. Allied abbreviation for "enemy boat," German or Italian motor torpedo boats. (*See also* S-Boat.)

EAKER, IRA CLARENCE (1896–   ). U.S. air commander.

In 1941 Eaker was sent to England to observe air combat there. He returned in 1942 with orders to select air bases for the American 8th Air Force. On August 17, 1942, he led the first American heavy bomber attack against targets in France. In December he was given command of the 8th Air Force, in which post he directed the destructive daylight precision bombing of German targets. The summer of 1944 he organized the first shuttle-bombing missions from Italy to the Soviet Union. He served as Air Commander-in-Chief of the Allied Air Force in *Operation Dragoon*, the invasion of southern France. He retired in 1947 to become an aircraft industry executive.

Bibliography. Eaker wrote three books with Gen. H. H. Arnold (*qq.v.*): *The Flying Game* (1936); *Winged Warfare* (1941); and *Army Flyer* (1942).

EAM. *See* NATIONAL LIBERATION MOVEMENT.

EASTERN FRONT, CAMPAIGNS ON THE. Also called the Russo-German campaigns. Operations in battles between Nazi Germany and the Soviet Union from June 22, 1941, the invasion of the USSR, to May 2, 1945, the fall of Berlin.

BACKGROUND. In *Mein Kampf* (*q.v.*), his autobiography, and in virtually all his speechs before 1939, Hitler designated Bolshevik Russia as Germany's major enemy. The world was astonished in the summer of 1939 when he made a direct about-face and signed a nonaggression pact with the Soviet Union. (*See* RUSSO-GERMAN NONAGGRESSION PACT.) But the German *Fuehrer* never forgot his ultimate goal of winning living space in the east at the expense of Bolshevik Russia. (*See LEBENSRAUM.*) Secretly, he intended to turn on his partner in the east at the first favorable opportunity.

DIRECTIVE NO. 21. On December 18, 1940, Hitler issued his War Directive No. 21, which outlined *Fall Barbarossa* (*Case Barbarossa*). (*See BARBAROSSA.*) He ordered German Armed Forces to prepare, even before the conclusion of the battle against England, "to crush Russia in a rapid campaign." The *Wehrmacht* (*q.v.*) was to employ all available formations to that end, with the reservation that the occupied territories were to be insured against surprise attack. The *Fuehrer* ordered Hermann Goering (*q.v.*) to make the *Luftwaffe* (*q.v.*), the air force, available for the Eastern campaign so that the army could bring land operations to a successful conclusion. Meanwhile, the main efforts of the navy would continue to be directed against England during the Eastern campaign.

PREPARATIONS. In his directive Hitler stated that he would issue orders for the deployment of *Barbarossa* eight weeks before the campaign was to begin. The bulk of the enemy force in western Russia was to be destroyed by "daring operations," led by deeply penetrating armored spearheads. The Russians were not to be allowed to withdraw into the depths of their country. The final objective was to erect a barrier against Asiatic hordes on the general line Volga-Archangel. The Russian Baltic Fleet would be deprived of its bases and rendered incapable of action.

Hitler counted on the active support of Rumania and Finland to protect the German flanks. Rumania would support the German southern flank, while Finland would cover the advance of the Northern Group of German forces moving down from Norway. Swedish railways and roads would be available for the movement of German troops in the North. Additional specific tasks were assigned to army, navy, and air force.

SECRECY. Hitler called for secrecy to be maintained for the entire operation. All orders by commanders were to be labeled "precautionary measures in case Russians should alter its present attitude toward us."

BARBAROSSA. On June 22, 1941, suddenly and without warning, the Nazi war machine surged across the borders of Poland and began the war with Soviet Russia. Along 1,800 miles of front was a veritable hell on earth—planes roared over the battlefields; artillery shells screamed; giant tanks ripped vicious holes in enemy lines; swift fluid maneuvers were held on open ground; deadly fighting took place in ruined streets and shattered buildings; everywhere were pincers, encirclement, entrapment, attrition. The Germans, using their previously successful *Blitzkrieg* (*q.v.*) technique pushed ahead in three massive drives—to the north under Field Marshal Wilhelm von Leeb, to the center under Field Marshal Fedor von Bock (*q.v.*), and to the south under Field Marshal Gerhard von Rundstedt (*q.v.*).

FROM POLISH TO RUSSIAN SOIL. The rampaging German *Panzers* sliced through Poland, taking Brest-Litovsk within two days. The Battle of Bialystok-Minsk resulted in a quick German victory. By September Hitler had won the Battle of the Ukraine. Kiev fell on September 19. The Germans completed a brilliant pincers movement and captured about 660,000 Russians.

SCORCHED EARTH. Once the shock of the attack wore off, the Russians called on their ancient allies—space, time, and winter. They carried out Stalin's so-called scorched-earth policy—smashing everything in the wake of their retreat. Living close to nature, they had a great capacity for enduring hardship. They destroyed factories, bridges, and dams, even their own homes. When hopelessly surrounded, they resisted all the more.

In mid-August 1941 the Russians evacuated Smolensk, just 200 miles from Moscow. The position in the center remained static. To the north at Leningrad and to the south in the Caucasus the German drives slowed to a halt. Nevertheless, there was great joy in Berlin. "Russia is broken!" Hitler shouted to the world. "She will never rise again." From London came the voice of Churchill: "Any man or state who fights against Nazism will have our aid."

BATTLE OF MOSCOW. At this junction Hitler made a critical and wrong decision. His generals favored a concentrated drive on Moscow with every ounce of German strength. The *Fuehrer,* convinced of his infallible military wisdom, decided instead for a super-Cannae, a vast encircling movement which would take Leningrad in the north and the Ukraine in the south, and only then would he turn on Moscow.

Hitler gave specific orders to von Bock on the central front. The general was to use his 17th Infantry Division, two motorized divisions, 1,000 tanks, and 900 aircraft to work out a series of smaller encirclements within the greater arc. One spearhead would drive northeast toward Kalinin, outflanking Moscow from the north; another would hit Tula and Orel to outflank Moscow from the south; and a third would push directly east through Vyazma and make a direct frontal attack on Moscow. Meanwhile, many of von Bock's veteran troops were shipped to the north and south, leaving him with mostly infantry for the attack on Moscow. Von Clausewitz, the great Prussian philosopher of war, would have been appalled.

Initially, the plan went well. In three weeks von Bock moved to within 70 miles of Moscow. The Soviet Government and the diplomatic corps fled to Kuibyshev, some 500 miles to the east, although Stalin himself remained in the capital. Hitler's generals asked for a halt in order to rest and resume the drive in the spring. The *Fuehrer* turned them down; he wanted immediate victory and called for a second great offensive against Moscow. That offensive began on November 15, 1941, and by December 2, advance elements had penetrated into the suburbs within sight of the Kremlin.

As the temperature dropped, so did the fortunes of the Germans. The whole countryside withdrew into white blankness. Water froze in the boilers of German locomotives; lubricants hardened in artillery weapons; tank engines froze and burst. Worst of all, the Germans were inadequately clad against the Russian winter. The Russians, clad in fur jackets, padded felt boots, woollen underclothes, and fur caps, struck back hard at the frostbitten, miserable German invaders.

COUNTERTHRUST. In December 1941 Gen. Georgi Zhukov (*q.v.*) began a blazing counterattack that stalled the Germans in the ice and snow. On December 8 Hitler announced that his offensive in the east was being suspended because of the weather. In six months he had lost 162,314 killed, 577,767 wounded, and 33,334 missing, by official German figures. He had come within sight of the Kremlin only to find his armies in the center pushed back for distances varying up to 200 miles.

LEVÉE EN MASSE AT LENINGRAD. Meanwhile, in the north the tremendous pressure of the German thrust on Leningrad was meeting stubborn resistance. The struggle for the key city soon reached an acute stage and the operations there overshadowed in scale and intensity those elsewhere on the eastern front. Eventually, the battle was transformed into a prolonged siege. (*See* LENINGRAD, SIEGE OF.) The Germans never successfully completed their mission on the northern front.

FALL OF SEVASTOPOL. On May 13, 1942, the Russians launched an offensive at Kharkov, west of Stalingrad. The next great battle was for Sevastopol, which began in June 1942 when the Germans strengthened their attack on the Crimean city. (*See* SEVASTOPOL, SIEGE OF.) It was Leningrad all over again with bombs, shellfire, air assaults, an inferno of fire and smoke. The struggle reached a roaring crescendo when the Germans hurled every ounce of their power on the burning city. The defenders finally capitulated on June 30, 1942, after some had blown themselves up with their last munitions. Everything else of military value to the Germans was destroyed.

VORONEZH AND ROSTOV. The next scene of operations was on the central front. Poised near the Don River was a massive German Army of 60 divisions, 1,000 tanks, and 3,000 first-lines planes. Its immediate target was Voronezh. (*See* CODE NAMES, GERMAN, *OPERATION BLAU*). In June 1942 the offensive began with the bombardment of Kursk. German forces crossed the Don and converged on Voronezh. So furious was the Red counterattack that the Germans decided instead to strike at Stalingrad in the southeast. Meanwhile, the Russians evacuated Rostov.

Hitler now divided his Rostov forces into two major parts. One he sent to the Black Sea coast and the Caucasus with the aim of clearing the area and driving on to the Baku oil fields. This spearhead won Maikop but fell short of the considerably larger oil fields at Grozny, and never reached the Caspian Sea. The second major force turned to Stalingrad.

BATTLE OF STALINGRAD. The epic struggle for Stalingrad—the Verdun of World War II—began in the summer of 1942. As days, weeks, and months went by, the battle increased in intensity. At first the Germans and Russians fought over portions of the city, then over streets, and finally in man-to-man combat. As winter approached, the German generals advised retreat, but an adamant Hitler again refused and insisted that he was on the Volga to stay. The result was that, in early February 1943, Gen. Friedrich Paulus (*q.v.*), trapped by the Soviet Army, surrendered. (*See* STALINGRAD, BATTLE OF.) That debacle broke the offensive power of the German Army and from then on the initiative was in the hands of the Russians. Stalingrad was a major turning point of the war.

BATTLE OF KURSK. Despite his shattering defeat at Stalingrad, Hitler was still reluctant to order a general retreat. Gen. Erich von Manstein (*q.v.*) launched a desperate counterattack and on March 11, 1943, again took Kharkov. On July 5, 1943, under the code name *Citadel,* an even heavier assault struck at Kursk, where the Russians occupied a massive bulge. The Germans struck with a great *Panzer* (*q.v.*) force, including new *Tiger* and *Panther* tanks. The defending Russians had 20,000 artillery pieces as well as many more, if less sophisticated, tanks of their own. The confrontation turned out to be one of the biggest and most vicious tank battles ever fought, with as many as 3,000 tanks engaged at the same time on the flat grasslands. In mid-July the Russians threw in seemingly endless reserves of men and tanks. Von Manstein had to withdraw or lose his entire armored force.

THRUST WESTWARD, 1943-1944. The Russians moved inexorably westward. Events on the eastern front from this point on must be judged in light of Hitler's Directive No. 51. His *Blitzkrieg* in Russia, which should have been over two years earlier, had foundered. The West was showing increasing power and was now rising against him. He ordered his defenses in the west to be strengthened even at the risk of giving up German conquests in the east.

After the Battle of Kursk, Russian armies fanned out and increased pressure on Kharkov. On September 25, 1943, the Germans, as a means of avoiding encirclement, abandoned Smolensk. By the end of September the Russians reached the banks of the Dnieper. In early November they took the city of Kiev, but the defending Germans escaped. A German counteroffensive took Zhitomir. The Russians then moved on the offensive in the Ukraine, utilizing equipment, food, and fuel left behind by the retreating Germans.

The Battle of the Ukraine lasted from December 1943 to May 1944. On December 24, 1943, the Russians launched their main winter offensive, recapturing Zhitomir. On January 4, 1944, advance elements of the Russian Army moved into Poland. South of Kiev the Russians encircled ten German divisions: in a vain attempt to save the ten divisions the Germans abandoned Nikopol, at the Dnieper in the south. A German counteroffensive on April 23 was unsuccessful. Odessa fell to the Red Army on April 10. On May 9, 1944, the Germans remaining in the Crimea, caught in a Soviet pincers movement, abandoned Sevastopol.

Additional confusion in the German ranks followed the July 20, 1944, attempt on the life of Hitler. (*See* JULY PLOT.) At this time the Russians commenced an offensive to clear Belorussia. One Russian triumph came after another: Battle of Jassy-Kishinev (August 1944); liberation of the Balkans (1944–1945); peace with Finland (1944); capture of East Prussia (1945); taking of Königsberg (April 1945); and the liberation of Hungary, Czechoslovakia, Austria, and East Germany (1944–1945). In the final drive the Russians entered Berlin. (*See* BERLIN, BATTLE OF.)

SIGNIFICANCE. These campaigns on the eastern front added up to a tremendous Russian victory. The initial Nazi *Blitz* had slowed down to a crawl on the Russian steppes in the face of firm Russian resistance and the worst weather in half a century. An embittered Hitler tried to explain it: "The Russians," he said, "are a cruel, bestial, and animal opponent. We made a mistake about one thing: We did not know how gigantic the preparations of this opponent against Germany were." The "invincible *Wehrmacht*" (*q.v.*) was battered all the way from Stalingrad to Berlin. Everything about this epic was on a massive scale. The German gains were erased, the boasting of Hitler proved a mockery, and the flower of German armies destroyed in forests, swamps, and steppes.

Bibliography. I. Ehrenburg, *Russia at War* (1943); W.E.D. Allen and P. Muratoff, *The Russian Campaigns of 1941-1943* (1944); E. Kuby, *The Russians and Berlin, 1945* (1968); A. Beloborodov, *They Did Not Pass (The Battle of Moscow)* (1968); P. Carell, *Scorched Earth: The Russo-German War, 1943-1944,* (1970); G. Jukes, *The Defense of Moscow* (1970); A. W. Turner, *Disaster at Moscow, 1941-1942* (1970); and A. Seaton, *The Russo-German War, 1941-1945* (1971).

EASTERN SOLOMONS, BATTLE OF THE. *See* GUADALCANAL CAMPAIGNS.

EBEN EMAEL, FORT. "Impregnable" Belgian fortress near Liège taken in only 30 hours by the Germans after the start of their *Blitzkrieg* (*q.v.*) in 1940.

BACKGROUND. The defensive hopes of the Belgians lay in obstacles of the Albert Canal and Eben Emael. The giant fortress, perched above the surrounding countryside near the German border, covered the bridges of the Meuse as well as the Albert Canal. Like the Maginot Line (*q.v.*), Eben Emael was a product of a defensive mentality. Constructed between 1931 and 1935, it was believed to be the single most fortified stronghold in the world, certainly powerful enough to hold off a German invasion until assistance came from the Western Allies.

PREPARATION. For the Germans, Eben Emael, although just a few miles across the border from Aachen, stood directly in the path to Brussels. Throughout the winter of 1939–1940, during the so-called Phony War (*see SITZKRIEG*) German units prepared for the assault. Using accurate reports furnished by spies, (*see* ESPIONAGE), they constructed a full-scale model of the Belgian fort. They trained engineers, demolition experts, and parachutists to familiarize themselves with every square inch of Eben Emael. They held exercises day after day until every man knew exactly what he was supposed to do. When the time came the troops reacted automatically and carried out the plan to perfection.

ASSAULT. Early on the morning of May 10, 1940, the Germans abruptly ended the Phony War and struck at both Holland and Belgium. One unit headed for Eben Emael. The operation was carried out exactly as planned. A dozen new *Luftwaffe* (*q.v.*) gliders took off carrying a lieutenant and 78 parachute engineers all bearing explosives, guns, and ammunition. These commandos landed on the flat roof of the fortress. They went to work like mechanical robots. Protected by smoke screens, they placed detonating charges into the barrels of the big defensive guns, dynamited observation posts, exits, and ventilator shafts, and threw hand grenades into ammunition elevators and dumps. Small commando units crawled from cupola to cupola, dropping explosive charges, and then scrambled to safety.

DEFENSE. The garrison of 1,200 Belgians was surprised by the swiftness and novelty of the attack. Soon most were trapped. The commander radioed for help to the nearby forts of Pontisse and Neuchâteau, which responded by mistakenly bombarding the superstructure of Eben Emael itself with shells. One astonished war correspondent could scarcely believe it: "The spectacle of one Belgian fort firing on another was the ultimate satire on immobile defense." At 12:30 A.M. on May 11, 1940, the garrison surrendered.

LOSSES. Casualties were light on both sides. The Belgians lost 60 dead and 40 wounded. The Germans lost only six men killed. What was supposed to be the most powerful fort in the world lay desolate and barren.

CONSEQUENCES. The success of the German attack was due to thorough training of the men, overwhelming air superiority, freight-carrying gliders, and use of a new highly intensive explosive. The feat opened the way for the German thrust to the Belgian capital and to the coast, while at the same time spearheads swept through the wooded mountains in the Ardennes to the southeast between the Meuse and the Moselle. The dispirited Belgians fell back to join the British Expeditionary Force (*q.v.*) between Brussels and Antwerp, only to see both cities abandoned to the enemy within five days.

As the Allies struggled desperately, King Leopold III (*q.v.*), deeming any further resistance useless, surrendered the Belgian Army on May 28, 1940. He gave no warning to the Allies and left their flank fatally exposed. The Allied forces in the north, now cut off, retreated to the one remaining port of Dunkirk (*q.v.*) (*See also* LOW COUNTRIES, CAMPAIGNS IN THE.)

Bibliography. I. Hay, *The Army at War: The Battle of Flanders* (1941); F. Ellis, *The War in France and Flanders, 1939-40* (1954); and J. E. Mrazek, *The Fall of Eben Emael: Prelude to Dunkirk* (1971).

ECONOMIC CONSEQUENCES OF THE WAR. The most costly conflict in history resulted in severe economic dislocations.

WAR COSTS. When the fighting ceased in Europe, the belligerent nations had to pause and take stock of the damage done. The enormous loss of life bled Europe of its young manhood. (*See* CASUALTIES, WAR.) The destruction of property was greater than in any previous war. There can be no accurate statistics on the value of material losses sustained during the war, but the following estimates, based primarily on the research of historian Geoffrey Bruun, indicate the tremendous war costs.

GOVERNMENTAL EXPENDITURES. The cost to the belligerent governments for war matériel and armaments added up to U.S. $1,154 billion. This represented an outlay of $120 billion for Britain, $317 billion for the United States, $192 billion for the Soviet Union, $94 billion for Italy, $272 billion for Germany, and lesser amounts for other nations.

DAMAGE TO CIVILIAN PROPERTY. Official reports of expenditures did not include any allowance for damage to civilian property. In the Soviet Union this amounted to at least U.S.$128 billion, in Britain to $5 billion. German losses were at least $50 billion to $75 billion. In other European countries an additional $230 million were added to the war costs.

Any attempt to give an accurate estimate of the value of destroyed property is futile. The astronomical figures cannot be grasped easily. Immense destruction of physical plants far exceeded that of World War I, where the desolation was confined mostly to battle areas. Material losses cut through the entire economic structure of Europe. Even a limited account gives a clue to the extent of the damage.

—The British had a third of their homes destroyed or damaged. For the French, Belgians, and Dutch the figure approached 20 percent.

—Allied merchant shipping losses were 5,150 vessels with a tonnage of

21,570,000, of which 2,828 were victims of Axis submarines, mostly German.

—Poland reported 30 percent of all its buildings destroyed, 60 percent of its school and administration buildings, 43 percent of its art, 35 percent of its farms, and 32 percent of its mines.

—In 49 of Germany's largest cities, 39 percent of the homes were destroyed or seriously damaged. Central business districts were reduced to rubble.

—Transportation was disrupted throughout Europe by the destruction of rail centers, locomotives, and bridges. Harbor areas everywhere were subjected to especially heavy bombardment.

—Agriculture suffered heavily from the loss of manpower, animals, machinery, and facilities.

WEAKENED ECONOMIC STRUCTURE. By 1945 the economic structures of countries everywhere were in chaos. Under the impact of war, the two great superpowers, the United States and the Soviet Union, harnessed their productive forces and reached unprecedented levels of war production. This economic fact, together with other factors, was responsible for a major change in the power relationship of the United States and the Soviet Union with Western Europe. (*See* POLITICAL CONSEQUENCES OF THE WAR.) The Kremlin limited its assistance to its areas of influence in Eastern Europe, while Washington turned its interest to the Western European democracies.

MARSHALL PLAN. Although the productive capacity of Europe had been severely damaged by the war, it was not completely destroyed. Recovery began almost at once. With American assistance, European production was able to recover its pre-war status. In the United States it was recognized that European prosperity was closely related to the security of Americans. Washington also wanted to prevent any further extension of Soviet military power. On June 5, 1947, in a commencement address at Harvard University, U.S. Secretary of State George C. Marshall (*q.v.*) outlined a plan for the economic rehabilitation of Europe, which came to be known as the Marshall Plan:

Europe's requirements for the next three or four years of foreign food and other essential products—principally from America—are so much greater than her present ability to pay that she must have substantial additional help or face economic, social and political deterioration of a very grave character. . . . It is logical that the United States do whatever it is able to assist in the return of normal economic health in the world, without which there can be no political stability and no assured peace.

British and French leaders received news of the Marshall Plan with enthusiasm. British Foreign Secretary Ernest Bevin (*q.v.*) called it "a lifeline to sinking men." Soviet Foreign Minister Vyacheslav Molotov (*q.v.*) rejected the plan as a U.S. scheme of "stretching capitalist tentacles into foreign markets." In the summer of 1947, representatives of 16 European countries met in Paris to discuss the Marshall Plan objectives for economic rehabilitation. In April 1948 the U.S. Congress appropriated $5.3 billion for the purchase of commodities, raw materials, machinery, and equipment.

Within three years the economic gains in Europe were impressive. Output of goods and services rose to new levels as the economic pump was primed, unemployment dropped, and trade between European states increased.

Western Europe was now able to stand on its own financial feet. In West Germany there was a *Wirtschaftswunder* ("economic miracle"); by 1952 its production reached 145 percent of its prewar level. The recovery of France, Britain, Italy, and smaller West European countries was less spectacular, but also impressive.

Bibliography. N. A. Buchanan and F.A. Lutz, *Rebuilding the World's Economy* (1947); S. E. Harris (ed.), *European Recovery Program* (1949); A. Settel (ed.), *This is Germany* (1950); L. Erhard, *Germany's Comeback in the World Market* (1954); H. C. Wallich, *Mainsprings of the German Revival* (1955); H. B. Price, *The Marshall Plan and Its Meaning* (1955); G. Bruun and V. S. Mamatey, *The World in the Twentieth Century* (1962); and R. A. Divine (ed.), *Causes and Consequences of World War II* (1970).

ECONOMIC WARFARE. World War II struggle between the Axis and the Allies to mobilize their resources, win superiority in war production, send supplies to the combat fronts, and diminish the enemy's capacity to wage war. It embraced every conceivable offensive or defensive measure taken against the enemy to destroy his economy, including the mobilization of financial and diplomatic means of cutting him off from vital strategic materials.

BACKGROUND. In World War II, as in World War I, the battle lines extended back to the industrial base of each belligerent. Both the Allies and the Axis set up special economic agencies to enforce blockades, negotiate trade agreements with neutrals, and arrange for the purchase of war materials. Fighting men in the combat zones were dependent upon the production of armaments factories and shipyards at home. Behind them the entire economic system was geared for war.

Added to the necessity for structuring its own industrial base, each belligerent attempted to disorganize the enemy by interrupting his productive capacity, cutting off essential supplies, and harrying transportation to the war fronts. This meant blockade by sea and air.

Both sides operated on the assumption that economic, as well as military, strategy had to be conceived on a global scale. It is probable that Hitler and his Axis partners never conceived of a global strategy, although this was assumed by the Allies during the war. He hoped originally to defeat the Russians, seize the Ukrainian heartland, and then turn south to the Mediterranean, strike at Britain's life line from Gibraltar-Malta-Suez, and then turn on the British Isles. His armies, advancing through the Balkans into Asia Minor, would link up with the *Afrika Korps* (*q.v.*) driving eastward from Libya across North Africa. Behind these drives was a combination of military and economic motives.

The Japanese also combined economic and military strategy. They would acquire control of the entire Pacific area with its vast supplies of raw materials, feed their own war machine, and deny the United States access to the area. While Hitler struck in the West, Japan would move into southern India from Indo-China and endanger the supply lines to and from British-controlled areas in the Far East.

ADJUNCT ECONOMIC WARFARE. There were three closely related battles in economic warfare between the Axis and Allies.

BATTLE FOR RESOURCES

Stockpiling access to critical war materials was of major importance. Combat strategy was often based on the need for holding areas rich in raw materials and denying them to the enemy. (*See* RESOURCES, BATTLE FOR.)

BATTLE OF PRODUCTION

The entire economy had to be geared for total war production. (*See* PRODUCTION, BATTLE FOR.)

BATTLE FOR SUPPLIES

A steady flow of food, fuel, and ammunition to combat zones was essential. It was also necessary to deny supplies to the enemy by aggressive action in the right place at the right time.

ALLIED BLOCKADE. Blockade was the cornerstone of Anglo-American economic warfare against the Axis. As in World War I, Allied economic strategy had the advantage of sea power but this was now tempered by the introduction of air power.

Immediately on the outbreak of war, the British Royal Navy began its blockade of Germany. It could not operate close to the Continent because of German air strength. The Germans were able to continue their coastal traffic, including a flow of iron ore from Sweden and Norway. Nevertheless, the British blockade was effective. In the first three months of the war the British captured or sank 1 million tons of German shipping, and seized 650,000 tons of cargo, including 250,000 tons of oil, 30,000 tons of copper, and 70,000 tons of iron ore.

NEUTRAL COUNTRIES. A problem for the British in 1939, as in 1914, was to prevent evasion of the blockade by use of neutral intermediaries. London set up control ports in England, Gibraltar, the Shetland Islands, and other strategic points. Although no formal blockade against Germany was declared, the British instituted a "paper blockade" with long lists of contraband, which included everything the Germans might import.

To control neutral loopholes, the British introduced the legal concept of "ultimate destination." Some military imports to neutrals were designated as imports into Germany. This "continuous voyage" could be interrupted by blockade at any point. Any imports in excess of normal requirements were designated as contraband.

Allied policy toward the neutrals stiffened as the war progressed. Both the British and Americans drew up "black lists," known officially as statutory lists, of Axis nationals or agents in neutral countries who gave assistance to the enemy. By law those whose names were on the black lists were considered economic lepers and were treated as such.

FINANCIAL BATTLEGROUND. In the field of finance, Anglo-American financial strength had an advantage by being able to outbid the Axis for strategic materials. The British pound sterling and the American dollar, with tremendous financial resources and institutions behind them, dominated the world money markets and dictated the patterns of war production. Even during the nadir of British military strength, the pound maintained its firm position in the world's markets. American financial power helped turned the tide against the Axis.

Germany's financial situation was eased considerably by its conquest of most of the Continent. Taking over intact virtually the entire financial structure of Europe, Hitler confiscated huge sums of gold and silver as well as foreign exchange from public banks and private sources. The Nazi looting technique was refined to the point of printing huge sums of money to flood the markets (*see* BERNHARD, OPERATION), seizing banks, insurance companies, factories, and commercial establishments, and gaining control of their overseas assets. The Germans extended their cartel system to the occupied countries and used neutral figureheads to mask cartel restrictions.

In financial warfare the Allies counterattacked by seeking to prevent the Germans and their collaborators from using sequestered funds outside occupied territories. They made it difficult for Germans to dispose of their foreign exchange in neutral countries and managed to forestall efforts to transfer and conceal assets. Both British and Americans used Trading-with-the-Enemy Acts to bar their citizens or representatives of subsidiaries in neutral countries from trading with the Axis without special governmental approval.

BRITISH WAR ECONOMY. The British war economy, as that of every belligerent, was geared totally to the war effort. Even in peacetime Britain was heavily dependent upon members of the Commonwealth and other countries for the importation of food, fuel, and raw materials. While blockading Germany, the British had to ensure a steady flow of imports to the home islands. The food supply—dairy products, bacon, eggs, and vegetables—came from Holland and the Scandinavian countries. British factories were dependent upon Swedish iron and ball bearings and upon Swiss machine tools.

British control of the seas was vital to provide the homeland with the tools of war. The great banking and insurance institutions of London assured the existence of global shipping and the flow of raw materials to the industrial complex. From the Middle East, Africa, and Latin-American countries came the strategic resources to maintain the British war effort. Scarce supplies were brought in from such neutrals as Spain and Switzerland. Victory for the British was possible only if they won the Battle of the Atlantic (*q.v.*). (*See also* BRITAIN AT WAR.)

GERMAN WAR ECONOMY. Germany had only a few of the 34 materials deemed necessary for carrying on war and was completely dependent on imports for 23 of them. This was partially compensated for in the immediate prewar years by careful stockpiling. The British blockade in the opening months of the war cut off imports to Germany on the high seas. To overcome deficiencies in raw materials and food, Hitler relied on a continuous flow of products from occupied countries in Europe. (*See also* GERMANY AT WAR.)

It was widely believed in Allied circles that the German economy, with its highly developed system of centralized control and its regulated transportation had so many bottlenecks it would soon collapse. It was assumed that the blockade and bombing would cut off such critical materials as ball bearings and cripple the production of planes and tanks.

The Allied goal of throttling the Nazi economy was not achieved until the closing days of the war. Throughout the early blockade and the later concentrated bombing from the air the Germans continued to receive and produce war materials of excellent quality. There were, indeed, temporary halts after giant raids but production resumed quickly after a cleanup. Until 1945 German industry was not completely handicapped by shortages of raw materials, with the single exception of petroleum.

There were several reasons for the Allied failure to cripple the German economy until late in the war: (1) Hitler had the advantage of five years of war preparation; (2) the full effect of the Allied blockade did not take effect until two years after the start of the war; (3) the early German campaigns were short and did not drain the economy; (4) valuable booty was taken from the conquered countries of Europe; and (5) German scientists provided adequate synthetics for materials in short supply.

Nevertheless, Germany's economy slowly deteriorated in confrontation with the Allies. The final defeat was due to the collapse of military, naval, and air power coupled with economic ruin.

RUSSIAN WAR ECONOMY. The Russian economy, weak even in peacetime, was severely taxed in the war. For a time it seemed that the German invasion would result in the dislocation of the Soviet economy. Stalin's scorched-earth policy of destroying everything in its path meant the loss of much Russian industry in the western regions. Some factories were uprooted and sent to the Urals and Siberia. (*See also* RUSSIA AT WAR.)

The Russian war economy was stimulated by the long-term measures of the

British and Americans to supply Russia with industrial equipment and raw materials on a basis sufficient to maintain its war industries. (*See* LEND-LEASE.)

AMERICAN WAR ECONOMY. Even before the war the United States had become the "arsenal of democracy." After the attack on Pearl Harbor the entire American economy, at that time the strongest in the world, was mobilized for war on the Axis. As in World War I, the weight of the American economy helped enormously in shifting the scales toward the Allied side. (*See* UNITED STATES AT WAR.)

JAPANESE WAR ECONOMY. Japan, like Britain, lacked most major raw materials and was dependent upon imports of food, fuel, and raw materials. In the first year of the war it could draw easily on the vast natural resources of the East Indies. (*See also* JAPAN AT WAR.)

The economic situation in the Far East was different from that of the European war. There were no neutrals in the Far East who could maintain commerce with both sides. The kind of "paper controls" that cut off German trade could not be applied here. In the Pacific it was a matter of sheer military, naval, and air power to isolate Japanese-occupied territory.

Allied economic warfare in the Pacific was slow, costly, and brilliantly effective. The American island-hopping campaign cut off Japanese shipping from the great resources in the southwest Pacific. As the campaigns progressed, Tokyo was reduced to the expedient of using cargo-carrying submarines and blockade runners to bring high precision instruments and technical information from its Axis partners in Europe. Late in the war this channel also dried up. Meanwhile, Japanese freighters loaded with raw materials from the Netherlands East Indies tried to run the Allied blockade.

Japanese forces in occupied China sent home whatever raw materials they could confiscate. They were thwarted by the Chinese, who moved strategic materials, such as tungsten, out of reach. Tokyo also found itself enmeshed in China in a bewildering kind of financial warfare with which it could not cope.

By 1945 the Japanese were hopelessly defeated in economic warfare with the Allies. Their once-powerful military, naval, and air forces no longer had a chance for victory.

Bibliography. E. V. Francis, *The Battle of Supplies* (1942); D. L. Gordon and R. Dangerfield, *The Hidden Weapon: The Story of Economic Warfare* (1947); E. L. Honze, *Foreign Labor in Nazi Germany* (1967); R. W. Oakley and R. M. Leighton, *Global Logistics and Strategy, 1943-1945* (1968); and A. S. Milward, *War, Economy and Society, 1939-1945* (1980).

EDEN, ROBERT ANTHONY (1897-1977). British statesman and war leader who worked closely with Churchill.

In 1939 Eden was recalled to the Cabinet as Secretary for the Dominions, and in May 1940 Churchill replaced Chamberlain as Prime Minister. The next

December the Prime Minister brought Eden back to his former post as Foreign Secretary. In this post Eden contributed much to forging the Grand Alliance against Hitler. Not only did he work closely with American envoys in London, but he also traveled to Washington to confer with Roosevelt and to Moscow to lead negotiations with Stalin. He was instrumental in concluding the wartime Anglo-Russian alliance and helped to consolidate Anglo-Russian collaboration after 1941. Closely connected with every conceivable civilian leadership activity, he attended all the fateful Big Three conferences. (*See* CONFERENCES, ALLIED WAR.)

Bibliography. Eden wrote *Foreign Affairs* (1939); *Freedom and Order: Days of Decision,* a collection of his speeches (1949); *Full Circle* (1960); *Facing the Dictators, 1932-1938* (1962); and *Another World, 1897-1917* (1977). *See also* biographies of Eden by L. Broad (1955); A. Campbell-Johnson (1955); D. Burden (1956); and R. Churchill (1959).

EDES. Greek Democratic Liberation Army. (*See* NATIONAL LIBERATION MOVEMENT.)

EHRENBURG, ILYA GRIGORIEVICH (1891-1967). Soviet author, writer of fiction, and best-known Russian journalist in World War II.

Ehrenburg went to Spain during the civil war and wrote dispatches for *Izvestia* accusing any Loyalist leader who opposed communism as a Fascist saboteur. In 1940 he moved to Moscow. After the invasion of the Soviet Union by Nazi Germany in 1941, Ehrenburg began to send dramatic front-line dispatches to Moscow. He played a large part in maintaining morale on the Russian home front and was generally considered, along with Konstantin Simonov, (*q.v.*) to be one of the outstanding Soviet war correspondents. (*See* REPORTING, WAR.).

A tall, gawky man, with disheveled hair and long arms, Ehrenburg was as ambitious as he was courageous. By American standards his reporting was lush and old fashioned. On occasion, he lapsed into stream-of-consciousness narration. But Russians were delighted with his staccato style and omniscient pronunciamentos.

Bibliography. Ehrenburg's *The Fall of Paris* (1942) treated French society just before World War II. His best-known novel was *The Thaw* (1954), which described Soviet life in the relatively liberal era after Stalin's death. His memoirs, *People, Years, Life* (1961-1965) are well-known and were translated into many languages. In these volumes he made an eloquent plea for the further liberalization of Soviet society.

EICHMANN, KARL ADOLF (1906-1962). German officer charged with the destruction of Jews under the Final Solution (*q.v.*).

In the early years of the war Eichmann was promoted to Chief of the subsection 4-B-4 of the RSHA, (*Reichssicherheitshauptamt*, "Reich" Security office). He was present at the Wannsee Conference on January 20, 1942, when it was decided to move all European Jews into extermination camps. He supervised the slaughter of Jews in gas chambers. In August 1944 he reported to Heinrich

Himmler (*q.v.*), powerful Reich Commissar for the Consolidation of German Nationhood, that 4 million Jews died in the extermination camps and 2 million more had been shot or otherwise eliminated by mobile units.

Eichmann escaped from an internment camp in the American zone in 1946. On May 11, 1960, Israeli agents found him in Argentina and smuggled him back to Israel. His trial, which took place in Jerusalem from April 11 to August 14, 1961, aroused global attention. Found guilty of crimes against the Jewish people and against humanity, he was executed by hanging at Ramle on May 31, 1962.

He was slightly built and thin, with a hatchet-like face. Eichmann had a melancholy childhood. Lonely, moody, and withdrawn, he was called "the little Jew" by his playmates because of his dark complexion. Later he developed into a talkative, hard-drinking extrovert. At his trial he insisted that he was only following orders and had no personal hatred of Jews. (*See also* WANNSEE CONFERENCE.)

Bibliography. M. A. Musmanno, *The Eichmann Commandos* (1961); H. Arendt, *Eichmann in Jerusalem: The Banality of Evil* (1963).

EIGHTH ARMY. British fighting force. The men of the 8th Army wore a patch showing a Crusader's Cross.

FORMATION. In the early stage of the war the British Middle Eastern forces were divided into a West Army, which included Egypt and the Western Desert, and an East Army stationed in Palestine and Syria. Both were led by Gen. Archibald Wavell (*q.v.*). In September 1941 the 8th Army was formed separating the forces in the Western Desert from those in Egypt. Called the Desert Army, it was originally under the command of Gen. Henry Maitland Wilson (*q.v.*). It included Britons, Australians, New Zealanders, and troops from India. One of its units, the 7th Armored Corps, took the name Desert Rats (*q.v.*).

CAMPAIGNS. On November 18, 1941, now under command of Gen. Alan Gordon Cunningham (*q.v.*), the 8th Army launched an offensive on the Egyptian frontier. From then on it played a key role in the seesaw battle with Axis forces in North Africa. Under Gen. Bernard Law Montgomery (*q.v.*), it turned back the Axis in the classic battle of El Alamein (*q.v.*).

Together with the U.S. 7th Army, the 8th Army took part in the first major assault on Fortress Europe (*q.v.*). (*See* SICILY, INVASION OF.) On September 3, 1943, it landed on the Italian mainland and fought its way up to Rome. (*See* ITALIAN FRONT, CAMPAIGNS ON THE.) In June 1944, combined units of the 8th Army, now including Polish troops, took part in *Operation Overlord.* (*See* NORMANDY INVASION.) The 8th Army ended its World War II fighting career in Austria. It was disbanded in July 1945.

SIGNIFICANCE. The performance of the 8th Army brought it the reputation of Britain's most effective fighting unit. From the sands of North Africa to the roads of Austria it struck repeatedly and successfully at the best of the German combat forces.

Bibliography. R. J. Crawford, *I Was an Eighth Army Soldier* (1944); and B. L. Montgomery, *El Alamein to the River Sangro* (1948).

EINSTEIN, ALBERT (1879–1955). German-born physicist, whose theory of relativity (1907) led indirectly to the development of the atomic bomb.

In contrast to other scientists, Einstein did not work directly on the project. In 1939, at the request of a group of scientists, including Niels Bohr (*q.v.*), he sent a letter to President Roosevelt emphasizing the urgency of investigating the possibility of using atomic energy in bombs. (*See* MANHATTAN PROJECT.) An ardent pacifist, Einstein later opposed use of the bomb and worked diligently in the cause of peace.

Bibliography. L. Barnett, *The Universe and Dr. Einstein* (1957); and R. W. Clark, *Einstein: The Life and Times* (1972).

EISENHOWER, DWIGHT DAVID (1890–1969). Supreme Commander of the Allied Expeditionary Forces in World War II. He was born in Denison, Texas, on October 14, 1890, the third of seven sons of a railroad worker. His father was of Bavarian Mennonite descent, his mother of Swiss extraction. Nicknamed Ike, he was raised in an atmosphere of strong religious training. He was graduated from the U.S. Military Academy at West Point in 1915, academically ranked 61 in a class of 174.

EARLY CAREER. Eisenhower spent the first years of his military career in almost total obscurity, following the standard career of an unknown army officer. He was about to sail for France when World War I ended in 1918. In the postwar era he settled into the life of a peacetime army officer. In September 1933 he was transferred to the Philippines to serve under Gen. Douglas MacArthur (*q.v.*), military adviser to the Philippines. The two officers, of vastly different temperaments, worked well together in building the defense of the islands.

WORLD WAR II. In 1939 Eisenhower held the rank of Lieutenant Colonel. In 1940 he was named Chief of Staff of the 3rd Division and the 9th Army Corps. Later he was appointed Chief of Staff of the 7th Army. In these assignments he played a leading role in the planning of the Louisiana war games, practice military maneuvers. Winning the attention of Gen. George C. Marshall (*q.v.*), who was looking for young officers for responsible posts, Eisenhower was promoted rapidly to Colonel and Brigadier General.

When the Japanese struck at Pearl Harbor on December 7, 1941, Marshall ordered Eisenhower to Washington to serve as Assistant Chief of War Plans, Division of the Army General Staff. In June 1942, after working on strategy for the invasion of Europe, Eisenhower was sent to London as Commanding General of the European Theater of Operations. He quickly demonstrated an unusual ability to bring together British and American officers of opposing views.

NORTH AFRICAN CAMPAIGN. In the fall of 1942 Eisenhower was given command of the Allied forces which were to implement *Operation Torch* (*q.v.*), the invasion of North Africa. With the cooperation of French Vichy (*q.v.*) leaders and with only limited resistance, he managed to bring North Africa under Allied control. (*See* NORTH AFRICA, CAMPAIGNS IN.)

SICILY AND ITALY. In the summer of 1943 Eisenhower captured Sicily and in the fall led the invasion of the Italian mainland. (*See* SICILY, INVASION OF; and ITALIAN FRONT, CAMPAIGNS ON THE.) His work in these campaigns was so outstanding that at the Teheran Conference (*q.v.*) in December 1943, he was chosen Supreme Commander of the Allied Expeditionary Forces (SCAEF) (*q.v.*).

OPERATION OVERLORD. The prospective role of the U.S. forces in the coming invasion of Europe led Churchill to agree that it should be led by an American instead of a British officer. Knowing that Gen. Marshall favored Eisenhower, Churchill gave his assent. Eisenhower began work on plans for a Second Front (*q.v.*) in January 1944. The invasion of Normandy, which began on June 6, 1944, was the largest single military action of its kind ever attempted. Eisenhower supervised an overwhelming force of troops, planes, warships, and landing craft in the successful operation. (*See* NORMANDY INVASION.)

VICTORY. Under Eisenhower's direction the Allied combined forces forged a bridgehead and made a wide sweep through France into Germany. He stopped the last German counterattack at the Battle of the Bulge (*q.v.*) in December 1944. He resumed the offensive in February 1945 and penetrated deeply into Germany. Churchill wanted to take Berlin and drive as far east as possible to keep the Russians from moving too far to the west. Eisenhower felt that a drive on the German capital would cost 100,000 American lives and furthermore that Berlin would have to be handed over to the Russians anyhow. Instead he sent his forces to south Germany and allowed the Russians to take Berlin. His decision was bitterly denounced later by critics. On May 8, 1945, the Germans surrendered unconditionally. (*See* GERMANY, BATTLE OF.)

POSTWAR. In the immediate postwar year Eisenhower served as Commander of the U.S. Occupation Forces. He retired in 1948 after 33 years of service. He served two terms as President of the United States (1953–1960). His presidency was marked by general prosperity on the domestic scene and an easing of tensions abroad. He died in Washington, D.C. on March 25, 1969.

PERSONALITY AND CHARACTER. Eisenhower was stockily built, a little above average height, with a bald head, prominent forehead, and broad mouth. His genial personality was that of the outgoing, gregarious, and friendly American. He possessed a combination of attractive qualities—sincerity, generosity, friendliness, and humility. His expressive face was unable to hide his emotions and his grin became famous.

Eisenhower's folksy, democratic ways endeared him to American troops. His gift for diplomacy made him a favorite with the upper echelons of the British military, with the exception of the crochety Gen. Bernard Law Montgomery (*q.v.*). Critics pointed to his mistrust of intellectuals and his preference for reading western novels. His concern to please everyone, they said, was naive and in the long run impossible.

Bibliography. Eisenhower's own account of the defeat of Germany was published in *Crusade in Europe* (1948), which became a best seller. For his role in World War II, *see* K. S. Davis, *A Soldier of Democracy: A Biography of Dwight Eisenhower* (1945); H. C. Butcher, *My Three Years with Eisenhower* (1946); R. G. Pogue, *The Supreme Command,* in K. R. Greenfield (ed.), *U.S. Army in World War II* (1954); W. B. Smith, *Eisenhower's Six Great Decisions* (1956); A. D. Chandler and E. E. Ambrose (eds.), *The Papers of Dwight D. Eisenhower. The War Years,* 4 vols., 1969–1970; and R. F. Weigler, *Eisenhower's Lieutenants* (1980).

EL ALAMEIN, BATTLE OF. Battle in the North African desert between the British 8th Army (*see* EIGHTH ARMY) and Italo-German forces from October 23 to November 4, 1942. It was one of the turning points of the war.

BACKGROUND. The first phase of the war in North Africa began in September 1940, when an Italian army under Marshal Rodolfo Graziani (*q.v.*) invaded Egypt from Libya. Two months later the British under Gen. Archibald Wavell (*q.v.*) drove the Italians back 500 miles into Libya. The second phase began in the spring of 1941 when Hitler sent Gen. Erwin Rommel and his *Afrika Korps* (*qq.v.*) to strike at the British. Rommel pushed the British back in a series of brilliant moves until he reached within 70 miles of Alexandria. The third phase began in early November 1942 when British and American forces invaded Morocco and Algeria in the west. The Germans were now caught between two giant pincer movements.

POSITION. The two rival armies were poised at El Alamein just 60 miles west of Alexandria on a line running between Tel el Eisa on the Mediterranean coast and the 600-foot pyramidal hill of Qyaret el Hemimat near the edge of the impassable Qattara Depression. El Alamein was the one area on the entire North African coast that could not be outflanked: The victor had to push straight through enemy lines. Both sides were unable to dig foxholes in the rocky soil and had to settle for little stone walls as defense spots.

The problem of supply was all important. Every day each armored division of the British 8th Army required 70,000 gallons of gasoline, 350 tons of ammunition, and 50 tons of spare parts. The British were only 200 miles from Suez, but their combat supplies had to be brought all the way around the Cape of Good Hope to Egypt. The buildup was slow. By early October 1942 a convoy of 18 Allied ships reached England with thousands of trucks and jeeps, hundreds of planes, and new *Sherman* (*q.v.*) tanks. The British were fortunate in holding the only freshwater springs in the vicinity of El Alamein.

The Axis seemed to be favored in the battle of supplies, but geography can be deceptive. German and Italian troops were 300 miles east of Tobruk, whose port capacity was inadequate. Axis supplies had to be unloaded at Benghazi, 600 miles to the west of El Alamein. Most transports setting out from Italian ports were sunk by the Allies. Water had to be brought in by ship because the British had salted, oiled, or blown up most of the wells around El Alamein. Rommel had 80,000 mixed German and Italians with 700 tanks, of which two-thirds were Italian. He also had a strong force of artillery and antitank guns.

PREPARATIONS. Both sides prepared for battle. In command of the 8th Army, Gen. Bernard Law Montgomery (*q.v.*) reorganized it completely. His fighting strength was 230,000 men, far beyond that of the Germans. He weeded out incompetent officers, dismissed generals as well as lieutenants, and visited his men to instill in them his own spirit of superconfidence. He scrapped all previous plans and ordered that no longer were dispersed units to be sent against the enemy to probe for weak points. In the midst of preparations he reversed his original plan and decided to attack the Axis on the flanks rather than attempt a central breakthrough. The code or cover name was *Operation Lightfoot.* "It seemed to me," he commented later, "that what Rommel liked was to get our armor to attack him. I was determined that would not happen this time. His tanks would come up against our tanks dug in hull-down positions."

OPERATION BERTRAM. Montgomery devised a series of ingenious tricks to persuade Rommel that the Allies were going one way (in the north) when actually they would take another route in the south. *Operation Bertram* was a gigantic bluff using a mass of deception tactics devised by a trained camouflage staff. Activities in the northern area, where Montgomery intended to attack, were carefully hidden. Combat vehicles, dumps of oil, lubricants, and stores were all thoroughly camouflaged.

In the south Montgomery built a 20-mile dummy pipeline to cause the enemy to believe that the main blow would be delivered on that flank. Five miles of dummy railway line were used for piping. There were also dummy pump houses. Thousands of men seemed to be at work unloading nonexistent supplies, covering tank traps, and rushing from one place to another. The troops, delighted by their new role as Thespians, discovered hidden talents in make-believe.

The deception of *Operation Bertram* was highly successful. German pilots discovered the tremendous activity in the south and duly reported a huge concentration of strength there.

CONFRONTATION. When the battle started the 8th Army had a total of 1,440 gun-armed tanks, of which 1,229 were ready for action. Rommel had just 200 German tanks, of which 20 were under repair, and 280 obsolete Italian tanks. The British had a 6 to 1 superiority in tanks and greater reserve strength.

At 9:40 P.M. on October 23, 1942, 1,000 British guns opened fire in a massive artillery barrage. There were ear-splitting crashes as Axis troops were smothered under dust and smoke. The barrage went on for four hours.

For a few minutes there was a strange silence. Then, suddenly, unearthly cries rose out of the desert as Allied fighters, including the famed 7th Armored Division Desert Rats, drove through the Axis lines.

Word of the attack was flashed to Hitler. Just before the assault Rommel had been ordered to return to Germany for medical treatment. He had been replaced by Gen. Georg von Stumme, who died of a heart attack on the battlefield. Hitler urged Rommel to return at once. The Desert Fox reached El Alamein on the evening of October 25. It was too late. His counterattack was stopped. Montgomery's tanks now outnumbered Rommel's 9 to 1.

The British 8th Army broke through on November 4. But two days later Rommel took advantage of rainy weather to escape into Tunisia. Montgomery might well have captured the entire *Afrika Korps,* but, afraid of extending his supply line too quickly, he began a cautious westward pursuit of the German and Italian forces.

LOSSES. The Axis suffered about 15,000 casualties and the Allies 13,500. The Allies took more than 30,000 prisoners, of whom about one-third were *Afrika Korps* troops, and captured 450 tanks and more than 1,000 guns. The Germans and Italians abandoned vast quantities of supplies. They were caught in a huge traffic jam as they retreated to Mersa Matruh.

AFTERMATH. It was a catastrophic Axis defeat. In the midst of the battle Hitler had ordered Rommel: "You can show your troops no other way than that which leads to victory or death." Among the prisoners was Gen. Ritter von Thomas, commander of the *Afrika Korps,* who denounced Hitler's order to hold fast as "unsurpassed madness." Soon after the debacle Rommel recommended to Hitler that the *Afrika Korps* be withdrawn from Tripolitania and that Tunisia be evacuated. (*See also* NORTH AFRICA, CAMPAIGNS IN.)

Bibliography. H.M. Stationery Office, *The Eighth Army* (1944); B. L. Montgomery, *El Alamein to the River Sangro* (1948); D. Young, *Rommel* (1950); F. W. von Mellenthin, *Panzer Battles, 1939–1945* (1955); and B. L. Montgomery, *Memoirs* (1958).

ELIOT, GEORGE FIELDING (1894–1971). American military writer and war commentator.

After serving in World War I in military intelligence, Eliot worked as a writer and lecturer, especially on military affairs. His books, articles, and lectures included analyses of problems of American defense. He served throughout World War II as military and naval correspondent for the *New York Herald Tribune* and as military analyst for the Columbia Broadcasting System. His semi-weekly articles were syndicated in 40 newspapers and his broadcasts were made nightly. His articles and broadcasts, presented in non-technical language for the layman made "Major George Fielding Eliot" America's most popular military analyst.

Bibliography. Among Eliot's many books were: *If War Comes* (with R. E. Dupuy) (1937); *Bombs Bursting in Air* (1939); *Hour of Triumph* (1944); and *Victory Without War* (1958).

ENIGMA CODING MACHINE. *See* ULTRA.

ENIWETOK. *See* MARSHALL ISLANDS, BATTLE FOR THE.

ESPIONAGE. Organized employment of secret agents or spies by belligerent countries in World War II to obtain information about enemies and also about allies or neutrals. Wartime espionage was recognized as a necessary function of the state in defense of its interests. National survival was regarded as the dominant goal.

SUBSIDIARY MEANINGS

COUNTERESPIONAGE, COUNTERINTELLIGENCE, OR SECURITY

Safeguarding a country's military secrets.

STRATEGIC ESPIONAGE OR INTELLIGENCE

Used for high-level planning of military operations.

TACTICAL ESPIONAGE OR INTELLIGENCE

Employed for combat actions by commanders and units on the war fronts.

BACKGROUND. Espionage is as old as recorded history. One of the earliest examples of spying is found in the Old Testament where Moses sent men out to "spy on the land of Canaan." Since then espionage has been geared in time of peace or war to: (1) gather information; (2) block attempts by others to gain national secrets; (3) disseminate false information; and (4) win military advantage. In World War I all the great powers had elaborate espionage systems. Dramatic examples of secret agents at work are Col. T. E. Lawrence, the famed Lawrence of Arabia, who operated in Egypt and Palestine, and Mata Hari, a Dutch-Javanese dancer who worked in France on behalf of Germany and was shot as a spy.

WORLD WAR II. Espionage reached a high peak in World War II as a result of new equipment and the fluid nature of military operations. This time there were few heavily manned front lines, and rival armies sometimes became inextricably mixed. The difficulty of distinguishing friend from foe made the work of spies and counterspies dangerous. New scientific developments, such as intricate ciphers and mechanical devices, were utilized. (*See* CODES and CODE

BREAKING.) Espionage was an important tool in frustrating enemy radar activities. (*See* RADAR, WARTIME.) Every operational staff, at both strategic and tactical levels, became adept at deception with skillfully prepared "cover plans" disseminated by secret agents.

BRITISH. As in World War I, British espionage functioned effectively. London became the key center of Allied intelligence. Special service agencies kept the government well informed of every major development in the Third Reich and German-occupied countries. Security was entrusted to Military Intelligence No. 5 (M.I. 5), an integral part of the War Office. M.I. 5 worked with Special Branch of Scotland Yard to promote counterintelligence. One of its main goals was to stop foreign agents or British citizens from consciously or unconsciously transmitting military and civilian secrets abroad. It had agents throughout the Continent.

British Special Operations Executive (SOE) (*q.v.*), like its American counterpart, the Office of Strategic Services (OSS) (*q.v.*), combined espionage with "special" or "strategic" operations that included sabotage, kidnapping, and assassination. British Security Coordination (BSC) (*q.v.*), headed by William Stephenson (*q.v.*), the man called Intrepid, had its headquarters in New York and acted as a hub for all branches of British intelligence.

British intelligence was especially efficient in creating bogus operational plans disseminated by its agents to the Axis. A typical example was the deception operation in April 1943 by which a corpse and secret agents were used to convince the Germans that the next Allied invasion would come in Corsica and Greece instead of Sicily. (*See* MINCEMEAT.) Similarly, British espionage agents spread false information before the great assault on the Continent in June 1944. (*See* NORMANDY INVASION.)

GERMAN. Before World War I the Germans had a well-developed secret service, including many agents operating in France. By 1939 Nazi spies were active in most major countries. The *Abwehr* (*q.v.*), secret intelligence and counterespionage agency of the German General Staff, seemed to function efficiently under Adm. Wilhelm Canaris (*q.v.*), who later became a leader of the conspiracy against Hitler. (*See* JULY PLOT.) The cooperation of fifth columns (*q.v.*) helped assure the rapid collapse of Poland, the Scandinavian and Low Countries, and France. As soon as Germans invaded a country, they recruited local collaborators to help maintain authority. The *Gestapo* (*q.v.*), ruthlessly efficient in internal espionage, generally bungled international spying.

German espionage scored some major successes. The sinking of the British battleship *Royal Oak* on October 14, 1939, by a German U-Boat was accomplished with the assistance of a German agent living in Kirkwall, Scotland. (*See ROYAL OAK;* and PRIEN, GÜNTHER.) Under the name "Cicero," (*q.v.*), a valet to the British Ambassador in Turkey provided much valuable information, although many of his reports were discounted in Berlin.

In general, however, despite intense activity, German espionage was less effective than that of the Allies. Again and again the Allies were triumphant in the battle of espionage. A Nazi attempt to sabotage the aluminum industry in the United States in mid-1942 turned out to be a fiasco. (*See PASTORIUS.*)

RUSSIAN. Before the 1917 Revolution, Russian espionage was grim and inefficient. It was concerned almost exclusively with uncovering dissenters from the Czarist regime. In the early 1930s the Communists created a highly skilled domestic and foreign espionage system, with spy networks covering the USSR and extending throughout the world.

The two main divisions of Soviet espionage were the Committee of State Security (Russian acronym, KGB), an independent security instrument of the Central Committee of the Communist Party, and the Chief Directorate of Military Intelligence (Russian acronym, GRU), subordinate to the Ministry of Defense. All intelligence activities were carefully organized and they functioned with efficiency.

Throughout the war, agents of the Red Orchestra (*q.v.*) fed information to Moscow even from inside the offices of the German High Command. From Switzerland a mysterious agent named Lucy sent streams of vital information. The Russians made use of secret defectors, notably Harry ("Kim") Philby, supposedly a British agent, who served the Kremlin throughout the war and in 1963 escaped to the Soviet Union. From Japan, Richard Sorge and his espionage unit kept Moscow fully informed of all German moves before and after Hitler's invasion of the Soviet Union. On May 12, 1941, five weeks before the invasion, Sorge reported to the Russians that the Germans had 170 divisions deployed on their borders.

AMERICAN. At first espionage in the United States was curtailed by counterespionage activities of the Federal Bureau of Investigation (FBI) under J. Edgar Hoover. In 1942 President Roosevelt created the first American espionage agency, the Office of Strategic Services (OSS) (*q.v.*) under William J. Donovan (*q.v.*). The OSS worked closely with the British, sending agents and spies into the occupied countries to help guerrillas and saboteurs. (*See MAQUIS;* PARTISANS; RESISTANCE MOVEMENTS; and UNDERGROUND). Among the OSS officials prominent in espionage was Allen W. Dulles (*q.v.*), whose office in Bern, Switzerland, became a center of European resistance to Hitler.

Bibliography. K. Reiss, *Total Espionage* (1941); R. Hirsch, *The Soviet Spies* (1947); I. Colvin, *Master Spy: The Incredible Story of Adm. Wilhelm Canaris* (1951); F. Leverkuehn, *German Military Intelligence* (1954); K. B. Abshagen, *Canaris* (1956); C. Wighton and G. Peis, *Hitler's Spies and Saboteurs* (1958); F. W. Deakin and R. Storry, *The Case of Richard Sorge* (1966); P. W. Blackstock, *The Secret Road to World War II* (1969); B. Whaley, *Stratagem: Deception and Surprise in War* (1969); S. Delmer, *The Counterfeit Spy* (1972); L. Fargo, *The Game of the Foxes* (1972); and D. Kahn, *Hitler's Spies* (1978).

ETAPPENDIENST. The secret supply and intelligence organization of the German Navy.

EXTERMINATION CAMPS. Nazi concentration camps converted into mass death camps with gas chambers and crematory ovens.

BACKGROUND. Shortly after his accession to political power, Hitler set up concentration camps to confine his many opponents and "people of inferior race" in "protective custody." (*See* CONCENTRATION CAMPS.) His *idée fixe* about superior and inferior races developed over the course of the years to a point where it was decided to liquidate millions in a massive biological cleansing campaign.

WORLD WAR II. Under the impact of the war the older idea of "preventive custody" gave way to a program of mass extermination. Several camps inside Germany, notably Dachau and Buchenwald, were transformed into extermination centers. To remove the slaughter as far as possible from sensitive German eyes, new death camps were constructed in Poland. The major ones were at Auschwitz, Maidanek, Treblinka, Chelmno, Belzec, and Sobibór.

Victims destined for extinction were gathered inside Germany and in occupied countries and sent to special labor camps as way stations. SS (*q.v.*) doctors on duty met the incoming transports hauling mostly Jews, and made instant decisions on life or death. Those fit for temporary work on war production were saved for a time, while others, including the elderly, women, and children, were dispatched immediately to the gas chambers. They expected to be cleaned by showers, but instead were asphyxiated by Zyclon-B, a crystallized poison acid dropped into death chambers through small openings. Death time for a group took from 3 to 15 minutes. Prisoners who were partially trusted then removed the gold rings and extracted gold teeth from the corpses.

The grisly system began in 1942 and continued to the winter of 1944, when advancing Russian troops began to threaten the extermination camp sites. By this time Heinrich Himmler (*q.v.*) and his SS colleagues were having difficulties in disposing of the great horde of victims sent to the death camps. Early in 1945 the extent of the holocaust became known.

ROLE OF THE EINSATSGRUPPEN. Special mobile formations called *EINSATZGRUPPEN* ("task forces") were charged with the task of carrying out liquidations in occupied countries. These groups were attached to *AMT* ("Office") *IV* of th RSHA (*Reichssicherheitshauptamt*, Reich Security Office). The individual detachment was termed an *Einsatzkommando,* the operations staff an *Einsatzstab,* and the smallest unit an *Einsatztrupp.* In general, the formations were assigned the task of supervising the Final Solution (*Endlösung*) of the Jewish problem by extermination. It is estimated that, with other elements of the Security Police the *Einsatzgruppen* were responsible for the death of at least 2 million Jews.

DACHAU. Situated in Bavaria, 12 miles northwest of Munich, Dachau was originally one of 3 camps set up in 1933 to form the nucleus of a concentration camp system. During the war it was made a death camp. Inmates were subjected to medical experiments, such as long immersion in cold water to test reaction on their bodies. Tens of thousands were slaughtered at Dachau.

AUSCHWITZ. On a marshy tract between the Vistula and the Sola, 160 miles southwest of Warsaw, Auschwitz was originally a military barracks and later the site of a tobacco factory. It was surrounded by stagnant pools and was smelly and pestilential.

Opened in 1940 after the defeat of Poland, Auschwitz was later greatly expanded. Bathhouses were installed for the gassing of inmates and corpse cellars for the storage of bodies. An experienced camp staff, composed of SS members, was sent to Auschwitz for the purpose of liquidating inmates. On May 1, 1940, Capt. Rudolf Franz Hoess (*q.v.*) was transferred from Sachsenhausen to Auschwitz as its commandant.

The first Jews arrived from Slovakia and Upper Silesia in 1941. Thereafter hundreds of thousands of victims were taken in transports to Auschwitz, where they were gassed and then burned in crematoria. It is estimated that several million prisoners died in this ghastly fashion at Auschwitz.

BUCHENWALD. One of the three original concentration camps set up in 1933, Buchenwald was situated on a wooden hill 4 miles from Weimar, the shrine of German culture. At the beginning of the war it was transformed into an armaments factory and later into a mass extermination camp. Inmates were subjected to starvation, beatings, tortures, incredibly crowded sleeping conditions, and final slaughter.

TREBLINKA. Situated at Malkinia Górna, on the Bug River in Poland, Treblinka was one of four main receiving centers for Jewish prisoners (the others were Chelmno, Belzec, and Sobibór). At first victims were asphyxiated by gas from internal combustion engines of captured tanks and trucks, but later the more efficient Zyclon-B gas was used on a major scale.

More than 80,000 prisoners were gassed at Treblinka in the six months preceding the spring of 1942. After the mass expulsion from Warsaw in late July 1942, Jews were brought to Treblinka at the rate of 5,000 a day. A mutiny took place on August 2, 1943, when about 150 inmates escaped, but they were hunted down one by one. Only a dozen survived. The knowledge of certain death at Treblinka led in part to the Warsaw uprising (*q.v.*).

SIGNIFICANCE. It is estimated that 11 million civilians were killed in Hitler's gas ovens. By far the largest proportion consisted of 6 million Jews from all parts of Europe, but the ovens also claimed Poles, Russians, Gypsies, and others. Nothing in history can be compared to this gigantic effort to purge Europe of "inferior races." It remained for a Polish scholar, Raphael Lemkin, to invent the word "genocide' to describe it. He called attention to Hitler's statement in *Mein Kampf* (*q.v.*): "The greatest of spirits can be liquidated if its bearer is beaten with a rubber truncheon."

Bibliography. E. Kogon, *The Theory and Practice of Hell* (1959); A. D. Morse, *While Six Million Died* (1968); A. Levin, *The Holocaust* (1968); M. Nyiszli, *Auschwitz* (1968); P. Lewinska, *Twenty Months at Auschwitz* (1968); G. Reitlinger, *The Final Solution* (1971); and M. J. Smith, *The Harrowing of Hell: Dachau* (1972).

F

F SECTION. The special section of Special Operations Executive (*q.v.*) concerned with Allied undercover operations against the Germans in France and all French territories. Its main work was concerned with deception tactics. (*See* ESPIONAGE.)

FAHNENEID. Military oath of allegiance required by all members of the German armed forces. This solemn declaration of loyalty to Hitler had to be taken by all officers and men. The order was issued on August 2, 1934, the day of the death of President Paul von Hindenburg, military hero of World War I. That same day Hitler took over the offices of President and Chancellor and announced the wording of the oath:

> I swear by God this sacred oath that I shall render unconditional obedience to Adolf Hitler, the *Fuehrer* of the German Reich, supreme commander of the armed forces, and that at all times I shall be prepared, as a brave soldier, to give my life for this oath.

For those officers who opposed Hitler this oath meant a severe conflict of conscience. They found it distasteful to break a pledge even though they had been forced to take it. At the Nuremberg Trials (*q.v.*) the moral question was posed to German generals as to whether they should obey orders of the *Fuehrer* to commit war crimes because they had taken the *Fahneneid*.

In discussing the Commissar Order (*q.v.*), calling for immediate liquidation of Russian commissars, Gen. Fritz Erich von Manstein (*q.v.*) told how he had found himself in conflict between his conscience and his duty to obey. "Actually, I should have obeyed [the Commissar Order] but I said to myself that as a solider I could not possibly cooperate in a thing like that. . . . It was against the honor of a soldier."

FALKENHAUSEN, ALEXANDER VON (1878–1966). German General of infantry.

Von Falkenhausen returned to Germany from China in 1939. From 1940 to 1944 he held commands in Belgium and northern France, where he supervised the taking and shooting of hostages as a means of enforcing orders. He showed some sympathy for the German Resistance movement, but he was discouraged by the conspirators because of his record in the execution of hostages. When the 1944 July Plot (*q.v.*) against Hitler misfired, von Falkenhausen was arrested by the *Gestapo* (*q.v.*) and sent to a concentration camp. Undoubtedly marked for execution, he was freed by the Americans in 1945.

Tough, militant, von Falkenhausen was a man of extraordinary courage (in World War I he was awarded the *Pour le Mérite,* Germany's highest military decoration). He was known by officers and troops for his dominating personality.

FALKENHORST, NIKOLAUS VON (1885–1968). German officer in World War I and World War II.

In the Polish invasion of 1939, von Falkenhorst served as a Lieutenant General in command of the 21st Army Corps. When Hitler decided to invade Norway before the British did, he belatedly appointed von Falkenhorst, then General of infantry, to command the forces that seized that country. When von Falkenhorst asked for troops, it turned out that Hitler had not even bothered to inform the German Army High Command of his plans for Norway. Nevertheless, von Falkenhorst expelled the British forces from Norway in May 1940. The next year he commanded the White Sea region in the Russian campaign, but returned to Norway as Commander-in-Chief of the considerable German forces there.

Von Falkenhorst was tried as a war criminal before a mixed British and Norwegian Military Court at Brunswick in 1946. He was sentenced to death on August 2 on charges of having turned over captured Commandos to the SS (*q.v.*) for execution. The sentence was commuted to one of life imprisonment, but he was released in 1953. He died in Holzminden on June 18, 1968.

"FAT MAN." Atomic bomb used at Nagasaki (*q.v.*) on August 9, 1945.

"Fat Man" was given its name because it was heavier and bulkier than the bomb dropped on Hiroshima (*q.v.*). "Fat Man" was a 20-kiloton weapon in which the U-235 charge was imploded to critical mass by an outer shell containing small explosive charges. It measured 10 feet 8 inches in length by 4 feet in diameter. The Hiroshima bomb was nicknamed the "Little Boy."

FERMI, ENRICO (1901–1954). Italian-American physicist and one of the architects of the atomic age.

The announcement in 1939 of the discovery in Germany of nuclear fission (*see* MEITNER, LISE), came at roughly the same time Fermi emigrated to the United States. He understood immediately the overriding importance and potential of nuclear fission. With colleagues at Columbia University, he worked assiduously on the realization of a chain reaction. In 1942 his project was transferred to the University of Chicago, where he supervised the construction of the first atomic reactor. It consisted of a pile of natural uranium embedded in layers of graphite and controlled by cadmium rods.

Fermi then worked at Los Alamos on the development of the atomic bomb. His path-breaking research on neutron bombardment of a large number of radioactive isotypes and his discovery of the effectiveness of slow neutrons in producing radioactivity were vital steps in the production of the atomic bombs used on Hiroshima and Nagasaki (*qq.v.*). (*See also* MANHATTAN PROJECT; and GROVES, LESLIE R.)

Bibliography. E. Fermi, *Collected Works*, 2 vols. (1962–1965), published posthumously; and E. Segré, *Enrico Fermi, Physicist* (1970).

FESTUNG EUROPA. German term for Fortress Europe. (*See* FORTRESS EUROPE.)

FIDO. British device used at airfields to dispel fog. With the assistance of Fido, heavy British bombers, including *Lancasters, Wellingtons,* and *Halifaxes* could take off and land in most kinds of weather.

FIELDS, GRACIE (1898–1979). British actress and a favorite of troops during the early days of World War II. She was born in the small cotton-manufacturing town of Rochdale, Lancashire, on January 9, 1898. She lived on a typically working-class street. Her education consisted of a public primary schooling. She worked in a cotton mill, a shop, and a paper factory, while establishing a reputation as a comedienne. In 1933 she celebrated the pressing of her 4-millionth record. She was the world's highest paid star in her heyday.

Gracie Fields enjoyed wide popularity during the war due to her combination of talents as a vocalist and comedienne, coupled with a brash, informal personality. The London *Times* wrote about her "large friendliness, cheerful common sense and persistent joy in what is ridiculous." *Time,* on the other hand, described her "sheer animal vulgarity, including flea-scratching and grimaces." (*See* BRITAIN AT WAR.)

Gracie Fields died on September 27, 1979, at her home on the Isle of Capri, Italy at the age of 81.

FIFTH COLUMN. Term used to describe subversion of a country's defenses during wartime. It was used especially to denote the Nazi network of supporters inside other countries.

The term *fifth column* originally referred to sympathizers of Gen. Francisco Franco (*q.v.*) inside Spain during the Spanish civil war. The Nationalist Gen. Queipo de Llano used it in a radio broadcast. In a radio talk on October 1, 1936, Gen. Emilio Mola, who was leading an attack by Nationalists on Madrid, also spoke of a "fifth column" of sympathizers inside the city who would supplement his own four columns of troops.

After he became Chancellor in 1933, Hitler ordered the organization of a global network of fifth columnists to assist in the conquest of other peoples. Swift defeats of Poland, the Scandinavian countries, the Low Countries, and France were accomplished with the help of fifth columns. German penetrations of Yugoslavia, Greece, and the Soviet Union were assisted by fifth columnists trained in espionage, sabotage, and subversion.

Much of fifth-column activity was exaggerated. It is probable that unreasoning fear of Hitler achieved more for the Nazis than the fifth column itself.

Bibliography. For typical fifth-column activity, see L. de Jong, The German Fifth Column in the Second World War (1956).

FILMS IN THE WAR. Use of motion pictures in belligerent countries as an integral part of the war effort.

BACKGROUND. In World War II, as in World War I, films became a potent instrument of national policy in the war effort. They served several purposes: (1) entertainment adapted to a wartime setting; (2) propaganda to promote morale; (3) stimulant to recruiting; and (4) military training. Audiences everywhere, faced with realities of war, sought escape, companionship, and moral comfort. Film makers gave them what they wanted plus a liberal dose of propaganda. The idea was to stimulate rather than to inform.

Film studios, like factories, were made over for war production. For audiences, war became an exciting adventure, death painless, heroism a blessing. Battles were portrayed as straightforward melodrama, with heroes and villains, and good soldiers setting out to defeat the villainous enemy. There was little originality. The emphasis was on entertainment adapted to a wartime milieu.

BRITISH. Until the outbreak of war, British films tended to be dull and unimaginative, but the war forced film making into an entirely new spirit of strenuous activity. Unlike Hollywood, Britain had limited production with budgets adapted to wartime conditions. British film output during the war was limited to 50 to 60 films a year as compared with 225 in 1937. War films tended to bring a sense of national identity, lower class barriers, and instill a quiet determination to preserve the British way of life. They stressed a new collective pride in being British and "ordinary."

The first war film, The Lion Has Wings, produced in November 1939 by Alexander Korda, portrayed British air defenses as unassailable. From then on, British films reflected the public's grim acceptance of the war. Convoy (1940), a film about a British cruiser engaging a German battleship, was an exciting account of the Royal Navy in action. After the Battle of Britain (q.v.), films about air combat became enormously popular, including Ships With Wings (1941), Target for Tonight (1941), and One of Our Aircraft is Missing (1942).

British war films reached maturity in 1942 with Noël Coward's classic *In Which We Serve,* inspired by the sinking of a British destroyer off Crete. Other films stressed such topics as careless talk, secret missions, spy stories, romantic interludes, and patriotism.

Throughout the war the British produced first-rate documentaries, including *The First Day* (1939), *London Can Take It* (1940), *Target for Tonight* (1941), *Words for Battle* (1941), *Coastal Command* (1942), and *The Big Blockade* (1942).

GERMAN. German films during the pre-war era, especially those of Leni Riefenstahl, reached a high degree of technical excellence. During the war German film making maintained its technical reputation but remained under strict ideological control. The film industry was placed under direction of Paul Joseph Goebbels (*q.v.*), Reich Minister for Public Enlightenment and Propaganda. Goebbels ruled the film industry firmly, abolishing critics and closely supervising production. He used studios in occupied Czechoslovakia to grind out films, most of which were devoted to straight propaganda and some to escapism.

Early German war films were filled with scenes of triumph, glorification of the fighting man, and denunciation of the enemy. Among them were *Baptism of Fire* (1940), a panegyric on the *Luftwaffe* (*q.v.*), *Campaign in Poland* (1940), *Victory in the West* (1940), and *Submarines Head West* (1941), which glamorized the U-Boat service. The themes were simple—the Germans were decent and chivalrous, the British were cowards who took advantage of other peoples. In deference to Hitler's monomania on Jews, Goebbels produced such anti-Semitic films as *The Eternal Jew* (1940) and *Jew Süss* (1941).

By late 1942 the German public seemed to become satiated with second-rate propaganda films. They were still impressed by *Die deutsche Wochenschau* (*The German Weekly Show*) a newsreel that retained its popularity to the end of the war. Audiences became smaller as the public stayed away from slapdash products, with their crude editing and weak scripts. From 1943 on, as the tide of battle began to change against the Germans, Goebbels used films in an effort to sustain morale. He transferred film studios from Berlin to Amsterdam, Budapest, and Rome, as Allied bombing crippled the Berlin film industry.

RUSSIAN. The entire Russian film industry was geared for "the moral, political, and military defeat of Fascism." Favorite themes were the indestructibility of the Russian people, victories of the Red Army, and German barbarism. Although there were many feature films, by far the greater stress was placed on documentaries, newsreels, and propaganda shorts. Hundreds of cameramen worked at the battle fronts to obtain scenes for the documentaries, and many of them were killed in the process.

Russian victories were celebrated in *Leningrad Fights* (1942), *The Story of Stalingrad* (1943), and *Berlin* (1945). *The Rainbow* (1944) gave a horrifying picture of the German occupation of a Ukrainian village. Some escapist films were made, such as *The Girl from Leningrad* (1941), and films depicting ancient Russian heroes or comparisons of Hitler and Napoleon.

AMERICAN. Hollywood remained the film capital of the world during World War II. What it lacked in quality the American film industry made up in quantity. Between 1942 and 1945 Hollywood produced 1,700 feature films, of which more than 500 were directly or indirectly concerned with the war. Added to this output was an enormous supply of documentaries and training films.

The American film industry, in wartime as in peace, was marked by extraordinary technical competence, the result of a division of labor by which each separate process was placed in the hands of specialized experts. Many actors, including Clark Gable and James Stewart, went into uniform, while others, such as Bob Hope (*q.v.*) and George Jessel, gave hundreds of performances on the battle fronts. Meanwhile, films poured from Hollywood, most of them shallow and trite, but some survived as works as art.

There was wide variety in Hollywood film production. Outright propaganda films were made, including *A Yank in the RAF* (1941), *Desperate Journey* (1941), *Songs of Russia* (1942), and *White Cliffs of Dover* (1944). Comedies entertained the bored servicemen in training camps and at the fronts, including *Buck Privates* (1941), *Road to Morocco* (1942), *This Is the Army* (1943), and *See Here, Private Hargrove* (1944). Servicemen also preferred such romantic films as *That Night in Rio* (1941) and *Cover Girl* (1944). Anti-Nazi films, the "hiss-and-boo" pictures, included *Hitler: Beast of Berlin*, *Hitler's Gang*, *Diary of a Nazi*, *Hitler's Children*, and *Der Fuehrer's Face*.

Documentaries and training films, directed by such experts as John Ford, William Wyler, John Huston, and Frank Capra, although consistently of high quality, intermingled entertainment with propaganda. Such films used combat footage of battles as well as newsreel shots. Frank Capra's "Why We Fight" series, explained American involvement in the war and why it was necessary to bring the war to a successful conclusion. Such actors as Cary Grant and George Murphy advised the armed services on training films. This type of visual education was an important factor in reducing the time devoted to training American fighting men.

Hollywood, as well as film-producing centers in other countries, was dedicated to the production of entertaining films planned to boost the morale and spirit of both civilians and soldiers. The aim was to keep the minds of both combat soldiers and civilians off the grim realities of clashes on the battlefields.

Bibliography. A. A. Hoehling, *Home Front U.S.A.* (1966); D. S. Hull, *Film in the Third Reich* (1969); I. Butler, *The War Film* (1974); C. Jeavons, *A Pictorial History of War Films* (1974); and F. Thorpe *et al.*, *British Official Films in the Second World War* (1980).

FINAL SOLUTION. German *Endlösung*. Nazi plan to destroy the Jews of Europe.

Although the "Final Solution" was aimed specifically at Jews, it also refers to the attempt to "purify Aryan blood" by elimination of other peoples, such as Poles, Russians, Gypsies, and Serbs. Altogether, 11 million civilians, including 6 million Jews, are believed to have lost their lives in mass extermination.

BACKGROUND. In his autobiography, *Mein Kampf* (*q.v.*), Hitler excoriated Jews as "parasites" and "destroyers of civilization." Hostility to Jews ran deeply into the German and European past, but Hitler made it a major, persistent tenet of Nazi creed. "The Jew," he said, "is the implacable enemy of all light, the hater of all true civilization."

The *Fuehrer* based his ideology on the supposed superiority of the Indo-European-Aryan-Nordic-Teutonic-Germanic "race." He resented the Jews on political and economic grounds and denounced Jewish newcomers who had moved into Germany from eastern Europe. Although the old Jewish community had proven its loyalty during World War I, it, too, was made the target of Hitler's abuse. His anti-Semitic line was promoted in such publications as *Der Stürmer* (*The Stormer*), edited by Julius Streicher (*q.v.*), and by Nazi orators and pamphleteers.

ANTI-JEWISH MEASURES. In the belief that the Jewish question called for a drastic solution, when in power Hitler decided to drive Jews from public life. He excluded most Jews from the administration, the press, and all agencies of German cultural life. "It suffices," read a Hitler statute in April 1933, "if one parent or grandparent is a non-Aryan." By a law of July 1933, a Jew or any person married to a Jew was debarred from government office. Jews were forced out of the universities, the legal profession, medicine, and dentistry. They were not allowed to enter military service or the Labor Front, nor could they own land. At first exceptions were made for Jewish war veterans, but later even they were driven from public life.

More and more disabilities were placed upon Germany's Jews. In 1935, by the so-called Nuremberg Racial Laws, Jews were deprived of German citizenship, prohibited from contracting marriage with German Aryans, and forbidden to take employment as domestic servants in so-called Aryan homes. Following the pogrom of November 1938, Jewish property was sold to non-Jews, synagogues destroyed, and a collective fine of 1 billion marks put on the Jewish community. All Jews were forced to wear a yellow Star of David as a distinguishing sign.

WORLD WAR II. Hitler's opposition to Jews turned to fanatical hatred after his invasion of the Soviet Union in June 1941. In his mind the Jews were responsible not only for the ills of capitalism but also for communism. At the Wannsee Conference held on January 20, 1942, the course of action was completed. The meeting was attended by 15 leading Nazi bureaucrats, headed by Reinhard Heydrich (*q.v.*), who declared that he was the plenipotentiary "for the final solution of the Jewish question." While no documentary evidence implicates Hitler personally in the work of this conference, it is clear that nothing of its importance could have taken place in the Third Reich without his knowledge and support. The Wannsee Protocol stated: "In the course of the execution of the Final Solution, Europe will be combed from west to east."

The Nazi death apparatus was placed in the hands of Heinrich Himmler (*q.v.*), who set up special mobile units called *Einsatzgruppen* to supervise the Final Solution. Several concentration camps inside Germany (Dachau, Belsen, and Buchenwald) were converted into death centers, while new extermination camps (*q.v.*) were constructed in Poland. Only the strongest prisoners could endure starvation, beatings, and disease. The Jewish community of Germany as well as other "undesirables," including Gypsies and Jehovah's Witnesses, became eligible for mass slaughter. When conventional methods of execution proved to be inadequate, camp authorities turned to asphyxiation in gas chambers under sadistic camp rulers. (*See* HOESS, RUDOLF FRANZ.) Millions were dispatched under inhumane conditions. Bodies of the victims were cremated, after their hair was shorn to make mattresses and their gold fillings extracted.

The macabre procedure was used in countries occupied by Germans. Nearly 3 million Jews disappeared in conquered Poland. At least 2 million Jews from Austria, Hungary, Belgium, Holland, Czechoslovakia, Yugoslavia, France, and Greece were put to death in German extermination camps. A million more from occupied Russia and the Baltic states are believed to have suffered the same fate.

Resistance to Nazi pressure saved the Jews in several countries. The small Jewish community in Italy, numbering fewer than 50,000, managed to maintain its existence even though Mussolini eventually had to accept Hitler's racial theories. Danes helped their 6,000 Jews to hide or escape to Sweden. The Dutch lost about 2,000 of their 16,000 Jews, including the young girl Anne Frank (*q.v.*) who hid in an Amsterdam house for two years. (*See also* EXTERMINATION CAMPS.)

SIGNIFICANCE. Although estimates vary, it is probable that at least 6 million Jews were annihilated in this Final Solution. The extermination campaign was unprecedented in history. European Jews found it difficult to escape from the planned industrialized murder. No identification with Nazism, no change of domicile inside Nazi Europe, seemed to help. Those who were sentenced to death without trial had committed the crime of having had Jewish grandparents. There had been violence against Jews for centuries, but nothing to compare with the Final Solution in magnitude and total configuration.

Bibliography. R. Hilberg, *The Destruction of the German Jews* (1961); N. Levin, *The Holocaust* (1968); J. Presser, *The Destruction of the Dutch Jews* (1969); H. Feinfold, *The Politics of Rescue* (1970); J. Yoors, *Crossing, A Journal of Resistance and Survival* (1971); G. Reitlinger, *The Final Solution* (1971); and L. S. Davidowicz, *The Holocaust and the Historians* (1981).

FINNISH-RUSSIAN WAR. *See* RUSSO-FINNISH WAR.

FLAME THROWERS. One of the most dramatic and effective weapons of the war.

Introduced during World War I, the flame thrower was changed very little during World War II. A simple weapon, it consisted of a fuel tank of mixed gasoline and oil, a pressure tank, and a hose with an adjustable nozzle. The ignited liquid emerged as a jet of flame, which was directed at the target. Although usually a one-man weapon, it was also mounted on tanks and used by British, German, and Americans in the closing months of the war in Europe.

The smaller flame throwers were effective against heavily armored targets, pillboxes, and tanks. Russians used them effectively for routing German troops out of dugout positions. The British "Ack Pack," weighing 49 pounds, was filled with 4 gallons of fuel and could be fired only 10 times, in 10 second shots, at a maximum range of 50 yards. Flame throwers were used by American troops against Japanese strongholds, particularly Iwo Jima, in the Pacific. (*See* IWO JIMA, BATTLE FOR.)

FLETCHER, FRANK JACK (1885–1973). American vice-admiral who worked with carrier-based air craft in the Pacific theater of war.

Rear Adm. Fletcher was at sea when Pearl Harbor (*q.v.*) was attacked by the Japanese. Fletcher was active in the decisive battles of the Coral Sea and Midway (*qq.v.*). At the Coral Sea his task force intercepted the Japanese fleet headed for Port Moresby and inflicted heavy damage on the Japanese during the battle in early May 1942. At Midway his flagship, the *Yorktown*, was sunk. Later, Fletcher's task force took part in the Guadalcanal campaign, during which he was wounded.

FLIP CORKIN. Cartoon character popular among American GIs (*q.v.*) during the war.

Flip Corkin was the main character in a cartoon strip created by Milton Caniff in 1942 and titled "Terry and the Pirates." Caniff modeled his hero on a friend, Col. Philip C. Cochran, a fighter-plane commander in Africa and the Orient. All during the war the fictional exploits of Flip Corkin were no less spectacular than the real ones of Philip Cochran. Flip Corkin bowed out as a cartoon character in 1947. (*See* STARS AND STRIPES, THE.)

FLYING FORTRESS (B-17). Main U.S. Air Forces bomber in the European theater of war. Regarded as the best defensive plane of its kind, the *B-17* was a four-engined, low-wing all-metal monoplane, with a long high fin and a wide span tail plane shaped like the wing.

PEDIGREE. Designed for high altitude, daytime precision bombing of restricted targets, the Boeing *B-17* was the first long-range American bomber.

The first *B-17,* completed in July 1935, flew non-stop from Seattle, Washington, to Dayton, Ohio, a distance of 2,100 miles, at an average speed of 250 miles per hour. Production was slow. By 1939, when World War II began in Europe, only 13 had been delivered to the U.S. Air Force.

WORLD WAR II. The *B-17* saw its first action with the Royal Air Force (*q.v.*) in 1941. Its performance was regarded as so slow and clumsy that the British abandoned it for daylight bombing and instead continued night air attacks with their own *Lancasters* and *Wellingtons.* American designers then radically altered the *B-17,* enlarged and redesigned the tail assembly and added heavy defensive armament, including power-operated turrets. The new *B-17s* quickly demonstrated that they could take more punishment than any other bomber.

The first all-American bombing raid by *Flying Fortresses* took place in August 1942 with an attack on Rouen. In succeeding months they rained thousands of tons of bombs on enemy targets, despite heavy losses. By now they were the outstanding bomber used on Allied daylight attacks on German targets. By early 1944 more than 1,000 *Flying Fortresses* were available for raids on Germany.

(For specifications *see* AIRCRAFT: AMERICAN AIRCRAFT DATA CHART.)

FLYING TIGERS. A volunteer force of mostly American pilots and mechanics, which won a series of victories against the Japanese from December 1941 to July 1942.

BACKGROUND. In the summer of 1937 the Japanese began large-scale military operations, accompanied by extensive air bombing, on the mainland of China. Japanese armies took most of the major cities, including Peking (Pei-p'ing), Nanking (Nan-jing), Shangai (Shang-hai), Canton (Guangzhou), and Hankow (Han-kou), but were unable to subdue the entire countryside. Terrorist methods resulted only in increased Chinese resistance. Fighting continued month after month with the Japanese unable to inflict a final overwhelming blow.

About a year after the outbreak of the war, Japan became a partner of Germany and Italy in the Tripartite Pact of September 1940, commonly called the Axis (*q.v.*). This step resulted in the merging of Far Eastern and European affairs. Meanwhile, the Chinese continued to resist with the intention of driving the last Japanese invader from their soil.

CHENNAULT. In the early days of the fighting against Japan, Chinese Nationalist leader Chiang Kai-shek (*q.v.*) engaged as civilian adviser for air training a slightly deaf, hard-bitten, recently retired officer, Claire L. Chennault (*q.v.*). The American was given the task of whipping the hodge-podge Chinese

Air Force into fighting trim. He also set up a series of air bases throughout the interior of China as well as what was generally recognized as a powerful striking force. At the same time he petitioned Washington for help. In 1940 he managed to obtain some bombers, pursuit planes, and even 100 *P-40 Warhawks,* which had been built for Sweden but now were allotted to China.

AMERICAN VOLUNTEERS. Short of pilots, Chennault returned to the United States in the summer of 1941 to recruit a force of volunteers to keep his planes flying. Without official sponsorship, he toured air base after air base, told the story about China and how desperately pilots were needed there. He offered a $600 a month salary plus $500 bonus for every Japanese plane shot down. Pilots, mechanics, and riggers set out for China.

Chennault set up his base camp 150 miles above Rangoon and proceeded to organize the American Volunteer Group, later to become the Flying Tigers. He began intensive training. He carefully compared the performance of the Japanese *Zero* and the American *P-40* in ten categories. He concluded that the American plane was superior in just two or three of these categories and he concentrated on these. Each pilot was required to work for at least six hours a day until he was letter perfect. Then the pilots were trained to work in formations as if every plane in the group were under single control. By November 1941 Chennault had two trained squadrons of 18 men each.

COMBAT ACTION. The American Volunteer Group struck at the Japanese throughout the fall and winter of 1941. Operating on their own, with no spit-and-polish or military discipline, they regarded their work as a deadly but satisfactory sport. Flying their *P-40s* with a shark's mouth painted under the nose, they engaged the Japanese wherever they could find them. The Chinese dubbed them the "Flying Tiger Sharks," while to the rest of the world they became known as the "Flying Tigers."

A few days before Christmas 1941, when Japanese bombers struck at the Kunming terminal of the Burma Road (*q.v.*), they were hit by the American volunteers. On the day before Christmas, Flying Tigers shot down 9 of 21 bombers on a mission to Rangoon. The engagement was typical of what happened the next three months. (*See* BURMA, CAMPAIGNS IN.)

PERFORMANCE. In the seven months after Pearl Harbor, by official count, the Flying Tigers destroyed 297 planes, racked up 300 probables, and killed 1,500 Japanese. They destroyed 20 enemy planes for every one of their own lost, and killed 92 enemy airmen for every American lost.

SIGNIFICANCE. The volunteer air force never had more than 49 combat planes in action at any one time nor more than 70 trained pilots. But the Flying Tigers exploded the myth of Japanese aerial supremacy. A thorn in the side of the Japanese, they operated for 65 days in two-plane teams to hold the Burma Road while tons of supplies were rushed to China. Most important of all, they kept the Japanese off balance at a critical time in their march of conquest.

AFTERMATH. In April 1942 Chennault was recalled to duty by the U.S. Army with the temporary rank of Colonel and ordered to continue his activities and relationship with the Chinese Government. Eventually, his Flying Tigers were incorporated into the U.S. 14th Air Force under Chennault. In this capacity he became responsible to Lt. Gen. Joseph W. Stilwell (*q.v.*), who for a time commanded the entire China-Burma-India theater of war. At once there were conflicts between the two, which ended with Chennault's retirement in July 1945.

Bibliography. T. L. Scott, *Flying Tiger: Chennault of China* (1959).

FORCED LABOR. Work or workers utilized to meet the needs of the Nazi military machine in World War II. Methods of recruitment and treatment of workers inside Germany and in occupied countries were such that the term "slave labor" is often used to describe the practice.

BACKGROUND. The forced labor system was implicit in Nazi racialism. Those accused of inferior ethnic origin were designated to serve the welfare of the master Aryan-Nordic-Germanic "race." As early as October 1, 1938, the High Command of the German Armed Forces indicated that it would be necessary to use the services of foreign civilians as well as prisoners of war to maintain the German military establishment. On May 23, 1939, Hitler reaffirmed this policy at a meeting with his top military leaders: "The population of non-Germans will perform no military service and will be available as a source of labor."

WORLD WAR II. From the beginning of the war the use of forced labor became a critical item for German administrators. On January 25, 1940, Hans Frank (*q.v.*), Governor-General of Poland, wrote to Hermann Goering (*q.v.*) that the supply and transport of at least 1 million Poles, male and female, of whom 640,000 were to be farm workers, must be arranged. By the end of 1940 a stream of Polish, French, and Dutch workers flowed into Germany. After the invasion of the Soviet Union in June 1941, tens of thousands of Russians were designated for forced labor. On March 21, 1942, Hitler signed a decree mobilizing both German and foreign workers, including prisoners of war, for placement on farms and in factories. For the remainder of the war German production of food and war matériel was dependent upon this system of forced labor.

RECRUITMENT. Responsibility for obtaining and handling of forced labor was given to Fritz Sauckel (*q.v.*), who held the title of Plenipotentiary for Labor Allocation. Sauckel carried out his assignment with tireless efficiency. He started his drive in relatively humane fashion: "All these people must be fed, housed, and treated in a way that with the least possible outlay the greatest possible results might be achieved." Early recruitment was comparatively mild. Those willing to work were supposed to be "treated correctly," with the understanding that the smallest sign of opposition "would be met with ruthless and energetic measures."

Opposition to recruitment soon led to severe retaliation. Millions had to be dragooned by force. Squads of SS (*q.v.*) officers would block off the entire area of a town and seize every able-bodied person caught in it. They corralled hundreds leaving moving picture theaters, often at gun point, stuffed the victims into boxcars, and shipped them like cattle to Germany. They separated wives and husbands and even kidnapped children old enough to work. A captured German document revealed that, in June 1944 in occupied Russian territory, apprehension of 40,000 to 50,000 youths from the ages of 10 to 14 was recommended for transportation to Germany to work as apprentices.

In the 12 months from April 1942 to April 1943, 3,636,056 workers were rounded up as forced labor for the German economy. An additional 1,622,820 prisoners of war were added to the supply. By 1944 more than 7.5 million civilians were designated for forced labor, of whom at least 500,000 were sent into the armament factories.

CONDITIONS OF WORK. The milieu of forced labor deteriorated to subhuman status. Workers were pushed to the breaking point by insatiable demands of the war machine. The situation in factories was deplorable, and living conditions even worse. With little food, less sanitation, and inadequate medical care, workers died quickly. Krupp laborers were housed in kennels, urinals, and baking houses, and were not allowed to enter restaurants or theaters. Those who protested were given "special treatment," a euphemism for hanging. The situation on the farms was little better. Farm workers were housed in stables and by official decree had to work as many hours as their masters wanted. Women were conscripted for work as domestics, maids, and cooks, and children also were required to work.

German officials made a distinction between Western and Eastern workers. British and French laborers received somewhat better treatment. Poles and Russians, considered racially inferior, were given severe treatment. They had to wear an "O" patch, signifying *Ostarbeiter,* or "Eastern worker." In Breslau, Polish workers had their identity cards stamped with the drawing of a pig. Eastern workers were given food pronounced tubercular by veterinarians. Tens of thousands were put to work to build fortifications or to carry ammunition to the front lines. As the German military situation worsened, thousands of workers disappeared to enter the Resistance or join guerrilla bands. (*See* RESISTANCE MOVEMENTS; UNDERGROUND; and PARTISANS.)

BUSINESS AND INDUSTRY. By 1943 demand for labor became insatiable by such corporations as Thyssen, Krupp, and IG Farbenindustrie. One Krupp official admitted: "Our new friendship with the SS is proving very profitable." Business and industrial leaders closed their eyes to methods of recruitment and conditions of work. They regarded forced labor as a matter of naked survival with no humanitarian or legal considerations.

AFTERMATH. Attention was given to forced labor in the judgments at the Nuremberg trials (*q.v.*). Hans Frank was judged guilty of "exploiting Poland in such a way which led to the deportation to Germany of over a million Poles." Fritz Sauckel was found guilty of deporting to Germany "more than five million human beings, many of them under terrible conditions of cruelty and suffering." Alfred Rosenberg (*q.v.*), Reich Minister for Eastern Occupied Territories, "helped formulate policies of German exploitation, forced labor, extermination of Jews and opponents of Nazi rule." Albert Speer (*q.v.*), Reich Minister of Armaments and Munitions, "knew when he made his demands on Sauckel they would be supplied by laborers serving under compulsion." Speer admitted his responsibility.

Bibliography. H. E. Kannapin, *Wirtschaft unter Zwang* (1966); E. L. Homse, *Foreign Labor in Nazi Germany* (1967); A. S. Milward, *The New Order and the French Economy* (1969); A. Speer, *Inside the Third Reich* (1970); and M. Kele, *Nazis and Workers* (1972).

FORRESTAL, JAMES VINCENT (1892–1949). Governmental official responsible for war procurement program.

In June 1940 President Roosevelt appointed Forrestal an administrative assistant. In the following August Forrestal was named Secretary of the Navy. On U.S. entry into the war he launched a procurement and industrial program that increased naval strength from 384 vessels to 1,500 combat ships and 50,000 auxiliary vessels, including landing craft. Under his direction naval personnel increased from 158,000 men to 3.6 million men and women. He organized the Office of Procurement and Matériel in the Navy Department, which placed military production into motion. He introduced the first efficient plan of priorities and allocations, and was instrumental in the production of destroyer escorts and landing craft used in the Normandy invasion and later in the Pacific. On the death of Frank Knox (*q.v.*) in May 1944, Forrestal was named Secretary of the Navy.

In September 1947 Forrestal became the first U.S. Secretary of Defense. In this post he worked to harmonize the three major services. He retired in March 1949. Depressed by what he considered to be unfair attacks on his integrity, he entered a naval hospital to be treated for nervous exhaustion. He appeared to be recovering, then had a relapse. He ended his life by leaping from a high window of the Navy Hospital at Bethesda, Maryland, on May 22, 1949.

Bibliography. J.V. Forrestal, *Diaries* (1951); and A. Rogow, *James Forrestal: A Study of Personality, Politics, and Policy* (1963).

FORTRESS EUROPE. German *Festung Europa.* Term used by Hitler to describe the European continent under German control.

The German dictator ordered that the Continent be defended against British, later Russian, and still later American attack. He fortified the Atlantic coastline from Norway to the Pyrenees and conscripted millions of men to protect conquered Europe. He regarded Fortress Europe as impregnable, but far overextended his lines of communication and transportation. It was a gross miscalculation. Cascading opposition to German occupation eventually broke down the entire structure. (*See also* NEW ORDER: RESISTANCE MOVE-MENTS; SIEGRIED LINE: and WEST WALL.)

Bibliography. F. Magdalany, *The Fall of Fortress Europe* (1968).

FOUR CHAPLAINS. Four U.S. Army chaplains who gave their life jackets to other men aboard a sinking troop transport in 1943.

BACKGROUND. On January 29, 1943, convoy *SG-19* left St. John, New-foundland, bound for Skovfjord. It consisted of two American merchant ships and the 5,649-ton U.S. Army transport *Dorchester,* built in 1926 as a passenger liner and outfitted in 1942 for Army service. The *Dorchester* carried 1,000 tons of cargo, a crew of 130 merchant marine seamen, an armed guard of 23, and 751 passengers, most of whom were U.S. Army reinforcements for Greenland. Three Coast Guard cutters served as escort.

The convoy quickly ran into cold and dirty weather. Escort vessels, bothered by icing, had difficulty in keeping up with the merchant ships. On February 2, 1943, a direction finder indicated the presence of U-Boats, whereupon the con-voy took evasive action.

ATTACK. Early the next day the convoy was steaming at 10 knots, reaching a point about 150 miles from Cape Farewell, when suddenly the *Dorchester* was torpedoed without warning by a German submarine, the *U-456.* After the master's order to abandon ship, the *Dorchester* began sinking by the bow. In the pitch black night the escort ships were unaware of what had happened.

There was panic on the doomed ship. Historian Samuel Eliot Morison reported that "both discipline and seamanship were wanting in the merchant crew." Only 2 of the 14 lifeboats were used; others capsized through over-crowding, fouling of the release gear, or poor handling in the water. Many passengers did not hear the abandon-ship signal because there was not enough steam to blow all six blasts. Escort ships rescued those who survived in the 34°F water. Of the 904 aboard the *Dorchester,* only 299 were saved. Hundreds of bodies were later seen floating on the water.

SACRIFICE. Four U.S. Army chaplains, all first lieutenants, were aboard the *Dorchester:* Clark V. Poling, of Schenectady, New York; John P. Washington, Newark, New Jersey; Alexander D. Goode, Washington, D.C.; and George L. Fox, Chicopee Falls, Massachusetts. Poling and Fox were Protestants; Washington was Catholic; and Goode was Jewish.

According to survivor affidavits released by the U.S. War Department, fear of icy water made many aboard almost helpless, convinced as they were that such a plunge could bring only death. The chaplains calmed their fears, and persuaded many to go overboard where there was a chance of rescue. Survivors reported seeing the chaplains standing together on the *Dorchester*'s forward deck, handing out life belts from a box. When the box was empty, each chaplain removed his own life jacket and gave it to another man. As the ship sank, the chaplains were seen linking arms and raising their voices in prayer. They were still on the deck together, praying, when the stricken ship made her final plunge.

The story of the four chaplains made a strong impression in the Allied World. On December 2, 1944, the U.S. War Department posthumously awarded the four chaplains the Distinguished Service Crosses. (*See* HERALDRY OF WORLD WAR II.)

Bibliography. Release by U.S. War Department, Bureau of Public Relations, Press Branch, December 3, 1944.

FOUR FREEDOMS. List of four aims proposed by President Franklin D. Roosevelt (*q.v.*) if peace were to be restored.

In his annual message to Congress on January 6, 1941, President Roosevelt recommended Lend-Lease (*q.v.*) for the Allies. He also stated that Four Freedoms should exist everywhere in the world—freedom of speech and expression, freedom of worship, freedom from want, and freedom from fear. In August 1941 these were incorporated substantially in the Atlantic Charter (*q.v.*). They represented Roosevelt's way of informing the world that the American people depended upon freedoms that were not associated generally with Nazi ideology. (*See also* WAR AIMS.)

FOUR HORSEMEN OF THE GERMAN APOCALYPSE. Russian name give to four Soviet generals who trapped Gen. Friedrich Paulus (*q.v.*) and his German 6th Army at Stalingrad (*see* STALINGRAD, BATTLE OF) in 1942. The four commanders were: Gens. Rodion Malinowsky, Konstantin Rokossovsky, Ivan Konev, and Fyodor Tolbukhin (*qq.v.*). When German Gen. Erich von Manstein (*q.v.*) tried to come to the aid of Paulus, the Four Horsemen combined to turn the German counteroffensive into a rout. (*See* EASTERN FRONT, CAMPAIGNS ON THE.)

FRANC TIREURS ET PARTISANS FRANÇAIS (FTP). Major Communist underground working in France during the German occupation.

FTP leaders had long experience in clandestine activity. Their practice of violence was expert, discipline severe, knowledge of underground warfare extensive. The FTP maintained that violence was the only way to strike back at the Nazis and lead to an eventual mass uprising. Its goal was to make the enemy insecure in occupied territory. Many of its leaders were executed by the Germans. (*See* RESISTANCE MOVEMENTS; and UNDERGROUND.)

FRANCE, FIRST BATTLE OF. Quick, unexpected defeat of France by Nazi Germany in June 1940.

BACKGROUND. While Poland was being crushed by the Nazi war machine in the *Blitzkrieg* (*q.v.*) of September 1939, France, her ally in the West, made no move to distract the German armies. French troops moved cautiously a few miles into German territory but retreated promptly when the main German forces were shifted from the east. At the beginning of the war, the French Army, consisting of 800,000 combat troops and trained reserves of 5.5 million was considered to be the most powerful fighting force in Europe. Chief of Staff Maurice Gamelin (*q.v.*) assured his people that his troops could smash any German assault.

PHONY WAR. Nothing of consequence happened during the winter of 1939–1940 when the western front settled down to the phony, or sit-down war. (*See SITZKRIEG.*) The French felt secure behind their Maginot Line (*q.v.*), while the Germans remained stationary behind their lightly built Siegfried Line (*q.v.*). Both sides were careful not to provoke the enemy into massive retaliation. The French, anesthetized by Hitler's war of nerves, even sent some of their troops home. The British Expeditionary Force (*q.v.*) sang a satirical song about hanging out their dirty wash on the Siegfried Line. (*See SIEGFRIED LINE, WE'RE GONNA HANG OUT THE WASHING ON THE.*)

On May 18, 1940, Premier Paul Reynaud (*q.v.*) removed Gamelin from command and replaced him with 72-year-old Gen. Maxime Weygand (*q.v.*), who gave orders to set up a new defensive line south of the Somme to be named the Weygand Line (*q.v.*). He placed 37 divisions in the line. But the best French troops had already been lost in Belgium or at Dunkirk (*see DUNKIRK EVACUATION*), and the French Air Force had been almost wiped out.

ASSAULT. On June 5, 1940, the day after the end of the Dunkirk evacuation, the *Luftwaffe* (*q.v.*) made its first raid on Paris. Two days later the Germans unleashed 120 divisions, with 23 held in reserve, in an overwhelming *Blitzkrieg* aimed at four points: (1) across the Somme into Normandy; (2) south of Amiens in a spearhead directed at Paris; (3) down the Oise River in another drive directed against Paris; and (4) around the northern flank of the Maginot Line. Thousands of German *Panzers* (*q.v.*) roared through the French countryside scattering the defense. The attempt to stop the tanks by concealed traps behind the lines failed.

The fast-moving Germans quickly pierced the crumbling Weygand Line above Beauvais and Reims. The French plunged into headlong retreat in a panic situation. A mass exodus on the roads south of Paris created chaos. Low-flying German planes strafed the desperate refugees clogging the roads.

By mid-June the French armies had been pushed back in confusion across the Marne. The government, regarding any defense of their capital city as suicidal, declared Paris an open city and fled first to Tours and then to Bordeaux. Disappointed by the debacle, Churchill ordered the evacuation of all remaining British troops from France.

ENTER MUSSOLINI. Motivated by the French disaster, Mussolini, who was becoming increasingly envious of German victories, suddenly decided to act. On June 10, 1940, he declared war on France and Britain and sent 400,000 Italian troops into the French Riviera. "We take the field against the plutocratic and reactionary democracies who always have blocked the march of and frequently plotted against the existence of the Italian people." "Italians! Rush to arms and show your tenacity, your courage, and your valor." From Roosevelt came a sarcastic indictment: "The hand that held the dagger has struck it into the back of its neighbor."

CHURCHILL'S PROPOSAL. On June 12, 1940, Churchill flew to Tours in a last-ditch attempt to persuade the French Cabinet to honor its promises not to sue for a separate peace and to carry on the war from North Africa. Desperately, he suggested that the French and British unite into one state, an astonishing proposal in view of the classic British policy of splendid isolation from the Continent. The French rejected the offer. Disillusioned and depressed, Weygand predicted: "England's neck will be wrung like a chicken's."

CAPITULATION. Although some units continued to fight tenaciously, the French were routed. Marshal Henri Pétain (*q.v.*), hero of World War I, asked for an armistice. The document was signed on June 22, 1940, at precisely the spot where the Germans had surrendered in 1918. (*See* COMPIÈGNE.)

SIGNIFICANCE. It was a tremendous victory for Hitler, who stamped his foot in joy on hearing of the capitulation. The German *Fuehrer* had demonstrated the power of his war machine against "Europe's finest army." For the French it was a catastrophe.

Dozens of factors interwoven in a maze of conflicting patterns contributed to the defeat. The notoriously exaggerated myth of French military strength was shattered. The Germans were superior in every department of war—leadership, manpower, stategy, tactics, and *esprit de corps*. The French neglected to fortify the critical Ardennes area and underrated the value of air power. Added to military weakness was political chaos. Year after year it had been the same —collapsing Cabinets, civic disunity, political corruption, extensive intrigues. With no effective leadership, the French were tired, dejected, demoralized, asking only to be let alone. The Germans were helped by many agents operating inside the country.

Gen. Charles de Gaulle (*q.v.*) had a word for it:

France lost the war for very definite reasons. First, our military system did not develop any mechanized strength in the air and on the ground; second, the panic paralyzed our civilian population while the German mechanized units advanced; third, the tangible effect the fifth column had on the minds of many of our leaders; and fourth, lack of coordination between us and our Allies.

Bibliography. A. Maurois, *Why France Fell* (1941); E. J. Boie, *Truth on the Tragedy of France* (1941); I. Hay, *The Battle of Flanders* (1941); A. Werth, *The Twilight of France 1933–1940* (1942); D. Vilfroy, *War in the West: The Battle of France, May–June 1940* (1942); Pertinax (Charles Joseph André Géraud) *The Gravediggers of France* (1944); M. Bloch, *Defeat* (1949); F. L. Ellis, *The War in France and Flanders, 1939–1940* (1953); A. Goutard, *The Battle of France* (1959); J. Williams, *The Ideas of May: The Defeat of France, May–June 1940* (1968); and W. L. Shirer, *The Collapse of the Third Republic* (1969).

FRANCE, SECOND BATTLE OF. Allied victory in Northern France in the summer of 1944.

BACKGROUND. Operation Overlord (q.v.), the most powerful amphibious landings in world history, took place with remarkably small losses. The Allies now had beachheads on Hitler's Fortress Europe (*q.v.*). (*See* NORMANDY INVASION.) The Allied Supreme Command committed its power to clearing France of Germans and then proceeding to the heart of the Third Reich itself. The Battle of Normandy began as vast supplies poured into the established beachheads.

CAPTURE OF CHERBOURG. The first major objective was the port of Cherbourg to the north of the beachheads. As the Americans advanced toward the city, the Germans withdrew into its fortifications. The overland approaches were mildly protected by a semicircle of wooded ridges and underground forts. On June 22, 1944, three American infantry divisions under Gen. J. Lawton ("Lightning Joe") Collins (*q.v.*) began an all-out attack on Cherbourg after an intense artillery and air bombardment. To the east British and Canadian forces pinned down four *Panzer* (*q.v.*) divisions and made it impossible for them to relieve the garrison at Cherbourg. On June 26 the German commander surrendered, and all resistance in the northern sector ended by July 1. Cherbourg, like Naples, bore mute witness to methodical German destruction. American engineers quickly repaired the smashed breakwaters and the damaged cranes. The occupation of Cherbourg blasted Hitler's hopes of driving the Allies into the sea.

BATTLE FOR CAEN. The center of gravity now shifted to southwest of Caen, where the 21st Army Group under Gen. Bernard Law Montgomery (*q.v.*) pressed on against bitter resistance. Here the Allies came up against strongly reinforced German forces in the battle for Caen, the hub of a critical network of communications. The Royal Air Force (*q.v.*) smothered Caen with bombs. On July 18, 1944, as the "carpet bombing" continued from the air, the Allies pushed into the town north and west of the Oise. The Germans, with their supplies cut off, broke, and ran. Montgomery was slow to take advantage of the victory.

AMERICANS AT ST. LÔ. Meanwhile, the Germans were fighting desperately to hold St. Lô, capital of the Department of La Manche. During most of July the Americans fought savagely for the strategic road center. It was one of the nastiest fights of the war, worse than D-Day (*q.v.*) itself. Gains were measured in yards. At every farmhouse the Germans had to be flushed out like protesting birds. In the Bocage country around St. Lô, U.S. tanks became snarled among the hedgerows—hundreds of thick banks of dirt, with thorn bushes on top, lining the roads and lanes of Normandy. Not until tanks were outfitted with new cutting devices could advances be made through the sticky hedgerow country. The Allies, with 30 divisions available, were now ready for a major offensive.

BREAKTHROUGH. With the gateway to the south and east open, American forces were ready to move out of Normandy, seal off the Germans in Brittany, and streak eastward and northeastward across the waist of France. Lt. Gen. George S. Patton, Jr. (*q.v.*) sent the bulk of his tank force eastward in company with the armor of Lt. Gen. Courtney H. Hodges (*q.v.*). As the rampaging tanks poured through Avranches the Battle of Normandy merged into the Second Battle of France. Racing through the fields at some 40 miles a day, the U.S. tank columns headed south and stormed into Rennes, the capital of Brittany. Three columns then turned westward and cut a corridor to the coast.

GERMAN COUNTERATTACK. For the normal military mind the situation obviously called for a prompt German withdrawal from Normandy. But a stubborn Hitler ordered four *Panzer* divisions of the German 7th Army to strike westward. The counterattack began on August 7, 1944, in the direction of Avranches. The Germans fought furiously, but it was a hopeless task. The Allies forged a four-pronged trap for them.

FALAISE POCKET. The German situation was precarious. The 5th and 7th *Panzer* Armies were trapped in the Falaise-Argentan pocket in a classic pincers movement. The encircling Allies relentlessly sewed up the area. Heavily battered from the air, the Germans staggered in disorder toward the Seine.

SIGNIFICANCE. The Second Battle of France ended in a resounding Allied victory. Since the start of the campaign, the equivalent of five *Panzer* divisions had been smashed and six severely mauled. More than 200,000 Germans were taken prisoner, including most of what was left of the 7th Army. The Allies destroyed 1,300 tanks, while the Germans lost 20,000 vehicles, and 500 assault guns. Straggling German units, homeward bound, crossed the Seine. The liberation of France and the Low Countries was near.

Bibliography. D.D. Eisenhower, *Report on the Operations in Europe, June 1944-May 1945* (1945); F. de Guingand, *Operation Victory* (1947); B. L. Montgomery, *Normandy to the Baltic* (1947); and D. Mason, *Breakout from Normandy* (1969).

FRANCE IN WARTIME. For defeated and humiliated France the period from 1940 to 1945 was a tragic era. Subjected to occupation by a detested enemy, the French suppressed their feelings and looked forward eagerly to Allied victory and their own liberation.

STRANGE DEFEAT. In the years immediately preceding the war, France was beset by a host of critical problems. Social reform lagged because its proponents attempted to right the wrongs of half a century with one blow. The economy was threatened by a combination of inflation and depression.

On one count the French public seemed to be assured, claiming they possessed "the finest army in Europe." The dominating position that France had maintained in Europe since the close of World War I had been due in large part to continental-wide respect for the French military arm. Frenchmen had positive faith in the strength of their modern and scientific Maginot Line (*q.v.*), which would protect them from any ill-advised aggression from the old enemy across the Rhine.

In September 1939, when France took up arms in defense of Poland, the French public was certain that its army would display its traditional élan and valor. Instead, it became a victim of Hitler's *Blitzkrieg* (*q.v.*). Total military collapse followed.

The defeat and the vengeful armistice at Compiègne astonished not only the French but the entire world as well. A combination of factors contributed to the unexpected defeat. While the French High Command placed its trust in old-fashioned defensive warfare, attack-minded Hitler created a strong military machine combining weight with mobility. French military leaders paid little attention to a young officer, Charles de Gaulle (*q.v.*), who called for a new type of mobile warfare. German experts appropriated his ideas in fashioning their *Blitzkrieg* tactics. Added to weak military leadership was the critical domestic situation, in which mutual class difficulties stultified social and economic reforms. The country's vitality was sapped by selfish activities of corrupt politicians. In the final analysis, however, France was defeated primarily because of the skill and boldness of German military leaders and their fighting men.

COLLAPSED MORALE. French morale caved in with military defeat. This time, as the Germans tore holes in French lines at Sedan, no taxicab army was shuttling from Paris to hold off the enemy, as in 1914. French bravery vanished against German tanks and punishing *Luftwaffe* (*q.v.*) planes. Every road leading from Paris was choked with a stream of bewildered refugees in cars, wagons, and carts. Traditional French confidence vanished in an atmosphere of misery.

END OF THE THIRD REPUBLIC. With German victory came the end of the Third French Republic, which had existed for nearly 70 years since it came to life in the turbulence of defeat in 1871. There was need for new leadership. Two dozen prominent politicians, among them Pierre Mendès-France and Édouard Daladier, attempted to set up a government-in-exile in Africa, but

Marshal Henri Pétain (*q.v.*), hero of World War I, ordered their arrest. From London Charles de Gaulle, professional soldier and Under Secretary of State just before the capitulation, summoned his countrymen to continue the fight. Discouraged and depressed, most Frenchmen turned to Pétain for salvation.

The French Parliament, both Senate and Chamber of Deputies, met at Vichy-les-Bains, a spa in the *département* of Allier, in central France, from July 9 to 10, 1940. The new government moved from Bordeaux to which it had retreated on June 10.

VICHY GOVERNMENT. The Vichy government was controlled by two men—Marshal Henri Pétain and Pierre Laval (*q.v.*). The "conqueror of Verdun" dedicated himself to the goal of reviving the confidence of the French. Both chambers voted Pétain by a majority of 569 to 80 the power to draw up a new constitution. The title of "republic" disappeared—it was now simply the French State. Although he was 84, Pétain was supported by almost all Frenchmen with blind confidence. But the attitude of the old war hero was essentially defeatist: he saw the war as irrevocably lost and was determined to make the best deal possible with Hitler.

Pierre Laval, named Vice-Premier, held the same view as Pétain on the finality of the defeat of France. He cunningly used the old marshal's prestige to convince the French people that it was to their interest to accept Nazi domination in the hope of preserving whatever remained of the country's sovereignty. France, he felt, must adapt to the new totalitarian age. Pétain had little use for Laval, yet he named him his political heir.

The two Vichy leaders persuaded Parliament to vote itself out of existence. The France of Liberty, Equality, and Fraternity was no more. Once democratic France was molded into a police state under Pétain as Chief of State. Pétain announced a *"Revolution Nationale,"* based on the slogan "Work, Family, Fatherland," as the means of providing "the sinews of the new national existence." His new regime, Pétain said, would be "national in foreign policy, hierarchical in domestic policy, coordinated and controlled in economy, and, above all, social in spirit."

In the new French state an administration was set up in consonance with the political philosophy of totalitarianism. Traditional French freedom of expression, in both press and radio, was ended. Many methods of coordination (*Gleichschaltung*) used in Nazi Germany were introduced into France. Labor unions, schools and universities, and youth organizations, all were now placed under rigid state control.

COLLABORATION. Behind their respectable front man, Pétain, there moved into power a combination of royalists, rightists, authoritarians, and opportunists, many of whom had been undermining the Third French Republic for years. Outspoken Fascists, including Jacques Doriot and Marcel Déat, went even farther than the men of Vichy and called for complete cooperation with

Hitler and Mussolini. Some who regarded Vichy as not extreme enough in its authoritarianism, deserted the new government, accepted German funds, and settled in Paris, where they intrigued against Pétain.

Most of the French people, astonished and shocked by their sudden defeat, believed at first that total collapse of the Allies was only a matter of weeks. Many felt that the collaboration tactics of Pétain and Laval had saved them from even a worse fate. Despairing, they accepted the "New Order" because they believed genuinely that there was no realistic alternative.

WARTIME ECONOMY. Economic conditions deteriorated rapidly following the defeat. Laval introduced a system of corporations similar to those in Fascist Italy and National Socialist Germany. He hoped to stimulate the economy by outlawing strikes and declaring lockouts illegal. His attempt to subject agriculture to state control was unsuccessful because by and large the peasantry evaded his regulations.

The French economy worsened after June 1941, when the drain of the war in the East against the Soviet Union forced Hitler to increase his demands on the French. He not only extracted financial tribute, but also required much of French industry, commerce, and agriculture to help meet his requirements. Worst of all was the steadily increasing inflation.

Hitler wanted to avoid a systematic policy of destroying France economically, as he had treated the Poles and other "inferior" peoples in the East, but at the same time his exacting demands on Laval weakened the economic structure of France. Laval did what he could to meet Hitler's wishes on the ground that the alternative would have been a German *Gauleiter,* who might well have crippled French economic life.

FOOD PROBLEM. With the country drained of foodstuffs, there was a marked decline in the standard of living. Even under nearly anarchic political conditions of the immediate pre-war years, the French had always maintained their interest in superb cooking. All basic food staples were in short supply and the result was a wave of melancholy among food lovers, which meant virtually the entire population. The Nazi requisitioning of food-stuffs from France was insatiable. From June 1940 to June 1944 the Germans sent home 2,845,000 tons of wheat, 845,000 tons of meat, 711,000 tons of potatoes, 220 million eggs, as well as 750,000 horses, enough to cripple the wants of the French public.

Hungry Frenchmen took to eating crows, pigeons, even cats. On October 31, 1941, several Parisian journals published a notice urging citizens not to eat cats because the animals harbored most dangerous germs and besides were useful when alive in ridding the city of its newly increased population of rats. Those who had money flocked to restaurants and complained of being reduced to "conditions of the Hindus." Most foods were on ration—from sugar to potatoes to wines. There were some food imports from African provinces, but not enough to appease the national hunger. The government encouraged people to "return to the soil," but this was a useless gesture. Small vegetable plots were set up everywhere in the cities. In Paris even the Tuileries were used to raise precious food.

SOCIAL PARALYSIS. Traditionally active French social life degenerated into a pall of gloom as the people muddled through the boring days of occupation. Life in Paris as well as in provincial towns and villages slowed to an unaccustomed pace. Once busy street traffic nearly vanished due to lack of petrol. Everything was on short supply—paper, tobacco, bicycle tires. The system of rationing was indifferently observed. People went to the cinemas for a few hours of entertainment. Lack of transportation meant that vacations could not be taken as in pre-war days.

Because Hitler was short of manpower in his factories, Laval had to agree to send a million Frenchmen to Germany to work under forced labor (*q.v.*). No single measure was more unpopular than this concession to Nazi power. Young men found myriad excuses to evade the trip to Germany. Many turned to the underground (*q.v.*) to avoid the degradation of working for the German war effort.

Forty million Frenchmen were ranged into two hostile camps, one calling for collaboration and the other for resistance. Apart from a handful of extreme pro-Germans, nearly everyone was anxious to see departure of the Germans. The main question was one of method. Meanwhile, there was uncertainty and dissatisfaction.

A glimmer of hope followed the Anglo-American landings in North Africa in November 1942. Hitler angrily ordered his troops across the demarcation line between occupied and unoccupied France, thereby placing the entire country under German control.

CULTURAL AND INTELLECTUAL LIFE. Despite the existence of an unpopular regime and the muted anger of a proud people under foreign domination, a vigorous cultural and intellectual life flourished in wartime France.

The traditionally free French press was muzzled by Vichy and German authorities, but clandestine underground Resistance papers were mimeographed in the tens of thousands, distributed and read throughout the country. Such newspapers as *Combat* kept alive the latent urge for liberation in all French social classes. Those who hoped for accurate war news listened to the British Broadcasting Corporation (BBC).

Because every phase of national education, from opening school years to university, was centralized, the Vichy-controlled Ministry of National Education saw to it that education reflected the needs of a puppet administration. University students were subjected to strict discipline. As always the universities formed a microcosm of national life. Students turned either to collaboration or resistance, but most of them, reconciled to what they deemed to be a hopeless situation, were content to await developments in difficult times.

Publication of books declined during the war years because of paper and other shortages, but the French still read books. The authorities banned books by "unreliable authors' such as Sigmund Freud and Emil Ludwig. The public eagerly read camouflaged philosophical works by Sartre, Beauvoir, and Camus. Much social and economic discontent was revealed in the popularity of existentialism, which blossomed in wartime France. (See LITERATURE IN THE WAR; and PSYCHOLOGICAL EFFECTS OF THE WAR.)

The French still retained their love for the theater. Whenever possible they went to see the productions of the Big Four—Louis Jouvet, Charles Dullin, Georges Pitoëff, and Gaston Baty. Among the most popular wartime productions were those by the mime Jean-Louis Barrault and Giraudoux's witty comedy, La Folle de Chaillot (The Madwoman of Chaillot).

As in pre-war years theatrical activity was centered in Paris. The great Opera edifice was busy catering to opera-loving Germans. The state theaters—the Comédie-Française, the Théâtre Nationale Populaire, the Théâtre des Nations (Sarah Bernhardt), and the Théâtre de l'Odéon (Salle Luxemburg)—were reorganized in 1944. State grants were given for local productions at Strasbourg, Toulouse, and other provincial cities.

The French, hungry for entertainment and anxious to keep warm, flocked to the cinema. Among the favorite film makers were René Clair, who had won his reputation with Sous les toits de Paris (1931); Jean Renoir, master of contrast, spontaneity, and critic of tradition; and Marcel Carné, who reflected the contemporary mood of love and happiness always beyond man's grasp in his Children of Paradise (1943-1945). (See FILMS IN THE WAR.)

Popular circuses were limited by shortages of food and transportation. Although heavily censored, the so-called theater of the absurd and theater of cruelty had a special place in a war society because the artists could comment on events and happenings.

GROWTH OF NATIONAL CONSCIOUSNESS. French anger increased as occupying Germans sent trainloads of booty home—furs, clothing, perfumes, and art works. By late 1942 it became clear that there was a possibility of Allied victory. French national consciousness was already awakened. Symptomatic of the change in morale was the scuttling of 73 ships of the French Mediterranean Fleet at Toulon on November 27, 1942. The French regarded this act as restoring their honor and as a signal of their own contribution to liberation.

RESISTANCE. The anti-German underground came into existence within weeks after the collapse of France in 1940. At first, opposition was limited to propaganda and intelligence by a few scattered groups who hated their German conquerors and who refused to accept defeat. These dissidents printed and distributed leaflets, listened to the BBC, organized escape routes for British airmen, spied on Germans, and sent important war information to London.

Gradually, the psychology changed from opposition to resistance to conspiracy. The movement intensified after Hitler invaded the Soviet Union in

June 1941. Until this time French Communists had kept themselves uninvolved in "the imperialist war," but now that Soviet Russia was being threatened they brought an infusion of strength into the French Resistance. They had the advantage of a tight and effective organization as well as experience in underground activities.

The Resistance now fell into two main groupings: Conservative recruits from the army allied with liberal bourgeois leaders in one group and Communist workers and intellectuals in the other. Communists organized shock units called *groupes francs,* of 30 men each, forming a kind of secret army. On a broader level the NAP (*Noyautage des administrations publiques*) infiltrated the civil service for recruits. Many French workers who were conscripted for labor in German factories, turned to the underground. (*See MAQUIS.*)

Members of the Resistance waged guerrilla warfare against Germans. They shot down German officers and executed traitors in their own ranks. Units called *sabotage fer* specialized in the destruction of railroad installations and other targets. Unwary German sentries fell victim to these guerrillas.

Resistance stiffened considerably when the Germans occupied Vichy France in November 1942. The Resistance movement in the south included army officers, liberationists (Unionists, Communists, Socialists), *Franc Tireurs* (intellectuals, mostly Communists), and the Catholic *Témoinage Chrétien.* Centers of Resistance activity were at Lyon and Toulouse.

In May 1943 all major Resistance groups were combined in one federation called the National Resistance Council. On February 1, 1944, all guerrilla and sabotage activities were placed under direction of the FFI (French Forces of the Interior), although Communists formed the FTP (Franc Tireurs et Partisans) inside the FFI. The Allied Supreme Council recognized the FFI as a regular combatant army and utilized it in the final invasion of June 1944.

LIFE AND DEATH FOR JEWS. For the Jews wartime France was a long period of martyrdom. In 1939 approximately 270,000 Jews were in France, of whom about 30,000 were refugees from Nazi Germany. In May 1940 some 40,000 more from Holland and Belgium sought refuge in France. Of the total more than one-half were foreign born and of these many were "stateless." Some naturalized Jews managed to escape.

The Vichy Government, recalling the anti-Dreyfusard coalition of the late 19th century, introduced anti-Jewish measures without prodding from Berlin. The *Statut des Juifs,* ("Jewish Statute") issued on October 4, 1940, ousted Jews from military, public, and administrative posts; forbade them to teach in schools and colleges; and required them to register. Later, Jews were forced to wear a distinguishing Jewish star. In April 1941 a special Commissariat for Jewish Questions was established under the direction of Xavier Vallat, a notorious French anti-Semite.

Despite protest by Jewish veterans, who enjoyed a privileged status, and opposition from the Christian clergy, including the Archbishops of Toulouse and

Lyon, anti-Jewish measures continued. By the end of 1942 more than 42,000
Jews were sent from France in cattle trains to extermination centers in the East.
By 1945 at least 80,000 Jews from France were killed in these death camps. (*See*
EXTERMINATION CAMPS.)

LIBERATION. By June 6, 1944, the day of the Normandy invasion, armed
French guerrilla units had grown large enough to play an important role in
liberation. While Anglo-American forces pressed forward, French sabotage
units destroyed railroads and bridges. Guerrillas ousted Vichy officials from one
town and village after another. On August 26, 1944, Resistance units joined de
Gaulle in a triumphant march down the Champs Élysées.

The outburst of patriotic enthusiasm on liberation was accompanied by
angry vengeance on those who had collaborated with the Germans. Women
who had fraternized with Germans were shorn of their hair and forced to march
through jeering crowds. Approximately 800 collaborators were executed and
more than 50,000 sentenced to prison and "national degradation."

NEW GOVERNMENTAL POLICIES. Gen. Charles de Gaulle (*q.v.*) became
temporary head of the newly proclaimed Fourth Republic. Like previous French
Governments, the provisional postwar regime of 1944–1946 turned out to be
unstable. Gen. de Gaulle remained conservative and somewhat authoritarian.
Many of the underground forces who aided in the defeat and expulsion of the
Germans were led by Communist organizers who wanted a turn to the left. Bitter factional strife took place between Communists and Popular Republicans,
and for a time it seemed that the Communists might win out. De Gaulle
retired from leadership in early 1946 in protest against factional strife.

Economic recovery was delayed by vexing political problems. A comprehensive economic program was introduced to improve French output. The defeat
of 1940, four years of German occupation, loss of population, and destruction
of property made it doubtful that France could ever recover its position as a
leading political and economic power, but the economy was gradually rebuilt.

During the remainder of the war British and Americans recognized valuable
services rendered by the Free French and by the underground forces. As a result
France was invited to have a part in peacemaking and a share in occupying German territory. The Russians objected but agreed when the British and
Americans created a French occupation zone in western Germany from
segments of the territory of their zones. Thus at the end of the war France
became one of the Big Four powers that undertook to disarm Germany and
bring those accused of being war criminals to justice.

Bibliography. A. Werth, *The Twilight of France* (1942); W. L. Langer, *Our Vichy Gamble* (1947);
M. Bloch, *Strange Defeat* (1949); H. Luethy, *France Against Herself* (1955); P. Farmer,
Vichy: Political Dilemma (1955); R. Aron, *The Vichy Regime* (1958); and R. O. Paxton,
Paradox and Politics at Vichy (1966).

FRANCO, FRANCISCO (1892–1975). Spanish head of state during the war.

In 1937 Franco, after a successful military revolt, declared himself Head of State, Prime Minister, and Commander-in-Chief of the Armed Forces, with the title of *Caudillo,* "leader" or "chief."

Although he sympathized openly with the Axis powers, which had helped him during the civil war, Franco refused to enter World War II. Taking a "non-belligerent" rather than a neutral position, he did send the Spanish Blue Division to fight alongside the Germans on the eastern front. As the Allies gradually won the upper hand, Franco drew back close to neutrality. He carefully steered a course between the belligerents without leaning too far in any direction.

Bibliography. S. Hoare, *Complacent Dictator* (1947); E. J. Hughes, *Report from Spain (1947)*; H. Feis, *The Spanish Story: Franco and the Nation at War* (1948); H. Thomas, *The Spanish Civil War* (1961); and J.W.O. Trythall, *El Caudillo* (1970).

FRANK, ANNE (1929–1945). German-Jewish girl, a victim of the Nazis in 1945. The story of her life is a poignant episode in a tragic war.

BACKGROUND. Anne Frank was born in Frankfurt am Main on June 12, 1929, the daughter of a businessman. She had a comfortable childhood in the secure love of her parents, sister, and relatives. Frightened by the advent of the Nazis, the Franks went to Amsterdam, where Otto Frank set up a produce business. But the family was not safe in Holland. When the Germans invaded the country in 1940, they began a roundup of Amsterdam's Jews with the intention of sending them to concentration camps in Germany.

SANCTUARY. Dutch citizens arranged for the safety of the Franks by hiding them in the rear annex of an upper floor in a warehouse on the Prinzengracht. The Franks were joined by the Van Dann family—father, mother, and son Peter who was, like Anne, about 12 years old—and an elderly dentist. For two years the small group remained in the secret hideout.

DISCOVERY. The dreaded knock on the door came on August 4, 1944. Alerted by informers, *Gestapo (q.v.)* agents rushed in, arrested the group, appropriated their property, and threw some innocent-looking papers on the floor. Anne was later taken to the Bergen-Belsen concentration camp, where she died in March 1945.

DIARY. A year later Otto Frank returned to the house on the Prinzengracht and found his daughter's notes lying on the floor where they had been thrown. Published as *The Diary of Anne Frank,* it became a sensation all over the world. It was translated into many languages and was a successful play and motion picture. The conscience of people everywhere was aroused by the story of a warm and sensitive girl passing through adolescence to her early death. Her words became famous: "In spite of everything, I believe that people are really good at heart. I simply cannot build up my hopes on a foundation consisting of confusion, misery, and death."

AFTERMATH. The little Jewish girl of Amsterdam became a legendary figure. Since the war thousands have visited the house on the Prinzengracht to see Anne's secret room with snippets of American movie stars pasted on the walls alongside her bed. Among the crowds have been many German teenagers who came to pay homage to the girl who believed that "bad is on the outside, good is on the inside." In late 1977 a statue of Anne Frank was unveiled around the corner from her secret hideout.

Bibliography. A. Frank, *The Diary of a Young Girl* (1952).

FRANK, HANS (1900–1946). German jurist and administrator and Governor-General of occupied Poland.

Soon after the conquest of Poland, Hitler in October 1939 named Frank Governor-General of the occupied country. Regarding Poles as an inferior race and as "slaves of the Greater German Empire," Frank began to take measures against the Polish people. He declared German the official language, eliminated the intelligentsia, and confiscated Polish property. He sentenced to death any Pole who tried to use force against a German official or damaged a public institution. He expropriated Polish-owned art for his own use, including a da Vinci and a Rembrandt. He was especially cruel to Polish Jews. By 1942 he had sent 82 percent of all Polish Jews to extermination camps.

NUREMBERG. Frank was one of the 22 major Nazis brought before the International Military Tribunal at Nuremberg (*see* NUREMBERG TRIALS). He announced his conversion to Catholicism, confessed his partial guilt, and begged the forgiveness of God and the court. Unimpressed, his judges found him guilty of war crimes and crimes against humanity. He was hanged at Nuremberg on October 16, 1946.

Bibliography. S. Pietrowski (ed.), *Hans Frank's Diary* (1961).

FRASER, BRUCE AUSTIN (1888–1981). British naval officer and Fleet Admiral.

At the outbreak of World War II Fraser was Third Sea Lord and Controller. In these posts he was responsible for the expansion of the Royal Navy. He supported the use of 14-inch guns on battleships and improved the accuracy of destroyers' antiaircraft fire power. In May 1941, after being knighted, he was returned to sea duty as Vice-Admiral and second in command of the Home Fleet. At this time Fraser was responsible for the safety of convoys to Murmansk, the Russian port. In 1943 he became Commander-in-Chief of the Home Fleet.

On December 26, 1943, Fraser, from his flagship *Duke of York,* directed the night engagement against the German battleship *Scharnhorst* (*q.v.*) when she was brought to action and sunk off North Cape, Norway. He commanded the blockade of Norway in 1943–1944. He was then transferred to the Far East as Commander-in-Chief of the British Pacific Fleet. As British representative, he signed the Japanese surrender documents aboard the USS *Missouri* in Tokyo Bay on September 2, 1945.

FREE FRANCE. French Resistance movement centered in London after 1940.

When the French Government capitulated in May 1940, Gen. Charles de Gaulle (*q.v.*) decided that the only place to continue the struggle against Hitler for a Free France was from London. He founded the Free French National Committee and assumed for himself the title of leader of all free Frenchmen. Relations between Free French and British leaders were strained severely throughout the war, due in large part, according to British authorities, to de Gaulle's arrogant behavior. From a position of relative weakness, they believed, he attempted to direct war strategy as he thought best. (*See also* FRENCH COMMITTEE OF NATIONAL LIBERATION; and *MAQUIS*.)

FREE FRENCH (FF). Name given to those who fought for a Free France (*q.v.*).

FREIKORPS DOENITZ. German volunteers who answered the call of Adm. Karl Doenitz (*q.v.*) to man his U-Boat fleet.

Most members of the *Freikorps Doenitz* were in their twenties and eager for battle and German victory. Doenitz testified at the Nuremberg Trials (*q.v.*): "Altogether, we had 40,000 men in the submarine force. Of these, 30,000 did not return and only 5,000 were taken prisoner. The majority of the submarines were destroyed from the air in the vast area of the Atlantic, where rescue was out of the question." (*See* ATLANTIC, BATTLE OF THE; and WOLF-PACK TACTICS.)

FRENCH COMMITTEE OF NATIONAL LIBERATION. Organization dedicated to work for the freedom of France from German control.

In October 1940, after rallying several French colonies to his movement, Gen. Charles de Gaulle (*q.v.*) formed the Council of Defense for the French Empire, which in September 1941 became the Free French National Committee. In June 1943 he became co-president with Gen. Henri Honoré Giraud (*q.v.*) at Algiers of the newly formed French Committee of National Liberation. After disagreement, de Gaulle managed to force Giraud out of the committee. The committee was proclaimed the Provisional Government of France in June 1944. (*See* FREE FRENCH.)

FRENCH FORCES OF THE INTERIOR (FFI). The French underground Resistance movement. (*See* FREE FRENCH; *MAQUIS*; RESISTANCE MOVEMENTS; and UNDERGROUND.)

FRENCH RESISTANCE. *See* FRANCE IN WARTIME.

FREYBERG, BERNARD CYRIL (1889–1963). New Zealand commander of the same division for most of the war.

Freyberg was recalled to duty at the beginning of World War II to command the 2nd New Zealand Expeditionary Force. His New Zealanders received their baptism of fire in Greece. He was among the last to board HMS *Ajax* for the planned withdrawal from Crete, after his troops inflicted heavy damage on the Germans.(*See* CRETE, BATTLE OF.) Later Freyberg fought against the Germans in North Africa. (*See* NORTH AFRICA, CAMPAIGNS IN.) At the end of the campaign there he and his troops were shipped to Italy to join the drive on Rome. Throughout the Italian campaign he was with his advance echelons as they rolled up the Italian Peninsula. He played a major role in the attack on Monte Cassino (*q.v.*) in February 1944 when many of his men were killed. (*See* ITALIAN FRONT, CAMPAIGNS ON THE.)

FRIEDEBURG, HANS GEORG VON (1895–1945.) German Admiral and the last Supreme Commander of the German Navy.

Friedeburg was appointed to the High Command in 1934 through the intercession of Heinrich Himmler (*q.v.*). He served throughout the war but came to prominence only during the final days. For just eight days, from May 1 to 9, 1945, he was Supreme Commander of the German Navy. In this capacity he was present at the unconditional surrender ceremony and was a signatory for defeated Germany. (*See* REIMS.) Depressed by the German defeat, Friedeburg committed suicide in Mürwick on May 23, 1945.

FRIEDMAN, WILLIAM FREDERICK (1891–1969). American cryptologist who led the army team that broke the Japanese code in 1940.

Born in Russia of parents who emigrated to the United States when he was three, Friedman got his first taste of military code breaking in 1918 during World War I at Gen. John J. Pershing's headquarters. His work on German codes and ciphers led to a governmental career, starting in 1921, of 34 years. In the period between the two World Wars, he headed the Army's Signal Intelligence Service, as a Colonel, monitoring world-wide messages. In 1934 he and his colleagues in the U.S. cryptographic service, used their first IBM machine for cryptanalysis (code breaking).

In the mid-1930s Japanese experts invented a new cipher machine that worked on the principle of a telephone switchboard and was based on the rebuilding of alphabets. Later dubbed *Purple*, the machine defied all efforts by U.S. experts to decode its messages. *Operation Magic* was the program designated to break the Japanese code. On September 25, 1940, Friedman and his small, dedicated group made a dramatic breakthrough by which the United States was able to decode simultaneously with their transmission, top secret messages being sent back and forth by Japan, her Allies, and her Ambassadors. It was of extraordinary advantage to the Allies during the war. The fact that American intelligence had cracked *Purple* was a closely guarded secret.

Col. Friedman suffered a nervous breakdown and played no part in the period immediately preceding Pearl Harbor (*q.v.*). On his death in 1969 he was buried in Arlington National Cemetery with full military honors. (*See also* CODES AND CODE BREAKING; and *ULTRA*.)

FROGMEN. Special units set up by most of the belligerent powers to attack enemy ships under water.

Suitably clothed and masked, frogmen were trained to swim for some time under water and fasten magnetic explosive charges called limpet mines against the hull of enemy ships. A notable example was the attempt by British frogmen to sink the *Tirpitz* in northern Norway in 1943. (*See TIRPITZ;* and ALTEN-FJORD RAID.)

FROMM, FRIEDRICH (1888–1945). German officer and Commander-in-Chief of the Reserve Army.

Fromm served throughout most of the war not only as head of the Reserve Army but also as Chief of Armaments. He was aware of the officers' plot against Hitler, but he refused to join it on the ground that the average German soldier would not march against the *Fuehrer*. He was in the Ministry of War headquarters on the Bendlerstrasse in Berlin when word came of the July 20, 1944, attempt on Hitler's life. He refused to take the word of Col. Claus Schenck Graf von Stauffenberg (*q.v.*) that Hitler was dead. In a comedy of errors, the conspirators arrested Fromm, who was able to turn the tables, and mindful of his own position, captured and executed the ringleaders. He also induced Gen. Ludwig Beck (*q.v.*), leader of the plot, to commit suicide. (*See* JULY PLOT.) The next day Fromm was arrested and imprisoned. He was tried before the People's Court on a charge of cowardice and executed by a firing squad on March 19, 1945.

Fromm's equivocal attitude toward the conspiracy against Hitler made him despicable in the eyes of the plotters. He was known as the ambitious officer ''who always heard the grass grow.''

FUEHRER'S BUNKER (FUEHRERBUNKER). Hitler's subterranean head-quarters below the new Reich Chancellery and its gardens in Berlin.

During the early days of the war, Hitler had his engineers build a set of underground rooms 50 feet below ground. From outside the bunker it gave the appearance of an ancient Egyptian tomb. It was a great windowless block of concrete, with no direct ventilation. Concrete walls 16½ feet thick separated Hitler and his entourage from the city above. A stairway led down to the bunker.

The *Fuehrerbunker* was built on several levels. On the top floor was a passageway separating the rooms on each side. On one side were the kitchens, on the other the servants' quarters and several guest rooms. At the end of the central passage a curved stairway led down to Hitler's bunker on the lower level. Here there were 17 small, cramped, and uncomfortable rooms. Three were reserved for Hitler.

In addition there were a map room used for conferences; the bedroom and dressing room of Eva Braun; quarters for Paul Joseph Goebbels (*q.v.*) and his family; rooms for physicians, lavatories, and bathrooms; an emergency telephone exchange; cloakrooms; guardrooms; and a special "dog bunker" for Hitler's dog Blondi. From the cloakroom an emergency exit led up four flights to the Chancellery garden.

In this bunker Hitler spent his last days from April 20 to 30, 1945, and here he committed suicide while Russian artillery shells reduced the buildings above the ground to a maze of rubble.

Bibliography. *See* H. R. Trevor-Roper, *The Last Days of Hitler* (1947); G. Blond, *The Death of Hitler's Germany* (1954); and L. Bezymenski, *The Death of Adolf Hitler: Unknown Documents from Soviet Archives* (1968).

FUEHRER'S   HEADQUARTERS   (*FUEHRERHAUPTQUARTIER*).
Various war headquarters occupied by Hitler, as Supreme Commander of the Armed Forces, and his staff. From these locations, in the manner of Napoleon, he personally conducted all major operations.

1. Special *Fuehrer* train parked at areas in Poland and Austria (1939–1941).

2. *Felsennest (Eyrie),* code or cover name for a bunker located at Münstereifel for the invasions of the West (May–June 1940). (*See* LOW COUNTRIES, CAMPAIGNS IN THE; and FRANCE, FIRST BATTLE OF.)

3. *Wolfsschlucht (Wolves' Den),* code or cover name for a bunker at Givet, Belgium (June 1940).

4. *Tannenberg,* code or cover name (after the World War I battlefield) for a bunker situated in the Black Forest (July 1940).

5. *Wolfsschanze (Wolf's Lair),* code or cover name for a barracks headquarters at Rastenburg, East Prussia, where Hitler directed the Russian campaign and where the 1944 attempt on his life took place. (*See* EASTERN FRONT, CAMPAIGNS ON THE; and JULY PLOT.)

6. *Werwolf (Wolf-Man).* Code or cover name for the headquarters at Vinnitsa in the Ukraine (summer 1942, winter 1942–1943).

7. *Adlerhorst (Eagle's Nest),* code or cover name for headquarters at Ziegenberg in the Taunus Mountains, south of Frankfurt (December 1944). (*See* ARDENNES, BATTLE OF THE.)

8. Bunker at the Reich Chancellery in Berlin (November 30, 1944–April 30, 1945) where Hitler committed suicide. (*See* FUEHRER'S BUNKER.)

At frequent intervals Hitler used his chalet Berghof at Berchtesgaden, Obersalzberg, for his military headquarters.

FULLER, JOHN FREDERICK CHARLES (1878–1966). British Army officer, military theoretician, and war historian, generally considered to be one of the fathers of modern armored warfare.

Fuller served as a reporter during the events leading to World War II. He covered the Italian invasion of Ethiopia in 1935, the Spanish civil war from 1936 to 1939, and Hitler's first war maneuvers in 1935. He saw his teachings largely vindicated during World War II, when armored warfare became the order of the day and affected all the belligerents.

Bibliography. Among Fuller's many works are: *Tanks in the Great War* (1920); *Future Warfare* (1938); *Field Service Regulations III* (1928), adopted for study by the German and Russian armies; *The Army in My Time* (1935); *Towards Armageddon* (1937); *Armaments and History* (1946); *The Second World War, 1939-1945* (1948); and *A Military History of the Western World*, 3 vols. (1954-1956).

FUSAG. 1st U.S. Army Group. A fictitious Allied force supposedly assembled in southeastern England for an invasion of France in the Pas de Calais area in 1944.

In the war of deception carried on by both sides, this was one of the ruses described in detail in documents allowed to be captured by the Germans. The idea was to keep the enemy off balance while preparations went on for invasion elsewhere. (*See also* NORMANDY INVASION.)

G

GALLAND, ADOLF (1912–   ). One of the most successful *Luftwaffe* (*q.v.*) fighting aces.

Galland served as a training officer in the early months of the war. Later he became active in almost every theater of operations, including France and Britain. He was credited with 103 air kills and was awarded many decorations. In November 1941 he succeeded Werner Moelders (*q.v.*) as General of Fighters. Because of disagreements with Hitler, he was removed from his post late in the war. He could not convince the *Fuehrer* to use the *Luftwaffe* as a strategic instead of a tactical force. He also called for greater emphasis on the fighter arm, but was again and again overruled by Hermann Goering (*q.v.*) and by the *Fuehrer,* who favored bombers in the latter stages of the war. As a lieutenant general, Galland led an elite fighter squadron in the closing days of the war.

In the postwar era Galland served as technical adviser to the Argentine Air Force.

GAMELIN, MAURICE GUSTAVE (1872–1958). French Commander-in-Chief of the Anglo-French forces during the German invasion of France in 1940.

Using his World War I experience Gamelin awaited a German attack rather than pursue the type of mobile warfare recommended by Charles de Gaulle (*q.v.*). Gamelin called for "courage, energy, confidence," but it was too late. His troops were in the wrong place at the wrong time. After the fall of France he was arrested by the Vichy authorities. He was tried at Riom in 1942 as one of the leaders responsible for the French collapse. Sent to Buchenwald concentration camp and later to a Tyrol prison, he was released by the Americans in May 1944.

GAULLE, CHARLES DE. French military and political leader. (*See* DE GAULLE, CHARLES ANDRÉ JOSEPH MARIE.)

GAVIN, JAMES MAURICE (1907–   ). U.S. Army officer.

In August 1940 Gavin, then a captain, was named instructor in tactics at West Point. As a student of the Nazi *Blitzkrieg* (*q.v.*), he became convinced of the importance of airborne operations. In December 1941 he was named plans and training officer of the provisional parachute group at Fort Benning, Georgia. In April 1942 he was appointed Chief of Military Operations of the Airborne Command at Fort Bragg, North Carolina.

On July 9, 1943, Gavin led the 505th Combat Team to spearhead the attack on Sicily. (*See* SICILY, INVASION OF.) On September 14, 1943, after the invasion of Italy, he led the regiment in a parachute drop to reinforce the American position at Salerno. (*See* SALERNO BEACHHEAD.) On August 15, 1944, after the Normandy invasion (*q.v.*), he was given command, at the age of 37, of the legendary 82nd Airborne Division, which played an important role in the Battle of Arnhem and the Battle of the Bulge (*qq.v.*).

Known as "Slim Jim" and "Jumpin' Jim," Gavin was an athletic type who achieved a brilliant record as a combat commander. His colleagues marveled at his calmness under fire. One of them described him by saying, "He could jump higher, shout louder, spit farther, and fight harder than any man I ever saw."

Bibliography. Gavin wrote *War and Peace in the Space Age* (1958).

GEE. A radio aid to navigation and target identification.

Soon after the ourbreak of war, the RAF (*q.v.*) Bomber Command became aware that normal methods of aerial navigation were inaccurate for night missions over Europe. One solution was a navigational aid called *Gee,* which was tested in 1941 and generally used in 1942. The *Gee* system brought together a master station in Britain and what was called a "slave station" with an airborne receiver that converted radio signals into a pulse which could be seen in a cathode ray tube. On the plane which housed the apparatus, the navigator would plot the time intervals between the master and slave stations and could then calculate his position relative to them.

Gee was an effective navigational aid until the Germans learned how to jam it. It was succeeded by *Oboe,* which was considerably more accurate as a navigation aid than *Gee.* (*See* OBOE; and RADAR, WARTIME.)

GEHLEN, REINHARD (1902–   ). Legendary spymaster-in-chief and Hitler's head military espionage in occupied areas of Soviet Russia during the war.

When Germany launched her *Blitzkrieg* (*q.v.*) against Poland in September 1939, Maj. Gehlen was operations officer with the 313th Infantry Division. He came to the attention of Gen. Franz Halder (*q.v.*), who on April 1, 1942, appointed him to the key post of intelligence chief of Foreign Armies East. In this post Gehlen was responsible for gathering intelligence information about the

Russians. He set up a massive organization employing hundreds of agents and analysts. Under his guidance the entire business of espionage was transformed. (*See* ESPIONAGE.) He sent back to Berlin a stream of information designed to reverse Hitler's obviously wrong decisions. The enraged *Fuehrer* declined to be convinced. Eventually, he threw Gehlen's charts and situation reports to the ground and suggested that his master spy belonged in an insane asylum.

Bibliography. Gehlen's memoirs were titled *The Service* (1972). *See also* C. Whiting, *Gehlen: Germany's Master Spy* (1972); E. H. Cookridge, *Gehlen: Spy of the Century* (1972); and H. Höhne and H. Zolling, *The General Was a Spy: The True Story of General Gehlen and His Spy Ring* (1972).

GEORGE II (1890–1947). King of the Hellenes.

In October 1940 George blocked Axis plans by driving Italian invaders from his country and occupying half of Albania. Hitler came to Mussolini's aid and by April 1941 bombed Greece into submission. George barely managed to reach the seacoast alive, while thousands of Greeks and Britons died in a defense rendered hopeless by lack of Allied airpower. (*See* GREECE, BATTLE FOR.) George formed a government-in-exile, at first in Crete, then Cairo, and finally in London.

In September 1946 George returned to Greece after obtaining a clear majority in a plebiscite, only to face a bitter civil war between left-wing and right-wing elements. Although supported by Great Britain and the United States, he failed to defeat the rebels. On April 1, 1947, only a few months after his return, he died in Athens and was succeeded by his brother Paul.

GEORGE VI (1895–1952). King of Great Britain, Ireland, and the British Dominions beyond the seas.

George VI and the royal family became symbols of national determination in the war against Hitler. With his country on the verge of defeat, he visited the bomb-damaged areas and encouraged the people to resist. He was instrumental in making London the headquarters for foreign allies. (*See* GOVERNMENTS-IN-EXILE.) He enjoyed a close and harmonious relationship with Churchill and also played a prominent role in establishing good relations with the United States.

George VI retained his royal impartiality during the strains of postwar reconstruction. He devoted every effort to maintaining the unity and morale of the nation as a whole. He died in Sandringham on February 6, 1952, and was succeeded by the elder of his two daughters, Elizabeth II.

Bibliography. See biographies by K. A. Enver (1937); C. W. Greatorex (1938); and J. W. Wheeler-Bennett (1958).

GEORGE CROSS. British medal for civilian bravery of both men and women in World War II. It replaced an older decoration, the Order of the British Empire for Gallantry.

DESIGN. The George Cross was a plain, four-armed silver cross with a circular medallion in the center showing St. George and the dragon surrounded by the words *For Gallantry.* The angle of each line showed the royal cipher *GVI.* The cross hung from a silver bar with laurel leaves. The ribbon was dark blue. Bearers were entitled to use the initials *G.C.* after their names.

AWARDS. Under German bombing in the summer of 1940 (*see* BRITAIN, BATTLE OF), British citizens performed such extraordinary feats of valor that it was decided to award a special decoration ''for acts of the greatest heroism or of the utmost conspicuous courage in circumstances of extreme danger.'' The George Cross, selected for this purpose, was considered to be one of the highest British decorations, ranking immediately after the Victoria Cross.

The George Cross was given primarily to individuals on the home front, but a military version was awarded to servicemen. In 1942 King George VI (*q.v.*) conferred the George Cross on the island of Malta to bear witness to the heroism of its inhabitants under attack. (*See* MALTA, SIEGE OF. *See also* HERALDRY OF WORLD WAR II).

GERMAN RESISTANCE. Activities of the German opposition to Hitler and the Nazi Third Reich.

BACKGROUND. Opposition to National Socialism began as soon as it emerged on the political scene. Many Germans were appalled by Hitler's policy of aggression and especially by his spurious racial theories. After the Nazis came to power in 1933, several attempts were made in governmental circles to discourage the more violent aspects of National Socialism. On June 17, 1934, Vice-Chancellor Franz von Papen made a speech at Marburg calling for greater freedom of thought and expression. On August 18, 1935, Dr. Hjalmar Schacht in a speech at Königsberg deplored Nazi violence against Jews. This kind of moderate criticism had no effect on either the *Fuehrer* or his followers.

Once established in power, Hitler had no intention of allowing any dissent. His policy of *Gleichschaltung* (co-ordination) was designed to bring every element of German life under control of centralized authority. The most consistent opposition at first came from the churches. Despite the Concordat of 1933 between the papacy and the Third Reich, Nazi authorities accused Catholic priests, monks, and nuns of currency violations. The papal encyclical, *Mit brennender Sorge* (*With Deep Anxiety*), issued on March 21, 1937, denounced the persecution of Catholics. A majority of Protestant pastors settled for political obedience, but a small group headed by Dr. Martin Niemoeller (*q.v.*) and Pastor Dietrich Bonhoeffer (*q.v.*) established the *Bekenntniskirche,* or Confessional Church, to defend Protestantism. Intellectuals, especially the Heidelberg group, led by Karl Jaspers, and the Freiburg Circle around the historian Gerhard Ritter, resisted the Nazi way of life. Added to these were the Christian- and socialist-oriented groups of the Kreisau Circle (*q.v.*).

This early opposition to Hitler was weak and ineffectual. Most Germans were impressed by the early accomplishments of the regime and supported it wholeheartedly. The opposition was driven underground. Those who were thoroughly disgusted by the New Order could protest only at the risk of their lives.

WORLD WAR II. During the first two years of the war, when Hitler was winning one victory after another, dissent remained muted. But gradually as the military and home front situations deteriorated, opposition grew into resistance and then into conspiracy. Religious leaders, both Protestant and Catholic, continued to criticize the regime. Socialists, Communists, and Syndicalists called for its overthrow. Gradually, several elements of opposition coalesced into the Resistance. The movement gathered strength when support came from inside the Foreign Office and even the *Wehrmacht* (*q.v.*). Among the government administrators were Christian Albrecht Ulrich von Hassell (*q.v.*), former German Ambassador to Italy, and Johannes Popitz, Prussian Minister of Finance. Among the civilian leaders were Dr. Carl Friedrich Goerdeler (*q.v.*), former Mayor of Leipzig, and Julius Leber, Social Democratic delegate to the *Reichstag*. Such church leaders as Jesuit Father Alfred Delp and Pastor Bonhoeffer joined the Resistance.

By far the most important development in the Resistance was support by military figures. Active on the technical side of the conspiracy were several high army officers, including Gen. Ludwig Beck (*q.v.*), chief of the Army General Staff; Field Marshal Erwin von Witzlebeen, one of the older officers; and several younger officers, notably Col. Claus Schenk Graf von Stauffenberg (*q.v.*). Added to these were two important intelligence officers, Maj. Gen. Hans Osler, chief of staff of the *Abwehr* (*q.v.*), and Adm. Wilhelm Canaris, director of the counterintelligence department of the High Command. Von Stauffenberg was the leader of the unsuccessful July Plot (*q.v.*) of 1944 on Hitler's life.

ESTIMATE. The German Resistance failed primarily because it never extended beyond a small group of conspirators and did not win mass support. It came too late to be effective. An additional unfavorable handicap was the inability of the conspirators to attract help outside the Third Reich.

The movement has been both exaggerated and underemphasized. One group of observers, notably Hans Rothfels, amplified the role of the German Resistance far beyond its actual status. Others deprecated the movement as weak and ineffectual. A fair judgment would pay tribute to a small number of courageous Germans who were willing to place their lives in jeopardy in the midst of an ironclad dictatorship. Aware that the Nazi regime was the most disgraceful era in German history and ashamed of Nazi practices in a civilized society, such Germans as Pastor Bonhoeffer, Carl Goerdeler, and Count von Stauffenberg paid with their lives for their beliefs. The hesitations and indecisions of opponents of the Hitler regime were all-too-human. No one who did not undergo the trials of the Hitler era has the right to criticize those of the German Resistance for the degree of courage necessary to oppose the Nazis.

Bibliography. H. Rothfels, *The German Opposition to Hitler* (1962); and R. Manvell and H. Fraenkel, *The July Plot* (1966).

GERMANY AT WAR.

Nearly twenty-one years after World War I, the German people were involved once again in a major conflict. The trauma of that defeat had scarcely worn off before the German home front was called on again to bear the tremendous burden of war.

BACKGROUND. Of all the belligerents the Third Reich was best prepared for war. Hitler and his generals knew exactly what kind of war they intended to fight and they believed they had the military power for it. For six years the German public had been made ready through an intensive propaganda campaign led by Paul Joseph Goebbels (*q.v.*). Germans were told that it was absolutely necessary to win *Lebensraum* (*q.v.*), living space without which they could not exist. There would be war and there would be hard discipline on the home front. This time there would be no *Dolchstoss,* no stab-in-the-back such as that in 1918 when, it was charged, Jews and Social Democrats in Berlin had brought about loss of the war by treason on the home front. (*See* PROPAGANDA, WAR.)

FIRST REACTIONS. In August 1914 all classes of Germans joined Kaiser Wilhelm II in a spontaneous outburst of patriotic enthusiasm. In September 1939, however, none of the German regiments marched off to war decorated with flowers as they had at the beginning of World War I. The old ecstasy of war spirit was lacking. Instead, with the exception of exuberant Nazis, there was a tired acceptance, a sullen sense of impending doom coupled with the hope that, perhaps, Hitler would confound his critics again and win great victories in a short war. A nameless dread was in the air. Nevile Henderson, British Ambassador to Germany from 1937 to 1939, who had worked zealously to prevent war, reported in his *Failure of a Mission* (1946):

My impression was that the mass of German people, that other Germany, was horror-struck at the whole idea of the war which was being thrust upon them. . . . But what I can say is that the whole general atmosphere in Berlin is one of utter gloom and depression (pp. 202ff).

ADJUSTMENT. The successful *Blitzkrieg* (*q.v.*) in Poland in 1939 and the conquest of France in 1940 (*see* POLAND, CAMPAIGN IN; and FRANCE, FIRST BATTLE OF) were received with satisfaction on the home front. There were few wild celebrations and most Germans hoped that the war would soon end. Throughout the first 2 years, when Hitler presented the Germans with a series of victories, sentiment gradually changed to nationwide support for the successful *Fuehrer*. The easy triumphs, the startling growth of greater Germany, the admitted superiority of German arms, all this pleased a people who had never forgotten the odium of defeat in World War I.

German casualties in the Polish and French campaigns had been light. True, there had been some air raids on German cities, but they were few and the public was not yet exposed to massive retaliation from the air.

SOCIAL CONDITIONS. During the period of Axis supremacy, social life in Germany went on much as before the war. Theaters, operas, and concerts were crowded; people still went to the movies; and athletic events drew large audiences. Goebbels's propaganda machine worked zealously to convince Germans that all was well. If anything, living conditions were improved with the exploitation of conquered lands, which permitted an increase in food rations and brought luxury items back on the market. Furs and perfumes flowed in from conquered France.

The average German was not too troubled. Now and then an acquaintance might disappear, presumably into a concentration camp. A Jewish family might be deported, but few Germans suffered in what seemed to be a winning war.

FINANCING THE WAR. A decree dated September 4, 1939, introduced for the duration of the war a 50 percent rise in income tax and an increased consumer tax. Other decrees called for excess profits to be absorbed by taxation. For propaganda reasons, against the advice of his General Staff, Hitler, attempted to prevent prices from rising and decreed an increase in production of consumer goods at the expense of armaments. He wanted to show the world that the German standard of living could remain higher than that of the British, and in fact it was during the early years of war.

To make up for deficits, Hitler drained the occupied countries of Europe, especially France, which contributed 40 percent of all the resources taken by Nazi Germany in conquered Europe. The average German now had even more purchasing power than before the war. At the same time the regime succeeded in maintaining stability of the currency. Strict regulations were imposed on distribution of vital commodities so that no one suffered. There was close supervision of wages and prices. Price increases of all kinds were subjected to heavy penalties.

In this stable economy of the early years of the war, Germans were called upon to subscribe heavily to war loans. Goebbels's patriotic propaganda made it difficult to refuse to contribute. At the same time, the German Government forced commercial and savings banks and insurance companies, all those holding capital funds, to make their money available for war purposes.

WAR ECONOMY. Germany was equipped to fight a short war at best, and this situation persisted during the first two years of Axis supremacy. On the surface the German war economy seemed to be of overwhelming strength, but underneath the organization of war, production was in trouble from the very beginning of the conflict. The vaunted German efficiency suffered under leadership of Hermann Goering (*q.v.*), who led the Four-Year Plan but who had little understanding of economics.

Hitler made a major error in issuing instructions of paralyzing effect. He was certain that he could achieve his military objectives without lowering the German standard of living, and he hoped to win the loyalty of German masses without sacrificing agricultural or consumer production. In the first two years of the war the civilian sectors of industry were allotted nearly as much steel as armaments factories.

At the beginning of the war Germany enjoyed an advantage in war matériel over her unprepared neighbors. A large part of the economy had been devoted since 1935 to military uses, but the war machine was not the iron colossus Nazi propaganda held it to be. The early contradiction of a war economy and a high standard of living was maintained during the two years of German victories. This situation could be retained as long as the enemy remained inferior in strength. But the Allied Powers gradually organized their superior economic potential, a development that was certain to slow the pace of Nazi triumphs.

LABOR SUPPLY. The war economy of the Third Reich was closely hinged to the problem of labor supply. In the early part of the war, when final victory seemed to be only a matter of weeks, Germans on the home front flocked to the factories to do their share for the war effort. The regime declared bonuses for night work and holidays as well as overtime. In some cases the work day was extended to ten hours. The lack of workers was compensated in part by the forced recruitment of foreign labor. (*See* FORCED LABOR.) The result was an increasing flow of war matériel from the factories. In 1941 alone workers in Germany produced 12,000 aircraft and 5,100 tanks.

In the matter of labor Hitler again made a basic error. Maintaining that the place of German women was in the home, he forbade employment of females in German factories until the closing months of the war. This Nazi ideological taboo undoubtedly was responsible for a drop in labor effectiveness. The war was becoming increasingly more protracted than Hitler had envisaged and it became necessary to turn to a new economic mobilization. Yet, contrary to the expectations of economists in the Allied countries, total German industrial production, despite Hitler's mistakes, was maintained for some time at a relatively high level.

RUSSIAN CRISIS. The Russo-German Nonaggression Pact (*q.v.*) of August 23, 1939, astonished the German public. After years of intensive anti-Russian propaganda, Germans were ordered to accept the Russians as allies. Then, on June 22, 1941, came another *volte face* with Hitler's invasion of the Soviet Union. There was consternation on the home front.

Most Germans hoped that the Russian campaign, like the earlier ones, would be short and decisive. The Red Army was supposed to be an undisciplined horde with out-dated weapons and a purged leadership. The defeat would be quick and smashing. First reports were optimistic. On October 3, 1941, Hitler announced to the world that the Russians were broken and would never rise again. It was, he boasted, "one of the mightiest victories in the history of the world." All that remained was a mopping-up-process to nail down the triumph.

Hitler's hope for a prompt victory in Russia soon turned to ashes. He had been so confident of victory that he had sent his troops into battle without proper winter clothing. Unluckily for him and the troops, the winter was one of the worst in European history. Moreover, Russian troops refused to capitulate, an attitude that mystified the *Fuehrer*. Adopting Fabian defense-in-depth tactics, they retreated slowly, scorching the earth, destroying supplies, and harrying the German flanks. (*See* EASTERN FRONT, CAMPAIGNS ON THE.)

PRODUCTION PROBLEMS. It became increasingly difficult to supply great armies strewn on a long amorphous line continually under attack by fanatical Russians. Oil reserves sank to a dangerous low. The mining of coal declined at a critical time when huge supplies were needed for long rail distances to the east. Miners had been conscripted for the armed services, leaving far too few to work the coal mines. Machines that had run at full capacity for years began to break down and replacements were hard to find. Now there were critical shortages of raw materials, engine parts, and food.

Hitler made belated attempts to increase the flow of war production. Until this time Goering was responsible for the Ministries of Economics, Labor, and Food, while Fritz Todt (*q.v.*) controlled the Ministry of Armaments as well as organization of major construction works. Both Goering and Todt valued their independence and worked at cross purposes. On February 15, 1942, Todt was killed in an air crash. Hitler replaced him with his architect, Albert Speer (*q.v.*), who became responsible for the central armaments program. From this time on priority was given to armaments in allocation of war matériel and manpower. Under the new program coal output, as well as production of steel, aluminum, and crude oil increased.

MANPOWER. The matter of manpower became critical after Stalingrad. In January 1942 Hitler initiated a national labor emergency program and appointed Fritz Sauckel (*q.v.*), Reich Plenipotentiary for Labor Allocation. Under Sauckel's direction a series of labor decrees was issued to put non-Germans and prisoners of war to work. Millions were imported for work in factories to stimulate war production. Methods of recruitment and treatment of workers in this program led to much resentment and criticism. (*See* FORCED LABOR.)

By the opening of 1943, the manpower situation on the home front had become so serious that Sauckel decreed mobilization "for compulsory labor" of every German male from 16 to 45 years of age who was not serving in combat and of all women from 17 to 45. Small industries were eliminated in favor of giant state-controlled cartels and workers thereby released were conscripted for the armed services. Several million children were mobilized for ''light work'' in small industries and on farms.

By 1944 the labor situation was even more critical. Additional attempts were made to conscript workers for industrial workshops and munitions factories. Germans were taken from schools and universities, from domestic service, and from the entertainment world to fill the pool of war labor. Inmates of concentration camps, where ability to work was a passport to life, were recruited for factory work.

GERMANY AT END OF THE WAR. With Stalingrad early German euphoria turned into dismay. The public was bewildered by the new propaganda line and despite efforts by the Propaganda Ministry, German morale began to sink. The public on the home front was shaken by endless reports of casualties from the Russian front. Rumors spread that more men were dying of exposure in the East than were killed by enemy action.

Although Hitler was drawing on occupied Europe, primarily France, Belgium, and Holland, for foodstuffs, raw materials, and manufactured goods, there were shortages of food and consumer goods. Slowly, it began to dawn on the German people that the days of Nazi triumph were over. Now, with American production at its peak, Germany's early advantages were lost. Hitler had brought his people into a war of attrition which they could not possibly win.

The war was being brought home to the Germans. Soon German cities were to be subjected to a rain of explosives. Allied aircraft bombed ceaselessly, the Americans by day and the British by night. German morale collapsed. Goebbels's propaganda could no longer have an effect on a people faced with the reality of Allied blockbusters (*q.v.*). Germans sank into semi-lethargy as the home front slid into chaos.

HUMAN LOSSES. The German people paid dearly for Hitler's adventure into aggression. Again accurate figures are not available, but it is estimated that the Germans, including Austrians and *Volksdeutsche,* incurred as many as 4.4 million battle deaths, three-quarters of them on the eastern front. About 2 million people survived with some degree of disablement. Many thousands of civilians were killed in Allied air raids. Many German nationals and most Jews died in concentration and extermination camps (*qq.v.*). At the end of hostilities tens of thousands of German prisoners were in Allied hands.

MATERIAL LOSSES. In May 1945, after nearly six years of war, Germany was a defeated, prostrate nation, its government dissolved and its economy shattered. Whole cities were reduced to heaps of rubble; bridges were blown up; roads were blocked. Railways, harbors, and canals were in chaos. More than half the locomotives and rolling stock could be used no longer. Production of coal, steel, and other key industries had dropped to the vanishing point. Agriculture was no longer able to provide food for the people. The public debt rose from 40,000,000,000 Reichsmarks in 1938 to nearly ten times that figure in 1946. Germany had ceased temporarily to be an industrial organism.

AFTERMATH. Under the Potsdam Agreement (*see* POTSDAM CON-FERENCE), the victorious powers divided defeated Germany into four zones of control—American, British, Russian, and French—cutting across provincial boundaries of the Third Reich. Occupation authorities began to purge Germany of Nazis and Nazism and destroyed the foundations of Hitler's structure. After 1947 attempts to demilitarize, decartelize, and democratize Germany were weakened by increasing friction between the Western Allies and the Soviet Union.

Theodor Heuss was elected first President of the Federal Republic of West Germany. The new republic embraced slightly more than half the area of pre-war Germany but nearly three-quarters of its population. The capital was established at the old university city of Bonn, where a federal parliament functioned under a new constitution based upon those of the Weimar Republic and the Western democracies. The Allies retained authority for the time being over demilitarization, reparations, decartelization, and foreign affairs. In 1951 West Germany was invited to create a military force and to unite it with the armies of the Western Allies. In 1952 it was integrated indirectly into the North Atlantic Treaty Organization (NATO) by signing a contract which included it in the community of free nations as an equal partner.

Subsidized heavily by its Western sponsors, especially the United States, and led by conservative Chancellor Konrad Adenauer, West Germany made a rapid economic recovery. German consumer goods began to flow in such quantities into the world markets that some countries, notably Britain, began to fear a price competition it could not meet. The German automotive industry, starting with gutted factories and scattered labor forces, began to sell not just cars but complete assembly plants as well. German gross national product achieved a spectacular increase in what some described as an economic miracle.

Even in its truncated condition West Germany eventually became the foremost economic, military, and political country on the European continent. As linchpin of the Atlantic Alliance, it was wooed by the Western democracies. The Soviet Union and the nations of Eastern Europe feared the rise of a new German power.

EAST GERMANY. A few weeks after the formation of the Federal Republic, the People's Republic of East Germany, with East Berlin as its capital, was formed. The East German Republic contained 27 percent of Germany's population and 31 percent of its area. It was ruled by the Communist Party under close collaboration with the Soviet Union. Non-Communist parties were allowed a nominal existence, but they were not permitted to oppose acts of the regime. Refugees by the thousands, dissatisfied with life in East Germany, crossed the "green border" into West Germany. In early August 1961 East Germany closed the border between East and West Berlin to stop the exodus. The East Germans built a wall dividing the city.

Bibliography. W. L. Shirer *Last Train from Berlin* (1941); W. Schultz, *The German Home Front* (1943); M. Seydewitz, *Civil Life in Wartime Germany* (1945); A. S. Milward, *The German Economy at War* (1965); B. A. Carroll, *Design for Total War* (1965); J. Remak (ed.), *The Nazi Years* (1969); and W. W. Schutz, *Pens Under the Swastika* (1971).

GERMANY, BATTLE OF. Final battle from February 1945 to May 1945 leading to the collapse of German resistance.

BACKGROUND. In January 1945 the Germans were caught in an enormous trap. The Allies were pressing against the entire German border in the west, while Russians were pushing steadily ahead in the east. Hitler made two public broadcasts again accusing Bolsheviks and Jews of attempting to bring Germany to slavery. "Almighty God will not abandon the man who throughout life wanted nothing but to preserve his people from a fate they did not deserve." "I expect every German to do his duty to the last. . . . Whoever stabs us in the back will die an ignominious death." Meanwhile, the Nazi cause went from critical to hopeless. The *Fuehrer* was being beaten with his own strategies—*Blitzkrieg* (*q.v.*) and divide-encircle-annihilate. Fortress Germany was shrinking more rapidly than Fortress Europe (*q.v.*).

The surging Russians had marched more than 1,000 miles from Stalingrad. By January 1945 they had three gigantic spearheads slashing onto German soil and headed for Berlin. They moved into Czechoslovakia, cut off East Prussia, and trampled the war industries of Silesia. They now marched from East Prussia to the Lower Vistula and from the upper Vistula. The target—Berlin. (*See* BERLIN, BATTLE OF.)

PREPARATIONS. The situation in the West was equally gloomy for the Germans. Hitler's offensive in the Ardennes had been contained and had become a retreat. (*See* BULGE, BATTLE OF THE.) Deployed along Germany's western frontier was a series of Allied concentrated strong points. There were to be three co-ordinated campaigns. In the north the Canadian 1st, the British 2nd, and the U.S. 9th Armies, under command of Gen. Bernard Law Montgomery (*q.v.*), were poised to squeeze the Germans in a triangle formed by the Maas and the Rhine and to clear the west bank of the Rhine facing the Ruhr. In the center, the U.S. 12th Army Group, under Gen. Omar N. Bradley (*q.v.*), was ready to move north of the Moselle between Cologne and Coblenz. In the south the U.S. 6th Army Group, under Lt. Gen. Jacob L. Devers (*q.v.*) was prepared to converge south of the Moselle, close in on the Rhine, and join the southern flank of the U.S. 3rd Army at Coblenz. Together these offensives aimed to clear the entire west bank of the Rhine.

ASSAULT. In early February 1945 the weather was still with the Germans. The thaw had melted the thick snows, turning rivers into torrents and fields into lakes. Nevertheless, on February 8, 1945, the Canadian 1st and British 2nd Armies jumped off on *Operation Veritable* and by February 21 were at the Rhine. On the next two days Allied planes flew 16,000 sorties and dropped 20,000 tons of bombs on the retreating Germans.

Meanwhile, the U.S. 9th Army, on the southern wing of the north flank, struck at two dams controlling the Roer River and two weeks later crossed the river in assault boats. By March 13, all the northern length of the west bank of the Rhine was in Allied hands.

It was the same story in the center. Here Germany's river barriers also began to collapse. The U.S. 1st and 3rd Armies surged ahead in *Operation Lumberjack* in simultaneous strikes, forcing the Germans to retreat across the Rhine. At the same time the U.S. 3rd Army reached the Rhine near Coblenz, as Maj. Gen. George S. Patton's (*q.v.*) 4th Armored Division raced 65 miles in 58 hours.

REMAGEN BRIDGE. On March 7, 1945, came one of those incredible strokes of fortune, one of the luckiest breaks in military annals. Neither the Allied Supreme Command nor the German High Command expected an easy crossing of the treacherous waters of the Rhine. No one had successfully crossed the river in war since Napoleon in 1805. But on that day Sgt. Alexander A. Drabik, a butcher from Holland, Ohio, led his platoon across the bridge. (*See* REMAGEN BRIDGE.)

Patton swung southward and rolled up the German forces west of the Rhine. By March 21 he swept the west bank clear of Germans along a 70-mile stretch between Coblenz and Mannheim. The great concentration of American tanks was now ready to join the airborne troops dropped behind German lines. To meet them the Germans had about 70 understrength and demoralized divisions. Hitler called for a counterattack but was told that no resources were available. The American advance into Germany now became a procession.

RUHR TRAP. After piercing the Rhine barrier, the Allies turned to the encirclement and reduction of the Ruhr, the industrial heart of Germany. During the third week of March 1945, Allied airmen flew 42,000 sorties and hit 18 major bridges and viaducts in the area. Hitler ordered that the Ruhr be made into another fortress. Again the Allies used the classic double envelopment technique. The U.S. 9th Army, led by Lt. Gen. William H. Simpson (*q.v.*), struck on the northern rim of the Ruhr against savage German resistance. At the same time the U.S. 1st Army, under Lt. Gen. Courtney H. Hodges (*q.v.*), advancing from the Remagen area, swung around the eastern flank of the Ruhr. The two powerful wings joined on April 1, 1945, near Paderborn, effectively enveloping the Ruhr. Field Marshal Walther Model's (*q.v.*) troops were now trapped inside a circle 80 miles in diameter. More than 400,000 Germans fell into Allied hands. Model committed suicide.

INTO THE HERZLAND. Hitler's Third Reich was now cracking and buckling at its seams. Twenty-one German divisions had been cut to ribbons. On the southern flank the Americans pushed eastward into Germany, taking Mannheim (March 29), Nuremberg, shrine of Nazism (April 20), and Munich (April 30). French troops crossed the Austrian border on April 30. In the center Bradley took Kassel (April 4), Hanover (April 10), and Leipzig (April 22).

Patton's 3rd Army moved with lightning speed over Hitler's superhighways. His tanks crossed the Salle River near Jena, while other units headed south, capturing Bayreuth, advanced to the Harz mountains, and reached the Czechoslovakian frontier (April 23). German towns toppled one after another under the impact of Patton's drive. In a display of remarkable teamwork, engineers cleared mine fields and road blocks ahead of the fast-moving tanks; artillery kept the way open with a blanket of protective fire; ordnance replaced or repaired the armored weapons; signalmen maintained the lines of communication; and the air arm cooperated from the skies. The Germans were helpless against this kind of combined warfare.

Meanwhile, in the north Montgomery stormed into Holland and the German coastal area. Bremen fell (April 8), and Amsterdam was occupied (April 18).

SIGNIFICANCE. Clearly, Hitler's Third Reich was now in its death throes. All along the great Allied front the armies began to halt roughly on the lines agreed with the Russians at the Yalta Conference (*q.v.*). Tens of thousands of German troops rushed to surrender to the Western Allies instead of to the dreaded Russians. On April 25, 1945, American and Russian troops met at Torgau (*q.v.*). The great trap was closed on Hitler.

Bibliography. D. D. Eisenhower, *Report on the Operations in Europe: June 1944 to May 1945* (1946); F. de Guingand, *Operation Victory* (1947); G. Blond, *The Death of Hitler's Germany* (1954); K. W. Hechler, *The Bridge at Remagen* (1957); C.B. MacDonald, *The Siegfried Line* (1963); C. Ryan, *The Last Battle* (1966); J. Toland, *The Last 100 Days* (1966); H. Essame, *The Battle for Germany* (1969); and F. M. Davis, *Across the Rhine* (1980).

GEROW, LEONARD TOWNSEND (1888–1972). U.S. Army officer.

Seventeen days after Pearl Harbor, Gerow was named Assistant Chief of Staff. In 1943 he was sent to England as Commander of the U.S. Field Forces in the European theater. At the age of 55 he was one of the youngest generals ever given so important a command. On June 6, 1944, he led the U.S. 5th Corps to Omaha Beach (*q.v.*) in the Normandy invasion in a brilliantly executed attack against heavily fortified enemy positions. He planned and led the drive across the flooded Cherbourg Peninsula, took part in the battle for Paris, led his troops across the Meuse, breached the Siegfried Line (*q.v.*), fought outside Cologne, and played a part in the Battle of the Bulge (*q.v.*) in December 1944.

Brown-haired, stern, distinguished by his southern drawl, Gerow was an officer of tremendous energy. Dispatches from combat fronts mentioned his unusual skill and ability. It was said that no American officer on the western front bore heavier responsibilities.

GESTAPO. Acronym for *Geheime Staats Polizei,* German secret state police.

FORMATION. The *Gestapo* was created by Hitler to protect the existence of the Third Reich by tracking down and eliminating all dissenters, complainers, and opponents of National Socialism. Under the leadership of Heinrich Himmler (*q.v.*), the *Gestapo* became an important security organization in Nazi Germany. Autonomous, it had its own legal system, with powers far exceeding that of any law court. It controlled the lives, freedom, and property of all Germans.

METHODS. In working for annihilation of its domestic enemies, the *Gestapo* used crude but effective methods. Anyone suspected of opposition to the regime ordinarily was given a warning. If that did not work, he was taken into custody as a threat to state security, interrogated under extreme brutality, and sometimes beaten to death. *Gestapo* agents hunted down Jews, Marxists, Gypsies, and "other enemies of the state." The average German dreaded the *Gestapo* because of rumors about what happened to victims in its headquarters.

During World War II, *Gestapo* agents were sent throughout occupied territories to control dissent and conspiracy. Everywhere it used its own tested methods to destroy any opposition to Nazi rule. It was generally regarded as one of the cruelest police forces of modern times.

NUREMBERG. The International Military Tribunal at Nuremberg (*q.v.*) declared the *Gestapo* to be criminal within the meaning of the Charter. Its members were found guilty of persecution and extermination of Jews, brutalities and killings in concentration camps, excesses in occupied territories, administration of the slave labor program, and mistreatment and murder of prisoners of war (*q.v.*).

Bibliography. E. Crankshaw, *The Gestapo* (1956).

GI. Acronym for Government Issue, applied to the American foot soldier.

Initially, the U.S. armed forces were built in a minimum time from varied material sent along by draft boards. At the base of the military system were the standard U.S. Government Issues, from uniforms to weapons to haircuts. So overwhelmed were the new draftees by omnipresent Government Issues of all kinds that they began referring to themselves also as GIs.

Bibliography. R. G. Martin, *The G.I. War, 1941-1945* (1967).

GIBSON, GUY (1918-1944). British leader of one of the war's most spectacular aerial attacks.

Gibson was one of the most experienced pilots of the Royal Air Force. He had already flown 173 successful missions when he was called in March 1943 to lead special Squadron No. 617, the mysterious "X-Squadron" or "Dam Busters Squadron" to carry out a mission against the Ruhr dams on the night of May 16-17, 1943. After intensively training his men, Gibson led them in the daring raid over the Möhne, Eder, and Sorpe dams in the Ruhr area. (*See* RUHR DAMS.) He was awarded the Victoria Cross for conspicuous gallantry during the dam-busting. He was then withdrawn from front-line operations, but soon he volunteered again. On September 19, 1944, while returning in a *Mosquito* (*q.v.*) from a raid on Rheydt, on which he was the marker bomber, he lost his life.

GILBERT ISLANDS, BATTLE FOR THE. Scene of the Allied advance to Japan along the Central Pacific route in November 1943.

BACKGROUND. After the successful conclusion of the Guadalcanal campaign (*q.v.*) the Joint Chiefs of Staff turned to the Central Pacific. They preferred a thrust at the Marshall Islands but dropped the plan because of lack of shipping and ground troops. Instead, they decided to begin with the Gilbert Islands, an archipelago of 16 small islands, 166 square miles in area, 2,500 miles from Pearl Harbor on the great circle route from Hawaii to Port Moresby in New Guinea. The Japanese had occupied the islands in 1941.

PREPARATIONS. Two attack forces were assigned for the operation. A northern one was to take Makin, with 6 transports carrying 7,000 troops, and a southern one with 16 transports carrying 18,000 marines would take Tarawa. In addition to escort carriers, the invasion was to be assisted by a task force of 6 fleet carriers, 5 light carriers, 6 new battleships, and many smaller warships. The assault would be covered by 850 aircraft in the carriers as well as 150 land-based U.S. Army bombers.

OPERATION GALVANIC. After preliminary bombing, the attack began on November 20, 1943. The U.S. 27th Infantry Division landed on Makin. The small garrison of 800 Japanese troops was overwhelmed within four days. Its defenders, stupefied with *saki* beer, sought death in a wild *banzai* (*q.v.*) charge. Makin was taken with the loss of only 65 men.

TARAWA. The twin part of *Operation Galvanic* began the same day with a heavy naval bombardment of Betio, a small island fortress off Tarawa. Tarawa itself was strongly defended with a garrison of more than 5,000 Japanese Imperial Marines. The defenders were dug in under pillboxes covered with 5 feet of concrete, 10-foot thick outer walls of sand and coral, and roofed with iron rails on coconut logs.

The naval bombardment hurled in 3,000 tons of shells in over two hours with little effect on the durable forts. It was believed that no one could survive this bombing. U.S. Marines stormed ashore only to meet a curtain of withering fire. Nearly a third of the Americans were hit as they waded between the coral reef and the beaches.

The Japanese defenders withdrew to two interior strong points. The withdrawal enabled the marines to spread over the island and trap the defenders. On the night of November 22 the Japanese began a series of counterattacks, as a result of which they were wiped out. By November 26 the Gilbert Islands were in Allied hands.

LOSSES. The Japanese lost their crack units garrisoned in the Gilberts. American casualties were heavy: 1,000 U.S. Marines and seamen killed and 2,100 wounded in the struggle for Tarawa.

AFTERMATH. The American public was shocked by the heavy casualties at Tarawa. In the controversy that followed the invasion, critics denounced the naval bombardment as inaccurate, the air strikes as badly timed, and the war matériel as unsatisfactory. Others claimed that priceless lessons were learned about the technique of amphibious operations. Naval historian Samuel E. Morison called Tarawa "the seed bed of victory in 1945."

Bibliography. P. A. Crowe and E. G. Lowe, *Seizure of the Gilberts and Marshalls* (1955); H. I. Shaw *et al.*, *Central Pacific Drive* (1966); and S. E. Smith (ed.), *The U.S. Marine Corps in World War II* (1969).

GILLARS, MILDRED. *See* AXIS SALLY.

GIRAUD, HENRI HONORÉ (1875–1949). French soldier who refused to bow to Nazi domination.

At the start of the war Giraud commanded the French 7th Army. When the Germans invaded Belgium on May 10, 1940, he led his men into that country to strike back. In World War I he had been captured by the Germans and had escaped. Once more he was taken by the Germans. This time his captors placed him in the heavily guarded fortress at Königstein in the district of Dresden. Although under vigilant surveillance, he managed to escape again. (*See* KÖNIGSTEIN FORTRESS.) The Germans offered a large reward for his recapture, but he reached unoccupied France.

When Giraud arrived in Vichy France, he was embraced by Marshal Henri Pétain (*q.v.*), who urged him to sign a pledge never again to take arms against the Germans. He refused. He escaped to North Africa in a British submarine to serve with Gen. Dwight D. Eisenhower's (*q.v.*) forces. After the Allies invaded North Africa, Giraud associated himself with Adm. Jean Darlan (*q.v.*). Following the murder of Darlan, the French Council chose Giraud unanimously to be High Commissioner in French North Africa, as well as French Commander-in-Chief there.

GIRAUD VERSUS DE GAULLE. In June 1943 Giraud and de Gaulle agreed to serve on the French Committee of National Liberation (*q.v.*) under a joint chairmanship. The arrangement did not work because of differences between the two generals. Both men wanted to lead the Free French (*q.v.*), but de

Gaulle already had a two-year start from London. Several high-level Allied attempts were made to reconcile the two, but they were unsuccessful. In the spring of 1944 Giraud's post as Commander-in-Chief in North Africa was abolished, primarily because the *Maquis* (*q.v.*), the French Resistance movement, distrusted him as a representative of the *ancien régime*.

Bibliography. R. Bouscat, *De Gaulle-Giraud* (1967).

GLEIWITZ RAID. Also called *Operation Himmler*. A simulated assault by "Polish" troops on a German radio station. It took place immediately before the outbreak of World War II.

BACKGROUND. In late August 1939 Hitler was anxious for an "incident" that would justify his intended invasion of Poland. Reinhard Heydrich, *Gestapo* (*q.v.*) leader, called in Alfred Helmut Naujocks (*q.v.*), a security agent, and outlined to him a plan for a fictitious Polish attack on a small German radio station at Gleiwitz, just one mile from the German border. An adventurous daredevil, Naujocks prepared his men carefully for the raid.

ASSAULT. At 7:30 P.M. on August 31, 1939, Naujocks and his commandos, dressed in Polish uniforms, stormed into the radio station, fired a fusillade of shots, and slugged the employees. A Polish-speaking German seized the transmitter and barked: "People of Poland! The time has come for war between Poland and Germany! Unite and smash down all Germans!" The commandos then fled, leaving behind them as "evidence" the blood-soaked body of a concentration camp inmate (previously killed and dressed in a Polish uniform).

SIGNIFICANCE. The next day a highly excited Hitler informed the German people that they were at war with Poland. He cited "the attack by regular Polish troops on the Gleiwitz transmitter." Few people outside Germany were fooled by this awkward schoolboy stunt.

GLIDING BOMB. New German device used in mid-1943. When the allies invaded Italy in September 1943, the Germans disabled the British warship *Warspite* by a direct hit from one of their new FX.1400 radio-guided gliding bombs.

GOEBBELS, (PAUL) JOSEPH (1897–1945). High-ranking Nazi politician and propaganda chief of the Third Reich.

It was Goebbels's task throughout the war to maintain public morale. (*See* PROPAGANDA, WAR.) His propaganda machine derided the British as decadent snobs and the Russians as subhumans. His assignment became more and more difficult as the tide of war changed against Nazi Germany. He reminded the German people of their fate if they surrendered. His assessment of the situation at the time of the 1944 July Plot (*q.v.*) against Hitler undoubtedly was responsible for halting the revolt in its tracks. Hitler rewarded him with the title of German General Plenipotentiary for the Mobilization of Total War.

Goebbels remained with Hitler in his Berlin bunker to share his final fate. He advised Hitler that only in a fiery *Götterdämmerung*, a "Twilight of the Gods," could the *Fuehrer* legend be maintained. He witnessed the last-day marriage of Hitler and Eva Braun as well as the burning of their bodies. He had his six children poisoned with lethal injections so that they would not have to grow up in a non-National Socialist Germany, and then ordered an SS (*q.v.*) officer to shoot his wife and himself.

Bibliography. *The Goebbels Diaries* (1948) are important for an understanding of the Third Reich. Among Goebbels's many books are several written during the war: *Die Zeit ohne Beispiel* (1941); *Kampf um Berlin* (1943); and *Vom Kaiserhof zur Reichskanzlei* (1944). For biographies *see* C. Reiss, *Joseph Goebbels* (1948); and R. Manvell and H. Fraenkel, *Doctor Goebbels: His Life and Death* (1960). *See also The Final Entries 1945: The Diaries of Joseph Goebbels* (1978).

GOERDELER, CARL FRIEDRICH (1884–1945). Lawyer and civilian leader of the Resistance movement against Hitler.

So great was Goerdeler's contempt for Hitler from the beginning of the war that he progressed from opposition to resistance to conspiracy. It was agreed among the conspirators that Goerdeler would become Chancellor after the fall of Hitler. Goerdeler even drew up a constitution for the hoped-for succession state. He was one of the main civilian leaders of the unsuccessful July Plot (*q.v.*) of 1944. He was arrested, brought before the dreaded People's Court, and sentenced to death. He was executed at Plötzensee Prison on February 2, 1945.

Bibliography. A. Lieber, *Conscience In Revolt* (1957).

GOERING, HERMANN WILHELM (1893–1946). No. 2 Nazi Hitler's heir apparent, head of the *Luftwaffe* (*q.v.*), and *Reichsmarschall,* the only German to hold such a rank.

Goering commanded Germany's air force in the *Blitzkrieg* (*q.v.*) assaults on Poland and France. (*See* POLAND, CAMPAIGN IN; and FRANCE, FIRST BATTLE OF.) On June 10, 1940, he was appointed Reich Marshal. The defeat of the *Luftwaffe* in the summer of 1940 (*see* BRITAIN, BATTLE OF) marked a radical change in his fortunes, for his failure there meant the abandonment of *Operation Sea Lion* (*q.v.*), Hitler's contemplated invasion of Britain. The power of his *Luftwaffe* thereafter declined in contrast to increasing Allied air strength. Goering tried to recoup his reputation in the campaign against the Soviet Union, but to no avail. Eventually, he was unable to defend German soil from Allied air bombardment.

Discredited, Goering turned his energy to stripping the occupied countries. He accumulated a vast hoard of art objects from all over Europe. In the closing days of the Third Reich, he aroused Hitler's hysterical anger when he sent word to the Berlin bunker that in accordance with previous understanding he was assuming the post of German Chancellor. The *Fuehrer* demanded that Goering be shot as a traitor, but the order was not carried out.

NUREMBERG. At the International Military Tribunal at Nuremberg (*see* NUREMBERG TRIALS), Goering defended himself with skill and aggressiveness. As highest ranking among the accused, he demanded obedience from his fellow prisoners. His judges were not impressed by his defense and found him guilty on all counts of the indictment. ''There is nothing to be said in mitigation. His guilt is unique in its enormity. The record discloses no excuse for this man.'' On October 15, 1946, only two hours before his scheduled execution, he swallowed a vial of poison and died instantly.

Bibliography. W. Frischauer, *The Rise and Fall of Hermann Goering* (1951); R. Manvell and H. Fraenkel, *Goering* (1962); C. H. Bowles, *Hermann Goering and the Third Reich* (1962); R. Lee, *Goering: Air Leader* (1972); and L. Mosley, *The Reich Marshal* (1974).

GOLD, JUNO, AND SWORD BEACHES. Three areas in Normandy assigned to British and Canadian troops during the landings on June 6, 1944. (*See* NORMANDY INVASION.) The three British beaches were to the east of the Americans. (*See* UTAH BEACH; and OMAHA BEACH.)

The British landings, in contrast to the Americans at Omaha Beach, went comparatively well. Supported by a Royal Navy bombardment, British and Canadian landing craft were brought in close to shore and accurate landings were made. The powerful armored force cleared mines, blasted pillboxes, and threw flames ahead of it. By nightfall the invaders had penetrated up to six miles inshore, where they came up against German infantry quartered in seaside hotels.

At the end of the first day 83,115 British and Canadians were on French soil. The men at Sword, Juno, and Gold Beaches suffered heavy casualties in the bloody chaos, but they were on the Continent to stay. (*See also* FRANCE, SECOND BATTLE OF.)

GOOSEBERRY. Allied code or cover name for an artificial breakwater constructed off the coast of Normandy in conjunction with *Operation Overlord* (*q.v.*) on June 6, 1944. (*See* NORMANDY INVASION.)

For the Allies the lack of port facilities on the shores of *Festung Europa* (*q.v.*) was a serious matter and had to be solved if a large army were to be landed on the beaches. Under the code name *Gooseberry,* Allied engineers constructed an anchorage by sinking old merchant ships in a line to be used as a breakwater to allow unloading of ships in relatively sheltered waters. This type of anchorage had been used before but never on this gigantic scale. (*See also* MULBERRIES.)

GORT, JOHN STANDISH SURTEES PRENDERGAST VEREKER (1886–1946). British Field Marshal and commander of the British Expeditionary Force (*q.v.*) in France early in World War II.

Immediately after the outbreak of World War II, Gort was made Commander-in-Chief of the British Expeditionary Force in France. In May 1940 his troops were driven westward by the driving German *Blitzkrieg* (*q.v.*) through the Ardennes, and his 10 divisions were hopelessly trapped in a small pocket at Dunkirk. (*See* DUNKIRK EVACUATION.) Gort directed the retreat and was one of the last to leave. The British press commended him for his brilliant generalship in a desperate situation.

Gort was then made Inspector General of the Forces for Training. From 1941 to 1942 he served as Governor and Commander-in-Chief of Gibraltar. From 1942 to 1944 he was Governor General of Malta (*q.v.*) and directed the spirited defense of the British dependency against heavy Axis assault. He was created a Field Marshal in 1943. He died in London on March 31, 1946.

Bibliography. J. R. Colville, *Man of Valour* (1972).

GOVERNMENTS-IN-EXILE. Countergovernments set up by exiled leaders of European countries absorbed by Hitler into his New Order (*q.v.*).

BACKGROUND. Hitler's conquest of European countries in the first two years of the war had been the most stunning coup since Napoleon. Nevertheless, he was faced with Resistance movements (*q.v.*) in countries conquered by his armies.

One after another governments-in-exile were established to retain a framework of organization for reestablishment of the old governments once the Nazi invaders were defeated. Most had their headquarters in London and all were recognized as bona fide members of the United Nations coalition against the Third Reich. They contributed special service units to the Allied cause. They supervised broadcasts to their people and maintained a steady flow of propaganda pointing to the day of liberation. They supplied homeland Resistance units with money, supplies, and agents.

POLAND. The Polish Government-in-exile was wrapped in complications. Shortly after the announcement of the Russo-German Nonaggression Pact (*q.v.*), signed on August 23, 1939, the Polish Government-in-exile was set up first in Paris and then in London. It was led by Gen. Wladyslaw Sikorski (*q.v.*), who furnished Polish troops, pilots, and seamen to fight on all fronts. After the Soviet Union joined the Western Allies in June 1941, a gradual deterioration of relations between Moscow and the Polish exile government ensued. Following the discovery in 1943 of the Katyn Forest massacre (*q.v.*), in which thousands of Polish officers were killed and buried near Smolensk, relations between the two governments were broken off.

Sikorski was killed in a plane crash at the height of the controversy. The rift between the Soviet Union and the Polish Government-in-exile caused serious concern in Washington and London. Efforts to heal the breach were unsuccessful. Without consulting the Allies, the Russians supported the Polish Communist Lublin administration.

The Polish underground in Warsaw, led by Gen. Tadeusz Bor-Komorowski, rebelled against its German captors. Many were massacred after nearby Russians failed to come to their assistance. London Poles denounced the incident as a shameless betrayal. In December 1944 Lublin Poles proclaimed themselves the Provisional Government of Poland. They were recognized by Moscow but not by Washington or London until the Yalta Conference (*q.v.*) of February 1945. It was clear now that Stalin was intent on imposing his own political pattern on the new Poland.

DENMARK AND NORWAY. King Christian X (*q.v.*) continued to govern Denmark during the German occupation, but a Danish Council was organized in London in late 1940 to cooperate with the Allies. The Danes maintained a strong Resistance movement against the Germans. Similarly, Norwegian King Haakon VII (*q.v.*) came to London in June 1940 after the Allied forces abandoned north Norway to lead a government-in-exile until the end of the war.

NETHERLANDS AND LUXEMBOURG. When Germans invaded the Netherlands on May 10, 1940, Queen Wilhelmina (*q.v.*), her family, and ministers reached London after a dramatic escape. From London the Dutch exile government cooperated with the Resistance inside Holland. Grand Duchess Charlotte of Luxembourg had a similar experience.

FRANCE. After the fall of France in June 1940, Gen. Charles de Gaulle (*q.v.*) organized the Free French (*see* FREE FRANCE) movement in London and headed the National Committe of Liberation. Although alienated by de Gaulle's haughty behavior, Churchill and Roosevelt eventually recognized his appeal to the French people and gave him their support. De Gaulle was recognized as provisional head of government after D-Day.

CZECHOSLOVAKIA. Soon after the war began, Eduard Beneš (*q.v.*), · former President, and Jan Masaryk (*q.v.*), son of the country's founder, formed a Czechoslovak Committee in London. Britain and France immediately recognized the Czech Government-in-exile, but Soviet Russia hedged until it was invaded by the Germans in June 1941.

YUGOSLAVIA. Yugoslavia was subjected to fratricidal clashes. On the one side was the monarchist Draja Mikhailovich (*q.v.*), leader of the Serbian Chetnik Resistance, and on the other Josip Tito's (*q.v.*) Communist Partisans (*q.v.*). At first the two fought together against the Germans, but eventually they became bitter enemies. Mikhailovich, deciding that there was little to choose between the Nazis and the Communists, began private talks with both the British and the Germans. The Yugoslav Government-in-exile appointed him war minister, but Churchill favored Tito's more aggressive force of Partisans. Mikhailovich was deposed and later executed by the Communists.

GREECE. When Greece fell in April 1941, King George II (*q.v.*) and his ministers fled from Athens to Crete, then to Cairo, and finally to London, where he established a Greek Government-in-exile. Clashes soon began inside Greece between the National Liberation Movement (Greek acronym, EAM), which was more pro-Communist than anti-Nazi, and the Greek Liberation Army (EDES), which was supported by the Greek Government-in-exile and the British. With British support, the EDES finally won out as the recognized Greek Government-in-exile.

SIGNIFICANCE. The governments-in-exile played an important role in the eventual overthrow of the Third Reich. Each one grew in strength as German power waned in the war.

Bibliography. W. Koht, *Norway: Neutral and Invaded* (1941); J. Karski, *Story of a Secret State* (1943); R. Aglion, *The Fighting French* (1943); D. Martin, *Ally Betrayed: The Uncensored Story of Tito and Mikhailovich* (1946); T. Bor-Komorowski, *The Secret Army* (1951); and D. Lampe, *The Danish Resistance* (1957).

GRABLE, BETTY (1916–1973). American motion picture actress.

Betty Grable was by far the most popular pin-up girl for American troops during the war. (*See* UNITED STATES AT WAR.) GIs talked exuberantly about her "billion-dollar gams," and sent her mail at the rate of many thousands a week. In some units her torso was photographically zoned off for instructions in map reading. Grable died in Santa Monica, California, on July 2, 1973.

GRAZIANI, RODOLFO, MARCHESE DE NEGHELII (1882–1955).
Italian Army officer and administrator, who was soundly defeated by the British in North Africa.

At the start of the war Graziani was commander of the Italian forces in Libya. When Italy declared war on Britain and France in 1940, he led Italian forces against the outnumbered British from Benghazi to Mersa Matruh. In his advance he constructed a series of strong fortifications all the way to Sidi Barrani. Then Gen. Archibald Wavell (*q.v.*), commanding the British forces in the winter of 1940–1941, inflicted a disastrous defeat on Graziani, one of the worst beatings of the war. Graziani attempted to evade responsibility by blaming his chief, Mussolini, for the strategy that went wrong. In the rout Graziani lost 100,000 men and vast quantities of supplies. Censured in March 1941, he was stripped of his title of Marshal.

When Italy surrendered in 1943, Graziani was appointed Defense Minister in Mussolini's new republican government. He was arrested by the Americans in 1945.

GREATER EAST ASIA CO-PROSPERITY SPHERE. Catchword used by
Japanese militarists to justify their plans for expansion.

Japan's warlords intended to establish a concentric defensive ring from the Aleutian Islands in the north to Burma in the south. They hoped that the United States, after vain efforts to break the ring, would agree eventually to a negotiated peace, accept Japan's conquests, and recognize the reality of Japanese hegemony in the Pacific.

Similar to Hitler's New Order (*q.v.*) in Europe, the Greater East Asia Co-Prosperity Sphere was won quickly. Its territorial boundaries were established within four months after Pearl Harbor.

GREECE, BATTLE FOR. Struggle between Allies and Axis for control of the Greek Peninsula in 1940–1941.

BACKGROUND. Hitler's early victories aroused the discomfort of Mussolini, his junior Axis partner. The latter needed a quick and decisive victory on the European mainland to supplement his North African campaign, which was going badly. By invading Greece he would challenge British sea power in the Mediterranean, remove threats to his own supply lines to North Africa, and ease the way for an assault on Egypt. He had no doubt that his modern, mechanized army could smash the ill-armed Greeks in short order. He had already occupied Albania in April 1939.

PREPARATIONS. Mussolini began preparing the way as early as mid-August 1940 when he demanded that Greece renounce the British guarantee (1939) of its independence. King George II (*q.v.*) indignantly refused. The *Duce* then denounced Greece as an "unneutral" country secretly sympathetic to Britain and indulging in terror tactics on the Albanian border. At a war council held in Rome on October 15, 1940, Italian generals rose one after another to declare their readiness. "Our troops are eager to fight and advance." "Enthusiasm is at its highest point." A participant later described it: "They spoke of seizing Greece or Yugoslavia in the same offhand way they would decide to order a cup of coffee."

Massing Italian forces on the Greek border, Mussolini soon found the border incident he had wanted. At 3 A.M. on October 28, 1940, the Italian minister at Athens presented a three-hour ultimatum listing Italian grievances and demanding occupation of several strategic Greek areas for the duration of the war.

DEFENSE. The Greeks had no mechanized equipment, no heavy arms, and only a few hundred antiquated planes. Their defensive Metaxas Line (*q.v.*), unfortunately for them, faced Bulgaria and not Albania, site of the coming Italian attack. But they were fortified with an indomitable fighting spirit. Help came immediately from the British, who mined Greek waters and dispatched 55,000 troops to the peninsula.

ASSAULT. Mussolini struck swiftly before expiration of the ultimatum. Happily confident, Italian troops crossed the border, only to bog down quickly in the mountainous, wooded terrain. Gen. John Metaxas (*q.v.*), the Greek commander, shrewdlly waited until the Italian columns were extended in the narrow valleys away from their supply lines. Then his seasoned mountain warriors, the *Evzones,* lobbed artillery shells down on the massed Italians and cut them to pieces. Meanwhile, British planes created havoc on the Italian supply lines. Mussolini committed a total of 25 divisions to the ill-fated invasion.

Demoralized, disheartened by bad weather, and with little stomach for this kind of fighting, the Italians broke ranks and retreated in disorder. By November 28, 1940, the advancing Greeks captured Ersek, thereby cutting off the main Italian lateral communications. The fighting ended on Greek territory and continued inside Albania. By the end of the year the Greeks held a fourth of Albania.

DEFEAT. For the Italian people, fed on a diet of Fascist invincibility, the news from Greece was a stunning blow. Mussolini still spoke confidently: "We'll break the back of the Greeks, and we don't need any help!" He ordered mass attacks, which were thrown back.

GERMAN INTERVENTION. Hitler was worried about the Italian debacle in Greece. Before attacking the Soviet Union, he wanted no hostile power endangering his southern flank. Bulgaria capitulated quickly to his threats, but Yugoslavia and Greece remained unintimidated. He decided to crush both in one blow. On April 6, 1941, German forces invaded Yugoslavia in a smashing *Blitzkrieg* (*q.v.*). In *Operation Punishment* the *Luftwaffe* (*q.v.*) pounded Belgrade, the Yugoslav capital, into a shattered ruin. (*See* BELGRADE, BOMBING OF.) Yugoslavia surrendered on April 17, 1941.

Simultaneously, German forces moved from Bulgaria, outflanked the Metaxas Line, isolated three Greek divisions, and captured Salonika in two days. Subsequent German assaults came from Yugoslavia and, together with remaining Italian units, through Albania.

BRITISH EVACUATION. A British Expeditionary Force (*q.v.*), consisting of some 56,637 veteran troops, mostly Australian and New Zealanders from the Army of the Nile, had been transferred to Greece. It could not possibly resist half a million seasoned German troops. Withdrawal was ordered. In another Dunkirk (*see* DUNKIRK EVACUATION), the British, pounded from the skies, retreated to the beaches, where they destroyed their big guns and supplies. The men were transferred to waiting ships of the Royal Navy. By April 23, 1941, the British had evacuated 43,000 troops, one-half to Crete and the remainder to Egypt. The Germans lost just over 5,000 men in the campaign.

SIGNIFICANCE. The Greek campaign ended in triumph for Hitler. He maintained the fiction of Italian control by allowing Mussolini to occupy portions of Greece. For the Greeks it was a heartbreaking tragedy. They had smashed the Italian invasion, only to succumb to German power. For the British the defeat in Greece meant an end for the time being to hold the key to the Balkans.

In the long run, however, British intervention in Greece was to have a profound strategic effect on the war. The time Hitler lost in the Yugoslav and Greek campaigns was critical for his coming assault on the Soviet Union. Had he not paused at the Acropolis, he might well have taken the Kremlin.

Bibliography. E. Wason, *Miracle in Hellas* (1943); L. S. Stavrianos, *Greece: The War and Aftermath* (1947); C. Buckley, *Greece and Crete, 1941* (1952); A. Heckstall-Smith and H. T. Baille-Gorman, *Greek Tragedy, 1941* (1961); and J. Tsatsos, *The Sword's Fierce Edge: A Journal of the Occupation of Greece, 1941–1944* (1969).

GREEK DEMOCRATIC LIBERATION ARMY (EDES). One of the two major Resistance movements inside Greece during the war.

Liberal and anti-Communist, the EDES opposed the Communist National Liberation Movement (EAM), and eventually, with support of the Greek Government-in-exile and the British, won out in the bitter internecine struggle. (*See* GOVERNMENTS-IN-EXILE; and RESISTANCE MOVEMENTS.)

Bibliography. C. de Loverdo, *Le bataillon sacré* (1968).

GREER **INCIDENT.** Clash between the U.S. destroyer *Greer* and the German U-Boat *U-652* before American entry into the war.

On September 4, 1941, the *U-652* encountered by the *Greer* near Iceland. The submarine commander, hearing depth charges nearby, assumed that they were from the U.S. destroyer. Actually a British plane had dropped the charges. He fired two torpedoes at the *Greer,* but both of them missed.

The skirmish was reported in the American press the next day as a major incident. President Roosevelt denounced "the rattlesnakes of the Atlantic." On September 11, 1941, he authorized attack on sight of any Axis ships or submarines in "U.S.-interested" waters. The *Greer* incident was one of the important incidents leading to U.S. participation in the war.

GREIF **("GRIFFIN").** German code or cover name for an operation in 1944 employing troops dressed in American uniforms to capture bridges at the Meuse River during the Ardennes campaign.

In the winter of 1944 Hitler's Third Reich was shrinking day by day and bleeding from every vein. After a chain of disasters, the *Fuehrer* ordered *Operation Herbstnebel* (Autumn Fog) (*see* CODE NAMES, GERMAN, HERBSTNEBEL), a strike at the Ardennes, where American troops were comparatively thin in numbers. *Greif* was designed as a subsidiary operation to assist the general breakthrough.

Commando Otto Skorzeny (*q.v.*), the SS (*q.v.*) colonel who had been instrumental in freeing Mussolini from the Gran Sasso, was charged with a plan to penetrate the American lines by using German troops disguised as GI's (*q.v.*). The unit was to capture the Meuse bridges before they could be blown up. For weeks preceding the operation, Skorzeny ran a "school for Americans" to train his men in American habits. He taught the commandos how Americans "smoked dry" and did not wet their lips as did Germans; that Americans lit their matches by striking inward not outward; and that American GIs knew all about Betty Grable (*q.v.*), the movie star, as well as the batting averages of baseball players.

Although Skorzeny's commandos managed to sneak past a score of American jeeps, they were unable to perform their assigned tasks. The plot was foiled when a German officer, who carried plans for the mission, failed the password and quiz tests. *Operation Greif* was a failure. (*See* BULGE, BATTLE OF THE.)

GROVES, LESLIE R. (1896–1970).

U.S. Army officer who directed the secrecy-shrouded project to develop the atomic bomb (1942–1945). (*See* MANHATTAN PROJECT.)

In 1941 then Col. Groves hoped for an assignment abroad, but instead he was selected for the super-secret project. In 1942 he was promoted to brigadier general and given command of the operation. Although he knew little about atomic physics, he knew much about the crash construction and operation of huge plants necessary for the project. In 1944 he was promoted to major general. By 1945 several hundred thousand scientists, technicians, mechanics, construction workers, and other personnel were busily at work in the creation of the super-secret bomb. One of his thorniest problems was the selection of J. Robert Oppenheimer (*q.v.*), as director of the Los Alamos, New Mexico, laboratory, which was opposed by Groves's own security men on the ground that Oppenheimer had associated, years before, with Communists. Groves, nevertheless, chose Oppenheimer.

The first atomic bomb was tested at Alamagordo, New Mexico, at 5:30 A.M. on July 15, 1945. (*See* HIROSHIMA and NAGASAKI for results of the first two atomic bombs.)

Bibliography. L. R. Groves, *Now It Can Be Told: The Story of the Manhattan Project* (1962).

GRUENTHER, ALFRED MAXIMILIAN (1899–   ).

U.S. Army officer whose work was an important factor in the surrender of Italian forces.

Gruenther came to the attention of his superior officers because of his efficient conduct during the September 1941 war games, the first large-scale military maneuvers in the United States for some time. He was appointed Deputy Chief of Staff of the 3rd Army under Gen. Dwight D. Eisenhower (*q.v.*) in October 1941. On August 1, 1942, he accompanied Eisenhower to London. He then went to North Africa for the campaign against the *Afrika Korps* (*q.v.*) in the desert war there. When Lt. Gen. Mark W. Clark (*q.v.*) formed his 5th Army, Gruenther was named his Chief of Staff. In this post he served with Clark through the North African, Sicilian, and Italian campaigns. As Chief of Staff with the 5th Army, he successfully adjusted the needs of a predominantly British unit to the requirements of an American Commander. He took care of the routine tasks of running an army, assembling information on which the commanding general could base his decisions, and giving orders to translate such decisions into action.

GUADALCANAL CAMPAIGNS. Among the most bitterly contested campaigns in American history, the Guadalcanal confrontations marked a changeover from defensive to offensive in the Pacific theater of war.

JAPANESE STRATEGY. For the Japanese Imperial GHQ, the Battle of the Coral Sea (*q.v.*) meant that its first thrust at Australia had been foiled. Moreover, the Battle of Midway (*q.v.*) put a block on Japanese expansion in the Central Pacific. Revising their overall strategy, the Japanese turned to the south to deliver two separate blows at Australia. The first thrust would be an overland drive over the Owen Stanley Mountains to take all of New Guinea. Simultaneously, the Solomon Islands would be seized. With their powerful air base at Rabaul (*q.v.*) in New Britain between New Guinea and the Solomons, and another at Tulagi in the midst of the Solomons, the Japanese could then mount an all-out offensive against Australia. Equally as important, control of the Solomons would cut the American life line to Australia.

ALLIED STRATEGY. The Joint Chiefs of Staff, after much discussion, agreed that the Japanese must not be permitted to consolidate their gains and that the Allies must go on the offensive. A compromise plan was to be carried out in three stages: (1) occupation of the Santa Cruz Islands and the eastern Solomons, including Tulagi and Guadalcanal; (2) capture of the rest of the Solomons; and (3) taking of Rabaul and the remainder of the Bismarck Archipelago.

The strategy was revised when on July 5, 1942, reconnaissance planes reported that the Japanese had moved troops from Tulagi to the larger nearby island of Guadalcanal and were building an airstrip at Lunga Point. To forestall the possibility of enemy bombers operating from this new airfield, the Joint Chiefs of Staff made Guadalcanal the primary objective.

The result was a series of clashes in the Guadalcanal area that comprised seven major naval engagements, nearly a dozen pitched land battles, and many additional bombardments and skirmishes.

PREPARATIONS. Guadalcanal, 90 miles long and 25 miles wide, lay in the midst of the volcanic archipelago of the Solomon Islands. The climate was hot and humid, the night mists filled with effluvia from putrescent matter in swamps and jungles, the whole area malaria-ridden. *Operation Watchtower* (July 2, 1942) was assigned to Vice-Adm. Robert L. Ghormley, with Rear Adm. Frank Fletcher as tactical commander and Lt. Gen. Alexander A. Vandegrift to lead the landing force. Several dozen carriers of varying size and reconstructed warships were made ready for the assault.

LANDINGS, AUGUST 7-8, 1942. Watchtower was the first amphibious operation undertaken by U.S. forces in the war. On August 7, 1942, three carrier groups, built around the carriers *Enterprise, Saratoga,* and *Wasp,* with transports and escorts, and covered by land-based air support from Port Moresby, moved on Guadalcanal. The pre-landing bombardment lasted only three hours.

U.S. Marines stormed ashore and by evening 11,000 were on the island. The next morning they captured the almost completed airfield and renamed it Henderson Field. The Japanese garrison of 2,200, mostly construction workers, fled into the jungle. There was stiffer resistance on the satellite islands of Tulagi, Florida, and Gavatu, but by midnight August 8–9 all four islands were secured.

BATTLE OF SAVO ISLAND. Meanwhile, Vice-Adm. Gunichi Mikawa at Rabaul received word of the American landings. His decision was prompt—to send reinforcements to the garrisons at Guadalcanal and Tulagi. He quickly assembled a task force of ships whose crews had never trained together. The force consisted of 5 heavy cruisers (*Chokai,* the flagship, *Kako, Aoba, Kimugasa,* and *Furutaka*); 2 light cruisers (*Tenryu* and *Yubari*); and 1 destroyer (*Yunagi*). In the early evening of August 7 the warships made rendezvous in St. George's Channel. The striking force steamed in full daylight down the Slot, the narrow waters between the two chains of the Solomons.

The Americans did not have the Slot properly covered by air search, a serious blunder. Two U.S. cruiser groups were moving at low speed on their monotonous patrol courses. Early on the morning of August 9 Adm. Mikawa summoned his crews to the battle station just off Savo Island. First he hit the southern and then the northern group. It was all over within an hour. The Japanese task force steamed back through the Slot.

The cost to the Allies was heavy—four heavy cruisers, including the Australian *Canberra,* sunk; one destroyer lost and one badly damaged; 1,270 officers and men killed and 709 wounded. It was one of the worst defeats ever inflicted on the U.S. Navy.

To the east, like so many sitting ducks, were loaded U.S. transports waiting to disembark their troops. Fortunately for them, Mikawa thought it best not to complete his mission.

JUNGLE WARFARE. On land U.S. Marines were getting their first taste of jungle warfare. They fought among a lush tangle of vines and brush, around huge hardwood trees buttressed by giant roots. From the moist ground came the stench of decaying vegetables, decomposition, and putrefaction. Everything was coated with dampness. The Americans waded through swamps and crossed rivers, always targets for Japanese snipers hidden in the underbrush or strapped to the tops of palm trees.

When the transports departed, some 16,000 marines were left on

Guadalcanal, but fewer than half their supplies and weapons had been unloaded. Through August 1942 the marines held a narrow strip 7 miles long and 4 miles wide on the shores of the island. Gradually, they began to fan out through the island.

BATTLE OF THE EASTERN SOLOMONS. To reinforce the several thousand men of the garrison on Guadalcanal, the Japanese Imperial GHQ assembled a great fleet during the third week of August 1942—3 carriers, 3 battleships, 9 cruisers, 13 destroyers, 36 submarines, and several auxiliary craft to run down the Slot and land additional troops. Meanwhile, another fleet carrier force, spearheaded by 2 carriers, 2 battleships, and 3 heavy cruisers, advanced into waters northeast of the Solomons. The light cruiser, Ryujo, moving ahead, was to be used as bait to attract American carrier planes into attacking her, while the heavier forces would strike at the enemy flattops.

The subsequent Battle of the Eastern Solomons did not turn out to be the trap that the Japanese had prepared. Alerted in time, the Americans sent a strong carrier force (Enterprise, Saratoga, Wasp) north to cover the sea lanes there. In the ensuing air battle the Americans destroyed at least 70 Japanese planes while losing only 17 of their own. The Enterprise took three bombs, which killed 74 men and caused severe deck and gun damage, but she was saved by good damage control. Both fleets retired after what was called an American victory, although it was not a clear-cut one.

TOKYO EXPRESS. Instead of sending in massive reinforcements to Guadalcanal, the Japanese were content with dribbles of troops one after another. They had now lost daytime control of the sea lanes, but at night they could land men and supplies without much difficulty. U.S. Marines called it the Tokyo Express because the destroyers brought in detachments regularly. By early September the Japanese had an additional 6,000 troops on Guadalcanal. In the Battle of Bloody Ridge, September 12–14, 1942, they lost 1,200 men, the Americans 40 marines.

Meanwhile, Japanese submarines attacked American warships, sinking the Wasp and badly damaging the Saratoga. With the Enterprise under repair, only the Hornet was left among the giant carriers to provide air cover.

BATTLE OF CAPE ESPERANCE. The next naval battle, Cape Esperance, was touched off by the dispatch of an American regiment to Guadalcanal in two large transports and 8 destroyers on October 9, 1942. A cruiser group ran interference. The Japanese countered by sending down the Slot a bombardment group of 3 heavy cruisers and 3 destroyers. The Americans added a task force of 2 heavy cruisers, 2 light cruisers, and 5 destroyers. The confrontation took place southwest of Savo Island and north of Cape Esperance.

Losses were relatively light on both sides, but this battle marked the nadir of misery for the Allies. During the battle the Japanese were able to reinforce their garrison on Guadalcanal, bringing the total there to 22,000 against 23,000 Americans.

BATTLE OF THE SANTA CRUZ ISLANDS. The Japanese now sent a huge fleet under Adm. Isoruku Yamamoto (*q.v.*), with 2 large carriers, 2 light carriers, 4 battleships, 14 cruisers, and 44 destroyers, to the Solomons. The great task force awaited news that Henderson Field had been taken by Japanese land forces. A considerably smaller U.S. task force, with 1 battleship against 4, moved to meet Yamamoto. The two fleets clashed on October 26, 1942, in a battle dominated by air action on both sides.

The Japanese suffered damage to 2 carriers and a loss of 200 planes. The Americans lost the *Hornet.* In terms of warships sunk, the Japanese could claim victory. The U.S. Navy now had only two carriers in the Pacific, the *Enterprise* and the *Saratoga*, both under repair.

NAVAL BATTLE OF GUADALCANAL. The action at Santa Cruz gave the Americans time to prepare for the next enemy onslaught. In the first 8 days of November 1942 the Japanese brought in 2 cruiser loads and 65 destroyer loads of reinforcements to Guadalcanal. By November 12 the Japanese garrison outnumbered the Americans on the island. Heavy American reinforcements were soon on the way.

The clash this time was one of the most furious sea battles ever fought. A Japanese task force, including at least one battleship of the *Konho* class, appeared off Guadalcanal to screen a new landing. The operation was protected by a great fleet gathered in a huge circle. An American task force, consisting of 2 heavy cruisers, 3 light cruisers, and 8 destroyers went to the attack.

American warships steamed ahead in a straight line of 3,000 yards directly at the enemy. They sped directly into the circle, which opened at one end like a mouth gaping with surprise. The Japanese were confused by the bold attack, which took place in the dark, punctuated by searchlights and flashes from big guns, streams of tracer bullets, and bursts from exploding ships. The Japanese began firing across empty space at their own ships. At proper range the great Japanese guns could have broken the smaller American ships like matches, but their gunners were unable to depress their weapons to fire at the small but speedy enemy craft.

A stronger American force allowed the Japanese to proceed to the north side of Savo Island, then speed up from the south to catch the enemy in a classic "T" maneuver. Nearly a dozen Japanese ships were left burning and exploding. The remainder of the Japanese fleet crawled westward away from disaster.

The Japanese had landed only 4,000 out of the 12,000 reinforcements and only 5 tons of their 10,000 tons of supplies.

JAPANESE EVACUATION. The Japanese were now in a hopeless position, having lost control of both sea and air. Their troops on Guadalcanal were reduced to eating grass and roots. There were two final naval engage-ments—the Battle of Tassafaronga on November 30, 1942, a sharp defeat of a superior American force by a Japanese destroyer force, and the Battle of Rennell Island on January 30, 1943, in which the Japanese sank the heavy cruiser *Chicago*. It was the last of seven naval battles of the Guadalcanal campaign.

By this time, however, the Japanese were almost out of Guadalcanal. Word came from Tokyo to abandon the island. During the first week in February 13,000 Japanese troops were evacuated, swiftly and efficiently, from the island.

SIGNIFICANCE. The Guadalcanal campaign ended in complete and total defeat for the Japanese. The Tokyo Express no longer had its terminus on the island. After six months of work and misery, the Americans had won 2,500 square miles of jungle-covered mountains and disease-ridden plains. But they had concluded their first major task in the Pacific—the climb to Rabaul. For the American public Guadalcanal was a morale booster of immense impor-tance. At long last sea lanes to Tokyo were pierced.

It was a serious defeat for the Japanese. There is no accurate count of casualties on both sides, but it is believed that the Japanese lost at least 25,000 of their best troops, including 9,000 from disease and hunger. Worse, they lost more than 600 planes plus their crews, all of which were difficult to replace. Each side lost 24 combatant ships, excluding smaller craft.

Bibliography. R. Tregaskis, *Guadalcanal Diary* (1943); J. Miller, *Guadalcanal: The First Offensive* (1949); S. E. Morison, *The Two-Ocean War* (1963); G. Cook, *The Battle of Cape Esperance* (1968); S. E. Smith (ed.), *The U.S. Marine Corps in World War II* (1969); R. J. O'Connor, *The Japanese Navy in World War II* (1970); S. Denlinger and C. Cary, *War in the Pacific* (1970); K. Kent, *Guadalcanal: Island Ordeal* (1971); and S. B. Griffith, *The Battle for Guadalcanal* (1980).

GUAM, 1944. *See* MARIANAS, BATTLE FOR THE.

GUDERIAN, HEINZ (1888–1954). General responsible for developing the German armored force and the technique of the *Blitzkrieg* (*q.v.*).

Against opposition Guderian devised the *Blitzkrieg* (*q.v.*) tactics used suc-cessfully at the start of the war. (*See* POLAND, CAMPAIGN IN.) His tanks destroyed thousands of enemy artillery pieces and demolished several Polish divisions. A grateful *Fuehrer* visited Guderian on the battlefield. In 1940 Guderian was transferred to the western front and once again his tactics resulted in brilliant victories. In May 1940 his tanks broke through at Sedan and headed for the English Channel, a move that resulted in the collapse of France. (*See* FRANCE, FIRST BATTLE OF.) He then set up his headquarters in Paris.

Guderian repeated his phenomenally successful tactics in the opening weeks of the invasion of Soviet Russia starting on June 22, 1941. When the campaign bogged down in wintry conditions and under Russian resistance, he ordered a strategic retreat against Hitler's orders. The angry *Fuehrer* forced him to resign in December 1941. He was made Inspector General of Armored Troops, evidently a demotion. Later he was assigned the task of designing new tanks, which were never put into production.

JULY PLOT. Guderian was inspecting troops in East Prussia when the attempt was made on Hitler's life on July 20, 1944. (*See* JULY PLOT.) He knew about the conspiracy, but he did not become an active member. At the same time he did not betray the plotters. After the failure of the plot, Guderian issued an order of the day denouncing the conspirators as cowards and weaklings "who preferred disgrace to duty and honor." Hitler made Guderian Chief of the Army General Staff and a member of the "Court of Honor," along with Gens. Wilhelm Keitel and Gerd von Rundstedt (*qq.v.*), to hear the *Gestapo* (*q.v.*) evidence against fellow officers in the plot. The accused were sent for trial before the notorious People's Court, which meant execution.

With restricted powers, Guderian held his post as Chief of the Army General Staff until the end of March 1945, when Hitler became incensed by his general's factual reports from the Russian front, and removed him from his post again.

Guderian was not brought to trial before the Nuremberg tribunal. (*See* NUREMBERG TRIALS.) He died at Schwangen, near Füssen, Bavaria, on May 14, 1954.

Bibliography. Guderian was one of the first military men to advocate *Blitzkrieg* tactics in his book *Achtung Panzer* (1938). His memoirs, *Erinnerungen eines Soldats,* appeared in 1951.

GUERRILLAS. *See* UNDERGROUND.

GUERNICA. Historic city in the Basque country of northern Spain considered holy by Spaniards.

Guernica was destroyed by planes of the German *Luftwaffe* (*q.v.*) in an annihilation raid on April 28, 1937. The indiscriminate bombing, which became a symbol of Fascist brutality, aroused world opinion at the time and became the subject of a masterly painting by Picasso.

H

HAAKON VII (1872–1957). King of Norway.

When Germany invaded Norway in April 1940, Haakon led the resistance of the Norwegian Army. He rejected Hitler's demands for surrender. After Vidkun Quisling's (*q.v.*) puppet government was formed, Haakon led the Norwegian Resistance Government from Trondheim. On the withdrawal of the Allies from Norway, he came to London to lead the Norwegian Government-in-exile there. (*See* GOVERNMENTS-IN-EXILE.) He retained communcation with the Norwegian Resistance and managed to solidify the previously divided ministry. He established favorable relations with neutral Sweden and helped the Russians in an attack from Finland on the Germans in late 1944.

Bibliography. A. L. Olson, *Scandinavia: The Background for Neutrality* (1940); and M. A. Michael, *Haakon, King of Norway* (1958).

HALDER, FRANZ, (1884–1972). German officer, Chief of the General Staff.

Despite his dislike for Hitler, Halder organized the opening German campaign of the war. (*See* POLAND, CAMPAIGN IN.) At the same time he continued to resist the *Fuehrer's* strategy in high-level conferences. He opposed Hitler's decision to strike at Moscow directly in late summer 1941. Hitler gave in and then dismissed Halder on September 24, 1942, when the Russian campaign failed. After the failure of the July Plot (*q.v.*) in 1944, Halder was arrested and kept in Dachau until the end of the war. He was liberated by American troops in April 1945.

Bibliography. Halder gave his assessment of Hitler as a military leader in *Hitler als Feldherr* (1949).

HALIFAX, EDWARD FREDERICK LINDLEY WOOD, 1st EARL (1881–1959). British statesman who was unsuccessful in efforts to head off war.

Halifax was Foreign Secretary in the Churchill Cabinet for seven months. In

1940 he was appointed Ambassador to the United States, scarcely an advancement for a Foreign Secretary. But in this post Halifax was successful in promoting a close Anglo-American relationship. He remained a member of the War Cabinet. He was made an earl in 1944.

Bibliography. See Halifax's autobiography, *Fullness of Days* (1957); and biographies by A. C. Johnson (1941) and S. Hodgson (1941).

HALSEY, WILLIAM FREDERICK, JR. (1882–1959). U.S. naval officer, outstanding leader in World War II. He was called "Bull" Halsey because of his aggressiveness.

Ten days before the Japanese struck at Pearl Harbor (*q.v.*), Halsey commanded a task force that set out for Wake Island to deliver planes. Returning to Hawaii on December 7, 1941, he found it necessary to keep his ships at sea. For two months the U.S. Pacific Fleet lay demoralized. Then Halsey was sent with a force of aircraft carriers, cruisers, and destroyers to make a surprise foray on five Japanese-held islands in the Marshalls and on Makin Island in the Gilberts. It was the first U.S. naval offensive of the war.

Invalided to Washington for a few months, Halsey returned to the Pacific as Commander of Carriers of the Pacific Fleet and of Carrier Division Two. He commanded the warships that escorted the carrier *Hornet* in the first U.S. air raid on Japan on April 18, 1942. (*See* DOOLITTLE RAID.)

On October 18, 1942, Halsey was given tactical command in the South Pacific. Eight days later, with his small "shoestring fleet," he fought at Santa Cruz. In mid-November he closed with the Japanese in a decisive engagement at Guadalcanal (*q.v.*), in which his force sunk at least 23 enemy vessels. He was named a full admiral. On June 17, 1944, serving in command of the 3rd Fleet, he directed the operations resulting in the capture of the Western Carolines.

Halsey's name was associated closely with the engagement at Leyte Gulf in 1944. (*See* LEYTE GULF, BATTLE OF; PACIFIC, CAMPAIGNS IN THE; and HALSEY CONTROVERSY.) He later led a series of brilliantly executed attacks on enemy installations in the Ryukus, Taiwan (Formosa), the Philippines, South China, and Indonesia. The formal Japanese surrender was signed on his flagship, the USS *Missouri* on September 1, 1945. (*See* SURRENDER, JAPANESE.)

Bibliography. W. F. Halsey, *Admiral Halsey's Story* (1947); B. M. Frank, *Halsey* (1974); and J. M. Merrill, *A Sailor's Admiral* (1976).

HALSEY CONTROVERSY. Dispute concerning the tactics of Adm. William F. Halsey, Jr., at the Battle of Leyte Gulf (*qq.v.*).

BACKGROUND. Of the three task forces that the Japanese Imperial Command committed to the battle, the third under Vice-Adm. Jisaburo Ozawa was assigned the mission of playing sacrificial decoy to lure the U.S. Third Fleet under Halsey north and away from the San Bernardino Strait north of Leyte.

The two main Japanese fleets would rendezvous at Leyte Gulf, annihilate the Americans, and isolate the U.S. troops already ashore.

The Japanese did, indeed, draw Halsey northward to strike at the diversionary force, leaving the San Bernardino Strait open for the main Japanese force, which soon abandoned the mission.

After the engagement and during the postwar era a controversy arose between the principals as well as among naval experts on whether in fact Halsey had made a major blunder.

KINKAID'S ARGUMENT. Vice-Adm. Thomas C. Kinkaid (q.v.), commander of the 7th Fleet, deplored Halsey's move.

His argument in summary:

1. Halsey relied too heavily on exaggerated claims of his pilots.

2. Halsey made a critical error of judgment when he dashed 300 miles to the north with all six of his battleships. With this decision he left behind too weak a force to make possible the destruction of the enemy fleet. Then, at the wrong time, he compounded the error by turning about and speeding south.

3. Kinkaid's own 7th Fleet had only old and slow battleships, was weak in firepower, and was supposed to provide support for the landing and not engage in major combat.

4. Halsey made the mistake of taking all six of his battleships north when he needed only two.

5. Halsey actually did exactly what the enemy wanted him to do. Kinkaid intimated that Halsey had foolishly fallen for the Japanese plan.

HALSEY'S DISSENT. Halsey entered a vigorous denial:

1. His decision to go north was not based solely on reports of his pilots. It was a calculated, aptly justified risk. He was playing the game on Saturday, and not "Monday-morning quarterbacking."

2. Halsey felt that Kinkaid's 7th Fleet could take care of Kurita's "battered forces." "I knew what I was doing at all times and deliberately took the risks, in order to get rid of the Jap carriers."

3. Halsey agreed that his decision in bowing to pressure and heading south was a mistake. "I consider this the gravest error I committed during the Battle of Leyte Gulf."

4. The difficulty lay in divided command and an unsatisfactory communication system. "Had either Admiral Kinkaid or I been put in supreme command, the battle would have been fought quite differently."

5. Halsey was not convinced that Ozawa's force in the north was supposed to be merely a lure. "The Japs had continually lied during the war, even to each other. Why believe them implicitly as soon as the war ends?"

These arguments were reinforced in *Admiral Halsey's Story* (1947), the admiral's autobiography. Here he stated that, given the same circumstances and the same information as he had then, he would have made the same decision. He had reason to believe that enemy forces in the central and southern sectors were being handled adequately by Kinkaid. He noted three alternatives:

1. He could guard San Bernardino with his whole fleet and wait for the Japanese Northern Force to strike him. He rejected this alternative because this would allow the enemy use of his airfields on Luzon as well as their carriers.

2. He could guard San Bernadino with Task Force 34 while striking the Northern Force with his carriers. Also rejected—it was necessary to keep the fleet intact.

3. He could leave San Bernadino unguarded and strike the Northern Fleet with all his power. This he accepted to preserve the integrity of his fleet. This alternative promised the greatest possibility of surprise. He, therefore, headed for the enemy 300 miles to the north.

Halsey further indicated that he was goaded to fury by dispatches from Commander-in-Chief of the Pacific Fleet Chester W. Nimitz with the message (Halsey's version): "THE WHOLE WORLD WANTS TO KNOW WHERE IS TASK FORCE 34." Halsey said that he was stunned as if struck in the face. He was so angered that he could not talk—unable to believe that Admiral Nimitz had sent such a message. Reacting in rage, he ordered the fleet split. At that moment, he wrote, the Northern Force, with its two remaining carriers crippled and dead in the water, was exactly 42 miles from the muzzle of Halsey's 15-inch guns. Halsey had to turn his back on an opportunity he had dreamed of since his days at Annapolis as a midshipman.

As a final clinching argument in his view, Halsey pointed out that the Japanese had lost 4 carriers, 1 light cruiser and 2 destroyers, and seen damage to 2 battleships, 2 light cruisers, and 4 destroyers.

SIGNIFICANCE. The controversy has not been resolved. The Battle of Leyte Gulf, despite Halsey's dash for the north, was as decisive as Salamis, when the Greek navies defeated Xerxes's fleet in 480 B.C.

Bibliography. W. F. Halsey, *Admiral Halsey's Story* (1947).

HAMBURG, BOMBING OF. Allied air assault on one of Germany's major cities in 1943. Under the code or cover name of *Gomorrah,* it was the most destructive air bombing before Hiroshima.

BACKGROUND. The Germans were the first to start mass bombardment of cities from the air with attacks on Warsaw (*q.v.*) (1939), Rotterdam (1940), London (1940), and Coventry (1940) (*q.v.*). (*See also* BRITAIN, BATTLE OF; and OPEN CITIES.) Once they consolidated their air power, the Allies began to strike back in kind.

TARGET. For the British Bomber Command, Hamburg was a target of prime importance. Just 64 miles from the mouth of the Elbe, it was the largest German seaport. Its major industries included shipbuilding, oil refining, metal and rubber goods, optical and electrical equipment, and footstuffs. It was easily identifiable to pilots who could fly across the open waters of the North Sea and then follow the Elbe River to the target.

PREPARATION. Raids on Hamburg were intensified in the spring of 1943. British bombers hammered the city by night, while American bombers struck during daylight. To put the port out of action, more than 100,000 men, air crews, and technicians were assembled for a knockout blow.

FIRESTORM. The massive raid came from July 24 to August 3, 1943. Exactly 2,353 heavy bombers of the Royal Air Force (*q.v.*) took part in three main attacks. Within the space of nine days, four night- and three American attacks were launched in 3,095 sorties during which a total of 9,000 tons of bombs were dropped, including both high explosives and incendiary bombs. For the first time the Allies used aluminum strips, known as *Window* (*q.v.*), which were dropped in large quantities to disrupt the enemy's radar warning system and thus blind the defense. (*See* RADAR, WARTIME.) The strips acted as a perfect shield against radar rays. German fighter planes and antiaircraft crews were confused and virtually helpless in the chaos.

Earlier attacks on Hamburg were innocuous when compared with this assault. German air-raid sirens were destroyed and the city's antiaircraft guns silenced. As the inhabitants streamed out of the stricken city, Allied planes hammered Hamburg without pause. In the center of the city a devastating firestorm snuffed out available oxygen and thousands perished.

Albert Speer described it:[*]

It had catastrophic consequences for us. The first attacks put the water supply pipes out of action. . . . Huge conflagrations created cyclone-like firestorms; the asphalt of the streets began to blaze; people were suffocated in their cellars or burned to death in the streets. The devastation of this series of air raids could be compared only with the effects of a major earthquake.

LOSSES. The casualties and material damage were greater than anything ex-

---

[*]Albert Speer, *Inside the Third Reich* (Avon: New York, 1971), pp. 369–370.

perienced in Germany. Statistics vary, but it is estimated that 30,482 inhabitants lost their lives in the deadly attack. The destruction caused by area conflagrations was between 60 and 98 percent. Half of Hamburg's dwelling houses were destroyed; four big shipbuilding yards were heavily hit; public services were paralyzed; more than 900,000 Germans became homeless fugitives. In addition, 180 tons of shipping were sunk in the harbor.

Allied losses were unusually low. In all only 57 planes were lost, or 2.4 percent of the total attacking force. Gen. Arthur T. Harris (*q.v.*), Commander-in-Chief of the British Bomber Command, reported: "On the first night of the attack . . . the radar-controlled searchlight waved aimlessly in all directions, the gunfire was inaccurate. . . . No raid ever known before had been so terrible."

AFTERMATH. The bombing of Hamburg, like that of Dresden in early 1945 (*see* DRESDEN, BOMBING OF), had a devastating effect on German morale. Germans denounced the raids as uncivilized, while Allied propagandists described them as a fitting response to earlier German attacks on open cities. The people of Hamburg spoke in awe and anger about the terrible event, which they called "*die Katastrophe*," and denounced "Bomber" Harris for the deadly assault.

Bibliography. A. T. Harris, *Bomber Offensive* (1947); M. Caidin, *The Night Hamburg Died* (1960); H. Rumpf, *The Bombing of Germany*, trans. by E. Fitzgerald (1963); and R. Jackson, *Bomber: Famous Bomber Missions of World War II* (1980).

HÄRÄ-KÏRI. Japanese term, from *härä* (belly) and *kïri* (cutting out). Traditional form of suicide by disembowelment, practiced under the *samurai* feudal code and carried into the 20th century. It was used by political figures and military men in accordance with the Japanese code of honor.

WORLD WAR II. Throughout the war Japanese military and naval officers who had been beaten in combat chose self-immolation as a way of atoning for the dishonor of defeat. A typical example took place on the island of Saipan in the Marianas in early July 1944. (*See* MARIANAS, BATTLE FOR THE.) The two senior officers on Saipan during the battle there were Gen. Yoshitsugu Saito, commander of the Japanese forces on the island, and Vice-Adm. Chuichi Nagumo, who had been demoted from his carrier command to a small area fleet with headquarters on Saipan. When defeat became inevitable, the two commanders ordered a mass suicidal *banzai* attack (*q.v.*) in which every remaining Japanese was to kill at least 10 Americans before taking his own life. More than 3,000 men tried to obey the order.

Meanwhile, the two commanders prepared to take their own lives in ceremonial *härä-kïri.* Saito sent a final message to his troops, informing them that he would die with them "to exalt true Japanese manhood." Then he sat down in his headquarters cave on a rock facing Tokyo. He shouted: "*Tenno Haika! Banzai!*" ("Hurrah for the Emperor. Ten Thousand Years, Forever!")

He then carefully opened an artery with his sword. He nodded to his adjutant who quickly shot him in the head.

In another cave Adm. Nagumo, commander of the Pearl Harbor striking force, killed himself with a pistol shot.

In each case Saito and Nagumo had varied the traditional *härä-kiri* procedure but the basic meaning was retained. In the common form, the individual would follow an accepted formula, at the end of which he would thrust his knife into his abdomen. Then a trusted aide would step forward and use his sword to cut off the suicide's head.

HARDING, ALLAN FRANCIS (JOHN) (1896–   ). British Army officer.

Harding was stationed in India at the start of World War II. In October 1939 he was transferred to the Middle East. In early 1942 he was named commander of the famed Desert Rats (*q.v.*), whom he led from El Alamein to Tripoli. He served in Italy as Chief of Staff to Gen. Harold Alexander (*q.v.*), and was credited with the plans used for the capture of Rome in 1944. Later he commanded the 13th Corps of the 8th Army.

Short, dapper, with a close-cropped sandy mustache, Harding was described as "an electric little man, only slightly taller than Napoleon's supposed five-feet-two inches." He was one of Britain's most respected officers during the war.

HARRIMAN, WILLIAM AVERELL (1891–   ). U.S. official, administrator, and diplomat active on delicate missions during the war.

In early 1941 Harriman was sent to London by Roosevelt with wide powers to expedite the new Lend-Lease (*q.v.*) program. He worked closely from then on with Churchill. In September–October 1941 he was sent, along with Lord Beaverbrook (*q.v.*), on a presidential mission to Moscow.

Harriman played a leading role in the American war effort. From 1943 to 1946 he served in the delicate post as Ambassador to the Soviet Union. He participated in the major war conferences (*see* CONFERENCES, ALLIED WAR), including those in Quebec, Cairo, and Teheran in 1943, and at Yalta and San Francisco in 1945 (*qq.v.*). Both Roosevelt and Churchill called upon him as an adviser. He warned of conflicting aspirations with Soviet Russia during the immediate postwar years and urged a posture of correct but firm relations with the USSR.

Bibliography. Harriman was the author of *Peace with Russia* (1959).

HARRIS, ARTHUR TRAVERS (1892–   ). British air marshal and Commander-in-Chief of the Bomber Command from the beginning of the war.

At the beginning of the war Harris commanded No. 5 Group of the Royal Air Force. He rose rapidly in rank: Air Vice-Marshal (1939); Air Marshal

(1941); Commander-in-Chief of the Bomber Command (1942); and Air Chief Marshal (1943). He strongly supported the production of heavy bombers and urged that attacks on enemy targets be eliminated in favor of saturation bombing. He won his point. The air offensive over Germany from 1942 on bore the Harris trademark. On May 30–31, 1942, he launched the first 1,000-plane raid on Cologne (*see* COLOGNE, BOMBING OF). He maintained the air offensive against Germany until April 1944, when despite his protests, the Bomber Command was placed under control of Gen. Dwight D. Eisenhower (*q.v.*) for the invasion of Normandy. In September 1944 Harris resumed the independent attacks on German cities, culminating in the raid on Dresden (*q.v.*) on February 13–14, 1945.

Bibliography. Harris gave a spirited defense of area bombing in his book *Bomber Command* (1946).

HASSELL, CHRISTIAN ALBRECHT ULRICH VON (1881–1944). German career diplomat.

At the start of the war von Hassell was already a member of the German Resistance movement. He promoted dissent among army officers and, as a monarchist, called for the restoration of the Hohenzollerns. Shadowed by the suspicious *Gestapo* (*q.v.*), he was arrested shortly after the unsuccessful 1944 July Plot (*q.v.*) on Hitler's life. Sent to Ravensbrück concentration camp, he was brought before the People's Court, sentenced to death and executed at Plötzensee Prison by hanging from piano wire on September 4, 1944.

Distinguished in bearing and manner, von Hassell was a diplomat of the old school. He was known for his trenchant humor, courteous demeanor, and unshakable political convictions.

Bibliography. The *Von Hassell Diaries* (1948), which were dug up from a tea chest in the garden of his home, is a main source of information about the German Resistance. The diaries give an extraordinary picture of the day-to-day activities of the small group of conspirators resolved to rid their country of Hitlerism.

HAYWORTH, RITA (1919–   ). American motion picture actress widely considered to be the most beautiful pin-up girl of World War II.

With her celebrated red hair, classic features, and sultry voice, Rita Hayworth was noted as the girl who "turned on" American troops in the war. Her most famous photograph—as Aphrodite in a black lace nightgown, smiling from the silk pillows of a huge bed—followed American GIs (*q.v.*) to every theater of operations in the war. It was said that millions of troops said their goodnights every night to the radiant redhead, the symbol for which every American was fighting. Her photograph by popular demand appeared again and again in *Yank, The Army Weekly* (*q.v.*).

HELLFIRE CORNER. Name given to the area of English coastal towns of Dover, Deal, and Folkstone, opposite Calais, all overlooking the important Strait of Dover. For four years the people living in this area were subjected to

incessant shellfire from German naval guns near Pas de Calais. Here the Germans had set up one of the most formidable fortresses in Europe.

Because of continued shelling, two-thirds of the people in Hellfire Corner were evacuated and most of those who remained took to the caves in the final days of the war. The area was relieved on October 3, 1944, when the Canadian 1st Army smashed its way to Calais.

HELLFIRE PASS. Name given by British troops to Halfaya Pass near Tobruk in North Africa.

On June 14, 1941, the British Western Desert Force began an attack on Gen. Erwin Rommel's *Afrika Korps* (*qq.v.*) at Halfaya Pass. Of the 13 British *Matilda* tanks, only one survived the tank trap of four 88s (*see* ARTILLERY WEAPONS: German Eighty-Eight Gun) placed by Rommel at Halfaya Pass. (*See also* NORTH AFRICA, CAMPAIGNS IN.)

HEPBURN REPORT. Official U.S. Navy report on the naval debacle at the Battle of Savo Island (*q.v.*).

BACKGROUND. On August 9, 1942, the U.S. Navy lost four heavy cruisers in 40 minutes at the hands of an inferior Japanese naval force at Savo Island in the Solomons. Severely shaken by the defeat, the U.S. Navy set about the task of finding out what had happened. In December 1942 Secretary of the Navy Frank Knox (*q.v.*) ordered Adm. Arthur J. Hepburn, former Commander-in-Chief of the U.S. Fleet, to investigate and determine "the primary and contributing causes of the losses and whether or not culpability attaches to any individual engaged in the operation." Adm. Hepburn, 64 years old and near retirement, was the navy's senior officer and highly regarded as a strategist and a tactician.

FINDINGS. The report was submitted on May 13, 1943, but was never made public. It concluded that the main cause of the defeat was "the complete surprise achieved by the enemy." "The surprise was due to unreadiness in the ships to meet sudden night attack; failure to understand the meaning of the enemy planes overhead just before the attack; too much confidence in radar; delay in contact reports; and withdrawal of the carrier groups on the evening before the battle." The report contained severe criticism of two relatively junior officers.

ADM. KING'S JUDGMENT. Adm. Ernest J. King, Commander-in-Chief United States Fleet, in a letter marked "secret" to Secretary of the Navy Knox, explained that the fact that the operation was not well executed "may have been due in part to lack of experience." The deficiencies "have long since been corrected." King recorded his approval of the decision and conduct of Rear Adm. R. K. Turner, U.S. Navy, and Rear Adm. C. Crutchley, Royal Navy. "In my judgment, these two officers were in no way inefficient, much less at fault in executing their parts of the operation. Both found themselves in awkward positions, and both did their best with the means at their disposal.'' King recommended that no part of his report be made public before the end of the war.

Bibliography. See S. E. Morison, *History of United States Naval Operations in World War II*, Vols. IV and V (1949 and 1951); and E. J. King and W. M. Whitehall, *Fleet Admiral King: A Naval Record* (1952).

HERALDRY OF WORLD WAR II. Use of medals, decorations, and symbols of distinction or honor.

BACKGROUND. The story of awards goes back to the laurel wreaths of ancient Greece and Rome and the heraldry of medieval chivalry. The practice of awarding decorations and medals was begun in the late 18th century. Decorations were given for gallantry or military service. Medals, on a slightly lower level of honor, were given for many types of military and civilian merit. Used as incentives to courageous conduct and good service, they were awarded both to individuals and units. They were surrounded by a special mystique. The practice carried through to World War II.

BRITISH. Great Britain and the United States led the field in the number and types of awards for gallantry. British medals were conferred not only in the United Kingdom but also in the Commonwealth and dependencies. Precedence was given to two medals: the Victoria Cross, abbreviated V.C., which was instituted by Queen Victoria in 1856, and the George Cross, abbreviated G.C., introduced by George VI in 1940. (*See* GEORGE CROSS.) The Distinguished Service Order was awarded only to commissioned officers. The Military Cross, instituted on December 31, 1914, was given to warrant officers and above. The Air Force Cross, the same as the DSC, was awarded for acts of bravery not necessarily in the face of the enemy. The Distinguished Conduct Medal was awarded to non-commissioned officers and men only. There were similar medals for other ranks.

During World War II the British awarded stars for medals covering special areas, such as the Atlantic Star, Africa Star, Air Crew Star, Europe Star, Italy Star, and France and Germany Star. The Defense Medal was awarded for Home Defense and the War Medal for all who served at least a month.

GERMAN. The basic German medal for gallantry in action was the Iron Cross, instituted in 1813 as a Prussian decoration for distinguished service in the War of Liberation. It was renewed in the Franco-Prussian War of 1870–1871 and in World War I in 1914. Hitler, who had been awarded the medal himself in 1918, revived it in 1939 but changed the design, ribbon, and grading. He set new conditions, abolished the decoration for non-combat service, and declared women eligible (only one woman, Hanna Reitsch, received the medal.) He introduced a new grade, the *Ritterkreuz* (Knight's Cross) to bridge the gap between the Iron Cross, First Class, and the Grand Cross.

Awards given in World War II included: Iron Cross, 6,793; Knight's Cross with Oak Leaves and Swords, 853; Knight's Cross with Oak Leaves, Swords, and Diamonds 27; Knight's Cross with Golden Oak Leaves, Swords, and Diamonds (awarded only to Col. Hans-Ulrich Rudel of the *Luftwaffe* [*q.v.*]; and the Grand Cross (given only to Gen. Hermann Goering [*q.v.*] in 1940 after the fall of France).

There were many additional older medals. Among the few new ones was a medal for service on the eastern front against Soviet Russia. For other theaters of war there were "shields" worn on the arm and indicating service at Narvik, Warsaw, and elsewhere. The War Merit Cross, instituted in 1939, was awarded to military and civilian personnel in three grades but was considered inferior to the Iron Cross.

RUSSIAN.   The highest awards of the Soviet Union in World War II were the Gold Star Medal presented to military and civilian "Heroes of the Soviet Union" (1939); and the Hammer and Sickle Gold Medal, a civilian honor for "Heroes of Socialist Labor" (1940). Both had similar five-pointed gold stars and brought with them automatic membership in the Order of Lenin (1930). At the top of the purely military decorations was the Order of Victory (1943), given only to high-ranking officers after outstanding victories. Numerous medals for military and naval merit were named after such national heroes as Prince Mikhail Illarionavich Kutuzov, who repelled Napoleon's invasion of Russia; Aleksandr Vasilevich Suvorov, hero of the Russo-Turkish War of 1887–1891; and Alexander Nevsky, the great military commander who repelled Swedish and German invasions in the 13th century. The Order of Glory was awarded for valor in battle and the Gold Star for service contributing to the honor and development of Russia.

Special medals were issued to commemorate service in various theaters of war, including defense of Leningrad, Sevastopol, Moscow, Stalingrad, and the Soviet Arctic. Special decorations were reserved for Partisans (*q.v.*), for those who helped liberate such cities in adjacent countries as Warsaw, Prague, and Belgrade, and for the capture of enemy cities, including Vienna and Berlin. The Order of the Patriotic War, was instituted in 1942 for all soldiers and guerrilla fighters who resisted the Germans in World War II.

AMERICAN. More than 50 types of U.S. service medals authorized since 1862 were awarded during World War II. Highest decoration for the armed forces was the Congressional Medal of Honor (navy 1861; army 1862). All recipients were granted a fund of $100 a month for life after being awarded the medal. Next in rank were the Distinguished Service Cross (1918 army) and the Navy Cross (1919), for extraordinary heroism in military operations against the enemy. The Distinguished Service Medal was designated for commanders not necessarily in combat.

Among many other American medals awarded during World War II were the Silver Star for conspicuous gallantry by members of all services; the Bronze Star Medal and the Air Medal for heroic or meritorious service; and the Purple Heart for wounded in action. In 1942 the Legion of Merit was established as a decoration for citizens of other countries. There were also campaign medals for such areas as Europe, Middle East, and Africa. All participants were presented with the Victory Medal.

JAPANESE WAR CULT. Medals and decorations did not play the same role in Japan as in other countries. For the Japanese fighting man combat was an act of worship for his Emperor and death in battle a sacrament. Everyone who served in the military adhered to the *busido* code of honor. Officers carried a *samurai* sword as well as a pistol in battle. Soliders wore the *senninbari,* a personal belt of 1,000 stitches made by his family, as well as a Japanese Rising Sun flag inscribed with Shinto prayers. Officers who considered themselves failures were expected to commit honorable suicide.

Bibliography. B. Fitzsimmons (ed.), *Heraldry of War: Medals, Badges, and Uniforms* (1973).

HERSEY, JOHN RICHARD (1914–   ). American novelist, journalist, and war correspondent.

In 1939 Hersey was sent to the Orient by *Time* magazine to report on the Far Eastern situation. Here he gained a firsthand knowledge of the Japanese character, which he used for his later books. In 1942 he reported the U.S. Marine attack on Guadalcanal and was commended for his work in removing wounded there. By this time he became one of the country's leading war correspondents. On four occasions, twice in the Pacific and twice in the Mediterranean, he survived airplane crashes. From Africa he accompanied the American invasion forces to Italy.

During the war Hersey began his career as a novelist. He stressed themes reflecting experiences as a war correspondent. His first novel, *A Bell for Adano* (1944), set in an American-occupied town in war-torn Italy, won the Pulitzer Prize for fiction in 1945, and had tremendous popularity as a book, film, and Broadway play.

In 1946 Hersey wrote *Hiroshima,* which originally appeared in the *New Yorker* magazine. A powerfully penetrating report on the effects of the atomic bombing, it won world-wide attention. Later novels included *The Wall* (1950), which depicted Nazi persecution of Polish Jews.

Tall and quiet in manner, Hersey was one of the most admired journalists of the war era. He was noted for an extraordinary respect for the printed word and for his sense of objectivity and integrity. He was also known for his coolness as a reporter under fire. His books are concerned primarily with the problem of man's inhumanity to man.

Bibliography. See also Hersey's books: *Men on Bataan* (1942); *Into the Valley* (1943); and *The War Lover* (1959).

HERSHEY, LEWIS BLAINE (1893–1977). U.S. Army officer who supervised the draft of millions of Americans in World War II.

Hershey became a key figure as Director of the Selective Service System in the mobilization of the United States against the armies of Germany and Japan. He presided over the induction of millions of soldiers, sailors, marines, and airmen. The system he helped create was built on a foundation of 4,000 local draft boards. In contrast to the universal military service in force in other countries, the boards selected only as many men by a draft lottery as were required by the armed services. Neighbors would decide whose "boy" would go off to war and whose would stay behind.

Although Hershey energetically defended his system as equitable, inevitably it encountered bitterness and charges of inequity. Some young men availed themselves of an elaborate system of deferments and exemptions on educational, occupational, or religious grounds. Others felt they had to bear the burden of the draft because they were poor, uneducated, black, unable to take advantage of the deferments, or otherwise marked for the military.

Tall, bespectacled, energetic and strong-willed, Hershey became a symbol of the draft. In the later stage of his career, he was one of the most hated men in the country by antiwar demonstrators, who denounced him as senile and autocratic. He was philosophical about criticism: "There isn't anything new about cussedness. I've seen quite a bit of this over the years." To the last he defended his draft system as the fairest version he could find. "For every boy who deserted or fled to avoid the draft, somebody else's boy had to go."

HESS, (WALTER RICHARD) RUDOLF (1894–   ). German National Socialist politician, deputy to Hitler, and in theory the *Fuhrer*'s successor after Hermann Goering (*q.v.*).

After the war began, Hess was gradually relegated into the background. To win back the attention of his worshipped *Fuehrer*, Hess in May 1941 flew alone to Scotland with personal proposals for a compromise peace with Britain. The flight, which astonished the world, was dismissed by Hitler as the act of a madman. (*See* HESS FLIGHT.) Hess was interned in Britain for the remainder of the war.

NUREMBERG. Brought before the International Military Tribunal in 1946 (*see* NUREMBERG TRIALS), Hess remained in a state of total or feigned amnesia throughout the trial. The tribunal found him guilty on two counts: conspiracy to commit crimes alleged in other courts, and crimes against peace.

He was sentenced to life imprisonment at Spandau. He was the last of the top two dozen Nazis judged at Nuremberg to remain in prison. The Russians insisted that his life sentence meant exactly that.

Bibliography. R. Manvell and H. Fraenkel, *Hess: A Biography* (1971); J. B. Hutton, *Hess: The Man and His Mission* (1970); and E. K. Bird, *Loneliest Man in the World* (1974).

HESS FLIGHT. Journey by plane to Scotland in 1941 by Rudolf Hess, deputy to Hitler, in a personal effort to win British collaboration against the Russians.

BACKGROUND. During the first year of the war, Hess believed he was being pushed into the background away from his beloved *Fuehrer.* Knowing of Hitler's plans for invasion of the Soviet Union, he decided to regain his patron's attention by a magnificent act of sacrifice. It was a tragedy, he believed, for Germans and British, "Aryan blood brothers," to fight one another. He would fly alone to the British Isles, be received as an important man in the Nazi hierarchy, and win British assistance in the coming war with the Bolshevik menace.

PREPARATION. Hess prepared himself thoroughly for his flight. Hitler had forbidden him to fly, but he induced Willi Messerschmitt (*q.v.*), the aircraft designer, to give him facilities for long-distance flying training. He learned navigation. His goal was the estate in Scotland of the Duke of Hamilton, whom he had met at the Berlin Olympic Games in 1936.

DEPARTURE. On May 10, 1941, Hess took off from Augsburg in an unarmed plane. Dressed as a *Luftwaffe* (*q.v.*) pilot, he carried a map on which he had pencilled his course. He reached his destination and bailed out over a Scottish farm to be taken prisoner by a farmer with a pitchfork. He had expected VIP treatment as a German stateman. Instead, high British officials declined to talk to him. To an officer of the Foreign Office he gave his message: If only the British would halt hostilities, they could join the German crusade against Bolshevism. Unfortunately, he said, Hitler would not negotiate with Churchill, and it would be best if the British Prime Minister resigned.

AFTERMATH. Churchill ordered that Hess be treated with dignity, as if he were an important general who had fallen by accident into British hands. From Germany came angry cries of disbelief and disavowal. Propaganda Minister Paul Joseph Goebbels (*q.v.*) informed the world press that Hess was insane and living "in a state of hallucination." The prisoner was eventually moved to the Tower of London, where he was held until October 6, 1945, the day of his transfer to a cell in Nuremberg. Later he was moved to Spandau, where he became a lone and final prisoner.

Bibliography. J. Leasor, *Rudolf Hess, The Uninvited Envoy* (1962); J. B. Hutton, *Hess: The Man and His Mission* (1970); and J. Douglas-Hamilton, *Motive for a Mission: The Story Behind Hess' Flight to Britain* (1971).

HEYDRICH, REINHARD (1904–1942). Main Nazi agent in the genocide campaign against the Jews.

Head of the Reich Security Service, Deputy Reich Protector of Bohemia and Moravia, administrator of concentration camps (*q.v.*), and specialist in Nazi terror, Heydrich was regarded in inner Nazi circles as a possible successor to Hitler. On January 20, 1942, in the midst of the war, he was chosen to administer the "Final Solution" (*q.v.*) of the Jewish question. His pacification measures in Czechoslovakia, carried out with extreme brutality, led to widespread resistance. Young men of the Czech Resistance, dropped by parachute in the vicinity of Prague, waited for Heydrich's automobile at the edge of the city, and threw a bomb which exploded under the vehicle. Heydrich was critically wounded and died a week later. An enraged Hitler, angered by his loss of "the man with an iron heart," saw to it that 860 Czechs were condemned to death at Prague and 395 at Brno. The entire village Lidice (*q.v.*) was obliterated and its inhabitants executed or scattered on the charge that they had harbored the assassins. A new intensified campaign against the Jews followed.

In his cold sadism, amorality, and greed for power, Heydrich ranks with the worst criminals of history. Cynical, brutal, suspicious, he trusted no one. Contemptuous of human life, he had no compassion, no sense of pity or decency. At the core of his character was a gnawing suspicion that his own body was tainted by Jewish blood. (*See also* WANNSEE CONFERENCE.)

HIMMLER, HEINRICH (1900–1945). National Socialist leader and ruthless practitioner of Nazi terror.

At the outbreak of war, Hitler made Himmler Reich Commissar for the Consolidation of German Nationhood. In this post he devised methods of mass murder based on a rationalized extermination process. He was responsible for the elimination of all "racial misfits," fifth columnists, and enemies of the Reich. He controlled the political administration of occupied territory. As Minister of the Interior in 1943, he strengthened his grip on the civil service and the courts. He organized a supply of expendable labor and enlarged the extermination camps. By mid-1944 he was a highly influential man in Germany, more powerful even than Goering, the No. 2 Nazi. On July 21, 1944, he was named Supreme Commander of the People's Army.

By early 1945, as the Russians closed in on Berlin, Himmler began to think in terms of his personal safety. His attempt to approach the Allies through a Swedish intermediary brought down Hitler's wrath on him. Infuriated by the news, Hitler ordered Himmler's arrest. In late May 1945 Himmler was captured by British troops near Bremen. In May 23, while being examined by doctors, he bit into a vial of cyanide and died almost instantly.

Bibliography. G. H. Combs, *Nazi Spider Man* (1942); W. Frischauer, *Himmler: The Evil Genius of the Third Reich* (1952); R. Manvell and H. Fraenkel, *Heinrich Himmler* (1965); and A. Wykes, *Himmler* (1972).

HIMMLER, OPERATION. Faked attack on the Gleiwitz radio station, the incident that provided the excuse to attack Poland. (*See* GLEIWITZ RAID.)

HIROHITO. 124th Emperor of Japan who served throughout the war.

Although Hirohito was known as Supreme Commander of the Japanese Army and Navy, with the power to declare war, determine the organization of the military, initiate and suspend legislation, and suspend the constitution, during the war, Japan was not ruled by him but in his name. Premier Gen. Hideki Tojo and the Japanese war party made all the pertinent decisions in the Emperor's name. Hirohito was a correct and conventional ruler, signing what he was expected to sign. His influence on the course of the war was negligible.
Bibliography. L. Mosley, *Hirohito, Emperor of Japan* (1966).

HIROSHIMA. Japanese city destroyed by the first atomic bomb in history. The bombing led to the unconditional surrender of Japan.

BACKGROUND. When scientist Albert Einstein sent his letter to President Roosevelt on August 2, 1939, pointing to the possibility of producing an atomic bomb, he stated that German scientists, like their American counterparts, were working with uranium. In the ensuing race to produce an atomic bomb, the Americans were successful. (*See* MANHATTAN PROJECT.)

Soon after Roosevelt's death in April 1945 Secretary of War Henry Stimson (*q.v.*) urged the new President, Harry S Truman, to appoint a committee on atomic policy. The committee recommended to the White House that the bomb be dropped on Japan as soon as possible. Truman had already come to the same conclusion independently. The President regarded the bomb as a military weapon that had to be used, and he ignored any moral questions raised by its use. Gens. George Marshall and Leslie Groves (*qq.v.*) advised him that Japan would not surrender and that the weapon be used especially after the negative response of the Japanese to the Potsdam Declaration. (*See* POTSDAM CONFERENCE.)

To achieve a maximum effect it was decided to use the atomic weapon over a city that had until then been untouched by bombing. Eventually, the list of primary targets narrowed down to one—the urban industrial area of Hiroshima.

THE BOMB. The U-235 bomb, known as "Little Boy," was about 14 feet long and 5 feet in diameter, weighing just under 10,000 pounds. The fissionable core, under .5 percent of this weight, was set in the interior. When the falling missile reached the altitude of 1,850 feet, its fuse would detonate an explosive charge that would thrust forward a small piece of U-235 at a speed of 5,000 feet a second until it collided with a larger piece of U-235 in the nose. The atomic explosion would occur at that instant.

PLANE CREW. A specialized unit of seven *Superfortresses B-29,* (*q.v.*) known as the 509th Composite Group, with pilots and crews ready, waited at Tinian in the Marianas for the order to strike. The pilot selected to carry the lethal charge was Col. Paul W. Tibbets, Jr., Captain of the *Enola Gay.* Only three of the crew were aware of the nature of the mission; the rest knew little beyond the fact that they were on a highly special flight.

STRIKE. At 2:45 A.M. on Monday, August 6, 1945, Tibbets's heavily loaded plane rolled down the coral runway. It was followed at two-minute intervals by three other *B-29s,* one to measure the blast and radiation, one to take photographs, and a third to transfer the bomb at Iwo Jima in the event that the *Enola Gay* developed trouble.

Everything seemed to be normal in Hiroshima. On the signal of an air-raid warning the people hurrying to work rushed to the safety of shelters. From the bomb bay of the *Enola Gay,* a large black object hurtled toward the earth. Suddenly, a piercing blind light, bright as the sun, burst over the city. There was an instant of deadly silence. Then an earth-shaking shock, crumbling everything in its range to rubble and dust as it thundered down violently over the center of the city.

Pilot Tibbets reported: "When the shock wave hit, the plane was in a bank. We were close enough to watch the cloud boil. It turned many different colors—orange and blue and gray. It was like looking over a tar barrel boiling."

DESTRUCTION. The violent blast crushed trees and telephones poles as if they were toothpicks, ripped sheets of metal from buildings, and lifted street cars from their tracks. When the great rolling cloud of dust and smoke, spiraling upward to form a long-necked mushroom, had lifted, the center of the city of 343,000 was flattened. Major industrial targets were obliterated. Hiroshima had become a trash heap.

Large drops of water the size of marbles began to fall; these were drops of condensed moisture spilling from the tower of dust, heat, and fision fragments. Streets were littered with fire-blackened parts of shattered houses. Sheets of flame whipped through the city. Panicky people fled in every direction. The eyebrows of some were burned off and skin hung loosely from their faces and hands. Others, in uncontrollable pain, held their arms forward as if they were carrying something. Some vomited as they staggered along. Throughout the area of impact was a strong odor of ionization, an electric smell given off by the bomb's fission.

CASUALTIES. About 68,000 people were killed outright, 10,000 missing were never found, and 37,000 were injured. These figures exclude those who later developed disease from exposure to the deadly gamma rays.

REACTION. President Truman reported the strike as "an overwhelming success," and added: "Let there be no mistake: we shall destroy completely Japan's power to make war." Churchill issued a statement saying that it was "by God's mercy" that American and British scientists, instead of German, had discovered the secret of atomic power. Stunned Japanese angrily denounced the attack as "inhumane, barbaric, and bestial. This diabolical weapon brands the United States for ages to come as a destroyer of peace and of mankind." The Japanese High Command ignored an ultimatum to surrender.

AFTERMATH. The use of the atomic bomb touched off a world-wide debate as to justification for its use. Those responsible for use of the weapon claimed that millions of both American and Japanese lives were saved by utilizing this "ultimate weapon." It was also, they said, a fitting response to Pearl Harbor (*q.v.*). Others were appalled and saddened by the use of this superhuman fireball of destruction. Still others denounced the attack in bitter terms as a ghastly mistake.

In Hiroshima a gutted section of the city was set aside as a "Peace City" to illustrate the effects of the atomic bomb. Since 1955 a world conference against nuclear weapons has been held at Hiroshima annually.

Bibliography. J. Hersey, *Hiroshima;* (1946); M. Kato, *The Lost War* (1946); R. Jungk, *Brighter Than a Thousand Suns* (1958); F. Knebel and C. W. Bailey II, *No High Ground* (1960); R. C. Bachelder, *The Irreversible Decision* (1962); and L. Giovannitti and F. Freed, *The Decision to Drop the Bomb* (1965).

HITLER, ADOLF (1889–1945).

Fuehrer ("Leader") and Chancellor of Nazi Germany. He was born in Braunau, on the Inn River between Germany and Austria, on April 20, 1889, the son of an Austrian customs official. He was educated in public schools at Fischlham and Leonding. He left the high school for science at Linz before being graduated.

EARLY CAREER. For two years, from age 16 to 18, young Hitler remained at home, spending hours in the public library reading German history and mythology. In October 1907 he went to Vienna, where he was refused admission to the Academy of Fine Arts, a blow to his pride from which he never recovered. For the next five years he lived on charity and the occasional sale of sketches. In Vienna he was influenced by the anti-Semitic and anti-Marxist milieu of the cafes. He found some relief in dreams of a great and glorious Germany that would take over from the weak Habsburg monarchy. Depressed and embittered, he left Vienna in May 1913 for Munich, a German city.

WORLD WAR I. Rejected in Austria as "unfit to bear arms," Hitler was accepted in 1914 by the 16th Bavarian Infantry (List Regiment) and served ably and courageously for four years, taking part in 47 battles and winning the Iron Cross (First and Second Classes). The war had a profound influence on him. It gave him a purpose in life and he learned about violence and its use.

RISE TO POLITICAL POWER. Returning to Munich, Hitler gave himself wholeheartedly to politics. He became member No. 7 of the German Workers' Party and soon transformed it into the National Socialist German Workers' Party, with himself as sole and unchallenged head. Convinced that the Weimar Republic was on the verge of collapse, he led an abortive Beer Hall *Putsch* on November 8–9, 1923, for which he was imprisoned at Landsberg am Lech. In prison he wrote the first volume of *Mein Kampf (q.v.),* his autobiography, which was to become the bible of the Nazi movement.

After the temporary collapse of the Nazi Party, Hitler helped rebuild it. A combination of insight into mass psychology and willingness to work with the conservative right eventually brought Hitler to the chancellorship on January 30, 1933.

THE THIRD REICH. In power Hitler used his mastery of Machiavellian tactics to consolidate his dictatorship. He turned to brutality to consolidate Nazi rule. He murdered or incarcerated opponents. He harried Jews and Communists, and deprived them of rights and of life. Pursuing expansionist and racist aims, he took supreme military command for himself and prepared the way for war. Many doubters were converted by his bold diplomat coups, beginning with German rearmament and culminating in the triumph of the Munich Agreement *(q.v.).* He bullied smaller nations and claimed that he was only trying to rectify the shame of Versailles. His tactics led straight to the outbreak of war. (*See* CAUSES OF WORLD WAR II.)

WORLD WAR II. In 1939 Hitler's life and career merged with the cascading events of World War II. He donned his soldier's tunic and announced that he would not change it until Germany was triumphant. For the first period of the war he was enormously successful with a sequence of *Blitzkriegs (q.v.)* against Poland, Belgium, the Netherlands, and France. His attempt to subjugate Britain by aerial bombardment was unsuccessful. (*See* BRITAIN, BATTLE OF.) He sent his *Afrika Korps (q.v.)* hurtling toward Egypt.

On June 22, 1941, Hitler turned on the Soviet Union, and from that day his fortunes began to decline. Unwilling to concede defeat, he ordered the mobilization of the German economy in an effort to extricate himself. He was not successsful—one crisis after another came to plague him. With the entry of the United States into the war his fate was sealed. He had overextended himself in Europe and found himself unable to maintain his New Order *(q.v.)* in the face of increasing resistance everywhere. Although the war was hopelessly lost by early 1945, Hitler insisted that the Germans fight on to death. On April 30, 1945, he committed suicide in his underground bunker at the chancellery in Berlin.

PERSONALITY AND CHARACTER. The personality and character of Hitler have been of such fascination to historians that literally hundreds of books have been written to throw light on one of the most extraordinary individuals of modern times. Emotionally frozen, he understood little of human kindness and decency. He indifferently sacrificed millions of victims to his naked lust for power. He was short, with an unruly hair lock, a puffy face, staring eyes, and a distinctive mustache; his personality was moody and indecisive. Although his education was erratic, he pretended to intellectual and cultural accomplishments. While not insane in the clinical sense, he had a paranoid fear of plots and persecutions.

The British historian Hugh R. Trevor-Roper caught the essence of Hitler's character in a remarkable sentence: "A terrible phenomenon, imposing indeed in its granite harshness' and yet infinitely squalid in its miscellaneous cumber—like some huge barbarian monolith, the expression of giant strength and savage genius, surrounded by a festering heap of refuse—old tins and dead vermin, ashes and eggshells and ordure—the intellectual detritus of centuries."*

SIGNIFICANCE. Hitler wielded enormous power. His ideas were old and shopworn, but his methods took on the trappings of modern technology. As a military leader he was a poor strategist: He operated under the principle of "Never retreat"—a foolish attitude in modern warfare. In the eyes of the world he became the incarnation of evil. A complex concatenation of circumstances elevated him from the soapbox to the seat of power in Germany. It took a coalition of powers to strike him down in the crucible of World War II.

Bibliography. The bibliography on Hitler is enormous and increasing steadily. Among the best works are H. R. Trevor-Roper, *The Last Days of Hitler* (1947); K. Heiden, *Der Fuehrer* (1948); A. Bullock, *A Study in Tyranny* (1953); W. L. Shirer, *The Rise and Fall of the Third Reich* (1960); J. C. Fest, *Hitler* (1974); J. Toland, *Hitler* (1977); and R.G.L. Waite, *The Psychopathic God: Adolf Hitler* (1977). D. Irving, *Hitler's War* (1977) presented the revisionist theory that Hitler knew little or nothing of the Final Solution (*q.v.*), a thesis rejected by most historians.

HITLER-STALIN PACT. Agreement between Germany and Soviet Russia signed on August 23, 1939, which opened the way to World War II. (*See* RUSSO-GERMAN NONAGGRESSION PACT.)

HO CHI MINH (1890?–1969). Leader of the national rebels in Southeast Asia against the Japanese.

When the Japanese occupied much of Southeast Asia after the outbreak of World War II Ho Chi Minh went to South China. There he organized Indo-Chinese Socialist and Nationalist exiles into the League for Independence of Vietnam, which came to be known as the Viet Minh. To assure national unity he temporarily dissolved the Vietnam Communist Party.

After the Japanese attacked Pearl Harbor (*q.v.*), Ho returned to Vietnam for

---

*From the introduction of H. R. Trevor-Roper in *Hitler's Secret Conversations* (1953), p. xxix.

the first time in three decades. He organized guerrilla units into combat units and led them against the Japanese occupying forces in his country. During the later phase of the war, he worked closely with the Allies, especially the United States, and his guerrillas rescued downed American flyers. He worked closely with the U.S. Office of Strategic Services (OSS), in return for which his liberation army received needed supplies. On August 19, 1945, his forces marched into Hanoi, driving out the Japanese and their puppet Emperor, Bao Dai.

Bibliography. A four-volume collection of Ho's writings was published in Hanoi in 1960–1962. See also B. B. Fall, *The Two Viet-Nams* (1963); and J. Cameron, *Here Is Your Enemy* (1966).

HODGES, COURTNEY HICKS (1887–1966). U.S. Army officer.

After the United States entered the war, Hodges was appointed Commanding General of the U.S. 10th Army Corps. During the preparations for *Operation Overlord* (*q.v.*), he commanded the U.S. 1st Army in England. On June 6, 1944, D-Day (*q.v.*), Hodges ranked immediately below Gen. Omar N. Bradley (*q.v.*). In the advance through Europe, Hodges's 1st Army formed the left flank of Bradley's 12th Army Group. Hodges's troops crossed the Seine to Liège, liberated Luxembourg, and captured Aachen. They took part in the Battle of the Bulge (*q.v.*) and later captured the vital Remagen Bridge (*q.v.*) across the Rhine. The 1st Army played an important role in the encirclement of the Ruhr.

After the liberation of Europe, Hodges was detailed to the Pacific area, where he took part in the battle for Okinawa.

A slender, somewhat shy man of medium height, Hodges was considered one of the army's ablest combat technicians. He was noted for his ability to handle troops in difficult situations. Far more reserved than many of his fellow officers, he surpassed them in achievements.

Bibliography. See F. C. Pogue, *The United States Army in World War II: The European Theater of Operations* (1960).

HOEPNER, ERICH (1886–1944). Germany Army officer and tank specialist.

Hoepner served in all *Blitzkrieg* (*q.v.*) campaigns as a *Panzer* (*q.v.*) or tank specialist. In 1941 he led the 4th Armored Group in the attack on the Soviet Union. Although his men came within sight of Moscow, they were unable to take the city. He urged Hitler to permit a temporary withdrawal, a request that so angered the *Fuehrer* that he ordered Hoepner's dismissal. Hitler's order of the day referred brusquely to "the *former* Colonel-General Hoepner."

Hoepner was an active member in the plot against Hitler. He was delegated to succeed Gen. Friedrich Fromm (*q.v.*) as Commander-in-Chief of the Reserve Army and to take over control of the entire armed forces after the elimination of Hitler. After the unsuccessful 1944 July Plot (*q.v.*) against Hitler, Hoepner was arrested and tried for treason before the People's Court. He was executed in

Berlin on August 8, 1944, under especially brutal circumstances. He was strangled slowly while hanging from a loop of piano wire on a meat hook.

Proud and defiant, Hoepner was an able combat leader who regarded Hitler and Nazism as a catastrophe for his country. When offered a pistol for a ceremonial suicide, he replied: "I am not a swine that I should have to condemn myself."

Bibliography. See R. Manvell and H. Fraenkel, *The July Plot* (1966).

HOESS, RUDOLF FRANZ (1900–1947). Nazi extermination camp commander.

In 1914, while not yet 15, Hoess managed to join the German Army. He was sent to the Turkish front, where he was wounded and won several decorations. In the postwar era he joined the Free Corps, a free-booting unit composed of veterans. In 1923 he was arrested for complicity in the murder of a teacher who had insulted the memory of Albert Leo Schlageter, who was to become a Nazi hero because of his opposition to French occupation of the Rhineland. Hoess served five years in prison and was released in 1928 under a general amnesty. A member of the SS (*q.v.*) he served as a corporal at Dachau and an adjutant at Sachsenhausen. He used this concentration camp training later to his own advantage.

In 1940 Hoess was assigned command of Auschwitz, one of the first extermination camps. Under his supervision more than 2.5 million inmates were executed, not counting a half million more who literally starved to death. A 1944 SS report commended him as "a true pioneer in this area because of his new ideas and educational methods." His new ideas and educational methods included the gassing of victims. By the end of the war he was made deputy to Gen. Richard Gluecke, head of the inspectorate of concentration camps.

Bibliography. Hoess told his own story in the posthumous *Commandant at Auschwitz* (1961).

HOLLANDIA. *See* NEW GUINEA, CAMPAIGNS IN.

HOLOCAUST. Hitler's destruction of 6,000,000 Jews during World War II. (*See* FINAL SOLUTION.)

HOME FRONTS. *See* BRITAIN AT WAR; FRANCE IN WARTIME; GERMANY AT WAR; JAPAN AT WAR; RUSSIA AT WAR; and UNITED STATES AT WAR.

HOMING TORPEDO. New German weapon introduced in mid-1943.

The homing torpedo was acoustically guided to ships' propellers. The device did not help much. In September and October 1942, when Adm. Karl Doenitz (*q.v.*) renewed his U-Boat campaign, only nine Allied merchant ships were destroyed in 64 North Atlantic convoys, while 25 U-Boats were sunk. (*See* ATLANTIC, BATTLE OF THE.)

HOMMA, MASAHARU (1888–1946). Japanese General who led the surprise attack on Luzon in the Philippines on December 10, 1941.

Homma forced the American-Filipino troops into the Bataan Peninsula, where they were forced to surrender in April 1942. (*See* BATAAN, BATTLE OF.) Unprepared for the massive surrender, Homma did little to relieve the conditions of the infamous Death March. Defeated in his early assaults on Bataan, he was relieved of his command.

In September 1945 Homma was arrested by American forces in Tokyo, taken to Manila, and tried as a war criminal. He was accused of responsibility for the Bataan Death March as well as other atrocities. He was executed by firing squad in April 1946. (*See* JAPANESE WAR CRIMINALS TRIAL.)

HONG KONG, FALL OF. Capture by the Japanese of the British colonial dependency on December 26, 1941.

TARGET. Hong Kong, the name derived from *Hiang-Kaing* ("Fragrant Harbor") is in the China Sea, separated from the coast of mainland China by a strait less than ½ mile in width. The island rises steeply to the north shore in a range of treeless hills of volcanic rock. It was strategically important because, together with Manila and Singapore, it formed a triangle of British power at the gateway to South China.

BACKGROUND. Because of the mountainous nature of the colony, the British optimistically believed that it could successfully resist any siege. They strengthened its defenses with a garrison of 12,000 men, including two Canadian battalions deployed there in 1941 before Pearl Harbor.

For the Japanese Imperial Command the seizure of Hong Kong was merely one of a number of targets to be taken by a rapid attack—like an exploding skyrocket. In addition to Pearl Harbor, the targets included simultaneous attacks on Guam, Midway, Wake Island, the Philippines, Kota Bahru in Malaya, and Singapore. Later attacks would be made in the South Pacific to win the oil of the Dutch East Indies.

ASSAULT. On December 8, 1941, a well-armed Japanese force more than a division strong (12 battalions), with air cover and artillery support, opened an attack from the mainland. The British fell back to the Kowloon Peninsula. Under hammer-like blows of the Japanese, the British withdrew to Hong Kong Island. Mark Young, the Governor of Hong Kong, declined the Japanese demand for surrender.

On the night of December 18, 1941, a Japanese force landed on the northeast corner of the island to meet a spirited British defense. Later that day they captured Victoria City as well as most of the island, which they now split in half. With 20,000 troops on the island and undisputed control of the air, the Japanese were on the verge of success.

SURRENDER. The critical factor for Hong Kong was shortage of water, for the Japanese controlled all possible sources. After a stand of 18 days, the garrison of 12,000 surrendered on Christmas Day, 1941. The Japanese suffered 3,000 casualties.

SIGNIFICANCE. The fall of Hong Kong ended a century of British rule. The small garrison had made a desperate defense against great odds, but it was unable to resist overwhelming Japanese power. Tokyo was well on its way to complete control of the Western Pacific.

AFTERMATH. Hong Kong remained in Japanese hands for 3½ years. During that time there was passive resistance in the colony and guerrilla activity in the surrounding area, all stimulated by the Allies. The Japanese authorities used severe punitive measures, but were never quite able to smother the Resistance movement. Hong Kong was liberated by units of the British Fleet on August 30, 1945.

Bibliography. On the fall of Hong Kong, *see* B. H. Liddell Hart, *History of the Second World War* (1971), pp. 219–221.

HOOD. British battle cruiser sunk by the Germans in 1941.

DESIGN. Constructed between May 1916 and March 1920, HMS *Hood,* for more than half the dreadnought era, was the largest warship in the world. Although her great size and beautiful lines gained her much attention, her deck armor was insufficient, and she was vulnerable to long-range fire. Her machinery was in an unsatisfactory state. She was due for modernization when she was called into action, even though the Director of Naval Construction warned that she was not fit for service.

SPECIFICATIONS.
   Standard Displacement. 42,100 tons.
   Maximum Speed. 31 knots.
   Armor. Belt 12 in.; turret 15 in.
   Armament. Eight 15 in. guns; twelve 5.5 in.; and four 4-in. antiaircraft.
   Complement. 1,419 officers and men on final voyage.

WORLD WAR II. The *Hood* served with Force H under Adm. James Somerville (*q.v.*) on July 3, 1940, when it opened fire on the French fleet in North Africa. (*See* ORAN NAVAL ENCOUNTER.) On May 24, 1941, she led the new battleship *Prince of Wales* into action against the German battleship *Bismarck* and the heavy cruiser *Prinz Eugen* just off the Denmark Strait. At the start of the action a shell from the *Bismarck* struck the *Hood* and apparently penetrated into her after-magazine. Split into two, with her back broken, the great warship sank in three minutes, taking with her all her officers and men with the exception of three survivors. (*See also* BISMARCK, SINKING OF THE.)

SIGNIFICANCE. Loss of the *Hood* was a shock to the British people. Churchill later spoke of it as a national calamity.

Bibliography. E. P. Van der Porten, *The German Navy in World War II* (1969).

HOOVER, J. EDGAR (1895-1972).

Head of the Federal Bureau of Investigation (FBI) before, during, and after the war.

In 1936 Hoover was designated by President Franklin D. Roosevelt to investigate sabotage and espionage. After Pearl Harbor his work was expanded to surveillance over Nazi infiltrators, the Communist Party in the United States, and civil rights groups.

HOPE, BOB (1903-   ).

The most popular American entertainer of the war.

In his film *Caught in the Draft* (1941), Hope convulsed audiences with his antics. After Pearl Harbor (*q.v.*) he was recruited as a morale-builder. With a troupe of entertainers he performed at bases around the world. His activity was unprecedented in scope, extraordinary in results. "It is impossible to see," said John Steinbeck, "how he can do so much, can cover so much ground, and can be so effective."

A genial comedian, with gimlet-like eyes and a ski slide nose, Hope had an uncanny ability to produce laughter with his one-liners deliverd with split-second timing. His popularity continued in the postwar era.

Bibliography. Hope's autobiography, *I Never Left Home* (1944) recounted how he and the GIs (*q.v.*) reacted to one another.

HOPKINS, HARRY LLOYD (1890-1946).

U.S. social reformer and adviser to Roosevelt.

Throughout the war Hopkins served as Roosevelt's personal liaison with governments overseas, making several trips to London and Moscow and arranging the war conferences at Casablanca, Cairo, Teheran, and Yalta (*qq.v.*). He was made head of the Lend-Lease Program (*q.v.*) in 1941 and negotiated with both Churchill and Stalin on supplying American armaments and munitions. He regularly attended sessions of the U.S. Joint Chiefs of Staff and in 1942 was made a member of the War Production Board.

Although his health deteriorated badly, Hopkins worked informally for the rest of the war from his post at the White House. He went to Moscow in the spring of 1945 to help arrange the Potsdam Conference (*q.v.*). After Roosevelt's death on April 12, 1945, the new President, Harry S Truman (*q.v.*), sent Hopkins to Moscow to confer with Stalin on the alarming conflicts in policy between the American and Russian delegates to the United Nations.

Bibliography. The best account of Hopkins's activities during the war years was written by Robert E. Sherwood, *Roosevelt and Hopkins* (1948). *See also* Sherwood's *The White House Papers of Harry L. Hopkins* (1948-1949).

HORE-BELISHA, LESLIE (1893–1957). British statesman.

As Minister of Transport from 1934 to 1937, Hore-Belisha installed the famous "Belisha Beacon," a yellow globe on a black and white post to mark pedestrian crossings. For this he was dubbed "the Archbeacon." In 1937, as Secretary of State for War, he introduced radical reforms "to democratize the Army." His campaign of military reform aroused such opposition that Prime Minister Neville Chamberlain (*q.v.*) reluctantly decided to remove him in January 1940. Hore-Belisha did not again hold office during the war. He, nevertheless, worked zealously to infuse a greater vigor into prosecution of the war.

A bachelor of flamboyant tastes, Hore-Belisha aroused conflicting estimates. Supporters called him "a second Disraeli" and praised him for his energy and imagination. Detractors denounced him as a publicity hound, too "foreign" to understand English traditions.

Bibliography. R. J. Minney, *The Private Papers of Hore-Belisha* (1960).

HORROCKS, BRIAN GWYNNE (1895–   ). British Army officer.

In the summer of 1941 Horrocks was promoted to Major General and sent to North Africa. Here he won a reputation in the defense of Egypt and the victory at El Alamein (*q.v.*). He was one of the key British officers who pitted their wits and tank-fighting genius against German Gen. Erwin Rommel (*q.v.*). After the Normandy invasion (*q.v.*) in June 1944, he commanded the British 3rd Army and led it in a dash from the Seine through Amiens to take Brussels and Antwerp, a distance of more than 200 miles covered in less than a week. The failure to hold Arnhem (*q.v.*) was not considered the fault of Horrock's ground forces but rather beyond his control. (*See* ARNHEM, BATTLE OF.)

Six-feet tall, slim, with blue eyes and hawk-like nose, Horrocks was known for his cool courage. He never wore a helmet even when under heavy shellfire. He was regarded as one of the best corps commanders in the British Army in World War II.

HORTHY DE NAGYBANYA, MIKLŎS (1868–1957). Hungarian Admiral and Regent of Hungary during most of World War II.

On the eve of war Hitler won over the reluctant Horthy by gifts of territory taken from Czechoslovakia and Rumania. Horthy brought Hungary into the Axis alliance and sent troops to fight with the Germans on the eastern front. In secret, however, he negotiated with the Allies to extract his country from the Axis alliance. In October 1944 he broadcast a plea to the Allies for an armistice. Hitler forced him to resign as regent and deported him to Austria. He was freed by American troops in May 1945.

Horthy carried himself as straight as a sentry. Recognizable by his thick black hair, he wore an admiral's uniform in a country that had no navy and was head of a kingdom which had no king. An important pawn in Hitler's plans for Europe, he found himself in an impossible position in trying to avoid war. It was said that he was the only head of a foreign country for whom Hitler had any respect.

Bibliography. M. Horthy, *Memoirs* (1957). *See also* P. Owen, *Regent of Hungary* (1939); and R. Forbes, *These Men I Know* (1940).

HOSSBACH PROTOCOL (HOSSBACH MEMORANDUM). Memorandum that revealed Hitler's intention of waging war almost two years before the outbreak of World War II. Most historians consider it a key document on responsibility for the war.

At a secret meeting of his top military advisers, held on November 5, 1937, Hitler outlined the steps he had in mind for undermining the territorial provisions of the Treaty of Versailles. Minutes of the meeting were recorded and five days later compiled from his notes by Col. Friedrich Hossbach, Hitler's *Wehrmacht* adjutant. Dated November 10, 1937, the memorandum was introduced in evidence before the International Military Tribunal at Nuremberg on November 24, 1945. (*See* NUREMBERG TRIALS.)

British revisionist historian A.J.P. Taylor claimed that it was historically inaccurate to attribute responsibility for the immediate outbreak of the war to Hitler, who, in Taylor's estimate, was a blunderer who was pressed into aggression by outsiders under circumstances utterly beyond his control. Taylor deprecated the importance of the Hossbach Conference and argued that this was merely an occasion on which Hitler dissimulated to confuse his opponents. Few scholars accept Taylor's interpretation on the origins of World War II.

Following is the complete text of the Hossbach protocol.* The reader can judge for himself the significance of this document.

Berlin, November 10, 1937

MINUTES OF THE CONFERENCE IN THE REICH CHANCELLERY, BERLIN, NOVEMBER 5, 1937, FROM 4:15 TO 8:30 P.M.

Present: The Führer and Chancellor,
Field Marshal von Blomberg, War Minister,
Colonel General Baron von Fritsch, Commander in Chief, Army.
Admiral Dr. h.c. Raeder, Commander in Chief, Navy,
Colonel General Göring, Commander in Chief, *Luftwaffe,*
Baron von Neurath, Foreign Minister,
Colonel Hossbach.

The Führer began by stating that the subject of the present conference was of such importance that its discussion would, in other countries, certainly be a matter for a full Cabinet meeting, but he—the Führer—had rejected the idea of making it a subject of discussion before the wider circle of the Reich Cabinet just because of the importance of the matter. His exposition to follow was the fruit of thorough deliberation and the ex-

---

*Germany, Auswärtiges Amt, *Documents on German Foreign Policy,* Series D, Government Printing Office, Washington, 1949, vol. 1, pp. 29–39.

periences of his 4½ years of power. He wished to explain to the gentlemen present his basic ideas concerning the opportunities for the development of our position in the field of foreign affairs and its requirements, and he asked, in the interests of a long-term German policy, that his exposition be regarded, in the event of his death, as his last will and testament.

The Führer then continued:

The aim of German policy was to make secure and to preserve the racial community [*Volksmasse*] and to enlarge it. It was therefore a question of space.

The German racial community comprised over 85 million people and, because of their number and the narrow limits of habitable space in Europe, constituted a tightly packed racial core such as was not to be met in any other country and such as implied the right to a greater living space than in the case of other peoples. If, territorially speaking, there existed no political result corresponding to this German racial core, that was a consequence of centuries of historical development, and in the continuance of these political conditions lay the greatest danger to the preservation of the German race at its present peak. To arrest the decline of Germanism [*Deutschtum*] in Austria and Czechoslovakia was as little possible as to maintain the present level in Germany itself. Instead of increase, sterility was setting in, and in its train disorders of a social character must arise in course of time, since political and ideological ideas remain effective only so long as they furnish the basis for the realization of the essential vital demands of a people. Germany's future was therefore wholly conditional upon the solving of the need for space, and such a solution could be sought, of course, only for a foreseeable period of about one to three generations.

Before turning to the question of solving the need for space, it had to be considered whether a solution holding promise for the future was to be reached by means of autarchy or by means of an increased participation in world economy.

Autarky

Achievement only possible under strict National Socialist leadership of the State, which is assumed; accepting its achievement as possible, the following could be stated as results:—

A. In the field of raw materials only limited, not total, autarky.

(1) In regard to coal, so far as it could be considered as a source of raw materials, autarky was possible.

(2) But even as regards ores, the position was much more difficult. Iron requirements can be met from home resources and similarly with light metals, but with other raw materials—copper, tin—this was not the case.

(3) Synthetic textile requirements can be met from home resources to the limit of timber supplies. A permanent solution is impossible.

(4) Edible fats—possible.

B. In the field of food the question of autarky was to be answered by a flat "No."

With the general rise in the standard of living compared with that of 30 to 40 years ago, there has gone hand in hand an increased demand and an increased home consumption even on the part of the producers, the farmers. The fruits of the increased agricultural production had all gone to meet the increased demand, and so did not represent an absolute production increase. A further increase in production by making greater demands on the soil, which already, in consequence of the use of artificial fertilizers, was showing signs of exhaustion, was hardly possible, and it was therefore certain that even with the maximum increase in production, participation in world trade was unavoidable. The not inconsiderable expenditure of foreign exchange to insure food supplies by imports, even when harvests were good, grew to catastrophic proportions with bad harvests. The possibility of a disaster grew in proportion to the increase in population, in which, too, the excess of births of 560,000 annually produced, as a consequence, an even further increase in bread consumption, since a child was a greater bread consumer than an adult.

It was not possible over the long run, in a continent enjoying a practically common standard of living, to meet the food supply difficulties by lowering that standard and by rationalization. Since, with the solving of the unemployment problem, the maximum consumption level had been reached, some minor modifications in our home agricultural production might still, no doubt, be possible, but no fundamental alteration was possible in our basic food position. Thus autarky was untenable in regard both to food and to the economy as a whole.

Participation in World Economy

To this there were limitations which we were unable to remove. The establishment of Germany's position on a secure and sound foundation was obstructed by market fluctuations, and commercial treaties afforded no guarantee for actual execution. In particular it had to be remembered that since the World War, those very countries which had formerly been food exporters had become industrialized. We were living in an age of economic empires in which the primitive urge to colonization was again manifesting itself; in the cases of Japan and Italy economic motives underlay the urge for expansion, and with Germany, too, economic need would supply the stimulus. For countries outside the great economic empires, opportunities for economic expansion were severely impeded.

The boom in world economy caused by the economic effects of rearmament could never form the basis of a sound economy over a long period, and the latter was obstructed above all also by the economic disturbances resulting from Bolshevism. There was a pronounced military weakness in those states which depended for their existence on foreign trade. As our foreign trade was carried on over the sea routes dominated by Britain, it was more a question of security of transport than one of foreign exchange, which revealed, in time of war, the full weakness of our food situation. The only remedy, and one which might appear to us as visionary, lay in the acquisition of greater living space—a quest which has at all times been the origin of the formation of states and of the migration of peoples. That this quest met with no interest at Geneva or among the satiated nations was understandable. If, then, we accept the security of our food situation as the principal question, the space necessary to insure it can only be sought in Europe, not, as in the liberal-capitalist view, in the exploitation of colonies. It is not a matter of acquiring population but of gaining space for agricultural use. Moreover, areas producing raw materials can be more usefully sought in Europe in immediate proximity to the Reich, than overseas; the solution thus obtained must suffice for one or two generations. Whatever else might prove necessary later must be left to succeeding generations to deal with. The development of great world political constellations progressed but slowly after all, and the German people with its strong racial core would find the most favorable prerequisites for such achievement in the heart of the continent of Europe. The history of all ages—the Roman Empire and the British Empire—had proved that expansion could only be carried out by breaking down resistance and taking risks; setbacks were inevitable. There had never in former times been spaces without a master, and there were none today; the attacker always comes up against a possessor.

The question for Germany ran: where could she achieve the greatest gain at the lowest cost?

German policy had to reckon with two hate-inspired antagonists, Britain and France, to whom a German colossus in the center of Europe was a thorn in the flesh, and both countries were opposed to any further strengthening of Germany's position either in Europe or overseas; in support of this opposition they were able to count on the agreement of all their political parties. Both countries saw in the establishment of German military bases overseas a threat to their own communications, a safeguarding of German commerce, and, as a consequence, a strengthening of Germany's position in Europe.

Because of opposition of the Dominions, Britain could not cede any of her colonial possessions to us. After England's loss of prestige through the passing of Abyssinia into Italian possession, the return of East Africa was not to be expected. British concessions could at best be expressed in an offer to satisfy our colonial demands by the appropriation of colonies which were not British possessions—e.g., Angola. French concessions would probably take a similar line.

Serious discussion of the question of the return of colonies to us could only be considered a moment when Britain was in difficulties and the German Reich armed and strong. The Führer did not share the view that the Empire was unshakable. Opposition to the Empire was to be found less in the countries conquered than among her competitors. The British Empire and the Roman Empire could not be compared in respect of permanence; the latter was not confronted by any powerful political rival of a serious order after the Punic Wars. It was only the disintegrating effect of Christianity, and the symptoms of age which appear in every country, which caused ancient Rome to succumb to the onslaught of the Germans.

Beside the British Empire there exist today a number of states stronger than she. The British motherland was able to protect her colonial possessions not by her own power, but only in alliance with other states. How, for instance, could Britain alone defend Canada against attack by America, or her Far Eastern interests against attack by Japan!

The emphasis on the British Crown as the symbol of the unity of the Empire was already an admission that, in the long run, the Empire could not maintain its position by power politics. Significant indications of this were:

(a) The struggle of Ireland for independence.

(b) The constitutional struggles in India, where Britain's half measures had given to the Indians the opportunity of using later on as a weapon against Britain, the nonfulfillment of her promises regarding a constitution.

(c) The weakening by Japan of Britain's position in the Far East.

(d) The rivalry in the Mediterranean with Italy who—under the spell of her history, driven by necessity and led by a genius—was expanding her power position, and thus was inevitably coming more and more into conflict with British interests. The outcome of the Abyssinian War was a loss of prestige for Britain which Italy was striving to increase by stirring up trouble in the Mohammedan world.

To sum up, it could be stated that, with 45 million Britons, in spite of its theoretical soundness, the position of the Empire could not in the long run be maintained by power politics. The ratio of the population of the Empire to that of the motherland of 9:1, was a warning to us not, in our territorial expansion, to allow the foundation constituted by the numerical strength of our own people to become too weak.

France's position was more favorable than that of Britain. The French Empire was better placed territorially; the inhabitants of her colonial possessions represented a supplement to her military strength. But France was going to be confronted with internal political difficulties. In a nation's life about 10 percent of its span is taken up by parliamentary forms of government and about 90 percent by authoritarian forms. Today, nonetheless, Britain, France, Russia, and the smaller states adjoining them, must be included as factors [*Machtfaktoren*] in our political calculations.

Germany's problem could only be solved by means of force and this was never without attendant risk. The campaigns of Frederick the Great for Silesia and Bismarck's wars against Austria and France had involved unheard-of risk, and the swiftness of the Prussian action in 1870 had kept Austria from entering the war. If one accepts as the basis of the following exposition the resort to force with its attendant risks, then there remain still to be answered the questions "when" and "how." In this matter there were three cases [*Fälle*] to be dealt with:

Case 1: Period 1943–1945

After this date only a change for the worse, from our point of view, could be expected.

The equipment of the army, navy, and *Luftwaffe*, as well as the formation of the officer corps, was nearly completed. Equipment and armament were modern; in further delay there lay the danger of their obsolescence. In particular, the secrecy of "special weapons" could not be preserved forever. The recruiting of reserves was limited to current age groups; further drafts from older untrained age groups were no longer available.

Our relative strength would decrease in relation to the rearmament which would by then have been carried out by the rest of the world. If we did not act by 1943–45, any year could, in consequence of a lack of reserves, produce the food crisis, to cope with which the necessary foreign exchange was not available, and this must be regarded as a "warning point of the regime." Besides, the world was expecting our attack and was increasing its countermeasures from year to year. It was while the rest of the world was still preparing its defenses [*sich abriegeln*] that we were obliged to take the offensive.

Nobody knew today what the situation would be in the years 1943–45. One thing only was certain, that we could not wait longer.

On the one hand there was the great *Wehrmacht*, and the necessity of maintaining it at its present level, the aging of the movement and of its leaders; and on the other, the prospect of a lowering of the standard of living and of a limitation of the birth rate, which left no choice but to act. If the Führer was still living, it was his unalterable resolve to solve Germany's problem of space at the latest by 1943–45. The necessity for action before 1943–45 would arise in cases 2 and 3.

Case 2

If internal strife in France should develop into such a domestic crisis as to absorb the French Army completely and render it incapable of use for war against Germany, then the time for action against the Czechs had come.

Case 3

If France is so embroiled by a war with another state that she cannot "proceed" against Germany.

For the improvement of our politico-military position our first objective, in the event of our being embroiled in war, must be to overthrow Czechoslovakia and Austria simultaneously in order to remove the threat to our flank in any possible operation against the west. In a conflict with France it was hardly to be regarded as likely that the Czechs would declare war on us on the very same day as France. The desire to join in the war would, however, increase among the Czechs in proportion to any weakening on our part and then her participation could clearly take the form of an attack toward Silesia, toward the north or toward the west.

If the Czechs were overthrown and a common German-Hungarian frontier achieved, a neutral attitude on the part of Poland could be the more certainly counted on in the event of a Franco-German conflict. Our agreements with Poland only retained their force as long as Germany's strength remained unshaken. In the event of German set-backs a Polish action against East Prussia, and possibly against Pomerania and Silesia as well, had to be reckoned with.

On the assumption of a development of the situation leading to action on our part as planned, in the years 1943–45, the attitude of France, Britain, Italy, Poland, and Russia could probably be estimated as follows:

Actually, the Führer believed that almost certainly Britain, and probably France as well, had already tacitly written off the Czechs and were reconciled to the fact that this question would be cleared up in due course by Germany. Difficulties connected with the Empire, and the prospect of being once more entangled in a protracted European war, were decisive considerations for Britain against participation in a war against Germany. Britain's attitude would certainly not be without influence on that of France. An attack by France without British support, and with the prospect of the offensive being brought to a standstill on our western fortifications, was hardly probable. Nor was a French march through Belgium and Holland without British support to be expected; this also was a course not to be contemplated by us in the event of a conflict with France, because it would certainly entail the hostility of Britain. It would of course be necessary to maintain a strong defense [*eine Abriegelung*] on our western frontier during the prosecution of our attack on the Czechs and Austria. And in this connection it had to be remembered that the defense measures of the Czechs were growing in strength from year to year, and that the actual worth of the Austrian Army also was increasing in the course of time. Even though the populations concerned, especially of Czechoslovakia, were not sparse, the annexation of Czechoslovakia and Austria would mean an acquisition of foodstuffs for 5 to 6 million people, on the assumption that the compulsory emigration of 2 million people from Czechoslovakia and 1 million people from Austria was practicable. The in-corporation of these two States with Germany meant, from the politico-military point of view, a substantial advantage because it would mean shorter and better frontiers, the freeing of forces for other purposes, and the possibility of creating new units up to a level of about 12 divisions, that is, 1 new division per million inhabitants.

Italy was not expected to object to the elimination of the Czechs, but it was impos-sible at the moment to estimate what her attitude on the Austrian question would be; that depended essentially upon whether the Duce were still alive.

The degree of surprise and the swiftness of our action were decisive factors for

Poland's attitude. Poland—with Russia at her rear—will have little inclination to engage in war against a victorious Germany.

Military intervention by Russia must be countered by the swiftness of our operations; however, whether such an intervention was a practical contingency at all was, in view of Japan's attitude, more than doubtful.

Should case 2 arise—the crippling of France by civil war—the situation thus created by the elimination of the most dangerous opponent must be seized upon *whenever it occurs* for the blow against the Czechs.

The Führer saw case 3 coming definitely nearer; it might emerge from the present tensions in the Mediterranean, and he was resolved to take advantage of it whenever it happened, even as early as 1938.

In the light of past experience, the Führer did not see any early end to the hostilities in Spain. If one considered the length of time which Franco's offensives had taken up till now, it was fully possible that the war would continue another 3 years. On the other hand, a 100 percent victory for Franco was not desirable either, from the German point of view; rather we were interested in a continuance of the war and in the keeping up of the tension in the Mediterranean. Franco in undisputed possession of the Spanish Peninsula precluded the possibility of any further intervention on the part of the Italians or of their continued occupation of the Balearic Islands. As our interest lay more in the prolongation of the war in Spain, it must be the immediate aim of our policy to strengthen Italy's rear with a view to her remaining in the Balearics. But the permanent establishment of the Italians on the Balearaics would be intolerable both to France and Britain, and might lead to a war of France and England against Italy—a war in which Spain, should she be entirely in the hands of the Whites, might make her appearance on the side of Italy's enemies. The probability of Italy's defeat in such a war was slight, for the road from Germany was open for the supplementing of her raw materials. The Führer pictured the military strategy for Italy thus: on her western frontier with France she would remain on the defensive, and carry on the war against France from Libya against the French North African colonial possessions.

As a landing by Franco-British troops on the coast of Italy could be discounted, and a French offensive over the Alps against northern Italy would be very difficult and would probably come to a halt before the strong Italian fortifications, the crucial point [*Schwerpunkt*] of the operations lay in North Africa. The threat to French lines of communication by the Italian Fleet would to a great extent cripple the transportation of forces from North Africa to France, so that France would have only home forces at her disposal on the frontiers with Italy and Germany.

If Germany made use of this war to settle the Czech and Austrian questions, it was to be assumed that Britain—herself at war with Italy—would decide not to act against Germany. Without British support, a warlike action by France against Germany was not to be expected.

The time for our attack on the Czechs and Austria must be made dependent on the course of the Anglo-French-Italian war and would not necessarily coincide with the commencement of military operations by these three States. Nor had the Führer in mind military agreements with Italy, but wanted, while retaining his own independence of action, to exploit this favorable situation, which would not occur again, to begin and carry through the campaign against the Czechs. This descent upon the Czechs would have to be carried out with "lightning speed."

In appraising the situation Field Marshal von Blomberg and Colonel General von

Fritsch repeatedly emphasized the necessity that Britain and France must not appear in the role of our enemies, and stated that the French Army would not be so committed by the war with Italy that France could not at the same time enter the field with forces superior to ours on our western frontier. General von Fritsch estimated the probable French forces available for use on the Alpine frontier at approximately twenty divisions, so that a strong French superiority would still remain on the western frontier, with the role, according to the German view, of invading the Rhineland. In this matter, moreover, the advanced state of French defense preparations [*Mobilmachung*] must be taken into particular account, and it must be remembered apart from the insignificant value of our present fortifications—on which Field Marshal von Blomberg laid special emphasis—that the four motorized divisions intended for the West were still more or less incapable of movement. In regard to our offensive toward the southeast, Field Marshal von Blomberg drew particular attention to the strength of the Czech fortifications, which had acquired by now a structure like a Maginot Line and which would gravely hamper our attack.

General von Fritsch mentioned that this was the very purpose of a study which he had ordered made this winter, namely, to examine the possibility of conducting operations against the Czechs with special reference to overcoming the Czech fortification system; the General further expressed his opinion that under existing circumstances he must give up his plan to go abroad on his leave, which was due to begin on November 10. The Führer dismissed this idea on the ground that the possibility of a conflict need not yet be regarded as so imminent. To the Foreign Minister's objection that an Anglo-French-Italian conflict was not yet within such a measurable distance as the Führer seemed to assume, the Führer put the summer of 1938 as the date which seemed to him possible for this. In reply to considerations offered by Field Marshal von Blomberg and General von Fritsch regarding the attitude of Britain and France, the Führer repeated his previous statements that he was convinced of Britain's nonparticipation, and therefore he did not believe in the probability of belligerent action by France against Germany. Should the Mediterranean conflict under discussion lead to a general mobilization in Europe, then we must immediately begin action against the Czechs. On the other hand, should the powers not engaged in the war declare themselves disinterested, then Germany would have to adopt a similar attitude to this for the time being.

Colonal General Göring thought that, in view of the Führer's statement, we should consider liquidating our military undertakings in Spain. The Führer agrees to this with the limitation that he thinks he should reserve a decision for a proper moment.

The second part of the conference was concerned with concrete questions of armament.

HOSSBACH

CERTIFIED CORRECT:
Colonel (General Staff)

HOSTAGE SYSTEM. Hitler's technique for maintaining control of his New Order (*q.v.*) in Europe.

BACKGROUND. The German hostage system was based on an old Frankish custom by which the value of a Frankish life was measured in terms of a greater number of the enemy. When a Belgian sniper took the life of a German soldier in World War I, local citizens who were held as hostages, including the mayor, schoolmaster, priest, and citizens picked at random, were promptly executed as a deterrent and warning.

WORLD WAR II. The pattern was repeated in World War II. Assaults on a German soldier, acts of sabotage, signs of resistance, often were quickly punished by execution of hostages. The practice began with the invasion of Poland. On the night of October 21–22, 1939, the home of a German official in a village was set afire by Poles. When the official died of heart failure, 10 Poles were shot as retribution because they were "known for their anti-German attitude."

Hitler's Night and Fog Decree (*q.v.*), issued on December 7, 1941, applied to any person anywhere in occupied Europe who endangered German security. Such individuals were to be seized by the SS or the *Gestapo* (*qq.v.*) and hustled away "in night and fog." On June 10, 1942, all men and older boys in the Czech village of Lidice (*q.v.*) were slaughtered in reprisal for the death of Reinhard Heydrich (*q.v.*). In late March 1944 the policy of 10 lives for 1 German was applied in Italy when 335 Italian hostages were killed after a bomb killed 32 Germans. (*See* ARDEATINE CAVES MASSACRE.) (The additional 15, rounded up by mistake, were also executed.)

No adequate records are available, but it is believed that among the hostages executed by the Germans were 30,000 Frenchmen, 8,000 Poles, and 2,000 Dutch citizens. Many thousands of hostages died in prisoner-of-war and concentration camps (*qq.v.*). Denmark was given special dispensation: Hitler ordered that only five Danes be shot for each German killed.

SIGNIFICANCE. German authorities regarded the hostage system as an absolute necessity for maintaining order. Other peoples, however, failed to understand the psychology and denounced the system as a barbaric practice alien to the "rules of warfare" and to simple justice. It was inhuman, they said, to take innocent lives in compensation or in reprisal.

HOWARD, LESLIE (1893–1943). Popular English stage and screen actor, killed as a civilian during the war.

In the spring of 1943 Howard went to Spain to promote British documentary films before groups of theater officials. He delayed his departure to attend the Lisbon premiere of his latest film, *The First of Few.* At 9:30 on the morning of June 1, 1943, he boarded a commercial British *DC-3* transport at Lisbon's international airport. He was accompanied by his business secretary, the portly Alfred Chenhalis, who bore a passing resemblance to Winston Churchill. At the time the British Prime Minister was returning home after a tour of Malta and British Mediterranean bases.

Minutes later, Lisbon air control received a message from the pilot of

Howard's airliner: "We are being attacked by several enemy planes." Then silence. Nothing was ever seen or heard of the twin-engine plane and its 16 occupants. It was widely believed that one of the many Nazi agents in Lisbon mistook Chenhalis for Churchill and sent word to *Luftwaffe* (*q.v.*) squadrons based in Spain, which responded by attacking the unarmed passenger plane. Churchill himself was convinced that he was the target and that the British film star died in a case of mistaken identity.

HOWE, QUINCY (1900–1977). U.S. newscaster.

After the start of World War II, Howe brought news of the conflict into the homes of Americans, joining such able radio journalists as Edward R. Murrow, Eric Sevareid, William L. Shirer, H. V. Kaltenborn, and Elmer Davis (*qq.v.*) He joined the Columbia Broadcasting System (CBS) in 1942. Previously, war news had been delivered as much as possible without comment. The new radio journalists presented not only the facts but their own interpretation as well.

After the war Howe and his colleagues made the transition to television. Howe left CBS in 1949 to teach journalism at the University of Illinois but continued to broadcast occasionally. From 1961 to 1965 he edited the journal *Atlas*. He died in New York on February 17, 1977.

A slight, pleasant-faced man, with a keen expressive face, Howe was a vital and restless reporter, always on the search for news. His Yankee twang added to a caustic tongue made him familiar to millions.

Bibliography. Among Howe's books are *World Diary, 1929-1934* (1934); *England Expects Every American To Do His Duty* (1937); *Blood is Cheaper Than Water* (1939); and *A World History of Our Times*, 2 vols. (1972).

HUFF-DUFF. Acronym for High Frequency Direction Finding.

Huff-Duff was a method of locating enemy naval and merchant craft by taking bearings on their radio broadcasting. The device was so successful that many sea captains preferred to maintain radio silence while in dangerous waters.

HULL, CORDELL (1871–1955). American statesman and U.S. Secretary of State during World War II.

As early as 1936 Hull foresaw the coming of war in the rise of the Axis dictatorships. When the European war broke out in 1939, he advocated the strongest possible rearmament and reaffirmed the U.S. foreign policy of maintaining the *status quo* in the Far East. He condemned Japanese moves in Indo-China. He played a prominent role in the Pan-American Congress in Havana in the summer of 1940, which aimed to present a united front against any threat from abroad.

Hull handled the delicate negotiations with Japan that culminated with the Pearl Harbor attack. He conducted the frustrating negotiations with Japanese envoys for some months while he tried to keep them going as long as possible in a situation that was clearly leading to war. He exploded in wrath on receiving the final Japanese message delivered after he knew of the attack on Pearl Harbor. (*See* PEARL HARBOR.)

To retain close relations with Soviet Russia, Hull attended the Moscow Conference of Foreign Ministers in October 1943. His diplomacy vastly improved U.S. wartime relations with the Kremlin. Meanwhile U.S. foreign policy was taken more and more into the hands of Roosevelt and his military advisers, a situation which undermined Hull's position. Hull continued to work on major problems, but ill-health forced his resignation as Secretary of State in November 1944.

Bibliography. Hull's *Memoirs* appeared in two volumes in 1948. *See also* J. W. Pratt, *Cordell Hull, 1933-1944* (2 vols., 1964).

HUMAN TORPEDOES. Italian two-man midget submarines.

In December 1941 these assault craft penetrated into Alexandria harbor to attack units of the British Fleet. Operators wearing Scuba gear and sitting astride their slender craft attached warheads to the keels of HMS *Queen Elizabeth* and *Valiant* and immobilized the battleships until 1943.

HUMBERT II (1904–   ). Crown Prince of Italy.

At the start of the war Humbert was given command of Italy's Northern Army in the Alpine frontier region, with the rank of Army Corps General. In October 1942 he was given the rank of Marshal. After the armistice of September 8, 1943, he and most of the royal family escaped to the Allied side. On June 5, 1944, Victor Emmanuel III retired from public life and made his son Regent of Italy.

Six-feet-two-inches tall, dashing, personable, Humbert built a reputation as a playboy with interest in fast cars, skis, and women. He was ridiculed by unimpressed Italians. Defenders praised his behavior under most difficult circumstances.

Bibliography. See G. Salvemini and G. La Piana, *What to Do with Italy* (1943).

HUMP, THE. Allied supply route to China over the Himalayas from 1942 to 1945.

LOCATION. The Hump, perpendicular to the east-west mass of the Himalaya Mountains, pointed southward to Malaysia and Indonesia. It consisted of great ridges and gorges, capped by peaks, including the 22,000-foot high mountain known as Tali.

BACKGROUND. In 1938 the only overland supply route from India to China was the Burma road, which ran from Mandalay to Lashio to Kunming in Yunnan Province. In 1942 Japanese penetration of Burma was so successful that the Burma Road was closed. For the Allies it became a matter of supreme importance to find new means of supplying the Chinese, who were keeping hundreds of thousands of Japanese troops deployed throughout the mainland.

Allied strategists envisioned the possibility of an airlift when in early 1942, a *DC-3*, operated by the China National Aviation Corporation (CNAC), successfully threaded its way through the Himalayas between India and China. In April 1942 the first U.S. military flight across the Hump was made. There followed the world's first great airlift.

BASES. The critical factor was the necessity for adequate bases at both ends of the airlift. In the southern area, after an agreement between London and Washington, six bases with concrete strips were built in the tea patches of Upper Assam by British engineers. Working in 140-degree heat, Indian natives constructed steel-mesh taxiways at Sookerating, Chabus, Misamari, and Mohanbari, all close to sea-level altitude.

Meanwhile, in the area around Kunming in China, hundreds of acres had to be covered with rock for an air base apron and revetments. For this work thousands of Chinese coolies were brought in from remote highlands to break rocks into little pieces. They built the bases more than a mile above sea level.

CARGOES. The U.S. Army Air Force's Ferry Command evolved into the Air Transport Command (ATC), which looked upon flights across the Hump as one of its most critical operations. Among the planes detailed for the operation were *C-46 Commandos; C-47 Skytrains; C-87* transports (converted *B-24 Liberator* bombers); and eventually *B-29 Superfortresses.*

Cargoes consisted of aviation fuel, bomb fuses, ammunition, metal ore, earth movers, and machinery of all kinds. Aircraft engines for the U.S. 14th Air Force in China were hauled over the Hump. On return trips, planes were often filled with troops on leave. Crews were housed at both ends for inspection, repairs, and maintenance of large aircraft.

CONDITIONS. As soon as flights over the Hump began, Japanese pilots from bases in conquered Burma did their best to thwart the airlift. It was difficult for Hump pilots to judge which was worst—enemy combat pilots or physical and meteorological conditions in the Himalayan area. Added to Japanese harassment were other dangers—the Himalayas themselves, fog and clouds, monsoons in the hot summer season, carburetor ice, and vapor lock. Pilots lived under primitive conditions in mud huts. They wore wet uniforms, ate unsatisfactory food, and were covered with blood because of leeches. They were subject to malaria and various forms of dysentery. They had to make fast turnabouts in flight. The service calling of *C-46s* was about 22,000 feet, just the height of some of the Himalayas, necessitating careful skirting of the ranges.

RESULTS. Month by month, tonnage flown over the Hump increased until it eventually surpassed what had been carried on the Burma Road. The operation went on every minute of the day and night, reaching 45,000 tons per month. From 1942 to 1945 a total of 650,000 tons were carried. As early as December 1943 the White House recognized the work of the India-China wing of the Air Transport Command by awarding it the Presidential Citation. All ATC personnel at both ends of the line began wearing the Distinguished Unit Badge.

The great airlift was a most important factor in the eventual defeat of the Japanese. Japanese were unable to compete with this extraordinarily effective operation.

Bibliography. B. K. Thorne, *The Hump* (1965); and A. L. White, *Ten Thousand Tons by Christmas* (1977).

HUON PENINSULA. *See* NEW GUINEA, CAMPAIGNS IN.

HURRICANE. Britain's standard fighter plane and the numerical mainstay of the Royal Air Force (*q.v.*) in the summer of 1940. (*See* BRITAIN, BATTLE OF.) The *Hurricane* was a single-engined, low-wing monoplane with pointed nose and large rounded fin and rudder.

DESIGN. The *Hurricane,* manufactured by Hawker, was originally planned in the mid-1930s and put into production in 1937. The designers wanted a fighter plane that could fly at a slow speed of 100 miles an hour and at a fast speed of more than 300 miles per hour. It had to be able to slow suddenly when attacked, forcing the enemy to pass, thus reversing the fighter roles when the pursuer became the pursued. For this purpose the designers rejected the idea of building a plane and getting an engine for it and instead constructed an engine and built a ship to fit it.

Initial plans called for a high-altitude interceptor, but eventually the *Hurricane* after successive modifications was used as fighter plane, tank-buster, interceptor, and catapult-launched sea escort. Subsequent models included the *Typhoon,* the *Tempest,* the *Hurribomber,* and the *Sea Hurricane.*

WORLD WAR II. The *Hurricane* was placed in full production as soon as the war began in 1939. Along with the *Spitfire* (*q.v.*), it played an outstanding role in the Battle of Britain, and with the *Spitfire* it was credited with saving Britain from defeat. *Hurricanes* shot down more German aircraft than all other British planes put together.

(For specifications *see* AIRCRAFT: BRITISH AIRCRAFT DATA CHART.)

HURTGEN FOREST. Scene of a savage battle in the winter of 1944.

The name Hurtgen Forest was applied to 1,300 square miles of densely wooded, roller-coaster land along the German-Belgian border south and southeast of Aachen. Actually, it embraced several forests—Roetgen, Wenau, Kinigl, and Hurtgen, the name that caught on with the Americans. Capture of the forest, followed by crossing of the Ruhr, would mean that the German West Wall (*q.v.*) had collapsed.

From mid-September to mid-December 1944 an American infantry division and part of the 5th Armored Division fought at one time or another in the Hurtgen Forest. It was a devastating, frustrating, and gory battle, regarded by military historians as the Argonne of World War II. The Americans finally won the battle, but at the expense of 28,000 casualties, including 8,000 who died from combat exhaustion and the weather. (*See also* GERMANY, BATTLE OF.)

Bibliography. P. Boesch, *Road to Hurtgen: Forest in Hell* (1962).

I

IFFY (IDENTIFICATION/FRIEND OR FOE). British device used on aircraft to notify radar guardians that the plane was a friendly one and was not to be fired on. (*See* RADAR, WARTIME.)

ILYUSHIN, SERGEI V. (1894–1977). Prominent Russian aircraft designer.

Young Ilyushin left home to make his way as a laborer. After two years of service in the Czarist army, he worked his way from mechanic to flight engineer to pilot. Expert in rebuilding damaged aircraft, he was graduated from the Khukivshy Air Force Engineering Academy in 1926. In the 1930s he emerged as one of Soviet Russia's finest aircraft designers. One of his planes, the *TsKB-30,* made a successful 5,000-mile flight across the North Pole to North America in 1930.

Ilyushin's most famous plane, which he developed just as the war began, was the *Il-2,* known as the *Stormovik* and dubbed "Black Death" by the Germans. It was, in effect, a flying tank. Military chiefs were at first skeptical, but Ilyushin won the support of Stalin. The performance of the *Stormovik* in combat was so exceptional that it was quickly put into mass production.

IMPERIAL RULE ASSISTANCE ASSOCIATION (IRAA). Japanese organization designed to involve all citizens in mobilization for war.

Founded on September 27, 1940, the IRAA was supposed to bring about national unity in a time of crisis. The association hoped to blunt military influence over politics. The army took control of IRAA after Pearl Harbor (*q.v.*). The association was formally dissolved on June 13, 1945.

INDO-CHINA. After the German conquest of France in 1940, the Japanese took advantage of France's defeat by forcing it to agree to the "protective occupation" of French Indo-China.

On July 24, 1941, President Roosevelt in reaction demanded that Tokyo withdraw its troops from Indo-China. Two days later he issued orders freezing all Japanese assets in the United States and placing an embargo on the oil supply. The incident precipitated a heated diplomatic exchange. The Japanese believed that such a paralyzing stroke would force them to fight in order to avoid a total economic collapse. Washington refused to lift the embargo unless Japan withdrew not only from Indo-China but also from China. The humiliated Japanese, losing face, began to prepare for Pearl Harbor, which followed five months later. (*See* PEARL HARBOR.)

No important developments occurred in Indo-China for the remainder of the war. Efforts by the French to organize a guerrilla campaign against the Japanese had little success. In the north national guerrillas, led by Ho Chi Minh (*q.v.*), moved into Vietnam to find bases for their underground activity. In early 1945 the Japanese deposed the French administration and took direct control of the country. Meanwhile, the French had announced plans for a federation of Indo-China inside the French union. The idea was accepted in Laos and Cambodia, but nationalists demanded the complete independence of Annam, Tonkin, and Cochin China as Vietnam. After the war these areas were plunged into bitter fighting between the French and extreme nationalists, resulting in the defeat of the French.

INFRA-RED TARGET DETECTION SYSTEMS. *See* TARGET DETECTION.

INTELLIGENCE AND COUNTERINTELLIGENCE, MILITARY. *See* ESPIONAGE.

INTREPID. Britain's master spy during the war. (*See* STEPHENSON, WILLIAM.)

INVASION—NORMANDY. *See* NORMANDY INVASION.

IRAN. *See* NEAR AND MIDDLE EAST, CAMPAIGNS IN THE.

IRAQ, OCCUPATION OF. *See* NEAR AND MIDDLE EAST, CAMPAIGNS IN THE.

IRONSIDE, WILLIAM EDMUND (1880–1959). British Field Marshal and Chief of the British Imperial General Staff (CIGS) from 1939–1940.

In 1939 Ironside was named to replace Gen. John Standish Gort (*q.v.*) as CIGS, the highest military post in Britain. In this post he found it difficult to work with Leslie Hore-Belisha, (*q.v.*), Secretary of State for War. In May 1940 Ironside visited Gen. Gort, Commander of the British Expeditionary Force (*q.v.*) in France, with the purpose of supervising a retreat southward, but finding it impossible he agreed to a withdrawal at Dunkirk (*q.v.*). Later that month he was replaced by Gen. John Greer Dill (*q.v.*) as CIGS. Ironside then became

Commander-in-Chief of Home Forces and in that post was responsible for drawing up plans for the defense of Britain against invasion. In July 1940 he was succeeded by Gen. Alan Brooke (*q.v.*). In the same year the baronies of Archangel and Ironside were conferred on him.

Six-feet-four-inches tall and weighing 250 pounds, Ironside was nicknamed "Tiny" by his troops, a title he bore with dignity. With his massive frame, long cigars, yellow corduroy trousers, and sport coat, as well as an ever-present bulldog, he was a rugged symbol of a 20th-century British fighter. It was said that during the Boer War he seized an enemy soldier in his arms and crushed him to death. Ironside became a central character in John Buchan's novels, *The Thirty-Nine Steps* and *Greenmantle*.

Bibliography. Ironside was the author of *Tannenberg: The First Thirty Days in East Prussia* (1925) and *Archangel* (1953). *The Ironsides Diaries, 1937-1940* appeared in 1961.

ISMAY, HASTINGS LIONEL (1887-1965). British soldier and administrator and leading military adviser to Churchill during the war.

In 1940 Ismay was appointed head of Churchill's new personal staff, serving simultaneously on the Chief of Staffs Committee and as Deputy Secretary of the War Cabinet. On November 6, 1942, he was promoted to Lieutenant General. In his two key posts Ismay became a vital link in Britain's machinery of high strategy. He was the main communication link between Churchill and the whole machinery of war. He accompanied his chief to the important Casablanca Conference (*q.v.*) from January 12 to 23, 1943, and also to other war conferences. Other Allied leaders considered his contribution to victory a major one.

Bibliography. H. L. Ismay, *Memoirs* (1960); and R. Wingate, *Lord Ismay: A Biography* (1970).

ITALIAN FRONT, CAMPAIGNS ON THE. Struggle for the Italian peninsula from 1943 to 1945.

BACKGROUND. On June 10, 1940, Italy declared war on Britain and France and invaded southern France. For the next three years Mussolini's Italy lost one battle after another. Its adventure in Greece in 1941 misfired (*see* GREECE, BATTLE FOR), and its defeat in North Africa was catastrophic (*see* NORTH AFRICA, CAMPAIGNS IN). At the Casablanca Conference (*q.v.*) in January 1943, the Allied Supreme Command made plans to eliminate Italy altogether. It would be attacked from North Africa in the British plan for an assault on the soft underbelly (*q.v.*) of Europe.

FALL OF MUSSOLINI. On July 17, 1943, Allied aircraft appeared over Rome and dropped leaflets with a message from Roosevelt and Churchill urging the Italians to surrender: "The time has come for you, the Italian people, to decide whether Italians shall die for Mussolini and Hitler—or live for Italy and civilization." The skillfully written message struck home. A few days earlier the Allies had invaded Sicily. (*See* SICILY, INVASION OF.) Mussolini appealed to Hitler for help only to be told: "Sicily must be made into a Stalingrad." Panic-stricken citizens of Rome surged into the sanctuary of Vatican City.

Five days later Mussolini summoned the Fascist Grand Council for its first meeting since the start of the war and in a passionate two-hour speech attempted to rally his weary collaborators. Stiffened by despair, the Council voted 19-7 with 2 abstentions for Mussolini to relinquish his command of the armed forces in favor of King Victor Emmanuel III (*q.v.*). The Duce resigned on July 26, 1943. He was replaced by Marshal Pietro Badoglio (*q.v.*), who as executive head under the king formed a new government.

ALLIED PREPARATIONS. The Allied Supreme Command was slow moving at the critical moment of Mussolini's deposition. Several days later Gen. Dwight D. Eisenhower (*q.v.*) issued a statement praising the Italian people for getting rid of their dictator. On September 3, 1943, Badoglio capitulated and signed the document of unconditional surrender. All Italian soldiers were required to lay down their arms. The Italian fleet surrendered at Malta, but the Germans were able to sink the battleship *Roma.* As the negotiations for surrender went on, the Allies prepared for a massive invasion.

SALERNO. At the beginning of September 1943 Allied warships shelled roads, power stations, and railways, while a great air offensive cut the Italian railway system. On September 3, 1943, came the great invasion at Salerno on the west coast south of Naples. The British 8th Army had a relatively easy time, but the U.S. 5th Army ran into trouble from the start. The Allies expected an easy landing, but it was not to be. Waiting on the high ground above Salerno the Germans zeroed in a great artillery barrage on the crowded beaches. For a time it seemed that the Americans would be driven into the sea, but they recovered as the Germans wavered and withdrew to Naples. (*See* SALERNO BEACHHEAD.)

BATTLE OF NAPLES. Allied men and supplies poured in. Within a month 135,000 men landed with 100,000 tons of supplies and 30,000 motor vehicles. The Americans were in Italy to stay. Led by Gen. Mark W. Clark (*q.v.*), they pushed back the German rear guard around Vesuvius, bypassed the ruins of Pompeii and Herculaneum, and entered Naples. They found the city in ruins, its people starving and racked by typhus. Allied engineers speedily repaired the harbor facilities. Simultaneously, the British 8th Army moving up the east coast seized the great system of airfields at Foggia. German Gen. Albert Kesselring (*q.v.*) retired to strong defensive positions on the north bank of the Volturno River.

BATTLE OF ANZIO. For the Allies only two routes to Rome were possible. They might drive along the Via Appia and the coastline or they might work their way along the Via Latina through the interior mountains around the key town of Cassino. Either way would be difficult. For the rest of 1943 they tried to push through the mud, dirt, and slush, as vehicles broke down and bridges were washed out by the incessant rains. From high ridges of almost solid rock the Germans poured down a withering fire. To defend Rome the Germans set up two lines of fortifications with Cassino at their center. (*See* DEFENSIVE LINES, GERMANY.)

On January 22, 1944, under an umbrella of air power, the Allies made a leapfrog jump to outflank the German fortifications. Although well planned, the operation came close to being a disaster. The attempt to relieve pressure from the main drive on Rome had failed. (*See* ANZIO BEACHHEAD.)

CASSINO. The failure at Anzio threw the main weight of the campaign on the town of Cassino, hinge of the Gustav Line. Allied bombing of the historic Abbey of Monte Cassino achieved little beyond a world-wide wave of protest. (*See* MONTE CASSINO.) Both sides fought through muddy days and freezing nights.

ROME. After a major reorganization, the Allies began a new offensive, code-named *Diadem* (*see* CODE NAMES, ALLIED, DIADEM), on May 12, 1944. They pushed across the Garigliano and Rapido rivers, pierced the Gustav Line, and entered Rome on June 4, 1944. (*See* ROME, LIBERATION OF.) The Germans retreated while the Romans received the Allies with a wave of hysteria.

The fall of Rome marked the beginning of the end of the last phase of the war in Europe. Two days later came the massive invasion in the north. (*See* NORMANDY INVASION.)

GOTHIC LINE. The Germans now moved behind their Gothic Line (*see* DEFENSIVE LINES, GERMAN), running from Pisa on the Tyrrhenian coast to Rimini on the Adriatic coast. On June 17, 1944, the American 5th Army entered Leghorn to find the docks demolished and the harbor clogged with a dozen wrecks. Meanwhile, Polish troops on the Adriatic coast straightened out the Allied lines by seizing Ancona, while the British 8th Army entered Perugia in the center. Probing through Tuscany, British patrols entered the outskirts of Florence on August 3, 1944, to find the magnificent city badly mangled.

END. On April 14, 1945, Clark's 5th Army began *Operation Grapefruit* for the final offensive. After a week of heavy fighting, the Americans entered Bologna from the west and south and approached the Po Valley. Meanwhile, the British 8th Army swept along the northeastern coastal plain, liberating Padua and Venice. The Americans then drove to the foothills of the Alps along the Brenner route. Racing to the valley of the Po, they reached Milan on April 29, 1945. On May 1 the Germans in Italy agreed to unconditional surrender.

SIGNIFICANCE. From Salerno to Milan it had been a long and bloody battle. It was a major victory but won at tremendous cost. Military critics held that it was folly to drive up the narrow mountainous peninsula where geography favored the defense. Historian Samuel Eliot Morison put it bluntly: "The unberbelly proved to be boned with the Apennines, plated with the hard scales of Kesselring's armor, and shadowed by the wings of the *Luftwaffe.*" Sunny Italy turned out to be Bloody Italy. No masses of troops were in this deadly slugging match. Armies did not "pour ahead" or "plunge through" or "sweep around." Instead, isolated units moved up and down inclines in what correspondent Eric Sevareid (*q.v.*) called "slow, spasmodic movement from one patch of silence to another." This was war in a chaos of muddy plains, snow-choked mountains, slushy mud, and nighttime freezing roads.

In response to criticism the Allied Supreme Command pointed out that 14 of the best German divisions, badly needed on the Russian front and in Normandy, were tied down by persistant Allied assault up the peninsula.

Bibliography. C. Buckley, *Road to Rome* (1945); B. L. Montgomery, *El Alamein to the Sangro* (1946); P. Badoglio, *Italy in the Second World War* (1947); M. Clark, *Calculated Risks* (1951); A. Kesselring, *Memoirs* (1953); F. Majdalanay, *Cassino* (1957); G. A. Shepperd, *The Italian Campaign, 1943-1945* (1968); and W.G.F. Jackson, *The Battle for Rome* (1969).

IWO JIMA, BATTLE FOR. Capture of island base on doorstep of Japan by U.S. Marines in mid-March 1945.

BACKGROUND. By early 1945 Allied sea and air power had moved close to the Japanese homeland. Allied strategists planned to strike at Japan from the Central Pacific. The attack would be made from the Marianas to Iwo Jima and then to Okinawa to provide advance air bases. Adm. Chester W. Nimitz (*q.v.*) was ordered to move on Iwo Jima in January 1945 and on Okinawa in early March.

LOCATION. The ugly little volcanic island of Iwo Jima was just eight miles square, situated in the Bonin Islands midway between Saipan and Tokyo. Its beaches were covered by soft, treacherous volcanic ash. The north end was a jungle of rocks, boulders, chasms, lava ledges, and steaming sulfur pits. At the southern end rose the slopes of Mount Suribachi, an extinct volcano.

This volcanic island was for both Japanese and Americans one of the most strategic areas in the entire Far East. It was the seat of Japanese "seeing-eye" devices to warn Tokyo of the approach of bombers. Japanese strategists transformed it into a rugged fortress, a kind of miniature Maginot Line (*q.v.*) in depth. Japanese workers combined the volcanic ash with cement to form a high quality concrete, which could be used to reinforce walls to a thickness of eight feet. They covered the island with interlocking underground strongholds, built thousands of blockhouses and pillboxes with steel-reinforced concrete, and fortified the caves, all cleverly camouflaged. Artillery and machine-gun nests covered nearly every inch of the island. The beaches and the interior were protected by heavy land mines. Fighter craft could rise from three airfields. To defend the bastion Tokyo had 23,000 experienced troops under command of Lt. Gen. Tadamichi Kuribayashi.

Iwo Jima was equally desirable for the Americans. U.S. air bases in the Marianas—Saipan, Tinian, and Guam—were 1,300 miles from Tokyo. A round trip of the *Superfortresses (B-29) (q.v.)* took 16 hours, leaving only a tiny amount of fuel. In rough weather the giant planes were doomed to dangerous crash landings in the Pacific. Iwo Jima would be a perfect refueling depot for returning *B-29*s, a haven for crippled craft, and an invaluable base for fighter planes to accompany the bombers.

PREPARATIONS. While Gen. Douglas MacArthur *(q.v.)* was pushing ahead in the Philippines and Lt. Gen. William J. Slim *(q.v.)* was driving the Japanese out of Burma, Americans concentrated their naval and air power on Iwo Jima. For 74 consecutive days the island was pounded from the air and sea. By January 15, 1945, nearly 7,000 tons of bombs and more than 20,000 shells had exploded on the island.

On February 17, 1945, massed U.S. sea power in the form of six battleships and a screen of cruisers and destroyers slowly circled the island and plastered it with tons of shells. Kuribayashi replied with a barrage of his own, but by this time the Americans were able to pinpoint their targets.

LANDINGS. At dawn on February 19, 1945, a great fleet of transports joined the bombarding warships. For more than two hours 25 U.S. warships fired shells, rockets, and mortars at the island, while aircraft dropped bombs and napalm. Packed aboard the vessels, which lay seven miles out in a great semi-circle, were 30,000 U.S. Marines. Inside the arc the landing craft churned the sea into foaming patterns. Scrambling down shipside nets into the landing craft, marines entered small boats and headed for the beaches.

INVASION. The invaders, including veterans of every landing since Guadalcanal, stormed ashore into one of the bloodiest operations of the war. Marines found themselves up to their ankles in loose volcanic ash while at the same time being swept by enveloping fire that seemed to come from nowhere. Automatic fire spat from apertures only a few inches above the ground. There were casualties for nearly every yard of progress. But within hours Marines carved out a beachhead about 4,500 yards long and averaging 500 yards deep.

For 48 hours the assault troops had no sleep as they fought their way in drenching rain up the rocky hillside to the plateau. Flame throwers *(q.v.)* were sent ahead to spearhead the attack. Americans had to blast concrete blockhouses again and again before the troops inside were silenced. In the ghastly slugging match the marines took more than three days to cover 700 yards up sloping ground through the flaming defenses. In an area 1,000 yards long and 200 yards deep they smashed more than 800 Japanese pillboxes one by one.

MOUNT SURIBACHI. At the end of the fourth day marines pushed their way to the base of Mount Suribachi. From the top of this key defensive position, the Japanese rained a torrent of shells on the beaches already littered with wrecked landing craft, tanks, and equipment. The congestion on the beaches was so great that almost every Japanese shell found a target. After a tremendous barrage from ships offshore and heavy bombing from the air, Americans pushed their way straight up the extinct volcano, sidestepping enemy mines, and systematically blew up dugouts, pillboxes, foxholes, and caves.

On the morning of February 23, 1945, a U.S. patrol reached the topmost ridge and within minutes had a flag-bearing pole in position. An Associated Press photographer, Joe Rosenthal, caught the scene of the flag-raising in what became one of the war's most famous photographs. Much of the island was still in Japanese hands with both sides fighting as hard as ever. Not until March 15, 1945, was the entire island taken.

CASUALTIES. It was a costly victory. The marines suffered nearly 26,000 casualties, including almost 6,000 killed—30 percent of the entire landing force. The navy lost 363 men. These were the highest American casualties of the Pacific war.

Japanese defenders fought almost to the last man. Of the original garrison of nearly 23,000, only 216 were taken prisoner. Nearly 3,000 remained in caves, where they died in mopping-up operations or in desperate *banzai* charges (*q.v.*). Gen. Kuribayashi committed suicide by *härä-kïri* (*q.v.*) on March 27, 1945.

SIGNIFICANCE. The capture of Iwo Jima, defended by Japan's most able troops, was one of the toughest and most costly of the war. The Americans, however, won their goal of a base close to the Japanese heartland. "The fighting," said Maj. Gen. Holland M. Smith, U.S. Marine commander in the Pacific, "was the toughest the Marines ran across in 168 years. American invaders overcame the most difficult defenses of both Nature and the Japanese."

Bibliography. R. Henri, *Iwo Jima* (1945); A. M. Joseph, *The Long and Short of It* (1945); W. S. Bartley, *Iwo Jima: Amphibious Epic* (1954); R. Sheeler, *The Bloody Battle of Iwo Jima* (1965); B. C. Nalty, *The United States Marines in Iwo Jima* (1967); R. F. Newcomb, *Iwo Jima* (1971); and M. Russell, *Iwo Jima* (1974).

J

JACKSON, ROBERT HOUGHWOUT (1892–1954). American lawyer and chief counsel for the United States at the Nuremberg War Crimes Trial (*see* NUREMBERG TRIALS).

In 1940 Jackson was named U.S. Attorney General and the next year was appointed to the U.S. Supreme Court. After the war he was assigned the duties of chief prosecuting officer for the United States at the Nuremberg Trial. He had the major role in drawing up indictments against 24 accused Germans and six Nazi organizations. On November 20, 1945, he delivered a masterly presentation at the opening of the trial. For ten and a half months he was responsible for the core of the indictments—the count charging defendants with conspiracy to wage war of aggression. Jackson died in Washington on October 9, 1954.

Bibliography. R. H. Jackson, *The Case Against the Nazi War Criminals* (1946); *The Nürnberg Case* (1947); and *The Supreme Court in the American System of Government* (1955). *See also* biography by E. C. Erhart (1958).

JAPAN AT WAR. As in other countries, the Japanese home front was geared for total war. Civilians were expected to match combat troops in sacrifices for victory.

TOTAL MOBILIZATION. Most Japanese were shocked and bewildered by the outbreak of war against the United States, but they recovered quickly and resolved to undergo any suffering in defense of the Imperial throne. Seventy-five million Japanese in the home islands had already undergone years of warfare, and now, despite increasing privations, they maintained their sense of unity and energetic zeal. A disciplined and regimented people, they accepted the necessity and reality of total mobilization. Every Japanese would do his share in the common cause.

WAR ECONOMY. The island empire of Japan depended on daily arrival and departure of merchant ships to maintain its economic life. Nipponese freighters plowed to and from some of the world's best sources of raw materials. Maintenance of the sea life line became the highest priority in the Japanese war effort.

The entire national economy was devoted to the war machine. There was to be no business as usual—industry, commerce, agriculture, all were committed to war production. The citadel of the Inner Empire, composed of Japan proper, Korea, Manchuria, and Formosa, was well supplied in the early days after the beginning of the war with strategic war materials, factories, and a cheap supply of labor. A coalition of militarists, office holders, and industrialists, called the *Gumbatsu,* was given access to raw materials, banking, finance, factories, and distribution centers to run the war machine.

The home islands had large coal resources, but lacked coke for the manufacture of steel. Vital coke was imported from Manchuria and Occupied China. Added to small home production of crude oil were major supplies from the conquered East Indian oil fields. Supplies of manganese, chromium, lead, copper, nickel, aluminum, all critical for the war effort, were stockpiled even before Pearl Harbor.

Although official prices and wages were frozen in 1939, the move was insufficient to avoid a rising inflation. From 1937 to 1943, by official figures, the cost of living rose 71 percent, food and clothing by 77 percent. During the war the cost of tobacco and tobacco products for public consumption rose 50 percent.

At first the Japanese economy appeared to be bolstered by the acquisition of a huge Asiatic empire, including China, Malaya, Burma, and the East Indies. This was to be the vaunted Greater East Asia Co-Prosperity Sphere (*q.v.*), a Japanese-run empire in which conquered nations would enjoy great economic advantages. Eventually, however, it became clear that Japan had extended itself beyond its capacity to govern or perform.

MANPOWER. The entire population of the Inner Empire was subjected to military and labor draft. At its strongest the army numbered at least 6 million troops, of whom more than 2 million were sent to China and Manchuria. At first many others could be drafted without seriously affecting war production. A large annual quota of new recruits was guaranteed by the nation's high birth rate.

All men, women, and children who did not serve in the armed forces were expected to engage in civilian activities supporting the war effort. A bureau called The Emergency Mobilization of National Labor required all males between 12 and 60 years of age and all unmarried females between 12 and 40 to register with the Labor Exchange for war duties. A centralized Ministry of Welfare, sitting in Tokyo, sent out conscription notices for workers needed in factories.

The entire personnel of the educational system was conscripted for war work. Schools and universities were turned into workshops for munitions and ammunitions. Children were encouraged to manufacture airplane parts. Even Shinto and Buddhist religious teachers were expected to work in armament factories.

RATIONING. Virtually every article useful or necessary for living was rationed, restricted, or controlled by official decree. Already accustomed to a relatively low standard of living, a stringent diet, and long working hours, the Japanese people willingly accepted the severe rationing system. War needs came first and what was left had to be shared. Such items of consumer goods as soap, matches, charcoal for heating fuel, and kerosene were rationed. Coal for private use and gas and electricity for heating were prohibited.

FOOD. Distribution of food was controlled by the government through central and local food corporations, which included food processors, dealers, and handling units. After the armed forces were supplied, the remaining food was allocated to neighborhood associations, each of which served 10 families.

All three diet staples—rice, fish, and beans—were in short supply. The basic ration of rice varied according to sex, age, and occupation. The monthly rice ration of 30 pounds per person in 1943 was reduced to 22.4 pounds in 1944. Fish became more and more difficult to obtain because many fishermen and fishing boats had gone to war. Soy beans were imported from Manchuria to provide proteins. The vegetable ration was set at 4 pounds per month per person, that of sugar at one-half pound per month.

Distribution of foodstuffs often broke down due to inadequate supplies, an overburdened transportation system, and ever-increasing Allied bombing. Often local committees had to stretch their rations of rice, fish, and vegetables.

CLOTHING. Nearly every item of clothing was rationed. For cotton and textiles the home front had to do with whatever was left after the combat forces had been clothed. Quality of clothing deteriorated rapidly because of widespread use of synthetics. People became used to *sufu,* a synthetic textile that shrank after two or three washings. Leather was banned for civilian use. Rationed shoes for the public were made of cloth, fishskin, paper, or wood, and usually fell apart after a short time.

GOVERNMENT CONTROLS. The Japanese were policed strongly during the war. Troops both at home and abroad on the fighting fronts were supervised by the *Kempei,* the military police. In Japan the *Kempei* cooperated with local authorities in arresting terrorists and political enemies of the regime; abroad they treated anti-Japanese guerrillas with special severity. Special higher police, called *Tokko,* were ordered to control "dangerous thoughts." Operating under the sponsorship of the home ministry, the *Tokko* suppressed all leftist movements, especially members of the Japan Communist Party. In addition, *Tokko* spies watched all religious and academic organizations and arrested those they believed were indulging in anti-war or anti-military activities. Those who were arrested often were subjected to brutal torture in prisons. Both *Kempei* and *Tokko* officers, despite their ruthless oppression, managed to get back into police work after the war.

CENSORSHIP. Censorship in Japan began as early as September 1937 after war broke out in China. For the next several years, using the pretext of conserving paper, the home ministry, in cooperation with local police, put hundreds of newspapers out of existence. The papers of many prefectures were consolidated into single regional papers. The idea was to abolish any dissent whatever. Publishing houses had to send in their proofs to be inspected before publication. Distinguished professors were driven from their university posts when they expressed the slightest objection to the war. The works of Marx, Engels, and Japanese Marxists were banned. Any author deemed unreliable was prevented from working.

Radio, a mainspring of Japanese psychological warfare, was censored. All stations were under the control of NHK, the Public Broadcasting Corporation. Radios were distributed free of charge to poor families in the villages. Short-wave sets were banned. Motion picture producers were cautioned to depict only "true Japanese emotions," and all movie scripts were censored in advance.

PROPAGANDA. History and tradition had already fashioned the Japanese public into highly disciplined citizens, regimented, skilled, self-sacrificing, and willing to endure hardships for the Emperor. Nevertheless, the government thought it best to maintain morale by an unceasing propaganda campaign. The entire life of the nation was committed to victory. Everyone was urged to fight on with relentless fanaticism. Heavy stress was placed on death in battle or in air raids as truly honorable. To the sense of honor was added inflexible pride, reverence for the glorious past, and willingness to endure hardships. A "National Total Stimulation Movement" was organized to increase the fighting spirit of the home front.

As part of the air defense program, Japanese were given a song to bolster their courage:

> *Why should we be afraid of air raids?*
> *The big sky is protected with iron defenses.*
> *For young and old it is time to stand up;*
> *We are loaded with the honor of defending*
> *the homeland.*
> *Come on, enemy planes! Come on many times!*

SOCIAL LIFE. Severely restricted social activities were adjusted to war conditions. Many restaurants, theaters, cafes, geisha houses, and bars were closed, their buildings converted into workshops and factories and their personnel assigned to war jobs. Every man, woman, and child was expected to sacrifice social life for victory.

Travel in private automobiles virtually disappeared and the number of trains was drastically reduced. Those who had to go on long trips required a special police permit. Morning newspapers were restricted to four pages; evening papers were no longer published. Anyone who migrated to cities for war jobs found overcrowded housing and little available food.

Despite heavy penalties, a black market emerged with prices three or four times those of the legal ceiling. Most Japanese, however, avoided the black market and accepted the rationing system as well as increased taxes as their proper contributions to victory.

CIVILIAN DEFENSE. Because of the tinder-box nature of Japanese houses (most were made of wood and paper), the authorities built underground shelters and expanded fire fighting and damage repair facilities. Construction of shelters in Tokyo was difficult because ground water was found within two or three feet. Food and fuel were stored for emergencies.

Every citizen was allotted a task in civilian defense. Each one was assigned to a neighborhood association responsible for his or her own home. Everyone was required to wear a tag around the neck giving name, address, and blood type. The elderly and children were evacuated to the provinces. Air-raid drills were held regularly, but workers were expected to remain at their jobs during alerts. The civilian defense equipment was mostly primitive, consisting of grappling hooks, buckets of sand, shovels, and barrels of water. Fire-fighting apparatus turned out to be inadequate.

ORDEAL BY FIRE. Allied air power hit hard at the Japanese home front. The public dismissed the Doolittle raid (q.v.) on April 18, 1942, as a propaganda stunt, especially because after the raid there was a recess from bombing that lasted nearly two years. On June 16, 1944, a flight of B-29s based in China bombed the Yawata steel plant in Kyushu, the beginning of a constantly mounting assault from the air. From then on, giant American planes bombed Japanese cities day and night in all kinds of weather. Apparently the Americans had accurate information about the location of Nipponese industrial sites. Japanese workers found little time to sleep.

In the long run, American air raids helped considerably to cripple Japan's war potential. Air warfare also accounted for the loss of freighters and for the damaging of external lines of communication. American aircraft also sowed mines throughout Japanese waters, cutting last links with the Chinese mainland.

DECLINING ECONOMY. Relentless bombing delivered grave blows to the Japanese economy. Industry reached its peak output of aircraft, ships, and munitions about mid-1944, but this was effected only by using stockpiles of raw materials and fuel oil amassed between 1937 and 1941. Now, in addition to bombing of industrial sites, American submarines struck hard at the Japanese Merchant Marine. In 1942, U.S. submarines sank 134 Japanese vessels; in 1943, 284; and in 1944, 492. The number declined eventually because of lack of quarry. By 1945 about 8 million tons of Japanese shipping had been sunk. The loss could be made good only by new construction and this was now impossible. The flow of such vital imports as oil, iron, coking coal, and bauxite was so drastically reduced that industrial output fell far below the minimum standards for maintaining either armed forces or national economy.

With the passage of time, the home front suffered even more privations. Supply of foodstuffs declined rapidly. The rice crop in 1945 was considerably smaller than in 1944, and the importation of sufficient supplies was no longer possible. Added to waning food was the manpower problem. By 1944 nearly 87 percent of the male population not serving in the armed forces had been drafted into food and munitions industries. Now many of these reservists were being called up for combat or home defense units. Already inadequate civil transport facilities had to be stretched to handle new formations. The home front was beset by a vicious cycle—if Japan were to be defended against invasion, new military formations had to be found, but the more they were raised the more the industrial structure would collapse.

As the military and economic situations both deteriorated, the traditional rivalry between the Japanese Army and Navy became even more intense. They vied with one another in buying up civilian supplies, for which each demanded priority. This practice tended to deepen friction between military and civilians.

JAPAN AT THE END OF THE WAR. From 1941 to 1943 the Japanese reveled in victory and prosperity as the Greater East Asia Co-Prosperity Sphere (*q.v.*) seemed to have become a reality. But in the dark summer days of 1945 the Japanese saw their cherished beliefs and myths go up in flames as their country was pounded systematically and indiscriminately. Schools were closed and pupils were sent to work on farms or in factories. There was famine in the land, unemployment, misery, poverty, even banditry. All that was left was Emperor Hirohito (*q.v.*). Japan was paying dearly for its adventure into aggression.

WANING MORALE. The worsening military situation and the battered home front resulted in intensified war weariness. Early in the war most Japanese had an unshakable faith in victory. It was unthinkable that the Emperor's armies could suffer defeat or that the navy would not be triumphant. But as the war dragged on, there was a distinct lowering of morale. There could be no sense of security anywhere as Allied strategy shifted attacks from one area to another. In off hours, workers had to go to the countryside to get food and then make their way home. Attendance at war plants was radically reduced. Travel by train became increasingly dangerous as Allied bombs hit the main lines. The old enthusiasm was dampened.

Masakatsu Nomura, who was drafted in August 1943 and sent to Burma, described his reactions to the home front when he returned. No words, he said, could express his feelings. He found the situation extremely bad. People were scraping together boards and steel sheets to build huts. He exchanged his military food certificate for some potato bread. It was all he could get. He prayed for the soul of all, friend and foe alike, who had lost their lives in the hell of war.

Morale on the home front was so seriously affected that in early 1945 Prince Konoye, former Premier and elder statesman, informed the Emperor that the situation in Japan was in every way favorable for a Communist revolution. He advised that Japan should try to end the war as soon as possible.

HIROSHIMA. The final argument came on August 6, 1945, when an American plane dropped an atomic bomb on the population of Hiroshima (*q.v.*). The stubbornness of Japanese soldiers on Okinawa foreshadowed the kind of war that had to be met in conquering the homeland. This tipped the scale in Washington for use of the new weapon. After the bomb was used with awesome results, the pace of Allied propaganda was redoubled. The Japanese were invited to surrender or face "utter devastation of the Japanese homeland."

HUMAN LOSSES. Casualty figures are lacking for Japan. Of the more than 6 million men in the armed forces at peak strength, there were 1.2 million to 2 million battle deaths, at least 280,000 civilian deaths, and at least 420,000 injured, many seriously, in Allied air raids. Among the missing were several hundred thousand Japanese captured by the Russians in Manchuria and Korea.

MATERIAL HAVOC. Material destruction was enormous. American raiders dropped an estimated 117,000 high explosive bombs and 4.7 million incendiaries on Japan during the war, for a total of about 1 missile for every 15 people in the country. Official Japanese figures list 2.3 million homes totally destroyed, 950,000 partly wrecked, and 9.5 million people homeless. Half of Tokyo and Hiroshima lay in ruins, and damage was tremendous in Nagoya and Osaka. More than 30,000 miles of railway track were destroyed; the merchant marine was crippled; and highly concentrated factories were paralyzed. War production was reduced to a third of that in 1943.

OCCUPATION. As soon as Japanese expansion was halted in the Pacific, Washington began to study problems that would be associated with the occupation of Japan. It was necessary to define the power of the coming military command and lay down principles of a new Pacific policy. The matter of territory came first. Japan, with its unconditional surrender, lost not only the territorial gains it had made in the early days of the war but also all its colonial possessions acquired since the mid-19th century.

Allied authorities hesitated for some time before determining what treatment would be accorded Emperor Hirohito, to whom the Japanese people looked as a god. It was decided to retain him on the throne, but keep him under close supervision and require him to delegate his power to American military authorities. The Americans rejected a Soviet proposal for a "Big Four" Control Commission, as in Germany, and instead set up a broader commission consisting of representatives of the 11 countries that had fought against Japan. Gen. Douglas MacArthur (*q.v.*), Supreme Commander of Allied Powers (SCAP) in Japan, was given the position of a kind of proconsul, who was subject, however, to the authority of the U.S. Government. Thus began an extraordinary co-existence between victors and vanquished.

Washington's goal was to transform Japan into a "peace-loving nation" by democratic reform. The armed forces were dissolved and their arms and equipment scrapped. Public life was purged of ultranationalists. Twenty-five old-line militarists and statesmen were placed on trial, of whom seven, including Gen. Hideki Tojo (*q.v.*), were executed. (*See* JAPANESE WAR CRIMINALS' TRIAL.)

PEACE TREATY. Work was started on a peace treaty, which went into effect on April 28, 1952. The brief and simple treaty deprived Japan of its overseas empire. It was required to renounce all rights to southern Sakhalin Island and to the Kurile Islands. Japan also concurred to a trusteeship administered by Washington of the Bonins and Ryukyus, including Okinawa. It was forced to give up claims to Formosa. Japan's sovereignty was limited to the four main home islands plus some minor islands. In effect, Japan was returned to the territorial status of 1854.

Bibliography. R. Brinew, *Until They Eat Stones* (1944); C. D. Carus and C. L. McNichols, *Japan: Its Resources and Industry* (1944); U.S. Office of War Information, *Enemy Japan* (1945); O. Tolischus, *Through Japanese Eyes* (1945); M. Kati, *The Lost War* (1945), and S. W. Kirby, *The War Against Japan* (5 vols., 1969).

JAPANESE SURRENDER. *See* SURRENDER, JAPANESE.

JAPANESE WAR CRIMINALS' TRIAL. Trial of 25 Japanese war leaders from 1947 to 1948, the Far Eastern equivalent of the Nuremberg Trials (*q.v.*).

BACKGROUND. Immediately after the war, Prince Konoye, three times Premier of Japan, declared that conflict with the Allies could have been averted and that Japanese militarists were guilty of starting it. Several war leaders, including Hajime Sugiyama, Chief of the Japanese General Staff to early 1944, committed suicide. When Americans came to arrest him, Gen. Hideki Tojo (*q.v.*), Japanese Prime Minister in 1941 and a staunch defender of the Axis, tried to kill himself.

In late 1946 an International Military Tribunal for the Far East was set up under the presidency of Sir William Webb. Its purpose was to try major Japanese war leaders for war crimes.

TRIAL. Of those Japanese statesmen and war leaders arrested immediately after the war, 25 were brought to trial in early 1947. Indictments accused them of conspiring to wage aggressive war to obtain military, naval, political, and economic domination of East Asia and the Pacific and Indian oceans; of allowing atrocities by the Japanese Army and Navy; of committing breaches of laws and customs of war; and of responsibility for other crimes. The trial lasted for 417 days and was finally adjourned on April 16, 1948.

VERDICTS. In its judgment delivered on November 21, 1948, the tribunal found all the defendants guilty. Seven, of whom six were generals and the seventh a foreign minister, were sentenced to death. The military men were Gens. Hideki Tojo, Kenji Doihara, Seishiro Itagaki, Heitaro Kimura, Iwane Matsui, and Akira Muto. The statesman was Koki Hirota, Foreign Minister from 1933 to 1936. The condemned men were hanged on December 23, 1948.

All the others accused were sentenced to life imprisonment, except Shigenori Togo, Foreign Minister during Tojo's administration, who was sentenced to 20 years' imprisonment, and Mamoru Shigemetsu, Foreign Minister from April 1943 to April 1945, who was given seven years' imprisonment.

REACTIONS. The sentences were greeted with satisfaction in the United States, where there was still much indignation over Pearl Harbor (*q.v.*). As in the case of the Nuremberg Trials, the verdicts touched off a continuing debate on the justice of the proceedings. Proponents admitted that crimes of the accused Japanese were far less heinous than those of their Nazi counterparts, but insisted that the proven atrocities were enough to convict the men on trial. Others claimed that the convicted men were victims of victor's justice.

Bibliography. P. R. Piccigallo, *The Japanese on Trial* (1979).

JAVA SEA, BATTLE OF THE. Japanese naval victory over the Allies in early 1942.

BACKGROUND. After victorious campaigns in Malaya and Burma, Japanese Imperial GHQ turned its attention to Australia. Its first objective was to capture the island of Java between the Java Sea on the north and the Indian Ocean on the south. Java was rich in such materials as rice, quinine, and manganese, but especially in oil. In peacetime Japan imported 88 percent of its oil and now the most important available oil fields were in the Dutch East Indies. The Dutch would probably destroy the installations, but these could be rebuilt quickly.

Java was defended by an unreliable force of 100,000 natives as well as several British, Dutch, and American warships, the latter remnants of the fleet that had escaped the Philippines. It seemed to be an easy target.

On December 24, 1941, a Japanese force landed at North Borneo and captured the oil fields there. On January 22–28, 1942, four American destroyers, assisted by elements of the Dutch Navy, inflicted serious losses on an enemy convoy, but the advantage was only momentary.

On February 15, 1942, a huge Japanese task force guarding 56 transports in a western group and 41 others in the eastward group, moved on Java. To meet the threat the Allies sent out their Combined Striking Force (CSF) of 5 cruisers (2 heavy and 3 light), and 10 destroyers (4 American, 3 British, 3 Dutch) under command of Rear Adm. Karel Doorman. There were no covering or reconnaissance aircraft. The crews had never worked together, but they were ordered to harass Japanese shipping, especially convoys, near Java and Sumatra.

CONFRONTATION. On February 27, 1942, as his ships were refueling, Doorman received word that a Japanese invasion force was spotted in the Makassar Straits. He moved to meet the enemy. Japanese heavy cruisers opened fire at a range of 16 miles while Doorman tried to close in with his light cruisers. Doorman's flagship and 3 other CSF ships were sunk. The admiral went down with his ship. The next day 2 Allied cruisers intercepted the transports and sank 2 of them before themselves falling victim to a strong Japanese naval escort group. Although damaged, the cruiser *Exeter* with 2 destroyers as escort engaged 4 heavy Japanese cruisers and 3 destroyers on February 29 in a battle that lasted for one and a half hours. All three Allied ships were sunk.

LOSSES. The Battle of the Java Sea was a distinct victory for the Japanese. Only 4 Allied warships survived the encounter. An Admiralty communiqué, issued on March 12, 1942, enumerated the losses as 5 cruisers (British *Exeter,* Australian *Perth;* U.S. *Houston;* Dutch *Java* and *de Ruyter*); 6 destroyers (British *Electra, Jupiter, Encounter,* and *Stronghold;* U.S. *Pope;* and Dutch *Kortenaer*); and one sloop, the *Yarra.*

AFTERMATH. Troops from the Japanese transports poured ashore at several points on the Java coastline. Within a week the whole of Java was in Japanese hands and Sumatra, too, was taken.

SIGNIFICANCE. The main factor in the defeat of the Allies was their lack of air cover. In addition, the Japanese displayed superiority in the use of torpedoes. The sea battle made it plain that defeat of the Japanese in the Pacific was to be no easy matter.

Bibliography. D. A. Thomas, *Battle of the Java Sea* (1968); R. J. O'Connor (ed.), *The Japanese Navy in World War II* (1970); W. G. Winslow, *USS Houston* (1971); and A. G. Watts and B. G. Gordon, *The Imperial Japanese Navy* (1972).

JEAN BART. French battleship gutted by the Allies in 1942.

DESIGN. The *Jean Bart,* sister ship of the *Richelieu,* was built from October 1933 to March 1940. She was unique both in appearance and proportion of displacement devoted to protection, with an armor weight of 14,000 tons.

SPECIFICATIONS.
  Standard Displacement. 35,000 tons.
  Maximum Speed. 30 knots.
  Armor. Belt 15¾ in.; turret 17 in.
  Armament. Eight 15-in. guns; nine 6 in.

BACKGROUND. On November 8, 1942, U.S. forces landed on either side of Casablanca. (*See* NORTH AFRICA, CAMPAIGNS IN.) There was unexpectedly strong French resistance. At Casablanca the *Jean Bart* lay in harbor along with cruisers and several smaller craft. Because its construction was unfinished, the *Jean Bart* was unable to move. Other warships and aircraft were sent out to engage the Americans.

ENCOUNTER. Though immobile, the *Jean Bart* fought back. She was ripped by the heavy guns of the U.S. battleship *Massachusetts* and sank in shallow water. Continuing the fight, the French crew struck back at Allied warships and landing craft until they were silenced by direct hits. Casablanca surrendered on November 11, 1942.

At the end of 1945 the *Jean Bart* was returned to France for repairs.

JEDBURGHS. Special three-man teams composed of one Briton, one American, and one Frenchman trained for sabotage on missions in Northern France. (*See* NORMANDY INVASION.)

Like similar units called Cooneys (*q.v.*), the Jedburghs were trained to impose discipline on the French Maquisards, members of the *Maquis* (*q.v.*), who were noted for their independence and undisciplined behavior. The Jedburghs probably took their name from their training headquarters at Jedburgh, a royal burg on the Jed River in Scotland's border country. British intelligence later claimed the name was picked from a schoolbook. The combination of three different nationalities for each team was considered necessary to avoid the charge of being agents for British imperialism. Each member of the team was expected to be an expert in demolition, guns, languages, poaching, and medicine, and had to be a man of reckless courage. All were given intensive training in physical fitness, silent killing, elementary Morse code, and railway demolition.

Some 80 Jedburgh teams were deployed before the Normandy landings to be included among 5,000 agents and soldiers to organize and lead French resistance. The sabotage carried out by these teams played an effective role in the success of the landings and the subsequent surge across French soil into the heart of Germany.

Bibliography. A. C. Brown, *Bodyguard of Lies* (1975).

JEEP. Military slang for a diminutive multipurpose, cross-country automotive vehicle used by the U.S. Armed Forces in World War II. Its name is derived from GP (general purpose) and also through association with the sound "jeep" made by a rodent character, Eugene the Jeep, in the comic strip "Popeye" by E. C. Segar. The vehicle was also called *bantam, blitzbuggy,* and (by the tank forces) the *peep.*

The term *jeep* was also used during the war to describe various individuals or objects distinguished by small size. It was often applied to a raw recruit or rookie. In U.S. Navy slang *jeep* referred to an escort carrier. For the U.S. Air Forces the *jeep* was a tiny 2,100-pound plane used for reconnaissance and liaison.

By the end of the war the *jeep* vehicle was being produced on the production lines in Detroit in enormous quantities. Many were sent to Soviet Russia, where they remained in use for many years after the war.

SPECIFICATIONS.
  Weight. 2,200 to 2,300 lbs.
  Maximum Speed. 60 m.p.h.
  Special Features. Four-wheel drive; standard transmission; wheel base 80 in.; capable of carrying five men.

JERVIS BAY. A British armed merchant cruiser sunk by the German pocket battleship *Admiral Scheer* (*q.v.*) in November 1940.

BACKGROUND. In early November 1940 the newly outfitted *Scheer* broke through the Denmark Strait between Iceland and Greenland in violent weather. Several days later her reconnaissance plane sighted a convoy of 38 ships. Capt. Theodor Krancke of the *Scheer* turned his battlewagon toward the convoy. Late on the afternoon of November 5, 1940, he saw the lines of merchant-ship hulls rising slowly over the horizon. There were no enemy warships in sight to protect the convoy. Krancke prepared for a wild duck shoot.

CLASH. Suddenly, one small merchant ship, trailing a smoke screen and firing red rockets, moved out of line and turned toward the *Scheer.* It was the 18-year-old former 14,000-ton pleasure liner *Jervis Bay,* which had been converted hurriedly into an armed merchant cruiser. Her captain, E. S. Fogarty Fegen, was sailing his vessel alone against the German battleship. He had no hope of inflicting any material damage on the big battlewagon, but he was determined to gain time to allow the ships of the convoy to escape.

At a range of 10 miles Capt. Krancke turned all his six 11-inch turret guns on the obstreperous auxiliary cruiser and methodically began to tear it to pieces. Meanwhile, Fegen kept his ship between the *Scheer* and the convoy as long as his engines and steering still worked. The first hit from the *Scheer* tore off Fegen's leg and damaged the other. With his stump bandaged, he dragged himself to the stern gun and continued firing. He was killed in a further explosion.

LOSSES. The crew of the *Jervis Bay* fought on for two hours. Her death toll was 190 as she rolled over and sank. Some 65 survivors were rescued.

AFTERMATH. The rest of the convoy disappeared into the growing darkness behind smoke screens. The *Scheer* turned her guns on other targets as they appeared briefly in the gathering darkness. With her radar seeking victims and her searchlights pinpointing targets, she cut through the scattered ships. When the three-hour carnage was over, five merchant ships had joined the *Jervis Bay* on the bottom of the sea and three more were damaged.

SIGNIFICANCE. The bold action forced the Germans to direct all their guns at the *Jervis Bay* and gained invaluable minutes for the threatened convoy. Thanks to this remarkable defense, the *Scheer's* score was relatively low. The convoy system was disorganized for two weeks, but it soon started again.

For his gallant sacrifice, Fegen was awarded the Victoria Cross posthumously. His feat became legendary in British naval annals.

Bibliography. T. Krancke and H. J. Brennecke, *The Battleship Scheer* (1956); and E. P. Von den Porten, *The German Navy in World War II* (1969).

JODL, ALFRED (1890–1946). German General and Chief of the Armed Forces Operational Staff for the duration of the war.

Jodl served as Hitler's adviser on strategic and operational matters throughout the war. He belonged to that group of high officers, including Gens. Wilhelm Keitel (*q.v.*) and Walther Warlimont, who resented the old-line Prussian military caste. "There is only one undisciplined element in the Army," he said, "and that is the generals, and in the last analysis that is because they are arrogant." Since his early days he had a Napoleonic hero complex and he remained loyal to Hitler until the *Fuehrer's* death. He denounced other officers for not believing in "the genius of Hitler."

Jodl was Gen. Keitel's most efficient and competent assistant. Much of the success of the early German campaigns in the war was due to Jodl's able direction. He was aware as early as 1940 that Hitler intended to attack the Soviet Union, and he was closely involved in the preliminary planning for that operation. The *Fuehrer,* he said, feared an attack by Russia and therefore moved first. In the latter stages of the Russian campaign Jodl made some faulty decisions that resulted in heavy losses.

Jodl was promoted to Colonel General in 1944, but his role in the later stages of the war was limited. He signed Germany's unconditional surrender at Reims on May 7, 1945.

NUREMBERG. Jodl was brought to trial before the International Military Tribunal. (*See* NUREMBERG TRIALS.) He was accused of discussing the Norway invasion with Hitler, planning the assaults on Greece and Yugoslavia, helping the preparations for the attack on Soviet Russia, and echoing Hitler's savage orders to the army. Jodl refused to admit his guilt. The most he would concede was that the Germans had not clung to justice as they should have in the conduct of the war. His defense was the doctrine of "superior orders."

The court found nothing in mitigation and pronounced Jodl guilty on all four counts of the indictment. The Court stated: "Participation in such crimes as these has never been required of a soldier and he cannot now shield himself behind a mystical requirement of soldierly obedience at all costs as his excuse for commission of these crimes." He was hanged at Nuremberg on October 16, 1946.

Bibliography. E. Davidson, *The Trial of the Germans: Nuremberg, 1945-1946* (1966); and G. Just, *Alfred Jodl: Soldat ohne Furcht und Tadel* (1971).

JOINT PLANNING STAFF (JPS). British military planning organization. One of its components was the London Controlling Section (LCS), which was concerned with the devising and coordination of deception schemes. (*See* ESPIONAGE; and *MINCEMEAT.*)

The United States also had its Joint Planning Staff, consisting of four members representing the army, navy, army air, and navy air. This unit served the U.S. Joint Chiefs of Staff in policy and strategic planning.

The two Joint Planning Staffs made up the Combined Planning Staff under the Combined Chiefs of Staff.

JOINT SECURITY CONTROL (JSC). U.S. organization under the Joint Chiefs of Staff responsible for the security of cryptanalytical and military operations.

The American counterpart of London Controlling Section (LCS), it was also concerned with the introduction, planning, and implementation of operations designed to deceive the enemy. (*See* ESPIONAGE.)

JONES, JAMES, (1921–1977). American novelist who specialized in war themes.

Jones served in the U.S. Army from 1939 to 1944. He became a Sergeant and received a Purple Heart. His part in the war gave him the background for his most famous novel, *From Here to Eternity,* which appeared in 1951 and which propelled him to the top of the American literary scene. The book was a highly realistic account of the U.S. Army in the immediate pre-war years. He portrayed the army as it existed at the end of the Depression as a refuge for the unemployed, misfits, and adventurers. He described the officer caste as waiting to be promoted in the next war. The novel ended with Pearl Harbor.

Jones replied to critics who complained that he had glorified combat by saying any accurate account had to reveal "the regimentation of souls, the systematic education of men to animal level, the horrors of pointless death, the exhaustion of living in constant fear."

Jones died in Southampton, Long Island, on May 9, 1977. He left an uncompleted novel titled *Whistle,* which he visualized as the final novel of a trilogy. "It will say everything that I have to say, or will ever have to say, on the human condition of war and what it means to us, as against what we claim it means to us." Willie Morris, a friend and neighbor in Bridgehampton, Long Island, finished the last three chapters. The book was published in 1977 posthumously.

JOSEPH STALIN TANK (JS) (STALIN TANK). See TANKS.

JOURNALISM IN WORLD WAR II. See REPORTING, WAR.

JOYCE, WILLIAM (1908–1946). Anglo-American propagandist for the Germans during the war, known in Britain and throughout the world as Lord Haw Haw because of his exaggerated drawl.

In 1933 Joyce joined the British Union of Fascists, led by Oswald Mosley, and became active in its ranks. Attracted by Nazi ideology, he moved to Germany in 1939.

Joyce quickly obtained employment in the Third Reich. He was regarded by Paul Joseph Goebbels (*q.v.*), Minister for Public Enlightenment and Propaganda, as a valuable asset in the propaganda war against the Allies. Joyce worked in a radio station in Berlin, from which he broadcast talks to England and combat areas in order to weaken Allied morale. In sarcastic tones he mocked British war efforts and urged Britons to lay down their arms and join their fellow Nordic-Aryans in a crusade to rid the world of democracy, liberalism, and (after June 1941) communism. Joyce succeeded only in earning the contempt of his listeners. There is no evidence that a single Allied soldier was influenced by his broadcasts.

FATE. On May 28, 1945, just three weeks after the German surrender, Joyce was arrested by British soldiers. Brought to trial at the Old Bailey in London, he disparaged his efforts as a propagandist. Furthermore, in an attempt to avoid British justice, he claimed American citizenship. Unfortunately for him, he carried a British passport, which made him subject legally to British jurisdiction. Sentenced to death, he appealed the verdict, but it was affirmed. He was hanged in London on January 3, 1946.

Bibliography. See R. West's *The Meaning of Treason* (1949), for a brilliant account of Joyce's career and trial. See also J. A. Cole, *Lord Haw Haw—and William Joyce: The Full Story* (1964).

JULY PLOT. Major unsuccessful attempt on Hitler's life on July 20, 1944.

BACKGROUND. Despite his early military successes, there was smoldering resentment inside Germany against Hitler. Discontent mounted in three stages—from opposition to resistance to conspiracy. Eventually, a small cadre of conspirators from military, diplomatic, and civilian sources combined in a plot to eliminate the man they regarded as a stain on the national honor.

There were several plots, all unsuccessful. On March 13, 1943, in *Operation Flash,* two officers placed a bomb on Hitler's plane (the so-called Smolensk Attentat [*q.v.*]). The device did not explode and the plotters were able to hide the evidence. Eight days later, on March 21, 1943, two bombs were to be placed in Hitler's overcoat pockets, but the plot failed when the *Fuehrer's* schedule was changed at the last moment. Again Hitler's luck held out, as on several occasions before the war when attempts had been made on his life.

PREPARATION. In early 1944 another major attempt was planned. At the center of the conspiracy was a group of senior officers, including Maj. Gen. Henning von Treschkow, Chief of Staff in Army Group Center on the Russian front; Col. Gen. Erich Hoepner (*q.v.*), head of the supply section of the Reserve Army; and Field Marshal Erwin von Witzleben, who had been retired from active service. Added to these were several junior officers, led by Col. Claus Schenck Graf von Stauffenberg, (*q.v.*), who was to play the central role in the conspiracy. Preparations were made for a bomb attack in Hitler's headquarters on the eastern front.

ATTENTAT. Early on the morning of July 20, 1944, Hitler called a conference of his close military advisers to be held at the *Wolfsschanze* ("Wolf's Lair") headquarters at Rastenburg at 12:30 P.M. The compound was protected by numerous devices, including electric fences, barbed wire, blockhouses, and check points. Von Stauffenberg, who was to report on the conditions of the Home Army, entered the frame wooden hut with a brief case holding a British plastic bomb. After greeting the *Fuehrer,* he placed the briefcase on the floor beside Hitler and excused himself "to make a phone call." One of the officers, feeling the brief case to be in his way, pushed it away from the chair in such a manner that it rested against the heavy upright support on the side farthest from the *Fuehrer.* That move saved Hitler's life.

At precisely 12:42 P.M. the bomb exploded with a tremendous blast, shattering the central table and wrecking the ceiling. Of the 24 men present, three were killed outright and three died later of their wounds. Shielded from the full blast, Hitler survived. His hair was set afire, his right arm partially paralyzed, his right leg burned, and his eardrums damaged.

AFTERMATH. Von Stauffenberg returned to Berlin believing that Hitler could not possibly have survived the blast. Arriving at the War Ministry, he learned to his dismay that his victim was still alive. The *Fuehrer* took terrible vengeance. All the conspirators were tracked down and killed in a massive blood purge. Many were strangled with piano wire and their bodies suspended like animal carcasses on huge metal hooks. Hitler had the scene filmed, and he watched the movies for hours throughout the night. Many young cadets, who were forced to view the films, fainted.

Bibliography. C. FitzGibbon, *20 July* (1956), and R. Manvell and H. Fraenkel, *The July Plot* (1966).

K

KAISER, HENRY JOHN (1882–1967). Prominent American industrialist who played a key role in U.S. production during the war.

In his early career Kaiser took an important part in the construction of Hoover, Bonneville, Grand Coulee, and Shasta dams. This experience was vital for his performance during the war. To help meet the need for ships, in 1940 he helped build in record time 60 cargo vessels for the British Admiralty. In 1941 he signed contracts with the U.S. Maritime Commission and the U.S. Navy. He built and operated seven shipyards. Speed was vital because so many ships were being sunk by German U-Boats that the survival of the Allies depended literally upon the rapidity with which Kaiser could construct ships. In May 1942 the average time it took to build a ship was 150 days. Kaiser cut it to 72 days, by the following August to 45 days, and by September to 27 days. Using mass production methods, Kaiser's men could assemble a pre-fabricated Liberty Ship (*q.v.*) in four and a half days.

During the war Kaiser produced 1,490 vessels, mostly Liberty Ships, Victory Ships, and aircraft carriers. In addition to accounting for almost one-third of the entire American production of shipping, he built 50 small 18,000-ton aircraft carriers. Navy experts said that the small aircraft carriers he designed could not be produced en masse, but his baby flattops contributed heavily to defeat of the Axis.

Kaiser's work did not stop at shipbuilding. He constructed a huge magnesium plant at Permanente, which produced more than 80 million pounds of magnesium incendiaries. In 1941–1942 he built in Fontana the first complete steel mill in California. In 1943 he took control of the Fleetwing Aircraft company at Bristol, Pennsylvania. In 1945 he became Chairman of Kaiser Industries, which included steel, aluminum, home building, and automobiles.

Bibliography. See B. C. Forbes (ed.), *America's Fifty Foremost Business Leaders* (1948); J. Gunther, *Inside U.S.A.* (1948); and D. Robinson, *The 100 Most Important Americans in the World Today* (1952).

KALTENBORN, HANS VON (1875–1965). American newscaster whose voice became familiar to millions in World War II.

In the summer of 1939 Kaltenborn spent three weeks in Europe interviewing key political figures in the increasingly dangerous situation. The war he predicted came in September. He reported the rest of the war as a news analyst from several European countries and later especially from the Pacific theater of war. In the postwar era he continued his broadcasts until his death in New York, on June 14, 1965.

Tall, ruddy-faced, and white-haired, Kaltenborn was widely known for his crisp, rapid tone while speaking on the air. He was one of the few broadcasters who went on the air without a script. Strong-willed, he never allowed himself to be interrupted by commercial announcements. His voice was so widely known that it was often imitated. On November 3, 1948, the morning after the presidential election, the winner Harry S Truman (*q.v.*) went on the air and gave a hilarious imitation of Kaltenborn's brisk delivery reporting Thomas E. Dewey's impending victory.

Bibliography. Among Kaltenborn's books were: *We Look At the World* (1930); *Kaltenborn Edits the News: Europe, Asia, America* (1937); *I Broadcast the Crisis* (1938); *Kaltenborn Edits the War News* (1942); *Europe Now* (1942); *Fifty Fabulous Years* (1950); and *It Seems Like Yesterday* (1956).

KALTENBRUNNER, ERNST (1903–1946). Austrian Nazi.

To win Hitler's approval, Kaltenbrunner stepped up the pace of Nazi activities in Austria. In early 1943 the *Fuehrer* chose Kaltenbrunner as successor to the assassinated Reinhard Heydrich (*q.v.*) as Reich Central Security Officer. Kaltenbrunner was energetic in hunting Jews for the gas chambers. He was responsible not only for the murdering of thousands of Jews but also Allied prisoners of war and parachutists as well as French prostitutes. In February 1944 he was appointed head of the *Abwehr* (*q.v.*), the counterintelligence service of the German High Command. In the last days of the war he attempted unsuccessfully to make contact with Allied officers for peace negotiations.

NURENBURG. At the postwar International Military Tribunal Kaltenbrunner angrily disputed evidence of his guilt in the murder of Jews and prisoners of war. "I have only done my duty and I refuse to serve as a substitute for Hitler." He was found guilty on count 3, war crimes, and count 4, crimes against humanity. He was executed at Nuremberg on October 16, 1946. His last words were: "Germany good luck!"

Tall, with a thick neck, piercing eyes, and a deep scar on the left side of his face, Kaltenbrunner was a man of consuming ambition. Utterly lacking in any sense of humanity, he hunted down Jews as if they were animals and was coldly indifferent to their slaughter.

Bibliography. Spiegelbild einer Verschwörung (1961).

KAMIKAZE. "Divine wind" in English, *kamikaze* suicide attack became an integral part of the Japanese war effort during the late days of the war.

BACKGROUND. Kamikaze tactics were regarded as suitable to the Japanese character and as motivated by tradition. Behind them was a combination of Japanese theology and psychology. The military code refused to recognize even the possibility of defeat. At a moment when the Empire was in a desperate situation a favorite old legend was revived, the story of a *kamikaze,* a providential typhoon sent by the Sun-Goddess to wreck the huge fleet of the Mongol conqueror Kublai Khan in 1281 in the hope that similar man-made strikes could be made to destroy the enemy and keep the home shores inviolable.

ORIGIN. After the Battle for Leyte Gulf (*q.v.*), Vice-Adm. Takijiro Onishi, commander of the Japanese Air Force in the Philippines, decided to send out his pilots on bomb laden *Zero* fighters or *Judy* bombers to crash on the decks of U.S. carriers. Gathering his pilots he told them of his plan for a glorious death for the Emperor: "Life is like a delicate flower. How can one expect the fragrance to last forever?" From that moment was born the *Kamikaze Tokubetsu Kogekitai* ("*Kamikaze* Special Attack Squad").

PILOTS. Kamikaze pilots regarded their suicidal missions as part of their duty. Almost all of Japan's flying aces were dead and most of its first-line planes had been destroyed. But it was believed that even an obsolete plane could be loaded with explosives and that young pilots could be taught quickly to fly a plane to the Allied fleet and then dive it into a ship. Most young pilots had minimal training for their last assignment. Before locking themselves in their cockpits for their last journey on earth, they held formal parties. They were given ceremonial belts inscribed with the code of *bushido* and then drank final toasts to the Emperor, the life of the Japanese Empire, and a glorious death. They sang the *Kamikaze Song of the Warrior:* "Let us die close by the side of our sovereign."

ATTACK. Spaced out for miles off the shores of Okinawa was a huge armada of 1,500 Allied vessels, chiefly American. Like angry wasps the *kamikazes* descended on the fleet below, most aiming for the prize carriers. The pilots used two methods of flight. In a low-altitude approach, one plane would fly close to the sea surface to prevent early detection by enemy radar. In a high-altitude approach the pilots had to be careful to see that the final dive angle was not too steep, because the aircraft could easily go out of control under the influence of gravity. The dive had to be made as shallow as possible with careful note of tail wind and any countermove by the target. The best point of aim against the carriers was the central elevator; against other ships the base of the bridge was preferred. To ensure a direct hit usually a single aircraft was sent against one warship.

RESULTS. Kamikaze pilots failed to sink any capital ships during the 82 days and nights of the assault. On May 15, 1945, they inflicted heavy damage on the giant American carrier, *Enterprise,* but quick work by the damage-control crew saved the warship. Statistically, the attacks took a heavy toll. It is believed that from 26 to 40 American ships were sunk, although none was larger than a destroyer. More than 165 were damaged, including carriers and battleships. It is estimated that several thousand U.S. Navy seamen were killed. At the height of the battle for the home islands the suicide missions caused so much damage that shipyards in California were filled with warships sent home for repairs, while others had to be moved to the East Coast. A U.S. Strategic Bombing Survey concluded that so much damage had been wrought that if the attacks had been sustained in great power and concentration "they might have been able to cause us to withdraw and revise our strategic plans."

The Japanese paid with losses variously estimated as from 1,220 to 4,000 planes and pilots. They were never able to improve their tactics because the doomed pilots never reported back. More success could have been achieved if four bomb-loaded planes attacked one target at once.

Eventually, Allied naval commanders developed techniques to deal with the *kamikazes.* In the late stage the Japanese found it difficult to find enough young men willing to die this way. Pilots began to return saying that they could not find the enemy.

Bibliography. I. Castro, *Kamikaze* (1970).

KASSERINE PASS. Scene of the worst U.S. defeat in North Africa in early 1943.

BACKGROUND. The land to the north and south of Kasserine and the narrow valleys hemmed in by rocky cliffs had been a battleground in North Africa for several thousand years. In early 1943 Kasserine Pass was behind the Allied lines. American forces took over the sector from the French 19th Corps. Ahead was a narrow gap between two mountains.

Meanwhile the Germans decided to mount a counteroffensive as soon as possible. They planned to attack the U.S. 2nd Corps head-on at Kasserine Pass, and then Gen. Erwin Rommel's *Afrika Korps* (*qq.v.*) would strike on the Americans' flank from Gafsa.

ATTACK. The German attack was launched on February 14, 1943. First, *Stukas* dived low from the eastern hilltops, bombing artillery units and machine-gunning the infantry. Then German tanks, including huge *Tigers,* roared out of the pass firing their new 88-mm. cannon. Inexperienced Americans fought bravely, but without air support and enough tanks, they could not halt the assault. Falling back to Kasserine, they dug into the hillside. There, without food or water, they held out for six days. Several of their attacks were forced back.

The Allied Supreme Command sent a flight of aircraft to assist the trapped infantry, but the bombardiers, confused by the cloudy weather, missed the target and killed Arabs on the ground 100 miles away. Surrounded troops had to surrender. The Americans lost 192 killed, 2,624 wounded, and 2,450 prisoners. The Germans had nearly 1,000 casualties; 535 Italians were captured.

SIGNIFICANCE. Kasserine Pass was a setback for the Americans. Insufficiently trained for this kind of warfare, they were no match for the Germans. Eisenhower attributed the defeat to faulty intelligence, inexperienced troops, and effective German leadership. Recovering quickly, Americans soon learned the essentials of desert warfare.

Despite their victory at Kasserine, the Germans did not exploit their success. Military historians believe that the Allies were fortunate that Rommel was not appointed theater commander until the day after the battle of Kasserine Pass ended.

Bibliography. B. H. Liddell Hart, *History of the Second World War* (1971), pp. 407–410.

KATYN FOREST MASSACRE. Controversial mass execution of Polish Army officers discovered in April 1943.

BACKGROUND. When Hitler and Stalin signed the Russo-German Nonaggression Pact (*q.v.*) on August 23, 1939, they agreed to a new partition of Poland. The country was taken by September 28, 1939. That same day Germany and Russia signed a treaty completing Poland's fourth partition. Germany took 71,000 square miles, Russia 75,000. The Germans admitted to having lost 10,572 men killed in the conquest. The Russians suffered almost no losses.

More than 240,000 Polish officers and men fell into Russian hands. Most were interned in Russian camps. After German invasion of the USSR on June 22, 1941, the Polish Government-in-exile (*q.v.*) in London and the Soviet Government agreed to repudiate the partition of 1939 and to form a Polish Army on Soviet territory. Poles in London requested that Polish prisoners of war, held in the Soviet Union, be used to form the nucleus of a new Polish Army. Moscow replied in December 1941 that this was impossible because most of the prisoners had escaped to Manchuria. The Poles insisted that they were mystified by the fate of 14,500 of their men, among them 8,000 officers, who were supposed to have been held since 1939 in camps near Smolensk.

DISCOVERY. In August 1941 the Germans captured the village of Katyn in central Western Russia. On April 13, 1943, Radio Berlin announced the discovery of a mass grave of 10,000 Polish officers in Katyn Forest near Smolensk. (The German report was inaccurate: There were actually 4,443.) The announcement stated that all had been shot in the back of the head by Soviet secret police. The Russian Government replied that Polish prisoners had been engaged in construction work and were massacred by Germans who controlled the area.

INVESTIGATIONS. The discovery of the mass slaughter caused international repercussions. The Polish Government-in-exile, dissatisfied with the Russian explanation, demanded an investigation by the International Red Cross, but Stalin refused. It was a German atrocity, he said, and no investigation was needed. The Germans then began their own inquiry. A German committee of experts examined documents found on the bodies as well as the age of the trees planted over the corpses, and concluded that the executions had taken place in early 1940 at a time when the entire Katyn area was under Russian control.

When Russians reoccupied the Smolensk area in September 1943, they set up their own inquiry. Their report held that because of the rapid German advance in 1941 it was impossible to evacuate the prisoner-of-war camps and all officers were systematically slaughtered by Germans. In 1951–1952 a U.S. Congressional investigation charged that the Russians had executed the Polish officers.

REPERCUSSIONS. For the remainder of the war after the discovery of the mass graves at Katyn, Allied leadership was reluctant to see the massacre used for internal quarrels. The Polish Government-in-exile was pressed to issue a statement generally condemning aggression against Polish citizens without specifying who were the actual Katyn criminals. On April 26, 1943, Stalin broke off relations with Poles in London, because they did not specifically exculpate the Russians in their statement.

The crime of Katyn was neither investigated at the Teheran Conference (*q.v.*) in late 1943 nor was it mentioned at the Nuremberg Trials (*q.v.*) after the war. Churchill took an ambivalent position. The Soviet Government, he wrote, in his history of the war, did not take the opportunity of clearing itself of the horrible and widely believed accusation against it. "Everyone is entitled to his own opinion."

The Soviet Government was reluctant to take the suggestion that it clear itself of the stain of Katyn. Instead, it preferred to disregard the matter. All mention of Katyn was ordered removed from textbooks. The reference to Katyn in the 1953 edition of the Soviet *Encyclopedia* was dropped in the 1973 edition.

AFTERMATH. Although the Katyn Massacre receives no further attention in Soviet Russia, it continues to occupy the interest of historians. Later research by Polish as well as independent authorities concluded that the Russians were responsible. If the Russian report of 1944 is to be believed, according to this research, 15,000 Polish officers and men passed into German hands from spring 1940 to summer 1941 and were killed by Germans without a single prisoner escaping, reporting to the Polish authorities, or joining the Polish underground. Observers who accuse Germans of atrocities at Lidice and Oradour-sur-Glans (*qq.v.*) are inclined to absolve them of the Katyn massacre and hold that the crime was the work of Russians, either by Stalin's personal command or by subordinates who panicked at the time of the German attack.

Bibliography. J. Mackiewicz, *The Katyn Wood Murders* (1951); J. K. Zawodny, *Death in the Forest* (1962); Z. Stahl, *The Crime of Katyn* (1965); L. FitzGibbon, *Katyn* (1971); and E. A. Komorowski, *Night Never Ending* (1974).

KEITEL, WILHELM (1882–1946). German General who was Hitler's military adviser during the war.

At the beginning of the war, Keitel was responsible for preparing the major German war moves beginning with the attack on Poland. Throughout the war he served as Hitler's closest military adviser. In June 1940 he was empowered by the *Fuehrer* to conclude an armistice with France at Compiègne (*q.v.*). On July 19, 1940, along with 11 other generals, he was promoted to Field Marshal by the triumphant Hitler.

In 1941 Keitel indicated to Hitler his opposition to the invasion of the Soviet Union. Although he threatened to resign, he was unable to prevent the attack on Russia. From then on his influence on Hitler waned. However, he remained loyal to his chief and continued to carry out all his orders. He signed operational papers requiring the shooting of hostages and committed other acts considered illegal under international law. The policy of killing hostages, which he carried out, led to the destruction of towns like Lidice and Oradour-sur-Glans (*qq.v.*). He served on the court of honor that decreed death sentences for those officers implicated in the attempt on Hitler's life on July 20, 1944. (*See* JULY PLOT.)

NUREMBERG. After the war Keitel was brought before the International Military Tribunal at Nuremberg (*see* NUREMBERG TRIALS) on charges of participating in conspiracy, crimes against peace, war crimes, and crimes against humanity. In his defense he stated that as an army officer he merely carried out orders of the state. The tribunal judged that the doctrine of immunity of heads of state did not apply when a state had violated international law. It also refused to recognize the defense that "superior orders" justified Keitel's actions. He was found guilty on all four counts and hanged at Nuremberg on October 16, 1946.

Bibliography. W. Goerlitz and D. Irving (eds.), *The Memoirs of Field-Marshal Keitel* (1966). *See also* chapters on Keitel in G. M. Gilbert, *Nuremberg Diary* (1947), pp. 237–255; E. Davidson, *The Trial of the Germans at Nuremberg, 1945–1946* (1966), pp. 328–342; and H. J. Schmeller, *Hitler and Keitel* (1970).

KELLY, COLIN P. (1915–1941). One of the first American war heroes.

Two days after Pearl Harbor, Captain Kelly took off in a *B-17* from Luzon, Philippine Islands, on a mission to bomb Japanese shipping. After scoring a hit on an enemy transport, he was attacked by the pilot of a Japanese *Zero*. With one of his crew killed, Kelly ordered the other six to bail out. The latter survived, but Kelly was killed when his plane exploded. Kelly was highly praised in the American press for his sacrifice in combat.

KENNEDY, JOHN FITZGERALD (1917–1963). Young naval officer who became thirty-fifth President of the United States.

In the spring of 1941 Kennedy tried to enlist in the U.S. Navy, but a spinal injury suffered in his sophomore year at Harvard University, delayed his acceptance until September 1941. In late 1942 he was assigned to a Motor Torpedo Squadron. In August 1943, as a Lieutenant Junior Grade, he was placed in command of *PT-109*. His torpedo boat was attacked by the Japanese while on patrol off the Solomon Islands in the South Pacific. His craft was cut in two by an enemy destroyer. Kennedy was credited with saving the lives of several of his seamen, one of whom he towed through the water for three miles by a lifebelt the rope of which he held in his mouth between his teeth. For the next several days he swam between islands to help rescue more of his seamen who had been helped by friendly natives. (*See also PT-109*).

Kennedy hoped to remain in the Pacific for more duty, but in December 1943 he was called back to the United States for medical attention. His exploits won him the Navy and Marine Corps medals.

Bibliography. J. M. Burns, *John Kennedy* (1960); J. MacCarthy, *The Remarkable Kennedys* (1960); and C. L. Markman and M. Sherwin, *John F. Kennedy: A Sense of Purpose* (1961).

KENNEDY, JOSEPH PATRICK (1888–1969). U.S. financier and governmental official.

In 1937 Kennedy was named U.S. Ambassador to Britain. When the war broke out in 1939, he expressed doubt about England's capacity to resist Hitler. He sent pessimistic reports to Washington on British morale and determination. "Democracy," he said, "is finished in Britian." In November 1940 he resigned his post saying that as a private citizen he wanted to keep his country out of the war. Despite his skepticism, he supported Lend-Lease (*q.v.*). His influence declined after the United States entered the war.

Three of Kennedy's sons became active in politics: John F. Kennedy, 35th President of the United States; Robert F. Kennedy, U.S. Senator and Attorney General; and Edward M. Kennedy, U.S. Senator. The elder Kennedy died in Hyannisport, Massachusetts, on November 18, 1969.

Red-faced, with receding sandy hair and blue eyes, Kennedy was known as a shrewd financial operator, harsh in business matters, and warm in family relations. One journalist described him as "athletic, unperplexed, easily pleased, hot-tempered, independent, impatient, and restless."

Bibliography. J. F. Dineen, *The Kennedy Family* (1960); R. J. Whalen, *The Founding Father: The Story of Joseph Patrick Kennedy* (1964); and D. E. Koskoff, *Joseph Patrick Kennedy: A Life and Times* (1974).

KESSELRING, ALBERT (1885–1960). Prominent German Field Commander noted for his performance in Italy and his superb conduct of the Italian campaign.

Kesselring commanded Air Fleet I in the invasion of Poland in 1939 and in this capacity ordered the bombing of Warsaw and Rotterdam (*qq.v.*). He was then sent to the western front as Commander of Air Fleet II. He ran the Flanders campaign and conducted the air attack on Dunkirk in the vain attempt to halt escaping British troops. (*See* DUNKIRK EVACUATION.) As a reward for success in the invasion of the Lowlands and France in May–June 1940, he was promoted to General Field Marshal of the *Luftwaffe* (*q.v.*) along with Erhard Milch and Hugo Sperrle (*qq.v.*).

Kesselring commanded the *Luftwaffe* during the summer of 1940. (*See* BRITAIN, BATTLE OF.) In 1941 he was sent to the Russian front, and in December 1941 was recalled to become Commander-in-Chief of Armed Forces South. In this post he took part in the campaigns in North Africa, as well as those in Sicily and Italy. He took countermeasures against Italians who had surrendered to the Allies. He was responsible for German operations in the closing days of the war. He surrendered the southern half of the German forces in Italy on May 7, 1945. (*See* ITALIAN FRONT, CAMPAIGNS ON THE.)

Bibliography. Kesselring wrote two books about his war experiences: *Soldat bis zum letzten Tag* (1953), translated as *Kesselring: A Soldier's Record* (1954); and *Gedanken zum Zweiten Weltkrieg* (Thoughts on World War II) (1955).

KHAN, NOOR INAYAT. British secret agent executed by the Germans in 1944. (*See* CODE NAMES, ALLIES, MADELEINE.)

KILROY WAS HERE. Favorite graffito slogan of American GIs (*q.v.*) in World War II.

American servicemen in every part of the world were conditioned to this inscription that appeared in the most unlikely places. Kilroy seemed to be everywhere at one and the same time. His scrawl in pencil, pen, chalk, or knife was found on the walls of most latrines from Oxford to Foggia, on fences, street signs, walls, store fronts, and in fresh cement work. In 1944–1945 it followed the onrushing Americans through France and Germany. It adorned German pillboxes at Cherbourg, the sewers of Paris, Notre Dame Cathedral, the bathrooms of war leaders at Potsdam, even Hitler's mirror at Berchtesgaden. On occasion the words were changed to "Kilroy slept here," or "Kilroy passed through." By 1945 the name was almost as familiar to Europeans as those of Roosevelt, Churchill, or Stalin.

Kilroy's identity was never revealed. He was variously said to be an AWOL (Absent-Without-Leave) army sergeant leaving false trails for pursuing MPs (Military Police); a Yankee secret agent setting a standard for mobility; a practical joker with a bemused sense of humor; or one of the 62 real Kilroys in the U.S. Army. The most recent claim was made by the widow of James J. Kilroy, a shipyard worker from Halifax, Mass. She recalled that her husband was a checker at the Fore River Shipyard in Quincy, just south of Boston, and that his job was to count the number of holes a riveter had filled. To see that the riveters were not paid twice for the same job, he used chalk to write the slogan: "Kilroy was here."

In all probability use of the name was the result of an indifferent gesture that caught the imagination of millions of bored GIs. For years after the war, Kilroy's trademark continued to appear on storefronts, in neglected air fields, deserted warehouses, and on the inside walls of old outhouses.

KIMMEL, HUSBAND EDWARD (1882-1968). U.S. naval officer and commander of the U.S. Pacific Fleet at the time of the bombardment of Pearl Harbor (q.v.).

On February 1, 1941, Kimmel was posted as Admiral in command of the U.S. Pacific Fleet. For this highest command in the U.S. Navy he was placed above 46 higher ranking officers. Then approaching his 59th birthday, he was known as an expert in gunnery, planning, and administration. Little more than 10 months later, his flagship, *Pennsylvania,* lay battered in dry dock among the ruins of Pearl Harbor. His career, along with that of Gen. Walter C. Short (q.v.), the Army commander in Hawaii, lay shattered as a result of the sudden disaster. Both officers were accused of "dereliction of duty." Ten days after the attack, Kimmel was released from his four-star command, and he retired from the Navy three months later. (*See* PEARL HARBOR CONTROVERSY.)

Bibliography. H. E. Kimmel, *Admiral Kimmel's Story* (1955).

KING, ERNEST JOSEPH (1878-1956). Commander-in-Chief of the U.S. fleet.

In February 1941 King was appointed commander of the Atlantic Fleet, with the rank of Admiral. Following the Japanese attack on Pearl Harbor (q.v.) on December 7, 1941, he succeeded Adm. Husband Edward Kimmel (q.v.) as Commander-in-Chief of the U.S. fleet (COMINCH). On March 26, 1942, he was also named to replace Adm. Harold R. Stark as Chief of Naval Operations. He was the first naval officer to hold both these offices simultaneously. Under his direction the U.S. Navy de-emphasized its reliance on battleships in favor of aircraft carriers, a decisive move in the war against the Japanese in the Far East.

Under ordinary circumstances, King would have retired on November 23, 1942, his 64th birthday, but the surge of events brought him to the top level of war strategists. For the remainder of the war he commanded the greatest aggregation of fighting ships, planes, and men in history: 1,849 ships, 23,380 operating aircraft, and 3,473,034 men. In a two-ocean war he sent his whole Pacific Fleet on the offensive in 1944 in an inexorable movement to the Japanese home islands. On December 14, 1944, he was promoted to the newly created post of Admiral of the Fleet, which was made permanent by the U.S. Congress in 1946.

Besides being responsible for naval strategy, King played an important diplomatic role in the war. He accompanied Roosevelt in an advisory capacity to the meeting resulting in the Atlantic Charter (1941) and succeeding war conferences at Casablanca (1943), Cairo (1943), Teheran (1943), Yalta (1945), and Potsdam (1945) (qq.v.)

Bibliography. W. M. Whitehead, *Fleet Admiral King* (1952).

KING, WILLIAM LYON MACKENZIE (1874–1950). Canadian Prime Minister and leader of the Canadian war effort.

Early in his career King was an isolationist, but once Canada was involved he played an important role in the war. In June 1940 he warned about the possibility of a German fleet crossing the ocean and introduced a measure conscripting all men between 18 and 45 years of age. In August of that same year he helped create a Permanent Joint Defense Board for Canada and the United States.

Canadian achievements in the war under King's leadership were impressive. Convoys sailed from Canadian ports bringing desperately needed supplies to Britain. Following the fiasco of the Dieppe raid (*q.v.*), Canadian troops performed valuable assistance for the Allies. After the Normandy invasion (*q.v.*) they swept across northern Europe to help consolidate the victory.

King also took part in the war conferences between Churchill and Roosevelt. (*See* QUEBEC CONFERENCES, FIRST: and QUEBEC CONFERENCE, SECOND.)

Bibliography. A well-known scholar in economics and political science, King wrote many books, including *Canada at Britian's Side* (1941) and *Canada and the Fight for Freedom* (1944). See also E. Ludwig, *Mackenzie King* (1944); B. Hutchinson, *The Incredible Canadian* (1953); B. Ostry, *The Age of Mackenzie King* (1955); and J. W. Pickersgill and D. F. Forster, *The Mackenzie King Record* (1968).

KINKAID, THOMAS C. (1888–1972). American admiral involved in many operations in the Pacific war.

Kinkaid commanded Task Force 16 in the Battle of Santa Cruz Islands. (*See* GUADALCANAL CAMPAIGNS.) Later he commanded Task Force 67, a squadron of cruisers ordered to prevent Japanese transports from reaching Guadalcanal. In May 1943 he commanded the Northern Pacific Forces in operations to retake the Aleutian Islands. His next assignment was in command of the 7th Fleet, a support fleet composed of old battleships and small escort carriers. His 7th Fleet took an important role in the Battle of Leyte Gulf (*q.v.*). (*See also* HALSEY CONTROVERSY.)

KLEIST, PAUL LUDWIG EWALD VON (1881–1954). German Field Marshal and expert in mechanical warfare.

Von Kleist was recalled to duty in August 1939 as Commanding General of the 2nd Corps. In 1940 he led a *Panzer* (''tank'') attack on the western front and made a decisive breakthrough at a canal near Abbeville. Sent to the Balkans in 1941, he captured Belgrade. He commanded the 1st *Panzer* Army in the invasion of the Soviet Union, but his tanks were halted before Rostov. In 1942 he was assigned to the Caucasus with orders to take the oil wells there before autumn. The Russians destroyed the wells before he could capture them. Hitler made him a General Field Marshal on January 31, 1943. Von Kleist was taken prisoner by the British in a small town in Yugoslavia before the end of the war.

Von Kleist was one of the few old-guard officers who found favor in Hitler's eyes. Though highly regarded as a tactician, he failed to bring victory in Russia.

Bibliography. See B. H. Liddell Hart, *The German Generals Talk* (1948).

KLUGE, HANS GÜNTHER VON (1882–1944). German General Field Marshal who was unable to stem the Allied invasion of Normandy.

At the start of the war von Kluge was recalled as the eighth ranking senior officer of the armed forces. He commanded Army Group VI during the campaign in Poland and in 1940 served on the western front. On July 19, 1940, he was one of the dozen generals promoted to Field Marshal by Hitler in a burst of enthusiasm over the fall of France. He served on the Russian front in 1941 and 1942. He was incapacitated for some months in 1943 after being injured in an automobile accident.

On July 2, 1944, Hitler, angered by the inability of Field Marshal Gerd von Rundstedt (*q.v.*) to halt the Allied assault on the Continent (*see* NORMANDY INVASION), replaced him with von Kluge. Unable to make a strategic retreat, von Kluge advised Hitler that all was lost and urged him to capitulate. The *Fuehrer* dismissed him and summoned Field Marshal Walther Model (*q.v.*) from the Russian front to succeed him.

Von Kluge was familiar with what was going on in the Resistance movement against Hitler, but he could not bring himself to move from opposition to conspiracy. He was flattered by the *Fuehrer's* attention (Hitler gave him a substantial amount of cash on his 60th birthday to improve his estate). He decided not to go along with the conspiracy. Distressed by his inability to contain the onrushing Allies, he committed suicide on August 18, 1944, on a field west of Metz used in battle in 1870.

KNOX, FRANK (1874–1944). U.S. Secretary of the Navy in World War II. He was born in Boston.

Knox enlisted in the army in World War I at the age of 43 as a private and won his majority in the field. In 1929 he became manager of the Hearst newspaper chain. He opposed Franklin D. Roosevelt's (*q.v.*) New Deal. In 1936 he ran for the vice-presidency but was defeated.

Before American entry into the war, Knox emphasized the need for naval supremacy. In a surprise move Roosevelt, seeking a coalition Cabinet, appointed Knox Secretary of the Navy. In this post Knox was charged with creating a strong two-front navy after the catastrophe of Pearl Harbor on December 7, 1941. He made the U.S. Navy the most powerful in history. He died in Washington on April 28, 1944.

Bibliography. Frank Knox, *American* (1936).

KNUDSEN, WILLIAM SIGNIUS (1879–1948). U.S. industrialist and director of war production.

In 1941 Knudsen was appointed Director General of the newly formed Office of Production Management. From 1941 to 1945 he served as a Lieutenant General in the U.S. Army directing production for the War Department. He contributed much to the mass-production processes that made the United States the arsenal for the Allied War effort.

Bibliography. N. Beasley, *Knudsen* (1947).

KOCH, ILSE (1906–1967). The so-called Witch (*Hexe*) of Buchenwald. (*See* EXTERMINATION CAMPS.)

Born in Saxony, the daughter of a laborer, Koch worked for a time as a librarian. In 1936, at the age of thirty, she married Karl Koch, a notorious criminal and then commandant of the concentration camp at Sachsenhausen. In 1939 she accompanied her husband to Buchenwald.

A strapping, red-haired woman of ample proportions, Koch liked to ride on horseback, with whip in hand, through the prison compound, lashing out at prisoners. Her hobby was collecting lampshades, book covers, and gloves made from the skin of dead inmates. She gave orders that new prisoners with "interesting tattoos" be reserved for her.

Karl Koch was sentenced to death and executed. In 1947 Ilse Koch was tried by an American military tribunal, found guilty, and sentenced to life imprisonment, but her term was reduced to four years. Rearrested in 1949, she was brought to trial before a West German court and sentenced to life imprisonment. Psychiatrists who examined her judged her to be "a perverted, nymphomaniacal, hysterical, power-mad demon." She committed suicide in prison on September 1, 1967, by using a bed-sheet latched to the door of her cell. "I cannot do otherwise," she wrote her son. "Death is the only deliverance."

KOGA, MINEICHI (1885–1944). Japanese Admiral who succeeded Adm. Yamamoto as Commander-in-Chief of the Japanese Combined Fleet.

A former Vice Chief of the Japanese Naval Staff Board, Koga had a prominent part in the seizure of Hong Kong and the Philippines. After commanding the Japanese fleet in Chinese waters, he was made head of the Yokohama naval base in November 1942. On May 20, 1943, Tokyo announced that Adm. Isoruko Yamamoto (*q.v.*) had been shot down and killed by American aircraft and that Adm. Koga had been named to succeed him as Commander-in-Chief of the Japanese Fleet.

In mid-July 1943, at a time when Koga had served only three months in his post, his flagship was attacked by Allied bombers in waters off the Duke of York Islands, near New Guinea. The Duke of York Islands was the old name for the New Ireland-New Britain group now generally known as the Bismarck Archipelago. The exact date of the incident is not known, but it took place during the Allied sea and air rollback offensive that sank or damaged 17 Japanese warships east of the archipelago in the Solomons during July 1943.

In 1944 Koga went to Singapore to prepare for a final confrontation with the U.S. Fleet, but was killed in a plane crash before he could complete his mission.

KOLOMBANGARA, BATTLE OF. Naval clash between the Japanese and Allies in the Central Solomons in mid-July 1943.

BACKGROUND. In the Battle of Kula Gulf (*q.v.*), the Allies were not successful in preventing the Japanese from bringing reinforcements to New Georgia down the Slot in the Central Solomons on the "Tokyo Express." On the night of July 12–13, 1943, Rear Adm. Walden L. Ainsworth was sent on his 15th mission up the Slot. The resulting Battle of Kolombangara was fought in almost the same area as that of Kula Gulf. The Allies had a force of 3 cruisers and 2 destroyer squadrons of 5 ships each.

CONFRONTATION. The Japanese support force consisted of the flagship *Jintsu*, 5 destroyers, and 4 destroyer transports. Both sides maneuvered for favorable position and got off their torpedoes at almost the same time. Concentrating on the biggest ship, the Americans smothered the *Jintsu* with 6-inch shells. She exploded and went down with all hands. A few minutes later a Japanese torpedo crashed into the New Zealand light cruiser *Leander* and put her out of the battle. In the darkness neither side could see the other except by the light of starshell fire. One American destroyer was sunk and 2 light cruisers damaged.

SIGNIFICANCE. Japanese seamen, as at Kula Gulf, showed great skill and verve with decided superiority in use of torpedoes and in night fighting. They had an advantage in their use of the long-lance torpedo, deadly when Allied ships closed in to 10,000 yards before opening fire. But the Americans used their radar-controlled guns to good advantage.

This battle, as that at Kula Gulf, did not succeed in breaking the outer perimeter of Japanese defenses. The Americans believed incorrectly that they had sunk at least a dozen enemy warships in the two battles.

Bibliography. S. E. Morison, *The Two-Ocean War* (1963).

KONEV, IVAN STEPANOVICH (1897–1973). Russian Marshal and hero of the Soviet Union.

In June 1940 Konev was promoted to Lieutenant General and was serving on the western front in Russia when Germany invaded the Soviet Union on June 22, 1941. Stalin gave him command of the central front after Gen. Semyon K. Timoskenko (*q.v.*) failed to halt the German drive toward Moscow in the fall of 1941. The next spring his 2nd Ukrainian Army recaptured 34 towns and villages on the Kalinin front within two days. In the summer of 1941 he conducted operations on the front west of Moscow, engaging German troops that otherwise would have been transferred to the Stalingrad front.

In 1943 Konev was promoted to army General. He defeated the Germans at Belgorod, the "second Stalingrad" in the Korsun-Schevschenki district at Lvov. He liquidated the pocket at Brody, cut through the whole of Poland to capture Upper Silesia, helped take Berlin, and drove the Germans out of Prague. Meanwhile, in February 1944, he was made a Marshal of the Soviet Union.

KÖNIGSTEIN FORTRESS. Grim, moated prison used by Germans for captured Allied officers.

Constructed by the King of Bohemia in the 12th century on a mountainside 750 feet above the Elbe River, 18 miles southeast of Dresden, the fortress was rebuilt early in World War II as an ''escape-proof'' prison.

GIRAUD'S ESCAPE. Königstein fortress received world-wide attention when in April 1942 Gen. Henri Giraud (*q.v.*), the French General, made a sensational escape from the prison. In World War I Giraud had managed to flee from German captivity, and now he repeated the feat. There are several conflicting versions of the episode. According to one story, he managed to obtain German maps and timetables in addition to materials for a ladder that he wove himself. After three unsuccessful attempts, he won his own way to freedom. Another version held that while on airings, he casually picked up strands of hemp that he wove into a rope of 60 feet by which he let himself down to the moat with the assistance of British confederates.

Posing as a Swiss traveling salesman, Giraud spent 11 days on obscure roads. He arrived in Switzerland on April 21, 1942. The Germans placed a price of 100,000 marks on his head, but he was never captured.

KONOYE, FUMIMARO (1891–1945). Prime Minister of Japan.

In 1919 Konoye attended the Paris Peace Conference. He then took his hereditary seat in the House of Peers and was President of that body from 1933 to 1937. In 1937 he formed a National Cabinet with himself as Premier, but resigned in 1939 because of his inability to control the militarists waging war in China.

Konoye was recalled in July 1940. During his tenure of office he announced that his government would follow a policy including Japanese domination in Asia. He signed the pact adhering to the Rome-Berlin-Tokyo Axis. At the same time he claimed that he was pro-American in attitude, indicating that he had been willing to discuss peace negotiations with authorities in the State Department at Washington. His inability to come to terms with the Americans again led to his resignation on July 16, 1941. But he returned to his post and again resigned on October 16, 1941, because of disagreement on national policies.

Konoye was named Vice-President in the first Japanese postwar Cabinet. He hoped to write a new constitution along democratic lines. Allied headquarters, however, named him as one of the major war criminals. On December 6, 1945, on the eve of surrendering, he left a social gathering at his lavish home in Tokyo, and took his life with poison. In a final note he wrote: ''I have been most gravely concerned with the fact that I have committed certain errors in the handling of affairs of state since the beginning of the China incident. I cannot, however, face the humiliation of being taken prisoner and being tried by an American court." He was posthumously condemned by a war crimes tribunal.

Tall for a Japanese, standing over six feet, dark, Konoye was known as a bundle of nerves. He was so fussy about hygiene that he would sprinkle alcohol on an apple before eating it. In his early career he was labeled a Marxist and later a liberal because he sent his son, "Butch," to Princeton to win a reputation as a golfer. Still later Konoye had to endure the epithet of a Fascist because he had to go along with Japanese war lords in their policy of territorial expansion. During his career he was called "the most popular statesman in Japan." As Premier he seldom slept in his own house, moving from one friend's house to another to avoid would-be assassins.

KRAMER, JOSEF (1906–1945). Concentration camp commander. He was an SS (*q.v.*) official who received his training under Rudolf Franz Hoess (*q.v.*) at Mauthausen, Dachau, and Birkenau.

In 1940 Kramer was delegated to accompany Hoess to Auschwitz to inspect it as a site for a synthetic oil and rubber plant. In August 1943, while at Netzweiler, he constructed a gas chamber and was personally responsible for killing 80 women in it. In May 1944 he was placed in charge of a section of Auschwitz.

In November 1944 Kramer arrived at Belsen in the village of Bergen near Hamburg. Until then Bergen-Belsen had been known as a camp where Jews were exchanged for extradited Germans. Kramer introduced a harsh rule. When he arrived, there were only 15,000 inmates, by March 1945 there were 42,000, by June 60,000. Hundreds died from typhus each day. By this time Kramer's administration was reduced to chaos. Inmates were left to their own fate; corpses were left rotting in the barracks where they were attacked by large rats.

When British troops burst into the camp, Kramer calmly led them on a "tour of inspection." More than 10,000 bodies lay in the compound; massed graves were filled in; huts were overcrowded with inmates in every stage of emaciation.

Kramer was tried by a military court at Lüneburg and on November 17, 1945, was sentenced to death. He was executed a short time later.

Bibliography. Trial of Joseph Kramer and 44 Others (The Belsen Trial) (1949). *See also* G. Reitlinger, *The Final Solution* (1953); and R. Hilberg, *The Destruction of the European Jews* (1961).

KREISAU CIRCLE (*Kreisauer Kreis*). Secret group of officers and civilians organized in 1933 to oppose the Hitler regime.

Led by Helmuth James Graf von Moltke and Peter Graf Yorck von Wartenburg, the members met at the Moltke estate in Kreisau, Silesia (now Kyzyzowa, Poland). By 1943 the Kreisau Circle contained more than 20 active members, including army officers, professors, Catholics, and Protestants. Proud of their

Christianity, the members called for the overthrow of Nazism and the substitute of a new political and social ethic. Several of the group who took part in the 1944 conspiracy against Hitler were executed. (*See* GERMAN RESISTANCE; and JULY PLOT.)

KRIEGSMARINE. The German war navy.

KRUPP VON BOHLEN UND HALBACH, ALFRIED FELIX (1907–1967).

German industrialist, son of Gustav Krupp von Bohlen und Halbach (*q.v.*).

During the war Krupp served as a Colonel in the Nazi flying corps. He was given charge of armaments and mining and was responsible for incorporating industries from occupied countries. He transported factories from as far away as the Urals and had them rebuilt. He imported thousands of Russians and other prisoners and prisoners of war to work in German coal mines and steel mills. He constructed factories close to concentration camps in order to use their labor. He was highly useful to Hitler, who awarded him many decorations.

In 1943, by the so-called Lex-Krupp, the *Fuehrer* gave the Krupp family the status of a dynasty, with Alfried as Chairman of the Board. At this time the Krupp factories covered five square miles and employed 160,000 workers, including slave labor.

Most of the Krupp factories were destroyed by Allied bombing. Alfried Krupp was arrested "for planning, preparing, initiating, and waging aggressive war." At first the charges were dismissed for lack of evidence, but in the spring of 1948 he was tried and sentenced to 12 months' imprisonment and confiscation of property. He was released in 1951 and the Krupp business expanded rapidly.

Bibliography. L. P. Lochner, *Tycoons and Tyrants* (1954); and T. Wilmowsky, *Warum wurde Krupp verurteilt?* (1950).

KRUPP VON BOHLEN UND HALBACH, GUSTAV (1870–1950).

German industrialist prominent in the war effort.

When Hitler began his rearmament policy in the mid-1930s, Krupp contributed to the production of weapons for the war machine. When the war began he was placed in charge of armaments and mining and the incorporation of industries of the occupied countries. The firm constructed a huge railway gun, known as the giant *Gustav* (*see* ARTILLERY WEAPONS, GERMAN GUSTAV), which fired enormous shells at Sevastopol. (*See* SEVASTOPOL, SIEGE OF.) Krupp imported thousands of civilians and used prisoners of war for work in his plants.

The Allies proposed to indict Krupp as a war criminal for his role in Germany's rearmament. He was never brought to trial because of ill health. He died in Blühnbach, near Salzburg, on January 16, 1950.

Bibliography. G. von Klass, *Krupps: The Story of an Industrial Empire* (1954).

KULA GULF, BATTLE OF. Naval battle between the Japanese and the Allies in the Central Solomons in the summer of 1943.

BACKGROUND. In early July 1943 Gen. Douglas MacArthur (*q.v.*) continued his Central Solomons campaign by landing 34,000 troops near Munda on New Georgia Island. At Munda the Japanese had an air base from which they could raid Guadalcanal and Tulagi. Imperial General Headquarters in Tokyo responded by sending in reinforcements to slow up the Allied advance. It ordered a convoy of 7 destroyers loaded with troops and supplies with an escort of 3 destroyers to move down the Slot in the mid-Solomons. Waiting for the convoy was a light cruiser task force of 3 cruisers and 4 destroyers commanded by Rear Adm. Walden L. Ainsworth.

SEA CLASH. The confrontation came on the night of July 5, 1943, in the Battle of Kula Gulf. Allied gunfire sank one destroyer and drove another ashore. The Japanese countered by sinking the cruiser *Helena* with their long-lance torpedoes. Rear Adm. Teruo Akiyama, losing 168 officers and men, managed to complete his mission by landing his troops.

Bibliography. S. E. Morison, *The Two-Ocean War* (1963).

KURSK, BATTLE OF. Clash between Germans and Russians in the summer of 1943 in one of the greatest land battles in history. (*See* EASTERN FRONT, CAMPAIGNS ON THE.)

KWAJALEIN. *See* MARSHALL ISLANDS, BATTLE FOR THE.

L

LACONIA. British transport torpedoed while crammed with passengers in South Atlantic waters in 1942.

BACKGROUND. In the fall of 1941 the war at sea reached its peak in favor of the Germans. (*See* ATLANTIC, BATTLE OF THE.) Available Allied tonnage was sinking rapidly despite new construction. Britain and the United States armed and converted passenger liners into troop-carriers and transports. German U-Boat commanders were ordered to keep a special lookout for such ships and sink them if possible. As the battle on the seas progressed incidents of mistaken judgment were increasing on both sides. The *Laconia* incident fell into this category.

LINER AND U-BOAT. The *Laconia* was a 19,695-ton, 20-year-old Cunard White Star passenger ship, launched in Newcastle in 1922. Her length was 600 feet and her width 74 feet. She was equipped with double-gear steam turbines and had a maximum speed of 16½ knots. She was converted into a transport and armed with 14 guns. In August 1942, under command of Capt. Rudolph Sharp, she formed part of a convoy of 17 vessels that headed around South Africa to Suez. For her return voyage to England she had on board, in addition to the crew, a complement of servicemen from various regiments; several badly wounded cases; British officers and families from Cairo or Middle East bases; Italian prisoners captured in Libya; and Polish guards for the prisoners. There were 2,732 people in all, including 463 officers and crew, 286 passengers from the army, navy, and air force, 1,800 Italian war prisoners, 103 Poles, and 80 civilians—men, women, and children.

The German submarine *U-156,* built and launched in Bremen in 1941, was on her fourth mission heading south 550 miles from Cape Palma, North-West Africa, to round the Cape of Good Hope. Her commander, Werner Hartenstein, and a crew of about 50 (the average was 20), were well-trained volunteers who had answered the call of Adm. Karl Doenitz (*q.v.*), Submarine

Commander-in-Chief (*BdU—Befehlshaber der U-Boote*), to man his submarine fleet. The young crewmen belonging to *Freikorps Doenitz* were jubilant at the brilliant victories the *Fuehrer* was winning on all fronts and were anxious to add to the toll of tonnage sunk. They knew all the figures by heart and discussed tonnages as if they were goals scored in football.

ATTACK. On the evening of September 12, 1942, just 500 miles south of the bulge of Africa, Hartenstein fired two torpedoes—or "eels" as the German sailors called them—at what he believed to be an enemy troopship. There was a thud as the first torpedo hit the *Laconia's* starboard side, exploded, and killed hundreds of Italian prisoners. Capt. Sharp ordered the ship abandoned. In the excitement of scoring a direct hit, the U-Boat commander did not at first realize that his success had resulted in a troublesome situation. Surfacing, he heard cries of "*Aiute!*" (Italian for "Help!"). He had sunk a ship with hundreds of Axis troops on board. He sent off a signal to Adm. Doenitz at headquarters in Paris: "Sunk British *Laconia*—unfortunately with 1,500 prisoners. 90 rescued so far."

At headquarters Doenitz was in a dilemma. Against the advice of his staff and fearful of Hitler's reaction, he radioed all U-Boats in the area to proceed to the scene immediately. Several were called back, but the *U-506* and *U-507* soon arrived. Meanwhile, Hartenstein packed his U-Boat with survivors and began to tow a string of lifeboats pending the arrival of the French warship *Gloire* and the sloop *Annamite* from Dakar, the Italian submarine *Cappellini* from her base at Bordeaux, and a British freighter.

AIR ATTACK. Three days later, as rescue activities went on, an American *B-24 Liberator* bomber, stationed at Freetown, West Africa, and probably in the service of the Royal Air Force (*q.v.*), passed over the rescue fleet and began bombing the *U-156*. Hartenstein radioed headquarters that he had been bombed five times by an American *Liberator* in low flight while he was towing four full boats in spite of a Red Cross flag on his bridge and in good visibility.

The *U-156* suffered severe damage and was forced to submerge to avoid destruction. The rescue fleet saved 1,100 lives out of the 2,732 of those on board the *Laconia*.

AFTERMATH. As a result of the disaster, Adm. Doenitz issued the Triton Null Order (also called the *Laconia* Order [*q.v.*]), which expressly forbade all U-Boat commanders to rescue survivors from torpedoed ships. From then on, German U-Boat commanders paid no attention to survivors of sunken ships.

Bibliography. L. Peillard, *The Laconia Affair*, (1963). *See also* Edward P. Von den Porten, *The German Navy in World War II* (1969).

LACONIA **ORDER.** Also known as the Triton Null Order. An order forbidding German U-Boat commanders to attempt rescue of survivors after sinkings at sea.

BACKGROUND. After the sinking of the British transport *Laconia* in the South Atlantic on September 12, 1942, Capt. Werner Hartenstein of the *U-156,* tried to rescue his victims. Attacked by an American *Liberator* based at Freetown, West Africa, he nearly lost his submarine. (*See LACONIA.*)

ORDER. On September 17, 1942, Adm. Karl Doenitz (*q.v.*), chief of the U-Boat Command, issued a top secret order for all U-Boat commanders:

1. No attempt of any kind must be made at rescuing members of ships sunk, and this includes picking up persons in the water and putting them in lifeboats, righting capsized lifeboats and handing over food or water. Rescue runs counter to the rudimentary demands of warfare for the destruction of enemy ships and crews.

2. Orders for bringing in captains and chief engineers still apply.

3. Rescue the shipwrecked only if their statements will be important for your boat.

4. Be harsh, bearing in mind that the enemy takes no regard of women and children in his bombing attacks on German cities.

RESULTS. The order had unfortunate consequences. After the *Laconia* tragedy, German U-Boat commanders were ruthless in dealing with survivors of sinkings. The controversial sentence: "Rescue runs counter to the rudimentary demands of warfare for the destruction of enemy ships and crews," was used against Doenitz at the Nuremberg Trials (*q.v.*).

Bibliography. See M. Maurer and L. J. Paszek, "Origins of the *Laconia* Order," in Air University Review, XV, March–April 1964, pp. 26–27; and D. Mason, *U-Boat: The Secret Menace* (1968).

LAMINETTA METHOD. German name for the British use of tinfoil in large quantities to thwart German radar. (*See* RADAR, WARTIME; and *WINDOW.*)

LANCASTRIA. British liner bombed at St. Nazaire in 1940 with heavy loss of life.

BACKGROUND. The British evacuation from Dunkirk (*q.v.*) ended on June 4, 1940, with heavy loss of life but with several hundred thousand troops rescued. On June 17, Marshal Henri Pétain (*q.v.*) asked the Germans for an armistice. That same day most of the remaining troops of the British Expeditionary Force (*q.v.*), numbering 156,000 British and 20,000 Polish soldiers, escaped at Cherbourg.

ATTACK. The evacuation was accompanied by a tragic note. German planes moving in to attack the British scored a direct hit on the liner *Lancastria,* which was moored in St. Nazaire. More than 3,000 perished in the bombing. Many were killed outright, others were drowned in the fuel oil burning in the harbor. Armed trawlers moved into the harbor and rescued hundreds of men from the foul-smelling black, treacly oil and water.

LANDING CRAFT. Shallow-draught vessels used especially for amphibious landings of men and cargoes many miles from staging areas.

BACKGROUND. Early in the war it became obvious that it would be necessary to establish beachheads in widely separated areas in order to transport men, equipment, fuel, and supplies in great quantities without the use of normal docking facilities. For this purpose Allied ship designers were ordered to plan new kinds of landing craft for amphibious service.

The British introduced landing-craft techniques in early raids on Norway and France. They used such vessels in the disastrous Dieppe raid (*q.v.*) on August 19, 1942. Every seaborne invasion in the Mediterranean theater for the remainder of the war was carried out with the use of landing craft of increasingly heavy design. They were a major factor in the assault on Europe in 1944. (*See* NORMANDY INVASION.)

American designers developed landing craft for use not only in the European theater but especially for island-hopping tactics in the Pacific. The vessels were necessary for assaults on hundreds of atolls, islands consisting of a belt of coral reef surrounding a central lagoon. From American shipyards came a succession of these strange-looking but practical vessels.

AMERICAN LANDING CRAFT

LCRS— Landing Craft, Rubber, Small: for transporting 6 men.

LCVP— Landing Craft, Vehicles and Personnel.

LCM— Landing Craft, Medium: 50-foot craft, carrying 60 men or 30 tons of supplies.

LCIL— Landing Craft, Infantry, Large: 158-foot craft, holding 200 men.

LVT— 25-foot amphibious-tracked vehicle, used as light tanks.

LSM— Landing Ship, Medium: 200-foot all-purpose craft, decks crammed with 4.5-inch rockets.

LST— Landing Ship, Tank: 327-foot craft carrying 175 troops, for transporting tanks and smaller landing craft; backbone of amphibious forces.

LSD— Landing Ship, Dock: huge 457-foot dry dock filled with power vehicles.

DUKW—heavy amphibious load-carrier used to disembark men, heavy vehicles, and supplies.

Bibliography. J. Kirk and R. Young, *Great Weapons of World War II* (1961).

LANGSDORFF, HANS (1890–1939). Captain of the pocket battleship *Admiral Graf Spee* who died with the scuttling of his ship. (*See ADMIRAL GRAF SPEE.*)

LAURENCE, WILLIAM LEONARD (1888–1977). American science reporter and the only newsman permitted to witness history's first nuclear blast.

In May 1940, after reading a few lines in the *Physical Review* about the successful isolation of uranium, Laurence wrote the first newspaper story of atomic fission and potential atomic power. He was also the first science reporter to write stories on penicillin and the sulfa drugs. Because of his astute reporting on the subject, U.S. officials told him in confidence about the Manhattan Project (*q.v.*) and invited him to view the first test in Alamagordo, New Mexico, on July 16, 1943. He was the only journalist to witness the first test of the atomic bomb.

NAGASAKI. Laurence was also the only journalist to witness the use of the second atomic bomb over Nagasaki. Flying as an observer in the *B-29* that bombed the Japanese city, Laurence wrote a dramatic account of the mission. Following are condensed excerpts from his remarkable story in *The New York Times,* September 9, 1945.

WITH THE ATOMIC-BOMB MISSION TO JAPAN, August 9 (Delayed)—We are on our way to bomb the mainland of Japan.

It is a thing of beauty to behold—this "gadget." Into its design went millions of man-hours of what is without doubt the most concentrated intellectual effort in history.

This atomic bomb is different from the bomb used three days ago with such devastating results on Hiroshima.

Does one feel any pity or compassion for the poor devils about to die? Not when one thinks of Pearl Harbor and of the Death March on Bataan.

Destiny chose Nagasaki as the ultimate target.

Out of the belly of *The Great Artiste* what looked like a black object went downward.

Despite the fact that it was broad daylight in our cabin, all of us became aware of a giant flash that broke through the dark barrier of our arc welder's lenses and flooded our cabin with intense light.

We removed our glasses after the first flash, but the light still lingered on, a bluish-green light that illuminated the entire sky around. A tremendous blast wave struck our ship and made it tremble from nose to tail. This was followed by four more blasts in rapid succession, each resounding like the boom of cannon fire hitting our plane from all directions.

Observers in the tail of our ship saw a giant ball of fire rise as though from the bowels of the earth, belching forth enormous white smoke rings. Next they saw a giant pillar of purple fire, ten thousand feet high, shooting skyward with enormous speed.

Only about fifty-five seconds had passed. Awestruck we watched (the purple fire) shoot upward like a meteor coming from the earth instead of from outer space, becoming ever more alive as it climbed.

Then, just when it appeared as though the thing had settled down into a state of permanence, there came shooting out of the top a giant mushroom that increased the height of the pillar to a total of forty-five thousand feet. The mushroom top was even more alive than the pillar, seething and boiling to a white fury of creamy foam, sizzling upward and then descending earthward, a thousand Old Faithful geysers rolled into one.

The quivering top of the pillar was protruding to a great height through the white clouds, giving the appearance of a monstrous prehistoric creature with a ruff around its neck, a fleecy ruff extending in all directions, as far as the eye could see.

For this story and a subsequent series of ten articles on the development of the atomic bomb, Laurence was awarded a second Pulitzer Prize. After the war Laurence continued to write about and analyze the most complex scientific ideas of the day. He died in Majorca, Spain, on March 19, 1977.

LAVAL, PIERRE (1883–1945). Prominent French political leader of the puppet Vichy regime.

After the defeat of France in June 1940, Laval became virtually the head of the Vichy Government as assistant to World War I hero Marshal Henri Pétain (*q.v.*), the official Head of State. On October 28, 1940, Laval became Foreign Minister. Convinced that the Germans would crush Britain, he urged his countrymen to collaborate with the invaders. He was dismissed in December 1940 but was recalled in April 1942. He took steps against the French Resistance, which deepened his unpopularity with the public. When the Allies moved toward victory, the Germans forced Laval to form a French Government-in-exile in Germany.

Laval managed to escape to Switzerland, but he was captured, returned to France, and tried for treason. He met his death before a firing squad on October 15, 1945.

Bibliography. P. Laval, *Unpublished Diary* (1948). *See also* A. Giraud (Pertinax), *The Grave-diggers of France* (1944); R. Aron, *The Vichy Regime* (1958); H. Cole, *Laval* (1963); C. Counelle, *Le dossier Laval* (1969); and G. Warner, *Pierre Laval and the Eclipse of France* (1969).

LEAHY, WILLIAM DANIEL (1875–1959). American Fleet Admiral.

Leahy served as Chief of Naval Operations from 1937 to 1939 and came out of retirement in 1940 to become Ambassador to Vichy France. Eventually, he became President Roosevelt's Personal Chief of Staff and in this position took part in virtually all the major decisions of the war, especially at the wartime international conferences. (*See* CONFERENCES, ALLIED WAR, and the entries on individual conferences.) In 1944 he was elevated to Fleet Admiral and became Personal Chief of Staff to President Truman. He also served as Chairman of the American Joint Chiefs of Staff. In 1946 he served briefly as Director of the Central Intelligence Group.

LEBENSRAUM. German term meaning "living space."

A slogan of German imperialism, *Lebensraum* was used before both world wars. There were two distinct meanings: 1) Germany did not have enough land for her people and needed expansion; and 2) Germany claimed territories on its borders as necessary for strategic or economic interests. Before World War I *Lebensraum* was used to denote the necessity for colonies throughout the world. Before World War II Hitler used the term to claim the extension of German living space mainly on the European continent.

LECLERC, JACQUES-PHILIPPE (1902–1947). French Army officer. Leclerc was the *nom de guerre* of Philippe, Comte de Hauteclerque.

In June 1940 Leclerc fought against the Germans (*see* FRANCE, FIRST BATTLE OF) and was taken prisoner at the Ailette River. He escaped from a chateau in butler's clothes and made his way to London to join the Free French (*see* FREE FRANCE). A week later he was sent to French Equatorial Africa to take command of the Free French forces there. From December 1942 to January 1943 he led a spectacular march from Lake Chad to Tripoli through 1,500 miles of enemy-held territory to join the British 8th Army. (*See* EIGHTH ARMY.) He then took part in the Tunisian campaign in North Africa. (*See* NORTH AFRICA, CAMPAIGNS IN.)

In June 1944 Leclerc commanded the French 2nd Armored Division. (*See* NORMANDY INVASION.) In August 1944 he was designated by Gen. Omar N. Bradley (*q.v.*) to lead his division into Paris. He accepted the formal German surrender. He subsequently captured Strasbourg. In August 1945 he was named French commander in the Far East and accepted the Japanese surrender at Tokyo for France.

In July 1946 Leclerc was appointed Inspector General of the French Forces in North Africa. He died on November 28, 1947, in a plane crash near Colomb-Bechehar, Algeria.

Short and blond, with straight hair and an aquiline nose, Leclerc was known for his soft-spoken modesty. Daring and imaginative, he was considered one of the most brilliant military figures to emerge in the war. One reporter called him "a combination of the courtly Lafayette and the reckless D'Artagnan." He was devoted to his family and assumed his pseudonym to protect his family from German reprisals.

LEDO ROAD. Supply road to China.

BACKGROUND. Supplying China, with its long coastline under Japanese occupation, was a difficult problem for the Allies. In the early stages, war matériel was sent by air over the "Hump," a range of mountains, some as high as 17,000 feet, between Allied bases in Northeast India and Kunming. To remedy this deficiency American engineers were instructed to build the Ledo Road running from India into North Burma to link up ultimately with the Burma Road (*q.v.*) to China.

CONSTRUCTION. The building of the Ledo Road was one of the most extraordinary achievements of the war. It was constructed while the campaigns in Burma raged in all their fury. Before the road could be built, supplies necessary for the project had to be transported hundreds of miles over a narrow-gauge railway to Ledo at the northeast corner of India.

An army of humans worked like ants, literally scratching the road out of jungles and mountains. Chinese coolies chipped away by hand at the earth and hauled the dirt away in baskets. They battled huge precipices, landslides, dust, rain, and the deadly mosquito. Inch by inch, foot by foot, mile by mile, they carved out a new life line over jagged mountain ranges.

The work began in December 1942 at the rate of three-quarters of a mile a day, but soon slowed down. By May 1943 only 47 miles had been built, with 431 to go. In the next three months only 10 miles were added. Then came the crippling monsoons, leaving rivers of mud, which had to be removed before work could be resumed. The road was completed on January 7, 1945, after two years and 23 days. At this time it was officially named the Stilwell Road by Generalissimo Chaing Kai-shek (*q.v.*) in honor of Gen. Joseph W. Stilwell (*q.v.*).

SIGNIFICANCE. The 478-mile Ledo Road, a masterpiece of human ingenuity, linked up with the Burma Road, main supply route to China. Sealed off by the Japanese in 1942, the Burma Road was now open for vast supplies to be sent to China.

LEE, JOHN CLIFFORD HODGES (1887–1958). U.S. Army officer.

Lee was one of the few high-ranking officers who achieved a general's status before the outbreak of hostilities. On May 23, 1942, he arrived in England to "stake out a claim" for the American forces. In July he was named to command the Services of Supply in the European theater of war. In January 1944 he was appointed deputy to Gen. Dwight D. Eisenhower (*q.v.*), Supreme Commander of the Allied Forces. Lee mobilized more than 700,000 different items for the massive assault on France in June 1944. (*See* NORMANDY INVASION.)

Of medium height, sturdy build, and with sparkling eyes, Lee was described as "the cherubic, bald, bee-busy U.S. supply chief in England." His feats as leader of the combat echelon of American industy were considered vital for Allied victory in the war.

LEIGH LIGHT. A powerful searchlight fitted in Allied planes assigned as convoy escorts and in anti-submarine patrols.

Named after its inventor, the Leigh Light was designed especially for night attacks on surfaced U-Boats. It was switched on as the bomber began its run on the target. (*See also* ATLANTIC, BATTLE OF THE.)

LEIGH-MALLORY, TRAFFORD (1892–1944). British Air Chief Marshal prominent in the Battle of Britain (*q.v.*).

When the German *Luftwaffe* (*q.v.*) attacked Britain in the summer of 1940, Leigh-Mallory commanded No. 12 Fighting Group of the RAF. In this post he shared operations control with the New Zealander Keith Park. He led a wing which destroyed 120 German aircraft in seven engagements. Together with Park he supervised the changeover of the Fighter Command from a defensive to an offensive role.

In August 1942 Leigh-Mallory won attention by the effective air umbrella he directed for the raid on Dieppe. (*See* DIEPPE RAID.) He was responsible for holding back the *Luftwaffe* and preventing it from bombing and strafing British troops on the ground. During the engagement his *Hurricanes* and *Spitfires* (*qq.v.*) brought down 91 enemy aircraft and scored 100 "probable" victories, while losing 98 planes. On November 28, 1942, Leigh-Mallory was appointed chief of the entire Fighter Command. On December 31, 1942 he was promoted to the post of Air Chief Marshal.

In June 1944 Leigh-Mallory was named Commander-in-Chief of the Allied Air Forces for the invasion of Europe. In this post he commanded 9,000 Royal Air Force and U.S. Army Air Forces (*qq.v.*) aircraft and provided the air power that made the assault possible. In October 1944 he was named Allied Air Commander-in-Chief in Southeast Asia. In November 1944, while flying on his way to his new post, he and his wife were reported missing. Their bodies were never found.

LeMAY, CURTIS EMERSON (1906–   ). U.S. Air Force commander.

Just after Pearl Harbor LeMay was the co-pilot of a *B-24 Liberator* that flew from Washington over the South Atlantic route to Africa and Asia Minor. The record-breaking 24,700 mile flight was designed to survey possible airports for the Ferrying Command.

In early 1942 LeMay took the 305th Bombardment Group to England for action against Germany. From October 1942 to November 1943 LeMay's group completed 25 missions over Germany, attacking U-Boat pens at Lorient (France), Wilhelmshaven, and Regensburg (*see* REGENSBURG RAID). He was a leading developer of precision bombing techniques used in flights over Germany. He eliminated the old V-formation of planes flying at the same altitude and substituted for it a staggered formation at different altitudes.

In July 1944 LeMay was transferred to the Burma-India-China theater of operations. He commanded the U.S. 21st Bomber Group in the Marianas in the Pacific. His men scored on missions to Singapore, Rangoon, Sumatra, Shanghai, and Japan. LeMay planned and carried out the devastating night raid over Tokyo on March 9–10, 1945, which destroyed nearly a quarter of the city and killed 84,000 people. (*See* TOKYO FIRE RAID.)

LEND-LEASE. Material aid extended by the United States to the Allies before and after American entry into World War II. President Roosevelt described it as one neighbor lending another neighbor a hose to put out a fire.

BACKGROUND. Without American assistance Britain would have been doomed at the beginning of the war. From September 1939 to August 1940 the British Commonwealth ordered 90 percent of all American exports of airplanes and airplane parts, as well as a large percentage of its munitions, ammunition, and weapons. During this period Britain bought 132 merchant ships. After the debacle at Dunkirk in May–June 1940 (*see* DUNKIRK EVACUATION), Britain was provided with 600,000 rifles, 80,000 machine guns, 316 trench mortars, and 900 field guns. More than $43 million in equipment was sent in the one month of June 1940.

All this was not enough. The British were in trouble because they lacked gold and were handicapped by the prevailing cash-and-carry American legislation. President Roosevelt urged Congress to act: "Let us say to the democracies: 'We Americans are vitally concerned in your defense of freedom. We are putting forth our energies, our resources and our organizing powers to give you the strength to regain and maintain a free world. We shall send you in ever-increasing numbers, ships, planes, tanks, guns. That is our purpose and our pledge.'"

LEND-LEASE ACT. The result was the Lend-Lease Act, which passed the Senate (March 8, 1941) by a vote of 60-31, and the House of Representatives (March 11, 1941), by a vote of 317-71. The law empowered the President to manufacture, sell, lend, transfer, lease, or exchange any war matériel to "the government of any country whose defense the President deems vital for the defense of the United States." Two weeks later Congress authorized an initial appropriation of $7 billion for Lend-Lease.

REACTIONS. American isolationists denounced the act. Senator Burton K. Wheeler of Montana asserted that Lend-Lease would "plow under every fourth American." Churchill, however, called it "an inspiring act of faith," and "the most unsordid act in history." Hitler was infuriated.

LEND-LEASE IN ACTION. Aid of almost every description—ammunition, munitions, food, tobacco, industrial raw stuffs—was sent across the Atlantic. By the summer of 1942 the flow reached huge proportions. By the end of the war the United States had advanced to its allies over $50 billion worth of supplies and services of all kinds. The British Empire was the largest benefactor of Lend-Lease. Soviet Russia was the next largest recipient of aid. Cargoes not only

Lend-Lease Aid Extended by the United States to Thirty-Eight Nations; to July 31, 1946*

AMERICAN REPUBLICS		OTHER GOVERNMENTS	
Bolivia	$5,633,989.02	Belgium	$148,394,457.76
Brazil	332,545,226.45	British Empire, including	
Chile	21,817,478.16	Australia, New Zealand,	
Colombia	7,809,732.58	India, South Africa	31,267,240,530.63
Costa Rica	155,022.73	China	1,548,794,965.99
Cuba	5,739,133.33	Czechoslovakia	413,398.78
Dominican Republic	1,610,590.38	Egypt (paid fully in cash)	1,019,169.14
Ecuador	7,063,079.96	Ethiopia	5,151,163.25
Guatemala	1,819,403.19	France and possessions	3,207,608,188.75
Haiti	1,449,096.40	Greece	75,475,880.30
Honduras	372,358.11	Iceland	4,795,027.90
Mexico	36,287,010.67	Iran	4,797,092.50
Nicaragua	872,841.73	Iraq (paid fully in cash)	4,144.14
Panama	83,555.92	Liberia	6,408,240.13
Paraguay	1,933,302.00	Netherlands and possessions	230,127,717.63
Peru	18,525,771.19	Norway	51,524,124.36
Salvador	892,358.28	Poland	16,934,163.60
Uruguay	7,148,610.13	U.S.S.R.	11,260,343,603.02
Venezuela	4,336,079.35	Saudi Arabia	17,417,878.70
Total	$456,094,634.58	Turkey	26,640,031.50
		Yugoslavia	32,026,355.58
		Total charge to foreign governments	$48,361,210,768.24
Aid not charged to foreign governments (including lost shipments, administrative costs, and Lend-Lease aid diverted to United States forces)			2,578,827,000.00
Total Lend-Lease aid			$50,940,037,768.24

*The New York Times, October 19, 1946.

had to be promised but safely delivered as well. To protect merchantmen on their errands in the early stages of Lend-Lease, the U.S. Navy set up "neutrality patrols" on water and in the air across the Atlantic. This vigilance was later increased.

SIGNIFICANCE. "Give us the tools and we'll finish the job," said Churchill in Britain's hour of danger. Lend-Lease was the American response—and more. It was probably the most important single innovation of the war, with the exception of the atomic bomb. The United States—as the Arsenal of Democracy—provided aid in sufficient quantities to help turn the scale against the Axis. The British reciprocated by giving bases and performing services later for American troops in England. The Russians gave little money in direct return for goods and services, but paid with lives and suffering by bearing the brunt of German aggressive power.

Bibliography. E. R. Stettinius, Jr., *Lend-Lease: Weapons for Victory* (1944); W. R. Kimball, "*The Most Unsordid Act*": *Lend-Lease, 1939–1941* (1969); and R. H. Jones, *The Roads to Russia: United States Lend-Lease to the Soviet Union* (1969).

LENINGRAD, SIEGE OF. Unsuccessful German attempt to take Leningrad beginning on August 21, 1941, and lasting for 890 days.

TARGET. Leningrad, the second largest city of the Soviet Union and second only to Moscow as an economic and cultural center, is situated at the head of the Gulf of Finland, on both sides of the Neva River. Built on a swamp, it was one of the best planned and most beautiful cities in the world. The old imperial city, originally called St. Petersburg, was founded by Peter the Great in 1703 as his Window to the West.

The magnificent metropolis housed such treasures as the Winter Palace, the Peter and Paul Fortress, the famed Hermitage Museum, castles, and cathedrals. Its network of canals and streams made it a northern Venice. Because of its German connotation, the name was changed to Petrograd in 1914. In 1924, after the successful Bolshevik Revolution of November 1917, it was renamed Leningrad in honor of Vladimir Ilyich Lenin.

HITLER'S STRATEGY. For the German dictator the capture of Leningrad would be historical justice. When Peter the Great built St. Petersburg and Kronstadt, the nearby island naval base in the Gulf of Finland, he began to extend Russian influence into the Baltic, an area that the Germans regarded as their own sphere of influence. Moreover, Leningrad had been the cradle of the Bolshevik Revolution. The *Fuehrer* held it to be his mission to destroy what he believed to be an abomination.

Leningrad, therefore, had a central place in Hitler's plan to smash the Soviet Union. *Operation Barbarossa* (*see* CODE NAMES, GERMAN, BARBAROSSA) envisioned a super-Cannae, a vast encircling action to take Moscow. Leningrad was the northern flank, the Ukraine the southern. Hitler would hit at both flanks and then turn inward and converge his forces on Moscow. For this task he assigned Field Marshal Wilhelm von Leeb (*q.v.*), who had smashed the Maginot Line (*q.v.*) in 1940, to take Leningrad.

Hitler ordered von Leeb to move on Leningrad in a series of sweeps and take the city within four weeks. Then he was to level Kronstadt and secure the Baltic coast while Soviet naval power was being destroyed. Only then was the final assault to take place. Hitler made this clear in his early war directive issued on December 18, 1940: "Only after the fulfillment of this first essential task, which must include the occupation of Leningrad and Kronstadt, will the attack be continued with the intention of occupying Moscow, an important center of communications and of the armaments industry." (*See* EASTERN FRONT, CAMPAIGNS ON THE.)

BLITZKRIEG. On June 22, 1941, Hitler began his assault on the Soviet Union from the Baltic in the north to the Black Sea in the south. The *Blitzkrieg* (*q.v.*) was a refined version of the earlier ones in Poland, the Scandinavian countries, the Low Countries, and France. First came pulverization from the air, then light forces pushed ahead, followed by swiftly moving armor, artillery, and infantry. Within hours the Soviet Air Force lost 1,200 of its first-line planes. The Germans advanced for 50 miles in 24 hours, taking 10,000 prisoners the first day.

Simultaneously, von Leeb moved toward Leningrad with 1,000 first-line aircraft, 1,000 tanks, a division of motorized infantry, and 300,000 troops. His Army Group North moved from East Prussia to the Baltic states of Latvia, Lithuania, and Estonia, which had been absorbed by the Soviet Union. A year earlier the Russians had set up a shield in the Baltic states. Von Leeb's left wing crashed through Estonia and trapped all Russian troops there, while the right wing turned on Leningrad. The main attack had met with little resistance. At this time the Russians had no tanks or long-range artillery.

RESISTANCE. For Stalin the invasion of his country came as a stunning surprise. He had been given ample warning by the British, Americans, and especially by the master spy Richard Sorge (*q.v.*), but he refused to believe them. (*See* ESPIONAGE.) The suspicious Russian leader believed that the warnings were only a trick to get him into the war against Germany. He even ordered Russian troops not to move and then went into a nervous collapse. Not until two weeks later did he recover and assume supreme command of the Soviet forces.

The first impact was catastrophic. Within three weeks 28 Soviet divisions, some 420,000 men, were wiped out. The situation at Leningrad was grave. Inside the city 500,000 People's Volunteers went to work building fortifications—trenches, tank traps, and gun emplacements. Old men, women, students, boys and girls, even prisoners, worked themselves to exhaustion.

Meanwhile, from July 10 to August 8, 1941, revived Russian troops managed to strike back and knock the *Blitzkrieg* off balance. The Germans were astonished and unprepared for fanatical resistance. Nevertheless, von Leeb kept hammering away at the gates of Leningrad. On August 30 his troops severed the last rail route to Moscow. Within a few days they captured Schlüsselburg, a great railway center on Lake Ladoga. Leningrad was now cut off from the rest of the country: Its only connection was by air or across Lake Ladoga to the northeast.

SIEGE. August 21, 1941, is generally considered the beginning of the siege of Leningrad. More than 200,000 Germans and soldiers of satellite countries had died on the approaches to the city. Unable to take the city by direct assault, Hitler was determined to choke it to death by siege warfare. Leningrad was now within artillery range. Meanwhile, the *Luftwaffe* (*q.v.*) began to attack it mercilessly from the air.

Stalin was dissatisfied with Gen. Kliment Yefrenovich Voroshilov (*q.v.*), who had military command of the northern third of the long front, including Leningrad. He replaced Voroshilov with Gen. Georgi Konstantinovich Zhukov (*q.v.*), a harsh and tough commander. "I have taken over," said Zhukov. "Tell the High Command that I propose to proceed more actively than my predecessor." He did.

Zhukov ordered the city to be defended to the last. He sent 500,000 Leningraders to work on antitank barriers, barbed-wire barricades, trench systems, and embrasures in buildings and houses. He put women and children to work in the factories; brought in water from rivers, wells, and canals; mined all bridges, factories, and institutions so that "the enemy will die in the ruins." He threatened any officer who did not move forward: "Attack or be shot!"

This active defense policy helped save Leningrad. Soviet aircraft bombed the German positions and struck at *Luftwaffe* bases in Finland and Estonia. The ground forces took a heavy tool.

LAKE LADOGA. By November–December 1941, transportation difficulties and German air raids brought the city to the verge of famine. Leningrad's only hope for survival lay in Lake Ladoga, the largest free-water lake in Europe, 125 miles long and nearly 80 miles across. The lake froze solid. Russians constructed a great ice highway across which convoys and horse-drawn sleighs were able to bring food and supplies into the stricken city.

RELIEF. In the spring of 1942 tens of thousands of weak and weary Leningraders appeared on the streets with shovels to clean up the city. The sewers and drains had been knocked out by German shells, and there was danger of an epidemic. Germans renewed the siege with the thaw of April 1942. They regained the German corridor between Tosno and Lake Ladoga. From Hitler came word that "there is not the slightest reason for the continued existence of this large city." But it was too late. Under bombing and shellfire the people of Leningrad continued working at their jobs.

Meanwhile, the blockade was pierced by combined operations. Heavy Russian tanks, which were brought across the Neva on pontoons, were put to use against the faltering Germans. Deadly low-flying *Stormoviks* hit German tanks and forced the enemy back to the edge of the forest. The battle continued until January 27, 1944, when a salute of cannon celebrated the final liberation of the city. The Germans had been driven more than 50 miles from Leningrad. The longest siege ever endured by a modern city had come to an end.

TOLL. There are no exact figures on the cost in lives. One estimate gave a total of 632,253 deaths of Leningraders, but there were probably many more. Another estimate places the figure at 1.5 million. More than 700,000 were deprived of their homes. Some 800 factories were destroyed as well as 71 bridges. Germans lost several hundred thousand men in the process.

SIGNIFICANCE. The relief of Leningrad was part of a massive Russian offensive along the entire eastern front. Hitler's failure to take the city contributed heavily to his eventual defeat in Soviet Russia. He had expected the city to collapse as easily as Warsaw, Rotterdam, Brussels, or Paris, but he was mistaken. The people of Leningrad refused to capitulate.

Bibliography. For a dramatic account *see* H. Salisbury, *The 900 Days: The Siege of Leningrad* (1959). *See also* L. Goure, *The Siege of Leningrad* (1962); A. Wykes, *The Siege of Leningrad* (1969); A. A. Fadeev, *Leningrad in the Days of the Blockade* (1971); and V. Inber, *Leningrad Diary* (1972).

LEOPOLD III (1901–   ). King of the Belgians and commander of the Belgian Army that capitulated to the Germans in 1940.

After Hitler started his *Blitzkrieg* (*q.v.*) on Belgium on May 10, 1940, Leopold took command of the Belgian Army and appealed in vain for Allied assistance. On May 28 he decided that further resistance would be useless and ordered a surrender to the Germans. The Belgian Government opposed capitulation, suspended allegiance to the crown, and called for further resistance. Leopold was taken prisoner by the Germans and confined at Laeken near Brussels. He was moved to Germany after the Allied invasion of Normandy (*q.v.*) on June 6, 1944. He was liberated by the Americans in May 1945.

After the war there was a public outcry when Leopold announced his intention of returning to Belgium. In 1946 he appointed a commission to examine his conduct during the war. Its report, issued in 1947, justified his conduct in capitulating to the Germans. In a referendum held in 1950, nearly 58 percent voted for his return. Leopold and his sons came back to Belgium only to meet rioting and strikes. He abdicated in favor of his son Baudouin in July 1951.

Bibliography. J. A. Goris, *Belgium in Bondage* (1943); and J. Pirenne, *Dossier du Léopold* (1970).

LEXINGTON. U.S. aircraft carrier (*CC-1*), known to navy men as "Queen of the Flat-Tops." She was the fourth ship of the U.S. Navy to bear the name *Lexington*.

DESIGN. Originally, the *Lexington* was one of 6 battle cruisers included in the naval construction program of 1916. Together with her sister ship, the *Saratoga* (*CC-3*), she was about one-third completed when the Washington Naval Conference was called in late 1921. At first all 6 ships were scrapped, but through the intercession of Adm. William A. Moffat, permission was granted to convert two of the battle cruisers into aircraft carriers. The old superstructure was eliminated, and the smokestack, bridge, and navigating office were concentrated in an island raised above the light deck and placed on the starboard side.

The designers used 600 separate compartments to make the *Lexington* supposedly unsinkable. Each compartment was locked from the others in watertight bulkheads, steel hatches, and heavy doors. The original battle-cruiser propulsion machinery was retained, consisting of 16 big oil-fired steam boilers supplying power for four electric turbine generator sets. The ship was also equipped with torpedo bulges, false hulls constructed below the water line to catch the impact of any torpedoes.

SPECIFICATIONS.
>*Measurements.* Length 888 ft.; breadth 106 ft.
>*Standard Displacement.* 43,500 tons.
>*Maximum Speed.* 33.9 knots.
>*Armament.* 100 2-mm. and 1.1-in. machine guns in batteries of four dispersed through the ship; also batteries of 5-in. guns.
>*Complement.* 2,951 officers and enlisted men on last mission.

COMBAT RECORD. The *Lexington* received its first test in World War II as early as February 10, 1942, when she was the main unit of a single carrier task force penetrating deeply into Japanese-held waters. In an engagement off Bougainville, a Japanese stronghold, her pilots downed 16 of 18 enemy bombers and 2 observation flying boats. In the spring of 1942, planes from the *Lexington* smashed Japanese forces at Lae and Salamau in New Guinea. The carrier was also part of the task force that engaged the Japanese off Tulagi in early May 1942, sinking 14 out of 15 ships found there (3 cruisers, 3 destroyers, 3 transports, 1 seaplane tender, 4 gunboats, and 8 aircraft). This was on the eve of the Battle of the Coral Sea.

END OF THE LEXINGTON. The *Lexington* was the flagship of Task Force 11 under Rear Adm. Aubrey W. Fitch when she took part in the Battle of the Coral Sea. On May 8, 1942, the task force was attacked by 69 Japanese aircraft from the carriers *Shokaku* and *Zuikaku.* The striking force consisted of *Kate* torpedo bombers and *Val* dive bombers.* In the ensuing battle the Japanese took a severe beating.

In the ensuing battle the *Lexington* was attacked by 103 Japanese planes within the space of 16 minutes. American gunners shot down 19 enemy planes and damaged many others. Despite the heavy antiaircraft fire, Japanese pilots came in without swerving and rammed one torpedo after another into the zig-zagging flat top. In the midst of the fighting, crews landed at least 30 planes. The first torpedoes exploded harmlessly against the *Lexington's* torpedo bulges, but others caused severe damage. Damage control crews went to work to shut off the compartments and repair the main hull. It was too late. One explosion followed another, mostly from volatile vapors of gas fumes. Aviation gas lines had been ruptured and fumes were distributed through the ventilation system.

---

*In order to identify the more important of the bewildering variety of Japanese planes, the U.S. War Department gave them names easily recognizable by American pilots. These included the fighters "Nate," "Zeke" (Zero), "Rufe," and "Hap"; the torpedo bomber "Kate"; the dive bomber "Val"; the medium bombers "Nell," "Sally," and "Betty"; the reconnaisance planes "Dave" and "Pete"; and the patrol bomber "Mavis."

When it became obvious that the *Lexington* could not be saved, Capt. Frederick C. Sherman gave orders to abandon ship. The entire complement of nearly 3,000 men was rescued by trailing destroyers. As the remainder of the task force pulled off, a lone destroyer, the USS *Phelps,* sent four torpedoes coursing into the side of the stricken flat top. Flames and clouds of steam hissed upward as the *Lexington* slowly settled under the water. There were 216 casualties; 36 aircraft were lost; and 2,735 men were saved by destroyers.

THE NEW LEXINGTON. The name *Lexington* was given to a new carrier of the Essex Class (*CV-16,* formerly the *Cabot*). Commissioned on February 17, 1943, she, too, had a notable combat record, participating in the invasions of Tarawa, Wake Island, the Gilberts, Truk, New Guinea, Iwo Jima, Okinawa, and the two battles of the Philippine Sea. (*See* PACIFIC, CAMPAIGNS IN THE.) She was damaged severely off Kwajalein in December 1943 and by *Kamikaze* (*q.v.*) pilots in late 1944. She was the first Navy craft to launch major air attacks against Tokyo in January 1945.

Bibliography. S. Johnston, *Queen of the Flat-Tops: The USS Lexington and the Coral Sea Battle* (1942).

LEY, ROBERT (1890–1945). National Socialist administrator and head of the German Labor Force during World War II.

During the war Ley ran the Nazi Labor Front. He controlled all the white-collar groups and management associations. It was his responsibility to obtain manpower for the war effort. As the war progressed and more and more workers were needed, Ley began to recruit prisoners, prisoners of war, and foreigners for his work program. (*See* FORCED LABOR.) Hitler never lost faith in Ley. In his final political testament the *Fuehrer* urged that Ley be retained in office.

On October 20, 1945, Ley went on trial before the International Military Tribunal. (*See* NUREMBERG TRIALS.) He became increasingly despondent when he learned the nature of the charges against him. On October 26, 1945, he was found strangled in his cell. In a suicide note he wrote that he was able no longer to bear the shame.

Bibliography. R. Ley, *Wir helfen den Fuehrer* (1940).

LEYTE GULF, BATTLE OF. Final battle fought by the Japanese Navy in World War II and considered by military historians to be one of the greatest naval clashes in history.

AMERICAN STRATEGY. Capture of Saipan, Guam, and Tinian in 1944 gave Americans control of the Marianas, from whose airfields they could not only strike at the Philippines but also at the Japanese home islands. (*See* MARIANAS, BATTLE FOR THE.) The overall U.S. strategy was working to perfection. Not only were the Gilberts, the Marshalls, and the Marianas in American hands, but Gen. Douglas MacArthur (*q.v.*) was also moving up the

New Guinea coastline. The Japanese strongholds at Truk and Rabaul were bypassed and immobilized.

The next goal was to take the Philippines. These islands stretched for 1,000 miles from Mindanao in the south to Luzon in the north. The first thrust would be at Leyte, one of the smaller central islands, in order to split the enemy's defense. To prepare the way U.S. aircraft hammered targets up and down the islands through the month of October 1944. Vice Adm. Mark A. Mitscher's (*q.v.*) Task Force 58 (*q.v.*) destroyed at least 500 Japanese aircraft in the process, while losing 79.

Americans gathered an imposing force for the coming showdown—166 warships and 1,289 planes. In the Leyte area they had the 7th Fleet under Vice-Adm. Thomas C. Kinkaid and the 3rd Fleet under Adm. William F. Halsey, Jr. (*q.v.*). (*See also* HALSEY CONTROVERSY.) Their mission was to defend the Leyte beachhead, come to grips with the enemy fleets, annihilate them, and thereby open the back door to Tokyo.

JAPANESE STRATEGY. Japanese Imperial Headquarters in Tokyo, even though it had been hit with one severe defeat after another, drew up plans for *Operation Sho-Go* as soon as it was informed that elements of MacArthur's army had landed on Leyte. It prepared for a "general decisive battle that would smash any American assault on the great island chain."

The operation provided for three separate commands. What was left of the Japanese Navy was committed to the all-out defense of the Philippines. A small force in the north, led by Vice-Adm. Jisaburo Ozawa (*q.v.*) and consisting mostly of carriers without aircraft, was to be a decoy to lure Halsey's 3rd Fleet northward and away from the action at Leyte beachhead. Ozawa could expect a mauling but he would draw American power from the two main fleets.

At the same time Vice-Adm. Takeo Kurita sailed from Singapore with his First Striking Force of heavy battleships and cruisers. His force was divided into two parts: Force A, under his own command, was composed of 5 battleships, 10 heavy cruisers, 2 light cruisers, and 15 destroyers. His task was to steam into the center area of the San Bernardino Strait north of Leyte Gulf, annihilate enemy warships there, and isolate U.S. troops already ashore.

The southern Force C. led by Vice-Adm. Ahoji Nishimura, composed of 2 battleships, 1 cruiser, and 4 destroyers, would enter Surigao Strait between Mindanao and Leyte. By this intended strategy, the American beachhead, with its ships being unloaded, would be caught between the two main Japanese fleets, while Kinkaid's 7th Fleet could be annihilated. Then when the decoyed Halsey returned, he in turn would be destroyed by superior forces.

CLASH IN THE CENTER. Kurita sent a detachment to push into Leyte Gulf from the southwest via Surigao Strait, while with his main force he came in from the northwest through the San Bernardino Strait. The plan did not work. On the night of October 23, 1944, 2 U.S. submarines, the *Darter* and the

Dace, detected the Japanese force, stalked it, and sank two cruisers while crippling another. The following day, at the Battle of the Sibuyan, the huge Japanese battleship, *Mushashi,* capsized and sank after 19 hits by torpedoes and 17 by bombs.

HALSEY'S DASH. At this point Halsey, assuming that Kurita was definitely in retreat, learned from his reconnaissance planes that Ozawa's force in the north was moving southward. Drawn by the decoy fleet, the aggressive admiral moved his entire available fleet north in pursuit of Ozawa, leaving San Bernardino Strait unguarded. Halsey's planes severely mauled Ozawa's ships, only to receive Kinkaid's urgent call for help. Instead of finishing off the enemy with his battleships, he turned his ships south, but he was so far north that he could not reach Leyte Gulf until the next morning. Halsey's breakaway action led to a bitter dispute with some historians claiming that he had damaged the Allied cause. (*See* HALSEY CONTROVERSY.)

CONFRONTATION IN THE SOUTH. In the meantime Kinkaid steamed south in the correct belief that another Japanese force might try to move through Surigao Strait. His destroyers and PT-Boats hit Nishimura's Southern Force hard as it moved through the strait. In the tense night battle the Americans made good use of their superior radar equipment. (*See* RADAR, WARTIME.)

It was a slaughter. Before dawn Nishimura lost both his battleships, 3 of his 4 destroyers, and his own life. The Japanese warships made the mistake of coming in line through the narrow stait, thereby exposing themselves to the concentrated fire of Adm. Jesse Oldendorf's 6 battle wagons, 4 heavy and 4 light cruisers, and a destroyer screen. The American admiral realized the dream of all naval commanders—the classic maneuver of crossing the enemy's *T.* Virtually the entire Japanese attacking force was wiped out.

ACTION IN THE CENTER. On October 25, 1944, Kurita brought his Central Force, still strong and consisting of 4 battleships, 6 cruisers, and many destroyers, through San Bernardino Strait. He soon found himself face to face with 16 escort carriers with destroyer escorts. In the bitter clash all 16 carriers sent their aircraft into action. Instead of moving in to shell the beaches, Kurita finally broke off the action and ordered his battleships to steam away. Intercepted radio messages made him believe that overpowering American reinforcements were on the way and that Halsey was farther south than he actually was. He was also worried about his lack of air cover.

LOSSES. The Japanese lost most of their battleships and all four of their carriers, the *Chitose, Chiyoda, Zuikaku,* and *Zuiho.* In addition, they lost 6 heavy cruisers, 3 light cruisers, 8 destroyers, and 4 submarines. The U.S. light carrier, *Princeton,* was sunk, as well as 2 escort carriers, 3 destroyers, and several smaller craft.

SIGNIFICANCE. The Battle of Leyte Gulf was far less a battle than a miniature 4-day war fought in three dimensions. It was a complicated engagement of naval fire, smoke screens, torpedo attacks, and air combat. A total of 282 warships were engaged in the encounter as well as hundreds of aircraft. During the clashes the Japanese introduced the first *Kamikaze* (*q.v.*) suicide planes.

A crucial blow was delivered to the Japanese by the sinking of their four aircraft carriers. Without them the remaining battleships were helpless. War reporters now began to speak of the huge monsters as "useless' and out-of-date.

Bibliography. C. V. Woodward, *The Battle of Leyte Gulf* (1947); J. A. Field, *The Japanese at Leyte Gulf* (1947); W. F. Halsey, *Admiral Halsey's Story* (1947); S. E. Morison, *History of U.S. Naval Operations in World War II,* 15 vols. (1947–1962); S. L. Falk, *Decision at Leyte* (1966); E. P. Hoyt, *The Battle of Leyte Gulf* (1972); and W. D. Dickson, *The Battle of the Philippine Sea* (1974).

LIBERTY SHIPS. Merchant-marine freighters mass produced in the United States to transport war matériel to war fronts.

BACKGROUND. The necessity for moving men and supplies across the Atlantic after U.S. entry into the war in December 1941 called for a radical reorganization of American shipping. By executive order on February 7, 1942, the War Shipping Administration was established under Rear Adm. Emory S. Land to supervise production of more ships.

CONSTRUCTION. Contracts were awarded to shipping firms, including one headed by industrialist Henry J. Kaiser (*q.v.*). Mass-production methods, including electrical welding, cut the time of production from months to weeks. Standardized Liberty Ships, from 10,000 to 14,000 tons, were capable only of a slow speed of 10 knots. The first one, the *Patrick Henry* was launched in September 1941. Later, with new turbines available, a second type, Victory ships, similar in size and capacity, were able to reach a speed of from 15 to 15 ½ knots. Altogether the American shipbuilding industry built nearly 6,000 Liberty and Victory ships during the war at a cost of $13 billion. Production of Liberty Ships rose from 746 in 1942 to 2,242 in 1943, and 2,161 in 1944.

PERFORMANCE. These new freighters, "workhorses of the seas," assured Allied supremacy on the high seas and made possible the survival of Britain and the eventual Normandy invasion (*q.v.*). Many were sunk by German U-Boats in the battle for supplies. Some split open while at sea after pipelines broke or storage tanks exploded. A contributory factor was poor welding during the quick construction, resulting in residual stress. Some were victims of faulty design.

POSTWAR. After the war those Liberty Ships that were not sunk by submarines were sold or stored. Hundreds sat rusting in silent immobilized fleets.

Millions of dollars were spent to store the ships and protect them from vandalism. Eventually, most were sold for scrap by the U.S. Federal Maritime Commission. One became a museum. In 1976, the 39 remaining Liberty Ships were given gratis to eight states for scuttling off their coasts to form fish habitats. The old ships served as congregation points and feeding sites for chains of marine life. Fewer than 10 of these wartime ships remain in Federal hands.

Bibliography. J. Bunker, *The Liberty Ship: The Ugly Ducklings of World War II* (1972).

LIDDELL HART, BASIL HENRY (1895–1970). British military strategist and historian known for his advocacy of mechanized warfare.

Liddell Hart served during World War I and was twice wounded in action. In the postwar era he began writing on military subjects. He presented strong arguments for the "expanding torrent" attack and accompanying infiltration tactics. An early advocate of air power and mechanized tank warfare, he stressed mobility and surprise. Before 1939 he served as military correspondent for London newspapers. His call for military reform won more interest in Germany than in his homeland.

Liddell Hart held no official appointment during World War II. German strategists utilized his theory of attack in crushing France. For the duration of the war he worked for the *Daily Mail.*

Skeptical of nuclear deterrence, Liddell Hart after the war urged conventional defense forces but at the same time advocated arms control. He was knighted in 1966. He died in Marlow, Buckinghamshire, on June 29, 1970.

Bibliography. Among Liddell Hart's prolific works are: *Paris, or The Future of War* (1925); *The Remaking of Modern Armies* (1927); *The Strategy of Indirect Approach* (1929); *The Defense of Britain* (1939); *A History of the World War, 1914–18* (1948); *The Other Side of the Hill* (1948); *The Tanks* (1959); *Deterrent or Defense* (1960); *Memoirs* (2 vols., 1965–1966); and *A History of the Second World War* (1970).

LIDICE. Czech village leveled by the Nazis in 1942.

BACKGROUND. Because the Czechs resented German control of their country, they were subjected to a policy of terror by *Gestapo* (*q.v.*) agents. In 1941 Hitler replaced Baron Constantin von Neurath with Reinhard Heydrich (*qq.v.*) as Reich Protector of Bohemia and Moravia. The goal was to bring recalcitrant Czechs into line with the ideology of the Third Reich. Heydrich went to extremes in his campaign to subjugate the Czechs. On May 27, 1942, he was critically wounded by a hand grenade. The assailants escaped. German authorities then decreed a state of emergency in the Protectorate. Heydrich died of his wounds on June 4. The Germans decided that the men who killed him had won sanctuary in the nearby village of Lidice.

REPRISAL. Six days later infuriated *Waffen-SS* (*q.v.*) squads took savage vengeance on the villagers. All the men and older boys, numbering 192, were summarily shot. Most of the 296 women and children were either killed or sent to the concentration camp at Chemnitz, where many were gassed. Other children were distributed to foster homes. The village itself was systematically destroyed and its name erased from official records.

AFTERMATH. People all over the world reacted with a mixture of shock and disgust. Nazi authorities, who believed the attack on Lidice to be fully justified, gave the same treatment to several other villages in Europe.

Bibliography. J. B. Hutak, *With Blood and Iron: The Lidice Story* (1957); and J. F. Bradley, *Lidice: Sacrificial Village* (1972).

LILI MARLEEN. Love song popular among both German and Allied troops during the war.

The song was based on a poem written by Hans Leip in Hamburg in 1923. In its original form the poem told the familiar story of the love of a soldier for his girl and how much he missed her. It was set to music in 1936 by Norbert Schultze and was introduced by the popular songstress Lala Anderson.

The song caught on with the *Afrika Korps* (*q.v.*) during the African campaign and became a favorite with German troops. Intrigued British servicemen adopted the melody and produced their own version with its title spelled a bit differently, *Lilli Marlene*. Henry Lamarchand wrote a French form, *Lily Marlène*. All three versions were equally sentimental with lyrics similar to thousands of other love songs.

In the United States the song was used in the film *Lili Marlene* (1944), starring Marlene Dietrich (*q.v.*), and in such films as John Hersey's (*q.v.*) *A Bell for Adano* (1945) and *Judgment at Nuremberg* (1961).

LINDBERGH, CHARLES AUGUSTUS, JR. (1902–1974). American aviator and prominent pre-war isolationist.

In 1925 Lindbergh became an officer in the Missouri National Guard and began to earn his living as a pilot in the government mail service between St. Louis and Chicago. On May 21, 1927, he astonished the world by completing the first non-stop air flight between New York and Paris in a single-engined plane, *The Spirit of St. Louis*. The flight brought him success and fame. He was far less successful in enduring the storms of public adulation.

At the request of the U.S. military attaché in Berlin, Lindbergh made several trips to Nazi Germany to report on the development of the *Luftwaffe* (*q.v.*). He unwittingly accepted a medal from Gen. Hermann Goering (*q.v.*) but later refused to give it back. Convinced of German air superiority, he became a strong isolationist. He opposed the policies of President Franklin D. Roosevelt (*q.v.*) and had scant confidence in Britain.

At the start of war Lindbergh maintained his isolationsim. On September 11, 1941, at an America First rally in Des Moines, Iowa, he said, "The three most important groups who have been pressing this country toward war are the British, the Jewish, and the Roosevelt Administration." His words lost him most of his popularity without diminishing his fame. Lindbergh later explained that he was not displaying anti-Semitism, but was merely being factual. Meanwhile, he had resigned his commission in the U.S. Air Corps.

Lindbergh abandoned his isolationism immediately on hearing the news of Pearl Harbor. He volunteered his services but he was informed that the White House would permit his commission only if he publicly admitted that he was wrong. He refused. In 1944, as a civilian "observer," he flew 50 combat missions, dropping bombs on Japanese targets and on one occasion shooting down a Japanese pilot over South Borneo. His war efforts were concentrated in the Pacific theater.

After the war Lindbergh resumed his scientific work (in 1936 he invented with Alexis Carrel a perfusion pump called an artificial heart). He also worked in commercial aviation and on conservation projects. He died in Maui, Hawaii, on August 26, 1974.

Tall, slender, serious in manner, Lindbergh was a proud individual who valued his privacy and hated the attention accorded him for his sensational flight. He stubbornly refused to admit mistakes and denied that he was pro-Nazi. Because of intense criticism he angrily quit the National Advisory Committee for Aeronautics.

Bibliography. Lindbergh wrote *We* (1927); *Of Flight and Life* (1948); and *The Spirit of St. Louis* (1953). *See also* B. Gill, *Lindbergh Alone* (1977).

LINDEMANN, FREDERICK ALEXANDER, LORD CHERWELL (1886–1957). Scientist, politician, and war adviser to Winston Churchill.

When Churchill became Prime Minister in 1940, he invited Lindemann to became his personal scientific adviser and to supervise all the varied scientific projects then under way. Much of the extraordinary scientific progress made during the war years in England was due to Lindemann's advice. Churchill had complete confidence in him.

A master of the art of presenting complicated matters with the greatest economy of words, Lindemann wrote memoranda for Churchill covering a vast range of topics. His advice was not only scientific. He also supervised a staff of economists, one of whose duties it was to produce charts and graphs for the Prime Minister so that he could visualize changes in weapon production, food imports, and shipping losses.

Lindemann was created a peer in 1941 with the title of Baron Cherwell of Oxford. In 1942 he was made Paymaster General, and in 1943 a Privy Councilor. Although never a member of the War Cabinet, he often attended its meetings.

Bibliography. See Lord Birkenhead, *The Prof. in Two Worlds* (1961).

LIST, WILHELM (1880–1971). Brilliant German tactician in the early days of the war.

List played an important role in the opening *Blitzkrieg* (*q.v.*) on Poland. He won Hitler's admiration by leading his 12th Army Group, "marching like the devil," through northern France. (*See* FRANCE, FIRST BATTLE OF.) On July 19, 1940, he was one of 12 generals named Field Marshal by a grateful Hitler. In February 1941 he led his forces through Bulgaria to smash Greece. (*See* GREECE, BATTLE FOR.) Hitler then named him Commander-in-Chief for the Southeast (Balkans).

In mid-1942 List was given command of Army Group A in the Caucasus region of the Russian front. For the first time in the war he was unable to breach an assigned barrier. An angry Hitler dismissed him from his command on September 9, 1942.

LITERATURE, WARTIME. In World War II, as in World War I, writers were conscripted for war service in all belligerent countries.

GENERAL. Writing during the war was of varying types in different countries. A large part of it was directly related to propaganda. Novelists, biographers, playwrights, and poets contributed their talents to maintenance of morale by stressing the positive quality of patriotism and urging an all-out effort for victory. (*See* PROPAGANDA, WAR.) Correspondents were sent to combat fronts to describe the valorous deeds of fighting men and to create instant heroes for an insatiable public. (*See* REPORTING, WAR.) Much of the writing was pedestrian, but a small portion of it was added to the world's outstanding literature.

Writers covered every possible phase of the war. Examples among the voluminous output were: ground combat—E. Waugh, *Men at Arms, Officers and Gentlemen,* and *Sword of Honour*; naval operations—C. S. Forester, *The Ship,* J. de Hartog, *The Captain,* and T. Heggen, *Mister Roberts*; air combat—M. Caiden, *The Last Dogfight,* and J. Heller, *Catch-22*; prisons and prisoners—J. Bor, *The Terezin Requiem,* and K. Vonnegut, *Slaughterhouse Five*; atrocities—A. Anatoli, *Babi Yar,* J. Hersey, *The Wall,* and E. Wiesel, *The Town Beyond the Wall*; Jews—E. M. Remarque, *The Night in Lisbon,* and H. Karmel-Wolfe, *The Baders of Jacob Street;* underground movements—A. Hall, *The Warsaw Document,* and S. de Gramont, *Lives to Give*; and children—G. Berto, *The Sky is Red,* and *The Diary of Anne Frank.*

FRENCH. Despite Vichy and German censorship, French literary forms—the novel, plays, poetry, non-fiction, and literally criticism—remained at a consistently high level throughout the war years. Until 1940 the novels of Romain Rolland, Marcel Proust, and André Gide continued to be read. Popular novelists in occupied France included Louis-Ferdinand Céline (*Guignold's Band,* 1943) and Antoine de Saint-Exupéry (*Vol de nuit,* 1931). New fiction tended to be "inspired newsreel," as indicated in the works of Jean Bruller (*Le Silence de la mer,* 1942); Roger Vailland (*Drôle de jeu,* 1945); Romain Gary; and Jules Roy.

The tendency to narrow the margin between fiction and documentary also appeared in the works of Jean-Paul Sartre, Simone de Beauvoir, and Albert Camus. All were philosophically inclined and continued to work despite German censorship and discouragement by Vichy collaborators. Sartre's wartime production, especially his *L'Être et le néant,* 1943 (*Being and Nothingness,* 1956), reflected much of the pessimism prevalent during the dark occupation years.

Sartre was the leading apostle of French existentialism, which became the vogue in France after the liberation in 1944. In effect, the philosophy expressed a revolt against traditional metaphysical approaches to man and his place in the universe. Existence, he said, precedes essence. There is no God and hence no fixed human nature which determines one to act. Man is totally free and is entirely responsible for what he makes of himself. Human life, in Sartre's estimation, is an "ineffective passion." (*See also* PSYCHOLOGICAL EFFECTS OF THE WAR.)

Sartre's existentialism appealed to Frenchmen who had lived under the heel of the Nazis and who were inclined to pessimism and despair. They were impressed by this moralist in the great French tradition, even if he was a clumsy novelist. Sartre's close friend, Simone de Beauvoir, added to his ideas an obsession with feminism and death.

Albert Camus, journalist and philosopher, was widely read during the war years. He deliberately moved to Paris from Algiers in 1940 at a time when many Frenchmen were leaving for North Africa. He founded the clandestine newspaper, *Combat,* which reflected the views of the French Resistance movement. His novel, *Étranger* (1942) was reminiscent of Kafka's work. His philosophical essay, *Le myth de Sisiphe* (1942), presented his concept of the absurd and urged his compatriots to live lucidly within it. Like Sartre, Camus wrote plays for the Parisian stage.

BRITISH. British writing maintained a generally high level throughout the war. The best-known British novel, which was also highly popular in the United States, was *Mrs. Miniver* by J. Struthers. Among many other novels were E. Waugh's *Put Out More Flags;* C. P. Snow's *Homecoming;* G. Greene's *The Ministry of Fear;* and N. Shute's *The Breaking Wave.* Several authors, including historian Hugh R. Trevor-Roper and journalist Malcolm Muggeridge, were recruited for intelligence work. The talented Noël Coward wrote plays and movies to bolster morale on the home front. In the immediate postwar years Winston Churchill published his six-volume *The Second World War.*

GERMAN. Outstanding literary figures, including Thomas Mann, Heinrich Mann, Ernst Toller, Lion Feuchtwanger, and Emil Ludwig, emigrated from Germany during the 1930s when Hitler consolidated his dictatorship. The only literary light of consequence to remain was the novelist and dramatist Gerhart Hauptmann, who in all probability was attracted by the mysticism and symbolism of Nazism. During the war, writing, along with films, radio, and sport, was coordinated by Paul Joseph Goebbels (*q.v.*) Minister of Public Enlighten-ment and Propaganda. Among novelists who later wrote about war subjects were H. Böll, *Absent Without Leave;* G. Grass, *War Years;* and H. H. Kirst, *Forward Gunner Asch!*

RUSSIAN. There was no place for dissent under Stalin's dictatorship. The great Russian literary tradition, epitomized in the work of Dostoievski, Gogol, Turgenev, and Tolstoy, gave way to mediocrity as novelists dutifully sang praise to Stalin, tractors, factories, and proletarian love. The process continued in World War II when writing was geared to needs of the state. Novelists K. Simonov and I. Ehrenburg went to combat fronts to extol the Great Patriotic War, with emphasis on Red heroes and Nazi monsters.

AMERICAN. Many American writers went to combat fronts (*see* REPORT-ING, WAR) or lent their talents to the Office of War Information (*q.v.*). The outstanding novelist of the war years was John Hersey, who wrote such classics as *A Bell for Adano.* Among other novels on World War II were E. Caldwell, *The Final Hour;* J. P. Marquand, *So Little Time;* and J. G. Cozzens, *Guard of Honor.*

LONDON CONTROLLING SECTION (LCS). British organization within the Joint Planning Staff (*q.v.*) at Churchill's headquarters. It was responsible for planning and coordinating ruses and deception schemes for the battle-fronts. One of its major successes was *Operation Mincemeat* (*q.v.*). (*See* ES-PIONAGE.)

LONG LANCE TORPEDO. Japanese oxygen-powered naval weapon.

The Navy Section of Imperial General Headquarters, contrary to American custom, insisted on the use of torpedo tubes on cruisers. As many as eight were used on Japanese heavy cruisers. Since the early 1930s, Japanese designers pro-duced the Long Lance torpedo, which was oxygen fueled and highly effective. Crews were minutely trained in use of the torpedo, which became a much-feared weapon on the seas. Japanese security measures kept the existence of the torpedoes secret until the latter part of the war. They were used in the sinking of four Allied heavy cruisers at the Battle of Savo Island. (*See* GUADAL-CANAL CAMPAIGNS.)

SPECIFICATIONS.
  Weight. 6,000 pounds.
  Diameter. 61 cm. (24 in.)
  Speed. 50 knots.
  Range. Nearly 4 mi.
  War Head. 1,210 lbs.

LONG RANGE DESERT GROUP (LRDG). Special British unit organized for long-range reconnaissance behind enemy lines in Libya.

Formed in June 1940 and consisting mostly of New Zealanders, the Long Range Desert Group later accepted British and Rhodesian volunteers. Operating 1,500 miles westward from the Nile and 500 miles inland, the men performed a variety of duties. Carrying supplies for a month and maintaining contact by radio, they raided enemy outposts, surveyed possible routes for the main desert forces, harassed German and Italian lines of communication, and supported local Partisan and guerrilla units.

Later the group increased its operations. In September 1942 it attacked the garrisons at Benghazi and Tobruk. (*See* NORTH AFRICA, CAMPAIGNS IN.) In 1943 it was reorganized for service in Greece, Yugoslavia, Albania, and Italy. In these theaters it used patrols of an officer and 20 men, including a navigator and wireless operator, and five unarmored vehicles. The LRDG often guided patrols of Special Air Service troops (that is, commandos) to designated targets and later picked them up again.

LONG-RANGE PENETRATION GROUP. Special Allied guerrilla unit set up in Burma to operate in Japanese-held areas.

The purpose of the long-range penetration group was to capture Japanese strongholds to serve as bases for obtaining information and planning attacks. (*See* BURMA, CAMPAIGNS IN; CHINDITS; and WINGATE, ORDE CHARLES.)

LONGSTOP HILL. British-held hill close to Medjez el Bab in the race for Tunis in late 1942. On December 25, 1942, German troops captured the hill and renamed it Christmas Hill. (*See* NORTH AFRICA, CAMPAIGNS IN.)

LORAN. Acronym for *l*ong *ra*nge *n*avigation, used by the U.S. Navy as an aid to navigation in the Pacific.

Developed in 1944, LORAN was a system by which radio signals were broadcast from two shore-based stations and received by a ship or plane using a receiver that measured the difference in time arrival of the two signals. Special charts were consulted for the LORAN fix. The system was helpful especially for night attacks on Japanese targets. In general it was similar to the British *Gee*. (*See also* OBOE.)

LORD HAW HAW. British turncoat who broadcast for the Germans during the war. (*See* JOYCE, WILLIAM.)

LOSSES, WAR. *See* CASUALTIES, WAR; and ECONOMIC CONSEQUENCES OF THE WAR.

LOTHIAN, PHILIP HENRY KERR, MARQUESS (1882–1940). British Ambassador to Washington who influenced American policy in the early stages of the war.

Lothian was sent to Washington as British Ambassador in August 1939 just preceding the start of World War II. Without diplomatic or political experience, he laid the foundation for close relations between the two countries. He won popularity with the American public by naming Abraham Lincoln his political saint, asserting that the United States had won World War I for the Allies, and adopting southern fried chicken as his favorite dish. In speeches he called Britain "the U.S. Maginot Line," and stated that "Britain stands at Armageddon in the battle for the Lord." He did much to swing American public support to the Allies. He died suddenly at the British Embassy in Washington on December 12, 1940.

With his broad forehead, high arched nose, and vested paunch, Lothian was said to look like a combination of a Roman Senator and a member of the House of Lords. He was always tactful: "I am not concerned today to attempt to tell you what you should do in this grave matter. That is your business." His approach was perfect for the American public, even if Senator William E. Borah denounced him as a British propagandist.

Bibliography. J.R.M. Butler, *Lord Lothian* (1966).

LOW COUNTRIES, CAMPAIGNS IN THE. Hitler's invasions of the northwestern European countries of Holland, Belgium, and Luxembourg in May 1940 before turning on France and Britain.

BACKGROUND. In 1939, German strategists considered the Maginot Line (*q.v.*) an unknown factor, but felt much respect for its defensive strength. Before attacking France, however, Hitler decided to strike at the Low Countries and thereby outflank the vaunted French fortifications. He would repeat the Schlieffen Plan of 1914 by striking a hammer blow on Paris through the old classic route of invasion.

For this purpose Hitler had some 89 divisions, including 2 armored, and a reserve of 47, a total of 136 divisions. His forces were divided into three army groups under Gens. Fedor von Bock, Gerd von Rundstedt (*qq.v.*), and Ritter Wilhelm von Leeb. Against this formidable German force the Allies had 149 divisions, including 106 French, 20 Belgian, 13 British, and 10 Dutch. The *Wehrmacht* (*q.v.*), already blooded in the Polish and Scandinavian campaigns (*see* POLAND, INVASION OF, and SCANDINAVIA, CAMPAIGNS IN) was superior in command, liaison, equipment, and training.

PREPARATIONS. The German campaign against Holland was prepared with traditional thoroughness. Nothing was left to chance. German "tourists, salesmen, and students," all carefully briefed, worked inside Holland, some using Dutch uniforms. There was help from the pro-Fascist followers of Anton

Mussert and Rost von Tonningen, Dutchmen sympathetic to fascism. The Dutch, neutral in World War I and untouched by war for a century, were not blind to German preparations, but there was little they could do with their modest four army corps, one dozen squadron of planes, and few antiaircraft guns. Where other countries relied on artillery and firepower for protection against invasion, the Dutch counted on their ability to flood extensive areas of their homeland by breaking strategic dikes.

ATTACK ON HOLLAND. At 4 A.M. on May 10, 1940, again without warning, German parachutists, some dressed in Allied uniforms, hurtled down at strategic points over the country. Simultaneously, screaming *Stukas* (*q.v.*) attacked bridges, railroad stations, and forts. The small Dutch air force was soon destroyed. It was *Blitzkrieg* (*q.v.*) all over again. Nazi tanks roared along the level terrain, slicing thin defense lines into segments and setting up islands behind the lines. Then came the swift-charging infantry to mop up resistance.

Two hours after the invasion began, the German minister at The Hague explained blandly that there was "irrefutable evidence" of a prepared Anglo-French invasion of the Low Countries and that the Germans had moved first to stop it. He gave the choice of capitulation or annihilation. The Dutch asked for British and French assistance, but it came far too late. The Dutch fought desperately as the Nazi *Blitz* rolled on.

DUTCH CAPITULATION. Within a few days the Germans penetrated into Gelder Valley and Fortress Holland, the eastern line from Muiden to Utrecht, and linked up with the parachutists who had already immobilized The Hague and Rotterdam. The Dutch declared Rotterdam an open city (*q.v.*) but Germans, nevertheless, subjected it to a heavy bombardment. (*See* ROTTERDAM, BOMBING OF.) Queen Wilhelmina (*q.v.*), members of the royal family, and government officials, managed to escape to England, where they set up a government-in-exile (*q.v.*).

Within five days, by May 15, 1940, it was all over. The little Dutch Army had suffered 100,000 casualties, a quarter of its strength. Hitler placed Holland under the harsh rule of Artur Seyss-Inquart (*q.v.*).

ASSAULT ON BELGIUM. On May 10, 1940, simultaneous with the attack on Holland, German forces hit the Low Countries all along the western front from the North Sea to Luxembourg. The Dutch capitulated in five days, the Belgians, better prepared, lasted for just 18 days.

The Belgians, like the Dutch, had been careful to avoid giving any excuse for attack, but it was useless. In 1937 Hitler had given his word to respect Belgian neutrality unless it took part in military action against Germany. His pledge was worthless.

Again there was the same spectacular pattern—ultimatum, *Blitzkrieg*—air attack, light armor, 2,000 tanks, infantry to mop up. Half the Belgian Air

Force was destroyed on the ground within a few hours. The "impregnable" Belgian fortress of Eben Emael, commanding the Albert Canal, was taken in 30 hours. (*See* EBEN EMAEL, FORT.) Casualties were light on both sides.

As soon as the Germans crossed the border, King Leopold III (*q.v.*) appealed to the Allies for help. All British forces on the Continent, plus a portion of the French Army, headed for Belgium at top speed. Although the Belgians, with Allied support, fought tenaciously, they could not contain the German assault. Within seven days German tanks reached the Channel and cut the Allied forces into two. When the Germans captured Calais and Boulogne, only the port of Dunkirk was left as a possible escape route for the British. (*See* DUNKIRK EVACUATION.)

BELGIAN CAPITULATION. At 5 P.M. on May 27, 1940, Leopold asked the Germans for an armistice. The next day nearly 400,000 weary and dispirited Belgian troops surrendered unconditionally. Leopold was placed in protective custody while his cabinet escaped to London.

FALL OF LUXEMBOURG. The tiny European Grand Duchy of Luxembourg, 999 square miles, was taken within a matter of hours. For Hitler the principality was important because of its strategic position on the route of his main thrust.

SIGNIFICANCE. Hitler's quick conquest of the Low Countries was expected. There was great rejoicing in Germany and corresponding gloom in London. On May 10, 1940, just as Hitler struck at the Low Countries, Neville Chamberlain (*q.v.*) resigned as Prime Minister and was succeeded by the more aggressive Winston Churchill (*q.v.*). After the campaigns in the Low Countries, the future looked bleak for embattled Britain.

Bibliography. E. N. Van Kleffen, *Juggernaut over Holland* (1941); Belgian Ministry of Foreign Affairs, *Official Account, 1939-1940* (1942); and W. Warmbrund, *The Dutch Under German Occupation* (1963); and W. P. Maass, *The Netherlands at War, 1940-1945* (1970).

LUCY. Espionage agent for the Russians.

Little is known about Lucy's activities other than that she operated from Switzerland and gave critical information to the Kremlin. She was especially effective in assisting the Russians after the German invasion of the Soviet Union. In the summer of 1942 her report to Moscow of German intentions gave the Russians time to reinforce the Stalingrad garrison against the army of Gen. Friedrich Paulus (*q.v.*). Her work was vital for the defense of the Volga region. (*See* ESPIONAGE.)

LUFTWAFFE. The German Air Force.

BACKGROUND. German airmen achieved a high reputation in World War I, when such aces as Baron Manfred von Richthofen, leader of the Flying Circus, won global attention. Under the terms of the Treaty of Versailles, defeated Germany was forbidden all military aircraft. The Germans promoted civil aviation and gliding clubs as a substitute. Meanwhile, the aircraft construction industry advanced spectacularly with the work of Focke Wulf at Bremen, Dornier at Friedrichsruh, Heinkel at Warnemünde, Junkers at Dessau, and Messerschmitt at Augsburg. While the Allies were flying obsolete planes, German designers developed all-metal monoplanes with cantilevered wings, retractable landing gear, and variable-pitch propellers.

LEADERSHIP. As soon as he became Chancellor, Hitler appointed his deputy, Gen. Hermann Goering (*q.v.*) Reich Commissioner for Air and gave him instructions to build a new *Luftwaffe*. With the able assistance of Gen. Erhard Milch (*q.v.*), Goering presented his chief with what he wanted—a powerful air striking force. Much of the work in building aircraft, airfields, and training schools was delegated to Gen. Walther Wever.

By 1935 the *Luftwaffe* had 1,188 planes of varying types and a cadre of 20,000 officers and men. In May 1936 Wever was killed in an air crash. He was succeeded by Gen. Albert Kesselring (*q.v.*), who continued the policy of expansion. In November 1936 Kesselring sent *Luftwaffe* pilots to Spain in a unit called the Condor Legion to obtain combat experience in the Spanish civil war.

ORGANIZATION. The basic tactical unit of the *Luftwaffe* was the 120-plane group (*Geschwader*). Each group was composed of three 40-plane wings (*Gruppen*). Each wing consisted of three 12 to 16-plane squadrons (*Staffeln*). There were further group divisions, including fighters, bombers, night fighters, fast bombers, dive bombers, transports, and special assignment groups.

WORLD WAR II. The *Luftwaffe* played a major role in the opening *Blitzkrieg* (*q.v.*) on Poland starting on September 1, 1939. (*See* POLAND, INVASION OF.) More than 1,600 aircraft, including the screaming *Stukas* (*q.v.*), smashed Polish airfields and attacked Polish ground troops. During the Sitdown War in the winter of 1939–1940 (*see SITZKREIG*), *Luftwaffe* pilots rested. They went back into action in Denmark, Norway, the Low Countries, and France. (*See* LOW COUNTRIES, CAMPAIGNS IN THE; and FRANCE, FIRST BATTLE OF.) Unable to prevent British retreat at Dunkirk, Goering turned his attention to support of ground units headed toward Paris. (*See* DUNKIRK EVACUATION.)

After defeat of France, Hitler ordered Goering to prepare for an all-out attack to drive the Royal Air Force (*q.v.*) from the skies as a preliminary to invasion of Britain. (*See* SEA LION.) On August 13, 1940, the *Luftwaffe* made 1,000 fighter sorties and 485 bombing runs over England, losing 45 planes in the process. On September 15, a critical day, it lost 60 planes in a daylight raid on London. It became obvious that the *Luftwaffe* was in serious trouble. It lost the struggle to subdue the British. (*See* BRITAIN, BATTLE OF.)

There were some local successes. On May 29, 1941, the *Luftwaffe* played a leading role in the successful German assault on Crete. (*See* CRETE, BATTLE OF.) But Hitler had gradually overextended his lines and his air force could not function effectively in Europe, North Africa, and the eastern front simultaneously. By spring 1945 the *Luftwaffe* was a beaten force. It still had 3,000 planes, but most of these remained on the ground without fuel and without an adequate supply of trained pilots.

LOSSES. From the start of the war the *Luftwaffe* lost 44,065 crewmen killed or missing, 28,200 wounded, and 27,610 prisoners of war. German statisticians claimed the destruction of 13,997 enemy planes, a staggering and certainly highly exaggerated claim.

SIGNIFICANCE. In building the *Luftwaffe* Hitler made a fundamental error. Convinced that he would wage only short, successful campaigns, he ordered the production of speedy fighter planes and at first gave comparatively little attention to heavy bombers. It was a serious miscalculation. Later he favored bombers but it was far too late. The prestige of the *Luftwaffe* plummeted precipitously until finally it was not even able to defend German cities and industrial centers. It was outgunned and outfought by the Royal Air Force and the U.S. Army Air Forces (*qq.v.*).

Bibliography. H. Hermann, *The Luftwaffe* (1943); A. Galland, *The First and the Last* (1954); W. Baumbach, *The Life and Death of the Luftwaffe* (1960); C. Bekker, *The Luftwaffe Diaries* (1968); J. Killen, *A History of the Luftwaffe;* A. Price, *The Luftwaffe* (1969); M. Schliephoke, *The Birth of the Luftwaffe, 1918-1939* (1971); D. Irving, *The Rise and Fall of the Luftwaffe* (1973); and *Luftwaffe Combat Planes* (1981).

M

M-4 (SHERMAN). See TANKS.

M-5. See TANKS.

M-26 (PERSHING). See TANKS.

MacARTHUR, DOUGLAS (1880–1964). Commander of the U.S. Armed Forces in the Far East (1941–1951). He was born at Little Rock, Arkansas, on January 26, 1880, the son of Arthur MacArthur, a professional army officer. He was graduated from the U.S. Military Academy at West Point in 1903, and was commissioned a 2nd Lieutenant in the Corps of Engineers.

EARLY CAREER. After graduation from West Point, MacArthur served in the Philippines and Japan. In 1906 he was made aide to President Theodore Roosevelt and from 1913 to 1917 was attached to the Army General Staff. In World War I he fought in France with the 42nd (Rainbow) Division and participated in several major campaigns, including the St. Mihiel and Meuse-Argonne offensives. He was promoted to Brigadier General in 1918 and served as Superintendent of West Point from 1919 to 1922. In 1935 he was appointed head of the American military mission to the Philippines, where he led a vast training program. He retired two years later but returned to duty in July 1941 to command the U.S. Armed Forces in the Far East.

WORLD WAR II. After the Japanese attack on Pearl Harbor (*q.v.*), MacArthur commanded the defense of the Philippines. When the Japanese landed large forces on December 22, 1941, north and south of Manila, MacArthur moved to Corregidor to lead its defense. (*See* CORREGIDOR, FALL OF.) In March 1942, he was ordered to Australia. On the trip he made his famous statement of determination: "I came through and I shall return." On April 18, 1942, he was named Supreme Commander of the Southwest Pacific Area.

411

NEW GUINEA CAMPAIGN. From this time on MacArthur persisted in his opinion that the first goal of the Allies should be to defeat Japan before Germany. Although MacArthur led all Allied forces in the Southwest Pacific, Adm. Chester Nimitz (*q.v.*) maintained his fleet as an independent force. While Nimitz struck in the Central Solomons, MacArthur began a "leapfrog" campaign starting on the northeast coast of New Guinea, by-passing Japanese troop concentrations. Taking the offensive, he led American and Australian troops in the long and difficult campaign to drive the enemy out of New Guinea. By February 1943 the Allies had won control of the eastern Papuan Peninsula and ended the Japanese threat to the sea lanes. (*See* NEW GUINEA, CAMPAIGNS IN.)

THE PHILIPPINES. MacArthur's triumph in New Guinea was one of the decisive steps that took the Allies westward toward the Philippines. The tempo of the Allied advance increased with the arrival of reinforcements and supplies from the United States. In early 1944 MacArthur's troops neutralized the Japanese stronghold at Rabaul (*q.v.*). Then they moved in leapfrog tactics along the northern coast of New Guinea, leaving by-passed Japanese troops to wither on the vine. While naval forces penetrated into the inner defenses of Japan by way of the Gilbert, Marshall, and Mariana islands (*qq.v.*), MacArthur moved on to attack the Philippines.

On October 20, 1944, MacArthur led the invasion of the central Philippines at Leyte. Wading ashore with his troops, he fulfilled the promise to return he had made two years earlier. On December 18, 1944, he was promoted to five-star General of the Army. In early January 1945 his troops invaded Luzon, the principal island of the Philippines and in late February captured Corregidor and Manila.

On August 14, 1945, after the atomic bombing of Hiroshima and Nagasaki (*qq.v.*), the Japanese accepted the Allied terms of unconditional surrender. On September 2, 1945, MacArthur received the formal surrender on board the battleship *Missouri.* (*See* SURRENDER, JAPANESE.)

POSTWAR. MacArthur was appointed Supreme Commander for the Allied Powers in Japan following the Japanese surrender. In 1950 he became commander of the U.S. Forces in Korea. Disagreement with President Harry S Truman (*q.v.*) on Far Eastern policy led to his removal from his posts. He died on April 5, 1964, in Washington, D.C.

PERSONALITY AND CHARACTER. Along with Gen. Bernard Law Montgomery (*q.v.*), MacArthur was one of the most controversial military figures of the war. Opinions on his personality and character vary widely. His ability as a strategist and tactician is seldom questioned. His war record was impressive. Again and again he made great advances with limited resources. His particular pride was the low casualty rate among his forces. Certain that he was a man of destiny, he seldom took advice and maintained a personal aloofness that irritated others. He preferred to use the pronoun "I" rather than "we" in all his reports and he was a masterly publicist. He did not hesitate to criticize his superiors but was allergic to criticism himself. Throughout the war he never retreated from his conviction that the Pacific theater of operations should be given priority in Allied planning.

Bibliography. J. Gunther, *The Riddle of MacArthur* (1951); R. H. Revere and A. M. Schlesinger, Jr., *The General and the President* (1951); C. Lee and R. Henschel, *Douglas MacArthur* (1952); F. Hunt, *The Untold Story of Douglas MacArthur* (1954); C. A. Willoughby and J. R. Chamberlain, *MacArthur, 1941–1951* (1954); C. Whitney, *MacArthur: His Rendezvous with History* (1956); D. MacArthur, *Reminiscences* (1964); and W. Manchester, *American Caesar: Douglas MacArthur, 1880–1964* (1979).

McAULIFFE, ANTHONY CLEMENT (1898–1975). U.S. Army officer known as the "Nuts General."

On the outbreak of World War II in September 1939, McAuliffe was ordered to Washington to attend the Army War College. In 1940 he was assigned as a Major to develop such new weapons as the *Jeep*, the *Sherman* medium tank, and the bazooka (*qq.v.*). In August 1942, after the entry of the United States into the war, he was given command as Brigadier General of the artillery division of the 101st Airborne Division, which was among the earliest divisions dispatched to Europe.

In April 1944, in a full dress rehearsal for *Operation Overlord* (*q.v.*), the coming invasion of Normandy, McAuliffe broke his back in a parachute fall. By June he was well enough to jump with his troops over Normandy on the night of D-Day. That same night he was appointed Deputy Division Commander and given the task of seizing Carenton.

BASTOGNE. McAuliffe commanded the glider echelon in the American airborne invasion of Holland beginning on September 18, 1944. He was with his troops in Reims when the Germans began their strong counteroffensive in the Battle of the Bulge (*q.v.*). Temporarily in command of the 101st Airborne Division, he rushed his men to defense of the little town of Bastogne, a crucial crossroad in the Ardennes forest.

When the Germans surrounded the American unit in Bastogne, they sent two officers to demand instant surrender. McAuliffe made his famous reply of "Nuts!" (*See* BASTOGNE.) According to one observer, McAuliffe's troops then fought on with renewed spirit and finally helped break the last great offensive of the war.

Gen. George Smith Patton, Jr. (*q.v.*) decorated McAuliffe with the Distinguished Service Cross. By this time McAuliffe became widely known as the Hero of Bastogne. He was promoted to Major General and given command of the 103d Infantry Division, which he led from Alsace through the Siegfried Line (*q.v.*) in March 1945. Later he took his division across Germany to Innsbruck, Austria, through the Brenner Pass to link up with the American 5th Army coming up from Italy.

Bibliography. F. Mackenzie, *The Men of Bastogne* (1968).

McNARNEY, JOSEPH TAGGART (1893–1972). U.S. Army officer.

In 1940 Col. McNarney was appointed a member of the Permanent Joint Defense Board for Canada and the United States. From December 1941 to January 1942 he served as a member of the Roberts Commission that investigated the Japanese attack on Pearl Harbor. In March 1942 he was appointed Department Chief of the General Staff with the responsibility of establishing policy and supervising budgetary affairs. In this post he gave special attention to the air force. In October 1942 he was named Deputy Supreme Commander of the Mediterranean Area and Commander of the U.S. Forces there. He was promoted to temporary General in March 1945.

Lean, of medium height, with thinning hair, McNarney was called "dour, taciturn, and officially ruthless." Gen. George Marshall (*q.v.*) spoke of him as "my right arm." McNarney successfully applied his great administrative talents to simplifying the structure of the U.S. Army.

MAGIC. Operation Magic was the code name for the overall American program dedicated to breaking Japanese codes.

BACKGROUND. The basic cipher machine in Germany, called *Enigma,* had been rebuilt in Britain to serve the *Ultra* (*q.v.*) organization. The Japanese version was called *Purple,* which worked on the principle of a telephone switchboard. At first the *Purple* machine defied all efforts of American cryptologists to crack Japanese messages.

CRACKING THE CODE. The U.S. Army Intelligence Service went to work on the *Purple* solution. On September 23, 1940, Col. William Friedman (*q.v.*), U.S. Army intelligence officer and a chief cryptanalyst of the War Department in Washington, successfully broke the Japanese code. The resultant recovery of Japanese ciphers was code named *Magic* from this point on.

The United States then set up three tracking stations that intercepted messages from Tokyo to Japanese embassies throughout the world. Special intelligence units went to work decoding Japanese messages. Both army and navy intelligence sections intercepted, decoded, and translated Japanese coded official communications.

SIGNIFICANCE. Magic gave Secretary of State Cordell Hull (*q.v.*) a decided advantage in his dealings with Adm. Kichisaburo Nomura (*q.v.*) early in December 1941. *Operation Magic* did not halt after the Japanese attack on Pearl Harbor (*q.v.*). The breaking of the Japanese codes played a major role, in the decisive defeat of the Japanese at the Battle of Midway (*q.v.*). Because of *Magic,* American naval commanders knew the approximate Japanese date of attack as well as the direction of Japanese warships. (*See also* CODES AND CODE BREAKING.)

MAGINOT LINE. Massive system of French fortifications stretching from Switzerland to the Belgian border. The Maginot Line was supposed to give security for France against any German attack.

BACKGROUND. Use of fixed ground fortifications had been traditional in France. Sébastian de Vauban built a series of fortresses for Louis XIV in the 17th century and Sère de Revière constructed similar defenses after the defeat of France by Prussia in 1871. In the era after World War I, French military leaders seemed to be fascinated by trench defenses of the late war and put their faith in elaborate fortifications. While political leaders set up a system of alliances in the name of security, military planners decided to build a permanent trench of concrete and steel in defense against Germans.

"WALL OF FRANCE." In the 1920s a Committee of Frontier Defense prepared the blueprint. The task was entrusted to André Maginot (1877–1932), who was Minister of War from 1929 to 1931 under Premier André Tardieu. Maginot was responsible for obtaining credits for the gigantic undertaking and carried out the first stages of the plan. His name became the symbol of the fixed fortification idea and the Maginot Line mentality which went along with it.

OPPOSITION. From the beginning there were vociferous critics. A young staff officer, Charles de Gaulle (*q.v.*), sarcastically denounced the "Maginot complex" as a gross mistake. In his book, *Vers l'armée de métier* (1934) (*The Army of the Future*, 1940), he ridiculed stationary defenses and called for an army of great mobility and striking power. He predicted with astonishing accuracy the German *Blitzkrieg* (*q.v.*) technique of World War II. There was similar skepticism in other countries. Maj. Gen. J.F.C. Fuller (*q.v.*), the British war expert, labeled the Maginot Line "the tombstone of France."

CONSTRUCTION. Into the Maginot Line went the services of a huge work force, costs running close to $1 billion, and more than 26 million cubic feet of cement. When the line was finished, it stretched in a series of gigantic pillboxes connecting old fortifications with two major new ones, Hackenberg and Hochwald. It covered the iron and industrial region of Lorraine. Alsace-Lorraine became a huge concrete molehill studded with gun turrets and dragon teeth.

Elevators led into underground passages that housed living quarters, hospitals, restaurants, ammunition dumps—all the paraphernalia of war. At points there were great underground forts on six levels, power stations for ventilation, miniature railroads, telephone exchanges—all immune to shells and bombs. Above ground were casemates served by elevators, with guns pointing only to the east.

AFTERMATH. In June 1940 the Germans skirted the Maginot Line and pushed through the fatal gap at Sedan, the old traditional route of invasion. The fault lay in inadequate military thinking. Maginot himself had conceived of his line as only a partial defense. He had not extended it through the flat Franco-Belgian frontier because the ground was not suitable for heavy underground fortifications. Moreover, the French High Command believed that the Belgian defenses anchored at Liège, Eben Emael (*q.v.*), and the Albert Canal were, in effect, a proper extension of the line. The French public, too, had an almost mystical faith in the Maginot Line and believed its defense to be absolute and total.

The Belgian surrender in 1940 gave the Germans an open invitation to the Sedan gap. When France signed the armistice at Compiègne (*q.v.*), the forts of the Maginot Line were intact. French military leaders, who neglected the development of planes and tanks in favor of their defensive line, had made a fatal error.

Bibliography. P. Belperon, *Maginot of the Line* (1940); and V. Rowe, *The Great Wall of France* (1961).

MAISKY, IVAN (1884–1975). Russian Ambassador to London during the early war years.

Because his experience as Ambassador to Britain at the start of the war gave him a profound knowledge of the British mentality, Maisky advised Moscow that the British would stand firm. In 1941 he informed Stalin of the upcoming assault on the Soviet Union by Hitler, but the Russian dictator refused to pay heed. Maisky was recalled in 1943 to serve as a Deputy Commissar for Foreign Affairs. In this post he passed on to the Allied Supreme Command Stalin's persistant calls for a Second Front (*q.v.*).

Bibliography. I. Maisky, *Memoirs of a Soviet Ambassador: The War, 1939–1943* (1968).

MALAYA, CAMPAIGN FOR. Japanese victory in Malaya in the early days of the war.

TARGET. The Malay Peninsula, an area of 50,690 square miles, protrudes from the southeast corner of Asia between India and China, jutting into the South China Sea. Nearly all of the country was covered by dense tropical jungle. The only cleared areas were stretches on the west coast, in the north, and along the main rivers, the Sungai Parak and the Sungai Paihang. Here was the greatest source of rubber in the world, as well as a huge supply of tin.

Malaya was of great strategic importance. At its tip lay Singapore, which along with Manila and Hong Kong, formed a triangle of Anglo-American power in the Far East. Singapore was guardian of the passage from the South China Sea to the Indian Ocean.

The British had not made adequate safeguards to counter possible land attacks on the Malay Peninsula. They had 19,000 of their own men there, added to 69,000 Indians, Malayans, and Australians, all poorly equipped and trained.

BACKGROUND. For Japanese Imperial Headquarters, Malaya was one of the first targets at the start of the war in the Pacific. To spearhead the attack, it designated the crack 25th Army. The plan called for initial overwhelming air bombing, landings on the northeast coast, and then a drive down the peninsula to take Singapore from the land side. The Japanese had about 35,000 men poised in Thailand and Indo-China for the task. Gen. Tomoyuki Yamashita was assigned to command the campaign.

ASSAULT. The Japanese plan was followed precisely. On December 7, 1941, the day of Pearl Harbor (*q.v.*), Japanese aircraft bombed Kota Bharu and British airfields in northern Malaya and within 24 hours established air superiority. Contingents of Yamashita's 25th Army landed on the beaches and soon overran four states—Kedah, Kelantan, Trengganu, and Perak. Japanese troops poured on land from vast numbers of sampans and small landing craft. Those who landed at Singora moved down the east coast of the Isthmus of Kra, while others crossed the borders from Siam and pressed down the west coast.

Helped by inside agents, the Japanese pushed ahead in a masterpiece of infiltration. The jungles were supposed to be impregnable, but the Japanese troops knifed through them in an amazing display of military power. They hacked their way through jungles, rice fields, rubber plantations, and forests; swam crocodile-infested waters; and won skirmish after skirmish with the enemy.

British, Australian, Indian, and Malayan troops attempted unsuccessfully to halt the march. Again and again Japanese troops appeared deep in their rear and on their flanks and often struck from all sides at once. The British sent out a few tanks of 1918 vintage to meet superbly trained troops.

The Japanese pushed steadily ahead, combining aggressive tactics with brilliant improvisations. By mid-January 1942 the British, outwitted and demoralized, staggered back the length of the peninsula and crossed the causeway to Singapore. Here there were no underground caverns as at Malta (*see* MALTA, SIEGE OF) or man-made tunnels as at Corregidor (*see* COR-REGIDOR, FALL OF) for a protracted defense. British reinforcements arrived just in time to share the defeat. The surrender came on February 15, 1942. (*See* SINGAPORE, FALL OF.) "There comes a stage," said Lt. Gen. Arthur E. Percival, British commander at Singapore, "when in the interests of the troops and civil population further bloodshed will serve no useful purpose."

LOSSES. It was estimated that 55,000 to 60,000 British and Imperial troops were made prisoners of war at Singapore alone, but many others were captured by the Japanese even before its fall. More than 3,500 British and Imperial troops were killed in action during the entire Malayan campaign, and 6,150 were wounded. It is not known exactly how many Japanese were killed or wounded, but it is believed that their total casualties were about 4,600.

The Japanese also captured a vast amount of booty, including 740 guns,

2,500 machine guns, 65,000 rifles, 200 armored cars, several thousand motor cars and trucks, 10 light planes, and 1,000 locomotives and railroad cars.

SIGNIFICANCE. It was a notable victory for the Japanese. They had given themselves 100 days to complete their campaign, and they had done it in 70. They now controlled the western Pacific and the South China Sea and could land their troops in any number anywhere in the Pacific with impunity. They had made their position in the Pacific seemingly impregnable. Yamashita's campaign had been so successful and so brilliantly executed that he thereafter bore the name Tiger of Malaya. Hirohito issued a glowing Imperial Rescript: "Britain's base of operations in the Far East is overthrown and annihilated. I deeply approve of this."

For the British it was a humiliating defeat. Churchill, saddened but still defiant, told the House of Commons: "I speak to you under the shadow of a heavy and far-reaching military defeat. All the Malay Peninsula has been overrun. This is one of those moments when the British race and nation can show their quality and their genius." Churchill explained that the Japanese success took place while British forces were heavily engaged in Europe, the Middle East, and North Africa.

Bibliography. F. S. Chapman, *The Jungle Is Neutral* (1948); A. E. Percival, *The War in Malaya* (1949); and M. Tsuji, *Singapore: The Japanese Version* (1960).

MALINOVSKY, RODION YAKOLEVITCH (1898–1967). Brilliant Russian tactician known as one of the Soviet's "Four Horsemen of the German Apocalypse" (*q.v.*).

On the German invasion of the Soviet Union in 1941, Malinovsky, as a Major General, defended Dnepropetrovsk. He was awarded the Order of Lenin for gallantry in action. In 1942 he was present at Stalingrad when Gen. Friedrich Paulus (*q.v.*) was caught in the city. He was among those Red generals responsible for trapping the German 6th Army in Stalingrad and turning the German counteroffensive into a rout.

In January 1943 Malinovsky was awarded the Order of Suvorov, 1st Degree, one of his country's highest honors. (*See* HERALDRY OF WORLD WAR II.) A month later he recaptured Rostov, the gateway to the Caucasus and the key to the entire Donetz River area. Early in 1944 his men were at the Dnieper bend, and on April 10, 1944, they captured Odessa. By mid-October his 2nd Ukrainian Army was in Hungary and driving on Budapest. Malinovsky won the rank of Marshal of the Soviet Union.

MALMÉDY MASSACRE. Slaughter of 101 American prisoners by German *Waffen-SS* (*q.v.*) troops in Belgium in late 1944.

BACKGROUND. On December 11, 1944, five days before the start of the German counteroffensive in the Ardennes (*see* BULGE, BATTLE OF THE),

Hitler issued a general order for the drive to be accompanied by a campaign of terror. German troops, he said, would have to act brutally and show no human inhibitions. A wave of fright was to precede the main assault and enemy resistance was "to be broken by terror."

Gen. Sepp Dietrich, noted for toughness, issued orders in the same vein the next day to divisional commanders of his 6th *Panzer SS* Army. Asked about what was to be done with prisoners, he replied: "You know what to do with them." Later he testified that he meant that provisions of the Hague Convention were to be respected. The order was passed down to lower echelons: The battle was to be conducted "stubbornly, with no regard for Allied prisoners of war, who will have to be shot if the situation makes it necessary and compels it."

Chosen to lead the advance was *Obersturmbannfuehrer* (Lt. Col.) Jochen Peiper (*q.v.*), commander of the *Leibstandarte,* Hitler's bodyguard. At 29 years of age, the youngest regimental commander in the German Army, Peiper had a reputation as a hard and ruthless leader of men on the Russian front. His 1st *Panzer* Regiment of the 1st SS Division consisted of picked men.

ASSAULT. At dawn on Sunday, December 17, 1944, camouflaged German tanks began to nose their way into the little Belgian border village of Büllingen in the Ardennes. Gathering speed, the *Panzer* (*q.v.*) unit pushed ahead and within minutes several hundred surprised American troops surrendered. Peiper and his men moved ahead to strike at vital American communications centers and supply dumps. They proceeded west to the crossroads village of Malmédy, where again several hundred Americans were taken prisoner. By this time the Americans were alerted. The U.S. 1st Army commander, Gen. Courtney Hodges (*q.v.*), had to flee from his headquarters.

Suddenly, at Malmédy, an atavistic fury seemed to overcome the German elite troops, what the Germans themselves called *Blutrausch,* or intoxication of the blood. Tank crews and combat engineers began to fire indiscriminately into ranks of defenseless prisoners. One after another the Americans began to fall. Those who tried to make a break were mowed down. Others, including Belgian civilians, were beaten over the head with rifle butts, lined up against walls and shot, or moved into gardens and killed one by one. The dead, dying, and wounded fell to the bloody grass. When it was over, 101 Americans lay dead at Malmédy. It was one of the worst atrocities of the war.

The Battle of the Bulge ended in mid-January 1945. Peiper and his men were surrounded and defeated by concentrated forces of just over two American divisions. Only 800 men of Peiper's battle group survived.

TRIAL. Appalled by the Malmédy massacre, the Judge Advocate branch of the U.S. Army was careful to collect evidence against Peiper's *Kampfgruppe* ("battle group"). Prisoners were segregated in a special camp in France and cross-examined. On May 16, 1946, the Allied War Command placed 74 of

Peiper's men on trial at Dachau. Fifty-four of their comrades agreed to testify against them. As the responsible officer, Gen. Dietrich was sentenced to 25 years' imprisonment. The verdict called for Peiper's death by hanging.

AFTERMATH. None of the defendants was executed because the war passions subsided. There was one stay of execution after another. A young U.S. senator, Joseph McCarthy of Wisconsin, initiated a new trial, which revealed that Peiper had been tortured by U.S. Intelligence to obtain a confession. The Senate Committee questioned the procedures under which the trials were conducted. Peiper's sentence was commuted to 12 years' imprisonment, after which he was released, first on parole and then on probation. The Belgians erected a monument at Malmédy bearing the names of the murdered Americans.

Bibliography. J. Toland, *Battle* (1959); and C. Whiting, *Massacre at Malmédy* (1971).

MALRAUX, ANDRÉ (1901–1976). Novelist, art critic, public official, and fighter in the French Resistance.

Malraux fought in the tank corps of the French Army at the start of the war. Wounded and captured by the Germans in June 1940, he escaped to Unoccupied France. He joined the French Resistance movement as ''Col. Berger'' and became a leader of the *Maquisards.* (*See MAQUIS.*) During the last days of the war he formed a close friendship with Gen. Charles de Gaulle (*q.v.*). Shortly before liberation he was again captured by the Germans and moved from one camp to another until he was freed finally by Free French (*see* FREE FRANCE) forces in Toulouse.

Bibliography. Among Malraux's works are *Man's Fate* (1933); *Man's Hope* (1937); *Voice of Silence* (1953); and *Anti-Memoirs* (1968). *See also* G. Picon, *Malraux par lui-même* (1958).

MALTA, SIEGE OF. Attempt by the Axis to take the British bastion in the Central Mediterranean from June 1940 to November 1942.

BACKGROUND. Malta (ancient Melita) was the principal island of a group of islands about 60 miles south of Sicily and about halfway between Gibraltar and Suez. Oval in shape, 17½ miles long and 8½ miles wide, it was 95 square miles in area. Its coastline was rocky and indented, its cliffs in the south rose to 400 feet.

The British regarded Malta as of major strategic importance. The Grand Harbor of Valletta, Malta's capital, was a base for the British Mediterranean Fleet and vital for the repair and refitting of warships. Hitler and Mussolini wanted the British naval and air bases at Malta to be destroyed before they could undertake a final drive into Egypt.

WORLD WAR II. As soon as the war began, it became obvious that North Africa would be the scene of a major conflict between the Allies and the Axis powers. It also became clear that the entire war there ran on gasoline. From their rocky base at Malta, the British had the task of hampering the flow of fuel and other war supplies from Italy to North Africa, where Gen. Erwin Rommel (*q.v.*) had begun to threaten the Nile Valley. The defenses of Malta were not strong—British airpower there consisted of only three outmoded biplanes named "Faith," "Hope," and "Charity." Churchill refused to heed the advice of his admirals to abandon the eastern Mediterranean to Mussolini. Instead, he ordered immediate strengthening of the island defenses and attacks on Axis convoys. He sent word to Gen. William Dobbie, Governor of Malta, to hold the island at all costs.

SIEGE. The Axis began its concentrated assault in the summer of 1940 immediately after Italy entered the war. For more than two years the garrison and Malta's people were subjected to continuous attack. There were heavy air attacks in January 1941. At that time the British aircraft carrier *Illustrious* moved to Malta for repairs. Germans used 500 aircraft, half of them bombers, in an effort to destroy the *Illustrious* as well as other warships in the harbor. On the night of February 7–8, 1941, the *Luftwaffe* (*q.v.*) again gave the island a merciless pounding. Despite such raids, the British managed to maintain their own supply lines to Malta while at the same time destroying a third of the war materials destined for Rommel.

On November 13, 1941, the British aircraft carrier *Ark Royal,* managed to deliver *Hurricanes* (*q.v.*) for the defense of Malta, but she was hit by torpedoes from the German submarine *U-81.* Taken in tow by other British vessels, she sank 25 miles from Gibraltar. (*See ARK ROYAL.*) In December 1941 Malta suffered 169 bombing raids by enemy aircraft. Hitler was prepared to take almost any losses in his effort to eliminate Malta as a threat to his supply lines.

German air strikes continued in 1942. In January alone the *Luftwaffe* made 262 raids on the island. The British managed to keep the island functioning, but enough Axis supplies got through to Rommel to enable him to drive the British Eighth Army (*q.v.*) back to the Gazala-Bir Hecheim Line. By March the siege escalated to a point where the people of Malta could expect daily attacks. In April Churchill asked Roosevelt to make the American carrier *Wasp* available to fly in assistance to the beleaguered island. The request was granted and 60 *Spitfires* (*q.v.*) were dispatched from the carrier to Malta. Within a few days all were destroyed.

Most of the people of Malta were able to save their lives by moving into the rock caves during air attacks. On April 15, 1942, King George VI conferred the George Cross collectively on all the people of the island in recognition of their heroism. The next month Governor William Dobbie, who had worked zealously since the beginning of the siege, was replaced by Gen. John Standish Gort (*q.v.*), the hero of the withdrawal from Dunkirk. (*See DUNKIRK EVACUATION.*) Strengthened by new supplies, Rommel took Tobruk on June 21 and captured huge dumps of British ammunition, a windfall for the Axis. Overjoyed, Hitler now decided to postpone any effort to take Malta and ordered Rommel to push on to Egypt.

On June 3 and 9, 1942, 59 *Spitfires* were delivered to Malta from carriers. In July the Royal Air Force (*q.v.*) sent Gen. Keith Park, one of its most dependable officers, to Malta with orders to take the offensive against the Axis. The situation in the besieged island began to improve as RAF power rose and that of the *Luftwaffe* dwindled. On August 11, 1942, a heavily escorted convoy of 13 Allied merchant ships, despite harassment by enemy U-Boats, reached Malta (*Operation Pedestal*). In the struggle the aircraft carrier *Eagle* sunk and the *Indomitable* was badly damaged. The carrier *Furious* managed to deliver 37 more *Spitfires*, however, and most of the merchant ships reached the island.

Meanwhile, the Italian fleet left Genoa and Spezia, and despite damage by attacking German planes, surrendered and moved into Malta for internment. By November 1942 the siege of Malta was lifted.

LOSSES. German aircraft dropped more than 14,000 tons of bombs on Malta but lost more than 1,000 planes in the process. The British Mediterranean Fleet was damaged, but it continued to function effectively. The RAF lost 568 aircraft in defending the island. There was great property damage: More than 35,000 buildings were destroyed or damaged; church spires were smashed; the Military Hospital of the Knights of Malta, with its 520-foot long ward, was badly damaged; and the dockyard area of Valetta was in ruins. The number of killed Maltese civilians was 1,436, a low figure due to effective use of air-raid shelters in the rocks.

CONSEQUENCES The unsuccessful siege of Malta cost the Axis supremacy of the Mediterranean area. The drive on Egypt lost its impetus due to lack of supplies. At the same time the Germans and Italians both lost most of their surface fleet, which contributed to growing Axis weakness. For the Allies the relief of Malta was a major victory. The bastion was kept alive by cooperation between the Royal Air Force, the Royal Navy, and the British merchant marine, added to the will of the island people. German failure at Malta contributed immeasurabaly to the final defeat of the Axis. (*See also* NORTH AFRICA, CAMPAIGNS IN.)

Bibliography. I. Hay, *The Unconquered Island: The Story of Malta* (1943); H.M.S.O., *Air Battle of Malta* and *East of Malta, West of Suez* (1944); F. S. de Domenico, *An Island Beleaguered* (1946); S. Perowne, *The Siege Within the Walls: Malta, 1940-1943* (1970); P. C. Smith, *Pedestal: The Malta Convoy of August, 1941* (1970); R. Jackson, *Malta Victory* (1980); and K. Poolman, *Night Strike from Malta* (1980).

MANHATTAN PROJECT. ALSO CALLED *MANHATTAN DISTRICT PROJECT.* Code or cover name *Trinity.* Wartime project to design and build a nuclear superexplosive by use of a fission process. The first two atomic bombs dropped on Japan put a quick end to the war in the Pacific.

BACKGROUND. Toward the end of the 19th century, physicists began to doubt the indivisibility of the atom, although the word itself, from the Greek *atomos,* means "indivisible." Antoine Henri Becquerel noted that a piece of uranium kept in a desk caused the blackening of some photographic plates nearby. The property of uranium to emit radiation was given the name radioactivity. Pierre and Marie Curie discovered the elements of polonium and radium. When kept enclosed, radium produced a gas that appeared to be helium. This was further evidence that atoms did not remain unchanged.

Max Planck's quantum theory (1900) and Albert Einstein's special theory of relativity (1905) provided formulas to determine the amount of energy released by the atom. Physicists everywhere worked on the task of splitting the atom and turning loose the energy in its core. Niels Bohr (*q.v.*), Danish physicist, described the structure of the atom. Ernest Rutherford, British scientist, found three different kinds of rays, *alpha, beta,* and *gamma,* shooting out from radium as if fired out of a gun barrel. In 1932 J. D. Cockcroft and E.T.S. Walton, built an "atom smasher" in the physics laboratory at the University of Cambridge. They were able to transform lithium and hydrogen into helium and in the process confirmed Einstein's equation of $E = mc^2$ (*E* being energy, *m* the mass in grams, and *c* the velocity of light in centimeters per second).

In 1932 James Chadwick discovered the electrically neutral particle in the atom, which he called the *neutron.* That same year Harold C. Urey isolated an isotope (radioactive version of common and harmless elements), which had been regarded as a theoretical necessity in splitting the atom. Also in 1932 J. Frédéric Joliot and his wife, Irène Curie, produced radioactivity artificially in splitting the atom. Two years later, Enrico Fermi, then at the University of Rome, began bombarding uranium with neutrons. Later, Fermi came to the United States. In the fall of 1938, a team of scientists at the Kaiser Wilhelm Institute in Berlin, composed of Otto Hahn, Fritz Strassmann, and Lise Meitner (*q.v.*), succeeded in splitting the uranium atom. They ascertained that neutron bombardment of uranium resulted in the formation of barium. Austrian-born Dr. Meitner, who was Jewish, was forced to leave Germany after the Nazi absorption of Austria.

A fantastic truth began to dawn on world physicists—uranium-235 would split when hit with a neutron and the fission of one such atom would release several free neutrons that would set off a chain reaction. It now became possible to produce a weapon of hitherto unheard of power.

THE EINSTEIN LETTER. In January 1939 Niels Bohr announced in Princeton, New Jersey, that the nuclear fission hypothesis of Lise Meitner and her nephew Otto R. Frisch, which interpreted the results of the recent discoveries of Otto Hahn and Fritz Strassmann in Germany, was the fission of uranium atoms when bombarded with neutrons with the consequent release of enormous amounts of energy. That spring a small group of scientists, mostly recent refugees from Nazi Germany and working at Columbia University in New York, attempted to arouse governmental interest in the possibility of military application of the new knowledge about splitting the atom. They were concerned with the possibility of Hitler devoting a major effort to fission development, which, if successful, would bring him global mastery.

On August 2, 1939, Einstein, encouraged by colleagues, sent a historic letter to President Roosevelt:

In the course of the last four months it has been made probable through the work of (Frédéric) Joliot, (Énrico) Fermi and (Leo) Szilard in America, that it may become possible to set up a nuclear chain reaction in a large mass of uranium, by which vast amounts of power and large quantities of new radium-like elements would be generated. Now it appears this could be achieved in the immediate future.

This phenomenon would also lead to the construction of bombs, and it is conceivable, though much less certain—that extremely powerful bombs of a new type may thus be constructed. A single bomb of this type, carried by boat and exploded in a port, might well destroy the whole port, together with some of the surrounding territory. . . .

GOVERNMENT SPONSORSHIP. Impressed by the letter from Einstein, Roosevelt immediately appointed an advisory committee on uranium. A few months later an initial grant of $6,000 was made to purchase uranium oxide. The project eventually expended $2.5 billion. Because of the necessity for secrecy, Roosevelt did not consult Congress for funds. Although the United States was not at war, American scientists worked closely with British counterparts who had already contributed to stages leading toward an atomic bomb. England was constantly exposed to bombing and possibility of invasion, while the United States, far from the range of enemy aircraft, had enormous industrial resources required for the job.

There was an uncomfortable feeling that the Germans might win the race to the atomic bomb. Although many Jewish physicists had left the country as refugees, the world-renowned Werner Heisenberg was still in Germany and he was familiar with all current developments. In 1942 it was known that German scientists were hard at work on a project which they hoped to add to the *V-1* flying bomb and *V-2* rocket (*qq.v.*) to rain destruction on Allied targets. A vital factor in the eventual outcome of the race was the raid by British and Norwegian commandos on the German heavy water (*deuterium*) installations in Norway during the winter of 1942–1943. At a cost of many lives, the raiders destroyed the Nazi source of heavy water, one of the important elements in the production of an atomic bomb.

In June 1940 Roosevelt appointed the National Defense Research Committee under the chairmanship of Vannevar Bush (*q.v.*). By November 1941 some 16 projects had been approved. The one for the production of the atomic bomb was enlarged and generally reorganized in December 1941.

MANHATTAN ENGINEER DISTRICT. In August 1942 the entire project was placed under U.S. Army control. The Manhattan Engineer District (MED) became the official name of what was later to be known as the Manhattan Project. Its commanding officer, Brig. Gen. Leslie R. Groves (*q.v.*), was given virtually unlimited powers over the entire American military, industrial, and scientific resources of the country for the express purpose of producing an atomic bomb. Enormous amounts of money had been expended to obtain necessary supplies of uranium-235 and plutonium-239.

Two gigantic plants were constructed to produce the bomb, one at Oak Ridge, Tennessee, and the other at the Hanford Engineer Works at the government-built town of Richland, in an isolated area 15 miles northwest of Pasco, Washington. Both plants were government-owned and operated. At Los Alamos, on an isolated high mesa near Santa Fe, New Mexico, a special laboratory was built under the direction of J. Robert Oppenheimer (*q.v.*) to handle technical problems. Among the key scientists at Los Alamos was Hans Albrecht Bethe, chief of the theoretical physics division.

There was no parallel in history for the scale of this undertaking. It took 125,000 workers to build the huge plants and 65,000 men and women to operate them. The work was completely compartmentalized so that no one worker was given any more information than was absolutely necessary to complete his special job. Only a few Americans knew anything about the Manhattan Project. The secrecy was so great that even the highest-ranking officials in Washington, including Harry S Truman, later to be President, was unaware of what was going on.

ALAMAGORDO TEST. On July 16, 1945, an experimental bomb was detonated in a desert area near Alamagordo, New Mexico, which generated an explosive power equivalent to 15,000–20,000 tons of TNT. In the secret test a steel tower holding the bomb was vaporized on explosion. A great cloud of cosmic fire and smoke rose more than eight miles to the stratosphere. The hard, solid desert was depressed to a depth of 25 feet, forming a huge saucer-shaped crater. "The spectacle," said an eyewitness, "was unprecedented, magnificent, beautiful, and terrifying. No man-made force of such tremendous power has ever occurred before. The whole countryside was lighted by a searching light with an intensity many times that of the mid-day sun."

Thirty seconds after the explosion came an air blast, followed almost immediately by a strong, sustained, awesome roar. At long last the secret weapon had been found to put an end to World War II. To do it, man, pygmy though he was, had to invade the cosmos.

The weapon was perfected too late to be used in the European theater of war. The first uranium bomb ("Little Boy") was delivered untested to the U.S. Army and dropped on Hiroshima (*q.v.*) on August 6, 1945, killing at least

68,000 people. Three days later a plutonium bomb was dropped on Nagasaki, (*q.v.*), killing 35,000. The Japanese surrender followed shortly thereafter.

Bibliography. J. W. Campbell, *The Atomic Story* (1947); S. Hecht, *Explaining the Atom* (1947); O. R. Frisch, *Meet the Atoms* (1947); L. R. Groves, *Now It Can Be Told* (1962); L. Lamont, *Day of Trinity* (1965); H. Feis, *The Atomic Bomb and the Eve of World War II* (1966); and E. R. Groueff, *The Manhattan Project* (1967).

MANNERHEIM, CARL GUSTAV EMIL, BARON VON (1867–1951).
Leader of the Finnish forces in the Russo-Finnish War of 1939–1940.

Mannerheim was on retired status when the Russians attacked Finland in 1939. He immediately returned to duty to lead the Finnish war effort in 1939–1940 and again in 1941–1944. In August 1944 he was elected President of Finland and the next month terminated hostilities with the Soviet Union. In 1946 he resigned the presidency because of ill health.

Six-feet tall, with jet black hair, Mannerheim was called "the Liberator of Finland." His friends regarded him as "a leader of truly heroic mold" and the one man responsible for the effectiveness of Finland's stand against Russia. Critics denounced his ruthlessness, stubbornness, and pride. His creed was: "We shall fight to the last old man and the last child. We shall burn our forests and houses, destroy our cities and industries, and what we yield will be cursed by the scourge of God."

Bibliography. Mannerheim wrote four textbooks on defensive tactics, as well as *Memoirs* (1953). *See also* P. Rodzianko, *Mannerheim* (1940); and T. Borenius, *Marshal Mannerheim* (1940).

MANNERHEIM LINE. Finnish defense system on the Karelian Isthmus set up against Soviet Russia.

The famous Mannerheim Line was built under the guidance of Marshal Carl Gustav von Mannerheim (*q.v.*). It was broken by the Russians in 1940 but only after it held up the Red Army for 13 weeks. The Mannerheim Line was subsequently dismantled.

MANSTEIN, FRIEDRICH ERICH VON LEWINSKI VON (1887–1973).
Outstanding German tactician in the successful operations of 1940.

From 1939 to 1940 von Manstein served as Chief of Staff to Gen. Gerd von Rundstedt (*q.v.*), and in that post showed himself to be a brilliant tactician. He was responsible for the successful operations plans in the West, as a result of which he was promoted by Hitler to General Field Marshal. In the 1941 invasion of the Soviet Union he commanded the 56th *Panzer* Corps in East Prussia and was later given command of the 11th Army. In November 1942 he was named to command Army Group Don. From 1943 to 1944 he led Army Group South. He was dismissed by Hitler in March 1944 when he repeatedly sent requests for temporary withdrawal of his forces.

Von Manstein was one of the senior officers approached by the German Resistance to eliminate Hitler. He informed Gen. Ludwig Beck (*q.v.*), military leader of the conspirators, that he would join the conspiracy as soon as Stalingrad fell to the Germans. But he was so disgusted with what he regarded as the inept and disloyal performance of Gen. Friedrich Paulus (*q.v.*) at Stalingrad (*see* STALINGRAD, BATTLE OF) that he reaffirmed his allegiance to Hitler.

In 1946 von Manstein was brought before a British court and sentenced to 18 years' imprisonment. He was released on parole in 1952. He died in Munich on June 21, 1973.

Bibliography. E. von Manstein, *Lost Victories* (1958). *See also* B. H. Liddell Hart, *The German Generals Talk* (1948).

MANSTEIN PLAN. The German plan of attack in the West in 1940. (*See* MANSTEIN, FRIEDRICH ERICH VON LEWINSKI VON.)

MAO TSE-TUNG (MAO ZE-DONG) (1893–1976). Leader and theoretician of the Communist movement in China during the war.

Mao initiated resourceful experiments in guerrilla warfare first against the Japanese and later against the Kuomintang. From 1942 to 1944 he pursued a far-reaching "rectification program" designed at tightening party discipline and purging dissident elements so that the Communists could take over after the war. In this goal he was singularly successful.

A brilliant strategist, Mao was able to mold China to his will as no emperor had ever succeeded in doing. Part scholar and part warrior, he always wore a simple uniform without insignia or rank. Communist propaganda made of him a living Buddha, "the people's great savior."

Bibliography. E. Snow, *Red Star Over China* (1968); and R. Payne, *Mao Tse-tung* (1969).

MAQUIS. Members of a major French Resistance movement during the German occupation.

The term *maquis* refers to dense thickets in the hot-dry regions of soil along the coasts of the Mediterranean Sea. By extension it was applied to bandits who, in evading the law, would hide in the maquis growth. Later, French guerrilla fighters adopted the name. The Allies often used *maquis* to designate French Forces of the Interior (*q.v.*) as a whole.

The defeat in 1940 sent a shock reverberating throughout France. Marshal Henri Pétain and his Vichy Government (*qq.v.*) were convinced that they had rescued the country from disaster, but many Frenchmen turned to opposition and then resistance. The pace of resistance increased in 1941 when veterans, civilians, students, clerks, and women joined the underground. Maquisard units were concentrated in mountainous regions of France bordering on Switzerland and Italy but later extended their activities elsewhere. They derailed trains, blew up bridges, slowed production, and cut communication lines.

By D-Day (*q.v.*), June 6, 1944, the *maquis,* who earlier had been organized mostly on a local basis, were playing a major role in the liberation of France.

Many paid with their lives in the guerrilla warfare. (*See also* FRANCE IN WAR-TIME; RESISTANCE MOVEMENTS; and UNDERGROUND.)

Bibliography. G. R. Miller, *Maquis* (1948); B. Ehrlich, *Resistance: France, 1940-1945* (1965).

MARETH LINE. German defensive line set up by Gen. Erwin Rommel (*q.v.*) 200 miles northwest of Tripoli in Tunisian territory during the campaign in North Africa.

In January 1943 Rommel reported to Hitler that British pressure was forcing him to fall back to the Mareth Line. This well-fortified position, originally built by the French, was just to the southeast of Gabès on the coast. There German engineers constructed what they believed to be an impenetrable position.

Hitler ordered Rommel not to withdraw from the Mareth Line under any circumstances. At the end of January 1943, Gen. Bernard Law Montgomery (*q.v.*) halted his British 8th Army (*q.v.*) just before the Mareth Line. He waited until March 21, 1943, and then sent a part of his army to attack the Mareth Line and another part in a wide-sweeping move on its flank. It was a spectacular victory as the *Afrika Korps* was forced back to the Cape Bon peninsula. (*See* NORTH AFRICA, CAMPAIGNS IN.)

MARIANAS, BATTLE FOR THE. Allied attack through the Central Pacific where the main objectives were the strategic islands of Saipan, Guam, and Tinian, June–August 1944.

BACKGROUND. After the Battle of the Philippine Sea (*q.v.*) in mid-June 1944 the fate of the Marianas was sealed but the Japanese refused to give in. Two weeks of heavy fighting were ahead on three principal islands of the Marianas. The great Allied counteroffensive was rolling. While Gen. Douglas MacArthur (*q.v.*) advanced along the New Guinea coast, Adm. Chester Nimitz (*q.v.*) moved to the north to win air and submarine bases in the southern Marianas for the final assault on Japan.

SAIPAN. On June 15, 1944, two U.S. Marine and one Army division, after a preliminary naval bombardment, landed on Saipan in *Operation Forager.* Saipan, a 12-mile-long island, was 3,800 miles west of Pearl Harbor and 1,385 miles south of Tokyo. Japanese resistance at first was as deadly as that at Tarawa, more protracted than that at Kwajalein. The invasion force of more than 125,000, of whom more than two-thirds were U.S. Marines, drove relentlessly forward and split the enemy into two groups. Then came suicidal counterattacks. (*See BANZAI* CHARGES.)

Casualties at Saipan were high on both sides. Of the Japanese garrison of 32,000, only 1,000 survived, and more than 20,000 civilians also lost their lives. Of the 125,000 Americans, 3,426 were killed or missing in action.

On June 19, 1944 four days after the landings at Saipan, came the biggest carrier battle of the war. (*See* PHILIPPINE SEA, BATTLE OF THE.) Although vastly outnumbered, the Japanese made their final vain attempt to destroy the U.S. Pacific Fleet.

GUAM. The next target in the Marianas was Guam, the southernmost island. On July 21, 1944, after days of heavy sea and air bombardment, American troops who had been turned back during the naval confrontation went ashore on Guam. In a campaign of just under three weeks Americans cleared the island of 19,000 enemy troops, most of whom were killed or died by suicide. Some survived to fight a desperate guerrilla campaign. Americans lost 1,435 killed or missing in action and 5,646 wounded. Work began immediately on a large air base.

TINIAN. The landing on Tinian, a tiny island on the southern tip of Saipan, began on July 24, 1944, and was executed successfully by the same units that had won Saipan. It was described as the most perfect amphibious operation of the Pacific war. The Japanese garrison of 9,000 men, taken by surprise, was almost entirely wiped out. The Americans lost 327 killed and 1,816 wounded.

SIGNIFICANCE. By mid-August 1944 the whole Marianas group had been won by the Allies. *Operation Forager* was completed in exactly two months after a brilliantly executed campaign. Although the three islands were as strongly defended as Guadalcanal and New Georgia, they were taken relatively quickly. Allied techniques in amphibious operations had been perfected by constant practice so that faultless landings were made over difficult reefs. The home islands of Japan were now within reach of U.S. bombers. The entire Allied strategy in the Mariana Islands was based on the need for bases from which American *Superfortresses (B-29) (q.v.)* could bomb the Japanese home islands.

Bibliography. P. A. Crowl, *Campaign in the Marianas* (1960); S. E. Morison, *The Two-Ocean War* (1963); H. I. Shaw, *et al., Central Pacific Drive* (1966); C. A. Lockwood and H. C. Adamson, *Battles of the Philippine Sea* (1967); and S. Denlinger and C. Cary, *War in the Pacific* (1970).

MARIANAS TURKEY SHOOT. *See* PHILIPPINE SEA, BATTLE OF THE.

MARKET-GARDEN. Code word for the double phases of an airborne-and-armored operation in September 1944. (*See* ARNHEM, BATTLE OF.)

MARSHALL, GEORGE CATLETT (1880–1959). President Roosevelt's chief strategic adviser throughout the war.

Marshall was promoted to General on September 1, 1939, the day the Germans invaded Poland. Chosen over the heads of 30 senior officers to become Chief of Staff, he served in that post for the remainder of the war. Under his command a wartime force was expanded from 200,000 men to 8.5 million by the end of the war. After the Japanese attack on Pearl Harbor on December 7,

1941, he became one of the foremost Allied military strategists. His staff and field officers were men he had tested in every possible way to ascertain their fitness for command.

It was largely due to Marshall's efforts that the plan to overrun Germany through France was adopted. In December 1944 he was promoted to General of the Army, the highest American military rank.

Marshall was regarded as a soldier's soldier. Although he would have preferred a field command, he followed orders without question and remained at his desk in Washington to direct the war. He was a perfectionist and strict disciplinarian. He is credited by most historians as being one of the main architects of Allied victory.

Churchill paid this tribute to Marshall:

In war he was as wise and understanding in counsel as he was resolute in action. In peace he was the architect who planned the restoration of our battered European economy and, at the same time, laboured tirelessly to establish a system of Western Defense. He has always fought victoriously against defeatism, discouragement and disillusion. Succeeding generations must not be allowed to forget his achievements and his example.

Bibliography. Marshall successfully resisted the urge to write his memoirs. For biographies *see* W. Frye, *Marshall: Citizen Soldier* (1947); F. C. Pogue, *General George C. Marshall* (1963); R. H. Ferrell, *George C. Marshall* (1966); and E. F. Puryear, *Nineteen Stars* (1971). *See also* K. T. Marshall, *Together: Annals of an Army Wife* (1946).

MARSHALL ISLANDS, BATTLE FOR THE. Next step in the island-hopping Allied campaign in the Central Pacific following the attack on the Gilbert Islands (*q.v.*).

BACKGROUND. Northwest of the Gilberts, athwart the Japanese life line between the Gilberts and Tokyo, lay the large archipelago of the Marshall Islands, consisting of hundreds of coral atolls. Acquired by Germany in 1885, the Marshalls were administered after World War I under a Japanese mandate.

At the insistence of Adm. Chester Nimitz (*q.v.*), the Joint Chiefs of Staff agreed to bypass the easterly islands of Jaluit and Wotje and make a direct leap to Kwajalein, the world's largest atoll, 66 milies long and 18 miles wide. Then Eniwetok, at the far end of the 700-mile chain of islands, would be seized.

PREPARATIONS. Two months before the projected assault on the Marshalls, aircraft based on the Gilberts started a softening-up process with more than 6,000 sorties over the islands. More than 150 Japanese planes were destroyed in the process. Meanwhile, a great force of 4 carrier groups, including 12 carriers and 8 battleships, moved in to transport 54,000 assault troops to the islands.

OPERATION FLINTLOCK. On January 31, 1944, U.S. Marines captured the undefended island of Majuro, thereby assuring a good anchorage for warships to bomb Kwajalein the next day. The main attack came on February 1.

The marines found the island in complete rubble, with no building standing. But again from inside the debris the Japanese garrison resisted fanatically. The invaders made a yard-by-yard advance, storming pillbox emplacements with flame throwers, bazookas (*q.v.*), and grenades. Again the Japanese made repeated suicidal *banzai* counterattacks. (*See BANZAI* CHARGES.) By February 7 Kwajalein Atoll was entirely American.

LOSSES. Exact casualty figures are not available, but it is believed that on the Japanese side 7,870 of the garrison of 8,675 men (of whom about 5,000 were combat troops) were wiped out. American losses were far less than at the Gilberts: Of the 54,000 assault troops committed to the invasion, 372 U.S. Marines and soldiers died.

AFTERMATH. On February 17–18, 1944, the U.S. 5th Fleet, under command of Adm. Raymond A. Spruance (*q.v.*), struck at Truk, the major Japanese base in the Carolines. The Japanese lost two cruisers, four destroyers, and more than 125,000 tons of merchant shipping. Caught off guard, the Japanese countered by land-based air attack without much effect. The Allies made no attempt to storm Truk itself, which was bypassed and its garrison rendered useless. (*See also* TRUK ISLANDS.)

On February 17–22, Adm. Nimitz sent a task force of 8,000 U.S. Marines 340 miles west to take over the enemy air base at Engebi on the Eniwetok atoll. Again the same pattern—assault followed by *banzai* suicide charges. The island was taken in four days with 339 men lost. Japanese killed numbered 2,677.

SIGNIFICANCE. The outer perimeter of the new Japanese Empire was now pierced. Enemy defenses were either captured, as at Kwajalein; left to starve, as at Jaluit and Wotje; or rendered impotent, as at Truk. Construction of new airfields began immediately in the Marshalls. Allied aircraft could now roam at will through the Western Pacific.

Bibliography. P. A. Crowe and E. G. Lowe, *Seizure of the Gilberts and Marshalls* (1955); H. I. Shaw *et al.*, *Central Pacific Drive* (1966); and S. E. Smith (ed.), *The U.S. Marine Corps in World War II* (1969).

MARSHALL PLAN. *See* ECONOMIC CONSEQUENCES OF THE WAR.

MASARYK, JAN GARRIGUE (1886–1948). Czechoslovak statesman.

In 1940 Masaryk was appointed by Eduard Beneš as Foreign Minister of the Czechoslovak Government-in-exile. Later he was made its Deputy Prime Minister. Throughout the early years of the war he was active in broadcasting to his homeland. At first he discouraged armed resistance to the Germans, knowing that it would have little success. But later, in April 1944, when the Russians were on the borders of Germany, he urged his people to join the armies of liberation against the Nazis. For most of the war he shuttled between London and Washington, lecturing and writing. Masaryk returned to Prague in 1945. When the city was forcibly conquered by the Russians in 1947, he resigned his post as Foreign Minister. He died in Prague on March 10, 1948, as a result of a fall from a window of the Foreign Ministry building. Communists called it a suicide, others termed it a new defenestration.

Six-feet-two-inches tall, partly bald, Marsaryk gave the appearance of a successful businessman or a political boss. A Czech patriot, proud of his Slavic background and culture, he was recognized as a worthy successor to his famous father. His upbringing and inclination led him to lean toward the West and its liberal philosophy. On a visit to the United States he was asked to fill in a form including the word "Race." He wrote down: "Human."

Bibliography. R.H.B. Lockhart, *Jan Masaryk* (1951); G. Bolton, *Czech Tragedy* (1955); and C. Sterling, *The Masaryk Case* (1969).

MASTER BOMBER TECHNIQUE. Method of night bombing devised by the British Bomber Command to supplement the Pathfinder technique (*q.v.*) of target lighting by flares.

The Master Bomber Technique was adopted after the Germans began to use dummy flares, flickering electric lights, and burning buildings to confuse British bombardiers. Two heavy *Lancaster* bombers, the first called the Master Bomber and the second the Deputy Master Bomber, would fly over the target 15 minutes ahead of the main body of attacking planes. They would drop either a 500- or a 250-pound bomb timed to explode in the air 300 feet above the target. The method was used with Sky Marking (*q.v.*), by which flares were exploded above cloud level. The combination of Pathfinder, Master Bombing, and Sky Marking, added to new radar (*see* RADAR, WARTIME) equipment, was highly successful for the Allies.

MASTERMAN, JOHN C. (1891–1977). British master spy.

Long associated as a student and as Vice-Chancellor of the University of Oxford, Masterman was recruited at the beginning of the war to direct British and later Allied counterintelligence units. (*See* ESPIONAGE.) As chairman of the XX-Committee (*q.v.*), he inaugurated a system by which German spies caught in England were converted into double agents (XX symbolizing double cross). Masterman trained his agents to feed carefully planned false information to confuse the Germans on the exact point of invasion of Fortress Europe (*q.v.*). His counterspies were the prime factor in tricking the Germans into stationing their troops to meet the 1944 invasion at Calais instead of Normandy. (*See* NORMANDY INVASION.)

Bibliography. In 1945 Masterman wrote a report on the activities of his XX-Committee. The British Government kept it secret for 27 years until its publication was allowed: *The Double-Cross System of the War of 1939–1945* (1972). *See also* A. C. Brown, *Bodyguard of Lies* (1975).

MATAPAN, BATTLE OF CAPE. Encounter between the British Mediterranean Fleet and the main Italian fleet in early 1941.

BACKGROUND. Despite the damage to his naval forces at Taranto (*see* TARANTO, BATTLE OF) on November 11, 1940, Mussolini hoped to recover his naval power and strike back at the British in the Mediterranean. By March 1941 the Axis buildup in North Africa was under way, while a large number of British troops were dispatched to hold Greece. Mussolini ordered his naval forces to intercept any British convoys headed for Greece. Aware of his intention, the British Admiralty dispatched a strong task force under Adm. Andrew Browne Cunningham (*q.v.*) to intercept the Italian fleet and bring it to battle.

CONFRONTATION. On March 27, 1941, British *Sunderland* patrol bombers sighted the Italian fleet putting to sea. Adm. Cunningham was then at Alexandria with the bulk of his Mediterranean Fleet. He ordered a light cruiser force to sail to a position south of Crete where it could intercept Italian ships headed for convoys to Greece. Cunningham, on his flagship *Warspite,* and accompanied by the aircraft carrier *Formidable,* the battleships *Valiant* and *Barham,* and several destroyers, steamed to the northwest in the afternoon in the hope of meeting the Italians. Meanwhile, the light cruiser *Orion,* one of the cruiser force and acting as a decoy, lured the unsuspecting Italians toward the main British fleet.

At 8 A.M. of the following day, British reconnaissance planes reported sighting an Italian force of one battleship, 6 cruisers, and 7 destroyers about 25 miles south of Crete. This force was soon joined by 2 more cruisers and 3 destroyers. The British light cruiser force was then about 40 miles away, Cunningham's stronger force about 95 miles. For a time the two fleets steamed on a parallel course. The Italians crossed the lines of the British fleet several times without suspecting its presence.

Planes from the carrier *Formidable* moved in, hitting a *Littorio*-class battleship three times, and scoring direct hits on a cruiser and a destroyer. The battleship had to reduce its speed, whereupon planes made further damaging attacks just as darkness fell. The Italian ships now turned and raced for port, pursued by the combined light and heavy forces of the British.

FINAL ACT. At 10 P.M. Cunningham ordered the bulk of his fleet to engage the cruiser *Pola,* which had been damaged and had stopped only three miles away. At the same time three more Italian ships came into view, just 100 miles southwest of Cape Matapan. As the Italian ships passed by the main British battle fleet, the destroyer *Greyhound* illuminated the scene with rocket flares. The British fleet now opened fire. With their guns directed by radar (*see* RADAR, WARTIME), British gunners covered the Italian ships with salvoes of accurate fire.

The Italians were bewildered by the sudden chaos that seemed to come from nowhere. Within seconds two Italian heavy cruisers were wrecked. Then British destroyers moved in to complete the destruction of the *Zara* and the *Pola*. At this point a force of Greek destroyers appeared on the scene, but the remainder of the Italian fleet was able to make its escape.

LOSSES. The score was extraordinarily one-sided. The British won the battle without any casualties and with no ship losses. One British plane was downed. The Italians, on the other hand, suffered a severe defeat. Their heavy cruisers *Pola, Zara,* and *Fiume* were sunk, as well as a cruiser of the *Colleone* class and two destroyers. A new battleship of the *Littorio* class was seriously damaged, as were other units of the Italian fleet.

The Italians lost 2,400 men in the battle, while 500 of their seamen were rescued by the British. British crewmen who boarded the *Pola* before she sank found a scene of incredible confusion. The warship was littered with packages of clothing that Italian seamen had hoped to salvage while being taken prisoner. Some crewmen in a drunken stupor jumped overboard. The *Pola* did not fire a gun in the battle.

SIGNIFICANCE. For the British the victory at Cape Matapan was good news after the depressing results of combat on land. For the Axis it was a debacle. Once again it was demonstrated that Mussolini did not have the naval power to make the Mediterranean "Our Sea" (*Mare Nostrum*). With his fleet paralyzed at Matapan, his armies defeated in Libya, East Africa, and Greece, the *Duce* was contributing little to Axis strength. Hitler decided to move into the Mediterranean theater by using his airpower to strike at British control of the sea.

Bibliography. S.W.C. Pack, *The Battle of Matapan* (1961), and *Night Action off Cape Matapan* (1972).

MAULDIN, WILLIAM H. (1921–   ). American cartoonist highly popular with GIs (*q.v.*) during the war.

In 1941, at the age of 20, Mauldin was sent overseas. For the next five years he served with the 45th Infantry Division and with the *Stars and Stripes* (*q.v.*), the Army daily newspaper, in campaigns in Sicily, Italy, and Germany.

Mauldin's cartoon characters Willie and Joe (*q.v.*) made him one of the best known and most admired GIs of the war. His rank-conscious wit appealed to enlisted men as much as it was detested by spit-and-polish officers. He depicted the dreary, often boring life of front-line infantrymen and emphasized their three choices: relief, wounds, or death.

Mauldin later described the GIs' life: "You wake up in the mud and your cigarettes are all wet and you have an ache in your joints and a rattle in your chest." A typical Mauldin cartoon showed battle-weary Uncle Willie being greeted effusively by a boyish nephew with pilot's wings and a colonel's eagles. The point was well understood in the ranks.

Bibliography. Mauldin wrote about his war experiences in *Star Spangled Banter* (1941); *Sicily Sketch Book* (1943); *Men, Mules and Mountains* (1943); *Up Front* (1945); and *Bill Mauldin's Army* (1951).

MEDITERRANEAN, CONTROL OF THE. Struggle between the Axis and the Allies in the early stages of the war for dominance in the Mediterranean area.

BACKGROUND. Italy's entrance into the war on June 10, 1940, at the time of the fall of France, changed the entire strategic picture. Until this time the Mediterranean had seen no major struggle, but now it was to become one of the major theaters of the war. For two decades Mussolini had dreamed of creating a new Roman Empire that would span the Mediterranean—*Mare Nostrum* ("Our Sea")—at the expense of Britain.

Mussolini was confident of success because the coming German assault on the British homeland (*see* BRITAIN, BATTLE OF) would necessitate recall of the bulk of the British fleet from the Mediterranean. From Italy the Axis would cut the Imperial life line between Britain and her bases in the Near and Middle East, India, and the Far East.

Britain countered by closing the Suez Canal to isolate the Italian Empire in East Africa and by strengthening the island fortress of Malta to strike at Axis convoys bearing supplies to Libya. (*See* MALTA, SIEGE OF.)

OPENING PHASE. The struggle for control of the Mediterranean merged into the battle for North Africa. (*See* NORTH AFRICA, CAMPAIGNS IN.) In September 1940, with the objective of reopening the Suez Canal, one Italian army moved northward from Italian East Africa and a second turned toward Egypt from Libya. Mussolini's plan was a classic pincers movement to force the British out of Africa. On the one side an army composed largely of 70,000 native troops under Italian command overran British Somaliland. The second army of 250,000 Italians and native troops moved into Egypt, taking Sidi Barrani, where it halted.

The British, under Gen. Archibald Wavell (*q.v.*) counterattacked vigorously and turned the Italian invasions into a rout. By early 1941 the British were in Benghazi, 500 miles to the west. By May 1942 they overwhelmed the Italian forces and smashed the Italian East African Empire. Angered by the Italian disaster, Hitler dispatched Gen. Erwin Rommel (*q.v.*), a master of tank warfare, and his specially trained *Afrika Korps* (*q.v.*) to Libya to stiffen Italian resistance.

BALKANS. The struggle for the Mediterranean was complicated by developments in the Balkans, where Hitler was seeking to establish his New Order (*q.v.*). Because of the British blockade, oil and food from the Balkans were vital for Germany. At first he sought to achieve his goal through pressure and threats. He was successful in Rumania, Bulgaria, Hungary, and Yugoslavia, but Greece remained strongly on the side of the British. (*See* BALKANS, CAMPAIGNS IN THE.)

When efforts to entice the Greeks into the Axis orbit failed, Mussolini decided on his own to subjugate the Greeks by force. Accustomed to mountain warfare, the Greeks turned on the Italians and thrust them back toward Albania in a disorganized retreat. (*See* GREECE, BATTLE FOR.)

Meanwhile, Germans continued their "diplomatic" offensive in the Balkans. German troops entered Bulgaria in March 1941. Dissatisfied with Yugoslav behavior, Hitler sent his mechanized divisions into the country on April 13, 1941, and took Belgrade, the capital. Two days later the Yugoslavs opened negotiations for surrender. (*See* BELGRADE, BOMBING OF.)

NORTH AFRICA. On the North African side of the Mediterranean, the German *Afrika Korps* and the British Eighth Army (*q.v.*) clashed in seesaw battles, which eventually ended in Axis defeat.

NAVAL SUPREMACY. The British Navy, meanwhile, was continuing its contributions to the general Italian rout. On July 3, 1940, a British task force blazed away at a large French squadron anchored at Oran, Algeria, and sank or damaged several ships. (*See* ORAN NAVAL ENCOUNTER.) On February 9, 1941, in broad daylight, Force H under Adm. James Fownes Somerville (*q.v.*), bombarded Genoa. On March 28, 1941, in a running engagement off Cape Matapan, the main Italian fleet suffered heavy damage. (*See* MATAPAN, BATTLE OF CAPE.) All Axis attempts to capture the strategic island of Malta were unsuccessful. (*See* MALTA, SIEGE OF.) The struggle for control of the Mediterranean Sea was clearly won by the British.

SIGNIFICANCE. Mussolini's dream of the Mediterranean as an Italian lake was exploded by British power on land and sea. His attempt to hold Italian Somiland, Eritrea, Ethiopia, and the North African coastline bordering the Mediterranean cost nearly 1 million casualties. The Allied triumph in North Africa reopened the Mediterranean life line to Egypt and the East. At the same time it exposed what Churchill had called Europe's "soft underbelly" (*q.v.*) to Allied attack.

Bibliography. R. de Belot, *The Struggle for the Mediterranean* (1951); M. Howard, *The Mediterranean Strategy in the Second World War* (1968); N. D. Orpen, *East African and Ethiopian Campaigns* (1969); S. Perowne, *The Siege Within the Walls: Malta, 1940–1943* (1970); and *La guerre en Méditerranée, 1939–1945* (1971).

MEIN KAMPF (MY STRUGGLE). Adolf Hitler's autobiography, in which he expressed his political-ideological *Weltanschauung* ("world view"). World War II historians regard it as an important document on the background of the war, expressing a philosophy that contributed to the outbreak of the conflict. (*See* CAUSES OF THE WAR.)

PRODUCTION. Part I of *Mein Kampf* was written in prison at Landsberg-am-Lech, where Hitler was incarcerated after his unsuccessful Beer-Hall *Putsch* in November 1923. He spent much of his time dictating portions of the manuscript to Emil Maurice and Rudolf Hoess (*q.v.*). Part II was written by Hitler from 1925 to 1926 after reconstitution of the National Socialist Party.

The original title was *Four-and-a-Half Years of Struggle against Lies, Stupidity, and Cowardice,* but the publisher, Max Amann, convinced Hitler to shorten it to the more saleable *Mein Kampf.*

CONTENT. The contents of *Mein Kampf* revealed the aggressive nature of a man altogether dissatisfied with the Treaty of Versailles and wholly dedicated to the task of remedying what he regarded as a shameful and unfair treatment of Germany. He became a German nationalist in his early years, although born in Austria: "When I look back now after so many years, I see two things of importance in my childhood. First, I became a nationalist. Second, I learned to understand and to grasp the real meaning of history. . . . When I was but 15 years old I understood the difference between 'dynamic patriotism' and 'racial nationalism.' " As a child he sang *Deutschland ueber Alles* with fervor and preferred it to the *Kaiserlied* despite the warnings of his teachers. "In short time I developed into a fervent nationalist."

What impressed the young Hitler most in Vienna was the lack of national pride (*Nationalstolz*) of its inhabitants. In Munich, the capital of Bavaria, he found his spiritual home: "A German city! What a difference from Vienna!" Here he became interested in politics and found his first taste of Social Democracy, which he regarded as "nationally unreliable." He studied the parliamentary system and found it wanting. "There is only one thing of importance for a nation—the general national necessity of existing (*"allgemeine nationale Lebensnotwendigkeiten"*).

In the First World War Hitler fought for Germany as a dispatch-bearer, was wounded and gassed, and was awarded the Iron Cross, First Class. The formation of the Weimar Republic left him embittered: "My brow burned with shame and I hated the men who brought about this crime. I, however, decided to become a politician."

After the war Hitler turned his attention to developing a new political philosophy. In an urgent tone he called on Germans to maintain the purity of their "race" in order to fulfill their destiny. He denounced the Weimar Republic as a monstrosity and insisted that a successful state must put race at the very core of its existence. The German race must be kept clean and the army must become the final and highest school.

Hitler's sense of aggressiveness was indicated in his conception of the state. "The German Reich, as a State, must include all Germans. Its task is to collect and maintain the most valuable primeval racial elements of this nation, which it must lead upward, slowly but surely, to a dominating position." It was the "business of the State" to:

1. Place race at the center of attention.

2. Keep the race clean.

3. Maintain birth control and allow no diseased or weak people to have children in order to prepare the German nation for future leadership.

4. Promote sport among youth to an unheard of proficiency.

5. Make the army the final and highest school.

6. Teach "racial knowledge" in all schools.

7. Awaken patriotism and national pride.

Hitler divided humanity into three classes: (1) founders of civilization; (2) bearers of civilization; and (3) destroyers of civilization. In page after page he denounced Jews as parasites and destroyers of civilization and called for their elimination from German life. He asserted that the Jews never had a culture of their own, that they had always borrowed their intellect from others. The Jewish race, he wrote, was "nakedly egoistic," without idealism. Jews were parasites on the bodies of other peoples, a people who made a state within the state and who refused to leave. The Jewish spirit was working for the ruin of Germany. Hitler retained this deep sense of hatred for Jews throughout his career and never relented in his desire to remove them from German national life. This hatred culminated in the tragic genocide of World War II.

Outlining a series of economic reforms based on the teachings of Gottfried Feder, Hitler called for a self-sufficient, economically independent, strongly national state. He would cut Germany off from the rest of Europe. Enough food could be raised in Germany and the eastern agricultural areas to insure the existence of the state. The "eastern agricultural areas" to which he referred, specifically the Ukraine, did not belong to Germany. But in the geopolitical views of Karl Haushofer, this was a European *Herzland* ("heartland") that was basic for Germany's existence. In Hitler's view, the principle of national autarky was essential if Germany were to right the wrongs of the Versailles Treaty.

The arguments presented in *Mein Kampf* were designed to appeal to all dissatisfied elements in Germany. The views were nationalistic, "truly socialist," and beyond those were dominantly negative—anti-Semitic, anti-Marxist, anti-parliamentary, anti-Catholic, anti-French, anti-Polish, and anti-Russian. Most of all they were aggressive: What Hitler wanted could not be attained without going to war. In this sense, *Mein Kampf* presented a political ideology that contributed to the outbreak of World War II.

SALES. The book was an enormous and profitable success. By 1939 it had sold 5.2 million copies and was translated into 11 languages. Every German couple about to be married was expected to buy a copy. Royalties made Hitler a multimillionaire.

CRITIQUE. In its original version *Mein Kampf* was filled with grammatical errors, which were corrected in subsequent editions. Much was an undigested repetition of the racial ideology of Count Arthur de Gobineau, a French racialist, and Houston Stewart Chamberlain, a British publicist. Hitler's book revealed the mind of a half-educated politician who hated intellectuals. Page after page gave evidence of a highly neurotic man with little sense of humanity or decency. Hitler praised the efficacy of the lie—the more a lie was told the more people would believe it.

SIGNIFICANCE. The importance of *Mein Kampf* lay in the fact that the intelligent German public, whose standards of literature were normally high, was so impressed by a book that objective reviewers dismissed as unmitigated nonsense. *Mein Kampf* was written in complete sincerity and presented the views of a man who intended to fulfill its ideology. It was a beacon for the tragic events of World War II

Bibliography. The unexpurgated edition of *Mein Kampf* in English translation was published by Houghton Mifflin, Boston, in 1943. The original German edition appeared in two volumes, the first in 1925 and the second in 1927.

MEITNER, LISE (1878–1968). Austrian physicist and mathematician and key figure in the introduction of the so-called Atomic Age.

After Hitler came to power in 1933, Meitner, although of Jewish extraction, managed to continue her work because she was an Austrian subject. But when Hitler absorbed Austria in the *Anschluss* of 1938, she was forced to flee to Stockholm. There, together with Otto Robert Frisch, her nephew, she published in January 1939 the idea that the uranium nucleus, when bombarded with neutrons, split in two (fission). Along with this suggestion went the prediction of the possibility of a chain reaction. The results of the study were communicated to Niels Bohr (*q.v.*), who immediately made known the discovery to the scientific world. It was of critical importance in the eventual production of the atomic bomb.

In releasing the report, Meitner and her co-workers had no thought of the destructive usage to which it could be put. In the United States the production of an atomic bomb became a project of the War Department, under the direction of Brig. Gen. Leslie R. Groves. (*See* MANHATTAN PROJECT: and GROVES, LESLIE R.) Inside Germany, scientists worked feverishly to solve the problem, only to lose the race to the Allies.

The news that the Allies had dropped an atomic bomb on Hiroshima (*q.v.*) on August 6, 1945, came as a shocking surprise to Meitner. Thrust into the world spotlight, she was reluctant to speak of her basic contribution to the development of the atomic bomb and the nuclear reactor.

MENZIES, ROBERT GORDON (1894–1978). Prime Minister of Australia at the outbreak of the war.

Menzies was chosen Prime Minister in April 1939 and held the post until August 1941. He initiated Australia's war program, including the construction of naval shipyards and docks, and the training of pilots. He sent supplies and troops to Britain. From January to May 1941 he represented Australia at London war conferences and visited battlefronts where Australian troops were stationed. He urged that measures be taken for the defense of Singapore as well as Australia, and openly expressed his dismay at the lack of comprehension about Japan's policy of aggression.

Returning to Australia, Menzies saw increasing opposition to his war policies by the Labor Party and he resigned on August 29, 1941. His call for an All-Party Government was turned down. In 1944 he became head of the newly organized Liberal Party. He died on May 15, 1978, at Melbourne at the age of 84.

Bibliography. R. G. Menzies, *To the People of Britain at War* (1941); and *The Forgotten People, and Other Studies in Democracy* (1943).

MERRILL'S MARAUDERS. American guerrillas of the 5307th Provisional Unit led by Maj. Gen. Frank D. Merrill in strikes behind Japanese lines in Burma. They were also known as Merrill's Raiders.

BACKGROUND. Impressed by the exploits of Gen. Orde C. Wingate (*q.v.*) in Burma, Gen. George C. Marshall (*q.v.*) sent Merrill and an American force to India to be trained in Wingate's novel ideas of guerrilla warfare. The unit comprised 3,000 officers and men, all volunteers, to form the 5307th Composite Unit (Provisional). It took on the name Galahad Force.

ACTION IN BURMA. Merrill's Marauders turned out to be tough jungle fighters. They had a specific mission: While Lt. Gen. Joseph W. Stilwell (*q.v.*) faced Japanese in the hill country around Myitkyna, the Marauders cut around enemy flanks and set up road blocks in their rear. Together with the Chindits (*q.v.*) they fought a succession of small but savage battles. They went on forced marches to sever enemy communications and strike at enemy supply lines.

The Marauders, like the Chindits, had to face not only Japanese bullets but also typhus, malaria, and dysentery. Wherever possible they forced their way through the jungle and ambushed Japanese who marched along the beaten tracks. Both Marauders and Chindits revealed an ability to meet the Japanese as equals in jungle warfare.

MESSERSCHMITT, WILLY (1898-1978). German aircraft designer.

In 1916 Messerschmitt designed his first plane. He established a manufacturing firm under his own name at Bamberg a few years after the war. In 1926 he produced his first all-metal plane. In 1937 he received the Lilienthal Prize for research in aviation.

Messerschmitt's *Me-109* (*q.v.*), first designed in 1935, was used throughout the war as the standard German single-seater fighter. Rated by experts one of the finest fighter planes in aircraft history, it flew and fought throughout the war in combat with the best Allied aircraft. Messerschmitt's twin-engined bomber, the *Me-110*, was also highly regarded in wartime aviation circles.

By this time Messerschmitt had achieved a world-wide reputation as one of the great aircraft designers of the 20th century. He died on September 15, 1978, at Munich.

MESSERSCHMITT-109 (Me-109).

MESSERSCHMITT-109 (Me-109). German standard fighter plane that saw action on every front during the war. Known to *Luftwaffe* (*q.v.*) pilots as "Emil," the *Me-109* was a single-engined low-wing monoplane with a single fin and rudder, and retractable landing gear.

DESIGN. When Hitler began to rearm Nazi Germany in 1934, he called for a fast monoplane to replace the obsolete biplane fighters of the past. A design contest was won by Willy Messerschmitt (*q.v.*). His *Me-109* was displayed publicly for the first time at the Berlin Olympic Games in 1936, and the next year was presented at the International Flying Meet in Zurich. In 1937 the plane was tested successfully in the Spanish civil war.

WORLD WAR II. With modifications the *Me-109* was used in the *Blitzkrieg* (*q.v.*) campaigns in Poland, Scandinavia, the Low Countries, and France (*qq.v.*). It was the backbone of the German fighter force during the days of German supremacy. During the Battle of Britain (*q.v.*) hundreds of *Me-109*s swarmed over England in an attempt to subjugate the British before invasion. But they met their match in the British *Spitfire* (*q.v.*), which had a greater diving speed, and a better rate of climb. The German plane proved to be less maneuverable at medium and low altitudes. Both planes were later improved, but the *Spitfire* maintained its supremacy.

(For specifications *see* AIRCRAFT: GERMAN AIRCRAFT DATA CHART.)

Bibliography. W. Green, *Augsburg Eagle: The Story of the Messerchmitt 109* (1972).

METAXAS, JOHN (1871-1941).

METAXAS, JOHN (1871-1941). Greek Army officer and dictator at the start of the war.

When George II returned to his throne in 1935, Metaxas was made Premier and by a coup in 1938 was proclaimed "Premier for Life." He was pro-German in domestic and foreign policies at the start of the war. When Mussolini attempted to violate Greek independence in October 1940, Metaxas led his country into war against the Axis. His armies struck viciously at the Italians and defeated them. In April 1941, German troops overran the Metaxas Line (*q.v.*), a fortified line of defense built in East Macedonia under his direction. (*See* GREECE, BATTLE FOR.) Metaxas's regime was ended by German occupation. He died in Athens on January 29, 1941.

Heavy-set, bespectacled, shabbily dressed, Metaxas had little of the flamboyant personality of fellow dictator Mussolini. Metaxas set the goal of his dictatorship: "I shall become a sort of modern monk. I shall renounce everything in the world and shall live only for Greece." He was a dictator without popular support until the outbreak of the war between his country and Italy.

Bibliography. See C. Buckley, *Greece and Crete, 1941* (1952).

METAXAS LINE. A defensive line of fortifications set up in Greece by dictator John Metaxas (*q.v.*) to defend his country from attack through Bulgaria. When the Germans invaded Greece on April 6, 1941, they outflanked the Metaxas Line and pushed on to capture Salonika in two days. (*See* GREECE, BATTLE FOR.)

MI-5. British counterintelligence and security service. (*See* ESPIONAGE.)

MIDDLE EAST, CAMPAIGNS IN THE. *See* NEAR AND MIDDLE EAST, CAMPAIGNS IN THE.)

MIDWAY, BATTLE OF. Naval and air battle between the Japanese and Americans in early 1942 and a major turning point in the war in the Pacific.

BACKGROUND. Japanese strategists were alarmed and angered by the Doolittle air assault on Tokyo. (*See* DOOLITTLE RAID.) It was clear that they would seek to save face by avenging this humiliation. For a decade Japanese war lords had won a series of great victories and now they had been challenged in their capital city. They had a choice of attacking in either of three directions—toward Australia, India, or Hawaii. Adm. Isoruku Yamamoto (*q.v.*), architect of Pearl Harbor (*q.v.*) and Commander-in-Chief, Combined Fleet, demanded that the target be Midway.

LOCATION. Midway Island, 1,135 miles northwest of Pearl Harbor, was the farthest outpost of the Hawaiian chain. Midway Atoll was only six miles in diameter and only a small part of it was dry land. For the Japanese it was a key point in the new outer defense perimeter set up after the attack on Pearl Harbor. Possession of the strategic island would give them an advance base for amphibious operations. Yamamoto proposed to use the area for the purpose of drawing out the U.S. fleet, or what remained of it in the Pacific, and destroying it in decisive battle.

PREPARATIONS. For a time strategists of the Japanese Combined Fleet and the Naval General Staff quarreled over details of the proposed Midway operation. The Doolittle raid put an end to the differences. On May 5, 1942, Imperial Headquarters issued the order for invasion and occupation of Attu and Kiska, strategic points in the Western Aleutians, and Midway Island. It was to be the most gigantic operation in the history of the Japanese Navy. More than

160 warships were assigned for the task, including 11 battleships, 8 carriers, 22 cruisers, 65 destroyers, and 21 submarines, all to be covered by an umbrella of 700 planes. The huge 64,000-ton battleship *Yamata* had nine 18-inch guns. Five major tactical forces would operate: Advance Expeditionary Force; Carrier Striking Force; Midway Occupation Force; Main Body; and Northern Area Force. All would be preceded by patrolling submarines ordered to cripple American naval countermoves.

The battle was to open in the Aleutians with air strikes against Dutch Harbor on June 3, 1942. The next day the First Carrier Striking Force, under Vice-Adm. Chuichi Nagumo (*q.v.*), with four fast carriers, *Kaga, Akagi, Soryu,* and *Hiryu,* would soften up Midway with its planes. Then the Main Body, with its great battlewagons, would move in, followed by the landing of 5,000 ground troops.

The comprehensive Japanese plan seemed perfect and the prognosis for success excellent. The Combined Fleet staff believed that there would be no American warships in the invasion area until after the landings at Midway. They expected the expedition to take two small islands in the Aleutians that would cause the U.S. Pacific Fleet to hurry northward. This would enable the Japanese to trap the Americans between their two carrier forces.

AMERICAN STRATEGY. The Japanese plan suffered from one vital defect—it expected the Americans to do exactly what Tokyo expected. The Japanese would pay heavily for their strategic inflexibility. They counted on complete tactical surprise, a serious miscalculation. U.S. Intelligence had broken the main Japanese code and Washington knew about the projected Midway attack. Plans were immediately set into motion for counteraction.

Adm. Chester W. Nimitz (*q.v.*), Commander-in-Chief U.S. Pacific Fleet, had to face a Japanese force superior to his own. Since the attack on Pearl Harbor no U.S. battleships were fit for action and after the Battle of Coral Sea (*q.v.*) only two U.S. carriers were ready, the *Hornet* and the *Enterprise.* These were increased to three by the addition of the *Yorktown,* which was repaired in two days instead of an estimated 90. Nimitz recalled Task Force 17, commanded by Rear Adm. Frank Jack Fletcher (*q.v.*), from the Southwest Pacific to the Midway area, and assigned Task Force 16, led by Rear Adm. Raymond A. Spruance (*q.v.*), for the operation. He deployed both forces to the northeast of Midway, so that they could make surprise flank attacks on the enemy. Nimitz correctly gauged the attack on Dutch Harbor as a diversionary move.

CONFRONTATION. On June 3, 1942, an American *Catalina* patrol bomber sighted the slow-moving Japanese transports about 600 miles west of Midway. The next morning 100 Japanese bombers and fighters bounced off their carriers and headed for the island. The U.S. fleet, several hundred miles to the east, could not then provide fighter protection, but from Midway 26 torpedo planes and dive bombers rose to meet the invaders. Only 9 returned.

Meanwhile the Japanese first wave did heavy damage to installations on Midway.

Thus far the Japanese seemed to have the best of it. One more thrust and Midway would be theirs. But the battle had only started and, as at Coral Sea, the planes did all the fighting. The big warships did not exchange a shot.

Of the first three successive waves of American torpedo bombers, Japanese fighters or antiaircraft guns shot down 35 of 41 planes. But minutes later 37 U.S. dive bombers from the *Enterprise* swooped down from 19,000 feet. Japanese fighters that had just countered the first three waves of torpedo bombers had no chance to climb and counterattack. The thunderous American attack was highly successful. Bombs and machine-gun bullets splashed over the zigzagging Japanese ships; internal explosions sent gushes of smoke and fire from the warships. Japanese planes overhead circled desperately with their frustrated pilots unable to land on battered carriers. Japanese destroyers sped around frantically trying to rescue the crews of battered capital ships. Planes from the three American carriers scored destructive hits on Japanese carriers, battleships, and cruisers. The next day *Flying Fortresses* (*q.v.*) from Hawaii joined the battle to plaster the Japanese warships.

RETREAT. Adm. Yamamoto, contemplating the loss of all four of his carriers, took advantage of the thick weather to break off the engagement. He abandoned his blazing ships and desperately turned homeward. The entire U.S. surface fleet in the vicinity joined to chase the beaten Japanese westward until shortage of fuel put an end to the action.

LOSSES. In four days the overconfident Japanese had lost all four of their carriers (*Kaga, Akagi, Soryu,* and *Hiryu,*) and the heavy cruiser *Mikuma;* the heavy cruiser *Mogani* was badly damaged, two destroyers were battered; and damage was done to other ships, including the battleship *Haruna.* They lost at least 250 aircraft, many on carriers when they were sunk. Several thousand Japanese lost their lives in the action.

The Americans paid heavily, too. They lost the aircraft carrier *Yorktown,* abandoned and sunk by an enemy submarine, the destroyer *Hammann,* and a total of 147 aircraft (109 carrier-based and 38 shore-based). The *Enterprise* alone lost 14 out of 37 dive bombers, 10 out of 14 torpedo bombers, and one smaller plane.

SIGNIFICANCE. Midway remained in American hands. The far stronger Japanese fleet had been outsmarted and outfought. American Intelligence had prepared the way for a stunning victory. "Had we lacked early information of the Japanese movements," Adm. Nimitz admitted, "and had we been caught with our carrier forces dispersed, the Battle of Midway would have ended differently." (*See MAGIC.*) In addition, American battle tactics were shrewd: American pilots stepped up their attacks as the Japanese were refueling their planes on the carriers. A bewildered Yamamoto headed back to Tokyo to bring bad news to the Emperor.

Midway was the first decisive defeat inflicted on the Japanese Navy in modern times. Despite carefully laid plans and superior gun power, Yamamoto had to abandon his mission. Tokyo now cancelled the proposed plans to conquer Fiji, New Caledonia, and New Zealand. Its long impressive sea offensive had reached a dead end.

Bibliography. S. E. Morison, *History of U.S. Naval Operations in World War II* (1948 ff.); W. Lord, *Incredible Victory* (1962); P.H.H. Frank and J.D. Harrington, *Rendezvous at Midway* (1967); and G. Bennett, *Naval Battles of World War II* (1975).

MIKAWA, GUNICHI (1888–   ). Japanese naval officer known for his aggressive tactics.

At the time of Pearl Harbor (*q.v.*) Mikawa was a Rear Admiral in command of a Support Force for Vice-Adm. Chuichi Nagumo (*q.v.*). Thereafter his force of battleships and cruisers prowled the Pacific in support of Nagumo's carriers.

In July 1942 Mikawa was given command of a new force, the 8th Fleet, known operationally as the Outer Sea Force, with headquarters at Rabaul, New Britain. On August 9, 1942, from the bridge of his flagship, the *Chokai,* he gave the order for an attack on the U.S. fleet in Savo Bay in the Solomon Islands. Although his force was inferior to that of the Americans, he moved in and within the space of 40 minutes sank four U.S. heavy cruisers. It was one of the most humiliating American defeats of World War II—a feat that nearly undid the recent triumph at Midway (*q.v.*) and nearly canceled the American landings at Guadalcanal and Tulagi.

Although soft spoken and giving the appearance of an intellectual, Mikawa was a man of action. His method of using battleships to cover fast carriers was copied by both the Americans and the British.

MIKHAILOVICH, DRAJA (1893–1946). Yugoslav guerrilla leader opposed to Tito's Communist Partisans.

When the Germans conquered Yugoslavia in April 1941, Mikhailovich retreated to the mountains near Belgrade and organized guerrilla forces known as *Chetniks* (Serbian *četnići*). So successful were his operations against the Germans that in January 1942 the Yugoslav Government-in-exile in London promoted him to General and Minister of War.

Meanwhile, Mikhailovich confronted another guerrilla group, the Partisans (*q.v.*), organized and led by Josip Broz, known as Tito (*q.v.*). The two found it impossible to agree on a common policy and began to fight each other. Tito's Partisans gradually gained the upper hand as Mikhailovich's forces dwindled. Mikhailovich lost Allied support and was reluctantly dismissed by King Peter from London. He continued to fight the Communist Partisans with the remnants of his forces. Captured by Tito's troops and tried on charges of collaboration with the Axis, Mikhailovich was executed on July 17, 1946.

Mikhailovich was an ardent Serbian patriot and a convinced royalist. He considered the Communists an even greater threat than the Nazis. It is probable that he did conspire with the Germans against his hated enemy Tito. He was executed by the Partisans as a matter of political expediency.

Bibliography. D. Martin, *Ally Betrayed: The Uncensored Story of Tito and Mikhailovich* (1946).

MIKOYAN, ANASTAS IVANOVICH (1895–1978). Russian Government and party official.

Following the Nazi attack on Soviet Russia in June 1941, Mikoyan became in effect the chief quartermaster for the armed forces. He supervised the procurement and transport of supplies for the Soviet war machine. He directed the conversion of consumer industry to war production and at the same time handled the intricate operations of the multibillion dollar war supply agreement with the United States and Britain. In 1943 he was awarded the title of Hero of Socialist Labor for his war services.

In 1946 Mikoyan served as Deputy Premier (Vice-Chairman of the Council of Ministers). He continued in this post after the death of Stalin in 1953. He was excluded from the Party's Presidium in 1966, but remained a member of the Central Committee.

Dark, stocky, with mustache and intense eyes, Mikoyan was known for his rapier-like mind. An American in Moscow called him "an intelligent and worldly-wise little Armenian." His leadership in commerce in the USSR was of vital importance to the Russian war effort.

Bibliography. A. Mikoyan, *Memoirs* (1970).

MILCH, ERHARD (1892–1972). German officer responsible for building the *Luftwaffe* (*q.v.*).

In 1933 Milch was named State Secretary of the Air Ministry as well as armaments chief of the *Luftwaffe*. Working closely with Gen. Hermann Goering (*q.v.*), he distributed management of armament production to capable technicians in industrial firms. Much of the effectiveness of the German Air Force was due to his efforts.

In the early months of the war Milch commanded German Air Fleet V in the Norwegian campaign. In 1940, after the fall of France, he was promoted to Field Marshal along with Albert Kesselring and Hugo Sperrle (*qq.v.*). From 1941 to 1944 he held the title of Air Inspector General. In 1942 he was appointed, along with Albert Speer (*q.v.*), as one of the two transportation dictators of Germany.

Milch was tried by an international military tribunal in 1947, found guilty, and sentenced to life imprisonment. He was released in 1954 and died in Wuppertal on January 25, 1972.

Milch's career in the Nazi regime was complicated by the accusation that he had a Jewish father, ordinarily an impossible situation for a Nazi leader. Goering, who regarded Milch as indispensable, solved the problem by having

Milch's mother certify that he was not a child of her marriage, but instead the son of her Aryan lover. Milch accepted this "evidence" of Aryanization.

Bibliography. See D. Irving, *The Rise and Fall of the Luftwaffe* (1973).

MILCH COWS. Popular nickname given to German supply submarines.

PROBLEM. At the beginning of the war Adm. Karl Doenitz (*q.v.*) had to refuel his U-Boats at sea by surface tankers. These supply ships steadily dwindled in numbers as British warships hunted them down. By the fall of 1942, losses had become so acute that use of surface tankers was discontinued. The most dangerous area for U-Boats, leaving and returning to their coastal bases after raids on convoy routes, was the water within range of the British Coastal Command aircraft and naval destroyers. With the surface tankers no longer useful, something had to be done to refuel U-Boats at sea.

SOLUTION. The answer to Doenitz's problem was the supply submarine to which the name Milch Cow was given. These Type XIV U-Boats were 1,688 tons, carried 720 tons of Diesel oil, and had a range of 12,300 miles. By 1942 a dozen were constructed and put to use. Milch Cows met the wolf packs (*see* WOLF-PACK TACTICS) at prearranged rendezvous and supplied them with fuel, torpedoes, ammunition, food, drinking water, and medical equipment. At the same time they removed sick or wounded members of the crews and provided replacements.

RESULTS. Milch Cows amply demonstrated their value for the Germans. No longer were operational U-Boats forced to return soon after reaching their patrol billets. The Allies met the new threat with a secret weapon of their own. Using information gathered from *Ultra* (*q.v.*), the secret decoding machine, they were able to find Milch Cows at sea and quietly send them to the bottom. Deprived of their supply submarines, German submarines began to lose their effectiveness. By mid-1943 the U-Boat domination of the Atlantic was broken. (*See* ATLANTIC, BATTLE OF THE.)

Bibliography. H. Busch, *U-Boats at War* (1955).

MILLER, GLENN (1909–1944). American band leader who disappeared in a plane flight in late 1944.

When the United States entered the war in 1941, Glenn Miller's music, with its combination of smooth strings plus skilled use of brasses and reeds, became highly popular with American GIs (*q.v.*). In late 1942, despite a lucrative contract with the Chesterfield program on the Columbia Broadcasting System, Miller broke up his band and accepted a captaincy in the Army Air Forces. He became director of the U.S. Air Forces Band.

In the third week of December 1944, Miller's Air Forces Band was playing in Paris and was scheduled for an "American Expeditionary Force Show" over the

British Broadcasting System (BBC) on Christmas eve from Paris. On the chilly evening of December 15, 1944, Miller boarded a single-engined liaison plane at an Air Force base near Abbotsripton, west of Cambridge in the Midlands. The small plane, a *UC-64A,* with its pilot and Miller inside the cramped cockpit, took off on a field choked with fog.

Nothing was ever heard of Miller or the aircraft again. No wreckage of the plane was found in England or in France. Possibly it fell or was shot down over the English Channel or the North Sea. On December 24, 1944, the Associated Press reported that "Major Glenn Miller is Missing on Flight From England to Paris."

MILNE BAY. *See* NEW GUINEA, CAMPAIGNS IN.

MINCEMEAT. British code or cover name for a deception operation in 1943 by which a corpse was used to bear false documents to mislead the Germans on an invasion area.

BACKGROUND. After the Allied invasion of North Africa and defeat of the *Afrika Korps* (*q.v.*), at a time when Soviet Russia was putting on more pressure, Hitler expected another strike from the West. Aware of Churchill's preference for the soft underbelly (*q.v.*) of Europe, Hitler believed the next major assault would come in the Balkans. For him this was the critical area, where Germany obtained its copper, bauxite, and chrome. He ordered the OKW, the German High Command, to counter this expected thrust.

At the Casablanca Conference (*q.v.*) in late January 1943 the Allied Supreme Command had already made its decision—it would attack Sicily. On June 11, 1943, the Allies captured the island of Pantelleria (*q.v.*), thereby giving a clear-cut signal of Allied intentions. Said Churchill: "Anyone but a damned fool would *know* that it was Sicily."

PREPARATION. The Allied Supreme Command decided to cloak *Operation Husky* (*see* CODE NAMES, ALLIED, HUSKY), the invasion of Sicily, by a very special strategy. Orders went to London Controlling Section (LCS), the organization inside Churchill's Joint Planning Staff (JPS) (*q.v.*) responsible for deception schemes. The orders were turned over to MI-5 (*q.v.*), the British counterintelligence and security service, which passed them on to its XX-Committee (*q.v.*). The latter controlled the activities of double agents.

The XX-Committee worked out a unique scheme. It was cryptogrammed *Trojan Horse,* after the most famous deception in history. The essential core was *Operation Mincemeat.* The idea was to convince the Germans that the next landings would be in Corsica, as a jumping-off place for southern France, and Greece, for the Balkans. That is what Hitler wanted to believe. He was proud of his knowledge of history and he knew about Churchill's ill-fated attempt to force the Dardanelles in 1915. Hitler was sure that the British would try it again in 1943.

From a mortuary in central London the XX-Committee obtained the body of a young man in his early 30s. It gave the corpse the name and identification of Captain (acting Major) William Martin, 09560, Royal Marines, a staff officer of Combined Operations Headquarters. Into his briefcase went fabricated letters from his father, his bank, and family solicitors, each dated and confirming the details of the others. There were receipted bills and ticket stubs. One letter contained a cryptic message obviously pointing to Sardinia: "He might bring sardines with him." Also included were falsified papers indicating that the Allies were, indeed, preparing for an invasion of Sicily but only as a cover for the real assault on Sardinia and Greece. This was the critical major deception.

IMPLEMENTATION. On the eve of April 19, 1943, the corpse of "Major Martin" left England in the submarine *Seraph*. Before dawn on April 30 the craft surfaced off the Spanish coast at Huelva in the Gulf of Cadiz. The body was removed from its container with the incriminating brief case attached to it, placed in a life jacket and lowered gently into the water. As the *Seraph* moved out to sea, the wash of its screws drove the body toward the shore.

RESULTS. What happened then was the outcome of careful planning and good fortune. A Spanish fisherman saw the corpse, hauled it aboard his craft, and returned to port. Spanish authorities immediately reported the find to the British vice-consul at Huelva, who knew nothing about it and asked for instructions from Madrid. At the same time the local *Abwehr* (*q.v.*), the German counterintelligence agency, was told that a British officer had died in an air crash and his body recovered with an interesting brief case. Within hours German agents had photocopied all the papers in the brief case and returned them. The British vice-consul arranged the burial of "Major Martin" with full military honors. Among the spectators was a German *Abwehr* agent who reported the proceedings to Berlin.

The documents were forwarded to Hitler. The *Fuehrer*, certain of his Balkan strategy, did not have the slightest doubt that they were genuine. As early as December 28, 1942, he had mentioned in a directive that "the situation in the Mediterranean makes it possible that an attack may be made in the foreseeable future on Crete and on German and Italian bases in the Aegean Sea and the Balkan peninsula." He could not dismiss the Balkans from his mind. Now he was certain. He ordered that "measures regarding Sardinia and the Peloponnesus take precedence over everything else."

Hitler's order resulted in immediate action. Commanders and units were dispatched to the critical areas. A general was dispatched to Athens to form an army group there. Despite the desperate need for the Kursk offensive in Russia, two *Panzer* (*q.v.*) divisions were withdrawn from the Russian front and sent to Greece. On the night of July 9–10, 1943, just as Rommel (*q.v.*) was setting up his headquarters in Athens, the Allies landed in Sicily. (*See* SICILY, INVASION OF.)

SIGNIFICANCE. The stratagem of *Operation Mincemeat* worked to perfection. All the belligerents at one time or another had used ruses and deceptions as an integral part of their war strategy. But *Mincemeat* was something special, one of the most effective operations of its kind in the history of warfare. It became the prototype for the stratagems used to cover the main operations of D-Day. (*See* NORMANDY INVASION.)

Bibliography. See A. C. Brown, *Bodyguard of Lies* (1975) for a dramatic account of *Mincemeat*.

MITCHELL (B-25). U.S. medium bomber used in both the Pacific and European theaters of war. It was a twin-engined, mid-wing monoplane with twin outboard rectangular fins.

DESIGN. The North American *B-25* was developed before U.S. entry into the war. From blueprint to production took less time than other comparable bombers. The designers wanted an all-purpose plane that could be used as a fighter bomber, an attack bomber, a photo-reconnaissance plane, and for submarine patrol. The plane was named after Col. William (Billy) Mitchell, the outspoken Army officer who had been court-martialed after World War I because of his strenuous defense of air power.

WORLD WAR II. The *B-25* won global attention when in April 1942 it was used in a sensational air raid on Tokyo. (*See* DOOLITTLE RAID.) It appeared throughout the Southwest Pacific battle areas, as well as on most European and African fronts. Beginning in 1943 the Royal Air Force used *B-25*s for tactical operations on the Continent. The Russians, too, bought 800 *B-25*s and were pleased by their performance. Their reaction: "It has all the good qualities of a good horse and an old-fashioned wife."

(For specifications *see* AIRCRAFT: AMERICAN AIRCRAFT DATA CHART.)

MITSCHER, MARC ANDREW (1887–1947). U.S. commander of Carrier Task Force 58 (*q.v.*) in the Pacific.

In October 1941 Capt. Mitscher commissioned the aircraft carrier *Hornet,* which he was to command for nearly two years. Three days before the Japanese attack on Pearl Harbor (*q.v.*), he was promoted to Rear Admiral, at the age of 54 and after 35 years in service. The *Hornet* was what President Roosevelt referred to as the "Shangri-La," from which the "impossible" Doolittle attack on Tokyo was made on April 18, 1942. (*See* DOOLITTLE RAID.) Six weeks after that sensational mission, Mitscher was in the Battle of Midway (*q.v.*), in which American naval power won an unmistakable victory over a larger and stronger Japanese force.

Between April and June 1943, Mitscher commanded the Allied Air Forces in the Solomons. As commander of Task Force 58 from June 10 to July 31, 1944, he led the force that destroyed 767 enemy planes, damaged many others, and sank 32 enemy vessels. His own losses were 157 aircraft and slight damage to three ships. As a result of his leadership and fighting spirit, the Central Pacific Force obtained and maintained complete control of the air throughout the vital area. He led Task Force 58 on most of the major sea and air battles for the remainder of the war.

MODEL, WALTHER (1891–1945). German officer regarded as a master of defensive warfare.

After taking part in the campaign in Poland, Model was named Chief of Staff with the 16th Army in the West in 1940. When the Soviet Union was invaded in 1941, he commanded the 3rd *Panzer* Division in the powerful onrushing German drive across the Dnieper. In 1942 Hitler gave him command of the 9th Army and in this post he played a leading role in the Kursk offensive. From 1943 to 1944 Model commanded in turn Army Groups North, South, and Center in Russia. In these campaigns Model showed himself to be a master of defensive warfare. Hitler called him "the saviour of the western front," despite the eventual German failure there.

Because of his success as a tactician in the East, Model was promoted by Hitler to General Field Marshal on March 1, 1944. When he received news of the unsuccessful July Plot (*q.v.*) on Hitler's life in 1944, Model congratulated the *Fuehrer* on his miraculous escape and vowed eternal loyalty. On August 16, 1944, Hitler issued an order forbidding any retreat in France. He was infuriated when he received word that Field Marshal Günther von Kluge (*q.v.*) had disobeyed his command and allowed his troops to fall back from the Falaise gap. The next day he dismissed von Kluge and appointed Model in his stead as Supreme Commander of Armed Forces in the West. This appointment only lasted until September 4, when Hitler appointed Field Marshal Gerd von Rundstedt (*q.v.*) in Model's place to plan and direct the Ardennes offensive in December 1944.

Meanwhile, Model directed Army Group B in the clash at Arnhem. (*See* ARNHEM, BATTLE OF.) Together with von Rundstedt he launched a surprising offensive in December. (*See* BULGE, BATTLE OF THE.) In early 1945 he retired to the Ruhr pocket, Germany's industrial area. Here more than 325,000 German troops and 30 generals were trapped by the Allies. On April 2, 1945, rather than face capture, Model shot himself.

Bibliography. See B. H. Liddell Hart, *The German Generals Talk* (1948).

MOELDERS, WERNER (1913–1941). Leading German fighter pilot.

Because of his combat experience in Spain, Moelders was given command of Fighter Group 53 at the outbreak of World War II. In the summer and fall of 1940 he commanded Fighter Group 51. (*See* FRANCE, FIRST BATTLE OF; and BRITAIN, BATTLE OF.) On the invasion of the Soviet Union in June 1941 he was transferred to the Eastern front, where he destroyed a large number of Russian aircraft. (*See* EASTERN FRONT, CAMPAIGNS ON THE.) He was promoted to General of Fighters and posted to the High Command of the *Luftwaffe* Inspector of Fighter Aircraft.

On November 17, 1941, Ernst Udet, another German fighter ace, committed suicide. Moelders was called home from the Crimea to attend the funeral of his fellow officer. On November 21, he took off in an *He-111* bomber, which developed engine trouble and crashed after hitting a cable while attempting to land at Breslau. Moelders was instantly killed.

According to *Luftwaffe* statisticians, not always reliable, Moelders had 115 confirmed air victories, of which 68 were in the Western theater and 47 in the East. He was the first German air pilot to be decorated with Hitler's special variation of the Knight's Cross (*Ritterkreuz*), with oak leaves, swords, and diamonds, for bravery in combat.

MOLOTOV, VYACHESLAV MIKHAILOVICH (1890–   ). Russian statesman and assistant to Stalin during the war years.

During the war Molotov was a member, along with Stalin, Lavrenti Beria, Kliment Voroshilov (*qq.v.*), and Georgi Malenkov of the five-man State Defense Committee. When Germany invaded the USSR in June 1941, Molotov attempted to negotiate a mutal aid pact with Britain. In the summer of 1942 he flew to Washington to arrange Lend-Lease (*q.v.*) supplies for his country. During the critical war years he took on many functions ordinarily assumed by Stalin. He played an important role in the high-level conferences among Allied war leaders, including those at Teheran, Yalta, Potsdam, and San Francisco (*qq.v.*).

Methodical and precise, Molotov was known for his extreme stubbornness. Lenin reportedly called him "the best file clerk in Russia." Churchill spoke of him as "above all men fitted to be the agent and instrument of an incalculable machine."

Bibliography. V. M. Molotov, *Stalin and Stalin's Leadership* (1950). *See also* G. Gay, *Molotov* (1940); J. Steel, *Men Behind the War* (1942); and B. Bromage, *Molotov: The Story of an Era* (1956).

MOLOTOV COCKTAIL. General term describing a crude hand grenade made of a bottle filled with an inflammable liquid such as gasoline, fitted with a wick or saturated rag taped to the bottom, and ignited at the time of hurling. Although its origin is not clear, it appears to have originated in the Russo-Finnish war (*q.v.*) in which it was used by the Finns. All belligerents in World War II used the weapon in varying forms. It was a favorite of guerrillas and combat troops in most theaters of war.

MOLOTOV-RIBBENTROP PACT. *See* RUSSO-GERMAN NONAGGRESSION PACT.

MONTE CASSINO, BOMBING OF. Allied assault on the historic Italian monastery in mid-February 1944.

BACKGROUND. The failure of the Allied campaign on the coastline at Anzio (*q.v.*) forced the main weight of the offensive to positions around the town of Cassino, hinge of Gen. Albert Kesselring's Gustav Line (*see* DEFENSIVE LINES, GERMAN, CASSINO LINE.) Cassino was situated 50 miles southeast of Anzio. On this spot Marc Antony, Roman consul in 44 B.C., once held orgies. The town, located along the Liri and Rapido rivers, dominated the narrow valley leading up to Rome. On the massif above Cassino was the site of ancient Roman fortifications, on which St. Benedict built the monastery of Monte Cassino in A.D. 520. It was considered the fountainhead of Western monasticism.

Despite its ecclesiastical importance, the monastery was merely Hill 516 on Allied war maps. Germans controlled the rocky, zigzag roadway twisting up one side to the stone buildings at the top. The 200-yard-long monastery itself was not occupied by the Germans, but Allied planners did not know it at the time. They saw it as a fortified mountain area from which deadly fire was being delivered on the troops below.

DECISION. The situation became critical in January 1944 when American troops were repulsed in a bloody engagement at the Rapido River. In early February Gen. Bernard Cyril Freyberg (*q.v.*) and his New Zealanders moved to capture several small hills north and northeast of Hill 516 as well as a part of Cassino. But deadly fire continued from the heights around the abbey. German 88s (*see* ARTILLERY WEAPONS, GERMAN EIGHTY-EIGHT GUN) picked off Allied armor, while *Nebelwerfer* rocket launchers, plastered the infantry.

Allied chances of taking Monte Cassino by direct assault were slim. On the other hand, if it were leveled, there would be condemnation by Catholics everywhere. The Allied Supreme Command concluded that the advantages held by the Germans at the monastery could no longer be ignored.

On February 14, 1944, American planes dropped leaflets addressed to "Italian Friends" and signed "The Fifth Army."

We have until now been careful to avoid bombarding Monte Cassino. The Germans have taken advantage of this. The battle is now closing in more and more around the sacred precincts. Against our will we are now obliged to direct our weapons against the Monastery itself. We warn you so that you may save yourselves. Leave the Monastery at once. This warning is urgent. It is given for your good.

In the monastery the 88-year-old Abbot Gregorio Diamare, monks, lay brothers, and refugees sought sanctuary in the subterranean chapel. German troops nearby paid no attention to the warning.

ATTACK. The attack began the next day when 142 *Flying Fortresses* (*B-17*) and 112 *Mitchells* (*B-25*) (*qq.v.*) dropped 576 tons of bombs on the monastery. Some of the bombardiers were Catholics who had volunteerd for the mission.

The interior of the monastery and five cloistered courtyards were reduced to rubble. An eyewitness reported that bright flames such as a giant might have produced by striking titanic matches on the mountainside, rose swiftly at half a dozen points. Then a pillar of smoke 500 feet high broke upward into the blue. The only two places to escape damage were the cell used by St. Benedict and the tomb in which his remains had rested for 1,400 years. It was a meaningful portent for the faithful.

AFTERMATH. The bombing of Monte Cassino achieved little in the way of strategic success. As expected, there was world-wide protest, which was carefully fanned by German propaganda. German troops moved into the shattered monastery and set up strong positions in the ruins. In his memoirs, Gen. Mark W. Clark (*q.v.*) called the bombing an unnecessary psychological mistake, as well as a tactical military mistake of the first magnitude. In the long run, he said, it only made the job more difficult, more costly in terms of men, machines, and time.

The work of reconstruction began shortly after the war. There were heavy Allied contributions for rebuilding the monastery according to old plans. It was formally reopened in 1956.

Bibliography. C. Buckley, *The Road to Rome* (1945); M.W. Clark, *Calculated Risk* (1950), T. Leccisotti, *Monte Cassino* (n.d.), and F. Majdalanay, *The Monastery* (1945).

MONTGOMERY, BERNARD LAW (1887–1976.) British Field Marshal regarded as one of the most colorful commanders of the war.

From 1939 to 1940 Montgomery led the 3rd Division in France and participated in the Dunkirk evacuation (*q.v.*). In 1942 he was sent to Egypt to command the British 8th Army (*q.v.*) under Gen. Harold Alexander (*q.v.*), Commander-in-Chief Middle East. Montgomery planned and won the critical victory at El Alamein (*q.v.*), when he routed Gen. Erwin Rommel's *Afrika Korps* (*qq.v.*) between October 23 and November 7, 1942, and drove the Germans retreating westward into Tunisia under continuous attack. In the winter of 1942 he pursued Rommel across Libya and Tripolitania and entered Tripoli to complete the conquest of Italy's African empire. (*See* NORTH AFRICA, CAMPAIGNS IN.)

Montgomery led the 8th Army in Sicily and Italy until December 1943. (*See* SICILY, INVASION OF; and ITALIAN FRONT, CAMPAIGNS ON THE.) He helped form the plans for the invasion of France in June 1944. (*See* NORMANDY INVASION.) He was named Field Commander of all ground forces until August 1944, when he was assigned to lead the 21st Army Group. At the German counterattack of December 1944 he temporarily commanded two American armies. (*See* BULGE, BATTLE OF THE.) He was promoted to Field Marshal in 1944.

A brilliant tactician, Montgomery had a keen sense of his own importance. He had a taste for picturesque uniforms and usually wore a black beret or an

Australian slouch hat covered with badges. As field commander he seldom moved until he was absolutely certain of near perfection in preparation. He became a highly controversial figure and was often criticized by fellow commanders.

Bibliography. Montgomery's writings, which often lauded his own achievements and criticized other commanders, included *Forward to Victory* (1946); *Normandy to the Baltic* (1947); *Forward From Victory* (1948); *El Alamein to the River Sangro* (1948); and *Memoirs* (1958). *See also* A. Morehead, *Montgomery* (1946); F. de Guingand, *Operation Victory* (1947); and R. W. Thompson, *Montgomery: The Field Marshal* (1969).

MOON PLANES. Special British aircraft used for landing British agents and saboteurs in German-occupied countries or rescuing important individuals from Nazi control.

Many Allied agents were dropped by parachute on enemy-held land, but special circumstances would make landing in a plane preferable. For this purpose British designers were asked for an aircraft that would be almost undetectable in the air, could land in a limited space, complete its mission quickly, and then disappear. The perfect plane for this purpose was the redesigned *Mosquito* (*q.v.*), made of plywood body to confuse enemy radar (*see* RADAR, WARTIME) and powered by two massive Rolls-Royce engines. Painted a dull black to be invisible in night skies, it could hedgehop speedily to its destination.

Moon squadrons were set up at secret airfields. Many of the planes were used on missions in which secrecy was a prime factor. (*See* ESPIONAGE.) On October 7, 1943, a Moon plane brought Dr. Niels Bohr, (*q.v.*), the famous Danish physicist, from Stockholm to Edinburgh to help in Allied atomic bomb research. (*See* BOHR MISSION.)

Bibliography. W. Stephenson, *A Man Called Intrepid* (1976).

MOORE, HENRY RUTHVEN (1886–1978). British naval officer.

As second in command of Britain's Home Fleet, the then Vice-Adm. Moore led a task force of warships and aircraft that delivered punishing blows to German ships, carriers, and freighters in waters supposed to be dominated by German U-Boats. On April 3, 1944, he commanded the task force that knocked out the German battleship *Tirpitz* temporarily. (*See* TIRPITZ).

Moore was known as a quiet, conscientious man who shunned publicity. Regarded as a naval hero by the British public, he was highly decorated for his strikes on the Nazis off Norway.

MORAVEC, FRANTISEK (1894–1966). Czechoslovak master spy.

Moravec served in the Austro-Hungarian Army throughout World War I on the Russian front. In the postwar era he was assigned to head the Czechoslovak Military Intelligence Department of the General Staff and was eventually promoted to General. In 1935 he obtained secret documents detailing plans for Hitler's *Luftwaffe* (*q.v.*). Over the next three years he worked at forecasting the war plans of the Third Reich and was able to predict accurately the Nazis' planned invasion of his country. With a dozen staff members, Moravec managed to flee from Czechoslovakia through Holland and thence to England. Working with British Intelligence in London, he continued reconnaissance throughout the rest of the war. It is believed that he was the master mind behind the assassination of Reinhard Heydrich (*q.v.*), the "Butcher of Prague." (*See* ESPIONAGE.)

Five-feet-ten-and-a-half inches tall, fair-haired, Moravec was known for his brilliant powers of deduction. He spoke many languages. His overriding characteristic was dedication to the cause of Czechoslovakia.

MORGENTHAU PLAN. Proposal by U.S. Secretary of the Treasury Henry Morgenthau (1891–1967) for controlling postwar Germany by converting the concentration of heavy industries to agriculture. The proposal was tentatively approved at the Second Quebec Conference (*see* QUEBEC CONFERENCE, SECOND), in September 1944, between President Roosevelt and Prime Minister Churchill. One statement not included in Morgenthau's original version was inserted in the communiqué signed by Roosevelt and Churchill: "The Allies were looking forward to converting Germany into a country primarily agricultural and pastoral in character."

A month later Roosevelt rejected the proposal, but damage had been done. Propaganda Minister Goebbels pointed to Morgenthau's "Program to Prevent Germany Starting World War III" as proof positive that defeat would finally seal the fate of all Germans. He urged Germans to fight on to the end to avoid the penalties supposed to be inflicted by the Morgenthau Plan.

Roosevelt's successor, President Harry S Truman (*q.v.*), was so opposed to the Morgenthau Plan that he requested Morgenthau to resign his post as Secretary of the Treasury.

Bibliography. J. M. Blum, *From the Morgenthau Diaries* (1959).

MOSCOW. Stirring war song in the Soviet Union during the war.

With music by Dan and Din Pokrass, the lyrics expressed the patriotism of the Russians in their stand for "dear Moscow's land." An English version with lyrics by Olga Paul similarly paid tribute to the ancient Kremlin walls.

MOSCOW CONFERENCE. Meeting of the Foreign Ministers of the United States, Britain, and Soviet Russia in late 1943 to discuss current and postwar problems.

BACKGROUND. The Russians did not take part in the First Quebec Conference (*see* QUEBEC CONFERENCE, FIRST) in August 1943, presumably because they were not at war with Japan. Both Roosevelt and Churchill (*qq.v.*) wanted talks with Stalin, but they decided it would be best at that time to have a meeting of chief aides. Moscow was chosen as the place for the conference.

PARTICIPANTS. The three main participants were U.S. Secretary of State Cordell Hull, British Foreign Secretary Anthony Eden, and Soviet Commissar for Foreign Affairs Vyacheslav Molotov (*qq.v.*). This was the first time during the war that the Russians had been host to so distinguished an array of diplomats. The delegates met from October 18 to November 1, 1943, at a time when Russian armed forces were surging forward against Germans.

DECISIONS. Sessions lasted 14 days and produced a number of agreements and understandings.

1. *Unconditional Surrender.* The pledge to obtain the unconditional surrender of the Germans was reaffirmed.

2. *United Nations.* The principal achievement of the conference was a mutual pledge to perpetuate the Grand Alliance after the war with the aim of achieving peace and security. A world authority would be set up for all peace-loving nations on a basis of national equality.

3. *Armaments.* It was agreed that the United Nations would confer in the future to regulate armaments.

4. *European Advisory Council.* A new Big Three council would be established in London to carry on the discussions started in Moscow.

5. *Frontiers and Economic Terms.* These were discussed and reviewed, but because of differences of opinion were left unresolved.

6. *Italy.* A special Advisory Council was set up for the purpose of destroying fascism in Italy and promoting a democratic regime with ordinary civil liberties.

7. *Austria.* It was agreed that Austria would be separated from Germany and restored to the list of free and independent states.

8. *Other Countries.* There were discussions on Poland, Finland, Czechoslovakia, Rumania, Yugoslavia, and Greece, but decisions were reserved for later meetings.

9. *Far East.* The Russians promised eventual participation in the war against Japan.

10. *Declaration of German Atrocities.* It was made clear that major war criminals would be tried ''on the scene of their crimes and judged on the spot by the people they have outraged.'' A special declaration denounced ''the recoiling Hitlerite Huns'':

DECLARATION OF GERMAN ATROCITIES

Released November 1, 1943

The United Kingdom, the United States and the Soviet Union have received from many quarters evidence of atrocities, massacres and cold-blooded mass executions which are being perpetrated by the Hitlerite forces in the many countries they have overrun and from which they are now being steadily expelled. The brutalities of Hitlerite domination are no new thing and all the peoples or territories in their grip have suffered from the worst form of government by terror. What is new is that many of these territories are now being redeemed by the advancing armies of the liberating Powers and that in their desperation the recoiling Hitlerite Huns are redoubling their ruthless cruelties. This is now evidenced with particular clearness by monstrous crimes of the Hitlerities on the territory of the Soviet Union which is being liberated from the Hitlerites, and on French and Italian territory.

Accordingly, the aforesaid three Allied Powers, speaking in the interests of the thirty-two [thirty-three] United Nations, hereby solemnly declare and give full warning of their declarations as follows:

At the time of the granting of any armistice to any government which may be set up in Germany, those German officers and men and members of the Nazi party who have been responsible for, or have taken a consenting part in the above atrocities, massacres and executions, will be sent back to the countries in which their abominable deeds were done in order that they may be judged and punished according to the laws of these liberated countries and of the free governments which will be created therein. Lists will be compiled in all possible detail from all these countries, having regard especially to the invaded parts of the Soviet Union, to Poland and Czechoslovakia, to Yugoslavia and Greece, including Crete and other islands, to Norway, Denmark, the Netherlands, Belgium, Luxemburg, France and Italy.

Thus, the Germans who take part in wholesale shootings of Italian officers or in the execution of French, Dutch, Belgian or Norwegian hostages or of Cretan peasants, or who have shared in the slaughters inflicted on the people of Poland or in territories of the Soviet Union which are now being swept clear of the enemy, will know that they will be brought back to the scene of their crimes and judged on the spot by the peoples whom they have outraged. Let those who have hitherto not imbrued their hands with innocent blood beware lest they join the ranks of the guilty, for most assuredly the three Allied Powers will pursue them to the uttermost ends of the earth and will deliver them to their accusers in order that justice may be done.

The above declaration is without prejudice to the case of the major criminals, whose offences have no particular geographical localisation and who will be punished by the joint decision of the Governments of the Allies.

ROOSEVELT
CHURCHILL
STALIN

SIGNIFICANCE. The Moscow Conference inaugurated another chapter in the history of the Grand Alliance against Hitler. In a euphoric atmosphere certain of coming victory, the Western Allies and the Soviet Union resolved their mutual suspicions for a time. The foreign ministers were anxious to disprove the Nazi charge that they could not possibly work together. Fears of a separate peace were dissipated as the Allies made a start for postwar reconstruction.

Bibliography. S. Arne, *United Nations Primer* (1945); and G. C. Marshall, *Moscow Meeting of the Committee of Foreign Ministers* (1947).

MOSQUITO. British bomber and fighter plane, one of the fastest aircraft used in the European theater of operations. The *Mosquito* was a twin-engined monoplane with pointed tail and solid nose and a dragon-fly appearance.

DESIGN. The *Mosquito* was built by the de Havilland Company on a revolutionary principle: A bomber could be effective when its only defense was an ability to outrun intercepting fighters. When used as a bomber, it carried no machine guns. The designers also departed from normal procedure by constructing the plane mostly of plywood to baffle enemy radar. (*See* RADAR, WARTIME.) For a time the Royal Air Force (*q.v.*) was reluctant to accept the plane, but it revised its attitude when the *Mosquito* demonstrated its phenomenal performance. Its speed was faster than most fighters; it was easily maneuverable; and it could be used as transport, night fighter, solitary bomber, or low-level attack plane. It served as a pathfinder for the big RAF nighttime bombers.

WORLD WAR II. The *Mosquito* soon won a legendary reputation in combat, both as fighter and bomber. It easily outdistanced the German *FW-190*s (*see AIRCRAFT: GERMAN AIRCRAFT DATA CHART*) sent out for interception. It played a central role in the opening daylight raids on Berlin. *Mosquitos* hammered the German capital by day and night, completing a total of 320 such raids in 1944–1945. Among its sensational exploits was the bombing of *Gestapo* (*q.v.*) headquarters in Copenhagen on March 3, 1945. Together with American *P-51 Mustangs* (*q.v.*), 18 *Mosquitos* flew in at roof-top height, and destroyed the building without taking the lives of all the prisoners on the top floor. (*See* SHELL HOUSE RAID.) Another *Mosquito* lobbed a 4,000-ton bomb into the mouth of a German railroad tunnel.

Mosquitos were also adapted as so-called Moon planes (*q.v.*) on special missions for landing British agents in German-occupied countries and in rescuing important individuals from Nazi control. In 1943 a *Mosquito* brought Niels Bohr, the Danish scientist, from an abandoned airfield near Stockholm to Edinburgh to work on Allied atomic bomb research. (*See* BOHR MISSION.) In the closing days of the war *Mosquitos* shot down many *V-1s* (*q.v.*), German flying bombs. (For specifications *see* AIRCRAFT: BRITISH AIRCRAFT DATA CHART.)

MOUNTBATTEN, LOUIS FRANCIS ALBERT VICTOR NICHOLAS (1900–1979). British naval officer active in Pacific commands.

At the opening of the war Mountbatten commanded the newly formed 5th Destroyer Flotilla. In December 1939 his flagship *Kelly* was damaged by mines in the North Sea, but he managed to bring her back to port. In April 1940 he took part in the Norwegian campaign and helped evacuate the British Expeditionary Force there. In mid-May 1940, the *Kelly* was sunk off Crete and Mountbatten was rescued by another destroyer.

On August 19, 1941, Mountbatten was assigned to command the aircraft carrier *Illustrious,* then under repairs in the United States. He was recalled in October to become Commodore of Combined Operations. In this post he supervised the raid on Nazaire in March 1942 and the giant raid by land, sea, and air on Dieppe in August 1942. He also took part in planning *Operation Torch* (*q.v.*), the Anglo-American invasion of North Africa.

Mountbatten was later appointed Supreme Allied Commander of South East Asia (SEAC). He served in this post from 1943 to 1946, leading forces that inflicted heavy land defeats on the Japanese.

On August 27, 1979, Mountbatten was killed by a bomb planted in all probability by a member or members of the Provisional wing of the Irish Republican Army.

Bibliography. A. Hatch, *The Mountbattens: The Last Royal Success Story* (1965).

MOWRER, EDGAR ANSEL (1892–1977). American journalist.

Mowrer received a Pulitzer Prize in 1933 for his dramatic reporting on Hitler's rise to power. He was expelled from Germany because of "unfriendly dispatches." In August 1940 he was assigned to Washington by his newspaper, the Chicago *Daily News.* From 1941 to 1943 he served as Deputy Director of the Office of Facts and Figures in the Office of War Information (*q.v.*).

Of medium height, with gray hair and black eyes, Mowrer was noted for his keen, incisive, and authoritative style of reporting. His colleagues regarded him as "a gallant fighter for the liberty of the press." Paul Joseph Goebbels (*q.v.*), Reich Minister for Public Enlightenment and Propaganda, was enraged by Mowrer's reports and said that he would expend an army division to capture him. Mowrer himself said that he "occupied a ringside seat at most of the major scenes of history" during his career.

Bibliography. Among Mowrer's books are: *Immortal Italy* (1922); *This American World Scene* (1928); *The Future of Politics* (1939); *Germany Puts the Clock Back* (1932); *Global War* (1942); *The Nightmare of American Foreign Policy* (1948); and *A Good Time To Be Alive* (1959).

MULBERRIES. Allied code and cover name for the main artificial harbors constructed outside the French coast in conjunction with *Operation Overlord* (*q.v.*) on June 6, 1944.

PREPARATION. Before D-Day (*q.v.*), 19,000 British workers were engaged in building enormous structures of reinforced concrete, resembling six-story buildings lying on their sides. The workmen had no idea what the contraptions were supposed to be, believing that perhaps they were grain elevators designed to feed the civilian population on the Continent. German secret agents passed the word to Berlin that the British were constructing huge piers for some special but unknown purpose. Actually, complete artificial piers were being built.

INVASION. Three days after the assault on France (*see* NORMANDY INVASION), giant sections of two *Mulberry* structures were towed piecemeal across the English Channel by dozens of straining tugs to form two substitute harbors. The outer breakwaters were built of partly sunken ships and concrete caissons. One faced the American Omaha Beach (*q.v.*) and the other the British front. The American *Mulberry* was wrecked in the worst Channel gale in 40 years.

The second *Mulberry* facing the British beachhead at Arromanches turned out to be an enormous success. It provided an outer roadstead in which ocean-going vessels could anchor, as well as an inner road in which the concrete caissons formed a fixed breakwater. Between the caissons and the shore ran steel piers over which men and supplies poured in a steady stream. From July 8, 1944, the *Mulberry* at Arromanches handled 6,000 tons of supplies daily. By that time a million Allied troops were in Normandy. (*See also* GOOSE-BERRY.)

SIGNIFICANCE. German leaders recognized the critical importance of the Mulberry harbors. Gen. Hans Speidel (*q.v.*) spoke of its "decisive significance." Albert Speer (*q.v.*), Minister of Armaments and War Production, called it "a single brilliant technical achievement," by which the Allies could bypass German defenses within two weeks after the first landing.

Bibliography. M. Harrison, *Mulberry: The Return to Triumph* (1965).

MÜLLER, HEINRICH (1896–?1945). Head of the Nazi *Gestapo* (*q.v.*) from 1936 to the end of the war and administrator of mass killing operations.

Both before and during the war, it was Müller's task as *Gestapo* chief to stop most anti-Nazi plots by an effective spy system. He was one of the 15 top-ranking Nazis present at the Wannsee Conference on January 20, 1942, when the Final Solution (*q.v.*), the destruction of European Jews, was planned. Efficient in his work, he was responsible for the elimination of hundreds of thousands. In January 1943 alone he rounded up 45,000 Jews from the Netherlands, 3,000 from Berlin, 30,000 from the Bialystok ghetto, and 10,000 from Theresienstadt to be sent to the extermination camp at Auschwitz. Not only Jews, but Russians and Poles in the hundreds of thousands were also slaughtered by direction of Müller. In this grisly work he acted as subordinate to Heinrich Himmler (*q.v.*) and as immediate superior to Adolf Eichmann (*q.v.*).

Müller was present at Hitler's bunker during the final days of the Third Reich. His task was to interrogate and condemn followers of the *Fuehrer* for last-minute desertion. Müller himself vanished. It was never established whether he was killed by the Russians or had escaped to South America, where it was rumored that he became a leader among escaped Nazi SS (*q.v.*) officers.

Like his superior, Himmler, Müller gave the appearance of a mild-mannered schoolteacher. Invariably polite, he was known as "*Gestapo* Müller." His name evoked dread throughout Germany and occupied countries of Europe.

MUNICH AGREEMENT. Pact between Germany, the United Kingdom, France, and Italy on September 29, 1938, by which signatories conceded to Hitler virtually everything for which he had asked in Czechoslovakia. The agreement is regarded as a major step on the road to World War II.

BACKGROUND. On September 12, 1938, Hitler, already master of Austria, announced that he demanded the right of self-determination for the Sudeten Germans of Czechoslovakia. Further, he said, if the Sudeten Germans could not defend themselves, "they will receive help from us." France and Russia were bound by treaty to defend the integrity of Czechoslovakia, while Britain was involved through commitments to France. It was clear that Hitler was prepared for war if his demands were not met in this most dangerous international crisis since World War I.

Prime Minister Neville Chamberlain (*q.v.*) of Great Britain was desperately anxious to prevent war. To appease Hitler, he took the unprecedented step of flying to Berchtesgaden and Bad Godesberg to discuss the situation. It was an extraordinary spectacle as the head of the British Government literally begged for peace. "Even if it should fail," said Chamberlain, "I should still say that it is right to attempt it. For the only alternative is war." He and French Premier Édouard Daladier (*q.v.*) were convinced that Hitler was not bluffing. They decided that the only way to avoid a general European war was to accept Hitler's terms.

The climax came at a meeting in Munich called by Hitler for the purpose of fixing the means by which the Sudetenland should be transferred to Germany. The agreement was signed on September 29, 1938.

TEXT. *

Germany, the United Kingdom, France and Italy, taking into consideration the agreement, which has been already reached in principle for the cession to Germany of the Sudeten German territory, have agreed on the following terms and conditions governing the said cession and the measures consequent thereon, and by this agreement they each hold themselves responsible for the steps necessary to secure its fulfilment:

1. The evacuation will begin on the 1st October.

2. The United Kingdom, France and Italy agree that the evacuation of the territory shall be completed by the 10th October, without any existing installations having been destroyed and that the Czechoslovak Government will be held responsible for carrying out the evacuation without damage to the said installations.

3. The conditions governing the evacuation will be laid down in detail by an international commission composed of representatives of Germany, the United Kingdom, France, Italy and Czechoslovakia.

Further Documents Respecting Czechoslovakia. Including the Agreement Concluded at Munich on September 29, 1938. Presented by the Secretary of State for Foreign Affairs to Parliament by Command of His Majesty, Misc. No. 8 Cmd. 5848 (His Majesty's Stationery Office, London, 1938), pp. 2, 3–6.

4. The occupation by stages of the predominantly German territory by German troops will begin on the 1st October. The four territories marked on the attached map will be occupied by German troops in the following order: the territory marked No. I on the 1st and 2nd of October, the territory marked No. II on the 2nd and 3rd of October, the territory marked No. III on the 3rd, 4th and 5th of October, the territory marked No. IV on the 6th and 7th of October. The remaining territory of preponderantly German character will be ascertained by the aforesaid international commission forthwith and be occupied by German troops by the 10th of October.

5. The international commission referred to in paragraph 3 will determine the territories in which a plebiscite is to be held. These territories will be occupied by international bodies until the plebiscite has been completed. The same commission will fix the conditions in which the plebiscite is to be held, taking as a basis the conditions of the Saar plebiscite. The commission will also fix a date, not later than the end of November, on which the plebiscite will be held.

6. The final determination of the frontiers will be carried out by the international commission. This commission will also be entitled to recommend to the four Powers, Germany, the United Kingdom, France and Italy, in certain exceptional cases minor modifications in the strictly ethnographical determination of the zones which are to be transferred without plebiscite.

7. There will be a right of option into and out of the transferred territories, the option to be exercised within six months from the date of this agreement. A German-Czechoslovak commission shall determine the details of the option, consider ways of facilitating the transfer of population and settle questions of principle arising out of the said transfer.

8. The Czechoslovak Government will within a period of four weeks from the date of this agreement release from their military and police forces any Sudeten Germans who may wish to be released, and the Czechoslovak Government will within the same period release Sudeten German prisoners who are serving terms of imprisonment for political offences.

Adolf Hitler
Neville Chamberlain
Édouard Daladier
Benito Mussolini

Munich, September 29, 1938

AFTERMATH. Chamberlain returned to London waving the text of the Munich Agreement and triumphantly announced that Munich meant "peace in our time." To critics the agreement simply "sold Czechoslovakia down the river." Munich was a diplomatic triumph of the first order for Hitler and it encouraged him to make further demands in Europe. The next step was Poland and that was too much for Chamberlain. It meant war.

Bibliography. L. B. Namier, *Diplomatic Prelude, 1938–39* (1948); J. W. Wheeler-Bennett *Munich: Prologue to Tragedy* (1948); and T. Taylor, *Munich: The Price of Peace* (1979).

MUNK, KAJ (1898–1944). Danish pastor and playwright murdered by the Nazis.

Munk was outstanding among the Nordic dramatists. His first success as a playwright came in 1931 with a drama on Henry VIII. His works always presented God as the supreme dictator and victor at the final curtain. He fought Nazism in his sermons and writings after the German occupation of his country. His popularity with his people was so great that the Nazis at first did not dare to arrest him, although they were angered by his work and forbade him to preach outside his own parish.

On January 5, 1944, four men pretending to be Danes and speaking Danish with a strong German accent called at Munk's house in the Jutland village of Jedersoe saying they had a warrant for his arrest. As his wife opened the door, Munk turned from the telephone and said: "The Germans are here to get me." The four abductors whisked him away before his wife and children could speak to him. Early the next morning a farmer found the pastor's body in a ditch 40 miles from his home.

The kidnapping and murder of Kaj Munk caused more public indignation in Denmark than any event since the deportation of Danish Jews. Danish members of the Resistance redoubled their efforts for liberation from the German occupation. (*See* RESISTANCE MOVEMENTS.)

Bibliography. See D. Lampe, *The Danish Resistance* (1957).

MURMANSK. Russian port on the Kola Peninsula in northwest Russia. An ice-free port on the Barents Sea, it was the terminus of the North Sea route—the Murmansk Run.

Lined by rail to Moscow and Leningrad, Murmansk was in a highly strategic position during the war. Supplies by American Lend-Lease (*q.v.*) went to Soviet Russia over the route to Murmansk. The city was bombed repeatedly by the German *Luftwaffe* (*q.v.*). German U-Boat commanders gave high priority to convoys moving to Murmansk. (*See also* CONVOY *PQ-17.*)

Bibliography. R. Carse, *A Cold Corner of Hell* (1969); and B. B. Schofield, *The Russian Convoys* (1964).

MURPHY, AUDIE (1924–1971). One of the most decorated American soldiers of World War II.

Murphy joined the army in June 1942 at the age of 18. Sent to Europe, he took part in all major American campaigns from North Africa to Germany. During the push up the Italian peninsula, he and a supply sergeant were the only ones of 235 in his company to survive the long bloody journey. (*See* ITALIAN FRONT, CAMPAIGNS ON THE.)

Promoted to Second Lieutenant, Murphy led a company on January 20, 1945, when it was caught in the Colmar pocket in eastern France. Ordering his men to take cover, he himself took refuge in a damaged American tank. Exposed on three sides, he grabbed a machine gun and killed or wounded 50 Germans. The incident was widely reported in the press and Murphy as awarded the Congressional Medal of Honor.

Bibliography. A. Murphy, *To Hell and Back* (1967).

MURPHY, ROBERT D. (1894–1978). U.S. diplomat.

A successful career diplomat, Murphy was credited with paving the way for the Allied invasion of North Africa. (*See TORCH.*) He conducted the secret negotiations necessary for success of the venture. As senior State Department officer in Africa, credited to Vichy since 1940, he was assigned the task of winning the support of the Free French in North Africa and to ease preparations for the Allied landings in early November 1942. He sent a stream of valuable reports to Washington and London on the temper of the military and civilian population, the names of officers with pro-Allied sympathies, and details of French military and naval strength in the area.

On one point Murphy miscalculated. He was convinced by French military leaders that the French in North Africa were ready to support Gen. Henri Giraud (*q.v.*), who had escaped from a German prison in World War I and duplicated the feat in World War II. The French generals claimed that he was the ideal leader, around whom the French of North Africa would rally and be led into the Allied camp. As events later showed, Murphy's advice was erroneous. Later, he served in the negotiations for the Italian armistice.

Bibliography. R. D. Murphy, *Diplomat Among Warriors* (1964).

MURROW, EDWARD R. (1908–1965). Most prominent and popular American broadcaster of the war.

Murrow's broadcasts from London in the early stage of the war were immensely popular. His opening words, "This is London," made him known to millions. During the German assault in the summer of 1940, he described the cool behavior of the British public. He told how the attack had resulted in a kind of revolution by consent, in which old power politics gave way to working for general welfare. His Columbia Broadcasting System (CBS) office was bombed twice as well as his British Broadcasting Company (BBC) studio.

Murrow continued his accurate and objective reporting from London after the United States entered the war. He flew on 25 bomber missions over Europe. On December 3, 1943, he broadcast a famous radio report about a massive raid by the Royal Air Force (*q.v.*) on Berlin. The German capital, he said, had become "an orchestrated hell, . . . a terrible symphony of light and flame."

Murrow's voice, next to those of Churchill and Roosevelt, was the best known in the United States during and after the war. The London *Telegraph* called him "America's unofficial Ambassador."

Bibliography. A selection of Murrow's broadcasts from 1939 to 1940 appeared in *This is London* (1941). "This book in the full sense is the stuff of history," commented *The New York Times. See also* E. R. Murrow, *In Search of Light* (1967); and A. Kendrick, *Prime Time* (1969).

MUSSOLINI, BENITO AMILCARE ANDREA (1883–1945). Italian dictator, founder of Fascism, and one of the leading figures of World War II. He was born in the village of Dovis on July 29, 1883, the son of a blacksmith and ardent labor leader. After an unruly childhood, he took his diploma as a schoolteacher at the age of 18.

EARLY CAREER. Mussolini taught briefly, went to Switzerland to avoid military service (1902–1904), and edited a newspaper in Trentino (1909). In World War I he was an Allied interventionist. His newspaper, *Popolo d'Italia,* was subsidized by the French to help win Italy's entry into the war on the Allied side.

In the postwar era Mussolini organized the Fascist movement and in 1922 won his way to power as Premier. Setting up a dictatorship, he stifled opposition, regimented the press, reorganized the state economy, and embarked on an expansionist foreign policy. In 1935 he promoted an attack on Ethiopia, and in 1936 interfered in the Spanish civil war. In 1936 he brought Italy into the Rome-Berlin Axis.

WORLD WAR II. Mussolini did not enter World War II, despite his alliance with Germany, until France fell in June 1940. Churchill denounced him as "a jackal" who hoped to seize pieces of French territory. During the course of the next two years Mussolini found himself at war with both the Soviet Union and the United States. After debacles in Libya and Greece, his country came under Hitler's control. The failure of Italian armies and the imminent invasion of the Italian peninsula itself caused a loss of prestige that Mussolini could not surmount.

In March 1943 Mussolini attempted to strengthen his control by reorganizing his party's directorate and demanding a personal pledge of loyalty from all party leaders. But with the fall of Tunisia his situation became even worse. In July 1943, when the Allied invasion of Sicily was well under way, he had to call on massive German help as the only way to save his country.

DECLINE AND FALL. Mussolini's enthusiasm for imperialistic expansion was diminishing rapidly. On July 24, 1943, the Fascist Grand Council, by a vote of 19 to 7, called for his resignation. He was arrested and imprisoned in the Abruzzi Mountains. His fall meant the end of the Fascist regime. In September 1943 Italy surrendered to the Allies. On September 12 Mussolini was rescued in a daring parachute raid by German commandos. (*See* SKORZENY, OTTO.) He set up a Fascist regime in the north of Italy, but it was without personal power, although he did manage to arrest some of his opponents, including his son-in-law Galeazzo Ciano (*q.v.*).

When the German defenses in the north collapsed, Mussolini, accompanied by his mistress, Clara Petacci, was betrayed to the Italian Partisans. On April 28, 1945, together with 12 members of his Fascist Cabinet and Petacci, he was shot. The bodies were carried to Milan, hung upside down in the public square to public ridicule, and buried in unmarked graves.

PERSONALITY AND CHARACTER. Five-feet-seven-inches tall, with a bald head, prominent nose, pugnacious chin, and hefty girth, Mussolini rolled his eyes while talking so that the white showed and his eyeballs popped with emotion. A political showman and flamboyant orator, he was a master rabble rouser. His vanity was legendary, yet he had intelligence, a talent for leadership, and, on occasion, a streak of sensitivity. Although not an original thinker, he acquired a hold over the Italian people by a combination of unscrupulous propaganda, exaggerated promises, and the support of the army and industrialists.

Unfortunately for his country, Mussolini operated in the wrong century at a time when Italy was a prisoner of its own geography. Like the legendary toad, he huffed and puffed until he exploded. Historians rate him as a "Sawdust Caesar."

Bibliography. Mussolini's *My Autobiography* (1939) is supplemented by *The Fall of Mussolini: His Own Story* (1948). *See also* biographies by G. Megaro (1938); G. Pini (1939); M. H. Macartney (1944); R. Dumbrowsky (1956); L. C. Fermi (1961); and R. Collier, *Duce* (1971).

MUSTANG (P-51). U.S. Air Forces aircraft considered by many experts to be the finest American fighter plane. A single-engined, low-wing monoplane, the *P-51* was easy to recognize with its square wing tips and long pointed nose.

DESIGN. The North American *Mustang* was originally produced at the request of the British. In early 1940 the Royal Air Force (*q.v.*) asked American assistance for a fast fighter with long range and good high-altitude performance. The response was the *P-51,* which was planned and constructed within eight months. With its propellers rotating in opposite directions, thus balancing torque, the aircraft turned out to be highly maneuverable.

WORLD WAR II. P-51s flown by British pilots saw combat action for the first time in August 1942 in support of ground commandos in the Dieppe raid (*q.v.*). Beginning in March 1944, *P-51s,* together with *P-47 Thunderbolts,* were used by American pilots to escort *Flying Fortresses (B-17)* (*q.v.*) and *B-24 Liberators* on daylight raids on Germany.

The *Mustang* proved to be superior to any German fighter sent against it and destroyed more enemy aircraft than any other fighter in the European theater of operations. A versatile plane, it was used for both low- and high-altitude fighting as well as photographic reconnaissance. It was especially successful in attacking trains and communications lines.

(For specifications *see* AIRCRAFT: AMERICAN AIRCRAFT DATA CHART.)

N

NACHT UND NEBEL. *See* NIGHT AND FOG DECREE.

NAGANO, OSAMI (1880-1947). Japanese Admiral, who gave the order for Japan's attack on Pearl Harbor (*q.v.*).

In April 1941 Nagano was Chief of the Naval General Staff in charge of fleet operations as well as naval member of the Supreme War Council. In these positions he gave the command for the attack on Pearl Harbor. Early in the occupation of Japan he accepted full responsibility for the assault on Pearl Harbor and for having broken a naval impasse on whether to strike there or toward the Netherlands East Indies. In February 1944, after a shake-up in the High Command because of war reverses, Nagano retired as chief Japanese naval strategist.

Nagano was one of 28 Japanese formally accused by the Allies in April 1946 of being part of a militaristic clique aiming for world power. The indictment included war crimes throughout the Pacific theater. He became ill in his Sugamo prison cell and died of a heart attack on January 5, 1947.

Nagano held most of the top posts in the Japanese Navy. Although in his early years he was regarded as a moderate and an opponent of military aggressiveness, he later threatened China: "Our mailed fist is ready."

NAGASAKI. Site of the second atomic bomb dropped on Japan.

BACKGROUND. The first atomic bomb dropped on Hiroshima (*q.v.*) on August 6, 1945, caused consternation and bewilderment in Japan, but the authorities gave little indication of immediate surrender. To speed up the will to surrender, Americans launched an intensive propaganda campaign, dropping some 16 million leaflets on 47 Japanese cities. A second atomic bomb strike was scheduled for August 11, but it was moved up to August 9, only three days after Hiroshima. The purpose was to convince the Japanese public that Hiroshima was by no means an isolated freakish incident.

THE BOMB. This time the bomb used plutonium and was the type that had been exploded in New Mexico. (*See* MANHATTAN PROJECT.) Named "Fat Man," it was considerably more powerful than the first bomb, which had used uranium.

TARGET. The primary target, Kokura, was closed in, and the pilot, Maj. Charles W. Sweeney, could not find the smallest hole in the clouds. Nagasaki, too, the alternate target, was also hidden by clouds. The final run was made by radar.

Nagasaki, a railroad terminal on Kyushu Island and a city of 250,000 was a major supply port for Japanese military and naval operations throughout the Pacific area. It was also an important shipbuilding and repair center for both warships and merchantmen.

BLAST. An eyewitness, William L. Laurence (*q.v.*) of *The New York Times,* who accompanied the mission, told how a great ball of fire from Nagasaki rose as though from the bowels of the earth, belching forth ominous white rings. "The entity assumed the form of a giant square totem pole, with its base about three miles long tapering off to about a mile at the top. Its bottom was brown, its center was amber, its top white. But it was like a living totem pole, carved with many grotesque masks grimacing at the earth."

Not even the range of protecting canyons and hills surrounding the city could save it from destruction. The bomb crushed Japan's largest torpedo factories and a huge steel mill, reducing these modern steel buildings to a mass of twisted girders. In the municipal area, three miles long and two miles wide, nothing was left except debris.

CASUALTIES. Estimates vary, but it is believed that at least 35,000 were killed, 6,000 injured, many seriously, and 5,000 were missing.

AFTERMATH. The next day the Japanese Cabinet sent a message through its emissaries in Switzerland accepting the terms of the Potsdam ultimatum. The proviso was added that the Emperor remain in power. Except for formalities, the war was ended.

Bibliography. *See* W. L. Laurence in *The New York Times,* September 9, 1945, who reported on "A thousand Old Faithful geysers rolled into one." *See also* F. Knebel and C. W. Bailey II, *No High Ground* (1960).

NAGUMO, CHUICHI (1887–1944). Japanese naval officer.

On December 7, 1941, Nagumo, then a Vice-Admiral, was in command of the Carrier Strike Force *Kido Butai,* which attacked Pearl Harbor (*q.v.*). On his flagship carrier, *Akagi,* he directed the two air strikes that caused devastating damage at the U.S. naval base and left the U.S. Pacific Fleet temporarily crippled. He decided against a third strike and headed for home waters.

Nagumo commanded the same carrier strike force in the Battle of Midway on June 4, 1942, when a force of 160 ships and 100,000 men received the first Japanese defeat in modern times. When his flagship, *Akagi,* was sunk, Nagumo was transferred to a cruiser. Adm. Isoruku Yamamoto (*q.v.*) ordered Nagumo, who had hoped for a night engagement, to withdraw. (*See* MIDWAY, BATTLE OF.)

Nagumo also commanded the task force in the Battle of the Eastern Solomons. At Guadalcanal he again lost his flagship. In the summer of 1944 he was sent to Saipan to help organize its defense. On July 6, 1944, as the battle drew to its close, he committed suicide by *härä-kïri (q.v.).* He could not endure the odium of defeat.

NATIONAL LIBERATION MOVEMENT (EAM). One of the two major Resistance movements inside Greece during the era of the German occupation.

The toughest and best-organized faction, the EAM was Communist-oriented. Consisting of 30,000 Partisans, the movement waged ferocious war against the Greek Democratic Liberation Army (EDES). (*See* GOVERNMENTS-IN-EXILE; PARTISANS; and RESISTANCE MOVEMENTS.)

NATIONAL REDOUBT. Supposed area of retreat in southern Germany, where Hitler was expected to make a final stand against the Allies in the late days of the war.

Allied strategists believed that Berchtesgaden, in southern Germany, far from being a harmless vacation spot for Hitler and his entourage, was designated as the center for a proposed desperate defense because it was well protected by mountain passes and fortifications. Here Hitler's Werewolf (*Werwolf [q.v.]*), composed of fanatical young guerrilla fighters, would give their lives for the *Fuehrer.*

Highly publicized, the National Redoubt caused grave concern for Gen. Dwight D. Eisenhower (*q.v.*). It was partly because of his belief in a final stand in the south that Eisenhower allowed the Russians to take Berlin in the north, a decision of enormous consequences for the postwar period. The vast network of Allied agents was never able to ascertain that the National Redoubt did not exist at all and was only a specter.

NAUJOCKS, ALFRED HELMUT (1911–   ). One of the most publicized of Nazi adventurers.

Naujocks's role in the Gleiwitz raid (*q.v.*) won him a reputation as "the man who started World War II." On November 8, 1939, he took part in the kidnapping by SS (*q.v.*) agents of two British agents in the Netherlands near the German border. (*See* VENLO INCIDENT.) In May 1940 he was involved in an undertaking in which German troops were disguised in Dutch and Belgian uniforms and carried false passports. He proposed a plan to drop forged bank notes from German planes flying over England. (*See* BERNHARD, OPERA-

TION). He later fought the Resistance in Belgium and Norway. On October 19, 1944, he deserted to the Americans.

Still leading a charmed life, Naujocks escaped from an internment camp in 1946. He was never brought to trial. He retired to Hamburg as a businessman and sold accounts of his exploits as "the man who started World War II."

NAVICERT SYSTEM. British system of inspecting cargoes of merchant ships flying neutral flags.

In World War I the British, in order to prevent war cargoes from reaching the enemy, began the practice of searching neutral ships either at their loading ports or at special contraband-control points. Those ships which passed inspection were given a certificate called for short a Navicert. The idea was to eliminate the necessity for at-sea inspections. This practice, in addition to stopping and searching American vessels on the high seas, resulted in sharp exchanges between Washington and London in the early months of the war.

NBBS. *See* NEW BRITISH BROADCASTING STATION.

NEAR AND MIDDLE EAST, CAMPAIGNS IN THE. Struggle in World War II for control of Islamic states between the Nile River and the Caspian Sea.

BACKGROUND. The situation in the spring of 1941 turned ominous for the British when the Germans invaded the Balkans. At the same time Gen. Erwin Rommel and his *Afrika Korps* (*qq.v.*) opened an offensive in Libya and drove the British, weakened by dispatch of a part of their forces to Greece and Crete, back into Egypt. (*See* NORTH AFRICA, CAMPAIGNS IN.) Hitler hoped for a series of revolts by Islamic peoples against the British in the Near and Middle East. He was encouraged by Egypt's refusal to declare war on the Axis. By strengthening his forces in Libya and by moving south from Crete, he would attain one of his major objectives—seizure of the Suez Canal.

IRAQ. In early May 1941 Rashid Ali, ruler of Iraq, who had strong pro-Axis leanings, requested the British to remove their troops from his country. Instead of complying, the British sent small forces from Palestine and Transjordan across the desert and defeated Rashid Ali with little difficulty. London installed a regime favorable to the Allies.

SYRIA. In French-mandated Syria, authorities representing Vichy France (*see* FRANCE IN WARTIME) indicated that they were willing to cooperate with the Axis. Allied strategists feared that Syria and neighboring Lebanon might be used as bases for operations against the Suez Canal. Accordingly, to forestall that possibility, British forces, assisted by Free French (*see* FREE FRANCE) units, invaded Syria in June 1941. Vichy administrators protested vehemently, but to no avail. French rule was ended in Syria.

IRAN. Reza Shah Pahlevi, ruler of Iran (Persia), made no secret of his pro-Axis sympathies and tolerated hundreds of Axis agents operating in his country. Although Iran had long been an area of bitter Russo-British rivalry, British and Russian troops combined in August 1941 to invade the strategic country. They deported the Shah to South Africa and replaced him with his son, Mohammed Reza Pahlavi (1919–1980).

In January 1942 Britain and Soviet Russia signed a treaty to "respect the territorial integrity and political independence of Iran" and to evacuate all their troops not later than six months after the cessation of hostilities. The United States also accepted this stipulation at the Teheran Conference (*q.v.*) in December 1943. In the immediate postwar years the subject of Iran again became a matter of dispute and the cause for a serious rift in the wartime Grand Alliance.

TURKEY. The Turks carefully nurtured their neutrality and sold their products indiscriminately to both sides. Although officially neutral, their attitude was ambivalent. Impressed with Hitler's victories in the Balkans (*see* BALKANS, CAMPAIGNS IN THE), the Turks on June 18, 1941, signed a treaty of "mutual trust" with Germany and began to send vital chrome and copper for the Axis war machine.

SIGNIFICANCE. By forceful, energetic steps, the British managed to reaffirm their control of the Near and Middle East. In taking over Iran they won a strategic "bridge of victory" over which supplies could be sent to the hard-pressed Russians. The main test of strength was to come later in Libya, but in the meantime the British effectively neutralized the direct route to Suez through Islamic countries.

Bibliography. G. Lenckowski, *Russia and the West in Iran, 1920-1948* (1948); M. N. Seton-Watson, *Britain and the Arab States* (1948); H. C. Cooke, *Challenge and Response in the Middle East* (1952); D. Orlow, *The Nazis in the Balkans* (1968); and B. M. Rubin, *The Great Powers in the Middle East, 1941-1947* (1980).

NEIGHBORHOOD ASSOCIATIONS. Community block groups formed in every city and village in wartime Japan to implement local administration on the home front.

Through the neighborhood associations, the people were organized to assure adequate sanitation, fair rations, and mutual aid during the American air assault on Japan. In July 1942 the Imperial Rule Assistance Association (*q.v.*) noted that there were more than 1.3 million neighborhood associations in Japan. Despite the dangerous air raids, the associations functioned well until the end of the war. During the American occupation they took charge of allocating scarce food and clothing.

NELSON, DONALD MARR (1888–1959). U.S. businessman who played an important role in war production.

In June 1940 Nelson was named Treasury Procurement Chief in charge of ordinary purchasing. A month later he was appointed coordinator of purchases
for the Defense Commission. In October 1940 he became administrator of the
Priorities Board. On creation of the Office of Production Management, the new
overall defense agency, Nelson headed its Division of Purchase. At this point
President Roosevelt made Nelson Chairman of the War Production Board, a
post he held for the remainder of the war. Immediately before Pearl Harbor,
Nelson was spending $3.5 billion a month on defense projects.

Bibliography. D. M. Nelson, *Arsenal of Democracy* (1946).

NEURATH, CONSTANTIN FREIHERR VON (1873–1956). Diplomat
and Hitler's adviser on foreign affairs.

Neurath entered government service in Berlin in 1901 and subsequently
devoted his career to diplomacy. On June 1, 1932, he was appointed by
Chancellor Franz von Papen to his "Cabinet of Barons," a post he retained
under Hitler. He was present at the Hossbach Conference (*see* HOSSBACH
PROTOCOL) in 1937, at which Hitler outlined his plans for aggression. His
protest against German expansion led to his temporary decline. On March 18,
1938, he was appointed Reich Protector of Bohemia and Moravia. In this post
he muzzled the press and abolished all opposition. He relinquished his office
on August 25, 1943. He was found guilty at the Nuremberg Trials (*q.v.*) and
sentenced to 15 years' imprisonment. Released from Spandau Prison in 1954
for reasons of health, he died on August 14, 1956.

Bibliography. J. L. Heinemann, *Hitler's First Foreign Minister: Constantin Freiherr von Neurath*
(1980).

NEUTRALS IN THE WAR. Only a few nations in Europe were able to maintain their neutrality in the great conflict, and these only because of favorable
geography or because Hitler preferred that they remain neutral. Either they had
a tight defensive system (Switzerland), possessed raw materials that they were
willing to sell to the Germans (Sweden), or had a persistent desire not to be
drawn into the war (Spain).

SWITZERLAND. With an army of 500,000 men permanently mobilized,
with older citizens trained for instant call, and all invasion routes mined, the
Swiss were certain of their invulnerability to invasion. Moreover, as bankers for
the world, they offered a safe repository for foreign funds, including Nazi
money. They sold to the Axis and Allies alike—as long as bills were paid. Swiss
factories went on a round-the-clock schedule to produce precision instruments,
fuses, clocks and watches, anything that could be sold to the belligerents at a
profit.

The Swiss also did business with Nazis, but their sympathies were on the
other side. It was said that they worked for Hitler six days a week and on the
seventh prayed for the Allies. Swiss citizens gave sanctuary to refugees from
both sides.

SWEDEN. On the northern periphery of Fortress Europe (*q.v.*), Swedes also made themselves indispensable to both sides, thereby maintaining a record of never having gone to war for more than a century. In September 1939 they warned the world and Hitler in particular that the first violation of their frontiers meant the self-destruction of every last factory, mine, and train in Sweden. There would be no more steel or ball bearings for sale. Hitler heeded the warning.

Meanwhile, Swedes maintained their contacts with the Allies. They sent food impartially to Poles, Norwegians, Danes, Dutch, and Czechs. They granted asylum to war survivors and took children into their homes. With fine impartially they allowed agents on both sides to function undisturbed in their cafes. Norwegians and Danes resented Swedish neutrality, but they could not convince Swedes to share their own subservient status.

SPAIN. Dictator Francisco Franco (*q.v.*) put on a dazzling virtuoso performance in keeping his country out of the war. Because of his vital assistance in the Spanish civil war, Hitler expected a *quid pro quo* from Franco, but he never got it. The Spanish leader duly signed the Anti-Comintern Pact in 1939 before the war, but on its start he refused to enter it. Spain, he said, had been devastated and needed time for recovery. He would be pro-Axis but non-belligerent. He helped the Axis powers in various ways—serviced their planes, sheltered their fleets, allowed their agents to operate in Madrid, and provided Germany with all-important wolframite (a source of tungsten used for making steel alloy).

Meanwhile, the Allies maintained a sizeable fleet at Gibraltar, a fair warning to Franco. In 1943, as the tide of war shifted to the Allied side, Franco moved from non-belligerence to benevolent neutrality. This meant that he could bargain with and sell to both sides. He now permitted interned Allied seamen to leave the country and allowed Allied espionage agents to operate in Spain. Eventually, as the outcome of the war became more certain, he halted the export of wolframite to Germany.

PORTUGAL. Under the dictatorship of Antonio de Oliveira Salazar (*q.v.*), dean of European autocrats, Portugal also sat out the war as a neutral. Although traditionally friendly to Great Britain, Portugal sold its precious supplies of wolframite indiscriminately to both sides. Agents of all belligerents operated openly in Lisbon. Portugal's neutrality paid dividends: It emerged from the war with a capital surplus, a hard currency, and a low public debt.

TURKEY. On the exposed southern flank of the Nazi-Soviet struggle, the Turks favored the Allies and simultaneously resisted the threats of the Axis powers. There was pressure on them from both sides. On February 23, 1945, Turkey declared war on Germany and Japan. The Turks were moved undoubtedly by the Allied decision not to invite to the forthcoming San Francisco Conference (*q.v.*) any nation that had not entered the war by March 1, 1945.

IRELAND. All parties in Ireland insisted upon strict neutrality. However, London complained that Ireland was a hotbed of Axis espionage, that the Irish extended greater liberties to Axis representatives in Dublin than ordinarily given to ambassadors, and that the German *Luftwaffe (q.v.)* used lighted Irish cities as checkpoints when attacking England. The Irish replied that, despite their neutrality, tens of thousands of their sons were fighting in British units or working in British factories.

Bibliography. W. Churchill, *History of World War II,* 6 vols. (1948–1953); H. C. O'Neill, *A Short History of the Second World War* (1950); and L.L. Snyder, *The War: A Concise History, 1939–1945* (1960).

NEW BRITISH BROADCASTING STATION (NBBS). Clandestine German broadcasting station operated in English during the "Phony War" in the winter of 1939–1940. *(See SITZKRIEG.)*

The NBBS was linked with *Operation Sea Lion (q.v.),* the projected invasion of England across the English Channel. Organized and administered by the Propaganda Section of the OKW *(q.v.),* the German High Command of the Armed Forces, NBBS was the equivalent of the *Voix de la Paix (q.v.),* a similar station in France. Both were designed for strategic deception and to subvert and demoralize listeners in England.

NBBS broadcasted varieties of cryptic messages supposed to contact espionage agents in London. Britons were urged to use hard physical force against "the shameless ruling class." "See that the war makers fear for their lives." Lists were read of prominent Englishmen and refugees living in England who would be held to account after the invasion. The station used *The Bonnie, Bonnie Banks of Loch Lomond* as a signature tune, and always ended its transmissions with the British national anthem.

Three other "black" stations broadcasted to England. The anticapitalistic *Workers Challenge* denounced British industrialists. The *Christian Peace Movement* urged all listeners not to help the war effort. *Caledonia* used a Scottish accent. All four stations hammered away at the theme that Britain was on the verge of collapse, that its industrial machine had been rendered impotent by sabotage, and that the country had fallen prey to fifth columnists. Churchill and other British leaders were described as in the pay of a global Jewish conspiracy.

German authorities believed that they were achieving good results with these four clandestine radio stations. Actually, reception was poor, and those Britons who did hear the broadcasts were amused. The British were clearly victors in the battle of wits. *(See PROPAGANDA, WAR.)*

NEW GUINEA, CAMPAIGNS IN. Series of Allied moves to wrest control of the second largest island in the world from the Japanese.

BACKGROUND. North of Australia, from which it is separated by the Torres Strait, New Guinea was on the outer perimeter of Japanese expansion and vital for possible control of Australia. In March 1942 a Japanese force moving from the stronghold at Rabaul (*q.v.*) in New Britain, landed at Lae on the northeastern coast of New Guinea. The seaborne expedition was supposed to capture strategic Port Moresby on the south coast of Papua below the Owen Stanley Mountains, but it had to turn back in May because of the indecisive Battle of the Coral Sea (*q.v.*). In the meantime Gen. Douglas MacArthur (*q.v.*) was appointed Allied Commander-in-Chief, Southwest Pacific. He commanded an initial force of 265,000 Australians and the 6th and 7th Divisions, which had returned from Europe, and 38,000 U.S. troops. After the Battle of Midway in June 1942, he was supplied with additional American strength for an amphibious advance westward along the coast of New Guinea.

BUNA. Both the Japanese and the Allies turned their attention to Buna on the northeastern coast at the head of the Kokoda trail that led southward through jungles and mountains to Port Moresby. On July 21, 1942, the Japanese landed 1,800 troops near Buna. Eight days later they were in possession of Kokoda in the mid-Papuan Peninsula on the way to Port Moresby. By mid-August some 13,000 men were committed to the task of forcing the Australians back through the jungle track. They were handicapped by overextended supply lines and continual harassment from the air.

By mid-September 1942 the Allies were ready to go on the offensive. On September 23, Gen. Thomas A. Blamey (*q.v.*), Australian Commander-in-Chief of the Allied Land Forces, Southwest Pacific, arrived in Port Moresby to take charge of the operation. By the end of October the Japanese were dislodged from their forward positions in the Owen Stanley Range. On November 2 the Australians reoccupied Kokoda and reopened the airfield there. The Japanese managed to hold an area around Buna through December.

MILNE BAY. Meanwhile the Japanese also struck at Milne Bay on the eastern tip of the peninsula, which could be used as a base for a sea and air assault on Port Moresby. At the end of August 1942 they landed 1,300 men on Goodenough Island and another 1,100 on the Papuan Peninsula. Australians and Americans resisted fiercely and after five days of fighting forced the enemy to disembark. It was the first Allied land victory of the war over the Japanese.

CASUALTIES. The first six months of fighting in New Guinea cost the Japanese more than 12,000 men. The Allies lost 8,500 (5,700 Australian and 2,800 American). Both sides suffered severely in the malaria-ridden jungles. Allied morale was stimulated by evidence that Australian and American troops could meet the enemy under appalling jungle conditions.

HUON PENINSULA. In August 1943 the Allies maintained pressure on Salamaua in order to divert Japanese attention from the Allied plan to attack Lae and the Huon Peninsula. Ports and airfields in this area were vital for future

Allied strategy. On September 7 the 503rd U.S. Parachute Regiment was dropped northwest of Lae in the first Allied airborne operation in the Pacific. Additional Australian troops were then flown in by transport aircraft. At the same time the overland advance on Salamaua was resumed.

Faced with superior forces, the Japanese evacuated Salamaua (September 11) and Lae (September 15) and soon found that they could not hold the port of Finschhafen at the end of the peninsula (October 2). They were then pushed back into mountainous country where they had no supplies. By the end of 1943 the Allies were planning a two-pronged advance along the coast to Madang.

HOLLANDIA AND WAKDE. After gaining control of the Huon Peninsula, the Allies halted to build up supplies and reinforcements. In the spring of 1944 they began a series of leapfrog attacks, advancing eventually 1,000 miles from Madang to the Vogelkop Peninsula at the western end of New Guinea. In April, while the Australians pushed westward from Madang, MacArthur's forces leapfrogged to Hollandia, the key base on Humboldt Bay, 200 miles west of Wewak, where the Japanese were cut off. The Allies now moved westward again to the offshore island of Wakde, where the enemy had built an airfield.

During these operations the Japanese were outnumbered in New Guinea. They had a total of 6 weak divisions to face the Allied 15 (8 American and 7 Australian), and were faced with heavy superiority on both sea and in the air. Japanese troopships heading for New Guinea were heavily damaged by U.S. submarines. In the Central Pacific the Japanese had their hands full in the Marianas and could not send reinforcements to New Guinea.

BIAK ISLAND. MacArthur's system of bypassing major enemy troop concentrations and leaving them without supplies was working to perfection. His next step came in May 1944 just a month after the capture of Hollandia. About 350 miles west of Hollandia and off the coast was Biak Island with vital airfields, where the Japanese maintained a garrison of 11,000 men. Initial landings were made after a naval bombardment. The Japanese then retreated to caves and entrenched positions on the high ground overlooking the airfields. Tokyo sent a strong convoy with reinforcements, but it was rushed back northward to meet the U.S. carrier threat in the Marianas. Fighting continued into August 1944. The Biak operation cost the Americans 474 killed and 2,400 wounded. The Japanese lost their entire garrison.

RECONQUEST OF NEW GUINEA. By mid-1944 the Allies had won the battle for New Guinea, although the fighting continued for another two months. With no air covering, remaining Japanese troops retreated to the western tip of the Vogelkop Peninsula. On July 30 the Allies put a division on shore near Cape Sansapor and started work on an airfield there.

SIGNIFICANCE. The reconquest of New Guinea prepared the way for a giant leap to the Philippines. By now the Allies had three groups of airfields in western New Guinea from which an assault could be mounted. The Japanese still had remnants of five weak divisions scattered over the peninsula, but without supplies and ammunition they posed no serious threat. Australian troops went systematically about the task of mopping up.

Bibliography. J. Vader, New Guinea: The Tide Is Stemmed (1971); B. H. Liddell Hart, History of the Second World War (1971); and W. Manchester, American Caesar: Douglas MacArthur (1979).

NEW ORDER. Hitler's reorganization of Europe under German control. He expected his New Order to last for 1,000 years.

BACKGROUND. For the Allies 1942 was a year of dismay. The Germans were on the way to enclosing the entire Mediterranean as well as the Near East in a great vise. Hitler hoped to move farther eastward, establish contact with the Japanese, and bring the war to a successful conclusion. He had special plans for Europe, which he could reorganize in a New Order of the Greater German Reich. As master of Europe, he would control a self-sufficient, self-sustaining continent, secure inside and unconquerable from outside. No longer would the German people be a *Volk ohne Raum* ("a people without room"). A self-confident Teutonic *Herrenvolk,* a monolithic ruling class, would control Continental life from factories to schools to theaters.

CATEGORIES. Hitler split his New Order into several categories. First were the territories annexed and incorporated into the Third Reich. Among these areas subjected to Nazi coordination (*Gleichschaltung*) were Austria, the Sudetenland, Alsace-Lorraine, Memel, Danzig, Teschen, Eupen, Malmédy, Luxembourg, parts of Slovenia, and sections of East and West Prussia.

Next were two territories, Czechoslovakia and Poland, neither of which was incorporated into Germany but each of which was regarded as a distinct part of Greater Germany. The core of Czechoslovakia became an autonomous area known as the Protectorate of Bohemia-Moravia, which was controlled by a Reich Protector and designated for future colonization. Hitler's contempt for Poles was even greater than for Czechs. To him the Poles were the scum of the earth, a subspecies of mankind, fit only for the role of slaves. He incorporated the western parts of Poland into Greater Germany and set up the central provinces as the Government-General of Poland, run by a whiplash administration under Hans Frank (*q.v.*).

For the next group of countries, considered to be of strategic importance, Hitler sent personal satraps. He placed Occupied France and the British Channel Islands under German administrators.

Another category included countries under semi-civilian, supposedly autonomous, rule. Norway was placed under Reich Commissioner Josef Terboven, assisted by collaborationist Vidkun Quisling (*qq.v.*); and Holland under Artur von Seyss-Inquart (*q.v.*).

German commissioners ruled the Ostland and the Ukraine while Denmark was allowed to retain its own monarch and Parliament, but both under German control. The general pattern of control was repeated in the Balkans.

TREATMENT. Throughout this patchwork of annexed, occupied, and controlled satellite states roamed Nazi raiding squads to maintain order and to recruit labor for the voracious German war machine. Huge supplies of materials and money flowed from Hitler's New Order to Nazi Germany—workers from France and Belgium, foodstuffs from Denmark, oil from Rumania, coal and grain from Poland. Men, horses, and machinery were piled into trains and sent to the homeland. In one year alone the Germans confiscated by seizure, fines, and reparations, money and property amounting to more than $36 billion. It was plundering on a massive scale. For the Jews of Europe the New Order was literally a hell on earth. (*See* HOLOCAUST.)

Bibliography. E. Jäckel, *La France dans l'Europe d'Hitler* (1968); A. S. Milward, *The New Order and the French Economy* (1969); E. Lund, *A Girdle of Truth* (1970); S. Grant Duff, *A German Protectorate* (1970); V. Mastny, *The Czechs under Nazi Rule* (1970); and M. Berwicj, *The Third Reich* (1971).

NIEMOELLER, MARTIN (1892–   ). German submarine commander and pastor who became an outspoken critic of the Nazis.

Serving in World War I as a U-Boat commander, Niemoeller was awarded the *Pour le Mérite* medal for bravery. After the war he served as pastor of the wealthy Berlin-Dahlem Church from 1931 to 1937. As a nationalist he, at first, welcomed Hitler and the National Socialist regime, but soon became disillusioned when the *Fuehrer* began to insist on the supremacy of state over religion. Niemoeller gave sermons criticizing racialism, concentration camps, and other Nazi practices. "No more," he said, "are we ready to keep silent at man's behest when God commands us to speak. We must obey God rather than man!" An infuriated Hitler saw to it that Niemoeller was sent to Moabit Prison in Berlin. The verdict called for only eight months, which angered the *Fuehrer* because of its leniency.

After the war Niemoeller resumed his active church career, which was distinguished by a firm opposition to atomic armament.

Bibliography. M. Niemoeller, *Here I Stand* (Chicago, 1937).

NIGHT AND FOG DECREE (*NACHT UND NEBEL ERLASS*). Decree issued by Hitler on December 7, 1941, to maintain discipline in his New Order (*q.v.*).

The *Fuehrer* ordered that those who had "endangered German security" were not to be executed immediately but were to vanish without a trace into night and fog. Such persons were to be seized by the *SS* or the *Gestapo* (*qq.v.*) late at night, hustled away, and no word was to be given to their families. It is not known how many Europeans vanished from their homes in this manner. There were few known survivors.

NIMITZ, CHESTER WILLIAM (1885-1966). Commander-in-Chief of the U.S. Pacific Fleet and Pacific Ocean areas.

Nimitz was in his home in Washington listening to a symphony on the radio when he heard the news that Pearl Harbor (*q.v.*) had been attacked. At this time he was chief of the Bureau of Navigation. Within the next few days he was appointed to command the U.S Pacific Fleet with the rank of Admiral. His orders were to win the 85 million square miles of the Pacific back from the Japanese. While waiting for U.S. shipyards to turn out the vessels he needed, he built up his combat teams, led by Adms. William F. Halsey, Jr., Marc A. Mitscher, Raymond A. Spruance, Richmond K. Turner, and Thomas C. Kinkaid (*qq.v.*). He was quick to see that American weakness lay in the lack of forward repair stations and maintenance squadrons. When these squadrons came into existence, he was prepared to take the fight to the Japanese.

Nimitz then sent his carrier forces into action. On May 8, 1942, the world's first naval battle was fought in the air. It was judged an American victory, although many U.S. planes were shot down. In June 1942 his shrewd positioning of U.S. carriers enabled dive bombers to sink four Japanese carriers. This naval victory brought U.S.-Japanese naval forces to near parity. The Allies could now shift to the offensive in the Solomons and New Guinea areas.

In late 1943 Nimitz exploited the growing U.S. amphibious strength in the Central Pacific. His forces captured positions in the Gilberts, the Marshalls, the Marianas, and the Palaus. The Japanese Navy was gradually reduced to a shadow of its former size. In 1945 his forces captured Iwo Jima and Okinawa (*qq.v.*), as his carrier forces began to raid Japan itself. On September 2, 1945, aboard the battleship USS *Missouri* in Tokyo Bay, Nimitz signed the instrument of surrender as representative of the United States.

Bibliography. Although he had commanded more than 2,000 ships and a million men in World War II, Nimitz resolutely refused to write his memoirs. *See* E. P. Hoyt, *How They Won the War in the Pacific: Nimitz and His Admirals* (1970).

NOMURA, KICHISABURO (1877-1964). Japanese diplomat and Ambassador to Washington at the time of the Japanese attack on Pearl Harbor (*q.v.*).

Adm. Nomura was named Japanese Foreign Minister in September 1939, at the outbreak of the war in Europe. His major task was to adjust Japanese-American relations, which had been strained badly by Japanese activities in China. He was appointed Ambassador to the United States in November 1940. He had "heart-to-heart" talks with President Roosevelt on means of improving the relations between the two countries despite the unprecedented state of tension. Always considered a good friend of the United States, Nomura had many conferences with Roosevelt and Secretary of State Cordell Hull (*qq.v.*).

On December 7, 1941, Nomura and Saburo Kurusu, special envoy, walked into Hull's office a few minutes after the Japanese bombs started falling on Pearl Harbor. Hull excoriated the two Japanese representatives in an unusual confrontation.

After Pearl Harbor Nomura protested that he was as "shocked and surprised as anyone" when his country's planes began bombing the Hawaiian naval base at the very moment when he was talking peace in Washington.

"I must have been the worst-informed ambassador in history," he said repeatedly. "I told the American authorities then that I might be called back at any time, but that there would only be talk and more talk. I said I was certain that there would be no attack."

NORDEN BOMBSIGHT. Accurate optical device with gyrostabilized automatic pilot designed to maintain level flight during a bomb run.

Invented and named after Carl L. Norden, a civilian working for the U.S. Navy, the Norden bombsight was tested and improved in the 1930s. With it American airmen performed miracles of precision from 25,000 feet during the war. It was said that they could "drop a bomb into a pickle barrel" because of the device. Successful use of the Norden bombsight, however, depended on clear weather and undisturbed bomb runs. (*See also* SPERRY BOMBSIGHT.)

NORMANDY INVASION. Assault on the former province of Normandy on June 6, 1944, in the campaign for the liberation of France and the overthrow of Nazi Germany.

BACKGROUND. From the early days of the war Allied strategists planned on a major invasion of Fortress Europe (*q.v.*) which was under Nazi control. The only questions were where and when. Plans were discussed for assaults on: (1) northern Norway; (2) the Balkans, the soft underbelly (*q.v.*) of Europe; (3) southern France; and (4) Normandy. The Cotentin Peninsula of Normandy, the area surrounding Cherbourg, was finally selected as the target for *Operation Overlord* (*q.v.*).

PREPARATION. Southern England was transformed for the coming attack into a vast military encampment. The greatest invasion fleet of all time—battleships, transports, landing craft, destroyers, mine sweepers—was at anchor in the ports. The docks were piled high with war equipment. Tens of thousands of troops were bivouacked in the fields. Assembled were 150,000 men (with many more in reserve), 1,500 tanks, 5,300 ships and craft, and 12,000 planes.

American strategists had wanted to undertake the invasion fully a year earlier, but they had to wait until it was prepared in the minutest detail. Techniques were studied and refined in North Africa and Sicily, and new contrivances were prepared to facilitate the invasion. (*See MULBERRIES;* and *GOOSEBERRY.*)

STRATEGY. Allied aircraft were to land three airborne divisions in Normandy, strike hard at German defenses, smash railroads and bridges, and isolate the beach defenses. Then five divisions, two American, two British, and one Canadian, would land from the sea in a 60-mile stretch between Caen and Cherbourg. The plan was to land 107,000 troops, 14,000 vehicles, and 14,500 tons of supplies within the first 48 hours.

DECEPTION. Meanwhile, the Germans would be thrown off balance by a game of deception. In southeast England, close to Dover, the Allies set up a phantom "First Army Group," which seemed to be a huge concentration of troops and craft always in movement. A special radio network busily sent out false orders. This ghost army pinned down 19 Nazi divisions for six weeks after the invasion. Equally effective tactics were utilized elsewhere. (*See* CODE NAMES, ALLIED, *BODYGUARD* and *ZEPPELIN.*) All exits from England were sealed off as well as a 10-mile strip in southern England.

FORTRESS EUROPE. Hitler's defense plan was rigidly linear. Although German cities were being bombed into ruins, North Africa had been lost, and his troops in Italy pushed back to Rome, he still had 60 divisions in France. His 7th Army was in place to defend the Normandy and Brittany beaches. He concentrated heavy power at Normandy despite reports by his Naval Intelligence that the coast there was unsuitable for a landing. German propaganda had depicted Hitler's Atlantic Wall (*q.v.*) as impregnable, but actually Hitler did not have enough manpower to hold a continuous line of fortifications. To meet the expected invasion, Hitler called in Field Marshal Erwin Rommel (*q.v.*), who worked energetically in the spring of 1944 to strengthen defenses.

PRELIMINARIES. The softening-up process began in February 1944 when Allied bombers in massive raids struck at targets inside Germany. The missions were designed not only to weaken German industrial production but especially to cut down available oil. Then the bombers concentrated on targets from Dunkirk westward to Cherbourg on the French coastline. German commanders sensed that an invasion was imminent, but they had no idea where it would fall. They relied on intelligence agents and spies who were aware of the buildup but were confused by rumors planted by Allied intelligence. The Germans strengthened their coastline defenses with additional barbed-wire fences, pillbox emplacements, and formidable underwater obstructions.

ASSAULT. Shortly after midnight on June 6, 1944, while a huge fleet moved silently across the English Channel, a thousand Royal Air Force (*q.v.*) bombers unloaded deadly cargoes on German coastal defenses at Normandy. At daylight came another thousand USAAF (*see* UNITED STATES ARMY AIR FORCES) bombers. It was an awesome demonstration of coordinated air attack. Outnumbered 50 to 1, the battered *Luftwaffe* (*q.v.*) had already withdrawn to air bases in the Paris area.

The first troops to land were American parachutists of the U.S. 9th Air Force assigned to Utah Beach and Omaha Beach. Within four hours 13,000 American paratroopers were on French soil. Farther to the east the British 6th Airborne Division landed 5,300 paratroopers and infantrymen near Caen behind Gold, Juno, and Sword Beaches.

Just as the sun rose over the French coast the naval bombardment began, the greatest duel of sea against shore in history. Destroyers and cruisers pushed in to rake the beaches. Offshore, heavy battleships hurled thunderous volleys into the interior. Under the hail of air and naval fire, mine sweepers surged in to clear the waters and mark out channels.

Backed across the Channel was a jumble of 5,300 ships of every tonnage—warships and transports. The invaders came ashore in a steady stream along a 60-mile line. On they came to be greeted by machine-gun fire from the defenders. All that day and night men poured ashore—35,250 on Utah Beach, 34,250 at Omaha Beach, 83,115 in the British-Canadian sector.

Despite careful planning, it was hard going. Thousands of troops became seasick in the miserable weather on the choppy English Channel. Some of the tanks, which were equipped with flotation devices, sank as they tried to make their way ashore. Troops with heavy equipment drowned when they left their landing craft too soon and found themselves in water over their heads. The attempt to knock out beach defenses was not altogether successful: The men who came ashore were greeted with deadly machine-gun fire. The price was high, estimated at 10,274 casualties, including 2,132 dead.

GERMAN REACTION. The Germans had incredibly bad luck. Rommel decided on June 4, because the weather was foul, to return to Germany to celebrate his wife's birthday. Field Marshal Gerd von Rundstedt (*q.v.*), over-all commander in the west, and Gen. Alfred Jodl (*q.v.*), Chief of Staff, did not respond quickly to the alert. A half-dozen other German generals were absent from their coastal commands. When the attack came Hitler was asleep and no one dared awaken him. Not until two o'clock that afternoon was he informed. He dismissed it as another Dieppe-style raid (*see* DIEPPE RAID) and ordered von Rundstedt to throw the invaders back into the sea. It was far too late.

SIGNIFICANCE. By D-Day plus 11, exactly 487,653 men and 89,728 vehicles were ashore. It was obviously a tremendous military, political, and psychological success for the Allies. All services cooperated successfully, and the Allied position on the Continent was consolidated. The Allies could not be dislodged and they held the initiative. It was the beginning of the end for Hitler and the Third Reich.

Bibliography. D. D. Eisenhower, *Crusade in Europe* (1948); H. Speidel, *Invasion 1944: Rommel and the Normandy Campaign* (1950); C. Ryan, *The Longest Day* (1959); S.L.A. Marshall, *Night Drop: The American Air-borne Invasion of Normandy* (1962); P. Gray, *D-Day* (1970); and J. M. Stagg, *Forecast for Overlord* (1971).

NORSTAD, LAURIS (1907–   ). U.S. Army Air Forces officer.

In December 1941, when the Air Forces established its first intelligence school at Langley Field, Virginia, Norstad was selected to head it. In February 1942 Gen. Henry H. Arnold (*q.v.*), the commanding officer of the Army Air Forces, chose Norstad as his personal advisor.

In October 1942 Norstad was sent to North Africa to plan the strategy for the coming Allied invasion. In the summer of 1943 he planned the air operations that accompanied the invasions of Italy and Sicily. In December 1943 he was appointed director of all the Allied Air Forces in the Mediterranean. He held this post until August 1944, when he was recalled to Washington to become Chief of Staff of the 20th Air Force and Deputy Chief of Staff for the entire Army Air Forces. In this post he organized the devastating attacks on the Japanese home islands and the atomic bomb raids on Hiroshima and Nagasaki.

Six-feet tall, slim, and curly-haired, Norstad was characterized as "a philosopher in uniform." His superiors praised his mind as "a precision instrument." Gen. Dwight D. Eisenhower (*q.v.*) said: "Norstad so impressed me by his alertness, grasp of problems, and personality that I never thereafter lost sight of him. He was and is one of those rare men whose capacity knows no limit."

NORTH AFRICA, ALLIED LANDINGS IN. *See* TORCH.

NORTH AFRICA, CAMPAIGNS IN. Defeat of the Axis in a seesaw confrontation in North Africa.

BACKGROUND. On the fall of France in June 1940, Italy's Mussolini saw an opportunity to acquire a great Mediterranean empire at the expense of Britain. "England," he said, "will be beaten, inexorably beaten." He would send his forces smashing into Egypt, seize the Suez Canal, cut the British life line, and revive the glory of ancient Rome. He believed himself to be well prepared: He had 500,00 troops in North Africa, a powerful fleet operating from strategic bases, and air squadrons based in Libya.

The British still held the arc from Gibraltar-Malta-Suez, but their defenses seemed pitifully weak. They had a small guard at Gibraltar, several divisions in Egypt, two fleets—one at Alexandria and another at Malta, and about 250 antiquated planes. The fall of France complicated matters. French troops were withdrawn from the Middle East, leaving the precious oil fields there open to Axis assault. French naval bases in the Mediterranean were denied to the British. Gen. Archibald Wavell (*q.v.*) had only 36,000 men in Egypt, 27,000 in Palestine, 9,000 in the Sudan, 8,500 in Kenya, and 1,500 in British Somaliland, all with little heavy equipment or antitank armament. The prognosis for the British in North Africa was not good.

BATTLE OF THE WESTERN DESERT. On August 5, 1940, the Duke of Aosta led an army of 70,000, mostly native troops, in three columns against

British Somaliland at the southern entrance to the Red Sea. The outnumbered British garrison had no choice but to withdraw. Mussolini had his first "great conquest." Then, with bugles blowing, Marshal Rodolpho Graziani (*q.v.*) sent 250,000 Italians and native troops on a drive from Libya toward Egypt and the Suez Canal. He quickly captured Solum and Sidi Barrani as the British retreated to Mersa Matruh, the railhead of the line to Alexandria. Here he halted to await reinforcements.

Although hard-pressed in the homeland, Churchill dispatched forces from England, India, Australia, and New Zealand. The Royal Air Force (*q.v.*) plastered Italian airfields while torpedo bombers from the aircraft carrier *Illustrious* smashed the Italian fleet at Taranto in early November 1940. (*See* TARANTO, BATTLE OF.) British tanks then moved forward to inflict a defeat on the Italians at Sidi Barrani, taking 38,000 prisoners and huge supplies at a cost of only 400 casualties. Bardua, Tobruk, and Benghazi fell in rapid succession. Mussolini had sustained his first setback and his threat to Egypt was gone.

STRUGGLE FOR LIBYA. The Italian setback in North Africa was disappointing to Hitler, who regarded the Suez Canal as vital to his overall strategic plan. He ordered elite troops of his *Afrika Korps* (*q.v.*) to be sent to Libya. Wavell's army there had been depleted to supply an expeditionary force for Greece. (*See* GREECE, BATTLE FOR.) The Germans, under the brilliant leadership of Gen. Erwin Rommel (*q.v.*), made their first appearance in the desert campaign in March 1941. They took Benghazi and pushed eastward five miles across the Egyptian frontier. Isolated Tobruk remained in British hands and its defense became an epic in British military annals. (*See* TOBRUK, SIEGE OF.) Meanwhile, British naval and air forces struck at Axis supply lines. For the Allies an additional goal was to divert pressure from the new Russian Front.

BATTLE OF SIDI RESEGH. The second major British offensive in Libya, code named *Operation Crusader,* started on November 17, 1941, when the newly created British 8th Army (*q.v.*), led by Alan Cunningham (*q.v.*), pushed 75 miles and captured the stronghold of Sidi Resegh, only 10 miles from Tobruk. The bloody tank battle was inconclusive as British light tanks held off heavier German armored vehicles. British pilots destroyed 120 Axis planes in the accompanying air battle.

TOBRUK RELIEVED. The intensive tank battle continued for the rest of November as the initiative gradually passed to the British. Tobruk was relieved on December 10, 1941. By January 1942 Rommel's front in Libya was broken and the British ended their second drive into Libya at El Agheila, 400 miles to the west.

ROMMEL'S COUNTEROFFENSIVE. The tide of battle soon turned against the British. Churchill weakened his forces in North Africa by sending contingents to the Far East, while at the same time the Germans poured in reinforcements and supplies to help Rommel. The German commander used his 88-mm. guns (see ARTILLERY WEAPONS: GERMAN EIGHTY-EIGHT GUN) in telling effect against the British. Starting slowly, he took Benghazi in late January 1942. For the next few months there was a lull in the fighting. Then the Desert Fox struck again. On June 11, 1942, German *Panzers* destroyed 224 out of 300 British tanks. The British began a retreat back to Egypt, leaving a garrison of 33,000 at Tobruk. It was a strategic mistake. On June 21, 1942, Rommel captured the city with its entire defense force.

BRITISH RETREAT. Rommel struck at the retreating British and took an additional 6,000 prisoners at Mersa Matruh. To bring the 8th Army into condition to resume the offensive, the British decided to make a stand at El Alamein, less than 75 miles from Alexandria. Here the desert narrowed to a passage of 30 miles at a point where Rommel could not make his favorite encircling movements. The British would make a stand between the Mediterranean on one side and the swampy, impenetrable Quattara Depression on the other. Rommel struck in full strength on July 1, 1942, but the British lines held.

In August Gen. Claude Auckinleck (*q.v.*), who had made the stand at El Alamein, was replaced by Gen. Bernard Law Montgomery (*q.v.*). The latter immediately made plans for a massive counteroffensive. Rommel, too, prepared for a major confrontation. "We did not advance into Egypt," he said, "merely to be thrown out. We propose to hold what we have." In September 1942 Montgomery defeated Rommel at Alam el Halfa.

BATTLE OF EL ALAMEIN. On October 23, 1942, Montgomery opened his counteroffensive with a tremendous artillery barrage. In the great battle that followed until November 7, the Germans lines were broken and their armor pushed all the way back to El Agheila in Libya. The retreat continued until the end of the year. (*See* EL ALAMEIN, BATTLE OF.)

ANGLO-AMERICAN LANDING. On November 8, 1942, U.S. and British forces under command of Gen. Dwight D. Eisenhower (*q.v.*) landed in French North Africa. They quickly captured the French naval base at Oran and took Algiers. Within a few days the vast coastline in the west was in Allied hands. Rommel was now caught in a powerful pincers movement. (*See* TORCH.)

BATTLE OF MARETH LINE. Pursuing Rommel westward, the British 8th Army took Tripoli by January 1943. The German general proposed to make a stand at the Mareth Line (*q.v.*), 200 miles northwest of Tripoli. Montgomery attacked on January 20, 1943, from the front and on both flanks. There was bitter resistance, but the British won through and pushed on to Tunis and Bizerte. Rommel escaped the final collapse. Axis troops threw down their arms and surrendered. A quarter of a million hard-bitten desert veterans were captured, including what was left of the vaunted *Afrika Korps*.

SIGNIFICANCE. The North African campaigns ended in disaster for Hitler. For Mussolini it meant the end of his new Roman Empire. He had lost all his African colonies with an area ten times that of Italy and a population of more than 15 million.

At long last the Allies were on the march. Now they had bases for the coming assault on Italy and the Balkans. The entire Mediterranean could be used by Allied ships instead of the long sea route around the Cape of Good Hope. "The troops that came out of this campaign," said Eisenhower, "are going to be battle wise and technically efficient." A giant trap was closing in on Hitler and his Third Reich.

Bibliography. A. Moorehead, *The End in Africa* (1943); HMSO, *The Eighth Army* (1944); B. L. Montgomery, *El Alamein to the Sangro* (1948); D. Young, *Rommel* (1950); B. Maugham, *Tobruk and El Alamein* (1968); W. Haupt, *North African Campaign, 1940-1943* (1969); J. Strawson, *The Battle for North Africa* (1970); J. Coggins, *The Campaign for North Africa* (1980); B. Pitt, *The Crucible of War* (1968); and K. Sainsbury, *The North African Landings, 1942* (1980).

NORTH CAPE, BATTLE OF. Sea battle on December 26, 1943, between the German battle cruiser *Scharnhorst* and the British Home Fleet.

The engagement took place between the northernmost tip of Norway and Bear Island in the Arctic and resulted in the sinking of the German capital ship. (*See SCHARNHORST.*)

NORTH SEA DUCKS. German U-Boats unsuitable for war service in the Atlantic.

At the outbreak of war the Germans had a total strength of 56 U-Boats, of which 10 were not fully operational. Of these, 30 were called North Sea Ducks because they were not equipped for oceanic operations. (*See ATLANTIC, BATTLE OF THE.*)

NORWAY CAMPAIGN, 1940. *See* SCANDINAVIA, CAMPAIGNS IN.

NOVIKOV, ALEKSANDR (1900-1976). Commander of the Soviet Air Force during World War II and Marshal of the Soviet Union.

Novikov was in charge of all operations over Leningrad in 1942 when he was designated head of the Red Air Force. His main task was to supervise the recovery of Russian air power after the heavy losses suffered during the German invasion starting on June 22, 1941. In the opening days the Russian Air Force was practically decimated. Novikov did a remarkable job in reviving Russia's strength in the air at Stalingrad in 1942 (*see* STALINGRAD, BATTLE OF) and at Kursk in 1943.

NUREMBERG TRIALS. Public trials of 22 German principals before an International Military Tribunal at Nuremberg, Germany, from November 1945 to October 1946.

BACKGROUND. Long before the end of the war the Allies considered what treatment should be accorded to Hitler and the hierarchy of Nazi leaders. They were determined that the same mistake would not be made that was made after World War I when the Kaiser escaped to Holland and was never tried. An International War Crimes Commission was appointed for the task of examining material concerned with individual war crimes. In the last year of the war four powers, the United States, the Soviet Union, Great Britain, and France, agreed to hold a court at Nuremberg. Although special courts had been arranged in the past to judge political crimes by extraordinary authority, no such court had ever obtained universal recognition. There never had been an effective tribunal to punish the transgressor in major conflicts.

INDICTMENT. The four counts of the indictment were: 1, conspiracy to commit crimes alleged in other counts; 2, crimes against peace; 3, war crimes; and 4, crimes against humanity. Not all defendants were indicted on all counts. The defendants were charged with the death of 12 million men, women, and children. The death penalty was demanded for all the accused. In addition, the prosecution asked that a number of organizations of the Third Reich be declared criminal and that membership in them meant liability for the death penalty. All defendants were represented by counsel selected by themselves.

PROSECUTION. The trials opened on November 20, 1945, under the presidency of a British judge, Lord Justice Geoffrey Lawrence (later Lord Oaksey). The chief American prosecutor, Justice Robert H. Jackson (*q.v.*), denounced National Socialist despotism and its "mad gamble for domination" with what it believed to be an invincible war machine. He charged that it took a union of the combined forces of imperilled civilization in a united effort to destroy the German war machine. Other prosecutors spoke in similar vein.

There were altogether 403 open sessions of the tribunal. Thirty-three witnesses appeared for the prosecution and testified on crimes committed by the defendants. A large part of the evidence consisted of documents captured by Allied armies from German headquarters buildings. The prosecution made intensive efforts to bolster its case by use of documents originally written by defendants. The authenticity of this evidence was seldom challenged.

DEFENSE. Some 61 witnesses testified for the defendants (Robert Ley [*q.v.*] committed suicide in prison on October 25, 1945, and Martin Bormann was tried *in absentia* under provisions of the charter). A further 143 witnesses gave evidence for the defense by deposition.

VERDICTS. Of the prisoners present at the trial three, Hjalmar Schecht Franz von Papen (*qq.v.*), and Hans Fritsche were acquitted. The Soviet judge, Lt. Col. R. A. Rudenko, dissented strongly on acquittals. Several formations of the Third Reich were declared criminal: (1) the Leadership Corps of the Nazi

Party; (2) the *Schutzstaffel* (SS), the elite guard and defense echelon; (3) the *Sicherheitsdienst* (SD), the security service; and (4) the *Geheime Staatspolizei* (*Gestapo*) (*qq.v.*), the secret police. The court refrained from declaring guilty three other groups named in the indictment: (1) the Reich Cabinet; (2) the *Sturm Abteilung* (SA), the militia of the Nazi Party; and (3) the German High Command. These were considered to be legitimate and not criminal groups.

AFTERMATH. The Allied Control Council rejected all appeals for clemency as well as requests by Goering, Jodl, and Keitel that they be given the privilege of being shot as soldiers instead of hanged. A short time before he was to be executed, Goering committed suicide by biting on a vial of poison. The remaining prisoners sentenced to death were hanged at Nuremberg on October 16, 1946.

LEGALITY. The legality of the trial troubled many jurists who were disturbed by the *ex post facto* implications of the proceedings. Others defended the new and important judgment laid down: that the principle of international law, which under certain circumstances protects the representatives of a state, cannot be applied to acts that are condemned as criminal by international law. In effect, this was a new kind of judgment of the world's conscience. If the Nuremberg judgment be valid, individual rulers could no longer violate the tenets of decency in relations between peoples. The subject aroused intense difference of opinion, and arguments on it persist to the present day.

Following are lists of the judges, the prosecution, and the accused (*see* individual biographies), verdicts, and punishments:

THE INTERNATIONAL MILITARY TRIBUNAL

President	Lord Justice Geoffrey Lawrence
British alternate member	Mr. Justice William Norman Birkett
United States member	Mr. Francis Biddle
United States alternate member	Judge John J. Parker
French member	Professor Henri Donnedieu de Vabre
French alternate member	M. Robert Falco
Russian member	Maj. Gen. I. T. Nikitchenko
Russian alternate member	Lieut. Col. A. F. Volchkov

THE PROSECUTION

American	Mr. Justice Robert H. Jackson
	Mr. T. J. Dodd
	Brig. Gen. Telford Taylor
British	Sir Hartley Shawcross
	Sir David Maxwell-Fyfe
	Mr. G. D. Roberts
	Col. H. J. Phillimore
	Col. J.M.G. Griffith-Jones
	Maj. F. Elwyn Jones
	Mr. J. Harcourt Barrington

French	M. François de Menthon (served until January 14, 1946)
	M. Edgar Faure
	M. Auguste Champetier de Ribes
	M. Charles Dubost
Russian	Col. R. A. Rudenko
	Col. Y. V. Pokrovsky

THE ACCUSED

Hermann Goering	Reich marshal and Commander-in-Chief of the *Luftwaffe*
Rudolf Hess	Deputy to the *Fuehrer*; top party official
Joachim von Ribbentrop	Reich Foreign Minister
Wilhelm Keitel	Chief of the High Command of the armed forces
Ernst Kaltenbrunner	Chief of the Security Police and SD and head of the RSHA
Alfred Rosenberg	Party philosopher and Reich Minister for the eastern occupied area
Hans Frank	Governor-General of occupied Polish territory
Wilhelm Frick	Former Minister of the Interior; brought the German nation under the complete control of the NSDAP
Julius Streicher	Founder of the anti-Semitic hate sheet, *Der Stürmer*
Walther Funk	President of the Reichsbank, 1939
Hjalmar Schacht	Minister of Economics, 1934–1937; president of the Reichsbank, 1933–1939
Karl Doenitz	Supreme Commander of the Navy, 1943; German Chancellor, 1945
Erich Raeder	Supreme Commander of the Navy, 1928–1943
Baldur von Schirach	*Fuehrer* of the Hitler Youth
Fritz Sauckel	Plenipotentiary for Labor Allocation
Alfred Jodl	Chief of the Operations Staff of the armed forces, 1939–1945
Franz von Papen	Chancellor, 1932; Minister and Ambassador in Vienna, 1934–1938; Ambassador in Turkey, 1939–1944
Artur Seyss-Inquart	Minister of the Interior and Reich Governor of Austria following fall of Von Schuschnigg; Reich Commissioner for the occupied Netherlands, 1940–1945
Albert Speer	Minister of Armaments and War Production; Inspector General of Highways
Constantin von Neurath	Minister of Foreign Affairs, 1932–1938; Reich Protector of Bohemia and Moravia, 1939–1943
Hans Fritzsche	Head of the Radio Division of the Propaganda Ministry
Martin Bormann (*in absentia*)	Deputy *Fuehrer* after Hess's flight to England

THE ACCUSED (AGE)	VERDICT	PUNISHMENT
Hermann Goering (53)	Guilty on all four counts	Death
Rudolf Hess (52)	Guilty on counts 1 and 2	Life imprisonment
Joachim von Ribbentrop (53)	Guilty on all four counts	Death
Wilhelm Keitel (64)	Guilty on all four counts	Death
Ernst Kaltenbrunner (43)	Guilty on counts 3 and 4	Death
Alfred Rosenberg (53)	Guilty on all four counts	Death
Hans Frank (46)	Guilty on counts 3 and 4	Death
Wilhelm Frick (69)	Guilty on counts 2, 3, and 4	Death
Julius Streicher (61)	Guilty on count 4	Death
Walther Funk (56)	Guilty on counts 2, 3, and 4	Life imprisonment
Hjalmar Schacht (69)	Not guilty	Acquitted
Karl Doenitz (55)	Guilty on counts 2 and 3	Ten years

Erich Raeder (70)	Guilty on counts 2, 3, and 4	Life imprisonment
Baldur von Schirach (39)	Guilty on count 4	Twenty years
Fritz Sauckel (51)	Guilty on counts 2 and 4	Death
Alfred Jodl (56)	Guilty on all four counts	Death
Franz von Papen (66)	Not guilty	Acquitted
Artur Seyss-Inquart (54)	Guilty on counts 2, 3, and 4	Death
Albert Speer (41)	Guilty on counts 3 and 4	Twenty years
Constantin von Neurath (73)	Guilty on all four counts	Fifteen years
Hans Fritzsche (46)	Not guilty	Acquitted
Martin Bormann (45; *in absentia*)	Guilty on counts 3 and 4	Death

Extracts from the Nuremburg Trials' Judgments
October 1, 1946

GOERING: From the moment he joined the party in 1922 and took command of the streetfighting organization, the S.A., Goering was the adviser, the active agent of Hitler and one of the prime leaders of the Nazi movement. As Hitler's political deputy he was largely instrumental in bringing the National Socialists to power in 1933, and was charged with consolidating this power and expanding German might. He developed the *Gestapo* and created the first concentration camps, relinquishing them to Himmler in 1934; conducted the Roehm purge in that year and engineered the sordid proceedings which resulted in the removal of von Blomberg and von Fritsch from the Army. . . .

Goering commanded the *Luftwaffe* in the attack on Poland and throughout the aggressive wars which followed. . . . The record is filled with Goering's admissions of his complicity in the use of slave labor. . . .

Goering persecuted the Jews, particularly after the November 1938 riots. . . .

There is nothing to be said in mitigation. . . . His guilt is unique in its enormity. The record discloses no excuse for this man.

VERDICT: GUILTY on all 4 counts.

SENTENCE: Death by hanging.

HESS: . . . As deputy to the *Fuehrer*, Hess was the top man in the Nazi party with responsibility for handling all party matters and authority to make decisions in Hitler's name on all questions of party leadership. . . . Hess was an informed and willing participant in German aggression against Austria, Czechoslovakia, and Poland. . . .

That Hess acts in an abnormal manner, suffers from loss of memory, and has mentally deteriorated during this trial, may be true. But there is nothing to show that he does not realize the nature of the charges against him, or is incapable of defending himself. He was ably represented at the trial by counsel, appointed for that purpose by the Tribunal. There is no suggestion that Hess was not completely sane when the acts charged against him were committed.

VERDICT: GUILTY on counts 1 and 2.

SENTENCE: Life imprisonment.

ROSENBERG: Recognized as the party's ideologist, he developed and spread Nazi doctrines in the newspapers *Völkischer Beobachter* and *N. S. Monatshefte*, which he edited, and in the numerous books he wrote. . . .

Rosenberg bears a major responsibility for the formulation and execution of occupation policies in the Occupied Eastern territories. . . . On July 17, 1941, Hitler appointed Rosenberg *Reich* Minister of the Eastern Occupied Territories, and publicly charged him with responsibility for civil administration. . . . He helped to formulate the policies of Germanization, exploitation, forced labor, extermination of Jews and opponents of Nazi rule, and he set up an administration which carried them out. . . . His subordinates engaged in mass killings of Jews, and his civil administrators considered that cleansing the Eastern Occupied Territories of Jews was necessary. . . . His signature of approval appears on the order of June 14, 1941, for the *Heu Aktion*, the apprehension of 40,000 to 50,000 youths, aged 10–14, for shipment to the Reich. . . .

VERDICT: GUILTY on all 4 counts.

SENTENCE: Death by hanging.

RIBBENTROP: Ribbentrop was not present at the Hossbach Conference held on November 5, 1937, but on January 2, 1938, while ambassador to England, he sent a memorandum to Hitler indicating his opinion that a change in the *status quo* in the East in the German sense could only be carried out by force and suggesting methods to prevent England and France from intervening in a European war fought to bring about such a change. . . . Ribbentrop participated in the aggressive plans against Czechoslovakia. . . .

Ribbentrop played a particularly significant role in the diplomatic activity which led up to the attack on Poland. He participated in a conference held on August 12, 1939, for the purpose of obtaining Italian support if the attack should lead to a general European war. . . .

He played an important part in Hitler's "final solution" of the Jewish question. In September 1942 he ordered the German diplomatic representatives accredited to various satellites to hasten deportation of the Jews to the East. . . . It was because Hitler's policy and plans coincided with his own ideas that Ribbentrop served him so willingly to the end.

VERDICT: GUILTY on all 4 counts.

SENTENCE: Death by hanging.

Bibliography. P. D. Mendelssohn, *The Nuremberg Documents* (1946); G. M. Gilbert, *Nuremberg Diary* (1947); D. M. Fyfe (ed.), *War Crimes Trials* (1948); and W. J. Bosch, *Judgment on Nuremberg* (1969).

"NUTS!" INCIDENT.

Reply of Gen. Anthony Clement McAuliffe to a German demand for surrender on December 21, 1944. (*See* BASTOGNE; BULGE, BATTLE OF THE; and McAULIFFE, ANTHONY CLEMENT.)

NYE, ARCHIBALD (1895–1967). British Army officer.

In 1940 Nye was promoted from Brigade Commander to Director of Staff Duties. He was then appointed Deputy Chief of the Imperial General Staff (Deputy CIGS), at 45 the youngest vice-chief in the history of the British Army. He served in this post as assistant to Field Marshal Alan Brooke (*q.v.*) throughout the war. He accompanied Anthony Eden (*q.v.*) to the Moscow Conference (*q.v.*) of foreign ministers in late October 1943. He was highly regarded by Churchill.

Nye was tall, mustached, soft-spoken, and popular with his men. With no family or political backing, without public school or Sandhurst training, he was one of the few to rise from the ranks to a military position of importance.

O

OBOE. Night navigational aid used by the Allied Bomber Command.

More successful as a navigational aid than *Gee,* which it succeeded, *Oboe* was a British device based on German models. A control station in Britain sent out a directional beam for the *Oboe*-equipped bomber, and tracked the plane by radar. The receiver-equipped plane flew along the end of this predetermined beam sent out by the transmitter. In effect, it was very much like a model plane flying in an arc at the end of a wire. When the plane equipped with *Oboe* met the point at which a signal intercepted the curve-flight beam, the aircraft was over the target and could release its bombs.

As the radar beam did not conform to the curvature of the earth, *Oboe* had limited range. It helped cause tremendous damage to German cities especially in the later stages of the war. (*See GEE;* and RADAR, WARTIME.)

ODESSA. Organization for *SS* members.

Organized shortly after the end of the war as a charitable institution for former *SS* (*q.v.*) members, Odessa was used to help many to escape Allied courts for war crimes.

OFFICE OF SCIENTIFIC RESEARCH AND DEVELOPMENT (OSRD). American agency charged with mobilization of the scientific resources of the nation.

The OSRD, established on June 28, 1941 under the direction of Dr. Vannevar Bush (*q.v.*), combined the facilities of the National Defense Research Committee and the Committee on Medical Research. During the war it let out contracts for the development of the proximity fuze (*q.v.*) and the atomic bomb (*see* MANHATTAN PROJECT).

OFFICE OF STRATEGIC SERVICES (OSS). Secret U.S. intelligence agency from 1942 to 1945 designed to obtain information about enemy nations and to sabotage their war potential and morale.

FORMATION. The OSS was created by executive order of President Roosevelt on June 13, 1942. He appointed William Joseph Donovan (*q.v.*) as its first and only director. The secret organization was charged with the task "of providing an intelligence service working behind enemy lines, sabotage, morale subversion, guerrilla organization, and aid to partisan resistance." (*See* ESPIONAGE.) "Whether we like it or not," said Donovan later in advocating its continuance after World War II, "we have many enemies in the world, and we must know exactly what they are doing." Although the "cloak-and-dagger agents" of the OSS received much publicity, a large part of its valuable work was done by the research and analysis section.

OPERATIONS. In the three years of its existence, the OSS employed 12,000 agents and spent $135 million on its activities. It had nearly 30,000 persons around the world on its roster. Representatives went into North Africa, Italy, occupied France, and Germany to send to home base reports on troop movements, bomb damage, sabotage, and resistance. There were scores of incidents in which OSS agents outwitted the enemy or caused him much damage. A full six months before the fall of Rome on June 4, 1944, OSS men infiltrated the city and prepared the way for its capture. In early 1944 the OSS sent its agents into southern France to set up 28 active radio stations operating before D-Day (*q.v.*).

OSS operatives mapped most of the French Mediterranean coast, and sent to London information on the location, trajectory, and range of 20 German batteries on each side of Marseilles, as well as the exact location of German observation posts. Working together with British agents, OSS men were responsible for the sinking of the 17,000-ton German troopship *Donau* in late December 1944, which prevented German reinforcements from reaching the Battle of the Bulge. (*See* BULGE, BATTLE OF THE.) These and other exploits of the intelligence and sabotage network undoubtedly played a role in the defeat of the Axis.

TERMINATION. On October 1, 1945, President Harry S Truman (*q.v.*) terminated the OSS by executive order. He transferred its research and analysis branch to the Department of State and the remainder of its units to the War Department. Donovan and others called for an independent intelligence agency with a civilian at its head to counter global Soviet activities and to take the offensive on the psychological front. Many functions of the OSS were later assumed by the Central Intelligence Agency (CIA.)

Bibliography. S. Alsop and T. Braden, *Sub Rosa: The O.S.S. and American Espionage* (1946); and H. H. Smith, *OSS: The Secret History of America's First Central Intelligence Agency* (1972).

OFFICE OF WAR INFORMATION (OWI). Washington agency dedicated to the task of gathering facts and figures to bolster the Allied war effort.

FORMATION. When President Roosevelt set up the Office of Strategic Services (OSS) (*q.v.*) on June 13, 1942, he also called for organization of a separate Office of War Information (OWI). Its purpose was to conduct political warfare "to reduce the cost of physical battle."

DOMESTIC BRANCH. The domestic branch was headed by journalist Elmer Davis (*q.v.*). It was his responsibility to provide war information to the American public.

OVERSEAS BRANCH. A London unit of the OWI was established in July 1942 under the direction of Robert E. Sherwood, the playwright. He worked with the OWI's British counterpart, the British Political Warfare Executive (PWE). Both agencies sent code messages to guerrillas inside the occupied countries with information on effective sabotage. To lower enemy morale OWI agents dropped millions of printed messages and photographs showing damage done to German cities by Allied bombings.

In 1943 Roosevelt ordered all propaganda outside the U.S. mainland to be under OWI control. By 1945 it was sending throughout the world more than 4,000 radio broadcasts in 45 languages each week.

OFFICES, AMERICAN WAR. Series of offices set up in the United States expressly for the civilian war front.

Office for Emergency Management (OEM). Established in 1940 inside the Executive Office of the President to coordinate and direct all emergency agencies.

Office of Civilian Defense (OCD). Agency set up in May 1941 to provide for cooperation with state and local governments for protection of the civilian population during emergencies. The initial director was Mayor Fiorello H. La Guardia of New York City, with Eleanor Roosevelt as assistant director.

Office of Defense Transportation (ODT). Organized in December 1941 to co-ordinate all forms of transportation.

Office of Economic Stabilization (OES). Agency inside the Office for Emergency Management, formed in October 1942, to stabilize wages and control living costs. The first Director was James F. Byrnes (*q.v.*), former Justice of the U.S. Supreme Court, who became Director of the Office of War Mobilization in May 1943.

Office of Price Administration (OPA). Set up as an independent agency in January 1942 with functions of rationing, price control, and rent control. Its first Director was Leon Henderson.

Office of Production Management (OPM). Agency for co-ordination of national defense purchases, industrial production, materials, and small business. The Director was William S. Knudsen (*q.v.*).

Office of Scientific Research and Development (OSRD). Agency responsible for the development of new equipment and war weapons. Its director was Dr. Vannevar Bush. This unit developed the proximity fuze (*q.v.*) and the atomic bomb. (*See* MANHATTAN PROJECT.)

Office of Strategic Services (OSS). Agency devoted to the collection and analysis of foreign information and charged with sabotaging enemy war potential and morale. Its director was Col. William J. "Wild Bill" Donovan (*q.v.*). (*See* OFFICE OF STRATEGIC SERVICES [OSS].)

Office of the Coordinator of Inter-American Affairs (OCIA). Agency devoted to relations with Latin America with special attention to lessening Axis influence there. Its first director was Nelson A. Rockefeller.

Office of War Information (OWI). Set up in June 1942, the OWI was authorized to direct war propaganda and control the flow of official information. It was headed by Elmer Davis (*q.v.*), the popular broadcaster. (*See* OFFICE OF WAR INFORMATION [OWI].)

Office of War Mobilization (OWM). Agency authorized to allocate civilian manpower and resources. Headed by James F. Byrnes (*q.v.*), in 1944 it was converted into the Office of War Mobilization and Reconversion.

OKH. *Oberkommando des Heeres.* German Army High Command.

OKINAWA, BATTLE FOR. Allied invasion of the final island base on the doorstep of Japan from April 1 to June 22, 1945. This was the last and costliest amphibious operation in the Central Pacific campaign.

LOCATION. While Japanese resisted fiercely in their fortified caves in the battle of Iwo Jima (*q.v.*), Allied strategists turned to another target closer to Tokyo. The main island of the southern part of the Ryuku Archipelago, malaria-ridden Okinawa was just 362 miles southwest of the home island of Kyushu. The Japanese regarded it as an integral part of Japan. It dominated the East China Sea and the Chinese coast from Foochow to Korea. It sat astride Japan's sea lanes to the supply-rich East Indies, already endangered by American occupation of the Philippines.

Okinawa was 67 miles long and 20 miles wide, its terrain cut up in a maze of ridges, cliffs, and limestone caves. The Japanese strengthened this already rugged natural defense with an ingenious system of interlocking tunnels, pillboxes, concrete blockhouses, and caves. They sent 77,000 combat troops and 20,000 service troops, to the island, later augmented by additional manpower, as well as 500 artillery guns. The garrison was expected to fight until the last man died.

For Americans, too, Okinawa was of prime strategic importance. They set aside an assault force of three marine and four army divisions, about 170,000 combat troops plus 115,000 service troops. They were attracted by airfield sites on the island which could handle up to 5,000 aircraft. Because of the large size of the island, the invaders would not be subject, as at Iwo Jima, to enfilading fire on one or two heavily defended beaches.

PREPARATIONS. On March 22, 1945, elements of the U.S. 5th Fleet began an intensive bombardment of Okinawa and the Ryukus. At the same time a force of *B-29s* stationed on Iwo Jima attacked enemy bases in the Kyushus. During the next week U.S. warships fired 27,000 shells of five inches or larger at Okinawa. At the same time British warships struck at the Sakishimas, the southernmost group of the Ryukus. Under cover of naval fire a preliminary landing force of the 77th Division landed on the Kerama Rotto group of islands on March 26, 1945, to set up an advance base.

Offshore lay the greatest invasion fleet ever assembled in the Pacific. There were 1,300 warships of all kinds and sizes and aboard them were more than 180,000 combat troops. This was the armada attacked by *kamikazes (q.v.).*

ASSAULT. Invasion of Okinawa began on Easter Sunday, April 1, 1945. At first the Japanese defenders were thrown into confusion by a series of feints against the southern tip and east coast. Surprisingly, the Japanese offered little resistance. U.S. troops swarmed ashore and made the landing beaches secure in the face of only sporadic defensive fire. Supplies came pouring in a seemingly endless movement.

Pushing from the coral beachheads up the slopes into the interior, U.S. Marines headed toward the mountainous terrain in the north against only slight resistance, while others moved across the island to the east coast. By the end of the first week the island was cut into two, and the central third was firmly in American hands. In the 85 square miles of the south, protected by a little "Siegfried Line" *(q.v.)* of blockhouses, pillboxes, and machine-gun nests, the Japanese elected to make their stand. Meanwhile, marines cleared the northern tip of the island and U.S. reinforcements poured in.

AIR AND NAVAL BATTLE. On April 6 the Japanese made a desperate attack on the invasion fleet assembled off Okinawa. More than 350 bombers and an equal number of *kamikaze* planes attacked the invasion fleet, but they were not able to cripple it. The next day U.S. planes located the Japanese Fleet and a carrier attack was immediately ordered.

The Japanese battleship *Yamato* was hit by bombs and 12 torpedoes and sank with the loss of nearly 3,000 seamen. Like the *Tirpitz (q.v.),* it never had a chance to fire its big guns at enemy battleships. Its fate gave further indication that the day of the battleship was past.

VICTORY ASHORE. After a stalemate of nearly two weeks, three U.S. divisions stormed the Japanese stronghold in the south. Screened by a heavy bombardment from the sea and a great umbrella of planes, Americans moved into one of the bloodiest battles of the war. Japanese fought from caves, pillboxes, even burial vaults, and had to be flushed out of fortified positions by flame throwers and demolition experts. Gains were reckoned by yards. It was mid-May before Americans broke into the suburbs of Naha, the western pivot of the Japanese position. On May 21, 1945, U.S. Marines took strategic Sugar Loaf Hill and Conical Hill. Three weeks later they captured Naha and its airfield. Japanese defenders were now reduced to 15,000 holding out in hills and caves.

SUICIDES. On the morning of June 22, 1945, Lt. Gen. Mitsuru Ushijima (*q.v.*), commander of the Japanese forces on Okinawa, and Lt. Gen. Isama Cho, dressed themselves in full uniform, with medals and insignia of rank, and went to a narrow ledge before their cave headquarters. Kneeling on a white sheet, symbol of death, and facing in the direction of the Imperial Palace of Tokyo, the two generals commited *seppuku* ("honorable suicide") by ripping open their bowels, after which a lieutenant struck off their heads. (*See HĀRĀ-KĪRI.*)

Simultaneously, groups of Japanese leaped to their deaths from the cliffs. Transfixed Americans watched the slaughter as naked Japanese ran out of their caves and either slit their throats, blew themselves up with grenades, or jumped off the cliffs. Others sought death in frenzied *banzai* charges (*q.v.*).

CASUALTIES. More than half a million men were involved in the fighting. On Okinawa the Japanese lost 109,629 killed and 7,871 taken prisoner. For the Americans it was the costliest of all Pacific engagements—12,520 killed and 36,631 wounded, more than twice the casualty rate of Iwo Jima.*

SIGNIFICANCE. It was a momentous victory for the Allies. All Japanese positions to the south were now cut off from the homeland. The Japanese situation in China, Burma, and the Netherlands East Indies now became untenable. Okinawa was set up as the final base for the invasion of Japan itself. Target date was November 1945, but the expected invasion never took place. (*See* MANHATTAN PROJECT; HIROSHIMA; and NAGASAKI.)

Bibliography. P. D. Carleton, *The Conquest of Okinawa* (1947); R. E. Appleman *et al., Okinawa: The Last Battle* (1948); and C. S. Nichols and H. I. Shaw Jr., *Okinawa: Victory in the Pacific;* and J. W. Belote and M. Williams, *Typhoon of Steel: The Battle for Okinawa* (1970).

OKW. *Oberkommando der Wehrmacht.* German High Command of the Armed Forces.

OLBRICHT, FRIEDRICH (1888–1944). German General and leader in the conspiracy against Hitler.

---

*All casualty losses here, as elsewhere, are approximate. Authorities differ widely on exact figures.

Olbricht served with his infantry division at the start of the war. In 1940 he was named Chief of the General Staff of the Army High Command. In 1943 he was appointed Deputy Commander of the Reserve Army. The latter post brought him to the War Office in the Bendlerstrasse in Berlin.

Alienated by Hitler's behavior, Olbricht entered the conspiracy against him. On July 15, 1944, the date originally set for the attempt, he ordered the troops in Berlin on a forced march as an "exercise." He was reprimanded by his superiors, but his part in the plot was not recognized at the time. When the bomb placed by Lt. Col. Claus Schenck Graf von Stauffenberg (*see* JULY PLOT) exploded on July 20, 1944, Olbricht gave the signal in the Bendlerstrasse to arrest Gen. Friedrich Fromm (*q.v.*). When it became known that Hitler was alive, Fromm turned the tables and arrested Olbricht. Along with Stauffenberg, Olbricht was shot by a firing squad.

Partially bald, thin-lipped, and bespectacled, Olbricht was an officer of the old school who believed the Nazi regime to be a disgrace to his Fatherland. A deeply religious man, he wagered his life to put an end to Nazism, and lost.

OMAHA BEACH. Along with Utah Beach (*q.v.*), the second main area in Normandy where the Americans stormed ashore on June 6, 1944.

American landings on Utah Beach, as well as those on Gold, Juno, and Sword Beaches (*q.v.*) by combined British-Canadian forces, went well, but there was stiff opposition at Omaha Beach. Germans hit the invaders with concentrated fury. The landing site itself gave little protection, for a concave strip of sand 50 to 300 yards wide ended in a steeply rising bluff, strongly fortified by the Germans. The beach exits were heavily mined. U.S. troops stormed fortified bluffs, and hugged the sand, while shrinking from the withering gunfire. Others huddled miserably under the sea wall. Casualties were high. Twenty-seven of 29 tanks were swamped before they could reach shore.

The landings had started too far offshore, as a result of which many craft sank while others went off course. Word soon came to land closer to the beaches. After a day of fighting 34,250 Americans were ashore at Omaha Beach. (*See* NORMANDY INVASION.)

OP-16-FE. Division of Naval Intelligence in Washington concerned with operations against Japan.

Lt. Commander Charles N. Spinks, a language specialist who had served in Japan until shortly before Pearl Harbor, was in charge of the Japanese desk at OP-16-FE in April 1943 when an American monitoring station in the Pacific intercepted a top-secret message from the Japanese. The incident led to the death of Adm. Isoruku Yamamoto (*q.v.*), who was shot down in his plane by American pilots.

OPEN CITIES. Public declaration by local authorities that a city was "open," that is, unarmed and undefended, as a means of saving it from enemy attack and possible destruction.

BACKGROUND. The open city declaration was a part of the attempt in modern times to devise a code calling for an absolute standard of humanity in warfare. But while civilized opinion grew more exacting, techniques of warfare became more murderous. Attempts to humanize warfare were made in the Geneva Conventions (1864 and 1906) and embodied in codes accepted at the Hague Conventions (1899 and 1907). Among the regulations were those concerned with prisoners of war (*q.v.*), wounded, and non-combatants. Belligerents were expected not "to attack or bombard towns, villages, habitations, or buildings which are not defended." The open-city concept, which had a long tradition behind it, thus became one of the so-called rules of war.

WORLD WAR II. At the opening of the war, Hitler ordered the bombing of Warsaw when word came that its inhabitants were determined to resist. (*See* WARSAW, BOMBING OF.) In early May 1940 the Dutch declared Rotterdam an open city, but Hitler, nevertheless, ordered a massive bombardment of its center. (*See* ROTTERDAM, BOMBING OF.) This attack set a standard for the rest of the war—and both sides paid little attention to open-city declarations.

Air power brought a new dimension to the war. Large cities were considered to be legitimate targets for bombing because they were centers of war production. The *Luftwaffe* (*q.v.*) struck hard at London (1940) (*see* BRITAIN, BATTLE OF), Coventry (1940), and Belgrade (1941) (*qq.v.*). In turn, the British Royal Air Force (*q.v.*), later assisted by Americans, hit Cologne (1942), Hamburg (1943) and Dresden (1945) (*qq.v.*). By the end of the war virtually all major German cities were under concentrated Allied air assault.

Two major cities, especially, escaped the holocaust from the air—Paris, due in part to Hitler's conception of himself as an artist; and Rome, the center of Catholic Christendom. On the other hand, the retreating Germans severely damaged the magnificent Italian city of Florence in 1944.

Bibliography. J. B. Scott (ed.), *The Hague Conventions and Declarations of 1899 and 1907* (1918).

OPPENHEIMER, JULIUS ROBERT (1904–1967). American physicist regarded as "father of the atomic bomb."

Because of his remarkable work in nuclear physics, Oppenheimer was selected by Brig. Gen. Leslie R. Groves (*q.v.*) to head the critical Manhattan Project (*q.v.*) at Los Alamos, New Mexico. The appointment was made despite the qualms of Army Counter-Intelligence over Oppenheimer's past associations, which included liberal, left-wing, and Communist individuals. To recruit a staff, he traveled all over the country and gathered top-notch physicists and other scientists who eventually numbered nearly 4,000. The staff lived in hastily built housing at Los Alamos under quasi-military conditions. Included among the co-workers were such brilliant physicists as Niels Bohr and Enrico Fermi (*qq.v.*).

For two years Oppenheimer and his staff worked under severe tension and at breakneck speed to construct the bomb. Oppenheimer's weight dropped to

115 pounds from the whiplash, but his genius in administration for handling a sensitive group of colleagues was instrumental in the final success of the project. (*See* HIROSHIMA; and NAGASAKI.)

THE OPPENHEIMER CASE. In 1954 Oppenheimer was relieved of his various advisory posts because of past associations and his reluctance to work on the hydrogen bomb. President Dwight D. Eisenhower ordered a "blank wall" to be erected between Oppenheimer and all government secrets. A special board of the Atomic Energy Commission found him to be a security risk although a "loyal citizen." He was charged with not taking the security system seriously enough; with exercising an "arrogant" judgment on the loyalty and reliability of other citizens; and with showing a lack of enthusiasm for the hydrogen bomb program. He was publicly rehabilitated in 1963 when the Atomic Energy Commission made him the recipient of the Fermi Award for his contributions to theoretical physics and administrative leadership.

Oppenheimer aroused strong convictions among both defenders and critics. Defenders spoke of his genius and deplored the branding as a security risk. Critics denounced him for overweening arrogance and "fundamental defects in his character." Secretary of War Henry Stimson (*q.v.*) stated: "The development of the bomb itself has been largely due to his genius and the inspiration and leadership he has given to his associates."

Bibliography. J. R. Oppenheimer, *Science and the Common Understanding* (1954); *The Open Mind* (1955); and *Some Reflections on Science and Culture* (1960). See also R. Jungk, *Brighter Than A Thousand Suns* (1958).

ORADOUR-SUR-GLANS. French village, scene of a tragic incident in 1944.

BACKGROUND. In both world wars German reprisal methods caused shock and resentment in Allied countries. In World War II the German military was infuriated by the activities of guerrillas throughout Europe. (*See* RESISTANCE MOVEMENTS.) In France fighting was serious between the *Maquisards* (*see MAQUIS*) and the Germans, especially in a village called Oradour-sur-Vayres. German authorities confused this village with Oradour-sur-Glans, which was in the department of Haute-Vienne, 12 miles southwest of Limoges. An order went out mistakenly to burn Oradour-sur-Glans on the excuse that an arms dump had been found there.

ATROCITY. On June 10, 1944, a detail of trucks bearing German *Waffen-SS* (*q.v.*) troops of the division *Der Fuehrer* came roaring into the center of Oradour-sur-Glans. All the men of the town were brought to a barn in batches of 20 and slaughtered. After all males were killed, women and children were herded into the church, the doors of which were locked after a large case of explosives was deposited inside. The case exploded within minutes and soon the building was in flames. The roof collapsed on the screaming victims.

Meanwhile, *SS* troops drenched all the rest of the houses and barns with incendiary materials and the entire village began to burn. Those who tried to escape from the flames were riddled with bullets. Estimates vary, but it is believed that from 650 to 800 people perished. Only seven escaped, including several who hid in a well and another who remained hidden in a hedge for several days.

AFTERMATH. The villagers of Oradour-sur-Glans were innocent of any anti-German behavior. No attacks on German soldiers had taken place there. No cache of weapons was ever discovered. Six days later the people of Limoges were summoned by their Bishop to a memorial service in the cathedral, in which the Bishop bitterly condemned the atrocity. Thousands of mourners attended the service, which was interrupted when time bombs, set by Vichy militia, were discovered in the crypt of the cathedral.

Exactly two years earlier, on June 10, 1942, the Germans had leveled the small village of Lidice in Czechoslovakia in another reprisal action. (*See* LIDICE.) Other villages in Soviet Russia, Poland, Greece, and Yugoslavia suffered similar terror tactics.

Bibliography. F. Delage, *Oradour, Ville Martyr* (1945); and J. Kruuse, *Madness at Oradour* (1969).

ORAN NAVAL ENCOUNTER. Code or cover name *Catapult.* Attack by a British task force in the summer of 1940 on French fleet units that had fled to the French North African port of Oran.

BACKGROUND. Because the British Fleet was spread throughout the Mediterranean and the German naval arm was still in a stage of full-scale preparation, the naval potential of France and Italy took on added importance at the beginning of the war. The British Admiralty was certain that it could deal with Italians later despite their speedy warships. But the disposition of the French fleet became a matter of prime importance. If Hitler could win control of French naval forces, he could swing the balance in the Mediterranean in favor of the Axis.

On July 3, 1940, a few days after the armistice between France and Germany at Compiègne (*q.v.*), the British took over the greater part of the French fleet lying in Portsmouth and Plymouth. Included were 2 battleships, 2 light cruisers, several submarines among which was the large *Surcouf,* 8 destroyers, and approximately 200 smaller craft such as mine sweepers and antisubmarine boats. The crews either joined the Royal Navy or returned to France.

Additional French warships at Alexandria were immobilized by a strong British battle fleet. According to the armistice, all French vessels were to be interned, and Hitler had promised not to make use of them. The *Fuehrer's* word was worthless. The Admiralty pondered what to do about the French war vessels.

TARGET. Important elements of the French fleet lay at anchor at Oran, a fortified Algerian seaport, and its adjacent military port of Mers-el-Kebir on the northern African shore of Morocco. Two of the finest vessels of the French fleet, the *Dunquerque* and the *Strasbourg,* modern battle cruisers, were at anchor there, as well as two battleships, several light cruisers, and a number of destroyers and submarines.

CONFRONTATION. Churchill hoped to settle matters at Oran without resistance or bloodshed. On July 3, 1940, a British task force composed of battleships, cruisers, and escort vessels, steamed into a position off Oran. In command was Vice-Adm. James F. Somerville (*q.v.*), one of Britain's oldest naval salts known for his aggressiveness. Somerville sent an officer to consult with Vice-Adm. Marcel B. Gensoul, the French commander. The parlays continued all day. The British offered several alternatives: (1) The French could join the British against the Axis; (2) Gensoul could sail his ships to a British port where his crews would be repatriated and his ships restored to France after the war; or (3) he could move to the British West Indies where his vessels would be either interned or entrusted to American care until the end of hostilities.

Gensoul refused to comply and announced his intention of fighting. Word was flashed back to London and the Admiralty ordered Somerville to complete his mission before darkness fell.

ACTION. At 5:50 P.M. British warships opened fire with deadly efficiency. A blaze of salvoes exploded in the midst of the French fleet. The attack, lasting 10 minutes, was followed by bombing from naval aircraft based on the carrier *Ark Royal* (*q.v.*).

While this action was being fought the battle cruiser *Strasbourg* managed to slip out of the harbor in an effort to reach Vichy-held Toulon or a North African port. The damaged vessel plus several other smaller ships proceeded to Toulon although she was pursued by aircraft and hit by at least one torpedo.

LOSSES. More than 1,300 French sailors were killed in the bombardment. There were only slight British casualties. A French battleship (*Bretagne* class) was sunk, another of the same class was heavily damaged, and two destroyers and a seaplane carrier were sunk or burned.

AFTERMATH. There was much distress in France when the tragic news became known. Nazi propagandists seized the opportunity to persuade the French to join the campaign against ''the perfidious British.'' The British considered the melancholy affair absolutely necessary. It was widely known that high-ranking officers of the French fleet were anti-British from the beginning of the war, and there was danger that they might join the Axis.

Churchill later explained: ''The genius of France enabled her people to comprehend the whole significance of Oran, and in her agony to draw new hope and strength from this additional bitter pang. General de Gaulle [*q.v.*], whom I did not consult beforehand, was magnificent in his demeanor, and France liberated and restored has ratified his conduct.''

ORDER OF BATTLE. The table below gives the Allied Order of Battle in 1945, with emphasis upon American commanders. (*See individual biographies.*)

European Theater (May 1945)

UNIT	COMMANDER	LOCATION
SHAEF (Supreme Headquarters, Allied Expeditionary Force)	General of the Army Dwight D. Eisenhower	Versailles
NORTHERN GROUP (21st Army Group)	Field Marshal Bernard Law Montgomery	Suchteln
1st Canadian Army	Gen. H. D. G. Crerar	Holland
2nd British Army	Lt. Gen. Miles C. Dempsey	Germany
XVIII Corps (Airborne)	Maj. Gen. M. B. Ridgeway	Germany
CENTRAL GROUP (12th Army Group)	Gen. Omar N. Bradley	Wiesbaden
9th Army	Lt. Gen. William H. Simpson	Braunschweig
XIII Corps	Maj. Gen. A. C. Gillen, Jr.	Germany
XVI Corps	Maj. Gen. J. B. Anderson	Germany
XIX Corps	Maj. Gen. R. S. McLain	Germany
1st Army	Gen. Courtney H. Hodges	Weimar
VII Corps	Lt. Gen. J. L. Collins	Germany
VIII Corps	Maj. Gen. Troy H. Middleton	Germany
3rd Army	Gen. George S. Patton, Jr.	Erlangen
III Corps	Maj. Gen. James A. Van Fleet	Germany
V Corps	Maj. Gen. Clarence R. Huebner	Germany
XII Corps	Maj. Gen. Stafford Leroy Irwin	Germany
XX Corps	Lt. Gen. Walton H. Walker	Germany
15th Army	Lt. Gen. Leonard T. Gerow	Bad Neunahr
XXII Corps	Maj. Gen. Ernest N. Harmon	Germany
XXIII Corps	Maj. Gen. Hugh J. Gaffey	Germany
SOUTHERN GROUP (6th Army Group)	Gen. Jacob L. Devers	Heidelberg
7th Army	Lt. Gen. Alexander M. Patch	Schwäbisch-Gmünd
XXI Corps	Maj. Gen. Frank W. Milburn	Germany
XV Corps	Lt. Gen. Wade H. Haislip	Germany
VI Corps	Maj. Gen. William H. H. Morris, Jr.	Austria
1st French Army	Gen. Jean J. Lattre de Tassigny	Lindau

European Theater (May 1945)

UNIT	COMMANDER	LOCATION
U.S. Strategic Air Forces in Europe	Gen. Carl A. Spaatz	Reims
8th Air Force	Lt. Gen. James A. Doolittle	High Wycomb
9th Air Force	Lt. Gen. Hoyt C. Vandenberg	Wiesbaden
1st Tactical Air Force	Maj. Gen. Robert M. Webster	Heidelberg
SHAEF RESERVE		
1st Allied Airborne	Lt. Gen. Louis H. Brereton	Maison LaFitte
13h Airborne Division	Maj. Gen. Elbridge G. Chapman, Jr.	France

Pacific Theater (August 1945)

UNIT	COMMANDER	LOCATION
General Headquarters, U.S. Army Forces in the Pacific	General of the Army Douglas MacArthur	Manila
6th Army	Brig. Gen. D. J. Myers	Panay
I Corps	Maj. Gen. I. P. Swift	Luzon
IX Corps	Maj. Gen. C. W. Ryder	Leyte
XI Corps	Lt. Gen. C. P. Hall	Luzon
8th Army	Lt. Gen. R. L. Eichelberger	Leyte
X Corps	Maj. Gen. F. C. Sibert	Mindanao
XV Corps	Lt. Gen. O. W. Griswold	Luzon
10th Army	Lt. Gen. J. W. Stilwell	Okinawa
U.S. Army Forces Middle Pacific	Lt. Gen. R. C. Richardson, Jr.	Oahu
U.S. Army Forces, Western Pacific	Lt. Gen. W. D. Steyer	Luzon
Far East Air Forces	Gen. G. C. Lenney	Okinawa

(For Order of Battle, U.S. Army Air Forces in the Pacific, August 1945. *see* UNITED STATES ARMY AIR FORCES.)

505

ORIGINS OF WORLD WAR II. *See* CAUSES OF WORLD WAR II.

OSLO LETTER. Document revealing secret weapons being developed in Germany before and during World War II.

BACKGROUND. After the outbreak of war in 1939, Hitler made a speech in which he spoke of "new and secret weapons" that would bring victory to the Third Reich. Allied authorities, reluctant to take the *Fuehrer* seriously, at first paid little attention to what they regarded as German war propaganda. But shortly after, British Intelligence agents received a mysterious "open letter" by way of the British consul in Oslo, Norway. The anonymous letter contained details of a variety of new German weapons, including long-range guns, rockets, and advanced aircraft. The information appeared to be so far-fetched that it was regarded at the time as a planted hoax designed to confuse Allied strategists.

THE LETTER. Gradually, as the war went on, it became obvious that the Oslo Letter was far from an unimportant crank letter. The identity of the writer was never established, but apparently he had a vast knowledge of what was going on at German research stations. The appearance of the *V-1* and *V-2* weapons (*qq.v.*) in the closing stage of the war proved the legitimacy of the Oslo Letter. Not until postwar Allied interrogation teams went into Germany to examine research stations was the extent of German work on secret weapons revealed. Eighty-six distinct rocket projects were in progress in 1945. Had these been centralized to function more smoothly, the German war effort would have been enhanced tremendously. American authorities speedily recruited German scientists for their own rocket development program. (*See* BRAUN, WERNHER VON; and *PEENEMÜNDE.*

Bibliography. V. Hogg and J. B. King, *German and Allied Secret Weapons of World War II* (1976).

OSS. Secret intelligence agency of the United States during World War II. (*See* OFFICE OF STRATEGIC SERVICES.)

OVERLORD, OPERATION. *See* NORMANDY INVASION.

OZAWA, JISABURO (1886–1966). Commander of the Japanese fleet at the Battle of Leyte Gulf (*See* LEYTE GULF, BATTLE OF.)

A graduate of the Japanese Naval Academy, Ozawa attained the rank of rear admiral in 1936. In 1937 he was made Chief of Staff of the Combined Fleet.

Promoted to vice admiral in 1940, he took part in Japan's seizure of Indonesia, Malaya, and the Philippines. At the Battle of Leyte Gulf, Ozawa's Mobile Fleet acted as a decoy and was successful in drawing Adm. William F. Halsey, Jr. (*q.v.*) away from the San Bernadino Strait. In 1944 Ozawa was appointed Vice-Chief of the Naval General Staff and president of the Naval War College.

P

PACIFIC, CAMPAIGNS IN THE. Series of naval, air, and ground attacks by the Allies intended to force the Japanese back to their home islands.

BACKGROUND. After their surprise attack on Pearl Harbor (*q.v.*) the Japanese war machine, in boldly aggressive movements, quickly captured the whole western and southwestern area of the Pacific and also penetrated into adjacent countries in southeast Asia. In two years Japan acquired a huge area, together with natural resources and supplies, running all the way from the Aleutians in the north to the Solomon Islands off Australia in the south. It surrounded its military vitals with layers of fat while setting up puppet governments in the conquered territory.

The second phase of the Pacific war saw the Japanese surge forward again in a major attempt to seize control of the American base in the Hawaiian Islands and simultaneously key British bases in Australia. They were halted by American air and sea power in the Battle of Midway (*q.v.*) and by the Allies in the series of bloody campaigns in Guadalcanal (*q.v.*) in the Solomon Islands. At Midway the Japanese suffered a crucial loss in the sinking of four aircraft carriers and off Guadalcanal they lost several battleships as well as hundreds of aircraft.

In the third phase of the Pacific war the Japanese were on the defensive. They ordered their troops in the Solomons and New Guinea to hold their positions while attempts were made in Burma to forestall a possible Allied attack from India. (*See* BURMA, CAMPAIGNS IN.)

ALLIED STRATEGY. The major goal of Allied strategy was to pierce the concentric rings of Japanese defense. There were problems. A move from the north was unlikely to be profitable because necessary bases were lacking and the weather was stormy and foggy. A thrust up from the south through China would bring with it insurmountable supply problems. Assault through distant Burma was not indicated because of British defeats there and the necessity for a long buildup. Little help could be expected from Stalin, who incessantly called for a Second Front (*q.v.*) in the European theater.

Faced with these difficulties, the Allied Joint Chiefs of Staff decided that it would be best to leave strategy in the Pacific to the Americans and to a route acceptable to them. Two alternate routes were available—along the southwestern Pacific from New Guinea to the Philippines, or through the central Pacific. Gen. Douglas MacArthur (*q.v.*), Commander-in-Chief, Southwest Pacific, argued for a thrust in the south, the quickest way, he contended, to deprive the Japanese of essential war materials. American naval chiefs opposed the MacArthur plan with the argument that the growing U.S. fleet of carriers was fully able to push ahead in the central Pacific.

A compromise plan agreed on at the Third Washington Conference (*q.v.*) of May 11–17, 1943, provided for a double-pronged thrust advancing along both routes. This would keep the Japanese guessing, make them disperse their forces, and prevent them from switching their strength from one route to the other. Both moves would converge in the Philippines.

ISLAND-HOPPING TECHNIQUE. At the core of the strategy was a series of leapfrog hops from one island to another by coordinated air, sea, and land attacks. Each successive conquest would yield airfield and harbor facilities from which strikes could be made at the next objective. Enemy shipping would be blocked and tens of thousands of enemy troops would be bypassed and left without reinforcements or supplies. Heavily defended bases, such as those at Rabaul and Truk (*qq.v.*), could be bombed frequently but never assaulted from the sea.

For this island-hopping strategy the Allies assembled in the Pacific the most powerful and diversified armada in naval history in addition to overwhelming air forces. Most of the sea and air power was American. By 1944 U.S. naval strength overshadowed that of Japan. Since December 1941 the Americans had increased their naval power from 383 to 613 warships and their air strength from 1,744 to 18,269 planes. In addition a vast number of troops, seamen, and airmen were committed to the task.

Vital to American strategy was the transfer to the Pacific of carrier strength. By the summer of 1944 the Americans had many carriers of all sizes in Pacific waters. There were floating bases in the form of supply and repair ships, making it unnecessary to send damaged warships to Australia or the West Coast for repairs. Thousands of landing craft (*q.v.*) poured from the shipyards. The way was prepared to cut off Japanese-held islands one by one.

(For *individual operations, see* ALEUTIAN ISLANDS CAMPAIGNS; BISMARCK SEA, BATTLE OF THE; BOUGAINVILLE; BURMA, CAMPAIGNS IN; CORAL SEA, BATTLE OF THE; GILBERT ISLANDS, BATTLE FOR THE; GUADALCANAL CAMPAIGNS; IWO JIMA, BATTLE FOR; JAVA SEA, BATTLE OF THE; KOLOMBANGARA, BATTLE OF; KULA GULF, BATTLE OF; LEYTE GULF, BATTLE OF; MARIANAS, BATTLE FOR

THE; MARSHALL ISLANDS, BATTLE FOR THE; MIDWAY, BATTLE OF; NEW GUINEA, CAMPAIGNS IN; OKINAWA, BATTLE FOR; PHILIPPINE SEA, BATTLE OF THE; RABAUL; TRUK ISLANDS; VELLA GULF, BATTLE OF; and YAMAMOTO, DEATH OF.)

Bibliography. K. Ayling, *Semper Fidelis: The U.S. Marines in Action* (1943); F. O. Hough, *The Island War* (1947); S. E. Morison, *History of U.S. Naval Operations in World War II* (1947–1962); C. A. Willoughby and J. Chamberlain, *Victory in the Pacific* (1951); Lord Mountbatten, *Report to the Combined Chiefs of Staff* (1951); B. Millot, *La Guerre de Pacifique* (1968); B. Collier, *The War in the Far East, 1941–1945* (1969); E. P. Hoyt, *How They Won the War in the Pacific* (1971); and W. Manchester, *Goodbye Darkness: A Memoir of the Pacific War* (1981).

PANTELLERIA. Strategic island in the Mediterranean occupied by the Allies in 1943.

BACKGROUND. Pantelleria, ancient Kossyra, is a volcanic island of 32 square miles situated near the narrow crossing between Sicily and Tunisia, 60 miles from Sicily and 44 miles from the African coast. At one time a colony of the Phoenicians and the Carthaginians, it passed successively to the Romans, Saracens, Normans, Turks, and Italians. About 10,000 people lived there and produced figs and also raisins for export. The Italians developed it as a base for E-Boats (*q.v.*). Allied strategists, attracted by its lone airfield, designated *Operation Corkscrew* for its occupation.

ASSAULT. In May 1943, simultaneous with the final conquest of Tunisia, Allied forces began an attack on Pantelleria. First came a preliminary bombardment from light and medium bombers. In early June American *Flying Fortresses (B-17) (q.v.)* and British *Wellingtons* began a daylight assault while warships bombed the island. In six days and nights the Allies dropped 5,000 tons of explosives. The strike was too much for the defending force.

On June 11, 1943, just as the invaders were about to enter their assault boats from larger ships, the garrison at Pantelleria capitulated. There were no Allied casualties. About 11,000 prisoners were taken. (*See also* SICILY, INVASION OF.)

Bibliography. M. Blumenson, *Sicily* (1969).

PANTHER. *See* TANKS.

PANZER. German term for armor. The word *Panzer* is defined as cuirass, coat of mail, iron-casing, or armor plating. In World War II *Panzerwagen*, or tank, was shortened to *Panzer*.

BACKGROUND. Protagonists of armored warfare, including Basil Liddell Hart and Charles de Gaulle (*qq.v.*), accurately predicted the nature of the war, but little attention was paid to them in Britain and France. In Germany, on the other hand, the memory of the devastating performance by tanks in World War I led to different conclusions. German tacticians remembered that British tanks had played an important part in forcing them into surrender in 1918. When Hitler rearmed Germany in the mid-1930s, he gave high priority to building a tank force second to none. He ordered *Panzer* elite troops to be trained to perfection.

WORLD WAR II. German *Panzers* went into action in the opening *Blitzkrieg (q.v.)* of the war, racing across northern Europe and ripping open Poland. In succeeding campaigns in the Low Countries, France, North Africa, and Russia, the *Panzers* remained at the core of the German war effort. However, they often overextended themselves, overran their supplies or fuel, and at times were in danger of being isolated from supporting arms. In North Africa, German *Panzer* units under the brilliant Gen. Erwin Rommel *(q.v.)* won the reluctant admiration of their opponents. Hitler himself, who was startled by the penetration capacity of his *Panzer* units, on occasion called a halt because he felt that they were being drawn into a trap.

Bibliography. J. Kirk and R. Young, *Great Weapons of World War II* (1961); K. J. Macksey, *Panzer Division: The Mailed Fist* (1968); and M. Cooper and J. Lucas, *Panzer: The Armored Force of the Third Reich* (1978).

PANZERFAUST. Popular term for *Faustpatrone*—mailed fist or tank destroyer. German hand weapon produced late in the war as a desperate measure to halt the Allied advance.

The *Panzerfaust,* modeled on the American *bazooka (q.v.),* was a small rocket shot fired by hand. German factories produced 997,000 in November 1944, 1,253,000 in December, and 1,200,000 in January 1945. They had little effect on the outcome of the war.

PAPEN, FRANZ VON (1879–1969). Politician and statesman who played a major role in Hitler's drive to power.

It was Franz von Papen who prevailed upon the aged President Paul von Hindenburg to make Adolf Hitler Chancellor on January 30, 1933. As Vice-Chancellor, he placed himself at the disposal of the Nazi regime, believing that he could control Hitler and once again assume a position of supreme political power. It was a gross miscalculation.

During World War II, from September 1939 to August 1944, von Papen served as Ambassador to Turkey. In April 1945 he was arrested in the Ruhr area by troops of the U.S. 9th Army. The next year he was brought to trial before the International Military Tribunal (*See* NUREMBERG TRIALS). Disassociating himself from Nazi guilt, he claimed to be astonished by the indictment: "I believe that paganism and the years of totalitarianism bear the main guilt. Through both of these Hitler became a pathological liar in the course of the years." The court denounced him for his "intrigue and bullying" in the campaign for *Anschluss* with Austria, but acquitted him on all counts because "such offenses against political morality, however bad they may be, were not criminal."

Bibliography. F. von Papen, *Memoirs* (1952) and *Vom Scheitern einer Demokratie* (1968); and T. Koeves, *Satan in Top Hat* (1941).

PARIS, LIBERATION OF. End of Nazi rule in the French capital on August 25, 1944.

BACKGROUND. After D-Day, June 6, 1944 (*See* NORMANDY INVASION), the Allied Supreme Command was careful to avoid bombing Paris and instead concentrated on railway bottlenecks outside the city. The idea was to save fuel and ammunition. Inside Paris the news from Normandy set off a revolt. In early August the Germans stationed in Paris began to panic and stampede into the countryside.

On August 19 more than 20,000 members of the French Forces of the Interior (*q.v.*), police of the gendarmerie, and assorted bands of civilians turned on the remaining German garrison. Enraged Frenchmen beat and killed collaborators and shaved the heads of women who had fraternized with the Germans and marched them through jeering crowds in the streets.

ENTRY. Gen. Dwight D. Eisenhower (*q.v.*) had intended to bypass Paris, but when word reached him of a revolt inside the city, he moved to its support. Led by lumbering *Sherman* tanks, two columns raced to the city. Gen. Jacques Leclerc (*q.v.*) was chosen for the honor of first entry. At 2 P.M. on August 25, 1944, he spoke in a baggage room at the Gare Montparnasse and announced the surrender of 10,000 Germans. The German commander, Gen. Dietrich von Choltitz, disobeyed Hitler and decided not to fight on to the last man or raze the city.

The next day Leclerc and Gen. Charles de Gaulle (*q.v.*), together with Resistance leaders, marched down the Champs Élysées amid ecstatic Parisians and down the aisle of Notre Dame Cathedral—despite sniper fire. De Gaulle considered it a personal victory: "Since each of these here had chosen Charles de Gaulle in his heart as the refuge against his agony and the symbol of his hopes, we must permit the man to be seen, familiar and fraternal, in order at this sight the national unity should shine forth."

SIGNIFICANCE. After four years Paris was liberated, the first Allied capital city to be reconquered from the Germans. A delirious celebration lasted three days, capped by a review of U.S. and French troops. After this temporary halt, the motorized Allied columns moved across the Seine to strike at the heart of Germany. (*See* GERMANY, BATTLE OF.)

Bibliography. B. Michael, *Les grandes énigmes de la Libération* (1969).

PARIS PEACE CONFERENCE. Meeting of the victorious powers at Paris in the summer of 1946 to make recommendations for peace treaties.

BACKGROUND. Once again it was demonstrated that wartime alliances seldom outlive victory. The United States, United Kingdom, and Soviet Union had combined in a common front against the Axis. When Germany was defeated, common interests between the United States and Britain remained, but little was left to hold the Western powers and the Soviet Union together. The wartime conferences were cordial because of fear of Hitler (*See* CONFERENCES, ALLIED WAR), but after 1945 the urge for cooperation weakened considerably.

It was decided at the Potsdam Conference (*q.v.*) to hold no additional Big Three conferences, but to create the Council of Foreign Ministers to prepare the peace treaties, first with Axis satellites and later with Germany. The first meeting of the Council was held in London from September 11 to October 3, 1945. A failure, it was adjourned after weeks of bitter wrangling. Later discussions took place in Moscow (December 16–20, 1945); London (April 25–May 16, 1946); and Paris (June 15–July 12, 1946), again with little agreement.

PARTICIPANTS. On July 29, 1946, 21 Allied nations, which had "actively waged war with substantial military forces against European enemy states," assembled in Paris. Present were delegates of the Big Four (Britain, France, the United States, and the Soviet Union) and smaller countries, the "Little Seventeen." There were 1,500 delegates. Georges Bidault, representing France, was host and chairman of the conference. Among the Americans were James F. Byrnes, Secretary of State; William Averell Harriman; and Gen. Walter Bedell Smith (*qq.v.*). British delegates included Clement Attlee, the new Prime Minister, and Ernest Bevin (*qq.v.*). The Russians were represented by Vyacheslav Molotov (*q.v.*) and Andrei Vyshinsky. Several well-known delegates belonged to smaller states, such as Paul-Henri Spaak of Belgium and Jan Masaryk of Czechoslovakia (*qq.v.*).

RESULTS. Despite the array of diplomatic talent and the urge for agreement, the outcome was meager and inconclusive. The delegates were embroiled in heated procedural discussions. The smaller states objected that the proposed two-thirds majority rule deprived them of a voice in actual decisions. The widening chasm between the West and Moscow was revealed by opposition from the "Soviet Six"—the Soviet Union, Czechoslovakia, Poland, the Ukraine, White Russia, and Yugoslavia—to non-Soviet delegates. The Russians sought to expand their power and influence, while representatives of Western democracies tried to contain the USSR. Whenever Soviet satellites called for treaty changes, the Soviet delegates supported the request; Soviet satellites automatically opposed suggestions of non-Soviet states. The result was endless debate, which degenerated into angry squabbles.

SATELLITE TREATIES. Finally, after more than six weeks of discussion, delegates approved drafts of treaties with Italy, Rumania, Bulgaria, Hungary and Finland, and then disbanded on October 15, 1946. The treaties were signed at the Quai d'Orsay in Paris on February 10, 1947. All these countries except Finland protested and began campaigns for revision.

In the Italian treaty, Italy accepted the creation of the Free State of Trieste and cession of small areas to France. The Italo-Austrian border was left unchanged. The Brenner Pass and southern Tyrol remained in Italian hands. Italy lost its African colonies, and its armed forces were severely limited. Italy was forced to pay reparations to victims of its aggressions. The terms were relatively mild because Italy had not acquired the sinister record of the Third Reich.

According to the Rumanian, Bulgarian, and Hungarian treaties, Rumania was allowed to hold Transylvania, but was required to cede Bessarabia and northern Bukovina to the Soviet Union. Bulgaria retained southern Dobrudja but failed to make good its claim to western Thrace against Greece. Hungary lost territory in southern Slovakia to Czechoslovakia. Similar armaments reductions were decreed, and all three had to pay reparations.

Under the Finnish treaty, the Finnish-Soviet frontier set in March 1940 was restored. The Finns were required to pay $300 million in reparations to the Soviet Union and Moscow was given considerable powers of interference in Finnish domestic affairs.

FAILURE OF GERMAN PEACE TREATY. A peace treaty with Austria was signed in Vienna on May 15, 1955. But there was no peace treaty with Germany. The Council of Foreign Ministers planned such a document, but it made little headway because of increasing difficulties over occupation policies in Germany. The Allies agreed on the punishment of war criminals. (*See* NUREMBERG TRIALS.) They also agreed on denazification procedures, but differed on methods of application. The Russians and French stripped their zones of occupation of every removable asset. The Council of Foreign Ministers met several times but ended in deadlock. The Western powers and the Soviet Union came to the conclusion that an agreement over Germany was impossible. Both proceeded to consolidate their zones of occupation into their own alliance systems.

Bibliography. T. V. Kalijarvi (ed.), *Peace Settlements of World War II* (1948); F. W. Pick, *Peacemaking in Perspective* (1950); and A. C. Leiss and R. Dennett (eds.), *European Peace Treaties after World War II* (1954).

PARTISANS. Members of underground Resistance movements during the war. Although the term was used to describe varied guerrilla and sabotage units, more often it referred specifically to Communist guerrillas.

ACTIVITIES. After the German invasion of the Soviet Union on June 22, 1941, Russian Partisans, despite severe reprisals, continued to operate behind enemy lines with considerable success. They endured hardships, but were able to hold out almost indefinitely. In Yugoslavia more than 100,000 Partisans were led by Tito (*q.v.*) in a campaign that resulted in heavy German loss of life. The Germans took harsh vengeance but were not able to suppress the guerrillas. Greek Partisans also waged effective internal warfare later in the war and well into the 1950s.

Italian Partisans in 1943 helped bring about the overthrow of Mussolini. On April 28, 1945, they captured the Italian *Duce,* together with his mistress, Clara Petacci and 12 members of his Cabinet. They carried the bodies of Mussolini, Petacci, and several others to Milan, where they were left hanging in a grisly display. (*See also* RESISTANCE MOVEMENTS; and UNDERGROUND.)

Bibliography. K. J. Macksey, *The Partisans of Europe in the Second World War* (1975); and G. Pesces, *And No Quarter: The Italian Partisans in World War II* (1971).

PASTORIUS. German code or cover name for an unsuccessful espionage operation in the United States in the summer of 1942.

BACKGROUND. In April 1942 the German Admiralty staff made plans to land German agents from U-Boats on the eastern coast of the United States to strike at a main bottleneck of the American war economy—aluminum production. Initiated by the *Abwehr* (*q.v.*), the counterintelligence agency, *Pastorius* was designed to use Germans who had spent many years in the United States and train them for sabotage. It was initiated by Adm. Wilhelm Canaris (*q.v.*), secret service chief, and directed by his right-hand man and top agent, Maj. Gen. Erwin von Lahousen-Vivrement, an Austrian aristocrat.

PREPARATION. Ten men were selected for the operation: Lt. Werner Kappe, a former German-American reporter; Georg John Dasch, a thin-faced, 40-year-old who had served in the U.S. Army; Edward Kerling, fanatical member of the German-American Bund; Hermann Otto Neubauer, a mechanic and ship's cook; Heinrich Heink, seaman; Richard Quirin, a Chicago petty racketeer; Werner Thiel, laborer and drifter; Hans Schmidt, a German-Canadian; Heinrich Wanner, Czech-born Sudeten German and a sergeant in the *Wehrmacht* (*q.v.*); and Herbert Haupt, a 19-year-old Chicagoan and Nazi sympathizer.

The ten were sent to a sabotage school to undergo intensive training on how to use fuses, make Molotov cocktails (*q.v.*), blow up railway lines, cut electrical supplies, wreck high tension wires, and destroy industrial potential. They were shown blueprints of such targets as power stations of the Tennessee Valley Authority, plants of the American Aluminum Company, and Hell Gate Bridge over the East River in New York City. On completing the training, Wanner withdrew and returned to his military unit. Dasch and Kerling were chosen leaders of two groups. All were provided with false identity papers and American-style clothes.

MISSION FAILURE. The saboteurs set out in two submarines from the French coast on May 26 and 28, 1942. The German *U-202,* which took a northern route, made the voyage without incident until it was detected by Allied sonar off the coast of Newfoundland and was nearly destroyed by depth bombs. Tossed up and down like a cork, it survived.

On June 12, 1942, the Dasch group, four men with Heink, Quirin, and replacement Burger, were landed in a dingy at Amagansett on the shores of Long Island. They were discovered by a young U.S. Coast Guardsman but managed to bluff their way to safety in New York City. Meanwhile, hundreds of miles to the south, the *U-170* landed the Kerling group not far from Jacksonville, Florida.

Dasch was the key figure in the incident. A native of Speyer, Rhineland, he had come to the United States in 1920 as a stowaway. After working as a dishwasher in a New York City luxury hotel, he made a vain effort to find work and then joined the U.S. Army. After discharge, he moved from job to job, married an American girl, and then became a left-wing agitator.

Whatever his motive, Dasch finally betrayed the saboteurs to the Federal Bureau of Investigation. One by one all eight spies were rounded up and the sensational news was given to the American public. On June 29, 1942, they were brought together in jail at Washington, D.C. Early in July President Roosevelt announced appointment of a special military court to try the accused men.

AFTERMATH. A secret trial was held in the Department of Justice building in Washington with Francis Biddle, who was active later at Nuremberg, prosecuting. (*See* NUREMBERG TRIALS.) The case rested largely on the confession of Dasch who insisted that he was serving as a double agent for the United States. Overwhelmed by the confession, the other eight had virtually no defense. All were found guilty and sentenced to death.

On August 12, 1942, Quirin, Heink, Kerling, Thiel, Neubauer, and Haupt went to the electric chair in Washington. Dasch and Burger, an SS (*q.v.*) officer acting under orders, had their sentences commuted to 30 years' imprisonment. Both were released on June 23, 1948. Dasch then served the East Germans until he lost the confidence of his Communist superiors. He escaped to West Germany.

SIGNIFICANCE. The unsuccessful mission illustrated the weakness of *Abwehr* operations and the comparatively more effective activity of American counterintelligence. (*See* ESPIONAGE.)

Bibliography. C. Wighton and G. Peis, *Hitler's Spies and Saboteurs* (1958).

PATHFINDER TECHNIQUE. Method of night bombing devised by the British Bomber Command for attacking German targets.

Introduced in late 1942, the technique used flares to light up targets on the ground. First, several aircraft flew ahead of the main body to drop their flares;

second, another small group of raiders dropped flares over a concentrated region; and finally, the heavy *Lancasters* came in to drop incendiaries over special targets. To counteract this procedure, the Germans began to light dummy fires in open country. They also used a network of flickering globes to simulate fallen bombs. The defensive measures were only partially successful. (*See* MASTER BOMBER TECHNIQUE.)

PATTERSON, ROBERT PORTER (1891–1952). U.S. statesman active in war procurement.

Patterson was named Under Secretary of War in December 1940 and in that post worked closely with his chief, Secretary of War Henry Stimson (*q.v.*). After American entry into the war in 1941, Patterson was given the responsibility for assuring the flow of supplies for the war effort. This meant the procurement of more than 7,000 different items. Patterson worked closely with both capital and labor, visited the fighting fronts to ascertain the needs of field commanders, and worked assiduously to obtain men, materials, and management for turning out planes and tanks. He contributed much to final Allied victory.

Patterson was noted for his quick decisions. "We need every man hour of production," he said, "and there should be no strikes or stoppages."

PATTON, GEORGE SMITH, JR. (1885–1945). U.S. Army commander known for his colorful personality.

In 1939 Patton was active in the training of armored units. He was named to command the 2nd Armored Division and later the 1st Armored Corps. In November 1942 he was assigned to *Operation Torch* (*q.v.*) and led the ground forces that entered Casablanca and French-occupied Morocco. In March 1943 he was appointed commander of the U.S. 2nd Corps in Tunisia. When the Germans tried frantically to shake the Americans off their flank, Patton stopped them with a concentration of firepower. Promoted to Lieutenant General, he was given command of the U.S. 7th Army for the campaign in Sicily, which took just 38 days. (*See* SICILY, INVASION OF.)

SLAPPING INCIDENT. During the campaign in Sicily, Patton became involved in a notorious incident that made his name known not only through the ranks of the U.S. Army but also throughout the world. As was his custom, he was making a round in a field hospital to cheer up the wounded men. Spotting an ambulatory patient, he asked the GI (*q.v.*) why he was there. The man replied: "General, I guess it is my nerves. I can't stand the shelling any more." Instantly Patton went into a rage, screaming a torrent of abuse at the startled GI: "Your nerves, hell," Patton shouted. "You're just a goddamned coward!" It was malingering, the general went on, and the man was unfit to be in the same hospital with wounded men. Losing control, Patton swung at the soldier's head, knocking off his helmet. "Shut up!" he yelled. "I won't have these brave men who've been shot at see a yellow bastard crying!"

Nearby doctors and nurses, embarrassed and helpless, looked on in dismay.

Patton stormed out of the hospital, still shouting imprecations about "psychoneurotics and cowards."

Word of the shocking performance soon spread through the battle units. On the home front a news commentator revealed the incident over the radio. Public clamor rose for Patton's dismissal. Gen. Dwight D. Eisenhower (*q.v.*), reluctant to lose a valuable combat commander, reprimanded Patton sharply and ordered him to apologize to the slapped man. In addition, he required Patton to appear before officers and enlisted men "to assure them that he had given way to impulse and really respected their positions as fighting soldiers of a democratic nation."

The affair became a major event in Patton's career. He never quite lived down the ignominy of his bizarre behavior in Sicily. Defenders attributed it to his reactions to the suffering he had seen in the campaign and declared that in any event the slapping was overpublicized. Gen. Omar N. Bradley (*q.v.*) explained Patton's conduct without condoning it: "I cannot believe that George was intentionally brutal. He simply sought to purge that soldier of 'cowardice' by shaming him. The private whose face he slapped did more to win the war in Europe than any other private in the army."

LATER CAREER. Patton went on to become one of the most dashing combat commanders of the war. He led the U.S. 3rd Army in the assault on France in June 1944. (*See* NORMANDY INVASION.) His armored units, moving swiftly and ruthlessly, exploited a critical breakthrough at Avranches and then, bypassing Paris, surged toward Germany. His tanks moved so fast that they outstripped their supply lines as they reached the German borders. (*See* FRANCE, SECOND BATTLE OF.)

Ordered to relieve the troops trapped at Bastogne, Patton led his men from their bridgehead on the Saar to the snow-covered Ardennes front in a matter of days and smashed at the southern flank of the Germans. (*See* BULGE, BATTLE OF THE.) He played a leading role in clearing the Palatinate. In the third week of April 1945 he led his tanks clear across southern Germany to the Czech border. He was less than 50 miles from Prague, when, for political reasons he was ordered to stop. (*See* GERMANY, BATTLE OF.)

Patton died in a Heidelberg military hospital on December 21, 1945, after an automobile accident near Mannheim. In its obituary *The New York Times* praised him as one of the outstanding military figures of World War II: "History has reached out and embraced General George Patton. His place is secure."

Despite a checkered career, Patton had an imaginative military mind. He was a keen student of the strategy of past wars, especially the American Civil War. He was always willing to commit himself to battle. A master technician, he invariably sought local superiority at one point before moving on to another. In this respect he was a commander in the image of Frederick the Great, Jeb Stuart, and Stonewall Jackson.

Bibliography. Patton's memoirs appeared posthumously under the title *War as I Knew It* (1947). *See* M. Blumenson, *The Patton Papers* (1947). Among the biographies are those by J. C. Wellard (1946); A. Hatch (1950); H. H. Semmes (1955); L. Farrago (1963); F. Ayer (1964); and C. Whiting (1970). *See also* B. G. Wallace, *Patton and His Third Army* (1980).

PAULUS, FRIEDRICH (1890–1957). German General whose name is associated with the defeat at Stalingrad.

At the outbreak of the war Paulus was Chief of Staff of the German 6th Army and retained that post in every major campaign in which he participated. In 1940 he served in the *Blitzkrieg* (*q.v.*), which smashed through Belgium and the Netherlands. On September 1, 1940, he was appointed Senior Quartermaster in the High Command of the Armed Forces. In this post he prepared a skeletal operational plan for an eventual offensive against the Soviet Union. In March 1941 he was sent to Budapest to coordinate military measures to be taken by the satellite forces against the isolated Yugoslavs. Enjoying Hitler's confidence, he assisted in the planning of *Operation Barbarossa* (*q.v.*) against the Soviet Union.

STALINGRAD. In August 1942, determined to deliver a knockout blow, Hitler ordered Paulus, in whom he had confidence, to lead the 6th Army against Stalingrad. Paulus pushed ahead in powerful thrusts and by November had taken nine-tenths of the city. But in reality he fell into a Soviet trap. With supplies cut off and ammunition dwindling, he was caught in the Russian winter, and his 6th Army was on the verge of a debacle.

Desperately, Paulus reported to Hitler that the situation was precarious and asked permission for a temporary retreat. The *Fuehrer's* reply meant inevitable defeat. His ego was so overwhelming that he could not admit the possibility of even a temporary halt or retreat. The lives of 330,000 German troops at Stalingrad meant little compared to the maintenance of his own prestige. "I have considered the situation carefully. My conclusion remains unaltered. The 6th Army stays where it is. I am not leaving the Volga."

Paulus's men suffered the agonies of frostbite, disease, and vanishing supplies. His appeals to Hitler were unsuccessful. The *Fuehrer* sent this message:

CAPITULATION IS IMPOSSIBLE. THE 6th ARMY WILL DO ITS HISTORIC DUTY AT STALINGRAD UNTIL THE LAST MAN.

On January 31, 1943, Hitler made Paulus a General Field Marshal. "The forces of the 6th Army," Hitler announced "will henceforth be known as Fortress Stalingrad." Paulus held his rank as a newly created Field Marshal for exactly one day. The next day he capitulated. From the cellars and caves of the besieged city streamed the last of the ragged and hungry German troops, now prisoners of the Russians. Infuriated, Hitler accused Paulus and his men of cowardice, asserting that all should have died to the last man. Later, Paulus aroused Hitler's contempt as well as that of German commanders by supporting the Russian-sponsored Free Germany movement, for which he broadcast appeals for German surrender.

POSTWAR. Paulus continued his work for what was now the National Committee for a Free Germany. In 1953, after release from a Russian prison, he settled in the German Democratic Republic (East Germany).

Bibliography. A. Werth, *The Year of Stalingrad* (1946); W. Goerlitz, *Paulus and Stalingrad* (1964); G. Jukes, *Stalingrad: The Turning Point* (1968); and W. Craig, *Enemy at the Gates: The Battle of Stalingrad* (1973).

PEARL HARBOR. Virtually land-locked harbor off the coast of Oahu Island, Hawaii, six miles west of Honolulu, and scene of an aerial attack by the Japanese on December 7, 1941.

One of the best natural harbors in the East Pacific Ocean, Pearl Harbor was made a naval base after the United States annexed Hawaii in 1900. In the vicinity were many military installations, including Hickam Air Force Base, Pearl Harbor Naval Air Station, and Camp H. M. Smith, headquarters of the U.S. Pacific Command.

BACKGROUND. Relations between the United States and Japan deteriorated rapidly from July 2, 1940, when the Export Control Act authorized the President to prohibit the export of war materials. Japan protested this "unfriendly act," which closed American markets for its war machine. In March 1941 Tokyo informed Washington of its increasing concern. In July 1941 the Japanese moved into southern Indo-China, thereby placing its armed forces within easy reach of the Philippines and vital American trade routes. On July 26, 1941, President Roosevelt issued an executive order freezing Japanese assets in the United States. Trade halted between the two countries. In mid-November 1941 Saburo Kurusu arrived in the United States as a special envoy to assist Ambassador Kichisaburo Nomura (*q.v.*) to find a peace formula.

Meanwhile, the decision for war had already been taken in Tokyo. The Cabinet and High Command of the Army and Navy, in the presence of the Emperor, proposed a surprise attack on Pearl Harbor to immobilize the U.S. Pacific Fleet there, to be followed by conquests throughout the Pacific area. If it could cripple the U.S. fleet, Japan could hold a vast Pacific empire.

TARGET. In 1939 the United States added fortifications and harbor improvements to the Pearl Harbor base. On the morning of December 7, 1941, many of the area's personnel were asleep, except the few on special Sunday duty. Seven great U.S. battleships were moored in the harbor, while another, the *Pennsylvania*, was in dry dock. Among the total of 86 warships were 7 cruisers, 28 destroyers, 5 submarines, and several auxiliaries. All three of the fleet's aircraft carriers were on missions elsewhere, the *Enterprise* and *Lexington* moving aircraft to Wake and Midway Islands, and the *Saratoga* in dry dock in California.

ATTACK. On November 26, 1941, while negotiations were held in Washington, a Japanese task force assembled secretly in the Kuriles departed for its mission and proceeded eastward in northern latitudes. The force was composed of 6 large aircraft carriers, 2 fast battleships, 2 cruisers, and several destroyers and tankers, all under command of Vice-Adm. Chuichi Nagumo (*q.v.*). The crews had been meticulously trained. Aircraft torpedoes were equipped with ailerons so that they could be used in the shallow depths of Pearl Harbor. The task force observed radio silence and encountered no shipping. The seas were rough; it was necessary to send back the light destroyers, while the rest of the force proceeded to its launching point.

At 6 A.M. on December 7, 1941, the fleet reached its goal 200 miles north of the Hawaiian Islands. Meanwhile, a force of 16 submarines moved to a rendez-vous just off Pearl Harbor and launched 5 midget submarines, 2 of which managed to get into the harbor on that morning. One was grounded on Oahu with its crew captured, the other did not return.

The first wave of 189 attacking planes, launched at 6 A.M., reached the northern point of Oahu at 7:50 A.M., without meeting any search aircraft. The air armada was detected by a U.S. Army radar operator, but the officer to whom he reported decided that this was a friendly squadron expected from the states. At Oahu the Japanese force split into two units, the dive bombers heading toward the air bases at Hickam Field, Wheeler Field, and Ford Island. Here the planes of the U.S. Army Air Forces were lined up neatly for supposed-ly greater protection against sabotage.

The second Japanese unit, consisting of 50 horizontal bombers, 40 torpedo planes, and 50 fighters, moved toward the battleships moored to concrete quays at Ford Island. The ships below, like sitting ducks, were soon enveloped in a crashing crescendo of destruction. The second wave of 171 aircraft arrived at 8:40 A.M., this time without torpedos. By this time all available antiaircraft guns were in action, bringing down a lone Japanese plane. There was a third minor attack at 9:15.

LOSSES. The damage was enormous. The *Arizona* was completely wrecked; the *West Virginia* and *California* were sunk; the *Oklahoma* lay capsized; the *Nevada* was heavily damaged. The *Maryland* and *Tennessee* were damaged but were able to move to the West Coast under their own power. In all 19 warships were hit, including cruisers, destroyers, and auxiliaries. Only 50 of the 200 naval aircraft escaped damage. Personnel casualties were heavy. Naval and Marine Corps casualties included 2,117 officers and men killed, 876 wounded, and nearly 1,000 missing. The army lost 226 officers and men, 396 wounded. The Japanese lost fewer than 100 men, 29 planes, 1 fleet submarine, and 5 midget subs.

SIGNIFICANCE. In less than 2 hours the Japanese had crippled the U.S. Pacific Fleet and undermined the American strategic position in the Pacific. It was, indeed, a brilliant tactical victory, prepared in minute detail and executed with dispatch—all surviving Japanese aircraft returned to their carriers before 1 P.M. that day. Adm. Nagumo, however, made a serious mistake by withdrawing before destroying the 4.5 million barrels of oil in the exposed tanks. This would have forced the entire Pacific Fleet back to California, isolated Hawaii, and cut communications to Australia. In the long run the Japanese attack was also a colossal political error.

AFTERMATH. At 2:05 P.M., eastern standard time, after the bombardment of Pearl Harbor had been under way for 46 minutes, Ambassador Nomura and Envoy Kurusu walked into the State Department in Washington to deliver to Cordell Hull (*q.v.*), the American Secretary of State, the Japanese reply to the American note of November 26, which set forth in detail the terms upon which the United States believed an amicable settlement of all the outstanding differences in the Pacific could be achieved. The proposals included withdrawal of all Japanese forces from China and Indo-China, relinquishment of Japan's Greater East Asia Co-Prosperity Sphere (*q.v.*), and future adherence to international law and order. After reading the note, Hull, in a voice choked with anger, informed the Japanese representatives that he already knew of the attack. "In all my fifty years of public service I have never seen a document that was more crowded with infamous falsehoods and distortions." Hull abruptly dismissed his callers.

The surprise attack resulted in an explosion of wrath by the American public. It wiped out immediately any isolationist sentiment. The entire country stood behind the President and gave him wholehearted support. On the following day the two houses of Congress met in joint session. The President read his message starting: "Yesterday, December 7, 1941—a date which will live in infamy." The Senate unanimously passed a formal declaration of war; the House passed it with one dissenting vote, cast by Jeanette Rankin of Montana, who had also voted against war in 1917. Britain quickly joined the United States in declaring war on Japan. Four days later Germany declared war on the United States and was followed immediately by Italy. The two wars now merged in a global conflict.

"Remember Pearl Harbor!" became the American war cry. Investigations of the tragedy began soon. (*See* PEARL HARBOR CONTROVERSY.) Today, Pearl Harbor is a national historic landmark with a memorial over the sunken *Arizona.*

Bibliography. W. Lord, *The Day of Infamy* (1957); W. Millis, *This is Pearl: The United States and Japan* (1947); H. L. Trefousse (ed.), *What Happened at Pearl Harbor* (1958); and R. Wohlstetter, *Pearl Harbor: Warning and Decision* (1962). *See* also bibliography for PEARL HARBOR CONTROVERSY.

PEARL HARBOR CONTROVERSY. Wartime and postwar dispute on fixing responsibility for the disaster at Pearl Harbor (*q.v.*).

BACKGROUND. The Japanese attack on Pearl Harbor (*q.v.*) on December 7, 1941, caused enormous damage and temporarily crippled the U.S. Pacific Fleet. The smoke had hardly cleared before Secretary of the Navy Frank Knox (*q.v.*) was sent to the scene on a mission of investigation. Angry Congressmen demanded punishment for Adm. Husband E. Kimmel (*q.v.*), Commander-in-Chief of the U.S. Navy and Pacific Fleet, and Gen. Walter C. Short (*q.v.*), Army commander in Hawaii. Both were relieved of their commands within ten days.

ROBERTS INVESTIGATION. President Roosevelt ordered a special investigating committee, headed by Associate Justice Owen J. Roberts of the U.S. Supreme Court, to look into the disaster and report its findings to the nation. The Roberts report was given to the President on January 24, 1942, and it was made public the next day. It was the first of eight public and private inquiries on the disaster.

The 51-page Roberts report stated: "The Japanese attack was a complete surprise to the commanders, and they failed to make suitable dispositions to meet such an attack. Each failed properly to evaluate the seriousness of the situation. These errors of judgment were the effective causes for the success of the attack." Both Kimmel and Short were charged with "dereliction of duty" in failing to consult with one another on imminence of hostilities and appropriate measures of defense. It was charged specifically that they had failed to communicate with one another.

CALL FOR COURTS-MARTIAL. The Roberts report added fuel to what was by this time a national controversy. Critics maintained that the report did not tell the whole story of Pearl Harbor, and that part of the responsibility went to higher echelons. Newspaper editorials demanded a prompt court-martial for both officers. Adm. Kimmel himself demanded trial to tell his side of the story. Army and navy officials, however, opposed any court-martial on the ground that it would hinder the war effort.

Both the War and Navy Departments announced on February 28, 1942, that Gen. Short and Adm. Kimmel would be tried by courts-martial "at such time as the public interest and safety permit;" on the charge of dereliction of duty. Meanwhile, on February 7, 1942, applications of both officers for retirement had been granted. Both waived the statute of limitations that would have prevented a court-martial after a lapse of two years.

CONGRESSIONAL INVESTIGATION, 1944. In June 1944 Congress passed legislation calling for an official investigation by the army and navy. Two boards represented both services. The Army Board, made up of three generals at or near retirement age, devoted three months to the inquiry, which produced 41 volumes of testimony and 70 exhibits. Among the facts revealed was that Short had been instructed by Chief of Staff Gen. George C. Marshall (*q.v.*) to end "old Army and Navy feuds," but that, nevertheless, there was not adequate army-navy liaison. "Had the equipment and material available been utilized, had there been in existence a detailed plan of operation of the staff and lower echelons and had sound judgment been exercised in the selection of the alert, the disaster at Pearl Harbor undoubtedly would have been materially mitigated, if not wholly avoided."

The report concluded by placing blame on Marshall and War Plans Chief Gen. Leonard Townsend Gerow for not keeping Short fully informed and for not investigating the readiness of his command. Short was blamed for his failure to place his command in a state of readiness for war. In an attached statement, Secretary of War Henry Stimson (*q.v.*) stated that Short's "error of judgment" was his own and not excused by circumstances, and that he had received adequate warning.

CONGRESSIONAL INVESTIGATION, 1945. On November 15, 1945, another congressional investigation of eight months' duration was begun. Gen. Short made his first public statement before the committee. He emphasized lack of information from Washington, the absence of an alert from Gen. Marshall, his own inadequate equipment, and his obvious inability to protect the fleet.

Adm. Kimmel testified that he had never received information that Washington had acquired. The Japanese code was broken and there were indications of the possibility of an attack on Hawaii. "Had I received it," he said, "the dispositions would have been very different. We might not have been able to deflect the attack, but we would have given them a very pretty party."

The majority report, issued in July 1946, held that overwhelming responsibility for the disaster lay with Adm. Kimmel and Gen. Short, but that their failures resulted from "errors of judgment" in officers of demonstrated ability and conscientiousness "and not derelictions of duty." At the same time the committee criticized the War and Navy Departments in Washington for their lack of unity of command.

CONGRESSIONAL INVESTIGATION, 1947. Another congressional investigation was held in January 1947. Gen. Short accused the War Department of making him the "scapegoat" for the disaster and maintained that even if his forces had been at the highest alert he could not possibly have protected the fleet from the tremendous damage inflicted by the Japanese. He admitted that he had erred in evaluating the possibility of hostile action, but he blamed Washington's policy of withholding information from him. Again the report was inconclusive.

AFTERMATH. Long after the end of the war both Adm. Kimmel and Gen. Short continued to maintain their innocence. Neither one ever appeared before a court-martial. In his 1955 book, *Admiral Kimmel's Story,* Kimmel recounted his congressional testimony and revealed numerous letters of abuse he had received as well as letters of sympathy. In a 1966 interview on the 25th anniversary of the attack he charged: "They made me the scapegoat. They wanted to get the United States into the war. That was President Roosevelt and Gen. George Marshall and others in the Washington High Command. He gave orders—I can't prove this categorically—that no word about Japanese fleet movements be sent to Pearl Harbor, except by Marshall, and then [Roosevelt] told Marshall not to send anything."

The elderly Gen. Short also asserted his innocence, pointing to his nearly 40 years of unblemished service. He declared that his conscience was clear that when all the facts were known he would be vindicated.

Exactly what happened before Pearl Harbor is still clouded in controversy. There is still no agreement on the causes for one of the greatest military disasters in U.S. history. The controversy still rages. Was the Pearl Harbor disaster a result of criminal negligence by military officers in the Pacific theater? On the one side, responsibility is directed to the officers in command; on the other, they are defended. Adm. William F. Halsey (q.v.) endorsed the accused officers: "I have always considered Admiral Kimmel and General Short to be splendid officers who were thrown to the wolves as scapegoats for something over which they had no control."

The best conclusion is that the disaster was due to a combination of unfortunate circumstances. Thomas C. Schelling, of Harvard University, presents a view of the "supremely ordinary blunder" at Pearl Harbor as cumulative and widespread. The surprise—complicated, diffuse, and bureaucratic—was due to: neglect of responsibility, but also responsibility poorly defined and ambiguously delegated; gaps in intelligence; an alarm that failed to work but also an alarm that had gone off so often it was disconnected; unalert watchmen; contingencies that occurred to no one; straightforward procrastination; decisions protracted by internal disagreement; inability of individuals to rise to the occasion; a measure of genuine novelty by the enemy; and possibly some sheer bad luck. *

Bibliography. R. A. Theobald, *The Final Secret of Pearl Harbor* (1954); H. E. Kimmel, *Admiral Kimmel's Story* (1955); H. L. Trefousse (ed.), *What Happened at Pearl Harbor* (1958); *Pearl Harbor: The Continuing Controversy* (1982); and R. Wohlstetter, *Pearl Harbor: Warning and Decision* (1962). In *Pearl Harbor and Its Aftermath* (1982), John Toland revives charges of Franklin D. Roosevelt's foreknowledge of the attack.

PEENEMÜNDE. German experimental center for the development of secret weapons.

LOCATION. Peenemünde was situated on a wooded island in the Baltic. Here, outdoor and underground workshops were built for advanced rocketry

---

*See Thomas C. Schelling, in the foreword to R. Wohlstetter, *Pearl Harbor: Warning and Decision* (1962), p. viii.

research. To this secret, out-of-the-way place, Hitler sent outstanding German scientists and engineers with instructions to draw up plans for new *Vergeltungswaffen* ("vengeance weapons"). Unfortunately for the German cause, he ordered relatively little money for this purpose, preferring instead to use his available funds for conventional weapons.

ALLIED REACTION. Allied espionage agents reported back to London about the work going on at Peenemünde. In May 1943, Allied photographic reconnaissance planes verified these reports. The Allied Bomber Command gave top priority to Peenemünde in its war strategy. In 1943 and 1944, concentrated air attacks were made on the experimental base. On August 7, 1943, some 597 bombers of the RAF (*q.v.*) bombed Peenemünde without inflicting heavy damage. Several important German scientists were killed in these raids. Additional attacks were made on landing sites on the French coast between Calais and Cherbourg. (*See* OSLO LETTER; BRAUN, WERNHER VON; *V-1;* and *V-2*).

Bibliography. See D. K. Huzel, *Peenemünde to Canaveral* (1962).

PEIPER, JOCHEN (1915–1976). Colonel in the SS (*q.v.*) and leader of the combat group that slaughtered 101 American prisoners in Belgium on December 17, 1944. (*See* MALMÉDY MASSACRE.)

At the beginning of the war, Peiper was assigned to the *Leibstandarte,* Hitler's bodyguard, for service with the 1st SS *Panzer* Division. He took part in the Polish campaign and was awarded the Iron Cross. As commander of a battalion he fought in France and the Balkans, and from 1942 to 1943 in Russia. In November 1943 he was assigned to command the 1st SS *Panzer* Regiment. His men pushed deeply into the enemy lines, broke up four Soviet divisions, and captured or destroyed 100 tanks and 75 antitank guns. He was rewarded with the coveted Knight's Cross.

At 29 years of age Peiper was one of the youngest regimental commanders in the German Army. In December 1944 he was chosen to lead 5,000 picked troops in the counteroffensive at Ardennes. (*See* BULGE, BATTLE OF THE.) After the Malmédy massacre, Peiper and his men were surrounded and captured by American forces. He was placed on trial at Dachau in May 1946 and condemned to death for his part in the slaughter of American prisoners. After a new trial his sentence was commuted to 12 years' imprisonment.

Bibliography. C. Whiting, *Massacre at Malmédy* (1971).

PERCIVAL, ARTHUR ERNEST (1887–1966). British commander of forces in Singapore at the time of the surrender to the Japanese in 1942.

Percival began his career as a private in the British Army. Early in the war he saw action in France. In April 1941 he was sent to the Far East to the Malaya Command. After the Japanese advance in Singapore, he was forced by a water shortage and lack of air cover to surrender the city of Singapore with 85,000 combatant troops and 15,000 foreign non-combatants.

Percival was interned in Manchuria. He was strongly criticized for his defense of both Malaya and Singapore, but he had been handicapped by prewar British military thinking which conceived of an attack on Singapore only from the sea. Percival was present at the formal surrender of the Japanese on the USS *Missouri* on September 2, 1945. (*See* SURRENDER, JAPANESE.)

PERSHING TANK. See TANKS.

PÉTAIN, HENRI PHILIPPE OMER JOSEPH (1856–1951). French soldier and statesman, hero of World War I, and head of the Vichy regime.

At the beginning of the war Pétain was venerated in France as the General whose name was associated with his promise in the earlier war: "They shall not pass!" In May 1940, with France on the brink of collapse, Premier Paul Reynaud (*q.v.*) recalled Pétain from Spain and made him Vice-Premier in an effort to bolster declining French morale. Pétain, however, was convinced that a German victory was inevitable and urged an immediate French capitulation in order to obtain the most favorable terms rather than risk a total collapse. On June 16, 1940, he succeeded Reynaud as Premier. At once he asked Hitler for an armistice, which was signed on June 22 at Compiègne (*q.v.*). It was not until June 25 that he informed the French people of its humiliating terms. More than half of France was occupied by the Germans.

VICHY. On July 10, 1940, the constitution of the Third Republic was suspended by a rump parliament and Pétain took office in unoccupied France as Chief of State. His Vichy Government, fascistic and authoritarian, collaborated with the Germans in what Pétain called "an honorable fashion." Again and again he yielded to German demands and obtained little in return. By 1942 his position became nominal when Pierre Laval (*q.v.*) took over control the next year. Hitler by then had occupied all of Vichy France.

FALL. When the Allies in June 1944 began the Normandy invasion (*q.v.*), Pétain advised his countrymen to remain quiescent. He was taken to Germany allegedly against his will. After Germany's defeat in 1945 he voluntarily returned to France to stand trial for treason. After his trial (July–August 1945), he was found guilty of collaborating with the enemy and was sentenced to death, "national indignity," and the loss of his property. Gen. Charles de Gaulle (*q.v.*) commuted the sentence to life imprisonment in a military fortress. Pétain was taken to the island of Yeu, where he died on July 23, 1951.

Seldom in history has so great a legendary hero fallen so far in the estimation of his people. From 1940 to 1942 many Frenchmen believed that Pétain had saved them from a worse fate, but his popularity plummeted under the harsh

German rule. At his trial he persisted in his sincere belief that he had served his country well: "The French people will not forget. They know that I defended them as I did at Verdun."

Bibliography. P. L. Michel, Le procès Pétain (1945); P. Farmer, Vichy Political Dilemma (1955); A. Werth, France, 1939–1945 (1955); R. Aron, The Vichy Regime (1958); S. M. Osgood, The Fall of France, 1940 (1965); and R. Griffiths, Marshal Pétain (1972).

PHILIPPINE SEA, BATTLE OF THE. Greatest carrier battle of the war on June 19, 1944.

BACKGROUND. When the Imperial GHQ in Tokyo learned of the invasion of Saipan (*See* MARIANAS, BATTLE FOR THE), it called for *Operation A-Go* committing its remaining warships to destruction of the U.S. fleet. Force A, commanded by Vice-Adm. Jisaburo Ozawa, was composed of 3 carriers, the *Taiho, Shokaku,* and *Zuikaku,* with 207 aircraft. Force B also had 3 carriers, the *Junyo, Hiyo,* and *Ryuku,* with 135 planes. Both forces were to be followed by Vice-Adm. Takeo Kurita's battleships.

To meet this formidable force the Allies sent Vice-Adm. Raymond A. Spruance (*q.v.*) in command of the assembled 5th Fleet of 15 carriers and 956 aircraft. This included Task Force 58 (*q.v.*), commanded by Vice-Adm. Marc A. Mitscher (*q.v.*). Although aware that the Allies had overwhelming superiority in the air, the Japanese counted on shore-based aircraft to even the power score.

GREAT MARIANAS TURKEY SHOOT. June 19, 1944, was a bright, warm day with few clouds to give cover for fighter pilots. For more than eight hours, from mid-morning to darkness, there was a desperate air battle over and around Guam. Early that morning American radar picked up an attack group to the west. This was the first of 4 massive raids from Ozawa's carriers. On the first raid 16 *Zeke* fighters, 46 *Zekes* carrying bombs, and 8 torpedo-carrying *Jills* were launched. U.S. *Hellcats* from the *Essex, Bunker Hill, Princeton,* and *Cowpens* rose to meet them. The bombers scattered at once, while the fighters went into acrobatics to avoid them, leaving the bombers vulnerable. Within minutes 45 of the 69 Japanese planes were destroyed. Not a single enemy aircraft reached the U.S. carriers.

The air battle that continued for the rest of the day turned out to be what an American aviator called "The Great Marianas Turkey Shoot." On Raid II the Japanese lost 98 of 130 planes; on Raid III 7 out of 47; and on Raid IV 73 out of 82. It was a fierce mêlée in which pilots went into zooms and sideslips, barrel rolls, and wingovers. Pilots maneuvered desperately to get on the tail of an enemy aircraft. Planes went into spirals, exploded in mid-air, or crashed flaming into the sea.

LOSSES. Estimates vary on Japanese air losses but it is believed that nearly all their planes, as many as 340, committed to battle were lost. Added to these were another 50 Guam-based planes, again with Japan's best remaining pilots. The Japanese also lost three carriers (*Shokaku, Taiho,* and *Hiyo*).

The U.S. Navy lost 30 planes. Of the 216 aircraft launched, many crashed into the sea in the dark as they struggled to find their carriers. Most of the crews were picked up, but 16 pilots and 33 crewmen were lost. Naval losses were only two small vessels.

SIGNIFICANCE. A crushing defeat for Japan, the air battle assured the success of the Allied operation in the Marianas. Japanese air power received a blow from which it never recovered. The contestants met on equal terms, but the Americans demonstrated their superiority in the air. After the battle the Japanese had so few remaining planes and pilots that their aircraft carriers were rendered useless.

Bibliography. R. R. Smith, *Triumph in the Philippines* (1963); S. E. Morison, *The Two-Ocean War* (1963); C. A. Lockwood and H. C. Adamson, *Battles of the Philippine Sea* (1967); and S. L. Falk, *Liberation of the Philippines* (1971).

PHONY WAR. Term popularized in the American press to describe the "sit-down war." (*See SITZKRIEG.*)

PIUS XII (*EUGENIO PACELLI*) (1876–1958). Roman Catholic Pope from 1939 through World War II.

In December 1939 Pius XII spoke out against "premeditated aggression" and the "barbarities of war." In his Christmas message 1942 he deplored the death and progressive extinction of those condemned because of their nation or race. In 1943 he denounced the persecution of non-Aryan or semi-Aryan Catholics. That same year he was instrumental in having Rome declared an open city, thereby preventing great damage to the capital. He used diplomatic immunity shielding victims from persecution, but when 3,000 Jews were rounded up in Rome he was accused of remaining silent.

POSTWAR CONTROVERSY. Pius XII died at Castel Gandolfo on October 9, 1958. After his death there arose a bitter controversy about his role in the Holocaust suffered by the Jews. (*See FINAL SOLUTION.*) Rolf Hochhuth, a German playwright, attacked Pius XII because of his alleged unwillingness to seek a halt to the persecution of Jews. Others produced documents to support the charge that he expressed no moral outrage or sense of urgency and did not go beyond acts of superficial charity. Defenders pointed out that any public defense by Pius XII would only have worsened the plight of Jews as well as Catholics in Nazi-occupied Europe. Here, too, documents were collected to show that the Pope had done what was possible to save Jews from Hitler's gas ovens.

Thin, bespectacled, ascetic, Pius XII was regarded as a master diplomat. He claimed that he was deeply distressed by the plight of the Jews, but "unhappily, in the present circumstances we cannot offer them effective help other than through our prayers.''

Bibliography. For a sympathetic biography, *see* N. Padellaro (1957). For a critical study, *see* S. Friedländer, *Pius XII and the Third Reich: A Documentation* (1966).

PLOESTI RAID. Allied air strike at the Ploesti oil fields in Rumania in 1943. The project was considered to be of such importance that it was given three successive code names: *Statesman* (May 19, 1943); *Soapsuds* (May 24, 1943); and *Tidal Wave* (July 1, 1943).

BACKGROUND. The German war machine could operate efficiently only as long as a sufficient supply of oil was maintained. On land fast-moving *Panzers* (*q.v.*) used petrol in huge quantities, while at sea, oil powered the turbines of German surface vessels and the diesels of U-Boats. The aircraft of the *Luftwaffe* (*q.v.*) had to have large supplies of the precious fluid. Much necessary oil was transported by rail tanker or pumped along pipelines from Rumania. German capital had played a major role in Rumania's industrial growth, and Germany was by far Rumania's largest customer for oil.

At the same time German U-Boats made deadly attacks on oil tankers in the shipping lanes from Venezuela and Texas to Britain in an attempt to deny oil to the enemy. The Allies were determined to retaliate by striking at synthetic oil plants inside Germany while at the same time seeking to cut off supplies to Germany from Rumania. The battle for oil became critical as the war went on.

TARGET. The Allied High Command was especially attracted by Ploesti (Ployeshti, or Ploesci), capital of Ploesti Province, in Rumania, 160 miles west of the Black Sea and 35 miles north of Bucharest. The town was dominated by oil refineries, which ringed it outside the surrounding railways. Germans regarded the area of such critical importance that they took careful measures for its defense. About 100 medium and heavy antiaircraft guns were manned by Rumanians and Germans, while the *Luftwaffe* was assigned six airfields near Ploesti. German technicians constructed two movable dummy towns of papier-mâché east and south of the town to confuse enemy aircraft.

FIRST STRIKE. On June 11, 1942, a preliminary attack was made on Ploesti by a small flight of 13 *B-24 Liberators* (*See* AIRCRAFT: AMERICAN AIRCRAFT DATA CHART), which took off from Near Eastern bases. Little damage was done. The raid encouraged Hitler to strengthen his Rumanian air defenses even further.

Meanwhile, the Allied Combined Chiefs of Staff instructed its planning staff to treat a major attack on Ploesti ''as a matter of emergency.'' Operations officers of the Royal Air Force (*q.v.*) argued that a low-level assault might be dangerous, but Gen. Henry H. Arnold (*q.v.*) judged it to be feasible. Plans crystallized for a major attack. The final decision to move was made at the Third Washington Conference (*q.v.*) in late May 1943.

TIDAL WAVE. Operation Tidal Wave began at dawn on August 1, 1943. From Benghazi, a seaport on the northern coast of Africa, 178 *Liberators* took off. Ahead of the air crews was a minimum of 12 hours flight, involving a 2,700-mile round trip, half of it directly over enemy-held territory. There was little margin for error—the extreme operating range of the *B-24*s was 3,500 miles. The air fleet took a northwest course for Corfu, passed 200 miles east of Crete, and then penetrated the Ionian Sea between Italy and Greece. Once across the Albanian coast the pilots had to negotiate mountains up to 8,000 feet. Then the planes crossed the German-occupied Balkans, flying at tree-top level to confuse radar defenses. The raiders had to fight off successive fighter attacks long before they reached their target.

Waves of *B-24*s flew in low to attack the seven refinery targets. Allied airmen dropped their bombs and soon had the refineries and oil tanks covered with flames and black smoke. At the same time the big *Liberators* began going down like stricken flies.

LOSSES. The final total of loss and damage made depressing reading for the Allies. Only 111 *Liberators* returned from the raid and more than half of these were damaged. The *Luftwaffe* claimed 48 shot down and 55 severely damaged, which was remarkably close to the final figures of 54 bombers lost, 41 shot down by the defenders. Of the 1,733 men sent on the mission, 446 were killed, 108 were taken prisoner in Rumania and Bulgaria, and others were lost in the Aegean as they tried to make their way back to Africa. Some found a haven in neutral Turkey.

AFTERMATH. Estimates varied on results of the raid. Allied war leaders professed satisfaction. Gen. Dwight D. Eisenhower (*q.v.*) pronounced the Ploesti attack "reasonably successful." An official U.S. Strategic Bombing Survey later declared that the raid was effective. "It was the Nazis' lack of gasoline, not the loss of plane production, that gave us air superiority." German sources, on the other hand, claimed that little damage was done, that full production started soon, and that their problem was not production of oil but its distribution. Neutral opinion had it that, although carefully planned and courageously carried out, *Operation Tidal Wave* was a costly failure.

Bibliography. W. F. Craven and J. L. Cate, *The Army Air Forces in World War II,* Vol. II (1949); L. Wolff, *Low Level Attack* (1957); J. Dugan, *Ploesti* (1963); R. A. Freeman, *The Mighty Eighth* (1970); J. Sweetman, *Ploesti Oil Strike* (1974); and R. Jackson, *Famous Bomber Raids of World War II* (1980).

PLUTO (PIPE LINES UNDER THE OCEAN). Acronym for fuel pipeline constructed under the English Channel in preparation for *Operation Overlord* (*q.v.*), the assault on Fortress Europe (*q.v.*) in June 1944.

Pluto, developed by Allied technicians, was a part of the enormous invasion buildup. Its purpose was to maintain supplies of gasoline to Allied troops on the Continent. A masterpiece of British ingenuity, the lines were wound on huge floating drums, shaped like a cotton reel, 60 feet long and 40 feet in diameter. Each drum was towed by a tug. The drum rested on the water and played out the line as it moved. (*See* NORMANDY INVASION.)

POLAND, CAMPAIGN IN. Opening invasion of World War II and the culminating step of Hitler's attempt to "right the wrongs of Versailles."

BACKGROUND. Although statesmen of the Weimar Republic bitterly resented the Treaty of Versailles after World War I, they, nevertheless, adopted a program of reconciliation. They cooperated in the system of collective security, obtained several drastic reductions in reparations, accepted membership in the League of Nations, and effected the evacuation of the Rhineland in 1930. Hitler rejected this approach and turned to a policy of aggression. He took Germany out of the League of Nations (1933), repudiated the military and naval clauses of the Treaty of Versailles (1935), began the rearming of Germany (1935), and won *Anschluss* (union) with Austria (1938).

Meanwhile, the generating causes for war were coming to a head. (*See* CAUSES OF WORLD WAR II.) In 1939 Hitler regarded Danzig (now Gdansk) and also the Polish Corridor to the sea as part of German *Lebensraum* (*q.v.*). In the Allied world, however, the belief that he was not ready to go to war continued. The situation changed in March 1939 when Hitler took all of Czechoslovakia. Then, when Germany began to mass troops along the Polish border, Poland was given a guarantee by Britain and France. On August 23, 1939, came the Russo-German Nonaggression Pact (*q.v.*), which gave Hitler the green light for his invasion of Poland. On August 29 he sent an ultimatum to Poland for acceptance before midnight, spelling out his demands to the British Ambassador in Berlin but never communicating them to the Poles.

PREPARATIONS. For the operation against Poland, Hitler selected his most experienced military leaders. He designated Gen. Walther von Brauchitsch (*q.v.*) as Supreme Commander, with Gen. Franz Halder (*q.v.*) as Chief of Staff, Gen. Gerd von Rundstedt (*q.v.*) to command three armies in the south, and Gen. Fedor von Bock (*q.v.*) to lead two armies in the north. For the operation, Hitler assigned 75 divisions, including reserve and occupation troops, totaling more than 1 million men.

POLISH DEFENSE. Against Germany's concentrated 54 front-line divisions, the Poles had 22 infantry divisions and 7 cavalry brigades. Of their 2 million first-line troops, only one-third were in the field at the time of the assault and these were no match against the avalanche of German power. Polish cavalry turned out to be helpless against German mechanized forces. The Polish Air Force had only a few first-line planes. Worst of all, the Poles would mistakenly try to defend their strategically indefensible western borders.

BLITZKRIEG. As justification for the German attack, Hitler used a trumped-up raid by ''Polish'' troops on a German radio station. (*See* GLEIWITZ RAID.) On September 1, 1939, without a declaration of war, nine German columns moved simultaneously from East Prussia, Pomerania, Silesia, and Slovakia across the Polish border. The clear autumn weather was ideal for air operations, the baked Polish plains were made to order for German tanks.

The opening *Blitzkrieg* (*q.v.*) was a stunning revelation of miliary adaptability to the machine age. Instead of static lines of World War I vintage (*see* MAGINOT LINE), the German drive stressed mobility, fluidity, and speed. The entire battlefield became an amorphous penetration, ''like a plague of vermin in a garden.''

The first strike came from the air. The *Luftwaffe* (*q.v.*), with 1,400 first-line planes based in Königsberg and Vienna, swooped down on Polish airfields and annihilated the enemy air force. At the same time, dive bombers demolished transportation facilities, bridges, and railroad stations, struck at communications, and trapped the Polish ground forces without the possibility of retreat. German *Stukas* (*q.v.*), with terror-provoking whistles in their wings, screamed down on Polish targets and strafed refugees cluttering the highways.

On the ground German armored forces pierced the 1,200-mile border at a dozen points. Trail-blazing motorized units, including motorcycles, light tanks, armored cars, and motorized artillery, were followed by heavy tanks. The columns headed for Polish nerve centers—roads, and railway junctions, bridges, telegraph stations, and airfields. As they moved they were supplied by air with gasoline, ammunition, and food. There were no opposing lines, no head-on clashes, but instead a succession of sudden and deep penetrations.

Finally, came the superbly trained infantry. Foot soldiers pushed ahead to join the extended *Panzer* (*q.v.*) tank divisions. The planned confusion worked perfectly. It was a classic example of the Cannae technique (pincers and encirclement) with an innovation—a greater outer encirclement plus an inner one. On the outer rim in the north, one German Army cut across the Polish Corridor and then split into two parts, one section moving still farther northward to reduce Gdynia, and the other heading above Warsaw. At the southern great semi-circle, other German spearheads swung around Krakow. Inside the great circle more armies formed a smaller arc around the capital. In a little over a week von Rundstedt was hammering at the gates of Warsaw.

RUSSIAN INVASION. On September 17, 1939, came additional bad news for the Poles. Without warning, Russian troops crossed the borders from the east into Poland. They came, Stalin said, ''to liberate and protect Ukrainian and White Russian minorities.'' Pushing ahead against only token resistance, Russians captured eastern Poland up to the Curzon Line, which had been set up in December 1919 by the Allied Supreme Council as the tentative eastern frontier of Poland. The Russians had cut off Germans from the rich oil fields of Galicia and also blocked the road to Rumania.

FALL OF WARSAW. By now Warsaw, the Polish capital 389 miles east of Berlin, was surrounded by German armies. The Poles, organized by Major Stefan Starzymski, "Stefan the Stubborn," set up fortifications and dug trenches zigzagging through the streets. From *Luftwaffe* planes came millions of pamphlets demanding surrender and promising "the brave Polish officers" that they could keep their swords. The response was contemptuous silence. The Germans then battered the city day and night from the air and from massed artillery. In ten days the city was reduced to piles of brick, rubble, and debris. Food ran low and water supplies were disrupted. On September 27, 1939, with no more ammunition and their cause hopeless, the defenders capitulated. (*See* WARSAW, BOMBING OF.)

LOSSES. Polish losses were heavy, but more than 70,000 Poles managed to flee to France and England. Later they performed valuable services for the Allies. It was not a cheap victory for Hitler. The Germans paid for it with 8,082 killed, 27,278 wounded, and 5,029 missing. They also lost 217 tanks and 400 aircraft.

SIGNIFICANCE. In one month Poland had been crushed in one of the speediest major campaigns in history. Again Hitler astounded his own people and the entire world by an extraordinary victory. It was clear now to the Western Allies that they faced a gigantic task in halting the Nazi avalanche.

AFTERMATH. On September 28, 1939, Hitler and Stalin divided the spoils of war. Poland, country of 150,000 square miles and a nation of 35,000,000 people, was partitioned for the fifth time (1772, 1793, 1795, 1815, and 1939). The Russians took all Poland to the Curzon Line, 77,000 square miles, including the major oil resources. The Germans appropriated 73,000 square miles, including the greater share of Poland's mining and manufacturing areas, with 22 million people. Of his share Hitler incorporated 36,000 square miles into Germany, and another 36,000 square miles in central Poland into a new General Government, with Krakow as its capital, and Hans Frank (*q.v.*), as Nazi administrator.

Bibliography. *The German New Order in Poland* (Polish Government White Paper) (1941); F. O. Miksche, *Attack: A Study of Blitzkrieg Tactics* (1942); J. T. Shotwell and M. M. Laserson, *Poland and Russia, 1919–1945* (1945); and A. Rossi, *The Russo-German Alliance, August, 1939 to June, 1941* (1949).

POLITICAL CONSEQUENCES OF THE WAR. The victory of the Allies in World War II resulted in significant changes in the political structure of Europe and the world.

ACCOUNTING. The war affected every phase of life. Up to 55 million people died in the crucible and millions were injured, scarred, or crippled. (*See*

CASUALTIES, WAR.) Added to this melancholy result was enormous property and material damage. (*See* ECONOMIC CONSEQUENCES OF THE WAR.) The technical brilliance of 20th-century scientists was displayed, but at the same time the war brought terror and misery to many millions of people and changed the nature of society. (*See* SOCIAL IMPACT OF THE WAR; and PSYCHOLOGICAL EFFECTS OF THE WAR.)

BASIC CHANGES. There were five fundamental political changes:

1. The old European state system, which had been dealt a shattering blow in World War I, was undermined still further.

2. The area of decisive global power shifted from its Western European habitat to the United States and the Soviet Union, each of which became a nucleus of world hegemony.

3. The nationalism born in Europe was extended to Asia and Africa, where colonial peoples demanded and obtained an end to the old imperialism.

4. There was a political swing to the Left in Western Europe.

5. Invention of new weapons altered past concepts of military geography. Industrial nations of the West became increasingly vulnerable in the new age of atomic power.

DECLINE OF EUROPE. In 1939 Britain and France went to war to maintain the traditional balance of power that Hitler wanted to change. Although the Allies won the war, they saw the destruction of the old balance of power. The process had been going on for some time. In 1918 four empires—German, Austrian, Russian and Turkish—collapsed. Britain and France were supposed to be strong victors, but actually their strength was an illusion. They were unable to impose a treaty on Turkey and had great difficulty in attempting to sort out Eastern European affairs. Both London and Paris conveniently forgot that their new status had been won in large part by American participation in the war and by Washington's quick withdrawal into isolation after World War I.

After 1919 the military balance was gradually restored as Russia and Germany recovered. The aggressive diplomacy of Hitler in the 1930s pushed the balance in Germany's favor. By the time Britain and France realized the extent of German expansionism in Central Europe, it was too late to restore the balance of power. In less than a year France capitulated and the British were driven from the Continent.

British success in World War II was due in large part to shrewd diplomacy. Churchill, an inspired war leader, refused to capitulate under any circumstances. He knew that Britain alone could not defeat the Axis, but he was certain that eventually the United States and the Soviet Union would be embroiled, whether they wanted to or not. With new powerful allies, Britain went on to victory, but was badly wounded by nearly six years of war. British interests were maintained, but the former equilibrium was lost. Germany, Italy, and France all lay prostrate and too weak to restore the balance of power.

AMERICAN AND SOVIET INFLUENCE. Two great superpowers, the United States and the Soviet Union, both outsiders, now controlled the European balance of power. As soon as World War I was ended in 1918, the United States retreated into isolationism, but the situation after 1945 was different. Washington and Moscow had worked together in the mighty effort to destroy Hitler, but now relations between the two deteriorated rapidly. Wartime unity evaporated as what Churchill called an Iron Curtain stretched from Stettin to Trieste. The Cold War had begun. Neither power dared to withdraw from Europe. Postwar Europe was cut in two with Western Europe under American sponsorship and Eastern Europe under the Soviet sphere. The old Europe, which for centuries had exercised global power, was now split into two areas of influence.

The war brought dramatic increases in American and Russian production. Their new political and diplomatic position in European affairs reflected this heightened economic status for the time being. Under the impact of war the United States, already the world's leading industrial power, reached amazing levels of production. Soviet Russia, too, after early losses, recovered and inaugurated a vastly expanded industrial plant. This rapid growth of industrial capacity by both the United States and the Soviet Union led to a temporary reversal of the political power relationship between Europe and the remainder of the world.

COLONIAL REVOLT. World War II furthered the decline of Western imperialism. The process had already started in World War I, which was called an anti-imperialist war and which put a temporary end to German ambitions for a great colonial empire. The victors divided among themselves the colonial inheritance of the vanquished, only to find the imperialist system wavering all over the world.

Nationalism and democracy, at one time operating exclusively in Europe and North America, were introduced into Eastern Europe following World War I. After 1945 they were further promoted in the colonial world. The development in Africa was typical of a global tendency. Africa, the second largest continent, three times the size of Europe and rich in natural resources, had been carved into colonies and protectorates by European conquerors in the 19th century. Now, in what was called "a revolution of rising expectations," all Africa from Cairo to the Cape of Good Hope exploded in a drive for political emancipation. The older map of Africa lost all meaning as a patchwork of independent states emerged.

There were varied reactions of colonial powers to the rising tide of nationalism. The United States, never comfortable in the role of colonial power, freed the Philippines, although it was the only country strong enough to retain possession of its colonies. The British, too, showed an understanding of the new trend and began the process of liquidating their colonial empire and transforming it into a commonwealth of independent nations. With some success they trained Africans for responsibilities of future self-government. They provided for steps to independence, encouraged mixed legislative councils, and delegated more and more power to local leaders. Eventually, the British were able to withdraw from most of Africa without the ignominy of being pushed out.

The French and Dutch, however, did not show the same understanding of what was happening in the colonial world. This may be attributed in part to their own isolation under German occupation and their intense preoccupation with winning liberation. For decades the French had centered in Paris the administration of their colonies and utilized a concept of assimilation by which the colonies were to be absorbed into the national French framework. The people who at one time had extended the gospel of nationalism and democracy to all corners of Europe now showed a lack of understanding for the aspirations of colonial peoples. Depressed by their humiliating defeat by the Germans, the French persisted in efforts to maintain control of their colonies by force. They encountered resistance and were embroiled in a series of colonial wars. It was far too late to extend their colonial empire into a French Community of Nations on the model of the British Commonwealth of Nations.

SWING TO LEFT. Military confrontations of World War II broke the back of Fascist aggression. At its close, due in part to the revulsion of the masses against Hitler and Mussolini, there was a strong political swing to the Left. There were major wartime and postwar changes in every belligerent government including an intensification of powerful leftward sympathies. This trend was indicated as early as 1945 by rise to political power of the Labour Party, Britain's champion of democratic socialism, and by the emergence of Christian Socialist parties in France, Germany, and Italy.

At the same time war achievements of the Soviet Union made a strong impression on the peoples of Western Europe. The prestige of the Kremlin was enhanced and growth of Communist ideology was promoted. Strong Communist parties appeared in both France and Italy. Later they drifted from Russian influence to what was called Eurocommunism.

DEFEATED GERMANY. At the Potsdam Conference (*q.v.*), held from July 17 to August 2, 1945, it was stipulated that "so far as practicable there shall be no uniformity of treatment of the German population throughout Germany." The defeated country was occupied by British, American, Russian, and French troops, and divided into four zones with four different policies of administration. The terms for Germany were: disarmament and demilitarization; dissolution of the National Socialist Party and its affiliates; elimination of militarism; provisions for democratization; trials for war criminals; and stiff reparations.

The Council of Foreign Ministers, representing the victorious Allies, met in

Paris in 1946, in Moscow in the spring of 1947, and in London in the winter of 1947. They remained deadlocked on precise terms of the proposed German and Austrian treaties of peace. Soviet representatives refused to yield or compromise on any of their views and repeatedly denounced other delegates as warmongers. (*See* PARIS PEACE CONFERENCE.)

NUREMBERG TRIALS. From November 1945 to October 1946, 21 Nazi war leaders were brought to trial at Nuremberg, scene of National Socialist Party rallies, and tried on four counts: 1, conspiracy to commit crimes alleged in other counts; 2, crimes against peace; 3, war crimes; and 4, crimes against humanity. After prolonged trials, 12 (including Martin Bormann [*q.v.*], tried in absentia), were sentenced to death. (*See* NUREMBERG TRIALS.)

ATOMIC AGE. As soon as the war was over it was recognized generally that the one major security problem underlying all others was control of atomic energy. At that stage the United States was the only country that had produced atomic bombs, although the Soviet Union and other countries possessed the basic scientific knowledge necessary for their production. The question of supervising scientific and technical uses of atomic energy through a system of licensing and control became a paramount issue among nations.

Relationships among nations was considerably altered by new nuclear weapons. It became clear now that a sufficient supply of such weapons was available to destroy all civilization if they were released in an all-out war. Although none of the great powers appeared to be contemplating aggression on a large scale, there was always the chance that a minor confrontation might result in a miscalculation that could develop rapidly into a major war.

Bibliography. B. Ward, *The West at Bay* (1948); R. K. Smith, *The State of Europe* (1949); H. Holborn, *The Political Collapse of Europe* (1951); C. Dawson, *The Movement of World Revolution* (1960); R. Emerson, *From Empire to Nation* (1960); J. Strachey, *The End of Empire* (1960); H. Kahn, *On Thermonuclear War* (1960); J. A. Lukacs, *A History of the Cold War* (1961); G. Barraclough, *Introduction to Contemporary History* (1965); L. L. Snyder, *The New Nationalism* (1968); and R. A. Divine, (ed.), *Causes and Consequences of World War II* (1970).

POLITICAL WARFARE EXECUTIVE (PWE). British agency organized to gather information for the Allied war effort. It worked hand in hand with the American OWI. (*See* OFFICE OF WAR INFORMATION.)

POPSKI'S PRIVATE ARMY. Independent unit serving the Allies.

Popski's Private Army was formed in October 1942 by Vladimir Peniakoff (Popski), who had been born in Belgium of Russian parents and educated in England. In 1940 Peniakoff joined the Long Range Desert Group (*q.v.*) and served with it for two years before establishing his own independent unit. Popski's Private Army served in North Africa behind enemy lines, obtaining important information, harassing lines of communication, and raiding in small, effective sorties. Later, it served in Italy, where it cooperated with Partisans (*q.v.*) behind the front lines. Its maximum strength was 120 men.

Bibliography. V. Peniakoff, *Private Army* (1950).

PORTAL, CHARLES FREDERICK ALGERNON (1893–1971). British officer responsible for the performance of the Royal Air Force. (*q.v.*)

In 1940 Portal was made Commander-in-Chief of the RAF Bomber Command, and then served as Chief of Air Staff for the remainder of the war. In this post he was responsible for directing the operations of the Royal Air Force (*q.v.*). He also attended the major war strategy conferences, especially at Casablanca (January 14–23, 1943), at Washington (May 11–27, 1943), and at Quebec (August 17–24, 1943) (*qq.v.*). He was respected and relied upon by Allied war leaders for his wide knowledge of air operations.

POTSDAM CONFERENCE. Code or cover name *Terminal*. Meeting of the chiefs of state of the Big Three, their principal advisers, and technical experts in Potsdam for two weeks in mid-summer 1945 to clarify and implement earlier agreements reached at the Yalta Conference (*q.v.*).

PARTICIPANTS. The conferees met from July 17 to August 2, 1945. Of the three leaders who made the decisions at Yalta, only Stalin remained. Negotiations were interrupted by parliamentary elections in Britain, in which the victory of the Labour Party resulted in replacement at Potsdam of Churchill by Clement R. Attlee (*q.v.*). The United States was represented by Roosevelt's successor, Harry S Truman (*q.v.*) Stalin spoke for the Soviet Union.

POTSDAM DECLARATION. A detailed blueprint for the future of defeated Germany emerged from the conference. "It is not the intention of the Allies," declared the representatives of the victorious nations, "to destroy or enslave the German people." The Germans, by amending their ways, would be able "in due course to take their place among the free and peaceful peoples of the world." At the same time, to assure that Germany would never again be able to threaten its neighbors or the peace of the world, the victorious nations would deprive it of the power to make war by abolishing all armed forces of the country and by forbidding manufacture of armaments. Nazism and its institutions would be abolished, the trial and punishment of war criminals pursued, and German education controlled by the inculcation of democratic ideas.

COUNCIL OF MINISTERS. It was agreed that a Council of Foreign Ministers, representing the five principal powers, would prepare peace treaties with Italy, and the Axis satellites—Bulgaria, Rumania, Hungary, and Finland. The body would also deal with other problems of general Allied concern. (*See* PARIS PEACE CONFERENCE.)

POLITICAL DECISIONS. Germany was carved into four administrative zones—Russian in the east and center; British in the northwest; French in the southwest; and American in the south. In each zone of occupation a distinctive pattern of administration was to be applied. Military rule would be displaced gradually by a local adminstration under foreign military control. This was an unprecedented attempt by four powers of divergent philosophies and methods to govern and reeducate in their own respective way a once highly integrated nation.

POLISH TERRITORY. Two territorial decisions were made for Eastern Europe. The northern portion of East Prussia, including the port of Königsberg, was "provisionally" allotted to the Soviet Union. What remained of East Prussia, including the free city of Danzig and an additional slice of German territory extending westward to the Oder and Neisse Rivers, was given to Poland, pending the final delimitation in a peace conference. The reason was to compensate the Poles for the eastern half of Poland, which the USSR had annexed in 1939.

In all, Germany was to lose about a quarter of its territory held in 1937. At the same time the conferees sought to mitigate the lot of Germans who were being driven out by Poles by calling for an "orderly transfer" of the German population. A similar formula was to be applied to those Germans forced to leave Czechoslovakia and Hungary.

ECONOMIC DECISIONS. Special attention was given to the effective deindustrialization of Germany. The economy would be decentralized, German external assets expropriated, and economic controls retained. Germany's industrial power would be curtailed sharply, leaving it for the time being an agricultural nation stripped of heavy industry. The standard of living would not be allowed to rise "above average European standards."

REPARATIONS. Defeated Germany was required to pay reparations as compensation for loss and suffering caused other peoples. The Soviet Union was awarded reparations in the form of goods and industrial equipment in the Russian zone of occupation, as well as a fourth of plant and machinery in the British and American zones. Thus, Stalin got what he wanted, on the ground that the Russians had borne the brunt of the battle against Germany and had suffered the greatest economic as well as human losses. Furthermore, the Russians were given complete control over German external assets in Finland, Hungary, Bulgaria, Rumania, and eastern Austria. The Russians promised to settle out of their own share of reparations Polish claims for reparations. The Western Allies agreed to collect their reparations from the remaining industrial wealth in their own zones of occupation.

AFTERMATH. Apart from these important decisions, the victors made little headway at Potsdam in dealing with many lesser issues in Eastern Europe, some of which involved implementation of decisions made at Yalta. In the months that followed the chasm between the West and the Soviets widened, as was revealed in stormy meetings between the representatives of the Foreign Ministers' Council in London, Paris, and New York. In February 1947, 18 months after Potsdam, treaties were finally signed with Italy, Rumania, Hungary, Finland, and Bulgaria.

Bibliography. F. W. Pick, *Peacemaking in Perspective: From Potsdam to Paris* (1950); H. Feis, *Between War and Peace: The Potsdam Conference* (1960); and J. L. Snell, *Illusion and Necessity* (1963).

POUND, ALFRED DUDLEY (1877–1943). British Admiral of the Fleet, who was largely responsible for many of the Royal Navy's successes in the first years of the war.

From June 1939 until his death Pound was First Sea Lord and Chief of the Naval Staff. During the next four years he played an important role in war leadership. He organized the naval strategy that brought about the victory over the Italians at Cape Matapan, the evacuation of British forces from Greece and Crete, the holding of Malta as a naval base, the Allied landings in North Africa, and the landing of the Allied forces in Sicily. In the Atlantic his strategy led to the scuttling of the *Admiral Graf Spee,* the sinking of the giant German battleship *Bismarck (qq.v.),* and the eventual defeat of the U-Boat campaign.

Early in September 1943 Pound informed Churchill that his health had deteriorated so much that he had to resign as First Sea Lord. Churchill was distressed but had to agree. Pound returned to England and on October 21, 1943 (Trafalgar Day) he died in a London hospital.

Experienced in naval operations, Pound was flexible in his thinking. Although 62 years of age when the war began, he displayed a toughness and spirit of mind during the intense strain of the next four years. He declined the peerage offered him in 1943. (*See* CAPE MATAPAN, BATTLE OF; GREECE, BATTLE FOR; CRETE, BATTLE OF; MALTA, SIEGE OF; NORTH AFRICA, CAMPAIGNS IN; and SICILY, INVASION OF.)

Bibliography. See W. S. Churchill, *The Second World War,* vols. I–IV (1948–1952); and T. K. Derry, *History of the Second World War* (1952).

PRIEN, GÜNTHER (1909–1941.) German U-Boat commander who sank the *Royal Oak (q.v.).*

Commanding the *U-47* on the night of October 13–14, 1939, Prien passed through the treacherous currents of the Kirk Sound, entered Scapa Flow, and sank the giant British battleship *Royal Oak.* His feat was hailed with joy throughout Germany. In other countries, too, there was praise for the energy and daring displayed by the U-Boat commander and his crew. The young skipper was received in a special audience with the *Fuehrer* and awarded the Iron Cross (First Class). Each member of the crew received the Iron Cross (Second Class).

Prien continued his services at sea, but on March 17, 1941, he was drowned while attacking a convoy.

PRINCE OF WALES. British battleship sunk along with the battlecruiser *Repulse* on December 10, 1941.

The new battleship, *Prince of Wales,* was the second of the *King George V* class to be commissioned. Displacing 45,000 tons, she had two widely spaced, tall, flat-sided stacks, with a massive tower bridge with tripod foremast. She was 740 feet long with a beam of 103 feet. She mounted ten 14-inch guns, sixteen 5.25-inch guns, and many smaller weapons. She was the fastest battleship in the British Navy.

On May 24, 1941, with dockyard workmen still aboard, the *Prince of Wales* followed her flagship, HMS *Hood* (*q.v.*), into action against the German battleship *Bismarck* (*q.v.*). As soon as the *Hood* blew up, the Germans turned their fire on the *Prince of Wales,* inflicting serious damage.

The *Prince of Wales* carried British Prime Minister Winston Churchill to his transatlantic meeting with President Franklin D. Roosevelt. (*See* ATLANTIC CHARTER.) On December 10, 1941, the *Prince of Wales* and the old battlecruiser *Repulse* (*q.v.*) were sent with the Royal Navy Force Z under Vice Adm. Tom Phillips in an ill-advised attempt to prevent the Japanese from attacking the British and Dutch possessions in the East Indies. Without air cover, both the *Prince of Wales* and the *Repulse* were sunk by Japanese aircraft. Phillips and 800 crewmen went down with the ship, but 2,000 men were saved.

PRISONERS OF WAR (POWs). The vast scale of operations on European fronts intensified the problem of how to deal with prisoners of war.

BACKGROUND. The Hague Conferences of 1899 and 1907 attempted to regulate warfare by providing for the protection of prisoners, wounded, and non-combatants. Regulations were adopted for humane treatment of prisoners. Their personal belongings were to remain their own property; they could be confined only as an indispensable measure of safety; their labor could be used according to rank and aptitude, with the exception of officers; their tasks could not be excessive and would have nothing to do with military operations; they were to receive the same food, clothing, and quarters as troops of the government that captured them; they would be subject to the same laws and regulations of the state into whose hands they had fallen; any liberated prisoner who again took up arms against the government that released him forfeited his rights as a prisoner of war and could be brought before the courts.

WORLD WAR II. These rules were not always observed properly in either World War I or World War II. At the start of World War II, efforts were made on all sides to follow regulations on treatment of prisoners of war. As intensity of conflict mounted, it became increasingly difficult to provide food, housing, and guards for prisoners taken in combat. With exceptions, the British and Americans were able to maintain reasonably fair standards, but both Germans and Russians accused each other of scandalous and barbaric treatment of their men captured by the enemy.

Accurate statistics on the numbers of prisoners of war in World War II are impossible to obtain. These rough estimates in round figures include the missing as well as prisoners of war: Britain, 214,000; Germany, 3,400,000; Italy, 350,000; USSR, 5,750,000; United States, 139,000.

BRITISH. Despite declining resources and lack of space, the British did what they could to maintain standards set by The Hague and Geneva Conventions. Like other belligerents, they were handicapped by inadequate shipping when hordes of enemy troops were captured. At the Battle of El Alamein (*q.v.*) in early November 1942, they had to contend with 30,000 Axis prisoners. In mid-May 1943 they were overwhelmed with 250,000 German and Italian prisoners of war in North Africa. Many of these POWs were transferred to Canadian camps.

GERMAN. Flushed with victory in the early days of the war, Germans treated their prisoners of war humanely, but later changed their attitude. At first, German U-Boat commanders made an attempt to rescue prisoners from ships they sank, but soon abandoned the effort when attacked from the air. (*See* LACONIA ORDER.)

The Germans made a distinction in their treatment of war prisoners. They transferred British and American POWs to prison camps where they received comparatively good treatment. They sent officers to special prisons, including Colditz and Königstein (*qq.v.*), from which many attempts were made to escape.

Poles and Russians, on the other hand, regarded as subhuman by Nazi racial logic, were treated with utmost severity. Of nearly 6 million Russians taken prisoner by Germans, only about 1 million survived the war. The remainder either disappeared, died, or were executed. During the Russian winter of 1941–1942, vast numbers of Russian POWs were left in the open without food or shelter to die in the miserable weather. Policy was changed in the latter stage of the war. On the principle that dead prisoners were useless, tens of thousands of Russians were assigned by German captors to armaments factories and mines, where they worked under most difficult conditions.

RUSSIANS. The Russians replied in kind. They gave little consideration to German prisoners of war and handled them with utmost cruelty. Russian treatment of POWs was enveloped by mystery and rumor. Tens of thousands of German prisoners literally disappeared into the Russian steppes. After August 1940, 4,443 Polish officers who had been taken prisoner were murdered and buried in the forest near Katyn. Russians and Germans mutually accused each other of the atrocity. (*See* KATYN MASSACRE.)

German troops were so intimidated by reports of what happened to their comrades taken prisoner that in the late stage of the war they hastened to surrender to Anglo-American troops rather than face Russian vengeance. They were convinced that capture by Russians meant instant or a slow, lingering death.

AMERICAN. The best treatment of POWs was undoubtedly provided by Americans. Although there were isolated instances of abuse by American guards, they were not allowed to become common. Americans had food, shipping, and space that other belligerents lacked. They transferred large batches of Axis prisoners to the U.S. mainland and treated them with fair regard for the conventions of war.

There were 425,871 POWs, mostly German, confined in the United States during the war. Most German prisoners were loyal to their Fatherland and resented efforts at interrogation. There were 2,803 escape attempts. About 50 were shot while trying to escape, of whom 34 died. Shortly after the end of the war, German prisoners were sent back to assist in the rebuilding of their country.

Bibliography. A.P. Higgins, *The Hague Peace Conferences* (1899); D. L. Sturgo, *The International Community and the Rights of War* (1929); H.M. Fehling, *One Great Prison* (1951); P. Brickhill, *The Great Escape* (1951); A Crawley, *Escape from Germany* (1970); S. A. Newman, *How to Survive as a Prisoner of War* (1970); J. M. Green, *From Colditz in Code* (1971); J. M. Gansberg, *Stalag U.S.A.* (1977); M. Kochan, *Prisoners of England* (1980); E. E. Williams, *The Wooden Horse* (1980); J. and C. Blair, *Return from the River Kwai* (1980); D. Thrower, *The Lonely Path to Freedom* (1980); and N. Crouter, *Forbidden Diary* (1980).

PRODUCTION, BATTLE OF. Struggle between the Allies and the Axis for supremacy in the production of tools and weapons of war.

WAR AND SCIENCE. In 20th-century warfare the issue of victory or defeat has come to depend to a large extent on the productive capacity of the nation at war. In turn war production is dependent upon the work of scientists. World War II revealed that scientific research for production could be a crucial factor in the outcome of the war.

The Allies placed great stress on scientific research. In Britain Professor Frederick Alexander Lindemann (*q.v.*), a close friend of Churchill, supervised varied research activities that were coordinated under the Ministry of Defense. On June 15, 1940, before U.S. entry into the war, President Franklin D. Roosevelt established the National Defense Research Committee, with Dr. Vannevar Bush(*q.v.*) as Chairman. In May 1941 this body was replaced by the Office of Scientific Research and Development. In Soviet Russia, scientific research was supervised by the Academy of Science.

Neither Germany, Italy, nor Japan could compete successfully with the Allies in the organization of scientific research. All Axis countries had national research councils, but they were given little authority and inadequate resources.

Counting on quick victories, Axis scientists lagged behind their Allied counterparts in using new approaches for war production.

TECHNOLOGICAL INNOVATIONS. The ordinarily slow pace of scientific research was speeded up dramatically to produce new and better weapons of war. Technology now conformed to the new nature of total war, in which not only armed forces struck at one another on land, sea, and air, but also in which civilian populations in great urban centers suddenly found themselves in the front lines.

Technological innovations changed the entire complexion of combat. Huge work forces in giant factories produced great quantities of tanks, improved artillery, and lighter, more accurate, and more deadly machine guns. Battleships were replaced by aircraft carriers. The new technology was explicit in the designing and development of aircraft. In the early days of the war bombers carried modest loads to be dropped on enemy targets. Later in the war *B-29 Flying Fortresses* were delivering bomb loads of 20,000 pounds from a height of 25,000 feet. The race to produce the atomic bomb was won by the Americans, who possessed the final and most destructive weapon of the war. (*See* MANHATTAN PROJECT; HIROSHIMA; and NAGASAKI.) This unexpected scientific development turned out to be a turning point in the history of mankind.

INDUSTRY GEARED FOR WAR. In all belligerent countries the entire industrial plant was geared to the production of war needs from wire nails to sophisticated aircraft. In a remarkably short period and by dint of enormous expenditure of wealth and self-sacrifice on the part of the people, each belligerent gave priority to accelerated production and produced war materials in huge quantities.

ALLIED SUPERIORITY. Despite early successes of the German war machine, it soon became obvious that Germany would be outstripped in production of food and materials of war for campaigns on war fronts and in manufacture of foodstuffs and consumer goods. There was an insatiable demand for agricultural, mineral, and forest raw materials and synthetic products for the manufacture of ammunition, munitions, guns, tanks, warships, aircraft, and transportation equipment. In the long run the Allies were better equipped to produce war materials on a scale hitherto believed impossible. It is estimated that at the height of the war the United Nations had a productive capacity at least 40 percent greater than that of the Axis powers.

BRITISH WAR PRODUCTION. Despite the feverish pace of German rearmament in the immediate prewar years, Britain was slow to convert its industry to armament production as an urgent priority. Soon after the outbreak of war, industrial establishments in the United Kingdom were converted to war production, and the construction of new plants increased the output of military equipment in British factories. In June 1940 industrial conscription was introduced by law. By July 1941 about 40 percent of the active population was either mobilized in the armed forces or conscripted for industry. There was no necessity for coercion; there were enough volunteers for every factory. The system of organizing labor was such that a worker could avoid military service only by being employed in war industry.

The great manufacturing regions in the United Kingdom were on or near coal fields and the seacoast. Most were within the range of *Luftwaffe* (*q.v.*) bombers and pursuit planes stationed along the mainland coast of Europe. Yet, despite bombings, the productive capacity of British industry was not seriously reduced. Arable farming was given priority over sheep and cattle breeding. Grain production doubled as 7,000,000 acres of pasture were plowed under. Production of iron and bauxite increased.

There were serious problems in British war production. Because of a shortage of skilled labor, it became necessary by 1942 to set a ceiling of 2 million men for the army. The lack of competent workers became worse even though in 1944 more than half the active adult population worked in war industries. There was a serious crisis in the coal industry due to antiquated equipment and the mistaken belief that the ban on coal exportation would leave an adequate amount for domestic needs. There were also increasing difficulties in transport.

Symptomatic of production problems was the output of tanks—626 in 1941; 8,611 in 1942; 7,476 in 1943; even fewer in 1944. By 1944, British productive capacity was diminishing. The deficit in war production was made up by assistance from the United States and the Commonwealth.

GERMAN WAR PRODUCTION. Albert Speer (*q.v.*), Hitler's Minister of Armaments and War Production, revealed that in 1936, three years before the start of the war, the *Fuehrer* issued a memorandum on a "Four-Year Plan," which candidly formulated his timetable for the war and the gearing of German war production. By means of centralized administration, the German economy was to be made capable of supporting a war within four years. Hitler ordered immediate production and stockpiling of synthetic fuel and artificial rubber, and increases in production of steel and explosives. With an efficient striking force and centralized control, he would conquer the immense eastern spaces and make Germany an economically self-sufficient world power.

With the outbreak of war Hitler placed all German factories on a round-the-clock production schedule. He did not really gear Germany for global war until after Soviet Russia and the United States were involved. Even then production in Nazi Germany was never very efficient.

Germany had enough coal for its needs, but had to import iron ore from Sweden through dangerous Norwegian waters. Despite the development of ersatz materials, the amounts of synthetic fuel and rubber were far from meeting needs of the German war machine. (*See* RESOURCES, BATTLE

FOR.) To keep the war factories at full production, workers were requisitioned for war work inside Germany. (*See* FORCED LABOR.)

For a time the situation in war production was eased by massive imports from conquered European countries. The practice of requisitioning goods of all kinds continued throughout the entire war. It was estimated that more than 25,000 French machine-tools were dismantled and taken to Germany. It became clear that Hitler was aiming at a monopoly of European industry after the war, especially in chemistry and metallurgy. For the time being he directed the output of conquered European countries to the needs of the German war economy.

Relentless pressure by the Allies eventually meant disaster for German war production. In the later stage of the war Allied bombing and the simultaneous lack of fuel brought German productive capacity to a perilous plight.

RUSSIAN WAR PRODUCTION. For several weeks after Hitler's invasion of the Soviet Union on June 22, 1941, Stalin was in a state of shock. He soon recovered and turned the country to war production. He ordered a gigantic evacuation of factories to the east. There was a sharp decline in output as machinery was reassembled and new factories built. Reconstruction went on day and night while Red armies were being defeated by the Nazi war machine. In 1942 the factories that had been moved were sent into production with an enormous labor force. Beginning in 1943, the development of war production became swift and steady. Output of armaments, a critical field, continued to rise. Special attention was given to production of the *T-34* medium tank, which Soviet leaders and many Allied military men considered to be the best in World War II.

It was clear that the Russians were bracing themselves for a long war. According to Soviet sources, in 1943 production figures rose to 34,900 aircraft, 24,000 tanks, and 130,000 guns. In 1944 the figures were 40,000 aircraft, 29,000 tanks, and 122,000 guns. Between 1941 and 1945, Russian factories produced 142,800 military aircraft, 102,500 tanks or armored cars, and 490,000 guns. These figures were second only to those of the United States and exceeded by far those of Great Britain and Germany.

JAPANESE WAR PRODUCTION. Like its army and navy, most of Japan's modern industry was of comparatively recent growth. In 1941 the industrial plant was geared to turn out all the country's war needs. For its war economy Japan had extensive deposits of strategic raw materials, sufficient sources of hydroelectric power, factories, and a great supply of cheap labor. Manpower from subjugated areas was drafted to supplement the native labor force. At the outbreak of war on December 7, 1941, more than 1,000,000 Koreans were employed in Japanese factories, and during the war 100,000 were added yearly from this single source.

Speedy Japanese successes in the opening months of the war gave the country access to some of the best strategic raw materials. These materials flowed back to the Inner Empire, either for manufacture or stockpiling. Production and prompt delivery of the myriad materials essential to conduct of war were major considerations for Japanese strategists. Fuel, shells, food, and gear for ships had to be on hand when needed. There were many problems, not the least of which were the great distances from the homeland to troops in the field and the critical shipping situation.

Japanese civilians were fashioned into instruments of total war. With regimented minds focused on victory for the Emperor, they were skilled and resourceful workers, motivated by religious fervor. Long conditioning made them willing to endure hardships in factories, privation, even hunger. Self-sacrifice was a cult that was presumed to carry the blessing of the gods.

Japanese production eventually was throttled as the Allies cut land and sea supplies leading from the sequestered treasure trove. Without access to its major oil supply, to rubber, and to sources of manganese, chromium, lead, copper, nickel, zinc, and aluminum, Japan was limited to its stockpiles, which quickly evaporated. With its war production crippled, Japan was on the verge of defeat even before Hiroshima and Nagasaki (*qq.v.*).

ALL-OUT AMERICAN PRODUCTION. There is little doubt that American war production was one of the major factors in the outcome of the war. In 1939 the war caught the United States almost completely unprepared with small stocks of arms or ammunition and scarcely a war industry, which represented only 2 percent of the total industrial production. The American economy was still experiencing the aftermath of the Depression and there were nearly 7 million unemployed. The country, however, had enormous potential with great reserves of raw materials, energy, and space.

The role of President Franklin D. Roosevelt (*q.v.*) was critical in the extraordinary transformation of the American economy to a war footing. Roosevelt took important tentative steps in co-ordinating and channeling production in the manufacture of armaments without imitating the harsh controls of totalitarian states. Faced with the choice of helping the democracies and rearming the American forces, he insisted emphatically that they were to be combined: "We shall allow the opponents of force the use of the material resources of our nation; and at the same time, we shall provide ourselves in America with equipment capable of meeting any defense needs."

In late May 1940, with the fall of France imminent, Roosevelt requested huge funds for the development of military and naval requirements. On December 20, 1940, he established the Office of Production Management, with industrial leader William S. Knudsen (*q.v.*) as Director. The President assigned tasks for co-ordinating defense production and speeding aid "short of war" to anti-Axis nations. On December 29, 1940, in a fireside chat on the radio, he called for a national production effort that would make the United States the world's "arsenal of democracy." Gradually, Roosevelt's four-point program became clear—increased defenses, all-out production, hemisphere solidarity, and lend-lease (*q.v.*) to the Allies. Promoting production, fixing the size of expenditures on armaments, and increasing manpower of the armed forces, Roosevelt designed what he called a "Victory Program."

The "Victory Program" was expanded after the attack on Pearl Harbor (*q.v.*) on December 7, 1941. At the beginning of 1942 Roosevelt announced a compulsory production program: "Let no one say that this cannot be done, and we are committed to doing it." He issued a clarion call for 60,000 planes, 45,000 tanks, 20,000 antiaircraft guns, 500,000 machine guns, and 8 million tons of merchant shipping *in one year*. The announcement astonished war chieftains, industrialists, and production economists in both Allied and Axis countries. Propaganda Minister Goebbels (*q.v.*) in Germany ridiculed the "bluff" and Hitler denounced the American President as "a sick brain."

The entire world was amazed by the pace of American production. By 1943 the production schedule was increased to 125,000 planes, 75,000 tanks, 35,000 antiaircraft guns, and 10 million tons of merchant shipping. By this time Axis military leaders were coming to the conclusion that their cause was hopeless. With tools and weapons of war flowing in an unending stream from American factories, it was becoming increasingly clear that the tide of war had changed in favor of the Allies.

During the course of the war the productive capacity of the United States gave the Allied coalition more than half its armaments, 35 percent of those used against Nazi Germany, and 86 percent of those employed against Japan. While providing the United Kingdom, the British Commonwealth, the Soviet Union, and Nationalist China with arms and loans, the United States at the same time more than doubled its industrial output. From 1941 to 1945 Americans constructed more industrial plants than during the preceding decade. The production of synthetic rubber alone went from 50,000 to 70,000 tons. By the end of the war the U.S. Army had at its service 96,000 tanks, 61,000 field guns, 7 million rifles, 2.3 million trucks, 1.2 million radio sets, and 20,000 radar units. Eleven million tons of munitions went overseas from American factories.

Nazi leader Hermann Goering (*q.v.*) had recommended "guns instead of butter." The American arsenal produced both guns and butter in such extraordinary quantities that Hitler's Third Reich was doomed to destruction.

Bibliography. E. V. Francis, *The Battle of Supplies* (1942); H. Brines, *Until They Eat Stones* (1944); C. D. Carus and C. L. McNichols, *Japan: Its Resources and Industries* (1944); O. Tolischus, *Through Japanese Eyes* (1945); D. Nelson, *The Arsenal of Democracy: The Story of the American War Production* (1946); J. D. Scott and R. Hughes, *Administration of War Production* (1950); M. M Postan, *British War Production* (1951); E. Janeway, *The Struggle for Survival: A Chronicle of Economic Mobilization in World War II* (1951); and A. Milward, *The German Economy at War* (1965).

PROPAGANDA, WAR. Battle of words in belligerent countries to maintain morale on both combat and home fronts. Both sides used every possible device to promote their own cause through psychological warfare.

BACKGROUND. Essentially a modern phenomenon, the preconditions for propaganda emerged in the late 18th century with the American and French revolutions, both of which emphasized the ideas of popular sovereignty, participation of citizens in public affairs, and primacy of public opinion. World War I saw the first sustained use of propaganda as an integral part of the war effort. The results were spectacular. Propaganda helped bring the United States into the war and drive Russia out of it. It contributed heavily to the smashing of the German, Austro-Hungarian, and Turkish empires.

WORLD WAR II. The propaganda of World War I was ideologically oriented from the Allied side as "a war to make the world safe for democracy." In World War II the Allied goal was "to rid the world of the menace of Hitlerisim." By this time propaganda became conterminous with psychological warfare—words were used to assist military operations. In this sense it was more tactical than ideological.

BRITISH. As in World War I the British proved themselves to be masters of propaganda. Their efforts were more subtle and refined than those of the Germans. Centered in London, British propaganda stressed themes of hope, vigorous action, and struggle for an attainable ideal. It called for continuous warfare against Hitler and Nazism, proclaimed the strength of U.S. and Soviet power, and predicted ultimate victory as certain.

As soon as the war began, a new Department of Propaganda to Enemy Countries was set up to function under the Foreign Office. At the same time a Ministry of Information was established. After Churchill became Prime Minister, he appointed a Special Operations Executive (SOE) (*q.v.*), a secret organization to arm, fund, and train patriot armies in German-occupied territories. One of its units was used exclusively for propaganda purposes. The British Broadcasting Corporation (BBC) was given funds to support a European-wide service, and it eventually broadcast in 23 languages. British propaganda was highly effective throughout the war.

GERMAN. The Germans regarded propaganda warfare as a critical appendage to their war machine. Centered in Berlin, German propaganda emphasized injustice of the Treaty of Versailles; world menace of Judaism; the Third Reich as the defender of Western civilization against Bolshevik communism; and inevitability of German victory. It was used on the domestic scene to bolster morale and in occupied countries to stir up religious and racial hatreds. Priority was given to South America, to which millions of Germans had emigrated.

At the start of the war, the *Oberkommando der Wehrmacht* (OKW), the High Command of the German armed forces (*See WEHRMACHT*) and the Foreign Ministry controlled their own propaganda systems. In 1940 Hitler combined both propaganda systems into one unit and at the same time placed responsibility for direction in the hands of Paul Joseph Goebbels (*q.v.*), Minister for Public Enlightenment and Propaganda. For Goebbels propaganda ceased to have any reliable informative value and became simply the science of moulding German public opinion by any means available. He made recognition of Nazi heroes nothing less than a religious cult. He hammered away at the theme that Germans were fighting for European culture and treated the war as if it were merely another election campaign. He boasted joyously about magnificent German victories. As the war progressed and the possibility of winning it waned, Goebbels shifted his emphasis and called for a choice between further sacrifice or slavery under the Jews.

German propaganda directed at the enemy in combat areas was as ponderous and ineffective as that used in World War I. American GIs (*q.v.*) laughed at the broadcasts of Axis Sally (*q.v.*) and paid but little attention to German leaflets with such messages as: "The Draft Dodgers at Home Expect Every Joe To Do His Duty" or "Who Is Cashing In On Huge War Profits?"

RUSSIAN. Before the outbreak of war the Russians had the best-organized propaganda machine of any European country. The Agitation and Propaganda section (*Agitprop*) of the Communist Party presented the cause of communism. The Communist International (*Comintern*), nominally independent but directed from Moscow, issued instructions for Communist propaganda activity.

At the start of the war, Russian propaganda scaled down the traditional furious onslaught on German fascism. It justified the Russo-German Nonaggression Pact (*q.v.*) of 1939 as a logical counterthrust to Western capitalism. After the German invasion on June 22, 1941, the Soviet propaganda machine was diverted from ideology to tactical operations. The all-embracing theme now became destruction of Hitlerism: Fight to the death against "the Fascist beast."

The effectiveness of Russian war propaganda was revealed by fanatical resistance shown by the masses against German invaders. That hatred was so intense that in the closing days of the war German troops desperately sought surrender to British and U.S. forces rather than face vengeance by the Russians.

JAPANESE. The Japanese attempted propaganda ploys throughout conquered lands in their "Greater East Asia Co-Prosperity Sphere" (*q.v.*). However, resentment was so great throughout Asia against Tokyo that Tokyo's clumsy efforts had little effect. Similarly, efforts by Tokyo Rose to lower their morale were received with amusement and ridicule by American GIs (*q.v.*), who enjoyed the jazz music but laughed at the propaganda. (*See* TOKYO ROSE.)

AMERICAN. American propaganda operated at a consistently effective level throughout the war. It stressed such themes as power and unity of the Allies, disadvantages of Nazi and Fascist dictatorships, advantages of democracy, and inevitability of Allied victory.

American organization of war propaganda was more complex than either British or German. In the summer of 1941, before U.S. entry into the war, President Roosevelt appointed Col. William J. Donovan (*q.v.*) as Chief Coordinator of Information. After Pearl Harbor this office was split into two parts, the new Office of Strategic Services (OSS) and the separate Office of War Information (*qq.v.*). The OSS, which was controlled by the Joint Chiefs of Staff, dealt with intelligence reports, sabotage, and support for Resistance movements (*q.v.*). The OWI, led by journalist Elmer Davis, had a domestic as well as overseas branch.

To improve morale at training camps and in combat areas, the government supported GI (*q.v.*) newspapers, including the *Stars and Stripes* (*q.v.*), which had European and Pacific editions, and such magazines as *Yank, The Army Weekly* (*q.v.*). American warplanes dropped accurate news reports in German to influence enemy troops as well as popular items for the public in occupied countries, such as soap, seeds, matches, needles, and thread, all with leaflets containing propaganda slogans. German combat troops also received Allied *Passierscheine*, ("safe-conduct passes"), signed by Gen. Dwight D. Eisenhower (*q.v.*), and promising fair treatment after surrender. These propaganda devices proved to be highly effective.

Bibliography. L. J. Margolin, *Paper Bullets* (1946); D. Lerner, *Sykewar* (1949); T. H. Qualter, *Propaganda and Psychological Warfare* (1962); E. K. Bramsted, *Goebbels and National Socialist Propaganda, 1925-1945* (1965); W. L. Cathcart, *The Role of Network Broadcasting in the Second World War* (1970); W. A. Boelcke, *The Secret Conferences of Dr. Goebbels* (1970); R. T. Hewell, *The Writer's War Board* (1971); J. W. Baird, *The Mythical World of Nazi War Propaganda* (1974); R. Herzstein, *The War Hitler Won* (1978); M. Wilkinson, *World War II Radio Broadcasts* (1978); and F. Thorpe *et al.*, *British Official Films in the Second World War* (1980).

PROXIMITY FUZE. Also called radio proximity fuze, variable time fuze, and VT fuze. Electronic device used with deadly effect by artillery in World War II.

The proximity fuze detonated a projectile or shell within range of the target by means of signals sent out from a tiny radio set in the nose of the projectile and reflected back to the set from the target. (*See also* RADAR, WARTIME; and OFFICE OF SCIENTIFIC RESEARCH AND DEVELOPMENT.)

PSYCHOLOGICAL EFFECTS OF THE WAR. The greatest war in history resulted in profound psychological consequences for the peoples of Europe and the world.

IMMEDIATE EFFECTS. The immediate, disintegrating effects of World War II upon the moral fabric of entire nations were devastating. From 1939 to 1945 armies in combat and civilian populations were subjected to death, famine, conquest, and slaughter—the dreaded Four Horsemen of the Apocalypse. While men on land, sea, and air killed one another with sophisticated weapons of warfare, the conflict changed the ordinary process of living and destroyed the familiar course of everyday existence. During six years of death and destruction, people everywhere were faced with an appalling lack of such basic necessities of life as food, clothing, and shelter.

The psychological result was almost universal discontent and restlessness. The minds and bodies of tens of millions of people were damaged beyond endurance. There was a decline in human decency as people hoarded and concealed food, patronized black markets, or struggled for means of adding to a skimpy starvation diet. Social differences and ideological tensions were sharpened during the seemingly endless struggle. Personality and character hardened in an atmosphere in which the urge for survival became more meaningful than ordinary human kindness and consideration.

NEW PESSIMISM. After the blood bath of 1914–1918, reflective Europeans judged that nothing could induce them to go to war on this vast scale again. They were not faced with the specter of a Nazi regime with which civilized men could not live. With heavy hearts they went on to fight what they deemed to be a "good war"—or as good as any war could be—"to rid the world of Hitler and the monstrous system associated with his name."

The necessity to strike back at Nazism brought with it a psychological descent into a new pessimism. In March 1944, before the end of the war, the Italian philospher Benedetto Croce wrote these uncomfortable words in his diary: "We must not expect the re-birth of that world [the pre-1914 world], its revival and improvement, but we must expect an interminable sequence of clashes, and upsets and ruin due to revolution and wars. . . . We must . . . get accustomed to a life without stability . . . so repugnant to us who were men who labored, who set themselves well through our programs and carried them calmly through. Upon this scene, faltering at every step, we must do the best we can to live with dignity."

Croce's pessimistic prophecy was proven correct in the immediate postwar years. Many thought that the healing influence of time would lighten the human miseries, but such was not the case. The psychological climate degenerated into resignation and indifference. Europeans began to feel that it was a hopeless vision to yearn for peace in a world in which force was worshiped as the ultimate solution to all major international problems. Added to these pessimists were advocates of the Malthusian law of populations, who saw war, along with famine, pestilence, and vice, as positive checks on the available food supply.

PHILOSOPHY OF DESPAIR. The terrible loss of life and property led many to despair of the human adventure. This kind of pessimism was expressed partly in a philosophy that became the vogue in France and spread through

Europe. In one of its many forms, existentialism stressed the absolute inanity of existence, the absurdity of human life, negation of all creation and therefore morale. (As Sartre put it, ''All human activities are equivalent, all are destined by principle, to defeat.'') One must be concerned with actual life, not with abstractions. There is no sublimity in man, only misery. The only solution for man was to follow blindly his own instincts and primitive impulses.

This form of existentialism was in part a response to the horror and frustration of the war years, a hell on earth, during which the cream of mankind perished on the battlefields. Millions of people, good and evil alike, had been slaughtered, millions of others had suffered extreme mental and physical suffering.

Existentialist ideas had been presented in the 19th century by the Danish philosopher Sören Aabye Kierkegaard (1813–1855). They were taken up in the immediate postwar period by Jean-Paul Sartre, representing left-wing intellectuals of the Latin quarter in Paris, and by the German philosopher Martin Heidegger. Existentialism became a popular philosophy in many countries during the postwar era. It took varying forms, from the atheism of Sartre and his followers to the religious approach of such theologians as Karl Barth, Martin Buber, Paul Tillich, and Reinhold Niebuhr. (*See also* LITERATURE, WARTIME.)

NEW DUALISM. Bolstering this pessimism was a new dualism that gave a schizophrenic tone to European life in general. Psychologically, Europe was cut in half and separated by institutional and ideological barriers. Wartime collaboration between Western European nations and the Soviet Union was dissolved within three years after the end of the war. The one-time fellowship was no longer possible. The break led on the Allied side to the Truman Doctrine, the Marshall Plan, and North Atlantic Treaty Organization. Moscow reacted by promoting the Warsaw Pact, a union of Communist countries. Churchill observed accurately that an ''Iron Curtain'' had descended on the Continent.

In addition to its economic, political, social, and cultural aspects, this new dualism had profound psychological undertones. As the gap between West and East widened, peoples on both sides looked to the ''new enemy.'' Contempt and hatred, which once were focused on Hitler, were now directed against others. The weak United Nations organization seemed unable to control fires of the new nationalism.

ATOMIC ENERGY. The atomic blast at Hiroshima (*q.v.*) was stunning notice to Europeans, as well as to the entire world, that a new psychological stage had been reached in history. The attitude of peoples began to change drastically once it was realized that a new weapon had come into existence which, if used in a future war, would mean almost certainly the end of life on this planet. The effort to control atomic energy proposed by Bernard M. Baruch in June 1946 failed when the Russians objected to any rigorous inspection system. In November 1947 the Kremlin announced that it now possessed the secret of atomic energy.

From this point on, atomic energy became a deterrent to the outbreak of a major war. But many Europeans, still pessimistic, pointed out that "new weapons" in the past had never prevented war. Now there were stockpiles of intercontinental guided missiles, radio controls, proximity fuzes, even biological warfare, all in addition to the ultimate weapon—the hydrogen bomb. Nations now had the power not only to annihilate their enemies but to destroy all life on earth as well. In the atomic age, the psychological reactions of human beings are being conditioned by a new attitude to life and death.

Bibliography. F. H. Heinemann, *Existentialism and the Modern Predicament* (1955); and R. C. Hewlett and O. E. Anderson, *The New World, 1939-1946* (1962).

PSYCHOLOGICAL WARFARE. *See* PROPAGANDA, WAR.

PT-109. U.S. motor torpedo boat sunk in the Central Solomons campaign in the summer of 1943.

During naval clashes between the Allies and Japan in the Central Solomons, U.S. *PT* Boats played an important role as auxiliaries to larger warships such as cruisers and destroyers. In New Georgia they were successful in attacking barges bringing Japanese reinforcements to the Solomons by way of the "Tokyo Express" through the Slot.

On the night of August 1–2, 1943, 15 U.S. PT-Boats, divided into four groups, attempted to block Blacker Strait south of Kolombangara. All their torpedoes missed the Japanese destroyers moving down the slot. The Japanese destroyer *Amagiri* ran down *PT-109,* commanded by Lt. John F. Kennedy (*q.v.*) and knifed it into two parts. Two men of the crew of 13 were lost.

Young Kennedy swam away, towing a wounded sailer, as the remainder of the crew held on to an improvised raft. The men managed to reach a small island in five hours. The next morning Kennedy sent a message on a coconut shell through a native to an Australian coastwatcher, who sent men to the rescue. The survivors were moved to safety.

Although the incident had little naval significance, it played a part in the election of Kennedy as 35th President of the United States.

PWE. A British agency organized to gather information for the Allied war effort. (*See* POLITICAL WARFARE EXECUTIVE.)

PYLE, ERNEST (ERNIE) TAYLOR (1900–1945). American journalist and war correspondent killed by Japanese sniper fire in April 1945.

In November 1940 Pyle flew via Lisbon to London and sent back vivid descriptions of the *Luftwaffe* bombing. His vivid, dramatic pieces excited much attention. In 1942 he accompanied American troops on the invasions of North

Africa and Italy. He was present at the Normandy invasion in June 1944 and returned to the United States three months later. His sensitive writing about the "little men" in combat won him much public attention as well as a Pulitzer Prize in 1943.

DEATH. In January 1945 Pyle went to the Pacific to continue his roving assignment. While observing the advance of American troops on Ie Shima, a small island west of Okinawa, he was killed instantly by a Japanese bullet. Disconsolate American fighting men, who had loved the reporter who so accurately pictured their worm's-eye view of the war, placed this inscription on a simple marker at the place where he was killed:

> At this Spot
> The
> 77th Infantry Division
> Lost a Buddy
> Ernie Pyle
> 18 April 1945

An inconspicuous little man, Pyle hated the dirty business of war, but he felt his place to be with the men at the front. His dispatches were filled with homey details about acts of kindness at the front, the loneliness of bored men behind the lines, and the raw courage of young soldiers. "I don't see," he wrote, "how any survivor of war can ever be cruel to anything ever again."

Bibliography. Selections from Pyle's columns were published in book form in *Ernie Pyle in England* (1941); *Here Is Your War* (1943); and *Brave Men* (1944).

PzKw-IV. See TANKS.

Q

QUEBEC CONFERENCE, FIRST. Under the code or cover name *Quadrant,* a conference of Allied leaders held in the summer of 1943 to discuss war plans.

BACKGROUND. In mid-1943, various war problems arose that required a new top-level conference. Among the issues were need for a final decision concerning Italy; naming of the COSSAC (Chief of Staff Supreme Allied Command); plans for *Operation Overlord,* the coming Normandy invasion, (*q.v.*); and the reorganization of strategy for the South Pacific.

PARTICIPANTS. The conference was attended by Roosevelt, Churchill, and their top-ranking advisers, including the Combined Chiefs of Staff. One notable was conspicuously absent—Stalin—technically because the Soviet Union was not at war with Japan. There were, indeed, discussions on relations with the Soviet Union, but nothing about them was mentioned in the decisions taken.

DECISIONS. The conference took place from August 17 to 24, 1943, at Quebec, Canada. The major decisions were:

ITALY

The most pressing matter at hand was a decision on whether the campaign in Sicily should be followed by an invasion of the Italian Peninsula. The issue was whether the Normandy invasion should be given "overriding priority." The U.S. Chiefs of Staff argued for *Overlord* first, and urged that the Normandy invasion be pursued even if the Germans were successful in concentrating forces to oppose it. British advisers insisted that a powerful Italian campaign was absolutely necessary to draw off enemy strength and that invasion of France should take place only if German fighting strength were reduced in the Normandy area. After heated discussions a compromise was reached, but priority would be given to Normandy.

OVERLORD

Available resources would be distributed with the main object of ensuring the success of *Overlord*. May 1, 1944 was reaffirmed as the target date. The assault force would be 25 percent larger than originally intended.

ANVIL

It was also agreed that the Normandy invasion would be supplemented by landings in southern France (*Anvil*, later *Dragoon* [*qq.v.*]).

COMMAND

Earlier it had been understood that *Overlord* would be led by a British commander. The British now conceded that because of preponderant American strength, the Normandy invasion should be led by an American. Roosevelt gratefully acquiesced. Gen. Dwight D. Eisenhower (*q.v.*) was appointed to the post.

SOUTHEAST ASIA

Agreement was reached on stepping up military operations in the Far East, especially in Burma. A Southeast Asia Command was established, with Lord Louis Mountbatten (*q.v.*) as Supreme Allied Commander in that theater of war.

SIGNIFICANCE. The First Quebec Conference revealed that the United States was playing an increasingly important role in Allied plans and operations. Churchill's preference for an assault on the "soft underbelly" (*q.v.*) of Europe had to give way to American desire for direct attack on Fortress Europe (*q.v.*) from the north. Therefore leadership for the Allied invasion of Normandy was assigned to an American general, in reciprocity a British officer was given top command in the Far East.

A short press communiqué issued at the end of the conference mentioned a "tripartite meeting which it may be able to arrange with Soviet Russia." This phrase revealed the eagerness of both the United States and Britain for collaboration with Soviet Russia. Soon the first meeting of the Big Three (*q.v.*) powers would take place. (*See* MOSCOW CONFERENCE.) Until this time the two Western Allies were on an uncertain footing with the third. Roosevelt, Churchill, and Stalin met three months later at Teheran. (*See* TEHERAN CONFERENCE.)

Bibliography. S. Arne, *United Nations Primer* (rev. ed. 1948).

QUEBEC CONFERENCE, SECOND. Under the code or cover name *Octagon*, a conference of Allied leaders held in the fall of 1944.

BACKGROUND. The German position deteriorated steadily in the summer of 1944. Allied fighting forces had pushed all the way to the German border, and in Italy they had penetrated as far north as Pisa. In the east the Russians were moving into Poland and the Baltic states. Bulgaria, Rumania, and Finland, once satellites, had deserted the Germans. The Nazi Third Reich was on the verge of collapse.

In this euphoric atmosphere of impending victory, the British called for a full-scale conference of war leaders. The Americans, believing that there was really little to discuss, consented only reluctantly, but they accepted the plan and the meeting was held in the Chateau Frontenac, high over the north bank of the St. Lawrence River at Quebec, Canada.

PARTICIPANTS. Present were Churchill, Roosevelt, and their large staffs of aides. They met from September 12 to 16, 1944.

DECISIONS. The main subjects for discussion were suggestions for the completion of the war in Europe and early plans for carrying on the war in the Pacific. Among the decisions were the following:

1. The Americans proposed to withdraw the U.S. 5th Army from Italy to France. When the British objected, it was decided to keep the 5th Army in Italy until the British completed their campaign against Field Marshal Albert Kesselring (*q.v.*).

2. The conferees agreed that command of Allied forces in France be transferred from Field Marshal Henry Maitland Wilson to Gen. Dwight D. Eisenhower (*qq.v.*).

3. At the suggestion of British experts, strategic bombing of Germany was placed under control of the Combined Chiefs of Staff.

4. For the coming occupation of Germany it was agreed that the British would take northwest Germany, and the Americans southwest Germany.

5. The port of Bremen would come under U.S. control.

6. Measures to prevent the rearmament of Germany were discussed.

7. U.S. Lend-Lease (*q.v.*) to Britain would continue.

8. A combined military mission would be sent to Moscow to represent the Chiefs of Staff of the Big Three (*q.v.*) in strategic and operational matters. (This project was abandoned because of Soviet delaying tactics.)

9. The conferees discussed the war with Japan.

10. The British promised to take part in the war in the Pacific.

SIGNIFICANCE. The Second Quebec Conference marked the transition from predominantly military matters to a political orientation. The cycle of military discussions on strategy was almost over. Plans that had been hammered out in preceding high-level meetings were to a large extent fulfilled. Former Anglo-American differences were resolved. Churchill informed a press conference: ''The fact that we have got to know each other so well, and understand each other so well makes for speed and full understanding in international deliberation.'' There was much good will in an atmosphere of impending victory. Churchill still spoke of British power and prestige, but by now major decisions were controlled by Americans.

At the same time it was obvious that Roosevelt and Churchill were also preparing for their next meeting to include Stalin, which took place in February 1945 at Yalta in the Crimea. (*See* YALTA CONFERENCE.)

Bibliography. S. Arne, *United Nations Primer* (rev. ed. 1948).

QUEEN ELIZABETH. Cunard Steamship Company passenger liner, which together with the *Queen Mary* (*q.v.*), carried a million and a half passengers on war service.

The *Queen Elizabeth* (83,673 tons; length 1031 feet, beam 118 feet) was at the time the world's largest passenger ship. She sailed in secrecy and without passengers on her maiden voyage to New York in 1940. Throughout the war she carried U.S. troops and supplies to Britain.

QUEEN MARY. Cunard Steamship Company passenger liner, which together with the *Queen Elizabeth* (*q.v.*) was used as a troopship on war service.

The *Queen Mary* (81,237 tons; length 1020 feet; beam 118 feet) began her service in 1936 and made record Atlantic crossings in that year, winning the Blue Riband* with a speed of 30.63 knots. In 1938 she set a record of 31.20 knots which was to stand for 14 years. The speeds of the *Queen Mary* and *Queen Elizabeth* were too fast for a destroyer escort except at the start and finish of their voyages. Speed, plus zigzagging and ever-changing routes, also gave the liners comparative safety from U-Boat attacks. No German submarine ever managed to intercept them on their many transatlantic crossings from August 1942 onward.

QUISLING, VIDKUN ABRAHAM (1887–1945). Norwegian Fascist politician and official, whose name became synonymous with traitor.

When World War II broke out, Quisling was quick to show his sympathy for the Nazi cause. In December 1939 he warned the Germans about the possibility of a British occupation of Norway and advised them to take over the

---

*The Blue Riband was awarded originally to prize bulls in Britain. A journalist one day awarded one to the fastest liner on the New York to Southampton run. The *Mauretania* won it in 1906 with an average of 26 knots for the trip. In 1929 the German liner *Europa* took the Blue Riband with an average of 29 knots. After the war the *United States* averaged 36 knots for the crossing.

country to forestall a British invasion. During the early months of April 1940, he collaborated with the Germans and after they landed in Norway on April 9 he used his authority as an army officer to hasten the collapse of his country. He proclaimed himself Prime Minister and formed a Nasjonal Samling (National Union Party) ministry.

Quisling's period of power lasted only a week. When German authorities gave him little support, he went to Berlin to seek Hitler's help. In September 1940 he was appointed sole political head of Norway and chief of a 13-man commission most of whom were his followers. On February 1, 1942 he was made Premier. He set up the *Hird,* a Norwegian version of the Nazi SS (*q.v.*) to seek out members of the Norwegian underground. In his puppet post he quarreled openly with Josef Terboven, the Nazi Commissar for Norway. He was merely tolerated by the Germans and despised by his own countrymen.

On May 9, 1945, Quisling was arrested and was brought to trial in August as a traitor. On September 10 he was found guilty of treason, of causing the death of many Norwegian patriots, and of incitement to mutiny. His appeal was denied. On October 24, 1945, he was shot at Akershus Fortress by a firing squad.

Quisling was a man who wore a perpetual frown. An admirer of Hitler's New Order (*q.v.*), he was a fanatical hater of communism. For the duration of the war he was a frustrated figurehead, a puppet who had to bow to Hitler's every wish. His name came to be associated with perfidy and treason not only in Norway but also throughout the world.

Bibliography. R. Hewins, *Quisling: Prophet Without Honor* (1965); H. F. Knudsen, *I Was Quisling's Secretary* (1967); H.-D. Loock, *Quisling, Rosenberg and Terboven* (1970); and P. M. Hayes, *The Career and Ideas of Vidkun Quisling* (1971).

R

RABAUL. Advance Japanese naval and air base in the southern Pacific.

LOCATION. The chief port of the Australian-mandated territory of New Guinea in northeast New Britain, Rabaul had a fine, landlocked port. The deep harbor, which may have once been a great volcano crater, offered excellent protection for ships of any kind. Around the harbor is a semi-circle of mountains.

BACKGROUND. Rabaul was the capital first of German New Guinea (1910–1920) and then of the Australian mandate (1920–1941). In 1937 it was nearly leveled by volcanic eruptions, which covered the town with mud and forced the inhabitants to flee. In 1941 it was superseded as the capital of New Guinea by Port Moresby.

WORLD WAR II. In their first expansionist drive, the Japanese occupied Rabaul on January 22, 1942, and began preparations to make it their advance naval and air base for the projected invasion of Australia. They sent a garrison of 100,000 men to hold the port, as well as two air armies of 600 aircraft. Units of the Japanese 8th Fleet were stationed there. To protect the town itself, the Japanese constructed strong defenses with the liberal use of land mines.

ALLIED STRATEGY. Allied strategy was to isolate Rabaul but avoid any direct attack on it. In the north, American sea and air power captured the Marshall Islands and eliminated Truk (*q.v.*) as a naval base. The struggle around Rabaul was long and hard. In the summer of 1943, the Allies took several islands near Rabaul and used them as air bases for attacks on the Japanese stronghold. Heavy air raids on the night of September 3, 1943, temporarily neutralized Rabaul.

By the beginning of 1944 the initiative in the South Pacific was entirely in Allied hands. Within a short time, after successes in the Admiralties, Rabaul's last supply route by sea was cut off. The Allies by-passed the base in their island-hopping strategy. (*See* PACIFIC, CAMPAIGNS IN THE.)

*STRANDED.*By-passed at Rabaul were 52,200 troops, 16,200 seamen, and 21,000 construction workers. The Japanese withdrew all their aircraft and ships from the base. Australians patrolled the area until the Japanese surrender.

RADAR, WARTIME. Acronym for *ra*dio *d*etection *a*nd *r*anging, the use of electronic tubes for radio detection.

Synonymous with radio location, radar revolutionized war on the ground, at sea, and in the air. As a technique it identified position, motion, and nature of an object in the distance by means of radio waves reflected from its surface.

PRINCIPLES. Radar was based on transmission of high-frequency pulses of electromagnetic energy by means of directional antenna. Following are the basic principles of radar operation during the war:

1. A transmitter sent out a short pulse of radio waves in a certain direction.

2. Some pulses impinged on an intercepting object and these reflections were picked up by a receiver in microcosm after emission.

3. The reflections were then converted into tiny dots (blips) on a fluorescent screen (part of a cathode ray tube). This screen was calibrated to give range, direction, and height (or altitude).

4. Range was measured by the time interval it took for the radar signal to reach the object and return.

5. Direction was determined by the area to which the antenna was pointed as the signal was transmitted.

6. The altitude was worked out by calibration of the time element of the signal by two antennae of different heights.

7. The same aerial was used for transmitting and receiving, and the intervals were so timed that a reflected pulse could be recorded before the next pulse was sent out.

8. A narrow beam of high power gave sharp definition.

9. Spiral spanning covered a solid angle of space in a fixed direction.

10. The antenna was rotated continuously at a constant speed.

INVENTION. Radar was developed independently in several countries between 1934 and 1940. Robert Watson-Watt, a Scottish physicist, devised one of the first viable systems of radar in 1934–1935. By 1939 a race was on in the belligerent countries to improve the use of radar as an adjunct to conventional weapons of war.

WORLD WAR II. As soon as war broke out, Churchill, realizing its critical importance, ordered an intensification of radar research. In response to his wishes, a Telecommunications Research Establishment was set up to which leading British physicists were sent to work on radar improvement. In 1940, before the entrance of the United States into the war, Roosevelt established a Microwave Commission under auspices of the National Research Defense Committee. British and American scientists worked together on problems of high power output, receiver sensitivity, timing, and signal-processing circuits. The British introduced the cavity magnetron, which profoundly affected radar by introducing microwave radio frequency power. American scientists on their part improved microwave radar to the point where it could be used for control of antiaircraft fire as well as aircraft navigation.

When they began bombing German targets, the British used two electronic systems as navigational aids—at first *Gee* (*q.v.*), which enabled planes to reach their targets with accuracy, and later by *Oboe* (*q.v.*), based on latest German methods. Variants and later refinements made for even greater accuracy in bombing. American refinements, especially *Loran* (*q.v.*), achieved spectacular results in long-range air navigation in the Pacific.

GROUND RADAR. When the British faced air attack by the German *Luftwaffe* (*q.v.*) in May 1940, they would have been helpless without some kind of warning system that would enable them to scramble their planes for defense. There was a chain of German airfields on the Continent only a few minutes flying time from British cities. Fortunately for the British, their radar was sufficiently well developed so that they could set up a series of radar bases to supply information about the approach of the raiders and their course. Radar was especially useful for day fighters. All the radar stations had to do was to send the Royal Air Force (*q.v.*) the general direction of the enemy formations. British pilots could then fly in by sight. Night flying was a different matter. Planes had to carry their own radar, which was not as well developed as the ground variety in the early stages of the war.

Radar proved to be invaluable for the British in the critical summer of 1940. (*See* BRITAIN, BATTLE OF.) The *Luftwaffe* lost 957 planes in August 1940, and 185 out of 500 on one day, September 15, 1940. Such heavy losses forced the Germans to change tactics and resort to night attacks.

AIRBORNE RADAR. Radar for air offensives was quickly perfected after the Battle of Britain. It became a highly useful navigational aid in the bombing of targets on the Continent and particularly in Germany. One of the most successful methods involved the exchange of signals with home bases. Ground stations in England sent out pulses to aircraft that carried an apparatus to pick up the signals. After a short time delay, the aircraft issued a response signal. The delay period gave the ground station the distance of the aircraft. Ground signals would then give the plane a position over the target within a few yards and could signal the exact instant for release of bombs. More than half the immense tonnage of bombs dropped on Germany was with radar aid.

Radar had many other uses during the closing two years of the war. It was employed in fights between air fleets, enormously simplifying the task of bringing fighters into conflict with bombers at appropriate times. It could be used to detect enemy flights and also to make accurate maps of ground targets. In 1945, radar units were placed on fast fighter planes to intercept German *V-1* and *V-2* (*qq.v.*) flying weapons over London.

SHIPBORNE RADAR. Radar also revolutionized naval warfare. By its use individual ships or entire fleets could identify one another even in fog or at night. The enemy could be engaged, even without seeing his ships, merely as blobs on a fluorescent screen. Shipborne radar played a major role in both the Mediterranean and the Atlantic. It was especially valuable for aircraft carriers in guiding fighters to their decks after sorties. The German battleship *Bismarck* (*q.v.*) was sunk with radar-directed gunfire. Convoys were often disturbed by two problems—collision and stragglers; radar prevented and solved both difficulties.

During the late days of World War I, convoys bound for Britain were protected by sonar, a sound-detecting system that prevented submarines from passing unobserved through the convoy. This device was highly successful in daylight but not at night. World War II radar discouraged U-Boats from attacking at night or in fog from the surface or from the sides of convoys. In 1943 nearly 100 U-Boats were sunk in three months, a feat that was considerably facilitated by the use of radar. The morale of German submarine crews declined precipitously.

GERMAN RADAR. Germany entered World War II with a viable long-wave radar system. Among the early models was the Freya, a ground-based warning set, which was modified repeatedly and which remained the backbone of the German radar system for the remainder of the war. The Würzburg, introduced in 1940, made accurate measurements of bearing and range as well as height. The Mannheim, a more complicated design, was used especially for antiaircraft defense. Progress was hindered by the lack of long-range electronic research and the tendency to freeze existing models into standard production. By early 1943 the Allies gained superiority in improvement of microwave radar. In December 1943 the Germans recovered a microwave radar set from an Allied bomber downed in the Netherlands. An attempt was made immediately to concentrate on production of similar units, but it was far too late. The first German microwave sets did not appear until a few months before the end of the war. Germany's defeat in the radar battle contributed much to its final loss of the war.

Bibliography. There is a vast literature, both scientific and popular, on radar. *See* especially U.S. Joint Board on Information Policy, *Radar: A Report on Science at War* (1945). British Information Service, *Radar* (1946); J.G. Crowther and R. Whiddington, *Science at War* (1948); B. Carroll Colby, *Operation Watchdog* (1956); A. H. Sullivan, Jr., "German Electronics in World War II," *Electrical Engineering,* 68 (1949), pp. 403–409; W. R. Hallows, *Radar Simply Explained* (1950); and H. E. Penrose and R.S.H. Boulding, *Principles and Practices of Radar* (rev. ed. 1959).

RAEDER, ERICH (1876–1960). Commander-in-Chief of the German Navy until his retirement in the midst of the war.

Raeder was much distressed when Germany went to war because he felt that its small surface fleet was no match for the British Navy and that there were too few U-Boats available. (*See* U-BOATS.) Nevertheless, once the step was taken, he gave his full cooperation. Convinced that Norwegian ports were vital, he urged Hitler to invade Norway on April 9, 1940. This gave him unlimited access to the Atlantic.

Again in 1941 Raeder opposed Hitler's plans for invasion of the Soviet Union, but once the decision was made he gave his cooperation. He sent naval forces to harass shipping in the Baltic, but he accomplished very little. The sinking of the *Bismarck* (*q.v.*) on May 27, 1941, was a blow from which Raeder never recovered. Gradually, his differences with Hitler grew unbearable. With the *Fuehrer's* assent, he retired at the end of January 1943.

NUREMBERG. After the war the International Military Tribunal at Nuremberg (*See* NUREMBERG TRIALS) accused Raeder of building and directing the German Navy in the 15 years he commanded it. Raeder, said his judges, admitted that his navy violated the Versailles Treaty, insisting that it was "a matter of honor for every man to do so." He was found guilty: "It is clear from evidence that Raeder participated in the planning and waging of aggressive war." He was sentenced to life imprisonment.

Raeder was released from Spandau prison in Berlin on September 26, 1955, at the age of nearly 80, on the ground of ill health. He died in Kiel on May 6, 1960.

Raeder tolerated no differences of opinion in naval matters. He sought to maintain the gentlemanly code of conduct he deemed necessary for the German Navy. He resisted Nazi attempts to determine naval policies in ideological matters, but cautiously gave in to Hitler after serious quarrels. Never self-seeking, he worked zealously for the navy. At Nuremberg he conducted himself with cool and calm courage.

Bibliography. For the story of Raeder's career, *see* his autobiography *Mein Leben* (2 vols., 1956-1957). For Raeder at the Nuremberg Trials, *see* G. M. Gilbert, *Nuremberg Diary* (1947), pp. 333–347 and *passim,* and E. Davidson, *The Trial of the Germans* (1966), pp. 368–392 and *passim.*

RAF. Air arm of the British combat forces during World War II. (*See* ROYAL AIR FORCE.)

RANGERS. U.S. commando unit. The Rangers were the first American foot soldiers to fight in North Africa and in Europe.

FORMATION. In the spring of 1942 Gens. George C. Marshall and Dwight D. Eisenhower (*qq.v.*) made the initial decision to organize the Rangers. They selected a young, aggressive West Pointer, Col. William O. Darby, to lead the outfit. Darby toured U.S. training camps in North Ireland for volunteers for commando training. The unit took its name from Roger's Rangers, crafty colonial frontiersmen who fought the French near the Canadian border.

TRAINING. The unit of 2,000 rangers was put through the British Commando school, with long forced marches, obstacle courses, exercises with live ammunition, and rough-and-tumble fighting. Chosen for their ability to use such weapons as daggers, grenades, mortars, and submachine guns, they underwent a rigid training. An Associated Press news report described it: "The men drilled at double time until their feet blistered and their lungs were bursting. Then they were trained in climbing, diving, crossing a bridge made of the seven-foot rope which each man carried. Then a 36 mile hike over bleak, trackless mountains, with only half rations and what the men could forage from the countryside."

PERFORMANCE. On August 14, 1942, Rangers joined Canadian, French, and British units in a combined operations attack on Dieppe. The raid was unsuccessful but the Allies learned much about invasion techniques to be used later. (*See* DIEPPE RAID.) After this baptism of fire, the Rangers fought in more actions, from North Africa to Sicily to Italy, than any other army unit. They also endured heavier casualties. Of the original unit of 2,000, just 199 came home. "The Rangers," said Gen. Omar N. Bradley (*q.v.*), "fought against the enemy's best, alongside the Allies' best: British Commandos and Guards, French Goums, the veteran American divisions."

RATIONS, U.S. ARMY. Rations for American servicemen, as in all the belligerent countries, were designed for use mostly under combat conditions.

A RATIONS. Used in most posts and army installations in the United States, A rations included fresh fruit and vegetables when they were available.

B RATIONS. Similar to A rations, with the exception that nonperishable foods replaced perishable items.

C RATIONS. Designed for the combat soldier who could carry a day's supply of food and who would be resupplied daily. It consisted of six 12-ounce cans, three of which contained combinations of meat and vegetables. The rest supplied biscuits, soluble coffee, cocoa, lemon powder, and cigarettes. C rations could be eaten hot or cold.

D RATION. Not a meal, but a food bar, originally designed as a survival ration. Also called the Logan Bar, it contained chocolate, oatmeal, sugar, and dried skim milk. Though nourishing, it was monotonous and led to many complaints of thirst and nausea.

K RATION. Designed for troops in combat, the K ration was derived from the American Indian's concentrated venison, or pemmican. It included meat as well as biscuits, coffee, cigarettes, chewing gum, and candy.

Bibliography. E. Risch, *The Quartermaster Corps: Organization, Supply and Services* (1953).

RED BALL EXPRESS. Allied improvised, one-way cross-country traffic movement after the invasion of Fortress Europe (*q.v.*) on June 6, 1944. (*See* NORMANDY INVASION.)

BACKGROUND. The Allied Supreme Command made elaborate and detailed plans to make the most efficient use of the French road system in the critical task of moving men and supplies after the invasion. Its major concern was to transform major highways into a one-way traffic leading eastward, with only limited access and exits. The system was inaugurated by Maj. Gen. Frank A. Ross, Chief of Transportation.

MOVEMENT. Along with this planning went the Red Ball Express, which turned out to be an extraordinary success. Thousands of trucks rolled at high speed across the countryside from Normandy toward Paris and beyond to German soil. They moved around the clock in all kinds of weather, without headlights but guided by trained traffic wardens. The speed with which Gen. George S. Patton, Jr. (*q.v.*) was able to lead his armored forces in the drive eastward was due in large part to the work performed by the Red Ball Express. It became known as one of the most famous war traffic movements in history. (*See also* GERMANY, BATTLE OF.)

RED DEVILS. Parachutist units organized for special airborne duties.

In 1941 Churchill ordered the formation of a new combat force for special assignments. He chose for its commander Maj. Gen. Frederick Browning (*q.v.*), an officer with a brilliant combat record. Browning trained his men carefully, including the Glider Pilot Regiment and parachute battalions and brigades. In 1942 one of his units took the name "Red Devils" from its emblem, a red beret. It took part in a number of engagements, especially at Arnhem. (*See* ARNHEM, BATTLE OF.)

Bibliography. G. G. Norton, *The Red Devils* (1971).

RED ORCHESTRA. German *Rote Kapelle*. Highly successful Soviet intelligence network operating outside of Russia.

The Red Orchestra managed to penetrate even into the offices of the German High Command and feed vital secrets to Moscow during the first three years of the war. Nazi authorities knew about its activities and used transmitters captured from it to confuse the enemy.

Clandestine activities of the Red Orchestra were directed by Leopold Leib Trepper, a Polish-born Jew and longtime Communist. The 290-member spy network was given its name, Red Orchestra, by the Germans. Nazi authorities smashed the organization in 1942–1943. A Hitler aide later estimated that the Trepper espionage ring had cost some 200,000 German soldiers' lives.

Trepper was betrayed and captured. He duped his German captors by feeding them mixed doses of true and false information. He managed to escape to Russia. At the end of the war he was punished by the soviets with a ten-year prison term. Released in 1955, he returned to Poland, from which he was allowed to emigrate to Israel in 1955. He died in late January 1982 in Jerusalem.

Bibliography. G. Perrault, *The Red Orchestra* (1968); H. Höhne, *Codeword Direktor: The Story of the Red Orchestra* (1972); and L. Trepper, *Memoirs of the Spy Hitler Couldn't Silence* (1977).

REGENSBURG RAID. Allied air strike at the Messerschmitt assembly works in Regensburg in southern Germany in 1943. Primarily an American operation, the raid took place in conjunction with a simultaneous strike at Schweinfurt's ball-bearing works. The code or cover name *Juggler* was given to the twin operation. (*See* SCHWEINFURT RAIDS.)

BACKGROUND. For Allied strategists the city of Regensburg (Ratisbon) was a target of high priority. It was situated in Bavaria at the confluence of the Danube and the Regen rivers, 65 miles northwest of Munich. Close to its outskirts, on a curve of the winding blue Danube, were great aircraft and engine assembly shops, where *Me-109s*, Germany's crack fighter planes, were produced. From these assembly lines came 30 percent of all the planes of the *Luftwaffe* (*q.v.*). A major concern of the Allied Bomber Command was to cut German aircraft production.

PLAN. The original plan was a combination of *Operation Tidal Wave*, a raid on the Rumanian oil fields at Ploesti (*See* PLOESTI RAID) and *Operation Juggler*, an attack on Regensburg. This plan was dropped in favor of a twin raid on Schweinfurt for the ball-bearing and Regensburg for the Messerschmitt assembly works. The combined force selected from the 8th Air Force would leave airfields in Anglia, cross Holland with an escort of fighters, and then split into two units, one heading for Schweinfurt and the other for Regensburg. The Schweinfurt raiders would hit their target and return to British bases, while the

Regensburg unit would bomb the Messerschmitt factories, then continue across the Alps, through the Brenner Pass to the coast of Italy, and land at desert airports in North Africa.

ATTACK. On August 17, 1943, a total of 363 American heavy bombers of the U.S. 1st Bombardment Wing (to Schweinfurt) and the U.S. 4th Bombardment Wing (to Regensburg) took off from English fields. They were accompanied as far as Holland by fighter escorts of American *P-47 Thunderbolts* and British *Spitfires* (*qq.v.*). The air fleet then separated into two parts. At this point German fighters rose to strike at the invaders. Each bomber had a heavy load of incendiary bombs in its belly and large fuel supplies in main and wingtip tanks in order to keep aloft for 11 hours. One after another the heavy bombers fell victim to German fighter attacks. Those planes that managed to keep flying went on to their target and dropped their load of bombs. The surviving planes of the Regensburg raiders flew on to North Africa.

LOSSES. The cost was heavy. When *B-17s* of the 4th Bombardment Wing flew back to British bases a week later, they had lost 63 aircraft. Some 60 others were not airworthy and were left in North African bases. Pilots reported that several *B-17s* were spotted gliding to safety in Switzerland 40 miles away.

RESULTS. Allied public relations officers spoke of "tremendous damage" and "great destruction" at Regensburg. Reconnaissance photographs showed that the bombing had been "concentrated and heavy." Undoubtedly, some damage was done, but scarcely enough to justify the great effort and the loss in lives. Despite the claims of greater accuracy by bomb sight, not all bombs landed on the target. Most of all, the twin Schweinfurt-Regensburg mission revealed that the decision to split the air fleet between the two targets was illconceived. The Allied Supreme Command did in fact gradually erode German strength in the air, but paid a high price for it.

Bibliography. J. Sweetman, *Schweinfurt: Disaster in the Skies* (1971).

REIMS. Also called Rheims, ancient Durocortorum. French city on the right bank of the Vesle in the *département* of the Marne. Site of the German unconditional surrender.

PARTICIPANTS. The delegates met on May 7, 1945, in a small room in a dismal brick schoolhouse, which for some months had been the Supreme Headquarters of Gen. Dwight D. Eisenhower (*q.v.*). On one side of the table sat three German emissaries: Adm. Hans Georg von Friedburg (*q.v.*), Commander-in-Chief of the German Navy; Field Marshal Alfred Gustav Jodl (*q.v.*), Chief of the German General Staff; and Jodl's aide, Maj. Gen. Wilhelm Oxenius. Opposite them were Allied officers of equivalent rank: Lt. Gen. Frederick Morgan, Staff Deputy; Gen. François Sevez; Adm. H. M. Burrough,

Commander of the Allied Naval Expeditionary Force; Lt. Gen. Walter Bedell Smith (*q.v.*), Chief of Staff to Eisenhower; Gen. Carl A. Spaatz (*q.v.*), Commander of the U.S. Strategic Air Forces; and Lt. Gen. Ivan Chermaiev and Gen. Ivan Suslaparov of the Soviet Union. Eisenhower and his Deputy, Air Chief Marshal Arthur Tedder (*q.v.*) were conspicuously absent. On May 8, at Berlin, Tedder signed the formal ratification (as Eisenhower's Deputy).

INSTRUMENT OF SURRENDER. The terms were simple and explicit:

We, the undersigned, acting by authority of the German High Command, hereby surrender unconditionally to the Supreme Commander, Allied Expeditionary Force, and simultaneously to the Soviet High Command, all forces on land, sea, and in the air who are at this date under German control.

REMAGEN BRIDGE. Scene of a major breakthrough for the Allies in March 1945. It was one of the most extraordinary strokes of good fortune in military history.

BACKGROUND. After the Germans were defeated in January 1945, they never again posed a serious threat on the western front. (*See* BULGE, BATTLE OF THE.) German reserves were exhausted, fuel supplies were virtually nonexistent, and the *Luftwaffe* (*q.v.*) almost disappeared from the skies. At the end of February the Allies were spread along the German border over most of its length. Their objective now was to force the enemy across the Rhine River. Six armies (three American, one British, one French, and one Canadian) were poised for the final offensive. What was now needed was a bridge across the Rhine. The Germans had blown up one span after another. No one had crossed the river in time of war since 1805. Gen. Dwight D. Eisenhower (*q.v.*) urged all units to seize any chance to cross the treacherous waters of the Rhine and shorten the war.

SEIZURE. On March 7, 1945, the U.S. 9th Armored Division rumbled toward the town of Remagen on the left bank of the Rhine just south of Cologne and 60 miles northwest of Mainz. A German prisoner warned his American captors that in 45 minutes the great bridge spanning the swollen Rhine at Remagen would be blown up. It was valuable information, for Capt. Willi Bratke had in fact been ordered to proceed with the demolition. Meanwhile, Sgt. Alexander A. Drabik, a butcher from Holland, Ohio, led his platoon through a hail of fire to the Remagen bridge. His orders were to hold a defensive position while troops to his north prepared for an assault crossing of the river.

At 3:30 P.M. a preliminary charge exploded, blowing a crater in the western flooring of the span. But the charge was too weak and the bridge remained intact. Twenty minutes later Drabik and his men reached the western end of the bridge. Without pausing, the platoon crossed in a cat-like line through a hail of bullets. Another explosion knocked out a main support, but strangely the 500 pounds of TNT failed to go off. Drabik later described it: "We ran down the middle of the bridge, shouting as we went. I didn't stop because I knew that if I kept moving they couldn't hit me. My men were in squad column and not one of them was hit. We took cover in some bomb craters. Then we just sat and waited for others to come. That's the way it was."

The bridge was captured intact despite the minor damage of two explosions. By 4 P.M., when the main charge set by German experts was supposed to go off, more than 100 Americans were across and ready to set up a strong position on the other side of the Germans' last natural defense in the west. Working speedily, American combat engineers installed heavy planking and supporting beams to allow heavy armor to cross. Within 24 hours more than 8,000 men and supporting hardware were on the other side of the Rhine. Nearby a pontoon bridge and a floating treadway were constructed.

REACTION. Hitler was infuriated by news of the disaster. He sent 25 of his new jet dive bombers to attack the Americans, but all except five were shot down or crashed. A dozen new *V-2* rockets (*q.v.*) exploded harmlessly nearby. Hitler ordered severe punishment for four officers he deemed responsible. All were brought before a drumhead court-martial and executed. Capt. Bratke survived because he had the good fortune to be captured by the Americans. The *Fuehrer* dismissed Field Marshal Gerd von Rundstedt (*q.v.*) and replaced him with Field Marshal Albert Kesselring (*q.v.*).

AFTERMATH. The capture of the Remagen bridge was of critical importance to the Allies. In a matter of days, 75,000 American combat engineers built 62 bridges, including 46 pontoon, 11 fixed highway, and 3 railway spans across the Rhine. By the end of March, seven Allied armies were across the river and were moving inexorably through the German countryside.

SIGNIFICANCE. Capture of the Remagen bridge made a long Rhine defense impossible and upset Hitler's entire defense system along the river. (*See* GERMANY, BATTLE OF.) For the Germans it was a depressing loss. Hitler later admitted that the Normandy bridgehead and the Remagen bridge sealed the fate of the Third Reich. Gen. Kesselring said, "Never was there more concentrated bad luck than at Remagen." The Allies were jubilant. Eisenhower called it "one of my happy moments in the war." Gen. George C. Marshall (*q.v.*) saw it as "demonstrating American initiative and adaptability at its best." "While the bridge lasted," said Lt. Gen. Walter Bedell Smith (*q.v.*), "it was worth its weight in gold."

Bibliography. R. W. Hechler, *The Bridge at Remagen* (1957); J.M. Zarish, *The Collapse of the Remagen Bridge* (1968); and P. Berber, *Remagen* (1970).

RENNELL ISLAND, BATTLE OF. *See* GUADALCANAL CAMPAIGNS.

REPORTING, WAR. Reportage of war news from both combat and home fronts was efficient on both sides.

GENERAL. World War II was the best reported war in history. Dedicated men from all belligerent countries recorded every conceivable event of the war years. Some of the reporting was officially inspired, but most of it came from a cadre of war correspondents roaming the battlefields. Women as well as men contributed their share, including American war correspondent Martha Gellhorn and photographer Margaret Bourke-White. Reporters endured the same hardships and perils as combat troops. They were exposed to enemy shellfire or strafing, bivouacked in dangerous spots to observe enemy action, or accompanied air crews on bombing missions. Most of them hated the bloody business of war, with its mud, filth, and ever-present specter of death, but they had a job to do and they did it well. Many, including 33 American reporters, lost their lives.

BRITISH. British war reporting was distinguished by its general tone of accuracy. Millions of people who lived in German-occupied countries on the Continent relied heavily for trustworthy news on the British Broadcasting Corporation (BBC), which sent its radio programs to every corner of Europe. Among the best examples of British war reportage were: Douglas Williams of the *Daily Telegraph* on the miracle at Dunkirk (*See* DUNKIRK EVACUATION) (1940); Rebecca West on the reaction of Britons to Hitler's air assault (*See* BRITAIN, BATTLE OF) (1940); A. B. Austin of the London *Daily Herald* on the raid on Dieppe (*See* DIEPPE RAID) (1942); and V. A. Pritchett on the last days of Berlin (*See* BERLIN, BATTLE OF) (1945).

GERMAN. In the totalitarian Third Reich the coordinated press was regarded as a propaganda weapon of the Nazi regime. Before the war Paul Joseph Goebbels (*q.v.*), Minister of Public Enlightenment and Propaganda, compiled a list of newsmen whom he considered to be suitable for war duty and gave them an eight-week training course in recommended techniques of war reporting. Before and during the war he supervised more than 3,600 newspapers and their reporting staffs. Each morning he received editors and gave them precise details on the news he wanted to be printed that day. He praised his combat reporters as "cold-blooded and fearless, as exposed to danger as the flame thrower." He assigned control of radio reporters to Hans Fritzsche, who was tried at Nuremberg. (*See* NUREMBERG TRIALS.)

During the opening years of Nazi war triumphs, German newsmen wrote glowing reports of magnificent victories in Poland, the Scandinavian countries, the Low Countries, and France. They described "brilliant victories" in Soviet Russia after the invasion of June 22, 1941, and later disparaged the strength of American forces while ridiculing Churchill and Roosevelt. Among the best German war reports were those by Karl Heinz Seiss on the invasion of the Soviet Union (1941); Heinz Werther Schmitt on El Alamein (*q.v.*) (1942); and

Heinz Schröter on Stalingrad (1943) (*See* STALINGRAD, BATTLE OF). A unique feature of German war reporting was the publication by the General Staff of the *Wehrmacht* (*q.v.*) of special dispatches from its own combat reporters.

RUSSIAN. Like German reportage, Russian war reports reflected the mores of a totalitarian state. One-sided and tendentious, Soviet reporting invariably boasted of magnificent victories by good Russians and the bestial behavior of evil Germans. Combat reports consisted primarily of panegyrics on Red fighters against monstrous Nazis. Two of Russia's outstanding novelists, Konstantin Simonov and Ilya Ehrenburg, went to the battle fronts to devote their talents to the building of morale.

Among outstanding Russian war reports were Simonov's classic story on the battle for Moscow (*See* EASTERN FRONT, CAMPAIGNS ON THE) (1942); Ehrenburg and Alexei Tolsoi on the German assault on Sevastopol (*see* SEVASTOPOL, SIEGE OF) (1941–1942); Nikolai Tikhonov on the German attempt to take Leningrad (*See* LENINGRAD, SIEGE OF) (1941–1944); and Vassili Grossman on the Red Army in Poland (1944).

JAPANESE. Japanese reportage during the early years of Japanese victories enthusiastically proclaimed the superiority of Nipponese arms. Even when the tide of victory receded, newspapers throughout the country continued the euphoric reporting of the early days. Much effort was devoted to attempts to lower American morale through English-language broadcasts from Tokyo. (*See* TOKYO ROSE.)

AMERICAN. In contrast to reportage in the Axis countries, American combat reporting was in general more accurate and less colored by propaganda. Some stories, indeed, were used for morale building, notably the account of the sacrifice of the Four Chaplains (*q.v.*). As in other countries, well-known authors served as war correspondents, among them Ernest Hemingway, John Hersey, John Steinbeck, Maurice Hindus, Irwin Shaw, Erskine Caldwell, and William Saroyan. (*See* LITERATURE, WARTIME.) Drama critics Brooks Atkinson and John Mason Brown managed to obtain front-line assignments. Most flamboyant of American war correspondents was Quentin Reynolds (*q.v.*), who was later involved in a lawsuit concerning in part his role in the war.

The New York Times sent a superb staff to the combat fronts, including Richard D. Macmillan, James Reston, Herbert L. Matthews, Gene Currivan, Otto Tolischus, Harrison Salisbury, Milton Bracker, C. Brooks Peters, and William L. Laurence (*q.v.*). Their dispatches provided important raw material for historians. Among classic American war reporters were Otto Tolischus on the German *Blitzkrieg* (*q.v.*) in Poland (1939); Leland Stowe of the Chicago *Daily News* on the defeat of the British Expeditionary Force in Norway (*see* SCANDINAVIA, CAMPAIGNS IN) (1940); M. W. Fodor of the Chicago

Daily News on the mass civilian exodus from Belgium (*see* LOW COUNTRIES, CAMPAIGNS IN THE) (1940); Larry Allen of the Associated Press on the sinking of the British warship *Barham* in the Mediterranean (1941); Richard D. Macmillan on the confrontation at El Alamein (*see* EL ALAMEIN, BATTLE OF) (1942); and Milton Bracker on the gruesome end of Benito Mussolini (1945).

Radio reporting was equally efficient. Among the outstanding American radio reports of the war were William L. Shirer's account from Compiègne on June 22, 1940, when a triumphant Hitler dictated armistice terms to a humiliated French commission; and Edward R. Murrow's (*q.v.*) broadcasts from London at the height of the Battle of Britain (*q.v.*) ("This is London calling!").

Bibliography. L. L. Snyder and R. B. Morris, *A Treasury of Great Reporting (1949, 1962);* and L. L. Snyder, *Masterpieces of War Reporting* (1962).

REPULSE. British Royal Navy battlecruiser sunk along with the new battleship *Prince of Wales* on December 10, 1941.

The battlecruiser *Repulse,* sister ship of the *Renown,* was built in 1915–1916 and twice modernized to correct her more striking deficiencies. Her length was 787 feet, her beam 102 feet. She carried six 150-inch guns, six 4-inch guns, and other guns. She was the only capital ship then in existence with three twin turrets, two forward and one aft. Her hull had cruiser lines when observed from the air.

In 1940 and 1941 the *Repulse* took part in the Norwegian campaign and served as escort for Atlantic convoys. In 1941, after cancellation of a proposed refit job in the United States, she was sent to the Far East to accompany the *Prince of Wales.* On December 10, 1941, off the east coast of Malaya, she was attacked by Japanese aircraft. She managed to dodge several torpedoes, but after one torpedo hit her steering gear, she was quickly finished off, rolled over, and sank. (*See* PRINCE OF WALES.)

RESISTANCE MOVEMENTS. Activities throughout occupied European countries during World War II to win freedom from Nazi control.

BACKGROUND. Hitler conceived of his New Order (*q.v.*) in Europe in terms of master and slave—rule of the great Indo-European-Aryan-Nordic-Germanic race over all other inferior peoples. For this purpose he hoped to use collaborators in each country. Unfortunately for him, collaborators were few and resisters many.

As soon as the shock of German occupation wore off, resistance increased. In every country where the *Gestapo* (*q.v.*), the German secret police, worked to subjugate the local population, bands of recalcitrants merged to strike back at Germans. A pattern of resistance began to appear. The Germans were given no rest. Armed bands struck from hills and forests. At night they derailed trains, blew up bridges, cleared roadblocks, and exploded ammunition dumps. Infiltrators sabotaged work in factories through go-slow signals, throwing sand or powdered glass into machine gears, making dud shells or dropping poison in food being canned for the armed forces. The resistance also played an important role in the gathering of military intelligence, especially on the *V-1* and *V-2* (*qq.v.*) weapons.

Most Resistance movements were run from London by governments-in-exile (*q.v.*) working with the British Special Operations Executive (SOE). The British Broadcasting Corporation (BBC) sent messages in many languages to underground fighters on where and when to strike. In return guerrillas and Partisans (*qq.v.*) supplied London with information of all kinds. Hundreds of Allied airmen and other prisoners of war were able to escape through underground railroads organized all over the Continent. Resistance newspapers, some printed, some mimeographed, kept alive the urge to liberation and issued warnings on collaborators.

POLAND. Polish Resistance matched the ferocity of German invaders. German sentries were found with their throat cuts. Factories were sabotaged, railroad lines severed, and ammunition dumps exploded. During the German occupation, Poland never had a Quisling (*q.v.*), that is a traitor. Poles by the hundreds escaped to fight with the Allies on many fronts. Inside Poland the Resistance faced the *Gestapo* with an effective espionage system of its own.

DENMARK. Denmark was supposed to be the show place of Nazism, a "happy" satellite state enjoying the benefits of German occupation. But the Danes did not respond as Hitler had hoped. Outwardly, from monarch to peasant, they treated the Germans with cold contempt. When occupation authorities urged the Danes to introduce the yellow badge to indicate Judaism, King Christian X (*q.v.*) was said to have replied: "The Jews are a part of the Danish nation. If the Jews are forced to wear the yellow star, I and my whole family shall wear it as a badge of honor." The story is probably apocryphal, but it indicates the nature of Danish resistance. When orders came from Berlin to transport all Jews to concentration camps, those Danes who had advance information smuggled many prospective victims to Sweden.

Danish resistance took many forms. When Hitler decreed confiscation of food from Danish farms for German use, Danes responded by eating themselves to exhaustion so that as little food as possible could be sent to Germany. More than 10,000 Danes escaped to join the British Army. Some 40,000 others, calling themselves "moles," joined the Danish underground.

NORWAY. Germans systematically plundered Norway of merchant ships, machinery, and movable goods. Collaborator Vidkun Quisling (*q.v.*) aroused the contempt of his own people. Norwegians, like the Danes, had little use for their Nazi "guests." The Norwegian Resistance transported an average of 20 people a day to Sweden. Ministers, teachers, workers, peasants, all struck back at Germans. The damage was so extensive that the Germans had to maintain an army of 300,000 men in Norway to prevent a possible Allied landing and to counteract acts of sabotage. More than 50,000 Norwegians escaped to Britain and Canada to serve in the Allied merchant marine.

BELGIUM. The Belgians, old hands at resistance, also struck back at the unwanted invaders. German officers found on their doorsteps copies of *Free Belgium* with the warning: "Belgians, never forget that the Germans are criminals, barbarians, murderers. Don't swallow their lies!" Copies were passed along in hollow cases, umbrellas, and false-bottomed suitcases. The paper never missed a deadline. Members of the Belgian underground brought silent death to many unsuspecting Nazi guards.

HOLLAND. Infuriated by the air assault on Rotterdam on May 10, 1940, (*See* ROTTERDAM, BOMBING OF), and the subsequent spoliation of their country, the Dutch hit back hard. Canals became watery graves for German sentries whose throats were slashed in the dark. Artur von Seyss-Inquart (*q.v.*), the Reich Commissioner for the Netherlands, could muster only an infinitesimal 5 percent of the people as collaborators.

FRANCE. Shocked into a coma by the defeat of 1940, the French soon recovered. Most Frenchmen rejected Marshal Henri Pétain and Pierre Laval (*qq.v.*), both of whom believed they were rescuing France from disaster. To avoid conscription, eligible Frenchmen resisted. More than 100,000 escaped to London to join Charles de Gaulle's (*q.v.*) Free French (*See* FREE FRANCE) (later Fighting French) movement. Others joined the *Maquis* (*q.v.*), one of the most effective of all Resistance organizations. (*See also* FRANCE IN WARTIME.)

YUGOSLAVIA. In Yugoslavia, the Chetniks (*q.v.*), mostly Serbians, fought against collaborators, hostile Croats, Communists, and Germans alike. Josip Broz, later known as Tito (*q.v.*), Croat and Communist, led some 100,000 Partisans (*q.v.*) against the Germans and by the end of 1943 was holding 20 German divisions at bay. The two Yugoslav Resistance movements clashed, after which the weight of Anglo-American aid went to Tito. (*See* GOVERNMENTS-IN-EXILE.)

GREECE. In Greece, too, opposition was hampered by internecine quarrels. The National Liberation Movement (EAM) (*q.v.*), with the best-organized and toughest fighters, clashed with the Greek Democratic Liberation Army (EDES), which was supported by the Greek Government-in-exile and by British authorities. In October 1944 the British sent 3,000 troops to defend the Greek Government against the EAM, who were driven to the hills.

COUNTERACTION. German authorities did everything possible to contain Resistance movements throughout Europe, but they were unsuccessful. They arrested thousands, held many others as hostages, and executed guerrillas and partisans, but nothing seemed to work. Trying to track down members of the Resistance was as frustrating as attempting to place a thumb on quicksilver. When resisters died, others took their place. Even the destruction of entire towns such as Lidice and Oradour-sur Glans (*qq.v.*) failed to stop the opposition. On occasion, 100 hostages, or 50, or 5 were executed in response to attacks on Germans. The *Gestapo* killed 8,000 hostages in Poland. More than 10,000 Dutch citizens were transported to concentration camps in Germany. In France nearly 30,000 hostages were murdered and an additional 40,000 died in *Gestapo* prisons. Nothing worked for German authorities in halting resistance.

SIGNIFICANCE. Part of Hitler's undoing may be attributed to his inability to realize that his brutal occupation policies were ineffective. Nazi behavior was abhorrent to all European peoples under German occupation. In the long run Hitler's lack of success in conquering Resistance movements contributed to his own collapse. (*See also* UNDERGROUND. For the movement inside Germany against Hitler, *see* GERMAN RESISTANCE.)

Bibliography. S. Siegel, *The New Order in Poland* (1942); P. Paulmer, *Denmark in Nazi Chains* (1942); L. De Jong and W. F. Stoppelman, *The Lion Rampant: The Story of Holland's Resistance to the Nazis* (1943); G. R. Miller, *Maquis* (1945); T. Bor-Komoroski, *The Secret Army* (1951); Survey of International Affairs, *Hitler's Europe* (1954); D. Lampe, *The Danish Resistance* (1957); M. J. Proudfoot, *European Refugees, 1939-1952* (1957); W. H. Weserübung, *Die deutsche Gesetzung von Dänemark und Norwegen, 1940* (1960); R. Manvell and H. Fraenkel, *The July Plot* (1966); H. Rothfels, *The German Opposition Against Hitler* (1962); H. Ehrlich, *Resistance: France 1940-1945* (1965); P. Novick, *The Resistance versus Vichy* (1968); R. R. Kedward, *Resistance in Vichy France* (1978); and A. and E. Praeger, *World War II Resistance Stories* (1979).

RESOURCES, BATTLE FOR. Struggle between the Allies and the Axis for supplies of raw materials to produce weapons of war.

BACKGROUND. To a greater extent than in previous conflicts, belligerents in World War II depended upon mineral, agricultural, and other raw materials, as well as synthetic products, for production of guns, tanks, warships, and aircraft. It was necessary to boost production to an enormous volume to meet the voracious demand for weapons. Military, naval, and air success depended upon superiority in fighting equipment, which in turn was dependent upon industrial capacity. No belligerent in the war, regardless of its resources in labor, capital, and engineering proficiency, could win superiority in military equipment without substantial power resources and abundant raw materials.

UNITED NATIONS. None of the Allies by itself possessed all the basic raw materials to wage a long war, but in combination they had access to necessary resources that could not be matched by the Axis. This was true even after Hitler had taken over much of continental Europe and after the Japanese had won control of a large part of southeastern Asia.

The Allies had the advantage of being able to call on the resources of most of the world for vital raw materials. Allied merchant ships plowed the sea lanes and continued to move in convoys despite U-Boat attacks. They brought oil from the Middle East and the Caribbean; rubber from Brazil, Africa, and Ceylon; wool from Australia; electrical equipment from Switzerland; leather from Argentina; tungsten and iron ore from Spain; and chrome ore from Caledonia.

The Allied Joint Chiefs of Staff considered it critically important to see that these and other raw materials and resources were denied to the Axis. A major part of Allied strategy was devoted to the task of throttling the flow of raw materials to Germany, Italy, and Japan.

AXIS. Soon after he came to power in 1933, Hitler initiated a program of stockpiling raw materials and rearming Germany. By 1939 he had Germany on a wartime footing for a short *Blitzkrieg* (*q.v.*) campaign. After successful invasion of other European countries, he began to drain their resources for benefit of his own war machine. At the same time he attempted to keep the neutrals, which were willing to sell to both sides, in line by the silent threat of occupation. He never successfully solved the problem of fighting a war on a global scale.

Mussolini, because of his lack of such basic raw materials as iron and coal, had to rely on his Axis partner for adequate resources to keep his war machine alive. In the early stage of their expansion the Japanese were able to acquire raw materials in occupied China and other parts of southeastern Asia, but the scorched-earth tactics (leaving nothing intact in the path of the invaders) by American, British, and Netherlands East Indies forces there denied to Japan the valuable raw materials of those areas.

ACCESS TO OIL. As in World War I, access to oil was of overwhelming importance in the strategy of World War II. Oil was an absolute necessity in mechanized warfare and those countries that had access to it had a tremendous advantage. The Allies together monopolized about 85 percent of the world's output. For the Axis the matter of oil supply was a continuous nightmare. Hitler regarded it as his first priority. He managed to win the Rumanian oil fields and a foothold in the oil fields of the Caucasus, but he was never able to penetrate into the Persian area. German scientists invented a process for extracting oil from liberal supplies of coal, but they never were able to produce enough for Hitler's war machine.

Allied strategists added to Hitler's oil problem by ordering the bombing of German refineries and extraction plants. Many of these targets were reduced to rubble before the end of the war.

The Italians, who were never able to solve the problem of oil supply, had to hold their ships in port and their planes on the ground because of insufficient petroleum. For a time the Japanese were in a far better position than their Axis partners in Europe. Soon after Pearl Harbor (*q.v.*) Japanese troops headed straight for the oil fields in the Netherlands East Indies and in British Malaya. These became major targets of the Allied counteroffensive.

RUBBER. Although of lesser critical importance than oil, rubber was high on the list of essential war commodities. The Japanese surge into the southern Pacific cut off a major source of rubber for the Allies. Both American and German scientists were successful in producing a substitute, synthetic rubber, which was in some respects superior to natural rubber because of its resistance to deterioration from oil. Natural rubber was the one resource the United States lacked.

TIN. Tin, which was useful for coating steel and for the accumulation of food reserves, was in short supply for both Allies and Axis. The Japanese cut off an important source from Malaya. There were alternatives, but the shortage was felt by both sides to the end of the war.

COAL. The belligerents, with the exception of Italy, had access to coal. Both the British and Americans had ample supplies for their needs. The Germans had enough coal deposits but they were hampered by a shortage of miners and by sabotage in conquered countries. The Russians had enough coal for their war machine. The Japanese had fairly large resources in the home islands, with additional supplies in Manchuria and Occupied China.

IRON ORE. Iron ore was the basic raw material for armaments and the metallurgical industry. The Allies had an advantage in plentiful supplies. Germans lacked high-grade ores and had to import more than two-thirds of their consumption. Japanese iron ore in the home islands was of low grade, better grade ores were imported from China, Manchuria, and Korea.

STEEL. All belligerents concentrated on production of steel. German and continental plants could produce 45 million tons a year, the Japanese 12.6 million, the Allies considerably more.

FERRO-ALLOYS. Certain ferro-alloys were essential for the production of steel for bearings, machine tools, guns, armor plate, and projectiles. Because of the shortage of ferro-alloys, the Axis countries could not exploit their full productive capacity. Chromium, for hardening steel, was plentiful in Turkey and most of it went to the United States. The main sources of tungsten were Portugal, China, and the United States. Molybdenum, a substitute for tungsten used to give elasticity to steel, was practically an American monopoly.

Vanadium, to toughen steel for use in gears, piston shafts, and gun barrels, was found mainly in the United States, Peru, Northern Rhodesia, and West Africa. Nickel, important for armaments because of the high tensile strength it gave to steel, was produced almost entirely in Canada for the Allies. Europe had no nickel. The European continent had only 10 percent of the world's supply of manganese, softening element to prepare steel in rails, forgings, and wire.

BAUXITE. Germany had no deposits of the raw material from which aluminum is produced. Aluminum was indispensable in the manufacturing of aircraft and it was also a useful substitute for copper in electric generating and transmission equipment. The largest producer of bauxite was France, but there were also supplies in Italy, Hungary, and Yugoslavia.

COPPER. Important for the production of ammunition and in the chemical industry, copper was found mostly in the neighborhood of Lake Superior, Cornwall, Siberia, Spain, and the Ural Mountains. Germany could produce less than 10 percent of its war needs.

LEAD. The United States produced more than one-third of the world's lead, vital for the manufacture of ammunition and batteries. Other important lead resources were found in Australia, Spain, and Mexico. Germany produced only about 40 percent of its needs.

ZINC. Used in galvanizing iron and in various alloys, zinc was found in rich supply in Australia, Mexico, Canada, Russia, France, and Sweden. The Germans produced about 70 percent of their war requirements.

PLATINUM. A catalyst in chemical industries and electrical manufacture, platinum was obtained in Soviet Russia, Brazil, Australia, Tasmania, and South Africa. Germany had no platinum.

MICA. The micas, complex silicates of aluminum and either alkali metals or iron and magnesium, were indispensable for such electrical equipment as radio and radar. Germany had no deposits of high-grade mica.

INDUSTRIAL DIAMONDS. The Allies had sources for industrial diamonds for use as abrasives and cutting tools. Germany had to import all its supplies.

SULFUR AND PYRITES. Essential for production of sulfuric acid, basic in the chemical industry, pulp making, and paper making, sulfur occurs in its free state chiefly in volcanic districts. Germany was seriously deficient in sulfur, but large supplies were available to its Axis partners, Italy and Japan. Important deposits were also in Texas and Louisiana.

OILS AND FATS. Necessary for the chemical industry, food, explosives, and soap making, oils and fats were imported by both Germans and Japanese.

LEATHER. The Allies had enormous supplies of leather, but the Germans were dependent on imports for most hides and skins.

TEXTILES. The Allies had access to large supplies of cotton, wool, hemp, and silk, but the Germans had no production of natural textile fibers.

FOODSTUFFS. Germans, sufficient only in potatoes, had to import most other foodstuffs and looked desperately to the Ukrainian breadbasket. Hitler ordered conquered Dutch, Danes, Belgians, French, and Norwegians to cultivate root and grain crops instead of dairy farming. He also conscripted peoples in Eastern Europe to raise soya beans, cotton, and grain—all for German consumption. (*See* FORCED LABOR.) Western Europeans lost meats and fats and had their dietary standards lowered in favor of Germans.

SYNTHETICS AND SUBSTITUTES. Because of insatiable demand for oil, rubber, steel, and many other materials by mechanized armies, all the belligerents pushed ahead with the production of synthetics and used substitute goods in production. The tempo of synthetic production was speeded up by new developments in industrial technology.

As in World War I, Germans were active in production of substitutes and synthetics. They managed the synthetic production of oil from coal, but could produce only a relatively small amount of lubricating oil and little 100-octane fuel. Importing huge quantities of oil from Rumania, they used their own synthetic plants for a safety margin of supplies. German production of synthetic Buna rubber was of high quality. In producing synthetic textiles, Germans made themselves almost independent of imported cotton and wool.

In World War I Germans had produced nitrates by the artificial fixation of atmospheric nitrogen to meet their requirements for explosives after the supply of Chilean nitrates had been cut off. In World War II their scientists created entirely new materials made of plastics and cellulose. Synthetic glass and plastic wood were used increasingly as a substitute in the building industries, and potato peelings became an important raw material for the making of pulp.

GERMAN DEFICIENCIES. Despite their conquests in Europe and despite the use of substitutes and synthetics, Germans were never able to overcome basic deficiencies in essential materials. They had adequate supplies of only 4 out of 34 raw materials considered necessary for the waging of modern war. However, they were not appreciably weakened by the Allied blockade and sabotage. German war production actually peaked in 1944: it was hit hard by bombing only in the latter stage of war.

JAPANESE DEFICIENCIES. The Japanese underwent a similar economic metamorphosis. Although they held on doggedly to territory that would give them access to vital raw materials, they eventually had to relinquish these areas. By late 1944 and early 1945 the Allies had clearly won the battle for resources. (*See also* ECONOMIC WARFARE; SUPPLIES, BATTLE FOR; and PRODUCTION, BATTLE OF.)

Bibliography. E. V. Francis, *The Battle of Supplies* (1942); U.S. Bureau of the Budget, *The United States at War* (1946); and D. L. Gordon and R. Dangerfield, *The Hidden Weapon: The Story of Economic Warfare* (1947).

RESPONSIBILITY, WAR. *See* WAR RESPONSIBILITY.

RESULTS OF THE WAR. *See* WAR CASUALTIES; ECONOMIC CONSEQUENCES OF THE WAR; POLITICAL CONSEQUENCES OF THE WAR; PSYCHOLOGICAL EFFECTS OF THE WAR; SOCIAL IMPACT OF THE WAR.

REUBEN JAMES. U.S. destroyer (*DD-245*) sunk by a German U-Boat in the Atlantic in 1941 during the undeclared war of the United States against Germany.

BACKGROUND. Before the attack on Pearl Harbor on December 7, 1941, brought the United States into the war, Britain fought to keep its supply channels open against savage U-Boat attacks. During this stage (*see* ATLANTIC, BATTLE OF THE), American warships, violating the technical definition of neutrality, assisted in escorting convoys from Newfoundland to the Irish Sea. In the summer of 1941 President Roosevelt ordered U.S. naval units to convoy duty.

Roosevelt and Churchill divided the North Atlantic between the United States and England: The ocean west of a dividing line in the center of the Atlantic was declared part of the U.S. defense system to be patrolled by the American Navy, while the area east of the line was to be guarded by the Royal Navy.

In mid-October 1941 the U.S. destroyer *Kearney* was hit by a torpedo, which killed 11 men, but the ship did not sink because of its watertight compartmentalization. Public opinion was outraged, but nothing was done.

SINKING. The *Reuben James* was an obsolete but trim World War I flush-deck U.S. destroyer assigned to duty with the British on the Atlantic. On October 31, 1941, more than a month before Pearl Harbor, "the Rube," was protecting a convoy headed for Iceland when her direction finder located U-Boat signals in the vicinity. Within moments she was struck by a torpedo fired from German U-Boat *U-562*. Her magazine exploded, and she was blown into two sections, both of which sank quickly. Some 115 seamen, more than two-thirds of those aboard the *Reuben James,* lost their lives, including the captain and all officers.

AFTERMATH. The *Reuben James* was the first American warship sunk— even before the United States entered the war. The incident caused comparatively little concern at the time, although it was one among many factors that led to American entry into the war. Folk singer Woody Guthrie made it the theme of a ballad about the names of the men on the *Reuben James.*
Bibliography. D. D. Lewis, *The Fight for the Sea* (1961).

REYNAUD, PAUL (1878–1966). French politician and Premier during the early days of the war.

On the outbreak of war Reynaud was Minister of Finance. He became Premier in 1940 and took over the Foreign and War Ministries. It was now far too late to win the military reforms he had advocated for many years. On the German invasion of France in May 1940, he proposed an Anglo-French union but was voted down. He was arrested by the Vichy Government and accused of "misappropriation of public funds." Found guilty, he was sent to a German prison in 1943 and remained there for the rest of the war.

Reynaud was known as a man of decision, imagination, and energy. Georges Clemenceau spoke admiringly of him: "This mosquito certainly can sting!"
Bibliography. Reynaud wrote *La problème militaire française* (1935); and *Au coeur de la mêlée, 1936–1945* (1952).

REYNOLDS, QUENTIN JAMES (1902–1965). U.S. correspondent and author.

At the start of the war Reynolds was sent to France on a roving commission for *Collier's* magazine. He was one of the last reporters to leave Paris and Bordeaux after the collapse of France. Later he covered the war fronts in North Africa, Italy and Palestine. In the fall of 1944 he made a tour of the southwest Pacific battle area.

In 1954 a Federal court jury in New York awarded Reynolds $175,001 in a suit against his old poker-playing crony, Westbrook Pegler. A Pegler column had called Reynolds "yellow" and an "absentee war correspondent." On the stand under the questioning of his attorney, Louis Nizer, Reynolds recounted his front-line record while a succession of witnesses and depositions testified to his heroism under fire. He died at Travis Air Base, California, on March 17, 1965.

Strapping, six-feet-one, 260 pounds, good-looking, and convivial, Reynolds was gregarious, hard-drinking, and a free-handed spender. His style of writing was swift running, dramatic, and enormously vivid. His admirers called him the World War II version of Richard Harding Davis (1864–1916), the most adventurous, the most read war correspondent of every war from the Greco-

Turkish War to World War I. His critics complained about the Rover-Boys quality of his writing.

Bibliography. Among Reynold's books are: *The Wounded Don't Cry* (1941); *London Diary* (1941); *Convoy* (1942); *Only the Stars Are Neutral* (1942); *Dress Rehearsal* (1943); *The Curtain Rises* (1944); and *Officially Dead* (1945).

RIBBENTROP, JOACHIM VON (1893–1946). German Foreign Minister in the pre-war period and throughout the war.

Before the outbreak of war Ribbentrop advised Hitler that the British would never go to war with Germany over Poland. His standing with Hitler declined precipitously after Britain entered the conflict. Throughout the war he played only a minor role, spending most of his energy in warding off the attacks of others in the Nazi hierarchy. On August 23, 1939, he revealed his skill as a diplomat when he signed in Moscow the critical Russo-German Nonaggression Plan Pact (*q.v.*). On September 28, 1939, he negotiated a second German-Soviet treaty readjusting the partition of Poland. He managed to extend the Rome-Berlin Axis (*q.v.*) into the Rome-Berlin-Tokyo Axis on September 27, 1940. (*See* AXIS.) Thereafter, his influence was negligible.

NUREMBERG. Ribbentrop was one of the major Nazi leaders brought before the International Military Tribunal at Nuremberg. He was accused of having participated in Hitler's aggressions and in anti-Jewish measures. Pale, stooped, and beaten, he sobbed and pleaded his innocence. Found guilty on all four counts, he was hanged at Nuremberg on October 16, 1946. (*See* NUREMBERG TRIALS.)

Critics accused Ribbentrop of arrogance and gave him such nicknames as Iago, The Wild Man, and Ribbensnob. His subservience to Hitler was notorious. At Nuremberg he boasted of his loyalty: "Even with all I know, if in this cell Hitler should come to me and say 'Do this!' I would still do it."

Bibliography. G. Von Gunther, *Von Ribbentrop* (1939); P. Schwartz, *This Man Ribbentrop* (1943); and *The Ribbentrop Memoirs* (1954).

RICHTHOFEN, WOLFRAM VON (1895–1945). German commander of the *Luftwaffe* (*q.v.*) in World War II.

In the opening days of the war in September 1939, von Richthofen led raids against Poland. For the air assault on Warsaw from September 21 to 27, 1939, he committed 400 bombers, many of which flew repeated sorties. (*See* WAR-SAW, BOMBING OF.) In July 1940, just before the air attack on England, he commanded a specialized corps of three squadrons of *Stukas* (*q.v.*) and reconnaissance aircraft. In the battle itself his *Fliegerkorps* ("Air Corps") suffered heavy damage. (*See* BRITAIN, BATTLE OF.) Later his men were moved to Calais to prepare for *Operation Sea Lion* (*q.v.*), which never took place.

The New York Times reported on March 22, 1945, that von Richthofen had been jailed "for defeatist attitude." Von Richthofen died on July 12, 1945. The place and circumstances of his death are not known.

RIDGEWAY, MATTHEW BUNKER (1895–   ). U.S. Army officer active in campaigns from North Africa to Normandy.

In 1939 Ridgeway was detailed to the War Department in Washington to work with the War Plans Division. In 1942 he was made Commanding General of the 82nd Infantry Division, which eventually became one of the army's first airborne units. He flew with this division in North Africa in April 1943. He planned the night airborne invasion of Sicily in July 1943, the first operation of its kind ever attempted by any army.

On June 6, 1944, D-Day, Ridgeway jumped with his troops in the Normandy strike to spearhead the assault on the Cotentin Peninsula. (*See* NORMANDY INVASION.) In August 1944 he was given command of the 18th Airborne Corps and in the ensuing months directed its operations in the Ardennes, the crossing of the Rhine, the surge to the Elbe, and the junction with Soviet troops on May 2, 1945. (*See* GERMANY, BATTLE OF.)

Ruggedly built, austere, and distinguished in appearance, Ridgeway was considered to be the typical American Army officer. *Time* magazine said, "He looks like a Roman senator and lives like a Spartan hoplite."

Bibliography. M. B. Ridgeway, *Soldier* (1956).

ROKOSSOVSKY, KONSTANTIN K. (1896–1968). Soviet Army officer and a top strategist.

Rokossovsky was called to duty after the German invasion of the Soviet Union on June 22, 1941. Promoted to Major General, he commanded the army that halted the Germans before they reached Moscow. He introduced the tactics by which Russian infantry and artillery held the enemy while tanks were kept in reserve. Then, when the Germans had just completed their breakthrough, Rokossovsky sent his armored units into action with devastating results. He also perfected the wide encircling movements that Soviet tank columns used successfully in attacking the enemy flanks. Rokossovsky worked out a plan for digging tanks into the ground so that only their turrets showed and used them as stationary artillery pieces.

In 1942–1943 Rokossovsky annihilated 22 German divisions at Stalingrad. (*See* STALINGRAD, BATTLE OF.) As Colonel General he directed the great Russian offensive on the Orel-Kursk arc in the summer of 1943. In 1944 he was promoted to Marshal of the Soviet Union. In the spring of 1945 he commanded the 2nd White Russian Army, which achieved final victory over the Germans with the capture of Berlin. (*See* EASTERN FRONT, CAMPAIGNS ON THE; and BERLIN, BATTLE FOR.)

Although a master of armored warfare, Rokossovsky was not always in favor with the Kremlin. Stalin suspected him of deviating, but regarded him as indispensable and spared him in the purge of army officers. Instead, he awarded him the Order of Suvorov, First Degree, one of the highest honors in the Soviet Union.

Bibliography. K. K. Rokossovskii, *A Soldier's Duty* (1970).

ROME, LIBERATION OF. End of Nazi rule in the Italian capital on June 4, 1944.

BACKGROUND. Rome was central to the planning of the Allied Supreme Command. Axis resistance was expected after the invasion of southern Italy on September 3, 1943, but the fighting for the next nine months was fiercer than expected. (*See* ITALIAN FRONT, CAMPAIGNS ON THE.) Allied forces were contained at Anzio (*see* ANZIO BEACHHEAD) and initially at Cassino (*q.v.*). An all-out effort to take Rome was ordered.

PREPARATIONS. The U.S. 5th Army was deployed on the west coast along the Tyrrhenian Sea, while the British 8th Army (*q.v.*) was moved to the Cassino area. *Operation Strangle* designed to block the three major rail lines and the roads to the north, was put into effect. Allied airmen systematically destroyed railroads, bridges, and aqueducts, flying 21,000 sorties in April 1944. The Germans were now forced to bring in supplies across waters guarded by the British fleet.

DEFENSE. To meet the assault Field Marshal Albert Kesselring (*q.v.*) had two fortified mountain barriers, the Gustav Line centered at Cassino and spread along the Garigliano and Rapido rivers, and behind it the Adolf Hitler Line stretched across the Liri Valley. (*See* DEFENSIVE LINES, GERMAN.) In early May 1944 he ordered the flooding of the Pontine Marches between Cassino and Anzio. Later that month he withdrew to the Caesar Line, 20 miles south of Rome.

ASSAULT. On May 11, 1944, Anglo-American forces moved in unison and within a week pierced the Gustav Line. British and Polish troops surrounded the ruined monastery at Cassino and took the town itself. The British 8th Army pushed north through the Hitler Line toward Rome, while the American 5th slugged its way to the relief of Anzio. Fighter bombers concentrated on German convoys as U.S. field guns battered Kesselring's troops. A dozen German counterattacks were thrown back. Fighting up and down extinct volcanoes, pierced the Caesar Line, and opened the road to the Italian capital.

ENTRY. Through the Vatican, Kesselring on June 4, 1944, declared Rome an open city to save it from bombardment. The advancing Allies, however, had no intention of destroying the sacred city of world Catholicism. That same day the 88th Division of the U.S. 5th Army, under Lt. Gen. Mark W. Clark (*q.v.*), entered Rome to be greeted with cheers, flowers, fruit, Chianti, and kisses. The British 8th Army received an equally joyous reception.

SIGNIFICANCE. Rome was the first of the Axis capitals to fall. Its capitulation moved Roosevelt to remark: "One down and two to go." Fascism was dead in the southern half of Italy. The Germans who still had 25 divisions in Italy, fell back 150 miles to the Gothic Line in the north.

Bibliography. W.G.F. Jackson, *The Battle for Rome* (1969).

ROME-BERLIN AXIS. *See* AXIS.

ROME-BERLIN-TOKYO AXIS. *See* BERLIN-ROME-TOKYO AXIS.

ROMMEL, ERWIN (1891–1944). Germany's best-known soldier in the war. The so-called Desert Fox held high German decorations for bravery.

In 1939 Hitler appointed Rommel to command his personal escort and through that post was given command of the 7th *Panzer* Division for the assault on France in 1940. He demonstrated his ability by crossing the Meuse. By the time the campaign in France was over, Rommel had established a reputation as a dashing tank leader.

Early in 1941 Hitler sent Rommel to North Africa to assist the Italians, who were taking a beating from the English. At the head of his new *Afrika Korps* (*q.v.*), Rommel won a highly publicized reputation not only as a theater commander but also as a tactician.

NORTH AFRICAN CAMPAIGN. In North Africa Rommel led his troops in outfighting forces larger than his own, but eventually was defeated. On March 21, 1941, he overcame the British at El Agheila and advanced to Tobruk. In the summer of 1942 he led a German advance from Gazala to El Alamein, for which he was promoted to Field Marshal and decorated. Meanwhile, Allied sea and air power, centered at Malta (*see* MALTA, SIEGE OF), began to strike at Rommel's supply lines. By September 1942 he was in serious trouble. Taken ill, he was flown home for medical treatment. On October 24, 1942, at the height of the battle of El Alamein (*q.v.*), he returned to the front to conduct the lost battle and the withdrawal to Tunisia.

Rommel was an ill man for the remainder of the North African campaign. Again and again he appealed to Hitler for support, which was not forthcoming. On February 22, 1943, he managed to inflict a severe defeat on the Americans at Kasserine Pass (*q.v.*), but his counterattack against the British 8th Army on March 5, 1943 failed. He was recalled to Germany at the end of March. (*See* NORTH AFRICA, CAMPAIGNS IN.)

NORMANDY INVASION. In mid-1943 Rommel commanded Army Group B in northern Italy with orders to prevent Italian defection and a possible Allied invasion of southern France. In January 1944 he was entrusted with the defense of a portion of the northern French coast where an Allied invasion was expected. He constructed formidable fortifications, but the coastline was long. When the Allied invasion began (*see* NORMANDY INVASION), Rommel was at home and it was two weeks before Hitler allowed him to move his *Panzer* (*q.v.*) divisions to the front. On July 17, 1944, Rommel was severely injured when his automobile was strafed by an RAF (*q.v.*) machine gunner.

RESISTANCE. By this time Rommel was thoroughly disillusioned by Hitler's unrealistic military leadership and also by the *Fuehrer's* conduct which had aroused world-wide disgust. He opposed any attempt on Hitler's life in the belief that this would create a martyr. He did not take an active part in the July Plot (*q.v.*) on July 20, 1944, although the conspirators hoped to make him head of state after the assassination.

When one of the plotters undergoing interrogation by the *Gestapo* (*q.v.*) blurted out Rommel's name, the fate of the General was sealed. Enraged, Hitler wanted revenge. On October 14, 1944, he sent two officers to Rommel's home to suggest suicide with a promise of safety for his family and "an honorable burial." Rommel chose death by poison. At his funeral service Field Marshal Gerd von Rundstedt (*q.v.*), his superior officer, stated sadly: "A pitiless destiny snatched him from us. His heart belonged to the *Fuehrer.*"

ROLE AS TACTICIAN. A stocky, cool Swabian with the daring of an adventurer and an engineer's eye for detail, Rommel was one of the legendary military commanders of the war. Genial and gregarious, he at the same time had an insatiable hunger for fame and glory. Churchill called him "a decent, honorable opponent." Nevertheless, he was, as the German High Command complained, a brilliant tactician but no strategist. His success depended not only in outsmarting the enemy but also on restraining his own General Staff. He sought to introduce a note of chivalry in a cruel war. An indifferent organizer, he had an uncanny ability to exploit inferior and demoralized troops. Despite his eventual defeat, he retained the prestige he had won in combat.

Bibliography. A. Moorehead, *African Trilogy* (1946); M. Schulman, *Defeat in the Vesy* (1947); D. Young, *Rommel: The Desert Fox* (1950); B. H. Liddell Hart (ed.) *The Rommel Papers* (1953); R. Lewin, *Rommel as Military Commander* (1968); and D. Irving, *The Trail of the Fox* (1977).

ROMULO, CARLOS PEÑA (1901–   ). Filipino officer and aide-de-camp to Gen. Douglas MacArthur (*q.v.*).

On the day of the Japanese surprise attack on the Philippines, Romulo, a pro-American Filipino head of a publishing company and a major in the Philippines Army Reserve, together with most of his staff resigned to serve with the Allies. A close friend of Gen. MacArthur, he became press aide to the Commander-in-Chief on December 10, 1941.

Romulo went to Bataan as a public relations man. He remained there for 14 weeks following the Japanese occupation of Manila. He described Manila, Corregidor, and Bataan as "three tight little components of hell." When the fall of Bataan became imminent, MacArthur arranged Romulo's rescue in a makeshift amphibian nicknamed The Duck. On April 8, 1942, Romulo made good his escape from Bataan, carrying letters from some of the doomed men trapped there.

Romulo returned to Australia as aide to MacArthur, a post he held until the end of the war. He was with MacArthur on his famous return to the Philippines on October 20, 1944.

Bibliography. C. P. Romulo, *I Saw the Fall of the Philippines* (1942); and *Mother America* (1943).

ROOSEVELT, ELEANOR (1884–1962). Wife of President Franklin D. Roosevelt, diplomat, and humanitarian.

After her husband became President in 1933, Eleanor Roosevelt embarked upon a precedent-breaking round of activities, which made her a controversial figure for the remainder of her career. Her peripatetic wanderings made her the object of much criticism and the object of "Eleanor jokes," but many Americans responded warmly to her compassion and humanitarian concerns. In September 1941 she was appointed Director of the Office of Civilian Defense.

Because of her husband's infirmity, Eleanor Roosevelt acted as his "eyes and ears" in travels to Britain, Australia, the South Pacific, and American military bases in the United States and elsewhere both before and during the war. She played an active role in keeping the morale of American military men and civilians as high as possible throughout the war. Winston Churchill praised her work as bolstering Anglo-American solidarity. After her husband's death on April 12, 1945, President Harry S Truman appointed Mrs. Roosevelt to the post of delegate to the United Nations (1945; 1949–1952; 1961), where she served as Chairman of the UN Commission on Human Rights (1946–1951).

Tall, with sparkling eyes and a high-pitched voice, Mrs. Roosevelt was noted for her indefatigable energy. Her efforts for global racial dignity and women's rights made her one of the most popular women of the 20th century.

Bibliography. See the two autobiographies, *This is My Story* (1937) and *On My Own* (1956). *See also* J. P. Lash, *Eleanor and Franklin* (1971) and *Eleanor: The Years Alone* (1972).

ROOSEVELT, FRANKLIN D. (1882–1945). Thirty-second U.S. President.

He was born in Hyde Park, New York, on January 30, 1882, the son of a country gentleman. He was educated at Groton and Harvard and studied law at Columbia University.

EARLY CAREER. Roosevelt was elected to the New York State Senate in 1910. He served as Assistant Secretary of the Navy from 1913 to 1920. In the latter year he lost the Vice-Presidency to Calvin Coolidge. The next year, while vacationing at Campobello Island, he was stricken with poliomyelitis and was thereafter paralyzed from the waist down. He was Governor of New York from 1928–1932 and in 1932 was elected President. His New Deal comprised a series of domestic reforms that brought him the wrath of his conservative opposition. He was reelected in 1936.

Roosevelt's foreign policy featured a "good neighbor" relationship with Latin America to achieve hemispheric solidarity. As Axis power increased, he spoke out against aggression and appealed to Hitler and Mussolini for a peaceful settlement of their demands.

WORLD WAR II. With the outbreak of war Roosevelt, certain that the United States would be involved eventually and sympathetic to Britain, began to speed up his plan to make the country the "arsenal of democracy." He declared U.S. neutrality. After the fall of France in June 1940, he lifted the ban on armaments and in 1941 supported Lend-Lease (*q.v.*) to the Allies. The two major political parties supported giving aid to Britain, but at this time both opposed U.S. entry into the war. Meanwhile, he broke with tradition and accepted a third term.

In January 1941 Roosevelt defined the Four Freedoms (*q.v.*) as the aims to be satisified if peace were to be restored. In August 1941 he met Churchill at sea and drafted the Atlantic Charter (*q.v.*). On December 7, 1941, the Japanese struck at Pearl Harbor and the United States plunged into the war.

WAR LEADER. The story of Roosevelt's third administration was essentially that of World War II as it touched upon the United States. He was one of the Big Three (*q.v.*) war leaders. As Commander-in-Chief of the armed forces, it was his task to lead an isolationist-minded people to victory and in this he succeeded brilliantly despite severe criticism. Together with Churchill he planned the major strategic moves that gradually turned the tide of war in favor of the Allies. In 1944 he was reelected for an unprecedented fourth term.

On April 12, 1945, less than a month before Germany surrendered to the Allies, Roosevelt died suddenly at Warm Springs, Georgia. There was worldwide mourning as he was buried in the family estate at Hyde Park.

PERSONALITY AND CHARACTER. Tall, with a statuesque head set on tremendous shoulders and with a massive chest, Roosevelt was known for his vibrant voice, flashing smile, and aristocratic ease. Exuding confidence and self-mastery, he had an electric effect on private and public audiences. He had an unusual ability to grasp details and an extraordinary memory. His wit was legendary. Despite his physical handicap, he worked long hours at critical times. Because of his leadership in time of economic crisis and in the crucible of war, his supporters rate him as one of the great American presidents.

At the same time his opponents accused him of extreme vanity, extravagance, and ruthless ambition. They described him as "a congenital prima donna" who "thrived on adulation and submission." Revisionist historians called him responsible for negligence at Pearl Harbor and even goading the Japanese into war. Others said that his misjudgment of Stalin and his hope to use his aristocratic charm to win over "Uncle Joe" laid the foundation for the postwar expansion of Soviet Russia and for the Cold War.

Bibliography. The literature on Roosevelt and the Roosevelt era is enormous. *See* B. D. Zevin (ed.), *Nothing to Fear: Selected Addresses of Franklin Delano Roosevelt* (1947). *See also* F. Perkins, *The Roosevelt I Knew* (1946); R. E. Sherwood, *Roosevelt and Hopkins* (1950); B. Bellush, *Franklin D. Roosevelt as Governor of New York* (1955); and A. M. Schlesinger, Jr., *The Age of Roosevelt* (1957 ff.) For biographies, *see* J. Gunther (1950); F. Freidel (3 vols. 1952–1956); R. G. Tugwell (1957); and J. M. Burns (1970).

ROOSEVELT'S WAR MESSAGE. Formal request by President Roosevelt that the U.S. Congress issue a declaration of war on Japan. On December 8, 1941, the day after the Japanese attack on Pearl Harbor, Roosevelt appeared before both houses of Congress to deliver his war message:

Yesterday, December 7, 1941—a date which will live in infamy—the United States of America was suddenly and deliberately attacked by naval and air forces of the Empire of Japan.

The United States was at peace with that nation and, at the solicitation of Japan, was still in conversation with its Government and its Emperor looking toward the maintenance of peace in the Pacific. . . .

No matter how long it may take us to overcome this premeditated invasion, the American people in their righteous might will win through to absolute victory.

I believe I interpret the will of the Congress and of the people when I assert that we will not only defend ourselves to the uttermost but will make very certain that this form of treachery shall never endanger us again.

Hostilities exist. There is no blinking at the fact that our people, our territory and our interests are in grave danger. With confidence in our armed forces—with the unbound determination of our people—we will gain the inevitable triumph—so help us God.

I ask that the Congress declare that since the unprovoked and dastardly attack by Japan on Sunday, December 7, a state of war has existed between the United States and the Japanese Empire.

ROSENBERG, ALFRED (1893–1946). Philosopher of National Socialist ideology.

Born in Estonia, the son of an Estonian mother and a Lithuanian father, Rosenberg settled in Munich in 1920. There he met Hitler and later became editor of the National Socialist newspaper, the *Völkischer Beobachter*.

Rosenberg's works, suffused with pseudoscientific verbiage, won him a reputation as the spiritual leader of National Socialism. In 1934 he was given responsibility for training all Nazi Party members in National Socialist ideology. On July 17, 1941, Hitler appointed him Reich Minister for the Eastern Occupied Territories. In that post Rosenberg brutally promoted the Germanization of Eastern peoples, supervised forced labor (*q.v.*), and arranged for the extermination of Jews.

At the Nuremberg Trials (*q.v.*) Rosenberg was found guilty on all four counts and sentenced to death by hanging. He was executed at Nuremberg on October 16, 1946.

Moody and retiring, but glibly persuasive, Rosenberg was also ruthlessly ambitious. He edged into Hitler's inner circle and managed to stay there. His *magnum opus*, *The Myth of the Twentieth Century* (1929), which stressed "the Myth of the Blood and the Soul of the Race," was a rehash of the racial ideology of Arthur Comte de Gobineau and Houston Stewart Chamberlain. It reflected the transition of German irrationalism to extreme Nazi mysticism.

Bibliography. A. Rosenberg, *Collected Works* (1970).

ROSIE THE RIVETER. Legendary woman factory worker on the home front in the United States.

Rosie the Riveter was reputed to have performed herculean feats in the battle of production (*q.v.*). Her real name was Rosina D. Bonavita. In June 1943, at the height of the war effort, she and a partner were credited with assembling an entire wing of a torpedo bomber in one shift, ramming in a record 3,345 rivets.

ROTTERDAM, BOMBING OF. Destructive German air assault on the Dutch city in 1940.

TARGET. Rotterdam was the most important port and second largest city of the Netherlands. It was strategically situated in the province of South Holland on the Rhine estuary 56 miles southwest of Amsterdam. For Hitler it was of great significance because of the transit trade to Germany and Switzerland along the Rhine. Before World War II it was considered the most important Atlantic port on the European continent.

BACKGROUND. Shortly before 5 A.M. on May 10, 1940, the German High Command signalled the end of the *Sitzkrieg* (*q.v.*), the sit-down war, and commenced the attack on Holland. Without advance notice, German parachutists, some dressed in Allied uniforms, and equipped with machine guns and radios, hurtled down on Dutch airfields across the country. Simultaneously, screaming *Stukas* of the *Luftwaffe* (*qq.v.*) struck at bridges, railroad stations, and forts. A new German *Blitzkrieg* (*q.v.*) was under way.

Overwhelmed by the sudden attack and fearful of the fate of Rotterdam, the Dutch declared it an open city. (*See* OPEN CITIES.) Rotterdam was undefended. The Germans issued a three-hour ultimatum for surrender, which the Dutch commander of the city accepted shortly after the deadline. But the German command, fearing that British help might be on the way, issued orders to go ahead.

ATTACK. On May 14, 1940, the *Luftwaffe* repeated the tactics it had used on the Polish capital in 1939. (*See* WARSAW, BOMBING OF.) Swarms of *Stukas,* their whistles shrieking, dived down on the city and released their bombs. Within a space of seven and a half minutes, 100 tons of high explosives were dropped dead center on the helpless city. Confused and terrorized, the people of Rotterdam could only pray for their lives. Added to the air attack were salvoes of artillery shells.

LOSSES. For years after the war it was estimated that as many as 30,000 were killed. This figure was exaggerated, but undoubtedly some 814 lost their lives in the sudden attack. Two square miles in the center of the city were reduced to rubble. More than 25,000 dwellings, 11,000 buildings, 2,400 shops, 1,200 factories and workshops, 69 schools, 24 churches, and 20 banks were destroyed. The 28,000-ton liner *Statendam,* one of the largest ships in the Dutch passenger fleet, lay smoldering in the harbor among other wrecks.

AFTERMATH. The Germans considered Rotterdam a legitimate target because it was a transportation and communications center and had important shipyards. At the same time it was Hitler's aim to cow his opponents by a display of *Schrecklichkeit* ("frightfulness"). The Dutch and the Allies regarded the bombing of an open city as senseless, brutal, and unnecessary—the city had already capitulated. Later, the Allied Bombing Command used Rotterdam as an excuse for its own vengeance raids on such German cities as Dresden and Hamburg (*see* DRESDEN, BOMBING OF; and HAMBURG, BOMBING OF). When the German public protested against the "barbarism" of Allied air attacks, they were told to "Remember Rotterdam." (*See also* LOW COUNTRIES, CAMPAIGNS IN THE.)

Bibliography. A. Price, *Luftwaffe* (1969); and R. Jackson, *Bomber! Famous Bomber Missions of World War II* (1980).

ROYAL AIR FORCE (RAF). Air arm of British combat forces in World War II. Youngest of the three services, the Royal Air Force was responsible for winning the Battle of Britain (*q.v.*), a key victory in determining the course of the war.

BACKGROUND. Forerunner of the Royal Air Force was the Royal Flying Corps, which was established on May 13, 1912. At the outbreak of World War I, squadrons of the Royal Flying Corps comprising 50 planes were sent to France, where they played a part in the battle of Mons. At that time there were only 250 officers in the air service with a maximum of 150 aircraft. The activities of this air unit gradually expanded until it was active in Belgium, France, the Mediterranean area, Palestine, Mesopotamia, and East Africa. Royal Flying Corps planes operated from carriers of the Royal Navy to bombard the Dardanelles.

By Act of Parliament in 1917 the Royal Flying Corps and the Royal Naval Air Service were amalgamated into what became the Royal Air Force on April 1, 1918. By the end of World War I the Royal Air Force was the most powerful air fleet in the world. There were now 30,000 officers in the service and 22,000 planes.

BETWEEN WARS. During the postwar era the Royal Air Force was reduced because of huge costs of maintenance. Winston Churchill (*q.v.*), Secretary of State for War and Air, was given responsibility for creating a small but highly efficient air arm, which could be expanded easily in case of necessity. He introduced a new training program and assigned pilots to survey air routes throughout the Commonwealth.

RAF pilots made many highly publicized flights, including one from Cairo to the Cape of Good Hope (1926) and another from England to Southwest Africa, a distance of 5,340 miles in 57 hours. RAF teams won the Schneider Trophy for speed three times (1927, 1929, and 1931). Planes developed for these contests eventually became the *Spitfires* and *Hurricanes* (*qq.v.*) of World War II. In the 1920s and 1930s RAF pilots gained experience in duties connected with tribal disorders and rebellions throughout the Commonwealth.

When Hitler began his energetic buildup of the *Luftwaffe* (*q.v.*), the German air arm, the British began to expand the RAF. Designers were ordered to plan new and powerful aircraft. A new training plan for pilots was organized with 360 schools in Canada, the United Kingdom, South Rhodesia, and the United States.

ORGANIZATION. The Royal Air Force was reorganized in 1937. The Fleet Air Arm was transferred to the Royal Navy and the RAF became a distinct unit. It was divided into several commands, each with its own headquarters: Bomber Command (High Wycomb); Fighter Command (Stanmore); Flying Training Command (Reading); Technical Training Command (Brampton); Maintenance Command (Andover); Transport Command (Upavon); Home Command (White Waltham); and Coastal Command (Northwood). Overseas headquarters were established also: Middle East Command (Cyprus); Air Headquarters Malta; RAF Gibraltar; Headquarters British Forces Aden; Air Headquarters Levant; Far East Air Force (Singapore); Air Headquarters Ceylon; and Air Headquarters Hong Kong. This organization was to be of extreme value in World War II operations.

LEADERSHIP. The British High Command assigned many of its best officers to commands in the Royal Air Force. Air Chief Marshal Hugh Dowding (*q.v.*) rescued a large part of the British Expeditionary Force (*q.v.*) from Dunkirk from May 26 to June 4, 1940. He also led the RAF in its brilliant performance in the Battle of Britain from June to September 1940. His successor, Air Marshal William Sholto Douglas (*q.v.*), supervised the transformation of the RAF Fighter Command from defensive to offensive operations. Air Vice-Marshal Arthur Coningham (*q.v.*) directed operations against the *Afrika Korps* (*q.v.*) in the desert campaign starting in 1941. Air Marshal Arthur Tedder (*q.v.*) served as Air Officer Commanding in the Middle East and later became Deputy Supreme Commander of the Allied Expeditionary Force for *Operation Overlord* (*q.v.*). Leadership of the RAF was matched by the will and energy of its pilots.

PERFORMANCE. At the start of World War II the RAF had 174,000 personnel and 2,600 operational aircraft. The fighter planes of the British air arm inflicted a stunning defeat on Hermann Goering's (*q.v.*) planes in the Battle of

Britain. The RAF played a decisive role in North Africa (*see* NORTH AFRICA, CAMPAIGNS IN) beginning in November 1941, culminating in the battle of El Alamein (*q.v.*) in November 1942, and ending with the cessation of fighting in North Africa in May 1943. It continued its important tasks in Sicily and Italy. (*See* SICILY, INVASION OF; and ITALIAN FRONT, CAMPAIGNS ON THE.)

While the Fighter Command of the RAF worked hand-in-hand with ground troops, the Coastal Command waged a spirited campaign against German U-Boats. Patrols by long-range British aircraft accounted for destruction of more than 300 German and Italian U-Boats at sea. RAF bombers, together with Royal Navy surface vessels, smashed another 66 in harbor. In addition, RAF planes sank more than 900 enemy surface vessels and another 770 by air-laid mines in North European waters. Fortified with radar-search devices, the RAF steadily whittled down the effectiveness of the German submarine menace. (*See* RADAR, WARTIME.)

As early as May 1940 the RAF Bomber Command sent its heavy bombers, *Lancasters* and *Halifaxes*, to strike first at German industries and then at German cities. By 1945 the RAF had dropped a half million tons of heavy bombs on German targets, laying waste industrial centers in the Ruhr and Rhineland. Steadily augmented raids of the RAF forced the *Luftwaffe*, or what remained of it, to remain in target areas. By the time of the great assault on France on June 6, 1944, the RAF, together with the U.S. Army Air Forces (*q.v.*), had complete control of the air.

By 1945 the RAF had become a gigantic enterprise. It now had 1,079,835 men and 9,200 operational aircraft. Nearly 200,000 men served in combat air crews; ground personnel reached nearly 900,000. There were 158,000 women serving in the Women's Auxiliary Air Force (WAAF) (*q.v.*).

SIGNIFICANCE. The RAF played a major role in the liberation of Europe from Hitler. After the fall of France in 1940, Joseph Kennedy, U.S. Ambassador to Great Britain, and Charles A. Lindbergh, American air hero, were both so impressed with German air power that they predicted British defeat. But the RAF, fighting with British backs to the wall, struck back and saved the country from invasion in a turning point of the war. "Never in the field of human conflict," said Churchill, "was so much owed by so many to so few." (*see* CHURCHILL'S WAR SPEECHES.)

Bibliography. See HMSO publications: H. St. G. Saunders, *The Battle of Britain* (1941); *Bomber Command* (1941); *Bomber Command Continues* (1942); *Coastal Command* (1942); and *Atlantic Bridge* (1944). See also N. Macmillan, *The RAF in the World War* (1950); and R. J. Overy, *The Air War, 1939-1945* (1980).

ROYAL OAK. British battleship sunk at Scapa Flow early in the war by German submarine *U-47* under command of *Kapitan-Leutnant* Günther Prien (*q.v.*).

DESIGN. One of the five units in the *Royal Sovereign* class, HMS *Royal Oak* was designed with a very wide quarterdeck with a stack set close to the bridge. A veteran of the Battle of Jutland in 1916, she bore a resemblance to the German battleships *Tirpitz* and *Scharnhorst* (*qq.v.*). She was little modified during her long life, although new antiaircraft guns and searchlights were added over the years.

SPECIFICATIONS.
   Measurements. Length 614½ ft.; beam 102½ ft.
   Standard Replacement. 29,150 tons.
   Maximum Speed. 21 knots.
   Main Armament. Fourteen 6 in. guns; eight 15 in. guns.

BACKGROUND. The port of Scapa Flow in the Orkney Islands, Scotland, was extraordinarily attractive for German naval strategy in both world wars. Toward the end of World War I two German U-Boats attempted to penetrate into Scapa Flow but were destroyed. In September 1939 Adm. Karl Doenitz (*q.v.*), head of the German U-Boat fleet, decided that an attack on Scapa Flow was feasible. German air intelligence revealed that entry was possible by way of the narrow Kirk Sound passage. For this task Doenitz called on one of his most trusted U-Boat commanders, the youthful *Kapitan-Leutnant* Günther Prien.

PASSAGE. On the morning of October 13, 1939, Prien's *U-47* lay on the sea bed near the Orkneys. Until this moment pledged to secrecy, he now briefed his crew on their daring assignment. That evening the U-Boat crept toward her target. There was no moon visible, but the path was lit by the Aurora Borealis.

Prien navigated his craft past the sunken ships that blockaded Kirk Sound. He ran aground once, but by 12:27 A.M. managed to get through. To the north he saw two battleships and several destroyers at anchor.

ATTACK. Moving in close, Prien fired four torpedoes. One torpedo failed to leave the tube; the other three missed. Prien turned his craft around and fired the main torpedo. Another miss. At the critical moment the torpedoes had proven faulty.

Prien was in the middle of Scapa Flow and his mission was still not accomplished. With his torpedo tubes empty, he gave the command to reload with reserve torpedoes. The order was carried out and after two hours two tubes were ready to fire again. He moved again to the attack. He fired a second salvo, this time with devastating effect. In 15 minutes HMS *Royal Oak* turned on her side and sank. With her went 24 officers and 809 men.

By this time the entire fleet at Scapa Flow was stirred into action. Prien's problem now was to escape to the open sea. He ordered full speed ahead. He managed to avoid British destroyers by holding to the coast to protect his silhouette. It was an incredible piece of good luck. The *U-47* reached the narrows of Kirk Sound and passed through safely. It reached Wilhelshaven three days later.

SIGNIFICANCE. For the British the loss of the *Royal Oak* was a stunning setback at the very beginning of the war. The German public hailed it with delight and made Prien and his crew national heroes.

Bibliography. A. McKee, *Black Saturday* (1959).

RUHR DAMS. The Möhne, Eder, and Sorpe dams in the Ruhr area of Germany attacked by air in May 1943 as part of the general air strategy of the British Bomber Command.

TARGETS. Three major dams controlled the industrial productive capacity of the Ruhr. The Möhne and Sorpe dams were about 10 miles apart in the Ruhr basin (*Ruhrgebiet*), one of the most important areas of heavy industry in Europe. The greater part of Germany's production of coal, iron, and steel was in the area. The Möhne dam held about 140 million tons of water in a great lake fed by the Ruhr River. Its purpose was to generate electricity, maintain both industrial and household water, and prevent flooding. Together with the Sorpe, the Möhne provided the Ruhr with 70 percent of its water for industrial purposes and all drinking water for 4.5 million people. The third dam, the Eder, the biggest of the three, served a similar purpose but also made the Weser River navigable and provided a number of important hydraulic stations.

These were attractive targets for British air power. British experts reasoned that if they attacked the dams in late spring or early summer, when the water level was at its highest, they could bring the industrial production of the Ruhr to a standstill. They could halt inland water transport on the Upper Weser for months and cripple the area by flooding.

PREPARATIONS. Training for the attack began in mid-March 1943. Special Barnes-Wallis time bombs were devised for the coming raid. Built like canisters, with a diameter of 10 feet, they held 2½ tons of explosives. To carry the bombs 23 *Lancasters* (*q.v.*) were stripped of every item of equipment not absolutely necessary and were adapted to carry the huge canisters athwart the bomb bay of the planes.

Wing Commander Guy Gibson (*q.v.*), a veteran Royal Air Force (*q.v.*) pilot, was designated leader of the mysterious "X" Squadron, also called the Dam Busters Squadron, for the mission. Gathering elite crews, he put them through six weeks of intensive training. Mock-ups were constructed on the Uppingham and Colchester reservoirs with a complete network of defense booms. Bombardiers flew in low and made 125 attempts with dummies and finally with real bombs. Five planes were lost during the training sessions.

OPERATION CHASTISE. On the night of May 16–17, 1943, Gibson and his men headed for the Ruhr. There were 18 *Lancasters* in all. Squadron No. 1, composed of nine planes, headed for Möhne and Eder dams. Squadron No. 2, consisting of five bombers, flew to the Sorpe dam. Squadron No. 3 of four bombers was held in reserve in England.

Gibson and his eight bombers flew in low over the Möhne dam, clearly visible in the moonlight, dropped their canisters, and heard tremendous explosions. He reported that his bombs had hit squarely on target and that he saw "the water of the damned lake rising like stirred porridge in the moonlight, rushing through a great breach."

LOSSES. There was heavy loss of life. Many Germans were caught asleep in their basements and drowned. No figures on German casualties were revealed, but it is estimated that at least 1,200 civilians died in the raid, including Ukrainian farm girls at a camp.

The RAF incurred much damage. Seven planes were lost over the targets, while another one crashed into the sea on the return trip. Of the crews on the *Lancasters* that were shot down only one man escaped with his life.

RESULTS. There was severe damage to power stations, waterworks, reservoirs, railway and road bridges, factories, and homes. Yet the carefully planned raid could not be accounted a success. British photo reconnaissance revealed that the high hopes of the British Bomber Command were not fulfilled. The Germans completed repair work within a comparatively short time. The goal of crippling the Ruhr was not reached.

SIGNIFICANCE. For the British the attack on the Ruhr dams was a morale builder of the first order. It was discouraging news for the Germans. Hitler was angered because the dams had been inadequately defended. There were no balloon barrages, no antiaircraft defenses, no camouflage, no dummy construction. For the average German, now thoroughly alarmed by the way the war was going, the attack on the Ruhr dams was disquieting news. Nazi officials played down the affair, thereby encouraging even more rumors about German losses.

Bibliography. G. Gibson, *Enemy Coast Ahead* (1946); P. Brickhill, *Dam Busters* (1951); G. Bowman, *Strategic Bombing* (1956); and H. Rumpf, *The Bombing of Germany* (1963).

RUNDSTEDT, KARL RUDOLF GERD VON (1875–1953). German General who failed to halt the Allies in the Normandy campaign (*see* NORMANDY INVASION).

In February 1938 Rundstedt was purged along with other old-line officers during the Blomberg-Fritsch crisis when Hitler decided to take control of the army himself. Von Rundstedt was recalled in 1939 to command Army Group South. He served as Commander-in-Chief in the West during the victory over France. (*See* FRANCE, FIRST BATTLE OF.) He was rewarded by promotion to Field Marshal on July 19, 1940, along with 11 other generals. During the invasion of the USSR in June 1941 he commanded Army Group South with orders to clear the Black Sea coast, take Rostov, seize the Makop oil fields, and then push on to the Volga to sever Stalin's last link with the Caucasus. After vainly urging Hitler to allow him a temporary withdrawal, he was relieved of his duties (November 1941). (*See* EASTERN FRONT, CAMPAIGNS ON THE.)

On March 1, 1942, von Rundstedt was named Commander-in-Chief of

Army West in command of the entire coast of West Europe. He failed to stop the Allied assault on Normandy in June 1944, and was replaced only to be reinstated in September. Skeptical about Hitler's counteroffensive in December, he nevertheless undertook it at the *Fuehrer's* command. (*See* BULGE, BATTLE OF THE.) He failed to stop the Allied advance into Germany. (*See* GERMANY, BATTLE OF.)

RESISTANCE. Von Rundstedt knew about the German Resistance movement from its inception, but he declined to commit himself wholeheartedly to it. He urged Gen. Erwin Rommel (*q.v.*) "as a young man popular with the people to do it." That was as far as he would go in the conspiracy. After the unsuccessful 1944 July Plot (*q.v.*), von Rundstedt decided to follow his oath of allegiance to Hitler (*see FAHNENEID*) and presided over the court of honor that found the conspirators guilty of treason.

Tall, thin, with large ears and set jaw, von Rundstedt was the epitome of a dedicated Prussian officer. He despised Hitler, but, like Günther von Kluge (*q.v.*) and others, he could not bring himself to violate his oath as an officer. He hoped for the success of the plot against the *Fuehrer,* but he was unwilling to pay the price for commitment.

Bibliography. G. Blumentritt, *Von Rundstedt, the Soldier and The Man* (1952). *See also* J. W. Wheeler-Bennett, *The Nemesis of Power* (1953).

RUSSIA AT WAR. For Russians, World War II was a People's War: first, a war waged by a people fighting for their lives at terrible odds, and later a war supported by a populace aroused to fury by Nazi methods and determined to demonstrate their own military superiority. The spirit of patriotic devotion and the urge to self-sacrifice shown by the Russians in World War II have few parallels in history. Like the British, they simply refused to be defeated.

BACKGROUND. After years of propaganda, Russians were convinced that the Western capitalistic world intended to destroy their experiment in communism. They accepted the Russo-German Nonaggression Pact (*q.v.*) of August 23, 1939, with a sense of relief, even though it meant agreement with a despised Fascist enemy. On September 17, 1939, Soviet troops moved into Poland. The Kremlin announced that the invasion was justified because the Polish state had ceased to exist after the German invasion: "Such a situation constitutes a threat to the USSR and makes it impossible to remain neutral any longer."

FIRST REACTIONS. When Hitler turned on the Soviet Union on June 22, 1941, Russians were left in a state of shock and dismay. Nevertheless, they resisted stiffly as Germans closed in on Moscow. The sense of panic soon wore off. Governmental offices were evacuated hurriedly to the east. A state of siege was proclaimed in Moscow. By the end of October 1941 more than 2 million people had left the capital. On the night of November 6, 1941, the 24th anniversary of the Bolshevik Revolution, Stalin made an extraordinary speech in which he called for a fanatical defense of the Holy Russian Motherland:

It is these people without honor or conscience, these people with the morality of animals, who have the effrontery to call for the extermination of the great Russian nation. . . . The German invaders want a war of extermination. Very well then, they shall have it! Our task now . . . will be to destroy every German, to the very last man, who had come to occupy our country. No mercy for the German invaders! Death to the German invaders!

It was an effective speech. Despite the oppressive Stalin regime, the people were motivated by a highly emotional determination to defend themselves as Hitler instituted his program of terror and brutalization of Slavs.

CIVILIAN MORALE. Convinced that they were fighting for their very survival, the Russians on the home front settled down to years of sacrifice. Once the shock of invasion wore off, the civilian population went to work with enthusiasm and iron will. While their front-line soldiers operated in defense-in-depth tactics (*see* EASTERN FRONT, CAMPAIGNS ON THE), people on the home front dedicated themselves wholeheartedly to war work. Old men, women, and children flocked to factories to work to the limit of their physical endurance to produce munitions, ammunition, and war matériel of all kinds.

Russians on the home front regarded the needs of the fighting man as paramount. Civilians accepted without complaint the almost total lack of consumer goods. There was extreme privation everywhere. Lack of food meant bare survival for most civilians. Those engaged in war production were given slightly larger rations to enable them to work at a breakneck pace. Most Russians accepted the reality of inadequate foodstuffs, insufficient clothing, lack of fuel, and a generally low standard of living.

It was the same throughout the Soviet Union. In Moscow thousands of women, mobilized by house committees, went by train, bus, and trucks into the outskirts to dig anti-tank ditches. In Stalingrad civilians joined Red troops to crawl through smashed buildings, fall on Germans, and kill them. (*See* STALINGRAD, BATTLE OF.) In the countryside, citizens joined guerrilla units to blow up bridges, dynamite dams, and destroy everything in the invaders' path. Civilian resistance and sabotage became an integral part of the military effort against the hated Germans.

There was one exception: Minority groups inside the Soviet Union, especially the Ukrainians, at first welcomed the Germans as deliverers from Soviet oppression. Hitler made the key mistake of treating the Ukrainians as conquered slaves, which led them, much against their will, to turn to Stalin and accept his plea for defense of the Motherland.

WAR ECONOMY. Hitler's sudden invasion and the early German successes on Russian soil caused tremendous losses for the Soviet economic system. It seemed impossible for the Russian economy to survive these early blows. The invading Germans seized industrial areas that produced 63 percent of the country's coal, 68 percent of its cast iron, and 58 percent of its steel. At the same time they expropriated more than half the country's livestock as well as the fertile land that produced a large part of its wheat. Added to these losses was the destruction caused by the Russians' own scorched-earth tactics, by which factories and warehouses were set on fire and railways and bridges as well as the giant Dnepropetrovsk dam, pride of Soviet engineering, were blown up in a campaign to make the invading enemy as uncomfortable as possible.

To meet its huge losses the country was placed on an all-out war economy. In contrast to other belligerents, the USSR, by the very nature of its society, controlled all the means of production. Soviet institutions remained in force: The Supreme Soviet of the USSR continued to approve the budget and ratified agreements, and the Councils of the People's Commissars made many decisions in routine matters. The actual conduct of the war, however, including control of the economy, was the responsibility of the State Defense Committee under the chairmanship of Stalin. It issued edicts having the force of law throughout the war and it was responsible only to itself. It sent delegates not only to the war fronts but also into industrial concerns. At lower levels, local soviets, trade unions, production co-operatives, and youth organizations spurred the people to satisfy war needs. Local soviets collected warm clothing for the troops and helped maintain the patriotic discipline regarded as necessary for victory.

RELOCATION OF FACTORIES EASTWARD. Because of huge losses at the start of the German invasion, the first goal was to move centers of industries and armament factories from the danger areas. Only three days after the invasion, the Party's Central Committee set up an evacuation unit to relocate factories from the west to the Urals, the Volga region, Siberia, and Kazakstan. It was a gigantic effort made easier because of the schemes followed by the Soviet economy before the war in the successive Five-Year Plans. Three groups were responsible for the transfer of: (1) factories; (2) personnel; and (3) transport. Soviet statistics, notoriously secret, reveal that between July and November 1941, 1,500,000 railway coaches were used to move 1,500 firms, including 1,300 large ones, to the east, as well as 10,000,000 people, more than 1,000,000 from the Moscow region. About 450 of these firms were set up in the Urals, 210 in western Siberia, and 250 in central Asia. A second, smaller wave, was stimulated by the German offensive in the summer of 1942. At the same time a tremendous effort went into the construction of new factories.

The new Commissariat for Munitions and Tanks functioned effectively. The Russians had an advantage in artillery weapons (*q.v.*) and here they made a special effort by developing branches of industry concerned with alloys and machine tools. Soviet military planners had produced effective rocket guns (*Katyushas*) even before the war. Now they turned to mass production of the

T-34 medium tank, which many military historians regard as the best of World War II. Hitler underestimated the number and quality of Soviet tanks, which played an important part in the eventual whittling down of German power. (*See* TANKS.)

The Russian economy began gradually to recover from its initial plight. Supplies began to come in from the United States, Britain, and Canada through the Arctic (despite considerable losses inflicted by German submarines), Iran, the Persian Gulf, and Alaska. Soviet factories were thus supplied with vital needs such as rubber and ball bearings without which they could not function. This flow of steel, aluminum, tin, copper, leather, and chemicals, despite official Soviet reluctance to admit it, meant survival for the Russians. (*See* LEND-LEASE.)

MANPOWER. The German invasion cut off 40 percent of the Russian population. With 170 million inhabitants, however, the Soviet Union could raise larger armies than Hitler would be able to raise and equip. The age of conscription was lowered and by the end of the war at least 12.5 million Russians, many of them very young, were serving in the armed forces. More than one-half the military consisted of card-carrying Communist Party members. At its peak the Red Army contained 209 infantry and 32 cavalry divisions. One of Hitler's gravest mistakes was his underestimating of Russian manpower and its quality.

HATRED FOR GERMANS. As the war went on, Russian hatred for Germans increased in intensity. A proud and sensitive people had never forgotten Hitler's public denunciation that placed them at subhuman level. Ilya Ehrenburg (*q.v.*), the journalist, struck back in kind. His strictures became a sort of thematic hatred that reflected public feeling:

The Germans are not human. "German" has become the most terrible swear word. Let us not speak. Let us not be indignant. Let us kill. If you do not kill the German, the German will kill you. He will carry away your family and torture them in his damned Germany. . . . If you have killed one German, kill another. There is nothing jollier than German corpses. (*Red Star,* August 13, 1942.)

Pravda echoed the line: "May holy hatred become our chief, our only feeling. This hatred combines a burning love of your country, anxiety for your family and children, and an unshakable will for victory."

SOCIAL LIFE. Every conceivable phase of Russian everyday life was nourished by this immeasurable hatred for Hitler, the Germans, and Germany. Victory on the economic front owed much to governmental organization and to the work of Soviet scientists, but it was made possible only by intense cooperation and suffering of the people. The war exacted a heavy toll of social life. All activity—from schools to theater, from athletics to family relationships—was bound up inextricably with the war effort. In 1943 the Government even officially recognized the Russian Orthodox Church again in order to give the war a religious sanction. The idea of class conflict was ignored for the time being. Throughout this mass human effort ran the backbone of an unquenchable patriotic sentiment.

The Russian people accepted without question orders by the Communist Party's Central Committee, no matter how harsh they might be. They were willing to relinquish even their rest hours if it meant advancement of the war effort against the Germans. Following a decision in Moscow in April 1942, factory workers uncomplainingly went to work on the land on their rest days. Workers unhesitatingly followed the decision to undertake market gardening on their own account. Millions of new gardens eased the critical food supply. Early in 1942, a decree mobilized all the able-bodied urban population, thereby bringing 12 million new workers, most of them women and children, to production lines.

Russian willingness to sacrifice social life for the war effort was illustrated during the siege of Leningrad beginning August 21, 1941, and lasting 890 days. The 3 million people of the city refused to cooperate with Hitler in his strategy to choke them to death. They dug in to meet the assault. Workmen dropped their tools, took up rifles and went into the trenches, their places in the factories taken by women and children. There was no fuel for cooking; water had to be brought from the river, wells, and canals; the food supply diminished to the vanishing point. Hitler had not counted on this unconquerable spirit. In the spring of 1942 tens of thousands weak and weary Russians appeared with shovels in the streets to clean snow and filth from sewers and drains. Despite gnawing hunger, the people pitched in to repair the ring of fortifications around the city. There was no German occupation of Leningrad. (*See* LENINGRAD, SIEGE OF.)

RUSSIA AT END OF THE WAR. While Soviet armies moved inexorably on Berlin, there was a wave of euphoria on the Russian home front. By this time most problems of war production had been solved. The shortage of workers in tank, aircraft, and ordnance factories was made up by mobilization of civilian workers. Despite weakness of the national economy, the development of war production was swift and steady. An enormous labor force worked steadily around the clock. The critical output of armaments continued to rise. Russian statistics claim that, between 1941 and 1945, Soviet factories produced 142,800 military aircraft, including 11,193 *Stormovik* planes; 102,500 tanks, including the deadly *T-34*s; and 490,000 guns, of which 92,000 were of more than 75-mm. caliber. This tremendous output was second only to that of the United States and ahead of both Britain and Germany. In the last months of the war the Red Army not only exceeded the Germans in manpower but also in quantity and quality of equipment.

The Russians won both the battle of production and the battle of morale.

They were convinced that their crusade against Hitler was a recapitulation of the Holy War against Napoleon. "Fascist beasts," they were sure, were attempting to drain the Soviet Union of its wealth, especially its oil and wheat, and they would fight for their possessions as well as for their lives and their self-respect. They reacted favorably to Stalin's judgment: "You are fighting a war of liberation, a just war, in which you can seek inspiration from our great forefathers." They took pride in the quality of their fighting men and sang songs exploiting the virtues of *Katyushas, T-34s,* and guerrillas. By the end of the war, Russians no longer sang the *Internationale*—they were fighting for the Motherland.

HUMAN LOSSES. The Russians paid a greater price for victory than any other belligerent. Accurate statistics are unavailable, but in 1947, G. M. Malenkov, a member of the Politburo, stated: "Seven million of our people were killed in action, perished during the occupation, or were forcibly driven off to Germany." This does not include the decline in population due to the falling birth rate. Another 20,000,000 or more were left homeless.

MATERIAL LOSSES. In addition to appalling loss of life, there was tremendous destruction of property, which presented the Soviet Government with an almost overwhelming problem. Economic losses for the country as a whole in private property and fixed and working capital were as much as one-quarter of the pre-war wealth. Soviet estimates, which may have been exaggerated as a basis for reparations claims, reported that 4,100 railroad stations and 13,000 bridges had been destroyed, 15,800 locomotives, 482,000 freight cars, and 65,000 kilometers of track. The Soviet War Damage Commission reported that the Germans had destroyed or burned 98,000 collective farms; 1,876 state farms; and 2,890 machine and tractor stations. At least 6 million buildings were destroyed throughout the country.

RECONSTRUCTION. The Russian Government faced a double task after 1945: It had to make good the stupendous losses incurred during the war and at the same time resume the program of industrialization that the war had interrupted. Within two years production was restored to 57 percent of the pre-war level. Coal mines were drained and mining operations improved. Rapid progress was also made in rehabilitating agriculture. Peasants went to work rebuilding collective farms and the government reopened the tractor stations. Rationing was terminated in December 1947. A fourth Five-Year Plan, covering the years 1946–1950, was inaugurated to restore and exceed pre-war levels in industry and agriculture.

POLITICAL AFTERMATH. Despite its enormous human and material losses, Soviet Russia emerged from the war with a prodigious improvement in prestige and international reputation. It was the only major Allied belligerent power that was able to extend its borders beyond their 1939 status. It kept all territories it had annexed as a result of its pact with Nazi Germany, including areas in Poland, the Baltic countries, Bessarabia, and northern Bukovina. Soviet Russia annexed East Prussia, Köningsberg, and sub-Carpathian Ruthenia. In Asia, it was able to acquire Port Arthur, Dairen, south Sakhalin, and the Kuriles. Its influence extended even farther. In Europe its armies occupied Poland, Rumania, Hungary, Bulgaria, and Czechoslovakia; in Asia they extended their influence into Manchuria and North Korea.

SIGNIFICANCE. In the early years of the war Soviet leaders were deeply apprehensive of its outcome, realizing the deep distrust in which their leadership was held by some citizens. Indeed, some German troops were greeted as liberators. But later the Russians learned well the meaning of Hitler's Commissar Order (*q.v.*), which stated that ''the war against Russia cannot be fought in knightly fashion.'' On both combat and home fronts, Russians reacted angrily to this dictum. They met German treatment with equal harshness when the tide of war changed. During the last days, German troops stampeded to be captured by British and Americans rather than face Russian vengeance.

Bibliography. J. Stalin, *On the Great Patriotic War of the Soviet Union* (1945); B. H. Liddell Hart, *The Other Side of the Hill* (1948); L. Goure, *The Siege of Leningrad* (1962); A. Werth, *Russia at War, 1941-1945* (1964); R. Campbell, *Soviet Economic Power* (1967); and R. Medvedev, *Let History Judge* (1972).

RUSSO-FINNISH WAR, 1939. Russo-Finnish confrontation at the start of World War II.

BACKGROUND. The Russo-German Nonaggression Pact (*q.v.*) of August 23, 1939, gave the signal for both partners to move militarily to satisfy their national aspirations. But there was little trust between Hitler and Stalin. For the German dictator the prognosis was good. Once Poland was out of the war and the Kremlin was posing no threat in the east, he could then concentrate his strength against the Western Allies. This would relieve him of the nightmare of war on two fronts.

It was also a time of decision for Stalin. The Russian dictator believed that he had foiled Anglo-French efforts to involve him in a destructive war with the Third Reich. He decided to strengthen his barriers in the north, where the key to Russian defense lay in the Baltic states. In his agreement with Hitler he had been careful to insist upon inclusion of a secret protocol designating the Baltic states as a Russian sphere of influence. He quickly pushed through treaties with three of them, Estonia, Latvia, and Lithuania, establishing military garrisons and naval and air bases on their soil. He planned eventual annexation.

Finland was another matter. The farthest north of the Baltic states, it held an important strategic position. Leningrad was only 20 miles from the Finnish frontier. The Finns had constructed a line of fortifications on the nearby Karelian Isthmus. (*See* MANNERHEIM LINE.) On October 14, 1939, Stalin "invited" the Finns to surrender a part of the Karelian Isthmus so that Leningrad would be out of artillery range of an enemy. In return Stalin promised that he would cede 2,135 square miles along the east-central border. The Finns were agreeable, but they balked at the provision for military bases as a violation of their sovereignty.

Stalin, annoyed by Finnish presumptions, ordered a campaign of abuse, holding that the Finns had fired on Russian border patrols. On November 30, 1939, Soviet planes bombed Helsinki. Stalin expected immediate capitulation.

ASSAULT. Soviet strategy called for a five-pronged invasion of Finland. The League of Nations acted with unaccustomed speed and formally ejected the Russians as unworthy of membership. More than 100,000 Russians crossed the borders. Expecting an easy victory, they were armed with propaganda leaflets, pennants, and banners. They were going to "liberate" the Finns from their "capitalistic oppressors." But the invaders were quickly disabused of their beliefs. Inadequately trained, badly briefed, with insecure supply lines, they came up against strong Finnish resistance.

DEFENSE. It was David against Goliath. The Finns, under Gen. Karl von Mannerheim (*q.v.*), refused to give in. They cleverly shifted their counterattacks from column to column. Heavily armed ski patrols, their white uniforms blending into the snowy countryside, crept silently behind the Russians and trapped them. It was a ghastly debacle as thousands of Red troops froze in the wreckage of war. By the end of 1939 the Russians had exhausted themselves in inconclusive fighting.

WORLD REACTION. The attention of the world was riveted on the little Baltic republic fighting for its life. From many countries came foodstuffs, medical supplies, and weapons of war. There was great sympathy in the United States for the Finns, "the only country to pay its World War I war debts." The intensity of American reaction was reflected in Robert E. Sherwood's famous play, *There Shall Be No Night,* which presented a sympathetic portrayal of the Finnish cause. In February 1940 Britain and France came close to declaring war on the Soviet Union. Norway and Sweden, cowed by the Kremlin, refused to allow the passage of Allied troops through their territory.

AFTERMATH. Stalin's "minor" engagement had misfired. To save face, he then sent in his best troops, finest artillery, and most modern equipment. He ordered a direct attack on the center of the Mannerheim Line. By now the Russians had an advantage of 50 to 1 in troops. The Finns resisted until March 1940.

The terms of the peace treaty were severe. The Finns had to cede the Karelian Isthmus, the western and northern shores of Lake Ladoga, and additional territory totaling 16,000 square miles and a half million people.

SIGNIFICANCE. The war revealed how badly prepared for war the Russian Army was. Their officers were inexperienced; they made no proper preparations for a powerful offensive; and their transport system was weak. The conflict cost them 200,000 men, nearly 700 aircraft, 1,600 tanks, and humiliation before world opinion. At the same time, Stalin got what he wanted—the Karelian Isthmus, "that dagger pointed at Leningrad." Its acquisition was to be of some importance later when Hitler tried to take Leningrad by siege.

The Finns sacrificed 25,000 lives but they had the satisfaction of preserving their independence.

Bibliography. H. B. Elliston, *Finland Fights* (1940); T. Barenius, *Field-Marshal Mannerheim* (1940); J. Langdon-Davies, *Invasion in the Snow* (1941); W. Strode, *Finland Forever* (1941); J. H. Wuorinen (ed.), *Finland and World War II* (1948); M. Jakobson, *The Diplomacy of the Winter War* (1961); P. H. Krosby, *Finland, Germany and the USSR, 1940-1941* (1968); and A. F. Upton, *Finland 1939-1940* (1980).

RUSSO-GERMAN NONAGGRESSION PACT. Agreement between Germany and Soviet Russia signed on August 23, 1939, which opened the way to World War II.

BACKGROUND. The possibility that Germany and Soviet Russia, sworn enemies, might sign a treaty of nonaggression seemed remote in the summer of 1939. But Hitler wanted to make sure that, in the event Britain and France came to the aid of Poland, he would not have to worry about fighting on two fronts. Later, after the Western nations had been defeated, he could accuse Moscow of broken faith.

Stalin, worried about German successes, wanted time to carry on the militarization of Russia. Both Hitler and Stalin in their own way were practicing their own versions of *Realpolitik.*

AGREEMENT. On August 23, 1939, Foreign Ministers Joachim von Ribbentrop and Vyacheslav Mikhailovich Molotov (*qq.v.*), acting respectively for Germany and Russia, signed a nonaggression pact at Moscow. The agreement, effective for 10 years, provided that the two countries would in no case resort to war against each other, would not support any third power that attacked either signatory, and would consult with each other on matters of common interest. In the secret protocol, Stalin obtained what he could not get from France and Britain. In effect, the pact prepared the way for the spoliation of Poland and its division between Germany and Soviet Russia.

*TEXT** Guided by the desire to strengthen the cause of peace between Germany and the Union of Socialist Soviet Republics, and basing themselves on the fundamental stipulations of the Neutrality Agreement concluded between Germany and the Union of

---

*German Library of Information, *Documents on the Events Preceding the Outbreak of the War,* compiled and published by the German Foreign Office (Berlin, 1939; New York, 1940), No. 348, pp. 370–371.

Socialist Soviet Republics in April, 1926, the German Government and the Government of the Union of Socialist Soviet Republics have come to the following agreement:

ARTICLE 1. The two contracting parties undertake to refrain from any act of force, any aggressive act, and any attacks against each other undertaken either singly or in conjunction with any other Powers.

ARTICLE 2. If one of the contracting parties should become the object of war-like action on the part of a third Power, the other contracting party will in no way support the third Power.

ARTICLE 3. The Governments of the two contracting parties will in future remain in consultation with one another in order to inform each other about questions which touch their common interests.

ARTICLE 4. Neither of the two contracting parties will join any group of Powers which is directed, mediately or immediately, against the other party.

ARTICLE 5. In case disputes or conflicts on questions of any kind should arise between the two contracting parties, the two partners will solve these disputes or conflicts exclusively by friendly exchange of views or if necessary by arbitration commissions.

ARTICLE 6. The present agreement is concluded for the duration of ten years with the stipulation that unless one of the contracting partners denounces it one year before its expiration, it will automatically be prolonged by five years.

ARTICLE 7. The present agreement shall be ratified in the shortest possible time. The instruments of ratification are to be exchanged in Berlin. The treaty comes into force immediately it has been signed.

Done in two original documents in the German and Russian languages, respectively.

Moscow, August 23, 1939

For the German Government
RIBBENTROP

As plenipotentiary of the Government of the Union of Socialist Soviet Republics

MOLOTOV

AFTERMATH. Announcement of the Hitler-Stalin Pact shocked the democracies. Two days later, on August 25, 1939, Britain replied by confirming its guarantee of support for Poland by a formal Anglo-Polish alliance. It was clear now that the democracies would reject another surrender to Hitler, which would have meant the final and irrevocable abdication of their position as Great Powers.

RYAN, CORNELIUS JOHN (1920–1974). U.S. author and historian of World War II.

Ryan's books on World War II have been read widely. Among them are *Minute to Ditch* (1957); *The Longest Day* (1959); (with Frank Kelley) *Star-Spangled Mikado* (1948); *MacArthur* (1951); *The Last Battle* (1965); and *A Bridge Too Far* (1974). Ryan's books are noted for their crisp writing style and dramatic impact. He died in New York City on November 24, 1974.

S

SABOTAGE. Destruction of railroads, bridges, and machinery by enemy agents in time of war. The term, originally meaning damage done to machinery by wooden shoes, came to be used to describe any deliberate obstruction of war work.

Throughout Hitler's New Order (*q.v.*) in Europe saboteurs worked to oppose the German war effort. Techniques varied from go-slow work in factories to the blowing up of railroads and bridges. In factories workers were courteous to their taskmasters, but performed their duties much too slowly and inefficiently. Germans were baffled by this technique and lacked the manpower to run the factories themselves. Railway workers throughout western Europe were often successful in crippling rail transportation for the Nazi war machine.

Britain's Special Operations Executive (SOE) (*q.v.*) directed sabotage operations in the occupied countries. Its special form of plastic bomb could put an entire factory out of action for weeks. In France the railroad system was rendered virtually useless to the Germans by SOE-directed sabotage teams. Important railway and bridge demolitions were carried out in Greece, Yugoslavia, Italy, and Norway. Throughout western Europe the sabotage of telephone systems was so extensive that the Germans had to use radio for most of their communications. SOE saboteurs played an important role in ending the German threat to produce an atomic bomb.

SACRED COW. President Frankin D. Roosevelt's personal transport plane during the war.

This aircraft, a *C-54C,* was outfitted with an electrically operated elevator that the polio-crippled President could board without leaving his wheelchair. In addition to accommodation for passengers, the *Sacred Cow* had a conference room. Bulletproof glass was used to protect the President.

SAD SACK Comic-strip character whose adventures appeared in the army magazine, *Yank, The Army Weekly (q.v.).*

Drawn by Sgt. George Baker, Sad Sack was the indestructible GI (*q.v.*), the little man who tried to cope in a world he never made. The character was highly popular among American servicemen, who saw in his antics a faithful depiction of their own experiences.

A typical strip in *Yank* showed Sad Sack being given a lesson in bayonet thrusting by a barking sergeant. In each panel the harassed GI gets more and more confused. At last, as the non-com walks away in disgust, Sad Sack in a burst of well-meant energy twirls his bayonet around and strikes the astonished sergeant in a rear-end action. The triumphant final scene shows a mob of cheering GIs carrying Sad Sack away on their shoulders.

SAIPAN, 1944. *See* MARIANAS, BATTLE FOR THE.

SALAZAR, ANTONIO DE OLIVEIRA (1889–1970). Portugese dictator who maintained his country's neutrality during the war.

In 1942 Portugal and Spain signed the Iberian Pact. Salazar announced that Portugal was remaining neutral during the war. Although Fascist in outlook, he made concessions to the United States and Britain in the Azores in 1943.

Bibliography. M. Detrick, *The Portugal of Salazar* (1938, 1972); F. C. Egerton, *Salazar* (1943); C. Garnier, *Salazar: An Intimate Portrait;* and H. Kay, *Salazar and Modern Portugal* (1970).

SALERNO BEACHHEAD. Allied strategists designed *Operation Avalanche* to take the city of Salerno in Campania, southern Italy, on the Gulf of Salerno.

On September 3, 1943, two divisions of Gen. Bernard Law Montgomery's (*q.v.*) 8th Army (*q.v.*), consisting of British and Canadians, crossed the Strait of Messina, and came ashore at Reggio de Calabria on the toe of the Italian boot. The invaders quickly turned northward.

Six days later, on September 9, the new U.S. 5th Army, half-American and half-British, under the command of Lt. Gen. Mark W. Clark (*q.v.*), and supported by an air umbrella and naval bombardment, stormed ashore on the Salerno beaches. The aim was to take Naples and then push northward. German defenders, who held the high ground to the north, east, and south of the beachhead, began a massive artillery barrage on the crowded beaches. The Allies replied with naval bombardments and heavy air assaults. Meanwhile, Montgomery's troops moving slowly from the south, forced the Germans to retire toward Naples.

Operation Avalanche was eventually successful, but it was carried out at heavy cost. (*See* ITALIAN FRONT, CAMPAIGNS ON THE.)

SAN FRANCISCO CONFERENCE. Meeting held in 1945 to set up a United Nations organization.

BACKGROUND. At Dumbarton Oaks (*q.v.*) in August-September 1944, tentative plans were made for creation of an international organization. With an Allied victory assured in the spring of 1945, a new conference was called at San Francisco for the same purpose. While plans were maturing, President Roosevelt died on April 12, 1945, at Warm Springs, Georgia. Allied leaders sorrowfully went ahead with the conference.

PARTICIPANTS. From April 25 to June 26, 1945, delegates of 50 nations with their staffs of experts met at San Francisco. The principal representatives were British Foreign Secretary Anthony Eden, U.S. Secretary of State Edward R. Stettinius, Jr., Russian Foreign Commissar Vyacheslav Molotov (*q.v.*), and T. V. Soong, spokesman for China. More than 2,535 press and radio reporters were present to spread word of what was regarded as one of the most momentous meetings of the 20th century. It was the first international conference in the modern era not dominated by Europe.

UN CHARTER. For nine weeks the delegates discussed what was to go into the Charter. Starting with the Dumbarton Oaks proposal, revisions and expansions were debated. The final UN Charter contained 111 articles under 19 chapters. Its goals were stated in the Preamble:

To save succeeding generations from the scourge of war which twice in our lifetime has brought sorrow to mankind, and

to reaffirm faith in fundamental human rights, in the dignity and worth of the human person, in the equal rights of men and women and of nations large and small, and

to establish conditions under which justice and respect for the obligations arising from treaties and other sources of international law can be maintained, and

to promote social progress and better standards of life in larger freedom,

AND FOR THESE ENDS

to practice tolerance and live together in peace with one another as good neighbors, and

to unite our strength to maintain international peace and security, and

to ensure, by the acceptance of principles and the institution of methods, that armed force shall not be used, save in the common interest, and

to employ international machinery for the promotion of the economic and social advancement of all peoples,

HAVE RESOLVED TO COMBINE OUR EFFORTS TO ACCOMPLISH THESE AIMS.

SIGNIFICANCE. In essence, the San Francisco conference was called to perpetuate the wartime coalition of the Big Three (*q.v.*) nations and to maintain security and an orderly world. Each signatory pledged to abstain from war or the threat of war and to work together to suppress violation of peace by military means if necessary. The new United Nations was an extension of the older League of Nations, with efforts made to eliminate the impractical features of the earlier world organization.

Bibliography. M. B. Schnapper (ed.), *United Nations Agreements* (1944); A. Vandenbosch and W. B. Hogan, *The United Nations* (1952); and L. N. Goodrich, *The United Nations* (1959).

SANTA CRUZ ISLANDS, BATTLE OF THE. *See* GUADALCANAL CAMPAIGNS.

SARTRE, JEAN-PAUL (1905–1980). French writer and philosopher.

World War II produced Sartrean existentialism. A philosophy of pessimism, it held that freedom of will determines all man's actions and that each individual exists only to confirm the existence of others. (*See* SOCIAL IMPACT OF THE WAR.)

Sartre joined the French Army as a private and was captured by the Germans. In prison camp he composed and directed plays for the inmates. Released in 1941, he returned to Paris, where he became active as a journalist in the French Underground (*q.v.*) movement. He contributed to such underground publications as *Les Lettres, Combat,* and others. In 1943 he wrote a play, *Les Mouches* (*The Flies*), on the Orestes theme, which the German censors unwittingly passed and which brought a message of hope to the French people.

Short, pale, wearing horn-rimmed glasses, Sartre had a sharp analytical mind. He was known for his harsh contempt for those who disagreed with him.

Bibliography. Among Sartre's works are *The Flies* (1943); *No Exit* (1944); and *The Age of Reason* (1945). *See also* studies by P. Thody (1960); M. Cranston (1962); and H. Peyre (1968).

SAS. British secret unit that went on raids behind enemy lines. (*See* SPECIAL AIR SERVICE.)

SAUCKEL, FRITZ (1894–1946). Nazi politician and head of slave labor recruitment.

On the outbreak of war Hitler appointed Sauckel a Reich defense commissioner with a special post as Plenipotentiary for Labor Allocation. In a decree dated March 21, 1942, the *Fuehrer* called for a mobilization of German and foreign workers. Responsible for this task, Sauckel at first ordered that foreign workers in Germany be treated with consideration. The assignment was a difficult one as the demands of the war machine became greater and greater. With Hitler's approval, Sauckel began to operate what became a system of forced labor. His "protection squads" rounded up thousands of men from the streets and from their homes to be sent to war factories. Millions of workers were drawn into Sauckel's labor system. (*See* FORCED LABOR.)

Sauckel was brought to trial before the International Military Tribunal together with 21 other Nazi leaders on November 20, 1945. (*See* NUREMBERG TRIALS.) He was indicted for his work as chief of slave labor recruitment. His defense was that he was only doing his duty for his fatherland in time of war. The conflict, he said he was led to believe, had been forced on Germany by the Bolshevik-Jewish-capitalist conspiracy, but now he realized that this was propaganda. He had only followed Hitler's orders: "I just supplied workers to places like the Krupp works at Hitler's command. It was like a seaman's agency. I am not responsible for the cruelty exercised without my knowledge."

Sauckel's judges were not convinced. He was found guilty on two counts: 3, war crimes; and 4, crimes against humanity. "The evidence shows that Sauckel was in charge of a program which involved deportation for slave labor of more than 5,000,000 human beings, many of them under terrible conditions of cruelty and suffering." Sauckel was hanged at Nuremberg on October 16, 1946.

A man of limited background but considerable energy, Sauckel was a rough-and-ready convert for the greatest labor roundup in history. Indefatigable and fervent in his Nazism, he was Hitler's choice as a man who would take orders. He was fanatical in his devotion to Hitler. A family man, he had 10 children, two of whom were killed in the course of the war. At Nuremberg he defended himself as a "good Christian" who always preferred honest work. On the gallows he screamed: "I am dying innocent! The sentence is wrong. God protect Germany and make her great again. God protect my family!"

Bibliography. See G. M. Gilbert, Nuremberg Diary (1947); and E. Davidson, The Trial of the Germans: Nuremberg, 1945-1946 (1966).

SAVO ISLAND, BATTLE OF. See GUADALCANAL CAMPAIGNS.

S-BOAT. German motor torpedo boat. The name *Schnellboote* was abbreviated *S-Boote*.

Able to achieve a speed of at least 42 knots, the S-Boats were armed with two fixed forward-firing torpedo tubes, as well as light automatic guns. Americans designated the S-Boats as E-Boats (enemy boats).

SCAEF. *S*upreme *C*ommander *A*llied *E*xpeditionary *F*orce.

The title was given to Gen. Dwight D. Eisenhower (*q.v.*) in December 1943 to prepare for the invasion of the European continent from the north in June 1944. (*See* NORMANDY INVASION.)

SCANDINAVIA, CAMPAIGNS IN. Hitler's strategy of strengthening his northern flank before attacking the Allies in the West in 1940.

BACKGROUND. The overwhelming defeat of Poland in September 1939 (*see* POLAND, CAMPAIGN IN) resulted in a wave of enthusiasm in Germany. The *Fuehrer* had done exactly what he had said he would do and he accomplished it with dispatch and low casualties. His credibility soared as his smiling legions returned from Warsaw to receive the victors' laurels. All that remained now was a prompt peace—but there was to be no peace.

On November 25, 1939, Hitler summoned his generals to a conference at the

Reich Chancellery. "My decision is unchangeable. I shall attack France and England at the most favorable and earliest moment. No one has ever achieved what I have achieved. I have to choose between victory and annihilation. I choose victory." There remained some unfinished business—the problem of supplies, especially iron ore. Swedish iron ore was carried westward from the mines by railroad to the Norwegian port of Narvik, loaded on German freighters, and brought down in territorial waters as far as the Skaggerak. The Norwegian Navy escorted the vessels on the principle that Norway was obliged to keep its waters "open to all legitimate traffic."

Hitler thought it best to take no chances. The British might well extend their blockade to cut off the supply of Swedish ore. Consequently, he ordered plans to be drawn up for the invasion of Norway and Denmark. He did not include cooperative Sweden. He had his *casus belli* on April 8, 1940, when London informed the Norwegians that it had decided to stop vessels carrying war contraband in Norwegian waters.

ATTACK ON DENMARK. At 5 A.M. on April 9, 1940 the Danish Government received a German note saying that it had "indubitable evidence" of Allied plans to make Scandinavia a battleground. Because the Scandinavian countries could not defend themselves adequately, Hitler would move in to "protect them." He paid no attention to his nonaggression treaty with Denmark, for which he himself had asked. He cut off Denmark's communications with the outside world, the usual preliminary step to invasion.

German forces rolled across Danish borders with only token resistance. Within a matter of hours they were in Copenhagen. King Christian X (*q.v.*) and Premier Thorvald Stauning had to accept the situation under protest. The king issued a proclamation urging his people to recognize a *fait accompli* and to maintain "a calm and controlled attitude." Denmark had fallen to Nazi power within 24 hours. Hitler allowed a Danish government to hold office until 1943, when he sent in a military administration.

CONQUEST OF NORWAY. At 1:30 A.M. on April 9, 1940, the commandant of three Norwegian warships stationed on the west coast of Oslo Fjord, received a telegram, supposedly from his government, not to fire on German warships that would be coming up the fjord. The message was really sent by the Germans. At 5 A.M. the German Minister at Oslo handed over a note demanding immediate Norwegian surrender because "the Allies were about to seize the country." The Norwegian Foreign Minister indignantly refused.

Within a few hours German forces were moving into Norway. *Luftwaffe* (*q.v.*) bombers swooped down on Oslo's airport. Swarms of German paratroopers dropped down near Oslo, Trondheim, Stavanger, and Narvik. Simultaneously, German warships and supply ships steamed into every important fjord, discharging their cargoes of men and machines. Caught unprepared, Norwegians fought back, but they were no match for the invaders. They were shocked by the invasion of Germans, who as hungry children had been taken into Norwegian homes after World War I and were now returning in Nazi uniforms as conquerors.

Soon every important harbor, all airfields, and five of the six divisional headquarters were overrun. German troops were in the streets of Oslo and in command of all governmental buildings. The conquest on land was decisive, but the Germans paid a stiff price at sea. Into Oslo Fjord moved the pocket battleship *Deutschland,* the 10,000-ton armored cruiser *Blücher,* the 5,600-ton light cruiser *Emden,* and a screen of mine sweepers, torpedo boats, and motor craft. Against this powerful force the Norwegians had only the mine layer *Olev Tryggvason* moored at a buoy, several smaller vessels, and four submarines. Before the city of Oslo were the Oscarborg defenses.

At 5:30 A.M. Norwegian lookouts sighted the *Blücher* towering over the escort vessels. The Norwegians fired their 11-inch guns at point-blank range. Two salvoes hit the warship and set it blazing. Then from the fixed torpedo defenses of the narrows two torpedos crashed into the side of the *Blücher,* which keeled over and sank, with the loss of more than 1,000 men. Both the *Deutschland* and the *Emden* were damaged. (*See also* BLÜCHER.)

CAPITULATION. The naval success was not enough to save Norway. The government and half the population retreated to the north. King Haakon VII (*q.v.*) fled to London and eventually set up a government-in-exile (*q.v.*) there. On the afternoon of April 9, 1940, the German press announced that all governmental power had been turned over to Maj. Vidkun Quisling (*q.v.*). That evening Quisling issued a radio proclamation ordering the people to cease resistance, avoid "criminal destruction of property," and to obey his National Government.

BRITISH REACTION. British intelligence was caught off guard by the suddenness and scope of the German operation. On and after April 16, 1940, some 13,000 British and French troops landed at Namsos and Andalsnes, ports flanking Trondheim, the key to central Norway. It was a dangerous maneuver for the area was beyond British fighter range. The catastrophic results were described by foreign correspondent Leland Stowe (*q.v.*), who in a famous dispatch to the Chicago *Daily News,* told the "bitter and most disillusioning story." The British had sent their young troops into the snow and mud without a single aircraft gun or a piece of artillery.

On June 7, 1940, the outnumbered and beaten British Expeditionary Force (*q.v.*) withdrew from Norway. "Fortune has been against us," said the new Prime Minister Winston Churchill. "Britain's finest troops . . . have been baffled by the vigor, enterprise, and training of Hitler's young men." The Allies had made a remarkable effort against great odds.

SIGNIFICANCE. A highly satisfied Hitler now had strategically located bases from which his *Luftwaffe* (*q.v.*) could dominate all Scandinavia, imperil

British shipping, and strike at Britain herself. With naval and submarine bases in Norway, he was no longer worried about attacks on his northern flank. Moreover, he had protection now for his iron-ore lifeline from Sweden. "By our action," said Foreign Minister Joachim von Ribbentrop (*q.v.*), "we have saved the countries and peoples of Scandinavia from annihilation, and will now guarantee true neutrality in the north until the war's end."

It was a disaster for the British, but they had learned some valuable lessons. Now they were aware that naval superiority meant little without air support and that *Blitzkrieg* (*q.v.*) could work even in mountainous and snowy areas. Most of the Norwegian merchant fleet, the fourth largest in the world, escaped to join the Allied pool of ships. They could be used now to supply Britain with the oil and food needed to carry on the war. To prevent seizure by Hitler, the British seized the Faroe Islands, Iceland, and Greenland, all formerly tied with Denmark.

Bibliography. C. J. Hambro, *I Saw It Happen in Norway* (1940); H. Koht, *Norway; Neutral and Invaded* (1941); P. Paulmer, *Denmark in Nazi Chains* (1942); A. Johnson, *Norway; Her Invasion and Occupation* (1948); and K. Derry, *The Campaign in Norway* (1952).

SCHACHT, (HORACE GREELEY) HJALMAR (1877-1970). German economist and financier who supervised the complicated program of exchange controls that enabled Hitler to rearm Germany.

Despite his important work for the German economy, Schacht played a relatively minor role during the war. He was retained as Minister without Portfolio until 1943 even though he opposed the elimination of Jews from economic life. His early defense of National Socialism made him only partially acceptable to the anti-Hitler plotters. On July 21, 1944, a day after the unsuccessful July Plot (*q.v.*) on Hitler's life, Schacht was arrested on suspicion of conspiracy, and sent to three successive concentration camps—Ravensbrück, Flossenbürg, and Dachau. (*See* CONCENTRATION CAMPS.) He was released by American troops in 1945.

NUREMBERG. Brought before the International Military Tribunal at Nuremberg (*q.v.*), Schacht protested his innocence. His judges acquitted him when they decided that the charge accusing him of planning aggressive war had not been proved beyond a reasonable doubt. A German People's Court sentenced him on May 13, 1947, to eight years' detention in a labor camp under the denazification laws, but he appealed and was released.

A brilliant economist and a man of many aptitudes, Schacht was also arrogant: At his trial, when films were shown of Nazi concentration camps, he folded his arms and angrily turned his back on the screen. He died in Munich on June 3, 1970.

Bibliography. Schacht wrote *Account Settled* (1949); and *Confessions of the Old Wizard* (1956). *See also* A. E. Simpson, *Hjalmar Schacht in Perspective* (1969).

SCHARNHORST. German battle cruiser sunk by the British in late 1943. She was named after Gerhard Johann David von Scharnhorst (1755-1813),

Prussian soldier who reorganized the army after the collapse of 1806–1807. A sister ship of the *Gneisenau,* she was a fast and deadly warship and the pride of the new German Navy.

DESIGN. Work on the *Scharnhorst* was begun on February 14, 1934, just a little more than a year after Hitler came to political power, and was completed on January 7, 1939. Her designers equipped her with nine 11-inch guns and powerful secondary armor. Her speed of 29 knots made her faster than any British warship. She was sufficiently compartmentalized to withstand heavy damage.

SPECIFICATIONS.
Measurements. Length 76 ft. 1 in.; beam 100 ft.
Displacement. 26,000 tons.
Draft. 24 ft. 8 in.
Maximum Speed. 29–31.5 knots.
Engines. 134,000 h.p.
Armor. Belt 12–13 in.; turrets 12 in.; decks 6 in.
Armament. Primary: Nine 11-in. guns in triple turrets; twelve 5.9-in. guns in twin turrets. *Secondary:* Numerous light and heavy AA guns, including fourteen 4.1-in., sixteen 37-mm., and twenty-eight 20-mm.
Complement. 1,461 men, 1,900 on operations.
Special Features. Carried two *Arado* aircraft on catapults; total aircraft—four; fired a comparatively light 650-lb. shell; equipped with auxiliary diesels for cruising purposes.

WORLD WAR II. The loss of the *Bismarck* on May 27, 1941 (*See* BISMARCK, SINKING OF THE), presented Hitler with a problem. Anxious to avoid losing any more capital ships, he ordered the U-Boat service to bear the brunt of fighting at sea. At this time the *Scharnhorst* and the *Gneisenau* were anchored in Brest harbor along with the *Prinz Eugen,* which had escaped in the *Bismarck* fiasco. Hitler decided to move his big warships to Norwegian waters, where they could protect his flank and simultaneously harry convoy routes to the Soviet Union.

CHANNEL DASH. At Brest the big warships were exposed to British air assault. How to get them to Norway was a problem. The route around Scotland was far too dangerous. The only practical way was to make a dash through the English Channel. In January German mine sweepers secretly cleared the way along the coastline to Heligoland Bight.

On February 12, 1942, the three warships, protected by a screen of destroyers, moved out of Brest at high speed and headed west in what was code named *Operation Cerberus.* Jamming British radar (*See* RADAR, WARTIME), the German force was already off the Belgian coast when London received the alarm. In the ensuing air battle over the fleets, the British lost 20 bombers and 16 fighters, while the Germans lost 15 fighters. The *Scharnhorst* struck a mine and was slowed down for several hours, but managed to reach Wilhelmshaven safely. German warships had run the gauntlet of enemy sea power in British-controlled waters.

CONVOY DUTY. The sister warships were sent on patrols to harass Allied convoys bound for Murmansk (*q.v.*). They would leave Norwegian fjords at the end of twilight, arrive at the convoy area at the start of twilight the next day, and attack before enemy planes could see them. On September 8–9, 1943, the *Scharnhorst* joined the *Tirpitz* (*q.v.*) in bombarding Spitzbergen. (*See* SPITZ-BERGEN RAID.)

TRAP. In October 1943 Churchill arranged a series of convoys to Murmansk. For the December convoy he provided an escort of 3 cruisers and 14 destroyers, but made certain to include an even stronger force some distance away under Adm. Bruce Austin Fraser (*q.v.*).

Germans fell into the trap. On receiving word from agents of the convoy sailing, Adm. Karl Doenitz (*q.v.*) ordered the *Scharnhorst,* escorted by 5 destroyers and several corvettes, to the attack.

BATTLE OF NORTH CAPE. The opposing fleets sighted one another 150 miles north of North Cape. By pre-arranged signal, the lumbering freighters scattered, while the British warships flung themselves on the *Scharnhorst.* It was early morning on December 26, 1943, with very little light. Illuminating the target with star shells, the British sent heavy shells screaming toward the German warship. Spinning around after being hit by a salvo, the *Scharnhorst* began to move away at noon, only to find British cruisers in its path. It turned and raced for Norwegian waters.

Meanwhile, the second British force moved south through the twilight to intercept the retreating *Scharnhorst,* which was unaware that she was being tracked. Fraser broke radio silence and ordered the enemy to be illuminated with star shells. Opening fire at 12,000 yards, the *Duke of York* sent three tons of hot steel charging through the air "like a maddened express train."

Four British destroyers moved in for the kill. Hit by four torpedoes, the *Scharnhorst* slowed down. Mortally wounded, a mass of flames, she turned on her side and went under. The British destroyers could save only 36 of the *Scharnhorst's* 1,900 officers and men.

SIGNIFICANCE. The Battle of North Cape was the first sea battle fought entirely by radar plotting. It was also the final major surface action of the war in European waters. A triumph for the British, it freed their Home Fleet from the task of watching German capital ships in northern waters.

Bibliography. C. S. Forester, *The Sinking of the Scharnhorst* (1965); J. D. Potter, *Fiasco: The Breakout of the German Battleships* (1970); and A. J. Watts, *The Loss of the Scharnhorst* (1970).

SCHIRACH, BALDUR VON (1907-1974). Nazi Youth leader.

In 1933 von Schirach was promoted to Youth Leader of the German Reich. Hitler was not altogether satisfied with von Schirach's work during the early days of the war. In July 1941 he sent the young man to Vienna to become district leader (*Gauleiter*) of the Nazi Party, in what was widely regarded as a demotion. To win his way back into the graces of his *Fuehrer,* von Schirach made speeches defending the deportation of Jews from Austria as "a contribution to European culture."

Before the International Military Tribunal (*See* NUREMBERG TRIALS), von Schirach denied knowledge of what went on in Vienna. His judges found him guilty on count 4, crimes against humanity. Among the evidence against him was a deportation order for 60,000 Jews. He was sentenced to 20 years' imprisonment. He was released in 1966.

Tall, plump, blond, round-faced, von Schirach was romantic and sentimental. He wrote flattering verses to "Germany's greatest son" and to "that genius grazing the stars, who remains a man like you and me." Other Nazis ridiculed his effeminate behavior and poked fun at his girlish "bedroom-in-white."

Bibliography. Von Schirach told why he believed in Hitler in his book *Ich glaube an Hitler* (1971).

SCHNÖRKEL (SNORT or SNORKEL). Air intake and diesel exhaust mast fitted to German U-Boats. *Schnörkel* is the German word for a spiral or twisted ornament, but it is also used in dialect satirically for the word "nose."

BACKGROUND. Before the use of this new device, U-Boats spent most of their time on the surface, diving only to attack or avoid enemy action. What was needed was some device that could enable submarines to charge their batteries while remaining at periscope depth. The answer was found in a Dutch contrivance of pre-1940 origin.

DESIGN. The *Schnörkel* consisted of two tubes, one for air intake and a second thinner one for removing gases from the U-Boat's engine. The tubes were raised or lowered by hydraulic pressure. With this device a submarine could stay submerged for weeks. There were some disadvantages. The crew had to keep a close watch by periscope when the *Schnörkel* was used in order to avoid attack by aircraft. From the air the mast was only a pinpoint, but the line it created while moving could be spotted. Moreover, staying under water for long periods of time was disadvantageous for crew morale.

WORLD WAR II. The *Schnörkel* was first used in mid-1943 and by the middle of the next year 30 U-Boats were fitted with it. Adm. Karl Doenitz (*q.v.*) hoped that the device would bolster his U-Boat record. But his losses mounted steadily until in June 1944 of the 16 submarines sent out to attack the Allied invasion fleet 7 were lost on the outward journey, while 1 of the 4 that reached the invasion fleet was destroyed.

SIGNIFICANCE. The *Schnörkel* was a useful device to help U-Boats remain at sea for longer periods. But added to other German devices introduced in mid-1943, such as the homing torpedo and the glider bomb (*qq.v.*), it did not turn the tide in the sea war. (*See* ATLANTIC, BATTLE OF.)

Bibliography. H. Busch, *U-Boats at War* (1955); and D. Mason, *U-Boat: The Secret Menace* (1968).

SCHWARZE KAPELLE ("BLACK ORCHESTRA"). Name used by Nazis to describe the conspirators against Hitler.

The *Schwarze Kapelle* included members of the *Abwehr* (*q.v.*), the counter-intelligence department of the High Command. (*See* JULY PLOT.)

SCHWEINFURT RAIDS. Allied air strikes at ball-bearing works of Schweinfurt in southern Germany in 1943.

BACKGROUND. World War II military weapons, especially aircraft and tanks, were dependent for smooth action on various types of ball bearings. The air frame of a single plane required more than 1,000 antifriction bearings, as did tanks and warships of all kinds. Germans received considerable supplies of ball bearings from Sweden, as well as from 40 plants of their own scattered throughout Germany and Austria. Allied military strategists were certain that a successful air raid on the ball-bearing industry in Germany would be effective in crippling enemy production. Their attention turned to Schweinfurt, a town in Bavaria 148 miles northeast of Munich and the hub of the ball-bearing industry.

TARGET. The original plan did not include Schweinfurt. It combined two contemplated operations, *Tidal Wave*, an attack on Rumanian oil fields at Ploesti (*see* PLOESTI RAID), and *Juggler,* a raid on the Messerschmitt assembly works at Regensburg in southern Germany. It was decided that the raids would be difficult to accomplish together. Instead, in final form, *Juggler* was planned as a twin attack on Schweinfurt for ball bearings and Regensburg for airplane assembly works. (*See* REGENSBURG RAID.)

The twin operation was to be primarily an American show of the 8th Air Force with fighter protection part of the way by American and British fighting planes. A large force of *Flying Fortresses (B-17)* (*q.v.*) would take off from East Anglian airfields, cross Holland, and then split into two major groups: one bombing Schweinfurt and then returning to England after a round trip of 800 miles, while the other would concentrate on Regensburg and then fly for another 1,000 miles to the safety of North African airfields. The mission to the targets would be over territory carefully protected by the Germans to deal with intruding bombers.

The day before *Juggler* was initiated came the disappointing news that the raid on Ploesti had resulted in serious Allied losses. Of the 178 *B-24 Liberators* that had flown unescorted from Benghazi to Ploesti, only 111 had returned safely. The mission to Schweinfurt and Regensburg was obviously a most dangerous one.

FIRST RAID. On August 17, 1943, a total of 363 American heavy bombers crossed the coast of Europe and headed for the two targets. One force, the U.S. 1st Bombardment Wing, flew toward Schweinfurt, while the second, the U.S. 4th Bombardment Wing, turned to Regensburg. The latter followed the first formation over the Dutch coast for 10 minutes. A smaller force turned away to create a diversion. At this point fighter escorts of American *P-47 Thunderbolts* and British *Spitfires* (*q.v.*) turned back and the huge bombers proceeded on their own. Fast *Me-109s* (*See* AIRCRAFT: GERMAN AIRCRAFT DATA CHART) of the German *Luftwaffe* (*q.v.*) whirled in to attack the bombing fleets. The raiders had to repel more than 200 separate fighter attacks. One after another *B-17s* were shot down, some of them disappearing in brilliant explosions as they disintegrated into small balls of fire. Over Schweinfurt the bombers had to face heavy enemy flak as they dropped pay loads.

LOSSES. Of the original 363 bombers on the two missions, the Americans lost 63 aircraft, an appalling ratio of 25 percent. More than 370 crew members were missing, although there were reports that many parachutes were seen during the raid.

SECOND RAID. Not discouraged, American strategists ordered another raid on October 14, 1943. This time 291 *B-17s* were sent to Schweinfurt on three simultaneous operations. Germans, expecting the new attack, sent out strong forces of *Ju-87 Stukas* and *He-111s* to meet the raiders. There was intense activity as the Germans coordinated their cannon and rocket fire with air-to-air bombing. A repetition of the first raid, this time 60 American bombers went down over enemy territory and 17 sustained heavy damage. This was "Black Thursday."

The damage done to Schweinfurt was greater than on the first raid. Yet, of the more than 1,000 bombs dropped, only 88 hit targets in the city, many others falling in open country.

RESULTS. There was wide disparity in Allied and German reports on results of the raids. American official sources claimed 80 direct hits on the two main ball-bearing plants of Schweinfurt after 424 short tons of bombs were dropped. It was also stated that 228 enemy aircraft had been shot down. Lt. Gen. Henry H. Arnold (*q.v.*), Commander-in-Chief of the U.S. Army Air Forces, asserted that high-altitude precision bombing had been triumphantly vindicated by the Schweinfurt and Regensburg raids.

German officials countered by describing the raids as unsuccessful. Albert Speer (*q.v.*), Hitler's Minister of Armaments and War Production, reported that production had been cut at Schweinfurt only 39 percent and that within four weeks repairs were carried out and the plants again were in full production. As for aircraft destroyed, the *Luftwaffe* reported accurately that it had lost only 25 fighters.

SIGNIFICANCE. In all there were 16 raids on Schweinfurt during the war. At the most the Allies could claim only a Pyrrhic victory. Some damage was done at the expense of tremendous losses in men and aircraft. The first raid suggested and the second raid proved that long-range penetration flights by unescorted bombers, no matter how strong their armament, were impractical. The strategy of splitting the forces between Schweinfurt and Regensburg meant that neither one had the power to complete its destructive mission. At most the Allied raids caused the redeployment of German ball-bearing facilities. By February 1944 about one-third of Schweinfurt's resources had been moved elsewhere. The most that could be claimed was that the Allied Bomber Command had paid a heavy price for a three-month indirect loss of production.

Bibliography. M. Caidin, *Black Thursday* (1960); J. Sweetman, *Schweinfurt: Disaster in the Skies* (1971); E. Jablonski, *Double Strike: The Epic Air Raids on Regensburg-Schweinfurt* (1974); and T. M. Coffey, *Decision Over Schweinfurt* (1977).

SCIENCE AND THE WAR. The accelerated development of science during World War II was a critical factor in the outcome of the conflict.

The dictum that necessity is the mother of invention held true for this war as for all others. In the belligerent countries scientists were put to work to produce more and more destructive weapons to counteract those of the enemy. (*See* PRODUCTION, BATTLE OF.) There was an important by-product of this scientific and technological activity—tremendous strides carried over into the postwar years brought benefits to those who survived. (*See* SOCIAL IMPACT OF THE WAR.)

RESEARCH. Authorities in all the Allied and Axis countries made intensive efforts to coordinate their research activities. Churchill ordered all British research in the early days of the war to be administered by the Ministry of Defense. At the same time he assigned his close friend Professor Frederick A. Lindemann (*q.v.*) to supervise various projects then under way. Similarly, in the United States, President Roosevelt established an Office of Scientific Research and Development in 1941 under the direction of Dr. Vannevar Bush (*q.v.*), electrical engineer and physicist, who took an important role in the eventual production of the atomic bomb. In Soviet Russia, too, all major military and civilian scientific research was entrusted to the Academy of Science.

The Allies were the winners in the battle of science. There were national research councils in both Germany and Italy, but they were given far too little support and encouragement. In Germany this was due in part to Hitler's misjudgment. He was so confident of early victory by the use of already developed weapons that he did not give enough attention to additional technological research.

German technology had been weakened by the brain drain from 1933 to 1939, when scores of scientists left their homeland in fear or disgust. Lise Meitner, physicist, mathematician, and professor at the University of Berlin from 1926 to 1933, left Germany in 1938. That same year she experimented in bombarding the uranium nucleus with slow-speed neutrons, a significant step in the development of the atomic bomb. (*See* MANHATTAN PROJECT.) The physicists who remained at home, notably Werner Heisenberg, were either discouraged by lack of governmental support, or deliberately engaged in a slowing down of work. By 1943 it had become too late to promote a successful national research program.

NEW PROJECTS. Among the critically important devices developed by the Allies was radar (acronym for *ra*dio *d*etection *a*nd *r*anging), which involved the use of electronic tubes for radio detection. Scientists in all major countries knew the principle of the device and worked feverishly to perfect it. (*See* RADAR, WARTIME.)

Another invention was the degaussing apparatus used to protect ships' hulls against magnetic mines. (The term *gauss* was derived from Karl Friedrich Gauss (1777–1855), German mathematician. It was used to describe a unit of magnetic flux density.)

In Germany important improvements were made in rockets. In the closing days of the war Hitler unleashed his *V-1* and *V-2* vengeance weapons on London. These were to be the *Wunderwaffen* ("wonder weapons") that would bring the British to their knees. It turned out to be an unfulfilled hope. (*See* *V-1; V-2;* PEENEMÜNDE; and BRAUN, WERNHER VON.)

MEDICINE. As in World War I, the proliferation of wounds on the battle fronts led to great strides in medicine, surgery, and rehabilitation procedures. Penicillin had been discovered by Alexander Fleming in 1928. During World War II it was extracted in relatively pure and stable form by pathologist Howard Walter Florey and biochemist Ernst Boris Chain and used for treatment of service personnel. There were also other innovations, such as the increased use of plasma for blood transfusions as well as advances in plastic surgery. Wartime pressures tended to transform medical and surgical procedures. All this work carried over into the postwar years.

ATOMIC RESEARCH. Sensational strides were made in the field of atomic energy. For years scientists all over the world had been seeking to split the atom in order to harness the energy released by fission. From small beginnings the research projects grew into a gigantic undertaking. The end result was the destruction of Hiroshima (*q.v.*) on August 6, 1945, an event which quickly ended the war and profoundly changed the history of civilization.

Bibliography. J. C. Crowther and H. Whiddington, *Science at War* (1946); O. Dunlap, *Radar: What It Is and How It Works* (1946); W. L. Laurence, *Dawn Over Zero: The Story of the Atomic Bomb* (1946); U.S. Joint Board on Scientific Information, *Electronic Warfare* (1945); G. Hartcup, *The Challenge of War: Britain's Scientific and Engineering Contributions in World War II* (1970); and B. J. Ford, *Allied Secret Weapons: The War of Science* (1971).

SEA LION. German *Seelöwe.* German code or cover name for Hitler's proposed invasion of the British Isles in 1940.

BACKGROUND. Britain had not been invaded by a foreign power since the Norman Conquest of 1066. Philip II of Spain attempted it in 1588 with his "Invincible Armada," only to lose 63 of his 128 ships to a combination of British resistance and catastrophic weather. Napoleon Bonaparte, with little affinity or appreciation for sea warfare, pleaded a tendency to seasickness and decided not to risk a repetition of his naval defeat at Trafalgar.

Certain about his historical acumen, Hitler stated categorically that "there are no more islands." He hoped that it would not be necessary, but he knew that eventually he would have to defeat the British in their homeland if he were to win the war. Unfortunately for him, in the period of Nazi rearmament starting in the mid-1930s, the Nazi *Fuehrer* paid most attention to strengthening his ground and air forces. The war came before his naval power was brought to the strength he wanted for it.

In the summer of 1940, with France fallen, most of Norway occupied, and Belgium and the Netherlands under German control, Hitler saw only one obstacle to the domination of Europe. He would have to invade England.

PREPARATIONS. On July 16, 1940, Hitler issued War Directive No. 16 on preparation for a landing operation against England. "Since England, in spite of her hopeless military situation, shows no signs of being ready to come to an understanding, I have decided to prepare a landing operation. . . . The aim of this operation will be to eliminate the English homeland as a base for the prosecution of the war against Germany, and, if necessary, to occupy it completely." He ordered a landing in the form of a surprise crossing on a wide front from about Ramsgate to the area west of the Isle of Wight, reduction of the Royal Air Force (*q.v.*), clearing of mines from the English Channel, sealing off the Strait of Dover, and tying down the British Navy. He issued precise instructions to army, navy, and *Luftwaffe* (*q.v.*).

Preparations went on through the summer of 1940. Ports along the French, Belgian, and Dutch coasts were crammed with small vessels of every description. A host of workers labored around the clock as German troops practised landing exercises. As Germans prepared for the invasion, British pilots rained bombs on enemy ports to discourage the project. There were rumors that the British intended to drop great supplies of gasoline among the concentrated craft and then fire a blazing inferno.

BATTLE OF BRITAIN. Hitler gave full instructions to Gen. Hermann Goering (*q.v.*) to smash the Royal Air Force (*q.v.*) as a preliminary to *Sea Lion.* Goering's pilots strove mightily to drive the British from the skies. But despite his promises Goering was unable to provide substantial air cover for the projected invasion. On August 19, 1940, Hitler changed the date of *Sea Lion* to late September. He declared in a speech on September 4: "If the people of England are puzzled and ask 'Why doesn't he come?' I shall put their minds at rest. He is coming!"

There were black days for Hitler in late August 1940. In one week Goering's *Luftwaffe* lost 256 aircraft. Nazi Germany was defeated in the war in the sky. (*See* BRITAIN, BATTLE OF.) The *Luftwaffe* never recovered from that beating.

ABANDONMENT. The disappointed *Fuehrer* again postponed the date for *Sea Lion.* On October 21, 1940, he put aside all plans for the rest of the year and set the next target date for the spring of 1941. It was a critically important decision: Britain had won the first round and, as it turned out, the decisive one.

On January 9, 1941, Hitler gave orders to discontinue preparations for *Sea Lion.* He mentioned the possibility of returning one day to his original plan, but he made the suggestion with little enthusiasm. On June 22, 1941, he turned on Soviet Russia. He dropped *Sea Lion* entirely and never referred to it again. Like Napoleon, he was destined never to cross the Channel.

SIGNIFICANCE. The failure of *Sea Lion* was an important factor in the defeat of Nazi Germany, as recognized by Field Marshal von Manstein (*q.v.*): "The conquest of Britain by Germany would have deprived the other side of the very base that was indispensable—in those days at any rate—for a seaborne assault on the continent of Europe. To launch an invasion from over the Atlantic without being able to use the island as a springboard was beyond the realm of possibility in those days." The survival of Britain and the entrance of the United States into the war meant ultimate defeat for the Third Reich.

Bibliography. P. Fleming, *Operation Sea Lion* (1957); R. Wheatley, *Operation Sea Lion* (1958); and W. Ansel, *Hitler Confronts England* (1960).

SECOND FRONT. Call by the Russians to their Western Allies to attack the Germans from the West and thereby relieve pressure on the Soviet armies.

BACKGROUND. On June 22, 1941, Hitler turned on the Soviet Union. (*See BARBAROSSA.*) He struck with a weight of armor and an accumulation of manpower rarely ever assembled. Swift blows in a new *Blitzkrieg* (*q.v.*) brought the Germans within 35 miles of Leningrad and Moscow, but by December 1941 they were caught in the Russian winter and no longer had the strength to press on. Then the Russians launched their first counteroffensive.

1942. In the spring of 1942 the Russians were more than holding their own, but at a terrible cost. At this time an anxious Stalin called on the West for assistance. The Russians, he said, had done more than their share of fighting, and it was high time to start a Second Front to relieve pressure on his exhausted troops. It was a mistaken military judgment, he said, for the Western Allies to concentrate their attacks by air on German industrial targets. Wars had to be won on the ground. Stalin suspected that his Western Allies secretly delayed a cross-Channel invasion in the hope that Germany and Russia would smash one another to death. He taunted British "reluctance" to fight the Germans.

Actually, war leaders in both Britain and the United States were wholly in favor of a Second Front and had been working on various plans for some time. But it was becoming increasingly obvious that they did not yet possess the technical equipment for such an effort with any chance of success. Allied planners continued to work on a future giant operation in France, but for the time being settled on a strong commando sortie against the French port of Dieppe. On August 19, 1942, just three days after Stalin's denunciation, 6,086 Allied commandos, mostly Canadian, attacked Dieppe in what turned out to be a disaster. (*See* DIEPPE RAID.)

In August 1942 Churchill flew to Moscow for a private talk with Stalin at the Kremlin to explain why an Allied landing in France had to be delayed in favor of an invasion of North Africa. A Second Front in 1942, Churchill said, was impossible without frightful loss of life. Dieppe had been a costly experiment, even though many valuable lessons had been learned for the future. He promised that the Western Allies would strike in due time with overwhelming force, but declared that neither he nor Roosevelt would risk Allied lives in a premature assault. He urged patience.

Churchill was rewarded with insults. "When are you going to start fighting?" Stalin asked. "Are you going to let us do all the work?" Relations grew dangerously strained.

1943. Churchill and Roosevelt agreed that it was best for the Big Three to meet face to face and solve the matter of a Second Front. Stalin turned down two urgent invitations. Finally, Churchill and Roosevelt met at the Casablanca Conference (*q.v.*) in January 1943 to decide what to do about a Second Front. Stalin declined to attend.

The two Allied war leaders decided that, although they recognized the necessity for a Second Front, it was best to wait—despite Stalin's injured feelings. There was still a shortage of Allied shipping, most of which was needed for the Far East. It was agreed to send vast supplies of war matériel to Russia via the Murmansk convoy route rather than have it stockpiled in Britain for the coming cross-Channel invasion.

IMPLEMENTATION. While satisfied with increased war supplies, Stalin grew even more insistent in his demand for a Second Front. Not until the Allies struck at northern France in early June 1944 in the greatest combined operation of its kind in history (*see* NORMANDY INVASION) did Stalin grant that Churchill and Roosevelt were serious in their contention that the Allies would move when they were fully prepared.

Bibliography. T. Higgins, *Winston Churchill and the Second Front* (1967); H. Feis, *Churchill, Roosevelt, Stalin: The War They Waged and the Peace They Sought* (1957); and E. L. Woodward, *British Foreign Policy in the Second World War* (1962).

SECTOR STATIONS. Local stations of the British Fighter Command organization.

Vital for operations of the British air arm, such stations as Biggin Hill, Kenley, and Hornchurch drew the attention of the *Luftwaffe* (*q.v.*) as preferred targets from the air. (*See* ROYAL AIR FORCE.)

SEE HERE, PRIVATE HARGROVE. Best-selling book on the life of a draftee in a U.S. training camp.

Written by Marion Hargrove, a GI (*q.v.*) from North Carolina, *See Here, Private Hargrove,* described in simple prose the trials of a new soldier in the U.S. Army. Draftees were quick to appreciate the stories of fast haircuts, inoculations, barking sergeants, and interminable crap games.

A typical passage:

At eight o'clock we put on our light packs and go for a tramp in the hills. The light pack includes guns, bayonet, canteen, fork, knife, spoon, meat cans, cup, shaving kit, pup tent, raincoat, cartridge belt, first aid kit, fire extinguisher, tent pins, rope, tent pole, hand ax, small spade, and a few other negligible items. Carrying my light pack, I weighed 217 ½ pounds. I weighed 131 pounds when I left home so you can see how easy it is to gain weight in the Army.

Bibliography. M. Hargrove, *See Here, Private Hargrove* (1942).

SEROV, IVAN ALEKSANDROVITCH (1905–   ). Russian police official active in security matters during the war.

Following the conquest of Poland in September 1939, Serov was assigned the task of eliminating all opposition there. He signed Order No. 00123 concerning executions and deportations in the newly annexed Baltic states. In 1940 he was named Commissioner of Internal Affairs for the Ukraine under Nikita Khrushchev and in this post sent many thousands of Ukrainians to Siberia. In July 1941 he was appointed First Deputy Commissar of State Security.

Serov played an active role in the defense of Moscow and Stalingrad. He executed hundreds of citizens accused of cowardice and desertion. He was awarded his country's highest military orders, including Hero of the Soviet Union, and was promoted to General of the Army.

Wiry, with gray-blue eyes, high forehead, and graying hair, Serov was a cold, ruthless, ambitious police chief completely dedicated to his work. Sinister guardian of an espionage network, he was convinced that the Soviet regime would collapse without his necessary work.

SEVAREID, ERIC (1912–   ). American journalist and one of the leading war correspondents of World War II.

In 1940 Sevareid traveled with the French Army. He left Paris just before the German occupation, and joined the staff of Edward R. Murrow (*q.v.*) in London. Returning to the United States, he was assigned to the CBS News Bureau at Washington, D.C., and served there from 1941 to 1943. In the summer of 1943 he went to the Far East on an assignment and had a miraculous escape when he had to bail out with 20 others from a plane flying over the Himalayas to India. Landing in a remote part of the Assam jungle, he lived with a head-hunting tribe of savages while making his way back to civilization.

In January 1944 Sevareid returned to the European theater of operations, reporting the Italian campaign, the activities of Marshal Tito's (*q.v.*) Yugoslavian Partisans, and the late stages of the war. He landed with the first wave of American troops in southern France, and accompanied the American drive through the Rhineland into Germany.

Tall and rangy, with an angular face and jutting jaw, Sevareid became one of the most familiar faces in American television history. He was widely praised for his dry wit, perceptiveness, and urbanity. Despite decades of broadcasting, he never conquered his nervousness on the air. "A lot of people," he said, "start blossoming when that little light goes on. I start to die."

Bibliography. Among Sevareid's books are: *Not So Wild a Dream* (1946); *One Ear* (1952); *Small Sounds in the Night* (1956); and *This is Eric Sevareid* (1964).

SEVASTAPOL, SIEGE OF. German assault on the Russian port in the southwest Crimea lasting more than seven months until its fall on July 3, 1942.

BACKGROUND. The German invasion of Soviet Russia starting in June 22, 1941, slowed down to a crawl during the last six months of that year. Hitler had failed to take either Leningrad on the northern front or Moscow in the center. (*See* EASTERN FRONT, CAMPAIGNS ON THE.) There was little doubt on both sides that he would launch another offensive somewhere in Russia. Because his attack on a mass front had misfired, he decided to make a major drive at one point—the southern flank.

From the rich Caucasus, Hitler could get badly needed oil, iron, manganese, food, and reinforcements. Strategically, he would split the northern and southern Red Armies while simultaneously depriving the Kremlin of its industrial basin. With control of the Black Sea, he could move to Egypt. He had three choices in the area: Voronezh in the north, Rostov in the center, and Sevastopol in the extreme south. He selected Sevastopol.

TARGET. Sevastopol, in the southwest Crimea and in the Southeast Ukrainian SSR, was a major port, naval base, and strategic strong point with shipyards, lumber mills, and processing industries. Founded in 1783 near the site of ancient Chersonesus, it was almost completely destroyed during the siege of 1854–1855 in the Crimean War. For Hitler it was an attractive prize.

ASSAULT. The German attack began in December 1941. The hard-pressed city received supplies and reinforcements from the Soviet Black Sea Fleet, which also shelled Germans from the sea. In early January 1942 Russians attempted to land troops behind the German lines north of the city, but these were quickly captured. Other Russian landings were also repulsed.

Early in May 1942, as a preliminary to summer operations, Hitler sent an army of 14 divisions under Gen. Erich von Manstein (*q.v.*) to take Sevastopol. It was Leningrad all over again. (*See* LENINGRAD, SIEGE OF.) *Luftwaffe* (*q.v.*) dive bombers screamed over the city, while artillery hurled massive shells into its center. The people of Sevastopol organized to fight in the inferno of fire and smoke.

SIEGE. By May 16, 1942, all the Crimea was in German hands except Sevastopol. Its defense was another epic in Russian history. On June 7 von Manstein mounted a major attack by land, sea, and air. Soviet ships sent reinforcements and evacuated the wounded. By day clouds of rock and dust were hurled up by German shells and bombs, by night the entire city was illuminated by flashes of gunfire. There was bitter struggle for each foot of ground, for every pillbox, every trench, in houses, streets, and railway tunnels. In vast cellars subdivided by metal screens, Russians worked at hundreds of lathes to produce grenades and ammunition. Thousands waited at the docks to be evacuated.

COLLAPSE. Hammered by air assault, conventional artillery, and a giant German siege gun called *Dora* (*See* ARTILLERY WEAPONS), Sevastopol finally capitulated on July 3, 1942. Russians blew up their last munitions and destroyed everything of military use. Von Manstein reported that 90,000 prisoners were taken as well as "booty so vast that it could not be calculated immediately."

SIGNIFICANCE. For Hitler it was a satisfying victory. He had won a naturally strong fortress, which had been reinforced, consolidated, and defended by an entire army. Now he had all the Crimea, and he could free thousands of troops for service elsewhere in Russia. He promoted von Manstein to Field Marshal.

AFTERMATH. The triumph was not permanent. Germans actually were in a vulnerable position. They were holding firm in the north and central fronts in Russia, but Army Group South was never able to form a proper defensive line. Russian counterattacks began to clear the Crimea and drive the Germans back into Sevastopol, where eventually they were cornered.

Bibliography. B. Voyetekhov, *The Last Days of Sevastopol* (1943); and E. von Manstein, *Lost Victories* (1943).

SEVERSKY, ALEXANDER D. (1894–1974). American aeronautical engineer, airplane designer, and strong advocate of air power.

Seversky was born in Tiflis, Russia, and was a graduate of the Imperial Naval Academy of Russia. In World War I he was assigned to a bombing squadron, was shot down, and lost his right leg. He emigrated to the United States in 1918, and became an American citizen in 1927 and test pilot for the U.S Government. As founder of the Seversky Aircraft Corporation (1931–1939) and Director of its successor firm the Republic Aircraft Corporation (1939–1940), he was responsible for a series of distinguished aircraft, including the Seversky *P35* and the famed Republic *P-47 Thunderbolt.*

Seversky was an energetic polemicist for air power, especially in his book, *Victory Through Air Power* (1942), adapted for the screen by Walt Disney (1943).

SEYSS-INQUART, ARTUR (1892–1946). Austrian Nazi and German High Commissioner of the Netherlands.

On October 12, 1939, Seyss-Inquart was named Deputy Governor-General of Poland. From 1940 to 1945 he served as High Commissioner of the occupied Netherlands. At first he announced that Dutch laws would remain in force. "We did not come here to oppress the people and to deprive the people of their freedom."

When Nazi soldiers were thrown into Dutch canals, Seyss-Inquart changed his attitude. He ordered brutal reprisals for acts of resistance. He drained the Dutch economy of wealth and art treasures, which he directed back to Germany. He ordered 5 million Dutch citizens sent to Germany as well as most of Holland's 140,000 Jews. Among his victims was Anne Frank (*q.v.*). Deprived of food in the last winter of the war, many Dutch civilians died of starvation.

NUREMBERG. After the war Seyss-Inquart was a defendant before the International Military Tribunal. (*See* NUREMBERG TRIALS.) In his final statement he admitted the "fearful excesses" of the Nazi regime and accepted partial responsibility for what had happened. He was found guilty on count 2, crimes against peace; count 3, war crimes; and count 4, crimes against humanity. He was hanged at Nuremberg on October 16, 1946.

Seyss-Inquart was a meek-looking Nazi with a heart of stone. Near-sighted, always well dressed, with an aristocratic appearance and impeccable manners, he had a brilliant mind and memory. Like many of his Nazi colleagues, he condoned brutality as a means of winning the approval of his *Fuehrer*.

Bibliography. A. Seyss-Inquart, *Vier Jahre in den Niederlanden* (1944); H. J. Meuman, *Artur Seyss-Inquart* (1967); and W. Rasar, *Deutsche Gemeinschaft* (1971).

SHAEF. *Supreme Headquarters, Allied Expeditionary Force.*

Leadership of SHAEF was entrusted in December 1943 to Gen. Dwight D. Eisenhower (*q.v.*) with headquarters in London.

SHELL HOUSE RAID. Sensational attack by the British Royal Air Force (*q.v.*) on *Gestapo* (*q.v.*) headquarters in Copenhagen in early 1945.

BACKGROUND. The Nazi *Gestapo* had three headquarters in occupied Denmark, one at Aarhus University in Jutland, which also housed a Nazi prison; a second at an agricultural college near Odense; and a third in Copenhagen in a new office building. In each were carefully guarded files concerning individual Danes and their Resistance activities. Danish underground fighters sent radio messages to London for assistance, describing the repositories and requesting help in attacking them. The Royal Air Force (*q.v.*) promised help. (*See* RESISTANCE MOVEMENTS.)

AARHUS BOMBING. The problem at Aarhus was that *Gestapo* headquarters were close to a hospital. Nevertheless, on October 31, 1944, *Mosquito* (*q.v.*) bombers flew to Aarhus and hurled missiles into the buildings. Astonished prisoners escaped from the rubble. A message went off to London from the Danish Underground:

BOMBING OF GESTAPO AARHUS O.K. GESTAPO HEADQUARTERS BUILDING COMPLETELY DESTROYED. ONLY ONE BOMB FAILED. LANGELANDSGADE BARRACKS IS BURNING. CONGRATULATIONS TO ALL CONCERNED.

PREPARATION. The *Gestapo* took over the Shell Petroleum Company's modern office building in the center of Copenhagen and converted it into an information center and a prison. Officials of the occupying force as well as Danish Nazis were given office space. The ground floor and the next two stories were filled with files giving information about the Danish Resistance. Only the sixth floor was empty because it lacked a heating system. The severe angle of its roof caused a problem. Workmen set up flimsy concrete block partitions to make the attic into prison cells.

Gestapo officers knew that every move was being reported to England by the Danish Resistance. They hoped that by placing prisoners in the 21 small cells in the attic they would discourage any attacks by the RAF. Ostentatiously, they selected members of the Danish Resistance elite for occupancy of the attic cells, knowing that this would be reported to London. If the Shell House were attacked, then loyal Danes would be killed in the process.

In December 1944 the Resistance radio in Copenhagen contacted London with word that all the hostages in Shell House probably soon would be executed. Would the RAF please attack the building and thereby destroy the dangerous *Gestapo* records? To London went complete plans of the building with details of its construction as well as photographs and maps. The Air Ministry was non-committal, but it ordered model makers to build a complete scale model of the center of the city and the Shell House.

RAID. The attack came on March 3, 1945. A British force composed of 18 *Mosquitos* and an American force of 28 *P-51 Mustangs* took off from airfields in England and crossed the North Sea in the direction of Jutland. When they reached the coast, the pilots zoomed across Denmark and flew to Copenhagen at tree-top height.

Then occurred one of the most remarkable exploits of the war. The raiders destroyed the target with minimum loss of life in Shell House itself. It was an astounding performance of pinpoint bombing.

LOSSES. Six prisoners in the attic died, while 27 escaped. Many thousands Nazis lost their lives in the raid. It was a successful mission for the Allies, but the cost was heavy. Four *Mosquitos* and two *Mustangs* with 10 men of their crews did not return to England. There was a coincidental tragic accident when a crashing *Mosquito* plunged into the Jeanne d'Arc School. Other bombardiers mistook the school for their target and dropped their lethal loads on it. There were 100 casualties, including nuns and 83 children.

AFTERMATH. Despite the severe loss of life, Danes welcomed the raid. A week after Copenhagen was liberated the British airmen who bombed the Shell House were received in the city as heroes.

Bibliography. D. Lampe, *The Danish Resistance* (1957).

SHERMAN **TANK.** *See* TANKS.

SHIRER, WILLIAM LAWRENCE (1894–   ). American journalist and war correspondent.

After the beginning of the war, Shirer reported regularly from Berlin as a CBS news analyst. Despite Nazi censorship, he managed to convey what he was thinking by his phrasing and use of American slang. On June 22, 1940, he scored a remarkable journalistic scoop by his broadcast of the Franco-German armistice proceedings at Compiègne (*q.v.*). He left Berlin in December 1940, after German censorship became stricter, and returned to the United States. He went to Europe on various assignments during the rest of the war.

After the war Shirer covered the Nuremberg Trials (*q.v.*), the San Francisco

Conference (*q.v.*) that established the United Nations, and also meetings of the United Nations. From 1947 to 1949 he was a commentator for the Mutual Broadcasting System.

Soft-spoken and mild-mannered, Shirer was known for his general excellence in radio reporting. His published works also indicate a wide background in history and political science.

Bibliography. Shirer's *Rise and Fall of the Third Reich* (1960) became the most successful study of its kind ever published. He also wrote *Berlin Diary* (1941); *End of a Berlin Diary* (1947); and *The Collapse of the Third Republic* (1969).

SHO. Japanese code or cover name for operations in the Pacific leading to expected victory. The term *Sho* means "Victory," *Sho Go* means "Victory Operation."

BACKGROUND. Japanese victories during the first six months of the war led to the formation of an outer defense perimeter within which the home islands felt secure. By April 1944, however, American land forces were pushing rapidly along the northern coast of New Guinea and moving ever closer to the Philippines. The loss of Saipan (*q.v.*) in July forced Japanese Imperial General Headquarters to take a new look at the Pacific conflict. There had to be major changes, especially concerning the Philippines, where defensive preparations were still half completed.

NEW STRATEGY. On July 24, 1944, a new and comprehensive "Plan for the Conduct of Future Operations," code named *Sho,* was accepted. The goal was a major defensive front embracing the Philippines, Formosa, the Ryukus, the four Japanese main islands, and the Kuriles. All Japanese air, sea, and land forces available would be concentrated on this new line to overwhelm the Americans in a final decisive battle which would determine the outcome of the war.

ALTERNATIVE PLANS. Japanese strategists expected the major American thrust to come in the Philippines. At the same time, they drew up four alternative plans:

1. *Sho-1:* Counterthrust against an expected attack on the Philippines.

2. *Sho-2:* Defense of Formosa and the Ryukus.

3. *Sho-3:* Defense of southern and central Japan.

4. *Sho-4:* Defense of northern Japan and the Kuriles.

All Japanese air, army, and naval forces were to be kept on alert in order to move in concentrated power against any target chosen by Imperial General Headquarters. Although it had incurred heavy losses, the Japanese Air Force was to be used to oppose any enemy landings. Similarly, the Japanese Navy, which had lost all but one flattop of its once powerful carrier force, would launch an attack at the moment of landing and also send units off to act as decoys. The Japanese Army was charged with the defeat of whatever U.S. troops managed to get ashore.

RESULTS. The *Sho* plan involved a major change in Japanese strategy from constant attack to desperate defense. On paper the prognosis was good. But Japanese air strength had been decimated by this time, naval power was radically reduced by defeat after defeat, and tens of thousands of the best Nipponese troops were by-passed and cut off on what were once Japanese strongholds. The critical step came with the struggle for Leyte in the Philippines. (*See* LEYTE, BATTLE OF.)

SHORT, WALTER CAMPBELL (1880–1949). U.S Army officer and commander in Hawaii when the Japanese attacked Pearl Harbor (*q.v.*).

On February 8, 1941, Short, a Lieutenant General, was posted as commander of the Hawaiian Department. Along with Rear Adm. Husband E. Kimmel (*q.v.*), he became the center of national controversy after the Japanese attacked Pearl Harbor. Both he and Kimmel were accused of laxity leading to the crippling of air, land, and naval defenses of the Hawaiian base.

President Roosevelt ordered a special investigating committee to look into the disaster and give its findings to the nation. The report held that the successful Japanese attack was due to the failure of Gen. Short and Adm. Kimmel to take adequate joint action to defend the Hawaiian Islands. Both were relieved of their commands ten days after Pearl Harbor. (*See* PEARL HARBOR CONTROVERSY.)

In February 1942 the War and Navy Departments announced that Gen. Short and Adm. Kimmel would be tried by court-martial. Both filed for retirement. Nearly two years later it was announced that both army and navy had found no evidence to justify a trial of the two commanders.

Short, like Kimmel, never ceased to proclaim his innocence. After an unblemished record for 40 years, the disaster at Pearl Harbor ended his career in disgrace.

SICILY, INVASION OF. Code or cover name *Operation Husky.* Allied campaign in the summer of 1943 preliminary to an attack on Italy, the "soft underbelly" (*q.v.*) of Europe.

BACKGROUND. With the costly desert war in North Africa won (*See* NORTH AFRICA, CAMPAIGNS IN), Allied war leaders met at the Casablanca Conference (*q.v.*) on January 14–23, 1943, to consider the next major operation. There were differences on locale. Americans preferred Sardinia and Corsica because of the favorable location on the flank of the Italian Peninsula.

The British insisted on a strike at Sicily because: (1) it would free Mediterranean shipping from Axis attacks; (2) it would divert German strength from the Russian front and thereby help satisfy Stalin; and (3) it would stimulate the Italians on the mainland to desert from the Germans. The British view prevailed.

TARGET. A gigantic triangular rock, 10,000 square miles with 600 miles of coastline, Sicily lies southwest of Italy, closely abutting both the Italian Peninsula and North Africa. In the north is a range of mountains and in the northeast the great volcano of Etna, 11,872 feet high. Among the good ports are Palermo on the north coast, Syracuse, Catania, and Messina on the east coast, the latter only two miles from the toe of Italy.

DEFENSE. German strategists expected an attack on Sicily. For its defense they had 13 divisions—9 Italian and 4 German, including, later the 15th *Panzer* Grenadier Division and the Hermann Goering *Panzer* Division, a total of about 350,000 Axis troops, all under the command of Field Marshal Albert Kesselring (*q.v.*). They also covered the island with a maze of fortifications including concrete pillboxes and barbed-wire entanglements. The *Luftwaffe* (*q.v.*) had about 1,400 planes available. "Smiling Albert Kesselring," relying on his crack Hermann Goering Division, had no doubt that he could throw any Allied invasion back into the sea.

PREPARATIONS. The Allied Supreme Command planned its first large-scale amphibious attack on Axis territory as a stupendous operation. With aircraft and landing boats rolling off the assembly lines, it ordered 3,000 ships of all kinds to a rendezvous south of the island. For the task it assigned 140,000 men, 3,700 aircraft, 600 tanks, 14,000 vehicles, and 1,800 big guns. The U.S. 7th Army with six divisions was led by Lt. Gen. George S. Patton, Jr. (*q.v.*); the British 8th Army (*q.v.*), with six divisions, including one Canadian and one airborne, was commanded by Gen. Bernard Law Montgomery (*q.v.*). Americans would provide 55 percent of the air power, the British 45 percent. The British Navy would make up 80 percent of naval strength. The Allies counted on the assistance of Sicilians, well-known for their contempt for Germans ("They eat all our chickens").

In early June 1943 the Allies struck at Pantalleria, a volcanic island 60 miles to the southwest of Sicily, and Italy's Heligoland in the central Mediterranean. After several days of naval and air bombardment, the garrison on the island surrendered. (*See* PANTELLERIA.)

ASSAULT. The great armada converged south of Malta on July 9, 1943. The weather turned foul, but during the night the wind eased, leaving moderate swells on Sicilian beaches. Weary Italians, alert for many nights, turned thankfully to their beds. They believed: "Tonight at any rate *they* cannot come," said Adm. Andrew Brown Cunningham (*q.v.*) later, "BUT THEY CAME!"

During the night Allied parachutists dropped inland to disrupt communications and occupy airfields. The next morning a powerful invasion force disembarked on five beaches along the southern coast in a bewildering array of landing craft, including the new American DUKWs, amphibious load carriers. Many British gliders, released too early by towing craft, were lost. At first there was little opposition with the beaches undefended and the pillboxes deserted. Germans had expected an invasion on the western end of the island, closest to North African ports in Allied hands, but the invaders came from the south and the east. Attack by the German *Panzer* divisions was driven off.

Italian troops offered only token resistance. Many donned civilian clothes and vanished. Sicilians reacted with joy, showering Allied troops with flowers, fruit, and wine. German commanders rushed tanks and planes to the scene, only to be met by deadly fire from the offshore armada.

BATTLE. By the end of July 11, 1943, the Allies had 80,000 troops and 8,000 vehicles ashore. But it was not to be an easy victory. This was rugged terrain, covered by stream beds so deep that tank breakthroughs were almost impossible. Movement on the narrow roads was slow and laborious. Fighting degenerated into a series of small engagements by artillery and infantry.

Montgomery's battle-wise 8th Army (*q.v.*) quickly took the eastern beaches and captured Syracuse. From here on to the north along the coast he had to pass along a precipitous narrow road on the seaward shoulder of Mount Etna toward Messina. On July 27, 1943, he was forced to halt on the Catania plain to await reinforcements. Meanwhile, Patton's 7th Army, which had landed at Gela and Licata on the southern coast, split into two units, one heading west to take Marsala and Palermo within two weeks, while the other raced straight up the center of the island.

The British and Americans linked their forces on July 30, 1943. They now held a line across Sicily to the south of Mount Etna. Fighting a powerful delaying action, Germans withdrew 3½ divisions to the security of the volcanic mountain. The Allies pressed on from one height to another. Traffic lunged forward in a groaning, pulsating stream over pulverized roads and bridges rebuilt over precipitous crags. Dozens of German counterattacks were thrown back in desperate fighting.

TRIUMPH. On August 17, the Allies took Messina and the island was theirs. In a new Dunkirk (*see* DUNKIRK EVACUATION) the Germans carried out a skillful operation in darkness and rescued some 39,000 men by plane and small boats. For once Allied air power failed, but enormous quantities of undamaged war matériel, including tanks, were captured.

LOSSES. The campaign in Sicily cost the Germans 12,000 men killed or wounded, the Italians 147,000, mostly prisoners. Allied casualties were 31,158 killed, wounded, or missing.

SIGNIFICANCE. "It was," said Roosevelt, "the beginning of the end." The conquest of Sicily demonstrated that the Allies could strike with tremendous power on one front. At the same time there was much criticism of both American and British commanders for what was said to be unimaginative leadership. With overwhelming superiority, they had allowed Germans to escape from the island. There was also dissatisfaction with Montgomery's go-slow tactics on the plains of Catania as well as with Patton for slapping a hospitalized GI. (*See* PATTON, GEORGE SMITH, JR.)

Bibliography. B. L. Montgomery, *El Alamein to the Sangro* (1946); *Memoirs of Field Marshal Kesselring* (1953); and M. Blumenson, *Sicily* (1969).

SIDI RESEGH, BATTLE OF. *See* NORTH AFRICA, CAMPAIGNS IN.

SIEGFRIED LINE. Term used by the Allies to describe the German West Wall (*q.v.*) in World War II. The Germans themselves never used the term *Siegfried Line* and regarded its use in the Allied countries as ridicule and polemic.

WORLD WAR I. In World War I the Siegfried Line was a portion of the Hindenburg Line, which stretched like a long serpent inside French territory between Switzerland and the North Sea. The Siegfried Line itself ran south from Dracourt near Lille to a point just south of Saint-Quentin. At the time the practice was to name sections of the line after such legendary figures in German mythology as Wotan, Hagen, Brunhilde, and Kriemhilde.

WORLD WAR II. The Siegfried, or Limes Line, was a lightly built triple line of fortifications supposed to run from Switzerland to Luxembourg. It was constructed from 1936 to 1940 as a partial response to the Maginot Line (*q.v.*). Nothing like its intricate, complex, and expensive French counterpart, it was largely only of psychological value. After victory over France in 1940, the Germans dismantled the Siegfried Line. Restored in part in 1944, it was unable to hold up the Allied advance.

Bibliography. W. Flack, *Wir bauen am Westwall* (1940); W. Pöschlinger, *Das Buch vom Westwall* (1940); and C. B. MacDonald, *The Siegfried Line Campaign* (1963).

"SIEGFRIED LINE, WE'RE GONNA HANG OUT THE WASHING ON THE." Popular British ditty during the fall and winter of 1939–1940.

When the French Army, seemingly secure behind the Maginot Line (*q.v.*), showed no desire to attack the German Siegfried Line (*q.v.*), and the Germans, too, showed no aggressiveness, the western front appeared to be in a stalemate. To the Germans it was a *Sitzkrieg* (*q.v.*), a "sitdown war." The British sent 150,000 men of the British Expeditionary Force (BEF) (*q.v.*) to serve in France during the first five months of the conflict.

In England the mood of non-belligerency encouraged songwriters Jimmy

Kennedy and Michael Carr to contribute a song about the boring days of the "phony war." The words:*

First Verse
Mother dear, I'm writing you from somewhere in
    France,
Hoping this finds you well,
Sergeant says I'm doing fine: "A soldier and
    a half"—
Here's the song that we'll all sing,
It'll sure make you laugh.

Chorus
We're gonna hang out the washing on the
    Siegfried Line,
Have you any dirty washing, Mother dear?
We're gonna hang out the washing on the
    Siegfried Line,
'Cos the washing day is here.
Whether the weather may be wet or fine,
We'll just rub along without a care,
We're gonna hang out the washing on the Siegfried
    Line,
If the Siegfried Line's still there.

Second Verse
Everybody's mucking in and doing their job,
Wearing a great big smile,
Everybody's got to keep their spirits up to-day!
If you want to keep in swing,
Here's the song to sing!

Chorus

SIKORSKI, WLADYSLAW (1881–1943). Premier of the Polish Government-in-exile.

When Poland was invaded by Germany and Russia, Sikorski, who had been refused a command, went to Paris to establish an expatriate "Capital of Poland." After Poland's defeat he was named Premier of the Provisional Polish Government-in-exile. Later, while in London, he became Commander-in-Chief of Polish forces in the war. After the invasion of the Soviet Union by Germany on June 22, 1941, he signed a treaty in Moscow, restoring diplomatic

---

*Copyright MCMXXXIX by Peter Maurice Music Co. Ltd. Copyright renewed. Sole selling agents—SKIDMORE MUSIC CO., INC., 10 East Fifty-third Street, New York, N.Y. 10022. Used by permission of Shapiro, Bernstein & Co., Inc.

relations between Russia and Poland and annulling the Russo-German partition of Poland.

The restored friendship did not last long between Poland and the Soviet Union. Sikorski hoped to form a large army made up of Polish prisoners of war and deportees held by Moscow. He was infuriated by discovery of the Katyn massacre (*q.v.*). In April 1943 Sikorski revealed information that the Russians had murdered thousands of Polish officers and had buried them in the Katyn forest.

On July 4, 1943, Sikorski was killed when his airplane crashed on take-off at Gibraltar. He was mourned in Poland as a fervent patriot and superb military organizer.

Bibliography. W. Sikorski, *Future War* (1926).

SIKORSKY, IGOR I. (1885–1972). Russian-American plane designer.

The Vought-Sikorsky-*300* was the forerunner of a long series of helicopters that bore Sikorsky's name. The U.S. Army bought its first helicopter in 1941. Throughout the rest of the war the only helicopters used by the U.S. Army Air Forces were those designed by Sikorsky. Originally called ''the mule pack of the air,'' Sikorsky's helicopters later gained the nicknames of ''Whirlybird,'' ''Egg Beater,'' and ''Chopper.''

Bibliography. I. I. Sikorsky, *The Story of the Winged-S: An Autobiography* (1938); and R. Bartlett, *Sky Pioneer* (1947).

SIM. *Servizio Informazione Segreto.* The Italian secret service. Its main duty was to maintain the existence of Mussolini's Fascist regime.

SIMONOV, KONSTANTIN (KYRILL) MICHAILOWITSCH (1915–   ). Soviet author, dramatist, and journalist.

During World War II Simonov served as a front-line correspondent and became, along with Ilya Ehrenburg (*q.v.*), one of Soviet Russia's most popular journalists. His dispatches glorified the courage of Red soldiers in the battles at the Volga in 1942. These reports were later incorporated into a book that achieved great popularity. His Stalingrad novel, *Days and Nights* (1943–1944) won a state prize (1946) and was made the subject of a film (1947). Simonov also became known during the war as a dramatist with such successes as *A Fellow From Our City* (1941) and *Russian People* (1942). His war reporting, like that of Ehrenburg, was by American standards highly subjective.

Bibliography. Simonov's works were published in Russian in 6 volumes (1966–1970).

SIMPSON, WILLIAM HOOD (1888–   ). U.S. Army officer.

In October 1941 Simpson was named Commanding General of the 35th Infantry Division. In September 1942 he was named to head the 12th Army Corps and in October 1943 commander of the 4th Army. In May 1944 he arrived in England to head the U.S. 8th Army, whose name was changed to 9th

Army to avoid confusion with the famous British 8th Army (*q.v.*). Under his leadership the 9th Army cleaned up Brittany after the Normandy invasion (*q.v.*), took 20,000 fully equipped German troops as prisoners, and captured the port of Brest on September 20, 1944.

Simpson led the 9th Army against Hitler's West Wall (*q.v.*). He pushed through the Aachen region, the Cologne plain, and the industrial Ruhr and Saar valleys. Simpson's men reached the vicinity of Berlin, only to be halted by the Allied Supreme Command at the Elbe. (*See* GERMANY, BATTLE OF.)

Simpson was considered a genius in military organization. Sharp featured, lean and completely bald, he was called "a Texas cowboy who got into the Army and never got out." Noted for his smartness of dress, he looked as if he had just stepped off the West Point parade grounds. German combat troops respected him as one of their most dangerous opponents.

SINCLAIR, MICHAEL. British Lieutenant killed while attempting to escape from the German prisoner-of-war fortress at Colditz (*q.v.*) in 1944. Known to the Germans as the Red Fox and the Great Escaper, Sinclair became a legendary figure of the war.

As a prisoner of war Sinclair regarded it as his first duty to return to his own forces. His first escape from a camp in northeastern Germany led him through Poland, Slovakia, Hungary, and Yugoslavia, only to be caught at the Bulgarian frontier. He was then transferred to Colditz (*q.v.*), which Germans regarded as virtually escape-proof, but he vanished for a short time while on the way and was again taken into custody. His third attempt from a Leipzig hospital ended when he was arrested in Cologne. He made a fourth effort in South Germany. Three additional attempts to escape were unsuccessful.

In October 1943 Sinclair, disguised as "Franz Josef," made his seventh escape attempt. Guards shot at him at a distance of three feet, but a bullet glanced off his ribs. He escaped with his life but was captured again. His eighth effort took place at Colditz on January 1944, and he got as far as the Dutch border before recapture. By the summer of 1944 the Third Reich was on the verge of collapse and escape from Colditz became almost meaningless. All Sinclair had to do was to await liberation by the onrushing Allied armies. But by this time the necessity for escape had become a compulsion for the young Briton.

On September 25, 1944, Sinclair suddenly broke away from a small group walking inside the wires of the interior park, bolted across the trip-wire, and reached the main fence. With thick gloves he began to mount the barbed wire and then fell down the other side. German guards, who by this time looked with disguised amusement on the brash young Briton, shouted for him to stop. But Sinclair went on down the ravine to a 10-foot wall. The sentries opened fire. One bullet glanced off the prisoner's elbow and entered his heart.

SINGAPORE, FALL OF. Japanese conquest of the British stronghold in the Far East in mid-February 1942.

BACKGROUND. Singapore Island was a British colony of about 21 square miles at the southern end of the Malay Peninsula. It is separated from the mainland by the three-quarter-mile-wide Strait of Johore. It is linked to the mainland by a causeway consisting of a road and a railway.

Strategically, Singapore was a corner of a triangle (Manila-Hong Kong-Singapore) of Anglo-American power in the Far East. Here the British constructed what was widely regarded as the strongest naval base in the world. From Singapore they could send a powerful task force into the waters of the Pacific. They protected it by strong fixed coastal defenses with big guns that could fire seaward as well as toward the mainland. It was little understood at the time that armor-piercing shells were effective against ships but nearly useless against troops advancing through the Malayan jungle. Japanese strategists, however, were well aware of it.

Singapore's vulnerability as a naval base without adequate air cover was demonstrated as early as December 9, 1941, when Vice Adm. Tom Philipps led a task force out of Singapore under low clouds and rain. Japanese airmen promptly attacked it and sent the *Prince of Wales* and *Repulse* (*qq.v.*) to the bottom of the sea.

PREPARATIONS. Singapore was a prime target of Japanese Imperial Headquarters. Its capture was to be the final step in the assault on Malaya. (*See* MALAYA, CAMPAIGN IN.) Knowing that the city was dependent on the mainland for its supply of water, the Japanese planned to take it from the land side. For this purpose Gen. Tomoyuki Yamashita (*q.v.*) had at his disposal three divisions of crack troops. Moreover, unlike the British, he could count on native support. The people of Malaya had resented British refusal to grant them Commonwealth status, and there was no force in Malaya comparable to the Filipino scouts trained by Americans.

For the defense of Singapore, Lt. Gen. Arthur Ernest Percival (*q.v.*) had 70,000 combatant and 15,000 non-combatant troops, but all his forces were understrength.

SIEGE. The Japanese campaign in Malaya came to a head in mid-January 1942, when British troops, outwitted, outfought, and demoralized, stumbled back to Singapore, crossed the causeway, blew up the bridges, and settled down to await either help or assault from the enemy. There were no underground caverns here as at Malta (*see* MALTA, SIEGE OF), nor any man-made tunnels as at Corregidor (*see* CORREGIDOR, FALL OF), nor was there any possibility of a rescue such as that at Dunkirk (*see* DUNKIRK EVACUATION). London rushed in reinforcements just in time to share defeat with the beleaguered garrison.

By the end of January 1942 the Japanese, in a highly successful jungle campaign, had pushed their way to the end of the Malayan Peninsula. By early February they were subjecting the great naval base to dive-bomber attacks and artillery barrages. For the next several weeks they converged on the city from three directions. On the night of February 8, 1942, the Japanese 5th and 18th Divisions landed and struck in an eight-mile stretch against three battalions of the 22nd Australian Brigade. Soon there were 30,000 Japanese troops at Singapore. On February 11 Yamashita called on the garrison to surrender, but there was no reply. The British abandoned the Jurong Line and fell back into the city. The Japanese captured the reservoirs and cut off the city's water supply.

SURRENDER. The British position was now hopeless. There was a serious shortage of water, food, petrol, and ammunition. It was senseless to hold out any longer. On February 15, 1942, in a highly dramatic meeting at which Yamashita issued a humiliating ultimatum, Percival surrendered the entire garrison.

LOSSES. About 85,000 Allied troops, including British, Australians, and Indians, as well as 15,000 foreign non-combatants, were taken prisoner. The Japanese had fewer than 10,000 casualties.

SIGNIFICANCE. The fall of the great bastion at Singapore was one of the most humiliating defeats ever suffered by British arms. Churchill pronounced it "a heavy and far-reaching military defeat." A turning point in the war in the Far East, it revealed that European power was no longer secure there. The entire relationship of Asia to Europe was now transformed. For the Japanese the fall of Singapore was a mighty triumph and a highly successful start of their Greater East Asia Co-Prosperity Sphere (*q.v.*).

Bibliography. A. E. Percival, *The War in Malaya* (1949); K. M. Tsuji, *Singapore: The Japanese Version* (1960); S. W. Kirby, *Singapore: The Battle That Changed the World* (1965); and J. Syth, *Percival and the Tragedy of Singapore* (1971).

SIT-DOWN WAR. Period of inactivity on the western front in the winter of 1939–1940. (*See SITZKRIEG.*)

SITZKRIEG (**"SIT-DOWN WAR"**). Derisive term used by the British as a takeoff on the German word *Blitzkrieg* (*q.v.*) to describe the period of inactivity on the western front from September 1939 to May 1940 (also called the Phony War).

BACKGROUND. While great events were unfolding in the East, the military situation in Western Europe was quiet. It was different from World War I, when great armies of the belligerents in the West were locked in indecisive trench warfare. Now the French remained behind their defensive Maginot Line (*q.v.*), secure in the belief that no German Army could crash through it. British Prime Minister Neville Chamberlain (*q.v.*) referred to the period of inactivity as the "twilight war," while the American press called it the "Phony War."

STALEMATE. Both sides were inactive, but the world awaited a clash between the seemingly irresistible German Army and the highly regarded French military forces. Suddenly, on May 10, 1940, the Germans invaded the Netherlands, Belgium, and Luxemburg in another *Blitzkrieg,* and six days later broke through at Sedan. Outflanking the Maginot Line, they captured Paris and forced the French to sign an armistice at Compiègne (*q.v.*) on June 22, 1940. (*See* FRANCE, FIRST BATTLE OF.) The *Sitzkrieg* vanished from the vocabulary of war.

Bibliography. E. S. Turner, *The Phoney War* (1962).

SKORZENY, OTTO (1908–1975). Highly publicized German adventurer, widely known as "the most dangerous man in Europe."

At the outbreak of World War II Skorzeny served in Hitler's personal bodyguard. Later he joined the *Waffen-SS* (*q.v.*) in the French and Russian campaigns. In April 1943 he commenced work as a Colonel with the Reich Central Security Office to direct secret agents in foreign and neutral countries. He soon won public attention by a series of sensational escapades.

RESCUE OF MUSSOLINI. At the end of July 1943 Hitler gave Skorzeny the mission of rescuing fellow-dictator Mussolini from the hands of the Allies. On September 12, 1943, Skorzeny led an airborne force of commandos by glider to a dangerous landing beside a mountainside hotel on the Gran Sasso d'Italia, high in the Abruzzi Appenines. Within a few minutes he had the astonished Italian *Duce* inside a tiny plane, took off from a rocky field, and landed safely with his guest in Rome. Skorzeny won instant fame by this daring rescue.

LATER EXPLOITS. When an attempt to assassinate Hitler was made on July 20, 1944, Skorzeny gave his assistance to the officers loyal to the *Fuehrer.* (*See* JULY PLOT.) In October 1944 he kidnapped Adm. Miklos Horthy (*q.v.*), Hungarian Regent, who was about to surrender his country to the advancing Russians. In December 1944 he was at the center of a proposed plot to kidnap Gen. Dwight D. Eisenhower (*q.v.*), but the attempt was never made. He had a leading part in *Operation Greif,* in which English-speaking Germans clad in U.S. uniforms tried to create havoc behind American lines at Ardennes in 1944. Most of his commandos were caught and shot. (*See* GRIEF.)

Arrested by U.S. troops in 1946, Skorzeny was brought before an American Military Tribunal at Dachau in 1947 and was acquitted. For a time he worked with the U.S. Army Historical Section. Arrested and imprisoned by the Germans, he escaped from a prison camp at Darmstadt in 1948. Later, as "Robert Steinbacher," he edited *Die Spinne* (*The Spider*), which led a campaign to help former SS (*q.v.*) members escape from Germany. He settled in Spain, where he ran an export-import business. He died in Madrid on July 5, 1975.

Bibliography. C. Whiting, *Otto Skorzeny* (1972).

SKY MARKING. Technique used by the British Bomber Command by which aircraft used flares above the cloud level to indicate target areas. (*See* MASTER BOMBER TECHNIQUE; and AIR RAIDS.)

SLAPPING INCIDENT. Assault by Gen. George Smith Patton, Jr., on a GI (*q.v.*) he believed to be malingering in a hospital in Sicily in August 1943. (*See* PATTON, GEORGE SMITH, JR.)

SLAVE LABOR. *See* FORCED LABOR.

SLIM, WILLIAM JOSEPH (1891-1970). British Army officer active in Burma.

At the start of World War II, Slim commanded an Indian brigade, and took part in the conquest of Italian East Africa in 1940. In 1941 he led the 10th Indian Division, marching his troops across Iraq into Syria. Here he assisted in the Allied campaign, which in June 1941 successfully ended the resistance of the Vichy Government. He then took part in the Anglo-Russian operations in Iran, and helped arrange the first junction of British Imperial troops with their new Russian allies.

By December 1941 Japan had entered the war and was threatening the British forces in Burma. Given command of the Burma Corps in March 1942, Slim retreated before superior Japanese forces who held control of the air. He managed to bring his men to the Indian frontier. In early 1944 the British offensive began. Although Slim won tactical victories, the Japanese did not collapse, and he had to fight his way through Burma before reaching Rangoon.

Slim led his men across the Irrawaddy and took Mandalay in late 1945. Using new tactics in guerrilla warfare, he eventually pushed the Japanese out of most of Burma. Rangoon fell on May 3, 1945. In June Slim became Supreme Allied Commander of Allied Ground Forces in Southeast Asia. The Japanese surrender cut short his plans for invasion of Malaya.

Sturdy, with a strong jaw and pleasant expression, Slim was said to have resembled an English farmer more than an outstanding general. A master of guerrilla warfare, he led his devoted troops through many miles of Japanese-infested mountain and jungle.

Bibliography. W. J. Slim, *Memoirs* (1956).

SLOVIK, EDDIE D. (1920-1945). U.S. Army private, the only American soldier since 1864 to be executed for desertion. He was born in Detroit, Michigan, on February 18, 1920, of Polish-American parentage. After attending Koscuisko and Pulaski schools, he became a dropout at the age of 15.

EARLY CAREER. Young Slovik's first police blotter entry was in 1932 after he and his friends broke into the basement of a brass foundry. He served prison terms from 1932 to 1937 for petty theft, breaking and entering, and disturbing the peace. He also was jailed from 1939 to 1942 for car stealing and violation of parole. He then seemed to settle down after marriage.

WORLD WAR II. Because of his criminal record Slovik was classified at first by the military as 4-F, unfit for service. On November 7, 1943, he was notified that his classification had been changed to 1-A and he was sent to Fort Sheridan, Illinois. On August 14, 1944, he landed in Scotland and after two days of instruction in hedgerow fighting, he was sent as a replacement to Omaha Beach, Normandy. (*See* NORMANDY INVASION.)

Slovik froze when he was first exposed to fire. He described it in a confession (with his own spelling):

They were shelling the town and we were told to dig in for the night. The following morning they were shelling us again. I was so scared nervos and trembling that at the time the other replacements moved out I couldn't move. I stayed in my foxhole till it was quite and I was able to move. I then walked to town.

Not seeing any of our troops so I stayed over night in a French hospital. The next morning I turned myself over to the Canadian Provost Corp. After being with them for six weeks I was turned over to an American MP. They turned me lose. I told my commanding officer my story and I said that if I had to go out their again I'd run away. He said their was nothing he could do for me if I ran away again. AND I'LL RUN AWAY AGAIN IF I HAVE TO GO OUT THEIR.

(Signed) Pvt. Eddie D. Slovik
ASN 36896415

It was a difficult time for the U.S. Army. The war was supposed to be almost over, but the Germans were fighting on. On November 11, 1944, Private Slovik was tried by court-martial, convicted of desertion under fire, and sentenced to death. Gen. Dwight D. Eisenhower (*q.v.*) confirmed the verdict despite Slovik's plea for mercy. The 25-year-old draftee was shot by a firing squad on January 31, 1945.

PERSONALITY AND CHARACTER. Five-feet-six-inches tall, weighing 138 pounds, with clear-blue eyes, sandy hair, and grotesquely bowed legs, Slovik was shy and introverted. Weak, frightened, and overcome by a sense of inferiority, he was poor combat material. He vowed that he would never fire his rifle, and he never did.

ATTITUDES. The execution of Private Slovik touched off an awkward debate. Critics point out that, of the more than ten million men inducted in the armed forces, only 2,864 were tried by court-martial for "bugging out missing" (went AWOL—absent without leave or deserted before the enemy in combat). Of these, only 49 were sentenced to death, and of the 49 only Private Slovik was executed. To critics this was unfair. Slovik himself went to his death convinced that he was being killed "only because I use to steal when I was a kid."

Defenders of the execution, such as Slovik's commanding officer, Gen. Norman D. Cote, held that the incident was unfortunate but that no military force could tolerate desertion. Slovik's death had to take place as a deterrent to others. In addition, it was said, the soldier who shirked combat placed an unfair burden on others.

President Roosevelt, remembering the unhappy experience of Abraham Lincoln, who was faced with decisions on executions in the Civil War, steered clear of the Slovik case. It was the responsibility, he said, of the theater commander.

AFTERMATH. In June 1977 Slovik's widow Antoinette, 63, epileptic, arthritic, and indigent, petitioned the army for payment of a $10,000 insurance policy on the life of her husband—in 1977, worth $70,000 including interest—and for Pvt. Slovik's reburial in a place of honor in a French cemetery. She contended that her husband had been singled out as an example to deserting troops and picked as a scapegoat. An Army Board for the correction of Military Records found that there was no reason to overturn the conviction. On August 12, 1977, Army Secretary Clifford L. Alexander formally rejected the appeal. On September 7, 1979, Mrs. Slovik died in a Detroit hospital less than a week before the U.S. Senate Judiciary Committee was to vote on a bill granting her Pvt. Slovik's GI insurance of $10,000 and $60,000 interest.

Bibliography. The case became famous in a dramatic and sympathetic book, W. B. Huie, *The Execution of Pvt. Slovik* (1947).

SMALL ARMS WEAPONS. The gigantic armory of World War II included small arms, the basic tools of the infantry used in every combat theater in tremendous quantities.

BACKGROUND. Every belligerent country went to great expense in reassessing firepower for its combat infantry and such special mission units as commandos and paratroopers. Efforts were made to improve automatic and semi-automatic shoulder weapons, to increase the cyclic rates of standard machine guns, and to introduce such new weapons as bazookas (*q.v.*) and rocket launchers. Many of the new small arms weapons had increased firepower but reduced accuracy.

BRITISH. The British stayed with the standard bolt-action rifle even though its rate of fire was moderate. The most widely used British gun of the war was the Lee Enfield rifle, the early design of which dated from the 1890s. It was refined again and again until it became the fastest operating bolt-action gun in use. Weighing 9 pounds, it fired two 5-round clips in just under a minute at a range of from 200 to 2,000 yards. An improved version, the Mark III, was fired from a box-type magazine jutting through the bottom of the stock just forward of the trigger guard.

The Lee Enfield retained its popularity among British troops, despite increasing use of automatic and semi-automatic weapons. They liked its superior locking system and the fact that the gun was easy to maintain in the field.

The best-known and most widely used British machine gun was the .303-caliber Vickers, based on the American Maxim. Belt-fed and liquid-cooled, it was usually mounted on a tripod. Weighing just under 10 pounds, it could fire at the rate of 500 rounds per minute with a range of 600 yards. Used as a standard infantry and aircraft weapon, it was so successful that its design was copied by ordnance experts of other countries.

GERMAN. Germans, too, stayed with the standard bolt-action rifle. The Walther pistol, considered to be the finest automatic hand gun of the war, was the only standard pistol with a double-action hammer. Called the P-38 by the Germans, it weighed 34 ounces, was 8.4 inches in length, and fired eight rounds from a handle clip. It was accurate up to 75 yards. So great was its reputation among Allied troops that it became one of the most sought-after souvenirs of the war.

The first light machine gun used by the Germans was the dual-purpose MG34, a blowback-operated automatic gun for searching fire. It was replaced by the 7.92 mm. MG-42 during the opening actions by the *Afrika Korps (q.v.)* in the North African campaign. Weighing 25 pounds with biped, it fired 900-1,200 round per minute at a maximum range of 4,000 yards. The MG-42 was fired like a rifle, with its barrel braced on a tripod mount. Mass produced, they were used on aircraft as well as on the ground.

RUSSIAN. The Russians preferred submachine guns, even though they were accurate only at short range. Submachine guns were often issued to infantrymen instead of the standard infantry rifle.

Most effective of Russian antitank weapons was the light 14.5-mm. Simonov. When fully assembled it was about seven feet long from shoulder stock to muzzle brake. It was usually worked by two men, one operating the rifle and the other handing him armor-piercing high explosive shells. Using bolt-action, it fired one round that could punch through 1.2 inches of armor plate at a distance of 500 yards. It was in every respect a crude weapon but was often effective against German armor.

AMERICAN. American small arms weapons were distinguished by their variety and effectiveness. Among his varied weapons the American infantryman preferred fast-firing, semi-automatic rifles.

The standard U.S. infantry weapon was the M-1, the Garand semi-automatic rifle. Weighing 9.5 pounds, the .30-caliber Garand differed from most bolt-action guns in that as soon as a shot was fired the hammer automatically cocked, the spent shell was ejected, and another instantly positioned for firing. Each shot required a separate squeeze of the trigger. A special feature of the Garand was that it could be converted to a grenade launcher.

The Thompson submachine gun, which had won its reputation as the "Chicago piano" used by gangsters in Prohibition days, was adapted for use on European as well as Asiatic fronts. Weighing just under 10 pounds, the .45-caliber Thompson was blowback-operated and fed its bullets from 50-round drum-type or 20-round box-type magazines. Its range was from 300 to 600 yards. Although it was expensive to produce and difficult to maintain in the field, it was often preferred by American troops to the lighter and more simple machine guns.

Equally popular among American troops was the BAR, the Browning automatic rifle. Weighing 17 pounds, the .30-caliber BAR fired 40 to 60 rounds per minute from a 20-round magazine at a range varying from 600 to 3,500 yards. Gas operated, it could be set to fire single rounds semi-automatically. Known for its versatility, it could be fired from the hip, from a prone position, or from a tripod mount. American troops were encouraged to mix BARs with other rifles to give their units more firepower.

The M-2, the Browning heavy machine gun, was designed for great range, accuracy, and shattering bullet impact. Weighing 81 pounds, the M-2 fired 400-500 rounds per minute at a maximum range of 7,200 yards. It used 100-round belts and its barrel was air-cooled. The M-2 could also be used as a light antiaircraft weapon. More than 2 million of these devastating weapons were produced during the war and used on all fronts.

The U.S. 2.36-inch antitank rocket launcher, a simple device of metal tubing open at both ends gave American infantry a hard-hitting weapon against the tank. (*See* BAZOOKA.)

Bibliography. J. Kirk and R. Young, Jr., *Great Weapons of World War II* (1961).

SMITH, WALTER BEDELL (1895–1961).

SMITH, WALTER BEDELL (1895–1961). U.S. Army officer and holder of one of the key staff positions in the joint United States-United Kingdom war effort.

During World War II Smith was involved in all major Allied operations in the European theater of war. After the United States entered the war, he was appointed U.S. Secretary of the Combined Chiefs of Staff (Anglo-American) in Washington, with additional duties as First Secretary of the Joint Board. After he came to the attention of Gens. George C. Marshall and Dwight D. Eisenhower (*qq.v.*), Smith was sent to England in September 1942 as Eisenhower's Chief of Staff. Later he served as Chief of Staff of the Allied Forces in North Africa and the Mediterranean theater.

In January 1944, when Eisenhower was chosen to command the Allied forces for the invasion of the European continent (*see* NORMANDY INVASION), Smith was made Chief of Staff at the Supreme Headquarters Allied Expeditionary Forces (SHAEF) (*q.v.*). In this post he was largely responsible for the cooperation of British, French, and U.S. units that made possible the success of the combined forces. On behalf of Eisenhower, he signed the Italian surrender document on September 1943, and on May 7, 1945, he headed the Allied group that accepted the unconditional surrender of Germany at Reims (*q.v.*).

Serious and hard working, Smith won widespread approval for his ability as a soldier. Eisenhower described him as ''the general manager of the war, a godsend, a master of detail with a clear comprehension of main issues.'' Churchill called him ''Bulldog'' because of his tenacity in handling problems. To his men Smith was known as ''Beetle,'' a designation he liked so much that he engraved his personal stationery with a small blue beetle.

Bibliography. Smith wrote *My Three Years in Moscow* (1950); and *Eisenhower's Six Great Decisions, 1944–1945* (1956).

SMOLENSK ATTENTAT. German code or cover name *Flash*. Unsuccessful attempt to assassinate Hitler in 1943 by German officers who placed a bomb aboard his aircraft.

PREPARATION. A number of officers took part in the plot, including Maj. Gen. Henning von Tresckow, Chief of Staff in the Central Army Group on the Eastern Front; First Lt. Fabian von Schlabrendorff, who worked with Tresckow; and Col. Freiherr von Gersdorff, who supplied the explosives. When in March 1943 Hitler announced his intention of visiting the Smolensk area, the conspirators decided to act. They would not shoot Hitler, but would eliminate him during the flight by smuggling a delayed-action bomb into his plane. The idea was to give the appearance of an air accident.

To make doubly sure the conspirators took not one but two explosives. They made one parcel, which by its shape seemed to contain two ordinary bottles.

ACTION. After lunch at Smolensk on March 13, 1943, Hitler returned by car to his plane. Von Schlabrendorff took the time bomb in another car to the airfield. He waited until Hitler had dismissed several officers, and when he saw the *Fuehrer* board the plane, he started the fuse. The bomb was timed to explode within half an hour. Von Schlabrendorff handed the parcel to a Col. Brandt, an officer of Hitler's staff, who had promised to take it to Supreme Headquarters. Brandt stepped into Hitler's plane, which took off in the direction of East Prussia.

MISFIRE. The explosion was expected shortly before Hitler's plane would reach Minsk in White Russia. After two hours of waiting, the conspirators received the news that Hitler had arrived safely in Rastenburg, his headquarters on the eastern front. The shaken plotters telephoned Col. Brandt, who was on the scene, and asked him whether the parcel had been delivered. Brandt replied that it was still in his keeping. He was told that there had been a mistake and to hold the parcel for a day. The next day von Schlabrendorff flew to headquarters, called on Brandt, and exchanged a parcel containing this time two genuine bottles of brandy.

Opening the packet on a sleeper train to Berlin, von Schlabrendorff dismantled the bomb and took out the detonator. The fuse had worked; the glass tube had broken; the corrosive liquid had consumed the retainer wire; the striker had operated; but the detonator cap had not reacted. Hitler never learned how close he had been to death. (*See also* JULY PLOT.)

Bibliography. C. FitzGibbon, *Officers' Plot to Kill Hitler* (1956).

SNOWFLAKE. Powerful illuminant rocket flare used as an important countermeasure by the Allies in defense against U-Boat attacks.

At first star-shells were used, but these were superseded by the far more efficient *Snowflake,* which could turn darkness into daylight. (*See* ATLANTIC, BATTLE OF THE; and WOLF-PACK TACTICS.)

SOCIAL IMPACT OF THE WAR. The deadliest conflict in history swept aside traditions rooted in the 19th century and brought about important changes in social relationships inside the belligerent countries as well as in world society.

BACKGROUND. Twentieth-century patterns of social change began after World War I. Defeat of four empires and Woodrow Wilson's vision of a democratic and peaceful world were supposed to result in the development of institutions more responsive to the people. However, the socio-economic status of the masses was not improved substantially after 1918. The old ruling elites, despite their professed regard for democracy, still managed to retain a privileged position in society.

In the so-called Long Armistice between wars from 1919 to 1939 the new democratic tendency was countered by rising dictatorships. Calling for territorial enhancement, aggressive dictators turned to war. The formation of a Grand Alliance and a long Second World War were necessary to halt the surge of Fascist aggression.

SOCIAL IMPLICATIONS. The six years of World War II not only claimed an appalling loss in lives and property, but they also transformed the nature of world society. Every important social development of the 20th century was accelerated by the conflict. The dictators were unable to win their objectives on the battlefields of the world, but the war they promoted resulted in profound economic, political, and social revolutions that made permanent changes in world society. The values of the 19th century, especially those of the Victorian era, were replaced by new social norms. In the major belligerent countries the war sparked a new social revolution by which personal horizons were expanded and new values appeared, in part a result of the movement of peoples. The collapse of colonial empires, followed by the emergence of underdeveloped nations, led to new social relationships. Seeds of social revolution were planted in Africa, India, Indonesia, and Indochina as the old colonial empires of Britain, France, Belgium, and the Netherlands disappeared.

MORAL HAVOC. Although World War II came to be known as the "last moral war," because of the necessity for smashing Nazism and Fascist aggression, the conflict revealed a thoroughly shattering collapse in morals. The concept that all is fair in war was carried to an extreme. The breakdown in morality began with Hitler's Nazi ideas that envisioned an ideological war as well as an international civil war. Nazis who blindly followed their *Fuehrer* believed themselves to be entrusted with a mission that was to be implemented by the armed forces. Nazi "law and order" were to be imposed on all Europeans who came under Hitler's jurisdiction. When the conquered peoples turned to resistance, the German Army applied its own system of hostages, which punished innocent people because no effort was made to ascertain who was guilty. (*See* HOSTAGE SYSTEM.) German occupation also resulted in a split into two camps—collaborators and resisters, with an accompanying decline in morality.

Not the least important evidence of moral rot during the war was the contempt shown by both sides for the civilian population. Hitler ordered indiscriminate bombing from the air of urban populations in an attempt to smash enemy morale. The bombing of Warsaw, Rotterdam, and London revealed contempt for ordinary laws of humanity. Later, angered Allies struck back a hundredfold, systematically destroying the main cities of Germany, Italy, and Japan. There were no aesthetic policies on either side: Germans destroyed parts of the magnificent Italian city of Florence, and Americans obliterated the monastery at Monte Cassino. The destruction of Hamburg and Dresden and the atomic bombs dropped on Hiroshima and Nagasaki (*qq.v.*) brought the moral issue to a peak. A distressed world society began to have a glimpse of what could take place in an uncertain future.

PERVERSION OF SCIENCE. An important social consequence of the war was the perversion of science in the desire for victory. Here, again, Hitler's Nazism paved the way. Scientists in every belligerent country put themselves entirely at the service of the state in the all-out effort to win the war. (*See* SCIENCE IN THE WAR.) In the United States, distinguished atomic scientists, many of them victims of Nazism, worked energetically to win the race to make an atomic bomb. (*See* MANHATTAN PROJECT.) Afterward, many of these scientists were appalled by what they had done and suffered pangs of conscience. This did not happen in the Third Reich: Nazi chemists produced Zyklon-B gas for use in concentration camps; Nazi "doctors" performed sadistic experiments on concentration camp victims—all apparently without any emotional distress.

SOCIAL CHAOS. The war had a deleterious effect for some years on world society. Henri Michel, the French historian, expressed it well:

The violence unleashed by the war took more overt forms in its usual aftermath: a wave of immorality, a mad urge to live after so many restrictions and alarms, the break-up of families after too long a separation of husband and wife, excessive profits made by black marketeers or collaborators, over-rapid promotion to adult responsibilities of insufficiently mature young people, exacerbated nationalism and ideological conflict, a thirst for money and pleasure, a heavy legacy. (Henri Michel, *The Second World War,* trans. by Douglas Parmee (1975), vol. 2, p. 825.)

REVOLT OF THE MASSES. At the close of World War II, due in part to the revulsion against Hitler and Mussolini, there was a political swing to the left in Western Europe. (*See* POLITICAL CONSEQUENCES OF THE WAR.) This trend had its counterpart in a kind of revolt of the masses. European recovery, stimulated by the American Marshall Plan (1948–1952), acted to the advantage of the working class. Workers shared in the new European prosperity and gained social advantages.

In Britain, a comprehensive system of social security, embodied in the Beveridge Report, was initiated in the midst of the war. (*See* BEVERIDGE, WILLIAM HENRY.) There was a general leveling effect in British society. The trend became European-wide after the war. Living standards rose dramatically. The highways of Europe, once restricted to the wealthy, became jammed with Volkswagens, Fiats, Volvos, and Fords, driven by common people. This improvement in economic means and social status took place at a time when European influence was declining in the rest of the world. The new prosperity brought with it a shift in working populations, as workers from the less-developed countries flocked to Germany, Holland, and Switzerland.

ROLE OF WOMEN. In World War I women demonstrated that they could perform virtually all civilian tasks as efficiently as men. This process carried over into World War II with even greater impact. To release men for combat, women in all belligerent countries worked on assembly lines in factories and shipyards. Millions served in the armed forces in non-combat roles.

The wartime status of women was illustrated by their role in American production. Before the United States entered the war, only 25 percent of the nation's work force was composed of women. For the first time in their lives millions of women were attracted to work. Rosie the Riveter (*q. v.*) became an honored name in American war production. The revelation that women could perform as well or better than men in factories and the professions resulted in a new social status for women in society. The notion that women were economically dependent on males and had to stay at home began to disappear as a social norm. The new freedom of women survived the war years and led to an ever-increasing demand for women's liberation.

BLACK REVOLUTION. One of the most sweeping changes brought on by the war was associated closely with the new mobility. In the United States racial groups once ghettoized in the big cities came into contact with Americans from the rural areas, with resulting changes in social patterns. The performance of blacks both in combat and on the home front led to changing attitudes toward ethnic minorities. Color was unimportant in combat. Many black veterans who returned from the war were in no mood to accept the old status of subservience. Voting restrictions were wiped out as blacks began to enter the mainstream of American life.

DISPLACED PERSONS. Shifting fortunes of war resulted in the movement or disapperance of millions of people. Contributory factors were : (1) forced or voluntary transfer of populations from one place to another; (2) flight of refugees from the war fronts; (3) exodus from bombed cities to the countryside; (4) escape of prisoners of war; and (5) search by the displaced for new homes. *(See* DISPLACED PERSONS.)

As they conquered one country after another, Germans rounded up able-bodied men and women and hauled them back to Germany to toil in the factories to produce weapons of war. Only by use of this pool of labor could Hitler continue the war. *(See* FORCED LABOR.)

The process of displacement continued in the immediate postwar years, as governments tried to make their ethnic boundaries coincide with new national boundaries. Millions of Germans were expelled from their ancestral homes in eastern Germany and the Sudetenland. The Kremlin ordered Germans out of territory annexed from Germany and Finland, and forced Poles out of their homes. Rumania was purged of a large German minority in Transylvania; Yugoslavia expelled its Germans and Italians; Bulgaria got rid of its Turks. At the Potsdam Conference *(q.v.)*, with the reluctant approval of the West, some 6,500,000 Germans were thrown out of Poland, Czechoslovakia, and Hungary.

These population changes, often accomplished with barbarous cruelty and disregard for human rights, formed the most intensive migration movement since the barbarian invasions at the dawn of modern times.

PRISONERS OF WAR. In the new mobile warfare, prisoners of war were taken by both sides on a gigantic scale. In the seesaw battles in North Africa, both Axis and Allied forces took prisoners in the tens of thousands. *(See* NORTH AFRICA, CAMPAIGNS IN.) How to care for captured troops became a major task for both sides. *(See* PRISONERS OF WAR.) The problem of returning prisoners became a thorny one. More than 500,000 Estonians, Latvians, Lithuanians, and Ukrainians, brought to Germany as prisoners of war or forced laborers, preferred a future in Germany to a return to Soviet rule.

CONCENTRATION CAMPS. The conscience of the world was aroused by news reports concerning concentration and extermination camps in Germany.

Concentration camps had been set up early in the Nazi regime. Their social implications followed logically from Hitler's racial ideology grounded in violence, power, coercion, and inhumanity. The system was intensified under the impact of war conditions. Wherever German arms were triumphant, the *SS* (*q.v.*) set up concentration camps for enemies of the Third Reich—primarily Jews, Communists, Gypsies, captured resisters, and pacifists. Millions of Europeans, most of them bewildered innocents—men, women, and children—disappeared in the gas ovens of Nazi Germany. (*See* CONCENTRATION CAMPS; EXTERMINATION CAMPS; and FINAL SOLUTION.)

ATROCITIES. The war produced horrifying evidence of the savagery latent in human beings. On June 10, 1942, the Germans systematically destroyed the Czech village of Lidice (*q.v.*). On June 10, 1944, they smashed the French village of Oradour-sur-Glans (*q.v.*) in a tragic error. On December 11, 1944, Germans killed 101 American prisoners. (*See* MALMÉDY MASSACRE.) By no means were the Germans alone in this kind of atrocity. It is probable that the Russians killed more than 4,000 Polish officers in the early days of the war. (*See* KATYN MASSACRE.) There were also instances in which Allied troops, including Americans, lost control of themselves and used barbaric methods in dealing with captured enemy soldiers.

WAR CRIMES. After the war Allied investigators were ordered to verify wartime crimes revealed by military reports and newspaper stories. Out of the probes came a depressing story of human degradation. For the first time in history war leaders of defeated countries were brought before International Military Tribunals in mass trials for atrocities and war crimes. (*See* NUREMBERG TRIALS; and JAPANESE WAR CRIMINALS' TRIAL.)

Bibliography. G. Frumkin, *Population Changes in Europe Since 1939* (1951); N. Levin, *Holocaust* (1968); E. Davidson, *The Trial of the Germans* (1968); A. D. Morse, *While Six Million Died* (1968); D. Collins, *P.O.W.* (1970); G. Moir (ed.) *Beyond Hatred* (1970); R. A. Divine (ed.) *Causes and Consequences of World War II* (1970); G. Reitlinger, *The Final Solution* (1971); R. Hilberg (ed.), *Documents of Destruction* (1971); R. A. Falk, K. Kolke, and H. J. Lifton (eds.), *Crimes of War* (1971); and C. W. Gregory, *Women in War Work* (1971).

SOE. British unit concerned with subversion and sabotage in German-occupied countries. (*See* SPECIAL OPERATIONS EXECUTIVE.)

SOFT UNDERBELLY. Strategy advocated by Winston Churchill (*q.v.*) during both World Wars. Germany, to be defeated, would be attacked through the "soft underbelly" from the south of Europe.

BACKGROUND. In both world wars Churchill was known for what was described as "eccentric" military ideas. His plans misfired in World War I in the bloody Gallipoli campaign of 1915–1916. The Allied forces sent through the "soft underbelly" had to be withdrawn eventually because of poor coordination, confused leadership, and opposition from non-British Allied commanders who believed that the outcome of the war could be decided only on the western front.

WORLD WAR II. The pattern was repeated in World War II. Although an inspired leader, Churchill again advocated and promoted "eccentric" enterprises, such as operations to open the Mediterranean, to secure Suez and Gibraltar, to take outposts in Norway and Africa, and to weaken the enemy through contrived attrition. Americans regarded these ideas as "periphery pecking" and opposed most of them.

From the start of the war Churchill and his strategists sought to divert the Allied battlefield away from an all-out cross-Channel invasion to a limited land offensive in the Mediterranean theater. The "soft underbelly" technique resulted in a near catastrophe in the attempt to defend Greece against the oncoming Germans. (*See* GREECE, BATTLE FOR.)

In subsequent operations, including campaigns in North Africa, Anglo-American landings in North Africa, invasion of Sicily, and beachheads at Salerno and Anzio (*qq.v.*), the British continued to put pressure on their American allies to keep the war as far as possible from France and the British homeland.

SIGNIFICANCE. The British eventually compromised with the Russian demand for a Second Front (*q.v.*) and the American insistence on a direct cross-Channel invasion. The soft-underbelly technique was pursued in conjunction with the Normandy invasion (*q.v.*). The strategy in southern Europe was eventually successful, but it was bought at considerable cost. The Allies had to fight a bloody campaign up the Italian Peninsula through rugged territory from Salerno to Anzio to Rome to Milan. (*See* ITALIAN FRONT, CAMPAIGNS ON.)

Historian Samuel Eliot Morison later described it: "The underbelly proved to be boned with the Apennines, played with the hard scales of Kesselring's armor, and shadowed by the wings of the *Luftwaffe.*"

Bibliography. T. Higgins, *Soft Underbelly* (1968).

SOMERVELL, BREHON BURKE (1892–1955). U.S. Army officer who directed American supply services during World War II.

At the beginning of the war Somervell was assigned to the office of the Quartermaster General in Washington, D.C. In March 1942 as a Lieutenant General, he was made head of the new Services of Supply, which later became the Army Service Forces. He was responsible for the supply of all major army services, including ordnance, engineering, medical, signal, and chemical warfare services. He worked closely with industry to produce the necessary supplies and to transport them to the war fronts. He was promoted to full General in May 1948, the first engineering officer in American history to achieve that rank.

Slim, gray, urbane, Somervell was an energetic officer in a critical post. He was known for his zeal in wearing out officers and civilians in a 17-hour work day. The tremendous success of the Normandy invasion (*q.v.*) was due in part to his driving personality.

SOMERVILLE, JAMES FOWNES (1882-1949). British naval officer noted for distinguished service in both world wars.

As soon as the war began, Churchill recalled Somerville and named him Commander-in-Chief of Royal Navy Force H operating out of Gibraltar. Somerville helped save the men at Dunkirk. (*See* DUNKIRK EVACUATION.) In July 1940 he helped immobilize the French fleet at Oran. (*See* ORAN NAVAL ENCOUNTER.) Early in February 1941 he commanded the battle cruiser *Renown* in a task force that swept through Italian waters to bomb Genoa. In May 1941 he participated in the destruction of the *Bismarck*. (*See* BISMARCK, SINKING OF THE.) In October 1941 he was knighted for "gallantry, determination, and resource" in escorting a convoy through Mediterranean waters.

In July 1942 Somerville was named Commander-in-Chief of the British Eastern Fleet, which was supposed to be based in Ceylon but which had to withdraw to East Africa because of Japanese naval superiority. In 1943 he took part in the capture of Madagascar from Vichy-French forces. From 1944 to 1945 he headed the British delegation to Washington to discuss the war in the Far East. He also served on the combined Chiefs of Staffs Committee under Gen. George C. Marshall (*q.v.*).

Square-jawed, with a firm mouth and determined eyes, Somerville was the picture of the naval hero. He was noted for his vigor and drive and for his outspoken nature. Nicknamed "Slim" Somerville, he was one of the old British naval salts in the Nelson tradition. Churchill described him as "an officer with an almost unrivalled experience of the conditions of modern war." Others regarded him as one of the best authorities on naval seamanship.

SONAR. Device used to detect submerged objects. (*See also* ASDIC.)

The term *sonar* is an acronym derived from *so*und *na*vigation *r*anging. Of pre-war origin it included all kinds of underwater devices for listening to echoes and locating obstacles. Throughout the war the Allies used sonar to detect German and Japanese submarines. Similar to radar (*See* RADAR, WARTIME), sonar was improved considerably during the course of the war by advances in the field of electronics.

In the summer of 1942, when shipping losses to U-Boats were becoming dangerous, the U.S. Navy Department introduced more effective training of sonar operators. Console sonars were developed to detect minefields and calculate U-Boat depths, as well as to indicate the presence of oncoming torpedoes. Together with refinements in the use of radar, these steps did much to extend the average of sinkings of enemy submarines.

SONGS OF WAR. Popular songs, folk songs, and ditties designed to maintain morale in combat areas and home fronts of all the belligerents.

BACKGROUND. Previous wars had brought with them classic war songs many of which lived long beyond their time. The legacy of the U.S. Civil War included such songs as "Battle Hymn of the Republic," "Tramp! Tramp! Tramp!" and "Dixie." There were many popular songs during World War I, including "It's a Long Way to Tipperary," "Keep the Home Fires Burning," "K-K-K-Katy," and "Over There."

WORLD WAR II. World War II was not a singing war. Although thousands of songs were written during the conflict, relatively few gained popularity. Axis successes during the early years of the war, as well as disgust with Hitler and Nazism, did not encourage much cheerfulness in Allied countries. The two outstanding hits of the war, the German "Lili Marlene" (*q.v.*) and the Australian "Waltzing Matilda," (*q.v.*), turned out to be songs-by-adoption in that they enjoyed wide popularity in other countries.

BRITISH. British lyricists and composers produced hundreds of war songs, but not one to compare with "Pack Up Your Troubles in Your Old Kit Bag," popular during World War I. Such entertainers as Gracie Fields and Vera Lynn relied on their own repertoires, some of them of World War I vintage. In the winter of 1940 appeared "We're Gonna Hang Out the Washing on the Siegfried Line," a song designed to ridicule the Germans during the boring days of the Sit-down War. (*See SIEGFRIED LINE, WE'RE GONNA HANG OUT THE WASHING ON THE;* and *SITZKRIEG.*)

GERMAN. Inspired by Nazi showmanship, Germans went to war fortified with songs of all kinds—traditional, marching, patriotic, humorous, and hymnal. The *Liederbuch* ("Song Book") became a standard part of troop equipment. Some preferred the old songs, including "Deutschland über Alles" (Germany Before All); "I Had a Comrade"; "No More Beautiful Death in the World"; or "My Regiment, My Fatherland." Others liked the sentimental "Do You Remember the Beautiful May Days?" or the humorous "Musketeers are Lusty Brothers." Fervent Nazis chose the "Horst Wessel Lied," the official Nazi song, or such marching songs as "Awake, German Fatherland" and "Tomorrow We March."

RUSSIAN. Red troops, noted for military choirs and deep bass voices, sang their way to victory with old Russian classics. Millions sang "Meadowland," which had been a favorite during the Russian Revolution, paying tribute to green meadows and fields in blossom and to the heroes of the great Red Army. Equally as popular were the stirring lyrics of "Moscow," which was written during the war. (*See MOSCOW.*)

AMERICAN. Composers and lyricists in New York's Tin Pan Alley worked overtime but produced little to compare with Irving Berlin's tunes of World War I. The mood of Americans was far from bouncy. The attitude of "Let's Get It Over With" left little room for happy songs. In the closing days of 1941 appeared "There'll be Bluebirds Over the White Cliffs of Dover," generally shortened to the last five words, a sentimental tribute to the British defiance of Nazi bombing. The song helped sell war bonds but had little rhythmic appeal for marching.

The most popular American song of 1942 was Frank Loesser's "Praise the Lord and Pass the Ammunition," based on a phrase supposedly uttered by a militant chaplain in the heat of battle. There were many attempts at patriotic songs, including, "There's a Star-Spangled Banner Waving Somewhere," "Johnny Doughboy Found a Rose in Ireland," and "He Wears a Pair of Silver Wings," but they had little appeal. Men in uniform preferred such non-belligerent songs as "Beer-Barrel Polka" and "Deep in the Heart of Texas." For marching songs they stayed with the old favorites such as "I've Been Working on the Railroad" and the British "I've Got Six Pence." Late in the war came the poignant ballad, "Roger Young," by Frank Loesser, which was not in any real sense a war song.

Bibliography. S. Spaeth, *A History of Popular Music in America* (1948); and W. W. Whitman (ed.), *Songs That Changed the World* (1969).

SORGE, RICHARD (1898–1944). German journalist, one of the master spies of World War II.

When World War II began, Sorge, using his contacts in Tokyo, served as a double agent. While presumably acting in the interests of Berlin, he worked for Moscow as a trusted agent. From Tokyo he sent the Russians a stream of information about German intentions. Four months before Hitler invaded the Soviet Union on June 22, 1941, Sorge informed Moscow of the exact date of *Operation Barbarossa* (*q.v.*). But Stalin, who had heard similar warnings from the Americans and British, refused to believe any of them.

On October 16, 1941, six weeks before Pearl Harbor, about which Sorge had also informed his superiors in Moscow, he was arrested in Tokyo along with a Japanese assistant. It was rumored that he was hanged in Tokyo on November 7, 1944, but no evidence has been produced about his execution. (*See also* ESPIONAGE.)

Sorge's name is surrounded by the mystique of the double agent. The Tokyo circles in which he moved regarded him as an eccentric. Tall and gaunt, generally clad in unkempt clothing, he was an alcoholic who lived in a slum district but was often seen in better surroundings. Possibly his odd behavior and drinking habits were designed deliberately to hide his activities as a double agent.

Bibliography. C. A. Willoughby, *A Partial Documentation of the Sorge Espionage Case* (1950); H. O. Meissner, *The Man with Three Faces* (1955); C. A. Johnson, *An Instance of Treason*

(1964); F. W. Deakin, *The Case of Richard Sorge* (1966); and R. de Toledano, *Spies, Dupes, and Diplomats* (1967).

SPAAK, PAUL-HENRI (1899-1972). Belgian statesman.

After the capitulation of the Belgian Army in May 1940, Spaak served as Foreign Minister of the Belgian Government-in-exile (*q.v.*) operating from London. In September 1944 he laid the foundations for Benelux, the postwar economic union between Belgium, the Netherlands, and Luxembourg.

Spaak was again Premier from 1947 to 1949, but resigned because of his opposition to the return of King Leopold III (*q.v.*). He acquired international stature as first President of the General Assembly of the United Nations. He was Secretary-General of NATO from 1957-1961. His principal goal was the political and economic unification of Western Europe.

Bibliography. P.-H. Spaak, *The Continuing Battle: Memoirs of a European, 1936-1966* (1972). See also J. H. Huizinga, *Mr. Europe* (1961).

SPAATZ, CARL ANDREW (1891-1974). U.S. Air Forces General and leading combat commander of the war.

At the start of the war Spaatz held the rank of Brigadier General. In 1941 he was appointed Chief of Air Staff, second in command to Maj. Gen. Henry H. Arnold (*q.v.*). After Pearl Harbor he was named commander of the U.S. 8th Air Force, which began bombing raids on Germany. Spaatz played a major role in the air offensive on German-occupied Europe. In 1943 he commanded the Northwest African Air Force in the Tunisian, Sicilian, and Italian campaigns. (*See* NORTH AFRICA, CAMPAIGNS IN; SICILY, INVASION OF; and ITALIAN FRONT, CAMPAIGNS ON THE.)

In January 1944 Spaatz was placed in command of the U.S. Strategic Air Forces in Europe, and in this capacity planned and executed the massive air raids on Germany. He was promoted to full General in 1945 and assigned to head the Strategic Air Forces against Japan. He was in command during the atomic attacks on Hiroshima and Nagasaki (*qq.v.*).

Sandy-haired, hard working, and vigorous, Spaatz was known as one of the most experienced officers in the U.S. Air Forces. His speed and skill in organization were legendary.

SPAM. U.S. Army food consisting of a meat compound.

Cooked in field kitchens or by the troops themselves, Spam was recalled with distaste by millions of GIs (*q.v.*). In a famous war cartoon, Sgt. George Baker showed his clumsy Sad Sack (*q.v.*) receiving this ration slammed on his plate by army cooks. Refusing another helping, Sad Sack went back disconsolately to his tent, where he delightedly found an overseas package from home. When he opened it, he discovered to his dismay that it contained two cans of Spam. (*See also* RATIONS, U.S. ARMY.)

SPARS. A unit of the U.S. Coast Guard composed of women. The purpose was to release men for combat duty at sea. (*See also* WACS; WAVES; and WOMEN MARINES.)

The term *Spars* was derived from *Semper Paratus,* "Always Ready." At its wartime peak, the unit consisted of 10,000 enlisted women and 1,000 officers (November 1944). It was demobilized in 1946.

SPECIAL AIR SERVICE (SAS). Secret Allied organization centered in London to promote sabotage missions of commandos behind enemy lines.

The SAS began its work as early as the spring of 1940. In July 1941 it sent out a brigade under the leadership of Lt. A. D. Stirling to operate in Egypt. Units were trained to pounce simultaneously on several targets behind enemy lines, smashing fuel dumps and destroying trains, vehicles, aircraft, and communications. Many of its tactics were derived from the activities of Lawrence of Arabia of World War I fame. Among its units was the desert group that worked behind the lines of Gen. Erwin Rommel and his *Afrika Korps* (*qq.v.*).

Later in the war the SAS was organized at regimental strength to take part in major engagements. It also worked in conjunction with foreign sabotage units, which it trained in its own methods. (*See also* BATTALION OF HEAVEN; and LONG RANGE DESERT GROUP.)

SPECIAL OPERATIONS EXECUTIVE (SOE). Secret unit set up by the British in 1940 to organize subversion and sabotage in German-occupied countries.

SOE agents worked with the underground (*q.v.*) in Poland, France, Belgium, Holland, and Norway to encourage resistance against the Germans. (*See* RESISTANCE MOVEMENTS.) Some were professional operators, others were adventurers who simply hated the Germans. They were careful to avoid striking at the main forces of the German occupation, and concentrated instead on weak defense points at the surface and edges. They were assisted by skillful propaganda broadcasts from the British Broadcasting Corporation (BBC). The recognition signal was the Morse code "V-for-Victory."

Bibliography. M.R.D. Foot, *SOE in France* (1968).

SPEER, ALBERT (1905–1981). Hitler's favorite architect and German Minister of Armaments during the war.

On February 8, 1942 Speer succeeded Fritz Todt (*q.v.*) as Minister of Armaments and War Production. He was also made director of the *Organisation Todt* (*See* ATLANTIC WALL), the semi-military organization responsible for construction of military installations and highways. For a time he was one of the most important leaders of the Third Reich and its war economy. His production miracles under heavy enemy bombing undoubtedly prolonged the war.

Speer showed some interest in the conspiracy to get rid of Hitler, but he never joined the 1944 attempt on the *Fuehrer's* life. (*See* JULY PLOT.) In the final weeks of the war he ignored Hitler's orders to leave chaos and destruction.

NUREMBERG. Brought before the International Military Tribunal (*see* NUREMBERG TRIALS), Speer admitted responsibility openly. "This trial is necessary," he said. "There is a common responsibility for such horrible crimes in an authoritarian system." Because of his participation in the slave-labor program (*see* FORCED LABOR), he was found guilty on count 3, war crimes, and count 4, crimes against humanity. He was sentenced to 20 years. He served his full term and was released in 1966.

Speer was the complete technocrat. Totally absorbed in his work, he was indifferent at first to the horrors it made possible. Later he was overwhelmed by realization of the extent of common German responsibility for the crimes of Hitler. He died in August 1981 at the age of 76.

Bibliography. Speer wrote two best sellers: *Inside the Third Reich* (1970), which historian Golo Mann described as "one of the foremost political memoirs of all time," and *Spandau* (1976).

SPEIDEL, HANS (1897–   ). German General charged with participation in the plot against Hitler.

Speidel served in France in the early stage of the war and later held a high post on the General Staff. In April 1944 he was summoned by Gen. Erwin Rommel (*q.v.*), an old comrade and fellow Württemberger, to serve as Chief of Staff for Army Group B. In this post he came into close contact with the anti-Hitler conspiracy, although he took no active part in it. In May 1944 he did what he could to obtain an armistice but with no results. When the Allies pushed on to Paris after the invasion of France (*see* NORMANDY INVASION), Speidel received orders from Hitler to destroy the city, but he paid no attention to the distraught *Fuehrer.*

After the failure of the 1944 July Plot (*q.v.*) on Hitler's life, Speidel was removed from his post and interrogated by the *Gestapo* (*q.v.*). He admitted nothing and did not betray comrades he knew were in the conspiracy. He was acquitted before a court of honor, although an infuriated Hitler believed him to be guilty.

Bibliography. H. Speidel, *Invasion 1944* (1949). *See also* J. W. Wheeler-Bennett, *The Nemesis of Power* (1953).

SPERRLE, HUGO (1885–1953). German Air Force officer.

In 1936 Sperrle commanded the Condor Legion in the Spanish civil war, in which he ordered his bombers to attack Spanish towns, including Guernica.

At the start of World War II, Sperrle commanded a *Luftflotte* ("Air Force") at Munich. His aircraft took part in the *Blitzkrieg* (*q.v.*) on France. (*See* FRANCE, FIRST BATTLE OF.) On July 19, 1940, as a result of his work in the victory over France, Sperrle, along with Erhard Milch (*q.v.*) was created a General Field Marshal of the *Luftwaffe.* Sperrle advised Hitler that the Royal

Air Force (*q.v.*) had to be destroyed before England could be invaded. He was detailed to Paris in 1944. The Allied Military Court in Nuremburg freed him on November 22, 1948. He died just before Easter 1953 and was buried in Munich on April 7, 1953.

A man of gigantic build, Sperrle was known for his energy and zeal. Although aware of the conspiracy against Hitler, he remained loyal to the *Fuehrer* and placed a close watch on the officers who were sympathetic to the plot.

Bibliography. See A. Price, *Luftwaffe* (1969).

SPERRY BOMBSIGHT. American precision device used for bombing during the war.

Named for its inventor, Elmer A. Sperry, the bombsight was introduced by the U.S. Army Air Corps in 1933. It was used by American pilots until the fall of 1943, when the Army decided not to purchase any more but to use those already produced. Results from high altitudes were disappointing. (*See also* NORDEN BOMBSIGHT.)

SPIES, WORLD WAR II. *See* ESPIONAGE.

SPITFIRE. British fighting plane. A single-engined, low-wing monoplane, it was the most famous fighter plane of World War II.

DESIGN. The prototype of the Vickers *Supermarine Spitfire* was an early racing plane, the *S-6B,* designed by Reginald Mitchell. In 1931 this plane won the Schneider Trophy for Britain with a speed of 406.9 miles per hour. The *Spitfire Mark I* was introduced immediately after the outbreak of the war in 1939 and quickly demonstrated its speed, climb, and maneuverability. In the evacuation of Dunkirk (*q.v.*) from May 26 to June 4, 1940, it provided the air umbrella that enabled the rescue of several hundred thousand troops.

WORLD WAR II. The *Spitfire* was used in every theater of operations in Europe and was produced in greater quantities than any other British aircraft (a total of 20,334 until 1947). During the war it underwent 40 major modifications from Mark I through Mark XXII, each change adding to its reputation as the best single-engined fighting plane. By the end of the war it was equipped with Rolls-Royce Merlin and Griffon engines that increased speed from 375 to 448 miles per hour. This late model was able to shoot down Hitler's *V-1s* (*q.v.*) as well as the first *Me-262* jet.

BATTLE OF BRITAIN. The performance of the *Spitfire,* added to that of the *Hurricane* (*q.v.*), was of decisive importance in the summer of 1940. (*See* BRITAIN, BATTLE OF.) Only by winning air control could Hitler hope to invade Britain across the English Channel. The ensuing duel between the German *Me-109*s and the British planes was won by the British. British pilots had the advantage of fighting on their home ground and, unlike their opponents, were unfettered by a range handicap.

When in August 1940 *Luftwaffe* chief Hermann Goering (*qq.v.*) asked Adolf Galland (*q.v.*), one of his leading aces, what he needed for victory, the pilot replied: "*Spitfires,* Herr Reichsmarschall, *Spitfires!*" For the British, pilots and public alike, the *Spitfire* was "our guardian angel." (For specifications *see* AIRCRAFT: BRITISH AIRCRAFT DATA CHART.)

SPITZBERGEN RAID. Successful German assault on a strategic Norwegian island in 1943.

TARGET. About 400 miles north of the Norwegian mainland, Spitzbergen housed a garrison that was holding out against Germans and provided the Allies with precious information and assistance on the convoy route to the Russian port of Murmansk (*q.v.*). Hitler regarded it as a prime goal to remove this thorn from his flank.

ASSAULT. At dawn on September 8, 1943, the *Tirpitz* (*q.v.*), Germany's mightiest warship since the loss of the *Bismarck* in May 1941 (*see* BISMARCK, SINKING OF THE), appeared out of the mist off Spitzbergen. Escorted by a powerful squadron of support ships, including the smaller battleship *Scharnhorst* (*q.v.*) and ten destroyers, the 43,000-ton *Tirpitz* trained her big guns on a wireless station behind the village of Barentsburg. A salvo of shells sped toward the target. Taken by surprise, the 150-man Norwegian garrison raced to the bunkers as buildings and fuel dumps exploded in searing flashes. The Norwegians used their small coastal guns to damage one of the attacking destroyers and killed or wounded assault troops ready to go ashore. Meanwhile, another destroyer pushed to the wharves and landed commandos.

RESULTS. German troops systematically destroyed everything of value on the island, including fuel dumps, a power plant, waterworks, supply depots, coal mines, and a weather station. The raiders had few losses. With mission accomplished, the *Tirpitz* led the convoy of battleships away from the fjord and within a day was back at her anchorage in German-occupied Norway.

SPRUANCE, RAYMOND AMES (1886-1969). U.S. naval officer and one of the outstanding commanders of aircraft carriers in the war.

After the Japanese bombed Pearl Harbor (*q.v.*) on December 7, 1941, Spruance was appointed commander of a cruiser division in the Pacific. In June 1942 he led one of the two carrier groups that inflicted the first decisive defeat on the Japanese Navy by an American naval task force. It was generally regarded as the turning point in the Pacific war. (*See* MIDWAY, BATTLE OF.) In 1943-1944 he commanded the Central Pacific Force, later known as the Fifth Fleet, in the invasion of the Gilbert and Marshall Islands.

In the Battle of the Philippine Sea (*q.v.*) in late June 1944, Spruance's planes scored important victories at extreme ranges against the Japanese fleet. In November 1945 he succeeded Adm. Chester A. Nimitz (*q.v.*) as Commander-in-Chief of the Pacific Fleet.

Naval historian Adm. Samuel Eliot Morison summarized Spruance's personality and character: "Power of decision and coolness in action were perhaps Spruance's leading characteristics. He envied no one, rivaled no man, won the respect of almost everyone with whom he came into contact and went ahead in his quiet way winning victories for his country."

Bibliography. E. P. Forrestel, *Admiral Raymond Spruance, USN: A Study in Command* (1966).

SS (*SCHUTZSTAFFEL*). Literally "defense echelon" or protection detachments—the elite guards of the Nazi Party.

ORIGINS. The *Schutzstaffel* was originally the black-shirted personal bodyguard of Hitler, but later it was transformed into a mass army responsible for the maintenance of the Nazi regime. The symbol *SS* was always presented not in Roman or Gothic letters but by two lightning flashes in imitation of ancient Gothic characters. Known as the Black Order, it was led for most of its existence by Heinrich Himmler (*q.v.*).

DEVELOPMENT. In the Blood Purge of 1934 Hitler eliminated Capt. Ernst Roehm's brown-shirted Storm Troopers, the *SA*. The *SS* then emerged as the most powerful limb (*Gliederung*) of the Nazi Party. Its purpose was to destroy all open and secret enemies of the *Fuehrer* and lead the fight for "our racial resurrection." In 1929 the *SS* numbered only 290 members; in 1939 it had grown into a corps of 240,000.

WORLD WAR II. The *SS* continued its existence throughout the war. With Hitler's agreement, Himmler formed an *SS* economic empire which controlled vast business and manufacturing enterprises. The *SS* was assigned to administer concentration and extermination camps (*qq.v.*). In May 1943 it played a major role in suppressing the Warsaw ghetto uprising, in which thousands of Jews were killed. The *Waffen-SS* (*q.v.*), special military branch of the *SS*, won a reputation for fanaticism in combat.

Bibliography. G. Reitlinger, *The SS—Alibi of a Nation* (1956); R. Grunberger, *Hitler's SS* (1970); and J. Keegan, *Waffen-SS: The Asphalt Soldiers* (1970).

STALAG. German term used to describe a prisoner-of-war detention camp. The acronym was derived from *Stammlager* (*Stamm*, "stem, trunk") and *Lager* ("camp").

Prisoners of war (*q.v.*) of many nationalities were held in these camps. After the war a stage play and film titled *Stalag 17* described conditions in a German detention camp.

Bibliography. See D. Bevan, *Stalag 17* (1951).

STALIN, JOSEPH VISSARIONOVICH (1879–1953). Russian dictator. Stalin was born in Gori, Georgia, on December 21, 1879, the son of a cobbler. His real name was Dzhugashvili, but he took the name of Stalin (''man of steel''). He was educated in a seminary at Tiflis, but was expelled in 1898 because of revolutionary views.

EARLY CAREER. Twice exiled to Siberia for revolutionary activities, Stalin escaped each time. He took an active role in the Bolshevik Revolution of 1917, and became Commissar for Nationalities in Lenin's new government. In 1923 he became Secretary of the Communist Party. After Lenin's death, Stalin emerged from a struggle with Leon Trotsky as undisputed victor. As dictator, he enforced his views by pitiless purging of opponents, including veteran Bolshevik comrades.

WORLD WAR II. When Germany attacked Soviet Russia on June 22, 1941, Stalin remained in the Kremlin to direct the war effort as Supreme Commander-in-Chief of the Soviet Armed Forces. Taking the rank of Marshal (1943) and later Generalissimo (1945), he interfered in the work of his leading military commanders. There is little doubt that much of the success of the Russian war effort was due to Stalin's leadership. He directed his attention to every phase of Russian participation in the war. He inspired a spirit of nationalism in his people by depicting the image of an endangered Motherland. He was able to obtain strong support from Britain and the United States during critical moments. He engendered a spirit of ruthlessness in battle which eventually brought Russian troops success against the Germans.

Stalin was well aware of the dependency of the West upon his opposition to Hitler. An astute diplomat, he used extraordinary cunning in his meetings with Roosevelt and Churchill at Teheran (1943) and Yalta (1943) and with Truman and Attlee at Potsdam (1945). He managed to win considerable advantages for the Soviet Union at comparatively little cost.

POSTWAR. After the war Stalin sought to retain as rigid a grip on the new Communist states as he had on the Russian political machine. He failed only in the case of Yugoslavia, where Marshal Tito (*q.v.*) successfully defied him. Stalin brought Russia out of the war as a vastly stronger and more influential country than he had ruled earlier. His last years were characterized by chauvinism, xenophobia, and anti-Semitism. He died in Moscow on March 5, 1953.

PERSONALITY AND CHARACTER. Five-feet-six-inches tall, weighing about 190 pounds, Stalin was built close to the ground, like a football tackle. With his crew cut, large nose, and prominent mustache, he was an austere and rugged figure in boots, stout baggy trousers, and snug-fitting blouse. He had huge hands and a harsh voice.

Historians agree in classifying Stalin, along with Hitler, as one of the cruelest rulers in history. A self-confident egoist, he believed himself to be an indispensable man destined by fate to consolidate socialism in Soviet Russia. He allowed nothing to stand in his way. He killed all opponents as well as those he mistrusted. No underling knew when the lightning would strike next in this milieu of Stalin terror. Millions of uncomprehending *kulaks,* Russian farmers, and old Bolshevik comrades innocent of disloyalty felt the weight of the tyrant's hand.

In 1956 Nikita S. Khrushchev delivered an unprecedented condemnation of Stalin in a "secret" report on "The Personality Cult and Its Consequences" to the 20th All-Union Party Congress. The excoriation came from inside Russia, not from the capitalist West. Stalin's body was removed to a less prominent place in the Kremlin.

Bibliography. Stalin wrote among other works *The Great Patriotic War of the Soviet Union* (1946). *See* the biographies by B. Souverine (1939); L. Trotsky (1946); B. D. Wolfe (1936); and I. Deutscher (1949). *See also* M. Djilas, *Conversations with Stalin* (1962); S. Bialer, *Stalin and His Generals* (1969); H. M. Hyde, *Stalin: The History of a Dictator* (1972); A.J.P. Taylor, *The War Lords* (1978); and W. O. McCagg, Jr., *Stalin Embattled, 1943-1948* (1978).

STALIN LINE. Russian defensive line that ran from the Gulf of Finland in the north through Lake Peipus along the frontiers of Latvia, Poland, and Rumania all the way down to Odessa and the Black Sea.

The Stalin Line, based roughly on the French Maginot Line (*q.v.*), combined a series of concrete works, tank traps, mine fields, and natural obstacles. By no means a continuous line (it utilized forests and lakes), it was thinly fortified, but at strategic points such as Minsk it was strengthened more than 50 miles. Germans were able to pierce it, but were never successful in maintaining their forces beyond it. (*See* EASTERN FRONT, CAMPAIGNS ON THE.)

STALIN ORGAN (*STALIN ORGEL*). German nickname for a Russian rocket launcher.

STALIN TANK (JS TANK, or *JOSEPH STALIN TANK) See* TANKS.

STALINGRAD, BATTLE OF. Defeat of the Germans in one of the major turning points of the war.

BACKGROUND. The struggle on the Russian front reached a roaring crescendo in the summer of 1942. After the Red troops evacuated Rostov, Hitler divided his forces into two parts. He sent one to the Caucasus to drive to the Baku oil fields. He ordered the second in the direction of Stalingrad and the Volga.

TARGET. The industrial city of Stalingrad stretched for 30 miles along the mile-wide Volga River. Between the city and onrushing Germans was only open steppe country broken by a few low hills. For Hitler, Stalingrad, with its great armament and tractor plants, was an attractive target. If he could take it he would cut off necessary supplies from Russian armies and at the same time place his own troops in a strong strategic position. The fall of Stalingrad would isolate Moscow and Leningrad and cut off the last important oil supplies from the Caspian Sea route to the Soviet Union. It would be a heavy psychological blow from which the Russians could not recover. The *Fuehrer* could look forward to the Volga as the easternmost boundary of the Greater German Reich.

PREPARATION. To lead the assault on Stalingrad, Hitler selected Gen. Friedrich Paulus (*q.v.*) and the 6th Army, with 330,000 of his best troops. There would be powerful *Panzer* and *Luftwaffe* (*qq.v.*) support. There had been severe setbacks for Germans at Moscow, Leningrad, and Voronezh, but the situation was still encouraging. Hitler had conquered a third of Russia's chemical industries as well as sources of its electrical power. So certain was he of taking Stalingrad that he moved his headquarters from East Prussia to a spot near Vinnitsa in the Ukraine. (*See FUEHRER'S* HEADQUARTERS.) He ordered that the city be taken by August 25, 1942.

Meanwhile, Russians braced for the attack. Orders came from Stalin in Moscow to hold the city at all costs.

FIRST PHASE. During July and August 1942 the German 6th Army advanced rapidly toward Stalingrad. The opening artillery bombardment by the Germans, starting on August 19, 1942, was one of the heaviest in history. Within three days a German spearhead penetrated into the northern suburb and reached the west bank of the Volga. The *Luftwaffe* then staged a devastating air attack on the night of August 23–24, using high explosives and incendiaries to destroy thousands of wooden homes dry from the summer heat. One raid of 600 planes killed 40,000 civilians and started huge fires.

DEFENSE. The Russian 62nd Army was pushed back into Stalingrad. As in other German attacks there were some desertions, but the majority of Russians refused to capitulate. A state of siege was declared. The Russian response was one of the most extraordinary stands in modern history. Russians bound grenades to their bodies and threw themselves under Nazi tanks. Others, armed with machine guns, bayonets, or knives, crawled through the streets and fell on the Germans. There was fighting in sewers, factories, and behind the walls of blasted buildings. Ironically, the Germans destroyed so much that the streets were impassable and they could not get their tanks through. There was hand-to-hand fighting not only for every building but also for every room. The Germans would clean out an entire block only to relinquish it a few hours later.

ENTRAPMENT. From Paulus came desperate pleas to Hitler to reinforce his battered 6th Army or allow him to withdraw a few hundred miles. Otherwise, he would have to face the cruel Russian winter. Hitler replied acidly: "Stay and fight! I am not leaving the Volga!"

On November 19, 1942, Russians launched a counterattack in two spearheads from points north and south of the German salient. They relied heavily on cold steel, a terrifying weapon to the machine-minded Germans. Caught in the Stalingrad pocket in one of the worst weather areas on earth were most of the 20 German and 2 Rumanian divisions. Under Russian pressure this great force was steadily compressed into a smaller and smaller area. With supply lines cut and ammunition dwindling, Germans had to eat horses, cats, and dogs.

Further appeals to Hitler were fruitless. The *Fuehrer* praised his 6th Army at "Fortress Stalingrad." All to no avail. The *Luftwaffe* was nowhere in sight. In mid-December Field Marshal Friedrich Erich von Lewinsky von Manstein (*q.v.*) led Army Group Don from the south in Operation *Winter Storm* to relieve Paulus. He fell short of his objective as the Russians struck back. By mid-January 1943 the Stalingrad pocket was reduced to an area about 15 miles long and 9 miles deep.

CAPITULATION. The great 6th Army, victorious in Holland and Belgium in 1940, was cut to pieces. In late January the last 12,000 ragged, hungry, and frostbitten Germans streamed out of cellars and caves. Paulus and his staff surrendered in the basement of a department store to a 27-year-old Russian lieutenant. More than 94,000 men, including 24 generals, surrendered with him.

LOSSES. The Battle of Stalingrad ended in the encirclement of what remained of a great German Army of 300,000 men. The Russians found 146,700 dead Germans in the city and buried them. An additional 100,000 Germans died outside the city. The Axis also lost one Italian, one Hungarian, and two Rumanian armies. Russian losses, although never announced, were heavy.

SIGNIFICANCE. It was a humiliating defeat for Hitler and the Third Reich. He had not wanted a second Verdun, but in many ways Stalingrad had the same elemental fury. The Germans had smashed through a wall of Russian steel, only to be shattered and thrust back. It was, said British historian J. W. Wheeler-Bennett, perhaps the most monumental isolated example in all military history of a deliberate and wasteful sacrifice of human life. From now on Hitler was on the defensive in eastern Europe. He denounced the Russians as "swamp animals" who refused to fight according to "normal" principles of war. He ordered four days of mourning for his lost legions.

For the Allies the successful Russian defense of Stalingrad was of major importance. In 1943 a sword of honor with a blade of hard-tempered steel was presented to the city with the inscription: "To the steel-hearted citizens of Stalingrad, the gift of King George VI, in token of the homage of the British people."

Bibliography. A. Werth, *The Year of Stalingrad* (1946); T. Plievier, *Stalingrad* (a novel) (1947); G. Jukes, *Stalingrad: The Turning Point* (1968); E. Ziemke, *Stalingrad to Berlin: The German Defeat in the East* (1968); and W. Craig, *Enemy at the Gates: The Battle of Stalingrad* (1973).

STARS AND STRIPES. Daily newspaper for the U.S. armed forces in all theaters of war.

Editions of the paper appeared in London, Paris, Nice, and elsewhere. The German edition was published late in the war at an auxiliary plant of the *Frankfurter Zeitung* at Pfungsstadt, Hesse.

No official control was exercised over the contents of the soldiers' newspaper. High military officials regarded it as an important morale builder for the ordinary GI (*q.v.*). In the inaugural issue, dated April 18, 1942, Gen. George C. Marshall (*q.v.*), Chief of Staff of the U.S. Army, was quoted in an interview: "A soldiers' newspaper, in these grave times, is more than a morale venture. It is a symbol of the thing we are fighting to preserve and spread in this threatened world. It represents the free thought and free expression of a free people."

The *Stars and Stripes* literally covered the globe. Its correspondents went directly to the battlefields, because its main interest was combat and combat troops. It also covered the home front because the men who were assigned overseas were interested in what went on back home. Its eight-page edition had sections devoted to war news, illustrations and maps, sporting news, pin-up girls, and the popular letters to the editor department, "Mail Call." A page of cartoons included *Li'l Abner, Terry and the Pirates, Gasoline Alley, Dick Tracy, Blondie*, and *Joe Palooka*. GIs were fascinated by Bill Mauldin's (*q.v.*) immortal *Willie and Joe*, the perennial GIs, and the drawings of Dave Breger and George Baker. (*See* MAULDIN, WILLIAM H.)

Among the top combat correspondents for *Stars and Stripes* were Irwin Shaw, Robert Meyer, Jr., Ernie Pyle (*q.v.*), Herbert Mitgang, Bill Jogan, Jack Foisie, Klaus Mann, and Bill Brinkley. Most of the writing in this professional soldier newspaper was of high caliber.

Bibliography. R. Meyer, Jr., *The Stars and Stripes Story of World War II* (1960).

STATE DEFENSE COMMITTEE (*Gosudarstvenny Komitet Oborony—GOKO, or GKO*). Supreme authority in the Soviet Union during World War II.

The State Defense Committee exercised unlimited power in every aspect of the war in combat areas and on the home front. Its chairman was Joseph Stalin with Vyacheslav Molotov as vice-chairman, and members including Kliment Voroshilov, Lavrenti Beria (*qq.v.*), and Georgi Malenkov. Other less prominent names were added later.

STAUFFENBERG, CLAUS SCHENK GRAF VON (1907–1944). Central figure among the conspirators of the July Plot (*q.v.*) on Hitler's life.

Born in Greifenstein Castle, Upper Franconia, on September 15, 1907, to a family that had served the royal houses of Württemberg and Bavaria, Claus von Stauffenberg was a strikingly handsome young man who was called the Bamberger Reuter because of his resemblance to the famous thirteenth-century statue in the cathedral of Bamberg. In the early part of World War II he served with distinction as an officer in the Bavarian cavalry regiment in Poland, France, and North Africa. In April 1943 he was wounded in the face, in both hands, and in the knee by fire from a low-flying plane.

Von Stauffenberg was obsessed by his utter contempt for Hitler and Nazism, calling Hitler the "Antichrist" and "Master of Vermin." He became closely connected with the Kreisau Circle (*q.v.*) in the conspiracy against Hitler. By the end of 1943 he was the true leader of the German Resistance. He prepared and executed the assassination attempt of July 20, 1944 without any thought of his own safety. The bomb he planted, however, did not end the *Fuehrer's* life, but merely shocked and blackened him. Von Stauffenberg paid with his life for the unsuccessful attentat.

Bibliography. K. Finker, *Stauffenberg und der 20 Juli 1944* (1967); and J. Kramark, *Stauffenberg: The Architect of the July 20th Conspiracy* (1967).

STEPHENSON, WILLIAM SAMUEL (1896–   ). Britain's super-spy, the man called Intrepid, who directed major Allied intelligence.

Shortly after the start of the war, Stephenson identified Norsk Hydro in Norway as the source of heavy water for German atomic experiments. In 1940 he came to the United States to discuss cooperation between the U.S. Federal Bureau of Investigation (FBI) and the British Security Coordination (BSC) (*q.v.*). Working closely with Gen. William J. Donovan of the Office of Strategic Services (OSS) (*qq.v.*), he was responsible for a number of intelligence coups. The two scored one of the most important intelligence victories of the war when they succeeded in delaying the Nazi invasion of Soviet Russia in 1941. In February 1942 Stephenson obtained details of the Heydrich conference on the "Final Solution of the Jewish Question." (*See* FINAL SOLUTION.)

With large forehead and strong chin, Stephenson was taciturn and soft-spoken. A shrewd and resourceful intelligence agent, he held no military rank and wore no uniform after 1918.

Bibliography. For a detailed account, *see* W. Stevenson, *A Man Called Intrepid* (1976).

STETTINIUS, EDWARD REILLY, JR. (1900–1949). U.S. industrialist and statesman who served as Secretary of State in the late days of the war.

From 1926 to 1934 Stettinius held several positions with General Motors Corporation, and in 1938 became Chairman of the Board of U.S. Steel. He resigned in 1940 to become a member of the National Defense Advisory Commission. Directly before and after the United States entered the war, he was appointed Lend-Lease (*q.v.*) administrator. From 1943 to 1944 he served as

Under Secretary of State and in December 1944 he succeeded Cordell Hull as Secretary of State. In this post he took part in the numerous international conferences. (*See* CONFERENCES, ALLIED WAR.)

Bibliography. E. R. Stettinius, Jr., *Lend-Lease: Weapons for Victory* (1944); *Roosevelt and the Russians* (1949); and *Diaries, 1943-46* (1975). For a biography, *see* R. L. Walker, *Edward R. Stettinius, Jr.* (1965).

STILWELL, JOSEPH WARREN (1883-1946). U.S. Army officer and commander of American forces in the China-Burma-India theater during World War II.

Soon after the Japanese attack on Pearl Harbor (*q.v.*), Stilwell was ordered to China on a special mission. On March 10, 1942, he was appointed Chief of Staff under Chiang Kai-shek (*q.v.*), and was placed in charge of the Chinese 5th and 6th Armies. In this position Stilwell inspected the Burma front. On March 20, 1942, he was given command of all American forces in India, Burma, and China. In April 1942 he directed the operations that freed the encircled Chinese garrison at Toungoo, India, on the road to Mandalay.

The Battle for Burma was finally lost by the Allies who got, in Stilwell's words, "a hell of a beating." (*See* BURMA, CAMPAIGNS IN.) On May 23, 1942, Stilwell arrived in New Delhi, India, after having retreated 140 miles through dense jungles. In 1943 he was named deputy commander of the Anglo-American Southeast Asia Command. The next year he returned to defeat the Japanese in Burma. Promoted to full General in August 1944, he was recalled to Washington after irreconcilable differences with Chiang Kai-shek.

In January 1945 Stilwell was named commander of the U.S. Army ground forces. On the defeat of Japan, he accepted the surrender of 100,000 Japanese troops in the Ryuku Islands.

Stilwell was known throughout the Pacific area as "Vinegar Joe" because of his acidulous opinions. "The United States means business," he said. "We won't be satisfied until we see American and Chinese troops in Tokyo together."

Bibliography. Stilwell's notes and wartimes diaries, not meant to be published, appeared in 1948 as the controversial *Stilwell Papers*. *See also* B. Tuchman, *Stilwell and the American Experience in China, 1941-1945* (1971).

STIMSON, HENRY LEWIS (1867-1950). U.S. Secretary of War throughout World War II.

When the war began in 1939, Stimson made known his opposition to Hitler and Mussolini, supported aid for Great Britain, and called for increased military training. In 1940, at the age of 73, and although a Republican, he was named Secretary of War by Democratic President Franklin D. Roosevelt (*q.v.*). In this post he argued for repeal of the Neutrality Act.

Stimson served as Secretaty of War throughout the conflict. He supervised the mobilization and training of the U.S. armed forces and played an important role in the conduct of general war operations. He supported an invasion of Europe in 1943, but Churchill adamantly opposed it at the time as premature. Stimson was especially concerned with nuclear fission and supported the atomic bomb project. In 1945 he recommended to President Harry S Truman (*q.v.*)

Single-minded, intense, and adamant in his views, Stimson was a controversial figure. He was called revolutionary and radical on some issues, bull-headed and militaristic on others. He was described as a strange mixture of conservatism and liberalism, of pacifism and militarism, of gentility and democracy. "I have abandoned everything except a consideration of the defense of the country."

Bibliography. Stimson was the author of *American Policy in Nicaragua* (1927); *The Far Eastern Crisis* (1936); *Democracy and Nationalism in Europe* (1943); *On Active Service in Peace and War* (with M. Bundy) (1948). *See also* biographies by R. N. Current (1954) and E. E. Morrison (1960).

STOWE, LELAND (1899–   ). American war correspondent.

Stowe was working in Paris in September 1939 when Germany invaded Poland and England declared war. When his paper told him that at 40 he was too old to cover the war, he resigned and moved to the Chicago *Daily News.* Assigned to Finland, he sent back eloquent dispatches on the Russo-Finnish situation.

On April 16, 1940 Stowe sent a report from Stockholm on the fantastically easy conquest of the Germans in Norway. He exposed the Trojan-horse treason and treachery by which the Germans were able to conquer Norway with incredible dispatch. Stowe's scoop became a classic of war reporting. His story put other European nations on guard against Fifth Column (*q.v.*) activities in their own territory. His revelations on the tragically mismanaged British expedition led to a shake-up of the British Cabinet and the ultimate ousting of Neville Chamberlain (*q.v.*) as Prime Minister.

Stowe covered the rest of the war in France, Belgium, and Holland (1944) and in Italy and Greece (1945). He was a radio commentator for the American Broadcasting Company and the Mutual Broadcasting System from 1945 to 1946.

Stowe was youthful and energetic despite his shock of white hair. An admiring colleague wrote that "when Stowe can't get a plane, a car or a horse, he starts out to walk." As a reporter he was known for his conscientious attention to detail.

Bibliography. L. Stowe, *Nazi Means War* (1933); *No Other Road to Freedom* (1941); *They Shall Not Sleep* (1944); and *While Time Remains* (1946).

STREICHER, JULIUS (1885–1946). Leading Nazi politician.

Streicher was a teacher in a Nuremberg suburb. He served in World War I and was awarded the Iron Cross (1st and 2nd Classes). After the war he formed his own anti-Semitic party, but joined the Nazis in 1921. In 1923 he founded

Der Stürmer (The Stormer), Germany's most virulent anti-Semitic organ. In 1929 he was elected to the Bavarian *Landtag* and in 1931 to the *Reichstag* as a delegate from Thuringia. Active in Nazi Party politics, he initiated the annual rallies at Nuremberg.

Streicher's campaign against the Jews at the start of the war was so hysterical and his general conduct so deplorable that even Hitler reprimanded him. The *Fuehrer* put him on a speaking ban *(Redeverbot)* on the ground that he was hurting the war effort. In 1940 he was investigated for illegal business transactions, as a result of which he was dismissed from various Party posts. Unrepentant, he continued his activities.

Brought to trial before the International Military Tribunal *(See* NUREMBERG TRIALS). Streicher was accused of the murder and the extermination of Jews on political and racial grounds "in connection with war crimes and [which] constitutes a crime against humanity." A restless, difficult prisoner, he denounced his trial as "a triumph of world Jewry." He was found guilty of crimes against humanity and sentenced to death. As he mounted the scaffold on October 16, 1946, he shouted: *"Purimfest!"* in reference to the Jewish festival celebrating the defeat of Haman, the oppressor of Jews in Biblical times. His last words were *"Heil Hitler!"*

Most historians agree that Streicher was one of the most evil characters in the Nazi gallery of rogues, ruffians, and blackmailers. Short, stocky, with bald head and hard mouth, he acquired a reputation as an eccentric. Brutal and violent, he advocated force as the solution to any problem. He was variously charged with assault, battery, libel, and rape.

Bibliography. An example of Streicher's strictures against the Jews is his *Kampf dem Weltfeind* (1938).

STRIKE OX. British code or cover name for a projected sabotage operation by which Nazi Germany would be denied certain critical supplies.

BACKGROUND. On December 16, 1939, Winston Churchill, then First Lord of the Admiralty, issued a "prayer," obviously an order, requiring British Naval Intelligence to prevent vital supplies from going to the Third Reich "by methods which will be neither diplomatic nor military." *Operation Strike Ox* was named after Oxeloesund, an ice-free port in Sweden about 60 miles from Stockholm. The purpose was to prevent tons of Swedish iron ore from reaching the Ruhr steel industry. By "vital supplies" Churchill also meant heavy water, which later was to become a necessary ingredient of the atomic bomb. Only Churchill and a small circle of scientists knew about the importance of heavy water.

CANCELLATION. When Foreign Secretary Lord Halifax *(q.v.)*, who was hoping for a negotiated peace if Britain did nothing further to annoy the *Fuehrer,* heard of the proposed sabotage, he denounced it as "an unprecedented violation of international law." *Operation Strike Ox* was cancelled.

STUELPNAGEL, KARL HEINRICH VON (1886-1944). German Army officer and opponent of Hitler.

After the fall of France in 1940, von Stuelpnagel was made Chairman of the German-French Armistice Commission. He commanded the 17th Army when Soviet Russia was invaded in June 1941 and took part in the encirclement of Kiev. In February 1942 he was named Military Governor of France. In May 1944 he urged Gens. Erwin Rommel and Hans Speidel (*qq.v.*) to join him in asking the Allies for an armistice, but his goal was not achieved.

Von Stuelpnagel moved from opposition to Hitler to resistance and finally to conspiracy. He made his Paris headquarters a center of the plot to kill Hitler. He was one of the leading figures of the July 1944 attempt on Hitler's life. (*See* JULY PLOT.) On receiving the false news of the *Fuehrer's* death, he immediately arrested 1,200 key *Gestapo* (*q.v.*) agents then in Paris. He was himself arrested and ordered back to Berlin.

On July 21, 1944, von Stuelpnagel and party set out by automobile. Thirty miles from Paris the car broke down. Von Stuelpnagel said that he wanted to go for a walk. He put a bullet into his head, destroying one eye and ruining the other. He was nursed back to health in Berlin and then brought before the People's Court. Sentenced to death, he was strangled in Plötzensee Prison on August 30, 1944.

STUKA (*JUNKERS-87; JU-87*). German ground attack and dive bomber. The *Stuka* was a single-engined, low-wing monoplane with big rounded radiator below the nose and fixed landing wheels with fairings.

DESIGN. The prototype of this most famous Junker plane appeared in 1929 at a time when the Germans were not allowed by the Treaty of Versailles to build military aircraft. It had its obscure beginnings in Malmö, Sweden. It was tested under battle conditions in the Spanish civil war, during which revisions in the design were worked out. Its record in Spain was so good that production of the plane was sharply increased.

WORLD WAR II. At the beginning of the war in 1939, *Stukas* were largely responsible for the destruction of the Polish air and tank forces on the ground. In early 1940, working closely with tank units, *Stukas* shattered Belgian forts in a matter of hours and harried Dutch and French supply and communication lines. In addition, the plane was used as an adjunct to German psychological warfare. It was fitted with "screamers" attached to the landing gear to help destroy enemy morale when it attacked from the air. The unearthly sound of the diving *Stukas* struck fear into the hearts of thousands.

The *Stuka* was also used for ground attack, strafing columns, and shooting up troop concentrations. Assisted by propaganda, its reputation rose to unusual proportions. It was reputed to be invincible, a weapon to defeat entire nations.

BATTLE OF BRITAIN. Despite its fearsome reputation, the *Stuka* was vulnerable to attack when in a dive. This was demonstrated in the summer of 1940 when it met Royal Air Force fighters in combat. (*See* BRITAIN, BATTLE OF.) The *Stuka's* relatively slow speed and light armament were severe handicaps. So many were lost that the *Luftwaffe* (*q.v.*) was forced to withdraw it from combat on that front. It continued to be used effectively in the Balkans, Crete, North Africa, the Soviet Union, and the Mediterranean and North Sea convoy routes. It supported every major German *Panzer* (*q.v.*) drive in the war.

The appearance of the *Stuka* was described by a British cartoonist in this jingle:

> A crooked wing, a square-cut tail,
> Fat legs below and a bomb to trail,
> Deep-jowled before a glasshouse hump,
> The *Stuka's* an unshapely lump.

(For specifications *see* AIRCRAFT: GERMAN AIRCRAFT DATA CHART.)

SULLIVAN BROTHERS. Five American brothers who lost their lives at the same time in the sinking of a U.S. warship in late 1942.

USS JUNEAU. The American light cruiser *Juneau* was laid down at Kearny, New Jersey, on May 27, 1940, and launched on October 25, 1941. After a hurried shakedown cruise along the Atlantic in the spring of 1942, she assumed blockade control in early May off Martinique and Guadaloupe to prevent the escape of Vichy French naval units. On August 22, 1942, she left for the Pacific theater of operations.

On September 15, 1942, while serving in a task force, which had a mission to ferry fighters to Guadalcanal, the crew of the *Juneau* rescued 1,810 survivors of the aircraft carrier *Wasp,* which had been torpedoed by Japanese submarine *I-19.* The *Juneau* then took part in several actions, repulsing Japanese thrusts at Guadalcanal: the Buin-Fasi-Tonolai Raid; the Battle of Santa Cruz Island; and the Naval Battle of Guadalcanal (*q.v.*).

THE SULLIVANS. Serving aboard the *Juneau* were five brothers, the sons of Thomas F. Sullivan of Waterloo, Iowa. The brothers, all of whom had been born in Waterloo, were:*

George Thomas (29), Gunners Mate 2/c, who had served in the Navy from 1937 to 1941 and reenlisted in 1942.

Francis Henry (26), Coxswain, who also served from 1937 to 1941 and reenlisted in 1942.

Joseph Eugene (23), Seaman 2/c, who started as an Apprentice Seaman.

---

*Details of the Sullivan brothers courtesy of the U.S. Navy.

Madison Abel (22), Seaman 2/c, who enlisted as an Apprentice Seaman.

Albert Leo (20), Seaman 2/c, also enlisted as an Apprentice Seaman.

All the brothers, including the two oldest who had previous navy service, enlisted on the same day, January 3, 1942. On February 3, 1942, at their own request to serve together, all were transferred to the receiving ship, *New York,* for duty on the *Juneau.* They took part in each combat action of the cruiser.

SEA BATTLE OF GUADALCANAL. On November 8, 1942, the *Juneau* left Noumea, New Caledonia, as a unit of Task Force 67 to escort reinforcements to Guadalcanal. Early the next morning she took her station in the protective screen around transports and cargo vessels off Guadalcanal. That afternoon 30 Japanese planes attacked the U.S. group. *Juneau* alone accounted for six enemy torpedo planes shot down. On November 13, a strong Japanese force of 18 to 20 warships, including two battleships, moved on Guadalcanal.

The outnumbered American forces immediately attacked. *Juneau,* teamed with *Atlanta,* sank a Japanese destroyer as the two forces slugged it out. During the exchange *Juneau* was struck on the port side by a torpedo, causing a severe list and necessitating withdrawal. Steaming on one screw, down 12 feet at the bow, she still managed to maintain a speed of 13 knots.

SINKING OF THE JUNEAU. At this point the Japanese submarine *I-26,* which was taking part in the battle, launched three torpedoes at the damaged *Juneau.* The crew of the *Juneau* successfully evaded two torpedoes, but the third struck her at the same point where she had been damaged in the surface action. There followed a terrific explosion, as the cruiser broke into two parts and sank within 20 seconds. Capt. Swanson and most of the crew, including the five Sullivan brothers, were lost. Only ten seamen survived the tragedy.

SIGNIFICANCE. The incident was the first instance of five brothers serving and dying together under the U.S. flag. During the American Civil War, five Judge brothers in the Confederate Army were also killed in battlefield action.

AFTERMATH. The shocking news saddened the entire country. President Roosevelt wrote a personal letter to the mother of the five brothers: "I am sure that we all take pride in the knowledge that they fought side by side. As one of your sons wrote, 'We will make a team together that can't be beat.' It is this spirit which in the end must triumph." U.S. Navy regulations were quickly revised to forbid service of siblings on the same warship.

On April 4, 1943, the USS *The Sullivans,* the first and only U.S. destroyer to bear such a unique and multiple name, was launched at San Francisco and christened by the mother of the five seamen. The destroyer served in nine combat engagements, starting with the invasion of the Marshalls and ending with the operations off Okinawa (*qq.v.*)

SUPERFORTRESS (B-29). U.S. Army heavy bomber. A four-engined, low-wing monoplane, it was by far the largest major heavy bomber of the war.

DESIGN. The Boeing *Superfortress* was designed to meet U.S. Army Air Forces (*q.v.*) specifications issued in the winter of 1939–1940 for a Hemisphere Defense Weapon to replace the *Flying Fortress (B-17)* (*q.v.*) and the *B-24 Liberator.* Its design was approved quickly and it went immediately into production. The superbomber was designed to carry a huge bomb load for thousands of miles at a speed approaching 400 miles-per-hour. It was given heavy defensive armor and armament as well as self-sealing fuel tanks. Altogether more than 2,000 *Superfortresses* were delivered by the end of the war.

WORLD WAR II. The *Superfortress* was first used against the Japanese homeland in June 1944 and thereafter was used against the Japanese exclusively. From bases in the Mariana Islands they began a sustained bombing offensive against Japan. On March 9, 1945, 334 *B-29*s made a low-level attack on Tokyo with devastating results, during which 75,000 Japanese died in the fire storms. By the end of July 1945 the raids reached huge proportions with as many as 800 *B-29*s attacking by night. Tokyo was gutted and smashed in the offensive. A single *B-29,* the *Enola Gay,* dropped the first atomic bomb, and a second, *Bock's Car,* delivered the second atomic bomb on Nagasaki. (*See* HIROSHIMA; and NAGASAKI.)

(For specifications *see* AIRCRAFT, AMERICAN AIRCRAFT DATA CHART.)
Bibliography. S. Birdsall, *Superfortress: The Boeing B-29* (1980).

SUPPLIES, BATTLE FOR. Efforts of the belligerents to send food, provisions, guns, ammunition, and munitions to their men on the combat fronts.

DEPENDENCE AND INTERDEPENDENCE. As in previous wars, supplies and provisions were of major importance in determining the outcome of the conflict. Nothing could have been achieved by any of the forces—on land, sea, or air—unless there was a constant flow of supplies of all kinds. Dependence on supplies was of critical importance on all fighting fronts in both European and Pacific theaters of war.

Supplies and provisions were also of utmost importance because of close interdependence of land, sea, and air forces. Land operations often depended on merchant seamen for supplies and on airmen for defense. This interdependence existed everywhere.

ROLE OF SEA POWER. Sea power was of major importance for the survival of Britain. Blockade by sea was necessary to reduce the German lead in war production. The German response was all-out U-Boat warfare in an effort to cripple British war production. The Battle of the Atlantic (*q.v.*) was in a very real sense a battle for supplies. Another example was the struggle for control of the northern sea route to Soviet Russia via Murmansk and Archangel—made dangerous by German planes, submarines, and warships operating off the coast of Norway.

ROLE OF AIR POWER. The flow of supplies to Britain and Soviet Russia was helped by the production of giant cargo planes. New airfields were constructed in Nova Scotia, Newfoundland, and Iceland on the North Atlantic route and in North Africa for sending supplies to the Near East.

LEND-LEASE. Of major importance in the battle for supplies was the assistance provided to Britain, the British Commonwealth, Soviet Russia, and China by the American Lend-Lease (*q.v.*) program. Billions of dollars in war materials, food, and services were given to the Allies by this program.

BRITISH. After winning control of the air in the Battle of Britain (*q.v.*), the British were faced with the formidable task of supplying their fighting men in North Africa and the Mediterranean area. At the start of the war the Mediterranean was a hazardous sea for British merchantmen. Supplies for troops in North Africa had to be brought the long way around the Cape of Good Hope. Only after the British Navy and the Royal Air Force had won control of the Mediterranean was the problem of providing supplies for North Africa solved.

GERMAN. To send supplies for the desert war in North Africa and later for the Russian front, both of which were some distance away, German trains, ships, and planes had to take into account guerrillas and Partisans (*q.v.*) along the route. They also had to run the gauntlet of Allied air and sea power. Later in the war the problem was complicated by intensive Allied day-and-night bombing of German factories.

To ensure a steady flow of supplies to his scattered armies, Hitler made use of forced labor (*q.v.*) on a massive scale. His agents rounded up able-bodied men in occupied countries and sent them back to Germany to help war production. On occasion the *Fuehrer* complicated the supply problem by erratic decisions. When he sent his armies surging across Soviet borders in June 1941, he was so confident of quick victory that he failed to equip his troops with winter clothing. Nor did he take into account the fact that German trains were unable to use the narrow tracks of Russian rail beds.

RUSSIAN. On the invasion of the Soviet Union in 1941, Stalin, with an eye toward Napoleon's invasion in 1812, ordered a scorched-earth policy of destroying everything to deprive the Germans of food and war supplies. To assure supplies for his own armies Stalin had factories moved east or built anew. Huge numbers of Russians worked around the clock to assure supplies for an effective stand against the Germans. Late in the war Soviet production began to outstrip that of the weakening enemy. Standardization of weapons, including tanks and artillery, was a key factor in Russian war production.

The Russian supply situation was considerably improved by British and American aid. The British sent several thousand tanks for Russian use, the Americans many thousands of *jeeps* (*q.v.*) as well as a myriad of other supplies.

AMERICAN. As the so-called arsenal of democracy, the United States produced vast supplies of every kind, foodstuffs, fuel, and weapons, for the Allied war effort. An essential element of the coalition against the Axis was the material assistance given by the United States. On Liberty Ships (*q.v.*) and by air American supplies went to every theater of war in constantly mounting size. American convoys moved across the Atlantic on the dangerous Murmansk route to the Soviet Union and through the vast expanses of the Pacific. (*See* UNITED STATES AT WAR; and LEND-LEASE.)

JAPANESE. The speedy building of her Greater East Asia Co-Prosperity Sphere (*q.v.*), a euphemism for the new Japanese Empire, brought a major headache to Japanese war leaders. The home islands were notoriously short of raw materials. Access to the southwestern Pacific area brought with it huge supplies of rubber and tin, both of which were denied to the Allies. These raw materials were cut off from Tokyo. The Allies gradually closed in on the home islands. The attempt to supply Japanese troops in Burma by air was frustrated by Allied air power. In the last stage of the war, American bombing from the air had a devastating effect on both Japanese production and the movement of supplies.

(*See also* ECONOMIC WARFARE; RESOURCES, BATTLE FOR; and PRODUCTION, BATTLE OF.)

Bibliography. E. V. Francis, *The Battle of Supplies* (1942); U.S. Office of War Information, *Enemy Japan* (1945); U.S. Bureau of the Budget, *The United States at War* (1946); D. L. Gordon and R. Dangerfield, *The Hidden Weapon: The Story of Economic Warfare* (1947); K. S. Davis, *Experience of War* (1965); A. Hezlet, *Aircraft and Sea Power* (1970); and R. B. Baldwin, *The Deadly Fuze* (1980).

SURIBACHI MOUNT. *See* IWO JIMA, BATTLE FOR.

SURRENDER, GERMAN. *See* "UNCONDITIONAL SURRENDER"; and REIMS.

SURRENDER, JAPANESE. The formal Japanese surrender took place on Sunday, September 2, 1945, exactly 3 years, 8 months, and 25 days since the attack on Pearl Harbor (*q.v.*).

BACKGROUND. As Americans made preparations in the summer of 1945 to invade the Japanese home islands, a peace faction in the Japanese Cabinet tried to begin negotiations with the Russians to end the war. On August 6 the first atomic bomb was dropped on Hiroshima (*q.v.*). Two days later the Russians declared war on Japan. On August 9 the second atomic bomb was dropped on Nagasaki (*q.v.*). The next day Emperor Hirohito (*q.v.*) informed the Cabinet that it must accept the Allied terms. There was some hesitation, but four days later the Cabinet gave in.

SCENE. While Allied seaborne troops were moving ashore and a stream of giant transport planes poured airborne troops on Japanese airfields, the formal surrender took place aboard the U.S. battleship *Missouri* in Tokyo Bay. Only a few weeks earlier the flagship of the U.S. Pacific Fleet was blasting the mainland with her 16-inch guns, but now she was anchored peacefully within sight of Mount Fujiyama. Her bow was directed toward the heart of Japan, her great guns pointed skyward to allow room for the proceedings. From her foremast flew the same flag that had waved over the Capitol in Washington on December 7, 1941, the day of Pearl Harbor. Also flying was the historic flag of Commodore Matthew Calbraith Perry, which, with its 31 stars, had been the first American flag to appear on Japanese soil 92 years before. Surrounding the *Missouri* was a gigantic array of American and British fighting strength. Along the battleship's decks were crewmen anxious to witness the historic ceremony.

CEREMONY. Nine members of the Japanese surrender delegation, three in formal clothes and top hat, and six in uniform, were piped aboard. All their faces showed strong muscular tension and deep emotion. Led by Foreign Minister Marmoru Shigemitsu, limping on his artificial leg, they were escorted to a table on the galley deck on which were two copies of the surrender documents, one bound in gold and the other in black.

Gen. Douglas MacArthur (*q.v.*), followed by Gen. Jonathan Wainwright (*q.v.*), who had surrendered at Corregidor (*q.v.*), then faced the microphone. The issues, he said, involving divergent ideals and ideologies, had been determined on the battlefields of the world and were not to be discussed or debated further. He expressed the hope that a better world would emerge out of the blood and carnage of the past. As Supreme Commander of the Allied Powers, he said that he intended to proceed in the discharge of his responsibilities with justice and tolerance, while taking all necessary dispositions to ensure that the terms of surrender were fully, promptly, and faithfully complied with. He then invited the representatives of the Emperor of Japan and the Japanese Government and the Japanese Imperial General Headquarters to sign the instrument of surrender at the places indicated. With these words came a pointing, triumphant gesture.

Shigemitsu stepped forward, removed his silk top hat, pulled off his long yellow gloves, checked two watches, took out his pen, and signed the two copies, varying his name in Japanese and English on the two documents. Then Gen. Yoshijiro Umezu, representing the Japanese General Staff, quickly signed for the Japanese Army and all the Japanese armed forces as personal representative of Emperor Hirohito.

It was now time for Allied signatures. Gen. MacArthur requested that two of his colleagues, Gen. Wainwright (*q.v.*) and Lt. Gen. Arthur Percival (*q.v.*), the British commander at the Singapore surrender, step forward. Both had been rescued only a few days before from Japanese prisoner-of-war camps. The two generals, gaunt but smiling, moved forward and saluted. MacArthur then used five silver-plated pens to sign, handing the first two to Wainwright and Percival.

There were additional signatures by Adm. Chester W. Nimitz (*q.v.*) for the United States; Adm. Bruce Fraser (*q.v.*) for Great Britain; Lt. Gen. K. Deryevyanko for the Soviet Union; Sir Thomas Blamey (*q.v.*) for Australia; and Gen. Hsu Yung Chang for the Chinese Republic. As the signatures were being recorded, the sun suddenly broke through the clouds and bathed the scene in brilliant light. MacArthur then said, "Let us pray for peace . . . and that God will preserve it always. These proceedings are closed."

DEMONSTRATION. After the ceremony a flight of 436 *Superfortresses* flew over Tokyo in a demonstration of U.S. air power for the Japanese people. At the same time, a 42-ship convoy steamed into Tokyo Bay and by nightfall landed 13,000 troops to augment the 20,000 already there.

AFTERMATH. In Washington President Harry S Truman (*q.v.*) told the American public by radio about the unconditional surrender. He proclaimed Sunday, September 2, 1945, as V-J Day, the Victory-over-Japan day. Two days later Emperor Hirohito, after worship at *Shinto* shrines in the grounds of the Imperial Palace, instructed his people to "win the confidence of the world by obeying the nation's commitments" (he pointedly ignored the word *surrender*). He ordered all Japanese field commanders forthwith to cease hostilities, to lay down their arms. On September 5, 1945, the U.S. flag was raised over Tokyo.

SIGNIFICANCE. The devastating defeat was the first in Japanese history. The military hierarchy, as well as the people, both conditioned by centuries of myth and tradition, had believed themselves to be invincible. After the initial successes in extending its power, Japan had been struck down and was on the verge of collapse when it surrendered.

The Japanese war party had made the fundamental mistake of challenging a country whose productive capacity at the time was ten times its own. It failed to understand that Japan's strategy was obsolete in the 20th century. Weak in scientific creativity, the Japanese relied on traditional weapons and could not match such new weapons as proximity fuzes, radar, aerial mines, and ground-to-air rockets. Above all they underestimated the role of air power. At the end of the war about half the Japanese fighter planes were essentially the same *Zeros* (*q.v.*) which had been used in China years before. It was, indeed, a powerful weapon, but it was soon outmoded in the crucible of combat. Nor did the Japanese succeed in developing mass-bombing techniques necessary for the vast spaces of the Pacific. They were out-gunned, out-guessed, and out-fought.

U.S. strategy, on the other hand, was brilliantly successful. The plan of chopping off the tentacles of the Japanese octopus worked to perfection. The Japanese were not able to supply their far-flung empire, nor could they import vast supplies needed to keep their war factories humming. (*See* SUPPLIES, BATTLE FOR.) American teamwork on ground, sea, and air gradually whittled down the Japanese merchant fleet as well as the Imperial Navy. Air power made a heap of ruins of Japanese cities and destroyed Japan's industry. U.S. ground forces met and defeated the enemy on land. The Japanese broke down under the impact of this concentrated power.

Bibliography. T. Kase, *Mission to the Missouri* (1950); R. T. Butow, *Japan's Decision to Surrender* (1954); and L. Brooks, *Behind Japan's Surrender* (1966).

SUZUKI, KANTARO (1867–1948). Japanese Premier in the late days of the war.

In the early years of Japan at war, Suzuki served in an honorary and traditional capacity. In August 1944 he became President of the Privy Council. In April 1945, during the rapidly deteriorating war situation, he was chosen Premier. Although 77 years old, he was considered to be the only compromise figure who would not be fiercely opposed by the many factions in the country. Although Suzuki continued to make warlike speeches, he worked to maneuver his cabinet into a situation in which the Emperor could call for peace. It was said that he persuaded the Emperor to accept the Allied surrender terms. On August 14, 1945, Suzuki tendered the resignation of his Cabinet because of "the new situation created by Japanese acceptance of the Potsdam Declaration."

As Premier Suzuki was noted for his delicate juggling act between factions. He spent much of his life avoiding assassination. Militarists blamed him for the surrender, and he had to live as a fugitive until the martial fever subsided.

SYKEWAR. Psychological warfare. (*See* PROPAGANDA, WAR.)

SYRIA, OCCUPATION OF. See NEAR AND MIDDLE EAST, CAMPAIGNS IN THE.

SZABO, VIOLETTE (1918–1945). A Briton of French extraction who served as contact agent with the French underground.

Violette Szabo was recruited by the British Special Operations Executive (SOE) for services in German-occupied France. On several occasions she was dropped by parachute with other agents to join French Resistance teams in sabotaging Nazi rule. Trapped by the *Gestapo* (*q.v.*), she fought back but was seized and taken to Paris. Later she was sent to Ravensbrück, a Nazi concentration camp 50 miles northeast of Berlin specializing in women inmates. She was executed in January 1945. (*See* RESISTANCE MOVEMENTS.)

T

T-34. See TANKS.

TALL BOY. A 12,000-pound bomb used by the Royal Air Force (*q.v.*) in raids on German targets. (*See* BLOCKBUSTERS.)

TANKS. Armor-plated, self-propelled vehicles moving on caterpillar treads, useful in combat for firepower and ability to operate over many kinds of terrain.

BACKGROUND. The first tanks were used by the British in World War I. The basic idea, mobility combined with offensive power, was not new. Centuries earlier the Chinese had employed war cars armored against projectiles. Battle-wagons and landships were used in European wars. The tank was made possible by invention of the internal combustion engine and the caterpillar track. The prototype of British tank had a speed of only four miles per hour, but its armor could resist any ordinary bullet.

British tanks went into action the first time on September 15, 1916, during the Battle of the Somme. They amazed German defenders, but they were not an unqualified success. Only a few of the 42 tanks proved to be effective. Many broke down with mechanical trouble, while others were immobilized in soft ground and shell holes. Despite the poor showing, the British continued to work on them. An improved version was used at the Battle of Cambrai on November 20, 1917.

WORLD WAR II. The new German *Blitzkrieg* (*q.v.*) technique took full advantage of the tank. The old Maginot Line (*q.v.*) mentality could not cope with new, fast-moving armored vehicles. Tanks were used not only in support of ground troops but also against enemy tank formations. There were confrontations throughout the war from the seesaw battles in North Africa to the Battle of the Bulge (*qq.v.*)

Both Axis and Allied forces used different forms of armored vehicles for combat. Heavily armored medium tanks proved to be the most effective. Light tanks were underarmored and giant tanks were too unwieldy.

BRITISH. Early British tanks used in World War II were inferior, especially in gun power and armor, to German counterparts. As soon as the British began to use American *Shermans* in quantity, they saw the balance in desert warfare change dramatically in their favor.

BRITISH CHURCHILL TANK

The *Churchill,* a British heavy tank, was named after Britain's wartime Prime Minister Winston Churchill (*q.v.*). The most famous of all British armored vehicles, it was conceived as early as 1938 as a means of breaking any possible trench warfare stalemate. Its design was an evolutionary link between the lozenge-shaped tanks of 1918 and the fast, low, heavily gunned vehicles that eventually emerged at the end of World War II. Mass production began in the middle of 1941 when there was a need for tanks in quantity.

Churchill tanks received their baptism of fire during the raid on Dieppe on August 19, 1942. (*See* DIEPPE RAID.) Some were knocked out quickly, and only a few managed to surmount the sea wall. They were used in desert fighting in North Africa in 1942. Here the American-built *Sherman* (*q.v.*) tank entered service and demonstrated its greater effectiveness. In Italy in 1943 the *Churchill* appeared in action against new German *Tigers* (*q.v.*). Large numbers of *Churchills* took part in the 1944 French campaign. (*See* NORMANDY INVASION) and in subsequent dashes across the Rhineland and Germany proper.

With its heavy armor, low silhouette, and maneuverability over almost any kind of terrain, the *Churchill* successfully punched holes in the German West Wall (*q.v.*). Among improved models was the *Crocodile,* of which 800 were produced. By the end of the war the *Churchill* was outgunned by German tactics.

> *SPECIFICATIONS* (Mk. VII).
> *Measurements.* Weight 47.2 tons; length 26 ft. 2 in.; width 10 ft. 11 in.; height 9 ft. 1½ in.
> *Maximum Speed.* 20 m.p.h.
> *Radius of Action:* 142 mi. (road).
> *Engine.* Flat 12-cyl., liquid-cooled, Bedford twin 6, 350 hp.
> *Armor.* Front 6 in.; sides 3.7 in.; rear 2 in.
> *Armament.* One 75 mm. gun; one 7.92 Besa machine gun; one .303 cal. Bren machine gun; one 2-in. bombthrower; one flame-gun.
> *Crew.* Five men.
> *Special Features.* Dual control system which allowed front gunner to drive in emergencies; transmission with four forward and one reverse speeds; small bogie wheels; triple helical springs.

GERMAN. In a war in which armor was king, Germans quickly demonstrated their efficiency in tank warfare. Much was due to the expertise of such

Panzer (*q.v.*) commanders as Gens. Heinz Guderian and Erwin Rommel (*qq.v.*), as well as technical superiority of their armor. Highly maneuverable tanks were the backbone of German armor in the first two years of the war in helping to overrrun Poland, the Low Countries, and France.

GERMAN *PzKW-IV* TANK

Mindful of German experience in World War I, Hitler called for a great tank force when he rearmed Germany in the mid-1930s. He commissioned Krupp, Daimler-Benz, and Rheinmetal-Borsig to produce tanks in the five-ton class. He also invited designs for early versions of the *PzKw* (*Panzerkraftwagen,* "tank"), Marks II and III. He tested these tanks in Spain in 1936 and again in Czechoslovakia and Austria.

Designed in 1936–1937, the *PzKw-IV* weighed about 20 tons, a weight believed by German experts to be ideal. Contrary to British practice, it was intended as a battle tank, a combat vehicle, instead of an armored car for close support of infantrymen. With a large turret for guns of ever-increasing velocity, it soon demonstrated its value in excellent cross-country performance.

By 1939 the *PzKw-IV* was purged of its many logistic defects. Used in early campaigns, it also led the advance into the Soviet Union in 1941, inflicted heavy casualties, and very nearly ensured German victory. But in the long run it was to meet its match in the Russian *T-34,* simply constructed but highly effective armored vehicle.

Because of its complicated design, the *PzKw-IV* could not be produced in quantity. Only 100 were built in German factories at a time when the Russians were producing 900 *T-34s.* By the end of the war the *PzKw-IV* was being replaced by the heavier *Tiger* and *Panther* tanks.

> *SPECIFICATIONS.*
> *Measurements.* Weight 18 tons (later increased to 25 tons); length 18 ft. 8 in.; width 9 ft. 4 in.; height 8 ft. 7 ½ in.
> *Maximum Speed.* 23 m.p.h.
> *Radius of Action.* 93.5 mi.
> *Engine.* 250 h.p. Maybach 12-cyl., with synchromesh transmission.
> *Armor.* ¾ in. front; 2 in. in turret.
> *Armament.* One 75-mm. (short) or 50 mm. (long) gun; two 7.9-mm. machine guns.
> *Crew.* Five men.
> *Special Features.* Eight road wheels each side grouped in four articulated pairs; four return rollers; elliptical spring suspension; gun mounted in shallow closed turret; chassis long and wide.

GERMAN *PANTHER* TANK

The German *Panther,* a medium tank, was considered by experts among the best armored vehicles of the war.

Its design was based on rugged experience. When Germans invaded the Soviet Union on June 22, 1941, they relied on their *PzKw-III* and *PzKw-IV* tanks as the backbone of their *Panzer* forces. They expected quick victory, but they had not counted on the formidable Russian *T-34*. German designers made an exhaustive study of the Russian tank and by 1943 came up with a satisfactory answer. The new *Panther* was faster and more heavily equipped than its predecessors.

In combat the *Panther* held its own in clashes with the Russian *T-34*, the British *Churchill*, and the American *Pershing*. It was constantly improved during the latter stages of the war. Later variations included the *Hunting Panther*, which used the standard *Panther* chassis as a base for a heavy 88-mm. PAK 43 gun. This improved version resulted in a formidable tank destroyer.

SPECIFICATIONS.

Measurements. Weight 43–49 tons; length 22 ft. 11 in.; width 11 ft., 5 in.; height 9 ft. 10 in.

Maximum Speed. 27–30 m.p.h.

Radius of Action. 105 mi.

Engine. 650 h.p. Maybach 12 cyl.

Armor. 4.3-in. on turret.

Armament. One 75-mm. gun fired at a muzzle velocity of 3,066 ft. per second; two 7.9-mm. machine guns.

Crew. Five men.

Special Features. Clutch and brake steering; hand and hydraulic power transverse; carried 21 liters of fuel.

GERMAN *TIGER* TANK

Clumsy but powerful, the *Tiger-1* was used effectively on all fronts in the European theater of operations.

The earliest version of the *Tiger*, known as *PzKw-VI*, was used first in the final phases of the North African campaign. Astonished Allied gunners saw their heavy shells bounce harmlessly off the *Tiger's* especially designed armored plate. The German tank was also used against Russians and later against Western Allies after June 1944. (*See* NORMANDY INVASION.) Although handicapped by its comparatively slow speed, it was regarded as a highly successful weapon. German *Panzer* units preferred to use it in a defensive role.

SPECIFICATIONS.

Measurements. Weight 55 tons; length 20 ft., 8 in.; width 12 ft. 5 in.; height 9 ft. 6½ in.

Maximum Speed. 23½ m.p.h.

Radius of Action. 62 mi.

Engine. 700 h.p. Maybach V-12.

Armor. 5.9-in. front and 7.3-in. turret. 110-mm. maximum.

Armament. One 88-mm. KwK 43 gun; two 7.9-mm. machine guns.

Crew. Five men.

Special Features. Hand and hydraulic power transverse; width could be reduced for rail travel.

German technicians worked to improve the earlier *Tiger-1* and produced later versions known as *Tiger-B* and *Royal Tiger*. Making their appearance in

1944, they were to be among the most powerful fighting vehicles of the war. On occasion, German tank experts dug pits, placed *King Tigers* inside them, and used them as stationary pillboxes.

RUSSIAN. Because of tremendous losses of equipment, the Russians had to produce tanks quickly and in quantity. They made a virtue of simplicity in production—and the idea was most successful. Russian tanks were more than a match for sophisticated German *Panzers.* Where German tanks broke down under harsh winter conditions, Soviet armored vehicles performed in all kinds of weather. Because of their generally low height, Russian tanks were poor targets for enemy tank destroyers.

RUSSIAN *T-34* TANK

The Russian *T-34,* a medium tank and the backbone of the Soviet armored forces, dominated German armor beginning in 1942. Armor experts judged it to be the best tank of the war.

Originally planned by Russian technicians in the early 1930s, the *T-34* was placed into mass production in 1939. Later it rolled off the assembly lines in enormous quantities. The designers struck an excellent balance of armor, gunpower, and speed. There was constant improvement in later models.

The *T-34* soon proved itself to be a match for German armor. By the middle of 1942 the Russians were successful in replacing their tank losses. They made special efforts to produce as many *T-34s* as possible. With its speed and mobility, the *T-34* could penetrate mud and snow. It hit the Germans with devastating effect at Stalingrad in the winter of 1942–1943. (*See* STALINGRAD, BATTLE OF.) At Kursk in July 1943, *T-34s* did much to stem the German offensive. So impressed were the Germans that they used the *T-34* as a model for their own new *Panther* tank.

> *SPECIFICATIONS.*
> *Measurements.* Weight 34 tons; length 20 ft.; width 9 ft. 10 in.; height 9 ft.
> *Maximum Speed.* 31 m.p.h.
> *Radius of Action.* 170 mi.
> *Engine.* 500 h.p., 12-cyl., water-cooled V-2-34 diesel.
> *Armor.* 1.8 in. front; 3.7 in. turret.
> *Armament.* One 85-mm. gun; two 7.62-mm. machine guns, one in bow and one with main armament.
> *Crew.* Five men.
> *Special Features.* Tracks two feet wide; used very little fuel; some *T-34s* had snorkeling capability in fording.

RUSSIAN *JS* TANK

Later the Russians produced in quantity the huge *Joseph Stalin* tank, the *JS,* which was effective against German armor.

Russian technicians were anxious to produce a weapon to challenge Germany's powerful new *Panther* and *Tiger* tanks. The new *Stalin,* or *JS,* marked a giant step beyond the all-successful *T-34*. With a high velocity gun mounted on a large turret set well forward on a wide chassis, it was a truly formidable weapon.

Weak in armored vehicles in 1941, within three years the Russians had built the world's leading tank force. The *JS* bore witness to this remarkable development. It appeared in large numbers in the spring of 1944 and was used effectively in hammering the Germans while Anglo-American forces hit them from the west. (*See* NORMANDY INVASION.) The *JS* was used also in Russian counteroffensives against the Germans in Poland, Czechoslovakia, Austria, and Germany. It knocked out Hitler's armor in the final battle for Berlin. (*See* BERLIN, BATTLE FOR.)

SPECIFICATIONS.
  Measurements. Weight 57 tons.
  Maximum Speed. 20 m.p.h.
  Engine. 600 h.p. cylinder V-12.
  Armor. 4.7-in. front armor.
  Armament. One 122-mm. gun; one 7.62-mm. machine gun; and one 12.7-mm. machine gun.
  Crew. Five men.
  Special Features. Gave appearance of a giant beetle.

AMERICAN. American tanks generally were successful on all fronts. Most effective were the medium ones which performed the functions of a heavy tank. The British credited their success in North Africa to the delivery of 400 American medium tanks at the critical moment. In later stages of the war Americans introduced heavy tanks with low silhouettes and heavy armor.

U.S. *M-5* LIGHT TANK

The *M-5*, an American light tank, was popular with U.S. troops at first, but its use dwindled later when the trend was to medium and heavy tanks.

The *M-1* to *M-5* series of American tanks were designed before the war for mobility to operate on the enemy's flanks and rear to force him to make detachments to guard his lines of communication. The design was redefined several times from 1937 on. Pilot models finished their trials in September 1939 just as Germany invaded Poland. Contracts were assigned to the American Car and Foundry Company for the tank, which required 14,000 separate parts. Production was accelerated later.

The *M-5* was essentially an unsophisticated vehicle that could be built quickly and easily maintained. It had a rear engine, front sprockets, and a bulkhead separating the engine from the fighting compartment. With its ample power, easy engine access, and sturdy rubber tracks, it was one of the most reliable tanks ever produced.

The first *M-5*s, easily transported across the Atlantic, went ashore in North Africa on November 7–8, 1942. Because they could be put on the beaches from small landing craft, they were used by Americans in all invasions for the remainder of the war, especially in Sicily, Italy, southern France, and Normandy. They were gradually replaced as *Shermans* rolled from production lines.

SPECIFICATIONS.
  Measurements. Weight 16.9 tons.
  Maximum Speed. 36 m.p.h.
  Engine. Two 130 h.p. Cadillac V-8s.
  Armor. 1.5-in. front and turret.
  Armament. One 37-mm. cannon in turret; two .30-cal. machine guns.
  Crew. Four men.
  Special Features. Automatic transmission; vertical spring suspension; gears and drive in nose with driver sitting to the left; fuel tanks in sponsons on either side of the fighting compartment.

U.S. *M-R* MEDIUM TANK

The *M-4,* named *Sherman* by the British after Gen. William Tecumseh Sherman (1820–1891), Union General in the American Civil War, proved to be one of the most effective armored vehicles of World War II.

In 1938 the *M-2* medium tank, which used a 37-mm. gun as its main armament, was designed for the U.S. Army. After the start of the war in Europe, the newly established National Defense Advisory Commission, made up of prominent industrialists, urged that more powerful tanks be produced by the American automobile industry "for a possible national emergency." American technicians, impressed by success of the German *PzKw-IV* in the *Blitzkrieg* (*q.v.*) on France in 1940, produced the *Sherman* as a rival for the German medium tank. The main requirements were mobility, reliability, and adequate armament, and the *Sherman* had all these qualities. By 1944, *Shermans* were rolling off the assembly lines in the Detroit Tank arsenal in great quantities.

In combat the *Sherman* proved equal to the *Blitzkrieg* role for which it was mainly used. Some 400 *Shermans* sent to the British 8th Army played a major part in defeating the Germans at the Battle of El Alamein (*q.v.*) from October 23 to November 3, 1943. With their low silhouette and welded hulls, they proved more than a match for German armor. In June 1944 (*See* NORMANDY INVASION), *Shermans* played a prominent role and later spearheaded the Allied attack across France and into Germany. This time the Germans were on the defensive and were using their heavy *Tigers* and *Panthers.* Actually, no *Sherman* could stand up to heavier German tanks, but Americans had the advantage of supporting air power, adequate reserves, and superb logistics.

In vast outflanking movements, the *Sherman* was used spectacularly as a weapon of advance and exploitation. By the end of the war it was among the best known and most widely produced tanks in the history of armored warfare.

SPECIFICATIONS.
  Measurements. Weight 18 tons; length 20 ft. 7. in.; width 8 ft. 9 in.
  Maximum Speed. 26 m.p.h.

Radius of Action. 120 mi.

Engine. 430 h.p., 6-cyl. Chrysler, with synchromesh transmission.

Armor. 2 in. in front; 3.2 in. in turret.

Armament. One 75-mm. gun M3; two .30-cal. machine guns.

Crew. Five men.

Special Features. Horizontal suspension system; periscope for each crew member; direct vision for driver; combination mount for gun and machine gun; operated by means of levers; maintenance comparatively easy.

U.S. *M-26* MEDIUM TANK

American tank technicians studied the German *Tiger-I* carefully when it was first used in 1942. Their purpose was to produce a medium tank with equivalent firepower and protection and which could hold its own with enemy *Panzers.* The *Pershing* turned out to be a reliable vehicle, mobile, and comfortable for the crew. It was placed into mass production at the Detroit Tank Arsenal (Chrysler operated) and the Grand Bank Tank Arsenal (Fisher Body Division of General Motors).

The *Pershing* was sent into combat late in the war to meet the German *Tiger-1, King Tiger-II,* and *Panther.* In March 1945, 210 *Pershings* were sent to the European theater of operations. However, American troops moved forward so rapidly that few *Pershings* could catch up with them. On VE-Day (*q.v.*) there were 300 in Europe, of which only 20 saw any action, most of them with the 9th Armored Division when it reached the Remagen bridge (*q.v.*) on March 7, 1945.

SPECIFICATIONS.

Measurements. Weight 35 tons; width 11 ft. 12 in.

Armor. Up to 89-mm.

Armament. 90-mm. M3 gun with muzzle velocity of 2,650 ft. per second.

Special Features. Low silhouette.

Bibliography. J. Kirk and R. Young, *Great Weapons of World War II* (1961); F. W. Mellenthin, *Panzer Battles* (1968); P. Chamberlain and C. Ellis, *The Sherman* (1969); Von Senger and F. M. Eyterlin, *German Tanks of World War II* (1969); G. Bradford, *Great Tank Battles of World War II* (1970); P. Chamberlain and C. Ellis, *British and American Tanks of World War II* (1970); J. Malsom, *Russian Tanks, 1900–1970* (1970); and R. J. Icks, *Famous Tank Battles* (1972).

TARANTO, BATTLE OF. Naval operation in the Mediterranean in late November 1940, when a British task force destroyed half the Italian battle fleet. The victory restored British naval supremacy in the Mediterranean.

BACKGROUND. When Mussolini brought Italy into the war against the Allies on June 10, 1940, he predicted that the British Mediterranean Fleet would quickly retreat before Italian numerical naval supremacy. Instead, British warships, under Adm. Andrew Browne Cunningham (*q.v.*), ranged the Mediterranean, struck at Italian supply lines to North Africa, and waited for a fight to the finish with the Italian Navy. To guard against an invasion on Italy's coastline, Mussolini kept the major part of his fleet at Taranto (ancient Tarentum), at the heel of the Italian boot, 49 miles southeast of Bari.

CONFRONTATION. On the evening of November 11, 1940, a British task force, part of the main Mediterranean Fleet, led by the the aircraft carrier, *Illustrious,* moved into position off the Bay of Taranto. From the decks of the *Illustrious* nine obsolete *Swordfish*, the oldest planes in the British service, rose in two waves and skimming over the surface of the gulf launched their torpedoes directly at the Italian warships. It was the first strike of its kind in history and it was most effective. Within minutes the harbor was a bowl of flames.

LOSSES. When the smoke cleared, the Italian naval force was cut in half. Three battleships were crippled, (the new *Littorio,* the *Conte di Cavour,* and the *Duilio*), in addition to two destroyers and two auxiliaires. The cost to the British was one plane shot down, one officer killed, and three men taken prisoner.

SIGNIFICANCE. For Mussolini the engagement was a tremendous blow. The attack shook his confidence. He ordered that Taranto be abandoned as a fleet base and sent his surviving vessels to Naples. News of the victory was received with great joy by embattled Greeks. Churchill pronounced the feat ''a crippling blow.'' It meant that Britain could now control its precious supply line through Gibraltar and Malta to Suez and at the same time strike at Axis supply lines to North Africa.

Bibliography. W. M. James, *The British Navies in the Second World War* (1947); J. Cresswell, *Sea Warfare, 1939-1945* (1949); and B. B. Schofield, *The Attack on Taranto* (1973).

TARAWA. *See* GILBERT ISLANDS, BATTLE FOR THE.

TARGET DETECTION. Infra-red systems used for locating targets at night. Both the Germans and the Allies did extensive research in this field.

GERMAN. The Germans preferred a method based on the emission of infrared beams from the target.

VAMPIRE

A combined lamp and telescope unit mounted on an assault rifle.

OBI

A searchlight director to detect bomber exhausts.

DONAU

A target locator for coast artillery. Built by Zeiss, it could detect targets at sea from the heat of their funnels at ranges up to seven miles.

SPANNER

Fitted to fighter planes to enable them to strike at planes at night.

ALLIED. Both British and American scientists worked on infra-red target seeking aids for night-driving vision units. They used the active method of throwing infra-red beams toward the target.

TABBY

A combination searchlight and viewer for night driving of tanks and motor vehicles.

SNIPERSCOPE

Mounted on machine guns or rifles.

TASK FORCE 58. Famed U.S. carrier task force that compiled an extraordinary record in the Pacific theater of war.

FORMATION. Task Force 58, the most mobile task force yet seen in warfare, was assembled in January 1944 under command of Vice-Adm. Mark A. Mitscher (*q.v.*). To it were assigned the latest and fastest carriers, battleships, cruisers, and destroyers of the U.S. Naval Fleet. Its carriers could launch more than 1,000 planes from 1.25 million feet of runway. Its warships could train 850 guns on enemy installations with the destructive power of 70 standard army field artillery units. It had its own vast fleet supply train, capable of providing food, fuel, ammunition, and replacement pilots wherever the task force might go. It was the strongest strike force of its kind ever assembled in the Pacific, so powerful that on occasion it was divided into several separate task forces.

RECORD. Task Force 58 provided air support for American invasions of Hollandia, Dutch New Guinea, and Australian New Guinea. It also took part in the fierce battles for Saipan and other Marianas Islands. Again and again Mitscher's carrier-based aircraft brought the fight to the now elusive Japanese. By August 1944 Task Force 58 was ranging the Pacific looking for the enemy.

An official résumé of Task Force 58's operations from January 29 through October 27, 1944, listed 795 Japanese naval and merchant vessels sunk or damaged and 4,426 Japanese planes destroyed, 2,569 in the air and 1,857 on the ground. Mitscher was known for the extreme care he took in air-rescue service for downed pilots under his command. In one major battle he broke the strict blackout to have searchlights guide his planes back to their carriers. He lost nearly 100 planes that night, but his destroyers rescued more than half that number of pilots and crewmen. (*See* PACIFIC, CAMPAIGNS IN THE.)

Bibliography. S. E. Morison, *History of U.S. Naval Operations in World War II* (1947–1960); and G. Bennett, *Naval Battles of World War II* (1975).

TASSAFARONGA, BATTLE OF. *See* GUADALCANAL CAMPAIGNS.

TAYLOR, MAXWELL DAVENPORT (1901–   ). Outstanding American paratroop commander.

In July 1942 Taylor was assigned as Chief of Staff to the 82nd Airborne Division, one of the army's first two air units. In March 1943 he went overseas with his division and fought in Sicily and Italy. (*See* SICILY, INVASION OF; and ITALIAN FRONT, CAMPAIGNS ON THE.) In September 1943 he undertook a dangerous mission to Rome behind enemy lines to determine if the recently surrendered Italians could give sufficient strength against Germans in the area. They could not. In March 1944 he was posted to the 101st Airborne Division. On D-Day, June 6, 1944, he parachuted with his men into Normandy (*See* NORMANDY INVASION), and became the first American General to fight in France. He took part in the battles at Arnhem and at the Bulge. (*See* ARNHEM, BATTLE OF; and BULGE, BATTLE OF THE.)

Bibliography. Taylor's book *The Uncertain Trumpet* (1959) called for a thorough reappraisal of
    U.S. military policy. *See also* his *Swords and Plowshares* (1972).

TAYLOR REVISIONIST THEORY. For British historian A.J.P. Taylor's revisionist theory on the origins of World War II, *see* WAR RESPONSIBILITY.

TAYLOR, TELFORD (1908–   ). Lawyer and writer, American presiding judge at the Nuremberg War Crimes Trial. (*See* NUREMBERG TRIALS.)

In October 1942 Taylor was commissioned in the army and was assigned to a special branch of Military Intelligence. In March 1943 he was promoted to Lieutenant Colonel and the following May was sent to take charge of the London office of the Special Branch of the War Department. In September 1944 he was promoted to Colonel and in April 1946 to Brigadier General.

NUREMBERG. In June 1945 Taylor was assigned to the Office of the Chief Counsel of the International War Crimes Trial in Nuremberg, Germany. He worked with U.S. Supreme Court Justice Robert H. Jackson (*q.v.*) in the joint four-power prosecution of Nazi officials. He was appointed to succeed Jackson as prosecutor in October 1946. The subsequent trials were held under the jurisdiction of the U.S. Military Government. Taylor obtained indictments against 23 German doctors, scientists, and medical administrators, and later against German industrialists who had financed Hitler's rise to power, 15 Nazi judges, 13 SS guards, and several Nazi generals.

Bibliography. Among Taylor's books are several standard works: *Sword and Swastika* (1952);
    The Breaking Wave (1967); and *Munich: The Price of Peace* (1979).

TEDDER, ARTHUR WILLIAM (1890–1967). British aviation officer and deputy to Gen. Dwight D. Eisenhower (*q.v.*) in June 1944. (*See* NORMANDY INVASION.)

At the start of the war Tedder was appointed Deputy Air Officer Commander-in-Chief for the Middle East. Following the disaster in Crete in May–June 1941 (*See* CRETE, BATTLE OF), Tedder became full air officer of the Middle East command, which covered the area from Malta to the Persian Gulf and extended south to Madagascar. In this post Tedder directed operations against Axis warships in the Mediterranean and submarines in the Persian Gulf; planned bombing raids on the cities and airdromes under Axis control; and supported the Royal Navy in the Mediterranean. In April 1942 he stepped up aid to Malta (*q.v.*), and in October of that year used the RAF as a front-line artillery against the Axis in Libya. His leadership in the coordination of air and ground forces helped defeat the Axis in North Africa, Sicily, and Italy.

OVERLORD. So impressed was Gen. Eisenhower with Tedder's performance that, when he organized his top team for the invasion of Europe, he chose Tedder as his deputy on December 28, 1943. This was the first time the Allied Supreme Command had given so important a post to an air officer. For the remainder of the war Tedder's strategic skill was an important factor in the liberation of Europe. As Eisenhower's deputy, he signed the formal surrender of Germany on May 9, 1945.

Tedder was considered one of the main architects of Allied victory. To his men he was always known as "The Chief." Known for his frank and biting wit, he was regarded by major Allied war leaders as probably the most experienced and skilled officer in the world in the use of the airplane as a tactical weapon.

Bibliography. A. W. Tedder, *With Prejudice: War Memoirs* (1966); and *Air Power in War* (1975).

TEHERAN CONFERENCE. Code or cover name *Eureka.* Allied war conference held to discuss final plans for the invasion of Western Europe. Teheran represented the climax of inter-Allied gatherings.

BACKGROUND. Roosevelt and Churchill had long wanted to talk with Stalin (*qq.v.*), but again and again the Russian leader declined on the ground that he was far too occupied with fighting the Germans. He finally agreed to come to Teheran, capital of Iran, for a high-level meeting.

PARTICIPANTS. The Big Three (*q.v.*), accompanied by their top military strategists and advisers, together with large staffs of assistants, met from November 28 to December 1, 1943, in an atmosphere of good fellowship. Roosevelt attempted to work his well-known charm on Stalin; Churchill displayed his mastery of the unexpected quip; and Stalin temporarily changed his cold exterior. At a birthday party for Churchill on November 30, 1943, no fewer than 50 toasts were proposed. Stalin approached Roosevelt, clinked glasses, and proposed: "My fighting friend Roosevelt!" Then he went to Churchill and said: "My fighting friend Churchill!" Then came an extraordinary admission from the Russian leader: "Without American production the United

Nations could never win the war." It was an astonishing statement from one who seldom expressed his gratefulness for American Lend-Lease (*q.v.*) supplies.

DECISIONS. Little was added to understandings already reached a month earlier at the Moscow Conference (*q.v.*) of Foreign Ministers. Disputes were shelved in the atmosphere of cordiality.

1. *Operation Overlord.* Stalin again called for a Second Front (*q.v.*), requesting categorical assurance that the invasion of France would take place in 1944. Roosevelt and Churchill tried to reassure him without yielding their reservations. Stalin agreed to a simultaneous major Russian counterattack to prevent Hitler from transferring large forces to the west.

2. *Operation Anvil.* Pleased by the plan for an additional landing in southern France, Stalin suggested that it be made two months ahead of *Overlord* in order to disrupt German plans. He opposed small-scale landings at the head of the Adriatic, which he said might detract from the main landings. It was obvious that he wanted to keep his Western Allies as far west as possible.

3. *German Settlement.* The Foreign Ministers at the Moscow Conference, uncertain about what to do about Germany, proposed that the matter be postponed for future consideration.

4. *Soviet Frontiers.* Stalin repeated his demand that the USSR should retain frontiers provided by the Russo-German Nonaggression Agreement (*q.v.*) of 1939 and the Russo-Finnish Treaty of 1940. He also put in a claim to the Baltic coast of East Prussia.

5. *Postwar International Organization.* It was decided to leave discussion on this matter for a later date, which turned out to be the Dumbarton Oaks Conference (*q.v.*) in the summer of 1944.

6. *Poland.* The conferees also opted for postponement on the problem of Poland, especially in view of Stalin's extreme distaste for the Polish Government-in-exile in London.

7. *Iran.* It was decided again that Allied soldiers stationed in Iran (Persia) would be evacuated after the war. As certification, a declaration was issued on December 1, 1944, guaranteeing postwar union and territorial integrity for Iran and promising economic assistance.

8. *Aid for Yugoslavia.* Substantial assistance was promised to Marshal Tito and his Partisans (*qq.v.*).

9. *Far East.* There was little discussion of the Far Eastern theater of operations because the Soviet Union was not yet engaged in war there. Roosevelt gave a description of operations in the Pacific Theater.

SIGNIFICANCE. The Teheran Conference revealed that the Allies were well on the way to victory. "We came here with hope and determination," read the closing communiqué. "We leave here, friends, in fact, in spirit, and in purpose." The Grand Alliance at long last was welded into a working union. After the war the euphoria of Teheran was to dissolve in an acidulous Cold War.

Bibliography. L. Havas, *The Long Jump* (1967), and *Hitler's Plot to Kill the Big Three* (1967); and R. Beitzell (ed.), *Tehran, Yalta and Potsdam* (1970).

TERBOVEN, JOSEF (1898–1945). Reich Commissioner for Norway.

On April 24, 1940, two weeks after the invasion of Norway, Hitler named Terboven Reich Commissioner for Norway and gave him powers superseding those of the collaborationist Vidkun Quisling (*q.v.*). At first Terboven acted with some consideration, but soon turned to brutality in dealing with recalcitrant Norwegians. Guerrillas derailed trains, blew up installations, and started landslides to engulf German troops.

As unrest mounted, Terboven declared a state of national emergency. He had three Norwegians shot by firing squad, the first cases of capital punishment in the history of modern Norway. He also shipped off Norwegian Jews to concentration camps inside Germany.

Terboven died in May 1945, presumably a suicide, to escape capture by the Allies.

Bibliography. H. D. Looch, *Quisling, Rosenberg and Terboven* (1970).

THIRD REICH (THIRD EMPIRE). Nazi designation for the National Socialist regime in power from January 1933 to May 1945.

Hitler regarded his government as the logical extension of two previous German empires. The First Reich was the Holy Roman Empire of the German Nations, which came into existence in A.D. 962 with the coronation of Otto the Great. The First Reich was abolished by Napoleon in 1806. The Second Reich was founded by Otto von Bismarck in 1871 and lasted until 1918 when the Hohenzollern dynasty fell at the end of World War I. Hitler regarded the Third Reich as the greatest of German empires and predicted confidently that it would last for 1,000 years.

THOMPSON, DOROTHY (1894–1961). U.S. journalist and newspaper columnist.

Thompson became a correspondent in Europe in the 1920s, reporting from Vienna and Berlin. An early critic of Hitler and the Nazis, she warned her readers of the dangers of the coming National Socialist regime. In 1928 she married the novelist Sinclair Lewis. In 1932 she wrote *I Saw Hitler,* in which she described him as "an insignificant little man." In 1934 she was expelled from Germany for her anti-Nazi writings. In 1939 she was evicted from a Nazi rally in Madison Square Garden, New York City, when she interrupted the speakers with loud, strident laughter.

Throughout the war Thompson expressed in biting prose her contempt for Hitler and the Third Reich, especially in her popular column, *On the Record,* for the Bell Syndicate. Originally an isolationist, she became an interventionist and called for the destruction of Nazism as a menace of civilization. Her broadcasts to Germany, titled "Listen Hans!" proved to be effective propaganda for the Allied cause.

Blond, later with soft gray hair, Dorothy Thompson was an aggressive and dynamic extrovert. One observer spoke of her "perpetual emotion." Another called her "greater than Eliza because not only does she cross the ice but also breaks it as she goes." Next to Eleanor Roosevelt, wife of the American President, Thompson had more recognition and prestige than any American woman of her time.

Bibliography. Among Dorothy Thompson's books are: *The New Russia* (1928); *A Political Guide* (1938); *Let the Record Speak* (1939); and *The Courage to Be Happy* (1957). *See also* V. Sheean, *Dorothy and Red* (1957).

TIGER. See TANKS.

TIMOSHENKO, SEMYON KONSTANTINOVICH (1895-1970). Soviet Field Marshal respected for his military talent.

When the Soviet Union invaded Finland on November 30, 1939, the Finns struck back viciously. After Soviet commanders made critical mistakes in the campaign, Stalin called on Timoshenko to extricate his army from its predicament. Timoshenko was responsible for retrieving the embarrassing situation.

Stalin rewarded Timoshenko with the rank of Marshal and the position of Minister of Defense. In this capacity Timoshenko arranged for the reorganization of the Red Army, which enabled the Russians to withstand Hitler's invasion starting on June 22, 1941. Taking command of the central front, he prevented the encirclement of Moscow. In August 1941 he directed the defense of Smolensk and delayed the German advance. Assigned to the Ukraine, he reconquered Rostov on November 26, 1941. But in May 1942 he failed to stop the Germans from taking the Crimea and advancing on Stalingrad. For this failure he was demoted to a staff assignment at Stalin's military headquarters. (*See also* EASTERN FRONT, CAMPAIGNS ON THE.)

Bibliography. E. W. Mehring, *Timoshenko: Soviet Marshal* (1942); and C. Cimorra, *Timoshenko* (1942).

TINIAN, 1944. See MARIANAS, BATTLE FOR THE.

TIRPITZ. German super battleship (*Schlachtschiff*). One of the most powerful warships afloat, she was crippled by British midget submarines in 1943 and eventually sunk by British planes on November 12, 1944.

DESIGN. German technicians began work on the *Tirpitz* in 1939. What emerged from the planning boards was one of the mightiest warships in naval history. Her designers gave her compartments that made her nearly immune from torpedo attack. To increase her structural strength they provided for no portholes except for a few at the extreme portions of the bow and stern. She was given deliberately a shallow draft of 28 feet so that she could be used as a raider in the North and Baltic Seas. With her catapult mounted atop a hanger amidships, she could accommodate 3 or 4 seaplanes for observation, and a second catapult could be mounted at the third turret on the quarterdeck. Her crewmen were proud of their sea monster, calling her "The Lonely Queen of the North."

SPECIFICATIONS.
  Measurements. Length approximately 800 ft.; beam 118 ft.
  Standard Displacement. 41,000 tons.
  Maximum Speed. 30½ knots.
  Armor. Not known, but probably equal to contemporaries—7.9-in. sides with 2-in. main deck.
  Armament. Eight 15-in. guns; twelve 5.9-in. guns; sixteen 4.1-in. AA guns.
  Complement. 2,000-plus.
  Special Features. Four seaplane scouts; hangar with two catapults; 150,000 h.p.; thin mainmast to give AA guns unobstructed view of sky.

WORLD WAR II. In May 1941 the *Bismarck* (*q.v.*), sister ship of the *Tirpitz*, was caught and sunk by the British. In January 1942 the *Tirpitz* completed her trials successfully. She was sent to Norwegian waters, where she was out of range of British bombers but close to the Arctic convoy routes to Soviet Russia. She quickly became a serious threat to the British Admiralty. Churchill was deeply worried. "The destruction or even crippling of this ship would be the greatest event at sea at the present time. The whole strategy of the war turns at this period on this ship, which is holding four times the number of British capital ships paralyzed. . . . I regard this matter as of the highest urgency and importance." For the British Admiralty it became a matter of the first priority to neutralize the *Tirpitz*.

On March 6, 1942, the *Tirpitz* moved out of her Norwegian anchorage for the first time to attack a convoy bound for Murmansk (*q.v.*). She was unable to find her prey and several days later was spotted by British planes. British pilots sent a score of torpedoes hurtling toward the German colossus, but all missed. From her four-barreled pom-poms the *Tirpitz* sent up a screen of fire that brought down a dozen British planes. The speedy warship slipped away and disappeared in the general direction of Narvik.

On March 12, 1942, the *Tirpitz* again tried to intercept a Murmansk-bound convoy, only to miss it because of the bad weather. The British Home Fleet sailed out to hunt for the German battleship, but was unable to find her due to the poor visibility. The *Tirpitz* returned to Trondheim. Merely by staying in Norwegian waters, she added to convoy dangers in the sea war. (*See* ATLANTIC, BATTLE OF THE.)

The following July the *Tirpitz* took part in the attack on convoy *PQ-17* (*q.v.*). At this time she was part of a large fleet that sailed out to meet the British, but she was quickly recalled by Hitler. On September 8, 1943, escorted by the *Scharnhorst* (*q.v.*) and 10 destroyers, the *Tirpitz* took part in a damaging raid on Allied installations at Spitzbergen. For the first time the *Tirpitz* fired her big 15-inch guns on a target. (*See* SPITZBERGEN RAID.)

On the night of September 23, 1943, 2 of 6 British midget submarines, called X-craft, slipped through the defenses of Altenfjord and frogmen (*q.v.*) managed to attach a limpet mine to the keel of the *Tirpitz*. (*See* ALTENFJORD RAID.) It took six months to repair the *Tirpitz* well enough so that she could be moved to a Baltic dockyard for refitting.

ENTRAPMENT. Then came a deadly cat-and-mouse game. British reconnaissance planes kept a careful watch as the Germans worked frantically to make the great ship seaworthy. The Admiralty waited until April 3, 1944, when there were signs that the *Tirpitz* was ready to move, and sent out a task force under Vice-Adm. Henry R. Moore. British bombers from aircraft carriers berthed at Archangel swooped down on the *Tirpitz* like a swarm of hornets and scored 15 hits in 11 minutes. Frustrated Germans towed the crippled battleship to Tromsöfjord. It was an invitation to disaster—the *Tirpitz* was now 200 miles closer to Britain and she had little or no air cover.

From July to October 1944 the British stepped up their attacks. On November 12, 1944, 60 British *Lancasters* (*q.v.*) flew from Scotland bearing six-ton Tall Boy (*q.v.*) bombs destined for the *Tirpitz*. The *Luftwaffe* (*q.v.*) detailed veteran *Me-109* (*q.v.*) fighters to intercept. Halfway to the target, half the British planes, without bombs, veered off sharply toward Bardufoss, a German airfield. The *Me-109*s dutifully followed. The remaining British planes, bearing their deadly bomb loads, headed toward Tromsöfjord and dropped their bombs on the *Tirpitz*. There were hits and near misses. The misses gouged out the sides of the fjord in such a way that the giant German warship was in danger of capsizing. Mortally wounded, she heeled over on her starboard side and sank.

TOLL. More than 1,400 German officers and men were killed or drowned. About 397 were saved. Of the complement, 400 men were on leave and lived to tell the story.

SIGNIFICANCE. The loss of the *Tirpitz* was a tremendous blow to the Germans. Both she and her sister ship, the *Bismarck,* had fallen to British power. The British were understandably elated. Now they could move their capital ships to the Far East, where they were desperately needed.

Bibliography. D. Woodward, *The Tirpitz and the Battle for the North Atlantic* (1953); L. Peillard, *Sink the Tirpitz* (1968); T. M. Gallagher, *The X-Raid* (1971); G. Frere-Cook, *The Attack on the Tirpitz* (1973); and L. Kennedy, *The Death of the Tirpitz* (1979).

TITO, JOSIP BROZ (1892-1981). Yugoslav leader of a victorious guerrilla army.

After the defeat and occupation of Yugoslavia by the Germans in April 1941, Tito, unlike other Communist leaders in Europe who sought safety in Moscow, emerged as leader of the Yugoslavian Partisan (*q.v.*) movement. His struggle was waged under great difficulties, for his antagonists included, in addition to the Germans, the followers of Draja Mikhailovich (*q.v.*) and Russian agents from Moscow. He organized the Yugoslav peasants into a triumphant guerrilla army, despite the opposition of the Yugoslav Government-in-exile. (*See* GOVERNMENTS-IN-EXILE.)

By 1943 Tito controlled a large part of Yugoslavia. Supported by Britain and the United States, he merged the royal Yugoslavian government and his own Council of National Liberation in November 1944, and became head of the new federal Yugoslav Government in March 1945.

Popular with all classes of the Yugoslav people, Tito managed to consolidate his government after the war despite bitter opposition from Moscow. In 1948 the Cominform expelled him for having deviated from "the correct Communist line." Tito set up his own secret police, purged dissident elements, and promoted his own form of communism. In 1963 his term as President was made unlimited. Tito died on May 4, 1981, 3 days before his 90th birthday.

Bibliography. H. F. Armstrong, *Tito and Goliath* (1951); L. White, *Balkan Caesar: Tito versus Stalin* (1951); V. Dedijer, *Tito Speaks* (1953); E. Halperin, *The Triumphant Heretic* (1957); P. Auty, *Tito: A Biography* (1970); H. M. Christman (ed.), *The Essential Tito* (1970); and W. R. Roberts, *Tito, Mihailovic and the Allies, 1941-1945* (1973).

TOBRUK, SIEGE OF. Attacks on the port in the province of Cyrenaica, Libya, in 1941-1942. The defense of Tobruk is an epic in British military history.

BACKGROUND. Because of its strategic position on Mediterranean routes, Tobruk was strongly fortified by Mussolini as a naval and air base. In November 1933 the *Duce* took over the Air Ministry and sent Italy's most popular soldier, Gen. Italo Balbo (*q.v.*), to supervise the fortifications of Tobruk. On June 28, 1940, two and a half weeks after Italy entered the war, Balbo was killed together with nine other occupants of a plane that crashed on Tobruk after an attack by the Royal Air Force (*q.v.*).

On January 22, 1941, after a heavy bombardment by the Royal Navy and the Australian Navy, Gen. Archibald Wavell (*q.v.*) defeated the Italians led by Gen. Rodolpho Graziani (*q.v.*), and entered Tobruk. In the fighting the British and Australians took more than 25,000 prisoners and 50 tanks, while their own casualties numbered only 500. The Allies settled in to hold Tobruk. When Gen. Erwin Rommel (*q.v.*) arrived in North Africa to engage the Allies, the British forces withdrew to the east, leaving the garrison Tobruk by-passed and isolated.

SIEGE. Gen. Wavell, backed by Churchill, made the decision to hold Tobruk and planned *Operation Battleaxe* to relieve it. For the next eight months some 23,000 of Wavell's men—British, Australians, New Zealanders, and Indians—defended Tobruk from German forces and dive bombers. Their refusal to surrender infuriated Hitler: Tobruk remained a thorn in his side no matter how many times he tried to remove it. He ordered Rommel to hammer away but the garrison held. Gen. Leslie J. Morshead, the Allied commanding officer at Tobruk, made it plain: "There'll be no Dunkirk here. If we should not have to get out, we shall fight our way out. There is to be no surrender and no retreat." (*See* DUNKIRK EVACUATION.)

German aircraft dropped bombs plus surrender leaflets on Tobruk:

THE GERMAN OFFICER COMMANDING THE GERMAN FORCES IN LIBYA RE-QUESTS THAT THE BRITISH TROOPS OCCUPYING TOBRUK SURRENDER THEIR ARMS. SINGLE SOLDIERS WAVING WHITE HANDKERCHIEFS ARE NOT FIRED ON. STRONG GERMAN FORCES HAVE ALREADY SURROUNDED TOBRUK AND IT IS USELESS TO ESCAPE.

The besieged garrison paid no attention to demands for surrender. They said that they were more worried about the famous desert fleas: "The fleas marched and countermarched up and down our writhing bodies until we thought we would go crazy." They pursued the fleas and named themselves the "Rats of Tobruk."

RELIEF. Meanwhile, Royal Navy and Royal Air Force (*q.v.*) kept the defenders supplied through the back door. In August 1941, British warships brought 6,000 fresh troops to Tobruk and took off 5,000 weary men. Another convoy in September brought in 6,000 more Australians and delivered several thousand tons of supplies. By the fall Tobruk had become the pivotal point of tank battles between Axis and Allies. At the end of November 1941 Gen. Claude Auchinleck's (*q.v.*) British forces near Sidi Rezegh launched an offensive to effect a junction with the isolated garrison at Tobruk. At the same time the besieged force broke out of Tobruk to threaten Rommel's rear.

Tobruk was relieved but only for a short time. Auchinleck's advance stopped at El Agheila and Rommel's counterthrust drove the British back to Gazala. Germans then smashed through to Tobruk again on December 2, 1941. The Allies counterattacked, forcing the Axis to withdraw and leave 36,000 prisoners and 40 tanks, as well as 25,000 dead and wounded. Tobruk was finally relieved on December 9, 1941, and Cyrenaica was once more in Allied hands. (*See also* NORTH AFRICA, CAMPAIGNS IN.)

AFTERMATH. The seesaw battle for Tobruk continued well into 1942. In mid-June the Germans again surrounded the city. After a devastating artillery barrage and air attacks, Germans, on June 21, 1942, penetrated Tobruk's defenses once again, forced the surrender of 35,000 Allied troops, and captured huge dumps of ammunition, gasoline, and food. Overjoyed, Hitler made Rommel a Field Marshal, postponed the projected invasion of Malta (*see* MALTA, SIEGE OF), and ordered his desert general to head for Egypt.

Germans did not hold Tobruk long this time. British victory at El Alamein (*q.v.*), October 23 to November 7, 1942, meant that Tobruk would eventually be taken. It was recaptured on November 13, 1942.

Bibliography. J. B. Devine, *The Rats of Tobruk* (1943); A. Morehead, *The End in Africa* (1943); HMSO, *The Eighth Army* (1944); D. Young, *Rommel* (1950); G. Landsborough, *Tobruk Commando* (1956); B. Maugham, *Tobruk and El Alamein* (1966); and J. W. Stork, *Tobruk: The Siege* (1973).

TODT, FRITZ (1891–1942). Reich Minister of Armaments and Munitions.

From 1940 to 1942 Todt served in the important post of Reich Minister of Armaments and Munitions. In this capacity he supervised the work of the so-called *Organisation Todt,* which was responsible for providing labor for work on the Siegfried Line (*q.v.*) and the submarine pens being built in defeated France. On February 8, 1942, he was killed in an airplane accident at Rastenburg, Hitler's field headquarters on the eastern front. He was succeeded by Albert Speer (*q.v.*), the *Fuehrer's* favorite architect.

Todt managed to steer clear of Nazi intrigues. The complete technician, he was interested only in his work and little else. According to Albert Speer, Hitler paid Todt and his accomplishments a respect bordering on reverence and gave him virtually total power over all road operations, navigable waterways, and power plants.

TOJO, HIDEKI (1884–1948). Japanese Premier and Army officer who ordered the attack on Pearl Harbor in 1941.

EARLY CAREER. Tojo was born in Tokyo in December 1884, the son of an army General. Following the military tradition of his family, he was graduated from the Military Staff College in 1915. Entering the army immediately after graduation, Tojo served in various posts, including Resident Officer in Germany, teaching at his Alma Mater, and sectional chief of the General Staff Office. In 1937 he was promoted to Lieutenant General and became Chief of Staff of the Japanese Army in China. For a time he organized a military inquiry that checked on the loyalty of every officer serving on the Chinese mainland. Meanwhile he became known as a hard-bitten advocate of total war. In May 1938 he was appointed Vice-Minister of War and the following December became Director of Military Aviation.

WORLD WAR II. As Japan's War Minister in 1940, Tojo drafted new mobilization plans and also concluded the Axis Pact with Germany and Italy. He disappointed Hitler and Mussolini by favoring Japanese expansion toward the south rather than collide head-on with the Soviet Union. On the resignation of Prince Fumimaro Konoye (*q.v.*) in October 1941, Tojo became Premier, while at the same time taking on the posts of war, industry, and education. In a speech at Osaka on October 26, 1941, he said: "Japan must go on and develop an ever-expanding program—there is no retreat! . . . If Japan's hundred millions merge and go forward, nothing can stop us. . . . Wars can be won with ease."

Tojo was virtual dictator of Japan from the time of Pearl Harbor and supported a declaration of war on the United States after the attack. At first a popular war leader, he began to lose influence with the series of setbacks starting with the battle of Midway (*q.v.*). Tojo resigned ten days after the American victory at Saipan on July 9, 1944.

POSTWAR. Depressed by the outcome of the war, Tojo attempted to shoot himself but his life was saved. He was tried by an International Military Tribunal and found guilty of crimes against humanity. As a last request he asked that he be served Japanese food on his final day on earth. On December 23, 1948, together with six others condemned to death, he was hanged at Sugamo Prison, Tokyo.

PERSONALITY AND CHARACTER. Short, bald, with sprawling mustache and horn-rimmed spectacles, Tojo was known for his nervous rapidity of speech. He was usually seen taking quick, jerky puffs from an ever-present cigar. Colleagues described him as smart, headstrong, resourceful, and contemptuous of compromise. Because of his edgy temperament, he was often referred to as *kamiseri* ("Razor Blade").

Bibliography. C. Browne, *Tojo: The Lazt Banzai* (1967).

TOKYO EXPRESS. *See* GUADALCANAL CAMPAIGNS.

TOKYO FIRE RAID. Devastating raid by heavy U.S. bombers over Tokyo in one of the most destructive single bombing missions of the war.

Tokyo, with its jerry-built houses, was especially vulnerable to incendiary attack, a fact of major importance to American strategists. High-altitude precision bombing of Japan proved to be ineffective, whereupon Gen. Henry H. Arnold (*q.v.*), commander of the U.S. Army Air Forces, turned to area bombing. Appointed for the task was Maj. Gen. Curtis E. LeMay (*q.v.*), who in January 1945 was given command of the 21st Bomber Command based on the Marianas.

On March 9–10, 1945, LeMay dispatched 334 B-29s from Guam, Saipan, and Tinian in a night raid. The pounding of Tokyo started during a high wind. Thousands of incendiaries created a vicious firestorm. Within half an hour the resulting flames were wholly out of control. A large portion of the city burned to ashes. Flames leapt hundreds of feet into the air with a solid wall of fire sweeping across the city. It was a devil's cauldron of twisting, seething fire as the huge bombers roared over the city in a seemingly endless stream.

The destruction matched the havoc caused later at Hiroshima and Nagasaki (*qq.v.*). Estimates of the damage vary, but the Tokyo fire department reported that 97,000 people were killed in the raid; 125,000 wounded; and 1.2 million left homelsss. Nearly a quarter of all buildings in Tokyo were consumed in the firestorm.

TOKYO ROSE. Collective name of a dozen women who broadcast Japanese propaganda from Radio Tokyo to Pacific-based U.S. troops during World War II. With the end of the war all Tokyo Roses lapsed into obscurity except for one. The others were Japanese citizens and were not brought to trial.

Iva Toguri was born in Los Angeles on July 4, 1916. In July 1941 she went to Japan to visit a sick aunt. She attempted to return home before Pearl Harbor, but her papers did not go through before the war broke out and she was precluded from returning to California. While in Japan, she married a Portuguese national and became Mrs. D'Aquino.

Because of her command of English, Mrs. D'Aquino was hired by the Japanese Broadcasting Corporation and paid about $40 a month for her daily 15-minute broadcasts. At first she identified herself on the air only as "Anna," short for announcer. Later she switched to "Orphan Ann," because she said she "felt adrift." Later she was identified by the name Tokyo Rose.

For millions of GIs in the South Pacific, Tokyo Rose became a normal part of their routine. In between familiar selections of American jazz music, she told the servicemen that their wives and girl friends were being appropriated by civilians who remained behind. There was no point in fighting, she said, because the Japanese were going to win anyway. (*See* PROPAGANDA, WAR.)

For most American soldiers and sailors the broadcasts were a pleasant joke, a break in the boredom of war, and not to be taken seriously. Many American officers even believed that Tokyo Rose contributed greatly to the morale of the armed forces in the Pacific.

POSTWAR. After the war Mrs. D'Aquino was held for two years without trial. She refused to renounce her American citizenship and was, therefore, the only one of the many Tokyo Roses brought to trial. She was tried on eight counts of treason, and was found guilty of one for stating in a broadcast: "Orphans of the Pacific, you are really orphans now. How will you get home now that your ships are sunk?" Mrs. D'Aquino contended that the statement was not intended seriously, that the Allies had just won a major sea victory, that she had been forced to do the broadcasts, and that, anyway, the talks never did any harm. She was convicted on October 6, 1949, and sentenced to ten years in prison and a $10,000 fine.

AFTERMATH. Mrs. D'Aquino was released from prison with credit for good behavior in 1956 and completed payment of her fine in 1975. On January 19,

1977, President Gerald Ford issued a pardon, without comment, for Tokyo Rose, now a 60-year-old clerk in an Oriental gift shop. "I have always maintained my innocence," she commented. "This pardon is a measure of vindication."

TOLAND, JOHN WILLARD, (1912–   ). U.S. author and historian of World War II.

Toland's books on World War II won great popularity. Among them are *Battle: The Story of the Bulge* (1959); *The Flying Tigers* (1963); *The Last Hundred Days* (1966), which won an Overseas Press Club citation; and *The Battle of the Bulge* (1966). His biography *Hitler* (1976), a best-seller, is considered one of the best works of its kind. Toland's style was distinguished by painstaking research with emphasis on interviews with survivors and a fast-paced narrative form.

TOLBUKHIN, FEDOR IVANOVICH (1894–1949). Soviet Army officer rated as one of the great tacticians of the war.

At the beginning of the war Tolbukhin was raised from obscurity to Major General. His military ability meant disaster for the Germans facing him on the southern flank of the eastern front. At Stalingrad he helped trap German troops in a devastating pincers movement. (*See* STALINGRAD, BATTLE OF.) He demoralized German forces by his blockage of the Crimean Peninsula and his clearance of the routes to the Black Sea. In 1944 he inflicted tremendous damage on the Germans in Bulgaria, Yugoslavia, Hungary, and Austria, and was instrumental in the final German capitulation. He was promoted to Marshal and awarded the Soviet Order of Victory, the Red Army's highest award.

With his broad, heavy face and stocky build, Tolbukhin resembled Churchill. His bulldog tactics dismayed the Germans. Russians include him among their "Four Horsemen of the German Apocalypse" (*q.v.*).

TORCH. Allied code or cover name for the simultaneous Anglo-American invasion of northwest Africa on November 8, 1942. The plan was worked out by Roosevelt and Churchill at the Casablanca Conference (*q.v.*). There were several objectives:

1. *Entrapment. Operation Torch* was designed to trap German Gen. Erwin Rommel (*q.v.*) and his desert troops between British forces moving from the east and Americans invading from the west.

2. *Base.* Success of the operation would provide a suitable base for action against southern Europe.

3. *Blockade.* From this base the blockade could be tightened against the Axis by concentrating on Mediterranean and South Atlantic sea routes.

4. *Soviet Alliance.* The move would help solidify the Allied alliance with Soviet Russia by taking some pressure from the Russian front.

5. *Spanish Neutrality*. It would prevent Gen. Francisco Franco (*q.v.*) from entering the war.

6. *Checkmate*. Finally, the success of *Operation Torch* would forestall any similar action by the Axis powers.

STRATEGY. The grand strategy for *Torch* was worked out in London by the Joint Chiefs of Staff. In a surprising move, Lt. Gen. Dwight D. Eisenhower (*q.v.*), then virtually unknown, was placed in overall command. A press commander identified him as "Lt. Col. D. D. Ersenbring." When news of *Torch* was communicated to Stalin, he enthusiastically agreed. He was still irked by Allied inaction in the matter of a Second Front (*q.v.*), but he was happy to note that a definite plan of action was under way to lift pressure from his weary troops. (*See also* NORTH AFRICA, CAMPAIGNS IN.)

LANDINGS. Three separate task forces made up the *Torch* invasion. Some 35,000 American troops left the United States for French Morocco; another 35,000 came from England to take Oran in western Algeria; and a third task force of 10,000 Americans and 23,000 British moved from England to take Algiers. The British and American naval forces transported all the troops in this undertaking.

The landings began on November 8, 1942. The British managed to get ashore with little difficulty, but the French forces at Oran and in Morocco did not surrender until November 10 and 11.

The operation was complicated by a confused political situation. The attempt to win a rapid French surrender was foiled when the anti-British Adm. Jean Darlan (*q.v.*) returned unexpectedly to North Africa two days before the invasion. He at first led a fierce French resistance. Some French forces in North Africa were loyal to Gen. Charles de Gaulle's (*q.v.*) liberation movement in England; others backed Gen. Henri Giraud (*q.v.*), who had just escaped to France from a German prison camp; and some were pledged to their commander, Gen. Henri Pétain (*q.v.*), head of the Vichy Government. Darlan broke with Pétain and ordered the surrender of Algiers on the evening of November 8th.

SIGNIFICANCE. The capitulation of the French forces in North Africa speeded up Hitler's long-planned total occupation of France. German troops advanced into southern France with the object of taking the powerful French fleet at Toulon. The British could not persuade the fleet to join the Allies. Within a few hours of the arrival of the Germans, the French scuttled 73 ships in Toulon Harbor (November 27). It was now clear that there would be a bitter struggle for possession of North Africa.

Bibliography. W. Haupt, *North African Campaign, 1940-1943* (1969); J. Strawson, *The Battle for North Africa* (1970); and M. MacCloskey, *TORCH and the Twelfth Air Force* (1971).

TORGAU. German town where advance patrols of Americans met Russian units for the first time in the war.

Torgau was about 30 miles northeast of Leipzig and 75 miles south of Berlin. On April 25, 1945, Russian troops of the 58th Guards' Division linked up with American patrols rolling in from the west. The meeting was a happy one for both Russians and Americans. The Russians displayed a large red banner reading: OUR GREETINGS TO THE BRAVE TROOPS OF THE AMERICAN FIRST ARMY. There were mutual toasts. Americans danced with Russian girls for the benefit of the press. The event signalled the doom of Nazi Germany.

TOTAL WAR. War in which all manpower and material resources are mobilized for the critical task of achieving victory.

Fought on land, sea, and air, total war makes no distinction between combatants and non-combatants, with the result that civilian deaths and injuries are substantial. World War II was an example of total war.

TRUK ISLANDS. Japanese naval and air base in the West Pacific.

LOCATION. Truk is a complex of 55 mountainous islands of volcanic origin comprising 39 square miles (100 sq. km.) in the East Caroline Islands. It is situated in a large lagoon enclosed by a coral reef and 87 low coral islets.

WORLD WAR II. Truk was a key Japanese naval and air base throughout World War II. A great stronghold was constructed on the six largest islands in the lagoon, 875 miles to the north of another powerful base at Rabaul (*q.v.*). In September 1942, the powerful 2nd and 3rd Japanese Fleets sailed from Truk to cover Japanese landings on Guadalcanal (*See* GUADALCANAL CAMPAIGNS). The Japanese warships were eventually recalled to Truk. In November 1943, after U.S. Marines landed on Bougainville (*q.v.*), the Japanese withdrew their warships and aircraft from the stronghold at Rabaul to Truk.

In February 1944, U.S. bombers made a devastating attack on Truk, destroying 275 aircraft, 2 destroyers, and a number of merchant ships. The assault enabled the Americans to invade Eniwetok (*see* MARSHALL ISLANDS, BATTLE FOR THE) without interference from Japanese aircraft. At this time Adms. Ernest King and Chester Nimitz (*qq.v.*) decided that Truk could be bypassed in much the same manner as Rabaul. For the remainder of the war, Truk, with its garrison of 50,000 lay useless.

Bibliography. See S. E. Morison, *History of U.S. Naval Operations in World War II* (1947–1960).

TRUMAN, HARRY S (1884–1972). 33rd President of the United States.

EARLY CAREER. Truman was born in Lamar, Missouri, on May 8, 1884, and was reared on a farm. He was educated at the high school in Independence, Missouri. He served in the field artillery in France during World War I. After a short period as a retail merchant, he turned to politics, and was elected judge (1922–1924 and 1926–1934). He was elected to the U.S. Senate in 1934.

WORLD WAR II. In 1941 Truman achieved national prominence through reports of his Senate Committee to investigate government expenditures. He accused the army of "fantastically poor judgment" in the choice of camp sites and in its policy of renting cars, trucks, and tractors instead of buying them in quantity. His inquiry was said to have saved the government $200 million.

In 1944 Truman was elected Vice-President, serving with Roosevelt, who was returned as President for a fourth term. The American people did not want to change leadership at a critical moment in the war. On the death of Roosevelt on April 12, 1945, Truman succeeded to the presidency after having been in office only 83 days as Vice-President.

PRESIDENCY. Truman continued most of his predecessor's policies including preparations for the United Nations. The war in Europe ended on May 8, 1945. In July Truman was in Berlin attending the Potsdam Conference (*q.v.*). He informed Stalin of the existence of the atomic bomb, but the Russian dictator seemed to show little interest. Churchill agreed that it should be used, but the final decision was made by Truman. He authorized its immediate use against Japan on August 6, 1945, and announced it to the world.

POSTWAR. The threatening advance of communism in Europe led Truman to abandon the policy of amicable conciliation with the Russians and to take a strong stand against further Communist expansion. To meet Soviet aggression in Turkey and Greece, he proposed the Truman Doctrine calling for economic and military assistance there (1947). In Europe he inaugurated the Marshall Plan to bring about the reconstruction of England and continental countries. Reelected in 1948, he supported the Fair Deal in domestic affairs and the North Atlantic Treaty Organization (NATO) in foreign policy. He died in Kansas City on December 26, 1972.

PERSONALITY AND CHARACTER. Five-feet-nine-and-three-quarter inches tall, weighing 167 pounds, Truman was smooth shaven and wore spectacles. He gave little evidence in his early career that he would turn out to be a strong-minded and decisive President. In his clipped Missouri accent he said that he had not lost a single night's sleep after making the decision to use the A-bomb. The American public rated him as among their outstanding Presidents.

Bibliography. Truman wrote *Year of Decision* (1955); *Years of Trial and Hope* (1956); and *Mr. Citizen* (1960). *See also* J. Daniels, *The Man of Independence* (1950); L. W. Koenig, *The Truman Administration* (1956); A. Steinberg, *The Man from Missouri* (1962); and H. F. Gosnell, *Truman's Crises: A Political Biography of Harry S. Truman* (1980).

TRUSCOTT, LUCIAN KING, JR. (1895–1965). U.S. Army officer and Field Deputy to Gen. Dwight D. Eisenhower (*q.v.*) in Tunisia.

Three weeks after the bombing of Pearl Harbor, Truscott was promoted to temporary Colonel. In May 1942, as a temporary Brigadier General, he was sent to England and attached to the Combined Operations staff there. He established the first American Ranger unit, a force of elite fighters patterned after the British Commandos. With them he developed his passion for rigorous training, which earned him the reputation of being "hard as hell." (*See* RANGERS). He was the principal U.S. observer on the raid on Dieppe, France, on August 19, 1942. (*See* DIEPPE RAID.) In November 1942 he landed in North Africa, where he led a special contingent to liberate Port Lyautey in French Morocco from Vichy troops. (*See* TORCH.)

During the battle of Tunisia, Truscott, as Field Deputy to Eisenhower, brought his harsh training methods to the troops in North Africa. He prided himself on having the fastest moving fighters by stepping up their march cadence. These marches were termed "Truscott Trots" by his grumbling troops. In July 1943 he headed the 3rd Division, which landed in Sicily and later took part in engagements on the Italian mainland. After the liberation of Rome he and his men were sent to take part in the amphibious landings in southern France.

In a succession of surprise attacks, Truscott led his troops to join the American thrust from Normandy. (*See* NORMANDY INVASION.) In December 1944 he was sent back to Italy to succeed Gen. Mark W. Clark (*q.v.*) as commanding General of the 5th Army. His troops took Bologna, Modena, and La Spezia, and together with British forces captured Genoa, Milan, and Turin. (*See* ITALIAN FRONT, CAMPAIGNS ON THE.)

Gray-haired, with strutting jaw and squinting eyes, Truscott, like Gen. George S. Patton, Jr. (*q.v.*), was regarded as an unorthodox and eccentric disciplinarian. His booming, throaty voice gave him an air of exceptional toughness. His dress, too, was outside the normal range. He wore a shiny, enameled helmet, a weather-stained jacket, a white silk scarf, and faded dress cavalry breeches and boots. He was widely regarded as one of the most efficient sea-to-land commander in the U.S. Army.

Bibliography. Truscott described his role in World War II in *Command Missions* (1954).

TUPOLEV, ANDREY N. (1888–1972). Russian aircraft designer.

Tupolev designed the *ANT-6,* a four-engined bomber with a bomb load of two tons, one of the oldest Soviet aircraft used in World War II. He also was responsible for the *SB-2,* a twin-engined medium bomber used in the Spanish civil war and in World War II as a night bomber until 1943. His *TU-2* carried some 5,000 pounds of bombs but was manufactured in only limited numbers. After the war he continued to design passenger planes.

TURNER, RICHMOND KELLY (1885–1961). U.S. naval officer who became the navy's leading expert in amphibious warfare.

In July 1942 Turner, at the age of 57, was ordered to the South Pacific. From mid-August to the end of 1942 he was in charge of task forces of occupation in the Solomon Islands. The forces under his command were subject to continual enemy submarine, surface, and air attack. Turner was held partly responsible for some disastrous losses (*See* SAVO ISLAND, BATTLE OF). He was, nevertheless, awarded the Navy Cross for his activities in the Solomons in fighting a new kind of war. At Rendova he had his flagship, *McCawley*, shot out from under him.

After the successful completion of the Solomons campaign, Turner was transferred to the Central Pacific area. It was his task to see that the men and equipment got off the ships and on to the beaches in the new type of island warfare. In November 1943 he led the forces that attacked the Gilbert Islands, which lay between Hawaii and New Guinea. His casualties at Tarawa (*q.v.*) were unexpectedly high when his landing crafts were caught on boat traps built among the reefs.

In February 1944 Turner's southern task force operating in the Marshall Islands captured all the immediate objectives on the strategic Kwajalein (*q.v.*) atoll. He moved on Eniwetok (*q.v.*), while Adm. Raymond Spruance (*q.v.*) directed a clever diversionary attack on the Japanese stronghold at Truk, in the Caroline Islands, about 750 miles to the east. He also took part in the Marianas campaign (*q.v.*) in June 1944, which began with the invasion of Saipan (*q.v.*). In August 1944 he established his land headquarters in Saipan.

Tall, with firm mouth and cold blue eyes under heavy eyebrows, Turner was described as hot-tempered, impatient of failure, and as abrasive as a file. He was not universally liked by the seamen; they resented his merciless denunciations of slack behavior. He fought interminably with other officers of equal or superior rank. Top navy brass, however, regarded him highly for his skilled organizing, dynamic leadership, executive ability, and personal fearlessness. He was, they said, "an old-line Navy man" with "the longest Irish upper lip in the Navy." He died in Monterey, California, on February 12, 1961.

TWENTY COMMITTEE. *See* XX-COMMITTEE; DOUBLE CROSS SYSTEM; and MASTERMAN, JOHN C.

TWILIGHT WAR. Term used by Prime Minister Neville Chamberlain (*q.v.*) to describe the "sit-down war." (*See SITZKRIEG.*)

U

U-BOATS. German submarine arm.

The term *U-Boat* was derived from *Unterseeboot,* or "underwater boat" and was used to describe German submarines in both world wars. Submarines were specifically banned by the Treaty of Versailles in 1919 after bitter Allied experience in World War I, but as early as 1922 plans were under way to promote research on future undersea craft. Early in his chancellorship Hitler placed secret orders for the expansion of the U-Boat arm even before he publicly renounced the Treaty of Versailles.

As in World War I, German U-Boats exacted a fearful toll of Allied shipping in the first months of the war. The Allies and neutral countries eventually lost more than 2,800 ships, totaling nearly 5 million tons, mostly to German U-Boats. (*See* WOLF-PACK TACTICS.)

Among the more noteworthy U-Boats were the following:

U-47. Type VIIB, this U-Boat, commanded by the then Lt. Günther Prien (*q.v.*), slipped into the great British naval base at Scapa Flow, north of Scotland, and sank the battleship *Royal Oak* (*q.v.*). Prien lost his submarine and his life on March 7, 1941, in the North Atlantic when attacked by two British corvettes.

U-48. Commanded by Herbert Schulze, the *U-48* compiled the highest record of victims in World War II, sinking 51 Allied ships between the outbreak of the war and June 1941.

U-110. Forced to the surface on May 9, 1941 by several British warships, the *U-110* was boarded by British seamen who obtained vital information about the *Enigma* coding machine (*see* ULTRA) as well as German U-Boat ciphers. The *U-110* sank while being towed.

U-132. U-Boat responsible for moving the sea war far westward. On July 6,

1942, it slipped into the Gulf of St. Lawrence in Canada and sank four ships before withdrawing two weeks later. (*See* ATLANTIC, BATTLE OF THE.)

U-166. On July 25, 1942, this U-Boat laid a barrage of mines off the estuary of the Mississippi River. She then moved into the Gulf of Mexico, where she torpedoed and sank four merchant ships.

U-201. Under command of *Kapitänleutnant* Schnee, the *U-201* roamed the mid-Atlantic in July 1944 and sank a British freight-carrying liner as well as a corvette.

U-505. One of Germany's larger type U-Boats, the *U-505* was captured and boarded by seamen from a U.S. task force northwest of Dakar. She was towed to the United States, where she became an object of public curiosity.

U-570. On August 28, 1941, the *U-570*, type VIIC of the German submarine force, surfaced, only to be bluffed into surrender by two British aircraft. The crew unsuccessfully tried to scuttle the craft, after which a boarding party took the U-Boat as a prize of war. Renamed the *Graph,* she underwent a series of exhaustive tests to devise countermeasures against U-Boats. After being used as a target, the *Graph* was wrecked off the Hebrides on March 20, 1944.

U-652. This U-Boat was involved in the "Greer Incident" (*q.v.*).
Bibliography. G. Bennett, *Naval Battles of World War II* (1975).

U-CRUISERS. New and larger U-Boats introduced by the Germans in mid-1942.
  Weighing 1,600 tons, with a radius of action of 30,000 miles, the U-Cruisers could dive to a depth of 600 feet and could be refueled in mid-ocean by new U-Tankers. (*See also* WOLF-PACK TACTICS.)

U-TANKERS. German ships used to refuel U-Boats in mid-ocean. (*See* MILCH COWS.)

ULTRA. Code or cover name for intelligence produced by deciphering German secret messages. Just before the start of World War II, *Ultra* enabled British Intelligence to break the German code. Throughout the war the British were able to intercept and decode wireless exchanges between Hitler and his generals in the field. The practice was an important element in Allied victory.

ENIGMA. Before 1939, German experts produced in quantity an electrically operated coding machine that they believed to be foolproof. Known as *Enigma,* the ancient Greek word for puzzle, it was considered of prime importance for successful military operations.

In 1939 a Polish mechanic, who had been employed in a factory in East Germany, guessed rightly that the Germans were making some sort of secret signaling machine. Despite activities of the *Gestapo* (*q.v.*) in Warsaw, the mechanic got in touch with a British agent, who reported his story to London. British agents secretly smuggled the young Pole to Paris under a false passport. There he constructed a wooden mock-up that convinced British Intelligence that it had something of vital importance.

With the help of the Polish Secret Service, and in utmost secrecy, a newly built *Enigma* machine was brought to London. Whether this was one of the many thousands manufactured in Germany or whether it was an exact copy is not clear. The machine consisted of electrically operated drums around which were placed letters of the alphabet. A typewriter fed messages into the machine, where they were scrambled in such a way that the contents were regarded as unbreakable code. German experts believed that the permutations were so complex that it would take many months to ascertain the meaning of any message.

CODE BREAKING. In early 1939 the *Enigma* machine was sent to a secluded country house near Bletchley Park (*q.v.*), home of the Government's Code and Cipher School. A team of Britain's top mathematicians and cryptanalysts was organized to break the supposedly unbreakable code. First the machine was dismantled. Then, using electronic computer techniques, and with the aid of another highly sophisticated machine, the scientists finally solved the problem of code breaking.

WORLD WAR II. Throughout most of the war, the British intercepted high-level German signals, processed them, and distributed them under complete security to Churchill, Roosevelt, and Allied commanders in the field. Allied civilian and military leaders in positions of command knew most German strategic and tactical moves before they began. Often Allied officers read Hitler's orders before his generals in the field received them.

From *Ultra* the British learned that *Case Yellow,* which originally envisaged an attack in the West through Belgium, Holland, and Luxembourg in 1940, had undergone considerable changes before it was placed into effect. It was *Ultra* that presented British airmen with information to keep the *Luftwaffe* at bay in the summer of 1940. (*See* BRITAIN, BATTLE OF.) The machine also gave London precise details of the development of *Sea Lion* (*q.v.*), the projected German invasion of England. It was responsible to a large extent for success of the North African campaign against Gen. Erwin Rommel's *Afrika Korps* (*qq.v.*). Rommel's every move was known in advance by quick decoding of messages between him and Hitler. (*See* NORTH AFRICA, CAMPAIGNS IN.)

Ultra gave the British precious information for their withdrawal from Crete on June 1, 1941. (*See* CRETE, INVASION OF.) In Sicily in the summer of 1943 it apprised Gen. George Smith Patton, Jr. (*q.v.*) of positions of German

Panzer (q.v.) units and made it possible for him to outflank them on the road to Messina. (*See* SICILY, INVASION OF.) *Ultra* helped the Allies trap German armies in the summer of 1944. (*See* NORMANDY INVASION.) It was ineffective as an Allied tool only in mid-December 1944 because Hitler for once ordered radio silence. (*See* BULGE, BATTLE OF THE.)

BATTLE OF THE ATLANTIC. Ultra was crucial for the war at sea. When the German battleship *Bismarck* sank the British battle cruiser *Hood* on May 24, 1941, the German commander, thinking that he was being shadowed by a British warship, sent a long message to Naval Headquarters in Germany complaining of loss of fuel and asking for orders. The *Bismarck* was ordered to return to Brest. British Intelligence learned the position of the German battleship by means of *Ultra.* Within two days the *Bismarck* was sunk. (*See* BISMARCK, SINKING OF THE.)

Ultra became the key to the war at sea. (*See* ATLANTIC, BATTLE OF THE.) It was valuable for reading German instructions to U-Boat captains and for enabling Allied convoys to elude attack. By mid-1943, German submarine domination of the Atlantic was broken, due in large part to information obtained by *Ultra.*

SECRECY. Throughout the war it was regarded as a matter of highest priority for Allied security to maintain secrecy about *Ultra.* On November 14, 1940, British Intelligence learned through *Ultra* that the midlands manufacturing city of Coventry was to be bombed. Curiously, instead of a code word, the Germans used the actual name "Coventry." Word was flashed to Churchill, who was presented with an agonizing choice. The attack would take place in four hours. If the Prime Minister ordered Coventry to be evacuated, he would arouse German suspicions that he had foreknowledge of the raid. Churchill most reluctantly made his tragic decision not to order evacuation, but instead alerted only the Royal Air Force (*q.v.*) and Coventry city services. This cost lives, but it safeguarded precious *Ultra.* (*See* COVENTRY, BOMBING OF.)

GERMAN SECURITY. Because they changed their code daily and because they used varying codes for the different armed forces, German military leaders believed their system of codes to be completely secure. Not until the end of the war did they learn how successful the British were with their special deciphering machine. The one major failure of *Ultra* was due to a stroke of German luck. Preparations for the Battle of the Bulge (*q.v.*) were so secret that no information was transmitted by wireless: The attack came as a complete surprise to the Allies.

Bibliography. For an excellent account of *Ultra* by a group captain who was in charge of security for this intelligence coup, *see* F. W. Winterbotham, *The Ultra Secret* (1974). *See also* A. C. Brown, *Bodyguard of Lies* (1975); R. Lewin, *Ultra Goes to War* (1980); R. Bennett, *Ultra in the West* (1980); P. Calvonessi, *The Secret Ultra* (1980); and J. Leasor, *Code Named Nimrod* (1981).

"UNCONDITIONAL SURRENDER." Term used by President Roosevelt in a press conference after the meeting of Allied war leaders at Casablanca. (*For details of the origin of the phrase, see* CASABLANCA CONFERENCE.)

The issue of "unconditional surrender" was of major importance. In Allied countries it was accepted widely as an official war aim. In Nazi Germany, Propaganda Minister Paul Joseph Goebbels (*q.v.*) used it to advise the German public that it had no alternative to fighting on until the end.

After the war some observers criticized Roosevelt's "unconditional surrender" formula as having contributed to unnecessary destruction in Germany and Japan as well as to bolstering the extension of Soviet influence.

UNDERGROUND. Clandestine groups of armed men and women who operated in countries conquered and occupied by the Germans. These irregular soldiers, usually volunteers, carried on warfare of their own.

BACKGROUND. The term *guerrilla* originated in Spain during the Peninsular War, 1808–1814, when bands of patriots retreated to the mountains to carry on war against the French invaders. The Hague Convention set up rules for guerrilla warfare in 1899 and confirmed them in 1907. Guerrillas were active in the Italian invasion of Ethiopia (1935) and in the Spanish civil war (1936–1939).

WORLD WAR II. The underground played a prominent part throughout World War II from the occupation of France in 1940 to the end of the war. Essentially a civilian movement, its goal was to strike back at Hitler's New Order (*q.v.*) and prepare the way for liberation. A kind of quasi-military organization, it operated in hostile territory. It carefully screened recruits, formed them into closely knit groups, and worked in high secrecy. Underground fighters kept in close touch with the local population to ensure food and shelter. Experts in sabotage, they blew up railway lines, destroyed ammunition dumps, and harried communication lines. They killed or kidnapped German sentries, gathered military information to be forwarded to London to governments-in-exile (*q.v.*), and smuggled Allied airmen back to London. They worked assiduously to discourage would-be collaborators.

One of the best-organized underground movements was the *Maquis,* French guerrillas who harried Germans during the occupation years in France and who cooperated with the Anglo-American invaders in 1944. (*See MAQUIS.*)

PARTISANS. Communist-led underground guerrilla units were known generally as Partisans (*q.v.*). Despite ferocious reprisals, they operated successfully behind German lines and held out until victory. Under the leadership of Josip Broz Tito (*q.v.*), Yugoslav Partisans struck at German invaders and by 1943 controlled much of the country. In 1944, Italian Partisans worked effectively for the overthrow of Mussolini and were responsible for his execution. (*See MUSSOLINI, BENITO.*)

SIGNIFICANCE. Underground guerrilla activity contributed much to final Allied victory. It played an important role in such war developments as the liberation of Paris in the summer of 1944. (*See* PARIS, LIBERATION OF.) (*See also FRANC TIREURS ET PARTISANS FRANÇAIS;* FRENCH FORCES OF THE INTERIOR; *MAQUIS;* PARTISANS and RESISTANCE MOVEMENTS.)

Bibliography. For a typical account of underground forces, see T. Bor-Komorowski, *The Secret Army* (1951).

UNITED NATIONS DECLARATION. Joint declaration by the Allies pledging themselves to continue the struggle against Nazi Germany.

On January 1, 1942, New Year's Day, 26 nations signed a United Nations Declaration agreeing to employ all their military and economic power to defeat the Axis. Each signatory promised not to make a separate peace. The idea of a postwar United Nations took hold at this time.

The text of the United Nations Declaration:

A joint declaration by the United States of America, the United Kingdom of Great Britain and Northern Ireland, the Union of Soviet Socialist Republics, China, Australia, Belgium, Canada, Costa Rica, Cuba, Czechoslovakia, Dominican Republic, El Salvador, Greece, Guatemala, Haiti, Honduras, India, Luxembourg, Netherlands, New Zealand, Nicaragua, Norway, Panama, Poland, South Africa, Yugoslavia.

The Governments signatory hereto,

Having subscribed to a common program of purposes and principles embodied in the Joint Declaration of the President of the United States of America and the Prime Minister of the United Kingdom of Great Britain and Northern Ireland dated August 14, 1941, known as the Atlantic Charter.

Being convinced that complete victory over their enemies is essential to defend life, liberty, independence and religious freedom, and to preserve human rights and justice in their own lands as well as in other lands, and that they are now engaged in a common struggle against savage and brutal forces seeking to subjugate the world, DECLARE:

(1) Each Government pledges itself to employ its full resources, military or economic, against those members of the Tripartite Pact and its adherents with which such government is at war.

(2) Each Government pledges itself to cooperate with the Governments signatory hereto and not to make a separate armistice or peace with the enemies.

The foregoing declaration may be adhered to by other nations which are, or which may be, rendering material assistance and contributions in the struggle for victory over Hitlerism.

Done at Washington.
January First, 1942

Bibliography. On the United Nations, *see* N. D. Bentwich, *From Geneva to San Francisco* (1946); J. E. Harley, *Documentary Textbook on the United Nations* (1947); G. Murray, *From the League to the U.N.* (1948); A. Vandenbosch and W. N. Hogan, *The United Nations* (1952); and C. N. Eichelberger, *U.N.: The First Twenty Years* (1965).

UNITED NATIONS MONETARY AND FINANCIAL CONFERENCE.
Meeting held in New Hampshire in the summer of 1944 to restore finan-

cial health and facilitate postwar reconstruction. (*See* BRETTON WOODS CONFERENCE.)

UNITED SERVICE ORGANIZATIONS (USO). War units that supplied social, recreational, welfare, and spiritual facilities for the U.S. armed services.

BACKGROUND. The United Service Organizations for National Defense was formed in February 1941, ten months before the attack on Pearl Harbor. Although incorporated as an independent agency, the USO was actually a combination of six national groups: the Young Men's Christian Association, Young Women's Christian Association, Salvation Army, National Catholic Community Service, National Jewish Welfare Board, and Traveler's Aid-International Social Service of America.

WORLD WAR II. The USO became a war agency shortly after the United States entered the war. In metropolitan centers and in towns near military posts, it provided relief from duty for members of the armed services. USO units specialized in dancing and entertainment, as well as in distribution of pastries, peanut butter sandwiches, coffee, and Coca-Cola.

In New York City the Stage Door Canteen, a branch of the USO, featured actresses of the Broadway stage, who served as volunteers in preparing food and offering entertainment. Abroad the USO sent volunteer celebrities, including Bing Crosby, George Jessel, Joe E. Brown, Jo Stafford, and Frances Langford, to perform for the armed forces. Bob Hope (*q.v.*), with his self-deprecating wit and officer jokes, was a special favorite. Entire units of lesser-known entertainers were flown to battle fronts by the U.S. Air Forces for the USO in all theaters of war.

The USO was supported by voluntary contributions, and thousands of volunteers assisted in its programs. Servicemen and women flocked to USO clubs and hospitality centers. More than 4,000 entertainers were sent to posts and hospitals around the world. USO officials claimed that they had entertained more than 1 billion persons throughout the war.

Bibliography. United Service Organizations for National Defense, *Operation USO* (1948); and J. M. Carson, *Home Away from Home: The Story of the USO* (c. 1948).

UNITED STATES ARMY AIR FORCES. American air arm in World War II. The American equivalent of the British Royal Air Force and the German *Luftwaffe* (*qq.v.*), it was responsible for combat against the Axis in the air, interdiction of German land forces, and strategic bombing of enemy targets in the Pacific.

BACKGROUND. On August 1, 1907, four years after the first flight of the Wright Brothers, the U.S. Army set up an aeronautical Division in the Office of the Chief Signal Officer. During World War I Americans manufactured

11,000 aircraft and purchased an additional 5,000 abroad. American pilots, including Capt. Eddie Rickenbacker, destroyed 781 enemy planes with a loss of 280. In May 1918 military aviation was removed from the Signal Corps and named the Air Service, a branch of the U.S. Army. In 1926 the Air Service became the Air Corps.

WORLD WAR II. German success in the *Blitzkrieg* (*q.v.*) against Poland, starting on September 1, 1939 (*see* POLAND, CAMPAIGN IN), stirred Washington into action. On January 3, 1940, President Roosevelt, in his annual message, called for the production of 50,000 planes a year, a figure that aroused amused but uncomfortable skepticism in Berchtesgaden. In the summer of 1941 the U.S. Army Air Corps became the U.S. Army Air Forces, responsible for the coordination of all air matters. In March 1942, after Pearl Harbor, the USAAF was granted equal status with the Army Ground Forces and the Services of Supply within the War Department. The air arm gradually achieved autonomy and retained its status during the war. Personnel increased from 150,000 to 2.4 million, and aircraft from 4,000 to approximately 230,000.

ORGANIZATION. The rough outlines of organization were set up during the war. Three major commands were combat oriented—Air Defense, Strategic Air, and Tactical Air Commands. Among the support commands were Air Material, Air Training, Military Air Transport Service, and Air Research and Development.

ORDER OF BATTLE. In mid-August 1945 the order of battle of the U.S. Army Strategic Air Forces in the Pacific area was as follows (*see* Order Of Battle for European Theater, May 1945).

Headquarters, USAAF, Guam, Mariana Islands:
    Commanding General   Gen. Carl Spaatz
    Deputy Commander   Lt. Gen. B. McK. Giles
    Chief of Staff   Maj. Gen. C. E. LeMay

9th Air Force, Okinawa, Ryuku Islands:
    Commanding General   Lt. Gen. James H. Doolittle

20th Air Force, Guam, Mariana Islands:
    Commanding General   Lt. Gen. Nathan F. Twining

PERFORMANCE. American air power played a major role in World War II. Bombers, including the *Flying Fortresses* (*B-17*) (*q.v.*) and the *Liberators* (*B-24*), flew more than 75,000 missions and dropped 395,000 tons of bombs on German targets. Fighter planes, including the *Lightning* (*P-38*), *Thunderbolt* (*P-47*), and *Mustang* (P-51), protected bombers on their raids and engaged in combat with the *Luftwaffe*. The USAAF destroyed more than 35,000 enemy aircraft, while losing 18,000.

Until May 1943 the bombing of Germany was done exclusively by the RAF. By then the U.S. 8th Air Force was strong enough to join in the systematic raids. Americans specialized in daylight attacks, while the RAF flew at night. U.S. pilots took part in the attack on the special targets (*see* RUHR DAMS) and helped make Berlin a modern Carthage. (*See* BERLIN, BATTLE FOR.) Performance of the USAAF in the Pacific was equally as impressive.

CASUALTIES. The USAAF suffered 115,382 battle casualties during the war.

Bibliography. D. Richards and D. Saunders, *The U.S. Strategic Bombing Survey* (1945); W. F. Craven and J. L. Cates, *The Army Air Forces in World War II* (1951–1954); and H. Rumpf, *The Bombing of Germany* (1961).

UNITED STATES AT WAR. For the second time in the 20th century the United States was at war with Germany. Once again American intervention played a crucial role in the conflict. Again the home front was geared for all-out war.

BACKGROUND. In 1914 American public opinion was divided, but gradually it swung to the Allied side. In 1939 most Americans were sympathetic to beleaguered Britain. Some isolationists, including national hero Charles A. Lindbergh (*q.v.*) and Senator Burton K. Wheeler, vehemently opposed American involvement in what they regarded as a European conflict. Others, notably President Franklin D. Roosevelt (*q.v.*), believed American intervention to be inevitable.

In the mid-1930s the U.S. Congress passed neutrality legislation, but within two months after the outbreak of war in Europe in 1939, the ban on arms was repealed. Roosevelt described Britain as "the spearhead of resistance to world conquest." In June 1940, just after the Dunkirk evacuation (*q.v.*), Washington sent a small supply of arms to Britain. A few months later came the much-disputed destroyer deal, by which 51 overage U.S. destroyers were given to Britain in exchange for American rights to maintain bases in Newfoundland and Bermuda. In addition, Roosevelt, took steps to protect American merchant ships at sea. The pendulum was swinging gradually to full support for Britain.

WASHINGTON AT WAR. Almost overnight after December 7, 1941, the day of Pearl Harbor, the national capital was transformed from a sleepy little southern town into the central metropolis of the free world. Only days earlier few uniforms were seen on the streets, but Washington soon was flooded with uniformed men and women. With London and Leningrad under siege and Paris occupied by Germans, the people of the Allied nations looked automatically to the American capital, far from the combat theaters, as the center of resistance against the Axis.

Washington became the focal point of the American war effort. The new Pentagon headquarters across the Potomac River in Virginia would become central for combat operations in all theaters of war. Washington offices regulated the flow of war production, set prices and wages, organized the ration system, allocated supplies, supervised civilian defense, informed the public, and issued a multitude of regulations.

This vast undertaking required the services of the country's best brains. Thousands of leaders from the industrial, business, and professional worlds were brought to the capital for critical war work. The Washington task force worked at multiple duties: writing regulations for the enforcement of rationing or price control (Office of Price Administration); working on bombing targets and blockades (Board of Economic Warfare); watching the mails for espionage (Office of Censorship); co-ordinating the use of rubber (War Production Board); or handling billions of dollars for war materials (Lend-Lease Program). There was much duplication and wastage of effort, but on the whole the management of the war from Washington was successful.

CIVILIAN MORALE. American morale remained consistently high throughout the war. Added to resentment against the Japanese was an increasing awareness of the nature of the Hitler regime and the belief that Nazism had to be destroyed. The American public was convinced that it was involved in a crusade for a decent world. Once committed, Americans pitched in with aggressive enthusiasm. They were willing to accept the deprivations of war. Those who were not drafted for the armed services—clerks, servants, nursemaids, cooks—went into the war plants to help produce the tools of war. Women drove cars, operated cranes, toiled in munitions factories. Children joined in war work. The entire country was united in an all-out effort for victory.

MOBILIZATION OF MANPOWER. In May 1940 the United States had only a small regular army, a one-ocean navy, in all a strictly limited military force. Soon after Pearl Harbor, necessary measures were taken to provide manpower. Roosevelt appointed a nine-man War Manpower Commission (WMC) for this purpose. The draft age was lowered to 18 and all males between 18 and 38 were made eligible for selective service, with deferments limited to war industries, agriculture, the clergy, and hardship cases.

Altogether during the war 31 million men were registered and almost 10 million were inducted into service. With voluntary enlistments, 15,145,115 men and women served in the armed forces—10.4 million in the army; 3.9 million in the navy; 600,000 in the marines; and 250,000 in the Coast Guard. The peak strength of the U.S. Army Air Forces was more than 2,400,000. The armed forces were bolstered eventually by 200,000 women. More than 4 million men and women were transported to battlefields scattered over the globe.

CONSCIENTIOUS OBJECTORS. According to the Selective Service Act of 1940, a person "who by means of religious training and belief was conscientiously opposed to participation in war in any form in place of being inducted could be assigned to work of national importance under civilian direction. More than 25,000 conscientious objectors served in the armed forces in noncombatant duty. Many, including Jehovah's Witnesses, refused to serve in any capacity and went to prison. Three times as many conscientious objectors were imprisoned in World War II as in World War I. There was no widespread public hostility to them, especially because conscientious objectors were respected for saving lives on the battlefronts.

SLACKERS. In a different category were the slackers, those who had no intention of serving in the armed forces and looked for methods of evading service. The vast majority of 132,000,000 Americans agreed that the war had to be fought, that Pearl Harbor had to be avenged, and that Hitler had to be stopped. But, as in World War I, there were those who used every possible means of evading service from working at war jobs to study at college to self-inflicting wounds. Tens of thousands turned to the shipyards, where they could earn high wages and at the same time get the draft status they wanted. Unlike its attitude to conscientious objectors, the public expressed its contempt for slackers.

STRATEGIC WAR MATERIALS. To a greater extent than in previous wars, World War II revealed dependence upon critical materials—mineral, agricultural, and forest—as well as synthetic production for the manufacture of adequate munitions, ammunition, guns, tanks, transportation, equipment, warships, and aircraft, without which the field forces could not carry out their assigned tasks. The joint Raw Materials Board of the United States and the British Empire extended its unity of actions primarily to raw materials. The task was a staggering one because of the desperate need for the bulk of the world's output of such critical raw materials as potash, mercury, rayon, staple fiber, natural silk, rubber, tin, bauxite, and kapok. Oil was the most critical of the major commodities, which also included food and rubber. The United States had lost its supplies in the Far East, the Germans were sinking tankers off the Atlantic shores. The crisis was met by sufficient development of petroleum reserves. (*See also* RESOURCES, BATTLE FOR.)

WAR PRODUCTION. Immediately after Pearl Harbor, the American war economy shifted into high gear. In an awesome example of economic planning and productive energy, the industrial establishment was placed on a firm war basis. The entire country was involved in a battle of production on a scale the world had never seen. (*See* PRODUCTION, BATTLE OF.)

On January 13, 1942, Roosevelt appointed Donald M. Nelson (*q.v.*) Chairman of the War Production Board (WPB) with powers to mobilize national resources for the war effort. Nelson was given virtual dictatorial control over industry, production, raw materials, factories, priorities, allocations, and rationing. Despite doubts to the contrary the country drove forward as a unit for war production. Slow processes of debate and consultative board action were abandoned in the smooth changeover to war conditions.

President Roosevelt astonished both production economists and industrial leaders by calling for 60,000 planes, 45,000 tanks, 20,000 antiaircraft guns, and 8 million tons of shipping in the single year 1942. The figures aroused amused but uncomfortable interest in Berlin's Nazi circles. By 1943, planes, ships, locomotives, tanks, and war weapons of all kinds were pouring from production lines.

PRODUCTION RECORDS. American productive capacity, larger than that of all enemy nations combined, shattered all records. From July 1940 to the end of the war, American factories and shipyards turned out more than 300,000 military aircraft; 89,000 tanks; 3 million machine guns; considerably more than 55 million tons of merchant shipping; and more tons of steel and aluminum than ever before in history. This enormous output was not only enough to supply the nation's own needs but also the needs of Britain and to some extent of Soviet Russia.

The enormous energy of a unified people was channeled into war production. New industries were created overnight, especially in the manufacture of several kinds of synthetic rubber. Great sums were poured into the construction and enlargement of war plants and emergency shipyards. Universities and industrial research laboratories developed hundreds of new techniques for production. Labor, management, capital, and government cooperated in this mighty endeavor, with strikes and lockouts eliminated for the duration.

FIGHT ON INFLATION. A key problem on the domestic front was the necessity of fighting inflation. On April 27, 1940, Roosevelt sent to Congress a seven-point program for preventing runaway inflation:

1. Increased taxation to keep personal and corporate profits at a reasonable rate;

2. Price ceilings for consumers, retailers, wholesalers, and manufacturers;

3. Pay stabilization;

4. Price stabilization;

5. Sale of war bonds;

6. Rationing of essential commodities;

7. Discouraging of credit and installment buying.

PRICE CONTROL. The Office of Price Administration was set up on January 30, 1942, to fix ceilings on all commodities except farm products, and at the same time introduce rent controls. Under successive administrators, Leon Henderson, Chester Bowles, and Prentiss M. Brown, the OPA was effective in the battle to avoid inflation.

RATIONING. The country was supposed to be abundantly supplied with food to yield variety, quality, and a balanced diet, but there were regions of local insufficiency which might have become vulnerable should the system of transportation break down. After the declaration of war, the Pacific sources of sugar, oil, fruit, and other foodstuffs were cut off and it became apparent that American agriculture had to be mobilized in a great productive effort. Shortages of meat, fats, oils, dairy products, and canned goods brought home to consumers the effect of war on food supply. New records were established in the production of such crops as peanuts, soybeans, and essential oils. Throughout the war, farmers used workers deferred from military service.

Washington issued ration stamps for butter and meat, as well as for gasoline, automobile tires, and cigarettes. The OPA authorized bakers to reduce the size of a loaf of bread but not the price, even though there was a shortage of smaller-sized baking pans.

Racketeers used the ration system for personal enrichment. There was a thriving black market for gasoline, tires, shoes, and food stamps, as well as a brisk trade in ration coupons. Counterfeit coupons were printed and used throughout the country. Crime syndicates turned to the ration system as an opportunity for quick riches. Ration boards of volunteer citizens were set up to meet desperate requests for fuel, food, and shoes, and to do what they could to eliminate widespread cheating.

These Eleven Commandments of Rationing were issued by one ration board:

1. Don't try to buy ration goods with loose stamps.

2. Don't lend your ration book to a friend.

3. Don't swap ration coupons.

4. Don't give your unused stamps to your dealer.

5. Don't try to buy rationed goods without coupons.

6. Don't try to use ration stamps after they have expired.

7. Don't try to use a ration book that doesn't belong to you or that should have been returned to your board.

8. Don't use a ration book that is a duplicate of one you already own in your own name.

9. Don't pay over top legal prices.

10. Don't let any dealer let you buy something you don't want to get something you do want.

11. Don't use your gasoline rations for anything except for the purpose for which intended.

ALLOCATING LABOR SUPPLY. In the early stage of the war, production had been limited primarily by shortages of raw materials. Later the labor supply began to set an ultimate limit on production. Some areas, notably on the Pacific coast, began to experience a lack of workers in almost all industries. The need was met by new allocations of labor by the War Manpower Commission and the War Production Board. Special deferment for workers was made by Selective Service. Emergency recruitment campaigns were inaugurated. Unemployment fell to a minimum. The number of women in the labor force reached a peak of 18.7 million in July 1943. The work week was increased by eight hours over pre-war standards.

On June 25, 1943, the Smith-Connally Anti-Strike Act made strikes illegal in government plants. Unions were held liable for damage suits or failure to give 30 days' notice of intention to strike in war industries.

The migration of blacks from rural sections of the country to industrial areas led to a call for the end of racial discrimination. The Fair Employment Practice Committee, originally set up in June 1941, was extended by executive order to end discrimination in war production and government employment.

SHIPPING. Shipping was placed on the critical list. "It is only by shipping," said Churchill in 1942, "that the United States or indeed ourselves can intervene either in the eastern or the western theaters." The War Shipping Administration (WSA), established by executive order on February 7, 1942, was placed under the direction of Rear Adm. Emory S. Land. Contracts were signed to replace warships lost at Pearl Harbor (*q.v.*). Liberty Ships and later Victory Ships (*qq.v.*) were produced in record time in shipyards under new mass-production methods. Workers flocked to shipyards in this crucial phase of war production.

WAR INFORMATION. The Government set up machinery for safeguarding information and for expanding facilities for the dissemination of information both at home and abroad. An executive order dated December 19, 1941, created the Office of War Censorship. Its objectives were: (1) to prevent transmission of information useful to the enemy; and (2) to obtain information for the prosecution of the war. The Office of War Information (OWI) was ordered to direct all agencies in dissemination of war information. The new agency was led by Elmer Davis, radio news commentator.

OTHER WAR AGENCIES. Several war agencies were established even before U.S. entry into the war. On June 28, 1941, the Office of Scientific Research and Development was set up, to be followed on July 30, 1941, by the Office of Coordinator of Inter-American Affairs under Nelson A. Rockefeller, and on October 8, 1941, by the Office of Lend-Lease Administration. (*See* LEND-LEASE.)

After Pearl Harbor the number of war agencies multiplied, including the Office of Defense Transportation (December 18, 1941); Office of Censorship (December 19, 1941); Office of Alien Property Custodian (March 11, 1942); Office of Strategic Services (*q.v.*) (June 13, 1942); and Office of Foreign Relief and Rehabilitation (December 4, 1942). On May 28, 1943, Supreme Court Justice James F. Byrnes was named to head the Office of War Mobilization (OWM) to unify all activities of Federal agencies engaged in production or distribution of civilian supplies. (*See also* OFFICES, AMERICAN WAR.)

RELOCATION OF ENEMY ALIENS. By order of President Roosevelt, certain military areas were prescribed to exclude unwanted persons. There was some concern on the West Coast about the Issei, born in Japan and ineligible for American citizenship, and the Nisei, second-generation American-born Japanese who held American citizenship. Some 110,000 of these Japanese-Americans living in California, Oregon, Washington, and Arizona, were transferred by March 29, 1942, to relocation camps in the interior. Although not to be compared to Nazi concentration or extermination camps (*qq.v.*), conditions in the relocation camps were far from satisfactory. This treatment of Japanese-Americans was criticized as ill-advised, unnecessary, and unfair, and as the most unjust disregard of personal rights in the nation's history since before the abolition of slavery. The U.S. Supreme Court never outlawed the camps. Military authorities insisted that relocation was necessary for the defense of the West Coast. With few exceptions, Japanese-Americans were loyal and handled themselves with dignity. Nisei troopers compiled an extraordinary combat record in Italian campaigns, and won praise for their service. On December 17, 1944, the mass exclusion of Japanese-Americans was terminated by the U.S. Army.

INTERNAL SECURITY. There was little to fear from American Communists now that the country had joined the USSR against the Axis. Internal security measures were taken on the East Coast, where Americans remembered the Black Tom explosions of World War I.* In June 1942, the Federal Bureau of Investigation (FBI) arrested eight Nazi saboteurs who landed by U-Boat on Long Island and Florida. All eight were convicted by military tribunal; six were executed and two were sentenced to long prison terms. (*See* PASTORIUS.)

---

*On July 30, 1916, a munitions explosion on Black Tom Island, New Jersey, attributed to German sabotage, resulted in property damage of $22 million.

On July 23, 1942, 28 persons, including George Sylvester Viereck, Gerald Winrod, and William Dudley Pelley, were indicted for sedition. The case never came to trial and the indictments were dismissed in 1946. The Communist Party of the United States was dissolved on May 20, 1944, but was reconstituted on July 27, 1945.

HOME FRONT. Virtually every phase of everyday American life was affected by the war effort. The entire nation adjusted quickly to war conditions. The mood of the American people was indicated in the most popular slogan of the day: "Remember Pearl Harbor!"

Though the country was to be spared the kind of bombing that decimated European cities, Civilian Defense and fire-fighting organizations were set up in major urban areas to cope with any emergencies. Many of those who were ineligible for the draft because of age or health surged to the shipyards and factories. Women, encouraged by publicity on Rosie the Riveter (*q.v.*), flocked to defense plants. Children cooperated by collecting heavy metals, lead, and aluminum.

The public accepted as necessary the rationing of food, fuel, and gasoline, although a flourishing black market arose. To save fuel, travel was discouraged with such slogans as "Is This Trip Necessary?" To prevent inflation and pay for weapons of war, Washington organized mass sales of war bonds, for which Hollywood stars offered their services.

Show business went to war. Stars of film, stage, and radio offered their services. Hitler, Mussolini, and Tojo were ridiculed in song and film. (*See* SONGS OF WAR, and FILMS IN THE WAR.) The entertainment world paid tribute to new American heroes. (*See* MURPHY, AUDIE; FOUR CHAPLAINS; and SULLIVAN BROTHERS.) In training camps throughout the country the USO (United Service Organizations [*q.v.*]) entertained servicemen and servicewomen. Among the most popular on both home and combat fronts were Bob Hope (*q.v.*), Bing Crosby, Jack Benny, Marlene Dietrich, Betty Grable (*q.v.*), and George Jessel, all of whom devoted their talents for victory. American families near training camps opened their homes to officers and enlisted men.

UNITED STATES AT END OF THE WAR. By the closing months of the war Americans knew that victory was near. The United States had seen its armies win brilliant victories, its own territory was unscarred, and its productive capacity had reached tremendous proportions. Morale was high—the people were united by anger over Pearl Harbor and by contempt for Hitler and Nazism.

Virtually all elements of the people—from farmers to laborers to businessmen and investors—were enjoying unprecedented prosperity. Americans, unlike others, generally ate as well or better than before the war. Employment was at an all-time high. Despite the growing housing shortage, most Americans lived as well as before 1941. Income of investors doubled, and corporations, without limit on profits, prospered. True, the national debt soared: From 1941 to 1945 it rose from $28 to $247 billion, but this was left for later generations to pay.

A united people had put aside temporarily its traditional quarrels. Where the Axis powers fought the war with weapons of tyranny and oppression, silencing and punishing nonconformity, American democratic processes went on almost uninterrupted. Criticism and independence were encouraged. Americans saw advantages in open debate, support by all segments of the people, and contributions of independent minds. Latin-Americans supported the Allies: 21 American republics broke off relations with the Axis, and only Argentina declined full cooperation. European influence in Latin American declined.

HUMAN LOSSES. As in World War I, American losses in World War II were considerably lower than those of other belligerents. Of the more than 12 million serving in the armed forces, there were one million casualties, including 292,131 killed in action, 115,185 other deaths, and 670,846 wounded.

AFTERMATH. The United States emerged from World War II vastly strengthened in power, wealth, and prestige, the richest and most powerful nation on earth. Within five years after 1945 it doubled its industrial output, tripled the amount of money circulating within its borders, and quadrupled its savings. Fears that quick demobilization of its fighting machine would result in a massive wave of unemployment proved to be groundless. At the same time, the American economy, burdened by war costs and financial assistance to other countries, was beset by rising prices, fear of inflation, and an increased national debt.

On the domestic American scene there was a greater concentration of federal powers. The government stepped into social services, public education, and other areas of national life. In foreign policy, the traditional preference of Americans for isolation gave way to acceptance of tasks to be shouldered as a global power. The growing threat of Russian expansion led to increasing realization that American responsibilities had not ceased with the victory of 1945. The United States in the postwar era committed itself to containment of Russian expansion and assistance for the free peoples of the world. By 1947 Europe had shown little signs of recovery from the war. The Marshall Plan, named after Gen. George C. Marshall (*q.v.*), was a momentous offer to aid Europe to recover its economic health. The U.S Congress appropriated $13 billion to assist the return to normal economic health, without which there could be no political stability or peace in the world.

America's entry into World War I marked the dawn of its world leadership. After 1945 the United States was thrust into a position of awesome global power.

Bibliography. S. Van Falkenberg, *America at War* (1942); F. Walton, *Miracle of World War II* (1958); H. T. Wade and R. A. Lively, *This Glorious Cause* (1958); A. R. Buchanan, *The*

United States and World War II, 2 vols. (1964); K. S. Davis, *Experience of War: The U.S. in World War II* (1965); A. A. Hoehling, *Home Front, U.S.A* (1966); R. Polenberg (ed.), *America at War: The Home Front, 1941–1945* (1968); R. R. Lingemann, *Don't You Know There is a War On? The American Front, 1941–1945* (1970); U.S. Bureau of the Budget, *The United States at War* (1972); R. Hoopes, *Americans Remember the Home Front* (1977); and T. R. Clark (ed.), *World Wars Remembered* (1980).

URQUHART, ROBERT ELLIOTT (1901–   ). British Army officer.

In the summer of 1942 Urquhart accompanied Gen. Bernard Law Montgomery (*q.v.*) to the Middle East and North Africa and fought with the 51st Highland Division from El Alamein (*q.v.*) to Tunisia. (*See also* NORTH AFRICA, CAMPAIGNS IN.) In September 1944 he commanded the 1st Airborne Division, the Red Devils (*q.v.*), who fought behind the German lines during nine days and nights in which three-fourths of his men were lost. (*See* ARNHEM, BATTLE OF.) At one time he was reported captured, although actually he was safe but had been cut off from his division for 36 hours.

Urquhart was criticized for leading his men into the Arnhem trap. He defended his heavy losses as due to the late arrival of airborne fighter reinforcements, lack of sufficient supplies, bad weather, and enemy flak. Montgomery also defended him: "There can be few episodes more glorious than the epic of Arnhem." Churchill told the House of Commons: "Not in vain may be the pride of those who survived and the epitaph of those who fell."

Six feet tall, of calm demeanor and efficient, Urquhart was described as a mustached version of Jack Dempsey. It was reported that, on returning from Arnhem, he showed up at his club wearing his red beret and swinging his walking stick as if he had just come back from a hike.

Bibliography. R. E. Urquhart, *Arnhem* (1958); and C. Hibbert, *The Battle of Arnhem* (1962).

USHIJIMA, MITSURU (1887–1945). Commander of Japanese forces in Okinawa in the final battle of the war.

Ushijima, a career officer, was appointed commandant of the Japanese Military Academy in 1942. After serving on Iwo Jima (*see* IWO JIMA, BATTLE FOR), he conducted a defensive campaign against the Allied troops which invaded the island in February and March 1945. On June 22, 1945, with Americans approaching his cave headquarters and with most of his troops already dead, he committed suicide. (*See* OKINAWA, BATTLE FOR.)

USO. Organization devoted to the morale of U.S. servicemen. (*See* UNITED SERVICE ORGANIZATIONS.)

UTAH BEACH. Area in northern France where American troops stormed ashore on June 6, 1944. (*See* NORMANDY INVASION.)

The first troops to land were parachutists from troop carriers and gliders of the U.S. 9th Air Force. Crossing the enemy coast a few minutes after midnight, they landed at Ste. Mère Église behind Utah Beach and outfought three German divisions. Then the U.S. 4th Infantry moved in to swamp the German defenses at the cost of only 197 casualties. All that day and night reinforcements poured ashore at Utah Beach until 35,250 men were on land. Utah Beach formed the western flank of the landings. (*See also* OMAHA BEACH.)

Bibliography. A. Renaud, *Utah Beach à Cherbourg* (1968).

UXB. Unexploded bomb. Name given by the British to a new German weapon introduced during the Battle of Britain in the summer of 1940.

The delayed-action bomb was dropped from the air and buried itself into the ground to be exploded later. For the harried British Civil Defense Service there was no effective way to ascertain whether the buried projectile was a UXB or an ordinary bomb that had failed to explode. Officers and men of the Royal Engineers, assigned the task of rendering the UXBs harmless, showed rare courage in grappling with the infernal machines that might have blown them to bits a⁺ any moment.

V

V-1 (VERGELTUNGSWAFFE-1—REPRISAL WEAPON-1). Also called FZG-76. First of two major weapons used by the Germans in the closing days of the war.

BACKGROUND. Shortly after the outbreak of war in 1939, Hitler promised that he had *Wunderwaffen* ("wonder weapons"), which he would unveil at the proper time. He put Germany's outstanding scientists and engineers to work at the Research Station at Peenemünde (*q.v.*), on an island in the Baltic. He instructed them to design, produce, and test new weapons. Engineers worked energetically on a round-the-clock basis on rockets and jet-propelled bombs that would win the war finally for the Third Reich. The first weapon was ready by the spring of 1944, but it was not yet in the mass production stage.

DESIGN. Dubbed by the British the "Buzz Bomb" or the "Doodlebug," the new weapon emitted a shrill, sputtering sound in flight. The *V-1* was actually a pilotless, mid-wing monoplane with a wing span of 17 feet 6 inches and a length of 25 feet 4 inches. It carried 150 gallons of fuel and a ton of explosives that exploded on impact. Most of its construction was wood and steel. Guidance to target was set before launch. The *V-1s* were mass produced before war ended.

TARGET. Hitler knew that there was a vast military buildup in the Portsmouth-Southampton area, but he decided that London was a better target for his new weapon. He would strike terror in the hearts of British civilians, destroy morale, and bring an end to the war. On the night of June 13–14, 1944, D-Day plus 7, Hitler's secret exploded on a startled London. From bases along the French coast in the Pas de Calais region, he sent *V-1s* hurtling toward London. The Buzz Bombs were visible as well as audible.

Not all flying bombs got off to target. Ironically, Hitler himself almost became one of the first victims of the *V-1s* on June 17, 1944. He expected to visit Cherbourg the next morning. Later that day the mechanism of a *V-1* intended for London failed, turned in the direction of the *Fuehrer's* compound, and exploded near it. Hitler cancelled his visit to Cherbourg and flew back to Berchtesgaden.

DEFENSE. The British quickly adopted countermeasures. They set up additional balloon barrages and strengthened antiaircraft defenses in Kent and Sussex. Busy pilots of the Royal Air Force (*q.v.*) soon became adept at hunting *V-1s* and shooting them down. At least 630 *V-1s* were exploded by pilots of speedy fighting planes that met the flying bombs as they crossed the English Channel.

RESULTS. Altogether the Germans fired 9,251 *V-1s* against England, of which 4,621 were destroyed. British losses were considerable. Estimates vary, but one accounting lists 5,470 killed, 15,994 wounded, and 25,000 buildings destroyed. Another estimate judged that at least 75,000 homes were destroyed or damaged. The results, however, were not crippling. The British public, refusing to be terrorized, met the new situation with grim determination.

Unfortunately for Hitler, he provided more funds in the early days of the war for conventional weapons than for research on his pilotless bombs. By the time he was ready to use them, it was too late. There were too few *V-1s*. Had these bombs been mass produced in the early years of the war, they might have led to a different outcome.

Bibliography. J. Kirk and R. Young, *Great Weapons of World War II* (1961); B. Collier, *The Battle of the V Weapons, 1944-45* (1964); B. Arct, *Poles Against the "V" Weapons* (1972); A. Kershaw (ed.), *Weapons of War* (1973); and V. Hogg and J. B. King, *German and Allied Secret Weapons of World War II* (1976).

V-2 (VERGELTUNGSWAFFE-2—REPRISAL WEAPON-2).

Also called the *A-4* rocket. Culmination of a series of rocket designs and the only rocket to be used by the Germans in the late days of the war. The *V-2* was a ballistic missile, more complex and deadly than the *V-1* (*q.v.*), the Buzz Bomb. The *V-1* was a jet-propelled plane, but the *V-2* was a more sophisticated supersonic rocket.

BACKGROUND. German rocket research began in the early 1930s at the Artillery Proving Ground at Kummersdorf. Later, Hitler transferred the work to the Peenemünde (*q.v.*) Research Station on the Baltic coast. There he put the country's outstanding scientists and engineers to work to design new *Wunderwaffen* ("wonder weapons"). Directed by Col. Walter Dornberger and led by the 25-year-old Wernher von Braun (*q.v.*), the scientists worked at rapid pace on the deadly weapon.

DESIGN. The *V-2* was designed as a rocket to replace heavy artillery. Aimed from fixed positions, it had a motor that used liquid oxygen, enabling it to fly above the earth's atmosphere. Weighing from 13 to 14 tons at launch, it carried a warhead of one ton of high explosives. The rocket hurtled down on its target at four times the speed of sound. Impact fuses set off the explosives when the rocket hit the ground. The weapon was launched on a pre-determined trajectory. The motor was shut off at a point that would take the rocket to its target.

SPECIFICATIONS.
   Measurements. Length 46 ft.; diameter 5 ft. 5 in.; weight 13-14 tons, including 1 ton of explosive warhead, 5 tons of liquid oxygen, and 4 tons of liquid alcohol.
   Maximum Speed. 3,500 m.p.h.
   Range. 225 mi.

PRODUCTION. The first test flight came in early October 1942. After Allied bombers struck at Peenemünde in the summer of 1943, production of *V-2*s was transferred to an underground factory in the Harz Mountains. Here production eventually reached nearly 5,000 *V-2*s a month.

TARGETS. On September 6, 1944, two *V-2*s were fired against Paris. Two days later, the bombardment of Britain began. A *V-2* descended on Chiswick and hurled itself into the ground before exploding.

DEFENSE. The *V-2* was a special problem for the British because, unlike the Buzz Bomb, it could not be seen or heard while in flight. It was difficult to shoot down in flight because of its altitude. Allied air power was used immediately in a campaign to smash the launching sites on the Continent. When ground troops finally overran most of the launching sites in northern France, the Germans began to direct *V-2*s on American Army installations at Liège and on the port of Antwerp. The attacks ceased only when all launching bases in France and the Netherlands were destroyed.

The reaction of the British public under the menace of this new and terrible weapon was extraordinary. Britons met the crisis with courage and endurance. Some helped rescue victims, others went into shelters or served as aircraft wardens or members of fire-fighting patrols.

RESULTS. It is estimtaed that about 10,000 *V-2*s were produced, of which about 1,300 were fired against England. Approximately 500 hit London. There were between 8,000 and 10,000 casualties, including 2,500 killed. Approximately 1,400 *V-2*s were fired against Antwerp, to disrupt Allied port operations, about 100 against Liège, and 15 against Paris. A dozen were directed at the Remagen bridge (*q.v.*) over the Rhine.

SIGNIFICANCE. In the long run, the *V-2* was an ineffective weapon for the already defeated Hitler. Albert Speer (*q.v.*), his Minister of Armaments and War Production, regarded the whole notion as absurd. Allied bombers were dropping an average of 3,000 tons of bombs a day on German targets, "and Hitler wanted to retaliate with 30 rockets that would have carried 24 tons of explosive to England daily." That would have been the equivalent of the bomb load of only 12 *Flying Fortresses*. The effort was on too small a scale and it was far too late. In the early days of the war Hitler was more interested in producing conventional weapons in quantity, and although he supported the experimentation at Peenemünde, he failed to order a massive assembly-line production of flying bombs and rockets.

The *V-2* was the forerunner of the long-range rockets used in both the American and Russian space programs. Scientists from Peenemünde, led by Wernher von Braun, were brought to the United States to work on the American space projects.

Bibliography. See bibliography for *V-1.*

VAAGSO RAID. First important British commando raid on a Norwegian port in late 1941.

BACKGROUND. The first two years of the war were a time of anxiety for the British despite their stubborn defense in 1940. (*See* BRITAIN, BATTLE OF.) Early raids on Norway deliberately avoided heavily defended sections of the enemy coast. British strategists decided in late 1941 to mount a major raid on a German fortified position in Norway to demonstrate an offensive spirit despite losses on the Continent.

TARGET. The selected port was Vaagsø, lying about halfway between Bergen and Trondheim in the Nordfjord, one of the most beautiful of the myriad Norwegian waterways. A special Service Brigade, composed of battalion-sized British and Norwegian commandos, was chosen to carry out *Operation Archery*. Naval and ground rehearsals took place through most of December 1941.

ASSAULT. At 9:15 P.M. on Christmas Eve 1941 a small force of British warships escorted two camouflaged excursion steamers, seven ships in all, out of Scapa Flow. After a stormy crossing of the North Sea, the invaders on December 27 sailed past a German lookout on Vaagsø Island into the fjord. The Commandos stormed ashore and immediately went to work demolishing fortifications, setting factories ablaze, and engaging the German defenders. Smoke-blackened and begrimed, the raiders returned to their ships bringing with them German prisoners and young Norwegians anxious to fight with the Free Norwegian Armed Forces.

LOSSES. Of the 525 commandos, 73 or about 14 percent, were casualties, lower than anticipated. Not a single Norwegian was killed at Vaagsø. The official German report listed 11 dead and 7 wounded plus 16 missing in action and presumably captured.

SIGNIFICANCE. For the British the Vaagsø raid was valuable experience for the later assaults on Dieppe (*see* DIEPPE RAID) and Normandy (*see* NORMANDY INVASION). It contributed distinctly to public morale. More important was the effect on Hitler back in Berlin. Angered by British resolve, he ordered, despite objections by his naval chiefs, massive preparations to defend Norway for a coming Allied assault. He sent the entire German fleet plus substantial land forces to Norway. This was exactly what the Allies wanted, for they had no intention of mounting a great assault on Norway. By June 6, 1944, D-Day (*q.v.*), when the Allies landed in Normandy, Hitler had 372,000 German troops sitting idly in Norway—all desperately needed on the western and eastern fronts.

Bibliography. J. H. Devins, *The Vaagsø Raid* (1967).

VANDEGRIFT, ALEXANDER ARCHER (1887–1973). U.S. Marine officer, and leader of the successful marine invasion of Guadalcanal and Bougainville in the Solomons. (*See* SOLOMONS, CAMPAIGNS IN THE.)

Vandegrift commanded the marines in August 1942 when they made their bold offensive move in the Solomons. Savage Japanese counterattacks were beaten off by reserves. Despite the naval defeat at the opening of the campaign, the marines held on. By the first anniversary of Pearl Harbor, Vandegrift announced that, since he and his marines had first landed four months earlier, the Japanese troop losses had exceeded that of his men by ten to one.

On his return to the United States, Vandegrift was awarded the Congressional Medal of Honor. He was the first marine in World War II to win both that medal and the Navy Cross, which he had been awarded in October 1942 at Guadalcanal.

Returning to the South Pacific the next summer, Vandegrift led the landings on Bougainville. On November 30, 1943, he was appointed the 18th commandant in Marine Corps history. The Japanese had announced erroneously that he had been killed in the Bougainville action.

Quiet and efficient, nicknamed Sunny Jim, Vandegrift was the opposite of the swashbuckling, grim-faced commandant usually associated with Leatherneck tradition. His unspectacular appearance hid a tough Marine Corps leader. Calm and even-tempered, modest and self-effacing, he compiled an extraordinary record in the Pacific war. He was the first Marine Corps officer to hold the rank of full General.

Bibliography. A. A. Vandegrift, *Once a Marine* (1964).

VASILEVSKY, ALEKSANDR M. (1895–1977). Chief of General Staff of the USSR Armed Forces.

During World War I Vasilevsky enlisted as a private and later served as an officer in the Russian Imperial Army. After the German invasion of the Soviet Union in 1941, he was chief of the operations directive of the General Staff, responsible for coordinating the different fronts at Stalingrad. A close friend of Stalin, he served continuously in the field and was eventually made a Marshal of the Soviet Union. In 1945 he served as Commander-in-Chief of the Soviet forces in the Far East. He took part in all major war conferences.

V-E DAY. Victory-in-Europe Day, May 8, 1945.

In early May 1945 sporadic resistance continued in Berlin, but it was disorganized and hopeless. At 2:41 A.M. on May 7, 1945, the Germans surrendered to the Americans and British in a schoolhouse at Reims in a brief ceremony. The next day, to symbolize unity among the Allies, Marshal Georgi Zhukov (*q.v.*) signed for the Soviet Union. May 8 thus became the official V-E Day. The event was greeted with an outpouring of joy in the Allied countries. There were frenzied celebrations in London, Paris, Moscow, and New York.

In a Victory Order of the Day, Gen. Dwight D. Eisenhower (*q.v.*) said: "Let us have no part in the pointless quarrels in which other men will inevitably engage as to what country, what service, won the European war. Every man, every woman, of every nation here represented has served according to his or her ability, and the efforts of each have contributed to the outcome."

In Moscow 1,000 guns fired 30 rounds each as a symbol for "complete and total victory." In a unique gesture, masses of Russians gathered in front of the American and British embassies to cheer their allies in victory.

Bibliography. P. Kecskemeti, *Unconditional Surrender* (1958); A. Armstrong, *Unconditional Surrender* (1961); and J. Toland, *The Last 100 Days* (1966).

V-FOR-VICTORY SIGNAL. "V" sign with the right hand to denote final victory. (*See* V-SYMBOL.)

V-MAIL. Special letter forms by which American troops could keep in touch with relatives and friends at home.

V-mail could reach even little-known destinations in about 10 days. The purpose of an efficient mail service was to maintain morale among servicemen in difficult situations.

V-SYMBOL. V-for-Victory signal that won great popularity during the late stages of the war.

In sound the symbol was used on the air by the British Broadcasting Company (BBC), which opened its programs in every European language with the opening bars of Beethoven's *Fifth Symphony*. The rhythm was translated into Morse code—dot-dot-dot-dash (V).

The dramatic signal was also used in the V-for-Victory sign, by which the right arm was extended high with the forefinger and middle finger forming the letter "V." This was Churchill's favorite greeting to the public and he was often photographed giving the V-sign.

VELLA GULF, BATTLE OF. Naval battle between the Japanese and the Allies in the Central Solomons in early August 1943.

BACKGROUND. The Allied capture of Munda on New Georgia Island on August 5, 1943, did not end the clashes in the Slot, where the Tokyo Express was bringing in reinforcements to Japanese garrisons in the Central Solomons. The next day the Allies received word that there would be another run this time to Kolombangara Island, just northeast of New Georgia. It was decided to send a small force of six destroyers whose captains had been clamoring to be "let loose from the cruisers' apron strings," to Vella Gulf to intercept the enemy.

CONFRONTATION. On the night of August 6–7, 1943, the Allied destroyer force clashed with 4 Japanese destroyers, 3 of which were carrying troops and supplies. From a range of 4000 yards the American destroyers sent a swarm of torpedoes hurtling toward the enemy craft. Three exploded with such force that sailors 30 miles distant believed that the volcano at Kolombangara had erupted. The fourth Japanese destroyer managed to escape. There were no Allied losses.

SIGNIFICANCE. This heavy blow led Imperial General Headquarters to cancel the Tokyo Express. It was now too dangerous to run the Slot any longer. (*See* GUADALCANAL CAMPAIGNS.)

Bibliography. S. E. Morison, *The Two-Ocean War* (1963).

VENLO INCIDENT. Clash between British and German intelligence agents at the start of the war.

BACKGROUND. In early September 1939, British agents in Holland learned from a German refugee that German officers, "appalled by losses in Poland," wanted to make contact with London. The British assigned Maj. R. H. Stevens and Capt. S. Payne Best to meet the Germans.

MEETING. On November 8, 1939, Stevens and Best arrived at the little Dutch border town of Venlo, where they were supposed to meet an important German General. Instead, they were kidnapped by a detachment of armed Germans from across the frontier and brought to Berlin. There they found to their dismay that the "Major Schaemel" they were to meet was actually Maj. Walter Schellenberg, chief of the counterespionage division of the *Gestapo* (*q.v.*). The British agents were held prisoners for the rest of the war until they were liberated by American troops.

SIGNIFICANCE. Hitler used the Venlo incident to claim that the Dutch were plotting against him. He charged that Holland obviously was violating neutrality, which gave him an excuse for later invasion.

Bibliography. S. P. Best, *The Venlo Incident* (1950).

VERONIKA DANKESCHÖN. Poster character used in occupied Germany to warn American GIs (*q.v.*) of dangers of fraternization with German girls.

Veronika Dankeschön. ("Veronica Thank-You-Very-Much") was presented to bored and lonely American troops as an attractive *Fräulein*, but their attention was directed to her initials "V.D." Throughout his army career the American GI was warned consistently about the dangers of venereal disease.

VIAN, PHILIP (1894–1968). British naval offficer.

Vian was captain of the destroyer HMS *Cossack*, which on February 16, 1940, dashed into Jössingfjord in Norway and rescued several hundred Allied seamen who were prisoners on the German supply ship *Altmark* (*q.v.*). He also commanded a destroyer in the trapping and sinking of the German battleship *Bismarck* on May 27, 1941. (*See BISMARCK, SINKING OF THE.*)

Promoted to Admiral in July 1941, Vian served with a task force that sailed from Scapa Flow to evacuate Norwegians and Russians from Spitzbergen. He was also active in the invasions of Sicily in July 1943 and Normandy in June 1944. (*See SICILY, INVASION OF; and NORMANDY INVASION.*) In 1945, before the end of the war in the Far East, he was transferred to the British Pacific Fleet.

VICTOR EMMANUEL III (1869–1947). King of Italy during World War II.

Victor Emmanuel was opposed to the war when it began. In September 1939 he announced: "While I am head of the House of Savoy, Italy will not take up arms against France." But on the Italian declaration of war on France after its fall in June 1940, Victor Emmanuel did not abdicate. He made no public objections to the Fascist dictatorship. Only when Italian defeat became inevitable did he try to disassociate himself from Mussolini (*q.v.*). When the Fascist Grand Council voted to depose Mussolini, Victor Emmanuel had the *Duce* arrested on July 25, 1943. Rebuffed in his attempt to take Italy out of the war with German consent, he tried to open negotiations with the Allies. He fled to southern Italy to take refuge under Allied protection. In June 1944 he declared his son Humbert regent.

Victor Emmanuel formally abdicated in 1946 in favor of his son, who reigned for just one month before Italy was declared a republic.

Short, with small, thin legs, Victor Emmanuel III had a small, close-cropped head with a receding chin. He was unpopular with his people, many of whom scorned him because of his toleration of fascism.

Bibliography. S. Berkson, *Their Majesties* (1938); and T. B. Morgan, *Spurs on the Boot* (1941).

VICTORY SHIPS. Later version of American freighters mass produced during the war. (*See LIBERTY SHIPS.*)

VOIX DE LA PAIX, LA **(THE VOICE OF PEACE).** German broadcasting station operated in France throughout the Phony War in the winter of 1939–1940. (*See SITZKRIEG.*)

Organized by the Propaganda Section of the OKW (*q.v.*), the High Command of the German Armed Forces, *La Voix de la Paix* was supposed to be run by Frenchmen from French territory. Its purpose was to subvert and demoralize the French before the coming *Blitzkrieg* (*q.v.*) on their country. (*See also* NEW BRITISH BROADCASTING STATION.)

VOLKSWAGEN. Most popular German vehicle of the war.

The early *Volkswagen* had a two-wheel drive and limited speed. For some years before the war Hitler had promised the Germans a car in every garage and deducted large sums from the pay of workers for the automobiles. The public never got them because the entire production of early *Volkswagens* was intended for the army from the start of the war. It was put to good use on every front on which the Germans fought.

After the war the *Volkswagen* was produced on assembly lines and soon became one of the most popular automobiles not only in Germany but throughout Europe and the world as well. Postwar German industry exported not only *Volkswagen* cars but also giant assembly plants for use in countries world-wide. It has remained one of the most successful automobiles in the history of transportation.

Bibliography. W. R. Nitske, *The Amazing Porsche and Volkswagen Story* (1958); W. H. Nelson, *Small Wonder* (1967); and A. H. Ransome, *Think Small* (1970).

VOROSHILOV, KLIMENT YEFREMOVICH (1881–1969). Soviet statesman, military leader, and member of the power group that led Russia's war effort.

In 1940, just after the Russian-Finnish War, Voroshilov was relieved of his post of Commissar of Defense, but he was appointed Deputy Premier. During the entire war he served as a member of the State Defense Committee (*q.v.*), which had unlimited powers to run the war. He directed, jointly with Marshal Georgi Zhukov (*q.v.*), the operations that broke the assaults on Leningrad in January 1943. (*See* LENINGRAD, SIEGE OF.)

Voroshilov attended many of the Allied war conferences as a member of the State Defense Committee. He acted as Soviet Russia's military spokesman in talks with other Allied war leaders. He attended the Teheran Conference (*q.v.*) in November 1943.

W

WAAF. The women's unit of the Royal Air Force (*q.v.*). (*See* WOMEN'S AUXILIARY AIR FORCE.)

WAC. Women's unit of the U.S. Army (*See* WOMEN'S ARMY CORPS.)

WAFFEN-SS **(ARMED SS).** Military arm and largest branch of the *Schutzstaffel*, Hitler's elite protection squads. (*See* SS.) (For Order of Battle, *see* pp. 741–742.)

BACKGROUND. Although Hitler regarded the *Wehrmacht* (*q.v.*) the armed forces, as indispensable, he at the same time suspected the loyalty of much of its leadership. Preferring to place his trust in a special armed force trained in Nazi ideology, he created the *Waffen-SS* as a separate military organization. Eventually, it numbered 39 divisions.

WORLD WAR II. Waffen-SS troops took part in a dozen major battles during the war and became noted for their tough fighting qualities. From the opening *Blitzkrieg* (*q.v.*) against Poland (*see also* POLAND, CAMPAIGN IN) to the late days of the war, *Waffen-SS* units played an important role in most major engagements. Foreign *Waffen-SS* units, consisting of Scandinavians, Yugoslavs, Ukrainians, Latvians, Estonians, Albanians, Dutch, Hungarians, Italians, Flemish, Walloons, Russians, and French, were organized for combat duty, but generally they counted for little in the overall military structure.

NUREMBERG. At the International Military Tribunal both the *SS* and the *Waffen-SS* were declared criminal organizations. (*See* NUREMBERG TRIALS.) *Wehrmacht* leaders insisted that atrocities in combat were committed by the *Waffen-SS* and not by regular army units.

The following table lists the order of battle of the *Waffen-SS* with details on origin, composition, and final disposition:

Bibliography. R. Grunberger, *Hitler's SS* (1970); J. Keegan, *Waffen SS: The Asphalt Soldiers* (1970); and D.D.V. Fosten and R. G. Manion, *Waffen-SS* (1971).

Order of Battle of the Waffen-SS

	TITLE[1]	DATE OF ORIGIN	COMPOSITION	FINAL DISPOSITION
I	SS-Panzerdivision-Leibstandarte Adolf Hitler	1933	Germans	Surrendered, 1945
II	SS-Panzerdivision-Das Reich	1939	Germans	Surrendered, 1945
III	SS-Panzerdivision-Totenkopf	1940	Germans	Surrendered, 1945
IV	SS-Polizei-Panzergrenadierdivision-Polizei Division	1940	Germans	Surrendered, 1945
V	SS-Panzerdivision-Wiking	1940	Germans	Surrendered, 1945
VI	SS-Gebirgsdivision-Nord	1940	Germans	Surrendered, 1945
VII	SS-Freiwilligen-Gebirgsdivision-Prinz Eugen	1942	Ethnic Germans	Surrendered, 1945
VIII	SS-Kavalleriedivision-Florian Geyer	1942	Germans/ethnic Germans	Surrendered, 1945
IX	SS-Panzerdivision-Hohenstaufen	1943	Germans	Surrendered, 1945
X	SS-Panzerdivision-Frundsberg	1943	Germans	Surrendered, 1945
XI	SS-Freiwilligen-Panzergrenadierdivision-Nordland	1942	Germans/Scandinavians	Surrendered, 1945
XII	SS-Panzerdivision-Hitler Jugend	1943	Germans	Surrendered, 1945
XIII	Waffen-Gebirgsdivision der SS-Handschar	1943	Yugoslavs	Dissolved, 1944
XIV	Waffen-Grenadierdivision der SS-Galizische No. 1	1943	Ukrainians	Surrendered, 1945
XV	Waffen-Grenadierdivision der SS-Lettische No. 1	1943	Latvians/Germans	Surrendered, 1945
XVI	SS-Panzergrenadierdivision-Reichsfuehrer-SS	1943	Germans/ethnic Germans	Surrendered, 1945
XVII	SS-Panzergrenadierdivision-Götz von Berlichingen	1943	Germans/ethnic Germans	Surrendered, 1945
XVIII	SS-Freiwilligen-Panzergrenadierdivision-Horst Wessel	1944	Germans/ethnic Germans	Surrendered, 1945
XIX	Waffen-Grenadierdivision der SS-Lettische No. 2	1944	Latvians	Surrendered, 1945
XX	Waffen-Grenadierdivision der SS-Estnische No. 1	1944	Estonians	Surrendered, 1945
XXI	Waffen-Gebirgsdivision der SS-Albanische No. 1-Skanderberg	1944	Albanians	Dissolved, 1944
XXII	SS-Freiwilligen-Kavalleriedivision-Maria Theresa	1944	Ethnic Germans/Germans	Surrendered, 1945
XXIII-a	Waffen-Gebirgsdivision der SS-Kama	1944	Yugoslavs	Dissolved, 1944
XXIII-b	SS-Freiwilligen-Panzerdivision-Nederland	1945	Dutch	Surrendered, 1945
XXIV	Waffen-Gebirgsdivision der SS-Karstjäger	1944	Italians/ethnic Germans	Dissolved, 1945
XXV	Waffen-Grenadierdivision der SS-Hunyadi No. 1	1944	Hungarians	Vanished
XXVI	Waffen-Grenadierdivision der SS-Hunyadi No. 2	1944	Hungarians	Vanished
XXVII	SS-Freiwilligen-Grenadierdivision-Langemarck	1945	Flemish/Belgians	Surrendered, 1945
XXVIII	SS-Freiwilligen-Grenadierdivision-Wallonie	1945	Walloons/Belgians	Surrendered, 1945

Order of Battle of the Waffen-SS (*Continued*)

	TITLE[1]	DATE OF ORIGIN	COMPOSITION	FINAL DISPOSITION
XXIX-a	*Waffen-Grenadierdivision der SS-Russische No. 1*	1944	Russians	Made part of Vlasov Army, 1944
XXIX-b	*Waffen-Grenadierdivision der SS-Italische No. 1*	1945	Italians	Vanished, 1945
XXX	*Waffen-Grenadierdivision der SS-Russische No. 2*	1944	Russians	Made part of Vlasov Army, 1945
XXXI	*SS-Freiwilligen-Grenadierdivision*	1945	Germans	Surrendered, 1945
XXXII	*SS-Freiwilligen-Panzerdivision-Böhmen-Mahren*	1945	Germans/ethnic Germans	Surrendered, 1945
XXXIII	*Waffen-Grenadierdivision der SS-January 30*	1945	Germans	Surrendered, 1945
XXXIV	*Waffen-Grenadierdivision der SS-Charlemagne*	1945	French	Defeated at Berlin, 1945
XXXV	*SS-Freiwilligen-Grenadierdivision-Landstorm Nederland*	1945	Dutch	Dissolved, 1945
XXXVI	*SS-Polizei-Grenadierdivision der SS*	1945	German policemen	Dissolved, 1945
XXXVII	*Waffen-Grenadierdivision-Dirlewanger*	1945	Germans	Surrendered, 1945
XXXVIII	*SS-Freiwilligen-Kavalleriedivision-Lützow*	1945	Ethnic Germans	Surrendered, 1945
XXXIX	*SS-Panzergrenadierdivision-Nibelungen*	1945	SS cadets	Surrendered, 1945

[1]Division titles often had a patriotic connotation and sometimes were based on ethnic composition. The *SS* Division was composed of German volunteers; the *SS-Freiwilligendivision*, of ethnic Germans or Germanic volunteers; the *Division der Waffen-SS*, of East Europeans. The main categories included the *Grenadierdivision* (infantry division); *Panzergrenadier-division* (motorized infantry division); *Gebirgsdivision* (mountain division); and *Kavalleriedivision* (cavalry division).

WAINWRIGHT, JONATHAN MAYHEW (1883–1953). U.S. Army officer who was forced to surrender at Corregidor.

In March 1942 Wainwright took command of the Philippines from Gen. Douglas MacArthur (*q.v.*), who had been ordered to Australia. He led combined American and Filipino troops fighting the Japanese in the Lingayen Gulf area. Throughout the peninsula campaign he fought with his troops against overwhelming odds. He turned down an ultimatum from the Japanese High Command.

After Bataan fell early in April 1942, Wainwright chose to continue the fight from Corregidor. At Corregidor he commanded a force of some 15,000 troops huddled under the almost incessant fire of the Japanese. On May 6, 1942, after a prolonged resistance, he was forced to surrender Corregidor and the survivors of the Philippines campaign to the Japanese.

As a prisoner of war of the Japanese, Wainwright had to go through the anguish of seeing his men mistreated by the victors. He often intervened on their behalf, but to no avail. He and other senior officers were starved and humiliated and made to do menial tasks so that they might "lose face," so important in the Orient. On August 25, 1945, he and his men were liberated.

On September 2, 1945, Wainwright participated in a place of honor behind Gen. MacArthur in the formal surrender ceremonies on the deck of the USS *Missouri*. He was then flown to the Philippines to receive the surrender of Lt. Gen. Tomoyuki Yamashita, the Japanese commander. On return to the United States the same month Wainwright was awarded the Congressional Medal of Honor, promoted to General, and assigned to head the Eastern Defense Command.

Known to his intimates as "Skinny," Wainwright was the typical tall, lean cavalryman. A War Department dispatch described him as "natural leader, magnetic personality, clipped speech, good disciplinarian, popular with officers and men, alert, forceful and has plenty of confidence in himself." President Dwight D. Eisenhower (*q.v.*) later (in 1953) spoke of "his example of courage, fortitude and unshakable patriotism, all exhibited in the face of the most discouraging conditions."

Bibliography. R. Considine (ed.), *General Wainwright's Story* (1946).

WAKDE. *See* NEW GUINEA, CAMPAIGNS IN.

WALDTEUFEL ("WOOD DEMON"). German code or cover name for a final offensive in the Balkans in the spring of 1945.

Following defeat at the Battle of the Bulge (*q.v.*), Hitler conceived an operation by which the 6th *SS Panzer* Army, although badly battered around Bastogne (*q.v.*), would reconquer the Sava-Danube triangle, and then advance through Hungary to the southeast. It was far too late for another German offensive.

WALLACE, HENRY AGARD (1888–1965). Vice-President of the United States during the war.

In 1940 Wallace was elected Vice-President and served in that capacity during Roosevelt's third term in office. He was sent on good-will tours of South America and the Far East. In December 1941, after American entry into the war, he was named to lead the War Cabinet as head of the Board of Economic Warfare. He suggested in this post that Roosevelt's Four Freedoms (*q.v.*) be implemented with Four Duties:

1. The duty of the people to produce to fullest capacity;

2. The duty of transporting war materials to combat areas as fast as possible;

3. The duty of citizens to fight with all their might and

4. The duty to build a peace that would be charitable and enduring.

In March 1945, after the nomination of Harry S Truman (*q.v.*) as Vice-President, Wallace was named Secretary of Commerce.

Wallace was considered by newspapermen to be casual, shy, and serious. His defenders regarded him as a great upholder of human welfare and as a friend of the common man. To critics he was a fuzzy-headed dreamer who allowed himself to be a tool of leftist ideologues. Deeply religious, he believed that the Bible was "heavily loaded on the side of the Progressive democrats." A brilliant plant geneticist, he developed hybrid corn as well as an improved strain of strawberries and gladiolas.

Bibliography. H. A. Wallace, *America Must Choose* (1934), and *Sixty Million Jobs* (1946). *See also* F. Kingdom, *An Uncommon Man* (1945), and R. Lord, *The Wallaces of Iowa* (1947).

WALTZING MATILDA. Australian song popular among troops.

A strange and haunting ballad, *Waltzing Matilda* was a 19th-century bush song and not a special war song, but it became enormously popular after it was introduced by Australians serving with the British 8th Army (*q.v.*) in North Africa. (*See* NORTH AFRICA, CAMPAIGNS IN.) Americans later heard it in the film *On the Beach*. The lyrics featured terms of Australian speech and slang unfamiliar to others.

WANNSEE CONFERENCE. Meeting called in Nazi Germany to discuss organizational problems of the genocide operation against the Jews in German occupied Europe. (*See also* FINAL SOLUTION.)

On January 20, 1942, fifteen leading Nazi bureaucrats were summoned by Karl Adolf Eichmann (*q.v.*) on behalf of Reinhard Heydrich (*q.v.*) to submit a comprehensive plan for "a final solution of the Jewish question." They met at Wannsee, a suburb of Berlin. Heydrich reviewed the emigration problem and stated that there was no longer any possibility of transporting Jews in this fashion. Jews would be evacuated to the east in huge labor columns. Undoubtedly, Heydrich said, a majority "would fall through natural diminution." The survivors would be "treated accordingly," for they were dangerous in that they might rebuild Jewish life.

SIGNIFICANCE. The 90-minute meeting at Interpol headquarters in wartime Berlin set the stage for the Nazi bid to exterminate the Jews of Europe. It marked the beginning of the three-year climax of the genocide program. The conference has been denounced both outside and inside Germany as one of the most shameful episodes in history. American historian Gordon A. Craig called it "the beginning of the most disgraceful era in German history." Denunciations in the contemporary Federal Republic of West Germany are equally harsh. An editorial in *Der Tagesspiegel* on January 20, 1982, judged the minutes of the Wannsee Conference as "probably the most dreadful document ever written in German." The editorial went on: "The way in which the final solution was planned and implemented showed how thin the veneer of civilization is and to what depths of hatred mankind can descend. That may well be the legacy that weights most heavily on all Germans capable of grasping the magnitude of their crimes and of being ashamed of them. No one can opt out of the history of his people."

WAR AIMS. Expressions by statesmen in belligerent countries about goals for which they were fighting.

BACKGROUND. In World War I the enunciation of war aims became a factor of critical importance not only in fighting the war but also in preparing for its end. On January 8, 1918, President Woodrow Wilson outlined in his Fourteen Points the principles upon which peace was to be restored. When the Germans asked for an armistice, they believed that peace would be made along the general lines of the Fourteen Points. Wilson later found it difficult to persuade the Allies of the wisdom and justice of his formula. The hard-bitten French statesman, Georges Clemenceau, put it bluntly at Versailles: "God Almighty had only Ten Points; Wilson had to have Fourteen!" Despite Clemenceau's sarcasm, the Wilsonian statement had an effect in ending the war.

WORLD WAR II. Axis leaders Hitler, Mussolini and Tojo expressed their aims before the outbreak of war. In one way or another the goal was *Lebensraum,* (*q.v.*), or living space, the overwhelming desire to gain additional territory as a necessity for the life of the nation. Soon after the outbreak of war, Allied leaders made it plain that they were fighting for elimination of Axis leaders as a menace to the peace of the world.

ANGLO-AMERICAN. The first major expression of British war aims came on May 13, 1940, from Churchill:

You ask what is our policy? I will say: It is to wage war, by sea, land, and air, with all our might, and with all the strength that God can give us: to wage war against a monstrous tyranny, never surpassed in the dark, lamentable catalogue of human crime. You ask, what is our aim? I can answer in one word: It is victory, victory at all costs, victory in spite of all terror, victory, however long and hard the road may be; for without victory there is no survival.

Anglo-American cooperation was established even before American entry into the war. On January 6, 1941, President Roosevelt enunciated his Four Freedoms (*q.v.*): freedom of speech and expression, freedom of worship, freedom from want, and freedom from fear. These indicated clearly the American attitude toward Axis ideology. On August 12, 1941, the Four Freedoms were embodied in the joint U.S.-British Declaration of the Atlantic Charter (*q.v.*).

In speech after speech Churchill stated British war aims. (*See* CHURCHILL'S WAR SPEECHES.) Following American entry into the war, Roosevelt also hammered away at the theme that the monstrous Hitler had to be destroyed if Western civilization were to survive. When criticized about the Allied alliance with the Communist Stalin, whose reputation for decency was low in the Western world, Churchill replied that he would ally himself with the devil if it meant the end of the German dictator.

On January 24, 1943, at a press conference after the Casablanca Conference (*q.v.*), Roosevelt used the term *unconditional surrender*, which had been thoroughly discussed at the conference. The term came to be accepted widely as the official Allied war aim. Nazi Propaganda Minister Paul Joseph Goebbels (*q.v.*) used it with telling effect to bolster German morale for a last-ditch fight against the Allies.

GERMAN. Hitler's war aims were explicit: (1) territorial revision of the Treaty of Versailles; and (2) expansion of the Third Reich to assure living space for the German people. He stated his immediate goals at a conference held on November 5, 1937, in which he called for "the greatest possible conquest at the lowest cost." Czechoslovakia and Austria were to be conquered simultaneously. (*See* HOSSBACH PROTOCOL.) On September 1, 1939, the day he began his *Blitzkrieg* (*q.v.*) against Poland, he stated: "Once again I have put on the tunic that was to me the holiest and most beloved garment. I shall take it off only after victory, or I shall not live to see the end." In later war speeches he called for annihilation of his accumulated enemies.

ITALIAN. By allying himself with Hitler, whom he regarded as invincible, Mussolini hoped to ensure the expansion of his Fascist empire. He would obtain territory in East and North Africa, drive the British Fleet from the Mediterranean to make it *Mare Nostrum* ("Our Sea"), and reestablish the glory of the old Roman Empire. He did not enter the war at its start, but on the fall of France he committed his country to the Axis cause. Rapid failures in Greece and North Africa led him to modify his war aims to mere survival of Italy as an appendage of the Third Reich.

RUSSIAN. In the late 1930s Stalin was convinced that the capitalist West was seeking to divert Hitler to an attack on the Soviet Union. To neutralize this possibility, he allied himself with Hitler to split Poland between them. (*See* RUSSO-GERMAN NONAGGRESSION PACT.) When Nazi Germany turned on him on June 22, 1941, Stalin enunciated a new war aim—rescue of the Motherland from "the Fascist beast" by "a great patriotic war." His goals were twofold: (1) to maintain the existence of the Soviet Communist state; and (2) to help smash Hitler, Nazism, and the Third Reich. He was successful on both counts. Not only were his war aims fulfilled, but also the USSR emerged from the war as one of the great global empires.

JAPANESE. During the latter half of the 19th century, after the United States opened feudal Japan to American trade, militant *samurai* inspired a revolution that placed Japan in competition with the West. A dynamic industrialism gave way to an enormous expansion drive that opened in China in 1931. Japanese militarists then turned to the oils and minerals of southern Asia. Aggressive designs had been proclaimed by Japanese militarists, who were said to have planned military conquest in the future.

Friction between Japan and the United States increased dramatically when President Roosevelt in July 1940 froze all Japanese assets in the United States and later put into effect a commercial blockade against Japan. Gen. Hideki Tojo (*q.v.*), leader of the Tokyo militarist clique, resolved on war "to assure Japan's existence." By this time the goal of a Greater East Asia Co-Prosperity Sphere (*q.v.*) had been set up to construct a huge Japanese Empire extending from Manchuria to Thailand.

Tojo carefully planned Japan's Pacific blueprint. First on the agenda was crippling of the U.S. fleet at Pearl Harbor. Then, with the United States unable to resist at sea, Japanese forces would overrun Southeast Asia and complete an impregnable perimeter around their conquests. This audacious program was endorsed at a Supreme War Council September 6, 1941. It was extraordinarily successful at first as the United States and the Allies suffered a series of overwhelming defeats in the Pacific.

Bibliography. L. W. Holborn (ed.), *War and Peace Aims of the United Nations* (2 vols., 1943–1948); H. Feis, *Churchill, Roosevelt, Stalin: The War They Waged and the Peace They Sought* (1957); E. Reves, *The Anatomy of Peace* (1969); G. Kolke, *The Politics of War* (1969); T. G. O'Connor, *Diplomacy for Victory* (1971); and N. Rich, *Hitler's War Aims* (1973).

WAR CRIMINALS, JAPANESE. *See* JAPANESE WAR CRIMINALS' TRIAL.

WAR RESPONSIBILITY. Historical dispute over assigning blame for the outbreak of World War II. The issue revolved not so much around the matter of fundamental causes, on which most historians agree, but on immediate guilt for lighting the fuse. (*See* CAUSES OF THE WAR.)

BACKGROUND. The controversy following World War I was repeated after World War II. After 1919, orthodox historical opinion, represented by Bernadotte Schmitt, attributed World War I to German aggression. He accused the German General Staff of preparing deliberately for war over the course of 40 years. He admitted that non-German as well as German statesmen made serious errors in diplomacy, but such mistakes were minor when compared with the German drive for war.

Revisionists, represented by Harry Elmer Barnes, disagreed. They explained that German statesmen did make moves that might have been interpreted as contributing to a war situation, but they did not plan and did not want war. Germany's pre-war record, they said, was not uniquely aggressive. In fact, its leaders were said to have worked energetically to prevent the conflict, because they knew that great gains already made in time of peace might be jeopardized.

A third approach held that responsibility should be distributed equally among the belligerents and that the war was the result of a combination of unresolved economic clashes, diplomatic intrigues, national rivalries, sword rattling, and a psychologically unsound conception of security. The blame, it was said, should be placed on the general institutional and cultural milieu, not on entire nations or individuals. Serious mistakes of judgment were made on all sides. Lloyd George explained it: "The more one reads of the memoirs and books written in the various countries of what happened before August 1, 1914, the more one realizes that no one at the head of affairs quite meant war. It was something into which they glided, or rather staggered or stumbled."

In 1961 more fuel was added to the controversy when Fritz Fischer, historian at the University of Hamburg, repeated the thesis that Germany in 1914 deliberately aimed at world domination. With minute documentation from both Western and German archives, he revealed how German aggression was pursued persistently. It was, he intimated, a nightmarish situation in which German war aims were placed above any other consideration.

WORLD WAR II. There is more general agreement that the blame for *starting* World War II rests primarily on Hitler. Most historians, represented by British scholars John H. Wheeler-Bennett and Lewis Namier and Americans William L. Langer, Norman Rich, and Gerhard Weinberg, see continuity in Hitler's thinking, which amounted to an ideology of aggression. They admit that the general economic, political, and psychological climate in the late 1930s was such that the war could be expected. But they also contend that Hitler's continued aggressions provided the spark that ignited the conflagration.

Some historians believe that the very existence of the Third Reich, with its goals outlined in Hitler's *Mein Kampf* (*q.v.*), was a threat to peace. They point to Hitler's writings, conversations, and captured secret reports as evidence.

"For the good of the German people we must wish for a war every 15 or 20 years. An army whose sole purpose it is to preserve peace leads only to playing at soldiers—compare Sweden and Switzerland." At the same time the *Fuehrer* informed the world: "I am not crazy enough to want a war. The German people have but one wish—to be happy in their own way and to be left in peace."

TAYLOR THESIS. Revisionism after World War II came to a head in 1961 when A.J.P. Taylor, a Fellow of Magdalen College, Oxford, published his *Origins of the Second World War.* According to Taylor, Hitler was not a maniac bent upon world conquest, but a traditional German statesman like Frederick the Great, Bismarck, and Stresemann. What the *Fuehrer* wanted was a revision of the Treaty of Versailles, not a war with Britain or France in 1939 or at any other time. The Hitler who turned on the Soviet Union in June 1941 was no longer the Hitler of the pre-war era. The only war Hitler desired in 1939 was a war of nerves, in which he excelled. He had no way of knowing that Britain and France would go to war over Danzig.

Taylor gave a different interpretation of the documentary evidence. *Mein Kampf,* he wrote, far from being a blueprint for war, was merely a grandiose daydream. Hitler's *Table Talk* was only fantasy. Documents produced at Nuremberg (*see* NUREMBERG TRIALS) were part of a "lawyer's brief," loaded against the defendants, and should be approached with caution. In biting satire Taylor challenged the consensus on war responsibility.

TREVOR-ROPER REACTION. Taylor's book created a stir when released in England. It was immediately denounced as a "whitewashing" of Hitler and an apology for appeasement. Hugh R. Trevor-Roper, Regius Professor of Modern History at Oxford, launched a powerful attack on his colleague. He charged Taylor with willfully misusing documents, acting as an apologist, and strengthening the forces of neo-fascism. According to Trevor-Roper, Taylor's thesis was illustrated "with all his old resources of learning, paradox, and *gaminerie.*" The entire thesis said Trevor-Roper, was "demonstrably false" and "utterly erroneous."

Where Taylor had described Hitler's "patience," Trevor-Roper saw indecision that had driven Hitler's followers wild. Trevor-Roper admitted that Hitler possessed "political genius," but his ultimate purpose was hardly that of traditional German statesmen. It aimed at "the destruction of European civilization by a barbarous empire in Central Europe." It was Hitler who provided the necessary and sufficient explanation of the origins of World War II.

HOSSBACH DOCUMENT. Critics of Taylor maintained that he had been unable to refute the evidence of the Hossbach Memorandum, which presented proof of Hitler's policy of aggression. At a secret meeting held on November 5, 1937, the *Fuehrer* outlined to his military leaders the practical items of aggression. This was nearly two years before the outbreak of war. (*See* HOSSBACH PROTOCOL.)

WILL TO WAR. On August 22, 1939, a day before the signing of the Russo-German Nonaggression Pact (*q.v.*) and one week before the invasion of Poland, Hitler spoke to his assembled generals: "The destruction of Poland has priority. . . . I shall give a propagandist reason for starting the war, no matter whether it is plausible or not. The victor will not be asked afterwards whether he told the truth or not. When starting and waging war it is not right that matters for victory."

The *Fuehrer* concluded: "Close your hearts to pity. Act brutally. Eighty million people must obtain what is their right. Their existence must be made secure. The strongest man is right. The greatest harshness." With these words Hitler dismissed his generals. *

CONSENSUS. Attribution of main war responsibility to Hitler is made not only by Allied scholars but also by historians and journalists in contemporary Germany. Karl-Heinz Janssen, in *Die Zeit* (August 31, 1979), in commenting on the 40th anniversary of the outbreak of World War II, wrote that the name of the man responsible for the war was Adolf Hiter. "No war since the campaign of Alexander had been planned more boldly, none started more frivolously and recklessly—with the exception perhaps that of King Pyrrhus."

Janssen pointed out that Hitler left his people in no doubt. In a speech in the *Reichstag* on September 1, 1939, the *Fuehrer* said he woud commit suicide if he were defeated. This "world power or destruction," "fight to be or not to be," this "all or nothing attitude," touched hidden chords in the German soul. According to Janssen, it was this combination of Hitler's driving force plus German receptivity which led straight to the war. The war did not come out of the blue. As every other human understanding, it had to be prepared and it required the cooperation and activity of many to become possible.

At this point Janssen spoke of the responsibility of the German people as a whole: "The majority of the German people was disposed for war before Hitler came to power. The dream of the glory of the Reich was fed from many traditions of thought—authoritarian, nationalist, militaristic, racist, economic." The German people had failed to learn that Europe tolerates no claim to hegemony, a lesson already learned by the French, Spanish, Dutch, and Swedes before them. The price of that lesson was appallingly high for both Germans and their victims.

CONTROVERSY ON JAPAN. After the war it was revealed that the American intelligence service had succeeded in decoding the Japanese

---

Documents on German Foreign Policy, 1918-1945. From the Archives of the German Foreign Ministry (H.M.S., London, 1948 ff.), D.VII, No. 193.

diplomatic code, thereby enabling the deciphering of messages between Tokyo and the Japanese Embassy in Washington. This led to a bitter historical controversy. The distinguished American historian Charles Beard, joined by others as well as the military and naval commanders at Pearl Harbor, contended that President Roosevelt had deliberately goaded the Japanese into war. The Pacific Fleet, it was charged, was kept at Pearl Harbor precisely to lure the Japanese into attacking it, an act of aggression that would shock the American public out of its isolationism.

Other equally eminent American historians rejected this new revisionism. Far from provoking the war, Roosevelt it was said, in his negotiations with Japanese emissaries, simply followed traditional principles of the open door policy of 1899 and the Stimson doctrine of 1931, which refused to recognize territories acquired by acts of aggression. These historians reject as utterly fallacious the thesis that Roosevelt was responsible in any way for the Japanese attack on Pearl Harbor. (*See also* PEARL HARBOR CONTROVERSY.)

Bibliography. J. W. Gantenbein (ed.), *A Documentary Background of World War II, 1931–1941* (1948); W. L. Langer and S. E. Gleason, *The World Crisis and American Foreign Policy*, 2 vols. (1952–1953); G. A. Craig and F. Gilbert (eds.), *The Diplomats, 1919–1939* (1953); L. B. Namier, *Europe in Decay, 1936–1940* (1953); R. J. Butow, *Tojo and the Coming of the War* (1961); A.J.P. Taylor, *The Origins of the Second World War* (1961); J. W. Wheeler-Bennett, *Munich: Prologue to Tragedy* (1966); J. V. Compton, *The Swastika and the Eagle* (1968); E.M. Robertson, *The Origins of the Second World War* (1971); N. Rich, *Hitler's War Aims* (1973); and G. C. Weinberg, *The Foreign Policy of Hitler's Germany: Starting World War II* (1981).

WAR ROOMS, BRITISH. Also called Churchill's Bunker. Headquarters in London for British war direction.

To Churchill it was a matter of some importance to remain in London despite incessant bombing by the Germans. Early in the war he arranged for the construction of a set of war rooms, a labyrinth of subterranean shelters just off Parliament Square. Engineers built a twisting maze of mole-like passages connecting chambers, conference rooms, kitchens, and sleeping quarters, all strengthened by low-hanging concrete roofs. Fresh air was pumped into the underground bunker, while sewage and debris were emptied into the Thames. Ventilation was good, but the bottom level was not electrified as a safety measure. There were no ordinary facilities for baths or showers, although very important people could take a "canary bath" from a shallow bowl. Public water closets were sanitized by heavy chemicals.

The war rooms were made to accommodate 150 people, although at times as many as 500 jammed the tiny cubicles. The Prime Minister was assigned a small bedroom, where he kept the two pairs of boots which he wore in public. Nearby was a little cubicle with a direct-line telephone to U.S. President Roosevelt.

Next to the bedroom and almost a part of it was the map room, the nerve center of the bunker. Large charts on the walls and blackboards displayed casualties, air missions, disposition of convoys, and location of submarine packs. In the map room were four different telephone circuits and a radio transmitter from which the Prime Minister broadcast his messages to the British people.

The central conference room was filled with old and worn furniture. In the center was a U-shaped table where the experts planned strategy and tactics. Conspicuous in the corners were two large cans that were supposed to catch the bouncing cigars discarded by Churchill in a backward motion over his shoulder.

WARSAW, BOMBING OF. Devastating assault on the capital of Poland by the *Luftwaffe* (*q.v.*) in the opening days of World War II.

TARGET. Warsaw, Russian Varshava, German Warschau, and French Varsovie, lay in the east central part of Poland. Standing on both banks of the Vistula, it was the center of rail and road connections with Soviet Russia and Western Europe. For the Germans it was especially important for the airport at Okevie as well as for such industries as metalworking, textiles, electrical goods, precision instruments, and motor cars.

BACKGROUND. For Hitler the pact with Soviet Russia signed on August 23, 1939 (*see* RUSSO-GERMAN NONAGGRESSION PACT) was the final step in his plans for attacking Poland. He could now move with no immediate concern for the Russian Army. On September 1, 1939, he started the first great *Blitzkrieg* (*q.v.*) of World War II. The Germans were superior in numbers, firepower, armor, and air strength. The *Luftwaffe* began the attack by destroying the Polish Air Force on the ground. Armored columns then smashed their way into the interior. By September 21 Western Poland was overrun and the only resistance left was in Warsaw. (*See* POLAND, CAMPAIGNS IN.)

Infuriated by word that Warsaw was holding, Hitler first tried the weapon of propaganda. German aircraft rained millions of leaflets on the city demanding surrender. Posters outside the besieged city informed ''brave officers'' that they would be allowed to keep their swords. Others read: ''Poles! Come to us. We will not hurt you. We will give you bread.''

DEFENSE. Although their city was surrounded, the people of Warsaw were determined to resist. Mayor Stefan Starzynski, nicknamed Stefan the Stubborn, urged his people to build trenches and fortifications. They constructed hundreds of tiny dugouts five yards apart from which two citizens could operate with rifles, hand grenades, and machine guns. Trenches zigzagged along streets in such profusion that it was possible to step from the front doors of apartment houses directly into the trenches. Polish officers who had retreated into the city formed new regiments.

ATTACK. On September 21, 1939, Hitler gave the order for a smashing assault from the air accompanied by massed artillery on the ground. For six days

400 German bombers, under command of Gen. Wolfram von Richthofen (*q.v.*), battered the city day and night. From a camouflaged command post nearby Hitler watched the orgy of destruction. Warsaw began to blaze from end to end while the water supply was disrupted. When their ammunition finally ran out, the people capitulated.

LOSSES. There is no adequate estimate of the loss of life in the bombardment. Most of the city was destroyed, including railroad stations, coal yards, hotels, and office buildings. The old Saxon palace in Pilsudski Square in the heart of the city burned to its foundations. Warsaw was reduced to smoking piles of brick, plaster, and debris. The cost to the Germans was minimal.

AFTERMATH. The bombing of Warsaw early in the war made it clear to the Allies how Hitler intended to fight his war. It was to be *Schrecklichkeit* ("frightfulness") with no regard for the civilian population. The *Luftwaffe* later repeated the tactics in the bombing of Rotterdam, London, and Coventry (*qq.v.*). The Allies replied in kind—and with more deadly effect—at Cologne, Hamburg, Dresden, and Berlin (*qq.v.*)

Bibliography. J.F.C. Fuller, *The Second World War, 1939-1945* (1948); C. Falls, *The Second World War* (1948); and G. W. Feuchter, *Geschichte des Luftkrieges* (1954).

WARSAW UPRISING. Rebellion by the Polish underground Home Army in the fall of 1944, first encouraged by Moscow, then denied Russian aid. It is to be distinguished from the Warsaw Ghetto Uprising of April-May 1943, in which thousands of Jews were killed.

BACKGROUND. The Russian onslaught against the citadel of Warsaw carried over into the last half of 1944. At the end of July, Marshal Konstantin Rokossovsky (*q.v.*), commanding a central Russian Army, approached Warsaw with the goal of passing over the Vistula and seizing the Polish capital before his Western Allies could cross the Rhine. Inside Warsaw, Polish Gen. Tadeusz Bor-Komorowski, head of the Polish underground Home Army, urged on by Moscow radio, began to fight against the Germans in the open. The Poles quickly captured several city districts. (*See* UNDERGROUND.)

MASSACRE. Rokossovsky suddenly brought his forces to a halt outside the city. Inside the city the Germans turned viciously on Polish defenders. It was a massacre. The Germans used heavy artillery and tanks on their trapped victims. For 60 days the Poles, fighting desperately in streets, cellars, and sewers, held out, only to be obliterated. More than 200,000 Poles are believed to have died in the assault.

SIGNIFICANCE. The deliberate Russian action revealed the extent to which Stalin would go for political ends. He did nothing to help the beleaguered

Poles because he believed that the Home Army leadership would prove troublesome when it came to establishing a Communist-controlled government in Poland. He ordered the Red Army not to cross the Vistula and enter the city until the Nazis had crushed the rebellion. He closed airfields behind Russian lines to Western Allied planes seeking to help the Poles. He then accused the Polish underground of acting too soon.

Bibliography. J. Radzymińska, *Dwa Razy Popiol* (1970).

WASHINGTON CONFERENCE, FIRST. Code or cover name *Arcadia.* Opening Anglo-American war council held after U.S. entry into the war.

BACKGROUND. Although there had been close cooperation between London and Washington during the first two years of the European war, Pearl Harbor (*q.v.*) brought full American participation in the conflict. A high-level conference was deemed necessary to give direction to the joint effort against the Axis.

PARTICIPANTS. Taking part in the First Washington Conference were President Roosevelt, Prime Minister Churchill (*qq.v.*), and their staffs of military and civilian advisers. The meetings were held from December 24, 1941, to January 14, 1942, in an atmosphere of grim but hopeful determination.

DECISIONS. The conferees solemnly agreed to wage war until victory. Several basic decisions were made with understanding that there would be later meetings.

ATLANTIC THEATER OF WAR

To the immense relief of the British, it was agreed that first priority would be given to the European-first principle. ''Only the minimum of force necessary for safeguarding of vital interests in other theaters [shall] be diverted from the operations against Germany.''

BRITISH STRATEGY

For the basic problem of how war was to be waged against Germany, the British introduced a plan which in general became the key to operations. Now that the Russians had resisted collapse, the Allies would forge a constricting ring around Axis Europe, starting on the Russian front, and moving in circular fashion across North Africa. Germany itself would be worn down by air attack, blockade, and its necessity of maintaining long lines of defense on the periphery of Europe.

SLEDGEHAMMER

If Soviet Russia were on the verge of collapse by September 1942, *Operation Sledgehammer* was designed as a limited plan to invade northwest Europe. Eventually, *Sledgehammer* was merged into *Operation Overlord* (*q.v.*).

GYMNAST

It was decided that combined Allied forces would land near Casablanca and move east to catch the Germans in North Africa in a classic pincers movement. *Operation Gymnast* would depend on developments on the Russian front. In June 1942 *Gymnast* was set aside in favor of *Torch* (*q.v.*).

COMBINED CHIEFS OF STAFF

On the U.S. side a Joint Chiefs of Staff Organization was established as a counterpart of the British Chiefs of Staff Committee. Members of both units would act in concert to plan operations in all theaters of war. All major decisions would be made in common.

DECLARATION OF UNITED NATIONS

A by-product of the meeting, this declaration embodied the war aims of the Allies in the spirit of the *Atlantic Charter* (*q.v.*)

SIGNIFICANCE. Understandings reached at the First Washington Conference indicated that, while there were differences of opinion regarding method, there was no misunderstanding about the goal—destruction of the Nazi Third Reich.

Bibliography. Foreign Relations of the United States, *The Conferences at Washington and Casablanca* (1968).

WASHINGTON CONFERENCE, SECOND. War conference held in 1942 to plan the next moves against the Axis.

BACKGROUND. The prognosis in the spring of 1942 was not altogether encouraging. Allied merchant ships were being sunk in American coastal waters at an alarming rate. In North Africa, Gen. Erwin Rommel (*q.v.*) and his *Afrika Korps* (*q.v.*) were poised at El Alamein (*q.v.*) for a breakthrough to the Suez Canal. Stalin was calling loudly for a Second Front (*q.v.*) while accusing the Western Allies of cowardly behavior. He hinted that Soviet Russia might not be able to remain in the war unless major pressure from the West relieved its overtaxed armies.

PARTICIPANTS. The Allied delegation included President Roosevelt, Prime Minister Churchill (*qq.v.*), and their staffs of experts. The meetings lasted only two days, from June 25 to 27, 1942.

DECISIONS. Discussions and decisions were limited to a few critical subjects.

WAR PRODUCTION

It was agreed that production was to be increased dramatically in both the United States and Britain. War matériel and supplies were to be produced on a round-the-clock basis. (*See* PRODUCTION, BATTLE OF; and SUPPLIES, BATTLE FOR.)

SHIPPING

Special efforts would be made to replace shipping lost through enemy action. Additional protection was to be given to North Atlantic convoys. (*See* ATLANTIC, BATTLE OF THE.)

AID TO CHINA

The conferees agreed to give additional help to Chiang Kai-shek (*q.v.*) and the Chinese in their struggle against Japan.

POSTPONEMENT OF *OVERLORD*

The projected invasion of Hitler's Fortress Europe (*q.v.*) across the English Channel was postponed until 1943 or later. Stalin, despite his complaints, would have to wait. *Overlord* (*q.v.*) would not be undertaken until the buildup was sufficient to forestall another Dunkirk. (*See* DUNKIRK EVACUATION.)

OPERATION TORCH

The conferees agreed to an operation designed to trap Gen. Erwin Rommel (*q.v.*) in North Africa between the British 8th Army (*q.v.*) and invading Allied forces from the west. *Operation Torch* would: (1) provide a durable base for action against southern Europe; (2) tighten the anti-Axis blockade; (3) provide bases from which the Mediterranean and South Atlantic water routes could be made safe; (4) forestall any similar action by the Germans; (5) help maintain Spanish neutrality; and (6) provide additional cement for the Western-Soviet alliance.

SIGNIFICANCE. The Second Washington Conference was designed to assure Stalin that a Second Front would be forthcoming eventually but that it would come when the West was ready and not before. Stalin was angered by the postponement of *Overlord* but he was also enthusiastic about plans for *Operation Torch*. For the first time at war conferences, the situation in the Far East was mentioned.

Bibliography. Foreign Relations of the United States, *The Conferences at Washington and Casablanca* (1968).

WASHINGTON CONFERENCE, THIRD. Code or cover name *Trident*. Meetings of Allied war leaders held in Spring 1943 to discuss problems of war and peace.

BACKGROUND. Less than a year had passed since the Second Washington Conference (*q.v.*) when *Operation Torch* (*q.v.*), the invasion of North Africa had been set up. In the preceding January the conference at Casablanca (*q.v.*)

had initiated *Operation Husky,* the invasion of Sicily (*q.v.*). These and other important events had altered the course of the war and another meeting was deemed essential.

PARTICIPANTS. The conferees, who met from May 11 to 27, 1943, included President Roosevelt, Prime Minister Churchill (*qq.v.*), and their staffs of experts. Among the Americans were Gen. George C. Marshall, Lt. Gen. Joseph T. McNarney, Adm. E. J. King, Adm. William D. Leahy, and Harry Hopkins (*qq.v.*). The British delegation included Field Marshal John Dill, Gen. Alan F. Brooke, Adm. of the Fleet A. Dudley Pound, Air Chief Marshal Charles F. A. Portal, and Lt. Gen. Hastings Ismay (*qq.v.*).

DECISIONS. The conferees discussed older problems and new questions of emphasis and priority.

MEDITERRANEAN

The immediate problem was where to move after the invasion of Sicily. It was decided to continue pressure to get Italy out of the war by whatever means might be best. Because it was likely that the Normandy invasion would not take place until Spring 1944, Churchill argued that further operations in Italy would keep the enemy occupied and make northern invasion easier. Roosevelt and the Americans pointed out that an Italian campaign would draw heavy forces from the Pacific theater. Specific means for the Italian campaign would be decided later by the Combined Chiefs of Staff.

INVASION OF FRANCE

The date of May 1, 1944, was set for the cross-Channel invasion of France. Churchill made it clear that full-scale operation would take place "as soon as a plan offering reasonable prospects for success could be made." The problems had not yet been solved: difficult beaches, large rise and fall of tide, strength of the enemy's defenses, and ease of his communications. But eventually, there would be relief for the armies of Soviet Russia.

SHIPPING

Attention would be given to the critical problem of shipping. This was to have first priority in the buildup of *Operation Overlord* (*q.v.*).

BOMBING OF GERMANY

It was agreed that there would be a stepped-up air assault on German cities and industrial centers. Heavy day and night raids would be increased.

PACIFIC STRATEGY. Much attention was given to operations in the Pacific theater. China would be reinforced by the establishment of Allied bases. There were differences between the British and Americans on how to fight the Burma campaign, but this was resolved in favor of an American-supported limited operation to open a supply route to China. It was agreed also to build up American air power in China.

SIGNIFICANCE. The conference indicated that the Allies now had the authority and prestige of approaching victory. It was considered important to redouble Allied efforts and grasp the fruits of success. The goal was to bring the war to an end as quickly as possible.

Bibliography. Foreign Relations of the United States, *The Conferences at Washington and Casablanca* (1968).

WATER WAGTAILS (*BACHSTELZE*). One-man observation kites used on German U-Boats in the war at sea.

Water wagtails were towed behind a surfaced U-Boat, which ordinarily had a poor range of vision. Submarine crews found it impossible to keep a close watch over a wide area from the low-lying bridge of their craft. They could extend the range of their vision by use of these kites. There was a serious handicap, for use of the water wagtails meant a loss of speed in submerging, which could be fatal. The contrivance was generally used only in areas where enemy aircraft were not on patrol. (*See* ATLANTIC, BATTLE OF THE.)

WAVELL, ARCHIBALD PERCIVAL (1883–1950). Leading British commander in the early stages of the war.

In 1939 Wavell held the Middle Africa command with the responsibility for operations in North Africa. For several years he led outnumbered forces in a delaying action against the Axis and sustained defeat after defeat. At the same time he disrupted the Axis timetable. From December 1940 to February 1941 he routed numerically superior Italians in Libya, a victory which eventually led to liquidation of the Italian Empire in East Africa.

In the spring of 1941 Wavell's strength was considerably weakened when he was ordered to send 60,000 of his troops, several Royal Air Force (*q.v.*) squadrons, and many tanks and guns for the defense of Greece. Nevertheless, he carried on his campaign against great odds in East Africa. Then came the counteroffensive by Gen. Erwin Rommel (*q.v.*), which British Intelligence had underestimated. After the Greek debacle and the loss of Cyrenaica, Wavell was sent to India in what was widely regarded as a demotion. In 1942 he was named to supreme command of Allied forces in the Southwest Pacific. Promoted to Field Marshal on January 1, 1943, he was appointed Viceroy and Governor-General of India in the same year.

Bibliography. J. H. Robertson, *Wavell, Scholar and Soldier* (1964), and *Wavell: Supreme Commander, 1941–1943* (1969).

WAVES. Unit of the U.S. Navy composed entirely of women. Its purpose was to release men for combat duty at sea. (*See also* WAACs; SPARS; and WOMEN MARINES.)

The term *WAVES* is an acronym for *W*omen *A*ccepted for *V*olunteer *E*mergency *S*ervice. The original unit was set up on July 30, 1942, so that women could enter the U.S. Naval Reserve. In 1944 the unit was renamed Women Reserves. Most WAVES performed shore duty in administrative work. Shortly before the end of the war the Women Reserves numbered about 90,000 women. After the war women were integrated into the regular U.S. Navy.

WEATHER BUOYS. Floating meteorological stations used by the German Navy and *Luftwaffe* (*q.v.*).

The weather buoy was a device about 15 yards long, which gave the impression of being a torpedo. Floating on the surface of the sea, its antenna automatically gave information by Morse code several times a day on temperature, wind direction and force, atmospheric pressure, and hygrometric state of the air. The buoys were towed into place by U-Boats.

WEDEMEYER, ALBERT COADY (1897–   ). Replacement for Gen. Joseph Stilwell as Chiang Kai-shek's (*qq.v.*) Chief of Staff.

In September 1940, as a Major, Wedemeyer was assigned to Washington to serve in the Training Section of the Office of the Chief of Infantry. Eight months later he became a member of the Plans Group of the War Department General Staff, serving under Gen. Dwight D. Eisenhower (*q.v.*). By this time he was regarded as one of the country's outstanding experts in war plans.

In September 1943, as a Major General, Wedemeyer was appointed American Deputy Chief of Staff of the Southeast Asia Command under Adm. Louis Mountbatten (*q.v.*). In October 1944 he was detailed to Chunking, China, as successor to Gen. Joseph W. Stilwell (*q.v.*). He remained in China until the end of the war.

WEHRMACHT. Literally "power for defense," the German term for war machine. The word was used to describe the German armed forces during the era of the Third Reich.

The *Wehrmacht* was Hitler's successor to the *Reichswehr,* the defensive land forces of the Weimar Republic (1919–1933). The Treaty of Versailles restricted Germany to a 100,000-man army. On May 31, 1935, Hitler issued a *Wehrgesetz* ("defense law"), which called for the formation of the new *Wehrmacht.* It included the combined Army, Navy, and Air Force (*Luftwaffe*) of the Third Reich. (*See* Chart on p. 760).

Bibliography. T. Taylor, *Sword and Swastika* (1952); W. Goerlitz, *History of the German General Staff* (1952); and J. W. Wheeler-Bennett, *The Nemesis of Power: The German Army in Politics, 1918–1945* (1953).

WELLES, SUMNER (1892–1961). American diplomat.

From 1937 to 1943 Welles served as Under Secretary of State, a post in which he helped lay the framework for the Latin-American Good Neighbor Policy. In

Organization of the Oberkommando Der Wehrmacht (High Command of the Armed Forces) in the Third Reich

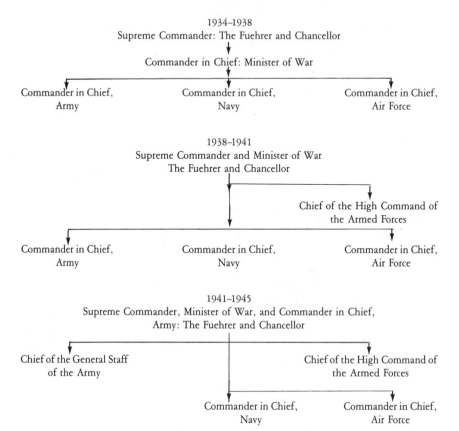

1934–1938
Supreme Commander: The Fuehrer and Chancellor

Commander in Chief: Minister of War

| Commander in Chief, Army | Commander in Chief, Navy | Commander in Chief, Air Force |

1938–1941
Supreme Commander and Minister of War
The Fuehrer and Chancellor

Chief of the High Command of the Armed Forces

| Commander in Chief, Army | Commander in Chief, Navy | Commander in Chief, Air Force |

1941–1945
Supreme Commander, Minister of War, and Commander in Chief, Army: The Fuehrer and Chancellor

| Chief of the General Staff of the Army | Chief of the High Command of the Armed Forces |

| Commander in Chief, Navy | Commander in Chief, Air Force |

1940 President Roosevelt sent him as his personal envoy on a diplomatic mission to Europe to discuss political and economic affairs with European leaders. His report to Roosevelt left scant hope "for the establishment of a just and lasting peace." He accompanied Roosevelt at his meeting at sea with Churchill in 1941 before the entry of the United States into the war. He served in the State Department until 1943.

After the war Welles devoted much of his time to writing. He died in Bernardsville, New Jersey, on September 24, 1961.

Tall, formal, with aquiline nose and clear blue eyes, Welles was the picture of the disciplined diplomat. Conservative in background and training, he had an inflexible will and defended his views vigorously.

Bibliography. Among Welles's books are *The World of the Four Freedoms* (1943); *The Time for Decision* (1944), which recounted the results of his mission to Europe; *The Intelligent American's Guide to Peace* (1945); *Where Are We Heading?* (1946); and *Seven Decisions that Shaped History* (1951).

WEREWOLF (*WERWOLF*). Hitler's field headquarters near Vinnitsa in the Ukraine. (*See FUEHRER'S* HEADQUARTERS.)

WEREWOLVES (WOLF-MEN). German organization of guerrilla fighters set up in the late days of the war to wrest victory from defeat.

Led by Gen. Hans Pruetzmann, the Werewolves modeled their activities on the Resistance fighters in German-occupied countries. (*See* RESISTANCE MOVEMENTS.) Because they wore uniforms, they claimed the rights of legitimate prisoners of war if captured. They regarded themselves as a paramilitary auxiliary of the regular German armed forces.

Rumors were started that the Werewolves intended to fight behind Allied lines. Members threatened vengeance on any German who refused to support them. Despite loud boasting, they never became an effective fighting force. Germany was too far on the road to defeat to be saved by grandiose braggadocio. Most Werewolves were fanatical youngsters.

When he became Chancellor on April 30, 1945, Adm. Karl Doenitz (*q.v.*) issued an order to all Werewolves to cease operations at once. The order was instantly obeyed, an indication of the movement's state of bankruptcy.

Bibliography. C. Whiting, *Hitler's Werewolves* (1972).

WEST WALL. German term used to describe the line of fortifications built along Germany's 1939 frontier from the Dutch boundary in the north to Switzerland in the south. It was designed as a "defense line" against attack from the west. The common name for the West Wall was Siegfried Line (*q.v.*), but Hitler preferred the term West Wall.

BACKGROUND. At the time of the Czechoslovak crisis in 1938, Hitler ordered his armed forces to prepare not only for an invasion of Czechoslovakia but also for a possible two-front war. At this time he called for the construction of a defense line opposite the Maginot Line. The work was entrusted to Fritz Todt (*q.v.*), then Inspector General of Highways, who mobilized 1 million men to expedite the work. Many families were evicted to make way for the fortifications. Hitler took a personal interest in the project and often visited the line on tours of inspection. The key point was the rebuilt fortress of *Listen*, opposite French Mulhouse.

Much of the West Wall was an elaborate hoax. Hitler had little faith in a defensive mentality and from the beginning opted for *Blitzkrieg* (*q.v.*), a fast mobile warfare of armored forces. He wanted merely to give the appearance of defense against possible assault from the west. He ordered a great show of activity. The Siegfried Line was never as elaborate as its French counterpart and much of it consisted merely of concrete teeth set in the earth, forbidding only in appearance.

WORLD WAR II. In a war directive issued on August 31, 1939, Hitler ordered: "The Army will occupy the West Wall and will take steps to secure it from being outflanked in the north by the Western Powers from Belgian or Dutch territory.'' Work on the West Wall was completed in May 1940 just north of Aachen. During that spring, Anglo-French troops in the Maginot Line faced Germans in the West Wall in what was popularly known at the time as the Sit-Down War (*See SITZKRIEG.*) The West Wall was dismantled partially and neglected after the defeat of France.

On August 24, 1944, the day before Paris fell to the Allies and when the whole German position was deteriorating, Hitler issued a directive calling for construction of a "new West Wall" for the defense of the Third Reich. It was far too late, however, to prevent a massive Allied assault on Germany. (*See* GERMANY, BATTLE OF.)

Bibliography. C. Sangiorgio (ed.), *Deutsche Gemeinschaftsarbeit: Geschichte, Idee und Bau des Westwalls* (1940); J. Poschlinger, *Das Buch vom Westwall* (1940); and W. Flack, *Wir bauen am Westwall* (1940).

WEYGAND, MAXIME (1867-1965). French Army officer active in the battle of France.

In September 1939 Weygand was recalled as a Commander-in-Chief of the Eastern Mediterranean theater at Beirut, Lebanon. On May 19, 1940, he was named Chief of Staff of all theaters of operation. After the First Battle of France (*q.v.*) (June 5–22, 1940) he asked the government to conclude an armistice. He served for three months in the Vichy Cabinet of Gen. Henri Pétain (*q.v.*) and was then sent to North Africa as the government's delegate-general. Because Weygand opposed German designs on French North African possessions, Hitler demanded his recall. In 1942 he was arrested by the *Gestapo* (*q.v.*) and held prisoner until his release in 1945.

In 1948 Weygand was tried before the French High Court of Justice and found innocent of all charges of collaboration with the Germans.

An advocate of the Maginot-Line (*q.v.*) mentality, Weygand did not understand the mobility of World War II. "I am a fireman," he said. "If a fire breaks out anywhere within my reach I shall try to put it out."

Bibliography. Weygand's works include *Foch* (1947); and *Recalled to Service: Memoirs* (1952). For a biography *see* P.C.F. Bankwitz, *Maxime Weygand and Civil-Military Relations in Modern France* (1967); and J. Weygand, *Weygand, mon père* (1970).

WEYGAND LINE. Hastily prepared defense line set up in 1940 to hold off the Germans.

Named after 73-year-old Gen. Maxime Weygand (*q.v.*), the line was prepared while the fighting at Dunkirk was still in progress. (*See* DUNKIRK EVACUATION.) Weygand gave orders for fortifications south of the Somme and Aisne rivers, from Abbeville to Montmédy, and called for its defense. He sent 37 of the 66 divisions available to him to the new line. But it was too late to prevent a German breakthrough. (*See* FRANCE, FIRST BATTLE OF.)

WILHELMINA, HELENA PAULINA MARIA (1880-1962). Queen of the Netherlands.

When the Germans invaded the Netherlands on May 10, 1940, Wilhelmina issued a spirited proclamation to her people: "I herewith direct a flaming protest against this unprecedented violation of good faith and violation of all that is decent in relations between cultured states. I am sure my Government will now do our duty." Together with her ministers she left for London. Here she headed the Dutch Government-in-exile for the rest of the war. She declared her intention of returning "as soon as possible to her people in their great distress and their heroic fight against overwhelming odds." In 1942 she visited the United States, where she addressed a joint meeting of Congress.

Bibliography. L.J.P. Power, *Royal Ladies of the Netherlands* (1939); and P. Paneth, *Queen Wilhelmina: Mother of the Netherlands* (1943).

WILLIE AND JOE. Legendary American GIs (*q.v.*), created by Bill Mauldin (*q.v.*) and appearing in the *Stars and Stripes* (*q.v.*), daily newspaper for the U.S. armed forces.

Cartoonist Mauldin depicted Willie and Joe as dirty, bone weary, and miserable, but at the same time as hilariously funny. They had little or no idea why they were in the army or in combat. Like many others, they fought as hard as they could while doing an inordinate amount of griping.

Mauldin captured the grim wit of combat conditions in a way that endeared him to millions of GIs. Willie and Joe had little use for their officers, and, like Willie and Joe, millions of GIs were not at all enthusiastic about the rigors of war. The most important thing in the world was to get the rotten job done and return home alive as soon as possible. One Mauldin cartoon showed Willie and Joe in a foxhole reading about the invasion of France while shells were bursting all around them. The caption: "Th' hell this ain't the most important hole in the world. I'm in it."

Spit-and-polish officers, notably Gen. George S. Patton, Jr. (*q.v.*), protested against Mauldin's characters because of their slovenly, unmilitary appearance. But higher echelons, aware that Willie and Joe were great morale builders, overruled the annoyed officers. Mauldin's characters, it was decided, provided a healthy release for GI frustrations.

Bibliography. R. Meyer, Jr., *The Stars and Stripes Story of World War II* (1960).

WILSON, HENRY MAITLAND (1881–1964). British officer who commanded troops in the Middle East.

At the outbreak of war in 1939 Wilson was GOC (General Officer Commanding) in Egypt under Gen. Archibald Wavell (*q.v.*). He led the British Army of the Nile when it virtually annihilated the Italians under Marshal Rodolpho Graziani (*q.v.*). In May 1941 he was sent to help the Greeks. In June 1941 he took Syria from Vichy France. In 1942 he was given the Persian-Iraq command to guard the Suez Canal. The next year he became Commander-in-Chief Middle East.

In 1944 Wilson succeeded Gen. Dwight D. Eisenhower (*q.v.*) as Supreme

Allied Commander in the Mediterranean. In that same year he was promoted to Field Marshal and sent to Washington as British Chief of Staff. He attended the war conferences at Yalta and Potsdam (*qq.v.*) as a British representative.

Bibliography. Wilson wrote *Eight Years Overseas* (1950).

WINANT, JOHN GILBERT (1889–1947). U.S. diplomat.

In 1941 Winant was named U.S. Ambassador to Britain and served in London through the remainder of the war. In this post he succeeded Joseph Kennedy (*q.v.*), who was skeptical about the ability of the British to withstand German power. Unlike Kennedy, Winant used every effort possible to help the British and give support to the Allied cause. He acted as intermediary between British leaders and President Roosevelt. Although he considered the position of the British extemely grave, he was confident that they would eventually be victorious.

Winant remained Ambassador in London until 1946, when he began work with the UN Economic and Social Council (UNESCO). He committed suicide in Concord, New Hampshire, on November 3, 1947.

Tall, dark, with prominent cheekbones, and jutting jaw, Winant gave the impression of a latter-day Lincoln. His critics contended that he carefully cultivated the Lincoln image by wearing unpressed suits despite his high income. His friends worried about his bouts of depression.

Bibliography. J. G. Winant, *Letter from Grosvenor Square* (1947), and *Our Greatest Harvest* (1950). For an excellent biography, *see* B. Bellush, *He Walked Alone* (1968).

WINDOW. British code or cover name for a method used by the Royal Air Force (*q.v.*) to drop bundles of tinfoil in large quantities in order to thwart German radar. (*See* RADAR, WARTIME.) The Germans dubbed it "the Laminetta Method."

The procedure was as primitive as it was effective. British heavy bombers and escorting aircraft dropped thin metallic strips of a length and width carefully attuned to German radar wave length. Drifting in the wind, the tinfoil fell slowly to the ground, forming a wall that could not be penetrated by enemy radar waves. German radar screens were blocked. The result was that the *Luftwaffe* (*q.v.*) was thrown into disarray because its fighter planes were in effect blinded. The night became as impenetrable as before the discovery of radar.

Window was used for the first time on the night of July 24–25, 1943, when 728 heavy bombers left England and in a succession of raids nearly obliterated Hamburg. Pilots of defensive aircraft were astonished by the sudden failure of their radar sets. (*See* HAMBURG, BOMBING OF.)

WINGATE, ORDE CHARLES (1903–1944). Controversial British Army officer.

In 1941 Wingate led a small army against the Italians in the Middle East. He entered Addis Ababa at the side of Emperor Haile Selassie, organized a force of 2,000 men, and in four months restored Haile Selassie to his throne.

In 1942 Wingate was sent to India to serve with Field Marshal Archibald Wavell in a campaign to drive the Japanese from Burma. He trained a force of British, Gurkhas, and Burmese in rigorous jungle warfare. In February–May 1943, he led his Imperial Commandos, known as the Ghost Army, on a sustained raid across the Chindwin River, destroying Japanese installations on the way. Every pound of supplies the troops needed was dropped to the raiders from the air. Wingate commanded his widely dispersed columns from a radio mounted on a mule. The radio was his only contact with the outside world.

In March 1944, Wingate, now a Major General, landed the largest Allied airborne force of the war 200 miles to the rear of the Japanese. Soon after the operation began, he was killed in a plane crash in Burma.

Burly, bearded, and handsome, Wingate was said to have had the eyes and bearing of an Old Testament prophet, the cunning of a hunted fox, and the endurance of an army mule. He couched his orders in biblical language and his personal magnetism fired the men who served under him. "You can't help but follow him," said one of his officers, "when you see him charge through the elephant grass in his old pith helmet. Out there in Burma there wasn't anything he couldn't do better than any man in the force."

Like Lawrence of Arabia, Wingate was a mystic and dreamer who enjoyed the intoxication of battle. With Colonel Philip ("Flip Corkin") Cochran (*q.v.*), who led the fleet of gliders landing Wingate's men in Burma, he formed a team that became known throughout the India-Burma theater as "the wing and the beard." (*See also* BURMA, CAMPAIGNS IN; CHINDITS; and LONG-RANGE PENETRATION GROUP.)

Bibliography. W. G. Burchett, *Wingate's Phantom Army* (1944); C. J. Rollo, *Wingate's Raiders* (1944); and L. O. Mosley, *Gideon Goes to War* (1955).

WINGATE'S RAIDERS. *See* CHINDITS.

"*WIR FAHREN GEGEN ENGELLAND*" ("*WE MARCH AGAINST ENGLAND*"). German patriotic ditty sung by individuals and massed choirs in the summer of 1940 when an invasion across the English Channel was expected. (*See SEA LION.*)

When the armistice with France was signed at Compiègne (*q.v.*) on June 22, 1940, the German radio concluded its account of the proceedings by broadcasting "*Wir fahren gegen Engelland.*" The song saw the waving Nazi flag as an emblem of the Reich and maintained that Germans could no longer endure the English making fun of it. Germans would sail away to conquer England.

WOLF-PACK TACTICS. New German U-Boat tactics introduced in the sea war.

BACKGROUND. The convoy system used by the Allies in World War I contributed much to overcoming the U-Boat menace. The method of group sailings protected by escorting warships was effective in reducing sea losses. The procedure was followed in the opening months of the war at sea. (*See* ATLAN-TIC, BATTLE OF THE.) During the winter of 1940–1941, the pressure of the U-Boat campaign diminished somewhat due to bad weather, but it was re-newed early in 1941.

OPERATION. In the spring of 1941 Adm. Karl Doenitz (*q.v.*), now able to put 32 U-Boats to sea, introduced his new wolf-pack tactics which had been prepared for several months. In the early days of the war the U-Boats would operate independently. The new method involved group instead of single attacks.

The standard operating procedure was simple. When the position of a con-voy was established, U-Boat Command Headquarters ashore would contact the nearest submarine group. The latter would assign one of its number to shadow the convoy and alert the others by radio. When all were assembled in the area, they would begin night attacks on the surface. During daylight hours the U-Boats would withdraw from the convoy and its escort. They would then go back in again for the kill.

These saturation attacks made it difficult for enemy escorting warships to strike back effectively. In battle the U-Boats ordinarily maintained radio silence and sought to intercept the signals of surface ships. On occasion U-Boat com-manders augumented their visual spotting technique by the use of *Bachstelle,* one-man observation kites trailed from submarines on the surface.

DEFENSE. The new wolf-pack tactics took the Allies by surprise. Hitherto they had been concerned mainly by attack from submerged submarines and had put their faith in Asdic (*q.v.*), an underwater detecting device. By trial and error they discovered that the best way to counter wolf-pack attacks was to locate the shadowing U-Boat, the "contact keeper," and drive it away. The idea was to make the submarine dive and thereby lose use of its periscope. Among other defensive measures were the use of *Snowflake* (*q.v.*), il-luminating devices, and powerful Leigh Lights (*q.v.*) placed on planes.

AFTERMATH. In July 1941, a month after the outbreak of the war with the Soviet Union, German headquarters detached a part of its Atlantic Fleet for operations in the Arctic. In September 1941 other U-Boats were ordered into the Mediterranean to support Gen. Erwin Rommel (*q.v.*) in his North African encounters. (*See* NORTH AFRICA, CAMPAIGNS IN.) Given a breathing spell, Allied strategists were able to refine their defense against wolf-pack tac-tics, especially by more effective air support and use of radar. (*See* RADAR, WARTIME.)

During the later months of the Pacific war, American submarines adopted wolf-pack tactics, but in much smaller groups.

Bibliography. J. Rohwer, *Die U-Boot-Erfolge der Achsenmächte, 1939, 1945* (1968); D. Mason, *U-Boat: The Secret Menace* (1968); and J.P.M. Showell, *U-Boats under the Swastika* (1973).

WOMEN MARINES. Unit of the U.S. Marine Corps composed entirely of women. The purpose was to release men for combat duty. (*See also* WACs; WAVES; and SPARS.)

WOMEN'S ARMY CORPS (WAC). Unit of the U.S. Army composed entirely of women.

On May 14, 1942, Congress passed a bill creating the Women's Army Auxiliary Corps (WAAC), which became the Women's Army Corps a year later. Young women who in normal times would still be under parental control were formed into non-combatant groups to perform services that would release men for combat duty. By the end of the war the unit reached its peak strength of 99,000 women under wartime director Col. Oveta Culp Hobby. WACs served in all theaters of war. After the war the unit was granted regular army status, and it was eventually dissolved. (*See also* WAVES; SPARS; and WOMEN MARINES.)

Bibliography. U.S. War Department, *WAC Life* (1940), and *The WAC Officer* (1945); and M. R. Treadwell, *The Women's Army Corps* (1968).

WOMEN'S AUXILIARY AIR FORCE (WAAF). Women's unit of the Royal Air Force (*q.v.*).

Set up on June 28, 1939, on a voluntary basis, the WAAF was granted military status in 1941. WAAF personnel, officers and enlisted women, were detailed to do much important groundwork, such as control tower operators, meteorologists, parachute packers, and plane mechanics. WAAF personnel wore uniforms similar to those of men in the RAF. By the summer of 1943 the unit numbered some 180,000 women. The first director, K. Jane Trefusis, was succeeded then by Air Commandant Lady Walsh. After the war the unit was absorbed into the RAF and became the Women's Royal Air Force (WRAF).

WOMEN'S ROYAL NAVAL SERVICE (WRNS). Women's unit of the Royal Navy.

Known as Wrens, British women served in shore posts to relieve men for combat duty at sea. In England, as in the United States (*see* WAVES), women played a far greater role in war then ever before, taking jobs as chauffeurs, workers, and ferry pilots. They asserted a new independence. Originally set up in World War I, the WRNS were reactivated in World War II under the direction of Vera Laughton Mathews as Superintendant, a rank corresponding to Colonel. The unit reached a peak wartime strength of 74,000 in 1944. After the war it became a part of the Royal Navy for shore duty only. (*See also* WAAF; and SOCIAL IMPACT OF THE WAR.)

WORKERS CHALLENGE. German clandestine broadcasting station used early in 1940 in conjunction with *Operation Sea Lion* (*q.v.*), the projected invasion of England. (*See* NEW BRITISH BROADCASTING STATION.)

WRNS. Women's unit of the Royal Navy. (*See* WOMEN'S ROYAL NAVAL SERVICE.)

X

X-2. Counterintelligence and agent-control branch of the American Office of Strategic Services (OSS) (*q.v.*).

X-CRAFT. British midget submarines designed especially for the raid on the German battleship *Tirpitz* in 1943.

X-Craft were 45 feet long and carried a crew of four. Of the six X-craft that set out to attack the *Tirpitz*, only the *X-6* and *X-7* succeeded in placing charges under the enemy warship. (*See TIRPITZ;* and ALTENFJORD RAID.)

Bibliography. T. M. Gallagher, *The X-Craft Raid* (1971).

X-GERÄT (**"X-APPARATUS"**). Special German radio-navigation device used by *Luftwaffe* (*q.v.*) bombers in the summer of 1940. (*See* BRITAIN, BATTLE OF.) The apparatus used in a bomber guided it along a beam aimed over the target. The bombs were released when the aircraft reached intersecting cross beams.

X-REPORT. Report issued in late October 1939 indicating Papal soundings had disclosed a willingness in London for a "soft" peace with a non-Nazi Germany.

BACKGROUND. Josef Müller, a Munich lawyer, devout Catholic, and confidant of Cardinal Faulhaber, reported to members of the German opposition to Hitler from Rome that Pope Pius XII was willing to go to surprising lengths to act as an intermediary between Germany and Britain on these terms:

1. Removal of the Nazi regime.
2. Formation of a new government in Germany and restoration of the *Rechtsstaat*.
3. No attack in the West by either side.
4. Settlement of the Eastern question in favor of Germany.

The information further stated that the British were ready to accept the conditions.

DISPOSITION. In late October 1939 the X-Report was submitted by Hans von Dohnanyi to Gen. Ludwig Beck (*q.v.*) and diplomat Ulrich von Hassell (*q.v.*), both leaders of the conspiracy against Hitler. The conspirators hoped to use the X-Report to influence Field Marshal Walther von Brauchitsch (*q.v.*) and other high German commanders to join the plot against the *Fuehrer.*

RESULTS. The X-Report was a monumental failure. Von Brauchitsch denounced it as "plain high treason." The generals thus lost their last chance for a negotiated peace favorable to themselves. Within a week after the final rejection of the X-Report, Hitler's troops swept into Denmark and Norway.

"X" SQUADRON. Special Squadron No. 617 of the Royal Air Force (*q.v.*) assigned to raid the Möhne, Eder, and Sorpe dams in the Ruhr district on May 16–17, 1943. (*See* RUHR DAMS; and GIBSON, GUY.)

XX-COMMITTEE. From the Roman numeral XX, signifying "double cross." Also called the Twenty Committee. Subsidiary unit of the British M-5 (*q.v.*), counterintelligence service.

The XX-Committee was responsible for the control and assignment of double agents. It recruited German spies who were caught in England and put them to work for the Allies. Through these spies the XX-Committee fed false information to the Germans. In 1943 it attempted to convince the Germans through an elaborate hoax that the Allies intended to land their forces in Corsica and Greece instead of Sicily. (*See* MINCEMEAT.) In 1944 it planted false reports that the Allied invasion of the Continent would take place at Calais instead of Normandy. (*See also* ESPIONAGE; DOUBLE CROSS SYSTEM; MASTERMAN, JOHN C.; and NORMANDY, INVASION OF.)

Bibliography. J. Masterman, *The Double Cross System of the War of 1939-1945* (1972).

Y

Y-DAY. The day (June 1, 1944) set for completion of all preparations for the invasion of Normandy. (*See* NORMANDY INVASION.)

YAKOVLEV, ALEKSANDR SERGEYEVICH (1906–   ). Russian aircraft designer.

In the years immediately before the war Yakovlev designed fighter planes that eventually turned out to be among the war's outstanding aircraft. Along with Sergei V. Ilyushin (*q.v.*), Andrei N. Tupolov, Artem L. Mikoyan, and Mikhail I. Gurevich, he was recognized as a top Russian plane designer.

Yakovlev's *Yak-1* fighter plane was usually teamed with Ilyushin's *Il-2* as mainstays of the Russian fighter force. Throughout the war and until 1948 Yakovlev was a Deputy People's Commissar (later Minister) of the aircraft industry. He was awarded the Stalin Prize six times and the Order of Lenin seven times.

YALTA CONFERENCE. Also called the Crimean Conference, code or cover name *Argonaut*. Meeting of Allied war leaders held at Yalta in the Crimea, February 4–12, 1945, as the first stage of peacemaking. One of the most important conferences of the war, it was also one of the most controversial.

PARTICIPANTS. Present at the conference were the Big Three—Roosevelt, Churchill, and Stalin (*qq.v.*). Among other participants were U.S. Secretary of State Edward R. Stettinius, Jr., British Foreign Secretary Anthony Eden, and Soviet Foreign Minister Vyacheslav M. Molotov (*qq.v.*). All Chiefs of Staff of the Big Three countries were there except U.S. Gen. Henry Harley Arnold (*q.v.*), who was ill. In addition, delegations of advisers and specialists attended from the three countries.

Roosevelt came to Yalta with several priorities. One of his main objectives was to win the cooperation of the Soviet Union in the work of building a

United Nations organization to establish security and preserve the peace. He wanted the USSR as a founding nation of the United Nations. He also wanted a firm commitment for Soviet entry into the war in the Pacific, permission for U.S. bombers to use bases in western Siberia, and continued Soviet support for the Chinese Nationalist Government. Churchill hoped to set limits for Soviet expansion in Western Europe.

Roosevelt and Churchill operated at Yalta under several handicaps. The war was still going on and that influenced the British and American attitude toward Stalin's demands. Soviet troops had already occupied Poland; British and American troops were just recovering from the Battle of the Bulge (*q.v.*); the Far East war was still raging and the Americans were taking heavy casualties; and it was not known at that time if the atom bomb would really work. Stalin, on his part, was willing to give firm assurance to join the war against Japan two to three months after the end of the war against Germany, but he was determined to ask a high price.

WORLD ORGANIZATION. It was decided that a United Nations Conference on a proposed world organization should be summoned on April 25, 1945, at San Francisco to prepare a Charter for a General International Organization for the maintenance of international peace and security. The basis would be the proposals made public in October 1944 at the Dumbarton Oaks Conference (*q.v.*). The nations to be invited would be the United Nations as they existed on February 8, 1945. In effect, this was a pointed invitation to those countries that had not yet entered the war to become belligerents as soon as possible. The United Kingdom and the United States agreed to support a proposal to admit to original membership two Soviet Socialist Republics, the Ukraine and White Russia.

Several organizational plans were made in advance. Each member of the Security Council was to have one vote. Decisions of the Security Council on procedural matters would be made by affirmative vote of seven members. On the matter of territorial trusteeship it was agreed that the five nations that would have permanent seats on the Security Council would consult with one another before the opening conference.

DECLARATION ON LIBERATED EUROPE. The conferees jointly declared their agreement to act together during the temporary period of instability in liberated Europe, and assist the peoples of the former Axis satellite states to solve by democratic means their pressing political and economic problems. Order in Europe would be established and economic life rebuilt by processes that would enable liberated peoples to destroy the last vestiges of Nazism and fascism and at the same time create democratic institutions of their own choice. The liberated countries or former Axis satellite states would be helped to establish conditions of internal peace; carry out emergency measures for the relief of distressed peoples; form interim governmental authorities broadly representative of all democratic elements of the population; allow free elections of governments responsive to the will of the people; and facilitate where necessary the holding of such elections.

The Declaration on Liberated Europe reaffirmed the principles of the Atlantic Charter (*q.v.*) as well as those enunciated in the Declaration of the United Nations. It expressed the determination of the signatories "to build in cooperation with other peace-loving nations a world order under law, dedicated to peace, security, freedom and general well-being of mankind."

DISMEMBERMENT OF GERMANY. At the time of the Yalta Conference, an early victory over the Germans seemed to be certain. The immediate concern was final defeat, to be followed by broad outlines for a German settlement. While military experts formulated the last combat plans, Roosevelt, Churchill, and Stalin discussed their ideas concerning the dismemberment of Germany. The subject had already been debated at the Second Quebec Conference (*q.v.*) on September 10, 1944, at which agreement was reached on broad principles concerning the form of military government soon to be set up in Germany.

An important decision concerned division of Germany into zones. Once Hitler's power was broken, Germany would be divided into four zones of occupation: one each for Britain, the Soviet Union, the United States, and France. Stalin for a time opposed the right of France to a zone on the ground that it "had opened the gates to the enemy," but later agreed when it was stipulated that the French zone was to be carved out of British and American sectors. Unity of administration was to be secured by means of a Central Control Commission.

REPARATIONS. It was agreed that Germany must pay in kind to the Allied nations for the losses it caused in the course of the war. Those countries that bore the main burden of the war and suffered the heaviest losses were to receive the first reparations, obviously a concession to the Russians. Reparations in kind were to be exacted in three forms: (1) destruction of Germany's war potential by removing within two years such national wealth as machine tools, equipment, ships, rolling stock, investments abroad, industrial, transport, and other enterprises inside Germany; annual deliveries of German reparations; and Allied use of German labor.

Stalin called for an exact sum of $20 billion of which the Soviet Union was to receive $10 billion. Churchill flatly refused. Roosevelt finally suggested that a Reparations Commission take the Russian figure as "a basis for discussion."

WAR CRIMINALS. The conferees agreed that the question of major war criminals should be the subject of inquiry by the three Foreign Secretaries for a report in due course after the Conference.

POLAND. The delicate question of Poland was the chief obstacle to accord among the Allies. Both Churchill and Roosevelt, fearing Soviet plans to dominate Eastern Europe, wanted the Poles to be allowed to choose by democratic means, not by outside pressure, the kind of government they desired. Stalin agreed that Poland was to be "free and sovereign," but added that for security reasons the government had to be friendly to the Soviet Union. He also agreed that there would be "free and unfettered elections as soon as possible on the basis of universal suffrage and the secret ballot."

Stalin had already set up his own Provisional Government in Poland, composed of the Lublin Polish group that had been sponsored by the Soviet Union. He did this without any consideration for the Polish Government-in-exile in London that had won the support of the Western Allies. (See GOVERN-MENTS-IN-EXILE.) It was agreed that the Provisional Government "now functioning in Poland" should be reorganized on a broader democratic basis with the inclusion of democratic leaders from Poland itself and from Poles abroad. The new government would then be called the Polish Provisional Government of National Unity.

On the critical matter of Poland's new boundaries, it was agreed to accept Stalin's request that the Curzon Line (*q.v.*), extending southward to the pre-war border of Czechoslovakia, be made the western boundary of the Soviet Union. This meant the inclusion of almost half of Poland's pre-war territory into the USSR. Both Roosevelt and Churchill finally approved the Curzon Line, but expressed the "hope" that the Soviet Union would make some concessions, such as awarding Lwow to the Poles. A discussion took place on how much territory from the north and east of Germany should be given to Poland, but the question was left open. When the Russians completed their military occupation of Germany, they arbitrarily made the Neisse River the Polish-German frontier.

YUGOSLAVIA. It was agreed to recommend to Marshall Tito (*q.v.*) that the new Yugoslav Government should declare that the anti-Fascist Assembly of National Liberation (AUNOJ) be extended to include members of the last Yugoslav *Skupstina* who had not compromised themselves by collaboration with the enemy, thus forming a temporary Parliament. Any legislative acts passed by the AUNOJ would be subject to subsequent ratification by the Constituent Assembly.

OTHER DECISIONS. Additional decisions were: Italo-Yugoslav and the Italo-Austria frontiers would be discussed later; Yugoslav-Bulgarian relations would be handled in Moscow; further matters, such as the Control Commission in Bulgaria, Greek claims upon Bulgaria, and oil equipment in Rumania, were postponed; the situation in Iran would be pursued through diplomatic channels; permanent machinery would be set up for meetings of the three Foreign Secretaries every three or four months; and the matter of the Montreux Convention and the Straits would be discussed by the three Foreign Secretaries later in London.

SECRET AGREEMENT REGARDING JAPAN. The approved Protocol was announced to the press of the world, but no mention was made of an additional secret agreement regarding Japan, by which Soviet Russia obtained the Kurile Islands in violation of the Atlantic Charter (*q.v.*). (*See* YALTA SECRET AGREEMENT.)

AFTERMATH. The end of the Yalta Conference found the Big Three in a happy mood. Roosevelt spoke to the American Congress: "I return from the Crimean Conference with a firm belief that we have made a good start on the road to world peace." Churchill said in the House of Commons: "The ties that bind the three great powers together, and their mutual comprehension of each other, have grown." Stalin said nothing, but there is little doubt that he was highly pleased by the outcome.

Undoubtedly, the meeting at Yalta represented an impressive step in the reconstruction of Europe as soon as hostilities ceased. Some tensions were eliminated. On paper it was a considerable agreement. Above all, Stalin had agreed to admit non-Communists to governments in Eastern Europe and had consented to the holding of free elections.

CRITICISM. It soon became obvious, however, that the substance differed from the form. Stalin believed that interpretation and implementation of the agreement depended upon relative bargaining power and that the Soviet Union could assert its point of view without any effective opposition. The Russian chief apparently had no intention of honoring the agreements made at Yalta. Almost immediately he began to violate its provisions. He paid no attention to the concept of an interim democratic government in Poland and threw his support to the Lublin Government as the legitimate government. The Russians allowed no "genuine coalition of democratic parties"; there were no elections for two years; when elections took place they were not "free and unfettered." In violation of the agreement reached at Yalta, the USSR intervened in Rumania to force King Michael to replace a coalition of moderates with a Soviet puppet regime.

Critics charged that Stalin's concept of "friendly governments" included only those dominated by the Soviet Union. Others believed that Roosevelt misjudged Stalin at Yalta and was not quite as successful as he thought in "charming Uncle Joe." Roosevelt was accused of making commitments from which the United States and the rest of the non-Communist world might never recover. Still other critics held Yalta responsible for many ills that the world suffered since the defeat of Germany. Special criticism was directed at the secret agreement regarding Japan, which was denounced as an unwarranted concession enabling Stalin to expand Soviet influence into the Far East.

Bibliography. V. M. Dean, *The Four Cornerstones of Peace* (1946); J. W. Snell and others, *The Meaning of Yalta: Big Three Diplomacy and the New Balance of Power* (1956); *The Tehran, Yalta, and Potsdam Conferences: Documents* (Moscow, 1969); R. Beitzell (ed.), *Tehran, Yalta, Potsdam: The Soviet Protocols* (1970); A. Conte, *Yalta* (1970); D.S. Clemens, *Yalta* (1970); and R. F. Fenno, *The Yalta Conference* (1972).

YALTA SECRET AGREEMENT. Secret Big Three (*q.v.*) understanding granting Soviet Russia special territorial acquisitions.

BACKGROUND. At the Teheran Conference (November 1943) Stalin assured Roosevelt and Churchill of his support in the Pacific war. At the Yalta Conference (February 4–11, 1945) the Soviet chief, in violation of the spirit of the Atlantic Charter (*q.v.*), demanded territorial compensation. "I only want to have returned to Russia what the Japanese have taken from my country." Eager to obtain the support of the Soviet Union at the time, Roosevelt and Churchill had to pay the price. A secret treaty was negotiated without the participation of either the U.S. State Department or the British Foreign Office. It was kept secret for months.

TEXT. The full text was released by the State Department on March 27, 1947:

Agreement Regarding Japan

The leaders of the three great powers—the Soviet Union, the United States of America, and Great Britain—have agreed that in two or three months after Germany has surrendered and the war in Europe has terminated, the Soviet Union shall enter into the war against Japan on the side of the Allies on condition that:

1. The *status quo* in Outer Mongolia (the Mongolian People's Republic) shall be preserved;

2. The former rights of Russia violated by the treacherous attack of Japan in 1904 shall be restored, viz.:

a. The southern part of Sakhalin as well as the islands adjacent to it shall be returned to the Soviet Union;

b. The commercial port of Dairen shall be internationalized, the preeminent interests of the Soviet Union in this port being safeguarded, and the lease of Port Arthur as a naval base of U.S.S.R. restored;

c. The Chinese Eastern Railroad and the South Manchurian Railroad, which provides an outlet to Dairen, shall be jointly operated by the establishment of a joint Soviet-Chinese company, it being understood that the preeminent interests of the Soviet Union shall be safeguarded and that China shall retain full sovereignty in Manchuria;

3. The Kurile Islands shall be handed over to the Soviet Union. It is understood that the agreement concerning Outer Mongolia and the ports and railroads referred to above will require concurrence of Generalissimo Chiang Kai-shek. The President [*Roosevelt*] will take measures in order to obtain this concurrence on advice from Marshal Stalin.

The heads of the three great powers have agreed that these claims of the Soviet Union shall be unquestionably fulfilled after Japan has been defeated.

YAMAMOTO, ISORUKU (1884–1943). Japanese Admiral who conceived the attack on Pearl Harbor.

Though he was personally opposed to war with the United States, Yamamoto, through his various assignments on the Japanese Naval General

Staff, planned the attack on Pearl Harbor. His report of the assault contained these words: "America has a full house, but we had a royal flush." Later a letter by Yamamoto was released containing these words: "I shall not be content merely to capture Guam and the Philippines and to occupy Hawaii and San Francisco, I am looking forward to dictating peace in the United States in the White House in Washington." That letter, widely publicized by American propaganda forces, had a strong effect on American morale.

Yamamoto later displayed his organizational ability in matters of naval support and supply in the conquests of Malaya, Java, the Philippines, and Burma. He incurred serious naval defeats in the Coral Sea, at Midway, and at Guadalcanal (*qq.v.*).

On April 18, 1943, while on an inspection visit by air to Japanese bases, Yamamoto was ambushed by American planes and shot down and killed. (*See* YAMAMOTO, DEATH OF.)

Yamamoto was said to have determined upon a naval career because he "intended to return the visit of Commodore Perry." In World War II his American opponents regarded him as the boldest, most imaginative, and unscrupulous of the Japanese combat commanders. In Japan he was venerated as a great national hero.

Bibliography. E. Sorimachi, *The Human Side of Isoruku Yamamoto* (1955); H. Agawa, *Isoruku Yamamoto* (1965); I. D. Potter, *Yamamoto* (1965); and B. Davis, *Get Yamamoto* (1969).

YAMAMOTO, DEATH OF. The ambush death of Adm. Isoruku Yamamoto, Commander-in-Chief of the Japanese Combined Fleet in mid-April 1943.

BACKGROUND. Yamamoto was the man who directed the attack on Pearl Harbor (*q.v.*) as well as conquests of Malaya, Java, the Philippines, and Burma. Known by his American opponents for his aggressiveness, he had been defeated in the Coral Sea, at Midway, and at Guadalcanal (*qq.v.*). (*See* YAMAMOTO, ISORUKU.)

REPORT OF DEATH. In late May 1943 Tokyo radio reported that Yamamoto had been killed in action while directing a naval operation from an airplane in mid-April 1943. The broadcast claimed that he had not been killed outright but had later died of injuries. It was further stated that Emperor Hirohito had elevated Yamamoto to Fleet Admiral. "This gracious gesture," the report went on, "failed to rally the condition of Admiral Yamamoto."

A later Japanese broadcast declared that the death of Admiral Yamamoto would stiffen the determination of Japan's armed forces. "Looking up to Fleet Admiral Yamamoto's fighting spirit as their example, the whole navy will heighten its intense fighting spirit and will stride forward toward the destruction of enemy American and Britian." The Admiral was given a state funeral. Tokyo radio announced that his successor would be Adm. Mineichi Koga (*q.v.*).

There was immediate speculation in the American press about the strange death of the Japanese Admiral. The Office of War Information (*q.v.*) hinted that he might have been killed in the crash of a passenger plane. Another report had it that he had committed suicide when he realized that Japan's far-flung seizures in the Pacific were beginning to be rolled back.

AMBUSH. Only later was it revealed how Yamamoto died. Appalled by the death of their naval leader, the Japanese attributed it to incredibly bad luck. What they did not know was that U.S. Naval Intelligence had cracked the Japanese naval code, and that Washington was aware of every detail of Yamamoto's inspection visit.

On April 17, 1943, a top-secret dispatch signed by Frank Knox (*q.v.*), Secretary of the Navy, was flashed from Washington to Henderson Field on Guadalcanal. The information was detailed: Adm. Yamamoto was leaving Rabaul, (*q.v.*), the Japanese stronghold in the Southwest Pacific, the following morning on the first leg of an inspection tour of Japanese bases. He would be traveling in a Mitsubishi *Betty,* a twin-engined bomber, and most of his staff would follow in another *Betty.* There would be an escort of six *Zero* (*q.v.*) fighters. All eight planes were scheduled to land at 9:45 A.M. at Kahili, an airport at the south end of Bougainville, about 300 miles from Rabaul. The dispatch ended with an order to exert maximum effort to destroy Yamamoto. "Intelligence stresses Admiral's exteme punctuality. President attaches extreme importance to this operation."

There was great excitement on Guadalcanal at the possibility of delivering a blow to avenge Pearl Harbor. The task of intercepting Yamamoto was assigned to a squadron of 18 Army *P-38 Lightnings* commanded by Maj. John W. Mitchell. Because of their limited gas supply, the planes would have to operate close to Kahili. Four *Lightnings* were to act as an attack group, while the remaining 14 would serve as a covering force to engage the enemy fighters expected to rise from Kahili to welcome the visiting Admiral.

On the morning of April 18, 1943, one of the *P-38s* on Henderson Field blew a tire and another was forced to turn back because of engine trouble. Immediately two substitute planes were assigned to the attack group, leaving a dozen for cover. To avoid detection the planes flew low, skimming over the water to Bougainville. A few minutes before the rendezvous, the four attack planes climbed to 10,000 feet while the cover group rose to 30,000 feet.

The success of the mission depended on a combination of American split-second timing and unwitting Japanese collaboration. A stiff martinet and stickler for promptness, Yamamoto arrived exactly on time—which meant a rendezvous with death. The Americans sighted the Japanese force just ten minutes before its scheduled landing.

It was over within minutes. The two dozen aircraft tangled in a deadly free-for-all. The Japanese bombers carrying Yamamoto and his staff went down for the safety of tree-top level, but it was too late. Both *Betty*s crashed in flames. It was reported that Yamamoto was found in his seat, his *samurai* sword still between his knees.

SIGNIFICANCE. Yamamoto's death was another victory for American Intelligence. At the time the Japanese were unaware that their code had been broken and that every phase of their combat communications was being monitored. For Americans the incident was regarded as another victory in the pledge to "Remember Pearl Harbor" and as a stimulant to American morale.
Bibliography. B. Davis, *Get Yamamoto* (1969). *See also* R. Vote, "The Death of Admiral Yamamoto," in *Retired Officer* (November, 1979), pp. 27–30.

YAMASHITA, TOMOYUKI (1885–1946). The "Tiger of Malaya," who won a decisive land victory there in early 1942.
A graduate of the Japanese War College in 1916, Yamashita served in various army posts and as military attaché in Switzerland, Germany, and Austria. He had a reputation as a shrewd strategist when appointed commanding general of the 25th Army in 1941. In mid-February 1942 he captured Singapore with scarcely any losses to his own forces. (*See* SINGAPORE, FALL OF.)
In July 1942 Yamashita was named to command the 1st Area Army in Manchuria. In 1944 he was appointed Supreme Commander of the Philippines, where he put up a spirited defense on Leyte. He continued fighting until he heard of the surrender of Japan on September 2, 1945.
After the war Yamashita was accused of war atrocities, which he heatedly denied. He was executed on February 23, 1946.

YANK, THE ARMY WEEKLY. American military magazine written "by and for the man in the service."
Yank appeared weekly throughout the participation of the United States in the war. Its purpose, like that of the daily *Stars and Stripes* (*q.v.*), was to boost the GI's (*q.v.*) morale on both home and combat fronts. Competition was strong for assignments to the publication. Staff writers included Sgts. Merle Miller, Debs Myers, Robert Bendiner, Ray Duncan, and Robert MacMillan.

FEATURES. The journalistic quality of the magazine was high. Each issue included a readable summary of news reports from all fronts. Feature articles gave GIs advice on problems of immediate concern to them. The weekly cartoon strip, *Sad Sack* (*q.v.*), by Sgt. George Baker, depicted the hilarious experiences of a draftee with whom the readers could identify. Individual cartoons had such one-line captions as:

"I need father advice, sir!"
"Merry Christmas! You're on KP!" [*Kitchen Police*]
"They call him Radar, he'll pick up anything!"
"Frankly, fellows, I need the extra dough for OCS!" [Officers' Candidate School]

A feature cherished by GI readers was the Mail Call column that appeared in each issue. These letters to the editor allowed the enlisted men to air their grievances, expecially against officers. An example:

Dear Yank:

This morning our company again formed for morning exercises. The exercises were again an example of the additional humiliation that is being heaped on us before discharge.

We were assigned a partner. Told to put our right hand around his neck. The order was tramp on your opponent's feet or he on yours. A despotic order. Failure to comply with same would bring you additional humiliation in front of the entire company. The second exercise was completed by placing heads against each other's shoulders, pushing forward, punching your opponent in the stomach.

The third routine was accomplished by placing the right hand on the opponent's neck while the left hand was placed against the opponent's right. The order was to wrestle until one man fell. As I didn't (get this chicken) "put enough into it," *I* was ordered to give a demonstration by our company commander (former West Point lad). The company witness same in silence while the officers watched laughing, as they had previously while the other boys pummeled themselves for fear of the consequences.

This is an example of what returning vets are going through before the great day when our points total discharge.

Camp Carson, Colo.   —(Name Withheld)

By far the most popular feature was the photographs of pin-up girls such as Betty Grable, Rita Hayworth, Marlene Dietrich (*qq.v.*), and Hollywood starlets, whose pictures could be cut to grace thousands of foot lockers.

HONORABLE DISCHARGE. The final issue, vol. 4, no. 28 (December 28, 1945), featured on the cover a replica of the GI's (*q.v.*) discharge paper:

ARMY OF THE UNITED STATES
This is to certify that
YANK
Army of the United States
is hereby Honorably Discharged from the military
service of the United States of America.
This certificate is awarded as a testimonial of
Honest and Faithful Service to this country.

Given at Washington, D.C.
Date 31 December 1945

(Signed) DWIGHT D. EISENHOWER
Chief of Staff

Bibliography. The Best From Yank (1945); and D. Myers, J. Kilbourn and R. Harrity, *Yank— The GI Story of the War* (c. 1947).

Z

Z-PLAN. German code or cover name for a plan to match Britain's naval power.

BACKGROUND. On April 1, 1939, at the launching of the new battleship *Tirpitz* (*q.v.*) at Wilhelmshaven, Hitler declared: "It is the Germans' most fervent wish never to go to war with Britain." On the same day the *Fuehrer* promoted Adm. Erich Raeder (*q.v.*), Commander-in-Chief of the German Navy, to Grand Admiral. In the preceding January, Raeder had presented his Z-Plan to Hitler. There were two possible alternatives for Germany, he said, emphasis on U-Boats or a powerful surface striking force. Hitler gave his consent for the second choice, while publicly speaking of peace and friendship for Britain. Within a few months he repudiated his naval treaty with Britain, and Germany was soon at war.

GOALS. The Z-Plan envisioned six super battleships powered by diesels and armed with 16-inch guns. Raeder projected two battleships of the *Gneisenau* class; 3 new speedy battle cruisers of 32,000 tons; two 23,000-ton aircraft carriers; five 10,000-ton heavy cruisers; 4 light cruisers; 9 patrol cruisers; 47 destroyers; 54 torpedo boats; and 228 U-Boats of various types. All these were to be completed by August 1948.

EXECUTION. The Z-Plan called for a tremendous construction effort. The *Tirpitz* was planned in 1936, launched in April 1939, and completed in early 1941. More building was contemplated, but the army and the *Luftwaffe* (*q.v.*) were given priority and most of the heavy ships remained in the blueprint stage.

At the outbreak of war the Z-Plan was in its early stages and soon had to be discarded in view of other commitments. In late 1939 Raeder was still attempting to justify his great program, but it was too late. His plan turned out to be a gigantic miscalculation. Once again he had to turn to U-Boat warfare as a means of striking at Britain.

Bibliography. See E. P. Von der Porten, *The German Navy in World War II* (1969).

ZEITZLER, KURT (1895–1963). Chief of the German General Staff from 1942 to 1944.

Zeitzler, a career officer, served in World War I as commander of the 72nd Infantry Regiment and held many important posts during the Hitler regime. On September 1942, disgusted with the performance of his military leaders in the Russian campaign, Hitler dismissed Gen. Franz Halder (*q.v.*) as Chief of the General Staff of the Army, and appointed Zeitzler in his place. Zeitzler did his best to convince Hitler that the German position in the Soviet Union was extremely precarious and that it was necessary to retreat temporarily. The *Fuehrer* refused to take his advice. After having threatened to resign several times, Zeitzler was retired in June 1944 "without the right to use the uniform." He was succeeded by Gen. Heinz Guderian (*q.v.*).

ZERO. Also known as *Zeke.* Japanese fighter plane and the mainstay of Japanese air power from the first to last during World War II. It was a single-engined, low-wing monoplane with single fin and rudder and retractable landing gear.

DESIGN. The Mitsubishi *A6M,* code named *Zero* by the Allies, was first ordered by the Japanese Navy in 1937 and placed into service two years later. Rather than use a folding wing with resulting heavy mechanism and complicated construction, the designers simply made the wing tips fold by using plain hinge joints. The land-based version was identical with the exception that the arrester gear was eliminated, thereby reducing weight and adding five miles per hour to the top speed. The entire plane was of light construction but was strong and well built.

Speed and maneuverability were due in large part to the omission of armor. Pilots were taped from waist to shoulders with feet strapped to the rudder.

WORLD WAR II. Within a few weeks after Pearl Harbor (*q.v.*), the Japanese controlled the skies over a vast area of the Pacific. This was due in large part to the versatile *Zero.* In the hands of proficient pilots, it quickly accounted for American, British, and Dutch aircraft in the area, and at the same time provided safe passage for the Japanese bombers in their attacks on land targets and shipping. The inability to cope with the Japanese fighter was a major factor in the conduct of the war during the first few months. In the first year of the war no Allied fighter could touch the *Zero.* In Japan, the *Zero-sen* became a symbol of Japanese success in the war.

This ideal state of affairs did not last. By 1943 the new American fighters gained ascendancy over the *Zero.* American pilots found its weakness: no armor protection for pilot or fuel tank. Of the more than 10,938 *Zeros* delivered to the Japanese Navy, large numbers were lost in combat. The *Zero* was used in the late days of the war, more than any other fighter plane, in the devastating *kamikaze* (*q.v.*) attacks. (For specifications *see* AIRCRAFT: JAPANESE AIRCRAFT DATA CHART.)

ZHUKOV, GEORGI KONSTANTINOVICH (1896–1974). Field Marshal and most prominent Soviet commander of the war.

Zhukov was Russian Chief of Staff in the final stages of the Russo-Finnish War. In this post he became Stalin's most trusted military trouble shooter. In 1940 he was promoted to full General. The next year he became Commissar for Defense and was made an alternate member of the Presidium. In October 1941 he was appointed to an important post as commander of the central front in the defense of Moscow. He was then sent to the Leningrad front to organize the defense against the German siege. (*See* LENINGRAD, SIEGE OF.)

By now Zhukov was virtual chief of the Soviet war effort. In 1942 he was given command of the southwest front. He reorganized the defense and in 1943 directed the Russian offensive against the Germans. He led his armies across Poland to the Czech border. He planned the final assault on Berlin (*See* BERLIN, BATTLE OF.) He headed the delegation that signed the formal declaration of surrender in Berlin on May 9, 1945.

Zhukov, a hard-bitten tough soldier who understood mobile warfare, was popular with the rank and file of the Red Army, but he was distrusted by political leaders. His war service in nearly every major Soviet campaign was of major importance.

Bibliography. G. K. Zhukov, *Marshal Zhukov's Greatest Battles* (1969), and *Memoirs* (1971). For a biography *see* O. P. Chaney, *Zhukov* (1972).

ZIEGENBERG. Hitler's headquarters, code named *Adlerhorst* ("Eagle's Nest"), during the closing days of the war.

Situated in the Taunus range near Bad Nauheim in Hesse, Ziegenberg was a manorial estate in the late 18th century. In 1939 Hitler ordered Albert Speer (*q.v.*) to set up a special field headquarters for him about a mile northwest of Ziegenberg at one end of a grassy valley. Speer constructed a fortified cluster of shelters hidden in the woods and camouflaged as blockhouses. He was careful to build the same massive ceilings and walls that Hitler favored.

Ziegenberg was supposed to serve as the *Fuehrer's* headquarters for the attack on the West in 1940. But after millions of marks were invested in the project, Hitler suddenly decided that it was too luxurious for him. He returned to Ziegenberg, however, during the final months of the war, after transferring his headquarters from the *Wolfsschanze* (*q.v.*) in the east. He directed the Ardennes offensive in the winter of 1944 from Ziegenberg. (*See* FUEHRER'S HEADQUARTERS.)

CHRONOLOGY OF WORLD WAR II

1939

Aug. 23	Russo-German Nonaggression Pact signed.
Sept. 1	Germany invades Poland. Ultimatum from Britain and France.
Sept. 3	Britain and France declare war on Germany.
Sept. 17	Soviet troops enter Eastern Poland.
Sept. 27	Warsaw surrenders.
Sept. 28	Poland partitioned by Germany and Russia.
Nov. 30	U.S.S.R. invades Finland.
Dec. 17	*Graf Spee* is scuttled at Montevideo.

1940

March 12	Peace signed in Moscow between USSR and Finland.
April 9	Nazis invade Denmark and Norway.
May 10	Nazis invade Netherlands, Belgium, and Luxembourg.
	Chamberlain resigns as British Prime Minister
	Churchill takes office.
May 12	Germans cross French frontier.
May 14	Dutch army capitulates.
May 16	French line broken at Sedan.
May 28	King Leopold of Belgium capitulates.
May 26–June 4	Dunkirk evacuation.
June 10	Italy declares war on Britain and France. Italy invades France.
June 14	Germans enter undefended Paris.
June 15–16	Russians occupy Lithuania, Latvia, and Estonia.
June 22	France and Germany sign armistice at Compiègne.
June 27	Rumania cedes Bessarabia and Northern Bukovina to Soviet Russia.
July 3	British attack French capital ships at Oran.
July 10	Beginning of Battle of Britain.
Sept. 3	U.S.–Great Britain destroyer-base exchange.
	Abdication of King Carol of Rumania.
Sept. 16	Selective Service Act in U.S.

Sept. 27	German-Italian-Japanese Tripartite Pact, 10-year agreement, signed in Berlin (Pact of Berlin).
Oct. 28	Italy invades Greece.
Nov. 11–12	Royal Air Force attacks Taranto.
Nov. 14–15	Germans raid Coventry.
Nov. 20–25	Hungary, Rumania, Slovakia join Tripartite Pact.

1941

Jan. 6	President Roosevelt's speech on the Four Freedoms.
Jan. 10	Lend-Lease Bill introduced into Congress.
	Soviet-German trade pact.
March 1	Bulgaria joins Tripartite Pact.
March 11	Lend-Lease Bill signed by President.
March 25	Yugoslavia joins Tripartite Pact.
March 27	Revolution in Yugoslavia. New cabinet does not ratify pact.
March 28	Battle of Cape Matapan.
March 30	German counteroffensive in North Africa.
April 6	Germans invade Greece and Yugoslavia.
April 11	Russo-Japanese Neutrality Treaty.
May 2–31	Revolution in Iraq suppressed by British.
May 10–11	Rudolf Hess flies to Scotland.
May 20	Germans invade Crete.
May 27	German battleship *Bismarck* sunk.
June 1	British withdraw from Crete.
June 8	Allies enter Syria.
June 14	Roosevelt freezes Axis funds in U.S.
June 18	Germany and Turkey sign treaty of friendship.
June 22	Hitler attacks Soviet Union.
July 12	British-Soviet mutual aid pact.
Aug. 12	Atlantic Charter. Roosevelt and Churchill meet at sea and agree on war aims.
Aug. 21	Beginning of siege of Leningrad.
Aug. 25	British and Russian troops enter Iran.
Sept. 19	Germans occupy Kiev.
Oct. 11	General Hideki Tojo becomes Premier of Japan.
Nov. 18	Eighth Army's desert offensive in Libya.
Nov. 26	Strong U.S. note to Japan.
Nov. 28	Russians retake Rostov.
Dec. 1	Russians counterattack at Tula.
Dec. 7	Japan attacks Pearl Harbor. Pacific Fleet crippled.
	Japan declares war on Britain and U.S.
Dec. 7–8	Britain declares war on Finland, Rumania, and Hungary.
Dec. 8	Japanese landings in Thailand and Malaya.
	U.S. and Great Britain declare war on Japan.
Dec. 10	H.M.S. *Prince of Wales* and H.M.S. *Repulse* sunk by Japanese air attacks off Malayan coast.
Dec. 10–11	Germany and Italy declare war on U.S. U.S. declares war on both those countries.

Dec. 13	Hungary and Bulgaria declare war on U.S.
Dec. 22	Japanese begin major attack on Philippines.
Dec. 24	First Washington Conference.
	Churchill in Washington.
Dec. 25	Hong Kong surrenders.

1942

Jan. 1	Twenty-six nations sign United Nations Declaration.
Jan. 10–11	Japanese invade Netherlands East Indies.
Jan. 21	German counteroffensive in North Africa.
Feb. 12	*Scharnhorst, Gneisenau,* and *Prinz Eugen* escape from Brest.
Feb. 15	British surrender Singapore.
March 7	Evacuation of Rangoon.
March 17	MacArthur arrives in Australia.
April 9	U.S. forces on Bataan surrender.
April 18	Tokyo bombed by U.S. Army Air Force planes.
May 4–8	Battle of the Coral Sea.
May 26	German counteroffensive in North Africa.
	Twenty-year Anglo-Soviet Treaty signed in London.
May 30–31	First R.A.F. 1,000-bomber raid on Cologne.
June 4–8	Battle of Midway Island.
June 21	Germans take Tobruk.
June 25–27	Second Washington Conference between Roosevelt and Churchill.
Aug. 7	U.S. Marines land on Guadalcanal.
Aug. 12	First Moscow Conference.
Aug. 19	Raid on Dieppe.
Oct. 23	Montgomery strikes at El Alamein.
Nov. 8	U.S. and Britain land great army in North Africa.
Nov. 11	German troops enter unoccupied France.
Nov. 19–22	Stalingrad counteroffensive.
Dec. 24	Admiral Darlan, Chief of State in North Africa, assassinated.

1943

Jan. 14–23	Casablanca Conference.
Jan. 23	Eighth Army enters Tripoli.
Feb. 2	German forces surrender at Stalingrad. Turning point of war in Russia.
March 3	Battle of the Bismarck Sea.
May 11–27	Third Washington Conference between Roosevelt and Churchill.
May 12	Organized Axis resistance in Tunisia ends.
May 15	Third International (Comintern) dissolved in Moscow. (Announced May 22.)
May 18	United Nations Food Conference at Hot Springs, Virginia.
May 20	Victory parade in Tunis.
July 9–10	Allied invasion of Sicily.
July 19	Bombing of Rome.
July 24	Beginning of saturation raid on Hamburg.
July 25	Mussolini replaced by Badoglio as Italian Premier.

Aug. 17–24	First Quebec Conference.
Aug. 28	Death of King Boris III of Bulgaria. Succeeded by son, 6-year-old Simeon II.
Sept. 3	Allied invasion of southern Italy.
Sept. 8	Italy surrenders.
Sept. 9	Allied landing at Salerno.
Sept. 10	Germans occupy Rome.
Oct. 13	Italy declares war on Germany.
Oct. 18–Nov. 1	Moscow Conference of foreign secretaries (Hull, Eden, Molotov).
Nov. 6	Recapture of Kiev by Russians.
Nov. 9	Establishment of the United Nations Relief and Rehabilitation Administration (U.N.R.R.A.)
Nov. 22–26	First Cairo Conference (Roosevelt, Churchill, Chiang Kai-shek).
Nov. 28–Dec. 1	Teheran Conference (Roosevelt, Churchill, Stalin).
Dec. 4–6	Second Cairo Conference (Roosevelt, Churchill, Inönü).
Dec. 12	Czecho-Soviet Alliance for mutual assistance.
Dec. 26	Nazi battleship *Scharnhorst* sunk off North Cape.

1944

Jan. 22	Allied troops land at Anzio behind German lines.
March 8	Finns reject Soviet armistice terms.
March 19	German troops cross Hungarian frontier.
April 10	Russians recapture Odessa.
May 23	Allied offensive from Anzio beachhead.
June 4	Rome recaptured by Anglo-American troops.
June 6	D-Day. Allied invasion of Normandy.
June 13–14	First *V-1* bombs fall on England.
June 15	First Superfortress raid on Japan.
July 1–22	International Monetary Conference at Bretton Woods.
July 3	Russians recapture Minsk.
July 20	Hitler wounded in bomb plot.
July 26	U.S. troops break through, west of St. Lô.
Aug. 11	U.S. forces complete conquest of Guam.
Aug. 15	Allied forces land on south coast of France.
Aug. 21–Sept. 28	Dumbarton Oaks Conference, Washington, D.C.
Aug. 23	Rumania accepts Russian armistice terms.
Aug. 25	Paris liberated.
Sept. 3	British liberate Brussels.
Sept. 4	End of Finnish-Russian fighting.
Sept. 5	The Soviet Union declares war on Bulgaria.
Sept. 8	First V-2 lands on London.
Sept. 9	Bulgarian armistice.
Sept. 12–16	Second Quebec Conference (Churchill and Roosevelt). Finnish armistice signed.
Sept. 17	Allied airborne army lands in Holland.
Oct. 14	Allies occupy Athens.

Oct. 20	Belgrade liberated by Russians and Yugoslavs.
	American troops invade Philippines.
Oct. 21–22	Battle of Leyte Gulf.
Nov. 12	*Tirpitz* sunk in Tromsö Fjord by RAF
Dec. 16	Germans launch counteroffensive. Battle of the Bulge.

1945

Jan. 9	U.S. forces land on Luzon on Philippines.
Jan. 17	Russians capture Warsaw.
Jan. 20	Provisional Government of Hungary signs armistice.
Jan. 27	Memel liberated.
Jan. 31	Churchill and Roosevelt meet at Malta.
Feb. 3	U.S. troops enter Manila.
Feb. 4–11	Yalta Conference (Roosevelt, Churchill, Stalin).
Feb. 13–14	Air raid on Dresden.
Feb. 19	U.S. Marines land on Iwo Jima.
March 4	Finland declares war on Germany as from September 15, 1944.
March 7	U.S. First Army crosses Rhine on bridge at Remagen.
April 1	U.S. invasion of Okinawa.
April 12	Death of President Roosevelt. Truman becomes President.
April 13	Vienna liberated by Soviet army.
April 25	United Nations parley opens at San Francisco.
	Russian and U.S. forces meet at Torgau on the Elbe.
April 28	Mussolini executed by Partisans.
April 30	Hitler commits suicide in bunker at Reich Chancellery in Berlin.
	33,000 inmates of Dachau concentration camp freed by U.S. forces.
	Soviet flag raised over *Reichstag* in Berlin.
May 1	Grand Admiral Doenitz takes command in Germany.
May 2	Fall of Berlin to Russians.
	German armies in Italy make complete surrender.
May 3	Rangoon captured.
May 7	Germany surrenders unconditionally to Western Allies and Russia.
May 8	V-E Day.
June 26	World Security Charter signed at San Francisco.
July 17–Aug. 2	Potsdam Conference (Truman, Stalin, Churchill and later Attlee).
Aug. 6	First atomic bomb dropped on Hiroshima.
Aug. 8	USSR declares war on Japan.
Aug. 9	Second atomic bomb dropped on Nagasaki.
Aug. 14	Japanese unconditional surrender.
Sept. 2	Japanese sign surrender terms on U.S.S. *Missouri* in Tokyo Bay.

TEN BASIC BOOKS ON WORLD WAR II

1. Bryant, Sir Arthur. *Triumph in the West* (New York, 1959).
2. Buchanan, A. Russell. *The United States and World War II*. 2 vols. (New York, 1964).
3. Churchill, Winston S. *The Second World War*. 6 vols. (London, 1953, 1962).
4. Falls, Cyril. *The Second World War* (London, 1948).
5. Fuller, John F. C. *The Second World War, 1939-1945* (New York, 1949).
6. Liddell Hart, B. H. *History of the Second World War* (London, 1980).
7. Matloff, Maurice *World War II* (New York, 1980).
8. Michel, Henri, *The Second World War*. Trans. by Douglas Parmee. 2 vols. (New York, 1975).
9. Morison, Samuel E. *History of the United States Naval Operations in World War II*. 15 vols. (Boston, 1947–1960).
10. Snyder, Louis L., *The War: A Concise History, 1939-1945*. 4th printing (New York, 1961).

INDEX

Due to the multiplicity of place names in this book, names of continents, countries, cities, towns, villages, mountains, bodies of water, et al., are listed only if they are of significance in the conduct of World War II. The page numbers set in **bold face** indicate the location of the main entry.

ABOUT THE AUTHOR

LOUIS L. SNYDER, Emeritus Professor of History at the City University of New York, is the author of nearly sixty books, including *The New Nationalism,* *Encyclopedia of the Third Reich,* and *Global Mini-Nationalisms: Autonomy or Independence?* (Greenwood Press, 1981).